# introduction TO
## MANAGERIAL ACCOUNTING

### 8TH EDITION

**PETER C. BREWER, Ph.D.**
Wake Forest University

**RAY H. GARRISON, D.B.A., CPA**
Professor Emeritus
Brigham Young University

**ERIC W. NOREEN, Ph.D., CMA**
Professor Emeritus
University of Washington
Accounting Circle Professor of Accounting
Temple University

Mc
Graw
Hill
Education

INTRODUCTION TO MANAGERIAL ACCOUNTING

Published by McGraw-Hill Education, 2 Penn Plaza, New York, NY 10121. Copyright © 2019 by McGraw-Hill
Education. All rights reserved. Printed in the United States of America. No part of this publication may be
reproduced or distributed in any form or by any means, or stored in a database or retrieval system, without the
prior written consent of McGraw-Hill Education, including, but not limited to, in any network or other
electronic storage or transmission, or broadcast for distance learning.

Some ancillaries, including electronic and print components, may not be available to customers outside the
United States.

This book is printed on acid-free paper.

1 2 3 4 5 6 7 8 9 LWI 21 20 19 18

ISBN 978-1-260-09175-5
MHID 1-260-09175-9

Cover Image: © Solomin Andrey/Shutterstock

mheducation.com/highered

# DEDICATION

*To our families and to our many colleagues who use this book.*

**Peter C. Brewer** is a lecturer in the Department of Accountancy at Wake Forest University. Prior to joining the faculty at Wake Forest, he was an accounting professor at Miami University for 19 years. He holds a BS degree in accounting from Penn State University, an MS degree in accounting from the University of Virginia, and a PhD from the University of Tennessee. He has published more than 40 articles in a variety of journals including: *Management Accounting Research;* the *Journal of Information Systems; Cost Management; Strategic Finance;* the *Journal of Accountancy; Issues in Accounting Education;* and the *Journal of Business Logistics.*

Professor Brewer has served on the editorial boards of the *Journal of Accounting Education* and *Issues in Accounting Education.* His article "Putting Strategy into the Balanced Scorecard" won the 2003 International Federation of Accountants' Articles of Merit competition, and his articles "Using Six Sigma to Improve the Finance Function" and "Lean Accounting: What's It All About?" were awarded the Institute of Management Accountants' Lybrand Gold and Silver Medals in 2005 and 2006. He has received Miami University's Richard T. Farmer School of Business Teaching Excellence Award.

Prior to joining the faculty at Miami University, Professor Brewer was employed as an auditor for Touche Ross in the firm's Philadelphia office. He also worked as an internal audit manager for the Board of Pensions of the Presbyterian Church (U.S.A.).

## Ray H. Garrison
is emeritus professor of accounting at Brigham Young University, Provo, Utah. He received his BS and MS degrees from Brigham Young University and his DBA degree from Indiana University.

As a certified public accountant, Professor Garrison has been involved in management consulting work with both national and regional accounting firms. He has published articles in *The Accounting Review, Management Accounting,* and other professional journals. Innovation in the classroom has earned Professor Garrison the Karl G. Maeser Distinguished Teaching Award from Brigham Young University.

## Eric W. Noreen
has taught at INSEAD in France and the Hong Kong Institute of Science and Technology and is emeritus professor of accounting at the University of Washington. Currently, he is the Accounting Circle Professor of Accounting, Fox School of Business, Temple University.

He received his BA degree from the University of Washington and MBA and PhD degrees from Stanford University. A Certified Management Accountant, he was awarded a Certificate of Distinguished Performance by the Institute of Certified Management Accountants.

Professor Noreen has served as associate editor of *The Accounting Review* and the *Journal of Accounting and Economics.* He has numerous articles in academic journals including: the *Journal of Accounting Research; The Accounting Review;* the *Journal of Accounting and Economics; Accounting Horizons; Accounting, Organizations and Society; Contemporary Accounting Research;* the *Journal of Management Accounting Research;* and the *Review of Accounting Studies.*

Professor Noreen has won a number of awards from students for his teaching.

# Pointing Students in the Right Direction

## "Why do I need to learn Managerial Accounting?"

Brewer's Introduction to Managerial Accounting has earned a reputation as the most accessible and readable book on the market. Its manageable chapters and clear presentation point students toward understanding just as the needle of a compass provides direction to travelers.

However, the book's authors also understand that everyone's destinations are different. Some students will become accountants, while others are destined for careers in management, marketing, or finance. Not only does the Brewer text teach students managerial accounting concepts in a clear and concise way, but it also asks students to consider how the concepts they're learning will apply to the real world situations they will eventually confront in their careers. This combination of conceptual understanding and the ability to apply that knowledge directs students toward success, whatever their final destination happens to be.

### Here's how your colleagues have described Brewer's *Introduction to Managerial Accounting*:

Great, readable text with streamlined coverage. the number of chapters combined with the readability make this a lean, up-to-date product.

Timothy Griffin, Hillsborough Community College

A simplified managerial accounting book.

Dan O'Brien, Madison College

A book with an appropriate level of coverage for students who may not all be majoring in accounting. This book has enough detail for accounting majors, with coverage that still keeps the interest and understanding of non-majors.

Dawn McKinley, Harper Community College

This is a thorough text that offers many well-structured exercises throughout.

Eric Weinstein, Suffolk Community College

The textbook is very good, with the Foundational 15 being my favorite feature. The Review Problems are also very thorough and serves as an outstanding study tool for students to use independently. The writing flows very well. If a student takes the time to read each chapter thoroughly, there is no excuse not to do well in the Managerial Accounting Course.

Randall Williams, Catawba Valley Community College

I really like the content and think it will be beneficial for all students. I especially like the highlighting of important concepts in the text, and the Guided examples that explain how to solve problems.

Diane Tanner, University of Northern Florida

## CONFIDENCE AT THE CORE

Your students want a text that is concise and that presents material in a clear and readable manner. Introduction to Managerial Accounting keeps the material accessible while avoiding advanced topics related to cost accounting. Students' biggest concern is whether they can solve the end-of-chapter problems after reading the chapter. Market research indicates that Brewer/Garrison/Noreen helps students apply what they've learned better than any other managerial accounting text on the market. Additionally, the key supplements are written and continually revised to ensure that students and instructors will work with clear, well-written supplements that employ consistent terminology. Author Pete Brewer examined each and every end of chapter question in Connect to guarantee accuracy and consistency.

## RELEVANCE AND DECISION MAKING

All students who pass through your class need to know how accounting information is used to make business decisions, especially if they plan to be future managers. That's why Brewer, Garrison, and Noreen make decision making a pivotal component of Introduction to Managerial Accounting. In every chapter you'll find the following key features that are designed to teach your students how to use accounting information: Each chapter opens with a Decision Feature vignette that uses real-world examples to show how accounting information is used to make everyday business decisions; Decision Point boxes within the chapters help students to develop analytical, critical thinking, and problem-solving skills; and end-of-chapter Building Your Skills cases challenge students' decision-making skills.

## A CONTEMPORARY APPROACH TO LEARNING

Today's students rely on technology more than ever as a learning tool, and Introduction to Managerial Accounting offers the finest technology package of any text on the market. From study aids like narrated, animated Guided Examples to online grading and course management, our technology assets have one thing in common: they make your class time more productive, more stimulating, and more rewarding for you and your students. McGraw-Hill Connect is an online assignment and assessment solution that connects students with the tools and resources they'll need to be successful. These resources include an online, media-rich, searchable version of the text in addition to access to Connect, giving students a convenient way to access everything they need to succeed in their course.

# BREWER / GARRISON / NOREEN'S

**Introduction to Managerial Accounting** is full of pedagogy designed to make studying productive and hassle-free. On the following pages, you'll see the kind of engaging, helpful pedagogical features that have made Brewer one of the best-selling Managerial Accounting texts on the market.

## NEW* INTEGRATION EXERCISES

We have added 12 new exercises located in the back of the text and in Connect that integrate learning objectives across chapters. These exercises will increase the students' level of interest in the course because they forge the connections across chapters. Rather than seeing each chapter as an isolated set of learning objectives, students begin to see how it all fits together to provide greater managerial insight and more effective planning, controlling, and decision making. The integration exercises are also tailor-made for flipping the classroom because they offer challenging questions that require students to work in teams to derive solutions that synthesize what they have learned throughout the semester.

## NEW* CONCEPT OVERVIEW VIDEOS

New for the 8th edition of Brewer, the Concept Overview Videos cover each learning objective through narrated, animated presentations. Formerly called Interactive Presentations, each Concept Overview Video has been enhanced for improved accessibility, and includes both the visual animations and transcripts to accommodate all types of learners. The Concept Overview Videos also pause frequently to check for comprehension with assignable, auto-graded Knowledge Check questions.

> **HELPFUL HINT**
>
> When students prepare variable costing income statements they often mistakenly assume that variable selling and administrative expense is a product cost. The confusion arises because variable selling and administrative expense is included in the calculation of contribution margin; however, it is not a product cost. Variable selling and administrative expense is always a period cost and the total amount of this expense included in the income statement is always derived by multiplying the variable selling and administrative expense per unit by the number of units sold—not the number of units produced.

## HELPFUL HINT

Helpful Hint boxes are found several times throughout each chapter and highlight a variety of common mistakes, key points, and "pulling it all together" insights for students.

> **DECISION POINT** — **The Pricing Decision**
>
> Each year Webb Company produces and sells 20,000 units of its only product. The selling price for this product is $100 per unit and its direct materials, direct labor, and variable manufacturing overhead costs per unit are $25, $15, and $10, respectively. Webb's annual fixed manufacturing overhead expenses and fixed selling and administrative expenses are $400,000 and $150,000, respectively. It does not have any variable selling and administrative expenses.
>
> The company's marketing manager believes a 10% price increase would lead to a 20% decline in the number of units sold. He claims that if the level of production stays at 20,000 units his price hike will increase gross margins and net operating income by $40,000. Would you support the price increase? Do you think it will increase profits?

"Very good conversation starters in a classroom or discussion board setting."

Randall Williams, Catawba Community College

## DECISION POINT

The Decision Point feature fosters critical thinking and decision-making skills by providing real-world business scenarios that require the resolution of a business issue. The suggested solution is located at the end of the chapter.

# POWERFUL PEDAGOGY

## THE FOUNDATIONAL 15

Each chapter contains one Foundational 15 exercise that includes 15 "building-block" questions related to one concise set of data. These exercises can be used for in-class discussion or as homework assignments. They are found before the Exercises and are available in **Connect.**

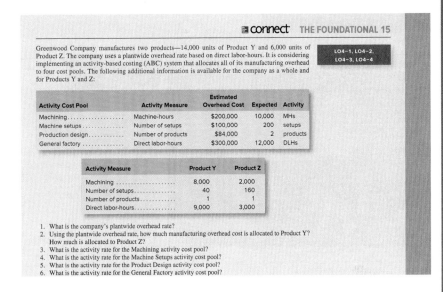

## CHAPTER OUTLINE

Each chapter opens with an **outline** that provides direction to the student about the road they can expect to traverse throughout the chapter. The **A Look Back/A Look at This Chapter/A Look Ahead** feature reminds students what they have learned in previous chapters, what they can expect to learn in the current chapter, and how the topics will build on each other in chapters to come.

**DECISION FEATURE**

University Tees: Serving Over
150 Campuses Nationwide

**University Tees** was founded in 2003 by two **Miami University** college students to provide screen-printing, embroidery, and promotional products for fraternities, sororities, and student organizations. Today, the company, which is headquartered in Cleveland, Ohio, employs as many as four Campus Managers on each of over 150 college campuses across America.

Accurately calculating the cost of each potential customer order is critically important to University Tees because the company needs to be sure that the sales price exceeds the cost associated with satisfying the order. The costs include the cost of the blank T-shirts themselves, printing costs (which vary depending on the quantity of shirts produced and the number of colors per shirt), screen costs (which also vary depending on the number of colors included in a design), shipping costs, and the artwork needed to create a design. The company also takes into account its competitors' pricing strategies when developing its own prices.

Given its success on college campuses, University Tees has introduced a sister company called **On Point Promos** to serve for-profit companies and nonprofit organizations.

Source: Conversation with Joe Haddad, cofounder of University Tees.

**LEARNING OBJECTIVES**

*After studying Chapter 2, you should be able to:*

**LO2–1** Compute a predetermined overhead rate.

**LO2–2** Apply overhead cost to jobs using a predetermined overhead rate.

**LO2–3** Compute the total cost and the unit product cost of a job using a plantwide predetermined overhead rate.

**LO2–4** Compute the total cost and the unit product cost of a job using multiple predetermined overhead rates.

## DECISION FEATURE

Each chapter opens with a **Decision Feature** feature that provides a real-world example for students, enabling them to see how the chapter's information and insights apply to the world outside the classroom. **Learning Objectives** alert students to what they should expect as they progress through the chapter.

---

**A Look at Bangladesh'S $20 Billion Garment Industry**   IN BUSINESS

In Bangladesh, the minimum wage is $38 per month. A highly-skilled sewing machine operator may earn as much as $100 per month before considering overtime. Companies such as **Fakir Apparels**, a T-shirt manufacturer in Bangladesh, can readily attract customers such as **Walmart**, **Gap**, and **Primark**, due to these low labor costs. However, in addition to serving mass market retailers, Fakir Apparels also makes T-shirts for premium brands such as **Tommy Hilfiger**, **Giorgio Armani**, **Hugo Boss**, and **G-Star Raw**. While the manufacturing cost for one of Fakir Apparels T-shirts ranges from $1.60 to $6.00, the retail selling prices for these T-shirts can vary from $6.00 (at Walmart) to as much as $91.00 (at G-Star Raw).

Source: Passariello, Christina et al., "Bangladesh's Tale of the T-Shirts," *The Wall Street Journal*, July 1, 2013, pp. B1 and B8.

## IN BUSINESS BOXES

These helpful boxed features appear in every chapter and they demonstrate how selected managerial accounting topics apply to real organizations and contexts.

---

3.  Which of the following statements is false with respect to the schedule of cost of goods manufactured? (You may select more than one answer.)
    a.  The beginning raw materials inventory plus raw materials purchases minus ending raw materials inventory equals the raw materials used in production.
    b.  Direct labor costs and actual manufacturing overhead costs are included in the schedule of cost of goods manufactured.
    c.  The cost of goods manufactured represents the amount that will be debited to Cost of Goods Sold during an accounting period.
    d.  If the finished goods inventory increases during an accounting period, it will decrease the cost of goods manufactured.

 CONCEPT CHECK

## CONCEPT CHECK

Concept Checks allow students to test their comprehension of topics and concepts covered at meaningful points throughout each chapter.

# END-OF-CHAPTER MATERIAL

*Introduction to Managerial Acounting* has earned a reputation for the best end-of-chapter review and discussion material of any text on the market. Our exercises and problems conform to AICPA, AACSB, and Bloom's Taxonomy categories, and they make a great starting point for class discussions and group projects. With review problems, discussion questions, Excel problems, the Foundational 15 set, exercises, problems, and Building Your Skills, Brewer offers students practice material of varying complexity and depth.

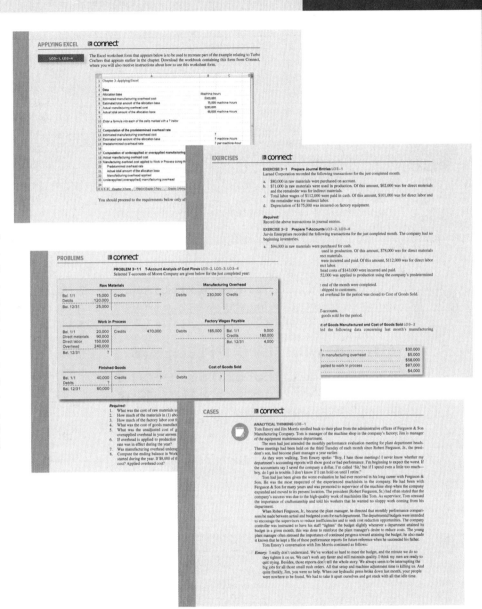

> **I think this text is more comprehensive in coverage and has excellent homework problems.**
>
> Robert Holtfreter, Central Washington University

## UTILIZING THE ICONS

 To reflect our service-based economy, the text is replete with examples from service-based businesses. A helpful icon distinguishes service-related examples in the text.

 The IFRS icon highlights content that may be affected by the impending change to IFRS and possible convergence between U.S. GAAP and IFRS.

 Ethics assignments and examples serve as a reminder that good conduct is vital in business. Icons call out content that relates to ethical behavior for students.

 The writing icon denotes problems that require students to use critical thinking as well as writing skills to explain their decisions.

## AUTHOR-WRITTEN SUPPLEMENTS

Unlike other managerial accounting texts, the book's authors write the major supplements such as the test bank and solution files, ensuring a perfect fit between text and supplements.

## ASSURANCE OF LEARNING READY

Many educational institutions today are focused on the notion of assurance of learning, an important element of some accreditation standards. *Introduction to Managerial Accounting,* 8e, is designed specifically to support your assurance of learning initiatives with a simple, yet powerful, solution.

Each question for *Introduction to Managerial Accounting,* 8e, maps to a specific chapter learning outcome/objective listed in the text. The reporting features of **Connect** can aggregate student to make the collection and presentation of assurance of learning data simple and easy.

## AACSB STATEMENT

McGraw-Hill Education is a proud corporate member of AACSB International. Recognizing the importance and value of AACSB accreditation, we have sought to recognize the curricula guidelines detailed in AACSB standards for business accreditation by connecting selected questions in *Introduction to Managerial Accounting,* 8e, to the general knowledge and skill guidelines found in the AACSB standards. The statements contained in *Introduction to Managerial Accounting,* 8e, are provided only as a guide for the users of this text. The AACSB leaves content coverage and assessment clearly within the realm and control of individual schools, the mission of the school, and the faculty. The AACSB does also charge schools with the obligation of doing assessment against their own content and learning goals. While *Introduction to Managerial Accounting,* 8e, and its teaching package make no claim of any specific AACSB qualification or evaluation, we have, within *Introduction to Managerial Accounting,* 8e, tagged questions according to the six general knowledge and skills areas. The labels or tags within *Introduction to Managerial Accounting,* 8e, are as indicated. There are, of course, many more within the test bank, the text, and the teaching package which might be used as a "standard" for your course. However, the labeled questions are suggested for your consideration.

> "I liked the way the LS (Learnsmart) assignments, homework, and quiz provided multiple interactions with the material for the students."
>
> Janet Jones, University of Minnesota-Duluth

> "Connect Accounting is a reliable and interesting system for learners to explore with"
>
> Chuo-Hsuan(Jason) Lee, SUNY Plattsburgh

> "The system is really user friendly and organized well (Connect)"
>
> Stacy Kline, Drexel University

# New in the Eighth Edition

Faculty feedback helps us continue to improve *Introduction to Managerial Accounting*. In response to reviewer suggestions, the authors have made the following changes to the text:

- We split the job-order costing chapter into two chapters to improve the students' ability to understand the material and to give professors greater flexibility in choosing how to cover the material.
- We reviewed all end-of-chapter exercises and problems and revised them as appropriate to better function within Connect.
- We added 12 Integration Exercises in the back of the book to help students connect the concepts. These exercises are suitable for both a flipped classroom model and an in-class active learning environment as they engage students and encourage critical thinking.
- In-Business boxes are updated throughout to provide relevant and current real-world examples for use in classroom discussion and to support student understanding of key concepts as they read through a chapter.

## Prologue
The Prologue has added coverage of the CGMA exam and an updated summary of the CMA exam content specifications.

## Chapter 1
The high-low method has been removed from this chapter. We added an exhibit to visually depict product and period cost flows. We also made various changes to further emphasize the chapter's unifying theme of *different cost classifications for different purposes*. We have created 11 new end-of-chapter exercises/problems.

## Chapter 2
This is a new chapter that explains how to use a job-order costing system to calculate unit product costs. It describes how to use plantwide and multiple overhead rates to apply overhead costs to individual jobs. The chapter has a strong managerial accounting orientation because it looks at how job-order costing systems serve the needs of internal managers.

## Chapter 3
This is a new chapter that explains how job-order costing systems can be used to determine the value of ending inventories and cost of goods sold for external reporting purposes. The chapter has a strong financial accounting orientation because it uses journal entries and T-accounts to explain the flow of costs in a job-order costing system. The chapter also has a new appendix that uses Microsoft Excel® to explain the flow of costs in a job-order costing system.

## Chapter 5
We revised the text in the main body of the chapter and in the online FIFO Supplement to better highlight the key concepts and steps needed to perform the weighted-average and FIFO process costing calculations.

## Chapter 6
We added a new appendix that explains how to analyze mixed costs using the high-low method and the least-squares regression method.

## Chapter 7
We added new text that better highlights this chapter's reliance on actual costing and contrasts it with the job-order costing chapters' reliance on normal costing.

## Chapter 8
The end-of-chapter materials include three new exercises/problems (8-17, 8-18, and 8-27).

## Chapter 9
We revised numerous end-of-chapter exercises and problems to better align them with Connect. We overhauled Appendix 9B to introduce students to a Microsoft Excel-based approach for creating an income statement using standard costing.

## Chapter 10
This chapter includes four new In Business boxes.

## Chapter 11
We revised the front-end of the chapter to better highlight the six key concepts that provide the foundation for effective decision making. We also revised the end-of-chapter exercises and problems to better dovetail with Connect and streamlined the coverage of sell or process further decisions to aid student comprehension.

## Chapter 12
We revised many end-of-chapter exercises and problems and extensively revised the formatting within Connect throughout all the chapters, (not just Chapter 13) to allow students greater flexibility for alternate methods of approaching a problem, such as performing net present value calculations.

## Chapter 13
We added three new In Business boxes.

**McGraw-Hill Connect®** is a highly reliable, easy-to-use homework and learning management solution that utilizes learning science and award-winning adaptive tools to improve student results.

## Homework and Adaptive Learning

- Connect's assignments help students contextualize what they've learned through application, so they can better understand the material and think critically.
- Connect will create a personalized study path customized to individual student needs through SmartBook®.
- SmartBook helps students study more efficiently by delivering an interactive reading experience through adaptive highlighting and review.

Over **7 billion questions** have been answered, making McGraw-Hill Education products more intelligent, reliable, and precise.

### Connect's Impact on Retention Rates, Pass Rates, and Average Exam Scores

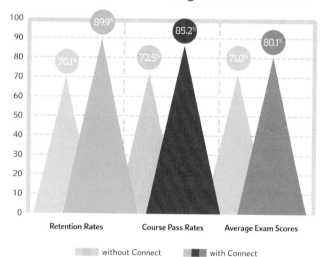

without Connect    with Connect

Using **Connect** improves retention rates by **19.8** percentage points, passing rates by **12.7** percentage points, and exam scores by **9.1** percentage points.

73% of instructors who use **Connect** require it; instructor satisfaction **increases** by 28% when **Connect** is required.

## Quality Content and Learning Resources

- Connect content is authored by the world's best subject matter experts, and is available to your class through a simple and intuitive interface.
- The Connect eBook makes it easy for students to access their reading material on smartphones and tablets. They can study on the go and don't need internet access to use the eBook as a reference, with full functionality.
- Multimedia content such as videos, simulations, and games drive student engagement and critical thinking skills.

# Robust Analytics and Reporting

- Connect Insight® generates easy-to-read reports on individual students, the class as a whole, and on specific assignments.

- The Connect Insight dashboard delivers data on performance, study behavior, and effort. Instructors can quickly identify students who struggle and focus on material that the class has yet to master.

- Connect automatically grades assignments and quizzes, providing easy-to-read reports on individual and class performance.

©Hero Images/Getty Images

## Impact on Final Course Grade Distribution

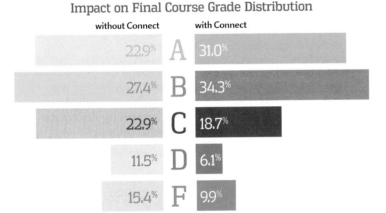

| without Connect | | with Connect |
|---|---|---|
| 22.9% | A | 31.0% |
| 27.4% | B | 34.3% |
| 22.9% | C | 18.7% |
| 11.5% | D | 6.1% |
| 15.4% | F | 9.9% |

More students earn **As** and **Bs** when they use **Connect**.

# Trusted Service and Support

- Connect integrates with your LMS to provide single sign-on and automatic syncing of grades. Integration with Blackboard®, D2L®, and Canvas also provides automatic syncing of the course calendar and assignment-level linking.

- Connect offers comprehensive service, support, and training throughout every phase of your implementation.

- If you're looking for some guidance on how to use Connect, or want to learn tips and tricks from super users, you can find tutorials as you work. Our Digital Faculty Consultants and Student Ambassadors offer insight into how to achieve the results you want with Connect.

**www.mheducation.com/connect**

# Acknowledgments

Suggestions have been received from many of our colleagues throughout the world who have used the prior edition of *Introduction to Managerial Accounting*. This is vital feedback that we rely on in each edition. Each of those who offered comments and suggestions has our thanks.

The efforts of many people are needed to develop and improve a text. Among these people are the reviewers and consultants who point out areas of concern, cite areas of strength, and make recommendations for change. We thank current and past reviewers who have provided feedback that was enormously helpful in preparing *Introduction to Managerial Accounting*.

## Previous Edition Reviewers

Melanie Anderson, *Slippery Rock University*
Pat Carter, *Green River Community College*
Ru-Fang Chiang, *California State University—Chico*
Gene Elrod, *University of North Texas*
Daniel J. Gibbons, *Waubonsee Community College*
Olen L. Greer, *Missouri State University*
Tom Hrubec, *Franklin University*
Robert L. Hurt, *California State Polytechnic University—Pomona*
Frank Ilett, *Boise State University*
Daniel Law, *Gonzaga University*
Marisa Lester, *University at Albany*
Candace Leuck, *Clemson University*
Diane Marker, *University of Toledo*
Lawrence Metzger, *Loyola University Chicago*
Susan Minke, *Indiana Purdue University at Fort Wayne*
Samir Nissan, *California State University—Chico*
Marilyn Pipes, *Tarleton State University*
Ronald O. Reed, *University of Northern Colorado*
Anwar Salimi, *California State Polytechnic University—Pomona*
Rex A. Schildhouse, *Miramar College, San Diego Community College District*
Pat Seaton, *University of Northern Colorado*
Randy Serrett, *University of Houston—Downtown*
Meghna Singhvi, *Loyola Marymount University*
Mike Slaubaugh, *Indiana University Purdue University Fort Wayne*
Joel Sneed, *University of Oregon*
Stephen Strand, *Southern Maine Community College*
Gloria Stuart, *Georgia Southern University*
Dominique Svarc, *Harper College*
Dorothy A. Thompson, *University of North Texas*
Clark Wheatley, *Florida International University*
Blair Arthur William, *Slippery Rock University*
Jan Workman, *East Carolina University*
Weihong Xu, *State University of New York at Buffalo*
Minna Yu, *Monmouth University*
Ronald Zhao, *Monmouth University*
L. M. Abney, *LaSalle University*
Nas Ahadiat, *Cal Poly Pomona*
Sol Ahiarah, *SUNY College at Buffalo*
Markus Ahrens, *St. Louis Community College—Meramec*
Natalie Allen, *Texas A&M University*
William Ambrose, *DeVry University*
Elizabeth M. Ammann, *Lindenwood University*
Robert J. Angell, *North Carolina A&T State University*
Robert Appleton, *University of North Carolina-Wilmington*
Thomas Arcuri, *Florida Community College at Jacksonville*
Rowland Atiase, *University of Texas at Austin*
Steven Ault, *Montana State University*
Leonard Bacon, *California State University, Bakersfield*
Roderick Barclay, *Texas A&M University*
Linda Batiste, *Baton Rouge Community College*
Benjamin W. Bean, *Utah Valley State College*
Debbie Beard, *Southeast Missouri State University*
Sarah Bee, *Seattle University*
Stephen Benner, *Eastern Illinois University*

Ramesh C. Bhatia, *Millersville University*
Kristen Bigbee, *Texas Tech University*
Larry Bitner, *Hood College*
Jay Blazer, *Milwaukee Area Technical College*
Nancy Bledsoe, *Millsaps College*
William Blouch, *Loyola College*
Eugene Blue, *Governor State University*
Rick Blumenfeld, *Sierra Community College*
Linda Bolduc, *Mount Wachusett Community College*
William J. Bradberry, *New River Community and Technical College*
Casey Bradley, *Troy State University*
Jim Breyley, Jr., *University of New England*
Betty Jo Browning, *Bradley University*
Marley Brown, *Mt. Hood Community College*
Myra Bruegger, *Southeastern Community College*
Barry S. Buchoff, *Towson University*
Robert Burdette, *Salt Lake Community College*
Francis Bush, *Virginia Military Institute*
Rebecca Butler, *Gateway Community College*
Leah Cabaniss, *Holyoke Community College*
June Calahan, *Redlands Community College*
John Callister, *Cornell University*
Annhenrie Campbell, *California State University, Stanislaus*
David G. Campbell, *Sierra Community College*
Elizabeth Cannata, *Stonehill College*
Dennis Caplan, *Iowa State University*
Kay Carnes, *Gonzaga University*
Suzanne Cercone, *Keystone College*
Gayle Chaky, *Dutchess Community College*
John Chandler, *University of Illinois-Champaign*
Chiaho Chang, *Montclair State University*
Siew Chan, *University of Massachusetts, Boston*
Chak-Tong Chau, *University of Houston*
Julie Chenier, *Louisiana State University-Baton Rouge*
Lawrence Chin, *Golden Gate University*
Carolyn Clark, *St. Joseph's University*
Darlene Coarts, *University of Northern Iowa*
Jay Cohen, *Oakton Community College*
Joanne Collins, *California State University-Los Angeles*
Judith Cook, *Grossmont College*
Mark Cornman, *Youngstown State University*
Debra Cosgrove, *University Of Nebraska-Lincoln*
Charles Croxford, *Merced College*
Kathy Crusto-Way, *Tarrant County College*
Richard Cummings, *Benedictine College*
Jill Cunningham, *Santa Fe Community College*
Alan Czyzewski, *Indiana State University*
Paul E. Dascher, *Stetson University*
Betty David, *Francis Marion University*
Deborah Davis, *Hampton University*
Peggy Dejong, *Kirkwood Community College*
Sandra Devona, *Northern Illinois University*
G. DiLorenzo, *Gloucester County College*
Jan Duffy, *Iowa State University*
Keith Dusenbery, *Johnson State College*
Terry Elliott, *Morehead State University*
Robert S Ellison, *Texas State U–San Marcos*
Gene B. Elrod, *University of North Texas*
Emmanuel Emenyonu, *Southern Connecticut State University*
James Emig, *Villanova University*
Denise M. English, *Boise State University*
Martin L. Epstein, *Central New Mexico Community College*
Diane Eure, *Texas State University*
Michael Farina, *Cerritos College*
John Farlin, *Ohio Dominican University*

Amanda Farmer, *University of Georgia*
Harriet Farney, *University of Hartford*
M. A. Fekrat, *Georgetown University*
W. L. Ferrara, *Stetson University*
Jerry Ferry, *University of North Alabama*
Kathleen Fitzpatrick, *University of Toledo-Scott Park*
Benjamin Foster, *University of Louisville*
Joan Foster, *Collge Misericordia*
James Franklin, *Troy State University Montgomery*
Joseph Galante, *Millersville University of Pennsylvania*
Ananda Roop Ganguly, *Purdue University*
Frank Gersich, *Monmouth College*
David Gibson, *Hampden-Sydney College*
Jackson Gillespie, *University of Delaware*
Lisa Gillespie, *Loyola University-Chicago*
John Gill, *Jackson State University*
Joe Goetz, *Louisiana State University*
Art Goldman, *University of Kentucky*
David Gorton, *Eastern Washington University*
Suzanne Gradisher, *University Of Akron*
James Gravel, *Husson College*
Linda Hadley, *University of Dayton*
Joseph Hagan, *East Carolina University*
Laurie Hagberg, *Trident Technical College*
Ron Halsac, *Community College of Allegheny County*
Michael R. Hammond, *Missouri State University*
Heidi Hansel, *Kirkwood Community College*
Dan Hary, *Southwestern Oklahoma State University*
Susan Hass, *Simmons College*
Robert Hayes, *Tennessee State University*
Annette Hebble, *University of St. Thomas*
James Hendricks, *Northern Illinois University*
Sheri L. Henson, *Western Kentucky University*
Youngwon Her, *University of Missouri–St. Louis*
Nancy Thorley Hill, *DePaul University*
Joan Van Hise, *Fairfield University*
Mary Hollars, *Vincennes University*
Joan Hollister, *State University of New York–New Paltz*
Jay Holmen, *University of Wisconsin-Eau Claire*
Norma C. Holter, *Towson University*
Anita Hope, *Tarrant County College*
Kathy Ho, *Niagra University*
Tom Hrubec, *Franklin University*
Susan B Hughes, *University of Vermont*
Ronald Huntsman, *Texas Lutheran University*
Robert L. Hurt, *Cal Poly Pomona*
Wayne Ingalls, *University of Maine College*
David Jacobson, *Salem State College*
Martha Janis, *University of Wisconsin-Waukesha*
Robyn Dawn Jarnagin, *Montana State University*
Agatha E. Jeffers, *Montclair State University*
John Savash-*Elmira College*
Holly Johnston, *Boston University*
Sanford Kahn, *University of Cincinnati*
Jai S. Kang, *San Francisco State University*
Sushila Kedia, *University of Southern Indiana*
Debra Kerby, *Truman State University*
Marsha Kertz, *San Jose State University*
Raj Kiani, *California State University, Northridge*
Ethan Kinory, *Baruch College, CUNY*
Bonnie K. Klamm, *North Dakota State University*
Michael Klimesh, *Gustav Adolphus University*
Mehmet Kocakulah, *University of Southern Indiana*
Greg Kordecki, *Clayton College and State University*
Michael Kulper, *Santa Barbara City College*

Christoper Kwak, *Ohlone College*
Thomas Largay, *Thomas College*
Cathy Larson, *Middlesex Community College*
Robert Larson, *Penn State University*
Chor Lau, *California State University, Los Angeles*
Dan Law, *Gonzaga University*
Chuo-Hsuan Lee, *SUNY Plattsburgh*
Minwoo Lee, *Western Kentucky University*
Angela Letourneau, *Winthrop University*
Barry Lewis, *Southwest Missouri State University*
Roger P. Lewis, *Saint Cloud State University*
Harold T. Little Jr., *Western Kentucky University*
Joan Litton, *Ferrum College*
Rebecca Lohmann, *Southeast Missouri State University*
Dennis M. Lopez, *University of Texas-San Antonio*
G. D. Lorenzo, *Gloucester Community College*
Catherine Lumbattis, *Southern Illinois University-Carbondale*
Nace Magner, *Western Kentucky University*
Bob Mahan, *Milligan College*
Leland Mansuetti, *Sierra College*
Ariel Markelevich, *Bernard M. Baruch College*
Lisa Martin, *Western Michigan University*
Raj Mashruwala, *University of Illinois-Chicago*
Jayne Mass, *Towson University*
Allen Mcconnell, *University of Northern Colorado*
Britton A McKay, *Georgia Southern University*
Dawn McKinley, *William Rainey Harper College*
Laurie B. McWhorter, *Mississippi State University*
Michael J. Meyer, *Ohio University*
Pam Meyer, *University of Louisiana at Lafayette*
Lorie Milam, *University of Northern Colorado*
Robert Milbrath, *University of Houston*
Valerie Milliron, *California State University, Chico*
Earl Mitchell, *Santa Ana College*
Arabian Morgan, *Orange Coast College*
Laura Morgan, *University of New Hampshire*
Anthony Moses, *Saint Anselm College*
Daniel Mugavero, *Lake Superior State University*
Matthew Muller, *Adirondack Community College*
Muroki Mwaura, *William Patterson University*
Presha Neidermeyer, *Union College*
Joseph M. Nicassio, *Westmoreland County Community College*
Lee Nicholas, *University of Northern Iowa*
Tracie Nobles, *Austin Community College-Northridge*
Eizabeth Nolan, *Southwestern Oklahoma State University*
Michael O'Neill, *Seattle Central Community College*
Omneya Abd-Elsalam, *Aston University*
Aileen Ormiston, *Mesa Community College*
George Otto, *Truman College*
Chei Paik, *George Washington University*
Abbie Gail Parham, *Georgia Southern University*
George Scott Pate, *Robeson Community College*
Paige Paulsen, *Salt Lake Community College*
Nori Pearson, *Washington State University*
Tamara Phelan, *Northern Illinois University*
Eustace Phillip, *Emmanuel College*
Anthony Piltz, *Rocky Mountain College*
H. M. Pomroy, *Elizabethtown College*
Alan Porter, *Eastern New Mexico University*
Barbara Prince, *Cambridge Community College*
Grant Pritchard, *Dominican University of California*

Ahmad Rahman, *La Roche College*
Vasant Raval, *Creighton University–Omaha*
Ronald Reed, *University of Northern Colorado*
Joan Reicosky, *University of Minnesota-Morris*
Jacci Rodgers, *Oklahoma City University*
Leonardo Rodriguez, *Florida International University*
Rick Roscher, *University of North Carolina-Wilmington*
Gary Ross, *College of the Southwest*
Luther Ross, *Central Piedmont Community College*
Anwar Salimi, *California State Polytechnic University-Pomona*
Martha Sampsell, *Elmhurst College*
Angela H. Sandberg, *Jacksonville State University*
Eldon Schafer, *University of Arizona*
Roger Scherser, *Edison Community College*
Henry Schulman, *Grossmont College*
Henry Schwarzbach, *University of Colorado*
Randall Serrett, *University of Houston Downtown*
Deborah Shafer, *Temple College*
Meghna Singhvi, *Florida International University*
Michael Skaff, *College of the Sequoias*
Henry C. Smith, III, *Otterbein College*
Ola Smith, *Michigan State University*
John Snyder, *Florida Technical*
Soliman Soliman, *Tulane University*
Patrick Stegman, *College of Lake County*
Alice Steljes, *Illinois Valley Community College*
Michael Stemkoski, *Utah Valley University Orem*
Dean Steria, *SUNY Plattsburgh*
Jane Stoneback, *Central Connecticut State University*
Jacqueline Stoute, *Baruch College, CUNY*
Arlene Strawn, *Tallahassee Community College*
Gloria Stuart, *Georgia Southern University*
Steve Swirsky, *Florida A&M University*
Frances Talavera, *California State University, San Marcos*
Diane Tanner, *University of North Florida*
Linda Tarrago, *Hillsborough Community College*
Joseph Ugras, *LaSalle University*
Leslie Vaughan, *University of Missouri-St. Louis*
Donna Viens, *Johnson & Wales University*
John M. Virchick, *Chapman University*
Edward Walker, *University of Texas-Pan American*
Frank Walker, *Lee College*
Sharon Walters, *Morehead State University*
Joseph Weintrop, *Baruch College*
James Weisel, *Georgia Gwinnett College*
Robert Weprin, *Lourdes College*
Clark Wheatley, *FLorida International University-Miami*
Janice White, *Kalamazoo Valley Community College*
Scott White, *Lindenwood University*
Brent Wickham, *Owens Community College*
Jane G. Wiese, *Valencia Community College*
George Williams, *Bergen Community College*
Lansing Williams, *Washington College*
Geri Wink, *University of Texas at Tyler*
James Wolfson, *Wilson College*
Lianzan Xu, *William Paterson University of New Jersey*
Weihong Xu, *State University of New York at Buffalo*
William Zahurak, *Community College of Allegheny County, Allegheny*
Judith Zander, *Grossmont College*
Mary Zenner, *College of Lake County*
Ronald Zhao, *Monmouth University*

# BRIEF CONTENTS

# CONTENTS

**CHAPTER SIX   216**

# Cost-Volume-Profit Relationships   216

**CHAPTER SEVEN   280**

# Variable Costing and Segment Reporting: Tools for Management   280

**A LOOK AT THE PROLOGUE**

The Prologue defines managerial accounting and explains why it is important to the future careers of all business students. It also explains how managerial accounting involves more than just quantitative calculations.

**A LOOK AHEAD**

Chapter 1 defines many of the cost terms that will be used throughout the textbook. It explains that in managerial accounting the term cost is used in many different ways depending on the immediate needs of management.

# Managerial Accounting: An Overview

PROLOGUE

## PROLOGUE OUTLINE

**What Is Managerial Accounting?**

- Planning
- Controlling
- Decision Making

**Why Does Managerial Accounting Matter to Your Career?**

- Business Majors
- Accounting Majors

**Managerial Accounting: Beyond the Numbers**

- An Ethics Perspective
- A Strategic Management Perspective
- An Enterprise Risk Management Perspective
- A Corporate Social Responsibility Perspective
- A Process Management Perspective
- A Leadership Perspective

The prologue explains why managerial accounting is important to the future careers of all business students. It begins by answering two questions: (1) What is managerial accounting? and (2) Why does managerial accounting matter to your career? It concludes by discussing six topics—ethics, strategic management, enterprise risk management, corporate social responsibility, process management, and leadership—that define the business context for applying the quantitative aspects of managerial accounting.

## WHAT IS MANAGERIAL ACCOUNTING?

Many students enrolled in this course will have recently completed an introductory *financial accounting* course. **Financial accounting** is concerned with reporting financial information to external parties, such as stockholders, creditors, and regulators. **Managerial accounting** is concerned with providing information to managers for use within the organization. Exhibit P–1 summarizes seven key differences between financial and managerial accounting. It recognizes that the fundamental difference between financial and managerial accounting is that financial accounting serves the needs of those

**EXHIBIT P–1**    Comparison of Financial and Managerial Accounting

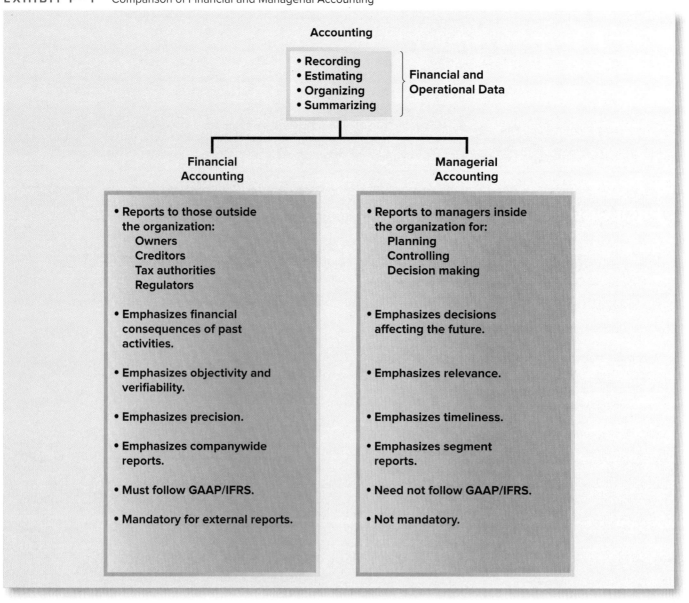

*outside* the organization, whereas managerial accounting serves the needs of managers employed *inside* the organization. Because of this fundamental difference in users, financial accounting emphasizes the financial consequences of past activities, objectivity and verifiability, precision, and companywide performance, whereas managerial accounting emphasizes decisions affecting the future, relevance, timeliness, and *segment* performance. A **segment** is a part or activity of an organization about which managers would like cost, revenue, or profit data. Examples of business segments include product lines, customer groups (segmented by age, ethnicity, gender, volume of purchases, etc.), geographic territories, divisions, plants, and departments. Finally, financial accounting is mandatory for external reports and it needs to comply with rules, such as generally accepted accounting principles (GAAP) and international financial reporting standards (IFRS), whereas managerial accounting is not mandatory and it does not need to comply with externally imposed rules.

As mentioned in Exhibit P–1, managerial accounting helps managers perform three vital activities—*planning, controlling,* and *decision making.* **Planning** involves establishing goals and specifying how to achieve them. **Controlling** involves gathering feedback to ensure that the plan is being properly executed or modified as circumstances change. **Decision making** involves selecting a course of action from competing alternatives. Now let's take a closer look at these three pillars of managerial accounting.

## Planning

Assume that you work for **Procter & Gamble (P&G)** and that you are in charge of the company's campus recruiting for all undergraduate business majors. In this example, your planning process would begin by establishing a goal such as: our goal is to recruit the "best and brightest" college graduates. The next stage of the planning process would require specifying how to achieve this goal by answering numerous questions such as:

- How many students do we need to hire in total and from each major?
- What schools do we plan to include in our recruiting efforts?
- Which of our employees will be involved in each school's recruiting activities?
- When will we conduct our interviews?
- How will we compare students to one another to decide who will be extended job offers?
- What salary will we offer our new hires? Will the salaries differ by major?
- How much money can we spend on our recruiting efforts?

### The Financial Side of Running a Community Theatre          IN BUSINESS

Formulating plans and creating budgets is an important part of running a community theater. For example, the **Manatee Players** is a theater group from Bradenton, Florida, that has seen its annual operating budget grow from $480,000 to $1.5 million over the last 10 years. The theater's ticket sales cover about 77% of its operating costs, with additional financial support coming from individual and corporate donors.

In addition to managing its revenues, the theater also seeks to control its costs in various ways—such as saving $3,000 per year by bringing the production of its programs in-house. Rather than promoting individual shows, the group has decided to focus its marketing dollars on touting the entire season of shows. It also shifted a portion of its marketing budget away from traditional methods to more cost-effective social-media outlets.

Source: Brass, Kevin, "Let's Put on a Show," *The Wall Street Journal,* November 3, 2014, p. D7.

©McGraw-Hill Education/Christopher Kerrigan, photographer

As you can see, there are many questions that need to be answered as part of the planning process. Plans are often accompanied by a *budget.* A **budget** is a detailed plan for the future that is usually expressed in formal quantitative terms. As the head of recruiting at P&G, your budget would include two key components. First, you would have to work with other senior managers inside the company to establish a budgeted amount of total salaries that can be offered to all new hires. Second, you would have to create a budget that quantifies how much you intend to spend on your campus recruiting activities.

## Controlling

Once you established and started implementing P&G's recruiting plan, you would transition to the control process. This process would involve gathering, evaluating, and responding to feedback to ensure that this year's recruiting process meets expectations. It would also include evaluating the feedback in search of ways to run a more effective recruiting campaign next year. The control process would involve answering questions such as:

- Did we succeed in hiring the planned number of students within each major and at each school?
- Did we lose too many exceptional candidates to competitors?
- Did each of our employees involved in the recruiting process perform satisfactorily?
- Is our method of comparing students to one another working?
- Did the on-campus and office interviews run smoothly?
- Did we stay within our budget in terms of total salary commitments to new hires?
- Did we stay within our budget regarding spending on recruiting activities?

As you can see, there are many questions that need to be answered as part of the control process. When answering these questions your goal would be to go beyond simple yes or no answers in search of the underlying reasons why performance exceeded or failed to meet expectations. Part of the control process includes preparing *performance reports.* A **performance report** compares budgeted data to actual data in an effort to identify and learn from excellent performance and to identify and eliminate sources of unsatisfactory performance. Performance reports can also be used as one of many inputs to help evaluate and reward employees.

Although this example focused on P&G's campus recruiting efforts, we could have described how planning enables **FedEx** to deliver packages across the globe overnight, or how it helped **Apple** develop and market the iPad. We could have discussed how the control process helps **Pfizer**, **Eli Lilly**, and **Abbott Laboratories** ensure that their pharmaceutical drugs are produced in conformance with rigorous quality standards, or how **Kroger** relies on the control process to keep its grocery shelves stocked. We also could have looked at planning and control failures such as **Takata**'s recall of more than 30 million defective driver-side air bags installed by a variety of automakers such as **Honda, Ford, Toyota**, and **Subaru**. In short, all managers (and that probably includes you someday) perform planning and controlling activities.

## Decision Making

Perhaps the most basic managerial skill is the ability to make intelligent, data-driven decisions. Broadly speaking, many of those decisions revolve around the following three questions. *What* should we be selling? *Who* should we be serving? *How* should we execute? Exhibit P–2 provides examples of decisions pertaining to each of these three categories.

The left-hand column of Exhibit P–2 suggests that every company must make decisions related to the products and services that it sells. For example, each year **Procter & Gamble** must decide how to allocate its marketing budget across numerous brands that each generates over $1 billion in sales as well as other brands that have promising growth potential. **Mattel** must decide what new toys to introduce to the market. **Southwest Airlines** must

**EXHIBIT P–2**   Examples of Decisions

| What should we be selling? | Who should we be serving? | How should we execute? |
|---|---|---|
| What products and services should be the focus of our marketing efforts? | Who should be the focus of our marketing efforts? | How should we supply our parts and services? |
| What new products and services should we offer? | Who should we start serving? | How should we expand our capacity? |
| What prices should we charge for our products and services? | Who should pay price premiums or receive price discounts? | How should we reduce our capacity? |
| What products and services should we discontinue? | Who should we stop serving? | How should we improve our efficiency and effectiveness? |

decide what ticket prices to establish for each of its thousands of flights per day. **General Motors** must decide whether to discontinue certain models of automobiles.

The middle column of Exhibit P–2 indicates that all companies must make decisions related to the customers that they serve. For example, **Sears** must decide how to allocate its marketing budget between products that tend to appeal to male versus female customers. **FedEx** must decide whether to expand its services into new markets across the globe. **Hewlett-Packard** must decide what price discounts to offer corporate clients that purchase large volumes of its products. A bank must decide whether to discontinue customers that may be unprofitable.

The right-hand column of Exhibit P–2 shows that companies also make decisions related to how they execute. For example, **Boeing** must decide whether to rely on outside vendors such as **Goodrich**, **Saab**, and **Rolls-Royce** to manufacture many of the parts used to make its airplanes. **Cintas** must decide whether to expand its laundering and cleaning capacity in a given geographic region by adding square footage to an existing facility or by constructing an entirely new facility. In an economic downturn, a manufacturer might have to decide whether to eliminate one 8-hour shift at three plants or to close one plant. Finally, all companies have to decide among competing improvement opportunities. For example, a company may have to decide whether to implement a new software system, to upgrade a piece of equipment, or to provide extra training to its employees.

This portion of the prologue has explained that the three pillars of managerial accounting are planning, controlling, and decision making. This book helps prepare you to become an effective manager by explaining how to make intelligent data-driven decisions, how to create financial plans for the future, and how to continually make progress toward achieving goals by obtaining, evaluating, and responding to feedback.

## WHY DOES MANAGERIAL ACCOUNTING MATTER TO YOUR CAREER?

Many students feel anxious about choosing a major because they are unsure if it will provide a fulfilling career. To reduce these anxieties, we recommend deemphasizing what you cannot control about the future; instead focusing on what you can control right now. More specifically, concentrate on answering the following question: What can you do now to prepare for success in an unknown future career? The best answer is to learn skills that will make it easier for you to adapt to an uncertain future. You need to become adaptable!

Whether you end up working in the United States or abroad, for a large corporation, a small entrepreneurial company, a nonprofit organization, or a governmental entity, you'll need to know how to plan for the future, how to make progress toward achieving goals, and how to make intelligent decisions. In other words, managerial accounting skills are useful in just about any career, organization, and industry. If you commit energy to this course, you'll be making a smart investment in your future—even though you cannot clearly envision it. Next, we will elaborate on this point by explaining how managerial accounting relates to the future careers of business majors and accounting majors.

**EXHIBIT P–3**    Relating Managerial Accounting to Three Business Majors

| | Marketing | Supply Chain Management | Human Resource Management |
|---|---|---|---|
| Planning | How much should we budget for TV, print, and Internet advertising? | How many units should we plan to produce next period? | How much should we plan to spend for occupational safety training? |
| | How many salespeople should we plan to hire to serve a new territory? | How much should we budget for next period's utility expense? | How much should we plan to spend on employee recruitment advertising? |
| Controlling | Is the budgeted price cut increasing unit sales as expected? | Did we spend more or less than expected for the units we actually produced? | Is our employee retention rate exceeding our goals? |
| | Are we accumulating too much inventory during the holiday shopping season? | Are we achieving our goal of reducing the number of defective units produced? | Are we meeting our goal of completing timely performance appraisals? |
| Decision Making | Should we sell our services as one bundle or sell them separately? | Should we transfer production of a component part to an overseas supplier? | Should we hire an on-site medical staff to lower our health care costs? |
| | Should we sell directly to customers or use a distributor? | Should we redesign our manufacturing process to lower inventory levels? | Should we hire temporary workers or full-time employees? |

## Business Majors

Exhibit P–3 provides examples of how planning, controlling, and decision making affect three majors other than accounting—marketing, supply chain management, and human resource management.

The left-hand column of Exhibit P–3 describes some planning, controlling, and decision-making applications in the marketing profession. For example, marketing managers make planning decisions related to allocating advertising dollars across various communication mediums and to staffing new sales territories. From a control standpoint, they may closely track sales data to see if a budgeted price cut is generating an anticipated increase in unit sales, or they may study inventory levels during the holiday shopping season so that they can adjust prices as needed to optimize sales. Marketing managers also make many important decisions such as whether to bundle services together and sell them for one price or to sell each service separately. They may also decide whether to sell products directly to the customer or to sell to a distributor, who then sells to the end consumer.

The middle column of Exhibit P–3 states that supply chain managers have to plan how many units to produce to satisfy anticipated customer demand. They also need to budget for operating expenses such as utilities, supplies, and labor costs. In terms of control, they monitor actual spending relative to the budget and closely watch operational measures, such as the number of defects produced relative to the plan. Supply chain managers make numerous decisions, such as deciding whether to transfer production of a component part to an overseas supplier. They also decide whether to invest in redesigning a manufacturing process to reduce inventory levels.

The right-hand column of Exhibit P–3 explains how human resource managers make a variety of planning decisions, such as budgeting how much to spend on occupational safety training and employee recruitment advertising. They monitor feedback related to numerous management concerns, such as employee retention rates and the timely completion of employee performance appraisals. They also help make many important decisions such as whether to hire on-site medical staff in an effort to lower health care costs, and whether to hire temporary workers or full-time employees in an uncertain economy.

For brevity, Exhibit P–3 does not include all business majors, such as finance, management information systems, and economics. Can you explain how planning, controlling, and decision-making activities would relate to these majors?

## Accounting Majors

Many accounting graduates begin their careers working for public accounting firms that provide a variety of valuable services for their clients. Some of these graduates will build successful and fulfilling careers in the public accounting industry; however, most will leave public accounting at some point to work in other organizations. In fact, the **Institute of Management Accountants** (IMA) estimates that more than 80% of professional accountants in the United States work in nonpublic accounting environments (www.imanet.org).

The public accounting profession has a strong financial accounting orientation. Its most important function is to protect investors and other external parties by assuring them that companies are reporting historical financial results that comply with applicable accounting rules. Managerial accountants also have strong financial accounting skills. For example, they play an important role in helping their organizations design and maintain financial reporting systems that generate reliable financial disclosures. However, the primary role of managerial accountants is to partner with their coworkers within the organization to improve performance.

Given the 80% figure mentioned above, if you are an accounting major there is a very high likelihood that your future will involve working for a nonpublic accounting employer. Your employer will expect you to have strong financial accounting skills, but more importantly, it will expect you to help improve organizational performance by applying the planning, controlling, and decision-making skills that are the foundation of managerial accounting.

### Professional Certification—A Smart Investment

If you plan to become an accounting major, the Certified Management Accountant (CMA) and Chartered Global Management Accountant (CGMA) designations are globally respected credentials that will increase your credibility, upward mobility, and compensation.

The CMA exam is sponsored by the Institute of Management Accountants (IMA) in Montvale, New Jersey. To become a CMA requires membership in the IMA, a bachelor's degree from an accredited college or university, two continuous years of relevant professional experience, and passage of the CMA exam. Exhibit P–4 summarizes the topics covered in the IMA's two-part CMA exam. For brevity, we are not going to define all the terms included in this exhibit. Its purpose is simply to emphasize that the CMA exam focuses on the planning, controlling, and decision-making skills that are critically

## A Networking Opportunity                                    IN BUSINESS

The **Institute of Management Accountants** (IMA) is a network of more than 70,000 accounting and finance professionals from over 120 countries. Every year the IMA hosts a student leadership conference that attracts 300 students from over 50 colleges and universities. Guest speakers at past conferences have discussed topics such as leadership, advice for a successful career, how to market yourself in a difficult economy, and excelling in today's multigenerational workforce. One student who attended the conference said, "I liked that I was able to interact with professionals who are in fields that could be potential career paths for me." For more information on this worthwhile networking opportunity, contact the IMA at the phone number and website shown below.

Source: Conversation with Jodi Ryan, the Institute of Management Accountants' Director, Education/Corporate Partnerships. (201) 474-1556 or visit its website at www.imanet.org.

**EXHIBIT P–4**  CMA Exam
Content Specifications

| | |
|---|---|
| Part 1 | *Financial Reporting, Planning, Performance and Control* |
| | External financial reporting decisions |
| | Planning, budgeting, and forecasting |
| | Performance management |
| | Cost management |
| | Internal controls |
| Part 2 | *Financial Decision Making* |
| | Financial statement analysis |
| | Corporate finance |
| | Decision analysis |
| | Risk management |
| | Investment decisions |
| | Professional ethics |

important to all managers. Information about becoming a CMA is available on the IMA's website (www.imanet.org) or by calling 1-800-638-4427.

The CGMA designaton is co-sponsored by the **American Institute of Certified Public Accountants** (AICPA) and the **Chartered Institute of Management Accountants** (CIMA), each of whom provides a distinct pathway to becoming a CGMA. The AICPA pathway requires a bachelor's degree in accounting (accompanied by a total of 150 college credit-hours), passage of the Certified Public Accountant (CPA) exam, membership in the AICPA, three years of relevant management accounting work experience, and passage of the CGMA exam—which is a case-based exam that focuses on technical skills, business skills, leadership skills, people skills, and ethics, integrity, and professionalism. Notice that the AICPA's pathway to becoming a CGMA requires passage of the multipart CPA exam, which emphasizes rule-based compliance—assurance standards, financial accounting standards, business law, and the tax code. Information on becoming a CGMA is available at www.cgma.org.

## IN BUSINESS

## How's the Pay?

The **Institute of Management Accountants** has created the following table that allows individuals to estimate what their salary would be as a management accountant.

| | | | Your Calculation |
|---|---|---|---|
| Start with this base amount . . . . . . . . . . . . . . . . . . . . . | | $48,990 | $48,990 |
| If you are top-level management . . . . . . . . . . . . . . . . | ADD | $58,043 | |
| OR, if you are senior-level management . . . . . . . . . . . | ADD | $35,855 | |
| OR, if you are middle-level management . . . . . . . . . . | ADD | $15,086 | |
| Number of years in the field _____ . . . . . . . . . . . . . | TIMES | $905 | |
| If you have an advanced degree . . . . . . . . . . . . . . . . | ADD | $14,509 | |
| If you hold the CMA . . . . . . . . . . . . . . . . . . . . . . . . . . | ADD | $15,308 | |
| If you hold the CPA . . . . . . . . . . . . . . . . . . . . . . . . . . . | ADD | $14,509 | |
| Your estimated salary level . . . . . . . . . . . . . . . . . . . . . | | | |

For example, if you make it to top-level management in 10 years, have an advanced degree and a CMA, your estimated salary would be $145,900 [$48,990 + $58,043 + (10 × $905) + $14,509 + $15,308].

Source: Krumweide, Kip, "IMA's Global Salary Survey," *Strategic Finance*, March 2017, pp. 29–39.

# MANAGERIAL ACCOUNTING: BEYOND THE NUMBERS

Exhibit P–5 summarizes how each chapter of the book teaches measurement skills that managers use on the job every day. For example, Chapter 8 teaches you the measurement skills that managers use to answer the question—how should I create a financial plan for next year? Chapter 9 teaches you the measurement skills that managers use to answer the question—how well am I performing relative to my plan? Chapter 4 teaches you measurement skills related to product and customer profitability. However, it is vitally important that you also understand managerial accounting involves more than just "crunching numbers." To be successful, managers must complement their measurement skills with six business management perspectives that "go beyond the numbers" to enable intelligent planning, control, and decision making.

| Chapter Number | The Key Question from a Manager's Perspective |
|---|---|
| Chapter 1 | What cost classifications do I use for different management purposes? |
| Chapter 2 | How much does it cost us to manufacture customized jobs for each of our customers? |
| Chapters 3 & 5 | What is the value of our ending inventory and cost of goods sold for external reporting purposes? |
| Chapter 4 | How profitable is each of our products and customers? |
| Chapter 6 | How will my profits change if I change my selling price, sales volume, or costs? |
| Chapter 7 | How should the income statement be presented? |
| Chapter 8 | How should I create a financial plan for next year? |
| Chapter 9 | How well am I performing relative to my plan? |
| Chapter 10 | What performance measures should we monitor to ensure that we achieve our strategic goals? |
| Chapter 11 | How do I quantify the financial impact of pursuing one course of action versus another? |
| Chapter 12 | How do I make long-term capital investment decisions? |
| Chapter 13 | What cash inflows and outflows explain the change in our cash balance? |
| Chapter 14 | How can we analyze our financial statements to better understand our performance? |

**EXHIBIT P–5**
Measurement Skills: A Manager's Perspective

## An Ethics Perspective

Ethical behavior is the lubricant that keeps the economy running. Without that lubricant, the economy would operate much less efficiently—less would be available to consumers, quality would be lower, and prices would be higher. In other words, without fundamental trust in the integrity of business, the economy would operate much less efficiently. Thus, for the good of everyone—including profit-making companies—it is vitally important that business be conducted within an ethical framework that builds and sustains trust.

**Code of Conduct for Management Accountants**    The **Institute of Management Accountants** (IMA) of the United States has adopted an ethical code called the *Statement of Ethical Professional Practice* that describes in some detail the ethical responsibilities of management accountants. Even though the standards were developed specifically for management accountants, they have much broader application. The standards consist of two parts that are presented in full in Exhibit P–6. The first part provides general guidelines

**EXHIBIT P–6**     Institute of Management Accountants (IMA) Statement of Ethical Professional Practice

Members of IMA shall behave ethically. A commitment to ethical professional practice includes: overarching principles that express our values and standards that guide our conduct.

### PRINCIPLES

IMA's overarching ethical principles include: Honesty, Fairness, Objectivity, and Responsibility. Members shall act in accordance with these principles and shall encourage others within their organizations to adhere to them.

### STANDARDS

A member's failure to comply with the following standards may result in disciplinary action.

#### I. COMPETENCE

Each member has a responsibility to:
1. Maintain an appropriate level of professional expertise by continually developing knowledge and skills.
2. Perform professional duties in accordance with relevant laws, regulations, and technical standards.
3. Provide decision support information and recommendations that are accurate, clear, concise, and timely.
4. Recognize and communicate professional limitations or other constraints that would preclude responsible judgment or successful performance of an activity.

#### II. CONFIDENTIALITY

Each member has a responsibility to:
1. Keep information confidential except when disclosure is authorized or legally required.
2. Inform all relevant parties regarding appropriate use of confidential information. Monitor subordinates' activities to ensure compliance.
3. Refrain from using confidential information for unethical or illegal advantage.

#### III. INTEGRITY

Each member has a responsibility to:
1. Mitigate actual conflicts of interest. Regularly communicate with business associates to avoid apparent conflicts of interest. Advise all parties of any potential conflicts.
2. Refrain from engaging in any conduct that would prejudice carrying out duties ethically.
3. Abstain from engaging in or supporting any activity that might discredit the profession.

#### IV. CREDIBILITY

Each member has a responsibility to:
1. Communicate information fairly and objectively.
2. Disclose all relevant information that could reasonably be expected to influence an intended user's understanding of the reports, analyses, or recommendations.
3. Disclose delays or deficiencies in information, timeliness, processing, or internal controls in conformance with organization policy and/or applicable law.

### RESOLUTION OF ETHICAL CONFLICT

In applying the Standards of Ethical Professional Practice, you may encounter problems identifying unethical behavior or resolving an ethical conflict. When faced with ethical issues, you should follow your organization's established policies on the resolution of such conflict. If these policies do not resolve the ethical conflict, you should consider the following courses of action:

1. Discuss the issue with your immediate supervisor except when it appears that the supervisor is involved. In that case, present the issue to the next level. If you cannot achieve a satisfactory resolution, submit the issue to the next management level. If your immediate superior is the chief executive officer or equivalent, the acceptable reviewing authority may be a group such as the audit committee, executive committee, board of directors, board of trustees, or owners. Contact with levels above the immediate superior should be initiated only with your superior's knowledge, assuming he or she is not involved. Communication of such problems to authorities or individuals not employed or engaged by the organization is not considered appropriate, unless you believe there is a clear violation of the law.
2. Clarify relevant ethical issues by initiating a confidential discussion with an IMA Ethics Counselor or other impartial advisor to obtain a better understanding of possible courses of action.
3. Consult your own attorney as to legal obligations and rights concerning the ethical conflict.

for ethical behavior. In a nutshell, a management accountant has ethical responsibilities in four broad areas: first, to maintain a high level of professional competence; second, to treat sensitive matters with confidentiality; third, to maintain personal integrity; and fourth, to disclose information in a credible fashion. The second part of the standards specifies what should be done if an individual finds evidence of ethical misconduct.

The ethical standards provide sound, practical advice for management accountants and managers. Most of the rules in the ethical standards are motivated by a very practical consideration—if these rules were not generally followed in business, then the economy and all of us would suffer. Consider the following specific examples of the consequences of not abiding by the standards:

- Suppose employees could not be trusted with confidential information. Then top managers would be reluctant to distribute such information within the company and, as a result, decisions would be based on incomplete information and operations would deteriorate.

- Suppose employees accepted bribes from suppliers. Then contracts would tend to go to the suppliers who pay the highest bribes rather than to the most competent suppliers. Would you like to fly in aircraft whose wings were made by the subcontractor who paid the highest bribe? Would you fly as often? What would happen to the airline industry if its safety record deteriorated due to shoddy workmanship on contracted parts and subassemblies?

- Suppose the presidents of companies routinely lied in their annual reports and financial statements. If investors could not rely on the basic integrity of a company's financial statements, they would have little basis for making informed decisions. Suspecting the worst, rational investors would pay less for securities issued by companies and may not be willing to invest at all. As a consequence, companies would have less money for productive investments—leading to slower economic growth, fewer goods and services, and higher prices.

Not only is ethical behavior the lubricant for our economy, it is the foundation of managerial accounting. The numbers that managers rely on for planning, controlling, and decision making are meaningless unless they have been competently, objectively, and honestly gathered, analyzed, and reported. As your career unfolds, you will inevitably face decisions with ethical implications. Before making such decisions, consider performing the following steps. First, define your alternative courses of action. Second, identify all of the parties that will be affected by your decision. Third, define how each course of action will favorably or unfavorably impact each affected party. Once you have a complete understanding of the decision context, seek guidance from external sources such as the IMA Statement of Ethical Professional Practice (see Exhibit P–6), the IMA Ethics Helpline at (800) 245-1383, or a trusted confidant. Before executing your decision ask yourself one final question—would I be comfortable disclosing my chosen course of action on the front page of *The Wall Street Journal?*

## A Strategic Management Perspective

Companies do not succeed by sheer luck; instead, they need to develop a *strategy* that defines how they intend to succeed in the marketplace. A **strategy** is a "game plan" that enables a company to attract customers by distinguishing itself from competitors. The focal point of a company's strategy should be its target customers. A company can only succeed if it creates a reason for its target customers to choose it over a competitor. These reasons, or what are more formally called *customer value propositions,* are the essence of strategy.

Customer value propositions tend to fall into three broad categories—*customer intimacy, operational excellence,* and *product leadership.* Companies that adopt a *customer intimacy* strategy are in essence saying to their customers, "You should choose us because we can customize our products and services to meet your individual needs better than our competitors." **Ritz-Carlton, Nordstrom,** and **Virtuoso** (a premium service travel agency) rely primarily on a customer intimacy value proposition for their success. Companies that pursue the second customer value proposition, called *operational excellence,* are saying to their target customers, "You should choose us because we deliver products and services faster, more conveniently, and at a lower price than our competitors." **Southwest Airlines, Walmart**, and **Google** are examples of companies that succeed first and foremost because of their operational excellence. Companies pursuing the third customer value proposition, called *product leadership,* are saying to their target customers, "You should choose us because we offer higher quality products than our competitors." **Apple, Cisco Systems**, and **W.L. Gore** (the creator of GORE-TEX® fabrics) are examples of companies that succeed because of their product leadership.[1]

The plans managers set forth, the variables they seek to control, and the decisions they make are all influenced by their company's strategy. For example, Walmart would not make plans to build ultraexpensive clothing boutiques because these plans would conflict with the company's strategy of operational excellence and "everyday low prices." Apple would not seek to control its operations by selecting performance measures that focus solely on cost-cutting because those measures would conflict with its product leadership customer value proposition. Finally, it is unlikely that **Rolex** would decide to implement drastic price reductions for its watches even if a financial analysis indicated that establishing a lower price might boost short-run profits. Rolex would oppose this course of action because it would diminish the luxury brand that forms the foundation of the company's product leadership customer value proposition.

## An Enterprise Risk Management Perspective

Every strategy, plan, and decision involves risks. **Enterprise risk management** is a process used by a company to identify those risks and develop responses to them that enable it to be reasonably assured of meeting its goals. The left-hand column of Exhibit P–7 provides 10 examples of the types of business risks that companies face. They range from risks that relate to the weather to risks associated with computer hackers, complying with the law, supplier strikes, and products harming customers. The right-hand column of Exhibit P–7 provides an example of a control that could be implemented to help reduce each of the risks mentioned in the left-hand column of the exhibit.[2] Although these types of controls cannot completely eliminate risks, they enable companies to proactively manage their risks rather than passively reacting to unfortunate events that have already occurred.

In managerial accounting, companies use controls to reduce the risk that their plans will not be achieved. For example, if a company plans to build a new manufacturing facility within a predefined budget and time frame, it will establish and monitor control measures to ensure that the project is concluded on time and within the budget. Risk management is also a critically important aspect of decision making. For example, when a company quantifies the labor cost savings that it can realize by sending jobs overseas, it should complement its financial analysis with a prudent assessment of the accompanying risks. Will the overseas manufacturer use child labor? Will the product's quality decline, thereby leading to more warranty repairs, customer complaints, and lawsuits? Will the elapsed time from customer order to delivery dramatically increase? Will terminating domestic employees diminish morale within the company and harm perceptions within the community? These are the types of risks that managers should incorporate into their decision-making processes.

---

[1]These three customer value propositions were defined by Michael Treacy and Fred Wiersema in "Customer Intimacy and Other Value Disciplines," *Harvard Business Review,* Volume 71 Issue 1, pp. 84–93.
[2]Besides using controls to reduce risks, companies can also choose other risk responses, such as accepting or avoiding a risk.

EXHIBIT P–7
Identifying and Controlling
Business Risks

| Examples of Business Risks | Examples of Controls to Reduce Business Risks |
|---|---|
| Intellectual assets being stolen from computer files | Create firewalls that prohibit computer hackers from corrupting or stealing intellectual property |
| Products harming customers | Develop a formal and rigorous new product testing program |
| Losing market share due to the unforeseen actions of competitors | Develop an approach for legally gathering information about competitors' plans and practices |
| Poor weather conditions shutting down operations | Develop contingency plans for overcoming weather-related disruptions |
| A website malfunctioning | Thoroughly test the website before going "live" on the Internet |
| A supplier strike halting the flow of raw materials | Establish a relationship with two companies capable of providing needed raw materials |
| A poorly designed incentive compensation system causing employees to make bad decisions | Create a balanced set of performance measures that motivates the desired behavior |
| Poor environmental stewardship causing reputational and financial damage | Create a reporting system that tracks key environmental performance indicators |
| Inaccurate budget estimates causing excessive or insufficient production | Implement a rigorous budget review process |
| Failing to comply with equal employment opportunity laws | Create a report that tracks key metrics related to compliance with the laws |

Companies also use controls in financial accounting to safeguard assets and minimize the risk of financial reporting errors. Exhibit P–8 describes seven types of controls that companies use to safeguard their assets and to reduce their financial reporting risks. Each item in the exhibit is labeled as a *preventive control* and/or a *detective control*. A **preventive control** deters undesirable events from occurring. A **detective control** detects undesirable events that have already occurred.

EXHIBIT P–8
Types of Internal Controls for
Financial Reporting

| Type of Control | Classification | Description |
|---|---|---|
| Authorizations | Preventive | Requiring management to formally approve certain types of transactions. |
| Reconciliations | Detective | Relating data sets to one another to identify and resolve discrepancies. |
| Segregation of duties | Preventive | Separating responsibilities related to authorizing transactions, recording transactions, and maintaining custody of the related assets. |
| Physical safeguards | Preventive | Using cameras, locks, and physical barriers to protect assets. |
| Performance reviews | Detective | Comparing actual performance to various benchmarks to identify unexpected results. |
| Maintaining records | Detective | Maintaining written and/or electronic evidence to support transactions. |
| Information systems security | Preventive/ Detective | Using controls such as passwords and access logs to ensure appropriate data restrictions. |

As shown in Exhibit P–8, requiring *authorizations* for certain types of transactions is a preventive control. For example, companies frequently require that a specific senior manager sign all checks above a particular dollar amount to reduce the risk of an inappropriate cash disbursement. *Reconciliations* are a detective control. If you have ever compared a bank statement to your checkbook to resolve any discrepancies, then you have performed a type of reconciliation known as a bank reconciliation. This is a detective control because you are seeking to identify any mistakes already made by the bank or existing mistakes in your own records. Another type of reconciliation occurs when a company performs a physical count of its inventory. The value of the physical inventory on hand is compared to the accounting records so that any discrepancies can be identified and resolved.

Exhibit P–8 also mentions *segregation of duties,* which is a preventive control that separates responsibilities for authorizing transactions, recording transactions, and maintaining custody of the related assets. For example, the same employee should not have the ability to authorize inventory purchases, account for those purchases, and manage the inventory storeroom. *Physical safeguards* prevent unauthorized employees from having access to assets such as inventories and computer equipment. *Performance reviews* are a detective control performed by employees in supervisory positions to ensure that actual results are reasonable when compared to relevant benchmarks. If actual results unexpectedly deviate from expectations, then it triggers further analysis to determine the root cause of the deviation. Companies *maintain records* to provide evidence that supports each transaction. For example, companies use serially numbered checks (a detective control) so that they can readily track all of their cash disbursements. Finally, companies maintain *information systems security* by using passwords (a preventive control) and access logs (a detective control) to restrict electronic data access as appropriate.

It bears reemphasizing that these types of controls may help a company reduce its risks, but they cannot guarantee that a company will achieve its objectives. For example, two or more employees may collude to circumvent the control system, or a company's senior leaders may manipulate financial results by intentionally overriding prescribed policies and procedures. This reality highlights the importance of having senior leaders (including the chief executive officer and the chief financial officer) who are committed to creating an ethical "tone at the top" of the organization.

## A Corporate Social Responsibility Perspective

Companies are responsible for creating strategies that produce financial results that satisfy stockholders. However, they also have a *corporate social responsibility* to serve other stakeholders—such as customers, employees, suppliers, communities, and

---

**IN BUSINESS** | **Managing Risks When Patients Go Under the Knife**

A study by researchers at **Johns Hopkins University** estimated that more than 4,000 claims are filed each year for what it referred to as never events—surgical errors that should never happen, such as operating on the wrong body part. The study found that over a 20-year period these never events led to death in 6.6% of patients and permanent injury in almost 33% of patients. The total payout from the ensuing lawsuits in these cases topped $1.3 billion.

Given these statistics, it is not surprising that many hospitals are paying greater attention to identifying risks and implementing controls to reduce those risks. For example, to reduce the risk that surgical objects are left inside a patient after the surgery concludes, hospitals are introducing controls such as counting instruments, needles, and sponges before and after each surgical procedure. Radio frequency identification tags are also being used to detect instruments inside a patient before wound closure.

Source: Landro, Laura, "How to Make Surgery Safer," *The Wall Street Journal*, February 17, 2015, pp. R1–R2.

environmental and human rights advocates—whose interests are tied to the company's performance. **Corporate social responsibility** (CSR) is a concept whereby organizations consider the needs of all stakeholders when making decisions. CSR extends beyond legal compliance to include voluntary actions that satisfy stakeholder expectations. Numerous companies, such as **Procter & Gamble, 3M, Eli Lilly and Company, Starbucks, Microsoft, Genentech, Johnson & Johnson, Baxter International, Abbott Laboratories, KPMG, PNC Bank, Deloitte, Southwest Airlines,** and **Caterpillar**, prominently describe their corporate social performance on their websites.

Exhibit P–9 presents examples of corporate social responsibilities that are of interest to six stakeholder groups.[3] If a company fails to meet the needs of these six stakeholder groups it can adversely affect its financial performance. For example, if a company pollutes the environment or fails to provide safe and humane working conditions for its employees, the negative publicity from environmental and human rights activists could cause the company's customers to defect and its "best and brightest" job candidates to apply elsewhere—both of which are likely to eventually harm financial performance. This explains why in managerial accounting a manager must establish plans, implement controls, and make decisions that consider impacts on all stakeholders.

## A Process Management Perspective

Most companies organize themselves by functional departments, such as the Marketing Department, the Research and Development Department, and the Accounting Department. These departments tend to have a clearly defined "chain of command" that

**EXHIBIT P–9**
Examples of Corporate Social Responsibilities

Companies should provide *customers* with:
- Safe, high-quality products that are fairly priced.
- Competent, courteous, and rapid delivery of products and services.
- Full disclosure of product-related risks.
- Easy-to-use information systems for shopping and tracking orders.

Companies should provide *suppliers* with:
- Fair contract terms and prompt payments.
- Reasonable time to prepare orders.
- Hassle-free acceptance of timely and complete deliveries.
- Cooperative rather than unilateral actions.

Companies should provide *stockholders* with:
- Competent management.
- Easy access to complete and accurate financial information.
- Full disclosure of enterprise risks.
- Honest answers to knowledgeable questions.

Companies and their suppliers should provide *employees* with:
- Safe and humane working conditions.
- Nondiscriminatory treatment and the right to organize and file grievances.
- Fair compensation.
- Opportunities for training, promotion, and personal development.

Companies should provide *communities* with:
- Payment of fair taxes.
- Honest information about plans such as plant closings.
- Resources that support charities, schools, and civic activities.
- Reasonable access to media sources.

Companies should provide *environmental and human rights advocates* with:
- Greenhouse gas emissions data.
- Recycling and resource conservation data.
- Child labor transparency.
- Full disclosure of suppliers located in developing countries.

[3]Many of the examples in Exhibit P–9 were drawn from Terry Leap and Misty L. Loughry, "The Stakeholder-Friendly Firm," *Business Horizons,* March/April 2004, pp. 27–32.

specifies superior and subordinate relationships. However, effective managers understand that *business processes,* more so than functional departments, serve the needs of a company's most important stakeholders—its customers. A **business process** is a series of steps that are followed in order to carry out some task in a business. These steps often span departmental boundaries, thereby requiring managers to cooperate across functional departments. The term *value chain* is often used to describe how an organization's functional departments interact with one another to form business processes. A **value chain**, as shown in Exhibit P–10, consists of the major business functions that add value to a company's products and services.

Managers need to understand the value chain to be effective in terms of planning, control, and decision making. For example, if a company's engineers plan to design a new product, they must communicate with the Manufacturing Department to ensure that the product can actually be produced, the Marketing Department to ensure that customers will buy the product, the Distribution Department to ensure that large volumes of the product can be cost-effectively transported to customers, and the Accounting Department to ensure that the product will increase profits. From a control and decision-making standpoint, managers also need to focus on process excellence instead of functional performance. For example, if the Purchasing Department focuses solely on minimizing the cost of purchased materials, this narrowly focused attempt at cost reduction may lead to greater scrap and rework in the Manufacturing Department, more complaints in the Customer Service Department, and greater challenges in the Marketing Department because dissatisfied customers are turning their attention to competitors.

Managers frequently use a process management method known as *lean thinking,* or what is called *Lean Production* in the manufacturing sector. **Lean Production** is a management approach that organizes resources such as people and machines around the flow of business processes and that only produces units in response to customer orders. It is often called *just-in-time* production (or *JIT*) because products are only manufactured in response to customer orders and they are completed just-in-time to be shipped to customers. Lean thinking differs from traditional manufacturing methods that organize

**EXHIBIT P–10**   Business Functions Making Up the Value Chain

| Research and Development | Product Design | Manufacturing | Marketing | Distribution | Customer Service |

work departmentally and that encourage departments to maximize their output even if it exceeds customer demand and bloats inventories. Because lean thinking only allows production in response to customer orders, the number of units produced tends to equal the number of units sold, thereby resulting in minimal inventory. The lean approach also results in fewer defects, less wasted effort, and quicker customer response times than traditional production methods.

## A Leadership Perspective

An organization's employees bring diverse needs, beliefs, and goals to the workplace. Therefore, an important role for organizational leaders is to unite the behaviors of their fellow employees around two common themes—pursuing strategic goals and making optimal decisions. To fulfill this responsibility, leaders need to understand how *intrinsic motivation, extrinsic incentives,* and *cognitive bias* influence human behavior.

**Intrinsic Motivation**　　Intrinsic motivation refers to motivation that comes from within us. Stop for a moment and identify the greatest accomplishment of your life. Then ask yourself what motivated you to achieve this goal? In all likelihood, you achieved it because you wanted to, not because someone forced you to do it. In other words, you were intrinsically motivated. Similarly, an organization is more likely to prosper when its employees are intrinsically motivated to pursue its interests. A leader, who employees perceive as *credible* and *respectful* of their value to the organization, can increase the extent to which those employees are intrinsically motivated to pursue strategic goals. As your career evolves, to be perceived as a credible leader you'll need to possess three attributes—technical competence (that spans the value chain), personal integrity (in terms of work ethic and honesty), and strong communication skills (including oral presentation skills and writing skills). To be perceived as a leader who is respectful of your co-workers' value to the organization, you'll need to possess three more attributes—strong mentoring skills (to help others realize their potential), strong listening skills (to learn from your co-workers and be responsive to their needs), and personal humility (in terms of deferring recognition to all employees who contribute to the organization's success). If you possess these six traits, then you'll have the potential to become a leader who inspires others to readily and energetically channel their efforts toward achieving organizational goals.

**Extrinsic Incentives**　　Many organizations use *extrinsic incentives* to highlight important goals and to motivate employees to achieve them. For example, assume a company establishes the goal of reducing the time needed to perform a task by 20%. In addition, assume the company agrees to pay bonus compensation to its employees if they achieve the goal within three months. In this example, the company is using a type of extrinsic incentive known as a bonus to highlight a particular goal and to presumably motivate employees to achieve it.

While proponents of extrinsic incentives rightly assert that these types of rewards can have a powerful influence on employee behavior, many critics warn that they can also produce dysfunctional consequences. For example, suppose the employees mentioned above earned their bonuses by achieving the 20% time reduction goal within three months. However, let's also assume that during those three months the quality of the employees' output plummeted, thereby causing a spike in the company's repair costs, product returns, and customer defections. In this instance, did the extrinsic incentive work properly? The answer is yes and no. The bonus system did motivate employees to attain the time reduction goal; however, it also had the unintended consequences of causing employees to neglect product quality, thereby increasing repair costs, product returns, and customer defections. In other words, what may have seemed like a well-intended extrinsic incentive actually produced dysfunctional results for the company. This example highlights an important leadership challenge that you are likely to face someday—designing financial compensation systems that fairly reward employees for their efforts without inadvertently creating extrinsic incentives that motivate them to take actions that harm the company.

**Cognitive Bias**   Leaders need to be aware that all people (including themselves) possess *cognitive biases,* or distorted thought processes, that can adversely affect planning, controlling, and decision making. To illustrate how cognitive bias works, let's consider the scenario of a television "infomercial" where someone is selling a product with a proclaimed value of $200 for $19.99 if viewers call within the next 30 minutes. Why do you think the seller claims that the product has a $200 value? The seller is relying on a cognitive bias called *anchoring bias* in an effort to convince viewers that a $180 discount is simply too good to pass up. The "anchor" is the false assertion that the product is actually worth $200. If viewers erroneously attach credibility to this contrived piece of information, their distorted analysis of the situation may cause them to spend $19.99 on an item whose true economic value is much less than that amount.

While cognitive biases cannot be eliminated, effective leaders should take two steps to reduce their negative impacts. First, they should acknowledge their own susceptibility to cognitive bias. For example, a leader's judgment might be clouded by optimism bias (being overly optimistic in assessing the likelihood of future outcomes) or self-enhancement bias (overestimating ones strengths and underestimating ones weaknesses relative to others). Second, they should acknowledge the presence of cognitive bias in others and introduce techniques to minimize their adverse consequences. For example, to reduce the risks of confirmation bias (a bias where people pay greater attention to information that confirms their preconceived notions, while devaluing information that contradicts them) or groupthink bias (a bias where some group members support a course of action solely because other group members do), a leader may routinely appoint independent teams of employees to assess the credibility of recommendations set forth by other individuals and groups.

## SUMMARY

The prologue defined managerial accounting and explained why it is relevant to business and accounting majors. It also discussed six topics—ethics, strategic management, enterprise risk management, corporate social responsibility, process management, and leadership—that define the context for applying the quantitative aspects of managerial accounting. The most important goal of the prologue was to help you understand that managerial accounting matters to your future career regardless of your major. Accounting is the language of business and you'll need to speak it to communicate effectively with and influence fellow managers.

## GLOSSARY

**Budget**   A detailed plan for the future that is usually expressed in formal quantitative terms. (p. 4)

**Business process**   A series of steps that are followed in order to carry out some task in a business. (p. 16)

**Controlling**   The process of gathering feedback to ensure that a plan is being properly executed or modified as circumstances change. (p.3)

**Corporate social responsibility**   A concept whereby organizations consider the needs of all stakeholders when making decisions. (p. 15)

**Decision making**   Selecting a course of action from competing alternatives. (p. 3)

**Detective control**   A control that detects undesirable events that have already occurred. (p. 13)

**Enterprise risk management**   A process used by a company to identify its risks and develop responses to them that enable it to be reasonably assured of meeting its goals. (p. 12)

**Financial accounting**   The phase of accounting that is concerned with reporting historical financial information to external parties, such as stockholders, creditors, and regulators. (p. 2)

**Lean Production**   A management approach that organizes resources such as people and machines around the flow of business processes and that only produces units in response to customer orders. (p. 16)

**Managerial accounting**   The phase of accounting that is concerned with providing information to managers for use within the organization. (p. 2)

**Performance report**   A report that compares budgeted data to actual data to highlight instances of excellent and unsatisfactory performance. (p. 4)

**Planning**   The process of establishing goals and specifying how to achieve them. (p. 3)

**Preventive control**   A control that deters undesirable events from occurring. (p. 13)

**Segment**   Any part or activity of an organization about which managers seek cost, revenue, or profit data. (p. 3)

**Strategy**   A company's "game plan" for attracting customers by distinguishing itself from competitors. (p. 10)

**Value chain**   The major business functions that add value to a company's products and services, such as research and development, product design, manufacturing, marketing, distribution, and customer service. (p. 16)

## QUESTIONS

| | |
|---|---|
| **P–1** | How does managerial accounting differ from financial accounting? |
| **P–2** | Pick any major television network and describe some planning and control activities that its managers would engage in. |
| **P–3** | If you had to decide whether to continue making a component part or to begin buying the part from an overseas supplier, what quantitative and qualitative factors would influence your decision? |
| **P–4** | Why do companies prepare budgets? |
| **P–5** | Why is managerial accounting relevant to business majors and their future careers? |
| **P–6** | Why is managerial accounting relevant to accounting majors and their future careers? |
| **P–7** | Pick any large company and describe its strategy using one of the three customer value propositions defined in the prologue. |
| **P–8** | Why do management accountants need to understand their company's strategy? |
| **P–9** | Pick any large company and describe three risks that it faces and how it responds to those risks. |
| **P–10** | Pick three industries and describe how the risks faced by companies within those industries can influence their planning, controlling, and decision-making activities. |
| **P–11** | Pick any large company and explain three ways that it could segment its companywide performance. |
| **P–12** | Locate the website of any company that publishes a corporate social responsibility report (also referred to as a sustainability report). Describe three nonfinancial performance measures included in the report. Why do you think the company publishes this report? |
| **P–13** | Why do companies that implement Lean Production tend to have minimal inventories? |
| **P–14** | Why are leadership skills important to managers? |
| **P–15** | Why is ethical behavior important to business? |
| **P–16** | If you were a restaurant owner, what internal controls would you implement to help maintain control of your cash? |
| **P–17** | As a form of internal control, what documents would you review prior to paying an invoice received from a supplier? |
| **P–18** | What internal controls would you implement to help maintain control of your credit sales and accounts receivable? |
| **P–19** | Why do companies take a physical count of their inventory on hand at least once per year? |
| **P–20** | Why do companies use sequential prenumbering for documents such as checks, sales invoices, and purchase orders? |

**connect** | **EXERCISES**

### EXERCISE P–1   Planning and Control

Many companies use budgets for three purposes. First, they use them to plan how to deploy resources to best serve customers. Second, they use them to establish challenging goals, or stretch targets, to motivate employees to strive for exceptional results. Third, they use them to evaluate and reward employees.

Assume that you are a sales manager working with your boss to create a sales budget for next year. Once the sales budget is established, it will influence how other departments within the company plan to deploy their resources. For example, the manufacturing manager will plan to produce enough units to meet budgeted unit sales. The sales budget will also be instrumental in determining your pay raise, potential for promotion, and bonus. If actual sales exceed the sales budget, it bodes well for your career. If actual sales are less than budgeted sales, it will diminish your financial compensation and potential for promotion.

*Required:*

1. Do you think it would be appropriate for your boss to establish the sales budget without any input from you? Why?
2. Do you think the company would be comfortable with allowing you to establish the sales budget without any input from your boss? Why?
3. Assume the company uses its sales budget for only one purpose—planning to deploy resources in a manner that best serves customers. What thoughts would influence your estimate of future sales as well as your boss's estimate of future sales?
4. Assume the company uses its sales budget for only one purpose—motivating employees to strive for exceptional results. What thoughts would influence your estimate of future sales as well as your boss's estimate of future sales?
5. Assume the company uses its sales budget for only one purpose—to determine your pay raise, potential for promotion, and bonus. What thoughts would influence your estimate of future sales as well as your boss's estimate of future sales?
6. Assume the sales budget is used for all three purposes described in questions 3–5. Describe any conflicts or complications that might arise when using the sales budget for these three purposes.

### EXERCISE P–2   Controlling

Assume that you work for an airline unloading luggage from airplanes. Your boss has said that, on average, each airplane contains 100 pieces of luggage. Furthermore, your boss has stated that you should be able to unload 100 pieces of luggage from an airplane in 10 minutes. Today an airplane arrived with 150 pieces of luggage and you unloaded all of it in 13 minutes. After finishing with the 150 pieces of luggage, your boss yelled at you for exceeding the 10 minute allowance for unloading luggage from an airplane.

*Required:*

How would you feel about being yelled at for taking 13 minutes to unload 150 pieces of luggage? How does this scenario relate to the larger issue of how companies design control systems?

### EXERCISE P–3   Decision Making

Exhibit P–2 from within the Prologue includes 12 questions related to 12 types of decisions that companies often face. In the prologue, these 12 decisions were discussed within the context of for-profit companies; however, they are also readily applicable to nonprofit organizations. To illustrate this point, assume that you are a senior leader, such as a president, provost, or dean, in a university setting.

*Required:*

For each of the 12 decisions in Exhibit P–2, provide an example of how that type of decision might be applicable to a university setting.

### EXERCISE P–4   Ethics and the Manager

Richmond, Inc., operates a chain of 44 department stores. Two years ago, the board of directors of Richmond approved a large-scale remodeling of its stores to attract a more upscale clientele.

Before finalizing these plans, two stores were remodeled as a test. Linda Perlman, assistant controller, was asked to oversee the financial reporting for these test stores, and she and other management personnel were offered bonuses based on the sales growth and profitability of these stores. While completing the financial reports, Perlman discovered a sizable inventory of outdated goods that should have been discounted for sale or returned to the manufacturer. She discussed the situation with her management colleagues; the consensus was to ignore reporting this inventory as obsolete because reporting it would diminish the financial results and their bonuses.

*Required:*

1. According to the IMA's Statement of Ethical Professional Practice, would it be ethical for Perlman *not* to report the inventory as obsolete?
2. Would it be easy for Perlman to take the ethical action in this situation?

Source: CMA, adapted

### EXERCISE P–5   Strategy

The table below contains the names of six companies.

*Required:*

For each company, categorize its strategy as being focused on customer intimacy, operational excellence, or product leadership. If you wish to improve your understanding of each company's customer value proposition before completing the exercise, review its most recent annual report. To obtain electronic access to this information, perform an Internet search on each company's name followed by the words "annual report."

| Company | Strategy |
|---|---|
| 1. Deere...................... | ? |
| 2. FedEx....................... | ? |
| 3. State Farm Insurance......... | ? |
| 4. BMW ....................... | ? |
| 5. Amazon.com ................. | ? |
| 6. Charles Schwab ............. | ? |

### EXERCISE P–6  Enterprise Risk Management

The table below refers to seven industries.

**Required:**

For each industry, provide an example of a business risk faced by companies that compete within that industry. Then, describe an example of a control that could be used to reduce the business risk that you have identified.

| Industry | Example of Business Risk | Example of Control to Reduce the Business Risk |
|---|---|---|
| 1. Airlines (e.g., **Delta Airlines**)...................... | | |
| 2. Pharmaceutical drugs (e.g., **Merck**)................. | | |
| 3. Package delivery (e.g., **United Parcel Service**) ....... | | |
| 4. Banking (e.g., **Bank of America**)..................... | | |
| 5. Oil & gas (e.g., **ExxonMobil**)........................ | | |
| 6. E-commerce (e.g., **eBay**)........................... | | |
| 7. Automotive (e.g., **Toyota**) ......................... | | |

### EXERCISE P–7  Ethics in Business

Consumers and attorney generals in more than 40 states accused a prominent nationwide chain of auto repair shops of misleading customers and selling them unnecessary parts and services, from brake jobs to front-end alignments. Lynn Sharpe Paine reported the situation as follows in "Managing for Organizational Integrity," *Harvard Business Review,* Volume 72 Issue 3:

> In the face of declining revenues, shrinking market share, and an increasingly competitive market . . . management attempted to spur performance of its auto centers. . . . The automotive service advisers were given product-specific sales quotas—sell so many springs, shock absorbers, alignments, or brake jobs per shift—and paid a commission based on sales. . . . [F]ailure to meet quotas could lead to a transfer or a reduction in work hours. Some employees spoke of the "pressure, pressure, pressure" to bring in sales.
>
> This pressure-cooker atmosphere created conditions under which employees felt that the only way to satisfy top management was by selling products and services to customers that they didn't really need.

Suppose all automotive repair businesses routinely followed the practice of attempting to sell customers unnecessary parts and services.

**Required:**

1. How would this behavior affect customers? How might customers attempt to protect themselves against this behavior?
2. How would this behavior probably affect profits and employment in the automotive service industry?

**EXERCISE P–8    Cognitive Bias**

In the 1970s, one million college-bound students were surveyed and asked to compare themselves to their peers. Some of the key findings of the survey were as follows:

a.   70% of the students rated themselves as above average in leadership ability, while only 2% rated themselves as below average in this regard.

b.   With respect to athletic skills, 60% of the students rated their skills as above the median and only 6% of students rated themselves as below the median.

c.   60% of the students rated themselves in the top 10% in terms of their ability to get along with others, while 25% of the students felt that they were in the top 1% in terms of this interpersonal skill.

*Required:*

1.   What type of cognitive bias reveals itself in the data mentioned above?
2.   How might this cognitive bias adversely influence a manager's planning, controlling, and decision-making activities?
3.   What steps could managers take to reduce the possibility that this cognitive bias would adversely influence their actions?

Source: Lovallo, Dan and Kahneman, Daniel, "Delusions of Success: How Optimism Undermines Executives' Decisions," *Harvard Business Review,* July 2003, pp. 56–63.

**EXERCISE P–9    Ethics and Decision Making**

Assume that you are the chairman of the Department of Accountancy at Mountain State University. One of the accounting professors in your department, Dr. Candler, has been consistently and uniformly regarded by students as an awful teacher for more than 10 years. Other accounting professors within your department have observed Dr. Candler's classroom teaching and they concur that his teaching skills are very poor. However, Dr. Candler was granted tenure 12 years ago, thereby ensuring him life-long job security at Mountain State University.

Much to your surprise, today you received a phone call from an accounting professor at Oregon Coastal University. During this phone call you are informed that Oregon Coastal University is on the verge of making a job offer to Dr. Candler. However, before extending the job offer, the faculty at Oregon Coastal wants your input regarding Dr. Candler's teaching effectiveness while at Mountain State University.

*Required:*

How would you respond to the professor from Oregon Coastal University? What would you say about Dr. Candler's teaching ability? Would you describe your answer to this inquiry as being ethical? Why?

**EXERCISE P–10    Corporate Social Responsibility**

In his book *Capitalism and Freedom,* economist Milton Friedman wrote on page 133: "There is one and only one social responsibility of business—to use its resources and engage in activities designed to increase its profits so long as it . . . engages in open and free competition, without deception or fraud."

*Required:*

Explain why you agree or disagree with this quote.

**EXERCISE P–11    Intrinsic Motivation and Extrinsic Incentives**

In a *Harvard Business Review* article titled "Why Incentive Plans Cannot Work," (Volume 71, Issue 5) author Alfie Kohn wrote: "Research suggests that, by and large, rewards succeed at securing one thing only: temporary compliance. When it comes to producing lasting change in attitudes and behavior, however, rewards, like punishment, are strikingly ineffective. Once the rewards run out, people revert to their old behaviors. . . . Incentives, a version of what psychologists call extrinsic motivators, do not alter the attitudes that underlie our behaviors. They do not create an enduring *commitment* to any value or action. Rather, incentives merely—and temporarily—change what we do."

*Required:*

1.   Do you agree with this quote? Why?
2.   As a manager, how would you seek to motivate your employees?
3.   As a manager, would you use financial incentives to compensate your employees? If so, what would be the keys to using them effectively? If not, then how would you compensate your employees?

**EXERCISE P–12    Cognitive Bias and Decision Making**

During World War II, the U.S. military was studying its combat-tested fighter planes to determine the parts of the plane that were most vulnerable to enemy fire. The purpose of the study was to identify the most vulnerable sections of each plane and then take steps to reinforce those sections to improve pilot safety and airplane durability. The data gathered by the U.S. military showed that certain sections of its combat-tested fighter planes were consistently hit more often with enemy fire than other sections of the plane.

***Required:***
1. Would you recommend reinforcing the sections of the plane that were hit most often by enemy fire, or would you reinforce the sections that were hit less frequently by enemy fire? Why?
2. Do you think cognitive bias had the potential to influence the U.S. military's decision-making process with respect to reinforcing its fighter planes?

Source: Denrell, Jerker, "Selection Bias and the Perils of Benchmarking," *Harvard Business Review,* Volume 83, Issue 4, pp. 114–119.

### EXERCISE P–13  Ethics and Decision Making

Assume that you just completed a December weekend vacation to a casino within the United States. During your trip you won $10,000 gambling. When the casino exchanged your chips for cash they did not record any personal information, such as your driver's license number or social security number. Four months later while preparing your tax returns for the prior year, you stop to contemplate the fact that the Internal Revenue Service requires taxpayers to report all gambling winnings on Form 1040.

***Required:***
Would you report your gambling winnings to the Internal Revenue Service so that you could pay federal income taxes on those winnings? Do you believe that your actions are ethical? Why?

**A LOOK BACK**

The Prologue defined managerial accounting and explained why it is important to the careers of all business students. It also explained how managerial accounting involves more than just quantitative calculations.

**A LOOK AT THIS CHAPTER**

This chapter defines many of the cost terms that will be used throughout the book. It explains that in managerial accounting the term cost is used in many different ways depending on the needs of management.

**A LOOK AHEAD**

Chapters 2, 3, 4, and 5 describe costing systems that are used to compute product costs. Chapters 2 and 3 describe job-order costing. Chapter 4 describes activity-based costing, an elaboration of job-order costing. Chapter 5 covers process costing.

# 1 Managerial Accounting and Cost Concepts

## CHAPTER OUTLINE

**Cost Classifications for Assigning Costs to Cost Objects**

- Direct Cost
- Indirect Cost

**Cost Classifications for Manufacturing Companies**

- Manufacturing Costs
- Nonmanufacturing Costs

**Cost Classifications for Preparing Financial Statements**

- Product Costs
- Period Costs

**Cost Classifications for Predicting Cost Behavior**

- Variable Cost
- Fixed Cost

- The Linearity Assumption and the Relevant Range
- Mixed Costs
- Cost Terminology—A Closer Look

**Cost Classifications for Decision Making**

- Differential Cost and Revenue
- Sunk Cost and Opportunity Cost

**Using Different Cost Classifications for Different Purposes**

- The Traditional Format Income Statement
- The Contribution Format Income Statement

## DECISION FEATURE

©Raymond Boyd/Getty Images

# Curbing Administrative Expenses

When Eric Kaler was appointed as the **University of Minnesota**'s president he promised to cut administrative expenses. Over an 11-year period, the university's administrative headcount had climbed by 1,000 employees, or 37%. This growth rate practically doubled the faculty and student growth rates during the same time period. Beyond the disparity in headcount growth rates, the executive administrators' pay raises exceeded the pay raises given to faculty members, while at the same time the university's in-state tuition and fees more than doubled.

Dr. Kaler's cost-cutting efforts included closing dozens of extension school offices, freezing or reducing salaries, eliminating 14 car allowances, restructuring health care and retirement benefits, and eliminating the Office of Academic Administration—a move that cut 5.5 full-time positions including a senior vice-president who earned more than $300,000.

Source: Belkin, Douglas and Thurm, Scott, "Dean's List: Hiring Spree Fattens College Bureaucracy—And Tuition," *The Wall Street Journal,* December 29–30, 2012, pp. A1 and A10.

LEARNING OBJECTIVES

*After studying Chapter 1, you should be able to:*

**LO1–1** Understand cost classifications used for assigning costs to cost objects: direct costs and indirect costs.

**LO1–2** Identify and give examples of each of the three basic manufacturing cost categories.

**LO1–3** Understand cost classifications used to prepare financial statements: product costs and period costs.

**LO1–4** Understand cost classifications used to predict cost behavior: variable costs, fixed costs, and mixed costs.

**LO1–5** Understand cost classifications used in making decisions: differential costs, sunk costs, and opportunity costs.

**LO1–6** Prepare income statements for a merchandising company using the traditional and contribution formats.

In accounting, costs can be classified differently depending on the needs of management. For example, the Prologue mentioned that **financial accounting** is concerned with reporting financial information to external parties, such as stockholders, creditors, and regulators. In this context, costs are classified in accordance with externally imposed rules to enable the preparation of financial statements. Conversely, **managerial accounting** is concerned with providing information to managers within an organization so that they can formulate plans, control operations, and make decisions. In these contexts, costs are classified in diverse ways that enable managers to predict future costs, to compare actual costs to budgeted costs, to assign costs to segments of the business (such as product lines, geographic regions, and distribution channels), and to properly contrast the costs associated with competing alternatives.

The notion of *different cost classifications for different purposes* is the most important unifying theme of this chapter and one of the key foundational concepts of the entire textbook. Exhibit 1–1 summarizes five types of cost classifications that will be used throughout the textbook, namely cost classifications (1) for assigning costs to cost objects, (2) for manufacturing companies, (3) for preparing financial statements, (4) for predicting cost behavior, and (5) for making decisions. As we begin defining the cost terminology related to each of these cost classifications, please refer back to this exhibit to help improve your understanding of the overall organization of the chapter.

**EXHIBIT 1—1**
Summary of Cost Classifications

| Purpose of Cost Classification | Cost Classifications |
|---|---|
| Assigning costs to cost objects | • Direct cost (can be easily traced)<br>• Indirect cost (cannot be easily traced) |
| Accounting for costs in manufacturing companies | • Manufacturing costs<br>  • Direct materials<br>  • Direct labor<br>  • Manufacturing overhead<br>• Nonmanufacturing costs<br>  • Selling costs<br>  • Administrative costs |
| Preparing financial statements | • Product costs (inventoriable)<br>• Period costs (expensed) |
| Predicting cost behavior in response to changes in activity | • Variable cost (proportional to activity)<br>• Fixed cost (constant in total)<br>• Mixed cost (has variable and fixed elements) |
| Making decisions | • Differential cost (differs between alternatives)<br>• Sunk cost (should be ignored)<br>• Opportunity cost (foregone benefit) |

# COST CLASSIFICATIONS FOR ASSIGNING COSTS TO COST OBJECTS

**LEARNING OBJECTIVE 1–1**

Understand cost classifications used for assigning costs to cost objects: direct costs and indirect costs.

Costs are assigned to cost objects for a variety of purposes including pricing, preparing profitability studies, and controlling spending. A **cost object** is anything for which cost data are desired—including products, customers, and organizational subunits. For purposes of assigning costs to cost objects, costs are classified as either *direct* or *indirect*.

## Direct Cost

A **direct cost** is a cost that can be easily and conveniently traced to a specified cost object. For example, if **Adidas** is assigning costs to its various regional and national sales offices, then the salary of the sales manager in its Tokyo office would be a direct cost of that office. If a printing company made 10,000 brochures for a specific customer, then the cost of the paper used to make the brochures would be a direct cost of that customer.

## Indirect Cost

An **indirect cost** is a cost that cannot be easily and conveniently traced to a specified cost object. For example, a **Campbell Soup** factory may produce dozens of varieties of canned soups. The factory manager's salary would be an indirect cost of a particular variety such as chicken noodle soup. The reason is that the factory manager's salary is incurred as a consequence of running the entire factory—it is not incurred to produce any one soup variety. *To be traced to a cost object such as a particular product, the cost must be caused by the cost object.* The factory manager's salary is called a *common cost* of producing the various products of the factory. A **common cost** is a cost that is incurred to support a number of cost objects but cannot be traced to them individually. A common cost is a type of indirect cost.

A particular cost may be direct or indirect, depending on the cost object. While the Campbell Soup factory manager's salary is an *indirect* cost of manufacturing chicken noodle soup, it is a *direct* cost of the manufacturing division. In the first case, the cost object is chicken noodle soup. In the second case, the cost object is the entire manufacturing division.

---

### The High Price of Selling on Manhattan's Fifth Avenue                    IN BUSINESS

The cost to buy retail real estate on Manhattan's Fifth Avenue exceeds $15,000 per square foot. Investors are willing to pay such a high price because they can turn around and rent their space to high-end retailers (such as **Dolce & Gabbana**, **Tommy Bahama**, and **Massimo Dutti**) for as much as $3,000 per square foot per year. **Abercrombie & Fitch**'s store at 720 Fifth Avenue is its single most profitable store—bringing in $100 million in annual sales while incurring annual rent of $12.5 million. When Abercrombie measures the profits earned at its Fifth Avenue location, the rental expense of $12.5 million is a direct cost of operating that particular store.

Source: Hudson, Kris and Mattioli, Dana, "Fifth Avenue's Eye-Popping Rents," *The Wall Street Journal*, November 21, 2012, pp. C1 and C10.

---

## COST CLASSIFICATIONS FOR MANUFACTURING COMPANIES

Manufacturing companies such as **Texas Instruments**, **Ford**, and **DuPont** separate their costs into two broad categories—manufacturing and nonmanufacturing costs.

> **LEARNING OBJECTIVE 1–2**
>
> Identify and give examples of each of the three basic manufacturing cost categories.

## Manufacturing Costs

Most manufacturing companies further separate their manufacturing costs into two direct cost categories, direct materials and direct labor, and one indirect cost category, manufacturing overhead. A discussion of these three categories follows.

**Direct Materials**     The materials that go into the final product are called **raw materials**. This term is somewhat misleading because it seems to imply unprocessed natural resources like wood pulp or iron ore. Actually, raw materials refer to any materials that are used in the final product; and the finished product of one company can become the raw materials of another company. For example, the plastics produced by **DuPont** are a raw material used by **Hewlett-Packard** in its personal computers.

**Direct materials** refers to raw materials that become an integral part of the finished product and whose costs can be conveniently traced to the finished product. This would include, for example, the seats that **Airbus** purchases from subcontractors to install in its commercial aircraft, the electronic components that **Apple** uses in its iPhones, and the doors that **Whirlpool** installs on its refrigerators.

---

## IN BUSINESS

## Cheap Part Costs General Motors a Fortune

A direct material component part, called a detent plunger, is used by **General Motors (GM)** in the manufacture of its automobile ignition switches. The part, which can be installed by direct laborers in a matter of minutes, costs GM between $2.00 and $5.00 per unit to manufacture. However, when this seemingly trivial component part caused ignition system failures that killed 12 people, its legal and financial impacts on GM became front-page news.

GM's troubles include a federal criminal probe that is investigating why the company did not act sooner to redesign, recall, and replace the flawed detent plunger. It appears as though GM learned of ignition switch failures in its Chevy Cobalt in 2004, but it did not redesign the detent plunger to eliminate the problem until 2007. Furthermore, the company did not issue a recall for cars that contained the faulty ignition switches until 2014. Beyond its legal matters, GM expects to spend $8 million replacing the ignition switches of 1.6 million recalled vehicles.

©Monty Rakusen/Getty Images RF

Source: Bennett, Jeff, "For GM, Cheap Part Now a Pricey Fix," *The Wall Street Journal*, March 13, 2014, pp. B1–B2.

---

**Direct Labor**   **Direct labor** consists of labor costs that can be easily traced to individual units of product. Direct labor is sometimes called *touch labor* because direct labor workers typically touch the product while it is being made. Examples of direct labor include assembly-line workers at **Toyota**, carpenters at the home builder **KB Home**, and electricians who install equipment on aircraft at **Bombardier Learjet**.

Managers occasionally refer to their two direct manufacturing cost categories as *prime costs*. **Prime cost** is the sum of direct materials cost and direct labor cost.

**Manufacturing Overhead**   **Manufacturing overhead**, the third manufacturing cost category, includes all manufacturing costs except direct materials and direct labor. For example, manufacturing overhead includes a portion of raw materials known as *indirect materials*, as well as *indirect labor*. **Indirect materials** are raw materials, such as the solder used to make electrical connections in a **Samsung** HDTV and the glue used to assemble an **Ethan Allen** chair, whose costs cannot be easily or conveniently traced to finished products. **Indirect labor** refers to employees, such as janitors, supervisors, materials handlers, maintenance workers, and night security guards, that play an essential role in running a manufacturing facility; however, the cost of compensating these people cannot be easily or conveniently traced to specific units of product. Since indirect materials and indirect labor are difficult to trace to specific products, their costs are included in manufacturing overhead.

Manufacturing overhead also includes other indirect costs that cannot be readily traced to finished products such as depreciation of manufacturing equipment and the utility costs, property taxes, and insurance premiums incurred to operate a manufacturing facility. Although companies also incur depreciation, utility costs, property taxes, and insurance premiums to sustain their nonmanufacturing operations, these costs are not included as part of manufacturing overhead. Only those indirect costs associated with *operating the factory* are included in manufacturing overhead.

In practice, managers use various names for manufacturing overhead, such as *indirect manufacturing cost, factory overhead,* and *factory burden.* All of these terms are synonyms for manufacturing overhead. Another term that managers frequently use in practice is *conversion cost.* **Conversion cost** refers to the sum of direct labor and manufacturing overhead. The term conversion cost is used to describe direct labor and manufacturing overhead because these costs are incurred to *convert* direct materials into finished products.

## Nonmanufacturing Costs

Nonmanufacturing costs are often divided into two categories: (1) *selling costs* and (2) *administrative costs.* **Selling costs** include all costs that are incurred to secure customer orders and get the finished product to the customer. These costs are sometimes called *order-getting* and *order-filling costs.* Examples of selling costs include advertising, shipping, sales travel, sales commissions, sales salaries, and costs of finished goods warehouses. Selling costs can be either direct or indirect costs. For example, the cost of an advertising campaign dedicated to one specific product is a direct cost of that product, whereas the salary of a marketing manager who oversees numerous products is an indirect cost with respect to individual products.

**Administrative costs** include all costs associated with the *general management* of an organization rather than with manufacturing or selling. Examples of administrative costs include executive compensation, general accounting, secretarial, public relations, and similar costs involved in the overall, general administration of the organization *as a whole.* Administrative costs can be either direct or indirect costs. For example, the salary of an accounting manager in charge of accounts receivable collections in the East region is a direct cost of that region, whereas the salary of a chief financial officer who oversees all of a company's regions is an indirect cost with respect to individual regions.

Nonmanufacturing costs are also often called selling, general, and administrative (SG&A) costs or just selling and administrative costs.

## COST CLASSIFICATIONS FOR PREPARING FINANCIAL STATEMENTS

When preparing a balance sheet and an income statement, companies need to classify their costs as *product costs* or *period costs.* To understand the difference between product costs and period costs, we must first discuss the matching principle from financial accounting.

**LEARNING OBJECTIVE 1–3**

Understand cost classifications used to prepare financial statements: product costs and period costs.

Generally, costs are recognized as expenses on the income statement in the period that benefits from the cost. For example, if a company pays for liability insurance in advance for two years, the entire amount is not considered an expense of the year in which the payment is made. Instead, one-half of the cost would be recognized as an expense each year. The reason is that both years—not just the first year—benefit from the insurance payment. The unexpensed portion of the insurance payment is carried on the balance sheet as an asset called prepaid insurance.

The *matching principle* is based on the *accrual* concept that *costs incurred to generate a particular revenue should be recognized as expenses in the same period that the revenue is recognized.* This means that if a cost is incurred to acquire or make something that will eventually be sold, then the cost should be recognized as an expense only when the sale takes place—that is, when the benefit occurs. Such costs are called *product costs.*

## Product Costs

For financial accounting purposes, **product costs** include all costs involved in acquiring or making a product. Product costs "attach" to a unit of product as it is purchased or manufactured and they stay attached to each unit of product as long as it remains in inventory awaiting sale. When units of product are sold, their costs are released from inventory as expenses (typically called cost of goods sold) and matched against sales on the income statement. Because product costs are initially assigned to inventories, they are also known as **inventoriable costs**.

For manufacturing companies, product costs include direct materials, direct labor, and manufacturing overhead.[1] A manufacturer's product costs flow through three inventory accounts on the balance sheet—*Raw Materials, Work in Process,* and *Finished*

---

[1]For internal management purposes, product costs may exclude some manufacturing costs. For example, see the discussion in Chapter 7.

*Goods*—prior to being recorded in cost of goods sold on the income statement. Raw materials include any materials that go into the final product. **Work in process** consists of units of product that are only partially complete and will require further work before they are ready for sale to the customer. **Finished goods** consist of completed units of product that have not yet been sold to customers.

When direct materials are used in production, their costs are transferred from Raw Materials to Work in Process. Direct labor and manufacturing overhead costs are added to Work in Process to convert direct materials into finished goods. Once units of product are completed, their costs are transferred from Work in Process to Finished Goods. When a manufacturer sells its finished goods to customers, the costs are transferred from Finished Goods to Cost of Goods Sold.

We want to emphasize that product costs are not necessarily recorded as expenses on the income statement in the period in which they are incurred. Rather, as explained above, they are recorded as expenses in the period in which the related products *are sold.*

## Period Costs

**Period costs** are all the costs that are not product costs. *All selling and administrative expenses are treated as period costs.* For example, sales commissions, advertising, executive salaries, public relations, and the rental costs of administrative offices are all period costs. Period costs are not included as part of the cost of either purchased or manufactured goods; instead, period costs are expensed on the income statement in the period in which they are incurred using the usual rules of accrual accounting. Keep in mind that the period in which a cost is incurred is not necessarily the period in which cash changes hands. For example, as discussed earlier, the cost of liability insurance is spread across the periods that benefit from the insurance—regardless of the period in which the insurance premium is paid.

Exhibit 1–2 summarizes the product and period cost flows for manufacturers that were just discussed. Notice that product costs flow through three inventory accounts on the

**EXHIBIT 1–2**    Cost Flows and Classifications in a Manufacturing Company

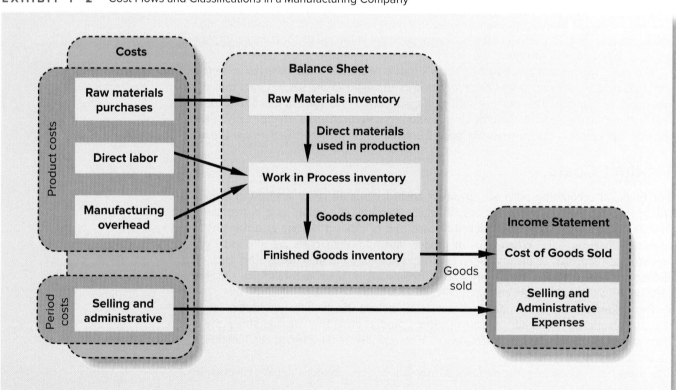

balance sheet prior to being recognized as part of cost of goods sold in the income statement. Conversely, period costs do not flow through the inventory accounts on the balance sheet and they are not included in cost of goods sold in the income statement. Instead, they are recorded as selling and administrative expenses in the income statement during the period incurred.

1. Which of the following statements is true? (You may select more than one answer.)
   a. Product costs are expensed on the income statement in the period incurred.
   b. Direct labor is a manufacturing cost and a product cost.
   c. Conversion costs include direct materials and direct labor.
   d. Nonmanufacturing costs are treated as period costs.
2. Which of the following statements is true? (You may select more than one answer.)
   a. Indirect materials and indirect labor are included in manufacturing overhead.
   b. Examples of selling costs include sales commissions, advertising, shipping, and the costs of operating finished goods warehouses.
   c. For financial accounting purposes, product costs include direct materials, direct labor, and manufacturing overhead.
   d. For financial accounting purposes, period costs are also referred to as inventoriable costs.

## COST CLASSIFICATIONS FOR PREDICTING COST BEHAVIOR

It is often necessary to predict how a certain cost will behave in response to a change in activity. For example, a manager at **Under Armour** may want to estimate the impact a 5 percent increase in sales would have on the company's total direct materials cost. **Cost behavior** refers to how a cost reacts to changes in the level of activity. As the activity level rises and falls, a particular cost may rise and fall as well—or it may remain constant. For planning purposes, a manager must be able to anticipate which of these will happen; and if a cost can be expected to change, the manager must be able to estimate how much it will change. To help make such distinctions, costs are often categorized as *variable, fixed,* or *mixed.* The relative proportion of each type of cost in an organization is known as its **cost structure**. For example, an organization might have many fixed costs but few variable or mixed costs. Alternatively, it might have many variable costs but few fixed or mixed costs.

> **LEARNING OBJECTIVE 1–4**
>
> Understand cost classifications used to predict cost behavior: variable costs, fixed costs, and mixed costs.

### Variable Cost

A **variable cost** varies, in total, in direct proportion to changes in the level of activity. Common examples of variable costs include cost of goods sold for a merchandising company, direct materials, direct labor, variable elements of manufacturing overhead, such as indirect materials, supplies, and power, and variable elements of selling and administrative expenses, such as commissions and shipping costs.[2]

For a cost to be variable, it must be variable *with respect to something.* That "something" is its *activity base.* An **activity base** is a measure of whatever causes the incurrence of a variable cost. An activity base is sometimes referred to as a *cost driver.* Some of the most common activity bases are direct labor-hours, machine-hours, units produced,

---

[2]Direct labor costs often can be fixed instead of variable for a variety of reasons. For example, in some countries, such as France, Germany, and Japan, labor regulations and cultural norms may limit management's ability to adjust the labor force in response to changes in activity. In this textbook, always assume that direct labor is a variable cost unless you are explicitly told otherwise.

and units sold. Other examples of activity bases (cost drivers) include the number of miles driven by salespersons, the number of pounds of laundry cleaned by a hotel, the number of calls handled by technical support staff at a software company, and the number of beds occupied in a hospital. *While there are many activity bases within organizations, throughout this textbook, unless stated otherwise, you should assume that the activity base under consideration is the total volume of goods and services provided by the organization. We will specify the activity base only when it is something other than total output.*

To provide an example of a variable cost, consider Nooksack Expeditions, a small company that provides daylong whitewater rafting excursions on rivers in the North Cascade Mountains. The company provides all of the necessary equipment and experienced guides, and it serves gourmet meals to its guests. The meals are purchased from a caterer for $30 a person for a daylong excursion. The behavior of this variable cost, on both a per unit and a total basis, is shown below:

| Number of Guests | Cost of Meals per Guest | Total Cost of Meals |
|---|---|---|
| 250.................... | $30 | $7,500 |
| 500.................... | $30 | $15,000 |
| 750.................... | $30 | $22,500 |
| 1,000 ................... | $30 | $30,000 |

While total variable costs change as the activity level changes, it is important to note that a variable cost is constant if expressed on a *per unit* basis. For example, the per unit cost of the meals remains constant at $30 even though the total cost of the meals increases and decreases with activity. The graph on the left-hand side of Exhibit 1–3 illustrates that the total variable cost rises and falls as the activity level rises and falls. At an activity level of 250 guests, the total meal cost is $7,500. At an activity level of 1,000 guests, the total meal cost rises to $30,000.

**EXHIBIT 1–3**     Variable and Fixed Cost Behavior

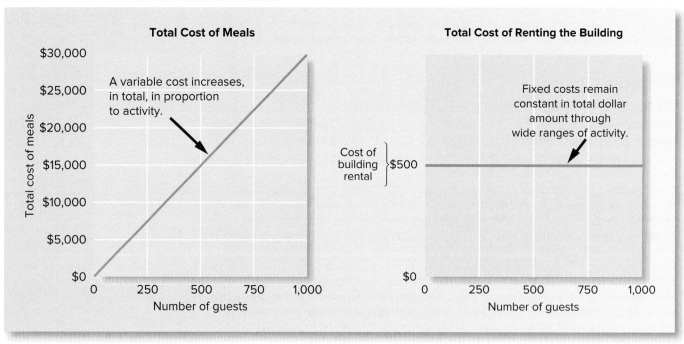

## Food Costs at a Luxury Hotel

The **Sporthotel Theresa** (http://www.theresa.at/), owned and operated by the Egger family, is a four star hotel located in Zell im Zillertal, Austria. The hotel features access to hiking, skiing, biking, and other activities in the Ziller alps as well as its own fitness facility and spa.

Three full meals a day are included in the hotel room charge. Breakfast and lunch are served buffet-style while dinner is a more formal affair with as many as six courses. The chef, Stefan Egger, believes that food costs are roughly proportional to the number of guests staying at the hotel; that is, they are a variable cost. He must order food from suppliers two or three days in advance, but he adjusts his purchases to the number of guests who are currently staying at the hotel and their consumption patterns. In addition, guests make their selections from the dinner menu early in the day, which helps Stefan plan which foodstuffs will be required for dinner. Consequently, he is able to prepare just enough food so that all guests are satisfied and yet waste is held to a minimum.

©Sandee Noreen

## Fixed Cost

A **fixed cost** is a cost that remains constant, in total, regardless of changes in the level of activity. Manufacturing overhead usually includes various fixed costs such as depreciation, insurance, property taxes, rent, and supervisory salaries. Similarly, selling and administrative costs often include fixed costs such as administrative salaries, advertising, and depreciation of nonmanufacturing assets. Unlike variable costs, fixed costs are not affected by changes in activity. Consequently, as the activity level rises and falls, total fixed costs remain constant unless influenced by some outside force, such as a landlord increasing your monthly rent. To continue the Nooksack Expeditions example, assume the company rents a building for $500 per month to store its equipment. The total amount of rent paid is the same regardless of the number of guests the company takes on its expeditions during any given month. The concept of a fixed cost is shown graphically on the right-hand side of Exhibit 1–3.

Because total fixed costs remain constant for large variations in the level of activity, the average fixed cost *per unit* becomes progressively smaller as the level of activity increases. If Nooksack Expeditions has only 250 guests in a month, the $500 fixed rental cost would amount to an average of $2 per guest. If there are 1,000 guests, the fixed rental cost would average only 50 cents per guest. The table below illustrates this aspect of the behavior of fixed costs. Note that as the number of guests increase, the average fixed cost per guest drops.

| Monthly Rental Cost | Number of Guests | Average Cost per Guest |
|---|---|---|
| $500 . . . . . . . . . . . | 250 | $2.00 |
| $500 . . . . . . . . . . | 500 | $1.00 |
| $500 . . . . . . . . . . | 750 | $0.67 |
| $500 . . . . . . . . . . | 1,000 | $0.50 |

As a general rule, *we caution against expressing fixed costs on an average per unit basis in internal reports because it creates the false impression that fixed costs are like variable costs and that total fixed costs actually change as the level of activity changes.*

For planning purposes, fixed costs can be viewed as either *committed* or *discretionary*. **Committed fixed costs** represent organizational investments with a *multiyear* planning horizon that can't be significantly reduced even for short periods of time without making fundamental changes. Examples include investments in facilities and equipment, as well as real estate taxes, insurance premiums, and salaries of top management. Even if operations are interrupted or cut back, committed fixed costs remain largely unchanged in the short term because the costs of restoring them later are likely to be far greater than any short-run savings that might be realized. **Discretionary fixed costs** (often referred to as *managed fixed costs*) usually arise from *annual* decisions by management to spend on certain fixed cost items. Examples of discretionary fixed costs include advertising, research, public relations, management development programs, and internships for students. Discretionary fixed costs can be cut for short periods of time with minimal damage to the long-run goals of the organization.

## HELPFUL HINT

Students often assume that fixed costs expressed on a per unit basis behave like variable costs. This is not true! If the average fixed cost per unit is $5 at an activity level of 100 units, it means the total amount of the fixed cost is $500. If the activity level increases to 101 units it does not mean that fixed costs will increase by $5. The total fixed cost remains constant at $500 within the relevant range of activity.

## The Linearity Assumption and the Relevant Range

Management accountants ordinarily assume that costs are strictly linear; that is, the relation between cost on the one hand and activity on the other can be represented by a straight line within a narrow band of activity known as the *relevant range*. The **relevant range** is the range of activity within which the assumption that cost behavior is strictly linear is reasonably valid.[3]

The concept of the relevant range is important in understanding fixed costs. For example, suppose the **Mayo Clinic** rents a machine for $20,000 per month that tests blood samples for the presence of leukemia cells. Furthermore, suppose that the capacity of the leukemia diagnostic machine is 3,000 tests per month. The assumption that the rent for the diagnostic machine is $20,000 per month is only valid within the relevant range of 0 to 3,000 tests per month. If the Mayo Clinic needed to test 5,000 blood samples per month, then it would need to rent another machine for an additional $20,000 per month. It would be difficult to rent half of a diagnostic machine; therefore, the step pattern depicted in Exhibit 1–4 is typical for such costs. This exhibit shows that the fixed rental cost is $20,000 for a relevant range of 0 to 3,000 tests. The fixed rental cost increases to $40,000 within the relevant range of 3,001 to 6,000 tests. The rental cost increases in discrete steps or increments of 3,000 tests, rather than increasing in a linear fashion per test.

This step-oriented cost behavior pattern can also be used to describe other costs, such as some labor costs. For example, the cost of compensating salaried employees can be characterized using a step pattern. Salaried employees are paid a fixed amount, such as $40,000 per year, for providing the capacity to work a prespecified amount of time, such as 40 hours per week for 50 weeks a year (= 2,000 hours per year). In this example, the total salary cost is $40,000 within a relevant range of 0 to 2,000 hours of work. The total salary cost increases to $80,000 (or two employees) if the organization's work requirements expand to a relevant range of 2,001 to 4,000 hours of work. Cost behavior patterns such as salaried employees are often called *step-variable costs*. Step-variable costs can often be adjusted quickly as conditions change. Furthermore, the width of the steps for

---

[3]Recent research has focused on how costs respond to changes in activity. That research is broadly consistent with the accountant's linear model, with anticipated activity outside of the relevant range often leading to adjustments in fixed costs. See Rajiv Banker and Dmitri Byzalov, "Asymmetric Cost Behavior," *Journal of Management Accounting Research,* 2014, Vol. 26, No. 2, pages 43–79, and Eric Noreen, "Capacity Constraints and Asymmetric Cost Behavior," working paper, 2014–5.

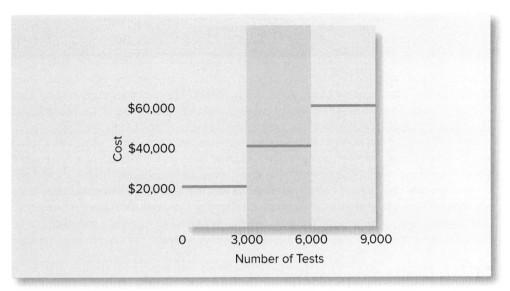

**EXHIBIT 1–4**
Fixed Costs and the Relevant
Range

step-variable costs is generally so narrow that these costs can be treated essentially as variable costs for most purposes. The width of the steps for fixed costs, on the other hand, is so wide that these costs should be treated as entirely fixed within the relevant range.

Exhibit 1–5 summarizes four key concepts related to variable and fixed costs. Study it carefully before reading further.

| | Behavior of the Cost (within the relevant range) | |
|---|---|---|
| **Cost** | **In Total** | **Per Unit** |
| Variable cost | Total variable cost increases and decreases in proportion to changes in the activity level. | Variable cost per unit remains constant. |
| Fixed cost | Total fixed cost is not affected by changes in the activity level within the relevant range. | Fixed cost per unit decreases as the activity level rises and increases as the activity level falls. |

**EXHIBIT 1–5**
Summary of Variable and Fixed
Cost Behavior

3. Which of the following cost behavior assumptions is true? (You may select more than one answer.)
   a. Variable costs are constant if expressed on a per unit basis.
   b. Total variable costs increase as the level of activity increases.
   c. The average fixed cost per unit increases as the level of activity increases.
   d. Total fixed costs decrease as the level of activity decreases.
4. Assume the following: (1) three people go to a restaurant, (2) each person orders a soda for $2 and the group of three orders a large pizza to share for a price of $12, and (3) a fourth person joins the group and orders one soda and is invited to share in eating the pizza. Which of the following statements is false? (You may select more than one answer.)
   a. The cost of the fourth person's soda will be $2.
   b. The total cost of the four sodas consumed by the group is $8.
   c. When the fourth person joined the group the total cost of the large pizza increased to $16.
   d. When the fourth person joined the group the average "pizza cost" per person dropped to $3.

CONCEPT
CHECK

## How Many Guides?

©Kuznetcov_Konstantin/Shutterstock. com RF

**Majestic Ocean Kayaking**, of Ucluelet, British Columbia, is owned and operated by Tracy Morben-Eeftink. The company offers a number of guided kayaking excursions ranging from three-hour tours of the Ucluelet harbor to six-day kayaking and camping trips in Clayoquot Sound. One of the company's excursions is a four-day kayaking and camping trip to The Broken Group Islands in the Pacific Rim National Park. Special regulations apply to trips in the park—including a requirement that one certified guide must be assigned for every five guests or fraction thereof. For example, a trip with 12 guests must have at least three certified guides. Guides are not salaried and are paid on a per-day basis. Therefore, the cost to the company of the guides for a trip is a step-variable cost rather than a fixed cost or a strictly variable cost. One guide is needed for 1 to 5 guests, two guides for 6 to 10 guests, three guides for 11 to 15 guests, and so on.

## Mixed Costs

A **mixed cost** contains both variable and fixed cost elements. Mixed costs are also known as semivariable costs. To continue the Nooksack Expeditions example, the company incurs a mixed cost called *fees paid to the state*. It includes a license fee of $25,000 per year plus $3 per rafting party paid to the state's Department of Natural Resources. If the company runs 1,000 rafting parties this year, then the total fees paid to the state would be $28,000, made up of $25,000 in fixed cost plus $3,000 in variable cost. Exhibit 1–6 depicts the behavior of this mixed cost.

Even if Nooksack fails to attract any customers, the company will still have to pay the license fee of $25,000. This is why the cost line in Exhibit 1–6 intersects the vertical cost axis at the $25,000 point. For each rafting party the company organizes, the total cost of the state fees will increase by $3. Therefore, the total cost line slopes upward as the variable cost of $3 per party is added to the fixed cost of $25,000 per year.

Because the mixed cost in Exhibit 1–6 is represented by a straight line, the following equation for a straight line can be used to express the relationship between a mixed cost and the level of activity:

$$Y = a + bX$$

In this equation,

$Y$ = The total mixed cost

$a$ = The total fixed cost (the vertical intercept of the line)

$b$ = The variable cost per unit of activity (the slope of the line)

$X$ = The level of activity

Because the variable cost per unit equals the slope of the straight line, the steeper the slope, the higher the variable cost per unit.

In the case of the state fees paid by Nooksack Expeditions, the equation is written as follows:

$$Y = \$25,000 + \$3.00X$$

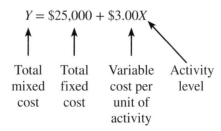

| Total mixed cost | Total fixed cost | Variable cost per unit of activity | Activity level |

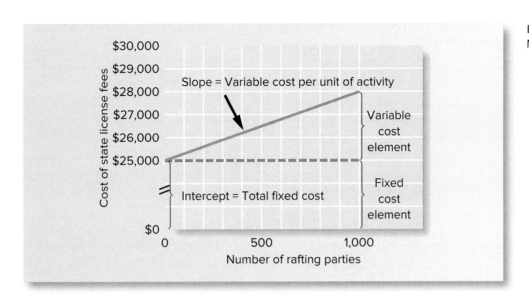

EXHIBIT 1–6
Mixed Cost Behavior

This equation makes it easy to calculate the total mixed cost for any activity level within the relevant range. For example, suppose that the company expects to organize 800 rafting parties in the next year. The total state fees would be calculated as follows:

$$Y = \$25,000 + (\$3.00 \text{ per rafting party} \times 800 \text{ rafting parties})$$
$$= \$27,400$$

## HELPFUL HINT

A mixed cost expressed on a per unit basis decreases as the activity level increases. Do you know why? Although the variable portion of a mixed cost stays constant on a per unit basis as the activity level increases, the fixed portion of a mixed cost decreases on a per unit basis as the activity level increases. This occurs because the fixed cost is being spread across more units.

## Cost Terminology—A Closer Look

To improve your understanding of some of the definitions and concepts introduced so far, consider the following scenario. A company has reported the following costs and expenses for the most recent month:

| | | |
|---|---:|---:|
| Direct materials | | $69,000 |
| Direct labor | | $35,000 |
| Variable manufacturing overhead | $15,000 | |
| Fixed manufacturing overhead | 28,000 | |
| Total manufacturing overhead | | $43,000 |
| Variable selling expense | $ 12,000 | |
| Fixed selling expense | 18,000 | |
| Total selling expense | | $30,000 |
| Variable administrative expense | $ 4,000 | |
| Fixed administrative expense | 25,000 | |
| Total administrative expense | | $29,000 |

These costs and expenses can be categorized in a number of ways, some of which are shown below:

| | | |
|---|---|---|
| Product cost | = | Direct materials + Direct labor + Manufacturing overhead |
| | = | $69,000 + $35,000 + $43,000 |
| | = | $147,000 |
| Period cost | = | Selling expense + Administrative expense |
| | = | $30,000 + $29,000 |
| | = | $59,000 |
| Conversion cost | = | Direct labor + Manufacturing overhead |
| | = | $35,000 + $43,000 |
| | = | $78,000 |
| Prime cost | = | Direct materials + Direct labor |
| | = | $69,000 + $35,000 |
| | = | $104,000 |
| Variable manufacturing cost | = | Direct materials + Direct labor + Variable manufacturing overhead |
| | = | $69,000 + $35,000 + $15,000 |
| | = | $119,000 |
| Total fixed cost | = | Fixed manufacturing overhead + Fixed selling expense + Fixed administrative expense |
| | = | $28,000 + $18,000 + $25,000 |
| | = | $71,000 |

# COST CLASSIFICATIONS FOR DECISION MAKING

Decisions involve choosing between alternatives. To make intelligent choices, it is essential to consider *relevant costs* (and benefits) while ignoring *irrelevant costs* (and benefits). More specifically, it important to understand the terms *differential cost* and *revenue, sunk cost,* and *opportunity cost.*

## Differential Cost and Revenue

In business decisions, each alternative will have costs and benefits that must be compared to the costs and benefits of other available alternatives. A future cost that differs between any two alternatives is known as a **differential cost**. Differential costs are always relevant costs. Future revenue that differs between any two alternatives is known as **differential revenue**. Differential revenue is an example of a relevant benefit. Any future cost or benefit that does not differ between the alternatives is irrelevant and should be ignored.

A differential cost is also known as an **incremental cost**. Although technically an incremental cost should refer only to an increase in cost from one alternative to another, whereas decreases in cost should be referred to as *decremental costs.* Differential cost is a broader term, encompassing both cost increases (incremental costs) and cost decreases (decremental costs) between alternatives.

The accountant's differential cost concept can be compared to the economist's marginal cost concept. In speaking of changes in cost and revenue, the economist uses the terms *marginal cost* and *marginal revenue.* The revenue that can be obtained from selling one more unit of product is called marginal revenue, and the cost involved in producing one more unit of product is called marginal cost. The economist's marginal concept is basically the same as the accountant's differential concept applied to a single unit of output.

Differential costs can be either fixed or variable. To illustrate, assume that Natural Cosmetics, Inc., is thinking about changing its marketing method from distribution through retailers to distribution by a network of neighborhood sales representatives. Present costs and revenues are compared to projected costs and revenues in the following table:

| | Retailer Distribution (present) | Sales Representatives (proposed) | Differential Costs and Revenues |
|---|---|---|---|
| Sales (*variable*) | $700,000 | $800,000 | $100,000 |
| Cost of goods sold (*variable*) | 350,000 | 400,000 | 50,000 |
| Advertising (*fixed*) | 80,000 | 45,000 | (35,000) |
| Commissions (*variable*) | 0 | 40,000 | 40,000 |
| Warehouse depreciation (*fixed*) | 50,000 | 80,000 | 30,000 |
| Other expenses (*fixed*) | 60,000 | 60,000 | 0 |
| Total expenses | 540,000 | 625,000 | 85,000 |
| Net operating income | $160,000 | $175,000 | $ 15,000 |

According to the above analysis, the differential revenue is $100,000 and the differential costs total $85,000, leaving a positive differential net operating income of $15,000 in favor of using sales representatives.

In general, only the differences between alternatives are relevant in decisions. Those items that are the same under all alternatives and that are not affected by the decision can be ignored. For example, in the Natural Cosmetics, Inc., example above, the "Other expenses" category, which is $60,000 under both alternatives, can be ignored because it has no effect on the decision. If it were removed from the calculations, the sales representatives would still be preferred by $15,000. This is an extremely important principle in management accounting that we will revisit in later chapters.

## Sunk Cost and Opportunity Cost

A **sunk cost** is a cost *that has already been incurred* and that cannot be changed by any decision made now or in the future. Because sunk costs cannot be changed by any decision, they are not differential costs. And because only differential costs are relevant in a decision, sunk costs should always be ignored.

To illustrate a sunk cost, assume that a company paid $50,000 several years ago for a special-purpose machine. The machine was used to make a product that is now obsolete and is no longer being sold. Even though in hindsight purchasing the machine may have been unwise, the $50,000 cost has already been incurred and cannot be undone. It would be folly to continue making the obsolete product in a misguided attempt to "recover" the original cost of the machine. In short, the $50,000 originally paid for the machine is a sunk cost that should be ignored in current decisions.

**Opportunity cost** is the potential benefit that is given up when one alternative is selected over another. For example, assume that you have a part-time job while attending college that pays $200 per week. If you spend one week at the beach during spring break without pay, then the $200 in lost wages would be an opportunity cost of taking the week off to be at the beach. Opportunity costs are not usually found in accounting records, but they are costs that must be explicitly considered in every decision a manager makes. Virtually every alternative involves an opportunity cost.

## Your Decision to Attend Class

**DECISION POINT**

When you make the decision to attend class on a particular day, what are the opportunity costs that are inherent in that decision?

CONCEPT CHECK ✓

5. Which of the following statements is true? (You may select more than one answer.)
   a. A common cost is one type of direct cost.
   b. A sunk cost is usually a differential cost.
   c. Opportunity costs are not usually recorded in the accounts of an organization.
   d. A particular cost may be direct or indirect depending on the cost object.

---

**IN BUSINESS**

## Navistar Closes Its Engine Plant in Alabama

When **Navistar International**'s share of the medium-size truck market dropped from 30% to 17%, the company decided to eliminate excess capacity by closing its engine plant in Alabama. The plant closure resulted in a loss of 280 jobs and an annual cost savings of about $22 million per year. When making this decision Navistar was essentially choosing between two alternatives—keep the Alabama plant open or close the plant. When Navistar analyzed the differential costs and revenues associated with these two alternatives, it opted to close the plant.

Source: Tita, Bob, "Truck Maker Navistar to Close Alabama Plant," *The Wall Street Journal*, February 21, 2014, p. B3.

---

# USING DIFFERENT COST CLASSIFICATIONS FOR DIFFERENT PURPOSES

**LEARNING OBJECTIVE 1–6**

Prepare income statements for a merchandising company using the traditional and contribution formats.

In this section of the chapter, we discuss how to prepare traditional and contribution format income statements for a merchandising company.[4] Merchandising companies do not manufacture the products that they sell to customers. For example, **Lowe's** and **Home Depot** are merchandising companies because they buy finished products from manufacturers and then resell them to end consumers.

Contrasting these two types of income statements enables us to illustrate the chapter's unifying theme of *different cost classifications for different purposes.* Traditional income statements are prepared primarily for *external reporting purposes.* They rely on cost classifications for preparing financial statements (product and period costs) to depict the financial consequences of *past* transactions. Contribution format income statements are prepared for *internal management purposes.* They use cost classifications for predicting costs behavior (variable and fixed costs) to better inform decisions affecting the *future.*

The two different purposes served by these income statements highlight what is arguably the most important difference between financial accounting and managerial accounting—an emphasis on recording past performance versus an emphasis on making predictions and decisions that affect future performance.

## The Traditional Format Income Statement

The left-hand side of Exhibit 1–7 shows a traditional income statement format for merchandising companies. This type of income statement organizes costs into two categories—cost of goods sold and selling and administrative expenses. Sales minus cost of goods sold equals the *gross margin.* The gross margin minus selling and administrative expenses equals net operating income.

---

[4] Subsequent chapters compare the income statement formats for manufacturing companies.

**EXHIBIT 1–7**  Comparing Traditional and Contribution Format Income Statements for Merchandising Companies (all numbers are given)

| Traditional Format | | | Contribution Format | | |
|---|---|---|---|---|---|
| Sales . . . . . . . . . . . . . . . . . . . . . . . . . . . | | $12,000 | Sales . . . . . . . . . . . . . . . . . . . . . . . . . . | | $12,000 |
| Cost of goods sold* . . . . . . . . . . . . . . | | 6,000 | Variable expenses: | | |
| Gross margin . . . . . . . . . . . . . . . . . . . | | 6,000 | Cost of goods sold . . . . . . . . . . . . | $6,000 | |
| Selling and administrative expenses: | | | Variable selling . . . . . . . . . . . . . . . | 600 | |
| Selling . . . . . . . . . . . . . . . . . . . . . . . | $3,100 | | Variable administrative . . . . . . . . . | 400 | 7,000 |
| Administrative . . . . . . . . . . . . . . . . | 1,900 | 5,000 | Contribution margin . . . . . . . . . . . . . . | | 5,000 |
| Net operating income . . . . . . . . . . . . | | $ 1,000 | Fixed expenses: | | |
| | | | Fixed selling . . . . . . . . . . . . . . . . . | 2,500 | |
| | | | Fixed administrative . . . . . . . . . . . | 1,500 | 4,000 |
| | | | Net operating income . . . . . . . . . . . | | $ 1,000 |

*For a manufacturing company, the cost of goods sold would include some variable costs, such as direct materials, direct labor, and variable overhead, and some fixed costs, such as fixed manufacturing overhead. Income statement formats for manufacturing companies will be explored in greater detail in a subsequent chapter.

The cost of goods sold reports the *product costs* attached to the merchandise sold during the period. The selling and administrative expenses report all *period costs* that have been expensed as incurred. The cost of goods sold for a merchandising company can be computed directly by multiplying the number of units sold by their unit cost or indirectly using the equation below:

$$\text{Cost of goods sold} = \text{Beginning merchandise inventory} + \text{Purchases} - \text{Ending merchandise inventory}$$

For example, let's assume that the company depicted in Exhibit 1–7 purchased $3,000 of merchandise inventory during the period and had beginning and ending merchandise inventory balances of $7,000 and $4,000, respectively. The equation above could be used to compute the cost of goods sold as follows:

$$\text{Cost of goods sold} = \text{Beginning merchandise inventory} + \text{Purchases} - \text{Ending merchandise inventory}$$
$$= \$7,000 + \$3,000 - \$4,000$$
$$= \$6,000$$

Although the traditional income statement is useful for external reporting purposes, it has serious limitations when used for internal purposes. It does not distinguish between fixed and variable costs. For example, under the heading "Selling and administrative expenses," both variable administrative costs ($400) and fixed administrative costs ($1,500) are lumped together ($1,900). Internally, managers need cost data organized by cost behavior to aid in planning, controlling, and decision making. The contribution format income statement has been developed in response to these needs.

## HELPFUL HINT

This chapter focuses on income statement formats for merchandisers rather than manufacturers. Therefore, within this chapter, the cost of goods sold shown in the traditional and contribution format income statements will always be a variable cost. It will not contain any fixed manufacturing overhead because merchandisers do not manufacture the products that they sell to customers.

## The Contribution Format Income Statement

The crucial distinction between fixed and variable costs is at the heart of the **contribution approach** to constructing income statements. The unique thing about the contribution approach is that it provides managers with an income statement that clearly distinguishes between fixed and variable costs and therefore aids planning, controlling, and decision making. The right-hand side of Exhibit 1–7 shows a contribution format income statement for merchandising companies.

The contribution approach separates costs into fixed and variable categories, first deducting all variable expenses from sales to obtain the *contribution margin*. For a merchandising company, cost of goods sold is a variable cost that gets included in the "Variable expenses" portion of the contribution format income statement. The **contribution margin** is the amount remaining from sales revenues after all variable expenses have been deducted. This amount *contributes* toward covering fixed expenses and then toward profits for the period. The contribution margin can also be stated on a per unit basis. For example, if the company depicted in Exhibit 1–7 sold 500 units, then its contribution margin per unit would be $10 per unit (= $5,000 ÷ 500 units).

The contribution format income statement is used as an internal planning and decision-making tool. Its emphasis on cost behavior aids cost-volume-profit analysis, management performance appraisals, and budgeting. Moreover, the contribution approach helps managers organize data pertinent to numerous decisions such as product-line analysis, pricing, use of scarce resources, and make or buy analysis. All of these topics are covered in later chapters.

CONCEPT CHECK

6.  Which of the following statements is true? (You may select more than one answer.)
    a. Traditional income statements include administrative expenses in the computation of gross margin.
    b. Contribution format income statements exclude variable selling expenses from the computation of contribution margin.
    c. Traditional income statements exclude fixed selling expenses from the computation of gross margin.
    d. Contribution format income statements exclude all fixed expenses from the computation of contribution margin.

**LO1–1 Understand cost classifications used for assigning costs to cost objects: direct costs and indirect costs.**

A direct cost such as direct materials is a cost that can be easily and conveniently traced to a cost object. An indirect cost is a cost that cannot be easily and conveniently traced to a cost object. For example, the salary of the administrator of a hospital is an indirect cost of serving a particular patient.

**LO1–2 Identify and give examples of each of the three basic manufacturing cost categories.**

Manufacturing costs consist of two categories of costs that can be conveniently and directly traced to units of product—direct materials and direct labor—and one category that cannot be conveniently traced to units of product—manufacturing overhead.

**LO1–3 Understand cost classifications used to prepare financial statements: product costs and period costs.**

For purposes of valuing inventories and determining expenses for the balance sheet and income statement, costs are classified as either product costs or period costs. Product costs are assigned to inventories and are considered assets until the products are sold. A product cost becomes an expense—cost of goods sold—only when the product is sold. In contrast, period costs are taken directly to the income statement as expenses in the period in which they are incurred.

In a merchandising company, product cost is whatever the company paid for its merchandise. For external financial reports in a manufacturing company, product costs consist of all manufacturing costs. In both kinds of companies, selling and administrative costs are considered to be period costs and are expensed as incurred.

**LO1–4 Understand cost classifications used to predict cost behavior: variable costs, fixed costs, and mixed costs.**

For purposes of predicting how costs will react to changes in activity, costs are classified into three categories—variable, fixed, and mixed. Variable costs, in total, are strictly proportional to activity. The variable cost per unit is constant. Fixed costs, in total, remain the same as the activity level changes within the relevant range. The average fixed cost per unit decreases as the activity level increases. Mixed costs consist of variable and fixed elements and can be expressed in equation form as $Y = a + bX$, where $X$ is the activity, $Y$ is the total cost, $a$ is the fixed cost element, and $b$ is the variable cost per unit of activity.

**LO1–5 Understand cost classifications used in making decisions: differential costs, sunk costs, and opportunity costs.**

The concepts of differential cost and revenue, sunk cost, and opportunity cost are vitally important for purposes of making decisions. Differential costs and revenues refer to the costs and revenues that differ between alternatives. Sunk cost is a cost that occurred in the past and cannot be altered. Opportunity cost is the benefit that is forgone when one alternative is selected over another. Differential costs and opportunity costs are relevant in decisions and should be carefully considered. Sunk costs are always irrelevant in decisions and should be ignored.

The various cost classifications discussed in this chapter are different ways of looking at costs. A particular cost, such as the cost of cheese in a taco served at **Taco Bell**, can be a manufacturing cost, a product cost, a variable cost, a direct cost, and a differential cost—all at the same time. Taco Bell essentially manufactures fast food. Therefore the cost of the cheese in a taco would be considered a manufacturing cost as well as a product cost. In addition, the cost of cheese would be considered variable with respect to the number of tacos served and would be a direct cost of serving tacos. Finally, the cost of the cheese in a taco would be considered a differential cost of the taco.

**LO1–6 Prepare income statements for a merchandising company using the traditional and contribution formats.**

The traditional income statement format is used primarily for external reporting purposes. It organizes costs using product and period cost classifications. The contribution format income statement aids decision making because it organizes costs using variable and fixed cost classifications. The contribution margin is the amount remaining from sales revenues after variable expenses have been deducted. This amount contributes toward covering fixed expenses and then toward profits for the period.

# GUIDANCE ANSWERS TO DECISION POINT

**Your Decision to Attend Class**

Every alternative involves an opportunity cost. Think about what you could be doing instead of attending class.

- You could have been working at a part-time job; you could quantify that cost by multiplying your pay rate by the time you spend preparing for and attending class.
- You could have spent the time studying for another class; the opportunity cost could be measured by the improvement in the grade that would result from spending more time on the other class.
- You could have slept in or taken a nap; depending on your level of sleep deprivation, this opportunity cost might be priceless.

## GUIDANCE ANSWERS TO CONCEPT CHECKS

1. **Choices b and d.** Product costs attach to units of production and are expensed on the income statement when the units are sold. Conversion costs do not include direct materials.
2. **Choices a, b, and c.** Product costs (rather than period costs) are referred to as inventoriable costs.
3. **Choices a and b.** The average fixed cost per unit decreases, rather than increases, as the level of activity increases. Total fixed costs do not change as the level of activity decreases (within the relevant range).
4. **Choice c.** When the fourth person joined the group the total cost of the large pizza held constant at $12.
5. **Choices c and d.** A common cost is one type of indirect cost, rather than direct cost. A sunk cost is not a differential cost.
6. **Choices c and d.** Traditional income statements exclude administrative expenses from the computation of gross margin. Contribution format income statements include variable selling expenses in the computation of contribution margin.

# REVIEW PROBLEM 1: COST TERMS

Many new cost terms have been introduced in this chapter. It will take you some time to learn what each term means and how to properly classify costs in an organization. Consider the following example: Porter Company manufactures furniture, including tables. Selected costs are given below:

1. The tables are made of wood that costs $100 per table.
2. The tables are assembled by workers, at a wage cost of $40 per table.
3. Workers assembling the tables are supervised by a factory supervisor who is paid $38,000 per year.
4. Electrical costs are $2 per machine-hour. Four machine-hours are required to produce a table.
5. The depreciation on the machines used to make the tables totals $10,000 per year. The machines have no resale value and do not wear out through use.
6. The salary of the president of the company is $100,000 per year.
7. The company spends $250,000 per year to advertise its products.
8. Salespersons are paid a commission of $30 for each table sold.
9. Instead of producing the tables, the company could rent its factory space for $50,000 per year.

*Required:*

Classify these costs according to the various cost terms used in the chapter. *Carefully study the classification of each cost.* If you don't understand why a particular cost is classified the way it is, reread the section of the chapter discussing the particular cost term. The terms *variable cost* and *fixed cost* refer to how costs behave with respect to the number of tables produced in a year.

**Solution to Review Problem 1**

| | Variable Cost | Fixed Cost | Period (Selling and Administrative) Cost | Direct Materials | Direct Labor | Manufacturing Overhead | Sunk Cost | Opportunity Cost |
|---|---|---|---|---|---|---|---|---|
| 1. Wood used in a table ($100 per table) .............. | X | | | X | | | | |
| 2. Labor cost to assemble a table ($40 per table) ......... | X | | | | X | | | |
| 3. Salary of the factory supervisor ($38,000 per year) ........................ | | X | | | | X | | |
| 4. Cost of electricity to produce tables ($2 per machine-hour) ................ | X | | | | | X | | |
| 5. Depreciation of machines used to produce tables ($10,000 per year) ............ | | X | | | | X | X* | |
| 6. Salary of the company president ($100,000 per year)............ | | X | X | | | | | |
| 7. Advertising expense ($250,000 per year)........... | | X | X | | | | | |
| 8. Commissions paid to salespersons ($30 per table sold) ........... | X | | X | | | | | |
| 9. Rental income forgone on factory space ($50,000 per year)..................... | | | | | | | | X† |

_____

*This is a sunk cost because the outlay for the equipment was made in a previous period.
†This is an opportunity cost because it represents the potential benefit that is lost or sacrificed as a result of using the factory space to produce tables. Opportunity cost is a special category of cost that is not ordinarily recorded in an organization's accounting records. To avoid possible confusion with other costs, we will not attempt to classify this cost in any other way except as an opportunity cost.

# REVIEW PROBLEM 2: INCOME STATEMENT FORMATS

McFarland, Inc., is a merchandiser that provided the following information:

| | Amount |
|---|---|
| Number of units sold .................... | 35,000 |
| Selling price per unit..................... | $40 |
| Variable selling expense per unit.......... | $3 |
| Variable administrative expense per unit ... | $1 |
| Total fixed selling expense ............... | $45,000 |
| Total fixed administrative expense......... | $28,000 |
| Beginning merchandise inventory ......... | $21,000 |
| Ending merchandise inventory............ | $35,000 |
| Merchandise purchases.................. | $805,000 |

*Required:*
1.  Prepare a traditional income statement.
2.  Prepare a contribution format income statement.

**Solution to Review Problem 2**
1.  Traditional income statement

| McFarland, Inc. Traditional Income Statement | | |
|---|---:|---:|
| Sales ($40 per unit × 35,000 units) | | $1,400,000 |
| Cost of goods sold ($21,000 + $805,000 − $35,000) | | 791,000 |
| Gross margin | | 609,000 |
| Selling and administrative expenses: | | |
| Selling expense (($3 per unit × 35,000 units) + $45,000) | $150,000 | |
| Administrative expense (($1 per unit × 35,000 units) + $28,000) | 63,000 | 213,000 |
| Net operating income | | $ 396,000 |

2.  Contribution format income statement

| McFarland, Inc. Contribution Format Income Statement | | |
|---|---:|---:|
| Sales | | $1,400,000 |
| Variable expenses: | | |
| Cost of goods sold ($21,000 + $805,000 − $35,000) | $791,000 | |
| Selling expense ($3 per unit × 35,000 units) | 105,000 | |
| Administrative expense ($1 per unit × 35,000 units) | 35,000 | 931,000 |
| Contribution margin | | 469,000 |
| Fixed expenses: | | |
| Selling expense | $ 45,000 | |
| Administrative expense | 28,000 | 73,000 |
| Net operating income | | $ 396,000 |

# GLOSSARY

**Activity base** A measure of whatever causes the incurrence of a variable cost. For example, the total cost of surgical gloves in a hospital will increase as the number of surgeries increases. Therefore, the number of surgeries is the activity base that explains the total cost of surgical gloves. (p. 31)

**Administrative costs** All executive, organizational, and clerical costs associated with the general management of an organization rather than with manufacturing or selling. (p. 29)

**Committed fixed costs** Investments in facilities, equipment, and basic organizational structure that can't be significantly reduced even for short periods of time without making fundamental changes. (p. 33)

**Common cost** A cost that is incurred to support a number of cost objects but that cannot be traced to them individually. For example, the wage cost of the pilot of a 747 airliner is a common cost of all of the passengers on the aircraft. Without the pilot, there would be no flight and no passengers. But no part of the pilot's wage is caused by any one passenger taking the flight. (p. 27)

**Contribution approach** An income statement format that organizes costs by their behavior. Costs are separated into variable and fixed categories rather than being separated into product and period costs for external reporting purposes. (p. 42)

**Contribution margin** The amount remaining from sales revenues after all variable expenses have been deducted. (p. 42)

**Conversion cost** Direct labor cost plus manufacturing overhead cost. (p. 28)

**Cost behavior** The way in which a cost reacts to changes in the level of activity. (p. 31)

**Cost object** Anything for which cost data are desired. Examples of cost objects are products, customers, geographic regions, and parts of the organization such as departments or divisions. (p. 26)

**Cost structure**    The relative proportion of fixed, variable, and mixed costs in an organization. (p. 31)

**Differential cost**    A future cost that differs between any two alternatives. (p. 38)

**Differential revenue**    Future revenue that differs between any two alternatives. (p. 38)

**Direct cost**    A cost that can be easily and conveniently traced to a specified cost object. (p. 28)

**Direct labor**    Factory labor costs that can be easily traced to individual units of product. Also called *touch labor*. (p. 28)

**Direct materials**    Materials that become an integral part of a finished product and whose costs can be conveniently traced to it. (p. 28)

**Discretionary fixed costs**    Those fixed costs that arise from annual decisions by management to spend on certain fixed cost items, such as advertising and research. (p. 34)

**Financial accounting**    The phase of accounting that is concerned with reporting historical financial information to external parties, such as stockholders, creditors, and regulators. (p.26)

**Fixed cost**    A cost that remains constant, in total, regardless of changes in the level of activity within the relevant range. If a fixed cost is expressed on a per unit basis, it varies inversely with the level of activity. (p. 33)

**Finished goods**    Units of product that have been completed but not yet sold to customers. (p. 30)

**Incremental cost**    An increase in cost between two alternatives. (p. 38)

**Indirect cost**    A cost that cannot be easily and conveniently traced to a specified cost object. (p. 27)

**Indirect labor**    The labor costs of janitors, supervisors, materials handlers, and other factory workers that cannot be conveniently traced to particular products. (p. 28)

**Indirect materials**    Small items of material such as glue and nails that may be an integral part of a finished product, but whose costs cannot be easily or conveniently traced to it. (p. 28)

**Inventoriable costs**    Synonym for product costs. (p. 29)

**Managerial accounting**    The phase of accounting that is concerned with providing information to managers for use within the organization. (p. 26)

**Manufacturing overhead**    All manufacturing costs except direct materials and direct labor. (p. 28)

**Mixed cost**    A cost that contains both variable and fixed cost elements. (p. 36)

**Opportunity cost**    The potential benefit that is given up when one alternative is selected over another. (p. 39)

**Period costs**    Costs that are taken directly to the income statement as expenses in the period in which they are incurred or accrued. (p. 30)

**Prime cost**    Direct materials cost plus direct labor cost. (p. 28)

**Product costs**    All costs that are involved in acquiring or making a product. In the case of manufactured goods, these costs consist of direct materials, direct labor, and manufacturing overhead. Also see *Inventoriable costs.* (p. 29)

**Raw materials**    Any materials that go into the final product. (p. 27)

**Relevant range**    The range of activity within which assumptions about variable and fixed cost behavior are valid. (p. 34)

**Selling costs**    All costs that are incurred to secure customer orders and get the finished product or service into the hands of the customer. (p. 29)

**Sunk cost**    A cost that has already been incurred and that cannot be changed by any decision made now or in the future. (p. 39)

**Variable cost**    A cost that varies, in total, in direct proportion to changes in the level of activity. A variable cost is constant per unit. (p. 31)

**Work in process**    Units of product that are only partially complete and will require further work before they are ready for sale to the customer. (p. 30)

## QUESTIONS

1–1    What are the three major types of product costs in a manufacturing company?

1–2    Define the following: (*a*) direct materials, (*b*) indirect materials, (*c*) direct labor, (*d*) indirect labor, and (*e*) manufacturing overhead.

1–3    Explain the difference between a product cost and a period cost.

1–4    Distinguish between (*a*) a variable cost, (*b*) a fixed cost, and (*c*) a mixed cost.

1–5    What effect does an increase in the activity level have on—
   a.    Unit fixed costs?
   b.    Unit variable costs?
   c.    Total fixed costs?
   d.    Total variable costs?

**1–6**   Define the following terms: (*a*) cost behavior and (*b*) relevant range.

**1–7**   What is meant by an *activity base* when dealing with variable costs? Give several examples of activity bases.

**1–8**   Managers often assume a strictly linear relationship between cost and the level of activity. Under what conditions would this be a valid or invalid assumption?

**1–9**   Distinguish between discretionary fixed costs and committed fixed costs.

**1–10**  Does the concept of the relevant range apply to fixed costs? Explain.

**1–11**  What is the difference between a traditional format income statement and a contribution format income statement?

**1–12**  What is the contribution margin?

**1–13**  Define the following terms: differential cost, sunk cost, and opportunity cost.

**1–14**  Only variable costs can be differential costs. Do you agree? Explain.

---

## APPLYING EXCEL     Mc Graw Hill Education **connect**

**LO1–6**

This Excel worksheet form is to be used to recreate Exhibit 1–7. Download the workbook containing this form from Connect, where you will also receive instructions.

| | A | B | C | D |
|---|---|---|---|---|
| 1 | **Chapter 1: Applying Excel** | | | |
| 2 | | | | |
| 3 | **Data** | | | |
| 4 | Sales | $12,000 | | |
| 5 | Variable costs: | | | |
| 6 |   Cost of goods sold | $6,000 | | |
| 7 |   Variable selling | $600 | | |
| 8 |   Variable administrative | $400 | | |
| 9 | Fixed costs: | | | |
| 10 |   Fixed selling | $2,500 | | |
| 11 |   Fixed administrative | $1,500 | | |
| 12 | | | | |
| 13 | *Enter a formula into each of the cells marked with a ? below* | | | |
| 14 | **Exhibit 1-7** | | | |
| 15 | | | | |
| 16 | **Traditional Format Income Statement** | | | |
| 17 | Sales | | ? | |
| 18 | Cost of goods sold | | ? | |
| 19 | Gross margin | | ? | |
| 20 | Selling and administrative expenses: | | | |
| 21 |   Selling | ? | | |
| 22 |   Administrative | ? | ? | |
| 23 | Net operating income | | ? | |
| 24 | | | | |
| 25 | **Contribution Format Income Statement** | | | |
| 26 | Sales | | ? | |
| 27 | Variable expenses: | | | |
| 28 |   Cost of goods sold | ? | | |
| 29 |   Variable selling | ? | | |
| 30 |   Variable administration | ? | ? | |
| 31 | Contribution margin | | ? | |
| 32 | Fixed expenses: | | | |
| 33 |   Fixed selling | ? | | |
| 34 |   Fixed administrative | ? | ? | |
| 35 | Net operating income | | ? | |
| 36 | | | | |

Chapter 1 Form / Filled in Chapter 1 Form

**Required:**

1.  Check your worksheet by changing the variable selling cost in the Data area to $900, keeping all of the other data the same as in Exhibit 1–7. If your worksheet is operating properly, the net operating income under the traditional format income statement and under the contribution format income statement should now be $700 and the contribution margin should now be $4,700. If you do not get these answers, find the errors in your worksheet and correct them.

    How much is the gross margin? Did it change? Why or why not?

2.  Suppose that sales are 10% higher as shown below:

| Sales | $13,200 |
|---|---|
| Variable costs: | |
| Cost of goods sold | $6,600 |
| Variable selling | $660 |
| Variable administrative | $440 |
| Fixed costs: | |
| Fixed selling | $2,500 |
| Fixed administrative | $1,500 |

Enter this new data into your worksheet. Make sure that you change all of the data that are different—not just the sales. Print or copy the income statements from your worksheet.

What happened to the variable costs and to the fixed costs when sales increased by 10%? Why? Did the contribution margin increase by 10%? Why or why not? Did the net operating income increase by 10%? Why or why not?

**≣connect**  THE FOUNDATIONAL 15

Martinez Company's relevant range of production is 7,500 units to 12,500 units. When it produces and sells 10,000 units, its average costs per unit are as follows:

LO1–1, LO1–2, LO1–3, LO1–4, LO1–5, LO1–6

| | Average Cost per Unit |
|---|---|
| Direct materials | $6.00 |
| Direct labor | $3.50 |
| Variable manufacturing overhead | $1.50 |
| Fixed manufacturing overhead | $4.00 |
| Fixed selling expense | $3.00 |
| Fixed administrative expense | $2.00 |
| Sales commissions | $1.00 |
| Variable administrative expense | $0.50 |

*Required:*
1.  For financial accounting purposes, what is the total amount of product costs incurred to make 10,000 units?
2.  For financial accounting purposes, what is the total amount of period costs incurred to sell 10,000 units?
3.  If 8,000 units are produced and sold, what is the variable cost per unit produced and sold?
4.  If 12,500 units are produced and sold, what is the variable cost per unit produced and sold?
5.  If 8,000 units are produced and sold, what is the total amount of variable costs related to the units produced and sold?
6.  If 12,500 units are produced and sold, what is the total amount of variable costs related to the units produced and sold?
7.  If 8,000 units are produced, what is the average fixed manufacturing cost per unit produced?
8.  If 12,500 units are produced, what is the average fixed manufacturing cost per unit produced?
9.  If 8,000 units are produced, what is the total amount of fixed manufacturing cost incurred to support this level of production?
10. If 12,500 units are produced, what is the total amount of fixed manufacturing cost incurred to support this level of production?
11. If 8,000 units are produced, what is the total amount of manufacturing overhead cost incurred to support this level of production? What is this total amount expressed on a per unit basis?
12. If 12,500 units are produced, what is the total amount of manufacturing overhead cost incurred to support this level of production? What is this total amount expressed on a per unit basis?

13. If the selling price is $22 per unit, what is the contribution margin per unit?
14. If 11,000 units are produced, what are the total amounts of direct and indirect manufacturing costs incurred to support this level of production?
15. What incremental manufacturing cost will Martinez incur if it increases production from 10,000 to 10,001 units?

## EXERCISES           Mc Graw Hill connect

### EXERCISE 1–1   Identifying Direct and Indirect Costs LO1–1

Northwest Hospital is a full-service hospital that provides everything from major surgery and emergency room care to outpatient clinics.

**Required:**

For each cost incurred at Northwest Hospital, indicate whether it would most likely be a direct cost or an indirect cost of the specified cost object by placing an *X* in the appropriate column.

| Cost | Cost Object | Direct Cost | Indirect Cost |
|---|---|---|---|
| Ex. Catered food served to patients | A particular patient | X | |
| 1. The wages of pediatric nurses | The pediatric department | | |
| 2. Prescription drugs | A particular patient | | |
| 3. Heating the hospital | The pediatric department | | |
| 4. The salary of the head of pediatrics | The pediatric department | | |
| 5. The salary of the head of pediatrics | A particular pediatric patient | | |
| 6. Hospital chaplain's salary | A particular patient | | |
| 7. Lab tests by outside contractor | A particular patient | | |
| 8. Lab tests by outside contractor | A particular department | | |

### EXERCISE 1–2   Classifying Manufacturing Costs LO1–2

The PC Works assembles custom computers from components supplied by various manufacturers. The company is very small and its assembly shop and retail sales store are housed in a single facility in a Redmond, Washington, industrial park. Listed below are some of the costs that are incurred at the company.

**Required:**

For each cost, indicate whether it would most likely be classified as direct materials, direct labor, manufacturing overhead, selling, or an administrative cost.
1. The cost of a hard drive installed in a computer.
2. The cost of advertising in the *Puget Sound Computer User* newspaper.
3. The wages of employees who assemble computers from components.
4. Sales commissions paid to the company's salespeople.
5. The salary of the assembly shop's supervisor.
6. The salary of the company's accountant.
7. Depreciation on equipment used to test assembled computers before release to customers.
8. Rent on the facility in the industrial park.

### EXERCISE 1–3   Classifying Costs as Product or Period Costs LO1–3

Suppose that you have been given a summer job as an intern at Issac Aircams, a company that manufactures sophisticated spy cameras for remote-controlled military reconnaissance aircraft. The company, which is privately owned, has approached a bank for a loan to help finance its growth. The bank requires financial statements before approving the loan.

**Required:**

Classify each cost listed below as either a product cost or a period cost for the purpose of preparing financial statements for the bank.
1. Depreciation on salespersons' cars.
2. Rent on equipment used in the factory.

3. Lubricants used for machine maintenance.
4. Salaries of personnel who work in the finished goods warehouse.
5. Soap and paper towels used by factory workers at the end of a shift.
6. Factory supervisors' salaries.
7. Heat, water, and power consumed in the factory.
8. Materials used for boxing products for shipment overseas. (Units are not normally boxed.)
9. Advertising costs.
10. Workers' compensation insurance for factory employees.
11. Depreciation on chairs and tables in the factory lunchroom.
12. The wages of the receptionist in the administrative offices.
13. Cost of leasing the corporate jet used by the company's executives.
14. The cost of renting rooms at a Florida resort for the annual sales conference.
15. The cost of packaging the company's product.

### EXERCISE 1–4    Fixed and Variable Cost Behavior LO1–4

Espresso Express operates a number of espresso coffee stands in busy suburban malls. The fixed weekly expense of a coffee stand is $1,200 and the variable cost per cup of coffee served is $0.22.

**Required:**
1.  Fill in the following table with your estimates of the company's total cost and average cost per cup of coffee at the indicated levels of activity. Round off the average cost per cup of coffee to the nearest tenth of a cent.

|  | Cups of Coffee Served in a Week | | |
|---|---|---|---|
|  | **2,000** | **2,100** | **2,200** |
| Fixed cost . . . . . . . . . . . . . . . . . . . . . . . . . . . . . . | ? | ? | ? |
| Variable cost. . . . . . . . . . . . . . . . . . . . . . . . . . . | ? | ? | ? |
| Total cost. . . . . . . . . . . . . . . . . . . . . . . . . . . . . . | ? | ? | ? |
| Average cost per cup of coffee served . . . . . . . . | ? | ? | ? |

2.  Does the average cost per cup of coffee served increase, decrease, or remain the same as the number of cups of coffee served in a week increases? Explain.

### EXERCISE 1–5    Differential, Sunk, and Opportunity Costs LO1–5

Northeast Hospital's Radiology Department is considering replacing an old inefficient X-ray machine with a state-of-the-art digital X-ray machine. The new machine would provide higher quality X-rays in less time and at a lower cost per X-ray. It would also require less power and would use a color laser printer to produce easily readable X-ray images. Instead of investing the funds in the new X-ray machine, the Laboratory Department is lobbying the hospital's management to buy a new DNA analyzer.

**Required:**
For each of the items below, indicate by placing an X in the appropriate column whether it should be considered a differential cost, a sunk cost, or an opportunity cost in the decision to replace the old X-ray machine with a new machine. If none of the categories apply for a particular item, leave all columns blank.

| Item | Differential Cost | Sunk Cost | Opportunity Cost |
|---|---|---|---|
| Ex. Cost of X-ray film used in the old machine . . . . . . . . . . . . . . | X | | |
| 1. Cost of the old X-ray machine . . . . . . . . . . . . . . . . . . . . . . . . . | | | |
| 2. The salary of the head of the Radiology Department . . . . . . | | | |
| 3. The salary of the head of the Laboratory Department . . . . . | | | |
| 4. Cost of the new color laser printer . . . . . . . . . . . . . . . . . . . . . | | | |
| 5. Rent on the space occupied by Radiology . . . . . . . . . . . . . . | | | |
| 6. The cost of maintaining the old machine. . . . . . . . . . . . . . . . | | | |
| 7. Benefits from a new DNA analyzer. . . . . . . . . . . . . . . . . . . . . | | | |
| 8. Cost of electricity to run the X-ray machines . . . . . . . . . . . . | | | |

**EXERCISE 1-6   Traditional and Contribution Format Income Statements LO1-6**

Cherokee Inc. is a merchandiser that provided the following information:

|  | Amount |
|---|---|
| Number of units sold ........................... | 20,000 |
| Selling price per unit............................ | $30 |
| Variable selling expense per unit............... | $4 |
| Variable administrative expense per unit ......... | $2 |
| Total fixed selling expense ..................... | $40,000 |
| Total fixed administrative expense ............. | $30,000 |
| Beginning merchandise inventory .............. | $24,000 |
| Ending merchandise inventory ................. | $44,000 |
| Merchandise purchases........................ | $180,000 |

**Required:**
1. Prepare a traditional income statement.
2. Prepare a contribution format income statement.

**EXERCISE 1-7   Direct and Indirect Costs LO1-1**

Kubin Company's relevant range of production is 18,000 to 22,000 units. When it produces and sells 20,000 units, its average costs per unit are as follows:

|  | Average Cost per Unit |
|---|---|
| Direct materials ............................. | $7.00 |
| Direct labor................................. | $4.00 |
| Variable manufacturing overhead ............ | $1.50 |
| Fixed manufacturing overhead................ | $5.00 |
| Fixed selling expense........................ | $3.50 |
| Fixed administrative expense ................ | $2.50 |
| Sales commissions .......................... | $1.00 |
| Variable administrative expense.............. | $0.50 |

**Required:**
1. Assume the cost object is units of production:
   a. What is the total direct manufacturing cost incurred to make 20,000 units?
   b. What is the total indirect manufacturing cost incurred to make 20,000 units?
2. Assume the cost object is the Manufacturing Department and that its total output is 20,000 units.
   a. How much total manufacturing cost is directly traceable to the Manufacturing Department?
   b. How much total manufacturing cost is an indirect cost that cannot be easily traced to the Manufacturing Department?
3. Assume the cost object is the company's various sales representatives. Furthermore, assume that the company spent $50,000 of its total fixed selling expense on advertising and the remainder of the total fixed selling expense comprised the fixed portion of the company's sales representatives' compensation.
   a. When the company sells 20,000 units, what is the total direct selling expense that can be readily traced to individual sales representatives?
   b. When the company sells 20,000 units, what is the total indirect selling expense that cannot be readily traced to individual sales representatives?
4. Are Kubin's administrative expenses always going to be treated as indirect costs in its internal management reports?

**EXERCISE 1–8  Product Costs and Period Costs; Variable and Fixed Costs LO1–3, LO1–4**
Refer to the data given in Exercise 1–7. Answer all questions independently.

**Required:**
1. For financial accounting purposes, what is the total amount of product costs incurred to make 20,000 units?
2. For financial accounting purposes, what is the total amount of period costs incurred to sell 20,000 units?
3. For financial accounting purposes, what is the total amount of product costs incurred to make 22,000 units?
4. For financial accounting purposes, what is the total amount of period costs incurred to sell 18,000 units?

**EXERCISE 1–9  Fixed, Variable, and Mixed Costs LO1–4**
Refer to the data given in Exercise 1–7. Answer all questions independently.

**Required:**
1. If 18,000 units are produced and sold, what is the variable cost per unit produced and sold?
2. If 22,000 units are produced and sold, what is the variable cost per unit produced and sold?
3. If 18,000 units are produced and sold, what is the total amount of variable cost related to the units produced and sold?
4. If 22,000 units are produced and sold, what is the total amount of variable cost related to the units produced and sold?
5. If 18,000 units are produced, what is the average fixed manufacturing cost per unit produced?
6. If 22,000 units are produced, what is the average fixed manufacturing cost per unit produced?
7. If 18,000 units are produced, what is the total amount of fixed manufacturing overhead incurred to support this level of production?
8. If 22,000 units are produced, what is the total amount of fixed manufacturing overhead incurred to support this level of production?

**EXERCISE 1–10  Differential Costs and Sunk Costs LO1–5**
Refer to the data given in Exercise 1–7. Answer all questions independently.

**Required:**
1. What is the incremental manufacturing cost incurred if the company increases production from 20,000 to 20,001 units?
2. What is the incremental cost incurred if the company increases production *and* sales from 20,000 to 20,001 units?
3. Assume that Kubin Company produced 20,000 units and expects to sell 19,800 of them. If a new customer unexpectedly emerges and expresses interest in buying the 200 extra units that have been produced by the company and that would otherwise remain unsold, what is the incremental manufacturing cost per unit incurred to sell these units to the customer?
4. Assume that Kubin Company produced 20,000 units and expects to sell 19,800 of them. If a new customer unexpectedly emerges and expresses interest in buying the 200 extra units that have been produced by the company and that would otherwise remain unsold, what incremental selling and administrative cost per unit is incurred to sell these units to the customer?

**EXERCISE 1–11  Cost Behavior; Contribution Format Income Statement LO1–4, LO1–6**
Harris Company manufactures and sells a single product. A partially completed schedule of the company's total costs and costs per unit over the relevant range of 30,000 to 50,000 units is given below:

| | Units Produced and Sold | | |
|---|---|---|---|
| | 30,000 | 40,000 | 50,000 |
| **Total costs:** | | | |
| Variable cost | $180,000 | ? | ? |
| Fixed cost | 300,000 | ? | ? |
| Total cost | $480,000 | ? | ? |
| **Costs per unit:** | | | |
| Variable cost | ? | ? | ? |
| Fixed cost | ? | ? | ? |
| Total cost per unit | ? | ? | ? |

**Required:**
1. Complete the above schedule of the company's total costs and costs per unit.
2. Assume that the company produces and sells 45,000 units during the year at a selling price of $16 per unit. Prepare a contribution format income statement for the year.

**EXERCISE 1–12    Product and Period Cost Flows LO1–3**

The Devon Motor Company produces automobiles. On April 1st the company had no beginning inventories and it purchased 8,000 batteries at a cost of $80 per battery. It withdrew 7,600 batteries from the storeroom during the month. Of these, 100 were used to replace batteries in cars being used by the company's traveling sales staff. The remaining 7,500 batteries withdrawn from the storeroom were placed in cars being produced by the company. Of the cars in production during April, 90 percent were completed and transferred from work in process to finished goods. Of the cars completed during the month, 30 percent were unsold at April 30th.

**Required:**
1. Determine the cost of batteries that would appear in each of the following accounts on April 30th.
   a. Raw Materials
   b. Work in Process
   c. Finished Goods
   d. Cost of Goods Sold
   e. Selling Expense
2. Specify whether each of the above accounts would appear on the balance sheet or on the income statement at the end of the month.

**EXERCISE 1–13    Variable and Fixed Cost Behavior LO1–4**

Munchak Company's relevant range of production is 9,000–11,000 units. Last month the company produced 10,000 units. Its total manufacturing cost per unit produced was $70. At this level of activity the company's variable manufacturing costs are 40% of its total manufacturing costs.

**Required:**

Assume that next month Munchak produces 10,050 units and that its cost behavior patterns remain unchanged. Label each of the following statements as true or false with respect to next month. Do not use a calculator to answer items 1 through 6. You can use a calculator to answer items 7 through 12. Record your answers by placing an X under the appropriate heading.

|  | True | False |
|---|---|---|
| 1. The variable manufacturing cost per unit will remain the same as last month. . . . | | |
| 2. The total fixed manufacturing cost will be greater than last month. . . . . . . . . . | | |
| 3. The total manufacturing cost will be greater than last month. . . . . . . . . . . . . . | | |
| 4. The average fixed manufacturing cost per unit will be less than last month. . . | | |
| 5. The total variable manufacturing cost will be less than last month. . . . . . . . . . | | |
| 6. The total manufacturing cost per unit will be greater than last month. . . . . . . . | | |
| 7. The variable manufacturing cost per unit will equal $28. . . . . . . . . . . . . . . . . . | | |
| 8. The total fixed manufacturing cost will equal $422,100. . . . . . . . . . . . . . . . . . | | |
| 9. The total manufacturing cost will equal $701,400. . . . . . . . . . . . . . . . . . . . . . | | |
| 10. The average fixed manufacturing cost per unit (rounded to the nearest cent) will equal $41.79. . . . . . . . . . . . . . . . . . . . . . . . . . . . . . . . . . . . . . . . . . . . . | | |
| 11. The total variable manufacturing cost will equal $280,000. . . . . . . . . . . . . . . . | | |
| 12. The total manufacturing cost per unit (rounded to the nearest cent) will equal $69.79 . . . . . . . . . . . . . . . . . . . . . . . . . . . . . . . . . . . . . . . . . . . . . . . . . . . | | |

**EXERCISE 1–14    Cost Classification LO1–2, LO1–3, LO1–4, LO1–5**

Wollogong Group Ltd. of New South Wales, Australia, acquired its factory building 10 years ago. For several years, the company has rented out a small annex attached to the rear of the building for $30,000 per year. The renter's lease will expire soon, and rather than renewing the lease, the company has decided to use the annex to manufacture a new product.

Direct materials cost for the new product will total $80 per unit. To have a place to store its finished goods, the company will rent a small warehouse for $500 per month. In addition, the company must rent equipment for $4,000 per month to produce the new product. Direct laborers will be hired and paid $60 per unit to manufacture the new product. As in prior years, the space in the annex will continue to be depreciated at $8,000 per year.

The annual advertising cost for the new product will be $50,000. A supervisor will be hired and paid $3,500 per month to oversee production. Electricity for operating machines will be $1.20 per unit. The cost of shipping the new product to customers will be $9 per unit.

To provide funds to purchase materials, meet payrolls, and so forth, the company will have to liquidate some temporary investments. These investments are presently yielding a return of $3,000 per year.

**Required:**
Using the table shown below, describe each of the costs associated with the new product decision in four ways. In terms of cost classifications for predicting cost behavior (column 1), indicate whether the cost is fixed or variable. With respect to cost classifications for manufacturers (column 2), if the item is a manufacturing cost, indicate whether it is direct materials, direct labor, or manufacturing overhead. If it is a nonmanufacturing cost, then select "none" as your answer. With respect to cost classifications for preparing financial statements (column 3), indicate whether the item is a product cost or period cost. Finally, in terms of cost classifications for decision making (column 4), identify any items that are sunk costs or opportunity costs. If you identify an item as an opportunity cost, then select "none" as your answer in columns 1–3.

| | Cost Classifications for: | | | |
|---|---|---|---|---|
| Cost Item | (1) Predicting Cost Behavior | (2) Manufacturers | (3) Preparing Financial Statements | (4) Decision Making |

### EXERCISE 1–15  Traditional and Contribution Format Income Statements LO1–6

The Alpine House, Inc., is a large retailer of snow skis. The company assembled the information shown below for the quarter ended March 31:

| | Amount |
|---|---|
| Sales | $150,000 |
| Selling price per pair of skis | $750 |
| Variable selling expense per pair of skis | $50 |
| Variable administrative expense per pair of skis | $10 |
| Total fixed selling expense | $20,000 |
| Total fixed administrative expense | $20,000 |
| Beginning merchandise inventory | $30,000 |
| Ending merchandise inventory | $40,000 |
| Merchandise purchases | $100,000 |

**Required:**
1. Prepare a traditional income statement for the quarter ended March 31.
2. Prepare a contribution format income statement for the quarter ended March 31.
3. What was the contribution margin per unit?

### EXERCISE 1–16  Cost Classifications for Decision Making LO1–5

Warner Corporation purchased a machine 7 years ago for $319,000 when it launched product P50. Unfortunately, this machine has broken down and cannot be repaired. The machine could be replaced by a new model 300 machine costing $313,000 or by a new model 200 machine costing $275,000. Management has decided to buy the model 200 machine. It has less capacity than the model 300 machine, but its capacity is sufficient to continue making product P50. Management also considered, but rejected, the alternative of dropping product P50 and not replacing the old machine. If that were done, the $275,000 invested in the new machine could instead have been invested in a project that would have returned a total of $374,000.

***Required:***
1. What is the total differential cost regarding the decision to buy the model 200 machine rather than the model 300 machine?
2. What is the total sunk cost regarding the decision to buy the model 200 machine rather than the model 300 machine?
3. What is the total opportunity cost regarding the decision to invest in the model 200 machine?

**EXERCISE 1–17  Classifying Variable and Fixed Costs and Product and Period Costs** LO1–3, LO1–4
Below are listed various costs that are found in organizations.
1. Hamburger buns in a Wendy's restaurant.
2. Advertising by a dental office.
3. Apples processed and canned by Del Monte.
4. Shipping canned apples from a Del Monte plant to customers.
5. Insurance on a Bausch & Lomb factory producing contact lenses.
6. Insurance on IBM's corporate headquarters.
7. Salary of a supervisor overseeing production of printers at Hewlett-Packard.
8. Commissions paid to automobile salespersons.
9. Depreciation of factory lunchroom facilities at a General Electric plant.
10. Steering wheels installed in BMWs.

***Required:***
Using the table shown below, describe each of the costs mentioned above in two ways. In terms of cost classifications for predicting cost behavior (column 1), indicate whether the cost is fixed or variable with respect to the number of units produced and sold. With respect to cost classifications for preparing financial statements (column 2), indicate whether the item is a product cost or period cost (selling and administrative cost).

| | Cost Classifications for: | |
| --- | --- | --- |
| Cost Item | (1) Predicting Cost Behavior | (2) Preparing Financial Statements |

**PROBLEMS**    ■ connect

**PROBLEM 1–18  Direct and Indirect Costs; Variable Costs** LO1–1, LO1–4
The following cost data pertain to the operations of Montgomery Department Stores, Inc., for the month of July.

| | |
| --- | --- |
| Corporate legal office salaries | $56,000 |
| Apparel Department cost of sales—Evendale Store | $90,000 |
| Corporate headquarters building lease | $48,000 |
| Store manager's salary—Evendale Store | $12,000 |
| Apparel Department sales commission—Evendale Store | $7,000 |
| Store utilities—Evendale Store | $11,000 |
| Apparel Department manager's salary—Evendale Store | $8,000 |
| Central warehouse lease cost | $15,000 |
| Janitorial costs—Evendale Store | $9,000 |

The Evendale Store is one of many stores owned and operated by the company. The Apparel Department is one of many departments at the Evendale Store. The central warehouse serves all of the company's stores.

***Required:***
1. What is the total amount of the costs listed above that are direct costs of the Apparel Department?
2. What is the total amount of the costs listed above that are direct costs of the Evendale Store?
3. What is the total amount of the Apparel Department's direct costs that are also variable costs with respect to total departmental sales?

**PROBLEM 1–19   Traditional and Contribution Format Income Statements LO1–6**

Todrick Company is a merchandiser that reported the following information based on 1,000 units sold:

| | |
|---|---|
| Sales ..................................... | $300,000 |
| Beginning merchandise inventory .......... | $20,000 |
| Purchases................................ | $200,000 |
| Ending merchandise inventory ............. | $7,000 |
| Fixed selling expense...................... | ? |
| Fixed administrative expense .............. | $12,000 |
| Variable selling expense .................. | $15,000 |
| Variable administrative expense............ | ? |
| Contribution margin ..................... | $60,000 |
| Net operating income..................... | $18,000 |

*Required:*

1. Prepare a contribution format income statement.
2. Prepare a traditional format income statement.
3. Calculate the selling price per unit.
4. Calculate the variable cost per unit.
5. Calculate the contribution margin per unit.
6. Which income statement format (traditional format or contribution format) would be more useful to managers in estimating how net operating income will change in responses to changes in unit sales? Why?

**PROBLEM 1–20   Variable and Fixed Costs; Subtleties of Direct and Indirect Costs LO1–1, LO1–4**

Madison Seniors Care Center is a nonprofit organization that provides a variety of health services to the elderly. The center is organized into a number of departments, one of which is the Meals-On-Wheels program that delivers hot meals to seniors in their homes on a daily basis. Below are listed a number of costs of the center and the Meals-On-Wheels program.

*example*   The cost of groceries used in meal preparation.

  *a.*   The cost of leasing the Meals-On-Wheels van.
  *b.*   The cost of incidental supplies such as salt, pepper, napkins, and so on.
  *c.*   The cost of gasoline consumed by the Meals-On-Wheels van.
  *d.*   The rent on the facility that houses Madison Seniors Care Center, including the Meals-On-Wheels program.
  *e.*   The salary of the part-time manager of the Meals-On-Wheels program.
  *f.*   Depreciation on the kitchen equipment used in the Meals-On-Wheels program.
  *g.*   The hourly wages of the caregiver who drives the van and delivers the meals.
  *h.*   The costs of complying with health safety regulations in the kitchen.
  *i.*   The costs of mailing letters soliciting donations to the Meals-On-Wheels program.

*Required:*

For each cost listed above, indicate whether it is a direct or indirect cost of the Meals-On-Wheels program, whether it is a direct or indirect cost of particular seniors served by the program, and whether it is variable or fixed with respect to the number of seniors served. Use the form below for your answer.

| | | Direct or Indirect Cost of the Meals-on-Wheels Program | | Direct or Indirect Cost of Particular Seniors Served by the Meals-on-Wheels Program | | Variable or Fixed with Respect to the Number of Seniors Served by the Meals-on-Wheels Program | |
|---|---|---|---|---|---|---|---|
| Item | Description | Direct | Indirect | Direct | Indirect | Variable | Fixed |
| Example | The cost of groceries used in meal preparation... | X | | X | | X | |

**PROBLEM 1–21**   **Traditional and Contribution Format Income Statements** LO1–6

Marwick's Pianos, Inc., purchases pianos from a large manufacturer for an average cost of $2,450 per unit and then sells them to retail customers for an average price of $3,125 each. The company's selling and administrative costs for a typical month are presented below:

| Costs | Cost Formula |
|---|---|
| **Selling:** | |
| Advertising..................... | $700 per month |
| Sales salaries and commissions...... | $950 per month, plus 8% of sales |
| Delivery of pianos to customers...... | $30 per piano sold |
| Utilities ........................ | $350 per month |
| Depreciation of sales facilities ....... | $800 per month |
| **Administrative:** | |
| Executive salaries ................. | $2,500 per month |
| Insurance ....................... | $400 per month |
| Clerical ......................... | $1,000 per month, plus $20 per piano sold |
| Depreciation of office equipment..... | $300 per month |

During August, Marwick's Pianos, Inc., sold and delivered 40 pianos.

**Required:**

1. Prepare a traditional format income statement for August.
2. Prepare a contribution format income statement for August. Show costs and revenues on both a total and a per unit basis down through contribution margin.
3. Refer to the income statement you prepared in (2) above. Why might it be misleading to show the fixed costs on a per unit basis?

**PROBLEM 1–22**   **Cost Terminology; Contribution Format Income Statement** LO1–2, LO1–4, LO1–6

Miller Company's total sales are $120,000. The company's direct labor cost is $15,000, which represents 30% of its total conversion cost and 40% of its total prime cost. Its total selling and administrative expense is $18,000 and its only variable selling and administrative expense is a sales commission of 5% of sales. The company maintains no beginning or ending inventories and its manufacturing overhead costs are entirely fixed costs.

**Required:**

1. What is the total manufacturing overhead cost?
2. What is the total direct materials cost?
3. What is the total manufacturing cost?
4. What is the total variable selling and administrative cost?
5. What is the total variable cost?
6. What is the total fixed cost?
7. What is the total contribution margin?

**PROBLEM 1–23**   **Cost Classification** LO1–1, LO1–3, LO1–4

Listed below are costs found in various organizations.

1. Property taxes, factory.
2. Boxes used for packaging detergent produced by the company.
3. Salespersons' commissions.
4. Supervisor's salary, factory.
5. Depreciation, executive autos.
6. Wages of workers assembling computers.
7. Insurance, finished goods warehouses.
8. Lubricants for production equipment.
9. Advertising costs.
10. Microchips used in producing calculators.
11. Shipping costs on merchandise sold.

12. Magazine subscriptions, factory lunchroom.
13. Thread in a garment factory.
14. Executive life insurance.
15. Ink used in textbook production.
16. Fringe benefits, materials handling workers.
17. Yarn used in sweater production.
18. Wages of receptionist, executive offices.

**Required:**

Prepare an answer sheet with column headings as shown below. For each cost item, indicate whether it would be variable or fixed with respect to the number of units produced and sold; and then whether it would be a selling cost, an administrative cost, or a manufacturing cost. If it is a manufacturing cost, indicate whether it is a direct cost or an indirect cost with respect to units of product. Three sample answers are provided for illustration.

| Cost Item | Variable or Fixed | Selling Cost | Administrative Cost | Manufacturing (Product) Cost | |
|---|---|---|---|---|---|
| | | | | Direct | Indirect |
| Direct labor . . . . . . . . . . . | V | | | X | |
| Executive salaries. . . . . . | F | | X | | |
| Factory rent. . . . . . . . . . . | F | | | | X |

**PROBLEM 1–24  Different Cost Classifications for Different Purposes** LO1–1, LO1–2, LO1–3, LO1–4, LO1–5

Dozier Company produced and sold 1,000 units during its first month of operations. It reported the following costs and expenses for the month:

| | | |
|---|---|---|
| Direct materials . . . . . . . . . . . . . . . . . . . . . . . . | | $69,000 |
| Direct labor. . . . . . . . . . . . . . . . . . . . . . . . . . . | | $35,000 |
| Variable manufacturing overhead . . . . . . . . . | $15,000 | |
| Fixed manufacturing overhead. . . . . . . . . . . . | 28,000 | |
| Total manufacturing overhead . . . . . . . . . . . . | | $43,000 |
| Variable selling expense . . . . . . . . . . . . . . . . | $12,000 | |
| Fixed selling expense. . . . . . . . . . . . . . . . . . . | 18,000 | |
| Total selling expense . . . . . . . . . . . . . . . . . . . | | $30,000 |
| Variable administrative expense. . . . . . . . . . . | $ 4,000 | |
| Fixed administrative expense . . . . . . . . . . . . . | 25,000 | |
| Total administrative expense. . . . . . . . . . . . . . | | $29,000 |

**Required:**

1. With respect to cost classifications for preparing financial statements:
   a. What is the total product cost?
   b. What is the total period cost?
2. With respect to cost classifications for assigning costs to cost objects:
   a. What is total direct manufacturing cost?
   b. What is the total indirect manufacturing cost?
3. With respect to cost classifications for manufacturers:
   a. What is the total manufacturing cost?
   b. What is the total nonmanufacturing cost?
   c. What is the total conversion cost and prime cost?

4.   With respect to cost classifications for predicting cost behavior:
  a.  What is the total variable manufacturing cost?
  b.  What is the total fixed cost for the company as a whole?
  c.  What is the variable cost per unit produced and sold?
5.   With respect to cost classifications for decision making:
  a.  If Dozier had produced 1,001 units instead of 1,000 units, how much incremental manufacturing cost would it have incurred to make the additional unit?

**PROBLEM 1–25   Traditional and Contribution Format Income Statements LO1–6**
Milden Company is a merchandiser that plans to sell 12,000 units during the next quarter at a selling price of $100 per unit. The company also gathered the following cost estimates for the next quarter:

| Cost | Cost Formula |
|---|---|
| Cost of good sold | $35 per unit sold |
| Advertising expense | $210,000 per quarter |
| Sales commissions | 6% of sales |
| Shipping expense | $28,000 per quarter + $9.10 per unit sold |
| Administrative salaries | $145,000 per quarter |
| Insurance expense | $9,000 per quarter |
| Depreciation expense | $76,000 per quarter |

*Required:*
1.   Prepare a contribution format income statement for the next quarter.
2.   Prepare a traditional format income statement for the next quarter.

## BUILDING YOUR SKILLS      connect

**ANALYTICAL THINKING LO1–1, LO1–2, LO1–3, LO1–4**
The Dorilane Company produces a set of wood patio furniture consisting of a table and four chairs. The company has enough customer demand to justify producing its full capacity of 2,000 sets per year. Annual cost data at full capacity follow:

| | |
|---|---|
| Direct labor | $118,000 |
| Advertising | $50,000 |
| Factory supervision | $40,000 |
| Property taxes, factory building | $3,500 |
| Sales commissions | $80,000 |
| Insurance, factory | $2,500 |
| Depreciation, administrative office equipment | $4,000 |
| Lease cost, factory equipment | $12,000 |
| Indirect materials, factory | $6,000 |
| Depreciation, factory building | $10,000 |
| Administrative office supplies (billing) | $3,000 |
| Administrative office salaries | $60,000 |
| Direct materials used (wood, bolts, etc.) | $94,000 |
| Utilities, factory | $20,000 |

*Required:*
1.   Prepare an answer sheet with the column headings shown below. Enter each cost item on your answer sheet, placing the dollar amount under the appropriate headings. As examples, this has been done already for the first two items in the list above. Note that each cost item is classified in two ways: first, as variable or fixed with respect to the number of units produced and sold; and second, as a selling and administrative cost or a product cost. (If the item is a product cost, it should also be classified as either direct or indirect as shown.)

| Cost Item | Cost Behavior | | Period (Selling or Administrative) Cost | Product Cost | |
| --- | --- | --- | --- | --- | --- |
| | Variable | Fixed | | Direct | Indirect* |
| Direct labor . . . . . . . . . . . . | $118,000 | | | $118,000 | |
| Advertising . . . . . . . . . . . . | | $50,000 | $50,000 | | |

*To units of product.

2. Total the dollar amounts in each of the columns in (1) above. Compute the average product cost of one patio set.

3. Assume that production drops to only 1,000 sets annually. Would you expect the average product cost per set to increase, decrease, or remain unchanged? Explain. No computations are necessary.

4. Refer to the original data. The president's brother-in-law has considered making himself a patio set and has priced the necessary materials at a building supply store. The brother-in-law has asked the president if he could purchase a patio set from the Dorilane Company "at cost," and the president agreed to let him do so.

   a. Would you expect any disagreement between the two men over the price the brother-in-law should pay? Explain. What price does the president probably have in mind? The brother-in-law?

   b. Because the company is operating at full capacity, what cost term used in the chapter might be justification for the president to charge the full, regular price to the brother-in-law and still be selling "at cost"?

### ETHICS CHALLENGE LO1–3

M. K. Gallant is president of Kranbrack Corporation, a company whose stock is traded on a national exchange. In a meeting with investment analysts at the beginning of the year, Gallant had predicted that the company's earnings would grow by 20% this year. Unfortunately, sales have been less than expected for the year, and Gallant concluded within two weeks of the end of the fiscal year that it would be impossible to report an increase in earnings as large as predicted unless some drastic action was taken. Accordingly, Gallant has ordered that wherever possible, expenditures should be postponed to the new year—including canceling or postponing orders with suppliers, delaying planned maintenance and training, and cutting back on end-of-year advertising and travel. Additionally, Gallant ordered the company's controller to carefully scrutinize all costs that are currently classified as period costs and reclassify as many as possible as product costs. The company is expected to have substantial inventories at the end of the year.

**Required:**

1. Why would reclassifying period costs as product costs increase this period's reported earnings?

2. Do you believe Gallant's actions are ethical? Why or why not?

### TEAMWORK IN ACTION LO1–4

Understanding the nature of fixed and variable costs is extremely important to managers. This knowledge is used in planning, making strategic and tactical decisions, evaluating performance, and controlling operations.

**Required:**

Form a team consisting of three persons. Each team member will be responsible for one of the following businesses:

   a. Dental clinic
   b. Fast-food restaurant
   c. Auto repair shop

1. For each business, decide what single measure best reflects the overall level of activity in the business and give examples of costs that are fixed and variable with respect to small changes in the measure of activity you have chosen.

2. Explain the relationship between the level of activity in each business and each of the following: total fixed costs, fixed cost per unit of activity, total variable costs, variable cost per unit of activity, total costs, and average total cost per unit of activity.

3. Discuss and refine your answers to each of the above questions with your group. For example, which of the above businesses seems to have the lowest ratio of variable to fixed costs? Which of the businesses' profits would be most sensitive to changes in demand for its services? Why?

**A LOOK BACK**

Chapter 1 defined many of the terms that are used to classify costs in an organization. Its central theme was that organizations should classify their costs differently depending on the needs of management.

**A LOOK AT THIS CHAPTER**

This chapter explains how job-order costing systems can be used to assign manufacturing costs to individual jobs. It illustrates how one plantwide predetermined overhead rate or multiple predetermined overhead rates can be used to apply overhead costs to jobs.

**A LOOK AHEAD**

Chapter 3 explains how job-order costing systems can be used to determine the value of ending inventories and cost of goods sold for external reporting purposes.

# Job-Order Costing: Calculating Unit Product Costs

## CHAPTER OUTLINE

**Job-Order Costing—An Overview**

**Job-Order Costing—An Example**

- Measuring Direct Materials Cost
- Job Cost Sheet
- Measuring Direct Labor Cost
- Computing Predetermined Overhead Rates
- Applying Manufacturing Overhead
- Manufacturing Overhead—A Closer Look
- The Need for a Predetermined Rate
- Computation of Total Job Costs and Unit Product Costs

**Job-Order Costing—A Managerial Perspective**

- Choosing an Allocation Base—A Key to Job Cost Accuracy

**Job-Order Costing Using Multiple Predetermined Overhead Rates**

- Multiple Predetermined Overhead Rates—A Departmental Approach
- Multiple Predetermined Overhead Rates—An Activity-Based Approach

**Job-Order Costing—An External Reporting Perspective**

- Overhead Application and the Income Statement
- Job Cost Sheets: A Subsidiary Ledger

**Job-Order Costing in Service Companies**

## DECISION FEATURE

Courtesy of University Tees, Inc.

# University Tees: Serving Over 150 Campuses Nationwide

**University Tees** was founded in 2003 by two **Miami University** college students to provide screen-printing, embroidery, and promotional products for fraternities, sororities, and student organizations. Today, the company, which is headquartered in Cleveland, Ohio, employs as many as four Campus Managers on each of over 150 college campuses across America.

Accurately calculating the cost of each potential customer order is critically important to University Tees because the company needs to be sure that the sales price exceeds the cost associated with satisfying the order. The costs include the cost of the blank T-shirts themselves, printing costs (which vary depending on the quantity of shirts produced and the number of colors per shirt), screen costs (which also vary depending on the number of colors included in a design), shipping costs, and the artwork needed to create a design. The company also takes into account its competitors' pricing strategies when developing its own prices.

Given its success on college campuses, University Tees has introduced a sister company called **On Point Promos** to serve for-profit companies and nonprofit organizations.

Source: Conversation with Joe Haddad, cofounder of University Tees.

## LEARNING OBJECTIVES

*After studying Chapter 2, you should be able to:*

**LO2–1** Compute a predetermined overhead rate.

**LO2–2** Apply overhead cost to jobs using a predetermined overhead rate.

**LO2–3** Compute the total cost and the unit product cost of a job using a plantwide predetermined overhead rate.

**LO2–4** Compute the total cost and the unit product cost of a job using multiple predetermined overhead rates.

Companies usually assign costs to their products and services for two main reasons. First, it helps them fulfill their planning, controlling, and decision-making responsibilities. For example, a company may use product cost information to better understand each product's profitability or to establish each product's selling price. Second, it helps them determine the value of ending inventories and cost of goods sold for external reporting purposes. The costs attached to products that have not been sold are included in ending inventories on the balance sheet, whereas the costs attached to units that have been sold are included in cost of goods sold on the income statement.

It is very common for external financial reporting requirements to heavily influence how companies assign costs to their products and services. Because most countries (including the United States) require some form of *absorption costing* for external financial reports, many companies use some form of absorption costing for product costing purposes. In **absorption costing**, all manufacturing costs, both fixed and variable, are assigned to units of product—units are said to *fully absorb manufacturing costs*. Conversely, all nonmanufacturing costs are treated as period costs and they are not assigned to units of product.

This chapter and the next explain a common type of absorption costing system known as *job-order costing*. In this chapter we'll discuss the role of job-order costing systems in planning, control, and decision making. Our focus will be on assigning manufacturing costs to individual jobs. In the next chapter, we will explain how job-order costing systems can be used to determine the value of ending inventories and cost of goods sold for external reporting purposes.

## JOB-ORDER COSTING—AN OVERVIEW

**Job-order costing** is used in situations where many *different* products, each with individual and unique features, are produced each period. For example, a **Levi Strauss** clothing factory would typically make many different types of jeans for both men and women during a month. A particular order might consist of 1,000 boot-cut men's blue denim jeans, style number A312. This order of 1,000 jeans is called a *job*. In a job-order costing system, costs are traced and allocated to jobs and then the costs of the job are divided by the number of units in the job to arrive at an average cost per unit. This average cost per unit is also referred to as the *unit product cost.*

Other examples of situations where job-order costing would be used include large-scale construction projects managed by **Bechtel International**, commercial aircraft produced by **Boeing**, greeting cards designed and printed by **Hallmark**, and airline meals prepared by **LSG SkyChefs**. All of these examples are characterized by diverse outputs. Each Bechtel project is unique and different from every other—the company may be simultaneously constructing a dam in Nigeria and a bridge in Indonesia. Likewise, each airline orders a different type of meal from LSG SkyChefs' catering service.

Job-order costing is also used extensively in service industries. For example, hospitals, law firms, movie studios, accounting firms, advertising agencies, and repair shops all use a variation of job-order costing to accumulate costs. Although the detailed example of job-order costing provided in the following section deals with a manufacturing company, the same basic concepts and procedures are used by many service organizations.

# JOB-ORDER COSTING—AN EXAMPLE

To introduce job-order costing, we will follow a specific job as it progresses through the manufacturing process. This job consists of two experimental couplings that Yost Precision Machining has agreed to produce for Loops Unlimited, a manufacturer of roller coasters. Couplings connect the cars on the roller coaster and are a critical component in the performance and safety of the ride. Before we begin our discussion, it bears reemphasizing that companies generally classify manufacturing costs into three broad categories: (1) direct materials, (2) direct labor, and (3) manufacturing overhead. As we study the operation of a job-order costing system, we will see how each of these three types of product costs is assigned to jobs for purposes of computing unit product costs.

Yost Precision Machining is a small company in Michigan that specializes in fabricating precision metal parts that are used in a variety of applications ranging from deep-sea exploration vehicles to the inertial triggers in automobile air bags. The company's top managers gather every morning at 8:00 A.M. in the company's conference room for the daily planning meeting. Attending the meeting this morning are: Jean Yost, the company's president; David Cheung, the marketing manager; Debbie Turner, the production manager; and Marc White, the company controller. The president opened the meeting:

**Jean:** The production schedule indicates we'll be starting Job 2B47 today. Isn't that the special order for experimental couplings, David?

**David:** That's right. That's the order from Loops Unlimited for two couplings for their new roller coaster ride for Magic Mountain.

**Debbie:** Why only two couplings? Don't they need a coupling for every car?

**MANAGERIAL
ACCOUNTING IN ACTION**
The Issue

**YOST**
Precision Machining

*David:*  Yes. But this is a completely new roller coaster. The cars will go faster and will be subjected to more twists, turns, drops, and loops than on any other existing roller coaster. To hold up under these stresses, Loops Unlimited's engineers completely redesigned the cars and couplings. They want us to make just two of these new couplings for testing purposes. If the design works, then we'll have the inside track on the order to supply couplings for the whole ride.

*Jean:*  We agreed to take on this initial order at our cost just to get our foot in the door. Marc, will there be any problem documenting our cost so we can get paid?

*Marc:*  No problem. The contract with Loops stipulates that they will pay us an amount equal to each coupling's unit product cost as determined by our job-order costing system. I can finalize each coupling's direct materials, direct labor, and manufacturing overhead costs on the day the job is completed.

*Jean:*  Good. Is there anything else we should discuss about this job at this time? No? Well then let's move on to the next item of business.

## Measuring Direct Materials Cost

The blueprints submitted by Loops Unlimited indicate that each experimental coupling will require three parts that are classified as direct materials: two G7 Connectors and one M46 Housing. Since each coupling requires two connectors and one housing, the production of two couplings requires four connectors and two housings. This is a custom product that is being made for the first time, but if this were one of the company's standard products, it would have an established *bill of materials*. A **bill of materials** is a document that lists the quantity of each type of direct material needed to complete a unit of product.

When an agreement has been reached with the customer concerning the quantities, prices, and shipment date for the order, a *production order* is issued. The Production Department then prepares a *materials requisition form* similar to the form in Exhibit 2–1. The **materials requisition form** is a document that specifies the type and quantity of materials to be drawn from the storeroom and identifies the job that will be charged for the cost of the materials. The form is used to control the flow of materials into production and also for making journal entries in the accounting records (as will be demonstrated in the next chapter).

The Yost Precision Machining materials requisition form in Exhibit 2–1 shows that the company's Milling Department has requisitioned two M46 Housings and four G7 Connectors for the Loops Unlimited job, which has been designated as Job 2B47.

**EXHIBIT 2–1**
Materials Requisition Form

| Materials Requistion Number | 14873 | | Date | March 2 |
|---|---|---|---|---|

| Job Number to Be Charged | 2B47 |
|---|---|

| Department | Milling |
|---|---|

| Description | Quantity | Unit Cost | Total Cost |
|---|---|---|---|
| M46 Housing | 2 | $124 | $248 |
| G7 Connector | 4 | $103 | 412 |
| | | | $660 |

## Job Cost Sheet

After a production order has been issued, the Accounting Department's job-order costing software system automatically generates a *job cost sheet* like the one presented in Exhibit 2–2. A **job cost sheet** records the materials, labor, and manufacturing overhead costs charged to that job.

**EXHIBIT 2–2**
Job Cost Sheet

After direct materials are issued, the cost of these materials are automatically recorded on the job cost sheet. Note from Exhibit 2–2, for example, that the $660 cost for direct materials shown earlier on the materials requisition form has been charged to Job 2B47 on its job cost sheet. The requisition number 14873 from the materials requisition form appears on the job cost sheet to make it easier to identify the source document for the direct materials charge.

## Measuring Direct Labor Cost

Direct labor consists of labor charges that are easily traced to a particular job. Labor charges that cannot be easily traced to specific jobs are treated as part of manufacturing overhead. As discussed in the previous chapter, this latter category of labor cost is called *indirect labor* and includes tasks such as maintenance, supervision, and cleanup.

Most companies rely on computerized systems to maintain employee *time tickets*. A completed **time ticket** is an hour-by-hour summary of the employee's activities throughout the day. One computerized approach to creating time tickets uses bar codes to capture data. Each employee and each job has a unique bar code. When beginning work on a job, the employee scans three bar codes using a handheld device much like the bar code readers at grocery store checkout stands. The first bar code indicates that a task is being started; the second is the unique bar code on the employee's identity badge; and the third is the unique bar code of the job itself. This information is fed automatically via an electronic network to a computer that notes the time and records all of the data. When the task is completed, the employee scans a bar code indicating the task is complete, the bar code on his or her identity badge, and the bar code attached to the job. This information is relayed to the computer that again notes the time, and a time ticket, such as the one shown in Exhibit 2–3, is automatically prepared. Because all of the source data is already in computer files, the labor costs can be automatically posted to job cost sheets. For example, Exhibit 2–3 shows $90 of direct labor cost related to Job 2B47. This amount is automatically posted to the job cost sheet shown in Exhibit 2–2. The time ticket in Exhibit 2–3 also shows $18 of indirect labor cost related to performing maintenance. This cost is treated as part of manufacturing overhead and does not get posted on a job cost sheet.

**EXHIBIT 2–3**   Employee Time Ticket

## Robots Replace Direct Laborers in China

**Suzhou Victory Precision Manufacture Company** is starting to replace its direct laborers with robots (which are part of manufacturing overhead) for three reasons. First, China's "one child policy" is decreasing the size of its labor force. The country's labor force peaked at 900 million in 2010 and will drop below 800 million by 2050. Second, the country's average labor rate has risen to $14.60 per hour, which is now 64% of the average hourly labor cost in the United States—up from 30% in 2000. Third, the cost of robots is declining while their capabilities continue to expand. Consequently, Chinese manufacturers are expected to buy at least 150,000 robots annually with the goal of eventually building more of their own robots.

Source: Whelan, Robbie and Fung, Esther, "China's Factories Turn to Robots," *The Wall Street Journal,* August 17, 2016, pp B1-B2.

**LEARNING OBJECTIVE 2–1**

Compute a predetermined overhead rate.

## Computing Predetermined Overhead Rates

Recall that in absorption costing, product costs include manufacturing overhead as well as direct materials and direct labor. Therefore, manufacturing overhead also needs to be recorded on the job cost sheet. However, assigning manufacturing overhead to a specific job is complicated by three circumstances:

1. Manufacturing overhead is an *indirect cost.* This means that it is either impossible or difficult to trace these costs to a particular product or job.

2. Manufacturing overhead consists of many different types of costs ranging from the grease used in machines to the annual salary of the production manager. Some of these costs are variable overhead costs because they vary in direct proportion to changes in the level of production (e.g., indirect materials, supplies, and power) and some are fixed overhead costs because they remain constant as the level of production fluctuates (e.g., heat and light, property taxes, and insurance).

3. Many companies have large amounts of fixed manufacturing overhead. Therefore, their total manufacturing overhead costs tend to remain relatively constant from one period to the next even though the number of units that they produce can fluctuate widely. Consequently, the average cost per unit will vary from one period to the next.

Given these circumstances, allocation is used to assign overhead costs to products. Allocation is accomplished by selecting an *allocation base* that is common to all of the company's products and services. An **allocation base** is a measure such as direct labor-hours (DLH) or machine-hours (MH) that is used to assign overhead costs to products and services. The most widely used allocation bases in manufacturing are direct labor-hours, direct labor cost, machine-hours, and (where a company has only a single product) units of product.

Manufacturing overhead is commonly assigned to products using a *predetermined overhead rate*. The **predetermined overhead rate** is computed by dividing the total estimated manufacturing overhead cost for the period by the estimated total amount of the allocation base as follows:

$$\text{Predetermined overhead rate} = \frac{\text{Estimated total manufacturing overhead cost}}{\text{Estimated total amount of the allocation base}}$$

The predetermined overhead rate is computed before the period begins using a four-step process. The first step is to estimate the total amount of the allocation base (the denominator) that will be required for next period's estimated level of production. The second step is to estimate the total fixed manufacturing overhead cost for the coming period and the variable manufacturing overhead cost per unit of the allocation base. The third step is to use the cost formula shown below to estimate the total manufacturing overhead cost (the numerator) for the coming period:

$$Y = a + bX$$

where,

$Y$ = The estimated total manufacturing overhead cost

$a$ = The estimated total fixed manufacturing overhead cost

$b$ = The estimated variable manufacturing overhead cost per unit of the allocation base

$X$ = The estimated total amount of the allocation base

The fourth step is to compute the predetermined overhead rate.[1] Notice the estimated amount of the allocation base is determined before estimating the total manufacturing overhead cost. This needs to be done because total manufacturing overhead cost includes variable overhead costs that depend on the amount of the allocation base.

---

[1]When there is more than one production department, each department may have a different variable manufacturing overhead cost per unit of the allocation base. In that case, the formula $Y = a + bX$ should be applied to each department separately. These departmental cost estimates ($Y$) can be combined in step 4 to calculate one overhead rate or they can be kept separate to calculate departmental overhead rates.

# Applying Manufacturing Overhead

To repeat, the predetermined overhead rate is computed *before* the period begins. The predetermined overhead rate is then used to apply overhead cost to jobs throughout the period. The process of assigning overhead cost to jobs is called **overhead application**. The formula for determining the amount of overhead cost to apply to a particular job is:

$$\text{Overhead applied to a particular job} = \text{Predetermined overhead rate} \times \text{Amount of the allocation base incurred by the job}$$

For example, if the predetermined overhead rate is $20 per direct labor-hour, then $20 of overhead cost is *applied* to a job for each direct labor-hour incurred on the job. When the allocation base is direct labor-hours, the formula becomes:

$$\text{Overhead applied to a particular job} = \text{Predetermined overhead rate} \times \text{Actual direct labor-hours worked on the job}$$

Note that the amount of overhead applied to a particular job is not the actual amount of overhead caused by the job. Actual overhead costs are not assigned to jobs—if that could be done, the costs would be direct costs, not overhead. The overhead assigned to the job is simply a share of the total overhead that was estimated at the beginning of the year. This approach to overhead application is known as *normal costing*. A **normal cost system** applies overhead costs to jobs by multiplying a predetermined overhead rate by the actual amount of the allocation base incurred by the jobs.

## Manufacturing Overhead—A Closer Look

To illustrate the steps involved in computing and using a predetermined overhead rate, let's return to Yost Precision Machining and make the following assumptions. In step one, the company estimated that 40,000 direct labor-hours would be required to support the production planned for the year. In step two, it estimated $640,000 of total fixed manufacturing overhead cost for the coming year and $4.00 of variable manufacturing overhead cost per direct labor-hour. Given these assumptions, in step three the company used the cost formula shown below to estimate its total manufacturing overhead cost for the year:

$$Y = a + bX$$
$$Y = \$640,000 + (\$4.00 \text{ per direct labor-hour} \times 40,000 \text{ direct labor-hours})$$
$$Y = \$640,000 + \$160,000$$
$$Y = \$800,000$$

In step four, Yost Precision Machining computed its predetermined overhead rate for the year of $20 per direct labor-hour as shown below:

$$\text{Predetermined overhead rate} = \frac{\text{Estimated total manufacturing overhead cost}}{\text{Estimated total amount of the allocation base}}$$

$$= \frac{\$800,000}{40,000 \text{ direct labor-hours}}$$

$$= \$20 \text{ per direct labor-hour}$$

The job cost sheet in Exhibit 2–4 indicates that 27 direct labor-hours (i.e., DLHs) were charged to Job 2B47. Therefore, a total of $540 of manufacturing overhead cost would be applied to the job:

$$\text{Overhead applied to Job 2B47} = \text{Predetermined overhead rate} \times \text{Actual direct labor-hours charged to Job 2B47}$$

$$= \$20 \text{ per DLH} \times 27 \text{ DLHs}$$

$$= \$540 \text{ of overhead applied to Job 2B47}$$

This amount of overhead has been entered on the job cost sheet in Exhibit 2–4.

EXHIBIT 2–4
A Completed Job Cost Sheet

**JOB COST SHEET**

| Job Number | 2B47 | | Date Initiated | March 2 |
| Department | Milling | | Date Completed | March 8 |
| Item | Special order coupling | | | |
| For Stock | | | Units Completed | 2 |

| Direct Materials | | Direct Labor | | | Manufacturing Overhead | | |
|---|---|---|---|---|---|---|---|
| Req. No. | Amount | Ticket | Hours | Amount | Hours | Rate | Amount |
| 14873 | $ 660 | 843 | 5 | $ 90 | 27 | $20/DLH | $540 |
| 14875 | 506 | 846 | 8 | 136 | | | |
| 14912 | 238 | 850 | 4 | 60 | | | |
| | $1,404 | 851 | 10 | 160 | | | |
| | | | 27 | $446 | | | |

| Cost Summary | | Units Shipped | | |
|---|---|---|---|---|
| Direct Materials | $ 1,404 | Date | Number | Balance |
| Direct Labor | 446 | March 8 | — | 2 |
| Manufacturing Overhead | 540 | | | |
| Total Product Cost | $ 2,390 | | | |
| Unit Product Cost | $ 1,195* | | | |

*$2,390 ÷ 2 units = $1,195 per unit.

## The Need for a Predetermined Rate

Instead of using a predetermined rate based on estimates, why not base the overhead rate on the *actual* total manufacturing overhead cost and the *actual* total amount of the allocation base incurred on a monthly, quarterly, or annual basis? If an actual rate is computed monthly or quarterly, seasonal factors in overhead costs or in the allocation base can produce fluctuations in the overhead rate. For example, the costs of heating and cooling a factory in Illinois will be highest in the winter and summer months and lowest in the spring and fall. If the overhead rate is recomputed at the end of each month or each quarter based on actual costs and activity, the overhead rate would go up in the winter and summer and down in the spring and fall. As a result, two identical jobs, one completed in the winter and one completed in the spring, would be assigned different manufacturing overhead costs.

Many managers believe that such fluctuations in product costs serve no useful purpose. To avoid such fluctuations, actual overhead rates could be computed on an annual or less-frequent basis. However, if the overhead rate is computed annually based on the actual costs and activity for the year, the manufacturing overhead assigned to any particular job would not be known until the end of the year. For example, the cost of Job 2B47 at Yost Precision Machining would not be known until the end of the year, even though the job will be completed and shipped to the customer in March. For these reasons, most companies use predetermined overhead rates rather than actual overhead rates in their cost accounting systems.

## Computation of Total Job Costs and Unit Product Costs

With the application of Yost Precision Machining's $540 of manufacturing overhead to the job cost sheet in Exhibit 2–4, the job cost sheet is complete except for two final steps. First, the totals for direct materials, direct labor, and manufacturing overhead are transferred to the Cost Summary section of the job cost sheet and added together to obtain the total cost for the job.[2] Then the total product cost ($2,390) is divided by the number of units (2) to obtain the unit product cost ($1,195). As indicated earlier, *this unit product cost is an average cost and should not be interpreted as the cost that would actually be incurred if another unit were produced.* The incremental cost of an additional unit is something less than the average unit cost of $1,195 because much of the actual overhead costs would not change if another unit were produced.

**MANAGERIAL ACCOUNTING IN ACTION**
**The Wrap-Up**

In the 8:00 A.M. daily planning meeting on March 9, Jean Yost, the president of Yost Precision Machining, once again drew attention to Job 2B47, the experimental couplings:

***Jean:*** I see Job 2B47 is completed. Let's get those couplings shipped immediately to Loops Unlimited so they can get their testing program under way. Marc, how much are we going to bill Loops for those two units?

***Marc:*** Because we agreed to sell the experimental couplings at cost, we will be charging Loops Unlimited just $1,195 a unit.

***Jean:*** Fine. Let's hope the couplings work out and we make some money on the big order later.

### Job-Order Costing in the Service Industry

**Accenture** is one of the world's largest consulting firms with annual revenues greater than $32 billion. Because the firm does not have any inventory on its balance sheet, it might be tempting to conclude that it does not need a job-order costing system. However, that is not true.

Accenture pays its consultants more than $22 billion per year to provide services for clients. Job-order costing enables the firm to compare each client's revenues to the costs of serving those clients. It also enables the firm to determine what portion of their consulting capacity was billable to clients and what portion was not billed to specific clients.

Source: Accenture 2016 Annual Report

---

[2]Notice we are assuming that Job 2B47 required direct materials and direct labor beyond the charges shown in Exhibits 2–1 and 2–3.

# JOB-ORDER COSTING—A MANAGERIAL PERSPECTIVE

Managers use job cost information to establish plans and make decisions. For example, managers may use job profitability reports to develop sales and production plans for next year. If certain types of jobs, such as low-volume engineering-intensive jobs, appear to be highly profitable, managers may decide to dedicate future advertising expenditures to growing sales of these types of jobs. Conversely, if other types of jobs, such as high-volume labor-intensive jobs, appear to be unprofitable, managers may take actions to reduce the projected sales and production of these types of jobs.

Managers may also use job cost information to make pricing decisions. For example, if Job A has a total manufacturing cost of $100, managers often use a predefined markup percentage, say 50%, to establish a markup of $50 (= $100 × 50%) and a selling price of $150 (= $100 + $50). Under this approach, known as cost-plus pricing, the managers establish a markup percentage that they believe will generate enough revenue to cover all of a job's manufacturing costs and a portion of the company's nonmanufacturing costs, while generating some residual profit.

If a company's job-order costing system does not accurately assign manufacturing costs to jobs, it will adversely influence the types of planning and decision-making scenarios just described. In other words, distorted job cost data may cause managers to use additional advertising dollars to pursue certain types of jobs that they believe are profitable, but in actuality are not. Similarly, inaccurate job costs may cause managers to establish selling prices that are too high or too low relative to the prices established by more savvy competitors.

At this point, you may be wondering, how can this happen? How can a job-order costing system inaccurately assign costs to jobs? The key to answering this question is to focus on *indirect* manufacturing costs, also called manufacturing overhead costs. While job-order costing systems can accurately trace *direct* materials and *direct* labor costs to jobs, they often fail to accurately allocate the manufacturing overhead costs used during the production process to their respective jobs. The root cause of the problem often relates to the choice of an allocation base.

## Choosing an Allocation Base—A Key to Job Cost Accuracy

Imagine going to a restaurant with three of your friends. The group orders an extra large pizza for $20 that is cut into ten slices. One of your friends eats five slices of pizza, your other two friends eat two slices each, and you eat one slice. When the bill arrives, the friend who ate five slices recommends paying the bill using "number of people seated at the table" as the allocation base, thereby requiring you to contribute $5 (= $20 ÷ 4) towards paying the bill. How would you feel about the accuracy of this cost allocation base? In all likelihood, you'd suggest distributing the bill among the four diners using another allocation base called "number of slices eaten." This approach would require each person seated at the table to pay $2 (= $20 ÷ 10) per slice consumed, thereby requiring you to contribute $2 towards paying the bill. While the distortion caused by using "number of people seated at the table" as the allocation base seems obvious, job-order costing systems often make the same error—they use allocation bases that do not reflect how jobs actually use overhead resources.

To improve job cost accuracy, the allocation base in the predetermined overhead rate should *drive* the overhead cost. A **cost driver** is a factor, such as machine-hours, beds occupied, computer time, or flight-hours, that causes overhead costs. If the base in the predetermined overhead rate does not "drive" overhead costs, it will not accurately measure the cost of overhead resources used by each job. Many companies use job-order costing systems that assume direct labor-hours (or direct labor cost) is the only manufacturing overhead cost driver. They use a single predetermined overhead rate, or what is called a **plantwide overhead rate**, to allocate all manufacturing overhead costs to jobs based on their usage of direct labor-hours. However, while direct labor-hours may indeed "drive" some of a company's manufacturing overhead costs, it is often overly simplistic and incorrect to assume that direct labor-hours is a company's *only* manufacturing overhead cost driver. When companies can identify more than one overhead cost driver they can improve job cost accuracy by using *multiple predetermined overhead rates.*

**CONCEPT CHECK**

1. Which of the following statements is false? (You may select more than one answer.)
   a. Absorption costing assigns fixed and variable manufacturing overhead costs to products.
   b. Job-order costing systems are used when companies produce many different types of products.
   c. A normal costing system assigns overhead costs to products by multiplying the actual overhead rate by the actual amount of the allocation base.
   d. A unit product cost represents the incremental cost that would be incurred if another unit were produced.
2. Assume that a company's total estimated fixed overhead cost for the coming year is $100,000 and its estimated variable overhead cost is $3.00 per direct labor-hour. If the company estimates that it will work 50,000 direct labor-hours in the coming year, what is its predetermined overhead rate per direct labor-hour?
   a. $2.00
   b. $3.00
   c. $4.00
   d. $5.00
3. Which of the following statements is true? (You may select more than one answer.)
   a. Manufacturing overhead is an indirect cost.
   b. Because manufacturing overhead includes fixed costs, the predetermined overhead rate tends to remain stable from period to period.
   c. Ideally, the allocation base in a predetermined overhead rate should be a cost driver.
   d. A unit product cost includes three types of manufacturing costs—direct materials, direct labor, and manufacturing overhead.

# JOB-ORDER COSTING USING MULTIPLE PREDETERMINED OVERHEAD RATES

**LEARNING OBJECTIVE 2–4**

Compute the total cost and the unit product cost of a job using multiple predetermined overhead rates.

A cost system with **multiple predetermined overhead rates** uses more than one overhead rate to apply overhead costs to jobs. For example, a company may choose to use a predetermined overhead rate for each of its production departments. Such a system, while more complex, is more accurate because it reflects differences across departments in terms of how jobs consume overhead costs. For example, in departments that are relatively labor-intensive, their overhead costs might be applied to jobs based on direct labor-hours and in departments that are relatively machine-intensive, their overhead costs might be applied to jobs based on machine-hours.

## Multiple Predetermined Overhead Rates—A Departmental Approach

Dickson Company has two production departments, Milling and Assembly. The company uses a job-order costing system and computes a predetermined overhead rate in each production department. The predetermined overhead rate in the Milling Department is based on machine-hours and in the Assembly Department it is based on direct labor-hours. The company uses cost-plus pricing (and a markup percentage of 75% of total manufacturing cost) to establish selling prices for all of its jobs. At the beginning of the year, the company made the following estimates:

| | Department | |
|---|---|---|
| | **Milling** | **Assembly** |
| Machine-hours. . . . . . . . . . . . . . . . . . . . . . . . . . . . . . . . . . . . . . | 60,000 | 3,000 |
| Direct labor-hours . . . . . . . . . . . . . . . . . . . . . . . . . . . . . . . . . . . | 8,000 | 80,000 |
| Total fixed manufacturing overhead cost . . . . . . . . . . . . . . . . | $390,000 | $500,000 |
| Variable manufacturing overhead per machine-hour . . . . . . | $2.00 | — |
| Variable manufacturing overhead per direct labor-hour . . . | — | $3.75 |

During the current month the company started and completed Job 407. It wants to use its predetermined departmental overhead rates and the information pertaining to Job 407 that is shown below to establish a selling price for this job:

| | Department | |
|---|---|---|
| **Job 407** | **Milling** | **Assembly** |
| Machine-hours. . . . . . . . . | 90 | 4 |
| Direct labor-hours . . . . . . | 5 | 20 |
| Direct materials . . . . . . . . | $800 | $370 |
| Direct labor cost . . . . . . . | $70 | $280 |

Exhibit 2–5 explains how Dickson would compute a selling price for Job 407 using a five-step process, the first of which is to calculate the estimated total manufacturing overhead cost in each department using the equation

$$Y = a + bX$$

where:

$Y$ = The estimated total manufacturing overhead cost
$a$ = The estimated total fixed manufacturing overhead cost
$b$ = The estimated variable manufacturing overhead cost per unit of the allocation base
$X$ = The estimated total amount of the allocation base

As shown in step 1 in Exhibit 2–5, this equation provides the Milling Department's estimated total manufacturing overhead cost of $510,000 and the Assembly Department's estimated total overhead cost of $800,000.

The second step is to calculate the predetermined overhead rate for each department using the following formula:

$$\text{Predetermined overhead rate} = \frac{\text{Estimated total manufacturing overhead cost}}{\text{Estimated total amount of the allocation base}}$$

Per step 2 in Exhibit 2–5, this formula results in predetermined overhead rates in the Milling and Assembly Departments of $8.50 per machine-hour and $10.00 per direct labor-hour, respectively.

The third step is to use the general equation shown below to calculate the amount of overhead applied from each department to Job 407.

$$\text{Overhead applied to Job 407} = \text{Predetermined overhead rate} \times \text{Actual amount of the allocation base used by Job 407}$$

**EXHIBIT 2–5**  Dickson Company: An Example Using Multiple Predetermined Overhead Rates

**Step 1: Calculate the estimated total manufacturing overhead cost for each department.**

| *Milling Department Overhead Cost (Y):* | *Assembly Department Overhead Cost (Y):* |
|---|---|
| = $390,000 + ($2.00 per MH × 60,000 MHs) | = $500,000 + ($3.75 per DLH × 80,000 DLHs) |
| = $390,000 + $120,000 | = $500,000 + $300,000 |
| = $510,000 | = $800,000 |

**Step 2: Calculate the predetermined overhead rate in each department.**

| *Milling Department Overhead Rate:* | *Assembly Department Overhead Rate:* |
|---|---|
| $= \dfrac{\$510{,}000}{60{,}000 \text{ machine-hours}}$ | $= \dfrac{\$800{,}000}{80{,}000 \text{ direct labor-hours}}$ |
| = $8.50 per machine-hour | = $10.00 per direct labor-hour |

**Step 3: Calculate the amount of overhead applied from both departments to Job 407.**

| *Milling Department: Overhead Applied to Job 407* | *Assembly Department: Overhead Applied to Job 407* |
|---|---|
| = $8.50 per MH × 90 MHs | = $10.00 per DLH × 20 DLHs |
| = $765 | = $200 |

**Step 4: Calculate the total job cost for Job 407.**

|  | Milling | Assembly | Total |
|---|---|---|---|
| Direct materials . . . . . . . . . . . . . . . . . | $800 | $370 | $1,170 |
| Direct labor. . . . . . . . . . . . . . . . . . . . . | $70 | $280 | 350 |
| Manufacturing overhead applied . . . | $765 | $200 | 965 |
| Total cost of Job 407 . . . . . . . . . . . . | | | $2,485 |

**Step 5: Calculate the selling price for Job 407.**

| | |
|---|---|
| Total cost of Job 407 . . . . . . . . . . . . . . . | $2,485.00 |
| Markup ($2,485 × 75%) . . . . . . . . . . . . . | 1,863.75 |
| Selling price of Job 407 . . . . . . . . . . . . | $4,348.75 |

As depicted in the middle of Exhibit 2–5, $765 of manufacturing overhead would be applied from the Milling Department to Job 407, whereas $200 would be applied from the Assembly Department to this same job.

Finally, Exhibit 2–5 also summarizes steps 4 and 5, which calculate the total job cost for Job 407 ($2,485) and the selling price of Job 407 ($4,348.75) using the markup percentage of 75%.

It is important to emphasize that using a departmental approach to overhead application results in a different selling price for Job 407 than would have been derived using a plantwide overhead rate based on either direct labor-hours or machine-hours. The appeal of using predetermined departmental overhead rates is that they presumably provide a more accurate accounting of the costs caused by jobs, which in turn, should enhance management planning and decision making.

## HELPFUL HINT

While using multiple predetermined overhead rates may seem more complex than the plantwide approach, the three-step process for applying overhead costs to jobs is the same for both methods. The first step is to use the equation $Y = a + bX$ to calculate the total overhead cost in the numerator of the predetermined rate. The second step is to calculate the predetermined overhead rate by dividing the numerator by the denominator. The third step is to apply overhead cost to jobs by multiplying the predetermined overhead rate by the actual amount of the allocation base used by the job.

# Multiple Predetermined Overhead Rates—An Activity-Based Approach

Using departmental overhead rates is one approach to creating a job-order costing system that includes multiple predetermined overhead rates. Another approach is to create overhead rates related to the activities performed within departments. This approach usually results in more overhead rates than a departmental approach because each department may perform more than one activity. When a company creates overhead rates based on the activities that it performs, it is employing an approach called *activity-based costing.*

For now, our goal is to simply introduce you to the idea of activity-based costing—an alternative approach to developing multiple predetermined overhead rates. Managers use activity-based costing systems to more accurately measure the demands that jobs, products, customers, and other cost objects make on overhead resources. Chapter 4 provides an in-depth discussion of activity-based costing and contrasts it with the plantwide approach described earlier in this chapter.

Ryan Company uses machine-hours as the allocation base in the Machining Department and direct labor-hours as the allocation base in the Assembly Department. At the beginning of the year, the company made the following estimates:

CONCEPT CHECK

| | Department | |
|---|---|---|
| | Machining | Assembly |
| Direct labor-hours ................................... | 8,000 | 25,000 |
| Machine-hours ...................................... | 40,000 | 5,000 |
| Total fixed manufacturing overhead cost ............... | $250,000 | $360,000 |
| Variable manufacturing overhead per machine-hour ...... | $2.50 | — |
| Variable manufacturing overhead per direct labor-hour ... | — | $4.25 |

4. What is Ryan's predetermined overhead rate in the Machining Department?
   a. $33.75
   b. $8.75
   c. $6.25
   d. $31.25
5. What is Ryan's predetermined overhead rate in the Assembly Department?
   a. $18.65
   b. $76.25
   c. $14.40
   d. $28.65
6. How much overhead cost would be applied to Job M assuming that it used five machine-hours in the Machining Department and 10 direct labor-hours in the Assembly Department?
   a. $188.25
   b. $210.25
   c. $277.45
   d. $230.25

## IN BUSINESS

## Cost System Design At Salmon River Foods

**Salmon River Foods'** largest product line is called Dream Chocolates. The company's cost system uses a plantwide overhead rate that allocates overhead costs based on the number of chocolate bars produced. The manufacturing process consists of seven steps: (1) receiving, (2) pouring, (3) inspection, (4) foiling, (5) labeling and custom label designs, (6) finished product storage, and (7) shipping. The company is considering implementing a new cost system that would include multiple predetermined overhead rates. Based on Salmon River Foods' seven-step manufacturing process, can you think of any reasons why using more than one overhead rate may make sense?

Source: Krumwiede, Kip R. and Walden, W. Darrell, "Dream Chocolate Company: Choosing a Costing System," *Issues in Accounting Education*, March 2013, pp. 637–652.

# JOB-ORDER COSTING—AN EXTERNAL REPORTING PERSPECTIVE

This chapter focuses on using job-order costing systems to compute unit product costs for internal management purposes. However, job-order costing systems are also often used to create a balance sheet and income statement for external parties, such as shareholders and lenders. While the next chapter will provide a detailed explanation of how job-order costing systems facilitate external financial reporting, we'd like to take a moment to highlight two important points related to overhead application and subsidiary ledgers that, in some sense, connect this chapter to the next.

## Overhead Application and the Income Statement

When a company uses predetermined overhead rates to apply overhead cost to jobs, it is almost a certainty that the amount of overhead applied to all jobs during a period will differ from the actual amount of overhead costs incurred during the period. When a company applies less overhead to production than it actually incurs, it creates what is known as *underapplied overhead*. When it applies more overhead to production than it actually incurs, it results in *overapplied overhead*.

The existence of underapplied or overapplied overhead has implications for how a company prepares its financial statements. For example, the cost of goods sold reported on a company's income statement must be adjusted to reflect underapplied or overapplied overhead. The adjustment for underapplied overhead increases cost of goods sold and decreases net operating income, whereas the adjustment for overapplied overhead decreases cost of goods sold and increases net operating income. The next chapter will provide a more in-depth numerical explanation of how to compute underapplied or overapplied overhead.

## Job Cost Sheets: A Subsidiary Ledger

A job cost sheet accumulates the total direct materials, direct labor, and manufacturing overhead costs assigned to a job. When all of a company's job cost sheets are viewed collectively they form what is known as a subsidiary ledger. In other words, a company's job costs sheets provide an underlying set of financial records that explain what specific jobs comprise the amounts reported in *Work-in-Process* and *Finished Goods* on the balance sheet as well as *Cost of Goods Sold* on the income statement.

To illustrate, assume Dixon Company started six jobs during its first month of operations and incurred no underapplied or overapplied manufacturing overhead. Jobs A and B were incomplete at the end of the month, Job C was finished, but unsold, and Jobs

D, E, and F, had been produced and sold during the month. In addition, assume the job cost sheets for these six jobs reported the following costs at the end of the month (in thousands):

| | Jobs | | | | | |
|---|---|---|---|---|---|---|
| | A | B | C | D | E | F |
| Direct materials ................. | $100 | $ 90 | $140 | $110 | $180 | $160 |
| Direct labor..................... | 80 | 60 | 90 | 70 | 120 | 100 |
| Manufacturing overhead applied .. | 96 | 72 | 108 | 84 | 144 | 120 |
| Total product cost ............... | $276 | $222 | $338 | $264 | $444 | $380 |

These six job costs would comprise Work in Process and Finished Goods on the balance sheet and Cost of Goods Sold on the income statement as follows:

| Work In Process | | Finished Goods | | Cost of Goods Sold | |
|---|---|---|---|---|---|
| Job A | $276 | Job C | $338 | Job D | $ 264 |
| Job B | 222 | Total | $338 | Job E | 444 |
| Total | $498 | | | Job F | 380 |
| | | | | Total | $1,088 |

This brief example illustrates the interrelationship between a company's job cost sheets and its financial statements. For example, the combined costs of Jobs A and B equal Work in Process ($498) on the balance sheet, whereas the combined costs of Jobs D, E, and F equal Cost of Goods Sold ($1,088) on the income statement.

# JOB-ORDER COSTING IN SERVICE COMPANIES

This chapter has focused on manufacturing companies; however, job-order costing is also used in service organizations such as law firms, movie studios, hospitals, and repair shops. In a law firm, for example, each client is a "job," and the costs of that job are accumulated day by day on a job cost sheet as the client's case is handled by the firm. Legal forms and similar inputs represent the direct materials for the job; the time expended by attorneys is like direct labor; and the costs of secretaries and legal aids, rent, depreciation, and so forth, represent the overhead.

In a movie studio such as **Columbia Pictures**, each film produced by the studio is a "job," and costs of direct materials (costumes, props, film, etc.) and direct labor (actors, directors, and extras) are charged to each film's job cost sheet. A share of the studio's overhead costs, such as utilities, depreciation of equipment, wages of maintenance workers, and so forth, is also charged to each film.

In sum, job-order costing is a versatile and widely used costing method that may be encountered in virtually any organization that provides diverse products or services.

## Treasurer, Class Reunion Committee

DECISION POINT

You've agreed to handle the financial arrangements for your high school reunion. You call the restaurant where the reunion will be held and jot down the most important information. The meal cost (including beverages) will be $30 per person plus a 15% gratuity. An additional $200 will be charged for a banquet room with a dance floor. A band has been hired for $500. One of the members of the reunion committee informs you that there is just enough money left in the

(continued)

class bank account to cover the printing and mailing costs. He mentions that at least one-half of the class of 400 will attend the reunion and wonders if he should add the 15% gratuity to the $30 per person meal cost when he drafts the invitation, which will indicate that a check must be returned with the reply card.

How should you respond? How much will you need to charge to cover the various costs? After making your decision, label your answer with the managerial accounting terms covered in this chapter. Finally, identify any issues that should be investigated further.

## SUMMARY

### LO2–1 Compute a predetermined overhead rate.
Manufacturing overhead costs are assigned to jobs using a predetermined overhead rate. The rate is determined at the beginning of the period so that jobs can be costed throughout the period rather than waiting until the end of the period. The predetermined overhead rate is determined by dividing the estimated total manufacturing overhead cost for the period by the estimated total amount of the allocation base for the period.

### LO2–2 Apply overhead cost to jobs using a predetermined overhead rate.
Overhead is applied to jobs by multiplying the predetermined overhead rate by the actual amount of the allocation base used by the job.

### LO2–3 Compute the total cost and the unit product cost of a job using a plantwide predetermined overhead rate.
The total cost of a job includes the actual direct materials and direct labor costs assigned to the job plus the applied overhead. The applied overhead is computed by multiplying the plantwide predetermined overhead rate by the actual amount of the allocation base used by a job. The unit product cost of a job is computed by dividing the total cost of the job by the number of units included in the job. Importantly, the unit product cost does not represent the incremental cost that would be incurred if another unit were produced.

### LO2–4 Compute the total cost and the unit product cost of a job using multiple predetermined overhead rates.
The total cost of a job includes the actual direct materials and direct labor costs assigned to the job plus the applied overhead. The applied overhead is computed by multiplying each predetermined overhead rate by the actual amount of its allocation base that is used by a job. The unit product cost of a job is computed by dividing the total cost of the job by the number of units included in the job.

## GUIDANCE ANSWER TO DECISION POINT

**Treasurer, Class Reunion Committee**
You should charge $38.00 per person to cover the costs calculated as follows:

| | |
|---|---|
| Meal cost . . . . . . . . . . . . . . . . . . . . . . . . . . . . . . . . . . . . . . . . . . | $30.00 Direct material cost |
| Gratuity ($30 × 0.15) . . . . . . . . . . . . . . . . . . . . . . . . . . . . . | 4.50 Direct labor cost |
| Room charge ($200 ÷ 200 expected attendees) . . . . . . | 1.00 Overhead cost |
| Band cost ($500 ÷ 200 expected attendees) . . . . . . . . . | 2.50 Overhead cost |
| Total cost. . . . . . . . . . . . . . . . . . . . . . . . . . . . . . . . . . . . . . . . . | $38.00 |

If exactly 200 classmates attend the reunion, the $7,600 of receipts (200 × $38) will cover the expenditures of $7,600 [meal cost of $6,000 (or 200 × $30) plus gratuity cost of $900 (or $6,000 × 0.15) plus the $200 room charge plus the $500 band cost]. Unfortunately, if less than 200 attend, the Reunion Committee will come up short in an amount equal to the difference between the 200 estimated attendees and the actual number of attendees times $3.50 (the total per person overhead charge). As such, you should talk to the members of the Reunion Committee to ensure that (1) the estimate is as reasonable as possible, and (2) there is a plan to deal with any shortage. On the other hand, if more than 200 attend, the Reunion Committee will collect more money than it needs to disburse. The amount would be equal to the difference between the actual number of attendees and the 200 estimated attendees times $3.50.

## GUIDANCE ANSWERS TO CONCEPT CHECKS

1. **Choices c and d.** A predetermined overhead rate rather than an actual overhead rate is used in a normal costing system. A unit product cost does not represent an incremental cost.
2. **Choice d.** At an activity level of 50,000 direct labor-hours, $Y = \$100{,}000 + (\$3$ per direct labor-hour)(50,000 direct labor-hours). Solving for $Y$ provides an estimated total manufacturing overhead cost of $250,000. The total manufacturing overhead ($250,000) divided by the total estimated direct labor-hours (50,000) equals the predetermined overhead rate of $5 per direct labor-hour.
3. **Choices a, c, and d.** Because manufacturing overhead includes fixed costs, the predetermined overhead rate tends to fluctuate from period to period.
4. **Choice b.** At an activity level of 40,000 machine-hours, $Y = \$250{,}000 + (\$2.50$ per machine-hour)(40,000 machine-hours). Solving for $Y$ provides an estimated total manufacturing overhead cost of $350,000. The total manufacturing overhead ($350,000) divided by the total estimated machine-hours (40,000) equals the predetermined overhead rate of $8.75 per machine-hour.
5. **Choice a.** At an activity level of 25,000 direct labor-hours, $Y = \$360{,}000 + (\$4.25$ per direct labor-hour)(25,000 direct labor-hours). Solving for $Y$ provides an estimated total manufacturing overhead cost of $466,250. The total manufacturing overhead ($466,250) divided by the total estimated direct labor-hours (25,000) equals the predetermined overhead rate of $18.65 per direct labor-hour.
6. **Choice d.** The amount of overhead applied from the Machining Department to Job M is calculated as follows: 5 machine-hours × $8.75 per machine-hour = $43.75. The amount of overhead applied from the Assembly Department to Job M is calculated as follows: 10 direct labor-hours × $18.65 per direct labor-hour = $186.50. The total overhead applied to Job M is calculated as follows: $43.75 + $186.50 = $230.25.

## REVIEW PROBLEM: CALCULATING UNIT PRODUCT COSTS

Redhawk Company has two manufacturing departments—Assembly and Fabrication. The company considers all of its manufacturing overhead costs to be fixed costs. The first set of data shown below is based on estimates that were made at the beginning of the year for the expected total output. The second set of data relates to one particular job completed during the year—Job A200.

| Estimated Data | Assembly | Fabrication | Total |
| --- | --- | --- | --- |
| Manufacturing overhead costs......... | $300,000 | $400,000 | $700,000 |
| Direct labor-hours.................... | 25,000 | 15,000 | 40,000 |
| Machine-hours....................... | 10,000 | 50,000 | 60,000 |

| Job A200 | Assembly | Fabrication | Total |
| --- | --- | --- | --- |
| Direct materials...................... | $110 | $50 | $160 |
| Direct labor......................... | $70 | $45 | $115 |
| Direct labor-hours.................... | 10 hours | 2 hours | 12 hours |
| Machine-hours....................... | 1 hour | 7 hours | 8 hours |

***Required:***

1.  If Redhawk uses a predetermined plantwide overhead rate with direct labor-hours as the allocation base, how much manufacturing overhead would be applied to Job A200?
2.  If Redhawk uses predetermined departmental overhead rates with direct labor-hours as the allocation base in Assembly and machine-hours as the allocation base in Fabrication, how much total manufacturing overhead cost would be applied to Job A200?
3.  Assume that Redhawk uses the departmental overhead rates mentioned in requirement 2 and that Job A200 includes 50 units. What is the unit product cost for Job A200?

**Solution to Review Problem**

1.  The predetermined plantwide overhead rate is computed as follows:

$$\text{Predetermined overhead rate} = \frac{\text{Estimated total manufacturing overhead cost}}{\text{Estimated total amount of the allocation base}}$$

$$= \frac{\$700,000}{40,000 \text{ direct labor-hours}}$$

$$= \$17.50 \text{ per direct labor-hour}$$

The manufacturing overhead applied to Job A200 is computed as follows:

$$\begin{array}{c}\text{Overhead applied to}\\ \text{Job A200}\end{array} = \begin{array}{c}\text{Predetermined}\\ \text{overhead rate}\end{array} \times \begin{array}{c}\text{Actual direct labor-hours}\\ \text{charged to Job A200}\end{array}$$

$$= \$17.50 \text{ per DLH} \times 12 \text{ DLHs}$$

$$= \$210 \text{ of overhead applied to Job A200}$$

2.  The predetermined departmental overhead rates are computed as follows:
    Assembly Department:

$$\text{Predetermined overhead rate} = \frac{\text{Estimated total manufacturing overhead cost}}{\text{Estimated total amount of the allocation base}}$$

$$= \frac{\$300,000}{25,000 \text{ direct labor-hours}}$$

$$= \$12 \text{ per direct labor-hour}$$

Fabrication Department:

$$\text{Predetermined overhead rate} = \frac{\text{Estimated total manufacturing overhead cost}}{\text{Estimated total amount of the allocation base}}$$

$$= \frac{\$400,000}{50,000 \text{ machine-hours}}$$

$$= \$8.00 \text{ per machine-hour}$$

The manufacturing overhead applied to Job A200 is computed as follows:

| Job A200 | (1)<br>Overhead Rate | (2)<br>Actual Hours Used | Applied Overhead<br>(1) × (2) |
|---|---|---|---|
| Assembly Department . . . . . . . . | $12 per DLH | 10 hours | $120 |
| Fabrication Department . . . . . . . | $8 per MH | 7 hours | 56 |
| Total applied overhead. . . . . . . . | | | $176 |

3.  The unit product cost for Job A200 is computed as follows:

| Job A200 | Assembly | Fabrication | Total |
|---|---|---|---|
| Direct materials . . . . . . . . . . . . . . . . . . . . . . . . | $110 | $50 | $160 |
| Direct labor. . . . . . . . . . . . . . . . . . . . . . . . . . . | $70 | $45 | 115 |
| Applied overhead . . . . . . . . . . . . . . . . . . . . . . | $120 | $56 | 176 |
| Total job cost (a). . . . . . . . . . . . . . . . . . . . . . . | | | $451 |
| Number of units in Job A200 (b). . . . . . . . . . . | | | 50 |
| Unit product cost (a) ÷ (b). . . . . . . . . . . . . . . | | | $9.02 |

# GLOSSARY

**Absorption costing** A costing method that includes all manufacturing costs—direct materials, direct labor, and both variable and fixed manufacturing overhead—in unit product costs. (p. 64)

**Allocation base** A measure of activity such as direct labor-hours or machine-hours that is used to assign costs to cost objects. (p. 69)

**Bill of materials** A document that shows the quantity of each type of direct material required to make a product. (p. 66)

**Cost driver** A factor, such as machine-hours, beds occupied, computer time, or flight-hours, that causes overhead costs. (p. 73)

**Job cost sheet** A form that records the direct materials, direct labor, and manufacturing overhead cost charged to a job. (p. 67)

**Job-order costing** A costing system used in situations where many different products, jobs, or services are produced each period. (p. 64)

**Materials requisition form** A document that specifies the type and quantity of materials to be drawn from the storeroom and that identifies the job that will be charged for the cost of those materials. (p. 66)

**Multiple predetermined overhead rates** A costing system with multiple overhead cost pools and a different predetermined overhead rate for each cost pool, rather than a single predetermined overhead rate for the entire company. Each production department may be treated as a separate overhead cost pool. (p. 74)

**Normal cost system** A costing system in which overhead costs are applied to a job by multiplying a predetermined overhead rate by the actual amount of the allocation base incurred by the job. (p. 70)

**Overhead application** The process of assigning overhead cost to specific jobs. (p. 70)

**Plantwide overhead rate** A single predetermined overhead rate that is used throughout a plant. (p. 73)

**Predetermined overhead rate** A rate used to charge manufacturing overhead cost to jobs that is established in advance for each period. It is computed by dividing the estimated total manufacturing overhead cost for the period by the estimated total amount of the allocation base for the period. (p. 69)

**Time ticket** A document that is used to record the amount of time an employee spends on various activities. (p. 67)

# QUESTIONS

2–1 What is job-order costing?
2–2 What is absorption costing?
2–3 What is normal costing?
2–4 How is the unit product cost of a job calculated?
2–5 Explain the four-step process used to compute a predetermined overhead rate.
2–6 What is the purpose of the job cost sheet in a job-order costing system?
2–7 Explain why some production costs must be assigned to products through an allocation process.
2–8 Why do companies use predetermined overhead rates rather than actual manufacturing overhead costs to apply overhead to jobs?
2–9 What factors should be considered in selecting an allocation base to be used in computing a predetermined overhead rate?
2–10 If a company fully allocates all of its overhead costs to jobs, does this guarantee that a profit will be earned for the period?
2–11 Would you expect the amount of applied overhead for a period to equal the actual overhead costs of the period? Why or why not?
2–12 What is underapplied overhead? Overapplied overhead?
2–13 What is a plantwide overhead rate? Why are multiple overhead rates, rather than a plantwide overhead rate, used in some companies?

 APPLYING EXCEL

This Excel worksheet relates to the Dickson Company example that is summarized in Exhibit 2-5. Download the workbook containing this form from Connect, where you will also find instructions about how to use this worksheet form.

LO2–1, LO2–2, LO2–3, LO2–4

| | A | B | C | D | E |
|---|---|---|---|---|---|
| 1 | Chapter 2: Applying Excel | | | | |
| 2 | | | | | |
| 3 | **Data** | | | | |
| 4 | Markup on job cost | 75% | | | |
| 5 | | | | | |
| 6 | | Department | | | |
| 7 | | Milling | Assembly | | |
| 8 | Machine-hours | 60,000 | 3,000 | | |
| 9 | Direct labor-hours | 8,000 | 80,000 | | |
| 10 | Total fixed manufacturing overhead cost | $390,000 | $500,000 | | |
| 11 | Variable manufacturing overhead per machine-hour | $2.00 | | | |
| 12 | Variable manufacturing overhead per direct labor-hour | | $3.75 | | |
| 13 | | | | | |
| 14 | Cost summary for Job 407 | Department | | | |
| 15 | | Milling | Assembly | | |
| 16 | Machine-hours | 90 | 4 | | |
| 17 | Direct labor-hours | 5 | 20 | | |
| 18 | Direct materials | $800 | $370 | | |
| 19 | Direct labor cost | $70 | $280 | | |
| 20 | | | | | |
| 21 | *Enter a formula into each of the cells marked with a ? below* | | | | |
| 22 | | | | | |
| 23 | **Step 1: Calculate the estimated total manufacturing overhead cost for each department** | | | | |
| 24 | | Milling | Assembly | | |
| 25 | Total fixed manufacturing overhead cost | ? | ? | | |
| 26 | Variable manufacturing overhead per machine-hour or direct labor-hour | ? | ? | | |
| 27 | Total machine-hours or direct labor-hours | ? | ? | | |
| 28 | Total variable manufacturing overhead | ? | ? | | |
| 29 | Total manufacturing overhead | ? | ? | | |
| 30 | | | | | |
| 31 | **Step 2: Calculate the predetermined overhead rate in each department** | | | | |
| 32 | | Milling | Assembly | | |
| 33 | Total manufacturing overhead | ? | ? | | |
| 34 | Total machine-hours or direct labor-hours | ? | ? | | |
| 35 | Predetermined overhead rate per machine-hour or direct labor-hour | ? | ? | | |
| 36 | | | | | |
| 37 | **Step 3: Calculate the amount of overhead applied from both departments to Job 407** | | | | |
| 38 | | Milling | Assembly | | |
| 39 | Predetermined overhead rate per machine-hour or direct labor-hour | ? | ? | | |
| 40 | Machine-hours or direct labor-hours for the job | ? | ? | | |
| 41 | Manufacturing overhead applied | ? | ? | | |
| 42 | | | | | |
| 43 | **Step 4: Calculate the total job cost for Job 407** | | | | |
| 44 | | Milling | Assembly | Total | |
| 45 | Direct materials | ? | ? | ? | |
| 46 | Direct labor cost | ? | ? | ? | |
| 47 | Manufacturing overhead applied | ? | ? | ? | |
| 48 | Total cost of Job 407 | | | ? | |
| 49 | | | | | |
| 50 | **Step 5: Calculate the selling price for Job 407** | | | | |
| 51 | Total cost of Job 407 | | | ? | |
| 52 | Markup | | | ? | |
| 53 | Selling price of Job 407 | | | ? | |
| 54 | | | | | |

Chapter 2 Form    Filled in Chapter 2 Form

You should proceed to the requirements below only after completing your worksheet.

*Required:*

1. Check your worksheet by changing the total fixed manufacturing overhead cost for the Milling Department in the Data area to $300,000, keeping all of the other data the same as in the original example. If your worksheet is operating properly, the total cost of Job 407 should now be $2,350. If you do not get this answer, find the errors in your worksheet and correct them.

   How much is the selling price of Job 407? Did it change? Why or why not?

2. Change the total fixed manufacturing overhead cost for the Milling Department in the Data area back to $390,000, keeping all of the other data the same as in the original example. Determine the selling price for a new job, Job 408, with the following characteristics. You need not bother changing the job number from 407 to 408 in the worksheet.

| | Department | |
|---|---|---|
| **Cost summary for Job 408** | **Milling** | **Assembly** |
| Machine-hours...................... | 40 | 10 |
| Direct labor-hours................... | 2 | 6 |
| Direct materials..................... | $700 | $360 |
| Direct labor cost.................... | $50 | $150 |

3. What happens to the selling price for Job 408 if the total number of machine-hours in the Assembly Department increases from 3,000 machine-hours to 6,000 machine-hours? Does it increase, decrease, or stay the same as in part 2 above? Why?

4. Restore the total number of machine-hours in the Assembly Department to 3,000 machine-hours. What happens to the selling price for Job 408 if the total number of direct labor-hours in the Assembly Department decreases from 80,000 direct labor-hours to 50,000 direct labor-hours? Does it increase, decrease, or stay the same as in part 2 above? Why?

**connect THE FOUNDATIONAL 15**

Sweeten Company had no jobs in progress at the beginning of March and no beginning inventories. The company has two manufacturing departments—Molding and Fabrication. It started, completed, and sold only two jobs during March—Job P and Job Q. The following additional information is available for the company as a whole and for Jobs P and Q (all data and questions relate to the month of March):

LO2–1, LO2–2, LO2–3, LO2–4

| | Molding | Fabrication | Total |
|---|---|---|---|
| Estimated total machine-hours used . . . . . . . . . . . . . . | 2,500 | 1,500 | 4,000 |
| Estimated total fixed manufacturing overhead. . . . . . . | $10,000 | $15,000 | $25,000 |
| Estimated variable manufacturing overhead per machine-hour. . . . . . . . . . . . . . . . . . . . . . . . . . . . . . . | $1.40 | $2.20 | |

| | Job P | Job Q |
|---|---|---|
| Direct materials . . . . . . . . . . . . . . . . . . . . . . . . . . . . . . . . . . . . . | $13,000 | $8,000 |
| Direct labor cost . . . . . . . . . . . . . . . . . . . . . . . . . . . . . . . . . . . . | $21,000 | $7,500 |
| Actual machine-hours used: | | |
| Molding. . . . . . . . . . . . . . . . . . . . . . . . . . . . . . . . . . . . . . . . . . | 1,700 | 800 |
| Fabrication . . . . . . . . . . . . . . . . . . . . . . . . . . . . . . . . . . . . . . . | 600 | 900 |
| Total . . . . . . . . . . . . . . . . . . . . . . . . . . . . . . . . . . . . . . . . . . . . | 2,300 | 1,700 |

Sweeten Company had no underapplied or overapplied manufacturing overhead costs during the month.

**Required:**

For questions 1–8, assume that Sweeten Company uses a plantwide predetermined overhead rate with machine-hours as the allocation base. For questions 9–15, assume that the company uses departmental predetermined overhead rates with machine-hours as the allocation base in both departments.

1. What was the company's plantwide predetermined overhead rate?
2. How much manufacturing overhead was applied to Job P and how much was applied to Job Q?
3. What was the total manufacturing cost assigned to Job P?
4. If Job P included 20 units, what was its unit product cost?
5. What was the total manufacturing cost assigned to Job Q?
6. If Job Q included 30 units, what was its unit product cost?
7. Assume that Sweeten Company used cost-plus pricing (and a markup percentage of 80% of total manufacturing cost) to establish selling prices for all of its jobs. What selling price would the company have established for Jobs P and Q? What are the selling prices for both jobs when stated on a per unit basis?
8. What was Sweeten Company's cost of goods sold for March?
9. What were the company's predetermined overhead rates in the Molding Department and the Fabrication Department?
10. How much manufacturing overhead was applied from the Molding Department to Job P and how much was applied to Job Q?
11. How much manufacturing overhead was applied from the Fabrication Department to Job P and how much was applied to Job Q?
12. If Job P included 20 units, what was its unit product cost?
13. If Job Q included 30 units, what was its unit product cost?

14. Assume that Sweeten Company used cost-plus pricing (and a markup percentage of 80% of total manufacturing cost) to establish selling prices for all of its jobs. What selling price would the company have established for Jobs P and Q? What are the selling prices for both jobs when stated on a per unit basis?

15. What was Sweeten Company's cost of goods sold for March?

## EXERCISES ▪ connect

**EXERCISE 2–1   Compute a Predetermined Overhead Rate LO2–1**

Harris Fabrics computes its plantwide predetermined overhead rate annually on the basis of direct labor-hours. At the beginning of the year, it estimated that 20,000 direct labor-hours would be required for the period's estimated level of production. The company also estimated $94,000 of fixed manufacturing overhead cost for the coming period and variable manufacturing overhead of $2.00 per direct labor-hour. Harris's actual manufacturing overhead cost for the year was $123,900 and its actual total direct labor was 21,000 hours.

**Required:**

Compute the company's plantwide predetermined overhead rate for the year.

**EXERCISE 2–2   Apply Overhead Cost to Jobs LO2–2**

Luthan Company uses a plantwide predetermined overhead rate of $23.40 per direct labor-hour. This predetermined rate was based on a cost formula that estimated $257,400 of total manufacturing overhead cost for an estimated activity level of 11,000 direct labor-hours.

The company incurred actual total manufacturing overhead cost of $249,000 and 10,800 total direct labor-hours during the period.

**Required:**

Determine the amount of manufacturing overhead cost that would have been applied to all jobs during the period.

**EXERCISE 2–3   Computing Total Job Costs and Unit Product Costs Using a Plantwide Predetermined Overhead Rate LO2–3**

Mickley Company's plantwide predetermined overhead rate is $14.00 per direct labor-hour and its direct labor wage rate is $17.00 per hour. The following information pertains to Job A-500:

| Direct materials | $231 |
|---|---|
| Direct labor | $153 |

**Required:**

1. What is the total manufacturing cost assigned to Job A-500?
2. If Job A-500 consists of 40 units, what is the unit product cost for this job?

**EXERCISE 2–4   Computing Total Job Costs and Unit Product Costs Using Multiple Predetermined Overhead Rates LO2–4**

Fickel Company has two manufacturing departments—Assembly and Testing & Packaging. The predetermined overhead rates in Assembly and Testing & Packaging are $16.00 per direct labor-hour and $12.00 per direct labor-hour, respectively. The company's direct labor wage rate is $20.00 per hour. The following information pertains to Job N-60:

|  | Assembly | Testing & Packaging |
|---|---|---|
| Direct materials | $340 | $25 |
| Direct labor | $180 | $40 |

**Required:**

1. What is the total manufacturing cost assigned to Job N-60?
2. If Job N-60 consists of 10 units, what is the unit product cost for this job?

**EXERCISE 2–5   Computing Total Job Costs and Unit Product Costs Using Multiple Predetermined Overhead Rates LO2–4**

Braverman Company has two manufacturing departments—Finishing and Fabrication. The predetermined overhead rates in Finishing and Fabrication are $18.00 per direct labor-hour and 110% of direct materials cost, respectively. The company's direct labor wage rate is $16.00 per hour. The following information pertains to Job 700:

| | Finishing | Fabrication |
|---|---|---|
| Direct materials | $410 | $60 |
| Direct labor | $128 | $48 |

**Required:**
1. What is the total manufacturing cost assigned to Job 700?
2. If Job 700 consists of 15 units, what is the unit product cost for this job?

**EXERCISE 2–6  Job-Order Costing for a Service Company** LO2–1, LO2–2, LO2–3

Tech Solutions is a consulting firm that uses a job-order costing system. Its direct materials consist of hardware and software that it purchases and installs on behalf of its clients. The firm's direct labor includes salaries of consultants that work at the client's job site, and its overhead consists of costs such as depreciation, utilities, and insurance related to the office headquarters as well as the office supplies that are consumed serving clients.

Tech Solutions computes its predetermined overhead rate annually on the basis of direct labor-hours. At the beginning of the year, it estimated that 80,000 direct labor-hours would be required for the period's estimated level of client service. The company also estimated $680,000 of fixed overhead cost for the coming period and variable overhead of $0.50 per direct labor-hour. The firm's actual overhead cost for the year was $692,000 and its actual total direct labor was 83,000 hours.

**Required:**
1. Compute the predetermined overhead rate.
2. During the year, Tech Solutions started and completed the Xavier Company engagement. The following information was available with respect to this job:

| | |
|---|---|
| Direct materials | $38,000 |
| Direct labor cost | $21,000 |
| Direct labor-hours worked | 280 |

Compute the total job cost for the Xavier Company engagement.

**EXERCISE 2–7  Job-Order Costing; Working Backwards** LO2–1, LO2–2, LO2–3

Hahn Company uses a job-order costing system. Its plantwide predetermined overhead rate uses direct labor-hours as the allocation base. The company pays its direct laborers $15 per hour. During the year, the company started and completed only two jobs—Job Alpha, which used 54,500 direct labor-hours, and Job Omega. The job cost sheets for the these two jobs are shown below:

| Job Alpha | |
|---|---|
| Direct materials | ? |
| Direct labor | ? |
| Manufacturing overhead applied | ? |
| Total job cost | $1,533,500 |

| Job Omega | |
|---|---|
| Direct materials | $235,000 |
| Direct labor | 345,000 |
| Manufacturing overhead applied | 184,000 |
| Total job cost | $764,000 |

**Required:**
1. Calculate the plantwide predetermined overhead rate.
2. Complete the job cost sheet for Job Alpha.

**EXERCISE 2–8  Applying Overhead Cost; Computing Unit Product Cost LO2–2, LO2–3**
Newhard Company assigns overhead cost to jobs on the basis of 125% of direct labor cost. The job cost sheet for Job 313 includes $10,000 in direct materials cost and $12,000 in direct labor cost. A total of 1,000 units were produced in Job 313.

*Required:*
What is the total manufacturing cost assigned to Job 313? What is the unit product cost for Job 313?

**EXERCISE 2–9  Job-Order Costing and Decision Making LO2–1, LO2–2, LO2–3**
Taveras Corporation is currently operating at 50% of its available manufacturing capacity. It uses a job-order costing system with a plantwide predetermined overhead rate based on machine-hours. At the beginning of the year, the company made the following estimates:

| | |
|---|---|
| Machine-hours required to support estimated production ....... | 165,000 |
| Fixed manufacturing overhead cost.......................... | $1,980,000 |
| Variable manufacturing overhead cost per machine-hour........ | $2.00 |

*Required:*
1. Compute the plantwide predetermined overhead rate.
2. During the year, Job P90 was started, completed, and sold to the customer for $2,500. The following information was available with respect to this job:
Compute the total manufacturing cost assigned to Job P90.

| | |
|---|---|
| Direct materials ......................................... | $1,150 |
| Direct labor cost ........................................ | $830 |
| Machine-hours used....................................... | 72 |

3. Upon comparing Job P90's sales revenue to its total manufacturing cost, the company's chief financial officer said "If this exact same opportunity walked through our front door tomorrow, I'd turn it down rather than making it and selling it for $2,500."
   a. Construct an argument (supported by numerical analysis) that refutes the chief financial officer's assertion.
   b. Construct an argument (accompanied by numerical analysis) that supports the chief financial officer's assertion.

**EXERCISE 2–10  Applying Overhead Cost to a Job LO2–2**
Sigma Corporation applies overhead cost to jobs on the basis of direct labor cost. Job V, which was started and completed during the current period, shows charges of $5,000 for direct materials, $8,000 for direct labor, and $6,000 for overhead on its job cost sheet. Job W, which is still in process at year-end, shows charges of $2,500 for direct materials and $4,000 for direct labor.

*Required:*
1. Should any overhead cost be applied to Job W at year-end? If so, how much? Explain.
2. How will the costs included in Job W's job cost sheet be reported within Sigma Corporation's financial statements at the end of the year?

**EXERCISE 2–11  Varying Plantwide Predetermined Overhead Rates LO2–1, LO2–2, LO2–3**
Kingsport Containers Company makes a single product that is subject to wide seasonal variations in demand. The company uses a job-order costing system and computes plantwide predetermined overhead rates on a quarterly basis using the number of units to be produced as the allocation base. Its estimated costs, by quarter, for the coming year are given below:

| | Quarter | | | |
|---|---|---|---|---|
| | First | Second | Third | Fourth |
| Direct materials .......................... | $240,000 | $120,000 | $ 60,000 | $180,000 |
| Direct labor.............................. | 128,000 | 64,000 | 32,000 | 96,000 |
| Manufacturing overhead ................... | 300,000 | 220,000 | 180,000 | ? |
| Total manufacturing costs (a).............. | $668,000 | $404,000 | $272,000 | $ ? |
| Number of units to be produced (b)......... | 80,000 | 40,000 | 20,000 | 60,000 |
| Estimated unit product cost (a) ÷ (b)........ | $8.35 | $10.10 | $13.60 | ? |

Management finds the variation in quarterly unit product costs to be confusing and difficult to work with. It has been suggested that the problem lies with manufacturing overhead because it is the largest element of total manufacturing cost. Accordingly, you have been asked to find a more appropriate way of assigning manufacturing overhead cost to units of product.

**Required:**
1. Assuming the estimated variable manufacturing overhead cost per unit is $2.00, what must be the estimated total fixed manufacturing overhead cost per quarter?
2. Assuming the assumptions about cost behavior from the first three quarters hold constant, what is the estimated unit product cost for the fourth quarter?
3. What is causing the estimated unit product cost to fluctuate from one quarter to the next?
4. How would you recommend stabilizing the company's unit product cost? Support your answer with computations.

**EXERCISE 2–12  Computing Predetermined Overhead Rates and Job Costs** LO2–1, LO2–2, LO2–3

Moody Corporation uses a job-order costing system with a plantwide predetermined overhead rate based on machine-hours. At the beginning of the year, the company made the following estimates:

| | |
|---|---|
| Machine-hours required to support estimated production ....... | 100,000 |
| Fixed manufacturing overhead cost.......................... | $650,000 |
| Variable manufacturing overhead cost per machine-hour........ | $3.00 |

**Required:**
1. Compute the plantwide predetermined overhead rate.
2. During the year, Job 400 was started and completed. The following information was available with respect to this job:

| | |
|---|---|
| Direct materials .......................................... | $450 |
| Direct labor cost ......................................... | $210 |
| Machine-hours used....................................... | 40 |

Compute the total manufacturing cost assigned to Job 400.
3. If Job 400 includes 52 units, what is the unit product cost for this job?
4. If Moody uses a markup percentage of 120% of its total manufacturing cost, then what selling price per unit would it have established for Job 400?
5. If Moody hired you as a consultant to critique its pricing methodology, what would you say?

**EXERCISE 2–13  Departmental Predetermined Overhead Rates** LO2–1, LO2–2, LO2–4

White Company has two departments, Cutting and Finishing. The company uses a job-order costing system and computes a predetermined overhead rate in each department. The Cutting Department bases its rate on machine-hours, and the Finishing Department bases its rate on direct labor-hours. At the beginning of the year, the company made the following estimates:

| | Department | |
|---|---|---|
| | Cutting | Finishing |
| Direct labor-hours....................................... | 6,000 | 30,000 |
| Machine-hours........................................... | 48,000 | 5,000 |
| Total fixed manufacturing overhead cost .................... | $264,000 | $366,000 |
| Variable manufacturing overhead per machine-hour ........... | $2.00 | — |
| Variable manufacturing overhead per direct labor-hour ........ | — | $4.00 |

**Required:**
1. Compute the predetermined overhead rate for each department.

2.  The job cost sheet for Job 203, which was started and completed during the year, showed the following:

|  | Department | |
|---|---|---|
|  | **Cutting** | **Finishing** |
| Direct labor-hours . . . . . . . . . . . . . . . . . | 6 | 20 |
| Machine-hours. . . . . . . . . . . . . . . . . . . . | 80 | 4 |
| Direct materials . . . . . . . . . . . . . . . . . . . | $500 | $310 |
| Direct labor cost . . . . . . . . . . . . . . . . . | $108 | $360 |

Using the predetermined overhead rates that you computed in (1) above, compute the total manufacturing cost assigned to Job 203.

3.  Would you expect substantially different amounts of overhead cost to be assigned to some jobs if the company used a plantwide predetermined overhead rate based on direct labor-hours, rather than using departmental rates? Explain. No computations are necessary.

**EXERCISE 2–14   Job-Order Costing for a Service Company** LO2–1, LO2–2, LO2–3

Yancey Productions is a film studio that uses a job-order costing system. The company's direct materials consist of items such as costumes and props. Its direct labor includes each film's actors, directors, and extras. The company's overhead costs include items such as utilities, depreciation of equipment, senior management salaries, and wages of maintenance workers. Yancey applies its overhead cost to films based on direct labor-dollars.

At the beginning of the year, Yancey made the following estimates:

| | |
|---|---|
| Direct labor-dollars to support all productions. . . . . . . . . . . | $8,000,000 |
| Fixed overhead cost. . . . . . . . . . . . . . . . . . . . . . . . . . . . . . . . . | $4,800,000 |
| Variable overhead cost per direct labor-dollar. . . . . . . . . . | $0.05 |

***Required:***

1.  Compute the predetermined overhead rate.
2.  During the year, Yancey produced a film titled *You Can Say That Again* that incurred the following costs:

| | |
|---|---|
| Direct materials . . . . . . . . . . . . . . . . . . . . . . . . . . . . . . . . . . . | $1,259,000 |
| Direct labor cost . . . . . . . . . . . . . . . . . . . . . . . . . . . . . . . . . . . | $2,400,000 |

Compute the total job cost for this particular film.

**EXERCISE 2–15   Plantwide and Departmental Predetermined Overhead Rates; Job Costs** LO2–1, LO2–2, LO2–3, LO2–4

Delph Company uses a job-order costing system and has two manufacturing departments—Molding and Fabrication. The company provided the following estimates at the beginning of the year:

| | **Molding** | **Fabrication** | **Total** |
|---|---|---|---|
| Machine-hours. . . . . . . . . . . . . . . . . . . . . . . . . . . . . . . . . . . . . . | 20,000 | 30,000 | 50,000 |
| Fixed manufacturing overhead cost. . . . . . . . . . . . . . . . . . . . | $700,000 | $210,000 | $910,000 |
| Variable manufacturing overhead cost per machine-hour. . . | $3.00 | $1.00 | |

During the year, the company had no beginning or ending inventories and it started, completed, and sold only two jobs—Job D-70 and Job C-200. It provided the following information related to those two jobs:

| **Job D-70** | **Molding** | **Fabrication** | **Total** |
|---|---|---|---|
| Direct materials cost. . . . . . . . . . . . . . . . . . . . . . . . . . . . . . . . . | $375,000 | $325,000 | $700,000 |
| Direct labor cost . . . . . . . . . . . . . . . . . . . . . . . . . . . . . . . . . . . | $200,000 | $160,000 | $360,000 |
| Machine-hours. . . . . . . . . . . . . . . . . . . . . . . . . . . . . . . . . . . . . . | 14,000 | 6,000 | 20,000 |

| Job C-200 | Molding | Fabrication | Total |
|---|---|---|---|
| Direct materials cost. | $300,000 | $250,000 | $550,000 |
| Direct labor cost | $175,000 | $225,000 | $400,000 |
| Machine-hours. | 6,000 | 24,000 | 30,000 |

Delph had no underapplied or overapplied manufacturing overhead during the year.

**Required:**
1. Assume Delph uses a plantwide predetermined overhead rate based on machine-hours.
   a. Compute the plantwide predetermined overhead rate.
   b. Compute the total manufacturing cost assigned to Job D-70 and Job C-200.
   c. If Delph establishes bid prices that are 150% of total manufacturing cost, what bid prices would it have established for Job D-70 and Job C-200?
   d. What is Delph's cost of goods sold for the year?
2. Assume Delph uses departmental predetermined overhead rates based on machine-hours.
   a. Compute the departmental predetermined overhead rates.
   b. Compute the total manufacturing cost assigned to Job D-70 and Job C-200.
   c. If Delph establishes bid prices that are 150% of total manufacturing costs, what bid prices would it have established for Job D-70 and Job C-200?
   d. What is Delph's cost of goods sold for the year?
3. What managerial insights are revealed by the computations that you performed in this problem? (*Hint:* Do the cost of goods sold amounts that you computed in requirements 1 and 2 differ from one another? Do the bid prices that you computed in requirements 1 and 2 differ from one another? Why?)

   **PROBLEMS**

**PROBLEM 2–16  Plantwide Predetermined Overhead Rates; Pricing LO2–1, LO2–2, LO2–3**
Landen Corporation uses a job-order costing system. At the beginning of the year, the company made the following estimates:

| | |
|---|---|
| Direct labor-hours required to support estimated production. | 140,000 |
| Machine-hours required to support estimated production | 70,000 |
| Fixed manufacturing overhead cost. | $784,000 |
| Variable manufacturing overhead cost per direct labor-hour | $2.00 |
| Variable manufacturing overhead cost per machine-hour. | $4.00 |

During the year, Job 550 was started and completed. The following information is available with respect to this job:

| | |
|---|---|
| Direct materials | $175 |
| Direct labor cost | $225 |
| Direct labor-hours | 15 |
| Machine-hours | 5 |

**Required:**
1. Assume that Landen has historically used a plantwide predetermined overhead rate with direct labor-hours as the allocation base. Under this approach:
   a. Compute the plantwide predetermined overhead rate.
   b. Compute the total manufacturing cost of Job 550.
   c. If Landen uses a markup percentage of 200% of its total manufacturing cost, what selling price would it establish for Job 550?
2. Assume that Landen's controller believes that machine-hours is a better allocation base than direct labor-hours. Under this approach:
   a. Compute the plantwide predetermined overhead rate.
   b. Compute the total manufacturing cost of Job 550.

c. If Landen uses a markup percentage of 200% of its total manufacturing cost, what selling price would it establish for Job 550?

3. Assume that Landen's controller is right about machine-hours being a more accurate overhead cost allocation base than direct labor-hours. If the company continues to use direct labor-hours as its only overhead cost allocation base what implications does this have for pricing jobs such as Job 550?

### PROBLEM 2–17    Plantwide and Departmental Predetermined Overhead Rates; Overhead Application LO2–1, LO2–2

Wilmington Company has two manufacturing departments—Assembly and Fabrication. It considers all of its manufacturing overhead costs to be fixed costs. The first set of data that is shown below is based on estimates from the beginning of the year. The second set of data relates to one particular job completed during the year—Job Bravo.

| Estimated Data | Assembly | Fabrication | Total |
|---|---|---|---|
| Manufacturing overhead costs..... | $600,000 | $800,000 | $1,400,000 |
| Direct labor-hours............... | 50,000 | 30,000 | 80,000 |
| Machine-hours................... | 20,000 | 100,000 | 120,000 |

| Job Bravo | Assembly | Fabrication | Total |
|---|---|---|---|
| Direct labor-hours............... | 11 | 3 | 14 |
| Machine-hours................... | 3 | 6 | 9 |

**Required:**

1. If Wilmington used a plantwide predetermined overhead rate based on direct labor-hours, how much manufacturing overhead would be applied to Job Bravo?
2. If Wilmington uses departmental predetermined overhead rates with direct labor-hours as the allocation base in Assembly and machine-hours as the allocation base in Fabrication, how much manufacturing overhead would be applied to Job Bravo?

### PROBLEM 2–18    Job-Order Costing for a Service Company LO2–1, LO2–2, LO2–3

Speedy Auto Repairs uses a job-order costing system. The company's direct materials consist of replacement parts installed in customer vehicles, and its direct labor consists of the mechanics' hourly wages. Speedy's overhead costs include various items, such as the shop manager's salary, depreciation of equipment, utilities, insurance, and magazine subscriptions and refreshments for the waiting room.

The company applies all of its overhead costs to jobs based on direct labor-hours. At the beginning of the year, it made the following estimates:

| | |
|---|---|
| Direct labor-hours required to support estimated output......... | 20,000 |
| Fixed overhead cost........................................ | $350,000 |
| Variable overhead cost per direct labor-hour................... | $1.00 |

**Required:**

1. Compute the predetermined overhead rate.
2. During the year, Mr. Wilkes brought in his vehicle to replace his brakes, spark plugs, and tires. The following information was available with respect to his job:

| | |
|---|---|
| Direct materials ............................................ | $590 |
| Direct labor cost ........................................... | $109 |
| Direct labor-hours used ..................................... | 6 |

Compute Mr. Wilkes' total job cost.
3. If Speedy establishes its selling prices using a markup percentage of 40% of its total job cost, then how much would it have charged Mr. Wilkes?

### PROBLEM 2–19    Multiple Predetermined Overhead Rates; Applying Overhead LO2–1, LO2–2, LO2–4

High Desert Potteryworks makes a variety of pottery products that it sells to retailers. The company uses a job-order costing system in which departmental predetermined overhead rates are used to apply manufacturing overhead cost to jobs. The predetermined overhead rate in the Molding Department is based on machine-hours, and the rate in the Painting Department is based on direct labor-hours. At the beginning of the year, the company provided the following estimates:

| | Department | |
| --- | --- | --- |
| | Molding | Painting |
| Direct labor-hours . . . . . . . . . . . . . . . . . . . . . . . . . . . . . . . . . . . . . . . | 12,000 | 60,000 |
| Machine-hours . . . . . . . . . . . . . . . . . . . . . . . . . . . . . . . . . . . . . . . . . | 70,000 | 8,000 |
| Fixed manufacturing overhead cost . . . . . . . . . . . . . . . . . . . . . | $497,000 | $615,000 |
| Variable manufacturing overhead per machine-hour . . . . . . . | $1.50 | – |
| Variable manufacturing overhead per direct labor-hour . . . . | – | $2.00 |

Job 205 was started on August 1 and completed on August 10. The company's cost records show the following information concerning the job:

| | Department | |
| --- | --- | --- |
| | Molding | Painting |
| Direct labor-hours . . . . . . . . . . . . . . . . . . . . . . . . . . . . . . . . . . . . | 30 | 84 |
| Machine-hours . . . . . . . . . . . . . . . . . . . . . . . . . . . . . . . . . . . . . . . | 110 | 20 |
| Direct materials . . . . . . . . . . . . . . . . . . . . . . . . . . . . . . . . . . . . . . | $770 | $1,332 |
| Direct labor cost . . . . . . . . . . . . . . . . . . . . . . . . . . . . . . . . . . . . . | $525 | $1,470 |

**Required:**
1. Compute the predetermined overhead rates used in the Molding Department and the Painting Department.
2. Compute the total overhead cost applied to Job 205.
3. What would be the total manufacturing cost recorded for Job 205? If the job contained 50 units, what would be the unit product cost?

**PROBLEM 2–20 Plantwide versus Multiple Predetermined Overhead Rates: Service Industry LO2–1, LO2–2, LO2–3, LO2–4**
McCullough Hospital uses a job-order costing system to assign costs to its patients. Its direct materials include a variety of items such as pharmaceutical drugs, heart valves, artificial hips, and pacemakers. Its direct labor costs (e.g., surgeons, anesthesiologists, radiologists, and nurses) associated with specific surgical procedures and tests are traced to individual patients. All other costs, such as depreciation of medical equipment, insurance, utilities, incidental medical supplies, and the labor costs associated with around-the-clock monitoring of patients are treated as overhead costs.

Historically, McCullough has used one predetermined overhead rate based on the number of patient-days (each night that a patient spends in the hospital counts as one patient-day) to allocate overhead costs to patients. Recently a member of the hospital's accounting staff has suggested using two predetermined overhead rates (allocated based on the number of patient-days) to improve the accuracy of the costs allocated to patients. The first overhead rate would include all overhead costs within the Intensive Care Unit (ICU) and the second overhead rate would include all Other overhead costs. Information pertaining to the hospital's estimated number of patient-days, its estimated overhead costs, and two of its patients—Patient A and Patient B—is provided below:

| | ICU | Other | Total |
| --- | --- | --- | --- |
| Estimated number of patient-days . . . . . . . . . . . . . . . . . | 2,000 | 18,000 | 20,000 |
| Estimated fixed overhead cost . . . . . . . . . . . . . . . . . . . . | $3,200,000 | $14,000,000 | $17,200,000 |
| Estimated variable overhead cost per patient-day . . . | $236 | $96 | |

| | Patient A | Patient B |
|---|---|---|
| Direct materials . . . . . . . . . . . . . . . . . . . . . . . . . . . . . . . . . . . . | $4,500 | $6,200 |
| Direct labor. . . . . . . . . . . . . . . . . . . . . . . . . . . . . . . . . . . . . . | $25,000 | $36,000 |
| Total number of patient-days (including ICU) . . . . . . . . | 14 | 21 |
| Number of patient-days spent in ICU. . . . . . . . . . . . . . | 0 | 7 |

**Required:**

1.  Assuming McCullough uses only one predetermined overhead rate, calculate:
    a.  The predetermined overhead rate.
    b.  The total cost, including direct materials, direct labor and applied overhead, assigned to Patient A and Patient B.
2.  Assuming McCullough calculates two overhead rates as recommended by the staff accountant, calculate:
    a.  The ICU and Other overhead rates.
    b.  The total cost, including direct materials, direct labor and applied overhead, assigned to Patient A and Patient B.
3.  What insights are revealed by the staff accountant's approach?

**PROBLEM 2–21   Plantwide Versus Multiple Predetermined Overhead Rates LO2–1, LO2–2**
Mason Company has two manufacturing departments—Machining and Assembly. The company considers all of its manufacturing overhead costs to be fixed costs. It provided the following estimates at the beginning of the year as well as the following information with respect to Jobs A and B:

| Estimated Data | Machining | Assembly | Total |
|---|---|---|---|
| Manufacturing overhead . . . . . . . . . . . . . . . . . | $500,000 | $100,000 | $600,000 |
| Direct labor-hours . . . . . . . . . . . . . . . . . . . . . . | 10,000 | 50,000 | 60,000 |
| Machine-hours. . . . . . . . . . . . . . . . . . . . . . . . . | 50,000 | 5,000 | 55,000 |

| Job A | Machining | Assembly | Total |
|---|---|---|---|
| Direct labor-hours . . . . . . . . . . . . . . . . . . . . . . | 5 | 10 | 15 |
| Machine-hours. . . . . . . . . . . . . . . . . . . . . . . . . | 11 | 2 | 13 |

| Job B | Machining | Assembly | Total |
|---|---|---|---|
| Direct labor-hours . . . . . . . . . . . . . . . . . . . . . . | 4 | 5 | 9 |
| Machine-hours. . . . . . . . . . . . . . . . . . . . . . . . . | 12 | 3 | 15 |

**Required:**

1.  If Mason Company uses a plantwide predetermined overhead rate with direct labor-hours as the allocation base, how much manufacturing overhead cost would be applied to Job A? Job B?
2.  Assume that Mason Company uses departmental predetermined overhead rates. The Machining Department is allocated based on machine-hours and the Assembly Department is allocated based on direct labor-hours. How much manufacturing overhead cost would be applied to Job A? Job B?
3.  If Mason multiplies its job costs by a markup percentage to establish selling prices, how might plantwide overhead allocation adversely affect the company's pricing decisions?

## BUILDING YOUR SKILLS    connect

**CASE LO2–1, LO2–2, LO2–3, LO2–4**
"Blast it!" said David Wilson, president of Teledex Company. "We've just lost the bid on the Koopers job by $2,000. It seems we're either too high to get the job or too low to make any money on half the jobs we bid."

Teledex Company manufactures products to customers' specifications and uses a job-order costing system. The company uses a plantwide predetermined overhead rate based on direct labor cost to apply its manufacturing overhead (assumed to be all fixed) to jobs. The following estimates were made at the beginning of the year:

| | Department | | | |
| | Fabricating | Machining | Assembly | Total Plant |
| --- | --- | --- | --- | --- |
| Manufacturing overhead . . . . . . | $350,000 | $400,000 | $90,000 | $840,000 |
| Direct labor. . . . . . . . . . . . . . . . | $200,000 | $100,000 | $300,000 | $600,000 |

Jobs require varying amounts of work in the three departments. The Koopers job, for example, would have required manufacturing costs in the three departments as follows:

| | Department | | | |
| | Fabricating | Machining | Assembly | Total Plant |
| --- | --- | --- | --- | --- |
| Direct materials . . . . . . . . . . . . . | $3,000 | $200 | $1,400 | $4,600 |
| Direct labor. . . . . . . . . . . . . . . . | $2,800 | $500 | $6,200 | $9,500 |
| Manufacturing overhead . . . . . . | ? | ? | ? | ? |

**Required:**
1. Using the company's plantwide approach:
   a. Compute the plantwide predetermined rate for the current year.
   b. Determine the amount of manufacturing overhead cost that would have been applied to the Koopers job.
2. Suppose that instead of using a plantwide predetermined overhead rate, the company had used departmental predetermined overhead rates based on direct labor cost. Under these conditions:
   a. Compute the predetermined overhead rate for each department for the current year.
   b. Determine the amount of manufacturing overhead cost that would have been applied to the Koopers job.
3. Explain the difference between the manufacturing overhead that would have been applied to the Koopers job using the plantwide approach in question 1 (b) and using the departmental approach in question 2 (b).
4. Assume that it is customary in the industry to bid jobs at 150% of total manufacturing cost (direct materials, direct labor, and applied overhead). What was the company's bid price on the Koopers job using a plantwide predetermined overhead rate? What would the bid price have been if departmental predetermined overhead rates had been used to apply overhead cost?

**COMMUNICATING IN PRACTICE LO2-1, LO2-2**

Search the Internet or contact your local chamber of commerce or local chapter of the Institute of Management Accountants to find the names of manufacturing companies in your area. Call or make an appointment to meet with the controller or chief financial officer of one of these companies.

**Required:**
Ask the following questions and write a brief memorandum to your instructor that addresses what you found out.
1. What are the company's main products?
2. Does the company use job-order costing or some other method of determining product costs?
3. How is overhead applied to products? What is the overhead rate? What is the basis of allocation? Is more than one overhead rate used?
4. Has the company recently changed its cost system or is it considering changing its cost system? If so, why? What changes were made or what changes are being considered?

**A LOOK BACK**

Chapter 2 described how job-order costing systems can be used to assign manufacturing costs to individual jobs and to calculate unit product costs.

**A LOOK AT THIS CHAPTER**

In Chapter 3, we explain how job-order costing systems can be used to determine the value of ending inventories and cost of goods sold for external reporting purposes.

**A LOOK AHEAD**

Chapter 4 continues the discussion of the allocation of manufacturing overhead costs, showing how these costs can be more accurately assigned using activity-based costing.

# Job-Order Costing: Cost Flows and External Reporting

## CHAPTER OUTLINE

**Job-Order Costing—The Flow of Costs**

- The Purchase and Issue of Materials

- Labor Cost

- Manufacturing Overhead Costs

- Applying Manufacturing Overhead

- Nonmanufacturing Costs

- Cost of Goods Manufactured

- Cost of Goods Sold

**Schedules of Cost of Goods Manufactured and Cost of Goods Sold**

**Underapplied and Overapplied Overhead—A Closer Look**

- Computing Underapplied and Overapplied Overhead

- Disposition of Underapplied and Overapplied Overhead Balances

- Comparing the Two Methods for Disposing of Underapplied or Overapplied Overhead

- A General Model of Product Cost Flows

**Appendix 3A: Job-Order Costing: A Microsoft Excel-Based Approach**

- Fundamental Accounting Equations

- Three Key Assumptions

- Sapphire Company—Setting the Stage

- Sapphire Company—Transaction Analysis

- Sapphire Company—Schedules of Cost of Goods Manufactured and Cost of Goods Sold

- Sapphire Company—Income Statement

©Pixtal/AGE Fotostock

LEARNING OBJECTIVES

*After studying Chapter 3, you should be able to:*

**LO3–1** Understand the flow of costs in a job-order costing system and prepare appropriate journal entries to record costs.

**LO3–2** Use T-accounts to show the flow of costs in a job-order costing system.

**LO3–3** Prepare schedules of cost of goods manufactured and cost of goods sold and an income statement.

**LO3–4** Compute underapplied or overapplied overhead cost and prepare the journal entry to close the balance in Manufacturing Overhead to the appropriate accounts.

**LO3–5** *(Appendix 3A)* Use Microsoft Excel to summarize the flow of costs in a job-order costing system.

# Inventory Accounting At Toll Brothers

**Toll Brothers** is one of America's largest home builders with annual revenues in excess of $5.1 billion. The company's inventory consists of land acquisition costs, land development costs, home construction costs, and overhead costs related to development and construction. In accordance with generally accepted accounting principles (GAAP), Toll Brothers treats its inventory as a long-lived asset rather than a current asset because its master planned communities can take up to 10 years to fully develop.

While Toll Brothers' industry has some unique attributes relative to most manufacturers, it is an industry well-suited for job-order costing. For example, each new home that the company builds can be accounted for as a job that gets assigned direct material costs (such as lumber, shingles, and bricks), direct labor (such as subcontracted electricians, plumbers, and roofers), and overhead costs (such as the costs of construction supervisors and the equipment that they use to perform their jobs).

Source: 2016 Toll Brothers Annual Report

Chapter 2 discussed how companies use job-order costing to assign manufacturing costs to individual jobs. This chapter describes how companies use job-order costing to prepare a balance sheet and an income statement for external reporting purposes.

Exhibit 3–1 summarizes seven important vocabulary terms that were introduced in the previous chapter. Please take a moment to review these terms, each of which is included in the Glossary at the end of this chapter, because it will help you understand the forthcoming learning objectives.

**EXHIBIT 3–1**    Summary of Important Vocabulary Terms

| Vocabulary Term | Definition |
|---|---|
| Job-order costing | A costing system used in situations where many different products, jobs, or services are produced each period. |
| Absorption costing | A costing method that includes all manufacturing costs—direct materials, direct labor, and both variable and fixed manufacturing overhead—in the cost of a product. |
| Allocation base | A measure of activity such as direct labor-hours or machine-hours that is used to assign costs to cost objects. |
| Predetermined overhead rate | A rate used to charge manufacturing overhead cost to jobs that is established in advance for each period. It is computed using the following equation: $$\text{Predetermined overhead rate} = \frac{\textbf{Estimated total manufacturing overhead cost}}{\textbf{Estimated total amount of the allocation base}}$$ |
| Overhead application | The process of assigning overhead costs to specific jobs using the following formula: $$\begin{array}{c}\textbf{Overhead applied to}\\\textbf{a particular job}\end{array} = \begin{array}{c}\textbf{Predetermined}\\\textbf{overhead rate}\end{array} \times \begin{array}{c}\textbf{Amount of the allocation base}\\\textbf{incurred by the job}\end{array}$$ |
| Normal costing | A costing system in which overhead costs are applied to a job by multiplying a predetermined overhead rate by the actual amount of the allocation base incurred by the job. |
| Job cost sheet | A form that records the direct materials, direct labor, and manufacturing overhead cost charged to a job. |

# JOB-ORDER COSTING—THE FLOW OF COSTS

In Chapter 1, we used Exhibit 1–2 to illustrate the cost flows and classifications in a manufacturing company. Now we are going to use a similar version of that exhibit, as shown in Exhibit 3–2, to introduce the cost flows and classifications in a manufacturing company that uses job-order costing.

Exhibit 3–2 shows that in job-order costing a company's *product costs* flow through three inventory accounts on the balance sheet and then on to cost of goods sold in the income statement. More specifically, raw materials purchases are recorded in the *Raw Materials* inventory account. **Raw materials** include any materials that go into the final product. When raw materials are used in production as direct materials, their costs are transferred to *Work in Process* inventory.[1] **Work in process** consists of units of product that are only partially complete and will require further work before they are ready for sale to the customer. To transform direct materials into completed jobs, direct labor cost is added to Work in Process and manufacturing overhead cost is applied to Work in Process by multiplying the predetermined overhead rate by the actual quantity of the allocation base consumed by each job.[2] When jobs are completed, their costs are transferred from Work in Process to *Finished Goods* inventory. **Finished goods** consist of completed units of product that have not yet been sold to customers.

---

[1]Indirect materials are accounted for as part of manufacturing overhead.
[2]For simplicity, Exhibit 3–2 assumes that Cost of Goods Sold does not need to be adjusted as discussed later in the chapter.

**EXHIBIT 3-2**   Cost Flows and Classifications in a Manufacturing Company That Uses Job-Order Costing

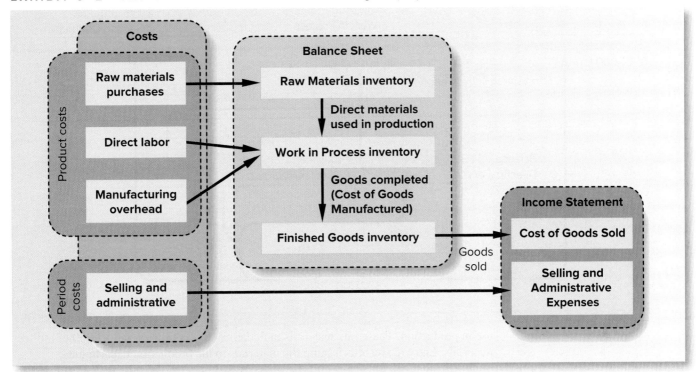

The amount transferred from Work in Process to Finished Goods is referred to as the *cost of goods manufactured*. The **cost of goods manufactured** includes the manufacturing costs associated with units of product that were finished during the period. As jobs are sold, their costs are transferred from Finished Goods to Cost of Goods Sold. At this point, the various costs attached to each job are finally recorded as an expense on the income statement. Until that point, these costs are in inventory accounts on the balance sheet. Period costs (or selling and administrative expenses) do not flow through inventories on the balance sheet. They are recorded as expenses on the income statement in the period incurred.

To illustrate the cost flows within a job-order costing system, we will record Ruger Corporation's transactions for the month of April. Ruger is a producer of gold and silver commemorative medallions and it worked on only two jobs in April. Job A, a special minting of 1,000 gold medallions commemorating the invention of motion pictures, was started during March and completed in April. As of March 31st, Job A had been assigned $30,000 in manufacturing costs, which corresponds with Ruger's Work in Process balance on April 1st of $30,000. Job B, an order for 10,000 silver medallions commemorating the fall of the Berlin Wall, was started in April and was incomplete at the end of the month.

## The Purchase and Issue of Materials

On April 1, Ruger Corporation had $7,000 in raw materials on hand. During the month, the company purchased on account an additional $60,000 in raw materials. The purchase is recorded in journal entry (1) below:

*(1)*

| | | |
|---|---|---|
| Raw Materials.................................. | 60,000 | |
|     Accounts Payable ......................... | | 60,000 |

Remember that Raw Materials is an asset account. Thus, when raw materials are purchased, they are initially recorded as an asset—not as an expense.

**Issue of Direct and Indirect Materials**   During April, *materials requisition forms* were prepared to authorize withdrawing $52,000 in raw materials from the storeroom for

**EXHIBIT 3–3**    Raw Materials Cost Flows

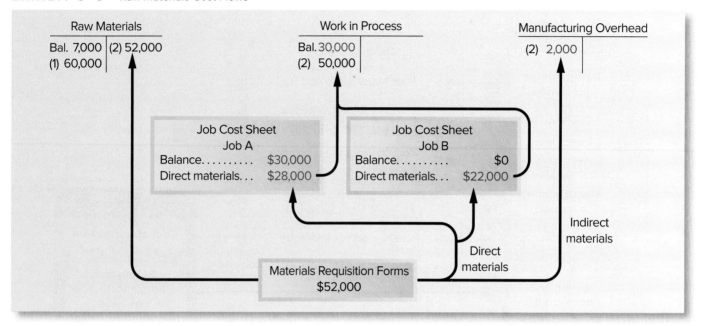

use in production. These raw materials included $50,000 of direct and $2,000 of indirect materials. Entry (2) records issuing the materials to the production departments.

|                                 | *(2)* |        |
| ------------------------------- | ------ | ------ |
| Work in Process ............................. | 50,000 |        |
| Manufacturing Overhead .................... | 2,000  |        |
|    Raw Materials ............................. |        | 52,000 |

The materials charged to Work in Process represent direct materials for specific jobs. These costs are also recorded on the appropriate job cost sheets. This point is illustrated in Exhibit 3–3, where $28,000 of the $50,000 in direct materials is charged to Job A's cost sheet and the remaining $22,000 is charged to Job B's cost sheet. (In this example, all data are presented in summary form and the job cost sheet is abbreviated.)

The $2,000 charged to Manufacturing Overhead in entry (2) represents indirect materials. The debit side of the Manufacturing Overhead account is always used to record the actual manufacturing overhead costs, such as indirect materials, that are incurred during the period. The credit side of this account, as you will see in transaction (7), is always used to record the manufacturing overhead applied to work in process.

Before leaving Exhibit 3–3, we need to provide one additional comment. Notice from the exhibit that the job cost sheet for Job A contains a beginning balance of $30,000. We stated earlier that this balance represents the cost of work done during March that has been carried forward to April. Also note that the Work in Process account contains the same $30,000 balance. Thus, the Work in Process account summarizes all of the costs appearing on the job cost sheets of the jobs that are in process. Job A was the only job in process at the beginning of April, so the beginning balance in the Work in Process account equals Job A's beginning balance of $30,000.

## Labor Cost

In April, the employee *time tickets* (which provide hourly summaries of each employee's activities throughout the day) included $60,000 recorded for direct labor and $15,000 for indirect labor. The following entry summarizes these costs:

|                                 | *(3)* |        |
| ------------------------------- | ------ | ------ |
| Work in Process ............................. | 60,000 |        |
| Manufacturing Overhead .................... | 15,000 |        |
|    Salaries and Wages Payable ................ |        | 75,000 |

**EXHIBIT 3-4**   Labor Cost Flows

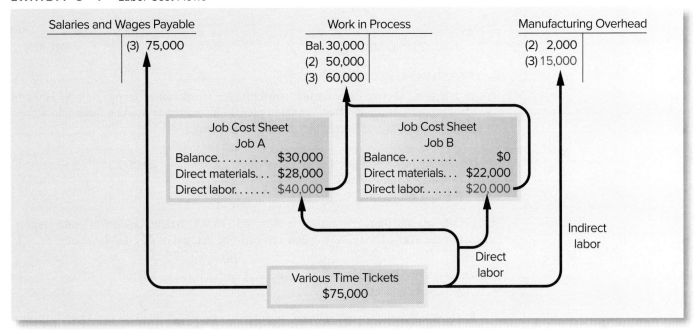

Only the direct labor cost of $60,000 is added to the Work in Process account. At the same time that direct labor costs are added to Work in Process, they are also added to the individual job cost sheets, as shown in Exhibit 3–4. During April, $40,000 of direct labor cost was charged to Job A and the remaining $20,000 was charged to Job B.

The $15,000 charged to Manufacturing Overhead represents the indirect labor costs of the period, such as supervision, janitorial work, and maintenance.

## A Look at Bangladesh'S $20 Billion Garment Industry          IN BUSINESS

In Bangladesh, the minimum wage is $38 per month. A highly-skilled sewing machine operator may earn as much as $100 per month before considering overtime. Companies such as **Fakir Apparels**, a T-shirt manufacturer in Bangladesh, can readily attract customers such as **Walmart**, **Gap**, and **Primark**, due to these low labor costs. However, in addition to serving mass market retailers, Fakir Apparels also makes T-shirts for premium brands such as **Tommy Hilfiger**, **Giorgio Armani**, **Hugo Boss**, and **G-Star Raw**. While the manufacturing cost for one of Fakir Apparels T-shirts ranges from $1.60 to $6.00, the retail selling prices for these T-shirts can vary from $6.00 (at Walmart) to as much as $91.00 (at G-Star Raw).

©Joerg Boethling/Alamy Stock Photo

Source: Passariello, Christina et al., "Bangladesh's Tale of the T-Shirts," *The Wall Street Journal*, July 1, 2013, pp. B1 and B8.

## Manufacturing Overhead Costs

Recall that all manufacturing costs other than direct materials and direct labor are classified as manufacturing overhead costs. These costs are entered directly into the Manufacturing Overhead account as they are incurred. To illustrate, assume that Ruger Corporation incurred the following general factory costs during April:

| | |
|---|---|
| Utilities (heat, water, and power) . . . . . . . . . . . . . . . . . . . | $21,000 |
| Rent on factory equipment . . . . . . . . . . . . . . . . . . . . . . . . | 16,000 |
| Miscellaneous factory overhead costs . . . . . . . . . . . . . . | 3,000 |
| Total . . . . . . . . . . . . . . . . . . . . . . . . . . . . . . . . . . . . . . . . | $40,000 |

The following entry records these costs:

*(4)*

| | | |
|---|---|---|
| Manufacturing Overhead...................... | 40,000 | |
|     Accounts Payable* ....................... | | 40,000 |

*Accounts such as Cash may also be credited

In addition, assume that during April, Ruger Corporation recognized $13,000 in accrued property taxes and that $7,000 in prepaid insurance expired on factory buildings and equipment. The following entry records these items:

*(5)*

| | | |
|---|---|---|
| Manufacturing Overhead...................... | 20,000 | |
|     Property Taxes Payable.................... | | 13,000 |
|     Prepaid Insurance ........................ | | 7,000 |

Finally, assume that the company recognized $18,000 in depreciation on factory equipment during April. The following entry records the accrual of this depreciation:

*(6)*

| | | |
|---|---|---|
| Manufacturing Overhead...................... | 18,000 | |
|     Accumulated Depreciation................. | | 18,000 |

In short, all actual manufacturing overhead costs are debited to the Manufacturing Overhead account as they are incurred.

## Applying Manufacturing Overhead

Because actual manufacturing overhead costs are charged to the Manufacturing Overhead account rather than to Work in Process, it begs the question how are manufacturing overhead costs assigned to Work in Process? The answer is, they are assigned by using the predetermined overhead rate—which is calculated by dividing the estimated total manufacturing overhead cost for the period by the estimated total amount of the allocation base. For example, if we assume that machine-hours is the allocation base, then overhead cost would be applied to jobs by multiplying the predetermined overhead rate by the number of machine-hours charged to each job.

To illustrate, assume that Ruger Corporation's predetermined overhead rate is $6 per machine-hour. Also assume that during April, 10,000 machine-hours were worked on Job A and 5,000 machine-hours were worked on Job B (a total of 15,000 machine-hours). Thus, $90,000 in overhead cost ($6 per machine-hour × 15,000 machine-hours = $90,000) would be applied to Work in Process. The following entry records the application of Manufacturing Overhead to Work in Process:

*(7)*

| | | |
|---|---|---|
| Work in Process ........................... | 90,000 | |
|     Manufacturing Overhead .................. | | 90,000 |

The flow of costs through the Manufacturing Overhead account is shown in Exhibit 3–5. The actual overhead costs on the debit side in the Manufacturing Overhead account in Exhibit 3–5 are the costs that were added to the account in entries (2)–(6). Observe that recording these actual overhead costs [entries (2)–(6)] and the application of overhead to Work in Process [entry (7)] represent two separate and entirely distinct processes.

**The Concept of a Clearing Account**    The Manufacturing Overhead account operates as a clearing account. As we have noted, actual manufacturing overhead costs are debited to the account as they are incurred throughout the year. When jobs are completed (or at the end of an accounting period), overhead cost is applied to the jobs using the predetermined overhead rate—Work in Process is debited and Manufacturing Overhead is credited. This sequence of events is illustrated below:

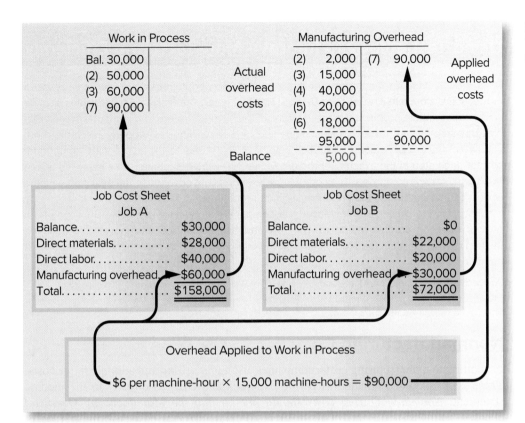

**Manufacturing Overhead
(a clearing account)**

| Actual overhead costs are charged to this account as they are incurred throughout the period. | Overhead is applied to Work in Process using the predetermined overhead rate. |
|---|---|

As we emphasized earlier, the predetermined overhead rate is based entirely on estimates of what the level of activity and overhead costs are *expected* to be, and it is established before the year begins. As a result, the overhead cost applied during a year will almost certainly turn out to be more or less than the actual overhead cost incurred. For example, notice from Exhibit 3–5 that Ruger Corporation's actual overhead costs for the period are $5,000 greater than the overhead cost that has been applied to Work in Process, resulting in a $5,000 debit balance in the Manufacturing Overhead account. We will reserve discussion of what to do with this $5,000 balance until later in the chapter.

For the moment, we can conclude from Exhibit 3–5 that the cost of a completed job consists of the actual direct materials cost of the job, the actual direct labor cost of the job, and the manufacturing overhead cost *applied* to the job. Pay particular attention to the following subtle but important point: *Actual overhead costs are not charged to jobs; actual overhead costs do not appear on the job cost sheet nor do they appear in the Work in Process account. Only the applied overhead cost, based on the predetermined overhead rate, appears on the job cost sheet and in the Work in Process account.*

**HELPFUL HINT**

Actual manufacturing overhead costs are recorded as debits to the Manufacturing Overhead account. The amount of manufacturing overhead applied to all jobs using the predetermined overhead rate is recorded on the credit side of the Manufacturing Overhead account. The manufacturing overhead cost added to all jobs during a period will equal the amount of the credits recorded in the Manufacturing Overhead account during that period.

**Using Technology to Improve Manufacturing Efficiency**

**Roland DG**, a Japanese manufacturer that employs 966 people, has developed an advanced production system that it refers to as D-shop. This technology-intensive system enables a single worker to assemble products from start to finish. Each worker refers to a computer screen that provides step-by-step instructions accompanied by 3-D drawings to properly assemble products. A computerized rotating parts rack automatically rotates to the appropriate component part for each step in the assembly process. Digital screwdrivers monitor how many times and how tightly screws are turned. The computer screen does not advance to the next step until the correct screws are turned the pre-specified number of times.

Thus far, the D-shop has increased the company's productivity by 60% with a long-term goal of doubling productivity. In essence, Roland has developed an innovative production method that invests in automated manufacturing overhead costs to reduce the direct labor cost per unit produced.

Source: Negishi, Mayumi, "No More Assembly Line," *The Wall Street Journal*, June 2, 2014, p. R3.

## Nonmanufacturing Costs

In addition to manufacturing costs, companies also incur selling and administrative costs. These costs should be treated as period expenses and charged directly to the income statement. *Nonmanufacturing costs should not go into the Manufacturing Overhead account.* To illustrate the correct treatment of nonmanufacturing costs, assume that Ruger Corporation incurred $30,000 in selling and administrative salary costs during April. The following entry summarizes the accrual of those salaries:

*(8)*

| | | |
|---|---|---|
| Salaries Expense............................. | 30,000 | |
| Salaries and Wages Payable ............... | | 30,000 |

Assume that depreciation on office equipment during April was $7,000. The entry is as follows:

*(9)*

| | | |
|---|---|---|
| Depreciation Expense ....................... | 7,000 | |
| Accumulated Depreciation................. | | 7,000 |

Pay particular attention to the difference between this entry and entry (6) where we recorded depreciation on factory equipment. In journal entry (6), depreciation on factory equipment was debited to Manufacturing Overhead and is therefore a product cost. In journal entry (9) above, depreciation on office equipment is debited to Depreciation Expense. Depreciation on office equipment is a period expense rather than a product cost.

Finally, assume that advertising was $42,000 and that other selling and administrative expenses in April totaled $8,000. The following entry records these items:

*(10)*

| | | |
|---|---|---|
| Advertising Expense......................... | 42,000 | |
| Other Selling and Administrative Expense ....... | 8,000 | |
| Accounts Payable*......................... | | 50,000 |

*Other accounts such as Cash may also be credited

The amounts in entries (8) through (10) are recorded directly into expense accounts—they have no effect on product costs. The same will be true of any other selling and administrative expenses incurred during April, including sales commissions, depreciation on sales equipment, rent on office facilities, insurance on office facilities, and related costs.

## Cost of Goods Manufactured

When a job has been completed, the finished output is transferred from the production departments to the finished goods warehouse. By this time, the accounting department will have charged the job with direct materials and direct labor cost, and manufacturing overhead will have been applied using the predetermined overhead rate. A transfer of costs is made within the costing system that *parallels* the physical transfer of goods to the finished goods warehouse. The costs of the completed job are transferred out of the Work in Process account and into the Finished Goods account. The sum of all amounts transferred between these two accounts represents the *cost of goods manufactured* for the period.

In the case of Ruger Corporation, remember that Job A was completed during April and Job B was incomplete at the end of the month. Thus, the following entry transfers the cost of Job A from Work in Process to Finished Goods:

*(11)*

| | | |
|---|---|---|
| Finished Goods . . . . . . . . . . . . . . . . . . . . . . . . . . . . . | 158,000 | |
| Work in Process . . . . . . . . . . . . . . . . . . . . . . . . . | | 158,000 |

The $158,000 represents the completed cost of Job A, as shown on the job cost sheet in Exhibit 3–5. Because Job A was the only job completed during April, the $158,000 also represents the cost of goods manufactured for the month.

Because Job B was not completed by the end of the month, its assigned costs will remain in Work in Process and carry over to the next month. If a balance sheet were prepared at the end of April, the cost accumulated thus far on Job B ($72,000) would appear in the asset account Work in Process.

## Cost of Goods Sold

As completed jobs are shipped to customers, their accumulated costs are transferred from Finished Goods to Cost of Goods Sold. If an entire job is shipped at one time, then the entire cost appearing on the job cost sheet is transferred to Cost of Goods Sold. However, sometimes only a portion of the units involved in a particular job will be immediately sold. In these situations, the unit product cost must be used to determine how much product cost should be removed from Finished Goods and charged to Cost of Goods Sold.

For Ruger Corporation, we will assume 750 of the 1,000 gold medallions in Job A were shipped to customers by the end of the month for total sales revenue of $225,000. Because 1,000 units were produced and the total cost of the job from the job cost sheet was $158,000, the unit product cost was $158. The following journal entries would record the sale (all sales were on account):

*(12)*

| | | |
|---|---|---|
| Accounts Receivable . . . . . . . . . . . . . . . . . . . . . . . . | 225,000 | |
| Sales. . . . . . . . . . . . . . . . . . . . . . . . . . . . . . . . . . | | 225,000 |

*(13)*

| | | |
|---|---|---|
| Cost of Goods Sold. . . . . . . . . . . . . . . . . . . . . . . . . | 118,500 | |
| Finished Goods. . . . . . . . . . . . . . . . . . . . . . . . . | | 118,500 |
| (750 units × $158 per unit = $118,500) | | |

**LEARNING OBJECTIVE 3–2**

Use T-accounts to show the flow of costs in a job-order costing system.

**EXHIBIT 3–6**
Summary of Journal
Entries—Ruger Corporation

Entry (13) completes the flow of costs through the job-order costing system. To pull the entire Ruger Corporation example together, journal entries (1) through (13) are summarized in Exhibit 3–6. In addition, Exhibit 3–7 presents the flow of costs through the accounts in T-account form.

**(1)**

| | | |
|---|---:|---:|
| Raw Materials | 60,000 | |
|    Accounts Payable | | 60,000 |

**(2)**

| | | |
|---|---:|---:|
| Work in Process | 50,000 | |
| Manufacturing Overhead | 2,000 | |
|    Raw Materials | | 52,000 |

**(3)**

| | | |
|---|---:|---:|
| Work in Process | 60,000 | |
| Manufacturing Overhead | 15,000 | |
|    Salaries and Wages Payable | | 75,000 |

**(4)**

| | | |
|---|---:|---:|
| Manufacturing Overhead | 40,000 | |
|    Accounts Payable | | 40,000 |

**(5)**

| | | |
|---|---:|---:|
| Manufacturing Overhead | 20,000 | |
|    Property Taxes Payable | | 13,000 |
|    Prepaid Insurance | | 7,000 |

**(6)**

| | | |
|---|---:|---:|
| Manufacturing Overhead | 18,000 | |
|    Accumulated Depreciation | | 18,000 |

**(7)**

| | | |
|---|---:|---:|
| Work in Process | 90,000 | |
|    Manufacturing Overhead | | 90,000 |

**(8)**

| | | |
|---|---:|---:|
| Salaries Expense | 30,000 | |
|    Salaries and Wages Payable | | 30,000 |

**(9)**

| | | |
|---|---:|---:|
| Depreciation Expense | 7,000 | |
|    Accumulated Depreciation | | 7,000 |

**(10)**

| | | |
|---|---:|---:|
| Advertising Expense | 42,000 | |
|    Other Selling and Administrative Expense | 8,000 | |
|    Accounts Payable | | 50,000 |

**(11)**

| | | |
|---|---:|---:|
| Finished Goods | 158,000 | |
|    Work in Process | | 158,000 |

**(12)**

| | | |
|---|---:|---:|
| Accounts Receivable | 225,000 | |
|    Sales | | 225,000 |

**(13)**

| | | |
|---|---:|---:|
| Cost of Goods Sold | 118,500 | |
|    Finished Goods | | 118,500 |

**EXHIBIT 3–7**    Summary of Cost Flows—Ruger Corporation

**Accounts Receivable**

| | | | |
|---|---|---|---|
| Bal. | XX | | |
| (12) | 225,000 | | |

**Prepaid Insurance**

| | | | |
|---|---|---|---|
| Bal. | XX | | |
| | | (5) | 7,000 |

**Raw Materials**

| | | | |
|---|---|---|---|
| Bal. | 7,000 | (2) | 52,000 |
| (1) | 60,000 | | |
| Bal. | 15,000 | | |

**Work in Process**

| | | | |
|---|---|---|---|
| Bal. | 30,000 | (11) | 158,000 |
| (2) | 50,000 | | |
| (3) | 60,000 | | |
| (7) | 90,000 | | |
| Bal. | 72,000 | | |

**Finished Goods**

| | | | |
|---|---|---|---|
| Bal. | 0 | (13) | 118,500 |
| (11) | 158,000 | | |
| Bal. | 39,500 | | |

**Accumulated Depreciation**

| | | | |
|---|---|---|---|
| | | Bal. | XX |
| | | (6) | 18,000 |
| | | (9) | 7,000 |

**Manufacturing Overhead**

| | | | |
|---|---|---|---|
| (2) | 2,000 | (7) | 90,000 |
| (3) | 15,000 | | |
| (4) | 40,000 | | |
| (5) | 20,000 | | |
| (6) | 18,000 | | |
| | 95,000 | | 90,000 |
| Bal. | 5,000 | | |

**Accounts Payable**

| | | | |
|---|---|---|---|
| | | Bal. | XX |
| | | (1) | 60,000 |
| | | (4) | 40,000 |
| | | (10) | 50,000 |

**Salaries and Wages Payable**

| | | | |
|---|---|---|---|
| | | Bal. | XX |
| | | (3) | 75,000 |
| | | (8) | 30,000 |

**Property Taxes Payable**

| | | | |
|---|---|---|---|
| | | Bal. | XX |
| | | (5) | 13,000 |

**Sales**

| | | | |
|---|---|---|---|
| | | (12) | 225,000 |

**Cost of Goods Sold**

| | | | |
|---|---|---|---|
| (13) | 118,500 | | |

**Salaries Expense**

| | | | |
|---|---|---|---|
| (8) | 30,000 | | |

**Depreciation Expense**

| | | | |
|---|---|---|---|
| (9) | 7,000 | | |

**Advertising Expense**

| | | | |
|---|---|---|---|
| (10) | 42,000 | | |

**Other Selling and Administrative Expense**

| | | | |
|---|---|---|---|
| (10) | 8,000 | | |

Explanation of entries:
 (1) Raw materials purchased.
 (2) Direct and indirect materials issued into production.
 (3) Direct and indirect factory labor cost incurred.
 (4) Utilities and other factory costs incurred.
 (5) Property taxes and insurance incurred on the factory.
 (6) Depreciation recorded on factory assets.
 (7) Overhead cost applied to Work in Process.
 (8) Administrative salaries expense incurred.
 (9) Depreciation recorded on office equipment.
(10) Advertising and other selling and administrative expense incurred.
(11) Cost of goods manufactured transferred to finished goods.
(12) Sale of Job A recorded.
(13) Cost of goods sold recorded for Job A.

CONCEPT
CHECK ✓

1. Which of the following statements is true? (You may select more than one answer.)
   a. Direct labor costs are debited to Work in Process and indirect labor costs are debited to Manufacturing Overhead.
   b. Raw material purchases are immediately debited to the Raw Materials account and recorded as an expense on the income statement.
   c. Administrative expenses are debited to the Manufacturing Overhead clearing account.
   d. Assume a company sells finished goods to a customer for $200 on credit. To record this transaction, the company would debit Accounts Receivable for $200 and credit Finished Goods Inventory for $200.
2. Which of the following statements is true with respect to the Manufacturing Overhead clearing account? (You may select more than one answer.)
   a. Actual manufacturing overhead costs are debited to Manufacturing Overhead.
   b. Applied manufacturing overhead costs are credited to Manufacturing Overhead.
   c. If the Manufacturing Overhead account has a debit balance at the end of an accounting period, it means that the actual overhead costs incurred throughout the period were less than the overhead applied to Work in Process during the period.
   d. The overhead cost applied to Work in Process during a period will usually equal the actual overhead cost incurred during the period.

---

**DECISION POINT**

## Would You Debit the Manufacturing Overhead Account?

Assume you are serving as an intern at a company that uses job-order costing. The company's chief financial officer (CFO) has asked you to review the costs that are shown below to determine which of them should be recorded as debits to the Manufacturing Overhead account. She has also asked you to provide explanations for your choices. What would you say?

| Type of cost: | Debit Manufacturing Overhead: Yes or No? |
|---|---|
| Sales commissions | ? |
| Utility expense, factory | ? |
| Direct materials | ? |
| Depreciation, office equipment | ? |
| Indirect labor | ? |
| Administrative salaries | ? |
| Direct labor | ? |

---

# SCHEDULES OF COST OF GOODS MANUFACTURED AND COST OF GOODS SOLD

This section uses the Ruger Corporation example to explain how to prepare schedules of cost of goods manufactured and cost of goods sold as well as an income statement. The **schedule of cost of goods manufactured** contains three elements of product costs—direct materials, direct labor, and manufacturing overhead—and it summarizes the portions of those costs that remain in ending Work in Process inventory and that are transferred out of Work in Process into Finished Goods. The **schedule of cost of goods sold** also contains three elements of product costs—direct materials, direct labor, and manufacturing overhead—and it summarizes the portions of those costs that remain in ending Finished Goods inventory and that are transferred out of Finished Goods into Cost of Goods Sold.

Exhibit 3–8 presents Ruger Corporation's schedules of cost of goods manufactured and cost of goods sold. We want to draw your attention to three equations that are embedded within the schedule of cost of goods manufactured. First, the *raw materials used in production* are computed using the following equation:

$$\text{Raw materials used in production} = \text{Beginning raw materials inventory} + \text{Purchases of raw materials} - \text{Ending raw materials inventory}$$

For Ruger Corporation, the beginning raw materials inventory of $7,000 plus the purchases of raw materials of $60,000 minus the ending raw materials inventory of $15,000 equals the raw materials used in production of $52,000. Second, the *total manufacturing costs* are computed using the following equation:

$$\text{Total manufacturing costs} = \text{Direct materials} + \text{Direct labor} + \text{Manufacturing overhead applied to work in process}$$

For Ruger Corporation, the direct materials of $50,000 plus the direct labor of $60,000 plus the manufacturing overhead applied to work in process of $90,000 equals the total manufacturing costs of $200,000. Notice, the direct materials used in production

**EXHIBIT 3−8**
Schedules of Cost of Goods Manufactured and Cost of Goods Sold

### Cost of Goods Manufactured

| | | |
|---|---:|---:|
| Direct materials: | | |
| Beginning raw materials inventory | $ 7,000 | |
| Add: Purchases of raw materials | 60,000 | |
| Total raw materials available | 67,000 | |
| Deduct: Ending raw materials inventory | 15,000 | |
| Raw materials used in production | 52,000 | |
| Deduct: Indirect materials included in manufacturing overhead | 2,000 | $ 50,000 |
| Direct labor | | 60,000 |
| Manufacturing overhead applied to work in process | | 90,000 |
| Total manufacturing costs | | 200,000 |
| Add: Beginning work in process inventory | | 30,000 |
| | | 230,000 |
| Deduct: Ending work in process inventory | | 72,000 |
| Cost of goods manufactured | | $158,000 |

### Cost of Goods Sold

| | | |
|---|---:|---:|
| Beginning finished goods inventory | | $ 0 |
| Add: Cost of goods manufactured | | 158,000 |
| Cost of goods available for sale | | 158,000 |
| Deduct: Ending finished goods inventory | | 39,500 |
| Unadjusted cost of goods sold | | 118,500 |
| Add: Underapplied overhead* | | 5,000 |
| Adjusted cost of goods sold | | $123,500 |

*Note that the underapplied overhead is added to cost of goods sold. If overhead were overapplied, it would be deducted from cost of goods sold.

($50,000) is included in total manufacturing costs instead of raw materials purchases ($60,000). The direct materials used in production will usually differ from the amount of raw material purchases when the raw materials inventory balance changes or indirect materials are withdrawn from raw materials inventory. You should also make a note that *this equation includes manufacturing overhead applied to work in process rather than actual manufacturing overhead costs.* For Ruger Corporation, its manufacturing overhead applied to work in process of $90,000 is computed by multiplying the predetermined overhead rate of $6 per machine-hour by the actual amount of the allocation base recorded on all jobs, or 15,000 machine-hours. *The actual manufacturing overhead costs incurred during the period are not added to the Work in Process account.*

The third equation included in the schedule of cost of goods manufactured relates to computing the cost of goods manufactured:

$$\text{Cost of goods manufactured} = \text{Total manufacturing costs} + \text{Beginning work in process inventory} - \text{Ending work in process inventory}$$

For Ruger, the total manufacturing costs of $200,000 plus the beginning work in process inventory of $30,000 minus the ending work in process inventory of $72,000 equals the cost of goods manufactured of $158,000. The cost of goods manufactured represents the cost of the goods completed during the period and transferred from Work in Process to Finished Goods.

The schedule of cost of goods sold shown in Exhibit 3–8 relies on the following equation to compute the unadjusted cost of goods sold:

$$\text{Unadjusted cost of goods sold} = \text{Beginning finished goods inventory} + \text{Cost of goods manufactured} - \text{Ending finished goods inventory}$$

The beginning finished goods inventory ($0) plus the cost of goods manufactured ($158,000) equals the cost of goods available for sale ($158,000). The cost of goods available for sale ($158,000) minus the ending finished goods inventory ($39,500) equals the unadjusted cost of goods sold ($118,500). Finally, the unadjusted cost of goods sold ($118,500) plus the underapplied overhead ($5,000) equals adjusted cost of goods sold ($123,500). The next section of the chapter takes a closer look at why cost of goods sold needs to be adjusted for the amount of underapplied or overapplied overhead.

Exhibit 3–9 presents Ruger Corporation's income statement for April. Notice that the cost of goods sold on this statement is carried over from Exhibit 3–8. The selling and administrative expenses (which total $87,000) did not flow through the schedules of cost of goods manufactured and cost of goods sold. Journal entries 8–10 show that these items were immediately debited to expense accounts rather than being debited to inventory accounts.

**EXHIBIT 3–9**
Income Statement

| Ruger Corporation<br>Income Statement<br>For the Month Ending April 30 | | |
|---|---:|---:|
| Sales ................................................. | | $225,000 |
| Cost of goods sold ($118,500 + $5,000) .................... | | 123,500 |
| Gross margin ........................................ | | 101,500 |
| Selling and administrative expenses: | | |
|   Salaries expense .................................. | $30,000 | |
|   Depreciation expense .............................. | 7,000 | |
|   Advertising expense ............................... | 42,000 | |
|   Other expense .................................... | 8,000 | 87,000 |
| Net operating income ................................. | | $ 14,500 |

3. Which of the following statements is false with respect to the schedule of cost of goods manufactured? (You may select more than one answer.)
   a. The beginning raw materials inventory plus raw materials purchases minus ending raw materials inventory equals the raw materials used in production.
   b. Direct labor costs and actual manufacturing overhead costs are included in the schedule of cost of goods manufactured.
   c. The cost of goods manufactured represents the amount that will be debited to Cost of Goods Sold during an accounting period.
   d. If the finished goods inventory increases during an accounting period, it will decrease the cost of goods manufactured.

**HELPFUL HINT**

The schedules of cost of goods manufactured and cost of goods sold use the same generic equation (Transferred out = Beginning balance + Additions − Ending balance) three times to track the flow of costs through raw materials, work in process, and finished goods inventories. The application of this general equation to each of the three inventory accounts is as follows:

**Raw materials:**

$$\text{Raw materials used in production} = \text{Beginning raw materials} + \text{Purchases of raw materials} - \text{Ending raw materials}$$

**Work in process:**

$$\text{Cost of goods manufactured} = \text{Beginning work in process} + \text{Total manufacturing costs} - \text{Ending work in process}$$

**Finished goods:**

$$\text{Cost of goods sold} = \text{Beginning finished goods} + \text{Cost of goods manufactured} - \text{Ending finished goods}$$

## UNDERAPPLIED AND OVERAPPLIED OVERHEAD—A CLOSER LOOK

This section explains how to compute underapplied and overapplied overhead and how to dispose of any balance remaining in the Manufacturing Overhead account at the end of a period.

### Computing Underapplied and Overapplied Overhead

Because the predetermined overhead rate is established before the period begins and is based entirely on estimated data, the overhead cost applied to Work in Process will generally differ from the amount of overhead cost actually incurred. In the case of Ruger Corporation, for example, the predetermined overhead rate of $6 per machine-hour was used to apply $90,000 of overhead cost to Work in Process, whereas actual overhead costs for April proved to be $95,000 (see Exhibit 3–5). The difference between the overhead cost applied to Work in Process and the actual overhead costs of a period is called either **underapplied overhead** or **overapplied overhead**. For Ruger Corporation, overhead was underapplied by $5,000 because the applied cost ($90,000) was $5,000 less than the actual cost ($95,000). If the situation had been reversed and the company had applied $95,000 in overhead cost to Work in Process while incurring actual overhead cost of only $90,000, then the overhead would have been overapplied.

What is the cause of underapplied or overapplied overhead? Basically, the method of applying overhead to jobs using a predetermined overhead rate assumes that actual overhead costs will be proportional to the actual amount of the allocation base incurred during the period. If, for example, the predetermined overhead rate is $6 per machine-hour, then it is assumed that actual overhead costs incurred will be $6 for every machine-hour that is actually worked. There are at least two reasons why this may not be true. First, much of the overhead often consists of fixed costs that do not change as the number of machine-hours incurred goes up or down. Second, spending on overhead items may or may not be under control. If individuals who are responsible for overhead costs do a good job, those costs should be less than were expected at the beginning of the period. If they do a poor job, those costs will be more than expected.

To illustrate these concepts, suppose that two companies—Turbo Crafters and Black & Howell—have prepared the following estimated data for the coming year:

| | Turbo Crafters | Black & Howell |
|---|---|---|
| Allocation base . . . . . . . . . . . . . . . . . . . . . . . . . . . . . . . . . . . . | Machine-hours | Direct materials cost |
| Estimated manufacturing overhead cost (a) . . . . . . . . . . . . . | $300,000 | $120,000 |
| Estimated total amount of the allocation base (b) . . . . . . . . | 75,000 machine-hours | $80,000 direct materials cost |
| Predetermined overhead rate (a) ÷ (b) . . . . . . . . . . . . . . . . . . | $4 per machine-hour | 150% of direct materials cost |

Note that when the allocation base is dollars (such as direct materials cost in the case of Black & Howell) the predetermined overhead rate is expressed as a percentage of the allocation base. When dollars are divided by dollars, the result is a percentage.

Now assume that because of unexpected changes in overhead spending and unit sales, the *actual* overhead cost incurred and the actual amount of the allocation base used during the year in each company are as follows:

| | Turbo Crafters | Black & Howell |
|---|---|---|
| Actual manufacturing overhead cost . . . . . . . . . . . . . . . . . . . . . | $290,000 | $130,000 |
| Actual total amount of the allocation base . . . . . . . . . . . . . . . . | 68,000 machine-hours | $90,000 direct materials cost |

Given this actual data and each company's predetermined overhead rate, the manufacturing overhead applied to Work in Process during the year would be computed as follows:

| | Turbo Crafters | Black & Howell |
|---|---|---|
| Predetermined overhead rate (a) . . . . . . . . . . . . . . . . . . . . . . . | $4 per machine-hour | 150% of direct materials cost |
| Actual total amount of the allocation base (b) . . . . . . . . . . . . | 68,000 machine-hours | $90,000 direct materials cost |
| Manufacturing overhead applied (a) × (b) . . . . . . . . . . . . . . | $272,000 | $135,000 |

This results in underapplied and overapplied overhead as shown below:

| | Turbo Crafters | Black & Howell |
|---|---|---|
| Actual manufacturing overhead cost . . . . . . . . . . . . . . . . . . . . . | $290,000 | $ 130,000 |
| Manufacturing overhead applied . . . . . . . . . . . . . . . . . . . . . . | 272,000 | 135,000 |
| Underapplied (overapplied) manufacturing overhead . . . . . | $ 18,000 | $ (5,000) |

**EXHIBIT 3–10**
Summary of Overhead Concepts

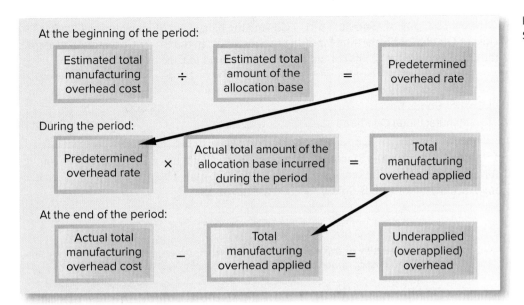

For Turbo Crafters, the overhead cost applied to Work in Process of $272,000 is less than the actual overhead cost for the year of $290,000; therefore, overhead is underapplied by $18,000.

For Black & Howell, the overhead cost applied to Work in Process of $135,000 is greater than the actual overhead cost for the year of $130,000, so overhead is overapplied by $(5,000).

A summary of these concepts is presented in Exhibit 3–10.

## Disposition of Underapplied or Overapplied Overhead Balances

The Turbo Crafters and Black & Howell examples demonstrate one way to calculate underapplied or overapplied overhead. However, another equivalent method of determining the amount of underapplied or overapplied overhead is to properly analyze the Manufacturing Overhead T-account. Explaining this second method also enables us to discuss the topic of preparing a journal entry to dispose of underapplied or overapplied overhead for financial reporting purposes.

If we return to the Ruger Corporation example and look at the Manufacturing Overhead T-account in Exhibit 3–7, you will see that there is a debit balance of $5,000. Remember that debit entries to this account represent actual overhead costs, whereas credit entries represent applied overhead costs. In this case, the applied overhead costs (the credits) are less than the actual overhead costs (the debits) by $5,000—hence, the debit balance indicates that manufacturing overhead is underapplied. In other words, if there is a *debit* balance in the Manufacturing Overhead account of X dollars, then the overhead is *underapplied* by X dollars. On the other hand, if there is a *credit* balance in the Manufacturing Overhead account of Y dollars, then the overhead is *overapplied* by Y dollars.

Once we have quantified the amount of underapplied or overapplied overhead, the corresponding amount remaining in the Manufacturing Overhead account at the end of a period must be disposed of in one of two ways:

1. It can be closed to Cost of Goods Sold.
2. It can be closed proportionally to Work in Process, Finished Goods, and Cost of Goods Sold.

**Closed to Cost of Goods Sold**   Closing the balance in Manufacturing Overhead to Cost of Goods Sold is the simpler of the two methods. In the Ruger Corporation example, the entry to close the $5,000 of underapplied overhead to Cost of Goods Sold is:

*(14)*

| | | |
|---|---|---|
| Cost of Goods Sold ......................... | 5,000 | |
|    Manufacturing Overhead .................. | | 5,000 |

Note that because the Manufacturing Overhead account has a debit balance, Manufacturing Overhead must be credited to close out the account. This has the effect of increasing April's Cost of Goods Sold by $5,000 as shown below:

| | |
|---|---|
| Unadjusted cost of goods sold [from entry (13)] ....... | $118,500 |
| Add underapplied overhead [from entry (14)] ......... | 5,000 |
| Adjusted cost of goods sold ....................... | $123,500 |

Ruger Corporation's adjusted cost of goods sold of $123,500 as shown here agrees with the company's income statement that was presented earlier in Exhibit 3–9.

Keep in mind that unadjusted cost of goods sold is based on the amount of manufacturing overhead cost applied to jobs, not the amount of actual manufacturing overhead cost incurred. So, when overhead is underapplied it means two things—not enough overhead cost was applied to jobs and the cost of goods sold is understated. Adding the underapplied overhead to the cost of goods sold corrects this understatement.

**Closed Proportionally to Work in Process, Finished Goods, and Cost of Goods Sold**   Closing underapplied or overapplied overhead proportionally to Work in Process, Finished Goods, and Cost of Goods Sold is more accurate than closing the entire balance into Cost of Goods Sold; however, it is also more complex. We'll explain the proportional allocation of underapplied or overapplied overhead using a three-step process.

The first step is to take the total overhead cost applied to production during the period and break it into three pieces—the portion included in Work in Process at the end of the period, the portion included in Finished Goods at the end of the period, and the portion applied to Cost of Goods Sold during the period. The second step is to state each of these three amounts as a percent of the total overhead cost applied to production during the period. The third step is to derive the amounts needed for the journal entry by multiplying the percentages from step two by the amount of underapplied or overapplied overhead.

Exhibit 3–11 illustrates this three-step process for Ruger Corporation. As you may remember, Ruger worked on only two jobs in April—Job A and Job B. Job A consisted of 1,000 gold medallions, 750 of which were sold to customers and 250 of which remained in Finished Goods at the end of the month. Job B consisted of 10,000 silver medallions and it was incomplete at the end of April.

In step 1 of Exhibit 3–11, Ruger takes its total manufacturing overhead applied to production from Exhibit 3–5 ($90,000) and splits it between Job A ($60,000) and Job B ($30,000). Because Job B was incomplete at the end of April, all of its applied overhead cost ($30,000) resides in Work in Process at the end of the month, whereas the $60,000 of overhead cost applied to Job A needs to be split into two accounts. A total of 25% of Job A's gold medallions (= 250 ÷ 1,000) were in Finished Goods at the end of April; therefore, 25% of Job A's applied overhead cost, or $15,000 (= $60,000 × 25%), also remains in Finished Goods. Similarly, 75% of Job A's gold medallions (= 750 ÷ 1,000) were sold during April; thus, 75% of Job A's applied overhead cost, or $45,000 (= $60,000 × 75%), is included in Cost of Goods Sold.

In step 2 of Exhibit 3–11, the amounts of applied overhead cost in Work in Process ($30,000), Finished Goods ($15,000), and Cost of Goods Sold ($45,000) are each stated

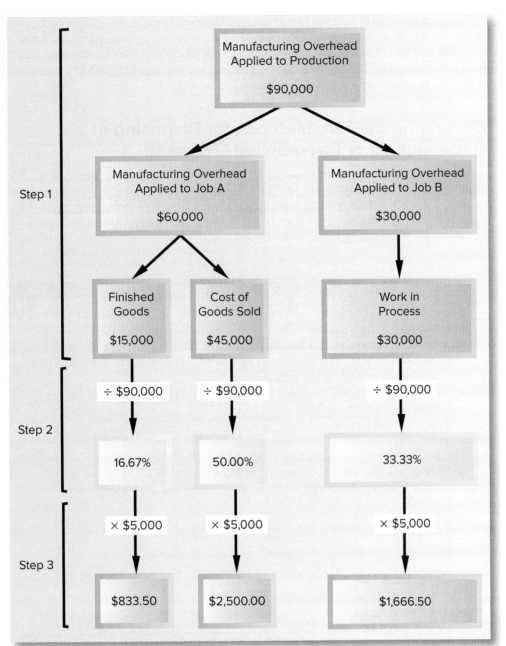

EXHIBIT 3–11
Ruger Corporation: Closing
Underapplied Overhead
Proportionally to Work in
Process, Finished Goods, and
Cost of Goods Sold

as a percent of the total manufacturing overhead cost applied to production during the period ($90,000). In other words, 33.33% of the period's total applied overhead cost resides in Work in Process at the end of April. Similarly, 16.67% of the total remains in Finished Goods and 50% is included in Cost of Goods Sold.

Step 3 from Exhibit 3–11 uses the percentages from step 2 to proportionally allocate the $5,000 of underapplied overhead to Work in Process, Finished Goods, and Cost of Goods Sold. Work in Process is allocated $1,666.50 of underapplied overhead, whereas Finished Goods and Cost of Goods Sold are allocated $833.50 and $2,500, respectively. Using these dollar amounts, the journal entry would be recorded as follows:

| | | |
|---|---:|---:|
| Work in Process . . . . . . . . . . . . . . . . . . . . . . . . . . . . | 1,666.50 | |
| Finished Goods . . . . . . . . . . . . . . . . . . . . . . . . . . . . | 833.50 | |
| Cost of Goods Sold . . . . . . . . . . . . . . . . . . . . . . . . | 2,500.00 | |
| Manufacturing Overhead . . . . . . . . . . . . . . . . . . . | | 5,000.00 |

Note that the $5,000 credit to Manufacturing Overhead ensures that this account concludes the month with a zero balance. Furthermore, it bears emphasizing that if Ruger's overhead had been overapplied rather than underapplied, the entry above would have been just the reverse. The Manufacturing Overhead account would have had a credit balance, thus necessitating a reversal of the debits and credits shown above.

## Comparing the Two Methods for Disposing of Underapplied or Overapplied Overhead

Closing the underapplied or overapplied overhead to Work in Process, Finished Goods, and Cost of Goods Sold is more accurate than the simpler approach of closing it out to Cost of Goods Sold. For example, the simpler approach overstates Ruger Corporation's Cost of Goods Sold by $2,500 (= $5,000 – $2,500) and understates its net operating income by the same amount.

CONCEPT CHECK ✔

4. The estimated total manufacturing overhead cost is $200,000. The estimated total amount of the allocation base is 40,000 direct labor-hours. The actual total manufacturing overhead cost for the period is $220,000 and the actual direct labor-hours worked on all jobs during the period is 41,000 hours. The total underapplied (overapplied) overhead for the period is:
   a. $20,000 underapplied
   b. $20,000 overapplied
   c. $15,000 underapplied
   d. $15,000 overapplied
5. The predetermined overhead rate is $50 per machine-hour, underapplied overhead is $5,000, and the actual amount of machine-hours is 2,000. What is the actual amount of total manufacturing overhead incurred during the period?
   a. $105,000
   b. $95,000
   c. $150,000
   d. $110,000

## HELPFUL HINT

Students struggle to understand two key points with respect to underapplied or overapplied overhead. First, underapplied or overapplied overhead is not computed for each job. It is computed for the company as a whole (if a plantwide overhead rate is used) or for each department (if departmental overhead rates are used). Second, students often fail to grasp the chronology of events in a normal costing system. Predetermined overhead rates are computed at the beginning of the period. Overhead is applied to jobs throughout the period. Underapplied or overapplied overhead is computed at the end of the period.

## A General Model of Product Cost Flows

Exhibit 3–12 presents a T-account model of the flow of manufacturing costs in a job-order costing system. This model can be very helpful in understanding how manufacturing costs flow through a normal costing system and finally end up as Cost of Goods Sold on the income statement.

**EXHIBIT 3–12**    A General Model of Cost Flows (Using Normal Costing)

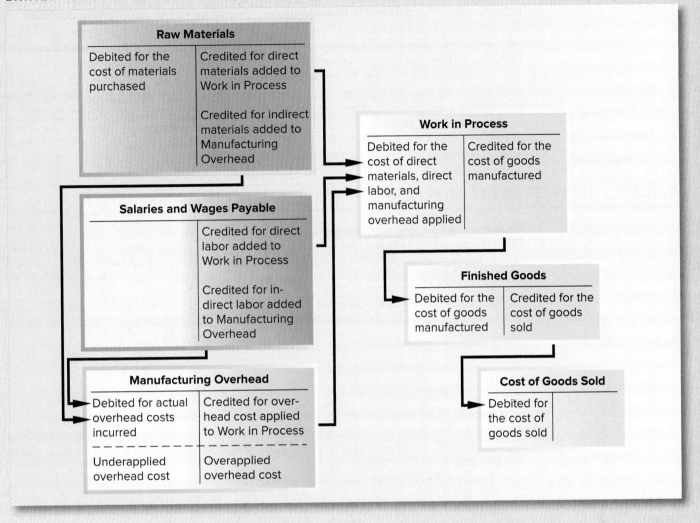

## SUMMARY

**LO3–1  Understand the flow of costs in a job-order costing system and prepare appropriate journal entries to record costs.**

Direct materials costs are debited to Work in Process when they are released for use in production. Direct labor costs are debited to Work in Process as incurred. Actual manufacturing overhead costs are debited to the Manufacturing Overhead account as incurred. Manufacturing overhead costs are applied to Work in Process using the predetermined overhead rate. The journal entry that accomplishes this is a debit to Work in Process and a credit to Manufacturing Overhead.

**LO3–2  Use T-accounts to show the flow of costs in a job-order costing system.**

See Exhibits 3–7 and 3–12 for summaries of the cost flows through the T-accounts.

**LO3–3  Prepare schedules of cost of goods manufactured and cost of goods sold and an income statement.**

The schedule of cost of goods manufactured calculates the cost of inventories that were completed and transferred from Work in Process to Finished Goods. The schedule of cost of goods sold calculates the cost of inventories that were transferred from Finished Goods to Cost of Goods Sold. See Exhibits 3–8 and 3–9 for an example of these schedules and an income statement.

**LO3–4  Compute underapplied or overapplied overhead cost and prepare the journal entry to close the balance in Manufacturing Overhead to the appropriate account.**
The difference between the actual overhead cost incurred during a period and the amount of overhead cost applied to production is referred to as underapplied or overapplied overhead. Underapplied or overapplied overhead is closed out to Cost of Goods Sold. When overhead is underapplied, the balance in the Manufacturing Overhead account is debited to Cost of Goods Sold. This has the effect of increasing the Cost of Goods Sold and occurs because costs assigned to products have been understated. When overhead is overapplied, the balance in the Manufacturing Overhead account is credited to Cost of Goods Sold. This has the effect of decreasing the Cost of Goods Sold and occurs because costs assigned to products have been overstated.

## GUIDANCE ANSWERS TO DECISION POINT

**Would You Debit the Manufacturing Overhead Account?**
The only costs that would be recorded as debits to the Manufacturing Overhead account are utility expense, factory and indirect labor. Both of these costs are indirect manufacturing costs that are properly classified as manufacturing overhead costs. Direct materials and direct labor are direct manufacturing costs rather than indirect manufacturing costs, so they would be debited to Work in Process rather than Manufacturing Overhead. Sales commissions, depreciation, office equipment, and administrative salaries are period costs rather than product costs, so they would be debited to expense accounts (rather than the Manufacturing Overhead account) that would flow through to the income statement in the period incurred.

## GUIDANCE ANSWERS TO CONCEPT CHECKS

1.  **Choice a.** Raw materials are not expensed when purchased. Administrative expenses are period costs; therefore, they are never recorded in the Manufacturing Overhead account. The debit to Accounts Receivable for $200 would be accompanied by a credit to Sales for $200.
2.  **Choices a and b.** If the Manufacturing Overhead account has a debit balance at the end of an accounting period, it means that the actual overhead costs incurred throughout the period were greater than (not less than) the overhead applied to Work in Process during the period. Also, the overhead cost applied to Work in Process during a period will usually differ from (rather than be equal to) the actual overhead cost incurred during the period.
3.  **Choices b, c, and d.** Applied manufacturing overhead costs are included in the schedule of cost of goods manufactured. The cost of goods manufactured represents the amount that will be debited to Finished Goods during an accounting period. A change in the Finished Goods inventory balance has no impact on the cost of goods manufactured.
4.  **Choice c.** Actual overhead of $220,000 minus applied overhead of $205,000 ($200,000 ÷ 40,000 direct labor-hours × 41,000 actual hours worked) equals $15,000 underapplied.
5.  **Choice a.** The amount of overhead applied to production is 2,000 hours multiplied by the $50 predetermined overhead rate, or $100,000. If overhead is underapplied by $5,000, the actual amount of overhead is $100,000 + $5,000 = $105,000.

## REVIEW PROBLEM: THE FLOW OF COSTS IN A JOB-ORDER COSTING SYSTEM

Hogle Corporation is a manufacturer that uses job-order costing. On January 1, the company's inventory balances were as follows:

| | |
|---|---|
| Raw materials ............................. | $20,000 |
| Work in process .......................... | $15,000 |
| Finished goods ........................... | $30,000 |

The company applies overhead cost to jobs on the basis of machine-hours worked. For the current year, the company's predetermined overhead rate was based on a cost formula that estimated $450,000 of total manufacturing overhead for an estimated activity level of 75,000 machine-hours. The following transactions were recorded for the year:

a.  Raw materials were purchased on account, $410,000.
b.  Raw materials were used in production, $380,000 ($360,000 direct materials and $20,000 indirect materials).
c.  The following costs were accrued for employee services: direct labor, $75,000; indirect labor, $110,000; sales commissions, $90,000; and administrative salaries, $200,000.
d.  Sales travel costs (on account) were $17,000.
e.  Utility costs (on account) in the factory were $43,000.
f.  Advertising costs (on account) were $180,000.
g.  Depreciation was recorded for the year, $350,000 (80% relates to factory assets, and 20% relates to selling and administrative assets).
h.  Insurance expired during the year, $10,000 (70% relates to factory operations, and the remaining 30% relates to selling and administrative activities).
i.  Manufacturing overhead was applied to production. Due to greater than expected demand for its products, the company worked 80,000 machine-hours on all jobs during the year.
j.  Jobs costing $900,000 to manufacture according to their job cost sheets were completed during the year.
k.  Jobs were sold on account to customers during the year for a total of $1,500,000. The jobs cost $870,000 to manufacture according to their job cost sheets.

**Required:**
1.  Prepare journal entries to record the preceding transactions.
2.  Post the entries in (1) above to T-accounts (don't forget to enter the beginning balances in the inventory accounts).
3.  Is Manufacturing Overhead underapplied or overapplied for the year? Prepare a journal entry to close any balance in the Manufacturing Overhead account to Cost of Goods Sold. Do not allocate the balance between Work in Process, Finished Goods, and Cost of Goods Sold.
4.  Prepare an income statement for the year.

**Solution to Review Problem**
1.

|   |   | | |
|---|---|---:|---:|
| a. | Raw Materials | 410,000 | |
|    | Accounts Payable | | 410,000 |
| b. | Work in Process | 360,000 | |
|    | Manufacturing Overhead | 20,000 | |
|    | Raw Materials | | 380,000 |
| c. | Work in Process | 75,000 | |
|    | Manufacturing Overhead | 110,000 | |
|    | Sales Commissions Expense | 90,000 | |
|    | Administrative Salaries Expense | 200,000 | |
|    | Salaries and Wages Payable | | 475,000 |
| d. | Sales Travel Expense | 17,000 | |
|    | Accounts Payable | | 17,000 |
| e. | Manufacturing Overhead | 43,000 | |
|    | Accounts Payable | | 43,000 |
| f. | Advertising Expense | 180,000 | |
|    | Accounts Payable | | 180,000 |
| g. | Manufacturing Overhead | 280,000 | |
|    | Depreciation Expense | 70,000 | |
|    | Accumulated Depreciation | | 350,000 |

*Continued*

*Continued*

| | | | |
|---|---|---|---|
| h. | Manufacturing Overhead | 7,000 | |
| | Insurance Expense | 3,000 | |
| | Prepaid Insurance | | 10,000 |

i.  The predetermined overhead rate for the year is computed as follows:

$$\text{Predetermined overhead rate} = \frac{\text{Estimated total manufacturing overhead cost}}{\text{Estimated total amount of the allocation base}}$$

$$= \frac{\$450,000}{75,000 \text{ machine-hours}}$$

$$= \$6 \text{ per machine-hour}$$

Based on the 80,000 machine-hours actually worked during the year, the company applied $480,000 in overhead cost to production: $6 per machine-hour × 80,000 machine-hours = $480,000. The following entry records this application of overhead cost:

| | | | |
|---|---|---|---|
| | Work in Process | 480,000 | |
| | Manufacturing Overhead | | 480,000 |
| j. | Finished Goods | 900,000 | |
| | Work in Process | | 900,000 |
| k. | Accounts Receivable | 1,500,000 | |
| | Sales | | 1,500,000 |
| | Cost of Goods Sold | 870,000 | |
| | Finished Goods | | 870,000 |

2.

### Accounts Receivable
| | | | |
|---|---|---|---|
| (k) | 1,500,000 | | |

### Prepaid Insurance
| | | | |
|---|---|---|---|
| | | (h) | 10,000 |

### Raw Materials
| | | | |
|---|---|---|---|
| Bal. | 20,000 | (b) | 380,000 |
| (a) | 410,000 | | |
| Bal. | 50,000 | | |

### Work in Process
| | | | |
|---|---|---|---|
| Bal. | 15,000 | (j) | 900,000 |
| (b) | 360,000 | | |
| (c) | 75,000 | | |
| (i) | 480,000 | | |
| Bal. | 30,000 | | |

### Finished Goods
| | | | |
|---|---|---|---|
| Bal. | 30,000 | (k) | 870,000 |
| (j) | 900,000 | | |
| Bal. | 60,000 | | |

### Manufacturing Overhead
| | | | |
|---|---|---|---|
| (b) | 20,000 | (i) | 480,000 |
| (c) | 110,000 | | |
| (e) | 43,000 | | |
| (g) | 280,000 | | |
| (h) | 7,000 | | |
| | 460,000 | | 480,000 |
| | | Bal. | 20,000 |

### Accumulated Depreciation
| | | | |
|---|---|---|---|
| | | (g) | 350,000 |

### Accounts Payable
| | | | |
|---|---|---|---|
| | | (a) | 410,000 |
| | | (d) | 17,000 |
| | | (e) | 43,000 |
| | | (f) | 180,000 |

### Salaries and Wages Payable
| | | | |
|---|---|---|---|
| | | (c) | 475,000 |

### Sales
| | | | |
|---|---|---|---|
| | | (k) | 1,500,000 |

### Cost of Goods Sold
| | | | |
|---|---|---|---|
| (k) | 870,000 | | |

### Sales Commissions Expense
| | | | |
|---|---|---|---|
| (c) | 90,000 | | |

### Administrative Salaries Expense
| | | | |
|---|---|---|---|
| (c) | 200,000 | | |

### Sales Travel Expense
| | | | |
|---|---|---|---|
| (d) | 17,000 | | |

### Advertising Expense
| | | | |
|---|---|---|---|
| (f) | 180,000 | | |

### Depreciation Expense
| | | | |
|---|---|---|---|
| (g) | 70,000 | | |

### Insurance Expense
| | | | |
|---|---|---|---|
| (h) | 3,000 | | |

3. Manufacturing overhead is overapplied for the year. The entry to close it out to Cost of Goods Sold is as follows:

| | | |
|---|---|---|
| Manufacturing Overhead .................... | 20,000 | |
| Cost of Goods Sold ...................... | | 20,000 |

4.

| Hogle Corporation Income Statement For the Year Ended December 31 | | |
|---|---|---|
| Sales ............................................... | | $1,500,000 |
| Cost of goods sold ($870,000 – $20,000) ........ | | 850,000 |
| Gross margin ....................................... | | 650,000 |
| Selling and administrative expenses: | | |
| Sales commissions expense .................... | $ 90,000 | |
| Administrative salaries expense ............... | 200,000 | |
| Sales travel expense ........................... | 17,000 | |
| Advertising expense ........................... | 180,000 | |
| Depreciation expense ......................... | 70,000 | |
| Insurance expense ............................. | 3,000 | 560,000 |
| Net operating income ............................. | | $  90,000 |

# GLOSSARY

**Absorption costing**   A costing method that includes all manufacturing costs—direct materials, direct labor, and both variable and fixed manufacturing overhead—in unit product costs. (p. 98)

**Allocation base**   A measure of activity such as direct labor-hours or machine-hours that is used to assign costs to cost objects. (p. 98)

**Cost of goods manufactured**   The manufacturing costs associated with units of product that were finished during the period. (p. 99)

**Finished goods**   Units of product that have been completed but not yet sold to customers. (p. 98)

**Job cost sheet**   A form that records the direct materials, direct labor, and manufacturing overhead cost charged to a job. (p. 98)

**Job-order costing**   A costing system used in situations where many different products, jobs, or services are produced each period. (p. 98)

**Normal costing**   A costing system in which overhead costs are applied to a job by multiplying a predetermined overhead rate by the actual amount of the allocation base incurred by the job. (p. 98)

**Overapplied overhead**   A credit balance in the Manufacturing Overhead account that occurs when the amount of overhead cost applied to Work in Process exceeds the amount of overhead cost actually incurred during a period. (p. 111)

**Overhead application**   The process of assigning overhead cost to specific jobs. (p. 98)

**Predetermined overhead rate**   A rate used to charge manufacturing overhead cost to jobs that is established in advance for each period. It is computed by dividing the estimated total manufacturing overhead cost for the period by the estimated total amount of the allocation base for the period. (p. 98)

**Raw materials**   Any materials that go into the final product. (p. 98)

**Schedule of cost of goods manufactured**   A schedule that contains three elements of product costs—direct materials, direct labor, and manufacturing overhead—and that summarizes the portions of those costs that remain in ending Work in Process inventory and that are transferred out of Work in Process into Finished Goods. (p. 108)

**Schedule of cost of goods sold**   A schedule that contains three elements of product costs—direct materials, direct labor, and manufacturing overhead—and that summarizes the portions of those costs that remain in ending Finished Goods inventory and that are transferred out of Finished Goods into Cost of Goods Sold. (p. 109)

**Underapplied overhead**   A debit balance in the Manufacturing Overhead account that occurs when the amount of overhead cost actually incurred exceeds the amount of overhead cost applied to Work in Process during a period. (p. 111)

**Work in process**   Units of product that are only partially complete and will require further work before they are ready for sale to the customer. (p. 98)

## QUESTIONS

**3–1**   What is the link that connects the schedule of cost of goods manufactured to the schedule of cost of goods sold?

**3–2**   What account is credited when overhead cost is applied to Work in Process? Would you expect the amount of overhead applied for a period to equal the actual overhead costs of the period? Why or why not?

**3–3**   What is underapplied overhead? Overapplied overhead? What disposition is made of these amounts at the end of the period?

**3–4**   Provide two reasons why overhead might be underapplied in a given year.

**3–5**   What adjustment is made for underapplied overhead on the schedule of cost of goods sold? What adjustment is made for overapplied overhead?

**3–6**   How do you compute the raw materials used in production?

**3–7**   How do you compute the total manufacturing costs within a schedule of cost of goods manufactured?

**3–8**   How do you compute the cost of goods manufactured?

**3–9**   How do you compute the unadjusted cost of goods sold?

**3–10**   How do direct labor costs flow through a job-order costing system?

## APPLYING EXCEL    connect

**LO3–1, LO3–4**

The Excel worksheet form that appears below is to be used to recreate part of the example relating to Turbo Crafters that appears earlier in the chapter. Download the workbook containing this form from Connect, where you will also receive instructions about how to use this worksheet form.

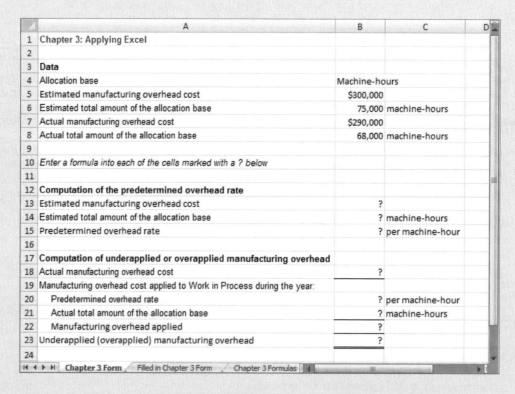

You should proceed to the requirements below only after completing your worksheet.

**Required:**

1. Check your worksheet by changing the estimated total amount of the allocation base in the Data area to 60,000 machine-hours, keeping all of the other data the same as in the original example. If your worksheet is operating properly, the predetermined overhead rate should now be $5.00 per machine-hour. If you do not get this answer, find the errors in your worksheet and correct them.

   How much is the underapplied (overapplied) manufacturing overhead? Did it change? Why or why not?

2. Determine the underapplied (overapplied) manufacturing overhead for a different company with the following data:

| | |
|---|---|
| Allocation base ..................................... | Machine-hours |
| Estimated manufacturing overhead cost ............. | $100,000 |
| Estimated total amount of the allocation base ......... | 50,000 machine-hours |
| Actual manufacturing overhead cost ................. | $90,000 |
| Actual total amount of the allocation base ............ | 40,000 machine-hours |

3. What happens to the underapplied (overapplied) manufacturing overhead from part (2) if the estimated total amount of the allocation base is changed to 40,000 machine-hours and everything else remains the same? Why is the amount of underapplied (overapplied) manufacturing overhead different from part (2)?

4. Change the estimated total amount of the allocation base back to 50,000 machine-hours so that the data look exactly like they did in part (2). Now change the actual manufacturing overhead cost to $100,000. What is the underapplied (overapplied) manufacturing overhead now? Why is the amount of underapplied (overapplied) manufacturing overhead different from part (2)?

**■connect** **THE FOUNDATIONAL 15**

LO3–1, LO3–2, LO3–3, LO3–4

Bunnell Corporation is a manufacturer that uses job-order costing. On January 1, the company's inventory balances were as follows:

| | |
|---|---|
| Raw materials ............... | $40,000 |
| Work in process ............. | $18,000 |
| Finished goods .............. | $35,000 |

The company applies overhead cost to jobs on the basis of direct labor-hours. For the current year, the company's predetermined overhead rate of $16.25 per direct labor-hour was based on a cost formula that estimated $650,000 of total manufacturing overhead for an estimated activity level of 40,000 direct labor-hours. The following transactions were recorded for the year:

a. Raw materials were purchased on account, $510,000.
b. Raw materials used in production, $480,000. All of of the raw materials were used as direct materials.
c. The following costs were accrued for employee services: direct labor, $600,000; indirect labor, $150,000; selling and administrative salaries, $240,000.
d. Incurred various selling and administrative expenses (e.g., advertising, sales travel costs, and finished goods warehousing), $367,000.
e. Incurred various manufacturing overhead costs (e.g., depreciation, insurance, and utilities), $500,000.
f. Manufacturing overhead cost was applied to production. The company actually worked 41,000 direct labor-hours on all jobs during the year.
g. Jobs costing $1,680,000 to manufacture according to their job cost sheets were completed during the year.
h. Jobs were sold on account to customers during the year for a total of $2,800,000. The jobs cost $1,690,000 to manufacture according to their job cost sheets.

**Required:**

1. What is the journal entry to record raw materials used in production?
2. What is the ending balance in Raw Materials?
3. What is the journal entry to record the labor costs incurred during the year?

4. What is the total amount of manufacturing overhead applied to production during the year?
5. What is the total manufacturing cost added to Work in Process during the year?
6. What is the journal entry to record the transfer of completed jobs that is referred to in item g above?
7. What is the ending balance in Work in Process?
8. What is the total amount of actual manufacturing overhead cost incurred during the year?
9. Is manufacturing overhead underapplied or overapplied for the year? By how much?
10. What is the cost of goods available for sale during the year?
11. What is the journal entry to record the cost of goods sold referred to in item h above?
12. What is the ending balance in Finished Goods?
13. Assuming that the company closes its underapplied or overapplied overhead to Cost of Goods Sold, what is the adjusted cost of goods sold for the year?
14. What is the gross margin for the year?
15. What is the net operating income for the year?

## EXERCISES

### EXERCISE 3–1   Prepare Journal Entries LO3–1

Larned Corporation recorded the following transactions for the just completed month.

a. $80,000 in raw materials were purchased on account.
b. $71,000 in raw materials were used in production. Of this amount, $62,000 was for direct materials and the remainder was for indirect materials.
c. Total labor wages of $112,000 were paid in cash. Of this amount, $101,000 was for direct labor and the remainder was for indirect labor.
d. Depreciation of $175,000 was incurred on factory equipment.

*Required:*
Record the above transactions in journal entries.

### EXERCISE 3–2   Prepare T-Accounts LO3–2, LO3–4

Jurvin Enterprises recorded the following transactions for the just completed month. The company had no beginning inventories.

a. $94,000 in raw materials were purchased for cash.
b. $89,000 in raw materials were used in production. Of this amount, $78,000 was for direct materials and the remainder was for indirect materials.
c. Total labor wages of $132,000 were incurred and paid. Of this amount, $112,000 was for direct labor and the remainder was for indirect labor.
d. Additional manufacturing overhead costs of $143,000 were incurred and paid.
e. Manufacturing overhead of $152,000 was applied to production using the company's predetermined overhead rate.
f. All of the jobs in process at the end of the month were completed.
g. All of the completed jobs were shipped to customers.
h. Any underapplied or overapplied overhead for the period was closed to Cost of Goods Sold.

*Required:*
1. Post the above transactions to T-accounts.
2. Determine the adjusted cost of goods sold for the period.

### EXERCISE 3–3   Schedules of Cost of Goods Manufactured and Cost of Goods Sold LO3–3

Primare Corporation has provided the following data concerning last month's manufacturing operations.

| | |
|---|---|
| Purchases of raw materials | $30,000 |
| Indirect materials included in manufacturing overhead | $5,000 |
| Direct labor | $58,000 |
| Manufacturing overhead applied to work in process | $87,000 |
| Underapplied overhead | $4,000 |

| Inventories | Beginning | Ending |
|---|---|---|
| Raw materials . . . . . . . . . . . . . . . . . . . . . . . . | $12,000 | $18,000 |
| Work in process . . . . . . . . . . . . . . . . . . . . . | $56,000 | $65,000 |
| Finished goods . . . . . . . . . . . . . . . . . . . . . | $35,000 | $42,000 |

**Required:**

1. Prepare a schedule of cost of goods manufactured for the month.
2. Prepare a schedule of cost of goods sold for the month. Assume the underapplied or overapplied overhead is closed to Cost of Goods Sold.

### EXERCISE 3–4    Underapplied and Overapplied Overhead LO3–4

Osborn Manufacturing uses a predetermined overhead rate of $18.20 per direct labor-hour. This predetermined rate was based on a cost formula that estimates $218,400 of total manufacturing overhead for an estimated activity level of 12,000 direct labor-hours.

The company actually incurred $215,000 of manufacturing overhead and 11,500 direct labor-hours during the period.

**Required:**

1. Determine the amount of underapplied or overapplied manufacturing overhead for the period.
2. Assume that the company's underapplied or overapplied overhead is closed to Cost of Goods Sold. Would the journal entry to dispose of the underapplied or overapplied overhead increase or decrease the company's gross margin? By how much?

### EXERCISE 3–5    Journal Entries and T-accounts LO3–1, LO3–2

The Polaris Company uses a job-order costing system. The following transactions occurred in October:

a. Raw materials purchased on account, $210,000.
b. Raw materials used in production, $190,000 ($178,000 direct materials and $12,000 indirect materials).
c. Accrued direct labor cost of $90,000 and indirect labor cost of $110,000.
d. Depreciation recorded on factory equipment, $40,000.
e. Other manufacturing overhead costs accrued during October, $70,000.
f. The company applies manufacturing overhead cost to production using a predetermined rate of $8 per machine-hour. A total of 30,000 machine-hours were used in October.
g. Jobs costing $520,000 according to their job cost sheets were completed during October and transferred to Finished Goods.
h. Jobs that had cost $480,000 to complete according to their job cost sheets were shipped to customers during the month. These jobs were sold on account at 25% above cost.

**Required:**

1. Prepare journal entries to record the transactions given above.
2. Prepare T-accounts for Manufacturing Overhead and Work in Process. Post the relevant transactions from above to each account. Compute the ending balance in each account, assuming that Work in Process has a beginning balance of $42,000.

### EXERCISE 3–6    Schedules of Cost of Goods Manufactured and Cost of Goods Sold; Income Statement LO3–3

The following data from the just completed year are taken from the accounting records of Mason Company:

| | |
|---|---|
| Sales . . . . . . . . . . . . . . . . . . . . . . . . . . . . . . . . . . . . . . . . . . . . . . . . . . . | $524,000 |
| Direct labor cost . . . . . . . . . . . . . . . . . . . . . . . . . . . . . . . . . . . . . . . . | $70,000 |
| Raw material purchases . . . . . . . . . . . . . . . . . . . . . . . . . . . . . . . . . | $118,000 |
| Selling expenses . . . . . . . . . . . . . . . . . . . . . . . . . . . . . . . . . . . . . . . | $140,000 |
| Administrative expenses . . . . . . . . . . . . . . . . . . . . . . . . . . . . . . . . | $63,000 |
| Manufacturing overhead applied to work in process . . . . . . . . . | $90,000 |
| Actual manufacturing overhead costs . . . . . . . . . . . . . . . . . . . . | $80,000 |

| Inventories | Beginning | Ending |
|---|---|---|
| Raw materials...................... | $7,000 | $15,000 |
| Work in process ................. | $10,000 | $5,000 |
| Finished goods ................. | $20,000 | $35,000 |

**Required:**
1. Prepare a schedule of cost of goods manufactured. Assume all raw materials used in production were direct materials.
2. Prepare a schedule of cost of goods sold. Assume that the company's underapplied or overapplied overhead is closed to Cost of Goods Sold.
3. Prepare an income statement.

**EXERCISE 3–7   Applying Overhead; Cost of Goods Manufactured LO3–3, LO3–4**
The following cost data relate to the manufacturing activities of Chang Company during the just completed year:

| Manufacturing overhead costs incurred: | |
|---|---|
| Indirect materials ........................................... | $  15,000 |
| Indirect labor .............................................. | 130,000 |
| Property taxes, factory ....................................... | 8,000 |
| Utilities, factory ............................................ | 70,000 |
| Depreciation, factory ........................................ | 240,000 |
| Insurance, factory .......................................... | 10,000 |
| Total actual manufacturing overhead costs incurred ............. | $473,000 |
| | |
| Other costs incurred: | |
| Purchases of raw materials (both direct and indirect) ............ | $400,000 |
| Direct labor cost ........................................... | $60,000 |
| Inventories: | |
| Raw materials, beginning ..................................... | $20,000 |
| Raw materials, ending ....................................... | $30,000 |
| Work in process, beginning .................................. | $40,000 |
| Work in process, ending ..................................... | $70,000 |

The company uses a predetermined overhead rate of $25 per machine-hour to apply overhead cost to jobs. A total of 19,400 machine-hours were used during the year.

**Required:**
1. Compute the amount of underapplied or overapplied overhead cost for the year.
2. Prepare a schedule of cost of goods manufactured for the year.

**EXERCISE 3–8   Applying Overhead; Journal Entries; Disposing of Underapplied or Overapplied Overhead LO3–1, LO3–2, LO3–4**
The following information is taken from the accounts of Latta Company. The entries in the T-accounts are summaries of the transactions that affected those accounts during the year.

| Manufacturing Overhead | | | | Work in Process | | | |
|---|---|---|---|---|---|---|---|
| (a) | 460,000 | (b) | 390,000 | Bal. | 15,000 | (c) | 710,000 |
| Bal. | 70,000 | | | | 260,000 | | |
| | | | | | 85,000 | | |
| | | | | (b) | 390,000 | | |
| | | | | Bal. | 40,000 | | |

| Finished Goods | | | | Cost of Goods Sold | | | |
|---|---|---|---|---|---|---|---|
| Bal. | 50,000 | (d) | 640,000 | (d) | 640,000 | | |
| (c) | 710,000 | | | | | | |
| Bal. | 120,000 | | | | | | |

The overhead that had been applied to production during the year is distributed among Work in Process, Finished Goods, and Cost of Goods Sold as of the end of the year as follows:

| | |
|---|---:|
| Work in Process, ending . . . . . . . . . | $ 19,500 |
| Finished Goods, ending . . . . . . . . . | 58,500 |
| Cost of Goods Sold . . . . . . . . . . . . | 312,000 |
| Overhead applied . . . . . . . . . . . . . | $390,000 |

For example, of the $40,000 ending balance in Work in Process, $19,500 was overhead that had been applied during the year.

**Required:**
1. Identify reasons for entries (a) through (d).
2. Assume that the underapplied or overapplied overhead is closed to Cost of Goods Sold. Prepare the necessary journal entry.
3. Assume that the underapplied or overapplied overhead is closed proportionally to Work in Process, Finished Goods, and Cost of Goods Sold. Prepare the necessary journal entry. Provide supporting computations.

**EXERCISE 3–9 Applying Overhead; T-accounts; Journal Entries** LO3–1, LO3–2, LO3–4

Harwood Company uses a job-order costing system that applies overhead cost to jobs on the basis of machine-hours. The company's predetermined overhead rate of $2.40 per machine-hour was based on a cost formula that estimates $192,000 of total manufacturing overhead for an estimated activity level of 80,000 machine-hours.

**Required:**
1. Assume that during the year the company works only 75,000 machine-hours and incurs the following costs in the Manufacturing Overhead and Work in Process accounts:

| | Manufacturing Overhead | | | Work in Process | |
|---|---:|---|---|---|---:|
| (Maintenance) | 21,000 | ? | (Direct materials) | 710,000 | |
| (Indirect materials) | 8,000 | | (Direct labor) | 90,000 | |
| (Indirect labor) | 60,000 | | (Overhead) | ? | |
| (Utilities) | 32,000 | | | | |
| (Insurance) | 7,000 | | | | |
| (Depreciation) | 56,000 | | | | |

Copy the data in the T-accounts above onto your answer sheet. Compute the amount of overhead cost that would be applied to Work in Process for the year and make the entry in your T-accounts.

2. Compute the amount of underapplied or overapplied overhead for the year and show the balance in your Manufacturing Overhead T-account. Prepare a journal entry to close the company's underapplied or overapplied overhead to Cost of Goods Sold.

3. Explain why the manufacturing overhead was underapplied or overapplied for the year.

**EXERCISE 3–10 Applying Overhead; Journal Entries; T-accounts** LO3–1, LO3–2

Dillon Products manufactures various machined parts to customer specifications. The company uses a job-order costing system and applies overhead cost to jobs on the basis of machine-hours. At the beginning of the year, the company used a cost formula to estimate that it would incur $4,800,000 in manufacturing overhead cost at an activity level of 240,000 machine-hours.

The company spent the entire month of January working on a large order for 16,000 custom-made machined parts. The company had no work in process at the beginning of January. Cost data relating to January follow:

a. Raw materials purchased on account, $325,000.
b. Raw materials used in production, $290,000 (80% direct materials and 20% indirect materials).
c. Labor cost accrued in the factory, $180,000 (one-third direct labor and two-thirds indirect labor).

d.   Depreciation recorded on factory equipment, $75,000.
e.   Other manufacturing overhead costs incurred on account, $62,000.
f.   Manufacturing overhead cost was applied to production on the basis of 15,000 machine-hours actually worked during the month.
g.   The completed job for 16,000 custom-made machined parts was moved into the finished goods warehouse on January 31 to await delivery to the customer. (In computing the dollar amount for this entry, remember that the cost of a completed job consists of direct materials, direct labor, and *applied* overhead.)

**Required:**
1.   Prepare journal entries to record items (a) through (f) above [ignore item (g) for the moment].
2.   Prepare T-accounts for Manufacturing Overhead and Work in Process. Post the relevant items from your journal entries to these T-accounts.
3.   Prepare a journal entry for item (g) above.
4.   If 10,000 of the custom-made machined parts are shipped to the customer in February, how much of this job's cost will be included in cost of goods sold for February?

## PROBLEMS          ▨ connect

### PROBLEM 3–11   T-Account Analysis of Cost Flows  LO3–2, LO3–3, LO3–4
Selected T-accounts of Moore Company are given below for the just completed year:

**Raw Materials**

| | | | |
|---|---|---|---|
| Bal. 1/1 | 15,000 | Credits | ? |
| Debits | 120,000 | | |
| Bal. 12/31 | 25,000 | | |

**Manufacturing Overhead**

| | | | |
|---|---|---|---|
| Debits | 230,000 | Credits | ? |

**Work in Process**

| | | | |
|---|---|---|---|
| Bal. 1/1 | 20,000 | Credits | 470,000 |
| Direct materials | 90,000 | | |
| Direct labor | 150,000 | | |
| Overhead | 240,000 | | |
| Bal. 12/31 | ? | | |

**Factory Wages Payable**

| | | | |
|---|---|---|---|
| Debits | 185,000 | Bal. 1/1 | 9,000 |
| | | Credits | 180,000 |
| | | Bal. 12/31 | 4,000 |

**Finished Goods**

| | | | |
|---|---|---|---|
| Bal. 1/1 | 40,000 | Credits | ? |
| Debits | ? | | |
| Bal. 12/31 | 60,000 | | |

**Cost of Goods Sold**

| | | |
|---|---|---|
| Debits | ? | |

**Required:**
1.   What was the cost of raw materials used in production during the year?
2.   How much of the materials in (1) above consisted of indirect materials?
3.   How much of the factory labor cost for the year consisted of indirect labor?
4.   What was the cost of goods manufactured for the year?
5.   What was the unadjusted cost of goods sold for the year? Do not include any underapplied or overapplied overhead in your answer.
6.   If overhead is applied to production on the basis of direct labor cost, what predetermined overhead rate was in effect during the year?
7.   Was manufacturing overhead underapplied or overapplied? By how much?
8.   Compute the ending balance in Work in Process. Assume that this balance consists entirely of goods started during the year. If $8,000 of this balance is direct labor cost, how much of it is direct materials cost? Applied overhead cost?

**PROBLEM 3-12  Predetermined Overhead Rate; Disposing of Underapplied or Overapplied Overhead LO3-4**

Luzadis Company makes furniture using the latest automated technology. The company uses a job-order costing system and applies manufacturing overhead cost to products on the basis of machine-hours. The predetermined overhead rate was based on a cost formula that estimates $900,000 of total manufacturing overhead for an estimated activity level of 75,000 machine-hours.

During the year, a large quantity of furniture on the market resulted in cutting back production and a buildup of furniture in the company's warehouse. The company's cost records revealed the following actual cost and operating data for the year:

| | |
|---|---|
| Machine-hours | 60,000 |
| Manufacturing overhead cost | $850,000 |
| Inventories at year-end: | |
| Raw materials | $30,000 |
| Work in process (includes overhead applied of $36,000) | $100,000 |
| Finished goods (includes overhead applied of $180,000) | $500,000 |
| Cost of goods sold (includes overhead applied of $504,000) | $1,400,000 |

**Required:**

1. Compute the underapplied or overapplied overhead.
2. Assume that the company closes any underapplied or overapplied overhead to Cost of Goods Sold. Prepare the appropriate journal entry.
3. Assume that the company allocates any underapplied or overapplied overhead proportionally to Work in Process, Finished Goods, and Cost of Goods Sold. Prepare the appropriate journal entry.
4. How much higher or lower will net operating income be if the underapplied or overapplied overhead is allocated to Work in Process, Finished Goods, and Cost of Goods Sold rather than being closed to Cost of Goods Sold?

**PROBLEM 3-13  Schedules of Cost of Goods Manufactured and Cost of Goods Sold; Income Statement LO3-3**

Superior Company provided the following data for the year ended December 31 (all raw materials are used in production as direct materials):

| | |
|---|---|
| Selling expenses | $140,000 |
| Purchases of raw materials | $290,000 |
| Direct labor | ? |
| Administrative expenses | $100,000 |
| Manufacturing overhead applied to work in process | $285,000 |
| Actual manufacturing overhead cost | $270,000 |

Inventory balances at the beginning and end of the year were as follows:

| | Beginning | Ending |
|---|---|---|
| Raw materials | $40,000 | $10,000 |
| Work in process | ? | $35,000 |
| Finished goods | $50,000 | ? |

The total manufacturing costs for the year were $683,000; the cost of goods available for sale totaled $740,000; the unadjusted cost of goods sold totaled $660,000; and the net operating income was $30,000. The company's underapplied or overapplied overhead is closed to Cost of Goods Sold.

**Required:**

Prepare schedules of cost of goods manufactured and cost of goods sold and an income statement. (*Hint:* Prepare the income statement and schedule of cost of goods sold first followed by the schedule of cost of goods manufactured.)

**PROBLEM 3–14    Schedule of Cost of Goods Manufactured; Overhead Analysis LO3–3, LO3–4**

Gitano Products operates a job-order costing system and applies overhead cost to jobs on the basis of direct materials *used in production* (*not* on the basis of raw materials purchased). Its predetermined overhead rate was based on a cost formula that estimated $800,000 of manufacturing overhead for an estimated allocation base of $500,000 direct material dollars to be used in production. The company has provided the following data for the just completed year:

| | |
|---|---:|
| Purchase of raw materials . . . . . . . . . . . . . . . . . . . | $510,000 |
| Direct labor cost . . . . . . . . . . . . . . . . . . . . . . . . . | $90,000 |
| Manufacturing overhead costs: | |
|    Indirect labor . . . . . . . . . . . . . . . . . . . . . . . . . . . | $170,000 |
|    Property taxes . . . . . . . . . . . . . . . . . . . . . . . . . . | $48,000 |
|    Depreciation of equipment . . . . . . . . . . . . . . . . | $260,000 |
|    Maintenance . . . . . . . . . . . . . . . . . . . . . . . . . . . | $95,000 |
|    Insurance . . . . . . . . . . . . . . . . . . . . . . . . . . . . . | $7,000 |
|    Rent, building . . . . . . . . . . . . . . . . . . . . . . . . . . | $180,000 |

| | Beginning | Ending |
|---|---:|---:|
| Raw Materials . . . . . . . . . . . . . . | $20,000 | $80,000 |
| Work in Process . . . . . . . . . . . . | $150,000 | $70,000 |
| Finished Goods . . . . . . . . . . . . . | $260,000 | $400,000 |

*Required:*

1.  Compute the predetermined overhead rate for the year.
2.  Compute the amount of underapplied or overapplied overhead for the year.
3.  Prepare a schedule of cost of goods manufactured for the year. Assume all raw materials are used in production as direct materials.
4.  Compute the unadjusted cost of goods sold for the year. Do not include any underapplied or overapplied overhead in your answer. What options are available for disposing of underapplied or overapplied overhead?
5.  Assume that the $70,000 ending balance in Work in Process includes $24,000 of direct materials. Given this assumption, supply the information missing below:

| | |
|---|---:|
| Direct materials . . . . . . . . . . . . . . . . . . . . . . | $24,000 |
| Direct labor . . . . . . . . . . . . . . . . . . . . . . . . . | ? |
| Manufacturing overhead . . . . . . . . . . . . . . | ? |
| Work in process inventory . . . . . . . . . . . . . | $70,000 |

**PROBLEM 3–15    Journal Entries; T-Accounts; Financial Statements LO3–1, LO3–2, LO3–3, LO3–4**

Froya Fabrikker A/S of Bergen, Norway, is a small company that manufactures specialty heavy equipment for use in North Sea oil fields. The company uses a job-order costing system that applies manufacturing overhead cost to jobs on the basis of direct labor-hours. Its predetermined overhead rate was based on a cost formula that estimated $360,000 of manufacturing overhead for an estimated allocation base of 900 direct labor-hours. The following transactions took place during the year:

a.  Raw materials purchased on account, $200,000.
b.  Raw materials used in production (all direct materials), $185,000.
c.  Utility bills incurred on account, $70,000 (90% related to factory operations, and the remainder related to selling and administrative activities).
d.  Accrued salary and wage costs:

| | |
|---|---:|
| Direct labor (975 hours) . . . . . . . . . . . . . . | $230,000 |
| Indirect labor . . . . . . . . . . . . . . . . . . . . . . . | $90,000 |
| Selling and administrative salaries . . . . . . | $110,000 |

e.  Maintenance costs incurred on account in the factory, $54,000.
f.  Advertising costs incurred on account, $136,000.
g.  Depreciation was recorded for the year, $95,000 (80% related to factory equipment, and the remainder related to selling and administrative equipment).
h.  Rental cost incurred on account, $120,000 (85% related to factory facilities, and the remainder related to selling and administrative facilities).
i.  Manufacturing overhead cost was applied to jobs, $ ? .
j.  Cost of goods manufactured for the year, $770,000.
k.  Sales for the year (all on account) totaled $1,200,000. These goods cost $800,000 according to their job cost sheets.
    The balances in the inventory accounts at the beginning of the year were:

| | |
|---|---|
| Raw Materials ....................... | $30,000 |
| Work in Process .................... | $21,000 |
| Finished Goods ..................... | $60,000 |

**Required:**
1.  Prepare journal entries to record the preceding transactions.
2.  Post your entries to T-accounts. (Don't forget to enter the beginning inventory balances above.) Determine the ending balances in the inventory accounts and in the Manufacturing Overhead account.
3.  Prepare a schedule of cost of goods manufactured.
4.  Prepare a journal entry to close any balance in the Manufacturing Overhead account to Cost of Goods Sold. Prepare a schedule of cost of goods sold.
5.  Prepare an income statement for the year.

**PROBLEM 3–16  Comprehensive Problem LO3–1, LO3–2, LO3–4**
Gold Nest Company of Guandong, China, is a family-owned enterprise that makes birdcages for the South China market. The company sells its birdcages through an extensive network of street vendors who receive commissions on their sales.

The company uses a job-order costing system in which overhead is applied to jobs on the basis of direct labor cost. Its predetermined overhead rate is based on a cost formula that estimated $330,000 of manufacturing overhead for an estimated activity level of $200,000 direct labor dollars. At the beginning of the year, the inventory balances were as follows:

| | |
|---|---|
| Raw materials ...................... | $25,000 |
| Work in process .................... | $10,000 |
| Finished goods ..................... | $40,000 |

During the year, the following transactions were completed:

a.  Raw materials purchased for cash, $275,000.
b.  Raw materials used in production, $280,000 (materials costing $220,000 were charged directly to jobs; the remaining materials were indirect).
c.  Cash paid to employees as follows:

| | |
|---|---|
| Direct labor ......................... | $180,000 |
| Indirect labor ....................... | $72,000 |
| Sales commissions .................. | $63,000 |
| Administrative salaries .............. | $90,000 |

d.  Cash paid for rent during the year was $18,000 ($13,000 of this amount related to factory operations, and the remainder related to selling and administrative activities).
e.  Cash paid for utility costs in the factory, $57,000.
f.  Cash paid for advertising, $140,000.
g.  Depreciation recorded on equipment, $100,000. ($88,000 of this amount related to equipment used in factory operations; the remaining $12,000 related to equipment used in selling and administrative activities.)
h.  Manufacturing overhead cost was applied to jobs, $ ? .
i.  Goods that had cost $675,000 to manufacture according to their job cost sheets were completed.
j.  Sales for the year (all paid in cash) totaled $1,250,000. The total cost to manufacture these goods according to their job cost sheets was $700,000.

**Required:**
1. Prepare journal entries to record the transactions for the year.
2. Prepare T-accounts for each inventory account, Manufacturing Overhead, and Cost of Goods Sold. Post relevant data from your journal entries to these T-accounts (don't forget to enter the beginning balances in your inventory accounts). Compute an ending balance in each account.
3. Is Manufacturing Overhead underapplied or overapplied for the year? Prepare a journal entry to close any balance in the Manufacturing Overhead account to Cost of Goods Sold.
4. Prepare an income statement for the year. (Do not prepare a schedule of cost of goods manufactured; all of the information needed for the income statement is available in the journal entries and T-accounts you have prepared.)

**PROBLEM 3–17   Cost Flows; T-Accounts; Income Statement** LO3–2, LO3–3, LO3–4
Supreme Videos, Inc., produces short musical videos for sale to retail outlets. The company's balance sheet accounts as of January 1, are given below.

| Supreme Videos, Inc.<br>Balance Sheet<br>January 1 | | |
|---|---:|---:|
| **Assets** | | |
| Current assets: | | |
| Cash ...................................... | | $ 63,000 |
| Accounts receivable ........................... | | 102,000 |
| Inventories: | | |
| Raw materials (film, costumes) ................. | $ 30,000 | |
| Videos in process ........................... | 45,000 | |
| Finished videos awaiting sale ................. | 81,000 | 156,000 |
| Prepaid insurance ............................. | | 9,000 |
| Total current assets .............................. | | 330,000 |
| Studio and equipment ............................. | 730,000 | |
| Less accumulated depreciation .................... | 210,000 | 520,000 |
| Total assets ...................................... | | $850,000 |
| **Liabilities and Stockholders' Equity** | | |
| Accounts payable ................................. | | $ 160,000 |
| Capital stock ..................................... | $420,000 | |
| Retained earnings ............................... | 270,000 | 690,000 |
| Total liabilities and stockholders' equity ............. | | $850,000 |

Because the videos differ in length and in complexity of production, the company uses a job-order costing system to determine the cost of each video produced. Studio (manufacturing) overhead is charged to videos on the basis of camera-hours of activity. The company's predetermined overhead rate for the year is based on a cost formula that estimated $280,000 in manufacturing overhead for an estimated allocation base of 7,000 camera-hours. The following transactions occurred during the year:

a. Film, costumes, and similar raw materials purchased on account, $185,000.
b. Film, costumes, and other raw materials used in production, $200,000 (85% of this material was considered direct to the videos in production, and the other 15% was considered indirect).
c. Utility costs incurred in the production studio, $72,000.
d. Depreciation recorded on the studio, cameras, and other equipment, $84,000. Three-fourths of this depreciation related to production of the videos, and the remainder related to equipment used in marketing and administration.
e. Advertising expense incurred, $130,000.
f. Costs for salaries and wages were incurred as follows:

| | |
|---|---:|
| Direct labor (actors and directors) ........................................... | $82,000 |
| Indirect labor (carpenters to build sets, costume designers, and so forth) ........ | $110,000 |
| Administrative salaries ................................................. | $95,000 |

g.  Prepaid insurance expired during the year, $7,000 (80% related to production of videos, and 20% related to marketing and administrative activities).

h.  Miscellaneous marketing and administrative expenses incurred, $8,600.

i.  Studio (manufacturing) overhead was applied to videos in production. The company used 7,250 camera-hours during the year.

j.  Videos that cost $550,000 to produce according to their job cost sheets were transferred to the finished videos warehouse to await sale and shipment.

k.  Sales for the year totaled $925,000 and were all on account. The total cost to produce these videos according to their job cost sheets was $600,000.

l.  Collections from customers during the year totaled $850,000.

m.  Payments to suppliers on account during the year, $500,000; payments to employees for salaries and wages, $285,000.

### Required:

1.  Prepare a T-account for each account on the company's balance sheet and enter the beginning balances.

2.  Record the transactions directly into the T-accounts. Prepare new T-accounts as needed. Key your entries to the letters (a) through (m) above. Compute the ending balance in each account.

3.  Is the Studio (manufacturing) Overhead account underapplied or overapplied for the year? Make an entry in the T-accounts to close any balance in the Studio Overhead account to Cost of Goods Sold.

4.  Prepare a schedule of cost of goods manufactured. If done correctly, the cost of goods manufactured from your schedule should agree with which of the above transactions?

5.  Prepare a schedule of cost of goods sold. If done correctly, the unadjusted cost of goods sold from your schedule should agree with which of the above transactions?

6.  Prepare an income statement for the year.

**connect** BUILDING YOUR SKILLS

### ETHICS CHALLENGE LO3-4

Terri Ronsin had recently been transferred to the Home Security Systems Division of National Home Products. Shortly after taking over her new position as divisional controller, she was asked to develop the division's predetermined overhead rate for the upcoming year. The accuracy of the rate is important because it is used throughout the year and any underapplied or overapplied overhead is closed out to Cost of Goods Sold at the end of the year. National Home Products uses direct labor-hours in all of its divisions as the allocation base for manufacturing overhead.

To compute the predetermined overhead rate, Terri divided her estimate of the total manufacturing overhead for the coming year by the production manager's estimate of the total direct labor-hours for the coming year. She took her computations to the division's general manager for approval but was quite surprised when he suggested a modification in the allocation base. Her conversation with the general manager of the Home Security Systems Division, Harry Irving, went like this:

*Ronsin:* Here are my calculations for next year's predetermined overhead rate. If you approve, we can enter the rate into the computer on January 1 and be up and running in the job-order costing system right away this year.

*Irving:* Thanks for coming up with the calculations so quickly, and they look just fine. There is, however, one slight modification I would like to see. Your estimate of the total direct labor-hours for the year is 440,000 hours. How about cutting that to about 420,000 hours?

*Ronsin:* I don't know if I can do that. The production manager says she will need about 440,000 direct labor-hours to meet the sales projections for the year. Besides, there are going to be over 430,000 direct labor-hours during the current year and sales are projected to be higher next year.

*Irving:* Teri, I know all of that. I would still like to reduce the direct labor-hours in the allocation base to something like 420,000 hours. You probably don't know that I had an agreement with your predecessor as divisional controller to shave 5% or so off the estimated direct labor-hours every year. That way, we kept a reserve that usually resulted in a big boost to net operating income at the end of the year in December. We called it our Christmas bonus. Corporate headquarters always seemed to be pleased that we could pull off such a miracle at the end of the year. This system has worked well for many years, and I don't want to change it now.

**Required:**

1.  Explain how shaving 5% off the estimated direct labor-hours in the allocation base for the predetermined overhead rate usually results in a big boost in net operating income at the end of the year.
2.  Should Terri Ronsin go along with the general manager's request to reduce the direct labor-hours in the predetermined overhead rate computation to 420,000 direct labor-hours?

**TEAMWORK IN ACTION LO3–1, LO3–2, LO3–4**

After a dispute concerning wages, Orville Arson tossed an incendiary device into the Sparkle Company's record vault. Within moments, only a few charred fragments were readable from the company's factory ledger, as shown below:

Sifting through ashes and interviewing selected employees has turned up the following additional information:

a.  The controller remembers clearly that the predetermined overhead rate was based on an estimated 60,000 direct labor-hours to be worked over the year and an estimated $180,000 in manufacturing overhead costs.
b.  The production superintendent's cost sheets showed only one job in process on April 30. Materials of $2,600 had been added to the job, and 300 direct labor-hours had been expended at $6 per hour.
c.  The accounts payable are for raw material purchases only, according to the accounts payable clerk. He clearly remembers that the balance in the account was $6,000 on April 1. An analysis of canceled checks (kept in the treasurer's office) shows that payments of $40,000 were made to suppliers during April. (All materials used during April were direct materials.)
d.  A charred piece of the payroll ledger shows that 5,200 direct labor-hours were recorded for the month. The personnel department has verified that there were no variations in pay rates among employees.
e.  Records maintained in the finished goods warehouse indicate that the finished goods inventory totaled $11,000 on April 1.
f.  From another charred piece in the vault, you are able to discern that the cost of goods manufactured for April was $89,000.

**Required:**

1.  Assign one of the following sets of accounts to each member of the team:
    a.  Raw Materials and Accounts Payable.
    b.  Work in Process and Manufacturing Overhead.
    c.  Finished Goods and Cost of Goods Sold.
    Determine the types of transactions that would be posted to each account and present a summary to the other team members. When agreement is reached, the team should work together to complete steps 2 through 4.
2.  Determine the company's predetermined overhead rate and the total manufacturing overhead applied for the month.
3.  Determine the April 30 balance in the company's Work in Process account.
4.  Prepare the company's T-accounts for the month. (It is easiest to complete the T-accounts in the following order: Accounts Payable, Work in Process, Raw Materials, Manufacturing Overhead, Finished Goods, Cost of Goods Sold.)

# APPENDIX 3A: JOB-ORDER COSTING: A MICROSOFT EXCEL-BASED APPROACH

In this appendix, we use Microsoft Excel to depict how the transactions in a job-order costing system impact a company's balance sheet. While the main body of the chapter focused on using journal entries to record transactions, the approach demonstrated in this appendix will help you develop a new and valuable managerial skill—analyzing how transactions affect the balance sheet without having to prepare formal journal entries.

To set the stage for the forthcoming example, we need to review your understanding of two fundamental accounting equations and we need to specify three important assumptions.

**Fundamental Accounting Equations**   A company's balance sheet is based on the following accounting equation that is the bedrock of double-entry bookkeeping:

$$\text{Assets} = \text{Liabilities} + \text{Stockholders' Equity}$$

In the Excel spreadsheets that we'll be using in this appendix, one column will always be populated with an "=" sign. The accounts on the left-hand side of the "=" sign will be asset accounts and the accounts on the right-hand side will be liability and stockholders' equity accounts. After we record every transaction, the amounts on the left-hand side of the "=" sign must equal the amounts on the right-hand side.

The second foundational equation relates to the Retained Earnings account on a company's balance sheet. The ending balance in retained earnings is computed using the following equation:

$$\text{Ending balance in retained earnings} = \text{Beginning balance in retained earnings} + \text{Net operating income} - \text{Dividends}$$

This equation highlights the connection between the balance sheet and the income statement. It recognizes the fact that net operating income from the income statement is embedded within retained earnings on the balance sheet. Thus, in our Microsoft Excel-based approach, any transactions involving sales or expenses will be recorded in the Retained Earnings column of the balance sheet.

**Three Key Assumptions**   The first assumption in the appendix is that we will always use only one predetermined overhead rate. In other words, we are going to use the same approach that was demonstrated in the main body of this chapter. This requires using an account titled Manufacturing Overhead within our Microsoft Excel spreadsheets that will serve the same purpose as the Manufacturing Overhead clearing account discussed earlier in the chapter.

The second assumption is that any underapplied or overapplied manufacturing overhead will always be closed to Cost of Goods Sold as reported in the income statement. Because the income statement is embedded in the Retained Earnings account on the balance sheet, we will always close underapplied or overapplied overhead to Retained Earnings.

Our third assumption is that we'll record transactions within Microsoft Excel by using positive numbers to increase balance sheet accounts and negative numbers (shown in parentheses) to decrease balance sheet accounts. This is a slightly different approach than we used in the main body of the chapter where all transactions were depicted using the language of debits and credits—in journal entry form and in T-account form. This appendix replaces the language of debits and credits with an equivalent alternative. Instead, it identifies the balance sheet accounts affected by each transaction and it determines if those account balances should increase or decrease.

**Sapphire Company–Setting the Stage**   Sapphire Company uses a job-order cost-ing system to assign manufacturing costs to jobs. Its balance sheet on January 1 is as follows:

| Sapphire Company Balance Sheet January 1 | | |
| --- | --- | --- |
| **Assets** | | |
| Cash ................................... | | $ 15,000 |
| Raw materials ........................... | $ 8,000 | |
| Work in process ......................... | 5,000 | |
| Finished goods .......................... | 13,000 | 26,000 |
| Prepaid expenses ....................... | | 3,000 |
| Property, plant, and equipment (net) ......... | | 240,000 |
| Total assets .............................. | | $284,000 |
| | | |
| **Liabilities and Stockholders' Equity** | | |
| Accounts payable......................... | | $  4,000 |
| Retained earnings ....................... | | 280,000 |
| Total liabilities and stockholders' equity ...... | | $284,000 |

Note: To reduce the number of columns contained in the Excel spreadsheets used throughout this appendix, we have excluded a Common Stock account from the balance sheets within this appendix.

Exhibit 3A–1 contains a Microsoft Excel spreadsheet that includes the beginning balances shown in the balance sheet above. Notice that column "J" of the spreadsheet contains "=" signs (see cells J5 and J6). This means that after we record each of the forth-coming transactions, the amounts on the left-hand side of column "J" will always need to equal the amounts on the right-hand side of column "J."

Also, notice that the spreadsheet contains all of the accounts shown in the January 1 balance sheet plus an account called Manufacturing Overhead. As discussed earlier in the chapter, Manufacturing Overhead is a clearing account that always has a beginning and ending balance of zero. This account is used to record two things—all actual overhead costs and the amount of manufacturing overhead applied to production using the prede-termined overhead rate. The difference between the actual overhead cost and the amount of overhead applied to production is the underapplied or overapplied overhead.

Finally, to conserve space, the Excel spreadsheet abbreviates Property, Plant, and Equipment (net) as PP&E (net). The term *net* implies that the acquisition cost of property, plant, and equipment is being reported *net* of accumulated depreciation.

**Sapphire Company–Transaction Analysis**   The remainder of the appendix proceeds in three steps. First, it lists Sapphire Company's transactions for the month of January. Second, it explains how each of these transactions is recorded in the Microsoft Excel spreadsheet. Finally, it explains how to use the information depicted in the spread-sheet to prepare a schedule of cost of goods manufactured, a schedule of cost of goods sold, and an income statement for the month of January.

**EXHIBIT 3A–1**   Sapphire Company: Transaction Analysis

| | A | B | C | D | E | F | G | H | I | J | K | L |
| --- | --- | --- | --- | --- | --- | --- | --- | --- | --- | --- | --- | --- |
| 1 | | | | | | Sapphire Company | | | | | | |
| 2 | | | | | | Transaction Analysis | | | | | | |
| 3 | | | | | | For the Month Ended January 31 | | | | | | |
| 5 | Transactions | | Cash | Raw Materials | Work in Process | Finished Goods | Manufacturing Overhead | Prepaid Expenses | PP&E (net) | = | Accounts Payable | Retained Earnings |
| 6 | Beginning balances @ 1/1 | | $ 15,000 | $ 8,000 | $ 5,000 | $ 13,000 | $    - | $ 3,000 | $240,000 | = | $ 4,000 | $280,000 |
| 7 | | | | | | | | | | | | |

Exhibit 3A-1 | Exhibit 3A-2 | Exhibit 3A-3 | Exhibit 3A-4 | Exhibit 3A-5

To begin our illustration, let's assume that Sapphire Company has a predetermined overhead rate of $25 per direct labor-hour that was based on a cost formula that estimated $100,000 in manufacturing overhead cost for an estimated allocation base of 4,000 direct labor-hours. During January, the company completed the following transactions:

a. Purchased raw materials on account, $80,000.
b. Raw materials used in production, $78,000 ($70,000 was direct materials and $8,000 was indirect materials).
c. Paid $135,000 of salaries and wages in cash ($68,000 was direct labor, $45,000 was indirect labor, and $22,000 was related to employees responsible for selling and administration).
d. Utility costs incurred (on account) to support production, $15,000.
e. Depreciation recorded on property, plant, and equipment, $40,000 (70% related to manufacturing equipment and 30% related to assets that support selling and administration).
f. Advertising expenses paid in cash, $18,000.
g. Prepaid insurance expired during the month, $1,000 (80% related to production, and 20% related to selling and administration).
h. Manufacturing overhead applied to production, $102,500. This amount was computed by multiplying 4,100 direct labor-hours worked in January by the predetermined overhead rate of $25 per direct labor-hour.
i. Cost of goods manufactured, $235,000.
j. Cash sales, $320,000.
k. Cost of goods sold, $245,000.
l. Cash payments to creditors, $92,000.
m. Close overapplied overhead of $5,700 to cost of goods sold.

Exhibit 3A–2 summarizes how each of the transactions just described would be recorded in the Microsoft Excel spreadsheet. The underlying explanations for each transaction are as follows (each transaction includes a parenthetical reference to its row within the Microsoft Excel spreadsheet):

a. (*row 7*) Purchasing raw materials on account for $80,000 will increase Raw Materials and Accounts Payable by $80,000.
b. (*row 8*) When raw materials are used in production, it decreases Raw Materials by $78,000. The direct materials of $70,000 are added to Work in Process, whereas the

**EXHIBIT 3A–2**   Sapphire Company: Completed Transaction Analysis

| | | Cash | Raw Materials | Work in Process | Finished Goods | Manufacturing Overhead | Prepaid Expenses | PP&E (net) | = | Accounts Payable | Retained Earnings |
|---|---|---|---|---|---|---|---|---|---|---|---|
| 6 | Beginning balances @ 1/1 | $ 15,000 | $ 8,000 | $ 5,000 | $ 13,000 | $ — | $ 3,000 | $240,000 | = | $ 4,000 | $280,000 |
| 7 | (a) Raw material purchases | | 80,000 | | | | | | = | 80,000 | |
| 8 | (b) Raw materials used in production | | (78,000) | 70,000 | | 8,000 | | | = | | |
| 9 | (c) Salaries and wages | (135,000) | | 68,000 | | 45,000 | | | = | | (22,000) |
| 10 | (d) Utility costs | | | | | 15,000 | | | = | 15,000 | |
| 11 | (e) Depreciation | | | | | 28,000 | | (40,000) | = | | (12,000) |
| 12 | (f) Advertising | (18,000) | | | | | | | = | | (18,000) |
| 13 | (g) Expiration of prepaid insurance | | | | | 800 | (1,000) | | = | | (200) |
| 14 | (h) Manufacturing overhead applied | | | 102,500 | | (102,500) | | | = | | |
| 15 | (i) Cost of goods manufactured | | | (235,000) | 235,000 | | | | = | | |
| 16 | (j) Sales | 320,000 | | | | | | | = | | 320,000 |
| 17 | (k) Cost of goods sold | | | | (245,000) | | | | = | | (245,000) |
| 18 | (l) Payments to creditors | (92,000) | | | | | | | = | (92,000) | |
| 19 | (m) Overapplied overhead | | | | | 5,700 | | | = | | 5,700 |
| 20 | Ending balances @ 1/31 | $ 90,000 | $ 10,000 | $ 10,500 | $ 3,000 | $ — | $ 2,000 | $200,000 | = | $ 7,000 | $308,500 |

Sapphire Company / Transaction Analysis / For the Month Ended January 31

Exhibit 3A-1  Exhibit 3A-2  Exhibit 3A-3  Exhibit 3A-4  Exhibit 3A-5 indirect materials of $8,000 are added to Manufacturing Overhead. Notice that actual manufacturing overhead costs, such as the $8,000 of indirect materials, *are not* added to Work in Process. As you will see in a later transaction, manufacturing overhead is applied to Work in Process using the predetermined overhead rate.

c. (*row 9*) The salaries and wages decrease Cash by $135,000. The direct labor cost of $68,000 increases Work in Process, whereas the indirect labor cost of $45,000 increases Manufacturing Overhead. The $22,000 paid to employees working in selling and administrative roles is a period cost that should be recorded on January's income statement. Because the income statement is embedded in Retained Earnings, we decrease Retained Earnings by $22,000.

d. (*row 10*) The utility costs support production, so they are treated as a product cost rather than a period cost. Thus, Manufacturing Overhead increases by $15,000 and Accounts Payable increases by the same amount.

e. (*row 11*) The depreciation reduces Property, Plant, and Equipment (net) by $40,000. This is equivalent to recording accumulated depreciation of $40,000. The depreciation on manufacturing equipment of $28,000 (a product cost) increases Manufacturing Overhead, whereas the depreciation on selling and administrative assets of $12,000 (a period cost) decreases Retained Earnings.

f. (*row 12*) Advertising is a period cost so Cash and Retained Earnings decrease by $18,000.

g. (*row 13*) The expired insurance coverage decreases Prepaid Expenses by $1,000. The insurance related to production (a product cost) increases Manufacturing Overhead by $800. The insurance related to selling and administration of $200 (a period cost) decreases Retained Earnings by $200.

h. (*row 14*) The manufacturing overhead applied increases Work in Process and decreases Manufacturing Overhead by $102,500. Notice that manufacturing overhead is applied to Work in Process using the predetermined overhead rate. Actual manufacturing overhead costs are not recorded in Work in Process. In a later transaction, the actual overhead costs will be compared to the applied overhead to determine the amount of underapplied or overapplied overhead for the month.

i. (*row 15*) The cost of goods manufactured refers to the cost of the goods that were transferred from work in process to finished goods during the period. This transaction decreases Work in Process by $235,000 and increases Finished Goods by the same amount.

j. (*row 16*) The sales will increase Cash by $320,000, and given that sales appear on the income statement, Retained Earnings will increase by the same amount.

k. (*row 17*) The cost of goods sold must be removed from finished goods; therefore, Finished Goods decreases by $245,000. Because cost of goods sold appears on the income statement, Retained Earnings decreases by the same amount.

l. (*row 18*) The cash payments to creditors decrease Cash and Accounts Payable by $92,000.

m. (*row 19*) The manufacturing overhead applied of $102,500 is $5,700 greater than the actual overhead costs incurred during the month of $96,800 (= $8,000 + $45,000 + $15,000 + $28,000 + $800). Therefore, manufacturing overhead is overapplied by $5,700. We record this transaction by increasing Manufacturing Overhead by $5,700 and increasing Retained Earnings by the same amount. The increase in Retained Earnings reflects the fact that we are decreasing Cost of Goods Sold (which increases net operating income).

Once we have recorded all transactions, the company's balance sheet at January 31 can be derived by summing each column in the spreadsheet (see row 20 for the ending balances that would be reported on Sapphire Company's balance sheet at January 31).

### Sapphire Company–Schedules of Cost of Goods Manufactured and Cost of Goods Sold

The transactions recorded in Exhibit 3A–2 can be used to create schedules of cost of goods manufactured and cost of goods sold. Exhibit 3A–3 shows

**EXHIBIT 3A-3**    Sapphire Company: Schedule of Cost of Goods Manufactured

| | A | B | C |
|---|---|---|---|
| 1 | **Sapphire Company** | | |
| 2 | **Schedule of Cost of Goods Manufactured** | | |
| 3 | **For the Month Ended January 31** | | |
| 5 | Direct materials: | | |
| 6 | Beginning raw materials inventory (D6) | $ 8,000 | |
| 7 | Add: Purchases of raw materials (D7) | 80,000 | |
| 8 | Total raw materials available | 88,000 | |
| 9 | Deduct: Ending raw materials inventory (D20) | 10,000 | |
| 10 | Raw materials used production | 78,000 | |
| 11 | Deduct: Indirect materials included in manufacturing overhead (G8) | 8,000 | $ 70,000 |
| 12 | Direct labor (E9) | | 68,000 |
| 13 | Manufacturing overhead applied to work in process (E14) | | 102,500 |
| 14 | Total manufacturing costs | | 240,500 |
| 15 | Add: Beginning work in process inventory (E6) | | 5,000 |
| 16 | | | 245,500 |
| 17 | Deduct: Ending work in process inventory (E20) | | 10,500 |
| 18 | Cost of goods manufactured | | $ 235,000 |
| 19 | | | |

H ◀ ▶ H   Exhibit 3A-1   Exhibit 3A-2   **Exhibit 3A-3**   Exhibit 3A-4   Exhibit 3A-5

Sapphire Company's schedule of cost of goods manufactured. Each row heading in this exhibit contains a cell reference that indicates where the number appears in Exhibit 3A–2.

Notice that the cost of goods manufactured of $235,000 as shown in Exhibit 3A–3 equals the cost of goods manufactured mentioned in transaction "i" and recorded in row 15 of Exhibit 3A–2.

Exhibit 3A–4 shows Sapphire Company's schedule of cost of goods sold. Each row heading in this exhibit contains a cell reference that indicates where the number appears in Exhibit 3A–2.

**EXHIBIT 3A-4**    Sapphire Company: Schedule of Cost of Goods Sold

| | A | B |
|---|---|---|
| 1 | **Sapphire Company** | |
| 2 | **Schedule of Cost of Goods Sold** | |
| 3 | **For the Month Ended January 31** | |
| 5 | Beginning finished goods inventory (F6) | $ 13,000 |
| 6 | Add: Cost of goods manufactured (F15) | 235,000 |
| 7 | Cost of goods available for sale | 248,000 |
| 8 | Deduct: Ending finished goods inventory (F20) | 3,000 |
| 9 | Unadjusted cost of goods sold | 245,000 |
| 10 | Deduct: Overapplied overhead (G19) | 5,700 |
| 11 | Adjusted cost of goods sold | $ 239,300 |
| 12 | | |

H ◀ ▶ H   Exhibit 3A-1   Exhibit 3A-2   Exhibit 3A-3   **Exhibit 3A-4**   Exhibit 3A-5

**EXHIBIT 3A-5**  Sapphire Company: Income Statement

| | A | B | C |
|---|---|---|---|
| 1 | **Sapphire Company** | | |
| 2 | **Income Statement** | | |
| 3 | **For the Month Ended January 31** | | |
| 5 | Sales (L16) | | $ 320,000 |
| 6 | Cost of goods sold | | 239,300 |
| 7 | Gross margin | | 80,700 |
| 8 | Selling and administrative expenses: | | |
| 9 | Salaries expense (L9) | $ 22,000 | |
| 10 | Depreciation expense (L11) | 12,000 | |
| 11 | Advertising expense (L12) | 18,000 | |
| 12 | Insurance expense (L13) | 200 | 52,200 |
| 13 | Net operating income | | $ 28,500 |
| 14 | | | |

Exhibit 3A-1 / Exhibit 3A-2 / Exhibit 3A-3 / Exhibit 3A-4 / Exhibit 3A-5

In the schedule of cost of goods sold, we subtract overapplied overhead of $5,700 from unadjusted cost of goods sold because overapplied overhead means that too much overhead was added to production during the period, and hence, the cost of goods sold was overstated. In Exhibit 3A–2, we add overapplied overhead to retained earnings (see row 19) because lowering cost of goods sold increases net operating income, which in turn increases retained earnings.

**Sapphire Company–Income Statement**  Exhibit 3A–5 shows Sapphire Company's income statement for the month of January. The sales and selling and administrative expenses come from the transaction analysis in Exhibit 3A–2 and they each contain a corresponding parenthetical cell reference. The cost of goods sold ($239,300) is carried over from the schedule of cost of goods sold in Exhibit 3A–4.

## APPENDIX 3A:          EXERCISES AND PROBLEMS

### EXERCISE 3A-1   Transaction Analysis LO3-5

Carmen Company is a manufacturer that completed numerous transactions during the month, some of which are shown below:

a.  Raw materials used in production as direct materials, $56,000.
b.  Paid direct laborers $40,000 in cash for their work on various jobs during the month.
c.  Applied $35,000 of manufacturing overhead to production during the month.
d.  Various jobs costing a total of $110,000 were completed during the month and transferred to Finished Goods.
e.  Various completed jobs costing a total of $90,000 were sold to customers.
f.  Cash sales for the month totaled $160,000.
g.  Selling and administrative expenses paid in cash, $18,000.

*Required:*

The table shown below includes a subset of Carmen Company's balance sheet accounts. Record each of the above transactions using the accounts that are given. If a transaction increases an account balance, then record the amount as a positive number. If it decreases an account balance, then record the amount in parentheses.

| Transaction | Cash | Raw Materials | Work in Process | Finished Goods | Manufacturing Overhead | | Retained Earnings |
|---|---|---|---|---|---|---|---|
| a. | | | | | | = | |
| b. | | | | | | = | |
| c. | | | | | | = | |
| d. | | | | | | = | |
| e. | | | | | | = | |
| f. | | | | | | = | |
| g. | | | | | | = | |

**EXERCISE 3A–2   Transaction Analysis LO3–5**

Adams Company is a manufacturer that completed numerous transactions during the month, some of which are shown below:

a.   Manufacturing overhead costs incurred on account, $80,000.

b.   Depreciation was recorded for the month, $35,000 (80% related to factory equipment, and the remainder related to selling and administrative equipment).

c.   Prepaid insurance expired during the month, $2,500 (75% related to production, and 25% related to selling and administration).

d.   Applied $115,000 of manufacturing overhead to production during the month.

e.   Closed $5,125 of overapplied overhead to cost of goods sold.

*Required:*

The table shown below includes a subset of Adams Company's balance sheet accounts. Record each of the above transactions using the accounts that are given. If a transaction increases an account balance, then record the amount as a positive number. If it decreases an account balance, then record the amount in parentheses.

| Transaction | Work in Process | Manufacturing Overhead | Prepaid Expenses | PP&E (net) | | Accounts Payable | Retained Earnings |
|---|---|---|---|---|---|---|---|
| a. | | | | | = | | |
| b. | | | | | = | | |
| c. | | | | | = | | |
| d. | | | | | = | | |
| e. | | | | | = | | |

**EXERCISE 3A–3   Transaction Analysis LO3–5**

Dixon Company is a manufacturer that completed numerous transactions during the month, some of which are shown below:

a.   Raw materials purchased on account, $100,000.

b.   Raw materials used in production, $78,000 direct materials, and $16,000 indirect materials.

c.   Sales commissions paid in cash, $45,000.

d.   Depreciation was recorded for the month, $60,000 (65% related to factory equipment, and the remainder related to selling and administrative equipment).

e.   Sales for the month, $450,000 (70% cash sales and the remainder were sales on account).

f.   Factory utilities paid in cash, $12,000.

g.   Applied $138,000 of manufacturing overhead to production during the month.

h.   Various jobs costing a total of $190,000 were completed during the month and transferred to Finished Goods.

i.   Cash receipts from customers who had previously purchased on credit, $115,000.

j.   Various completed jobs costing a total of $220,000 were sold to customers.

k.   Cash paid to raw material suppliers, $90,000.

*Required:*

The table shown below includes only one account from Dixon Company's balance sheet—Retained Earnings. For each of the above transactions, select "No" if it would not affect Retained Earnings. Conversely if the transaction would affect Retained Earnings, then record the amount of the increase or (decrease) to this account under the "Yes" column.

| | Retained Earnings | |
|---|---|---|
| Transaction | Yes | No |
| a. . . . . . . . . . . . . . . . . . . | | |
| b. . . . . . . . . . . . . . . . . | | |
| c. . . . . . . . . . . . . . . . . | | |
| d. . . . . . . . . . . . . . . . . | | |
| e. . . . . . . . . . . . . . . . | | |
| f. . . . . . . . . . . . . . . . | | |
| g. . . . . . . . . . . . . . . | | |
| h. . . . . . . . . . . . . . . | | |
| i. . . . . . . . . . . . . . . | | |
| j. . . . . . . . . . . . . . . | | |
| k. . . . . . . . . . . . . . | | |

**PROBLEM 3A–4    Transaction Analysis LO3–5**

Morrison Company uses a job-order costing system to assign manufacturing costs to jobs. Its balance sheet on January 1 is as follows:

| Morrison Company Balance Sheet January 1 | | |
|---|---|---|
| **Assets** | | |
| Cash . . . . . . . . . . . . . . . . . . . . . . . . . . . . . . . . . . . . . | | $ 32,000 |
| Raw materials . . . . . . . . . . . . . . . . . . . . . . . . . . . | $ 9,000 | |
| Work in process . . . . . . . . . . . . . . . . . . . . . . . . . | 4,000 | |
| Finished goods . . . . . . . . . . . . . . . . . . . . . . . . . . | 17,000 | 30,000 |
| Prepaid expenses . . . . . . . . . . . . . . . . . . . . . . . | | 2,000 |
| Property, plant, and equipment (net) . . . . . . . . . . . | | 190,000 |
| Total assets . . . . . . . . . . . . . . . . . . . . . . . . . . . . . | | $254,000 |
| | | |
| **Liabilities and Stockholders' Equity** | | |
| Accounts payable . . . . . . . . . . . . . . . . . . . . . . . . . | | $   7,000 |
| Retained earnings . . . . . . . . . . . . . . . . . . . . . . . . | | 247,000 |
| Total liabilities and stockholders' equity . . . . . . . . . | | $254,000 |

During January the company completed the following transactions:
a.  Purchased raw materials on account, $74,000.
b.  Raw materials used in production, $77,000 ($67,000 was direct materials and $10,000 was indirect materials).
c.  Paid $167,000 of salaries and wages in cash ($95,000 was direct labor, $35,000 was indirect labor, and $37,000 was related to employees responsible for selling and administration).
d.  Various manufacturing overhead costs incurred (on account) to support production, $33,000.
e.  Depreciation recorded on property, plant, and equipment, $90,000 (70% related to manufacturing equipment and 30% related to assets that support selling and administration).
f.  Various selling expenses paid in cash, $27,000.
g.  Prepaid insurance expired during the month, $1,200 (80% related to production, and 20% related to selling and administration).
h.  Manufacturing overhead applied to production, $132,000.
i.  Cost of goods manufactured, $288,000.
j.  Cash sales to customers, $395,000.
k.  Cost of goods sold (unadjusted), $285,000.
l.  Cash payments to creditors, $62,000.
m.  Underapplied or overapplied overhead ___ $? ___ .

**Required:**

1. Calculate the ending balances that would be reported on the company's balance sheet on January 31. You can derive your answers using Microsoft Excel and Exhibit 3A–2 as your guide, or you can use paper, pencil, and a calculator. (*Hint:* Be sure to calculate the underapplied or overapplied overhead and then account for its effect on the balance sheet.)

2. What is Morrison Company's net operating income for the month of January?

**PROBLEM 3A–5   Transaction Analysis** LO3–5

Star Videos, Inc., produces short musical videos for sale to retail outlets. The company's balance sheet accounts as of January 1 are given below.

| Star Videos, Inc. Balance Sheet January 1 | | |
|---|---|---|
| **Assets** | | |
| Cash ......................................... | | $ 73,000 |
| Accounts receivable ............................. | | 96,000 |
| Inventories: | | |
| Raw materials (film, costumes) ................... | $33,000 | |
| Videos in process ............................ | 47,000 | |
| Finished videos awaiting sale ................... | 78,000 | 158,000 |
| Prepaid insurance ............................. | | 8,000 |
| Studio and equipment (net) ....................... | | 530,000 |
| Total assets .................................... | | $865,000 |
| | | |
| **Liabilities and Stockholders' Equity** | | |
| Accounts payable ................................ | | $150,000 |
| Retained earnings .............................. | | 715,000 |
| Total liabilities and stockholders' equity .............. | | $865,000 |

Because the videos differ in length and in complexity of production, the company uses a job-order costing system to determine the cost of each video produced. Studio (manufacturing) overhead is charged to videos on the basis of camera-hours of activity. The company's predetermined overhead rate for the year ($40 per camera-hour) is based on a cost formula that estimated $280,000 in manufacturing overhead for an estimated allocation base of 7,000 camera-hours. Any underapplied or overapplied overhead is closed to cost of goods sold. The following transactions were recorded for the year:

a. Film, costumes, and similar raw materials purchased on account, $183,000.
b. Film, costumes, and other raw materials issued to production, $210,000 (85% of this material was considered direct to the videos in production, and the other 15% was considered indirect).
c. Utility costs incurred (on account) in the production studio, $78,000.
d. Depreciation recorded on the studio, cameras, and other equipment, $82,000. Three-fourths of this depreciation related to actual production of the videos, and the remainder related to equipment used in marketing and administration.
e. Advertising expense incurred (on account), $131,000.
f. Salaries and wages paid in cash as follows:

| | |
|---|---|
| Direct labor (actors and directors) ................................ | $84,000 |
| Indirect labor (carpenters to build sets, costume designers, and so forth) ....................................... | $105,000 |
| Administrative salaries ....................................... | $95,000 |

g. Prepaid insurance expired during the year, $7,000 (70% related to production of videos, and 30% related to marketing and administrative activities).
h. Miscellaneous marketing and administrative expenses incurred (on account), $9,600.

i.  Studio (manufacturing) overhead was applied to videos in production. The company recorded 7,250 camera-hours of activity during the year.

j.  Videos that cost $565,000 to produce according to their job cost sheets were transferred to the finished videos warehouse to await sale and shipment.

k.  Sales for the year totaled $930,000 and were all on account.

l.  The total cost to produce the videos that were sold according to their job cost sheets was $610,000.

m.  Collections from customers during the year totaled $880,000.

n.  Payments to suppliers on account during the year, $515,000.

o.  Underapplied or overapplied overhead $ _____?_____.

**Required:**

1.  Using Exhibit 3A–2 as your guide, prepare a transaction analysis that records all of the above transactions. Calculate the ending balances at December 31 for all balance sheet accounts.

2.  Using Exhibit 3A–3 as your guide, prepare a schedule of cost of goods manufactured for the year. If done correctly, your cost of goods manufactured should equal what amount mentioned in the transactions above?

3.  Using Exhibit 3A–4 as your guide, prepare a schedule of cost of goods sold for the year. If done correctly, your unadjusted cost of goods sold should equal what amount mentioned in the transactions above?

4.  Using Exhibit 3A–5 as your guide, prepare an income statement for the year.

**PROBLEM 3A–6    Transaction Analysis LO3–5**

Brooks Corporation uses a job-order costing system to apply manufacturing costs to jobs. The company closes its underapplied or overapplied overhead to cost of goods sold. Its balance sheet on March 1 is as follows:

| Brooks Corporation Balance Sheet March 1 | | |
|---|---|---|
| **Assets** | | |
| Cash ........................................... | | $ 83,000 |
| Raw materials ................................... | $18,000 | |
| Work in process ................................ | 14,000 | |
| Finished goods .................................. | 22,000 | 54,000 |
| Prepaid expenses ............................... | | 1,800 |
| Property, plant, and equipment (net) ................ | | 175,000 |
| Total assets ..................................... | | $313,800 |
| | | |
| **Liabilities and Stockholders' Equity** | | |
| Accounts payable ................................ | | $ 12,000 |
| Retained earnings ............................... | | 301,800 |
| Total liabilities and stockholders' equity ............. | | $313,800 |

During March the company completed the following transactions:

a.  Purchased raw materials for cash, $69,000.

b.  Raw materials used in production, $77,000 ($67,000 was direct materials and $10,000 was indirect materials).

c.  Paid $178,000 of salaries and wages in cash ($102,000 was direct labor, $23,000 was indirect labor, and $53,000 was related to employees responsible for selling and administration).

d.  Various manufacturing overhead costs paid in cash to support production, $41,000.

e.  Depreciation recorded on property, plant, and equipment, $35,000 (85% related to manufacturing equipment and 15% related to assets that support selling and administration).

f.  Various selling expenses incurred on account, $27,000.

g.  Prepaid insurance expired during the month, $450 (60% related to production, and 40% related to selling and administration).

h.  Manufacturing overhead applied to production, $101,000.

i.  Cost of goods manufactured, $____?____. (*Hint:* The Work in Process balance on March 31 is $5,000.)
j.  Cash sales to customers, $429,000.
k.  Cost of goods sold (unadjusted), $____?____. (*Hint:* The Finished Goods balance at March 31 is $6,000.)
l.  Cash payments to creditors, $35,000.
m.  Underapplied or overapplied overhead $____?____.

### Required:

1.  Calculate the ending balances that would be reported on the company's balance sheet at March 31. You can derive your answers using Microsoft Excel and Exhibit 3A–2 as your guide, or you can use paper, pencil, and a calculator. (*Hint:* Be sure to calculate the underapplied or overapplied overhead and then account for its effect on the balance sheet.)
2.  Prepare Brooks Corporation's schedule of cost of goods manufactured for the month ended March 31. You can derive your answers using Microsoft Excel and Exhibit 3A–3 as your guide, or you can use paper, pencil, and a calculator.
3.  Prepare Brooks Corporation's schedule of cost of goods sold for the month ended March 31. You can derive your answers using Microsoft Excel and Exhibit 3A–4 as your guide, or you can use paper, pencil, and a calculator.
4.  Prepare Brooks Corporation's income statement for the month ended March 31. You can derive your answers using Microsoft Excel and Exhibit 3A–5 as your guide, or you can use paper, pencil, and a calculator.

**A LOOK BACK**

Chapter 3 explained how job-order costing systems are used to value ending inventories and cost of goods sold for external reporting purposes.

**A LOOK AT THIS CHAPTER**

Chapter 4 describes how activity-based costing systems are used to allocate overhead costs to products. It contrasts activity-based overhead cost allocation with the plantwide approach to overhead cost allocation that was discussed in earlier chapters.

**A LOOK AHEAD**

Chapter 5 compares job-order costing to process costing. It also explains how process costing systems assign direct materials, direct labor, and manufacturing overhead costs to units of production.

# 4 Activity-Based Costing

## CHAPTER OUTLINE

**Assigning Overhead Costs to Products**

- Plantwide Overhead Rate
- Departmental Overhead Rates
- Activity-Based Costing (ABC)

**Designing an Activity-Based Costing System**

- Hierarchy of Activities
- An Example of an Activity-Based Costing System Design

**Using Activity-Based Costing**

- Comtek Inc.'s Basic Data

- Direct Labor-Hours as a Base
- Computing Activity Rates
- Computing Product Costs
- Shifting of Overhead Cost

**Targeting Process Improvements**

**Evaluation of Activity-Based Costing**

- The Benefits of Activity-Based Costing
- Limitations of Activity-Based Costing
- Activity-Based Costing and Service Industries

©Kevin Clark/Alamy Stock Photo RF

*After studying Chapter 4, you should be able to:*

**LO4–1** Understand the basic approach in activity-based costing and how it differs from conventional costing.

**LO4–2** Compute activity rates for an activity-based costing system.

**LO4–3** Compute product costs using activity-based costing.

**LO4–4** Contrast the product costs computed under activity-based costing and conventional costing methods.

# Airline Fuel Cost Drivers

Stop for a moment to identify as many airline fuel cost drivers as you can. Perhaps you readily thought of two important cost drivers—the number of flights and the number of miles flown. However, did you consider the weight of the plane in flight given the fact that heavier planes consume more fuel? While you may have overlooked weight as a cost driver, rest assured that the airline industry has not. Regulators have given airlines clearance for its pilots to replace the bulky navigation charts and manuals that they have hauled around for years with an iPad. **American Airlines** estimates that the switch to iPads will eliminate 3,000 pages of paper per pilot, which translates to annual savings of 400,000 gallons of fuel and $1.2 million dollars.

In this chapter, you'll learn how companies implement activity-based costing systems to better understand and manage the cost drivers that influence the profitability of their products.

Source: Carey, Susan, "Airlines Jettison a Costly Load of Paper," *The Wall Street Journal*, June 27, 2013, p. B6.

As discussed in earlier chapters, direct materials and direct labor costs can be directly traced to products. Overhead costs, on the other hand, cannot be easily traced to products. Some other means must be found for assigning them to products for financial reporting and other purposes. In the previous chapter, overhead costs were assigned to products using a plantwide predetermined overhead rate. This method is simpler than the methods of assigning overhead costs to products described in this chapter, but this simplicity has a cost. A plantwide predetermined overhead rate spreads overhead costs uniformly over products in proportion to whatever allocation base is used—most commonly, direct labor-hours. This procedure results in high overhead costs for products with a high direct labor-hour content and low overhead costs for products with a low direct labor-hour content. However, the real causes of overhead may have little to do with direct labor-hours and as a consequence, product costs may be distorted. Activity-based costing attempts to correct these distortions by more accurately assigning overhead costs to products.

# ASSIGNING OVERHEAD COSTS TO PRODUCTS

**LEARNING OBJECTIVE 4–1**

Understand the basic approach in activity-based costing and how it differs from conventional costing.

Companies use three common approaches to assign overhead costs to products. The simplest method is to use a plantwide overhead rate. A slightly more refined approach is to use departmental overhead rates. The most complex method is activity-based costing, which is the most accurate of the three approaches to overhead cost assignment.

## Plantwide Overhead Rate

The preceding chapter assumed that a single overhead rate, called a *plantwide overhead rate,* was used throughout an entire factory. This simple approach to overhead assignment can result in distorted unit product costs, as we shall see below.

When cost systems were developed in the 1800s, cost and activity data had to be collected by hand and all calculations were done with paper and pen. Consequently, the emphasis was on simplicity. Companies often established a single overhead cost pool for an entire facility or department as described in earlier chapters. Direct labor was the obvious choice as an allocation base for overhead costs. Direct labor-hours were already being recorded for purposes of determining wages. In the labor-intensive production processes of that time, direct labor was a large component of product costs—larger than it is today. Moreover, managers believed direct labor and overhead costs were highly correlated. (Two variables, such as direct labor and overhead costs, are highly correlated if they tend to move together.) And finally, most companies produced a very limited variety of similar products, so in fact there was probably little difference in the overhead costs attributable to different products. Under these conditions, it was not cost-effective to use a more elaborate costing system.

Conditions have changed. Many companies now sell a large variety of products that consume significantly different amounts of overhead resources. Consequently, a costing system that assigns essentially the same overhead cost to every product may no longer be adequate. Additionally, factors other than direct labor often drive overhead costs.

On an economywide basis, direct labor and overhead costs have been moving in opposite directions for a long time. As a percentage of total cost, direct labor has been declining, whereas overhead has been increasing. Many tasks previously done by hand are now done with largely automated equipment—a component of overhead. Furthermore, product diversity has increased. Companies are introducing new products and services at an ever-accelerating rate. Managing and sustaining this product diversity requires many more overhead resources such as production schedulers and product design engineers, and many of these overhead resources have no obvious connection with direct labor. Finally, computers, bar code readers, and other technology have dramatically reduced the costs of collecting and processing data—making more complex (and accurate) costing systems such as activity-based costing much less expensive to build and maintain.

Nevertheless, direct labor remains a viable base for applying overhead to products in some companies—particularly for external reports. Direct labor is an appropriate allocation base for overhead when overhead costs and direct labor are highly correlated. And indeed, most companies throughout the world continue to base overhead allocations on direct labor or machine-hours. However, if factorywide overhead costs do not move in tandem with factorywide direct labor or machine-hours, product costs will be distorted.

## Departmental Overhead Rates

Rather than use a plantwide overhead rate, many companies use departmental overhead rates with a different predetermined overhead rate in each production department. The nature of the work performed in a department will determine the department's allocation base. For example, overhead costs in a machining department may be allocated on the basis of machine-hours. In contrast, the overhead costs in an assembly department may be allocated on the basis of direct labor-hours.

Unfortunately, even departmental overhead rates will not correctly assign overhead costs in situations where a company has a range of products and complex overhead costs. The reason is that the departmental approach usually relies on a single measure of activity as the base for allocating overhead cost to products. For example, if the machining department's overhead is applied to products on the basis of machine-hours, it is assumed that the department's overhead costs are caused by, and are directly proportional to, machine-hours. However, the department's overhead costs are probably more complex than this and are caused by a variety of factors, including the range of products processed in the department, the number of batch setups that are required, the complexity of the products, and so on. A more sophisticated method like *activity-based costing* is required to adequately account for these diverse factors.

HELPFUL HINT

Conventional cost systems that use plantwide predetermined overhead rates suffer from an important limitation. They tend to inaccurately assign too much overhead to high-volume products and too little overhead to low-volume products. This distortion occurs because conventional cost systems rely exclusively on allocation bases, such as direct labor-hours and machine-hours, that are highly correlated with (or move in tandem with) the volume of production. Make a point of noticing a recurring theme throughout this chapter—activity-based costing systems usually reveal that low-volume (high-volume) products cost more than (less than) reported by conventional cost systems.

## Activity-Based Costing (ABC)

**Activity-based costing (ABC)** is a technique that attempts to assign overhead costs more accurately to products than the simpler methods discussed thus far. The basic idea underlying the activity-based costing approach is illustrated in Exhibit 4–1. A customer order triggers a number of activities. For example, if **Nordstrom** orders a line of women's skirts from **Calvin Klein**, a production order is generated, patterns are created, materials are ordered, textiles are cut to pattern and then sewn, and the finished products are packed for shipping. These activities consume resources. For example, ordering the appropriate materials consumes clerical time—a resource the company must pay for. In activity-based costing, an attempt is made to trace these costs directly to the products that cause them.

EXHIBIT 4–1
The Activity-Based Costing
Model

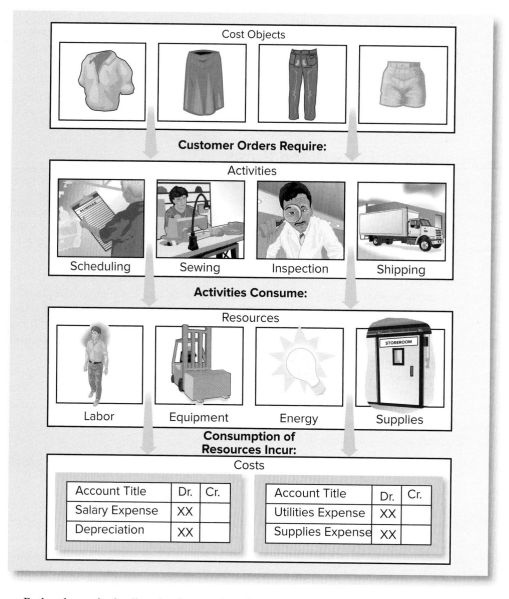

Rather than a single allocation base such as direct labor-hours or machine-hours, in activity-based costing a company uses a number of allocation bases for assigning costs to products. Each allocation base in an activity-based costing system represents a major *activity* that causes overhead costs. An **activity** in activity-based costing is an event that causes the consumption of overhead resources. Examples of activities in various organizations include the following:

- Setting up machines.
- Admitting patients to a hospital.
- Scheduling production.
- Performing blood tests at a clinic.
- Billing customers.
- Maintaining equipment.
- Ordering materials or supplies.
- Stocking shelves at a store.
- Meeting with clients at a law firm.
- Preparing shipments.
- Inspecting materials for defects.
- Opening an account at a bank.

Activity-based costing focuses on these activities. Each major activity has its own overhead cost pool (also known as an *activity cost pool*), its own *activity measure,* and its own overhead rate (also known as an *activity rate*). An **activity cost pool** is a "cost bucket" in which costs related to a particular activity measure are accumulated. The **activity measure** expresses how much of the activity is carried out and it is used as the allocation base for assigning overhead costs to products and services. For example, *the number of patients admitted* is a natural choice of an activity measure for the activity *admitting patients to the hospital.* An **activity rate** is an overhead rate in an activity-based costing system. Each activity has its own activity rate that is used to assign overhead costs to cost objects.

For example, the activity *setting up machines to process a batch* would have its own activity cost pool. Products are ordinarily processed in batches. And because each product has its own machine settings, machines must be set up when changing over from a batch of one product to another. If the total cost in this activity cost pool is $150,000 and the total expected activity is 1,000 machine setups, the activity rate for this activity would be $150 per machine setup ($150,000 ÷ 1,000 machine setups = $150 per machine setup). Each product that requires a machine setup would be charged $150. Note that this charge does not depend on how many units are produced after the machine is set up. A small batch requiring a machine setup would be charged $150—just the same as a large batch.

Taking each activity in isolation, this system works exactly like the job-order costing system described in the previous chapters. An activity rate is computed for each activity and then these rates are used to assign costs to jobs and products based on the amount of activity consumed by the job or product.

## DESIGNING AN ACTIVITY-BASED COSTING SYSTEM

The most important decisions in designing an activity-based costing system concern what activities will be included in the system and how the activities will be measured. In most companies, hundreds or even thousands of different activities cause overhead costs. These activities range from taking a telephone order to training new employees. Setting up and maintaining a complex costing system that includes all of these activities would be prohibitively expensive. The challenge in designing an activity-based costing system is to identify a reasonably small number of activities that explain the bulk of the variation in overhead costs. This is usually done by interviewing a broad range of managers in the organization to find out what activities they think are important and that consume most of the resources they manage. This often results in a long list of potential activities that could be included in the activity-based costing system. This list is refined and pruned in consultation with top managers. Related activities are frequently combined to reduce the amount of detail and record-keeping cost. For example, several actions may be involved in handling and moving raw materials, but these may be combined into a single activity titled *material handling.* The end result of this stage of the design process is an *activity dictionary* that defines each of the activities that will be included in the activity-based costing system and how the activities will be measured.

Some of the activities commonly found in activity-based costing systems in manufacturing companies are listed in Exhibit 4–2. In the exhibit, activities have been grouped into a four-level hierarchy: *unit-level activities, batch-level activities, product-level activities,* and *facility-level activities.* This cost hierarchy is useful in understanding the difference between activity-based costing and conventional approaches. It also serves as a guide when simplifying an activity-based costing system. In general, activities and costs should be combined in the activity-based costing system only if they fall within the same level in the cost hierarchy.

### Hierarchy of Activities

**Unit-level activities** are performed each time a unit is produced. The costs of unit-level activities should be proportional to the number of units produced. For example, providing

| Level | Activities | Activity Measures |
|---|---|---|
| *Unit-level* | Processing units on machines<br>Processing units by hand<br>Consuming factory supplies | Machine-hours<br>Direct labor-hours<br>Units produced |
| *Batch-level* | Processing purchase orders<br>Processing production orders<br>Setting up equipment<br>Handling material | Purchase orders processed<br>Production orders processed<br>Number of setups; setup hours<br>Pounds of material handled;<br>    number of times material moved |
| *Product-level* | Testing new products<br>Administering parts inventories<br>Designing products | Hours of testing time<br>Number of part types<br>Hours of design time |
| *Facility-level* | General factory administration<br>Plant building and grounds | Direct labor-hours*<br>Direct labor-hours* |

*Facility-level costs cannot be traced on a cause-and-effect basis to individual products. Nevertheless, companies that choose to use activity-based absorption costing will allocate these costs to products using some arbitrary allocation base such as direct labor-hours.

power to run processing equipment is a unit-level activity because power tends to be consumed in proportion to the number of units produced.

**Batch-level activities** consist of tasks that are performed each time a batch is processed, such as processing purchase orders, setting up equipment, packing shipments to customers, and handling material. Costs at the batch level depend on *the number of batches processed* rather than on the number of units produced. For example, the cost of processing a purchase order is the same no matter how many units of an item are ordered.

**Product-level activities** (sometimes called *product-sustaining activities*) relate to specific products and typically must be carried out regardless of how many batches or units of the product are manufactured. Product-level activities include maintaining inventories of parts for a product, issuing engineering change notices to modify a product to meet a customer's specifications, and developing special test routines when a product is first placed into production.

**Facility-level activities** (also called *organization-sustaining activities*) are activities that are carried out regardless of which products are produced, how many batches are run, or how many units are made. Facility-level costs include items such as factory management salaries, insurance, property taxes, and building depreciation. These costs cannot be traced on a cause-and-effect basis to individual products. Therefore, companies that choose to implement an activity-based absorption costing system will be required to arbitrarily allocate facility-level cost to products. As we will see later in the book, these types of arbitrary allocations can lead to bad decisions.

## HELPFUL HINT

Students often struggle to grasp the meaning of unit-level, batch-level, and product-level activities. Imagine a professor who teaches one section of managerial accounting that includes 35 students and one section of financial accounting that includes 25 students. In this example, the two courses represent two separate products. The activity "preparing a syllabus" would be a product-level activity because it needs to be performed once for each course regardless of the number of class meetings during the semester or the number of enrolled students per class. The activity "preparing a lesson plan" would be a batch-level activity because it needs to be performed once for each class session regardless of the number of enrolled students in each class. The activity "grading exams" would be a unit-level activity because it needs to be performed once for each student enrolled in each class.

## Dining in the Canyon

**Western River Expeditions** (www.westernriver.com) runs river rafting trips on the Colorado, Green, and Salmon rivers. One of its most popular trips is a six-day trip down the Grand Canyon, which features famous rapids such as Crystal and Lava Falls as well as the awesome scenery accessible only from the bottom of the Grand Canyon. The company runs trips of one or two rafts, each of which carries two guides and up to 18 guests. The company provides all meals on the trip, which are prepared by the guides.

In terms of the hierarchy of activities, a guest can be considered as a unit and a raft as a batch. In that context, the wages paid to the guides are a batch-level cost because each raft requires two guides regardless of the number of guests in the raft. Each guest is given a mug to use during the trip and to take home at the end of the trip as a souvenir. The cost of the mug is a unit-level cost because the number of mugs given away is strictly proportional to the number of guests on a trip.

What about the costs of food served to guests and guides—is this a unit-level cost, a batch-level cost, a product-level cost, or an organization-sustaining cost? At first glance, it might be thought that food costs are a unit-level cost—the greater the number of guests, the higher the food costs. However, that is not quite correct. Standard menus have been created for each day of the trip. For example, the first night's menu might consist of shrimp cocktail, steak, cornbread, salad, and cheesecake. The day before a trip begins, all of the food needed for the trip is taken from the central warehouse and packed in modular containers. It isn't practical to finely adjust the amount of food for the actual number of guests planned to be on a trip—most of the food comes prepackaged in large lots. For example, the shrimp cocktail menu may call for two large bags of frozen shrimp per raft and that many bags will be packed regardless of how many guests are expected on the raft. Consequently, the costs of food are not a unit-level cost that varies with the number of guests actually on a trip. Instead, the costs of food are a batch-level cost.

Source: Conversations with Western River Expeditions personnel.

©Sandee Noreen

# An Example of an Activity-Based Costing System Design

The complexity of an activity-based costing system will differ from company to company. In some companies, the activity-based costing system will be simple with only one or two activity cost pools at the unit, batch, and product levels. For other companies, the activity-based costing system will be much more complex.

Under activity-based costing, the manufacturing overhead costs at the top of Exhibit 4–3 are allocated to products via a two-stage process. In the first stage, overhead costs are assigned to the activity cost pools. In the second stage, the costs in the activity cost pools are allocated to products using activity rates and activity measures. For example, in the first-stage cost assignment, various manufacturing overhead costs are assigned to the production-order activity cost pool. These costs could include the salaries of engineers who modify products for individual orders, the costs of scheduling and monitoring orders, and other costs that are incurred as a consequence of the number of different orders received and processed by the company. We will not go into the details of how these first-stage cost assignments are made. In all of the examples and assignments in this book, the first-stage cost assignments have already been completed. Once the amount of cost in the production-order activity cost pool is known, the activity rate for the cost pool is computed by dividing the total cost in the production-order activity cost pool by the anticipated number of orders for the upcoming year. For example, the total cost in the production-order activity cost pool might be $450,000 and the company might expect to process a total of 1,200 orders. In that case, the activity rate would be $375 per order. Each order would be charged $375 for production-order costs. This is no different from the way overhead was assigned to products in earlier chapters except that the number of orders is the allocation base rather than direct labor-hours.

**EXHIBIT 4–3**   Graphic Example of Activity-Based Costing

1. Which of the following statements is false? (You may select more than one answer.)
   a. In recent years, most companies have experienced increasing manufacturing overhead costs in relation to direct labor costs.
   b. Batch-level costs do not depend on the number of units produced in a batch.
   c. Facility-level costs are not caused by particular products.
   d. Product-level costs are larger for high-volume products than for low-volume products.
2. Which of the following statements is true? (You may select more than one answer.)
   a. The costs of a unit-level activity should be proportional to the number of units produced.
   b. Unit-level activities are performed each time a unit is produced.
   c. Setting up equipment is an example of a unit-level activity.
   d. Activity-based costing systems may use direct labor-hours and/or machine-hours to assign unit-level costs to products.

## USING ACTIVITY-BASED COSTING

Different products place different demands on resources. This is not recognized by conventional costing systems, which assume that overhead resources are consumed in direct proportion to direct labor-hours or machine-hours. The following example illustrates the distortions in product costs that can result from using a traditional costing system.

Comtek Inc. makes two products, a GPS system and a Phone system, that are both sold to automobile manufacturers for installation in new vehicles. Recently, the company has been losing bids to supply GPS systems because competitors have been bidding less than Comtek has been willing to bid. At the same time, Comtek has been winning every bid it has submitted for its Phone system, which management regards as a secondary product. The marketing manager has been complaining that at the prices Comtek is willing to bid, competitors are taking the company's high-volume GPS business and leaving Comtek with just the low-volume Phone business. However, the prices competitors quote on the GPS systems are below Comtek's manufacturing cost for these units—at least according to Comtek's conventional accounting system that applies manufacturing overhead to products based on direct labor-hours. Production managers suspected that the conventional costing system might be distorting the relative costs of the GPS system and the Phone system—the Phone system takes more overhead resources to make than the GPS system and yet their manufacturing overhead costs are identical under the conventional costing system. With the enthusiastic cooperation of the company's accounting department, a cross-functional team was formed to develop an activity-based costing system to more accurately assign overhead costs to the two products.

## Comtek Inc.'s Basic Data

The ABC team gathered basic information relating to the company's two products. A summary of some of this information follows. For the current year, the company's budget provides for selling 50,000 Phone systems and 200,000 GPS systems. Both products require two direct labor-hours to complete. Therefore, the company plans to work 500,000 direct labor-hours (DLHs) during the current year, computed as follows:

| | |
|---|---:|
| Phone: 50,000 units × 2 DLHs per unit . . . . . . . . . . . . . | 100,000 |
| GPS: 200,000 units × 2 DLHs per unit . . . . . . . . . . . . . . | 400,000 |
| Total direct labor-hours . . . . . . . . . . . . . . . . . . . . . . . . . | 500,000 |

Costs for direct materials and direct labor for one unit of each product are given below:

| | Phone | GPS |
|---|:---:|:---:|
| Direct materials. . . . . . . . . . . . . . . . . . . . . . . . . . . . . | $90 | $50 |
| Direct labor (at $10 per DLH) . . . . . . . . . . . . . . . | $20 | $20 |

The company's estimated manufacturing overhead costs for the current year total $10,000,000. The ABC team discovered that although the same amount of direct labor time is required for each product, the more complex Phone system requires more machine time, more machine setups, and more testing than the GPS system. Also, the team found that it is necessary to manufacture the Phone systems in smaller batches; consequently, they require more production orders than the GPS systems.

The company has always used direct labor-hours as the base for assigning overhead costs to its products.

With these data in hand, the ABC team was prepared to begin the design of the new activity-based costing system. But first, they wanted to compute the cost of each product using the company's existing cost system.

As you continue to read through the Comtek Inc., example, keep the following "big picture" insight in mind. The company's existing cost system and the ABC system will both assign a total of $10 million in manufacturing overhead costs to the two products. In other words, the total amount of the "pie" being assigned to GPS systems and Phone systems will be the same in both cost systems. However, the two cost systems will assign different portions of the pie to each product. The existing cost system will assign $8,000,000 (= 200,000 units × $40 per unit) of manufacturing overhead cost to the high-volume GPS systems and $2,000,000 (= 50,000 units × $40 per unit) of overhead cost to the low-volume Phone systems. The ABC system will correct this inaccuracy by assigning $5,110,000 of overhead to GPS systems and $4,890,000 of overhead to Phone systems. Again, both cost systems will be assigning a total $10 million in manufacturing overhead to the GPS and Phone systems. They will simply apportion the pie differently.

## Direct Labor-Hours as a Base

Under the company's existing costing system, the predetermined overhead rate would be $20 per direct labor-hour, computed as follows:

$$\text{Predetermined overhead rate} = \frac{\text{Estimated total manufacturing overhead}}{\text{Estimated total amount of the allocation base}}$$

$$= \frac{\$10,000,000}{500,000 \text{ DLHs}} = \$20 \text{ per DLH}$$

Using this rate, the ABC team computed the unit product costs as given below:

|  | Phone | GPS |
|---|---|---|
| Direct materials . . . . . . . . . . . . . . . . . . . . . . . . . . . . . . . . . . . . . . . . . . . . . . . . . . | $ 90 | $ 50 |
| Direct labor. . . . . . . . . . . . . . . . . . . . . . . . . . . . . . . . . . . . . . . . . . . . . . . . . . . . . . . | 20 | 20 |
| Manufacturing overhead (2 DLHs × $20 per DLH). . . . . . . . . . . . . . . . . . . . | 40 | 40 |
| Unit product cost. . . . . . . . . . . . . . . . . . . . . . . . . . . . . . . . . . . . . . . . . . . . . . . . . | $150 | $110 |

The problem with this costing approach is that it relies entirely on direct labor-hours to assign overhead cost to products and does not consider the impact of other factors—such as setups and testing—on the overhead costs of the company. Even though these other factors suggest that the two products place different demands on overhead resources, under the company's conventional costing system, the two products are assigned the same overhead cost per unit because they require equal amounts of direct labor time.

While this method of computing costs is fast and simple, it is accurate only in those situations where other factors affecting overhead costs are not significant. These other factors *are* significant in the case of Comtek Inc.

## Computing Activity Rates

**LEARNING OBJECTIVE 4–2**

Compute activity rates for an activity-based costing system.

The ABC team then analyzed Comtek Inc.'s operations and identified six major activities to include in the new activity-based costing system. Cost and other data relating to the activities are presented in Exhibit 4–4. That exhibit shows the amount of overhead cost for each activity cost pool, along with the expected amount of activity for the current year. The machine setups activity cost pool, for example, was assigned $1,600,000 in overhead cost. The company expects to complete 4,000 setups during the year, of which 3,000 will be for Phone systems and 1,000 will be for GPS systems. Data for other activities are also shown in the exhibit.

The ABC team then computed an activity rate for each activity. (See the middle panel in Exhibit 4–4.) The activity rate of $400 per machine setup, for example, was computed by dividing the total estimated overhead cost in the activity cost pool, $1,600,000, by the expected amount of activity, 4,000 setups. This process was repeated for each of the other activities in the activity-based costing system.

## HELPFUL HINT

Students often make the mistake of trying to compute an activity rate for each product. This is incorrect because you should compute only one activity rate for each activity cost pool. The activity rate is then multiplied by the amount of the activity measure used by each product to assign overhead costs to that product.

**EXHIBIT 4-4**    Comtek's Activity-Based Costing System

### Basic Data

| Activity Cost Pools and Activity Measures | Estimated Overhead Cost | Expected Activity | | |
|---|---|---|---|---|
| | | Phone | GPS | Total |
| Labor-related (direct labor-hours). . . . . . . . . . | $    800,000 | 100,000 | 400,000 | 500,000 |
| Machine-related (machine-hours). . . . . . . . . | 2,100,000 | 300,000 | 700,000 | 1,000,000 |
| Machine setups (setups) . . . . . . . . . . . . . . . . | 1,600,000 | 3,000 | 1,000 | 4,000 |
| Production orders (orders). . . . . . . . . . . . . . . | 3,150,000 | 800 | 400 | 1,200 |
| Parts administration (part types) . . . . . . . . . . | 350,000 | 400 | 300 | 700 |
| General factory (machine-hours) . . . . . . . . . | 2,000,000 | 300,000 | 700,000 | 1,000,000 |
| | $10,000,000 | | | |

### Computation of Activity Rates

| Activity Cost Pools | (a) Estimated Overhead Cost | (b) Total Expected Activity | (a) ÷ (b) Activity Rate |
|---|---|---|---|
| Labor-related . . . . . . . . . . . . . . . . . . | $800,000 | 500,000 DLHs | $1.60 per DLH |
| Machine-related. . . . . . . . . . . . . . . | $2,100,000 | 1,000,000 MHs | $2.10 per MH |
| Machine setups . . . . . . . . . . . . . . | $1,600,000 | 4,000 setups | $400.00 per setup |
| Production orders . . . . . . . . . . . . . . | $3,150,000 | 1,200 orders | $2,625.00 per order |
| Parts administration . . . . . . . . . . . . | $350,000 | 700 part types | $500.00 per part type |
| General factory . . . . . . . . . . . . . . . | $2,000,000 | 1,000,000 MHs | $2.00 per MH |

### Computation of the Overhead Cost per Unit of Product

| Activity Cost Pools and Activity Rates | Phone | | GPS | |
|---|---|---|---|---|
| | Expected Activity | Amount | Expected Activity | Amount |
| Labor-related, at $1.60 per DLH. . . . . . . . . . . . . . . . . | 100,000 | $    160,000 | 400,000 | $    640,000 |
| Machine-related, at $2.10 per MH. . . . . . . . . . . . . . . | 300,000 | 630,000 | 700,000 | 1,470,000 |
| Machine setups, at $400 per setup . . . . . . . . . . . . . | 3,000 | 1,200,000 | 1,000 | 400,000 |
| Production orders, at $2,625 per order . . . . . . . . . . | 800 | 2,100,000 | 400 | 1,050,000 |
| Parts administration, at $500 per part type . . . . . . . . | 400 | 200,000 | 300 | 150,000 |
| General factory, at $2.00 per MH. . . . . . . . . . . . . . . | 300,000 | 600,000 | 700,000 | 1,400,000 |
| Total overhead costs assigned (a) . . . . . . . . . . . . . . . | | $4,890,000 | | $5,110,000 |
| Number of units produced (b). . . . . . . . . . . . . . . . . . | | 50,000 | | 200,000 |
| Overhead cost per unit (a) ÷ (b) . . . . . . . . . . . . . . . . | | $97.80 | | $25.55 |

## Computing Product Costs

Once the activity rates were calculated, it was easy to compute the overhead cost that would be allocated to each product. (See the bottom panel of Exhibit 4–4.) For example, the amount of machine setup cost allocated to Phone systems was determined by multiplying the activity rate of $400 per setup by the 3,000 expected setups for Phones during the year. This yielded a total of $1,200,000 in machine setup costs to be assigned to the Phone systems.

Note from the exhibit that the use of an activity approach has resulted in $97.80 in overhead cost being assigned to each Phone system and $25.55 to each GPS system. The ABC team then used these amounts to determine unit product costs under activity-based

> **LEARNING OBJECTIVE 4–3**
>
> Compute product costs using activity-based costing.

EXHIBIT 4-5
Comparison of Unit Product
Costs

| | Activity-Based Costing | | Direct-Labor-Based Costing | |
|---|---|---|---|---|
| | Phone | GPS | Phone | GPS |
| Direct materials.................. | $ 90.00 | $ 50.00 | $ 90.00 | $ 50.00 |
| Direct labor ...................... | 20.00 | 20.00 | 20.00 | 20.00 |
| Manufacturing overhead........... | 97.80 | 25.55 | 40.00 | 40.00 |
| Unit product cost ................ | $207.80 | $ 95.55 | $150.00 | $110.00 |

costing, as presented in Exhibit 4–5. For comparison, the exhibit also shows the unit product costs derived earlier when direct labor-hours were used as the base for assigning overhead costs to the products.

The ABC team members summarized their findings as follows in the team's report:

> In the past, the company has been charging $40.00 in overhead cost to a unit of either product, whereas it should have been charging $97.80 in overhead cost to each Phone system and only $25.55 to each GPS system. Thus, unit costs have been badly distorted as a result of using direct labor-hours as the allocation base. The company may even have been suffering a loss on the Phone systems without knowing it because the cost of these units has been so vastly understated. Through activity-based costing, we have been able to more accurately assign overhead costs to each product.

> Although in the past we thought our competitors were pricing below their cost on the GPS systems, it turns out that we were overcharging for these units because our costs were overstated. Similarly, we always used to believe that our competitors were overpricing the Phone systems, but now we realize that our prices have been way too low because the cost of our Phone systems was being understated. It turns out that we, not our competitors, had everything backwards.

The pattern of cost distortion shown by the ABC team's findings is quite common. Such distortion can happen in any company that relies on direct labor-hours or machine-hours in assigning overhead cost to products and ignores other significant causes of overhead costs.

## IN BUSINESS

### IKEA Redesigns Products to Lower Shipping Costs

©jipen/123RF

**IKEA**'s product designs are a cost driver that influences the company's shipping costs. For example, when IKEA redesigned its Ektorp sofa from one solid piece into several detachable components, it reduced the product's package size by 50%. This decrease in packaging size enabled the company to remove 7,477 delivery trucks from the road per year and to share the associated cost savings with customers by lowering the sofa's price by 14%.

The company also reduced the number of components in its Textur lamp from 33 to nine. The simpler design reduced the product's packaging weight by 28% and increased the number of units that could be transported on a pallet from 80 to 128. IKEA shared these savings with customers by dropping the price of the lamp by 34%.

Source: Chaudhuri, Saabira, "Ikea's Favorite Design Idea: Shrink the Box," *The Wall Street Journal*, June 18, 2015, p. B10.

**LEARNING OBJECTIVE 4–4**

Contrast the product costs computed under activity-based costing and conventional costing methods.

## Shifting of Overhead Cost

When a company implements activity-based costing, overhead cost often shifts from high-volume products to low-volume products, with a higher unit product cost resulting for the low-volume products. We saw this happen in the Comtek example, where the product cost of the low-volume Phone systems increased from $150.00 to $207.80 per unit. This increase in cost resulted from batch-level and product-level costs, which shifted from the high-volume product to the low-volume product. For example, consider the cost of issuing production orders, which is a batch-level activity. As shown in Exhibit 4–4, the average cost to Comtek to issue a single production order is $2,625. This cost is assigned to a production order regardless of how many units are processed in that order. The key here is to realize that fewer Phone systems (the low-volume product) are processed per production order than GPS systems.

|  | Phone | GPS |
|---|---|---|
| Number of units produced per year (a) | 50,000 | 200,000 |
| Number of production orders issued per year (b) | 800 | 400 |
| Average number of units processed per production order (a) ÷ (b) | 62.5 | 500 |

Spreading the $2,625 cost to issue a production order over the number of units processed per order results in the following average cost per unit:

|  | Phone | GPS |
|---|---|---|
| Cost to issue a production order (a) | $2,625 | $2,625 |
| Average number of units processed per production order (see above) (b) | 62.5 | 500 |
| Average production order cost per unit (a) ÷ (b) | $42.00 | $5.25 |

Thus, the production order cost for a Phone system (the low-volume product) is $42, which is *eight times* the $5.25 cost for a GPS system.

Product-level costs—such as parts administration—have a similar impact. In a conventional costing system, these costs are spread more or less uniformly across all units that are produced. In an activity-based costing system, these costs are assigned more accurately to products. Because product-level costs are fixed with respect to the number of units processed, the average cost per unit of an activity such as parts administration will be higher for low-volume products than for high-volume products.

## Activity-Based Costing in a Governmental Organization

**IN BUSINESS**

Activity-based costing is often studied in the context of for-profit companies; however, it can also be applied by governmental organizations. For example, the city of **Somerville, MA**, used activity-based costing to help manage its Traffic Unit Department. It assigned the Traffic Unit Department's operating costs to six activities: (1) investigate accidents, (2) manage tow companies, (3) traffic enforcement, (4) staff and supervise crossing guard posts, (5) process data, and (6) organize special events. The city also applied an activity-based costing perspective to the Electric, Water, and Building and Grounds programs within its Public Works Department. For example, the five activities within the Water Program included (1) maintain water quality and pressure, (2) maintain gate valves, (3) maintain and read meters, (4) track and issue water permits, and (5) maintain hydrants.

Source: Bilmes, Linda J., "City of Somerville: Using Activity-Based Budgeting to Improve Performance in the Somerville Traffic Units," *Harvard Business School Publishing*, August 2013, pp. 1–29.

# TARGETING PROCESS IMPROVEMENTS

Activity-based costing can be used to identify activities that would benefit from process improvements. When used in this way, activity-based costing is often called *activity-based management*. Basically, **activity-based management** involves focusing on activities to eliminate waste, decrease processing time, and reduce defects. Activity-based management is used in organizations as diverse as manufacturing companies, hospitals, and the U.S. Marine Corps.

The first step in any improvement program is to decide what to improve. The activity rates computed in activity-based costing can provide valuable clues concerning where there is waste and opportunity for improvement. For example, looking at the activity rates in Exhibit 4–4, Comtek's managers may conclude that $2,625 to process a production order is far too expensive for an activity that adds no value to the product. As a consequence, they may target production-order processing for a process improvement project.

*Benchmarking* is another way to leverage the information in activity rates. **Benchmarking** is a systematic approach to identifying the activities with the greatest room for improvement. It is based on comparing the performance in an organization with the performance of other, similar organizations known for their outstanding performance. If a particular part of the organization performs far below the world-class standard, managers will target that area for improvement.

# EVALUATION OF ACTIVITY-BASED COSTING

Activity-based costing improves the accuracy of product costs, helps managers to understand the nature of overhead costs, and helps target areas for improvement through benchmarking and other techniques. These benefits are discussed in this section.

## The Benefits of Activity-Based Costing

Activity-based costing improves the accuracy of product costs in three ways. First, activity-based costing usually increases the number of cost pools used to accumulate overhead costs. Rather than accumulating all overhead costs in a single, plantwide pool, or accumulating them in departmental pools, the company accumulates costs for each major activity. Second, the activity cost pools are more homogeneous than departmental cost pools. In principle, all of the costs in an activity cost pool pertain to a single activity. In contrast, departmental cost pools contain the costs of many different activities carried out in the department. Third, activity-based costing uses a variety of activity measures to assign overhead costs to products, some of which are correlated with volume and some of which are not. This differs from conventional approaches that rely exclusively on direct labor-hours or other measures of volume such as machine-hours to assign overhead costs to products.

Because conventional costing systems typically apply overhead costs to products using direct labor-hours, it may appear to managers that overhead costs are caused by direct labor-hours. Activity-based costing makes it clear that batch setups, engineering change orders, and other activities cause overhead costs rather than just direct labor. Managers thus have a better understanding of the causes of overhead costs, which should lead to better decisions and better cost control.

Finally, activity-based costing highlights the activities that could benefit most from process improvement initiatives. Thus, activity-based costing can be used as a part of programs to improve operations.

## Limitations of Activity-Based Costing

Any discussion of activity-based costing is incomplete without some cautionary warnings. First, the cost of implementing and maintaining an activity-based costing system may outweigh the benefits. Second, it would be naïve to assume that product costs provided even by an activity-based costing system are always relevant when making decisions. These limitations are discussed below.

### The Cost of Implementing Activity-Based Costing

Implementing ABC is a major project that requires substantial resources. First, the cost system must be designed—preferably by a cross-functional team. This requires taking valued employees away from other tasks for a major project. In addition, the data used in the activity-based costing system must be collected and verified. In some cases, this requires collecting data that has never been collected before. In short, implementing and maintaining an activity-based costing system can present a formidable challenge, and management may decide that the costs are too great to justify the expected benefits. Nevertheless, it should be kept in mind that the costs of collecting and processing data have dropped dramatically over the last several decades due to bar coding and other technologies, and these costs can be expected to continue to fall.

When are the benefits of activity-based costing most likely to be worth the cost? Companies that have some of the following characteristics are most likely to benefit from activity-based costing:

1. Products differ substantially in volume, batch size, and in the activities they require.
2. Conditions have changed substantially since the existing cost system was established.
3. Overhead costs are high and increasing and no one seems to understand why.
4. Management does not trust the existing cost system and ignores cost data from the system when making decisions.

### Limitations of the ABC Model

The activity-based costing model relies on a number of critical assumptions.[1] Perhaps the most important of these assumptions is that the cost in each activity cost pool is strictly proportional to its activity measure. What little evidence we have on this issue suggests that overhead costs are less than proportional to activity.[2] Economists call this increasing returns to scale—as activity increases, the average cost drops. As a practical matter, this means that product costs computed by a traditional or activity-based costing system will be overstated for the purposes of making decisions. The product costs generated by activity-based costing are almost certainly more accurate than those generated by a conventional costing system, but they should nevertheless be viewed with caution. Managers should be particularly alert to product costs that contain allocations of facility-level costs. As we shall see later in the book, product costs that include facility-level or organization-sustaining costs can easily lead managers astray.

### Modifying the ABC Model

The discussion in this chapter has assumed that companies use an absorption costing approach when they design an activity-based costing system. If the product costs are to be used by managers for internal decisions, some modifications should be made to the absorption approach. For example, for decision-making purposes, the distinction between manufacturing costs on the one hand and selling and administrative expenses on the other hand is unimportant. Managers need to know what costs a product causes, and it doesn't matter whether the costs are manufacturing costs or selling and administrative expenses. Consequently, for decision-making purposes, some selling and administrative expenses should be assigned to products as well as manufacturing costs. Moreover, as mentioned above, facility-level and organization-sustaining costs should be removed from product costs when making decisions. Nevertheless, the techniques covered in this chapter provide a good basis for understanding the mechanics

---

[1]Eric Noreen, "Conditions under Which Activity-Based Cost Systems Provide Relevant Costs," *Journal of Management Accounting Research,* Fall 1991, pp. 159–168.

[2]Eric Noreen and Naomi Soderstrom, "The Accuracy of Proportional Cost Models: Evidence from Hospital Service Departments," *Review of Accounting Studies* 2, 1997; and Eric Noreen and Naomi Soderstrom, "Are Overhead Costs Proportional to Activity? Evidence from Hospital Service Departments," *Journal of Accounting and Economics,* January 1994, pp. 253–278.

of activity-based costing. For a more complete coverage of the use of activity-based costing in decisions, see more advanced texts.[3]

## Bakery Owner

You are the owner of a bakery that makes a complete line of specialty breads, pastries, cakes, and pies for the retail and wholesale markets. A summer intern has just completed an activity-based costing study that concluded, among other things, that one of your largest recurring jobs is losing money. A local luxury hotel orders the same assortment of desserts every week for its Sunday brunch buffet for a fixed price of $975 per week. The hotel is quite happy with the quality of the desserts the bakery has been providing, but it would seek bids from other local bakeries if the price increased.

The activity-based costing study conducted by the intern revealed that the cost to the bakery of providing these desserts is $1,034 per week, resulting in an apparent loss of $59 per week or over $3,000 per year. Scrutinizing the intern's report, you find that the weekly cost of $1,034 includes facility-level costs of $329. These facility-level costs include portions of the rent on the bakery's building, your salary, depreciation on the office personal computer, and so on. The facility-level costs were arbitrarily allocated to the Sunday brunch job on the basis of direct labor-hours.

Should you demand an increase in price from the luxury hotel for the Sunday brunch desserts to at least $1,034? If an increase is not forthcoming, should you withdraw from the agreement and discontinue providing the desserts?

## Activity-Based Costing and Service Industries

Although initially developed as a tool for manufacturing companies, activity-based costing is also being used in service industries. Successful implementation of an activity-based costing system depends on identifying the key activities that generate costs and tracking how many of those activities are performed for each service the organization provides. Activity-based costing has been implemented in a wide variety of service industries including railroads, hospitals, banks, and data services companies.

**CONCEPT CHECK**

3.   Which of the following explain why activity-based costing improves product cost accuracy when compared to traditional methods? (You may select more than one answer.)
   a.  Activity-based costing typically uses more cost pools than traditional methods.
   b.  Activity-based costing assigns direct labor costs to products, whereas traditional methods do not.
   c.  Activity-based costing often uses a plantwide overhead allocation, whereas traditional methods do not.
   d.  Activity-based costing uses a variety of activity measures to assign overhead costs to products, some of which are correlated with volume and some of which are not.
4.   Which of the following statements is false? (You may select more than one answer.)
   a.  Activity-based costing systems usually shift costs from low-volume products to high-volume products.
   b.  Benchmarking can be used to identify activities with the greatest potential for improvement.
   c.  Activity-based costing is most valuable to companies that manufacture products that are similar in terms of their volume of production, batch size, and complexity.
   d.  Activity-based costing systems are based on the assumption that the costs included in each activity cost pool are strictly proportional to the cost pools activity measure.

---

[3]See, for example, Chapter 7 and its Appendix 7A in Ray Garrison, Eric Noreen, and Peter Brewer, *Managerial Accounting,* 16th edition, McGraw-Hill Education © 2018.

**LO4–1 Understand the basic approach in activity-based costing and how it differs from conventional costing.**

Activity-based costing was developed to more accurately assign overhead costs to products. Activity-based costing differs from conventional costing as described in earlier chapters in two major ways. First, in activity-based costing, each major activity that consumes overhead resources has its own cost pool and its own activity rate, whereas the plantwide approach described in earlier chapters relied on a single overhead cost pool and a single predetermined overhead rate. Second, the allocation bases (or activity measures) in activity-based costing are diverse. They may include machine setups, purchase orders, engineering change orders, and so on, in addition to direct labor-hours or machine-hours.

**LO4–2 Compute activity rates for an activity-based costing system.**

Each activity in an activity-based costing system has its own cost pool and its own activity measure. The activity rate for a particular activity is computed by dividing the total cost in the activity's cost pool by the total amount of activity.

**LO4–3 Compute product costs using activity-based costing.**

Product costs in activity-based costing, as in conventional costing systems, consist of direct materials, direct labor, and overhead. In the case of an activity-based costing system, each activity has its own activity rate. The activities required by a product are multiplied by their respective activity rates to determine the amount of overhead that is assigned to the product.

**LO4–4 Contrast the product costs computed under activity-based costing and conventional costing methods.**

Under conventional costing methods, overhead costs are applied to products using some measure of volume such as direct labor-hours or machine-hours. This results in most of the overhead cost being applied to high-volume products. In contrast, under activity-based costing, some overhead costs are assigned on the basis of batch-level or product-level activities. This change in allocation bases shifts overhead costs from high-volume products to low-volume products. Accordingly, product costs for high-volume products are commonly lower under activity-based costing than under conventional costing methods, and product costs for low-volume products are higher.

## GUIDANCE ANSWERS TO DECISION POINT

**Bakery Owner**

The bakery really isn't losing money on the weekly order of desserts from the luxury hotel. By definition, facility-level costs are not affected by individual products and jobs—these costs would continue unchanged even if the weekly order were dropped. Recalling the discussion in Chapter 1 concerning decision making, only those costs and benefits that differ between alternatives in a decision are relevant. Because the facility-level costs would be the same whether the dessert order is kept or dropped, they are not relevant in this decision and should be ignored. Hence, the real cost of the job is $705 ($1,034 − $329), which reveals that the job actually yields a weekly profit of $270 ($975 − $705) rather than a loss.

No, the bakery owner should not press for a price increase—particularly if that would result in the hotel seeking bids from competitors. And no, the bakery owner certainly should not withdraw from the agreement to provide the desserts.

## GUIDANCE ANSWERS TO CONCEPT CHECKS

1. **Choice d.** Product-level costs are unrelated to the amount of a product that is made.
2. **Choices a, b, and d.** Setting up equipment is an example of a batch-level activity.
3. **Choices a and d.** Traditional methods assign direct labor costs to products and they often rely on plantwide overhead allocation.
4. **Choices a and c.** Activity-based costing systems usually shift costs from high-volume products to low-volume products. Activity-based costing is most valuable for companies with highly diverse products rather than with similar products.

# REVIEW PROBLEM: ACTIVITY-BASED COSTING

Aerodec, Inc., manufactures and sells two types of wooden deck chairs: Deluxe and Tourist. Annual sales in units, direct labor-hours (DLHs) per unit, and total direct labor-hours per year are provided below:

| | |
|---|---|
| Deluxe deck chair: 2,000 units × 5 DLHs per unit. | 10,000 |
| Tourist deck chair: 10,000 units × 4 DLHs per unit. | 40,000 |
| Total direct labor-hours | 50,000 |

Costs for direct materials and direct labor for one unit of each product are given below:

| | Deluxe | Tourist |
|---|---|---|
| Direct materials | $25 | $17 |
| Direct labor (at $12 per DLH) | $60 | $48 |

Manufacturing overhead costs total $800,000 each year. The breakdown of these costs among the company's six activity cost pools is given below. The activity measures are shown in parentheses.

| Activity Cost Pools and (Activity Measures) | Estimated Overhead Cost | Expected Activity Deluxe | Tourist | Total |
|---|---|---|---|---|
| Labor-related (direct labor-hours) | $ 80,000 | 10,000 | 40,000 | 50,000 |
| Machine setups (number of setups) | 150,000 | 3,000 | 2,000 | 5,000 |
| Parts administration (number of parts) | 160,000 | 50 | 30 | 80 |
| Production orders (number of orders) | 70,000 | 100 | 300 | 400 |
| Material receipts (number of receipts) | 90,000 | 150 | 600 | 750 |
| General factory (machine-hours) | 250,000 | 12,000 | 28,000 | 40,000 |
| | $800,000 | | | |

**Required:**
1. Classify each of Aerodec's activities as either a unit-level, batch-level, product-level, or facility-level activity.
2. Assume that the company applies overhead cost to products on the basis of direct labor-hours.
   a. Compute the predetermined overhead rate.
   b. Determine the unit product cost of each product, using the predetermined overhead rate computed in (2)(a) above.
3. Assume that the company uses activity-based costing to compute overhead rates.
   a. Compute the activity rate for each of the six activities listed above.
   b. Using the rates developed in (3)(a) above, determine the amount of overhead cost that would be assigned to a unit of each product.
   c. Determine the unit product cost of each product and compare this cost to the cost computed in (2)(b) above.

**Solution to Review Problem**
1.

| Activity Cost Pool | Type of Activity |
|---|---|
| Labor-related | Unit-level |
| Machine setups | Batch-level |
| Parts administration | Product-level |
| Production orders | Batch-level |
| Material receipts | Batch-level |
| General factory | Facility-level |

2.   a.   Predetermined overhead rate $= \dfrac{\text{Estimated total manufacturing overhead}}{\text{Estimated total amount of the allocation base}}$

$= \dfrac{\$800,000}{50,000 \text{ DLHs}} = \$16 \text{ per DLH}$

b.

|  | Deluxe | Tourist |
|---|---|---|
| Direct materials.......................... | $ 25 | $ 17 |
| Direct labor ............................... | 60 | 48 |
| Manufacturing overhead applied: |  |  |
| Deluxe: 5 DLHs × $16 per DLH.............. | 80 |  |
| Tourist: 4 DLHs × $16 per DLH .............. |  | 64 |
| Unit product cost ......................... | $165 | $129 |

3.   a.

| Activity Cost Pools | (a) Estimated Overhead Cost | (b) Total Expected Activity | (a) ÷ (b) Activity Rate |
|---|---|---|---|
| Labor-related............ | $80,000 | 50,000 DLHs | $1.60 per DLH |
| Machine setups ......... | $150,000 | 5,000 setups | $30.00 per setup |
| Parts administration...... | $160,000 | 80 parts | $2,000.00 per part |
| Production orders........ | $70,000 | 400 orders | $175.00 per order |
| Material receipts......... | $90,000 | 750 receipts | $120.00 per receipt |
| General factory.......... | $250,000 | 40,000 MHs | $6.25 per MH |

b.

| Activity Cost Pools and Activity Rates | Deluxe Expected Activity | Deluxe Amount | Tourist Expected Activity | Tourist Amount |
|---|---|---|---|---|
| Labor-related, at $1.60 per DLH ........... | 10,000 | $ 16,000 | 40,000 | $ 64,000 |
| Machine setups, at $30 per setup.......... | 3,000 | 90,000 | 2,000 | 60,000 |
| Parts administration, at $2,000 per part..... | 50 | 100,000 | 30 | 60,000 |
| Production orders, at $175 per order....... | 100 | 17,500 | 300 | 52,500 |
| Material receipts, at $120 per receipt....... | 150 | 18,000 | 600 | 72,000 |
| General factory, at $6.25 per MH .......... | 12,000 | 75,000 | 28,000 | 175,000 |
| Total overhead cost assigned (a)........... |  | $316,500 |  | $483,500 |
| Number of units produced (b).............. |  | 2,000 |  | 10,000 |
| Overhead cost per unit, (a) ÷ (b)........... |  | $158.25 |  | $48.35 |

c.

|  | Deluxe | Tourist |
|---|---|---|
| Direct materials ............................. | $ 25.00 | $ 17.00 |
| Direct labor................................ | 60.00 | 48.00 |
| Manufacturing overhead (see above) .......... | 158.25 | 48.35 |
| Unit product cost........................... | $243.25 | $113.35 |

Under activity-based costing, the unit product cost of the Deluxe deck chair is much greater than the cost computed in (2)(b), and the unit product cost of the Tourist deck chair is much less. Using volume (direct labor-hours) in (2)(b) to apply overhead cost to products results in too little overhead cost being applied to the Deluxe deck chair (the low-volume product) and too much overhead cost being applied to the Tourist deck chair (the high-volume product).

## GLOSSARY

**Activity**   An event that causes the consumption of overhead resources. (p. 150)

**Activity-based costing (ABC)**   A two-stage costing method in which overhead costs are assigned to products on the basis of the activities they require. (p. 149)

**Activity-based management**   A management approach that focuses on managing activities as a way of eliminating waste and reducing delays and defects. (p. 160)

**Activity cost pool**   A "bucket" in which costs are accumulated that relate to a single activity measure in an activity-based costing system. (p. 151)

**Activity measure**   An allocation base in an activity-based costing system; ideally, a measure of whatever causes the costs in an activity cost pool. (p. 151)

**Activity rate**   An overhead rate in activity-based costing. Each activity cost pool has its own activity rate which is used to assign overhead to products and services. (p. 151)

**Batch-level activities**   Activities that are performed each time a batch of goods is handled or processed, regardless of how many units are in a batch. The amount of resources consumed depends on the number of batches run rather than on the number of units in the batch. (p. 152)

**Benchmarking**   A systematic approach to identifying the activities with the greatest room for improvement. It is based on comparing the performance in an organization with the performance of other, similar organizations known for their outstanding performance. (p. 160)

**Facility-level activities**   Activities that are carried out regardless of which products are produced, how many batches are run, or how many units are made. (p. 152)

**Product-level activities**   Activities that relate to specific products that must be carried out regardless of how many units are produced and sold or batches run. (p. 152)

**Unit-level activities**   Activities that arise as a result of the total volume of goods and services that are produced, and that are performed each time a unit is produced. (p. 151)

## QUESTIONS

**4–1**   What are the three common approaches for assigning overhead costs to products?

**4–2**   Why does activity-based costing appeal to some companies?

**4–3**   Why do departmental overhead rates sometimes result in inaccurate product costs?

**4–4**   What are the four hierarchical levels of activity discussed in the chapter?

**4–5**   Why is activity-based costing described as a "two-stage" costing method?

**4–6**   Why do overhead costs often shift from high-volume products to low-volume products when a company switches from a conventional costing method to activity-based costing?

**4–7**   What are the three major ways in which activity-based costing improves the accuracy of product costs?

**4–8**   What are the major limitations of activity-based costing?

## APPLYING EXCEL    ■ connect

**LO4–1, LO4–2, LO4–3, LO4–4**

A form for using Excel to recreate the Review Problem related to Aerodec, Inc., is shown below. For simplicity, the form excludes the Parts Administration and Material Receipts activities that were included in the Review Problem. Download the workbook containing this form in the *Connect Library*. On the website *you will also receive instructions about how to use this worksheet form.*

| | A | B | C | D | E | F | G |
|---|---|---|---|---|---|---|---|
| 1 | Chapter 4: Applying Excel | | | | | | |
| 2 | | | | | | | |
| 3 | Enter a formula into each of the cells marked with a ? below | | | | | | |
| 4 | Review Problem: Activity-Based Costing | | | | | | |
| 5 | | | | | | | |
| 6 | Data | | | | | | |
| 7 | | Deluxe | Tourist | | | | |
| 8 | Annual sales in units | 2,000 | 10,000 | | | | |
| 9 | Direct materials per unit | $25 | $17 | | | | |
| 10 | Direct labor-hours per unit | 5 | 4 | | | | |
| 11 | | | | | | | |
| 12 | Direct labor rate | $12 per DLH | | | | | |
| 13 | | | | | | | |
| 14 | | Estimated | | | | | |
| 15 | | Overhead | | Expected Activity | | | |
| 16 | Activities and Activity Measures | Cost | Deluxe | Tourist | Total | | |
| 17 | Labor-related (direct labor-hours) | $ 80,000 | ? | ? | ? | | |
| 18 | Machine setups (setups) | 150,000 | 3,000 | 2,000 | ? | | |
| 19 | Production orders (orders) | 70,000 | 100 | 300 | ? | | |
| 20 | General factory (machine-hours) | 250,000 | 12,000 | 28,000 | ? | | |
| 21 | | ? | | | | | |
| 22 | | | | | | | |
| 23 | Compute the predetermined overhead rate | | | | | | |
| 24 | Estimated total manufacturing overhead (a) | | ? | | | | |
| 25 | Estimated total amount of the allocation base (b) | | ? DLHs | | | | |
| 26 | Predetermined overhead rate (a) ÷ (b) | | ? per DLH | | | | |
| 27 | | | | | | | |
| 28 | Compute the manufacturing overhead applied | | Deluxe | | Tourist | | |
| 29 | Direct labor-hours per unit (a) | | ? DLHs | | ? DLHs | | |
| 30 | Predetermined overhead rate (b) | | ? per DLH | | ? per DLH | | |
| 31 | Manufacturing overhead applied per unit (a) × (b) | | ? | | ? | | |
| 32 | | | | | | | |
| 33 | Compute traditional unit product costs | Deluxe | Tourist | | | | |
| 34 | Direct materials | ? | ? | | | | |
| 35 | Direct labor | ? | ? | | | | |
| 36 | Manufacturing overhead applied | ? | ? | | | | |
| 37 | Traditonal unit product cost | ? | ? | | | | |
| 38 | | | | | | | |
| 39 | Compute activity rates | Estimated | | | | | |
| 40 | | Overhead | | | | | |
| 41 | Activities | Cost | Total Expected Activity | | Activity Rate | | |
| 42 | Labor-related | ? | ? DLHs | | ? per DLH | | |
| 43 | Machine setups | ? | ? setups | | ? per setup | | |
| 44 | Production orders | ? | ? orders | | ? per order | | |
| 45 | General factory | ? | ? MHs | | ? per MH | | |
| 46 | | | | | | | |
| 47 | Compute the ABC overhead cost per unit | | Deluxe | | Tourist | | |
| 48 | | Activity | Expected | | Expected | | |
| 49 | Activities | Rate | Activity | Amount | Activity | Amount | |
| 50 | Labor-related | ? | ? | ? | ? | ? | |
| 51 | Machine setups | ? | ? | ? | ? | ? | |
| 52 | Production orders | ? | ? | ? | ? | ? | |
| 53 | General factory | ? | ? | ? | ? | ? | |
| 54 | Total overhead cost assigned (a) | | | ? | | ? | |
| 55 | Number of units produced (b) | | | ? | | ? | |
| 56 | ABC overhead cost per unit (a) ÷ (b) | | | ? | | ? | |
| 57 | | | | | | | |
| 58 | Compute the ABC unit product costs | Deluxe | Tourist | | | | |
| 59 | Direct materials | ? | ? | | | | |
| 60 | Direct labor | ? | ? | | | | |
| 61 | ABC overhead cost per unit (see above) | ? | ? | | | | |
| 62 | ABC unit product cost | ? | ? | | | | |
| 63 | | | | | | | |

You should proceed to the requirements below only after completing your worksheet.

**Required:**
1. Check your worksheet by reducing the direct labor-hours per unit to 2 for the Deluxe model in cell B10. The Data area of the worksheet should look like this:

| Data | Deluxe | Tourist |
|---|---|---|
| Annual sales in units | 2,000 | 10,000 |
| Direct materials per unit | $25 | $17 |
| Direct labor-hours per unit | 2 | 4 |
| Direct labor rate | $12 per DLH | |

| Activity Cost Pools and (Activity Measures) | Estimated Overhead Cost | Expected Activity | | |
|---|---|---|---|---|
| | | Deluxe | Tourist | Total |
| Labor-related (direct labor-hours) ... | $ 80,000 | 4,000 | 40,000 | 44,000 |
| Machine setups (setups) . . . . . . . . . . . | 150,000 | 3,000 | 2,000 | 5,000 |
| Production orders (orders) . . . . . . . . . | 70,000 | 100 | 300 | 400 |
| General factory (machine-hours) . . . . | 250,000 | 12,000 | 28,000 | 40,000 |
| | $550,000 | | | |

The Deluxe model's unit product cost under traditional costing should now be $74.00 and the ABC unit product cost should be $143.89. If you do not get these results, find the errors in your worksheet and correct them.

    a. What happened to the predetermined overhead rate when the direct labor-hour requirement for the Deluxe model dropped from 5 hours to 2 hours? Explain.

    b. Compare the unit product costs for the *Tourist* model before and after changing the direct labor-hour requirements for the *Deluxe* model. The traditional unit product cost of the Tourist model increased from $109 to $115 when the direct labor-hour requirement for the Deluxe model changed from 5 to 2 hours per unit. In contrast, the ABC unit product cost of the Tourist model increased from $100.15 to $101.02. Which costing method do you trust more for making decisions? Explain.

2.   Change the direct labor-hour requirement for the Deluxe model back to 5 hours in cell B10. Assume that the production orders change so that the Deluxe model will have 300 orders in cell C19 and the Tourist model will have 100 orders in cell D19. The Data area should now look like this:

| Data | Deluxe | Tourist |
|---|---|---|
| Annual sales in units. . . . . . . . . . . . . . . . . | 2,000 | 10,000 |
| Direct materials per unit. . . . . . . . . . . . . . | $25 | $17 |
| Direct labor-hours per unit. . . . . . . . . . . . | 5 | 4 |
| Direct labor rate. . . . . . . . . . . . . . . . . . . . | $12 per DLH | |

| Activity Cost Pools and (Activity Measures) | Estimated Overhead Cost | Expected Activity | | |
|---|---|---|---|---|
| | | Deluxe | Tourist | Total |
| Labor-related (direct labor-hours) ... | $ 80,000 | 10,000 | 40,000 | 50,000 |
| Machine setups (setups) . . . . . . . . . . . | 150,000 | 3,000 | 2,000 | 5,000 |
| Production orders (orders) . . . . . . . . . | 70,000 | 300 | 100 | 400 |
| General factory (machine-hours) . . . . | 250,000 | 12,000 | 28,000 | 40,000 |
| | $550,000 | | | |

    a. What effect does this change have on the traditional unit product costs? Explain.

    b. What effect does this change have on the ABC unit product costs? Explain.

    c. Which method, the traditional direct labor-based costing system or the ABC costing system, apparently provides more accurate costs? Explain.

3.   Change the data in red so that the Data area looks like this:

| Data | Deluxe | Tourist |
|---|---|---|
| Annual sales in units. . . . . . . . . . . . . . . . . | 1,000 | 9,000 |
| Direct materials per unit. . . . . . . . . . . . . . | $20 | $20 |
| Direct labor-hours per unit. . . . . . . . . . . . | 1 | 1 |
| Direct labor rate. . . . . . . . . . . . . . . . . . . . | $10 per DLH | |

| Activity Cost Pools and (Activity Measures) | Estimated Overhead Cost | Expected Activity | | |
|---|---|---|---|---|
| | | Deluxe | Tourist | Total |
| Labor-related (direct labor-hours) . . . | $ 33,000 | 1,000 | 9,000 | 10,000 |
| Machine setups (setups) . . . . . . . . . . . | 120,000 | 20 | 80 | 100 |
| Production orders (orders) . . . . . . . . . | 70,000 | 15 | 35 | 50 |
| General factory (machine-hours) . . . . | 150,000 | 10,000 | 10,000 | 20,000 |
| | $373,000 | | | |

a. Are the traditional unit product costs for the two products the same or different? Explain.
b. Are the ABC unit product costs for the two products the same or different? Explain.
c. Which method, the traditional direct labor-based costing system or the ABC costing system, apparently provides more accurate costs? Explain.

**connect**  THE FOUNDATIONAL 15

Greenwood Company manufactures two products—14,000 units of Product Y and 6,000 units of Product Z. The company uses a plantwide overhead rate based on direct labor-hours. It is considering implementing an activity-based costing (ABC) system that allocates all of its manufacturing overhead to four cost pools. The following additional information is available for the company as a whole and for Products Y and Z:

LO4–1, LO4–2, LO4–3, LO4–4

| Activity Cost Pool | Activity Measure | Estimated Overhead Cost | Expected Activity | |
|---|---|---|---|---|
| Machining. . . . . . . . . . . . . . . . . . . | Machine-hours | $200,000 | 10,000 | MHs |
| Machine setups . . . . . . . . . . . . . . | Number of setups | $100,000 | 200 | setups |
| Production design. . . . . . . . . . . | Number of products | $84,000 | 2 | products |
| General factory . . . . . . . . . . . . . | Direct labor-hours | $300,000 | 12,000 | DLHs |

| Activity Measure | Product Y | Product Z |
|---|---|---|
| Machining . . . . . . . . . . . . . . . . . . . | 8,000 | 2,000 |
| Number of setups. . . . . . . . . . . . . | 40 | 160 |
| Number of products. . . . . . . . . . . | 1 | 1 |
| Direct labor-hours. . . . . . . . . . . . | 9,000 | 3,000 |

1. What is the company's plantwide overhead rate?
2. Using the plantwide overhead rate, how much manufacturing overhead cost is allocated to Product Y? How much is allocated to Product Z?
3. What is the activity rate for the Machining activity cost pool?
4. What is the activity rate for the Machine Setups activity cost pool?
5. What is the activity rate for the Product Design activity cost pool?
6. What is the activity rate for the General Factory activity cost pool?
7. Which of the four activities is a batch-level activity? Why?
8. Which of the four activities is a product-level activity? Why?
9. Using the ABC system, how much total manufacturing overhead cost would be assigned to Product Y?
10. Using the ABC system, how much total manufacturing overhead cost would be assigned to Product Z?
11. Using the plantwide overhead rate, what percentage of the total overhead cost is allocated to Product Y? What percentage is allocated to Product Z?
12. Using the ABC system, what percentage of the Machining costs is assigned to Product Y? What percentage is assigned to Product Z? Are these percentages similar to those obtained in question 11? Why?

13. Using the ABC system, what percentage of Machine Setups cost is assigned to Product Y? What percentage is assigned to Product Z? Are these percentages similar to those obtained in question 11? Why?

14. Using the ABC system, what percentage of the Product Design cost is assigned to Product Y? What percentage is assigned to Product Z? Are these percentages similar to those obtained in question 11? Why?

15. Using the ABC system, what percentage of the General Factory cost is assigned to Product Y? What percentage is assigned to Product Z? Are these percentages similar to those obtained in question 11? Why?

## EXERCISES          connect

**EXERCISE 4–1   ABC Cost Hierarchy LO4–1**
The following activities occur at Greenwich Corporation, a company that manufactures a variety of products:

a.  Various individuals manage the parts inventories.
b.  A clerk in the factory issues purchase orders for a job.
c.  The personnel department trains new production workers.
d.  The factory's general manager meets with other department heads to coordinate plans.
e.  Direct labor workers assemble products.
f.  Engineers design new products.
g.  The materials storekeeper issues raw materials to be used in jobs.
h.  The maintenance department performs periodic preventive maintenance on general-use equipment.

*Required:*
Classify each of the activities above as either a unit-level, batch-level, product-level, or facility-level activity.

**EXERCISE 4–2   Compute Activity Rates LO4–2**
Rustafson Corporation is a diversified manufacturer of consumer goods. The company's activity-based costing system has the following seven activity cost pools:

| Activity Cost Pool | Estimated Overhead Cost | Expected Activity |
|---|---|---|
| Labor-related . . . . . . . . . . | $52,000 | 8,000 direct labor-hours |
| Machine-related. . . . . . . . | $15,000 | 20,000 machine-hours |
| Machine setups . . . . . . . . | $42,000 | 1,000 setups |
| Production orders . . . . . . | $18,000 | 500 orders |
| Product testing. . . . . . . . . | $48,000 | 2,000 tests |
| Packaging. . . . . . . . . . . . | $75,000 | 5,000 packages |
| General factory . . . . . . . . | $108,800 | 8,000 direct labor-hours |

*Required:*
1.  Compute the activity rate for each activity cost pool.
2.  Compute the company's predetermined overhead rate, assuming that the company uses a single plantwide predetermined overhead rate based on direct labor-hours.

**EXERCISE 4–3   Compute ABC Product Costs LO4–3**
Larner Corporation is a diversified manufacturer of industrial goods. The company's activity-based costing system contains the following six activity cost pools and activity rates:

| Activity Cost Pool | Activity Rates |
|---|---|
| Labor-related . . . . . . . . . . . . . . . . | $7.00 per direct labor-hour |
| Machine-related. . . . . . . . . . . . . . | $3.00 per machine-hour |
| Machine setups . . . . . . . . . . . . . . | $40.00 per setup |
| Production orders . . . . . . . . . . . . | $160.00 per order |
| Shipments. . . . . . . . . . . . . . . . . . | $120.00 per shipment |
| General factory . . . . . . . . . . . . . . | $4.00 per direct labor-hour |

Cost and activity data have been supplied for the following products:

|  | J78 | B52 |
|---|---|---|
| Direct materials cost per unit ......... | $6.50 | $31.00 |
| Direct labor cost per unit ............. | $3.75 | $6.00 |
| Number of units produced per year.... | 4,000 | 100 |

|  | Total Expected Activity | |
|---|---|---|
|  | J78 | B52 |
| Direct labor-hours ................. | 1,000 | 40 |
| Machine-hours..................... | 3,200 | 30 |
| Machine setups ................... | 5 | 1 |
| Production orders ................. | 5 | 1 |
| Shipments......................... | 10 | 1 |

**Required:**
Compute the unit product cost of each product listed above.

**EXERCISE 4–4  Contrast ABC and Conventional Product Costs LO4–4**
Pacifica Industrial Products Corporation makes two products, Product H and Product L. Product H is expected to sell 40,000 units next year and Product L is expected to sell 8,000 units. A unit of either product requires 0.4 direct labor-hours.
   The company's total manufacturing overhead for the year is expected to be $1,632,000.

**Required:**
1.   The company currently applies manufacturing overhead to products using direct labor-hours as the allocation base. If this method is followed, how much overhead cost would be applied to each product? Compute both the overhead cost per unit and the total amount of overhead cost that would be applied to each product. (In other words, how much overhead cost is applied to a unit of Product H? Product L? How much overhead cost is applied in total to all the units of Product H? Product L?)
2.   Management is considering an activity-based costing system and would like to know what impact this change might have on product costs. For purposes of discussion, it has been suggested that all of the manufacturing overhead be treated as a product-level cost. The total manufacturing overhead would be divided in half between the two products, with $816,000 assigned to Product H and $816,000 assigned to Product L.
If this suggestion is followed, how much overhead cost per unit would be assigned to each product?
3.   Explain the impact on unit product costs of the switch in costing systems.

**EXERCISE 4–5  Assigning Overhead to Products in ABC LO4–2, LO4–3**
Sultan Company uses an activity-based costing system.
   At the beginning of the year, the company made the following estimates of cost and activity for its five activity cost pools:

| Activity Cost Pool | Activity Measure | Expected Overhead Cost | Expected Activity |
|---|---|---|---|
| Labor-related................. | Direct labor-hours | $156,000 | 26,000 DLHs |
| Purchase orders .............. | Number of orders | $11,000 | 220 orders |
| Parts management............ | Number of part types | $80,000 | 100 part types |
| Board etching ............... | Number of boards | $90,000 | 2,000 boards |
| General factory.............. | Machine-hours | $180,000 | 20,000 MHs |

**Required:**
1.   Compute the activity rate for each of the activity cost pools.
2.   The expected activity for the year was distributed among the company's four products as follows:

| Activity Cost Pool | Expected Activity | | | |
| --- | --- | --- | --- | --- |
| | Product A | Product B | Product C | Product D |
| Labor-related (DLHs)................... | 6,000 | 11,000 | 4,000 | 5,000 |
| Purchase orders (orders) ............... | 60 | 30 | 40 | 90 |
| Parts management (part types).......... | 30 | 15 | 40 | 15 |
| Board etching (boards)................. | 500 | 900 | 600 | 0 |
| General factory (MHs)................. | 3,000 | 8,000 | 3,000 | 6,000 |

Using the ABC data, determine the total amount of overhead cost assigned to each product.

**EXERCISE 4–6   Cost Hierarchy and Activity Measures LO4–1**

Various activities at Companhia de Textils, S.A., a manufacturing company located in Brazil, are listed below. The company makes a variety of products in its plant outside São Paulo.
a.   Preventive maintenance is performed on general-purpose production equipment.
b.   Products are assembled by hand.
c.   A security guard patrols the company grounds after normal working hours.
d.   Purchase orders are issued for materials to be used in production.
e.   Modifications are made to product designs.
f.   New employees are hired by the personnel office.
g.   Machine settings are changed between batches of different products.
h.   Parts inventories are maintained in the storeroom. (Each product requires its own unique parts.)
i.   Insurance costs are incurred on the company's facilities.

**Required:**
1.   Classify each of the activities as either a unit-level, batch-level, product-level, or facility-level activity.
2.   Where possible, name one or more activity measures that could be used to assign costs generated by the activity to products or customers.

**EXERCISE 4–7   Contrast ABC and Conventional Product Costs LO4–2, LO4–3, LO4–4**

Kunkel Company makes two products and uses a conventional costing system in which a single plantwide predetermined overhead rate is computed based on direct labor-hours. Data for the two products for the upcoming year follow:

| | Mercon | Wurcon |
| --- | --- | --- |
| Direct materials cost per unit ........ | $10.00 | $8.00 |
| Direct labor cost per unit............ | $3.00 | $3.75 |
| Direct labor-hours per unit .......... | 0.20 | 0.25 |
| Number of units produced .......... | 10,000 | 40,000 |

These products are customized to some degree for specific customers.

**Required:**
1.   The company's manufacturing overhead costs for the year are expected to be $336,000. Using the company's conventional costing system, compute the unit product costs for the two products.
2.   Management is considering an activity-based costing system in which half of the overhead would continue to be allocated on the basis of direct labor-hours and half would be allocated on the basis of engineering design time. This time is expected to be distributed as follows during the upcoming year:

| | Mercon | Wurcon | Total |
| --- | --- | --- | --- |
| Engineering design time (in hours) ....... | 4,000 | 4,000 | 8,000 |

Compute the unit product costs for the two products using the proposed ABC system.
3.   Explain why the product costs differ between the two systems.

**EXERCISE 4–8 Computing ABC Product Costs** LO4–2, LO4–3

Performance Products Corporation makes two products, titanium Rims and Posts. Data regarding the two products follow:

|  | Direct Labor-Hours per Unit | Annual Production |
|---|---|---|
| Rims ................. | 0.40 | 20,000 units |
| Posts................. | 0.20 | 80,000 units |

Additional information about the company follows:

a. Rims require $17 in direct materials per unit, and Posts require $10.
b. The direct labor wage rate is $16 per hour.
c. Rims are more complex to manufacture than Posts and they require special equipment.
d. The ABC system has the following activity cost pools:

| Activity Cost Pool | Activity Measure | Estimated Overhead Cost | Rims | Posts | Total |
|---|---|---|---|---|---|
| Machine setups...................... | Number of setups | $21,600 | 100 | 80 | 180 |
| Special processing .................... | Machine-hours | $180,000 | 4,000 | 0 | 4,000 |
| General factory ...................... | Direct labor-hours | $288,000 | 8,000 | 16,000 | 24,000 |

*Required:*
1. Compute the activity rate for each activity cost pool.
2. Determine the unit product cost of each product according to the ABC system.

**EXERCISE 4–9 Compute and Use Activity Rates to Determine the Costs of Serving Customers** LO4–2, LO4–3

Med Max buys surgical supplies from a variety of manufacturers and then resells and delivers these supplies to dozens of hospitals. In the face of declining profits, Med Max decided to implement an activity-based costing system to improve its understanding of the costs incurred to serve each hospital. The company broke its selling and administrative expenses into four activities as shown below:

| Activity Cost Pool | Activity Measure | Total Cost | Total Activity |
|---|---|---|---|
| Customer deliveries............................. | Number of deliveries | $ 400,000 | 5,000 deliveries |
| Manual order processing ........................ | Number of manual orders | 300,000 | 4,000 orders |
| Electronic order processing ..................... | Number of electronic orders | 200,000 | 12,500 orders |
| Line item picking................................ | Number of line items picked | 500,000 | 400,000 line items |
| Total selling and administrative expenses ........... | | $1,400,000 | |

Med Max gathered the data below for two of the many hospitals that it serves—City General and County General:

| Activity Measure | City General | County General |
|---|---|---|
| Number of deliveries ..................... | 10 | 20 |
| Number of manual orders ................. | 0 | 40 |
| Number of electronic orders............... | 10 | 0 |
| Number of line items picked............... | 100 | 260 |

*Required:*
1. Compute the activity rate for each activity cost pool.
2. Compute the total activity costs that would be assigned to City General and County General.
3. Describe the purchasing behaviors that are likely to increase Med Max's cost to serve its customers.

**EXERCISE 4–10  Contrasting ABC and Conventional Product Costs** LO4–2, LO4–3, LO4–4
Rocky Mountain Corporation makes two types of hiking boots—Xactive and Pathbreaker. Data concerning these two product lines appear below:

|  | Xactive | Pathbreaker |
|---|---|---|
| Direct materials per unit . . . . . . . . . . . . . . . . . | $64.80 | $51.00 |
| Direct labor cost per unit. . . . . . . . . . . . . . . . | $18.20 | $13.00 |
| Direct labor-hours per unit . . . . . . . . . . . . . . | 1.4 DLHs | 1.0 DLHs |
| Estimated annual production and sales . . . . . | 25,000 units | 75,000 units |

The company has a conventional costing system in which manufacturing overhead is applied to units based on direct labor-hours. Data concerning manufacturing overhead and direct labor-hours for the upcoming year appear below:

| | |
|---|---|
| Estimated total manufacturing overhead . . . . . . . | $2,200,000 |
| Estimated total direct labor-hours . . . . . . . . . . . . | 110,000 DLHs |

*Required:*
1. Compute the predetermined overhead rate based on direct labor-hours. Using this rate and other data from the problem, determine the unit product cost of each product.
2. The company is considering replacing its conventional costing system with an activity-based costing system that would assign its manufacturing overhead to the following four activity cost pools:

| | | Expected Activity | | |
|---|---|---|---|---|
| Activity Cost Pools and (Activity Measures) | Estimated Overhead Cost | Xactive | Pathbreaker | Total |
| Supporting direct labor (direct labor-hours) . . . . . . | $  797,500 | 35,000 | 75,000 | 110,000 |
| Batch setups (setups) . . . . . . . . . . . . . . . . . . . . . . . . . | 680,000 | 250 | 150 | 400 |
| Product sustaining (number of products) . . . . . . . . | 650,000 | 1 | 1 | 2 |
| General factory (machine-hours). . . . . . . . . . . . . . . | 72,500 | 2,500 | 7,500 | 10,000 |
| Total manufacturing overhead cost . . . . . . . . . . . . | $2,200,000 | | | |

Determine the activity rate for each of the four activity cost pools.
3. Using the activity rates and other data from the problem, determine the unit product cost of each product.
4. Explain why the conventional and activity-based cost assignments differ.

**EXERCISE 4–11  Contrasting Activity-Based Costing and Conventional Product Costing** LO4–2, LO4–3, LO4–4
Rusties Company recently implemented an activity-based costing system. At the beginning of the year, management made the following estimates of cost and activity in the company's five activity cost pools:

| Activity Cost Pool | Activity Measure | Expected Overhead Cost | Expected Activity |
|---|---|---|---|
| Labor-related. . . . . . . . . . . . . . | Direct labor-hours | $18,000 | 2,000 DLHs |
| Purchase orders . . . . . . . . . . . | Number of orders | $1,050 | 525 orders |
| Product testing . . . . . . . . . . . . | Number of tests | $3,500 | 350 tests |
| Template etching . . . . . . . . . . | Number of templates | $700 | 28 templates |
| General factory . . . . . . . . . . . . | Machine-hours | $50,000 | 10,000 MHs |

*Required:*
1. Compute the activity rate for each of the activity cost pools.
2. The expected activity for the year was distributed among the company's four products as follows:

|                                          | Expected Activity |           |           |           |
| Activity Cost Pool                       | Product A | Product B | Product C | Product D |
|------------------------------------------|-----------|-----------|-----------|-----------|
| Labor-related (DLHs)....................  | 500       | 100       | 700       | 700       |
| Purchase orders (orders) ...............  | 80        | 105       | 180       | 160       |
| Product testing (tests)..................  | 200       | 60        | 0         | 90        |
| Template etching (templates) ...........  | 0         | 14        | 10        | 4         |
| General factory (MHs)...................  | 3,400     | 2,200     | 1,800     | 2,600     |

Using the ABC data, determine the total amount of overhead cost assigned to each product.

3. Assume that prior to implementing ABC, Rusties used a conventional cost system that applied all manufacturing overhead to products based on direct labor-hours. Explain how the conventional overhead cost assignments would differ from the activity-based cost assignments with respect to Product B.

## PROBLEMS

### PROBLEM 4–12  Contrasting ABC and Conventional Product cost LO4–2, LO4–3, LO4–4

Precision Manufacturing Inc. (PMI) makes two types of industrial component parts—the EX300 and the TX500. It annually produces 60,000 units of EX300 and 12,500 units of TX500. The company's conventional cost system allocates manufacturing overhead to products using a plantwide overhead rate and direct labor dollars as the allocation base. Additional information relating to the company's two product lines is shown below:

|                        | EX300     | TX500     | Total     |
|------------------------|-----------|-----------|-----------|
| Direct materials.....................  | $366,325  | $162,550  | $528,875  |
| Direct labor .......................  | $120,000  | $42,500   | $162,500  |

The company is considering implementing an activity-based costing system that distributes all of its manufacturing overhead to four activities as shown below:

|                                             | Manufacturing Overhead |    | Activity |    |
| Activity Cost Pool (and Activity Measure)   |          | EX300    | TX500    | Total     |
|---------------------------------------------|----------|----------|----------|-----------|
| Machining (machine-hours) ..................  | $198,250 | 90,000   | 62,500   | 152,500   |
| Setups (setup hours).......................  | 150,000  | 75       | 300      | 375       |
| Product-level (number of products) ...........  | 100,250  | 1        | 1        | 2         |
| General factory (direct labor dollars) .........  | 60,125   | $120,000 | $42,500  | $162,500  |
| Total manufacturing overhead cost ...........  | $508,625 |          |          |           |

*Required:*

1. Compute the plantwide overhead rate that would be used in the company's conventional cost system. Using the plantwide rate, compute the unit product cost for each product.
2. Compute the activity rate for each activity cost pool. Using the activity rates, compute the unit product cost for each product.
3. Why do the conventional and activity-based cost assignments differ from one another?

### PROBLEM 4–13  ABC Cost Hierarchy LO4–1

Mitchell Corporation manufactures a variety of products in a single facility. Consultants hired by the company to do an activity-based costing analysis have identified the following activities carried out in the company on a routine basis:

a. Milling machines are used to make components for products.
b. A percentage of all completed goods are inspected on a random basis.

c.  Production orders are issued for jobs.
d.  The company's grounds crew maintains planted areas surrounding the factory.
e.  Employees are trained in general procedures.
f.  The human resources department screens and hires new employees.
g.  Purchase orders are issued for materials required in production.
h.  Material is received on the receiving dock and moved to the production area.
i.  The plant controller prepares periodic accounting reports.
j.  The engineering department makes modifications in the designs of products.
k.  Machines are set up between batches of different products.
l.  The maintenance crew does routine periodic maintenance on general-purpose equipment.

**Required:**
1.  Classify each of the above activities as a unit-level, batch-level, product-level, or facility-level activity.
2.  For each of the above activities, suggest an activity measure that could be used to allocate its costs to products.

**PROBLEM 4–14   Compute and Use Activity Rates to Determine the Costs of Serving Customers LO4–2, LO4–3, LO4–4**
Gino's Restaurant is a popular restaurant in Boston, Massachusetts. The owner of the restaurant has been trying to better understand costs at the restaurant and has hired a student intern to conduct an activity-based costing study. The intern, in consultation with the owner, identified the following major activities:

| Activity Cost Pool | Activity Measure |
|---|---|
| Serving a party of diners | Number of parties served |
| Serving a diner | Number of diners served |
| Serving drinks | Number of drinks ordered |

A group of diners who ask to sit at the same table is counted as a party. Some costs, such as the costs of cleaning linen, are the same whether one person is at a table or the table is full. Other costs, such as washing dishes, depend on the number of diners served.
    Data concerning these activities are shown below:

|  | Serving a Party | Serving a Diner | Serving Drinks | Total |
|---|---|---|---|---|
| Total cost ..... | $32,800 | $211,200 | $69,600 | $313,600 |
| Total activity... | 8,000 parties | 32,000 diners | 58,000 drinks | |

Prior to the activity-based costing study, the owner knew very little about the costs of the restaurant. She knew that the total cost for the month was $313,600 and that 32,000 diners had been served. Therefore, the average cost per diner was $9.80 ($313,600 ÷ 32,000 diners = $9.80 per diner).

**Required:**
1.  Compute the activity rates for each of the three activities.
2.  According to the activity-based costing system, what is the total cost of serving each of the following parties of diners?
    a.  A party of four diners who order three drinks in total.
    b.  A party of two diners who do not order any drinks.
    c.  A lone diner who orders two drinks.
3.  Convert the total costs you computed in part (2) above to costs per diner. In other words, what is the average cost per diner for serving each of the following parties?
    a.  A party of four diners who order three drinks in total.
    b.  A party of two diners who do not order any drinks.
    c.  A lone diner who orders two drinks.
4.  Why do the costs per diner for the three different parties differ from each other and from the overall average cost of $9.80 per diner?

**PROBLEM 4–15   Contrasting ABC and Conventional Product Costs LO4–2, LO4–3, LO4–4**
Marine, Inc., manufactures a product that is available in both a flexible and a rigid model. The company has made the rigid model for years; the flexible model was introduced several years ago to tap a new segment of the market. Since introduction of the flexible model, the company's profits have steadily declined,

and management has become concerned about the accuracy of its costing system. Sales of the flexible model have been increasing rapidly.

Overhead is applied to products on the basis of direct labor-hours. At the beginning of the current year, management estimated that $600,000 in overhead costs would be incurred and the company would produce and sell 1,000 units of the flexible model and 10,000 units of the regular model. The flexible model requires 2.0 hours of direct labor time per unit, and the regular model requires 1.0 hours. Direct materials and labor costs per unit are given below:

|  | Flexible | Rigid |
|---|---|---|
| Direct materials cost per unit .......... | $110.00 | $80.00 |
| Direct labor cost per unit.............. | $30.00 | $15.00 |

**Required:**
1. Compute the predetermined overhead rate using direct labor-hours as the basis for allocating overhead costs to products. Compute the unit product cost for one unit of each model.
2. An intern suggested that the company use activity-based costing to cost its products. A team was formed to investigate this idea. It came back with the recommendation that four activity cost pools be used. These cost pools and their associated activities are listed as follows:

| Activity Cost Pool and Activity Measure | Estimated Overhead Cost | Expected Activity | | |
|---|---|---|---|---|
|  |  | Flexible | Rigid | Total |
| Purchase orders (number of orders) .......... | $ 20,000 | 100 | 300 | 400 |
| Rework requests (number of requests) ........ | 10,000 | 60 | 140 | 200 |
| Product testing (number of tests) ............ | 210,000 | 900 | 1,200 | 2,100 |
| Machine-related (machine-hours)............. | 360,000 | 1,500 | 2,500 | 4,000 |
|  | $600,000 |  |  |  |

Compute the activity rate for each of the activity cost pools.
3. Using activity-based costing, do the following:
   a. Determine the total amount of overhead that would be assigned to each model for the year.
   b. Compute the unit product cost for one unit of each model.
4. Can you identify a possible explanation for the company's declining profits? If so, what is it?

**PROBLEM 4–16  Contrasting ABC and Conventional Product Costs** LO4–2, LO4–3, LO4–4

For many years, Thomson Company manufactured a single product called LEC 40. Then three years ago, the company automated a portion of its plant and at the same time introduced a second product called LEC 90 that has become increasingly popular. The LEC 90 is a more complex product, requiring 0.80 hours of direct labor time per unit to manufacture and extensive machining in the automated portion of the plant. The LEC 40 requires only 0.40 hours of direct labor time per unit and only a small amount of machining. Manufacturing overhead costs are currently assigned to products on the basis of direct labor-hours.

Despite the growing popularity of the company's new LEC 90, profits have been declining steadily. Management is beginning to believe that there may be a problem with the company's costing system. Direct material and direct labor costs per unit are as follows:

|  | LEC 40 | LEC 90 |
|---|---|---|
| Direct materials..................................................... | $30.00 | $50.00 |
| Direct labor (0.40 hours and 0.80 hours @ $15.00 per hour)........ | $6.00 | $12.00 |

Management estimates that the company will incur $912,000 in manufacturing overhead costs during the current year and 60,000 units of the LEC 40 and 20,000 units of the LEC 90 will be produced and sold.

**Required:**
1. Compute the predetermined overhead rate assuming that the company continues to apply manufacturing overhead cost on the basis of direct labor-hours. Using this rate and other data from the problem, determine the unit product cost of each product.

2. Management is considering using activity-based costing to assign manufacturing overhead cost to products. The activity-based costing system would have the following four activity cost pools:

| Activity Cost Pool | Activity Measure | Estimated Overhead Cost |
|---|---|---|
| Maintaining parts inventory............ | Number of part types | $225,000 |
| Processing purchase orders........... | Number of purchase orders | 182,000 |
| Quality control...................... | Number of tests run | 45,000 |
| Machine-related .................... | Machine-hours | 460,000 |
| | | $912,000 |

| | Expected Activity | | |
|---|---|---|---|
| Activity Measure | LEC 40 | LEC 90 | Total |
| Number of part types ...................... | 600 | 900 | 1,500 |
| Number of purchase orders ................ | 2,000 | 800 | 2,800 |
| Number of tests run ....................... | 500 | 1,750 | 2,250 |
| Machine-hours............................ | 1,600 | 8,400 | 10,000 |

Determine the activity rate for each of the four activity cost pools.
3. Using the activity rates you computed in part (2) above, do the following:
   a. Determine the total amount of manufacturing overhead cost that would be assigned to each product using the activity-based costing system. After these totals have been computed, determine the amount of manufacturing overhead cost per unit of each product.
   b. Compute the unit product cost of each product.
4. From the data you have developed in parts (1) through (3) above, identify factors that may account for the company's declining profits.

**PROBLEM 4–17  Contrast Activity-Based Costing and Conventional Product Costing** LO4–2, LO4–3, LO4–4
Puget World, Inc., manufactures two models of television sets, the N 800 XL model and the N 500 model. Data regarding the two products follow:

| | Direct Labor-Hours per Unit | Annual Production | Total Direct Labor-Hours |
|---|---|---|---|
| Model N 800 XL ................... | 3.0 | 3,000 units | 9,000 |
| Model N 500 ...................... | 1.0 | 12,000 units | 12,000 |
| | | | 21,000 |

Additional information about the company follows:
a. Model N 800 XL requires $75 in direct materials per unit, and Model N 500 requires $25.
b. The direct labor wage rate is $18 per hour.
c. The company has always used direct labor-hours as the base for applying manufacturing overhead cost to products.
d. Model N 800 XL is more complex to manufacture than Model N 500 and requires the use of special equipment. Consequently, the company is considering the use of activity-based costing to assign manufacturing overhead cost to products. Three activity cost pools have been identified as follows:

| Activity Cost Pool | Activity Measure | Estimated Overhead Cost |
|---|---|---|
| Machine setups..................... | Number of setups | $ 360,000 |
| Special processing................... | Machine-hours | 165,000 |
| General factory..................... | Direct labor-hours | 1,260,000 |
| | | $1,785,000 |

| Activity Measure | Expected Activity | | |
|---|---|---|---|
|  | Model N 800 XL | Model N 500 | Total |
| Number of setups .................. | 100 | 200 | 300 |
| Machine-hours....................... | 16,500 | 0 | 16,500 |
| Direct labor-hours .................. | 9,000 | 12,000 | 21,000 |

**Required:**
1. Assume that the company continues to use direct labor-hours as the base for applying overhead cost to products.
   a. Compute the predetermined overhead rate.
   b. Compute the unit product cost of each model.
2. Assume that the company decides to use activity-based costing to assign manufacturing overhead cost to products.
   a. Compute the activity rate for each activity cost pool and determine the amount of overhead cost that would be assigned to each model using the activity-based costing system.
   b. Compute the unit product cost of each model.
3. Explain why manufacturing overhead cost shifts from Model N 500 to Model N 800 XL under activity-based costing.

**PROBLEM 4–18  Contrasting Activity-Based Costing and Conventional Product Costing LO4–2, LO4–3, LO4–4**

Adria Company recently implemented an activity-based costing system. At the beginning of the year, management made the following estimates of cost and activity in the company's five activity cost pools:

| Activity Cost Pool | Activity Measure | Expected Overhead Cost | Expected Activity |
|---|---|---|---|
| Labor-related ................ | Direct labor-hours | $35,000 | 7,000 DLHs |
| Purchase orders ............. | Number of orders | $4,000 | 2,000 orders |
| Material receipts ............. | Number of receipts | $10,450 | 950 receipts |
| Relay assembly .............. | Number of relays | $7,000 | 1,000 relays |
| General factory .............. | Machine-hours | $240,000 | 40,000 MHs |

**Required:**
1. Compute the activity rate for each of the activity cost pools.
2. The expected activity for the year was distributed among the company's four products as follows:

| Activity Cost Pool | Expected Activity | | | |
|---|---|---|---|---|
|  | Product A | Product B | Product C | Product D |
| Labor-related (DLHs)................... | 2,400 | 500 | 3,500 | 600 |
| Production orders (orders).............. | 100 | 350 | 800 | 750 |
| Materials receipts (receipts)............ | 400 | 208 | 342 | 0 |
| Relay assembly (relays) ............... | 170 | 170 | 300 | 360 |
| General factory (MHs)................. | 12,000 | 7,000 | 8,000 | 13,000 |

Using the ABC data, determine the total amount of overhead cost assigned to each product.
3. Assume that prior to implementing ABC, Adria used a conventional cost system that applied all manufacturing overhead to products based on machine-hours. Explain how the conventional cost assignments would differ from the activity-based cost assignments with respect to Product C.

# BUILDING YOUR SKILLS  ■ connect

### COMMUNICATING IN PRACTICE LO4–1

You often provide advice to Maria Graham, a client who is interested in diversifying her company. Maria is considering the purchase of a small manufacturing company that assembles and packages its many products by hand. She plans to automate the factory and her projections indicate that the company will once again be profitable within two to three years. During her review of the company's records, she discovered that the company currently uses direct labor-hours to allocate overhead to its products. Because of its simplicity, Maria hopes that this approach can continue to be used.

*Required:*

Write a memorandum to Maria that addresses whether or not direct labor should continue to be used as an allocation base for overhead.

### TEAMWORK IN ACTION LO4–1

Your team should visit and closely observe the operations at a fast-food restaurant.

*Required:*

Identify activities and costs at the restaurant that fall into each of the following categories:

a.  Unit-level activities and costs.
b.  Customer-level activities and costs. (This is like a batch-level activity at a manufacturing company.)
c.  Product-level activities and costs.
d.  Facility-level activities and costs.

### ETHICS CHALLENGE LO4–1

You and your friends go to a restaurant as a group. At the end of the meal, the issue arises of how the bill for the group should be shared. One alternative is to figure out the cost of what each individual consumed and divide up the bill accordingly. Another alternative is to split the bill equally among the individuals.

*Required:*

Which system for dividing the bill is more equitable? Which system is easier to use? How does this issue relate to the material covered in this chapter?

### CASE LO4–2, LO4–3, LO4–4

Coffee Bean, Inc. (CBI), is a processor and distributor of a variety of blends of coffee. The company buys coffee beans from around the world and roasts, blends, and packages them for resale. CBI offers a large variety of different coffees that it sells to gourmet shops in one-pound bags. The major cost of the coffee is raw materials. However, the company's predominantly automated roasting, blending, and packing processes require a substantial amount of manufacturing overhead. The company uses relatively little direct labor. Some of CBI's coffees are very popular and sell in large volumes, while a few of the newer blends sell in very low volumes.

For the coming year, CBI's budget includes estimated manufacturing overhead cost of $3,000,000. CBI assigns manufacturing overhead to products on the basis of direct labor-hours. The expected direct labor cost totals $600,000, which represents 50,000 hours of direct labor time.

The expected costs for direct materials and direct labor for one-pound bags of two of the company's coffee products appear below.

|                                      | Mona Loa | Malaysian |
|--------------------------------------|----------|-----------|
| Direct materials.....................| $4.20    | $3.20     |
| Direct labor (0.025 hours per bag) ..| $0.30    | $0.30     |

CBI's controller believes that the company's traditional costing system may be providing misleading cost information. To determine whether or not this is correct, the controller has prepared an analysis of the year's expected manufacturing overhead costs, as shown in the following table:

| Activity Cost Pool | Activity Measure | Expected Activity for the Year | Expected Cost for the Year |
|---|---|---|---|
| Purchasing............................. | Purchase orders | 1,710 orders | $ 513,000 |
| Material handling .................... | Number of setups | 1,800 setups | 720,000 |
| Quality control....................... | Number of batches | 600 batches | 144,000 |
| Roasting.............................. | Roasting hours | 96,100 roasting hours | 961,000 |
| Blending.............................. | Blending hours | 33,500 blending hours | 402,000 |
| Packaging ............................ | Packaging hours | 26,000 packaging hours | 260,000 |
| Total manufacturing overhead cost...... | | | $3,000,000 |

Data regarding the expected production of Mona Loa and Malaysian coffee are presented below. There will be no raw materials inventory for either of these coffees at the beginning of the year.

| | Mona Loa | Malaysian |
|---|---|---|
| Expected sales ...................... | 100,000 pounds | 2,000 pounds |
| Batch size.......................... | 10,000 pounds | 500 pounds |
| Setups.............................. | 3 per batch | 3 per batch |
| Purchase order size ................. | 20,000 pounds | 500 pounds |
| Roasting time per 100 pounds......... | 1.0 roasting hours | 1.0 roasting hours |
| Blending time per 100 pounds ........ | 0.5 blending hours | 0.5 blending hours |
| Packaging time per 100 pounds ....... | 0.1 packaging hours | 0.1 packaging hours |

**Required:**

1. Using direct labor-hours as the base for assigning manufacturing overhead cost to products, do the following:
   a. Determine the predetermined overhead rate that will be used during the year.
   b. Determine the unit product cost of one pound of the Mona Loa coffee and one pound of the Malaysian coffee.
2. Using activity-based costing as the basis for assigning manufacturing overhead cost to products, do the following:
   a. Determine the total amount of manufacturing overhead cost assigned to the Mona Loa coffee and to the Malaysian coffee for the year.
   b. Using the data developed in part (2a) above, compute the amount of manufacturing overhead cost per pound of the Mona Loa coffee and the Malaysian coffee. Round all computations to the nearest whole cent.
   c. Determine the unit product cost of one pound of the Mona Loa coffee and one pound of the Malaysian coffee.
3. Write a brief memo to the president of CBI explaining what you have found in parts (1) and (2) above and discussing the implications to the company of using direct labor as the base for assigning manufacturing overhead cost to products.

(CMA, adapted)

**ANALYTICAL THINKING\* LO4–2, LO4–3, LO4–4**

"Two dollars of gross margin per briefcase? That's ridiculous!" roared Roy Thurmond, president of First-Line Cases, Inc. "Why do we go on producing those standard briefcases when we're able to make over $11 per unit on our specialty items? Maybe it's time to get out of the standard line and focus the whole plant on specialty work."

---

\*Adapted from Harold P. Roth and Imogene Posey, "Management Accounting Case Study: Carry All Company," *Management Accounting Campus Report,* Institute of Management Accountants, Fall 1991, p. 9. Used by permission from the IMA, Montvale, NJ, USA, www.imanet.org.

Mr. Thurmond was referring to a summary of unit costs and revenues that he had just received from the company's accounting department:

| | Standard Briefcases | Specialty Briefcases |
|---|---|---|
| Selling price per unit ................. | $26.25 | $42.50 |
| Unit product cost .................... | 24.25 | 31.40 |
| Gross margin per unit ............... | $ 2.00 | $11.10 |

FirstLine Cases produces briefcases from leather, fabric, and synthetic materials in a single plant. The basic product is a standard briefcase that is made from leather lined with fabric. The standard briefcase is a high-quality item and has sold well for many years.

Last year, the company decided to expand its product line and produce specialty briefcases for special orders. These briefcases differ from the standard in that they vary in size, they contain the finest leather and synthetic materials, and they are imprinted with the buyer's name. To reduce labor costs on the specialty briefcases, automated machines do most of the cutting and stitching. These machines are used to a much lesser degree in the production of standard briefcases.

"I agree that the specialty business is looking better and better," replied Beth Mersey, the company's marketing manager. "And there seems to be plenty of demand out there, particularly because the competition hasn't been able to touch our price. Did you know that Velsun Company, our biggest competitor, charges over $50 a unit for its specialty items? Now that's what I call gouging the customer!"

A breakdown of the manufacturing cost for each of FirstLine Cases' products is given below:

| | Standard Briefcases | Specialty Briefcases |
|---|---|---|
| Units produced each month........................... | 10,000 | 2,500 |
| Direct materials: | | |
| Leather........................................... | $ 8.00 | $12.00 |
| Fabric............................................ | 2.00 | 1.00 |
| Synthetic ........................................ | 0 | 7.00 |
| Total materials..................................... | 10.00 | 20.00 |
| Direct labor (0.5 DLH and 0.40 DLH @ $12.00 per DLH) .... | 6.00 | 4.80 |
| Manufacturing overhead (0.5 DLH and 0.4 DLH @ $16.50 per DLH) .............. | 8.25 | 6.60 |
| Total cost per unit..................................... | $24.25 | $31.40 |

Manufacturing overhead is applied to products on the basis of direct labor-hours. The rate of $16.50 per hour was determined by dividing the total manufacturing overhead cost for a month by the direct labor-hours:

$$\text{Predetermined overhead rate} = \frac{\text{Manufacturing overhead}}{\text{Direct labor-hours}} = \frac{\$99,000}{6,000 \text{ DLHs}} = \$16.50 \text{ per DLH}$$

The following additional information is available about the company and its products:

a. Standard briefcases are produced in batches of 1,000 units, and specialty briefcases are produced in batches of 100 units. Thus, the company does 10 setups for the standard items each month and 25 setups for the specialty items. A setup for the standard items requires one hour, whereas a setup for the specialty items requires two hours.

b. All briefcases are inspected to ensure that quality standards are met. Each month a total of 200 hours is spent inspecting the standard briefcases and 400 hours is spent inspecting the specialty briefcases.

c. A standard briefcase requires 0.5 hours of machine time, and a specialty briefcase requires 1.2 hours of machine time.

d. The company is considering the use of activity-based costing as an alternative to its traditional costing system for computing unit product costs. The activity-based costing system has already been designed and costs have been allocated to the activity cost pools. The activity cost pools and activity measures are detailed below:

| Activity Cost Pool | Activity Measure | Estimated Overhead Cost |
|---|---|---|
| Purchasing...................... | Number of orders | $15,000 |
| Material handling ................. | Number of receipts | 16,000 |
| Production orders and setups ...... | Setup-hours | 6,000 |
| Inspection ....................... | Inspection-hours | 18,000 |
| Frame assembly ................. | Assembly-hours | 12,000 |
| Machine-related ................. | Machine-hours | 32,000 |
| | | $99,000 |

| | Expected Activity | | |
|---|---|---|---|
| Activity Measure | Standard Briefcases | Specialty Briefcases | Total |
| Number of orders: | | | |
| Leather ......................... | 50 | 10 | 60 |
| Fabric ......................... | 70 | 20 | 90 |
| Synthetic material ............... | 0 | 150 | 150 |
| Number of receipts: | | | |
| Leather ......................... | 70 | 10 | 80 |
| Fabric ......................... | 85 | 20 | 105 |
| Synthetic material ............... | 0 | 215 | 215 |
| Setup-hours ...................... | ? | ? | ? |
| Inspection-hours .................. | 200 | 400 | 600 |
| Assembly-hours.................... | 700 | 800 | 1,500 |
| Machine-hours.................... | ? | ? | ? |

**Required:**
1. Using activity-based costing, determine the amount of manufacturing overhead cost that would be assigned to each standard briefcase and each specialty briefcase.
2. Using the data computed in part (1) above and other data from the case as needed, determine the unit product cost of each product line from the perspective of the activity-based costing system.
3. Within the limitations of the data that have been provided, evaluate the president's concern about the profitability of the two product lines. Would you recommend that the company shift its resources entirely to the production of specialty briefcases? Explain.
4. Beth Mersey stated that "the competition hasn't been able to touch our price on specialty business." Why do you suppose the competition hasn't been able to touch FirstLine Cases' price?

**A LOOK BACK**

We described job-order costing systems in Chapters 2 and 3 and then looked at activity-based costing in Chapter 4. Activity-based costing uses a larger variety of allocation bases to assign overhead costs to products than conventional approaches.

**A LOOK AT THIS CHAPTER**

Chapter 5 covers process costing, which is an important alternative to job-order costing. In process costing, departmental costs are applied uniformly to the products processed through the department during the period.

**A LOOK AHEAD**

Chapter 6 describes the basics of cost-volume-profit analysis, a tool that helps managers understand the interrelationships among cost, volume, and profit.

# 5 Process Costing

## CHAPTER OUTLINE

**Comparison of Job-Order and Process Costing**

- Similarities between Job-Order and Process Costing

- Differences between Job-Order and Process Costing

**Cost Flows in Process Costing**

- Processing Departments

- The Flow of Materials, Labor, and Overhead Costs

- Materials, Labor, and Overhead Cost Entries

**Process Costing Computations: Three Key Concepts**

- Key Concept #1

- Key Concept #2

- Key Concept #3

**The Weighted-Average Method: An Example**

- Step 1: Compute the Equivalent Units of Production

- Step 2: Compute the Cost per Equivalent Unit

- Step 3: Assign Costs the Units

- Step 4: Prepare a Cost Reconciliation Report

**Operation Costing**

## SUPPLEMENT: PROCESS COSTING USING THE FIFO METHOD
### (available in Connect)

- Step 1: Compute the Equivalent Units of Production

- Step 2: Compute the Cost per Equivalent Unit

- Step 3: Assign Costs the Units

- Step 4: Prepare a Cost Reconciliation Report

- A Comparison of Costing Methods

©Kristoffer Tripplaar/Alamy Stock Photo

### LEARNING OBJECTIVES

*After studying Chapter 5, you should be able to:*

**LO5–1** Record the flow of materials, labor, and overhead through a process costing system.

**LO5–2** Compute the equivalent units of production using the weighted-average method.

**LO5–3** Compute the cost per equivalent unit using the weighted-average method.

**LO5–4** Assign costs to units using the weighted-average method.

**LO5–5** Prepare a cost reconciliation report using the weighted-average method.

# Costing the "Quicker-Picker-Upper"

If you have ever spilled milk, there is a good chance that you used Bounty paper towels to clean up the mess. **Procter & Gamble (P&G)** manufactures Bounty in two main processing departments—Paper Making and Paper Converting. In the Paper Making Department, wood pulp is converted into paper and then spooled into 2,000 pound rolls. In the Paper Converting Department, two of the 2,000 pound rolls of paper are simultaneously unwound into a machine that creates a two-ply paper towel that is decorated, perforated, and embossed to create texture. The large sheets of paper towels that emerge from this process are wrapped around a cylindrical cardboard core measuring eight feet in length. Once enough sheets wrap around the core, the eight foot roll is cut into individual rolls of Bounty that are sent down a conveyor to be wrapped, packed, and shipped.

In this type of manufacturing environment, costs cannot be readily traced to individual rolls of Bounty; however, given the homogeneous nature of the product, the total costs incurred in the Paper Making Department can be spread uniformly across its output of 2,000 pound rolls of paper. Similarly, the total costs incurred in the Paper Converting Department (including the cost of the 2,000 pound rolls that are transferred in from the Paper Making Department) can be spread uniformly across the number of cases of Bounty produced.

P&G uses a similar costing approach for many of its products such as Tide detergent, Crest toothpaste, and Dawn dishwashing liquid.

Source: Conversation with Brad Bays, formerly a Procter & Gamble financial executive.

**J**ob-order costing and process costing are two common methods for determining unit product costs. As explained in previous chapters, job-order costing is used when many different jobs or products are worked on each period. Examples of industries that use job-order costing include furniture manufacturing, special-order printing, ship-building, and many types of service organizations.

By contrast, **process costing** is used most commonly in industries that convert raw materials into homogeneous (i.e., uniform) products, such as bricks, soda, or paper, on a continuous basis. Examples of companies that would use process costing include **Reynolds Consumer Products** (aluminum ingots), **Scott Paper** (paper towels), **General Mills** (flours), **ExxonMobil** (gasoline and lubricating oils), **Coppertone** (sunscreens), and **Kellogg's** (breakfast cereals). In addition, process costing is sometimes used in companies with assembly operations. A form of process costing may also be used in utilities that produce gas, water, and electricity.

Our purpose in this chapter is to explain how product costing works in a process costing system.

## COMPARISON OF JOB-ORDER AND PROCESS COSTING

In some ways process costing is very similar to job-order costing, and in some ways it is very different. In this section, we focus on these similarities and differences to provide a foundation for the detailed discussion of process costing that follows.

### Similarities between Job-Order and Process Costing

Much of what you learned in previous chapters about costing and cost flows applies equally well to process costing in this chapter. We are not throwing out all that we have learned about costing and starting from "scratch" with a whole new system. The similarities between job-order and process costing are as follows:

1. Both systems have the same basic purposes—to assign material, labor, and manufacturing overhead costs to products and to provide a mechanism for computing unit product costs.
2. Both systems use the same basic manufacturing accounts, including Manufacturing Overhead, Raw Materials, Work in Process, and Finished Goods.
3. The flow of costs through the manufacturing accounts is basically the same in both systems.

As can be seen from this comparison, much of what you have already learned about costing is applicable to a process costing system. Our task now is to refine and extend your knowledge to process costing.

### Differences between Job-Order and Process Costing

Exhibit 5–1 summarizes three differences between job-order and process costing. First, job-order costing is used when a company produces many different jobs that have unique production requirements. Process costing is used when a company produces a continuous flow of units that are indistinguishable from one another. Second, job-order costing uses job cost sheets to accumulate costs for individual jobs. Process costing accumulates costs by department (rather than by job) and assigns these costs uniformly to all identical units that pass through the department during a period. Third, job-order costing uses job cost sheets to compute units costs for each job. Process costing systems compute unit costs by department.

| Job-Order Costing | Process Costing |
|---|---|
| 1. Many different jobs are worked on during each period, with each job having unique production requirements. | 1. A single product is produced either on a continuous basis or for long periods of time. All units of product are identical. |
| 2. Costs are accumulated by individual job. | 2. Costs are accumulated by department. |
| 3. Unit costs are computed *by job* on the job cost sheet. | 3. Unit costs are computed *by department*. |

**EXHIBIT 5–1**
Differences between Job-Order and Process Costing

# COST FLOWS IN PROCESS COSTING

Before going through a detailed example of process costing, it will be helpful to see how, in a general way, manufacturing costs flow through a process costing system.

## Processing Departments

A **processing department** is an organizational unit where work is performed on a product and where materials, labor, or overhead costs are added to the product. For example, a **Nalley's** potato chip factory might have three processing departments—one for preparing potatoes, one for cooking, and one for inspecting and packaging. A brick factory might have two processing departments—one for mixing and molding clay into bricks and one for firing the molded bricks. Some products and services may go through a number of processing departments, while others may go through only one or two. Regardless of the number of processing departments, they all have two essential features. First, the activity in the processing department is performed uniformly on all of the units passing through it. Second, the output of the processing department is homogeneous; in other words, all of the units produced are identical.

Products in a process costing environment, such as bricks or potato chips, typically flow in sequence from one department to another as in Exhibit 5–2.

## The Flow of Materials, Labor, and Overhead Costs

Cost accumulation is simpler in a process costing system than in a job-order costing system. In a process costing system, instead of having to assign costs to hundreds of different jobs, costs are assigned to only a few processing departments.

**EXHIBIT 5–2**    Sequential Processing Departments

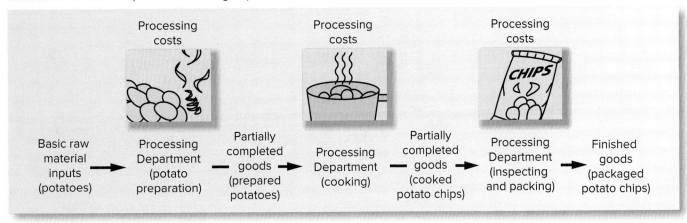

## Get the Door! It's Papa Johns

©A.Penkov/Shutterstock.com RF

On Super Bowl Sunday 12.5 million pizzas are delivered to American households. Each pizza comes in a box, many of which are manufactured in one of 17 plants owned by **Rock-Tenn Company** in Norcross, Georgia. The company's Atlanta plant uses a production line that spans more than one and a half football fields to convert "58-inch diameter rolls of heavy paper into a ribbon of corrugated cardboard that runs through a printing press and then through high-speed die cutters that crease, cut and trim it into individual boxes." A total of 50 employees keep this production line churning out 400 unfolded boxes per minute for 24 hours a day and seven days a week.

This type of manufacturing process is conducive to process costing because the pizza boxes being produced at 400 units per minute are indistinguishable from one another. It stands in stark contrast to job-order manufacturing where customized outputs are produced in response to unique customer demands.

Source: Tita, Bob, "It's Crunch Time for Pizza Boxes," *The Wall Street Journal,* January 30, 2015, pp. B1 and B6.

Exhibit 5–3 shows a T-account model of materials, labor, and overhead cost flows in a process costing system. Several key points should be noted from this exhibit. First, note that a separate Work in Process account is maintained for *each processing department.* In contrast, in a job-order costing system the entire company may have only one Work in Process account. Second, note that the completed production of the first processing department (Department A in the exhibit) is transferred to the Work in Process account of the second processing department (Department B). After further work in Department B, the completed units are then transferred to Finished Goods. (In Exhibit 5–3, we show only two processing departments, but a company can have many processing departments.)

**EXHIBIT 5–3**     T-Account Model of Process Costing Flows

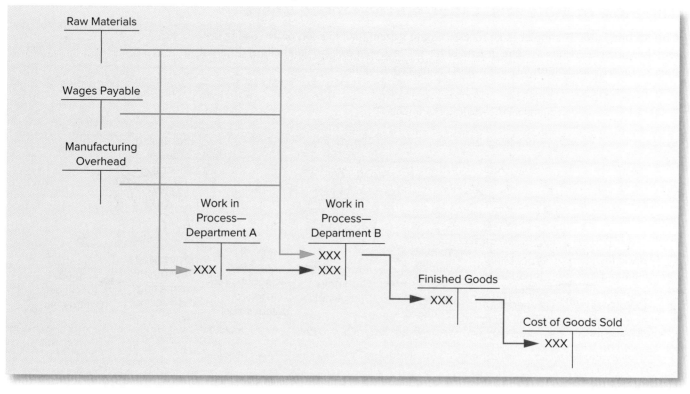

Finally, note that materials, labor, and overhead costs can be added in *any* processing department—not just the first. Costs in Department B's Work in Process account consist of the materials, labor, and overhead costs incurred in Department B plus the costs assigned to the units transferred in from Department A (called transferred-in costs).

## Materials, Labor, and Overhead Cost Entries

To complete our discussion of cost flows in a process costing system, in this section we show journal entries relating to materials, labor, and overhead costs at Megan's Classic Cream Soda, a company that has two processing departments—Formulating and Bottling. In the Formulating Department, ingredients are checked for quality and then mixed and injected with carbon dioxide to create bulk cream soda. In the Bottling Department, bottles are checked for defects, filled with cream soda, capped, visually inspected again for defects, and then packed for shipping.

**LEARNING OBJECTIVE 5–1**

Record the flow of materials, labor, and overhead through a process costing system.

**Materials Costs**  As in job-order costing, materials are drawn from the storeroom using a materials requisition form. Materials can be added in any processing department, although it is not unusual for materials to be added only in the first processing department, with subsequent departments adding only labor and overhead costs.

At Megan's Classic Cream Soda, some materials (i.e., water, flavors, sugar, and carbon dioxide) are added in the Formulating Department and some materials (i.e., bottles, caps, and packing materials) are added in the Bottling Department. The journal entry to record the materials used in the first processing department, the Formulating Department, is as follows:

| | | |
|---|---|---|
| Work in Process—Formulating................................ | XXX | |
| Raw Materials .......................................... | | XXX |

The journal entry to record the materials used in the second processing department, the Bottling Department, is as follows:

| | | |
|---|---|---|
| Work in Process—Bottling................................... | XXX | |
| Raw Materials .......................................... | | XXX |

**Labor Costs**  In process costing, labor costs are traced to departments—not to individual jobs. The following journal entry records the labor costs in the Formulating Department at Megan's Classic Cream Soda:

| | | |
|---|---|---|
| Work in Process—Formulating................................ | XXX | |
| Salaries and Wages Payable................................ | | XXX |

A similar entry would be made to record labor costs in the Bottling Department.

**Overhead Costs**  In process costing, as in job-order costing, predetermined overhead rates are usually used. Manufacturing overhead cost is applied according to the amount of the allocation base that is incurred in the department. The following journal entry records the overhead cost applied in the Formulating Department:

| | | |
|---|---|---|
| Work in Process—Formulating................................ | XXX | |
| Manufacturing Overhead................................... | | XXX |

A similar entry would be made to apply manufacturing overhead cost in the Bottling Department.

**Completing the Cost Flows**   Once processing has been completed in a department, the units are transferred to the next department for further processing, as illustrated in the T-accounts in Exhibit 5–3. The following journal entry transfers the cost of the units that have been completed within the Formulating Department to the Bottling Department:

| | | |
|---|---|---|
| Work in Process—Bottling. . . . . . . . . . . . . . . . . . . . . . . . . . . . . . . . . . . | XXX | |
| Work in Process—Formulating . . . . . . . . . . . . . . . . . . . . . . . . . . . . | | XXX |

After processing has been finished in the Bottling Department, the costs of the completed units are transferred to the Finished Goods inventory account:

| | | |
|---|---|---|
| Finished Goods . . . . . . . . . . . . . . . . . . . . . . . . . . . . . . . . . . . . . . . . . | XXX | |
| Work in Process—Bottling . . . . . . . . . . . . . . . . . . . . . . . . . . . . . . . | | XXX |

Finally, when a customer's order is filled and units are sold, the cost of the units is transferred to Cost of Goods Sold:

| | | |
|---|---|---|
| Cost of Goods Sold . . . . . . . . . . . . . . . . . . . . . . . . . . . . . . . . . . . . . | XXX | |
| Finished Goods . . . . . . . . . . . . . . . . . . . . . . . . . . . . . . . . . . . . . . . | | XXX |

To summarize, the cost flows between accounts are basically the same in a process costing system as they are in a job-order costing system. The only difference at this point is that in a process costing system each department has a separate Work in Process account.

CONCEPT CHECK

1. Which of the following statements is true? (You may select more than one answer.)
   a. Job-order costing and process costing systems both use the same basic manufacturing accounts, including Manufacturing Overhead, Raw Materials, Work in Process, and Finished Goods.
   b. Process costing is used when a company produces a continuous flow of units that are indistinguishable from one another.
   c. Process costing systems accumulate costs by customer order rather than by department.
   d. Job-order costing and process costing systems both provide a mechanism for computing unit product costs

IN BUSINESS

## Junk Food Goes on a Health Kick

Candy manufacturers are feeling pressure from customers to remove unhealthy ingredients from their snack food. For example, **Nestlé** has been working on removing artificial colors (such as Red 40 and Yellow 5) and artificial flavors (such as Vanillin) from its more than 250 chocolate products. The company plans to use Annatto (which comes from achiote trees) instead of artificial food colors and it intends to replace vanillin with natural vanilla flavor. While these natural ingredients cost more, Nestlé says that it will not offset these higher material costs with higher prices. In addition to Nestlé, **Mondelez International**, the makers of Oreo cookies and Cadbury chocolate, plans to reduce the saturated fat and sodium in its products by 10% by 2020.

Source: Gasparro, Annie, "Nestle Bars Artificial Color, Flavors," *The Wall Street JournaL*, February 18, 2015, p. B6.

©Ryan Remiorz/The Canadian Press/ AP Images

# PROCESS COSTING COMPUTATIONS: THREE KEY CONCEPTS

In process costing, each department needs to calculate two numbers for financial reporting purposes—the cost of its ending work in process inventory and the cost of its completed units that were transferred to the next stage of the production process. The key to deriving these two numbers is calculating *unit costs* within each department. On the surface, these departmental unit cost calculations may seem very straightforward—simply divide the department's costs (the numerator) by its outputs, or units produced (the denominator). However, to set the stage for correctly performing this seemingly simple computation, you will need to understand three key foundational concepts.

## Key Concept #1

There is more than one way to calculate departmental unit costs. This chapter explains two methods for performing these calculations, the *weighted-average method* and the *FIFO method*. The **weighted-average method** of process costing, which will be explained in the main body of the chapter, calculates unit costs by combining costs and outputs from the current and prior periods. The **FIFO method** of process costing, which will be covered in the Chapter 5 Supplement, calculates unit costs based solely on the costs and outputs from the current period.

## Key Concept #2

Each department needs to calculate a separate unit cost for each type of manufacturing cost that it incurs. For example, if a given department adds materials cost, labor cost, and overhead cost to the production process it would need to compute a unit cost for each of these three cost categories. To simplify things, companies often consolidate these three cost categories into two groups by combining labor and overhead costs into a category called *conversion costs* (or conversion for short). **Conversion cost**, as defined in an earlier chapter, is direct labor cost plus manufacturing overhead cost.

## Key Concept #3

Quantifying each department's number of units produced during a period is complicated by the fact that most departments usually have some partially completed units on hand at the end of the period. Because it would be an overstatement to count these partially completed units as equivalent to fully completed units when counting the department's output, these partially completed units are translated into an *equivalent* number of fully completed units. In process costing, this translation is done using the following formula:

Equivalent units = Number of partially completed units × Percentage completion

As the formula states, **equivalent units** is the product of the number of partially completed units and the percentage completion of those units with respect to the processing in the department. Roughly speaking, the equivalent units is the number of complete units that could have been obtained from the materials and effort that went into the partially complete units.

For example, suppose Department A has 500 units in its ending work in process inventory that are 60% complete with respect to processing in the department. These 500 partially complete units are equivalent to 300 fully complete units (500 × 60% = 300). Therefore, Department A's ending work in process inventory would contain 300 equivalent units that are included within its output for the period.

**DECISION POINT**

## Writing Term Papers

Assume your professors assigned four separate five-page papers that were all due on the same day. You turned in two complete papers and two incomplete papers—one of which was two pages long and the other was three pages long. Assuming that each page requires the same time and effort, how many complete papers could you have turned in with the same expenditure of time and effort?

## THE WEIGHTED-AVERAGE METHOD: AN EXAMPLE

We now turn our attention to Double Diamond Skis, a company that manufactures a high-performance, deep-powder ski, and that uses process costing to determine its unit product costs. The company's production process is illustrated in Exhibit 5–4. Skis go through a sequence of five processing departments, starting with the Shaping and Milling Department and ending with the Finishing and Pairing Department.

We will use the Double Diamond Skis example to explain the weighted-average method of process costing in four steps:

Step 1: Compute the equivalent units of production.
Step 2: Compute the cost per equivalent unit.
Step 3: Assign costs to units.
Step 4: Prepare a cost reconciliation report.

### Step 1: Compute the Equivalent Units of Production

**LEARNING OBJECTIVE 5–2**

Compute the equivalent units of production using the weighted-average method.

The *equivalent units of production* is the name we use for the denominator in unit cost calculations. Each processing department calculates the equivalent units of production for each of its manufacturing cost categories. In the weighted-average method, the **equivalent units of production** for a department is the number of completed units transferred to the next department (or to finished goods) plus the equivalent units in the department's ending work in process inventory. This definition in equation form is as follows:

**WEIGHTED-AVERAGE METHOD**
**(a separate calculation is made for each cost category in each processing department)**

$$\text{Equivalent units of production} = \text{Units transferred to the next department or to finished goods} + \text{Equivalent units in ending work in process inventory}$$

To better understand this formula, consider the Shaping and Milling Department at Double Diamond Skis. This department uses computerized milling machines to precisely shape the wooden core and metal sheets that will be used to form the backbone of the ski. Exhibit 5–5 summarizes the Shaping and Milling Department's production data for the month of May for its two manufacturing cost categories, materials and conversion.

The first thing to note about Exhibit 5–5 is the flow of units through the department (focus on the data under the Units heading). The department started with 200 units in beginning work in process inventory. During May, 5,000 units were started into production. This made a total of 5,200 units. Of this total, 4,800 units were completed during May and transferred to the next department and 400 units were still in the department's ending work in process inventory. In general, the units in beginning work in process inventory plus the units started into production must equal the units

**EXHIBIT 5–4**   The Production Process at Double Diamond Skis*

**Shaping and Milling Department**

Computer-assisted milling machines shape the wood core and aluminum sheets that serve as the backbone of the ski.

**Graphics Application Department**

Graphics are applied to the back of clear plastic top sheets using a heat-transfer process.

**Molding Department**

The wooden core and various layers are stacked in a mold, polyurethane foam is injected into the mold, and then the mold is placed in a press that fuses the parts together.

**Grinding and Sanding Department**

The semi-finished skis are tuned by stone grinding and belt sanding. The ski edges are beveled and polished.

**Finishing and Pairing Department**

A skilled technician selects skis to form a pair and adjusts the skis' camber.

**Finished Goods**

*Adapted from Bill Gout, Jesse James Doquilo, and Studio M D, "Capped Crusaders," *Skiing*, October 1993, pp. 138–144.

EXHIBIT 5–5
Shaping and Milling Department
Production Data for May

| | | Percent Complete | |
|---|---|---|---|
| **Shaping and Milling Department** | **Units** | **Materials** | **Conversion** |
| Beginning work in process inventory . . . . . . . . . . . . . . . . | 200 | 55% | 30% |
| Units started into production during May. . . . . . . . . . . . . | 5,000 | | |
| Units completed during May and transferred to the next department. . . . . . . . . . . . . . . | 4,800 | 100%* | 100%* |
| Ending work in process inventory . . . . . . . . . . . . . . . . . . | 400 | 40% | 25% |

*We always assume that units transferred out of a department are 100% complete with respect to the processing done in that department.

in ending work in process inventory plus the units completed and transferred out. In equation form, this is:

$$\begin{matrix}\text{Units in beginning} \\ \text{work in process} \\ \text{inventory}\end{matrix} + \begin{matrix}\text{Units started into} \\ \text{production or} \\ \text{transferred in}\end{matrix} = \begin{matrix}\text{Units in ending} \\ \text{work in process} \\ \text{inventory}\end{matrix} + \begin{matrix}\text{Units completed} \\ \text{and transferred out}\end{matrix}$$

A second point worth mentioning about Exhibit 5–5 is that its beginning work in process inventory was 55% complete with respect to materials and 30% complete with respect to conversion. This means that 55% of the materials cost required to complete the units in beginning work in process inventory had already been incurred. Likewise, 30% of the conversion costs required to complete the units in beginning work in process inventory had already been incurred. However, when using the weighted-average method to compute the equivalent units of production, these two completion percentages pertaining to the beginning work in process inventory (55% for materials and 30% for conversion) will be ignored.

The third point to highlight from Exhibit 5–5 is that the Shaping and Milling Department's ending work in process inventory is 40% complete with respect to materials and 25% complete with respect to conversion. This means that 40% of the materials cost and 25% of the conversion costs required to complete the units in ending work in process inventory have already been incurred. Under the weighted-average method, these two completion percentages pertaining to the ending work in process inventory (40% for materials and 25% for conversion) will be included in the computation of equivalent units of production.

Exhibit 5–6 summarizes the equivalent units of production calculations within the Shaping and Milling Department for materials and conversion. Notice that these calculations ignore the fact that the units in the beginning work in process inventory were partially complete with respect to materials and conversion. For example, the 200 units in beginning inventory were already 30% complete with respect to conversion costs. However, the weighted-average method is concerned only with the 100 equivalent units that are in ending inventories and the 4,800 units that were transferred to the next department (for a total of 4,900 equivalent units of production); it is not concerned with the fact that the beginning work in process inventory was already partially complete. In other words, the 4,900 equivalent units of production computed using the weighted-average method include work that was accomplished in the prior period. This is a key point concerning the weighted-average method and it is easy to overlook.

EXHIBIT 5–6
Equivalent Units of Production:
Weighted-Average Method

| **Shaping and Milling Department** | **Materials** | **Conversion** |
|---|---|---|
| Units transferred to the next department. . . . . . . . . . . . . . . . . . . . | 4,800 | 4,800 |
| Equivalent units in ending work in process inventory: | | |
| Materials: 400 units × 40% complete . . . . . . . . . . . . . . . . . . . . . | 160 | |
| Conversion: 400 units × 25% complete . . . . . . . . . . . . . . . . . . . | | 100 |
| Equivalent units of production . . . . . . . . . . . . . . . . . . . . . . . . . . . . | 4,960 | 4,900 |

**EXHIBIT 5–7**
Visual Perspective of Equivalent
Units of Production

Exhibit 5–7 provides another way of looking at the computation of equivalent units of production. It depicts the computations for conversion costs. Study it carefully before going on.

You need to perform separate equivalent units of production calculations for each manufacturing cost category, such as materials and conversion. When using the weighted-average method to compute equivalent units of production for a cost category you should ignore the completion percentage for the units in beginning inventory. The units transferred to the next department plus the units in ending work in process inventory multiplied by their percentage completion equals the equivalent units of production.

## Step 2: Compute the Cost per Equivalent Unit

**LEARNING OBJECTIVES 5–3**

Compute the cost per equivalent unit using the weighted-average method.

In step 2 we need to determine the total cost to include in the numerator and then divide it by the equivalent units of production that we already calculated in step 1 to derive the cost per equivalent unit for materials and conversion. To help us with this step, Exhibit 5–8 displays the Shaping and Milling Department's cost data for the Month of May.

**EXHIBIT 5–8**
Shaping and Milling Department
Cost Data for May

|  | Materials | Conversion | Total |
|---|---|---|---|
| Cost of beginning work in process inventory . . . . . . . | $ 9,600 | $ 5,575 | $ 15,175 |
| Costs added during the period . . . . . . . . . . . . . . . . . . | 368,600 | 350,900 | 719,500 |
| Total cost . . . . . . . . . . . . . . . . . . . . . . . . . . . . . . . . . . | $378,200 | $356,475 | $734,675 |

Given this cost data, we can now compute the Shaping and Milling Department's cost per equivalent unit for materials and conversion using the following equation:

**WEIGHTED-AVERAGE METHOD**
**(a separate calculation is made for each cost category in each processing department)**

$$\text{Cost per equivalent unit} = \frac{\text{Cost of beginning work in process inventory} + \text{Cost added during the period}}{\text{Equivalent units of production}}$$

Note that the numerator is the sum of the cost of beginning work in process inventory and of the cost added during the period. Thus, the weighted-average method blends together costs from the prior and current periods. That is why it is called the weighted-average method; it averages together costs and outputs from the current and prior periods.

Using this equation, the Shaping and Milling Department's costs per equivalent unit for materials and conversion for May are computed as follows:

| Shaping and Milling Department Costs per Equivalent Unit | Materials | Conversion |
|---|---|---|
| Cost of beginning work in process inventory | $ 9,600 | $ 5,575 |
| Costs added during the period | 368,600 | 350,900 |
| Total cost (a) | $378,200 | $356,475 |
| Equivalent units of production (see Exhibit 5–6) (b) | 4,960 | 4,900 |
| Cost per equivalent unit (a) ÷ (b) | $76.25 | $72.75 |

**CONCEPT CHECK** ✓

2.  Which of the following statements is false? (You may select more than one answer.)
    a.  The activity in a processing department is performed uniformly on all units passing through the department.
    b.  The output of a processing department is heterogeneous; in other words, all of the units produced are distinct from one another.
    c.  Equivalent units are calculated by taking the number of partially completed units on hand and multiplying those units by their percentage of completion.
    d.  The weighted-average method of computing the cost per equivalent unit averages together units and costs from the current and prior periods.

## Step 3: Assign Costs to Units

**LEARNING OBJECTIVE 5–4**

Assign costs to units using the weighted-average method.

In step 3 we use the costs per equivalent unit to value the equivalent units in ending inventory and the completed units that are transferred to the next department. For example, each unit transferred out of Double Diamond's Shaping and Milling Department to the Graphics Application Department, as depicted in Exhibit 5–4, will carry with it a cost of $149.00 ($76.25 for materials and $72.75 for conversion). Because 4,800 units were transferred out in May to the next department (see Exhibit 5–5), the total cost assigned to those units would be $715,200 (= 4,800 units × $149.00 per unit).

A complete accounting of the costs of both ending work in process inventory and the units transferred out appears below:

| Shaping and Milling Department Costs of Ending Work in Process Inventory and the Units Transferred Out | Materials | Conversion | Total |
|---|---|---|---|
| **Ending work in process inventory:** | | | |
| Equivalent units (see Exhibit 5–6) (a) | 160 | 100 | |
| Cost per equivalent unit (b) | $76.25 | $72.75 | |
| Cost of ending work in process inventory (a) × (b) | $12,200 | $7,275 | $19,475 |
| **Units completed and transferred out:** | | | |
| Units transferred to the next department (see Exhibit 5–6) (a) | 4,800 | 4,800 | |
| Cost per equivalent unit (b) | $76.25 | $72.75 | |
| Cost of units transferred out (a) × (b) | $366,000 | $349,200 | $715,200 |

For materials and conversion, the equivalent units in ending work in process inventory and the completed units transferred to the next department are multiplied by the cost per equivalent unit to determine the cost assigned to the units. For example, the 100 equivalent units of conversion in ending work in process inventory are multiplied by the cost per equivalent unit of $72.75 to determine the conversion costs included in ending work in process inventory of $7,275. Similarly, the 4,800 units completed and transferred out are multiplied by the conversion cost per equivalent unit of $72.75 to determine the conversion costs attached to the completed units transferred out of $349,200.

## Step 4: Prepare a Cost Reconciliation Report

The costs assigned to the equivalent units in ending work in process inventory and to the completed units transferred out reconcile with the costs we started with in Exhibit 5–8 as shown below:

**LEARNING OBJECTIVE 5–5**

Prepare a cost reconciliation report using the weighted-average method.

| Shaping and Milling Department Cost Reconciliation | |
|---|---|
| Costs to be accounted for: | |
| Cost of beginning work in process inventory (Exhibit 5–8) . . . . . . . . . . . . . . . . | $ 15,175 |
| Costs added to production during the period (Exhibit 5–8) . . . . . . . . . . . . . . . . | 719,500 |
| Total cost to be accounted for . . . . . . . . . . . . . . . . . . . . . . . . . . . . . . . . . . . . . . . | $734,675 |
| | |
| Costs accounted for as follows: | |
| Cost of ending work in process inventory (see above) . . . . . . . . . . . . . . . . . . . . | $ 19,475 |
| Cost of units transferred out (see above) . . . . . . . . . . . . . . . . . . . . . . . . . . . . . . | 715,200 |
| Total cost accounted for . . . . . . . . . . . . . . . . . . . . . . . . . . . . . . . . . . . . . . . . . . . . | $734,675 |

The $715,200 cost of the units transferred to the next department, Graphics Application, will be accounted for in that department as "costs transferred in." It will be treated in the process costing system as just another category of costs like materials or conversion costs. The only difference is that the costs transferred in will always be 100% complete with respect to the work done in the Shaping and Milling Department. Costs are passed on from one department to the next in this fashion, until they reach the last processing department, Finishing and Pairing. When the products are completed in this last department, their costs are transferred to finished goods.

## HELPFUL HINT

To help you understand the logic of a cost reconciliation report, imagine that you have a non-interest bearing checking account with a balance on March 1 of $200. Also, assume that during March you earned paychecks totaling $1,000. On March 31, you would have $1,200 to be accounted for. At the end of the month, each of your $1,200 dollars must be accounted for in one of two ways. Either it remains in your checking account as of March 31 or it has been transferred out during the month (perhaps to your landlord, to the supermarket, or to your savings account). The ending balance in your checking account plus the total amount of cash transferred out during the month must equal $1,200.

The same concepts apply to the cost reconciliation report in this chapter. The cost of beginning work in process inventory plus the costs added to production during the period equals the total cost to be accounted for. The cost of ending work in process inventory plus the cost of units transferred out equals the total cost accounted for.

CONCEPT
CHECK ✔

3. Beginning work in process includes 400 units that are 20% complete with respect to conversion and 30% complete with respect to materials. Ending work in process includes 200 units that are 40% complete with respect to conversion and 50% complete with respect to materials. If 2,000 units were started during the period, what are the equivalent units of production for the period according to the weighted-average method?
   a. Conversion equivalent units = 2,280 units; Material equivalent units = 2,100 units
   b. Conversion equivalent units = 1,980 units; Material equivalent units = 2,080 units
   c. Conversion equivalent units = 2,480 units; Material equivalent units = 1,980 units
   d. Conversion equivalent units = 2,280 units; Material equivalent units = 2,300 units
4. Assume the same facts as above in Concept Check 3. Also, assume that $9,900 of material costs and $14,880 of conversion costs were in the beginning inventory and $180,080 of materials and $409,200 of conversion costs were added to production during the period. What is the total cost per equivalent unit using the weighted-average method?
   a. $268.60
   b. $267.85
   c. $280.00
   d. $265.00

# OPERATION COSTING

Job-order costing and process costing represent the two ends of a continuum. On one end is job-order costing, which is used by companies that produce many different products in one facility. On the other end is process costing, which is used by companies that produce homogeneous products in large quantities. Between these two extremes there are many hybrid systems that include characteristics of both job-order and process costing. One of these hybrids is called *operation costing*.

**Operation costing** is used in situations where products have some common characteristics and some individual characteristics. Shoes, for example, have common characteristics in that all styles involve cutting and sewing that can be done on a repetitive basis, using the same equipment and following the same basic procedures. Shoes also have individual characteristics—some are made of expensive leathers and others may be made using inexpensive synthetic materials. In a situation such as this, where products have some common characteristics but also must be processed individually, operation costing may be used to determine product costs.

As mentioned above, operation costing is a hybrid system that employs aspects of both job-order and process costing. Products are typically processed in batches when operation costing is used, with each batch charged for its own specific materials. In this sense, operation costing is similar to job-order costing. However, labor and overhead costs are accumulated by operation or by department, and these costs are assigned to units as in process costing. If shoes are being produced, each shoe is charged the same per unit conversion cost, regardless of the style involved, but it is charged with its specific materials cost. Thus, the company is able to distinguish between styles in terms of materials, but it is able to employ the simplicity of a process costing system for labor and overhead costs.

Examples of other products for which operation costing may be used include electronic equipment (such as semiconductors), textiles, clothing, and jewelry (such as rings, bracelets, and medallions). Products of this type are typically produced in batches, but they can vary considerably from model to model or from style to style in terms of the cost of materials.

# SUMMARY

**LO5–1 Record the flow of materials, labor, and overhead through a process costing system.**

The journal entries to record the flow of costs in process costing are basically the same as in job-order costing. Direct materials costs are debited to Work in Process when the materials are released for use in production. Direct labor costs are debited to Work in Process as incurred. Manufacturing overhead costs are applied to Work in Process by debiting Work in Process. Costs are accumulated by department in process costing and by job in job-order costing.

**LO5–2 Compute the equivalent units of production using the weighted-average method.**

To compute unit costs for a department, the department's output in terms of equivalent units of production must be determined. In the weighted-average method, the equivalent units of production for a period are the sum of the units transferred out of the department during the period and the equivalent units in ending work in process inventory at the end of the period.

**LO5–3 Compute the cost per equivalent unit using the weighted-average method.**

The cost per equivalent unit for a particular cost category in a department is computed by dividing the sum of the cost of beginning work in process inventory and the cost added during the period by the equivalent units of production for the period.

**LO5–4 Assign costs to units using the weighted-average method.**

The cost per equivalent unit is used to value units in ending inventory and units transferred to the next department. The cost assigned to ending inventory is determined by multiplying the cost per equivalent unit by the equivalent units in ending inventory. The cost assigned to the units transferred to the next department is determined by multiplying the cost per equivalent unit by the number of units transferred.

**LO5–5 Prepare a cost reconciliation report using the weighted-average method.**

The costs to be accounted for consist of beginning work in process inventory plus the cost added to work in process. These costs must equal the cost of ending work in process inventory plus the cost of the units transferred out.

# GUIDANCE ANSWER TO DECISION POINT

**Writing Term Papers**

Each complete paper is five pages long and, by assumption, each page requires the same time and effort to write. Therefore, the time and effort that went into writing one incomplete two-page paper and one incomplete three-page paper could have been used to write one complete five-page paper. Added to the two complete papers that were turned in, this would have resulted in three complete papers.

# GUIDANCE ANSWERS TO CONCEPT CHECKS

1. **Choices a, b, and d.** Process costing systems accumulate costs by department.
2. **Choice b.** The output of a processing department is homogeneous, meaning that all of the units are indistinguishable from one another.
3. **Choice d.** Material equivalent units are 2,200 units completed and transferred to the next department plus 100 equivalent units in ending work in process inventory (200 units × 50%). Conversion equivalent units are 2,200 units completed and transferred to the next department plus 80 equivalent units in ending work in process inventory (200 units × 40%).
4. **Choice a.** ($189,980 ÷ 2,300 equivalent units) + ($424,080 ÷ 2,280 equivalent units) = $268.60.

# REVIEW PROBLEM: PROCESS COST FLOWS AND COSTING UNITS

Luxguard Home Paint Company produces exterior latex paint, which it sells in one-gallon containers. The company has two processing departments—Base Fab and Finishing. White paint, which is used as a base for all the company's paints, is mixed from raw ingredients in the Base Fab Department. Pigments are then added to the basic white paint, the pigmented paint is squirted under pressure into one-gallon containers, and the containers are labeled and packed for shipping in the Finishing Department. Information relating to the company's operations for April follows:

a.  Raw materials used in production: Base Fab Department, $851,000; and Finishing Department, $629,000.

b.  Incurred direct labor costs: Base Fab Department, $330,000; and Finishing Department, $270,000.

c.  Applied manufacturing overhead cost: Base Fab Department, $665,000; and Finishing Department, $405,000.

d.  Transferred basic white paint from the Base Fab Department to the Finishing Department, $1,850,000.

e.  Transferred paint that had been prepared for shipping from the Finishing Department to Finished Goods, $3,200,000.

**Required:**

1.  Prepare journal entries to record items (a) through (e) above.

2.  Post the journal entries from (1) above to T-accounts. The balance in the Base Fab Department's Work in Process account on April 1 was $150,000; the beginning balance in the Finishing Department's Work in Process account was $70,000. After posting entries to the T-accounts, find the ending balance in each department's Work in Process account.

3.  Compute the Base Fab Department's cost of ending work in process inventory for materials, labor, overhead, and in total for April. Also, compute the Base Fab Department's cost of the completed units transferred to the next department for materials, labor, overhead, and in total for April. The following additional information is available regarding production in the Base Fab Department during April:

| Production data: | |
| --- | --- |
| Units (gallons) in process, April 1: materials 100% complete; labor and overhead 60% complete.................................... | 30,000 |
| Units (gallons) started into production during April ...................... | 420,000 |
| Units (gallons) completed and transferred to the Finishing Department ..... | 370,000 |
| Units (gallons) in process, April 30: materials 50% complete; labor and overhead 25% complete.................................... | 80,000 |

| Cost data: | |
| --- | --- |
| Work in process inventory, April 1: | |
| Materials ............................................... | $ 92,000 |
| Labor .................................................. | 21,000 |
| Overhead............................................... | 37,000 |
| Total cost of work in process inventory ................................ | $150,000 |
| Cost added during April: | |
| Materials ............................................... | $ 851,000 |
| Labor .................................................. | 330,000 |
| Overhead............................................... | 665,000 |
| Total cost added during April........................................ | $1,846,000 |

4.  Prepare a cost reconciliation report for April.

**Solution to Review Problem**

1.

| | | | |
| --- | --- | --- | --- |
| a. | Work in Process—Base Fab Department.................... | 851,000 | |
| | Work in Process—Finishing Department ................... | 629,000 | |
| | Raw Materials ....................................... | | 1,480,000 |
| b. | Work in Process—Base Fab Department.................... | 330,000 | |
| | Work in Process—Finishing Department ................... | 270,000 | |
| | Salaries and Wages Payable ............................ | | 600,000 |
| c. | Work in Process—Base Fab Department.................... | 665,000 | |
| | Work in Process—Finishing Department ................... | 405,000 | |
| | Manufacturing Overhead ............................... | | 1,070,000 |
| d. | Work in Process—Finishing Department ................... | 1,850,000 | |
| | Work in Process—Base Fab Department................... | | 1,850,000 |
| e. | Finished Goods....................................... | 3,200,000 | |
| | Work in Process—Finishing Department ................ | | 3,200,000 |

2.

| Raw Materials | | | |
|---|---|---|---|
| Bal. | XXX | (a) | 1,480,000 |

| Salaries and Wages Payable | | | |
|---|---|---|---|
| | | (b) | 600,000 |

**Work in Process—
Base Fab Department**

| | | | |
|---|---|---|---|
| Bal. | 150,000 | (d) | 1,850,000 |
| (a) | 851,000 | | |
| (b) | 330,000 | | |
| (c) | 665,000 | | |
| Bal. | 146,000 | | |

**Manufacturing Overhead**

| | | | |
|---|---|---|---|
| (Various actual costs) | | (c) | 1,070,000 |

**Work in Process—Finishing
Department**

| | | | |
|---|---|---|---|
| Bal. | 70,000 | (e) | 3,200,000 |
| (a) | 629,000 | | |
| (b) | 270,000 | | |
| (c) | 405,000 | | |
| (d) | 1,850,000 | | |
| Bal. | 24,000 | | |

**Finished Goods**

| | | | |
|---|---|---|---|
| Bal. | XXX | | |
| (e) | 3,200,000 | | |

3. First, we must compute the equivalent units of production for each cost category:

**Base Fab Department
Equivalent Units of Production**

| | Materials | Labor | Overhead |
|---|---|---|---|
| Units transferred to the next department. . . . . . . . . . . . . . . . . . . . | 370,000 | 370,000 | 370,000 |
| Equivalent units in ending work in process inventory (materials: 80,000 units × 50% complete; labor: 80,000 units × 25% complete; overhead: 80,000 units × 25% complete) . . . . | 40,000 | 20,000 | 20,000 |
| Equivalent units of production . . . . . . . . . . . . . . . . . . . . . . . . . . . . . | 410,000 | 390,000 | 390,000 |

Then we must compute the cost per equivalent unit for each cost category:

**Base Fab Department
Costs per Equivalent Unit**

| | Materials | Labor | Overhead |
|---|---|---|---|
| Costs: | | | |
| Cost of beginning work in process inventory . . . . . . . . . . . . | $ 92,000 | $ 21,000 | $ 37,000 |
| Costs added during the period . . . . . . . . . . . . . . . . . . . . . . . | 851,000 | 330,000 | 665,000 |
| Total cost (a) . . . . . . . . . . . . . . . . . . . . . . . . . . . . . . . . . . . . . | $943,000 | $351,000 | $702,000 |
| Equivalent units of production (b) . . . . . . . . . . . . . . . . . . . . . | 410,000 | 390,000 | 390,000 |
| Cost per equivalent unit (a) ÷ (b) . . . . . . . . . . . . . . . . . . . . . | $2.30 | $0.90 | $1.80 |

The costs per equivalent unit can then be assigned to the units in ending work in process inventory and the units transferred out as follows:

**Base Fab Department
Costs of Ending Work in Process Inventory and the Units Transferred Out**

| | Materials | Labor | Overhead | Total |
|---|---|---|---|---|
| Ending work in process inventory: | | | | |
| Equivalent units . . . . . . . . . . . . . . . . . . . . . . . . . . | 40,000 | 20,000 | 20,000 | |
| Cost per equivalent unit . . . . . . . . . . . . . . . . . . | $2.30 | $0.90 | $1.80 | |
| Cost of ending work in process inventory . . . . . | $92,000 | $18,000 | $36,000 | $146,000 |
| Units completed and transferred out: | | | | |
| Units transferred to the next department. . . . . | 370,000 | 370,000 | 370,000 | |
| Cost per equivalent unit . . . . . . . . . . . . . . . . . . | $2.30 | $0.90 | $1.80 | |
| Cost of units completed and transferred out . . . | $851,000 | $333,000 | $666,000 | $1,850,000 |

4.

| Base Fab Department Cost Reconciliation | |
| --- | --- |
| **Costs to be accounted for:** | |
| Cost of beginning work in process inventory . . . . . . . . . . . . . . . . . . . . . . . . . . . . . . | $  150,000 |
| Costs added to production during the period. . . . . . . . . . . . . . . . . . . . . . . . . . . . . | 1,846,000 |
| Total cost to be accounted for . . . . . . . . . . . . . . . . . . . . . . . . . . . . . . . . . . . . . . . . | $1,996,000 |
| | |
| **Costs accounted for as follows:** | |
| Cost of ending work in process inventory . . . . . . . . . . . . . . . . . . . . . . . . . . . . . . . | $  146,000 |
| Cost of units transferred out. . . . . . . . . . . . . . . . . . . . . . . . . . . . . . . . . . . . . . . . . . | 1,850,000 |
| Total cost accounted for . . . . . . . . . . . . . . . . . . . . . . . . . . . . . . . . . . . . . . . . . . . . . | $1,996,000 |

# GLOSSARY

**Conversion cost**   Direct labor cost plus manufacturing overhead cost. (p. 191)

**Equivalent units**   The product of the number of partially completed units and their percentage of completion with respect to a particular cost. Equivalent units are the number of complete whole units that could be obtained from the materials and effort contained in partially completed units. (p. 191)

**Equivalent units of production (weighted-average method)**   The units transferred to the next department (or to finished goods) during the period plus the equivalent units in the department's ending work in process inventory. (p. 192)

**FIFO method**   A process costing method that calculates unit costs based solely on the costs and outputs from the current period. (p. 191)

**Operation costing**   A hybrid costing system used when products have some common characteristics and some individual characteristics. (p. 198)

**Process costing**   A costing method used when essentially homogeneous products are produced on a continuous basis. (p. 186)

**Processing department**   An organizational unit where work is performed on a product and where materials, labor, or overhead costs are added to the product. (p. 187)

**Weighted-average method**   A process costing method that calculates unit costs by combining costs and outputs from the current and prior periods. (p. 191)

# QUESTIONS

**5–1**   Under what conditions would it be appropriate to use a process costing system?

**5–2**   In what ways are job-order and process costing similar?

**5–3**   Why is cost accumulation simpler in a process costing system than it is in a job-order costing system?

**5–4**   How many Work in Process accounts are maintained in a company that uses process costing?

**5–5**   Assume that a company has two processing departments—Mixing followed by Firing. Prepare a journal entry to show a transfer of work in process from the Mixing Department to the Firing Department.

**5–6**   Assume that a company has two processing departments—Mixing followed by Firing. Explain what costs might be added to the Firing Department's Work in Process account during a period.

**5–7**   What is meant by the term *equivalent units of production* when the weighted-average method is used?

**5–8**   Watkins Trophies, Inc., produces thousands of medallions made of bronze, silver, and gold. The medallions are identical except for the materials used in their manufacture. What costing system would you advise the company to use?

**APPLYING EXCEL**

This exercise relates to the Double Diamond Skis' Shaping and Milling Department that was discussed earlier in the chapter. The Excel worksheet form that appears below consolidates data from Exhibits 5–5 and 5–8. Download the workbook containing this form from Connect, where you will also receive instructions about how to use this worksheet form.

**LO5–2, LO5–3, LO5–4, LO5–5**

| | A | B | C | D | E |
|---|---|---|---|---|---|
| 1 | Chapter 5: Applying Excel | | | | |
| 2 | | | | | |
| 3 | **Data** | | | | |
| 4 | Beginning work in process inventory: | | | | |
| 5 | Units in process | 200 | | | |
| 6 | Completion with respect to materials | 55% | | | |
| 7 | Completion with respect to conversion | 30% | | | |
| 8 | Costs in the beginning work in process inventory: | | | | |
| 9 | Materials cost | $9,600 | | | |
| 10 | Conversion cost | $5,575 | | | |
| 11 | Units started into production during the period | 5,000 | | | |
| 12 | Costs added to production during the period: | | | | |
| 13 | Materials cost | $368,600 | | | |
| 14 | Conversion cost | $350,900 | | | |
| 15 | Ending work in process inventory: | | | | |
| 16 | Units in process | 400 | | | |
| 17 | Completion with respect to materials | 40% | | | |
| 18 | Completion with respect to conversion | 25% | | | |
| 19 | | | | | |
| 20 | Enter a formula into each of the cells marked with a ? below | | | | |
| 21 | | | | | |
| 22 | **Weighted Average method:** | | | | |
| 23 | | | | | |
| 24 | *Equivalent Units of Production* | | | | |
| 25 | | Materials | Conversion | | |
| 26 | Units transferred to the next department | ? | ? | | |
| 27 | Equivalent units in ending work in process inventory: | | | | |
| 28 | Materials | ? | | | |
| 29 | Conversion | | ? | | |
| 30 | Equivalent units of production | ? | ? | | |
| 31 | | | | | |
| 32 | *Costs per Equivalent Unit* | | | | |
| 33 | | Materials | Conversion | | |
| 34 | Cost of beginning work in process inventory | ? | ? | | |
| 35 | Costs added during the period | ? | ? | | |
| 36 | Total cost | ? | ? | | |
| 37 | Equivalent units of production | ? | ? | | |
| 38 | Cost per equivalent unit | ? | ? | | |
| 39 | | | | | |
| 40 | *Costs of Ending Work in Process Inventory and the Units Transferred Out* | | | | |
| 41 | | Materials | Conversion | Total | |
| 42 | Ending work in process inventory: | | | | |
| 43 | Equivalent units | ? | ? | | |
| 44 | Cost per equivalent unit | ? | ? | | |
| 45 | Cost of ending work in process inventory | ? | ? | ? | |
| 46 | | | | | |
| 47 | Units completed and transferred out: | | | | |
| 48 | Units transferred to the next department | ? | ? | | |
| 49 | Cost per equivalent unit | ? | ? | | |
| 50 | Cost of units transferred out | ? | ? | ? | |
| 51 | | | | | |
| 52 | *Cost Reconciliation* | | | | |
| 53 | Costs to be accounted for: | | | | |
| 54 | Cost of beginning work in process inventory | ? | | | |
| 55 | Costs added to production during the period | ? | | | |
| 56 | Total cost to be accounted for | ? | | | |
| 57 | Costs accounted for as follows: | | | | |
| 58 | Cost of ending work in process inventory | ? | | | |
| 59 | Cost of units transferred out | ? | | | |
| 60 | Total cost accounted for | ? | | | |
| 61 | | | | | |

◄ ► ... **Chapter 5 Form** Chapter 5 Fo ... ⊕

You should proceed to the requirements below only after completing your worksheet.

*Required:*
1. Check your worksheet by changing the beginning work in process inventory to 100 units, the units started into production during the period to 2,500 units, and the units in ending work in process inventory to 200 units, keeping all of the other data the same as in the original example. If your worksheet is operating properly, the cost per equivalent unit for materials should now be $152.50 and

the cost per equivalent unit for conversion should be $145.50. If you do not get these answers, find the errors in your worksheet and correct them.

How much is the total cost of the units transferred out? Did it change? Why or why not?

2.  Enter the following data from a different company into your worksheet:

| Beginning work in process inventory: | |
|---|---|
| Units in process..................................... | 200 |
| Completion with respect to materials ................... | 100% |
| Completion with respect to conversion ................. | 20% |
| Costs in the beginning work in process inventory: | |
| Materials cost ...................................... | $2,000 |
| Conversion cost ................................... | $800 |
| Units started into production during the period ............ | 1,800 |
| Costs added during the period: | |
| Materials cost ...................................... | $18,400 |
| Conversion cost ................................... | $38,765 |
| Ending work in process inventory: | |
| Units in process .................................... | 100 |
| Completion with respect to materials .................. | 100% |
| Completion with respect to conversion ................. | 30% |

What is the cost of the units transferred out?

3.  What happens to the cost of the units transferred out in part (2) above if the percentage completion with respect to conversion for the beginning inventory is changed from 20% to 40% and everything else remains the same? What happens to the cost per equivalent unit for conversion? Explain.

## THE FOUNDATIONAL 15         connect

> **LO5–1, LO5–2, LO5–3, LO5–4, LO5–5**

Clopack Company manufactures one product that goes through one processing department called Mixing. All raw materials are introduced at the start of work in the Mixing Department. The company uses the weighted-average method of process costing. Its Work in Process T-account for the Mixing Department for June follows (all forthcoming questions pertain to June):

| Work in Process—Mixing Department | | | |
|---|---|---|---|
| June 1 balance | 28,000 | Completed and transferred to Finished Goods | ? |
| Materials | 120,000 | | |
| Direct labor | 79,500 | | |
| Overhead | 97,000 | | |
| June 30 balance | ? | | |

The June 1 work in process inventory consisted of 5,000 units with $16,000 in materials cost and $12,000 in conversion cost. The June 1 work in process inventory was 100% complete with respect to materials and 50% complete with respect to conversion. During June, 37,500 units were started into production. The June 30 work in process inventory consisted of 8,000 units that were 100% complete with respect to materials and 40% complete with respect to conversion.

*Required:*

1.  Prepare the journal entries to record the raw materials used in production and the direct labor cost incurred.
2.  Prepare the journal entry to record the overhead cost applied to production.
3.  How many units were completed and transferred to finished goods during the period?

4. Compute the equivalent units of production for materials.
5. Compute the equivalent units of production for conversion.
6. What is the cost of beginning work in process inventory plus the cost added during the period for materials?
7. What is the cost of beginning work in process inventory plus the cost added during the period for conversion?
8. What is the cost per equivalent unit for materials?
9. What is the cost per equivalent unit for conversion?
10. What is the cost of ending work in process inventory for materials?
11. What is the cost of ending work in process inventory for conversion?
12. What is the cost of materials transferred to finished goods?
13. What is the amount of conversion cost transferred to finished goods?
14. Prepare the journal entry to record the transfer of costs from Work in Process to Finished Goods.
15. What is the total cost to be accounted for? What is the total cost accounted for?

  **EXERCISES**

**EXERCISE 5–1   Process Costing Journal Entries LO5–1**
Quality Brick Company produces bricks in two processing departments—Molding and Firing. Information relating to the company's operations in March follows:
a. Raw materials used in production: Molding Department, $23,000; and Firing Department, $8,000.
b. Direct labor costs incurred: Molding Department, $12,000; and Firing Department, $7,000.
c. Manufacturing overhead was applied: Molding Department, $25,000; and Firing Department, $37,000.
d. Unfired, molded bricks were transferred from the Molding Department to the Firing Department. According to the company's process costing system, the cost of the unfired, molded bricks was $57,000.
e. Finished bricks were transferred from the Firing Department to the finished goods warehouse. According to the company's process costing system, the cost of the finished bricks was $103,000.
f. Finished bricks were sold to customers. According to the company's process costing system, the cost of the finished bricks sold was $101,000.

**Required:**
Prepare journal entries to record items (a) through (f) above.

**EXERCISE 5–2   Equivalent Units of Production—Weighted-Average Method LO5–2**
Clonex Labs, Inc., uses the weighted-average method in its process costing system. The following data are available for one department for October:

|  | | Percent Completed | |
| --- | --- | --- | --- |
|  | Units | Materials | Conversion |
| Work in process, October 1 ............ | 30,000 | 65% | 30% |
| Work in process, October 31 ........... | 15,000 | 80% | 40% |

The department started 175,000 units into production during the month and transferred 190,000 completed units to the next department.

**Required:**
Compute the equivalent units of production for October.

**EXERCISE 5–3   Cost per Equivalent Unit—Weighted-Average Method** LO5–3

Superior Micro Products uses the weighted-average method in its process costing system. Data for the Assembly Department for May appear below:

|  | Materials | Labor | Overhead |
|---|---|---|---|
| Work in process, May 1............................. | $18,000 | $5,500 | $27,500 |
| Cost added during May............................. | $238,900 | $80,300 | $401,500 |
| Equivalent units of production.................... | 35,000 | 33,000 | 33,000 |

**Required:**

Compute the cost per equivalent unit for materials, labor, overhead, and in total.

**EXERCISE 5–4   Assigning Costs to Units—Weighted-Average Method** LO5–4

Data concerning a recent period's activity in the Prep Department, the first processing department in a company that uses process costing, appear below:

|  | Materials | Conversion |
|---|---|---|
| Equivalent units in ending work in process inventory.......... | 2,000 | 800 |
| Cost per equivalent unit...................................... | $13.86 | $4.43 |

A total of 20,100 units were completed and transferred to the next processing department during the period.

**Required:**

1.  Compute the cost of ending work in process inventory for materials, conversion, and in total.
2.  Compute the cost of the units completed and transferred out for materials, conversion, and in total.

**EXERCISE 5–5   Cost Reconciliation Report—Weighted-Average Method** LO5–5

Maria Am Corporation uses the weighted-average method in its process costing system. The Baking Department is one of the processing departments in its strudel manufacturing facility. In June in the Baking Department, the cost of beginning work in process inventory was $3,570, the cost of ending work in process inventory was $2,860, and the cost added to production was $43,120.

**Required:**

Prepare a cost reconciliation report for the Baking Department for June.

**EXERCISE 5–6   Equivalent Units of Production—Weighted-Average Method** LO5–2

Highlands Company uses the weighted-average method in its process costing system. It processes wood pulp for various manufacturers of paper products. Data relating to tons of pulp processed during June are provided below:

|  | Tons of Pulp | Percent Completed | |
|---|---|---|---|
|  |  | Materials | Labor and Overhead |
| Work in process, June 1............... | 20,000 | 90% | 80% |
| Work in process, June 30.............. | 30,000 | 60% | 40% |
| Started into production during June... | 190,000 |  |  |

**Required:**

1.  Compute the number of tons of pulp completed and transferred out during June.
2.  Compute the equivalent units of production for materials and for labor and overhead for June.

**EXERCISE 5–7   Process Costing Journal Entries** LO5–1

Chocolaterie de Geneve, SA, is located in a French-speaking canton in Switzerland. The company makes chocolate truffles that are sold in popular embossed tins. The company has two processing departments—Cooking and Molding. In the Cooking Department, the raw ingredients for the truffles are mixed and then cooked in special candy-making vats. In the Molding Department, the melted chocolate and other ingredients from the Cooking Department are carefully poured into molds and decorative flourishes are applied by hand. After cooling, the truffles are packed for sale. The company uses a process costing system. The T-accounts below show the flow of costs through the two departments in April:

**Work in Process—Cooking**

| | | | |
|---|---|---|---|
| Balance 4/1 | 8,000 | Transferred out | 160,000 |
| Direct materials | 42,000 | | |
| Direct labor | 50,000 | | |
| Overhead | 75,000 | | |

**Work in Process—Molding**

| | | | |
|---|---|---|---|
| Balance 4/1 | 4,000 | Transferred out | 240,000 |
| Transferred in | 160,000 | | |
| Direct labor | 36,000 | | |
| Overhead | 45,000 | | |

**Required:**
Prepare journal entries showing the flow of costs through the two processing departments during April.

**EXERCISE 5–8 Equivalent Units; Cost per Equivalent Unit; Assigning Costs to Units—Weighted-Average Method LO5–2, LO5–3, LO5–4**

Helix Corporation uses the weighted-average method in its process costing system. It produces prefabricated flooring in a series of steps carried out in production departments. All of the material that is used in the first production department is added at the beginning of processing in that department. Data for May for the first production department follow:

| | | Percent Complete | |
|---|---|---|---|
| | Units | Materials | Conversion |
| Work in process inventory, May 1 . . . . . . | 5,000 | 100% | 40% |
| Work in process inventory, May 31 . . . . . | 10,000 | 100% | 30% |
| Materials cost in work in process inventory, May 1 . . . . . . . . . . . . | | $1,500 | |
| Conversion cost in work in process inventory, May 1 . . . . . . . . . . | | $4,000 | |
| Units started into production . . . . . . . . . . . . . . . . . . . . . . . . . . . . . . | | 180,000 | |
| Units transferred to the next production department . . . . . . . . . . | | 175,000 | |
| Materials cost added during May . . . . . . . . . . . . . . . . . . . . . . . . . . | | $54,000 | |
| Conversion cost added during May . . . . . . . . . . . . . . . . . . . . . . . . | | $352,000 | |

**Required:**
1. Calculate the first production department's equivalent units of production for materials and conversion for May.
2. Compute the first production department's cost per equivalent unit for materials and conversion for May.
3. Compute the first production department's cost of ending work in process inventory for materials, conversion, and in total for May.
4. Compute the first production department's cost of the units transferred to the next production department for materials, conversion, and in total for May.

**EXERCISE 5–9 Equivalent Units and Cost per Equivalent Unit—Weighted-Average Method LO5–2, LO5–3**

Pureform, Inc., uses the weighted-average method in its process costing system. It manufactures a product that passes through two departments. Data for a recent month for the first department follow:

| | Units | Materials | Labor | Overhead |
|---|---|---|---|---|
| Work in process inventory, beginning. . . . . | 5,000 | $4,320 | $1,040 | $1,790 |
| Units started in process . . . . . . . . . . . . . . . | 45,000 | | | |
| Units transferred out . . . . . . . . . . . . . . . . . . | 42,000 | | | |
| Work in process inventory, ending . . . . . . . | 8,000 | | | |
| Cost added during the month . . . . . . . . . . | | $52,800 | $21,500 | $32,250 |

The beginning work in process inventory was 80% complete with respect to materials and 60% complete with respect to labor and overhead. The ending work in process inventory was 75% complete with respect to materials and 50% complete with respect to labor and overhead.

**Required:**

1. Compute the first department's equivalent units of production for materials, labor, and overhead for the month.
2. Determine the first department's cost per equivalent unit for materials, labor, and overhead for the month.

**EXERCISE 5–10   Equivalent Units of Production—Weighted-Average Method LO5–2**

Alaskan Fisheries, Inc., processes salmon for various distributors and it uses the weighted-average method in its process costing system. The company has two processing departments—Cleaning and Packing. Data relating to pounds of salmon processed in the Cleaning Department during July are presented below:

|  | | Percent Completed | |
| --- | --- | --- | --- |
|  | Pounds of Salmon | Materials | Labor and Overhead |
| Work in process inventory, July 1 . . . . . . . | 20,000 | 100% | 30% |
| Work in process inventory, July 31 . . . . . . | 25,000 | 100% | 60% |

A total of 380,000 pounds of salmon were started into processing during July. All materials are added at the beginning of processing in the Cleaning Department.

**Required:**

Compute the Cleaning Department's equivalent units of production for materials and for labor and overhead in the month of July.

**EXERCISE 5–11   Comprehensive Exercise; Second Production Department—Weighted-Average Method LO5–2, LO5–3, LO5–4, LO5–5**

Scribners Corporation produces fine papers in three production departments—Pulping, Drying, and Finishing. In the Pulping Department, raw materials such as wood fiber and rag cotton are mechanically and chemically treated to separate their fibers. The result is a thick slurry of fibers. In the Drying Department, the wet fibers transferred from the Pulping Department are laid down on porous webs, pressed to remove excess liquid, and dried in ovens. In the Finishing Department, the dried paper is coated, cut, and spooled onto reels. The company uses the weighted-average method in its process costing system. Data for March for the Drying Department follow:

|  | | Percent Completed | |
| --- | --- | --- | --- |
|  | Units | Pulping | Conversion |
| Work in process inventory, March 1 . . . . . . . . . . . . . . . . . . . | 5,000 | 100% | 20% |
| Work in process inventory, March 31 . . . . . . . . . . . . . . . . . . | 8,000 | 100% | 25% |
| Pulping cost in work in process inventory, March 1 . . . . . . . . . . . . . . . | | $4,800 | |
| Conversion cost in work in process inventory, March 1 . . . . . . . . . . | | $500 | |
| Units transferred to the next production department . . . . . . . . . . . . | | 157,000 | |
| Pulping cost added during March . . . . . . . . . . . . . . . . . . . . . . . . . . . . | | $102,450 | |
| Conversion cost added during March . . . . . . . . . . . . . . . . . . . . . . . . | | $31,300 | |

No materials are added in the Drying Department. Pulping cost represents the costs of the wet fibers transferred in from the Pulping Department. Wet fiber is processed in the Drying Department in batches; each unit in the above table is a batch and one batch of wet fibers produces a set amount of dried paper that is passed on to the Finishing Department.

**Required:**

1. Compute the Drying Department's equivalent units of production for pulping and conversion in March.
2. Compute the Drying Department's cost per equivalent unit for pulping and conversion in March.
3. Compute the Drying Department's cost of ending work in process inventory for pulping, conversion, and in total for March.
4. Compute the Drying Department's cost of units transferred out to the Finishing Department for pulping, conversion, and in total in March.
5. Prepare a cost reconciliation report for the Drying Department for March.

## EXERCISE 5–12 Equivalent Units; Assigning Costs; Cost Reconciliation—Weighted-Average Method LO5–2, LO5–4, LO5–5

Superior Micro Products uses the weighted-average method in its process costing system. During January, the Delta Assembly Department completed its processing of 25,000 units and transferred them to the next department. The cost of beginning work in process inventory and the costs added during January amounted to $599,780 in total. The ending work in process inventory in January consisted of 3,000 units, which were 80% complete with respect to materials and 60% complete with respect to labor and overhead. The costs per equivalent unit for the month were as follows:

|  | Materials | Labor | Overhead |
|---|---|---|---|
| Cost per equivalent unit . . . . . . . . . . . . . . . . . . . . . . . . . . . | $12.50 | $3.20 | $6.40 |

**Required:**

1. Compute the equivalent units of materials, labor, and overhead in the ending work in process inventory for the month.
2. Compute the cost of ending work in process inventory for materials, labor, overhead, and in total for January.
3. Compute the cost of the units transferred to the next department for materials, labor, overhead, and in total for January.
4. Prepare a cost reconciliation for January. (Note: You will not be able to break the cost to be accounted for into the cost of beginning work in process inventory and costs added during the month.)

 **connect**                                                 **PROBLEMS**

## PROBLEM 5–13 Comprehensive Problem; Second Production Department—Weighted-Average Method LO5–2, LO5–3, LO5–4, LO5–5

Old Country Links, Inc., produces sausages in three production departments—Mixing, Casing and Curing, and Packaging. In the Mixing Department, meats are prepared and ground and then mixed with spices. The spiced meat mixture is then transferred to the Casing and Curing Department, where the mixture is force-fed into casings and then hung and cured in climate-controlled smoking chambers. In the Packaging Department, the cured sausages are sorted, packed, and labeled. The company uses the weighted-average method in its process costing system. Data for September for the Casing and Curing Department follow:

|  | Units | Percent Completed | | |
|---|---|---|---|---|
|  |  | Mixing | Materials | Conversion |
| Work in process inventory, September 1 . . . . . . . . . . . | 1 | 100% | 90% | 80% |
| Work in process inventory, September 30 . . . . . . . . . . | 1 | 100% | 80% | 70% |

|  | Mixing | Materials | Conversion |
|---|---|---|---|
| Work in process inventory, September 1 . . . . . . . . . . . . . . . . . | $1,670 | $90 | $605 |
| Cost added during September . . . . . . . . . . . . . . . . . . . . . . . . | $81,460 | $6,006 | $42,490 |

Mixing cost represents the costs of the spiced meat mixture transferred in from the Mixing Department. The spiced meat mixture is processed in the Casing and Curing Department in batches; each unit in the above table is a batch and one batch of spiced meat mixture produces a set amount of sausages that are passed on to the Packaging Department. During September, 50 batches (i.e., units) were completed and transferred to the Packaging Department.

**Required:**

1. Determine the Casing and Curing Department's equivalent units of production for mixing, materials, and conversion for the month of September. Do not round off your computations.
2. Compute the Casing and Curing Department's cost per equivalent unit for mixing, materials, and conversion for the month of September.

3.   Compute the Casing and Curing Department's cost of ending work in process inventory for mixing, materials, conversion, and in total for September.
4.   Compute the Casing and Curing Department's cost of units transferred out to the Packaging Department for mixing, materials, conversion, and in total for September.
5.   Prepare a cost reconciliation report for the Casing and Curing Department for September.

**PROBLEM 5–14    Analysis of Work in Process T-account—Weighted-Average Method LO5–1, LO5–2, LO5–3, LO5–4**

Weston Products manufactures an industrial cleaning compound that goes through three processing departments—Grinding, Mixing, and Cooking. All raw materials are introduced at the start of work in the Grinding Department. The Work in Process T-account for the Grinding Department for May is given below:

| Work in Process—Grinding Department | | | |
|---|---|---|---|
| Inventory, May 1 | 21,800 | Completed and transferred to the Mixing Department | ? |
| Materials | 133,400 | | |
| Conversion | 225,500 | | |
| Inventory, May 31 | ? | | |

The May 1 work in process inventory consisted of 18,000 pounds with $14,600 in materials cost and $7,200 in conversion cost. The May 1 work in process inventory was 100% complete with respect to materials and 30% complete with respect to conversion. During May, 167,000 pounds were started into production. The May 31 inventory consisted of 15,000 pounds that were 100% complete with respect to materials and 60% complete with respect to conversion. The company uses the weighted-average method in its process costing system.

*Required:*
1.   Compute the Grinding Department's equivalent units of production for materials and conversion in May.
2.   Compute the Grinding Department's costs per equivalent unit for materials and conversion for May.
3.   Compute the Grinding Department's cost of ending work in process inventory for materials, conversion, and in total for May.
4.   Compute the Grinding Department's cost of units transferred out to the Mixing Department for materials, conversion, and in total for May.

**PROBLEM 5–15    Comprehensive Problem—Weighted-Average Method LO5–2, LO5–3, LO5–4, LO5–5**

Sunspot Beverages, Ltd., of Fiji uses the weighted-average method in its process costing system. It makes blended tropical fruit drinks in two stages. Fruit juices are extracted from fresh fruits and then blended in the Blending Department. The blended juices are then bottled and packed for shipping in the Bottling Department. The following information pertains to the operations of the Blending Department for June.

| | | Percent Completed | |
|---|---|---|---|
| | Units | Materials | Conversion |
| Work in process, beginning ......... | 20,000 | 100% | 75% |
| Started into production ............ | 180,000 | | |
| Completed and transferred out ..... | 160,000 | | |
| Work in process, ending ........... | 40,000 | 100% | 25% |

| | Materials | Conversion |
|---|---|---|
| Work in process, beginning ........ | $25,200 | $24,800 |
| Cost added during June ........... | $334,800 | $238,700 |

*Required:*
1.   Calculate the Blending Department's equivalent units of production for materials and conversion in June.
2.   Calculate the Blending Department's cost per equivalent unit for materials and conversion in June.
3.   Calculate the Blending Department's cost of ending work in process inventory for materials, conversion, and in total for June.

4. Calculate the Blending Department's cost of units transferred out to the Bottling Department for materials, conversion, and in total for June.
5. Prepare a cost reconciliation report for the Blending Department for June.

**PROBLEM 5–16  Comprehensive Problem—Weighted-Average Method LO5–2, LO5–3, LO5–4, LO5–5**
Builder Products, Inc., uses the weighted-average method in its process costing system. It manufactures a caulking compound that goes through three processing stages prior to completion. Information on work in the first department, Cooking, is given below for May:

```
Production data:
    Pounds in process, May 1; materials 100% complete;
        conversion 80% complete ..............................   10,000
    Pounds started into production during May ...................  100,000
    Pounds completed and transferred out .......................      ?
    Pounds in process, May 31; materials 60% complete;
        conversion 20% complete ..............................   15,000
Cost data:
    Work in process inventory, May 1: ..........................
        Materials cost .......................................   $1,500
        Conversion cost ......................................   $7,200
    Cost added during May:
        Materials cost .......................................  $154,500
        Conversion cost ......................................  $90,800
```

**Required:**
1. Compute the equivalent units of production for materials and conversion for May.
2. Compute the cost per equivalent unit for materials and conversion for May.
3. Compute the cost of ending work in process inventory for materials, conversion, and in total for May.
4. Compute the cost of units transferred out to the next department for materials, conversion, and in total for May.
5. Prepare a cost reconciliation report for May.

**PROBLEM 5–17  Cost Flows LO5–1**
Lubricants, Inc., produces a special kind of grease that is widely used by race car drivers. The grease is produced in two processing departments—Refining and Blending. Raw materials are introduced at various points in the Refining Department.

The following incomplete Work in Process account is available for the Refining Department for March:

**Work in Process—Refining Department**

| | | | |
|---|---|---|---|
| March 1 balance | 38,000 | Completed and transferred to Blending | ? |
| Materials | 495,000 | | |
| Direct labor | 72,000 | | |
| Overhead | 181,000 | | |
| March 31 balance | ? | | |

The March 1 work in process inventory in the Refining Department consists of the following elements: materials, $25,000; direct labor, $4,000; and overhead, $9,000.

Costs incurred during March in the Blending Department were: materials used, $115,000; direct labor, $18,000; and overhead cost applied to production, $42,000.

**Required:**
1. Prepare journal entries to record the costs incurred in both the Refining Department and Blending Department during March. Key your entries to the items (a) through (g) below.
   a. Raw materials used in production.
   b. Direct labor costs incurred.
   c. Manufacturing overhead costs incurred for the entire factory, $225,000. (Credit Accounts Payable.)
   d. Manufacturing overhead was applied to production using a predetermined overhead rate.
   e. Units that were complete with respect to processing in the Refining Department were transferred to the Blending Department, $740,000.

f. Units that were complete with respect to processing in the Blending Department were transferred to Finished Goods, $950,000.

g. Completed units were sold on account, $1,500,000. The Cost of Goods Sold was $900,000.

2. Post the journal entries from (1) above to T-accounts. The following account balances existed at the beginning of March. (The beginning balance in the Refining Department's Work in Process is given in the T-account shown above.)

| | |
|---|---|
| Raw Materials. . . . . . . . . . . . . . . . . . . . . . . . . . . . . . . . . . . | $618,000 |
| Work in Process—Blending Department . . . . . . . . . . . | $65,000 |
| Finished Goods . . . . . . . . . . . . . . . . . . . . . . . . . . . . . . . | $20,000 |

After posting the entries to the T-accounts, find the ending balance in the inventory accounts and the Manufacturing Overhead account.

**PROBLEM 5–18  Interpreting a Report—Weighted-Average Method** LO5–2, LO5–3, LO5–4

Cooperative San José of southern Sonora state in Mexico makes a unique syrup using cane sugar and local herbs. The syrup is sold in small bottles and is prized as a flavoring for drinks and for use in desserts. The bottles are sold for $12 each. The first stage in the production process is carried out in the Mixing Department, which removes foreign matter from the raw materials and mixes them in the proper proportions in large vats. The company uses the weighted-average method in its process costing system.

A hastily prepared report for the Mixing Department for April appears below:

| | |
|---|---|
| **Units to be accounted for:** | |
| Work in process, April 1 (materials 90% complete; conversion 80% complete) . . . . . . . . . . . . . . . . . . . . . . . . . . . | 30,000 |
| Started into production . . . . . . . . . . . . . . . . . . . . . . . . . . . . . . | 200,000 |
| Total units to be accounted for . . . . . . . . . . . . . . . . . . . . . . . . | 230,000 |
| **Units accounted for as follows:** | |
| Transferred to next department . . . . . . . . . . . . . . . . . . . . . . . . | 190,000 |
| Work in process, April 30 (materials 75% complete; conversion 60% complete) . . . . . . . . . . . . . . . . . . . . . . . . . . . | 40,000 |
| Total units accounted for . . . . . . . . . . . . . . . . . . . . . . . . . . . . . | 230,000 |
| **Cost Reconciliation** | |
| Cost to be accounted for: | |
| Work in process, April 1 . . . . . . . . . . . . . . . . . . . . . . . . . . . . . | $ 98,000 |
| Cost added during the month . . . . . . . . . . . . . . . . . . . . . . . . . | 827,000 |
| Total cost to be accounted for . . . . . . . . . . . . . . . . . . . . . . . . . | $925,000 |
| Cost accounted for as follows: | |
| Work in process, April 30 . . . . . . . . . . . . . . . . . . . . . . . . . . . . | $119,400 |
| Transferred to next department . . . . . . . . . . . . . . . . . . . . . . . . | 805,600 |
| Total cost accounted for . . . . . . . . . . . . . . . . . . . . . . . . . . . . . | $925,000 |

Management would like some additional information about Cooperative San José's operations.

**Required:**

1. What were the Mixing Department's equivalent units of production for materials and conversion for April?

2. What were the Mixing Department's cost per equivalent unit for materials and conversion for April? The beginning inventory consisted of the following costs: materials, $67,800; and conversion cost, $30,200. The costs added during the month consisted of: materials, $579,000; and conversion cost, $248,000.

3. How many of the units transferred out of the Mixing Department in April were started and completed during that month?

4. The manager of the Mixing Department stated, "Materials prices jumped from about $2.50 per unit in March to $3 per unit in April, but due to good cost control I was able to hold our materials cost to less than $3 per unit for the month." Should this manager be rewarded for good cost control? Explain.

## BUILDING YOUR SKILLS

**ANALYTICAL THINKING LO5–2, LO5–3, LO5–4**

"I think we goofed when we hired that new assistant controller," said Ruth Scarpino, president of Provost Industries. "Just look at this report that he prepared for last month for the Finishing Department. I can't understand it."

| Finishing Department costs: | |
| --- | --- |
| Work in process inventory, April 1, 450 units; materials 100% complete; conversion 60% complete . . . . . . . . . . . . . . . . . . . . . . . | $  8,208* |
| Costs transferred in during the month from the preceding department, 1,950 units . . . . . . . . . . . . . . . . . . . . . . . . . . . . | 17,940 |
| Materials cost added during the month . . . . . . . . . . . . . . . . . . . . . . . . . . | 6,210 |
| Conversion costs incurred during the month . . . . . . . . . . . . . . . . . . . . . . | 13,920 |
| Total departmental costs . . . . . . . . . . . . . . . . . . . . . . . . . . . . . . . . . . . . . | $46,278 |
| | |
| Finishing Department costs assigned to: | |
| Units completed and transferred to finished goods, 1,800 units at $25.71 per unit . . . . . . . . . . . . . . . . . . . . . . . . . . . . . | $46,278 |
| Work in process inventory, April 30, 600 units; materials 0% complete; conversion 35% complete . . . . . . . . . . . . . . . | 0 |
| Total departmental costs assigned . . . . . . . . . . . . . . . . . . . . . . . . . . . . . | $46,278 |

*Consists of cost transferred in, $4,068; materials cost, $1,980; and conversion cost, $2,160.

"He's struggling to learn our system," replied Frank Harrop, the operations manager. "The problem is that he's been away from process costing for a long time, and it's coming back slowly."

"It's not just the format of his report that I'm concerned about. Look at that $25.71 unit cost that he's come up with for April. Doesn't that seem high to you?" said Ms. Scarpino.

"Yes, it does seem high; but on the other hand, I know we had an increase in materials prices during April, and that may be the explanation," replied Mr. Harrop. "I'll get someone else to redo this report and then we can see what's going on."

Provost Industries manufactures a ceramic product that goes through two processing departments—Molding and Finishing. The company uses the weighted-average method in its process costing.

*Required:*
1. Prepare a report for the Finishing Department showing how much cost should have been assigned to the units completed and transferred to finished goods, and how much cost should have been assigned to ending work in process inventory in the Finishing Department.
2. Explain to the president why the unit cost on the new assistant controller's report is so high.

**ETHICS CHALLENGE LO5–2, LO5–3, LO5–4**

Gary Stevens and Mary James are production managers in the Consumer Electronics Division of General Electronics Company, which has several dozen plants scattered in locations throughout the world. Mary manages the plant located in Des Moines, Iowa, while Gary manages the plant in El Segundo, California. Production managers are paid a salary and get an additional bonus equal to 5% of their base salary if the entire division meets or exceeds its target profits for the year. The bonus is determined in March after the company's annual report has been prepared and issued to stockholders.

Shortly after the beginning of the new year, Mary received a phone call from Gary that went like this:

*Gary:* How's it going, Mary?

*Mary:* Fine, Gary. How's it going with you?

*Gary:* Great! I just got the preliminary profit figures for the division for last year and we are within $200,000 of making the year's target profits. All we have to do is pull a few strings, and we'll be over the top!

*Mary:* What do you mean?

*Gary:* Well, one thing that would be easy to change is your estimate of the percentage completion of your ending work in process inventories.

*Mary:* I don't know if I can do that, Gary. Those percentage completion figures are supplied by Tom Winthrop, my lead supervisor, who I have always trusted to provide us with good estimates. Besides, I have already sent the percentage completion figures to corporate headquarters.

*Gary:* You can always tell them there was a mistake. Think about it, Mary. All of us managers are doing as much as we can to pull this bonus out of the hat. You may not want the bonus check, but the rest of us sure could use it.

The final processing department in Mary's production facility began the year with no work in process inventory. During the year, 210,000 units were transferred in from the prior processing department and 200,000 units were completed and sold. Costs transferred in from the prior department totaled $39,375,000. No materials are added in the final processing department. A total of $20,807,500 of conversion cost was incurred in the final processing department during the year.

*Required:*

1.  Tom Winthrop estimated that the units in ending work in process inventory in the final processing department were 30% complete with respect to the conversion costs of the final processing department. If this estimate of the percentage completion is used, what would be the cost of goods sold for the year?

2.  Does Gary Stevens want the estimated percentage completion to be increased or decreased? Explain why.

3.  What percentage completion would result in increasing reported net operating income by $200,000 over the net operating income that would be reported if the 30% figure were used?

4.  Do you think Mary James should go along with the request to alter estimates of the percentage completion? Why or why not?

### A LOOK BACK

We provided overviews of the systems that are used to accumulate product costs in Chapters 2 and 3 (job-order costing), Chapter 4 (activity-based costing), and Chapter 5 (process costing).

### A LOOK AT THIS CHAPTER

Chapter 6 describes the basics of cost-volume-profit analysis, an essential tool for decision making. Cost-volume-profit analysis helps managers understand the interrelationships among cost, volume, and profit.

### A LOOK AHEAD

Chapter 7 contrasts variable costing and absorption costing income statements for manufacturers and it explains how the contribution format can be used to measure the profitability of business segments.

# Cost-Volume-Profit Relationships

## CHAPTER OUTLINE

**The Basics of Cost-Volume-Profit (CVP) Analysis**

- Contribution Margin
- CVP Relationships in Equation Form
- CVP Relationships in Graphic Form
- Contribution Margin Ratio (CM Ratio) and the Variable Expense Ratio
- Additional Applications of CVP Concepts

**Break-Even and Target Profit Analysis**

- Break-Even Analysis
- Target Profit Analysis
- The Margin of Safety

**CVP Considerations in Choosing a Cost Structure**

- Cost Structure and Profit Stability
- Operating Leverage

**Structuring Sales Commissions**

**Sales Mix**

- The Definition of Sales Mix
- Sales Mix and Break-Even Analysis

**Appendix 6A: Analyzing Mixed Costs**

- Diagnosing Cost Behavior with a Scattergraph Plot
- The High-Low Method
- The Least-Squares Regression Method
- Comparing the High-Low and Least-Squares Regression Methods

©Everett Collection Inc/Alamy Stock Photo

# Kid Rock and Live Nation Entertainment Pull the CVP Levers

**Live Nation Entertainment (LNE)** owns and operates outdoor amphitheaters. When hosting music concerts the company usually pays a large amount of guaranteed upfront compensation to musical artists to safeguard them from poor attendance. However, rapper-turned-country rocker Kid Rock suggested a different financial arrangement. In exchange for bypassing his up-front fee (which usually ranged between $250,000 and $350,000) and agreeing to share a portion of his ticket revenues with LNE, Kid Rock asked for a share of the revenues from food, drinks, and parking. He then lowered his ticket prices to $20 in an effort to increase attendance and the amount of discretionary spending per customer for food, drinks, and his $20 concert T-shirts. Kid Rock's ultimate goal was to design a financial model that gave fans a more affordable evening of entertainment while still providing his band and LNE adequate profits.

Source: Jurgensen, John, "Kid Rock's Plan to Change the Economics of Touring," *The Wall Street Journal*, June 7, 2013, pp. D1–D8.

*After studying Chapter 6, you should be able to:*

**LO6–1** Explain how changes in activity affect contribution margin and net operating income.

**LO6–2** Prepare and interpret a cost-volume-profit (CVP) graph and a profit graph.

**LO6–3** Use the contribution margin ratio (CM ratio) to compute changes in contribution margin and net operating income resulting from changes in sales volume.

**LO6–4** Show the effects on net operating income of changes in variable costs, fixed costs, selling price, and volume.

**LO6–5** Determine the break-even point.

**LO6–6** Determine the level of sales needed to achieve a desired target profit.

**LO6–7** Compute the margin of safety and explain its significance.

**LO6–8** Compute the degree of operating leverage at a particular level of sales and explain how it can be used to predict changes in net operating income.

**LO6–9** Compute the break-even point for a multiproduct company and explain the effects of shifts in the sales mix on contribution margin and the break-even point.

**LO6–10** *(Appendix 6A)* Analyze a mixed cost using a scattergraph plot and the high-low method.

**LO6–11** *(Appendix 6A)* Analyze a mixed cost using a scattergraph plot and the least-squares regression method.

**217**

Cost-volume-profit (CVP) analysis helps managers make many important decisions such as what products and services to offer, what prices to charge, what marketing strategy to use, and what cost structure to maintain. Its primary purpose is to estimate how profits are affected by the following five factors:

1. Selling prices.
2. Sales volume.
3. Unit variable costs.
4. Total fixed costs.
5. Mix of products sold.

To simplify CVP calculations, managers typically adopt the following assumptions with respect to these factors[1]:

1. Selling price is constant. The price of a product or service will not change as volume changes.
2. Costs are linear and can be accurately divided into variable and fixed components. The variable costs are constant per unit and the fixed costs are constant in total over the entire relevant range.
3. In multiproduct companies, the mix of products sold remains constant.

While these assumptions may be violated in practice, the results of CVP analysis are often "good enough" to be quite useful. Perhaps the greatest danger lies in relying on simple CVP analysis when a manager is contemplating a large change in sales volume that lies outside the relevant range. However, even in these situations the CVP model can be adjusted to take into account anticipated changes in selling prices, variable costs per unit, total fixed costs, and the sales mix that arise when the estimated sales volume falls outside the relevant range.

To help explain the role of CVP analysis in business decisions, we'll now turn our attention to the case of Acoustic Concepts, Inc., a company founded by Prem Narayan.

**MANAGERIAL
ACCOUNTING IN ACTION
THE ISSUE**

ACOUSTIC
concepts
inc

Prem, who was a graduate student in engineering at the time, started Acoustic Concepts, Inc., to market a radical new speaker he had designed for automobile sound systems. The speaker, called the Sonic Blaster, uses an advanced microprocessor and proprietary software to boost amplification to awesome levels. Prem contracted with a Taiwanese electronics manufacturer to produce the speaker. With seed money provided by his family, Prem placed an order with the manufacturer and ran advertisements in auto magazines.

The Sonic Blaster was an immediate success, and sales grew to the point that Prem moved the company's headquarters out of his apartment and into rented quarters in a nearby industrial park. He also hired a receptionist, an accountant, a sales manager, and a small sales staff to sell the speakers to retail stores. The accountant, Bob Luchinni, had worked for several small companies where he had acted as a business advisor as well as accountant and bookkeeper. The following discussion occurred soon after Bob was hired:

*Prem:* Bob, I've got a lot of questions about the company's finances that I hope you can help answer.

*Bob:* We're in great shape. The loan from your family will be paid off within a few months.

*Prem:* I know, but I am worried about the risks I've taken on by expanding operations. What would happen if a competitor entered the market and our sales slipped? How far could sales drop without putting us into the red? Another question I've been trying to resolve is how much our sales would have to increase to justify the big marketing campaign the sales staff is pushing for.

---

[1]One additional assumption often used in manufacturing companies is that inventories do not change. The number of units produced equals the number of units sold.

*Bob:* Marketing always wants more money for advertising.

*Prem:* And they are always pushing me to drop the selling price on the speaker. I agree with them that a lower price will boost our sales volume, but I'm not sure the increased volume will offset the loss in revenue from the lower price.

*Bob:* It sounds like these questions are all related in some way to the relationships among our selling prices, our costs, and our volume. I shouldn't have a problem coming up with some answers.

*Prem:* Can we meet again in a couple of days to see what you have come up with?

*Bob:* Sounds good. By then I'll have some preliminary answers for you as well as a model you can use for answering similar questions in the future.

# THE BASICS OF COST-VOLUME-PROFIT (CVP) ANALYSIS

Bob Luchinni's preparation for his forthcoming meeting with Prem Narayan begins with the contribution format income statement that was introduced in an earlier chapter. The contribution income statement emphasizes the behavior of costs and therefore is extremely helpful to managers in judging the impact on profits of changes in selling price, cost, or volume. Bob will base his analysis on the following contribution income statement he prepared last month:

**Acoustic Concepts, Inc.**
**Contribution Income Statement**
**For the Month of June**

|  | Total | Per Unit |
|---|---|---|
| Sales (400 speakers) . . . . . . . . . . . . | $100,000 | $250 |
| Variable expenses . . . . . . . . . . . . . . | 60,000 | 150 |
| Contribution margin . . . . . . . . . . . . | 40,000 | $100 |
| Fixed expenses . . . . . . . . . . . . . . . . | 35,000 | |
| Net operating income . . . . . . . . . . | $ 5,000 | |

Notice that sales, variable expenses, and contribution margin are expressed on a per unit basis as well as in total on this contribution income statement. The per unit figures will be very helpful to Bob in some of his calculations. Note that this contribution income statement has been prepared for management's use inside the company and would not ordinarily be made available to those outside the company.

## HELPFUL HINT

Students often struggle to derive the selling price per unit and the variable expense per unit when they are not explicitly stated in a problem. Therefore, remember that the total sales and total variable expenses can each be divided by the quantity of units sold to derive the selling price per unit and the variable expense per unit.

## Contribution Margin

Contribution margin is the amount remaining from sales revenue after variable expenses have been deducted. Thus, it is the amount available to cover fixed expenses and then to provide profits for the period. Notice the sequence here—contribution margin is used *first* to cover the fixed expenses, and then whatever remains goes toward profits. If the contribution margin is not sufficient to cover the fixed expenses, then a loss occurs for the

**LEARNING OBJECTIVE 6–1**

Explain how changes in activity affect contribution margin and net operating income.

period. To illustrate with an extreme example, assume that Acoustic Concepts sells only one speaker during a particular month. The company's income statement would appear as follows:

| Contribution Income Statement Sales of 1 Speaker | Total | Per Unit |
|---|---|---|
| Sales (1 speaker) | $ 250 | $250 |
| Variable expenses | 150 | 150 |
| Contribution margin | 100 | $100 |
| Fixed expenses | 35,000 | |
| Net operating loss | $(34,900) | |

For each additional speaker the company sells during the month, $100 more in contribution margin becomes available to help cover the fixed expenses. If a second speaker is sold, for example, then the total contribution margin will increase by $100 (to a total of $200) and the company's loss will decrease by $100, to $34,800:

| Contribution Income Statement Sales of 2 Speakers | Total | Per Unit |
|---|---|---|
| Sales (2 speakers) | $ 500 | $250 |
| Variable expenses | 300 | 150 |
| Contribution margin | 200 | $100 |
| Fixed expenses | 35,000 | |
| Net operating loss | $(34,800) | |

If enough speakers can be sold to generate $35,000 in contribution margin, then all of the fixed expenses will be covered and the company will *break even* for the month—that is, it will show neither profit nor loss but just cover all of its costs. To reach the break-even point, the company will have to sell 350 speakers in a month because each speaker sold yields $100 in contribution margin:

| Contribution Income Statement Sales of 350 Speakers | Total | Per Unit |
|---|---|---|
| Sales (350 speakers) | $87,500 | $250 |
| Variable expenses | 52,500 | 150 |
| Contribution margin | 35,000 | $100 |
| Fixed expenses | 35,000 | |
| Net operating income | $ 0 | |

Computation of the break-even point is discussed in detail later in the chapter; for the moment, note that the **break-even point** is the level of sales at which profit is zero.

*Once the break-even point has been reached, net operating income will increase by the amount of the unit contribution margin for each additional unit sold.* For example, if 351 speakers are sold in a month, then the net operating income for the month will be $100 because the company will have sold 1 speaker more than the number needed to break even:

| **Contribution Income Statement**<br>**Sales of 351 Speakers** | | |
|---|---|---|
| | Total | Per Unit |
| Sales (351 speakers) . . . . . . . . . . . . | $87,750 | $250 |
| Variable expenses . . . . . . . . . . . . . . | 52,650 | 150 |
| Contribution margin . . . . . . . . . . . . | 35,100 | $100 |
| Fixed expenses . . . . . . . . . . . . . . . . | 35,000 | |
| Net operating income . . . . . . . . . . | $ 100 | |

If 352 speakers are sold (2 speakers above the break-even point), the net operating income for the month will be $200. If 353 speakers are sold (3 speakers above the break-even point), the net operating income for the month will be $300, and so forth. To estimate the profit at any sales volume above the break-even point, multiply the number of units sold in excess of the break-even point by the unit contribution margin. The result represents the anticipated profits for the period. Or, to estimate the effect of a planned increase in sales on profits, simply multiply the increase in units sold by the unit contribution margin. The result will be the expected increase in profits. To illustrate, if Acoustic Concepts is currently selling 400 speakers per month and plans to increase sales to 425 speakers per month, the anticipated impact on profits can be computed as follows:

| | |
|---|---|
| Additional speakers to be sold . . . . . . . . . . . . . . . . . | 25 |
| Contribution margin per speaker . . . . . . . . . . . . . . . . | × $100 |
| Increase in net operating income . . . . . . . . . . . . . . . | $2,500 |

These calculations can be verified as follows:

| | **Sales Volume** | | | |
|---|---|---|---|---|
| | **400**<br>**Speakers** | **425**<br>**Speakers** | **Difference**<br>**(25 Speakers)** | **Per Unit** |
| Sales (@ $250 per speaker) . . . . . . . . | $100,000 | $106,250 | $6,250 | $250 |
| Variable expenses | | | | |
| (@ $150 per speaker) . . . . . . . . . . | 60,000 | 63,750 | 3,750 | 150 |
| Contribution margin . . . . . . . . . . . . . . | 40,000 | 42,500 | 2,500 | $100 |
| Fixed expenses . . . . . . . . . . . . . . . . . | 35,000 | 35,000 | 0 | |
| Net operating income . . . . . . . . . . . . | $ 5,000 | $ 7,500 | $2,500 | |

To summarize, if sales are zero, the company's loss would equal its fixed expenses. Each unit that is sold reduces the loss by the amount of the unit contribution margin. Once the break-even point has been reached, each additional unit sold increases the company's profit by the amount of the unit contribution margin.

1.  Which of the following statements is a common assumption underlying cost-volume-profit analysis? (You may select more than one answer.)
    a.  The variable cost per unit remains constant.
    b.  The selling price per unit remains constant.
    c.  Total fixed costs are constant within the relevant range.
    d.  The total variable costs remain constant as the level of sales fluctuates.
2.  Once a company hits its break-even point, net operating income will
    a.  Increase by an amount equal to the selling price per unit multiplied by the number of units sold above the break-even point.
    b.  Increase by an amount equal to the contribution margin ratio multiplied by the number of units sold above the break-even point.
    c.  Increase by an amount equal to the contribution margin per unit multiplied by the number of units sold above the break-even point.
    d.  Increase by an amount equal to the variable cost per unit multiplied by the number of units sold above the break-even point.

## CVP Relationships in Equation Form

The contribution format income statement can be expressed in equation form as follows:

$$\text{Profit} = (\text{Sales} - \text{Variable expenses}) - \text{Fixed expenses}$$

For brevity, we use the term *profit* to stand for net operating income in equations.

When a company has only a *single* product, as at Acoustic Concepts, we can further refine the equation as follows:

$$\text{Sales} = \text{Selling price per unit} \times \text{Quantity sold} = P \times Q$$
$$\text{Variable expenses} = \text{Variable expenses per unit} \times \text{Quantity sold} = V \times Q$$

$$\text{Profit} = (P \times Q - V \times Q) - \text{Fixed expenses}$$

We can do all of the calculations of the previous section using this simple equation. For example, earlier we computed that the net operating income (profit) at sales of 351 speakers would be $100. We can arrive at the same conclusion using the above equation as follows:

$$\text{Profit} = (P \times Q - V \times Q) - \text{Fixed expenses}$$
$$\text{Profit} = (\$250 \times 351 - \$150 \times 351) - \$35,000$$
$$= (\$250 - \$150) \times 351 - \$35,000$$
$$= (\$100) \times 351 - \$35,000$$
$$= \$35,100 - \$35,000$$
$$= \$100$$

It is often useful to express the simple profit equation in terms of the unit contribution margin (Unit CM) as follows:

$$\text{Unit CM} = \text{Selling price per unit} - \text{Variable expenses per unit} = P - V$$
$$\text{Profit} = (P \times Q - V \times Q) - \text{Fixed expenses}$$
$$\text{Profit} = (P - V) \times Q - \text{Fixed expenses}$$

$$\text{Profit} = \text{Unit CM} \times Q - \text{Fixed expenses}$$

We could also have used this equation to determine the profit at sales of 351 speakers as follows:

$$\text{Profit} = \text{Unit CM} \times Q - \text{Fixed expenses}$$
$$= \$100 \times 351 - \$35,000$$
$$= \$35,100 - \$35,000$$
$$= \$100$$

For those who are comfortable with algebra, the quickest and easiest approach to solving the problems in this chapter may be to use the simple profit equation in one of its forms.

## CVP Relationships in Graphic Form

The relationships among revenue, cost, profit, and volume are illustrated on a **cost-volume-profit (CVP) graph**. A CVP graph highlights CVP relationships over wide ranges of activity. To help explain his analysis to Prem Narayan, Bob Luchinni prepared a CVP graph for Acoustic Concepts.

**Preparing the CVP Graph**  In a CVP graph (sometimes called a *break-even chart*), unit volume is represented on the horizontal ($X$) axis and dollars on the vertical ($Y$) axis. Preparing a CVP graph involves the three steps depicted in Exhibit 6–1:

1. Draw a line parallel to the volume axis to represent total fixed expense. For Acoustic Concepts, total fixed expenses are $35,000.
2. Choose some volume of unit sales and plot the point representing total expense (fixed and variable) at the sales volume you have selected. In Exhibit 6–1, Bob Luchinni chose a volume of 600 speakers. Total expense at that sales volume is:

| | |
|---|---|
| Fixed expense | $ 35,000 |
| Variable expense (600 speakers × $150 per speaker) | 90,000 |
| Total expense | $125,000 |

After the point has been plotted, draw a line through it back to the point where the fixed expense line intersects the dollars axis.
3. Again choose some sales volume and plot the point representing total sales dollars at the activity level you have selected. In Exhibit 6–1, Bob Luchinni again chose a volume of 600 speakers. Sales at that volume total $150,000 (600 speakers × $250 per speaker). Draw a line through this point back to the origin.

The interpretation of the completed CVP graph is given in Exhibit 6–2. The anticipated profit or loss at any given level of sales is measured by the vertical distance between the total revenue line (sales) and the total expense line (variable expense plus fixed expense).

The break-even point is where the total revenue and total expense lines cross. The break-even point of 350 speakers in Exhibit 6–2 agrees with the break-even point computed earlier.

When sales are below the break-even point—in this case, 350 units—the company suffers a loss. Note that the loss (represented by the vertical distance between the total expense and total revenue lines) gets bigger as sales decline. When sales are above the break-even point, the company earns a profit and the size of the profit (represented by the vertical distance between the total revenue and total expense lines) increases as sales increase.

**EXHIBIT 6–1**
Preparing the CVP Graph

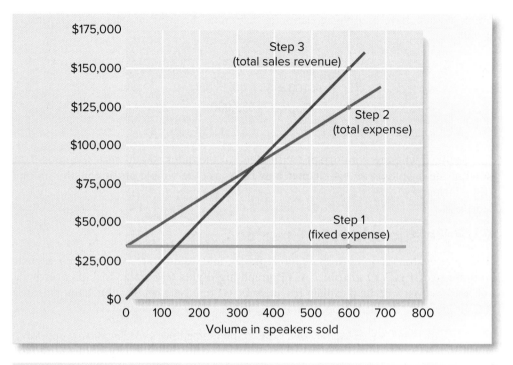

**EXHIBIT 6–2**
The Completed CVP Graph

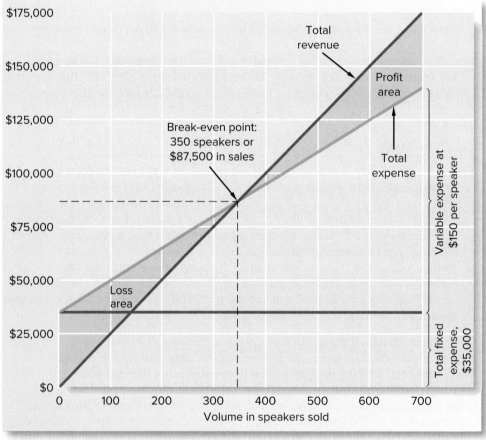

An even simpler form of the CVP graph, which we call a profit graph, is presented in Exhibit 6–3. That graph is based on the following equation:

$$\text{Profit} = \text{Unit CM} \times Q - \text{Fixed expenses}$$

In the case of Acoustic Concepts, the equation can be expressed as:

$$\text{Profit} = \$100 \times Q - \$35,000$$

Because this is a linear equation, it plots as a single straight line. To plot the line, compute the profit at two different sales volumes, plot the points, and then connect them with a

**EXHIBIT 6–3** The Profit Graph

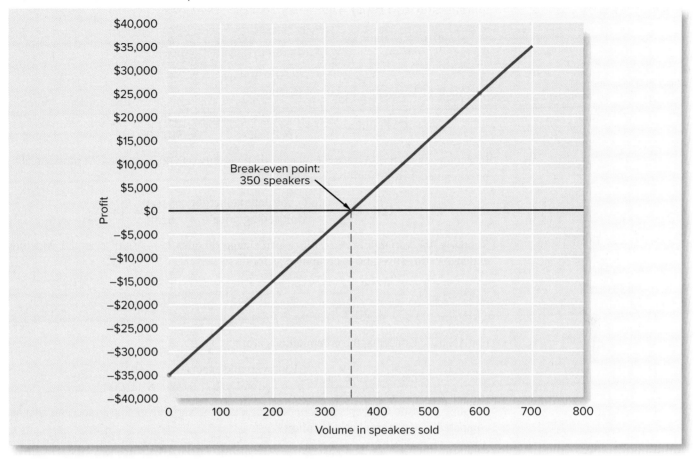

straight line. For example, when the sales volume is zero (i.e., $Q = 0$), the profit is − $35,000 (= $100 × 0 − $35,000). When $Q$ is 600, the profit is $25,000 (= $100 × 600 − $35,000). These two points are plotted in Exhibit 6–3 and a straight line has been drawn through them.

The break-even point on the profit graph is the volume of sales at which profit is zero and is indicated by the dashed line on the graph. Note that the profit steadily increases to the right of the break-even point as the sales volume increases and that the loss becomes steadily worse to the left of the break-even point as the sales volume decreases.

## Contribution Margin Ratio (CM Ratio) and the Variable Expense Ratio

In the previous section, we explored how CVP relationships can be visualized. This section begins by defining the *contribution margin ratio* and the *variable expense ratio*. Then it demonstrates how to use the contribution margin ratio in CVP calculations.

As a first step in defining these two terms, we have added a column to Acoustic Concepts' contribution format income statement that expresses sales, variable expenses, and contribution margin as a percentage of sales:

|  | Total | Per Unit | Percent of Sales |
|---|---|---|---|
| Sales (400 speakers) .................... | $100,000 | $250 | 100% |
| Variable expenses ...................... | 60,000 | 150 | 60% |
| Contribution margin ..................... | 40,000 | $100 | 40% |
| Fixed expenses ......................... | 35,000 | | |
| Net operating income ................... | $ 5,000 | | |

The contribution margin as a percentage of sales is referred to as the **contribution margin ratio (CM ratio)**. This ratio is computed as follows:

$$\text{CM ratio} = \frac{\text{Contribution margin}}{\text{Sales}}$$

For Acoustic Concepts, the computations are:

$$\text{CM ratio} = \frac{\text{Total contribution margin}}{\text{Total sales}} = \frac{\$40,000}{\$100,000} = 40\%$$

In a company such as Acoustic Concepts that has only one product, the CM ratio can also be computed on a per unit basis as follows:

$$\text{CM ratio} = \frac{\text{Unit contribution margin}}{\text{Unit selling price}} = \frac{\$100}{\$250} = 40\%$$

Similarly, the variable expenses as a percentage of sales is referred to as the **variable expense ratio**. This ratio is computed as follows:

$$\text{Variable expense ratio} = \frac{\text{Variable expenses}}{\text{Sales}}$$

For Acoustic Concepts, the computations are:

$$\text{Variable expense ratio} = \frac{\text{Total variable expenses}}{\text{Total sales}} = \frac{\$60,000}{\$100,000} = 60\%$$

Because Acoustic Concepts has only one product, the variable expense ratio can also be computed on a per unit basis as follows:

$$\text{Variable expense ratio} = \frac{\text{Variable expense per unit}}{\text{Unit selling price}} = \frac{\$150}{\$250} = 60\%$$

Having defined the two terms, it bears emphasizing that the contribution margin ratio and the variable expense ratio can be mathematically related to one another:

$$\text{CM ratio} = \frac{\text{Contribution margin}}{\text{Sales}}$$
$$\text{CM ratio} = \frac{\text{Sales} - \text{Variable expenses}}{\text{Sales}}$$
$$\text{CM ratio} = 1 - \text{Variable expense ratio}$$

So, in the case of Acoustic Concepts, this relationship would be as follows:

$$\text{CM ratio} = 1 - \text{Variable expense ratio}$$
$$= 1 - 60\%$$
$$= 40\%$$

## Applications of the Contribution Margin Ratio

The CM ratio shows how the contribution margin will be affected by a change in total sales. Acoustic Concepts' CM ratio of 40% means that for each dollar increase in sales, total contribution margin will increase by 40 cents ($1 sales × CM ratio of 40%). Net operating income will also increase by 40 cents, assuming that fixed costs are not affected by the increase in sales. Generally, the effect of a change in sales on the contribution margin is expressed in equation form as:

$$\text{Change in contribution margin} = \text{CM ratio} \times \text{Change in sales}$$

As this illustration suggests, *the impact on net operating income of any given dollar change in total sales can be computed by applying the CM ratio to the dollar change.* For example, if Acoustic Concepts plans a $30,000 increase in sales during the coming month, the contribution margin should increase by $12,000 ($30,000 increase in sales × CM ratio of 40%). As we noted above, net operating income also will increase by $12,000 if fixed costs do not change. This is verified by the following table:

| | Sales Volume | | | Percent of Sales |
| --- | --- | --- | --- | --- |
| | Present | Expected | Increase | |
| Sales ...................... | $100,000 | $130,000 | $30,000 | 100% |
| Variable expenses ........... | 60,000 | 78,000* | 18,000 | 60% |
| Contribution margin ......... | 40,000 | 52,000 | 12,000 | 40% |
| Fixed expenses ............. | 35,000 | 35,000 | 0 | |
| Net operating income ....... | $ 5,000 | $ 17,000 | $12,000 | |

*$130,000 expected sales ÷ $250 per unit = 520 units. 520 units × $150 per unit = $78,000.

The relation between profit and the CM ratio can also be expressed using the following equation[2]:

$$\text{Profit} = \text{CM ratio} \times \text{Sales} - \text{Fixed expenses}$$

or, in terms of changes,

$$\text{Change in profit} = \text{CM ratio} \times \text{Change in sales} - \text{Change in fixed expenses}$$

For example, at sales of $130,000, the profit is expected to be $17,000 as shown below:

$$\begin{aligned}
\text{Profit} &= \text{CM ratio} \times \text{Sales} - \text{Fixed expenses} \\
&= 0.40 \times \$130,000 - \$35,000 \\
&= \$52,000 - \$35,000 \\
&= \$17,000
\end{aligned}$$

Again, if you are comfortable with algebra, this approach will often be quicker and easier than constructing contribution format income statements.

The CM ratio is particularly valuable in situations where the dollar sales of one product must be traded off against the dollar sales of another product. In this situation, products that yield the greatest amount of contribution margin per dollar of sales should be emphasized.

3. The contribution margin ratio always increases when (you may select more than one answer):
   a. Sales increase.
   b. Fixed costs decrease.
   c. Total variable costs decrease.
   d. Variable costs as a percent of sales decrease.

CONCEPT CHECK

---

[2] This equation can be derived using the basic profit equation and the definition of the CM ratio as follows:

$$\text{Profit} = (\text{Sales} - \text{Variable expenses}) - \text{Fixed expenses}$$
$$\text{Profit} = \text{Contribution margin} - \text{Fixed expenses}$$
$$\text{Profit} = \frac{\text{Contribution margin}}{\text{Sales}} \times \text{Sales} - \text{Fixed expenses}$$
$$\text{Profit} = \text{CM ratio} \times \text{Sales} - \text{Fixed expenses}$$

## Additional Applications of CVP Concepts

Having demonstrated how to use the contribution margin ratio in CVP calculations, Bob Luchinni, the accountant at Acoustic Concepts, wanted to offer the company's president, Prem Narayan, five additional examples of how CVP analysis can be used to answer the types of questions that their company is facing. So, he began by reminding Prem that the company's fixed expenses are $35,000 per month and he restated the following key pieces of data:

|  | Per Unit | Percent of Sales |
|---|---|---|
| Selling price . . . . . . . . . . . . . . . . | $250 | 100% |
| Variable expenses . . . . . . . . . . | 150 | 60% |
| Contribution margin . . . . . . . . . | $100 | 40% |

## HELPFUL HINT

The picture below may improve your understanding of Learning Objective 6–4. It highlights the four variables that impact net operating income—the number of units sold (also called sales volume), the selling price per unit, the variable expense per unit, and total fixed expenses. Once you input the proper amounts for each of these variables in the tan boxes shown below, follow four steps to compute the new net operating income. First, multiply the number of units sold by the selling price per unit to derive total sales. The second step is to multiply the number of units sold by the variable expense per unit to derive total variable expenses. The third step is to subtract the total variable expenses from total sales to derive the contribution margin. The fourth step is to subtract total fixed expenses from the contribution margin to derive the new net operating income.

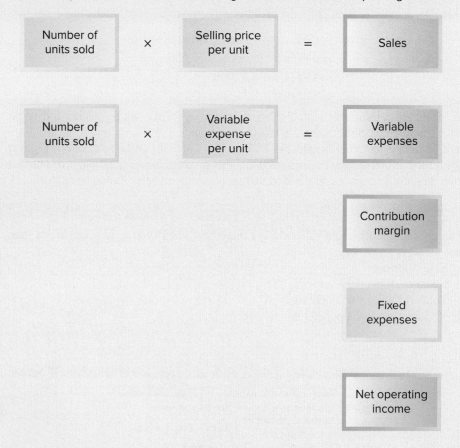

**Example 1: Change in Fixed Cost and Sales Volume**   Acoustic Concepts is currently selling 400 speakers per month at $250 per speaker for total monthly sales of $100,000. The sales manager feels that a $10,000 increase in the monthly advertising budget would increase monthly sales by $30,000 to a total of 520 units. Should the advertising budget be increased? The table below shows the financial impact of the proposed change in the monthly advertising budget.

| | Current Sales | Sales with Additional Advertising Budget | Difference | Percent of Sales |
|---|---|---|---|---|
| Sales ..................... | $100,000 | $130,000 | $30,000 | 100% |
| Variable expenses .......... | 60,000 | 78,000* | 18,000 | 60% |
| Contribution margin .......... | 40,000 | 52,000 | 12,000 | 40% |
| Fixed expenses ............. | 35,000 | 45,000† | 10,000 | |
| Net operating income ........ | $  5,000 | $  7,000 | $  2,000 | |

*520 units × $150 per unit = $78,000.
†$35,000 + additional $10,000 monthly advertising budget = $45,000.

Assuming no other factors need to be considered, the increase in the advertising budget should be approved because it would increase net operating income by $2,000. There are two shorter ways to arrive at this solution. The first alternative solution follows:

### Alternative Solution 1

| | |
|---|---|
| Expected total contribution margin: | |
| $130,000 × 40% CM ratio ................... | $52,000 |
| Present total contribution margin: | |
| $100,000 × 40% CM ratio ................... | 40,000 |
| Increase in total contribution margin ............. | 12,000 |
| Change in fixed expenses: | |
| Less incremental advertising expense .......... | 10,000 |
| Increased net operating income ................ | $ 2,000 |

Because in this case only the fixed costs and the sales volume change, the solution can also be quickly derived as follows:

### Alternative Solution 2

| | |
|---|---|
| Incremental contribution margin: | |
| $30,000 × 40% CM ratio ..................... | $12,000 |
| Less incremental advertising expense ............ | 10,000 |
| Increased net operating income ................ | $ 2,000 |

Notice that this approach does not depend on knowledge of previous sales. Also note that it is unnecessary under either shorter approach to prepare an income statement. Both of the alternative solutions involve **incremental analysis**—that is, they consider only the costs and revenues that will change if the new program is implemented. Although in each case a new income statement could have been prepared, the incremental approach is simpler and more direct and focuses attention on the specific changes that would occur as a result of the decision.

**Example 2: Change in Variable Costs and Sales Volume**   Refer to the original data. Recall that Acoustic Concepts is currently selling 400 speakers per month. Prem is considering the use of higher-quality components, which would increase variable costs (and thereby reduce the contribution margin) by $10 per speaker. However, the sales manager predicts that using higher-quality components would increase sales to 480 speakers per month. Should the higher-quality components be used?

The $10 increase in variable costs would decrease the unit contribution margin by $10—from $100 down to $90.

**Solution**

| | |
|---|---:|
| Expected total contribution margin with higher-quality components: | |
| 480 speakers × $90 per speaker .............. | $43,200 |
| Present total contribution margin: | |
| 400 speakers × $100 per speaker ............. | 40,000 |
| Increase in total contribution margin  ............. | $ 3,200 |

According to this analysis, the higher-quality components should be used. Because fixed costs would not change, the $3,200 increase in contribution margin shown above should result in a $3,200 increase in net operating income.

**Example 3: Change in Fixed Cost, Selling Price, and Sales Volume**   Refer to the original data and recall again that Acoustic Concepts is currently selling 400 speakers per month. To increase sales, the sales manager would like to cut the selling price by $20 per speaker and increase the advertising budget by $15,000 per month. The sales manager believes that if these two steps are taken, unit sales will increase by 50% to 600 speakers per month. Should the changes be made?

A decrease in the selling price of $20 per speaker would decrease the unit contribution margin by $20 down to $80.

**Solution**

| | |
|---|---:|
| Expected total contribution margin with lower selling price: | |
| 600 speakers × $80 per speaker ................... | $48,000 |
| Present total contribution margin: | |
| 400 speakers × $100 per speaker ................ | 40,000 |
| Incremental contribution margin  ....................... | 8,000 |
| Change in fixed expenses: | |
| Less incremental advertising expense .............. | 15,000 |
| Reduction in net operating income ................... | $ (7,000) |

According to this analysis, the changes should not be made. The $7,000 reduction in net operating income that is shown above can be verified by preparing comparative contribution format income statements as shown here:

| | Present 400 Speakers per Month | | Expected 600 Speakers per Month | | |
|---|---:|---:|---:|---:|---:|
| | Total | Per Unit | Total | Per Unit | Difference |
| Sales ...................... | $100,000 | $250 | $138,000 | $230 | $38,000 |
| Variable expenses ........... | 60,000 | 150 | 90,000 | 150 | 30,000 |
| Contribution margin .......... | 40,000 | $100 | 48,000 | $ 80 | 8,000 |
| Fixed expenses .............. | 35,000 | | 50,000* | | 15,000 |
| Net operating income (loss) .... | $ 5,000 | | $ (2,000) | | $ (7,000) |

*35,000 + Additional monthly advertising budget of $15,000 = $50,000.

**Example 4: Change in Variable Cost, Fixed Cost, and Sales Volume**   Refer to Acoustic Concepts' original data. As before, the company is currently selling 400 speakers per month. The sales manager would like to pay salespersons a sales commission of $15 per speaker sold, rather than the flat salaries that now total $6,000 per month. The sales manager is confident that the change would increase monthly sales by 15% to 460 speakers per month. Should the change be made?

**Solution**   Changing the sales staff's compensation from salaries to commissions would affect both variable and fixed expenses. Variable expenses per unit would increase by $15, from $150 to $165, and the unit contribution margin would decrease from $100 to $85. Fixed expenses would decrease by $6,000, from $35,000 to $29,000.

| | |
|---|---:|
| Expected total contribution margin with sales staff on commissions: | |
| 460 speakers × $85 per speaker | $39,100 |
| Present total contribution margin: | |
| 400 speakers × $100 per speaker | 40,000 |
| Decrease in total contribution margin | (900) |
| Change in fixed expenses: | |
| Add salaries avoided if a commission is paid | 6,000 |
| Increase in net operating income | $ 5,100 |

According to this analysis, the changes should be made. Again, the same answer can be obtained by preparing comparative contribution income statements:

| | Present 400 Speakers per Month Total | Per Unit | Expected 460 Speakers per Month Total | Per Unit | Difference |
|---|---:|---:|---:|---:|---:|
| Sales | $100,000 | $250 | $115,000 | $250 | $15,000 |
| Variable expenses | 60,000 | 150 | 75,900 | 165 | 15,900 |
| Contribution margin | 40,000 | $100 | 39,100 | $ 85 | 900 |
| Fixed expenses | 35,000 | | 29,000 | | (6,000)* |
| Net operating income | $ 5,000 | | $ 10,100 | | $ 5,100 |

*Note: A reduction in fixed expenses has the effect of increasing net operating income.

**Example 5: Change in Selling Price**   Refer to the original data where Acoustic Concepts is currently selling 400 speakers per month. The company has an opportunity to make a bulk sale of 150 speakers to a wholesaler if an acceptable price can be negotiated. This sale would not alter the company's regular sales and would not affect the company's total fixed expenses. What price per speaker should be quoted to the wholesaler if Acoustic Concepts is seeking a profit of $3,000 on the bulk sale?

**Solution**

| | |
|---|---:|
| Variable cost per speaker | $150 |
| Desired profit per speaker: | |
| $3,000 ÷ 150 speakers | 20 |
| Quoted price per speaker | $170 |

Notice that fixed expenses are not included in the computation. This is because fixed expenses are not affected by the bulk sale, so all of the additional contribution margin increases the company's profits.

## IN BUSINESS

## Newspaper Circulars: Still Worth The Investment

In the digital era, it might be easy to assume that retailers should abandon the advertising inserts (called newspaper circulars) that accompany print newspapers. However, **Wanderful Media** estimates that 80% of people who read print newspapers look at the circulars inside, whereas only 1% of online readers click through to digital circulars. **Walmart** acquainted itself with these statistics when it discontinued print circulars in Fargo, North Dakota, Madison, Wisconsin, and Tucson, Arizona and redirected its advertising dollars in those markets to digital media. The ensuing drop in sales motivated Walmart to immediately reinstate its circular ads in print newspapers.

**Kohl's** hopes to decrease the cost of producing and distributing its circulars by 40% while largely retaining its existing sales volumes. Its plan is to use data from past purchases to identify the zip codes with the highest concentrations of loyal Kohl's shoppers and then to limit its distribution of circulars to the most profitable zip codes (rather than relying on more expensive mass distribution in all zip codes). The company will probably use cost-volume-profit analysis to determine if its plan increases profits.

Source: Kapner, Suzanne, "Retailers Can't Shake Their Circular Habit," *The Wall Street Journal*, March 12, 2015, p. B8.

# BREAK-EVEN AND TARGET PROFIT ANALYSIS

Managers use break-even and target profit analysis to answer questions such as how much would we have to sell to avoid incurring a loss or how much would we have to sell to make a profit of $10,000 per month? We'll discuss break-even analysis first followed by target profit analysis.

## Break-Even Analysis

**LEARNING OBJECTIVE 6–5**

Determine the break-even point.

Earlier in the chapter we defined the break-even point as *the level of sales at which the company's profit is zero.* To calculate the break-even point (in unit sales and dollar sales), managers can use either of two approaches, the equation method or the formula method. We'll demonstrate both approaches using the data from Acoustic Concepts.

**The Equation Method**    The equation method relies on the basic profit equation introduced earlier in the chapter. Because Acoustic Concepts has only one product, we'll use the contribution margin form of this equation to perform the break-even calculations. Remembering that Acoustic Concepts' unit contribution margin is $100, and its fixed expenses are $35,000, the company's break-even point is computed as follows:

$$\text{Profit} = \text{Unit CM} \times Q - \text{Fixed expense}$$
$$\$0 = \$100 \times Q - \$35,000$$
$$\$100 \times Q = \$0 + \$35,000$$
$$Q = \$35,000 \div \$100$$
$$Q = 350$$

Thus, as we determined earlier in the chapter, Acoustic Concepts will break even (or earn zero profit) at a sales volume of 350 speakers per month.

**The Formula Method**    The formula method is a shortcut version of the equation method. It centers on the idea discussed earlier in the chapter that each unit sold provides a certain amount of contribution margin that goes toward covering fixed expenses. In a single product situation, the formula for computing the unit sales to break even is[3]:

$$\text{Unit sales to break even} = \frac{\text{Fixed expenses}}{\text{Unit CM}}$$

In the case of Acoustic Concepts, the unit sales needed to break even is computed as follows:

$$\begin{aligned}
\text{Unit sales to break even} &= \frac{\text{Fixed expenses}}{\text{Unit CM}}\\
&= \frac{\$35,000}{\$100}\\
&= 350
\end{aligned}$$

Notice that 350 units is the same answer that we got when using the equation method. This will always be the case because the formula method and equation method are mathematically equivalent. The formula method simply skips a few steps in the equation method.

4.  Assume the selling price per unit is $30, the contribution margin ratio is 40%, and the total fixed cost is $60,000. What is the break-even point in unit sales?
    a.  2,000
    b.  3,000
    c.  4,000
    d.  5,000

CONCEPT CHECK

**Break-Even in Dollar Sales**    In addition to finding the break-even point in unit sales, we can also find the break-even point in dollar sales using three methods. First, we could solve for the break-even point in *unit* sales using the equation method or formula method and then simply multiply the result by the selling price. In the case of Acoustic Concepts, the break-even point in dollar sales using this approach would be computed as 350 speakers × $250 per speaker, or $87,500 in total sales.

Second, we can use the equation method to compute the break-even point in dollar sales. Remembering that Acoustic Concepts' contribution margin ratio is 40% and its fixed expenses are $35,000, the equation method calculates the break-even point in dollar sales as follows:

$$\begin{aligned}
\text{Profit} &= \text{CM ratio} \times \text{Sales} - \text{Fixed expenses}\\
\$0 &= 0.40 \times \text{Sales} - \$35,000\\
0.40 \times \text{Sales} &= \$0 + \$35,000\\
\text{Sales} &= \$35,000 \div 0.40\\
\text{Sales} &= \$87,500
\end{aligned}$$

Third, we can use the formula method to compute the dollar sales needed to break even as shown below[4]:

$$\text{Dollar sales to break even} = \frac{\text{Fixed expenses}}{\text{CM ratio}}$$

---

[3]This formula can be derived as follows:
$$\begin{aligned}
\text{Profit} &= \text{Unit CM} \times Q - \text{Fixed expenses}\\
\$0 &= \text{Unit CM} \times Q - \text{Fixed expenses}\\
\text{Unit CM} \times Q &= \$0 + \text{Fixed expenses}\\
Q &= \text{Fixed expenses} \div \text{Unit CM}
\end{aligned}$$

[4]This formula can be derived as follows:
$$\begin{aligned}
\text{Profit} &= \text{CM ratio} \times \text{Sales} - \text{Fixed expenses}\\
\$0 &= \text{CM ratio} \times \text{Sales} - \text{Fixed expenses}\\
\text{CM ratio} \times \text{Sales} &= \$0 + \text{Fixed expenses}\\
\text{Sales} &= \text{Fixed expenses} \div \text{CM ratio}
\end{aligned}$$

In the case of Acoustic Concepts, the computations are performed as follows:

$$\text{Dollar sales to break even} = \frac{\text{Fixed expenses}}{\text{CM ratio}}$$

$$= \frac{\$35,000}{0.40}$$

$$= \$87,500$$

Again, you'll notice that the break-even point in dollar sales ($87,500) is the same under all three methods. This will always be the case because these methods are mathematically equivalent.

## Target Profit Analysis

**LEARNING OBJECTIVE 6–6**

Determine the level of sales needed to achieve a desired target profit.

*Target profit analysis* is one of the key uses of CVP analysis. In **target profit analysis**, we estimate what sales volume is needed to achieve a specific target profit. For example, suppose Prem Narayan of Acoustic Concepts, Inc., would like to estimate the sales needed to attain a target profit of $40,000 per month. To determine the unit sales and dollar sales needed to achieve a target profit, we can rely on the same two approaches that we have been discussing thus far, the equation method or the formula method.

**The Equation Method**    To compute the unit sales required to achieve a target profit of $40,000 per month, Acoustic Concepts can use the same profit equation that was used for its break-even analysis. Remembering that the company's contribution margin per unit is $100 and its total fixed expenses are $35,000, the equation method could be applied as follows:

$$\text{Profit} = \text{Unit CM} \times Q - \text{Fixed expense}$$
$$\$40,000 = \$100 \times Q - \$35,000$$
$$\$100 \times Q = \$40,000 + \$35,000$$
$$Q = \$75,000 \div \$100$$
$$Q = 750$$

Thus, the target profit can be achieved by selling 750 speakers per month. Notice that the only difference between this equation and the equation used for Acoustic Concepts' break-even calculation is the profit figure. In the break-even scenario, the profit is $0, whereas in the target profit scenario the profit is $40,000.

**The Formula Method**    In general, in a single product situation, we can compute the sales volume required to attain a specific target profit using the following formula:

$$\text{Unit sales to attain the target profit} = \frac{\text{Target profit} + \text{Fixed expenses}}{\text{Unit CM}}$$

In the case of Acoustic Concepts, the unit sales needed to attain a target profit of $40,000 is computed as follows:

$$\text{Unit sales to attain the target profit} = \frac{\text{Target profit} + \text{Fixed expenses}}{\text{Unit CM}}$$

$$= \frac{\$40,000 + \$35,000}{\$100}$$

$$= 750$$

**Target Profit Analysis in Terms of Dollar Sales**    When quantifying the dollar sales needed to attain a target profit we can apply the same three methods that we used for calculating the dollar sales needed to break even. First, we can solve for the *unit* sales needed to attain the target profit using the equation method or formula method and then simply multiply the result by the selling price. In the case of Acoustic Concepts, the dollar sales to attain its target profit would be computed as 750 speakers × $250 per speaker, or $187,500 in total sales.

Second, we can use the equation method to compute the dollar sales needed to attain the target profit. Remembering that Acoustic Concepts' target profit is $40,000, its contribution margin ratio is 40%, and its fixed expenses are $35,000, the equation method calculates the answer as follows:

$$\text{Profit} = \text{CM ratio} \times \text{Sales} - \text{Fixed expenses}$$
$$\$40,000 = 0.40 \times \text{Sales} - \$35,000$$
$$0.40 \times \text{Sales} = \$40,000 + \$35,000$$
$$\text{Sales} = \$75,000 \div 0.40$$
$$\text{Sales} = \$187,500$$

Third, we can use the formula method to compute the dollar sales needed to attain the target profit as shown below:

$$\text{Dollar sales to attain the target profit} = \frac{\text{Target profit} + \text{Fixed expenses}}{\text{CM ratio}}$$

In the case of Acoustic Concepts, the computations would be:

$$\text{Dollar sales to attain the target profit} = \frac{\text{Target profit} + \text{Fixed expenses}}{\text{CM ratio}}$$
$$= \frac{\$40,000 + \$35,000}{0.40}$$
$$= \$187,500$$

Again, you'll notice that the answers are the same regardless of which method we use. This is because all of the methods discussed are simply different roads to the same destination.

## Would You Pay $800 For A Pair Of Sneakers?                  IN BUSINESS

Some companies rely on sales volume to drive profits whereas others rely on scarcity to increase margins and profits. **Buscemi** sneakers burst on to the market for $760 a pair and soon climbed to $865 a pair. The company purposely limits production to drive up its prices. It initially produced a batch of 600 pairs of sneakers that sold out in days. Then the company released 4,000 additional pairs that were sold out by the time pop star Justin Bieber posted a picture of his gold-colored Buscemis on Instagram. Its next step was to release 8,000 more pairs to about 50 stores. Although Buscemi could almost certainly increase production and unit sales, the company chooses to limit availability to add to the mystique (and price) of the brand.

©Astrid Stawiarz/Goodman's Men's Store/Getty Images

Source: Karp, Hannah, "An $800 Sneaker Plays Hard to Get," *The Wall Street Journal*, July 28, 2014, pp. B1 and B7.

## The Margin of Safety

The **margin of safety** is the excess of budgeted or actual sales dollars over the break-even volume of sales dollars. It is the amount by which sales can drop before losses are incurred. The higher the margin of safety, the lower the risk of not breaking even and incurring a loss. The formula for the margin of safety is:

Margin of safety in dollars = Total budgeted (or actual) sales − Break-even sales

The margin of safety also can be expressed in percentage form by dividing the margin of safety in dollars by total dollar sales:

$$\text{Margin of safety percentage} = \frac{\text{Margin of safety in dollars}}{\text{Total budgeted (or actual) sales in dollars}}$$

The calculation of the margin of safety for Acoustic Concepts is:

| | |
|---|---|
| Sales (at the current volume of 400 speakers) (a)............ | $100,000 |
| Break-even sales (at 350 speakers)...................... | 87,500 |
| Margin of safety in dollars (b) ........................... | $ 12,500 |
| Margin of safety percentage, (b) ÷ (a) ..................... | 12.5% |

This margin of safety means that at the current level of sales and with the company's current prices and cost structure, a reduction in sales of $12,500, or 12.5%, would result in just breaking even.

In a single-product company like Acoustic Concepts, the margin of safety also can be expressed in terms of the number of units sold by dividing the margin of safety in dollars by the selling price per unit. In this case, the margin of safety is 50 speakers ($12,500 ÷ $250 per speaker = 50 speakers).

## DECISION POINT

### Loan Officer

Steve Becker owns Blue Ridge Brewery, a microbrewery in Arden, North Carolina. He charges distributors $100 per case for his premium beer. The distributors tack on 25% when selling to retailers who in turn add a 30% markup before selling the beer to consumers. In the most recent year, Blue Ridge's revenue was $8 million and its net operating income was $700,000. Becker reports that the costs of making one case of his premium beer are $32 for raw ingredients, $20 for labor, $4 for bottling and packaging, and $12 for utilities.

Assume that Becker has approached your bank for a loan. As the loan officer, you should consider a variety of factors, including the company's margin of safety. Assuming that other information about the company is favorable, would you consider Blue Ridge's margin of safety to be comfortable enough to extend a loan?

**MANAGERIAL ACCOUNTING IN ACTION**
**THE WRAP-UP**

ACOUSTIC concepts inc

Prem Narayan and Bob Luchinni met to discuss the results of Bob's analysis.

***Prem:*** Bob, everything you have shown me is pretty clear. I can see what impact the sales manager's suggestions would have on our profits. Some of those suggestions are quite good and others are not so good. I am concerned that our margin of safety is only 50 speakers. What can we do to increase this number?

***Bob:*** Well, we have to increase total sales or decrease the break-even point or both.

***Prem:*** And to decrease the break-even point, we have to either decrease our fixed expenses or increase our unit contribution margin?

***Bob:*** Exactly.

***Prem:*** And to increase our unit contribution margin, we must either increase our selling price or decrease the variable cost per unit?

***Bob:*** Correct.

***Prem:*** So what do you suggest?

***Bob:*** Well, the analysis doesn't tell us which of these to do, but it does indicate we have a potential problem here.

***Prem:*** If you don't have any immediate suggestions, I would like to call a general meeting next week to discuss ways we can work on increasing the margin of safety. I think everyone will be concerned about how vulnerable we are to even small downturns in sales.

5.  Assume a company produces one product that sells for $55, has a variable cost per unit of $35, and has fixed costs of $100,000. How many units must the company sell to earn a target profit of $50,000?
    a.  7,500 units
    b.  10,000 units
    c.  12,500 units
    d.  15,000 units
6.  Given the same facts as in question 5 above, if the company exactly meets its target profit, what will be its margin of safety in sales dollars?
    a.  $110,000
    b.  $127,500
    c.  $137,500
    d.  $150,000
7.  Which of the following statements is false with respect to the margin of safety? (You may select more than one answer.)
    a.  The total budgeted (or actual) sales minus sales at the break-even point equals the margin of safety in dollars.
    b.  The margin of safety in dollars divided by the total budgeted (or actual) sales in dollars equals the margin of safety percentage.
    c.  In a single product company, the margin of safety in dollars divided by the variable cost per unit equals the margin of safety in units.
    d.  The margin of safety in dollars can be a negative number.

# CVP CONSIDERATIONS IN CHOOSING A COST STRUCTURE

Cost structure refers to the relative proportion of fixed and variable costs in an organization. Managers often have some latitude in trading off between these two types of costs. For example, fixed investments in automated equipment can reduce variable labor costs. In this section, we discuss the choice of a cost structure. We also introduce the concept of *operating leverage.*

## Cost Structure and Profit Stability

Which cost structure is better—high variable costs and low fixed costs, or the opposite? No single answer to this question is possible; each approach has its advantages. To show what we mean, refer to the following contribution format income statements for two blueberry farms. Bogside Farm depends on migrant workers to pick its berries by hand, whereas Sterling Farm has invested in expensive berry-picking machines. Consequently, Bogside Farm has higher variable costs, but Sterling Farm has higher fixed costs:

|  | Bogside Farm | | Sterling Farm | |
| --- | --- | --- | --- | --- |
|  | Amount | Percent | Amount | Percent |
| Sales .......................... | $100,000 | 100% | $100,000 | 100% |
| Variable expenses .............. | 60,000 | 60% | 30,000 | 30% |
| Contribution margin ............ | 40,000 | 40% | 70,000 | 70% |
| Fixed expenses ................. | 30,000 | | 60,000 | |
| Net operating income .......... | $ 10,000 | | $ 10,000 | |

Which farm has the better cost structure? The answer depends on many factors, including the long-run trend in sales, year-to-year fluctuations in the level of sales, and the attitude of the owners toward risk. If sales are expected to exceed $100,000 in the future, then Sterling Farm probably has the better cost structure. The reason is that its CM ratio is higher, and its profits will therefore increase more rapidly as sales increase. To illustrate, assume that each farm experiences a 10% increase in sales without any increase in fixed costs. The new contribution income statements would be as follows:

|  | Bogside Farm | | Sterling Farm | |
|---|---|---|---|---|
|  | Amount | Percent | Amount | Percent |
| Sales | $110,000 | 100% | $110,000 | 100% |
| Variable expenses | 66,000 | 60% | 33,000 | 30% |
| Contribution margin | 44,000 | 40% | 77,000 | 70% |
| Fixed expenses | 30,000 |  | 60,000 |  |
| Net operating income | $ 14,000 |  | $ 17,000 |  |

Sterling Farm has experienced a greater increase in net operating income due to its higher CM ratio even though the increase in sales was the same for both farms.

What if sales drop below $100,000? What are the farms' break-even points? What are their margins of safety? The computations needed to answer these questions are shown below using the formula method:

|  | Bogside Farm | Sterling Farm |
|---|---|---|
| Fixed expenses | $ 30,000 | $ 60,000 |
| Contribution margin ratio | ÷ 0.40 | ÷ 0.70 |
| Dollar sales to break even | $ 75,000 | $ 85,714 |
| Total current sales (a) | $100,000 | $100,000 |
| Break-even sales | 75,000 | 85,714 |
| Margin of safety in sales dollars (b) | $ 25,000 | $ 14,286 |
| Margin of safety percentage (b) ÷ (a) | 25.0% | 14.3% |

Bogside Farm's margin of safety is greater and its contribution margin ratio is lower than Sterling Farm. Therefore, Bogside Farm is less vulnerable to downturns than Sterling Farm. Due to its lower contribution margin ratio, Bogside Farm will not lose contribution margin as rapidly as Sterling Farm when sales decline. Thus, Bogside Farm's profit will be less volatile. We saw earlier that this is a drawback when sales increase, but it provides more protection when sales drop. And because its break-even point is lower, Bogside Farm can suffer a larger sales decline before losses emerge.

To summarize, without knowing the future, it is not obvious which cost structure is better. Both have advantages and disadvantages. Sterling Farm, with its higher fixed costs and lower variable costs, will experience wider swings in net operating income as sales fluctuate, with greater profits in good years and greater losses in bad years. Bogside Farm, with its lower fixed costs and higher variable costs, will enjoy greater profit stability and will be more protected from losses during bad years, but at the cost of lower net operating income in good years. Moreover, if the higher fixed costs in Sterling Farm reflect greater capacity, Sterling Farm will be better able than Bogside Farm to profit from unexpected surges in demand.

# Operating Leverage

A lever is a tool for multiplying force. Using a lever, a massive object can be moved with only a modest amount of force. In business, *operating leverage* serves a similar purpose. **Operating leverage** is a measure of how sensitive net operating income is to a given percentage change in dollar sales. Operating leverage acts as a multiplier. If operating leverage is high, a small percentage increase in sales can produce a much larger percentage increase in net operating income.

**LEARNING OBJECTIVE 6–8**

Compute the degree of operating leverage at a particular level of sales and explain how it can be used to predict changes in net operating income.

Operating leverage can be illustrated by returning to the data for the two blueberry farms. We previously showed that a 10% increase in sales (from $100,000 to $110,000 in each farm) results in a 70% increase in the net operating income of Sterling Farm (from $10,000 to $17,000) and only a 40% increase in the net operating income of Bogside Farm (from $10,000 to $14,000). Thus, for a 10% increase in sales, Sterling Farm experiences a much greater percentage increase in profits than does Bogside Farm. Therefore, Sterling Farm has greater operating leverage than Bogside Farm.

The **degree of operating leverage** at a given level of sales is computed by the following formula:

$$\text{Degree of operating leverage} = \frac{\text{Contribution margin}}{\text{Net operating income}}$$

*The degree of operating leverage is a measure, at a given level of sales, of how a percentage change in sales volume will affect profits.* To illustrate, the degree of operating leverage for the two farms at $100,000 sales would be computed as follows:

$$\text{Bogside Farm}: \frac{\$40,000}{\$10,000} = 4$$

$$\text{Sterling Farm}: \frac{\$70,000}{\$10,000} = 7$$

Because the degree of operating leverage for Bogside Farm is 4, the farm's net operating income grows four times as fast as its sales. In contrast, Sterling Farm's net operating income grows seven times as fast as its sales. Thus, if sales increase by 10%, then we can expect the net operating income of Bogside Farm to increase by four times this amount, or by 40%, and the net operating income of Sterling Farm to increase by seven times this amount, or by 70%. In general, this relation between the percentage change in sales and the percentage change in net operating income is given by the following formula:

$$\begin{array}{c}\text{Percentage change in} \\ \text{net operating income}\end{array} = \begin{array}{c}\text{Degree of} \\ \text{operating leverage}\end{array} \times \begin{array}{c}\text{Percentage} \\ \text{change in sales}\end{array}$$

Bogside Farm : Percentage change in net operating income = 4 × 10% = 40%

Sterling Farm : Percentage change in net operating income = 7 × 10% = 70%

What is responsible for the higher operating leverage at Sterling Farm? The only difference between the two farms is their cost structure. If two companies have the same total revenue and same total expense but different cost structures, then the company with the higher proportion of fixed costs in its cost structure will have higher operating leverage. Referring back to the original data, when both farms have sales of $100,000 and total expenses of $90,000, one-third of Bogside Farm's costs are fixed but two-thirds of Sterling Farm's costs are fixed. As a consequence, Sterling's degree of operating leverage is higher than Bogside's.

The degree of operating leverage is not a constant; it is greatest at sales levels near the break-even point and decreases as sales and profits rise. The following table shows the degree of operating leverage for Bogside Farm at various sales levels. (Data used earlier for Bogside Farm are shown in color.)

| Sales | $75,000 | $80,000 | $100,000 | $150,000 | $225,000 |
|---|---|---|---|---|---|
| Variable expenses | 45,000 | 48,000 | 60,000 | 90,000 | 135,000 |
| Contribution margin (a) | 30,000 | 32,000 | 40,000 | 60,000 | 90,000 |
| Fixed expenses | 30,000 | 30,000 | 30,000 | 30,000 | 30,000 |
| Net operating income (b) | $ 0 | $ 2,000 | $ 10,000 | $ 30,000 | $ 60,000 |
| Degree of operating leverage, (a) ÷ (b) | ∞ | 16 | 4 | 2 | 1.5 |

Thus, a 10% increase in sales would increase profits by only 15% (10% × 1.5) if sales were previously $225,000, as compared to the 40% increase we computed earlier at the $100,000 sales level. The degree of operating leverage will continue to decrease the farther the company moves from its break-even point. At the break-even point, the degree of operating leverage is infinitely large ($30,000 contribution margin ÷ $0 net operating income = ∞).

The degree of operating leverage can be used to quickly estimate what impact various percentage changes in sales will have on profits, without the necessity of preparing detailed contribution format income statements. As shown by our examples, the effects of operating leverage can be dramatic. If a company is near its break-even point, then even small percentage increases in sales can yield large percentage increases in profits. *This explains why management will often work very hard for only a small increase in sales volume.* If the degree of operating leverage is 5, then a 6% increase in sales would translate into a 30% increase in profits.

## IN BUSINESS

©MachineHeadz/Getty Images RF

### Comparing The Cost Structures Of Two Online Grocers

Perhaps the biggest flop of the dot.com era was an online grocer called **Webvan**. The company burned through $800 million in cash before filing for bankruptcy in 2001 and halting operations. Part of Webvan's downfall was a cost structure heavily skewed toward fixed costs. For example, Webvan stored huge amounts of inventory in refrigerated warehouses that cost $40 million each to build. The company had 4,500 salaried employees with benefits (including warehouse workers and delivery personnel) and a fleet of its own delivery trucks.

Fast forward more than 15 years, and now **Instacart Inc.** is trying to become a profitable online grocer. Only this time Instacart is avoiding the kinds of huge fixed cost investments that plagued Webvan. Instead of hiring salaried employees with benefits, Instacart uses drivers who are independent contractors to deliver groceries to customers. The company pays its drivers $10 per order delivered plus additional compensation based on order size and delivery speed. Since the drivers use their own vehicles to pick up groceries directly from the supermarket, it eliminates the need for a fleet of delivery trucks, as well as the need for expensive refrigerated warehouses and the associated working capital tied up in perishable inventories.

Source: Benninger, Greg, "Rebuilding History's Biggest Dot-Com Bust," *The Wall Street Journal,* January 13, 2015, pp. B1–B2.

## STRUCTURING SALES COMMISSIONS

Companies usually compensate salespeople by paying them a commission based on sales, a salary, or a combination of the two. Commissions based on sales dollars can lead to lower profits. To illustrate, consider Pipeline Unlimited, a producer of surfing equipment. Salespersons sell the company's products to retail sporting goods stores throughout

North America and the Pacific Basin. Data for two of the company's surfboards, the XR7 and Turbo models, appear below:

|  | Model | |
|---|---|---|
|  | **XR7** | **Turbo** |
| Selling price . . . . . . . . . . . . . . . . . . . | $695 | $749 |
| Variable expenses . . . . . . . . . . . . . | 344 | 410 |
| Contribution margin . . . . . . . . . . . . | $351 | $339 |

Which model will salespeople push hardest if they are paid a commission of 10% of sales revenue? The answer is the Turbo because it has the higher selling price and hence the larger commission. On the other hand, from the standpoint of the company, profits will be greater if salespeople steer customers toward the XR7 model because it has the higher contribution margin.

To eliminate such conflicts, commissions can be based on contribution margin rather than on selling price. If this is done, the salespersons will want to sell the mix of products that maximizes contribution margin. Providing that fixed costs remain constant, maximizing the contribution margin will also maximize the company's profit.[5] In effect, by maximizing their own compensation, salespersons will also maximize the company's profit.

# SALES MIX

Before concluding our discussion of CVP concepts, we need to consider the impact of changes in *sales mix* on a company's profit.

> **LEARNING OBJECTIVE 6–9**
>
> Compute the break-even point for a multiproduct company and explain the effects of shifts in the sales mix on contribution margin and the break-even point.

## The Definition of Sales Mix

The term **sales mix** refers to the relative proportions in which a company's products are sold. The idea is to achieve the combination, or mix, that will yield the greatest profits. Most companies have many products, and often these products are not equally profitable. Hence, profits will depend to some extent on the company's sales mix. Profits will be greater if high-margin rather than low-margin items make up a relatively large proportion of total sales.

Changes in the sales mix can cause perplexing variations in a company's profits. A shift in the sales mix from high-margin items to low-margin items can cause total profits to decrease even though total sales may increase. Conversely, a shift in the sales mix from low-margin items to high-margin items can cause the reverse effect—total profits may increase even though total sales decrease. It is one thing to achieve a particular sales volume; it is quite another to sell the most profitable mix of products.

## Sales Mix and Break-Even Analysis

If a company sells more than one product, break-even analysis is more complex than discussed to this point. The reason is that different products will have different selling prices, different costs, and different contribution margins. Consequently, the break-even point depends on the mix in which the various products are sold. To illustrate, consider Virtual Journeys Unlimited, a small company that sells two DVDs: the Monuments DVD, a tour

---

[5]This also assumes the company has no production constraint. If it does, the sales commissions should be modified.

**Virtual Journeys Unlimited**
**Contribution Income Statement**
**For the Month of September**

| | Monuments DVD | | Parks DVD | | Total | |
|---|---|---|---|---|---|---|
| | Amount | Percent | Amount | Percent | Amount | Percent |
| Sales | $20,000 | 100% | $80,000 | 100% | $100,000 | 100% |
| Variable expenses | 15,000 | 75% | 40,000 | 50% | 55,000 | 55% |
| Contribution margin | $ 5,000 | 25% | $40,000 | 50% | 45,000 | 45% |
| Fixed expenses | | | | | 27,000 | |
| Net operating income | | | | | $ 18,000 | |

Computation of the break-even point:

$$\frac{\text{Fixed expenses}}{\text{Overall CM ratio}} = \frac{\$27,000}{0.45} = \$60,000$$

Verification of the break-even point:

| | Monuments DVD | Parks DVD | Total |
|---|---|---|---|
| Current dollar sales | $20,000 | $80,000 | $100,000 |
| Percentage of total dollar sales | 20% | 80% | 100% |
| Sales at the break-even point | $12,000 | $48,000 | $60,000 |

| | Monuments DVD | | Parks DVD | | Total | |
|---|---|---|---|---|---|---|
| | Amount | Percent | Amount | Percent | Amount | Percent |
| Sales | $12,000 | 100% | $48,000 | 100% | $60,000 | 100% |
| Variable expenses | 9,000 | 75% | 24,000 | 50% | 33,000 | 55% |
| Contribution margin | $ 3,000 | 25% | $24,000 | 50% | 27,000 | 45% |
| Fixed expenses | | | | | 27,000 | |
| Net operating income | | | | | $ 0 | |

of the United States' most popular National Monuments; and the Parks DVD, which tours the United States' National Parks. The company's September sales, expenses, and break-even point are shown in Exhibit 6–4.

As shown in the exhibit, the break-even point is $60,000 in sales, which was computed by dividing the company's fixed expenses of $27,000 by its overall CM ratio of 45%. However, this is the break-even only if the company's sales mix does not change. Currently, the Monuments DVD is responsible for 20% and the Parks DVD for 80% of the company's dollar sales. Assuming this sales mix does not change, if total sales are $60,000, the sales of the Monuments DVD would be $12,000 (20% of $60,000) and the sales of the Parks DVD would be $48,000 (80% of $60,000). As shown in Exhibit 6–4, at these levels of sales, the company would indeed break even. But $60,000 in sales represents the break-even point for the company only if the sales mix does not change. *If the sales mix changes, then the break-even point will also usually change.* This is illustrated by the results for October in which the sales mix shifted away from the more profitable Parks DVD (which has a 50% CM ratio) toward the less profitable Monuments DVD (which has a 25% CM ratio). These results appear in Exhibit 6–5.

Although sales have remained unchanged at $100,000, the sales mix is exactly the reverse of what it was in Exhibit 6–4, with the bulk of the sales now coming from the

**EXHIBIT 6–5**    Multiproduct Break-Even Analysis: A Shift in Sales Mix (see Exhibit 6–4)

**Virtual Journeys Unlimited**
**Contribution Income Statement**
**For the Month of October**

| | Monuments DVD | | Parks DVD | | Total | |
|---|---|---|---|---|---|---|
| | **Amount** | **Percent** | **Amount** | **Percent** | **Amount** | **Percent** |
| Sales ............................... | $80,000 | 100% | $20,000 | 100% | $100,000 | 100% |
| Variable expenses ................... | 60,000 | 75% | 10,000 | 50% | 70,000 | 70% |
| Contribution margin ................. | $20,000 | 25% | $10,000 | 50% | 30,000 | 30% |
| Fixed expenses...................... | | | | | 27,000 | |
| Net operating income ............... | | | | | $  3,000 | |

Computation of the break-even point:

$$\frac{\text{Fixed expenses}}{\text{Overall CM ratio}} = \frac{\$27,000}{0.30} = \$90,000$$

less profitable Monuments DVD. Notice that this shift in the sales mix has caused both the overall CM ratio and total profits to drop sharply from the prior month even though total sales are the same. The overall CM ratio has dropped from 45% in September to only 30% in October, and net operating income has dropped from $18,000 to only $3,000. In addition, with the drop in the overall CM ratio, the company's break-even point is no longer $60,000 in sales. Because the company is now realizing less average contribution margin per dollar of sales, it takes more sales to cover the same amount of fixed costs. Thus, the break-even point has increased from $60,000 to $90,000 in sales per year.

In preparing a break-even analysis, an assumption must be made concerning the sales mix. Usually the assumption is that it will not change. However, if the sales mix is expected to change, then this must be explicitly considered in any CVP computations.

8.  Which of the following statements is true? (You may select more than one answer.)
    a. One minus the contribution margin ratio equals the variable expense ratio.
    b. Incremental analysis focuses only on the costs and revenues that change as a result of a decision.
    c. Sales commissions based on sales dollars can lead to lower profits than commissions based on contribution margin.
    d. If a company's total sales remain constant, then its net operating income must remain constant even if the sales mix fluctuates.

CONCEPT
CHECK

**SUMMARY**

**LO6–1 Explain how changes in activity affect contribution margin and net operating income.**

The unit contribution margin, which is the difference between a unit's selling price and its variable cost, indicates how net operating income will change as the result of selling one more or one less unit. For example, if a product's unit contribution margin is $10, then selling one more unit will add $10 to the company's profit.

**LO6–2 Prepare and interpret a cost-volume-profit (CVP) graph and a profit graph.**

A cost-volume-profit graph displays sales revenues and expenses as a function of unit sales. The break-even point on the graph is the point at which the total sales revenue and total expense lines intersect. A profit graph displays profit as a function of unit sales. The break-even point on the profit graph is the point at which profit is zero.

**LO6–3 Use the contribution margin ratio (CM ratio) to compute changes in contribution margin and net operating income resulting from changes in sales volume.**

The contribution margin ratio is computed by dividing the unit contribution margin by the unit selling price, or by dividing the total contribution margin by the total sales.

The contribution margin shows how much a dollar increase in sales affects the total contribution margin and net operating income. For example, if a product has a 40% contribution margin ratio, then a $100 increase in sales should result in a $40 increase in contribution margin and in net operating income.

**LO6–4 Show the effects on net operating income of changes in variable costs, fixed costs, selling price, and volume.**

Contribution margin concepts can be used to estimate the effects of changes in various parameters such as variable costs, fixed costs, selling prices, and volume on net operating income.

**LO6–5 Determine the break-even point.**

The break-even point is the level of sales at which profit is zero. This is just a special case of solving for the level of sales needed to achieve a desired target profit—in this special case the target profit is zero.

**LO6–6 Determine the level of sales needed to achieve a desired target profit.**

The level of sales needed to achieve a desired target profit can be computed using several methods. The answer can be derived using the fundamental profit equation and simple algebra or formulas can be used. In either approach, the unit sales required to attain a desired target profit is ultimately determined by summing the desired target profit and the fixed expenses and then dividing the result by the unit contribution margin.

**LO6–7 Compute the margin of safety and explain its significance.**

The margin of safety is the difference between the total budgeted (or actual) sales dollars of a period and the break-even sales dollars. It expresses how much cushion there is in the current level of sales above the break-even point.

**LO6–8 Compute the degree of operating leverage at a particular level of sales and explain how it can be used to predict changes in net operating income.**

The degree of operating leverage is computed by dividing the total contribution margin by net operating income. The degree of operating leverage can be used to determine the impact a given percentage change in sales would have on net operating income. For example, if a company's degree of operating leverage is 2.5, then a 10% increase in sales from the current level of sales should result in a 25% increase in net operating income.

**LO6–9 Compute the break-even point for a multiproduct company and explain the effects of shifts in the sales mix on contribution margin and the break-even point.**

The break-even point for a multiproduct company can be computed by dividing the company's total fixed expenses by the overall contribution margin ratio.

This method for computing the break-even point assumes that the sales mix is constant. If the sales mix shifts toward products with a lower contribution margin ratio, then more total sales are required to attain any given level of profits.

# GUIDANCE ANSWERS TO DECISION POINT

**Loan Officer**

To determine the company's margin of safety, you need to determine its break-even point. Start by estimating the company's variable expense ratio:

$$\text{Variable cost per unit} \div \text{Selling price per unit} = \text{Variable expense ratio}$$
$$\$68 \div \$100 = 68\%$$

Then, estimate the company's variable expenses:

$$\text{Sales} \times \text{Variable expense ratio} = \text{Estimated amount of variable expenses}$$
$$\$8,000,000 \times 0.68 = \$5,440,000$$

Next, estimate the company's current level of fixed expenses as follows:

$$\text{Sales} = \text{Variable expenses} + \text{Fixed expenses} + \text{Profits}$$
$$\$8,000,000 = \$5,440,000 + X + \$700,000$$
$$X = \$8,000,000 - \$5,440,000 - \$700,000$$
$$X = \$1,860,000$$

Use the equation approach to estimate the company's break-even point:

$$\text{Sales} = \text{Variable expenses} + \text{Fixed expenses} + \text{Profits}$$
$$X = 0.68X + \$1,860,000 + \$0$$
$$0.32X = \$1,860,000$$
$$X = \$5,812,500$$

Finally, compute the company's margin of safety:

$$\text{Margin of safety} = (\text{Sales} - \text{Break-even sales}) \div \text{Sales}$$
$$= (\$8,000,000 - \$5,812,500) \div \$8,000,000$$
$$= 27.3\%$$

The margin of safety appears to be adequate, so if the other information about the company is favorable, a loan would seem to be justified.

## GUIDANCE ANSWERS TO CONCEPT CHECKS

1. **Choices a, b, and c.** The total variable costs will change as the level of sales fluctuates.
2. **Choice c.** Choice *a* fails to consider variable costs. Choice *b* is invalid because it is not stated in terms of dollars. Choice *d* excludes the selling price per unit.
3. **Choice d.** The contribution margin ratio equals 1.0 – Variable costs as a percent of sales.
4. **Choice d.** The contribution margin per unit is $12 (40% of $30). Therefore, the break-even point in units sold = $60,000 ÷ $12 = 5,000.
5. **Choice a.** ($100,000 + $50,000) ÷ $20 contribution margin per unit = 7,500 units.
6. **Choice c.** 7,500 units is 2,500 units above the break-even point. Therefore, the margin of safety is 2,500 units × $55 per unit = $137,500.
7. **Choice c.** The margin of safety in dollars divided by the selling price per unit equals the margin of safety in units.
8. **Choices a, b, and c.** If a company's total sales remain constant, its net operating income may change if the sales mix fluctuates.

## REVIEW PROBLEM: CVP RELATIONSHIPS

Voltar Company manufactures and sells a specialized cordless telephone for high electromagnetic radiation environments. The company's contribution format income statement for the most recent year is given below:

| | Total | Per Unit | Percent of Sales |
|---|---|---|---|
| Sales (20,000 units) | $1,200,000 | $60 | 100% |
| Variable expenses | 900,000 | 45 | ? % |
| Contribution margin | 300,000 | $15 | ? % |
| Fixed expenses | 240,000 | | |
| Net operating income | $ 60,000 | | |

Management is anxious to increase the company's profit and has asked for an analysis of a number of items.

**Required:**

1.  Compute the company's CM ratio and variable expense ratio.
2.  Compute the company's break-even point in both unit sales and dollar sales. Use the equation method.
3.  Assume that sales increase by $400,000 next year. If cost behavior patterns remain unchanged, by how much will the company's net operating income increase? Use the CM ratio to compute your answer.
4.  Refer to the original data. Assume that next year management wants the company to earn a profit of at least $90,000. How many units will have to be sold to earn this target profit?
5.  Refer to the original data. Compute the company's margin of safety in both dollar and percentage form.
6.  a. Compute the company's degree of operating leverage at the present level of sales.
    b. Assume that through a more intense effort by the sales staff, the company's sales increase by 8% next year. By what percentage would you expect net operating income to increase? Use the degree of operating leverage to obtain your answer.
    c. Verify your answer to (b) by preparing a new contribution format income statement showing an 8% increase in sales.
7.  Refer to the original data. In an effort to increase sales and profits, management is considering the use of a higher-quality speaker. The higher-quality speaker would increase variable costs by $3 per unit, but management could eliminate one quality inspector who is paid a salary of $30,000 per year. The sales manager estimates that the higher-quality speaker would increase annual sales by at least 20%.
    a. Assuming that changes are made as described above, prepare a projected contribution format income statement for next year. Show data on a total, per unit, and percentage basis.
    b. Compute the company's new break-even point in both unit sales and dollar sales. Use the formula method.
    c. Would you recommend that the changes be made?

### Solution to Review Problem

1.
$$\text{CM ratio} = \frac{\text{Unit contribution margin}}{\text{Unit selling price}} = \frac{\$15}{\$60} = 25\%$$

$$\text{Variable expense ratio} = \frac{\text{Variable expense}}{\text{Selling price}} = \frac{\$45}{\$60} = 75\%$$

2.
$$\text{Profit} = \text{Unit CM} \times Q - \text{Fixed expenses}$$
$$\$0 = \$15 \times Q - \$240,000$$
$$\$15Q = \$240,000$$
$$Q = \$240,000 \div \$15$$
$$Q = 16,000 \text{ units; or, at } \$60 \text{ per unit, } \$960,000$$

3.

| | |
|---|---|
| Increase in sales ............................... | $400,000 |
| Contribution margin ratio ....................... | × 25% |
| Expected increase in contribution margin ........ | $100,000 |

Because the fixed expenses are not expected to change, net operating income will increase by the entire $100,000 increase in contribution margin computed above.

4.  Equation method:
$$\text{Profit} = \text{Unit CM} \times Q - \text{Fixed expenses}$$
$$\$90,000 = \$15 \times Q - \$240,000$$
$$\$15Q = \$90,000 + \$240,000$$
$$Q = \$330,000 \div \$15$$
$$Q = 22,000 \text{ units}$$

Formula method:
$$\frac{\text{Unit sales to attain}}{\text{the target profit}} = \frac{\text{Target profit} + \text{Fixed expenses}}{\text{Contribution margin per unit}} = \frac{\$90,000 + \$240,000}{\$15 \text{ per unit}} = 22,000 \text{ units}$$

5.  Margin of safety in dollars = Total sales − Break-even sales

$$= \$1,200,000 − \$960,000 = \$240,000$$

$$\text{Margin of safety percentage} = \frac{\text{Margin of safety in dollars}}{\text{Total sales}} = \frac{\$240,000}{\$1,200,000} = 20\%$$

6.  a.  $\text{Degree of operating leverage} = \dfrac{\text{Contribution margin}}{\text{Net operating income}} = \dfrac{\$300,000}{\$60,000} = 5$

    b.

| | |
|---|---|
| Expected increase in sales ......................... | 8% |
| Degree of operating leverage ...................... | × 5 |
| Expected increase in net operating income ......... | 40% |

    c.  If sales increase by 8%, then 21,600 units (20,000 × 1.08 = 21,600) will be sold next year. The new contribution format income statement would be as follows:

| | Total | Per Unit | Percent of Sales |
|---|---|---|---|
| Sales (21,600 units) ............ | $1,296,000 | $60 | 100% |
| Variable expenses ............. | 972,000 | 45 | 75% |
| Contribution margin ............ | 324,000 | $15 | 25% |
| Fixed expenses ................ | 240,000 | | |
| Net operating income ......... | $  84,000 | | |

Thus, the $84,000 expected net operating income for next year represents a 40% increase over the $60,000 net operating income earned during the current year:

$$\frac{\$84,000 − \$60,000}{\$60,000} = \frac{\$24,000}{\$60,000} = 40\% \text{ increase}$$

Note that the increase in sales from 20,000 to 21,600 units has increased *both* total sales and total variable expenses.

7.  a.  A 20% increase in sales would result in 24,000 units being sold next year: 20,000 units × 1.20 = 24,000 units.

| | Total | Per Unit | Percent of Sales |
|---|---|---|---|
| Sales (24,000 units) ............ | $1,440,000 | $60 | 100% |
| Variable expenses ............. | 1,152,000 | 48* | 80% |
| Contribution margin ............ | 288,000 | $12 | 20% |
| Fixed expenses ................ | 210,000† | | |
| Net operating income ......... | $  78,000 | | |

*$45 + $3 = $48; $48 ÷ $60 = 80%.
†$240,000 − $30,000 = $210,000.

Note that the change in per unit variable expenses results in a change in both the per unit contribution margin and the CM ratio.

    b.  $\text{Unit sales to break even} = \dfrac{\text{Fixed expenses}}{\text{Unit contribution margin}}$

$$= \frac{\$210,000}{\$12 \text{ per unit}} = 17,500 \text{ units}$$

$$\text{Dollar sales to break even} = \frac{\text{Fixed expenses}}{\text{CM ratio}}$$

$$= \frac{\$210,000}{0.20} = \$1,050,000$$

c. Yes, based on these data, the changes should be made. The changes increase the company's net operating income from the present $60,000 to $78,000 per year. Although the changes also result in a higher break-even point (17,500 units as compared to the present 16,000 units), the company's margin of safety actually becomes greater than before:

$$\text{Margin of safety in dollars} = \text{Total sales} - \text{Break-even sales}$$
$$= \$1,440,000 - \$1,050,000 = \$390,000$$

As shown in (5), the company's present margin of safety is only $240,000. Thus, several benefits will result from the proposed changes.

## GLOSSARY

**Break-even point**   The level of sales at which profit is zero. (p. 220)

**Contribution margin ratio (CM ratio)**   A ratio computed by dividing contribution margin by sales. (p. 226)

**Cost-volume-profit (CVP) graph**   A graphical representation of the relationships between an organization's revenues, costs, and profits on the one hand and its sales volume on the other hand. (p. 223)

**Degree of operating leverage**   A measure, at a given level of sales, of how a percentage change in sales will affect profits. The degree of operating leverage is computed by dividing contribution margin by net operating income. (p. 239)

**Incremental analysis**   An analytical approach that focuses only on those costs and revenues that change as a result of a decision. (p. 229)

**Margin of safety**   The excess of budgeted or actual dollar sales over the break-even dollar sales. (p. 235)

**Operating leverage**   A measure of how sensitive net operating income is to a given percentage change in dollar sales. (p. 239)

**Sales mix**   The relative proportions in which a company's products are sold. Sales mix is computed by expressing the sales of each product as a percentage of total sales. (p. 241)

**Target profit analysis**   Estimating what sales volume is needed to achieve a specific target profit. (p. 234)

**Variable expense ratio**   A ratio computed by dividing variable expenses by sales. (p. 226)

## QUESTIONS

6–1   What is the meaning of *contribution margin ratio*? How is this ratio useful in planning business operations?

6–2   Often the most direct route to a business decision is an incremental analysis. What is meant by an *incremental analysis?*

6–3   In all respects, Company A and Company B are identical except that Company A's costs are mostly variable, whereas Company B's costs are mostly fixed. When sales increase, which company will tend to realize the greatest increase in profits? Explain.

6–4   What is the meaning of *operating leverage?*

6–5   What is the meaning of *break-even point?*

6–6   In response to a request from your immediate supervisor, you have prepared a CVP graph portraying the cost and revenue characteristics of your company's product and operations. Explain how the lines on the graph and the break-even point would change if (*a*) the selling price per unit decreased, (*b*) fixed cost increased throughout the entire range of activity portrayed on the graph, and (*c*) variable cost per unit increased.

6–7   What is the meaning of *margin of safety?*

6–8   What is meant by the term *sales mix?* What assumption is usually made concerning sales mix in CVP analysis?

6–9   Explain how a shift in the sales mix could result in both a higher break-even point and a lower net operating income.

The Excel worksheet form that appears below is to be used to recreate portions of the Review Problem relating to Voltar Company. Download the workbook containing this form from Connect, where you will also receive instructions about how to use this worksheet form.

**LO6–5, LO6–7, LO6–8**

| | A | B | C | D |
|---|---|---|---|---|
| 1 | Chapter 6: Applying Excel | | | |
| 2 | | | | |
| 3 | **Data** | | | |
| 4 | Unit sales | 20,000 | units | |
| 5 | Selling price per unit | $60 | per unit | |
| 6 | Variable expenses per unit | $45 | per unit | |
| 7 | Fixed expenses | $240,000 | | |
| 8 | | | | |
| 9 | *Enter a formula into each of the cells marked with a ? below* | | | |
| 10 | **Review Problem: CVP Relationships** | | | |
| 11 | | | | |
| 12 | ***Compute the CM ratio and variable expense ratio*** | | | |
| 13 | Selling price per unit | ? | per unit | |
| 14 | Variable expenses per unit | ? | per unit | |
| 15 | Contribution margin per unit | ? | per unit | |
| 16 | | | | |
| 17 | CM ratio | ? | | |
| 18 | Variable expense ratio | ? | | |
| 19 | | | | |
| 20 | ***Compute the break-even*** | | | |
| 21 | Break-even in unit sales | ? | units | |
| 22 | Break-even in dollar sales | ? | | |
| 23 | | | | |
| 24 | ***Compute the margin of safety*** | | | |
| 25 | Margin of safety in dollars | ? | | |
| 26 | Margin of safety percentage | ? | | |
| 27 | | | | |
| 28 | ***Compute the degree of operating leverage*** | | | |
| 29 | Sales | ? | | |
| 30 | Variable expenses | ? | | |
| 31 | Contribution margin | ? | | |
| 32 | Fixed expenses | ? | | |
| 33 | Net operating income | ? | | |
| 34 | | | | |
| 35 | Degree of operating leverage | ? | | |
| 36 | | | | |

Chapter 6 Form   ...   ⊕

You should proceed to the requirements below only after completing your worksheet.

*Required:*
1. Check your worksheet by changing the fixed expenses to $270,000. If your worksheet is operating properly, the degree of operating leverage should be 10. If you do not get this answer, find the errors in your worksheet and correct them. How much is the margin of safety percentage? Did it change? Why or why not?
2. Enter the following data from a different company into your worksheet:

| | |
|---|---|
| Unit sales . . . . . . . . . . . . . . . . . . . . . . . . . . . | 10,000 |
| Selling price per unit . . . . . . . . . . . . . . . . . | $120 |
| Variable expenses per unit . . . . . . . . . . . . | $72 |
| Fixed expenses . . . . . . . . . . . . . . . . . . . . . . | $420,000 |

What is the margin of safety percentage? What is the degree of operating leverage?
3. Using the degree of operating leverage and without changing anything in your worksheet, calculate the percentage change in net operating income if unit sales increase by 15%.

4.  Confirm the calculations you made in part (3) above by increasing the unit sales in your worksheet by 15%. What is the new net operating income and by what percentage did it increase?

5.  Thad Morgan, a motorcycle enthusiast, has been exploring the possibility of relaunching the Western Hombre brand of cycle that was popular in the 1930s. The retro-look cycle would be sold for $10,000 and at that price, Thad estimates that he could sell 600 units each year. The variable cost to produce and sell the cycles would be $7,500 per unit. The annual fixed cost would be $1,200,000.

    a.  Using your worksheet, what would be the unit sales to break even, the margin of safety in dollars, and the degree of operating leverage?

    b.  Thad is worried about the selling price. Rumors are circulating that other retro brands of cycles may be revived. If so, the selling price for the Western Hombre would have to be reduced to $9,000 to compete effectively. In that event, Thad also would reduce fixed expenses by $300,000 by reducing advertising expenses, but he still hopes to sell 600 units per year. Do you think this is a good plan? Explain. Also, explain the degree of operating leverage that appears on your worksheet.

# THE FOUNDATIONAL 15   ■ connect

**LO6–1, LO6–3, LO6–4, LO6–5, LO6–6, LO6–7, LO6–8**

Oslo Company prepared the following contribution format income statement based on a sales volume of 1,000 units (the relevant range of production is 500 units to 1,500 units):

| | |
|---|---:|
| Sales .......................................... | $20,000 |
| Variable expenses ........................... | 12,000 |
| Contribution margin ......................... | 8,000 |
| Fixed expenses .............................. | 6,000 |
| Net operating income ....................... | $ 2,000 |

**Required:**

(Answer each question independently and always refer to the original data unless instructed otherwise.)

1.  What is the contribution margin per unit?
2.  What is the contribution margin ratio?
3.  What is the variable expense ratio?
4.  If sales increase to 1,001 units, what would be the increase in net operating income?
5.  If sales decline to 900 units, what would be the net operating income?
6.  If the selling price increases by $2 per unit and the sales volume decreases by 100 units, what would be the net operating income?
7.  If the variable cost per unit increases by $1, spending on advertising increases by $1,500, and unit sales increase by 250 units, what would be the net operating income?
8.  What is the break-even point in unit sales?
9.  What is the break-even point in dollar sales?
10. How many units must be sold to achieve a target profit of $5,000?
11. What is the margin of safety in dollars? What is the margin of safety percentage?
12. What is the degree of operating leverage?
13. Using the degree of operating leverage, what is the estimated percent increase in net operating income of a 5% increase in sales?
14. Assume that the amounts of the company's total variable expenses and total fixed expenses were reversed. In other words, assume that the total variable expenses are $6,000 and the total fixed expenses are $12,000. Under this scenario and assuming that total sales remain the same, what is the degree of operating leverage?
15. Using the degree of operating leverage that you computed in the previous question, what is the estimated percent increase in net operating income of a 5% increase in sales?

# EXERCISES   ■ connect

## EXERCISE 6–1   The Effect of Changes in Activity on Net Operating Income LO6–1

Whirly Corporation's contribution format income statement for the most recent month is shown below:

| | Total | Per Unit |
|---|---|---|
| Sales (10,000 units) . . . . . . . . . . . . . . . . | $350,000 | $35.00 |
| Variable expenses . . . . . . . . . . . . . . . . . | 200,000 | 20.00 |
| Contribution margin . . . . . . . . . . . . . . . . | 150,000 | $15.00 |
| Fixed expenses . . . . . . . . . . . . . . . . . . . . | 135,000 | |
| Net operating income . . . . . . . . . . . . . . | $ 15,000 | |

**Required:**
(Consider each case independently):
1.  What would be the revised net operating income per month if the sales volume increases by 100 units?
2.  What would be the revised net operating income per month if the sales volume decreases by 100 units?
3.  What would be the revised net operating income per month if the sales volume is 9,000 units?

### EXERCISE 6–2    Prepare a Cost-Volume-Profit (CVP) Graph LO6–2

Karlik Enterprises distributes a single product whose selling price is $24 per unit and whose variable expense is $18 per unit. The company's monthly fixed expense is $24,000.

**Required:**
1.  Prepare a cost-volume-profit graph for the company up to a sales level of 8,000 units.
2.  Estimate the company's break-even point in unit sales using your cost-volume-profit graph.

### EXERCISE 6–3    Prepare a Profit Graph LO6–2

Jaffre Enterprises distributes a single product whose selling price is $16 per unit and whose variable expense is $11 per unit. The company's fixed expense is $16,000 per month.

**Required:**
1.  Prepare a profit graph for the company up to a sales level of 4,000 units.
2.  Estimate the company's break-even point in unit sales using your profit graph.

### EXERCISE 6–4    Computing and Using the CM Ratio LO6–3

Last month when Holiday Creations, Inc., sold 50,000 units, total sales were $200,000, total variable expenses were $120,000, and fixed expenses were $65,000.

**Required:**
1.  What is the company's contribution margin (CM) ratio?
2.  What is the estimated change in the company's net operating income if it can increase total sales by $1,000?

### EXERCISE 6–5    Changes in Variable Costs, Fixed Costs, Selling Price, and Volume LO6–4
Data for Hermann Corporation are shown below:

| | Per Unit | Percent of Sales |
|---|---|---|
| Selling price . . . . . . . . . . . . . . . . | $90 | 100% |
| Variable expenses . . . . . . . . . . | 63 | 70 |
| Contribution margin . . . . . . . . . | $27 | 30% |

Fixed expenses are $30,000 per month and the company is selling 2,000 units per month.

**Required:**
1.  How much will net operating income increase (decrease) per month if the monthly advertising budget increases by $5,000 and monthly sales increase by $9,000?
2.  Refer to the original data. How much will net operating income increase (decrease) per month if the company uses higher-quality components that increase the variable expense by $2 per unit and increase unit sales by 10%.

### EXERCISE 6–6    Break-Even Analysis LO6–5

Mauro Products distributes a single product, a woven basket whose selling price is $15 per unit and whose variable expense is $12 per unit. The company's monthly fixed expense is $4,200.

*Required:*
1. Calculate the company's break-even point in unit sales.
2. Calculate the company's break-even point in dollar sales.
3. If the company's fixed expenses increase by $600, what would become the new break-even point in unit sales? In dollar sales?

**EXERCISE 6–7   Target Profit Analysis LO6–6**
Lin Corporation has a single product whose selling price is $120 per unit and whose variable expense is $80 per unit. The company's monthly fixed expense is $50,000.

*Required:*
1. Calculate the unit sales needed to attain a target profit of $10,000.
2. Calculate the dollar sales needed to attain a target profit of $15,000.

**EXERCISE 6–8   Compute the Margin of Safety LO6–7**
Molander Corporation is a distributor of a sun umbrella used at resort hotels. Data concerning the next month's budget appear below:

| | |
|---|---|
| Selling price per unit .......... | $30 |
| Variable expense per unit ...... | $20 |
| Fixed expense per month ...... | $7,500 |
| Unit sales per month .......... | 1,000 |

*Required:*
1. What is the company's margin of safety?
2. What is the company's margin of safety as a percentage of its sales?

**EXERCISE 6–9   Compute and Use the Degree of Operating Leverage LO6–8**
Engberg Company installs lawn sod in home yards. The company's most recent monthly contribution format income statement follows:

| | Amount | Percent of Sales |
|---|---|---|
| Sales ............................ | $80,000 | 100% |
| Variable expenses ................ | 32,000 | 40% |
| Contribution margin ............... | 48,000 | 60% |
| Fixed expenses .................... | 38,000 | |
| Net operating income ............. | $10,000 | |

*Required:*
1. What is the company's degree of operating leverage?
2. Using the degree of operating leverage, estimate the impact on net operating income of a 5% increase in sales.
3. Verify your estimate from part (2) above by constructing a new contribution format income statement for the company assuming a 5% increase in sales.

**EXERCISE 6–10   Multiproduct Break-Even Analysis LO6–9**
Lucido Products markets two computer games: Claimjumper and Makeover. A contribution format income statement for a recent month for the two games appears below:

| | Claimjumper | Makeover | Total |
|---|---|---|---|
| Sales ......................... | $30,000 | $70,000 | $100,000 |
| Variable expenses ............... | 20,000 | 50,000 | 70,000 |
| Contribution margin .............. | $10,000 | $20,000 | 30,000 |
| Fixed expenses .................. | | | 24,000 |
| Net operating income ............ | | | $ 6,000 |

*Required:*
1. What is the overall contribution margin (CM) ratio for the company?
2. What is the company's overall break-even point in dollar sales?

3. Verify the overall break-even point for the company by constructing a contribution format income statement showing the appropriate levels of sales for the two products.

**EXERCISE 6–11  Missing Data; Basic CVP Concepts LO6–1, LO6–9**

Fill in the missing amounts in each of the eight case situations below. Each case is independent of the others. (*Hint:* One way to find the missing amounts would be to prepare a contribution format income statement for each case, enter the known data, and then compute the missing items.)

a. Assume that only one product is being sold in each of the four following case situations:

| Case | Units Sold | Sales | Variable Expenses | Contribution Margin per Unit | Fixed Expenses | Net Operating Income (Loss) |
|---|---|---|---|---|---|---|
| 1 .......... | 15,000 | $180,000 | $120,000 | ? | $50,000 | ? |
| 2 .......... | ? | $100,000 | ? | $10 | $32,000 | $8,000 |
| 3 .......... | 10,000 | ? | $70,000 | $13 | ? | $12,000 |
| 4 .......... | 6,000 | $300,000 | ? | ? | $100,000 | $(10,000) |

b. Assume that more than one product is being sold in each of the four following case situations:

| Case | Sales | Variable Expenses | Average Contribution Margin Ratio | Fixed Expenses | Net Operating Income (Loss) |
|---|---|---|---|---|---|
| 1 ................ | $500,000 | ? | 20% | ? | $7,000 |
| 2 ................ | $400,000 | $260,000 | ? | $100,000 | ? |
| 3 ................ | ? | ? | 60% | $130,000 | $20,000 |
| 4 ................ | $600,000 | $420,000 | ? | ? | $(5,000) |

**EXERCISE 6–12  Multiproduct Break-Even Analysis LO6–9**

Olongapo Sports Corporation distributes two premium golf balls—Flight Dynamic and Sure Shot. Monthly sales and the contribution margin ratios for the two products follow:

| | Product | | |
|---|---|---|---|
| | Flight Dynamic | Sure Shot | Total |
| Sales ............. | $150,000 | $250,000 | $400,000 |
| CM ratio ........... | 80% | 36% | ? |

Fixed expenses total $183,750 per month.

*Required:*

1. Prepare a contribution format income statement for the company as a whole. Carry computations to one decimal place.
2. What is the company's break-even point in dollar sales based on the current sales mix?
3. If sales increase by $100,000 a month, by how much would you expect the monthly net operating income to increase? What are your assumptions?

**EXERCISE 6–13  Changes in Selling Price, Sales Volume, Variable Cost per Unit, and Total Fixed Costs LO6–1, LO6–4**

Miller Company's contribution format income statement for the most recent month is shown below:

| | Total | Per Unit |
|---|---|---|
| Sales (20,000 units) ............ | $300,000 | $15.00 |
| Variable expenses ............. | 180,000 | 9.00 |
| Contribution margin ............ | 120,000 | $ 6.00 |
| Fixed expenses ............... | 70,000 | |
| Net operating income .......... | $ 50,000 | |

*Required:*

(Consider each case independently):

1. What is the revised net operating income if unit sales increase by 15%?
2. What is the revised net operating income if the selling price decreases by $1.50 per unit and the number of units sold increases by 25%?
3. What is the revised net operating income if the selling price increases by $1.50 per unit, fixed expenses increase by $20,000, and the number of units sold decreases by 5%?
4. What is the revised net operating income if the selling price per unit increases by 12%, variable expenses increase by 60 cents per unit, and the number of units sold decreases by 10%?

**EXERCISE 6–14   Break-Even and Target Profit Analysis** LO6–3, LO6–4, LO6–5, LO6–6

Lindon Company is the exclusive distributor for an automotive product that sells for $40 per unit and has a CM ratio of 30%. The company's fixed expenses are $180,000 per year. The company plans to sell 16,000 units this year.

*Required:*

1. What are the variable expenses per unit?
2. What is the break-even point in unit sales and in dollar sales?
3. What amount of unit sales and dollar sales is required to attain a target profit of $60,000 per year?
4. Assume that by using a more efficient shipper, the company is able to reduce its variable expenses by $4 per unit. What is the company's new break-even point in unit sales and in dollar sales? What dollar sales is required to attain a target profit of $60,000?

**EXERCISE 6–15   Operating Leverage** LO6–1, LO6–8

Magic Realm, Inc., has developed a new fantasy board game. The company sold 15,000 games last year at a selling price of $20 per game. Fixed expenses associated with the game total $182,000 per year, and variable expenses are $6 per game. Production of the game is entrusted to a printing contractor. Variable expenses consist mostly of payments to this contractor.

*Required:*

1. Prepare a contribution format income statement for the game last year and compute the degree of operating leverage.
2. Management is confident that the company can sell 18,000 games next year (an increase of 3,000 games, or 20%, over last year). Given this assumption:
   a. What is the expected percentage increase in net operating income for next year?
   b. What is the expected amount of net operating income for next year? (Do not prepare an income statement; use the degree of operating leverage to compute your answer.)

**EXERCISE 6–16   Break-Even Analysis and CVP Graphing** LO6–2, LO6–4, LO6–5

The Hartford Symphony Guild is planning its annual dinner-dance. The dinner-dance committee has assembled the following expected costs for the event:

| | |
|---|---|
| Dinner (per person) | $18 |
| Favors and program (per person) | $2 |
| Band | $2,800 |
| Rental of ballroom | $900 |
| Professional entertainment during intermission | $1,000 |
| Tickets and advertising | $1,300 |

The committee members would like to charge $35 per person for the evening's activities.

*Required:*

1. What is the break-even point for the dinner-dance (in terms of the number of persons who must attend)?
2. Assume that last year only 300 persons attended the dinner-dance. If the same number attend this year, what price per ticket must be charged in order to break even?
3. Refer to the original data ($35 ticket price per person). Prepare a CVP graph for the dinner-dance from zero tickets up to 600 tickets sold.

**EXERCISE 6–17   Break-Even and Target Profit Analysis** LO6–4, LO6–5, LO6–6

Outback Outfitters sells recreational equipment. One of the company's products, a small camp stove, sells for $50 per unit. Variable expenses are $32 per stove, and fixed expenses associated with the stove total $108,000 per month.

*Required:*
1. What is the break-even point in unit sales and in dollar sales?
2. If the variable expenses per stove increase as a percentage of the selling price, will it result in a higher or a lower break-even point? Why? (Assume that the fixed expenses remain unchanged.)
3. At present, the company is selling 8,000 stoves per month. The sales manager is convinced that a 10% reduction in the selling price would result in a 25% increase in monthly sales of stoves. Prepare two contribution format income statements, one under present operating conditions, and one as operations would appear after the proposed changes. Show both total and per unit data on your statements.
4. Refer to the data in (3) above. How many stoves would have to be sold at the new selling price to attain a target profit of $35,000 per month?

**EXERCISE 6–18   Break-Even and Target Profit Analysis; Margin of Safety; CM Ratio** LO6–1, LO6–3, LO6–5, LO6–6, LO6–7

Menlo Company distributes a single product. The company's sales and expenses for last month follow:

|  | Total | Per Unit |
|---|---|---|
| Sales | $450,000 | $30 |
| Variable expenses | 180,000 | 12 |
| Contribution margin | 270,000 | $18 |
| Fixed expenses | 216,000 | |
| Net operating income | $ 54,000 | |

*Required:*
1. What is the monthly break-even point in unit sales and in dollar sales?
2. Without resorting to computations, what is the total contribution margin at the break-even point?
3. How many units would have to be sold each month to attain a target profit of $90,000? Verify your answer by preparing a contribution format income statement at the target sales level.
4. Refer to the original data. Compute the company's margin of safety in both dollar and percentage terms.
5. What is the company's CM ratio? If sales increase by $50,000 per month and there is no change in fixed expenses, by how much would you expect monthly net operating income to increase?

**connect** PROBLEMS

**PROBLEM 6–19   Break-Even Analysis; Pricing** LO6–1, LO6–4, LO6–5

Minden Company introduced a new product last year for which it is trying to find an optimal selling price. Marketing studies suggest that the company can increase sales by 5,000 units for each $2 reduction in the selling price. The company's present selling price is $70 per unit, and variable expenses are $40 per unit. Fixed expenses are $540,000 per year. The present annual sales volume (at the $70 selling price) is 15,000 units.

*Required:*
1. What is the present yearly net operating income or loss?
2. What is the present break-even point in unit sales and in dollar sales?
3. Assuming that the marketing studies are correct, what is the maximum annual profit that the company can earn? At how many units and at what selling price per unit would the company generate this profit?
4. What would be the break-even point in unit sales and in dollar sales using the selling price you determined in (3) above (e.g., the selling price at the level of maximum profits)? Why is this break-even point different from the break-even point you computed in (2) above?

**PROBLEM 6–20   CVP Applications: Break-Even Analysis; Cost Structure; Target Sales** LO6–1, LO6–3, LO6–4, LO6–5, LO6–6, LO6–8

Northwood Company manufactures basketballs. The company has a ball that sells for $25. At present, the ball is manufactured in a small plant that relies heavily on direct labor workers. Thus, variable expenses are high, totaling $15 per ball, of which 60% is direct labor cost.

Last year, the company sold 30,000 of these balls, with the following results:

| | |
|---|---:|
| Sales (30,000 balls) | $750,000 |
| Variable expenses | 450,000 |
| Contribution margin | 300,000 |
| Fixed expenses | 210,000 |
| Net operating income | $ 90,000 |

**Required:**
1. Compute (a) last year's CM ratio and the break-even point in balls, and (b) the degree of operating leverage at last year's sales level.
2. Due to an increase in labor rates, the company estimates that next year's variable expenses will increase by $3 per ball. If this change takes place and the selling price per ball remains constant at $25, what will be next year's CM ratio and the break-even point in balls?
3. Refer to the data in (2) above. If the expected change in variable expenses takes place, how many balls will have to be sold next year to earn the same net operating income, $90,000, as last year?
4. Refer again to the data in (2) above. The president feels that the company must raise the selling price of its basketballs. If Northwood Company wants to maintain the same CM ratio as last year (as computed in requirement 1a), what selling price per ball must it charge next year to cover the increased labor costs?
5. Refer to the original data. The company is discussing the construction of a new, automated manufacturing plant. The new plant would slash variable expenses per ball by 40%, but it would cause fixed expenses per year to double. If the new plant is built, what would be the company's new CM ratio and new break-even point in balls?
6. Refer to the data in (5) above.
   a. If the new plant is built, how many balls will have to be sold next year to earn the same net operating income, $90,000, as last year?
   b. Assume the new plant is built and that next year the company manufactures and sells 30,000 balls (the same number as sold last year). Prepare a contribution format income statement and compute the degree of operating leverage.
   c. If you were a member of top management, would you have been in favor of constructing the new plant? Explain.

**PROBLEM 6–21　Sales Mix; Multiproduct Break-Even Analysis LO6–9**
Gold Star Rice, Ltd., of Thailand exports Thai rice throughout Asia. The company grows three varieties of rice—White, Fragrant, and Loonzain. Budgeted sales by product and in total for the coming month are shown below:

| | White | | Fragrant | | Loonzain | | Total | |
|---|---|---|---|---|---|---|---|---|
| Percentage of total sales | 20% | | 52% | | 28% | | 100% | |
| Sales | $150,000 | 100% | $390,000 | 100% | $210,000 | 100% | $750,000 | 100% |
| Variable expenses | 108,000 | 72% | 78,000 | 20% | 84,000 | 40% | 270,000 | 36% |
| Contribution margin | $ 42,000 | 28% | $312,000 | 80% | $126,000 | 60% | 480,000 | 64% |
| Fixed expenses | | | | | | | 449,280 | |
| Net operating income | | | | | | | $ 30,720 | |

$$\text{Dollar sales to break-even} = \frac{\text{Fixed expenses}}{\text{CM ratio}} = \frac{\$449,280}{0.64} = \$702,000$$

As shown by these data, net operating income is budgeted at $30,720 for the month and the estimated break-even sales is $702,000.

Assume that actual sales for the month total $750,000 as planned. Actual sales by product are: White, $300,000; Fragrant, $180,000; and Loonzain, $270,000.

**Required:**

1. Prepare a contribution format income statement for the month based on the actual sales data. Present the income statement in the format shown above.
2. Compute the break-even point in dollar sales for the month based on your actual data.
3. Considering the fact that the company met its $750,000 sales budget for the month, the president is shocked at the results shown on your income statement in (1) above. Prepare a brief memo for the president explaining why the net operating income (loss) and the break-even point in dollar sales are different from what was budgeted.

**PROBLEM 6-22   CVP Applications; Contribution Margin Ratio; Break-Even Analysis; Cost Structure**
LO6-1, LO6-3, LO6-4, LO6-5, LO6-6

Due to erratic sales of its sole product—a high-capacity battery for laptop computers—PEM, Inc., has been experiencing financial difficulty for some time. The company's contribution format income statement for the most recent month is given below:

| | |
|---|---|
| Sales (19,500 units × $30 per unit) | $585,000 |
| Variable expenses | 409,500 |
| Contribution margin | 175,500 |
| Fixed expenses | 180,000 |
| Net operating loss | $ (4,500) |

**Required:**

1. Compute the company's CM ratio and its break-even point in unit sales and dollar sales.
2. The president believes that a $16,000 increase in the monthly advertising budget, combined with an intensified effort by the sales staff, will result in an $80,000 increase in monthly sales. If the president is right, what will be the increase (decrease) in the company's monthly net operating income?
3. Refer to the original data. The sales manager is convinced that a 10% reduction in the selling price, combined with an increase of $60,000 in the monthly advertising budget, will double unit sales. If the sales manager is right, what will be the revised net operating income (loss)?
4. Refer to the original data. The Marketing Department thinks that a fancy new package for the laptop computer battery would grow sales. The new package would increase packaging costs by 75 cents per unit. Assuming no other changes, how many units would have to be sold each month to attain a target profit of $9,750?
5. Refer to the original data. By automating, the company could reduce variable expenses by $3 per unit. However, fixed expenses would increase by $72,000 each month.
   a. Compute the new CM ratio and the new break-even point in unit sales and dollar sales.
   b. Assume that the company expects to sell 26,000 units next month. Prepare two contribution format income statements, one assuming that operations are not automated and one assuming that they are. (Show data on a per unit and percentage basis, as well as in total, for each alternative.)
   c. Would you recommend that the company automate its operations? Explain.

**PROBLEM 6-23   CVP Applications; Contribution Margin Ratio: Degree of Operating Leverage** LO6-1, LO6-3, LO6-4, LO6-5, LO6-8

Feather Friends, Inc., distributes a high-quality wooden birdhouse that sells for $20 per unit. Variable expenses are $8 per unit, and fixed expenses total $180,000 per year. Its operating results for last year were as follows:

| | |
|---|---|
| Sales | $400,000 |
| Variable expenses | 160,000 |
| Contribution margin | 240,000 |
| Fixed expenses | 180,000 |
| Net operating income | $ 60,000 |

*Required:*

Answer each question independently based on the original data:
1.  What is the product's CM ratio?
2.  Use the CM ratio to determine the break-even point in dollar sales.
3.  If this year's sales increase by $75,000 and fixed expenses do not change, how much will net operating income increase?
4.  a. What is the degree of operating leverage based on last year's sales?
    b. Assume the president expects this year's sales to increase by 20%. Using the degree of operating leverage from last year, what percentage increase in net operating income will the company realize this year?
5.  The sales manager is convinced that a 10% reduction in the selling price, combined with a $30,000 increase in advertising, would increase this year's unit sales by 25%. If the sales manager is right, what would be this year's net operating income if his ideas are implemented? Do you recommend implementing the sales manager's suggestions? Why?
6.  The president does not want to change the selling price. Instead, he wants to increase the sales commission by $1 per unit. He thinks that this move, combined with some increase in advertising, would increase this year's sales by 25%. How much could the president increase this year's advertising expense and still earn the same $60,000 net operating income as last year?

**PROBLEM 6–24   Break-Even and Target Profit Analysis LO6–5, LO6–6**
The Shirt Works sells a large variety of tee shirts and sweatshirts. Steve Hooper, the owner, is thinking of expanding his sales by hiring high school students, on a commission basis, to sell sweatshirts bearing the name and mascot of the local high school.

These sweatshirts would have to be ordered from the manufacturer six weeks in advance, and they could not be returned because of the unique printing required. The sweatshirts would cost Hooper $8 each with a minimum order of 75 sweatshirts. Any additional sweatshirts would have to be ordered in increments of 75.

Since Hooper's plan would not require any additional facilities, the only costs associated with the project would be the costs of the sweatshirts and the costs of the sales commissions. The selling price of the sweatshirts would be $13.50 each. Hooper would pay the students a commission of $1.50 for each shirt sold.

*Required:*
1.  What level of unit sales and dollar sales is needed to attain a target profit of $1,200?
2.  Assume that Hooper places an initial order for 75 sweatshirts. What is his break-even point in unit sales and dollar sales?

**PROBLEM 6–25   Changes in Fixed and Variable Costs; Break-Even and Target Profit Analysis LO6–4, LO6–5, LO6–6**
Neptune Company produces toys and other items for use in beach and resort areas. A small, inflatable toy has come onto the market that the company is anxious to produce and sell. The new toy will sell for $3 per unit. Enough capacity exists in the company's plant to produce 16,000 units of the toy each month. Variable expenses to manufacture and sell one unit would be $1.25, and fixed expenses associated with the toy would total $35,000 per month.

The company's Marketing Department predicts that demand for the new toy will exceed the 16,000 units that the company is able to produce. Additional manufacturing space can be rented from another company at a fixed expense of $1,000 per month. Variable expenses in the rented facility would total $1.40 per unit, due to somewhat less efficient operations than in the main plant.

*Required:*
1.  What is the monthly break-even point for the new toy in unit sales and dollar sales.
2.  How many units must be sold each month to attain a target profit of $12,000 per month?
3.  If the sales manager receives a bonus of 10 cents for each unit sold in excess of the break-even point, how many units must be sold each month to attain a target profit that equals a 25% return on the monthly investment in fixed expenses?

**PROBLEM 6–26   CVP Applications; Break-Even Analysis; Graphing LO6–1, LO6–2, LO6–4, LO6–5**
The Fashion Shoe Company operates a chain of women's shoe shops that carry many styles of shoes that are all sold at the same price. Sales personnel in the shops are paid a sales commission on each pair of shoes sold plus a small base salary.

The following data pertains to Shop 48 and is typical of the company's many outlets:

| | Per Pair of Shoes |
|---|---|
| Selling price . . . . . . . . . . . . . . . . . . . | $30.00 |
| Variable expenses: | |
| Invoice cost . . . . . . . . . . . . . . . . . | $13.50 |
| Sales commission . . . . . . . . . . . . . | 4.50 |
| Total variable expenses . . . . . . . . . . | $18.00 |

| | Annual |
|---|---|
| Fixed expenses: | |
| Advertising . . . . . . . . . . . . . . . . . | $ 30,000 |
| Rent . . . . . . . . . . . . . . . . . . . . . . | 20,000 |
| Salaries . . . . . . . . . . . . . . . . . . . . | 100,000 |
| Total fixed expenses . . . . . . . . . . . | $150,000 |

**Required:**
1. What is Shop 48's annual break-even point in unit sales and dollar sales?
2. Prepare a CVP graph showing cost and revenue data for Shop 48 from zero shoes up to 17,000 pairs of shoes sold each year. Clearly indicate the break-even point on the graph.
3. If 12,000 pairs of shoes are sold in a year, what would be Shop 48's net operating income (loss)?
4. The company is considering paying the Shop 48 store manager an incentive commission of 75 cents per pair of shoes (in addition to the salesperson's commission). If this change is made, what will be the new break-even point in unit sales and dollar sales?
5. Refer to the original data. As an alternative to (4) above, the company is considering paying the Shop 48 store manager 50 cents commission on each pair of shoes sold in excess of the break-even point. If this change is made, what will be Shop 48's net operating income (loss) if 15,000 pairs of shoes are sold?
6. Refer to the original data. The company is considering eliminating sales commissions entirely in its shops and increasing fixed salaries by $31,500 annually. If this change is made, what will be Shop 48's new break-even point in unit sales and dollar sales? Would you recommend that the change be made? Explain.

**PROBLEM 6–27   Sales Mix; Break-Even Analysis; Margin of Safety LO6–7, LO6–9**

Island Novelties, Inc., of Palau makes two products—Hawaiian Fantasy and Tahitian Joy. Each product's selling price, variable expense per unit, and annual sales volume are as follows:

| | Hawaiian Fantasy | Tahitian Joy |
|---|---|---|
| Selling price per unit . . . . . . . . . . . . . . . . . | $15 | $100 |
| Variable expense per unit . . . . . . . . . . . . . | $9 | $20 |
| Number of units sold annually . . . . . . . . . . | 20,000 | 5,000 |

Fixed expenses total $475,800 per year.

**Required:**
1. Assuming the sales mix given above, do the following:
   a. Prepare a contribution format income statement showing both dollar and percent columns for each product and for the company as a whole.
   b. Compute the company's break-even point in dollar sales. Also, compute its margin of safety in dollars and its margin of safety percentage.
2. The company has developed a new product called Samoan Delight that sells for $45 each and that has variable expenses of $36 per unit. If the company can sell 10,000 units of Samoan Delight without incurring any additional fixed expenses:
   a. Prepare a revised contribution format income statement that includes Samoan Delight. Assume that sales of the other two products does not change.
   b. Compute the company's revised break-even point in dollar sales. Also, compute its revised margin of safety in dollars and margin of safety percentage.

3.  The president of the company examines your figures and says, "There's something strange here. Our fixed expenses haven't changed and you show greater total contribution margin if we add the new product, but you also show our break-even point going up. With greater contribution margin, the break-even point should go down, not up. You've made a mistake somewhere." Explain to the president what has happened.

**PROBLEM 6–28   Sales Mix; Commission Structure; Multiproduct Break-Even Analysis** LO6–9

Carbex, Inc., produces cutlery sets out of high-quality wood and steel. The company makes a Standard set and a Deluxe set and sells them to retail department stores throughout the country. The Standard set sells for $60, and the Deluxe set sells for $75. The variable expenses associated with each set are given below.

|  | Standard | Deluxe |
|---|---|---|
| Variable production costs . . . . . . . . . . . . . . . . . . . . . . . . | $15.00 | $30.00 |
| Sales commissions (15% of sales price) . . . . . . . . . . . . . . | $9.00 | $11.25 |

The company's fixed expenses each month are:

| Advertising . . . . . . . . . . . . . . . . . . . | $105,000 |
|---|---|
| Depreciation . . . . . . . . . . . . . . . . . . | $21,700 |
| Administrative . . . . . . . . . . . . . . . . . | $63,000 |

Mary Parsons, the financial vice president, watches sales commissions carefully and has noted that they have risen steadily over the last year. For this reason, she was shocked to find that even though sales have increased, profits for the current month—May—are down substantially from April. Sales, in sets, for the last two months are given below:

|  | Standard | Deluxe | Total |
|---|---|---|---|
| April . . . . . . . . . . . . . . . | 4,000 | 2,000 | 6,000 |
| May . . . . . . . . . . . . . . . | 1,000 | 5,000 | 6,000 |

***Required:***

1.  Prepare contribution format income statements for April and May. Use the following headings:

|  | Standard | | Deluxe | | Total | |
|---|---|---|---|---|---|---|
|  | Amount | Percent | Amount | Percent | Amount | Percent |
| Sales . . . . . . |  |  |  |  |  |  |
| Etc. . . . . . . . |  |  |  |  |  |  |

Place the fixed expenses only in the Total column. Do not show percentages for the fixed expenses.

2.  Explain the difference in net operating incomes between the two months, even though the same total number of sets was sold in each month.

3.  What can be done to the sales commissions to improve the sales mix?
    a.  Using April's sales mix, what is the break-even point in dollar sales?
    b.  Without doing any calculations, explain whether the break-even point in May would be higher or lower than the break-even point in April. Why?

**PROBLEM 6–29   Changes in Cost Structure; Break-Even Analysis; Operating Leverage; Margin of Safety** LO6–4, LO6–5, LO6–7, LO6–8

Morton Company's contribution format income statement for last month is given below:

| Sales (15,000 units × $30 per unit) . . . . . . . | $450,000 |
|---|---|
| Variable expenses . . . . . . . . . . . . . . . . . . . . | 315,000 |
| Contribution margin . . . . . . . . . . . . . . . . . . . | 135,000 |
| Fixed expenses . . . . . . . . . . . . . . . . . . . . . . . | 90,000 |
| Net operating income . . . . . . . . . . . . . . . . . | $ 45,000 |

The industry in which Morton Company operates is quite sensitive to cyclical movements in the economy. Thus, profits vary considerably from year to year according to general economic conditions. The company has a large amount of unused capacity and is studying ways of improving profits.

*Required:*

1. New equipment has come onto the market that would allow Morton Company to automate a portion of its operations. Variable expenses would be reduced by $9 per unit. However, fixed expenses would increase to a total of $225,000 each month. Prepare two contribution format income statements, one showing present operations and one showing how operations would appear if the new equipment is purchased. Show an Amount column, a Per Unit column, and a Percent column on each statement. Do not show percentages for the fixed expenses.

2. Refer to the income statements in (1). For the present operations and the proposed new operations, compute (a) the degree of operating leverage, (b) the break-even point in dollar sales, and (c) the margin of safety in dollars and the margin of safety percentage.

3. Refer again to the data in (1). As a manager, what factor would be paramount in your mind in deciding whether to purchase the new equipment? (Assume that enough funds are available to make the purchase.)

4. Refer to the original data. Rather than purchase new equipment, the marketing manager argues that the company's marketing strategy should be changed. Rather than pay sales commissions, which are currently included in variable expenses, the company would pay salespersons fixed salaries and would invest heavily in advertising. The marketing manager claims this new approach would increase unit sales by 30% without any change in selling price; the company's new monthly fixed expenses would be $180,000; and its net operating income would increase by 20%. Compute the company's break-even point in dollar sales under the new marketing strategy. Do you agree with the marketing manager's proposal?

**PROBLEM 6–30   Graphing; Incremental Analysis; Operating Leverage** LO6–2, LO6–4, LO6–5, LO6–6, LO6–8

Angie Silva has recently opened The Sandal Shop in Brisbane, Australia, a store that specializes in fashionable sandals. In time, she hopes to open a chain of sandal shops. As a first step, she has gathered the following data for her new store:

| | |
|---|---:|
| Sales price per pair of sandals . . . . . . . . . . . . . . . . . . . | $40 |
| Variable expenses per pair of sandals . . . . . . . . . . . . | 16 |
| Contribution margin per pair of sandals . . . . . . . . . . | $24 |
| Fixed expenses per year: | |
| Building rental . . . . . . . . . . . . . . . . . . . . . . . . . . . . . . . . | $15,000 |
| Equipment depreciation . . . . . . . . . . . . . . . . . . . . . | 7,000 |
| Selling . . . . . . . . . . . . . . . . . . . . . . . . . . . . . . . . . . . . . . | 20,000 |
| Administrative . . . . . . . . . . . . . . . . . . . . . . . . . . . . . . . | 18,000 |
| Total fixed expenses . . . . . . . . . . . . . . . . . . . . . . . . . . | $60,000 |

*Required:*

1. What is the break-even point in unit sales and dollar sales?

2. Prepare a CVP graph or a profit graph for the store from zero pairs up to 4,000 pairs of sandals sold each year. Indicate the break-even point on your graph.

3. Angie has decided that she must earn a profit of $18,000 the first year to justify her time and effort. How many pairs of sandals must be sold to attain this target profit?

4. Angie now has two salespersons working in the store—one full time and one part time. It will cost her an additional $8,000 per year to convert the part-time position to a full-time position. Angie believes that the change would increase annual sales by $25,000. Should she convert the position? Use the incremental approach. (Do not prepare an income statement.)

5. Refer to the original data. During the first year, the store sold only 3,000 pairs of sandals and reported the following operating results:

| | |
|---|---:|
| Sales (3,000 pairs) . . . . . . . . . . . . . . | $120,000 |
| Variable expenses . . . . . . . . . . . . . . | 48,000 |
| Contribution margin . . . . . . . . . . . . . | 72,000 |
| Fixed expenses . . . . . . . . . . . . . . . . . | 60,000 |
| Net operating income . . . . . . . . . . . | $ 12,000 |

a.  What is the store's degree of operating leverage?
b.  Angie is confident that with a more intense sales effort and with a more creative advertising program she can increase sales by 50% next year. Using the degree of operating leverage, what would be the expected percentage increase in net operating income if Angie is able to increase sales by 50%?

**PROBLEM 6–31   Interpretive Questions on the CVP Graph** LO6–2, LO6–5
A CVP graph such as the one shown below is a useful technique for showing relationships among an organization's costs, volume, and profits.

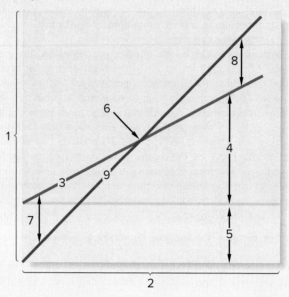

**Required:**
1.  Identify the numbered components in the CVP graph.
2.  State the effect of each of the following actions on line 3, line 9, and the break-even point. For line 3 and line 9, state whether the action will cause the line to:
    Remain unchanged.
    Shift upward.
    Shift downward.
    Have a steeper slope (i.e., rotate upward).
    Have a flatter slope (i.e., rotate downward).
    Shift upward *and* have a steeper slope.
    Shift upward *and* have a flatter slope.
    Shift downward *and* have a steeper slope.
    Shift downward *and* have a flatter slope.
    In the case of the break-even point, state whether the action will cause the break-even point to:
    Remain unchanged.
    Increase.
    Decrease.
    Probably change, but the direction is uncertain.
    Treat each case independently.
    x.  *Example.*   Fixed expenses are reduced by $5,000 per period.
        *Answer* (see choices above):   Line 3: Shift downward.
                                        Line 9: Remain unchanged.
                                        Break-even point: Decrease.
    a.  The unit selling price is increased from $18 to $20.
    b.  Unit variable expenses are decreased from $12 to $10.
    c.  Fixed expenses are increased by $3,000 per period.
    d.  Two thousand more units are sold during the period than were budgeted.
    e.  Due to paying salespersons a commission rather than a flat salary, fixed expenses are reduced by $8,000 per period and unit variable expenses are increased by $3.
    f.  Due to an increase in the cost of materials, both unit variable expenses and the selling price are increased by $2.
    g.  Advertising costs are increased by $10,000 per period, resulting in a 10% increase in the number of units sold.
    h.  Due to automating an operation previously done by workers, fixed expenses are increased by $12,000 per period and unit variable expenses are reduced by $4.

### ANALYTICAL THINKING LO6–5, LO6–9

Cheryl Montoya picked up the phone and called her boss, Wes Chan, the vice president of marketing at Piedmont Fasteners Corporation: "Wes, I'm not sure how to go about answering the questions that came up at the meeting with the president yesterday."

"What's the problem?"

"The president wanted to know the break-even point for each of the company's products, but I am having trouble figuring them out."

"I'm sure you can handle it, Cheryl. And, by the way, I need your analysis on my desk tomorrow morning at 8:00 sharp in time for the follow-up meeting at 9:00."

Piedmont Fasteners Corporation makes three different clothing fasteners in its manufacturing facility in North Carolina. Data concerning these products appear below:

|  | Velcro | Metal | Nylon |
|---|---|---|---|
| Annual sales volume .................... | 100,000 | 200,000 | 400,000 |
| Unit selling price ........................ | $1.65 | $1.50 | $0.85 |
| Variable expense per unit ................ | $1.25 | $0.70 | $0.25 |

Total fixed expenses are $400,000 per year.

All three products are sold in highly competitive markets, so the company is unable to raise prices without losing an unacceptable numbers of customers.

The company has an extremely effective lean production system, so there are no beginning or ending work in process or finished goods inventories.

**Required:**
1.  What is the company's over-all break-even point in dollar sales?
2.  Of the total fixed expenses of $400,000, $20,000 could be avoided if the Velcro product is dropped, $80,000 if the Metal product is dropped, and $60,000 if the Nylon product is dropped. The remaining fixed expenses of $240,000 consist of common fixed expenses such as administrative salaries and rent on the factory building that could be avoided only by going out of business entirely.
    a.  What is the break-even point in unit sales for each product?
    b.  If the company sells exactly the break-even quantity of each product, what will be the overall profit of the company? Explain this result.

### CASE LO6–4, LO6–5, LO6–6

Pittman Company is a small but growing manufacturer of telecommunications equipment. The company has no sales force of its own; rather, it relies completely on independent sales agents to market its products. These agents are paid a sales commission of 15% for all items sold.

Barbara Cheney, Pittman's controller, has just prepared the company's budgeted income statement for next year as follows:

**Pittman Company**
**Budgeted Income Statement**
**For the Year Ended December 31**

| | | |
|---|---|---|
| Sales ..................................... | | $16,000,000 |
| Manufacturing expenses: | | |
|    Variable ............................... | $7,200,000 | |
|    Fixed overhead ........................ | 2,340,000 | 9,540,000 |
| Gross margin ............................. | | 6,460,000 |
| Selling and administrative expenses: | | |
|    Commissions to agents ................. | 2,400,000 | |
|    Fixed marketing expenses .............. | 120,000* | |
|    Fixed administrative expenses ............ | 1,800,000 | 4,320,000 |
| Net operating income ..................... | | 2,140,000 |
| Fixed interest expenses ................... | | 540,000 |
| Income before income taxes .............. | | 1,600,000 |
| Income taxes (30%)....................... | | 480,000 |
| Net income ............................ | | $ 1,120,000 |

*Primarily depreciation on storage facilities.

As Barbara handed the statement to Karl Vecci, Pittman's president, she commented, "I went ahead and used the agents' 15% commission rate in completing these statements, but we've just learned that they refuse to handle our products next year unless we increase the commission rate to 20%."

"That's the last straw," Karl replied angrily. "Those agents have been demanding more and more, and this time they've gone too far. How can they possibly defend a 20% commission rate?"

"They claim that after paying for advertising, travel, and the other costs of promotion, there's nothing left over for profit," replied Barbara.

"I say it's just plain robbery," retorted Karl. "And I also say it's time we dumped those guys and got our own sales force. Can you get your people to work up some cost figures for us to look at?"

"We've already worked them up," said Barbara. "Several companies we know about pay a 7.5% commission to their own salespeople, along with a small salary. Of course, we would have to handle all promotion costs, too. We figure our fixed expenses would increase by $2,400,000 per year, but that would be more than offset by the $3,200,000 (20% × $16,000,000) that we would avoid on agents' commissions."

The breakdown of the $2,400,000 cost follows:

| Salaries: | |
|---|---:|
| Sales manager . . . . . . . . . . . . . . . . . | $ 100,000 |
| Salespersons . . . . . . . . . . . . . . . . . . | 600,000 |
| Travel and entertainment . . . . . . . . . . | 400,000 |
| Advertising . . . . . . . . . . . . . . . . . . . . . | 1,300,000 |
| Total . . . . . . . . . . . . . . . . . . . . . . . . . . | $2,400,000 |

"Super," replied Karl. "And I noticed that the $2,400,000 equals what we're paying the agents under the old 15% commission rate."

"It's even better than that," explained Barbara. "We can actually save $75,000 a year because that's what we're paying our auditors to check out the agents' reports. So our overall administrative expenses would be less."

"Pull all of these numbers together and we'll show them to the executive committee tomorrow," said Karl. "With the approval of the committee, we can move on the matter immediately."

***Required:***
1.  Compute Pittman Company's break-even point in dollar sales for next year assuming:
    a.  The agents' commission rate remains unchanged at 15%.
    b.  The agents' commission rate is increased to 20%.
    c.  The company employs its own sales force.
2.  Assume that Pittman Company decides to continue selling through agents and pays the 20% commission rate. Determine the dollar sales that would be required to generate the same net income as contained in the budgeted income statement for next year.
3.  Determine the dollar sales at which net income would be equal regardless of whether Pittman Company sells through agents (at a 20% commission rate) or employs its own sales force.
4.  Compute the degree of operating leverage that the company would expect to have at the end of next year assuming:
    a.  The agents' commission rate remains unchanged at 15%.
    b.  The agents' commission rate is increased to 20%.
    c.  The company employs its own sales force.
    Use income *before* income taxes in your operating leverage computation.
5.  Based on the data in (1) through (4) above, make a recommendation as to whether the company should continue to use sales agents (at a 20% commission rate) or employ its own sales force. Give reasons for your answer.

**TEAMWORK IN ACTION LO6–1, LO6–4**
Revenue from major intercollegiate sports is an important source of funds for many colleges. Most of the costs of putting on a football or basketball game may be fixed and may increase very little as the size of the crowd increases. Thus, the revenue from every extra ticket sold may be almost pure profit.

Choose a sport played at your college or university, such as football or basketball, that generates significant revenue. Talk with the business manager of your college's sports programs before answering the following questions:

*Required:*

1.  What is the maximum seating capacity of the stadium or arena in which the sport is played? During the past year, what was the average attendance at the games? On average, what percentage of the stadium or arena capacity was filled?
2.  The number of seats sold often depends on the opponent. The attendance for a game with a traditional rival (e.g., Nebraska vs. Colorado, University of Washington vs. Washington State, or Texas vs. Texas A&M) is usually substantially above the average. Also, games against conference foes may draw larger crowds than other games. As a consequence, the number of tickets sold for a game is somewhat predictable. What implications does this have for the nature of the costs of putting on a game? Are most of the costs really fixed with respect to the number of tickets sold?
3.  Estimate the variable cost per ticket sold.
4.  Estimate the total additional revenue that would be generated in an average game if all of the tickets were sold at their normal prices. Estimate how much profit is lost because these tickets are not sold.
5.  Estimate the ancillary revenue (parking and concessions) per ticket sold. Estimate how much profit is lost in an average game from these sources of revenue as a consequence of not having a sold-out game.
6.  Estimate how much additional profit would be generated for your college if every game were sold out for the entire season.

(CMA, adapted)

# APPENDIX 6A: ANALYZING MIXED COSTS

The main body of Chapter 6 assumed that all costs could be readily classified as variable or fixed. In reality, many costs contain both variable *and* fixed components—they are *mixed costs*. The purpose of this appendix is to describe various methods that companies can use to separate mixed costs into their variable and fixed components, thereby enabling cost-volume-profit (CVP) analysis.

Mixed costs are very common in most organizations. For example, the overall cost of performing surgeries for patients at the **Harvard Medical School Hospital** is a mixed cost. The costs of equipment depreciation and surgeons' and nurses' salaries are fixed, but the costs of surgical gloves, power, and other supplies are variable. At **Southwest Airlines**, maintenance costs are a mixed cost. The company incurs fixed costs for renting maintenance facilities and for keeping skilled mechanics on the payroll, but the costs of replacement parts, lubricating oils, tires, and so forth, are variable with respect to how often and how far the company's aircraft are flown.

The fixed portion of a mixed cost represents the minimum cost of having a service *ready and available* for use. The variable portion represents the cost incurred for *actual consumption* of the service, thus it varies in proportion to the amount of service actually consumed.

Managers can use a variety of methods to estimate the fixed and variable components of a mixed cost such as *account analysis,* the *engineering approach,* the *high-low method,* and *least-squares regression analysis.* In **account analysis**, an account is classified as either variable or fixed based on the analyst's prior knowledge of how the cost in the account behaves. For example, direct materials would be classified as variable and a building lease cost would be classified as fixed because of the nature of those costs. The **engineering approach** to cost analysis involves a detailed analysis of what cost behavior should be, based on an industrial engineer's evaluation of the production methods to be used, the materials specifications, labor requirements, equipment usage, production efficiency, power consumption, and so on.

The high-low method and least-squares regression method estimate the fixed and variable elements of a mixed cost by analyzing past records of cost and activity data. Throughout the remainder of this appendix, we will define these two cost estimation methods and use an example from Brentline Hospital to illustrate how they each derive their respective fixed and variable cost estimates. The least-squares regression computations will be explained using Microsoft Excel because it can perform the underlying mathematics much faster than using a pencil and a calculator.

## Diagnosing Cost Behavior with a Scattergraph Plot

Assume that Brentline Hospital is interested in predicting future monthly maintenance costs for budgeting purposes. The senior management team believes that maintenance cost is a mixed cost and that the variable portion of this cost is driven by the number of patient-days. Each day a patient is in the hospital counts as one patient-day. The hospital's chief financial officer gathered the following data for the most recent seven-month period:

| Month | Activity Level: Patient-Days | Maintenance Cost Incurred |
|---|---|---|
| January ............... | 5,600 | $7,900 |
| February.............. | 7,100 | $8,500 |
| March................. | 5,000 | $7,400 |
| April ................. | 6,500 | $8,200 |
| May.................. | 7,300 | $9,100 |
| June ................. | 8,000 | $9,800 |
| July ................. | 6,200 | $7,800 |

The first step in applying the high-low method or the least-squares regression method is to diagnose cost behavior with a scattergraph plot. The scattergraph plot of maintenance costs versus patient-days at Brentline Hospital is shown in Exhibit 6A–1. Two things should be noted about this scattergraph:

1.  The total maintenance cost, $Y$, is plotted on the vertical axis. Cost is known as the **dependent variable** because the amount of cost incurred during a period depends on the level of activity for the period. (That is, as the level of activity increases, total cost also will ordinarily increase.)

2.  The activity, $X$ (patient-days in this case), is plotted on the horizontal axis. Activity is known as the **independent variable** because it causes variations in the cost.

From the scattergraph plot, it is evident that maintenance costs do increase with the number of patient-days in an approximately *linear* fashion. In other words, the points

**EXHIBIT 6A–1**
Scattergraph Method of Cost Analysis

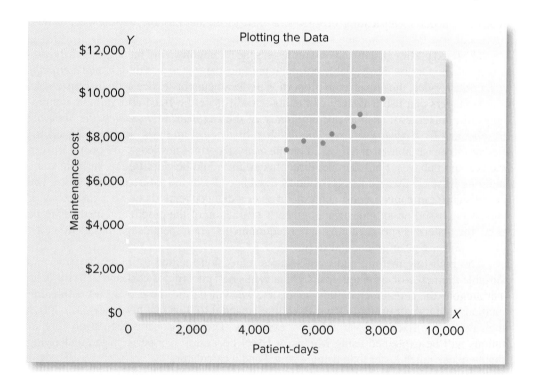

lie more or less along a straight line that slopes upward and to the right. **Linear cost behavior** exists whenever a straight line is a reasonable approximation for the relation between cost and activity.

Plotting the data on a scattergraph is an essential diagnostic step that should be performed before performing the high-low or least-squares regression calculations. If the scattergraph plot reveals linear cost behavior, then it makes sense to perform the high-low or least-squares regression calculations to separate the mixed cost into its variable and fixed components. If the scattergraph plot does not depict linear cost behavior, then it makes no sense to proceed any further in analyzing the data.

Once we determine that the dependent and independent variables have a linear relationship, the high-low and least-squares regression methods both rely on the following equation for a straight line (as introduced in Chapter 1) to express the relationship between a mixed cost and the level of activity:

$$Y = a + bX$$

In this equation,

$Y$ = The total mixed cost
$a$ = The total fixed cost (the vertical intercept of the line)
$b$ = The variable cost per unit of activity (the slope of the line)
$X$ = The level of activity

**The High-Low Method**    The high-low method is based on the rise-over-run formula for the slope of a straight line. Assuming that the relation between cost and activity can be represented by a straight line, then the slope of the straight line is equal to the variable cost per unit of activity. Consequently, the following formula can be used to estimate the variable cost:

$$\text{Variable cost} = \text{Slope of the line} = \frac{\text{Rise}}{\text{Run}} = \frac{Y_2 - Y_1}{X_2 - X_1}$$

To analyze mixed costs with the **high-low method**, begin by identifying the period with the lowest level of activity and the period with the highest level of activity. The period with the lowest activity is selected as the first point in the above formula and the period with the highest activity is selected as the second point. Consequently, the formula becomes:

$$\text{Variable cost} = \frac{Y_2 - Y_1}{X_2 - X_1} = \frac{\text{Cost at the high activity level} - \text{Cost at the low activity level}}{\text{High activity level} - \text{Low activity level}}$$

or

$$\text{Variable cost} = \frac{\text{Change in cost}}{\text{Change in activity}}$$

Therefore, when the high-low method is used, the variable cost is estimated by dividing the difference in cost between the high and low levels of activity by the change in activity between those two points.

To return to the Brentline Hospital example, using the high-low method, we first identify the periods with the highest and lowest *activity*—in this case, June and March. We then use the activity and cost data from these two periods to estimate the variable cost component as follows:

|  | Patient-Days | Maintenance Cost Incurred |
|---|---|---|
| High activity level (June) .............. | 8,000 | $9,800 |
| Low activity level (March) ............. | 5,000 | 7,400 |
| Change ......................... | 3,000 | $2,400 |

$$\text{Variable cost} = \frac{\text{Change in cost}}{\text{Change in activity}} = \frac{\$2,400}{3,000 \ \ \text{patient-days}} = \$0.80 \ \ \text{per patient-day}$$

Having determined that the variable maintenance cost is 80 cents per patient-day, we can now determine the amount of fixed cost. This is done by taking the total cost at *either* the high or the low activity level and deducting the variable cost element. In the computation below, total cost at the high activity level is used in computing the fixed cost element:

Fixed cost element = Total cost − Variable cost element

= \$9,800 − (\$0.80 per patient-day × 8,000 patient-days)

= \$3,400

Given that we have estimated the variable and fixed cost elements, the maintenance cost can now be expressed as \$3,400 per month plus 80 cents per patient-day, or as:

$$Y = \$3,400 + \$0.80X$$

Total
maintenance
cost

Total
patient-days

The data used in this illustration are shown graphically in Exhibit 6A–2. Notice that a straight line has been drawn through the points corresponding to the low and high levels of activity. In essence, that is what the high-low method does—it draws a straight line through those two points.

Sometimes the high and low levels of activity don't coincide with the high and low amounts of cost. For example, the period that has the highest level of activity may not have the highest amount of cost. Nevertheless, the costs at the highest and lowest levels of *activity* are always used to analyze a mixed cost under the high-low method. The reason is that the analyst would like to use data that reflect the greatest possible variation in activity.

The high-low method is very simple to apply, but it suffers from a major (and sometimes critical) defect—it utilizes only two data points. Generally, two data points are

**EXHIBIT 6A–2**   High-Low
Method of Analyzing a Mixed
Cost

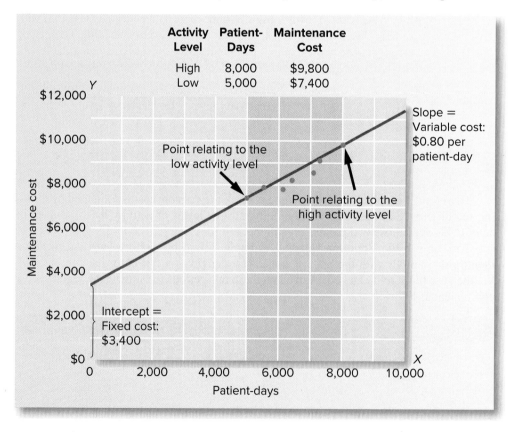

not enough to produce accurate estimates. Additionally, the periods with the highest and lowest activity tend to be unusual. A cost formula that is estimated solely using data from these unusual periods may misrepresent the true cost behavior during normal periods. Such a distortion is evident in Exhibit 6A–2. The straight line should probably be shifted down somewhat so that it is closer to more of the data points. For these reasons, least-squares regression will generally be more accurate than the high-low method.

### The Least-Squares Regression Method

The **least-squares regression method**, unlike the high-low method, uses all of the data to separate a mixed cost into its fixed and variable components. A *regression line* of the form $Y = a + bX$ is fitted to the data, where $a$ (the intercept) represents the total fixed cost and $b$ (the slope) represents the variable cost per unit of activity. The basic idea underlying the least-squares regression method is illustrated in Exhibit 6A–3 using hypothetical data points. Notice from the exhibit that the deviations from the plotted points to the regression line are measured vertically on the graph. These vertical deviations are called the regression errors. There is nothing mysterious about the least-squares regression method. It simply computes the regression line that minimizes the sum of these squared errors.

**LEARNING OBJECTIVE 6–11**

Analyze a mixed cost using a scattergraph plot and the least-squares regression method.

**EXHIBIT 6A–3**   The Concept of Least-Squares Regression

While the basic idea underlying least-squares regression analysis is pretty simple, the formulas that calculate $a$ (the intercept) and $b$ (the slope) are quite complex as shown below:

$$b = \frac{n(\Sigma XY) - (\Sigma X)(\Sigma Y)}{n(\Sigma X^2) - (\Sigma X)^2}$$

$$a = \frac{(\Sigma Y) - b(\Sigma X)}{n}$$

where:
$X$ = The level of activity (independent variable)
$Y$ = The total mixed cost (dependent variable)
$a$ = The total fixed cost (the vertical intercept of the line)
$b$ = The variable cost per unit of activity (the slope of the line)
$n$ = Number of observations
$\Sigma$ = Sum across all $n$ observations

Fortunately, Microsoft Excel can be used to estimate the fixed cost (intercept) and variable cost per unit (slope) that minimize the sum of the squared errors. Excel also provides a statistic called the $R^2$, which is a measure of "goodness of fit." The $R^2$ tells us the percentage of the variation in the dependent variable (cost) that is explained by variation in the independent variable (activity). The $R^2$ varies from 0% to 100%, and the higher the percentage, the better.

As mentioned earlier, you should always plot the data in a scattergraph, but it is particularly important to check the data visually when the $R^2$ is low. A quick look at the scattergraph can reveal that there is little relation between the cost and the activity or that the relation is something other than a simple straight line. In such cases, additional analysis would be required.

Exhibit 6A–4 uses Excel to depict the Brentline Hospital data that we used earlier to illustrate the high-low method. We'll be using this same data set to illustrate how Excel can be used to create a scattergraph plot and to calculate the intercept *a,* the slope *b,* and the $R^2$ using least-squares regression.[6]

To prepare a scattergraph plot in Excel, begin by highlighting the data in cells B4 through C10 (as shown in Exhibit 6A–4). From the Charts group within the Insert tab, select the "Scatter" subgroup and then click on the choice that has no lines connecting the data points. This should produce a scattergraph plot similar to the one shown in Exhibit 6A–5. Notice that the number of patient-days is plotted on the $X$–axis and the

**EXHIBIT 6A–4**   The Least-Squares Regression Worksheet for Brentline Hospital

|    | A | B | C |
|----|------|---------|-------------|
|    |   | Patient | Maintenance |
| 1  |   | Days    | Cost        |
| 2  |   |         |             |
| 3  | *Month* | X | Y |
| 4  | January | 5,600 | $    7,900 |
| 5  | February | 7,100 | $    8,500 |
| 6  | March | 5,000 | $    7,400 |
| 7  | April | 6,500 | $    8,200 |
| 8  | May | 7,300 | $    9,100 |
| 9  | June | 8,000 | $    9,800 |
| 10 | July | 6,200 | $    7,800 |
| 11 |   |         |             |

Least-squares regression

**EXHIBIT 6A–5**   A Scattergraph Plot for Brentline Hospital Using Microsoft Excel

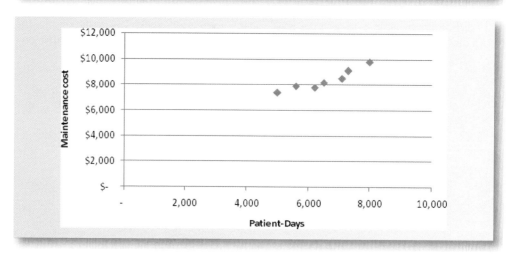

⁶ The authors wish to thank Don Schwartz, Professor of Accounting at National University, for providing suggestions that were instrumental in creating this appendix.

maintenance cost is plotted on the $Y$–axis.[7] As we saw verified earlier in Exhibit 6A–1, the data is approximately linear, so it makes sense to proceed with estimating a regression equation that minimizes the sum of the squared errors.

To determine the intercept $a$, the slope $b$, and the $R^2$, begin by right clicking on any data point in the scattergraph plot and selecting "Add Trendline." This should produce the screen that is shown in Exhibit 6A–6. Notice that under "Trend/Regression Type" you should select "Linear." Similarly, under "Trendline Name" you should select "Automatic." Next to the word "Backward" you should input the lowest value for the independent variable, which in this example is 5000 patient-days. Taking this particular step instructs Excel to extend your fitted line until it intersects the $Y$–axis. Finally, you should check the two boxes at the bottom of Exhibit 6A–6 that say "Display Equation on chart" and "Display R-squared value on chart."

Once you have established these settings, then click "Close." As shown in Exhibit 6A–7, this will automatically insert a line within the scattergraph plot that minimizes the sum of the squared errors. It will also cause the estimated least-squares regression equation and $R^2$ to be inserted into your scattergraph plot. Instead of depicting the results using the form $Y = a + bX$, Excel uses an equivalent form of the equation depicted as $Y = bX + a$. In other words, Excel reverses the two terms shown to the right of the equals sign. So, in Exhibit 6A–7, Excel shows a least-squares regression equation of $y = 0.7589x + 3,430.9$. The slope $b$ in this equation of \$0.7589 represents the estimated variable maintenance cost per patient-day. The intercept $a$ in this equation of \$3,430.90 (or approximately \$3,431) represents the estimated fixed monthly maintenance cost. Note that the $R^2$ is approximately 0.90, which is quite good and indicates that 90% of the variation in maintenance cost is explained by the variation in patient-days.

**EXHIBIT 6A–6** Trendline Options in Microsoft Excel

---

[7] To insert labels for the $X$–axis and $Y$–axis, go to the Layout tab in Excel. Then, within the Labels group, select Axis Titles.

**EXHIBIT 6A–7** Brentline
Hospital: Least-Squares
Regression Results Using
Microsoft Excel

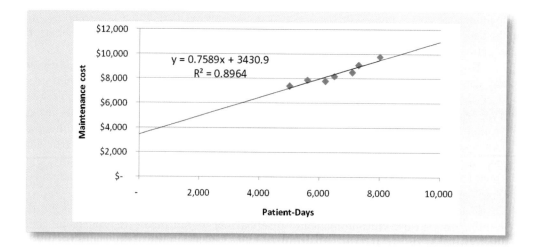

## Comparing the High-Low and Least-Squares Regression Methods

The table below compares Brentline Hospital's cost estimates using the high-low method and the least-squares regression method:

|  | High-Low Method | Least-Squares Regression Method |
|---|---|---|
| Variable cost estimate per patient-day . . . . . . . . . | $0.800 | $0.759 |
| Fixed cost estimate per month . . . . . . . . . . . . . . . | $3,400 | $3,431 |

When Brentline uses the least-squares regression method to create a straight line that minimizes the sum of the squared errors, it results in estimated fixed costs that are $31 higher than the amount derived using the high-low method. It also decreases the slope of the straight line resulting in a lower variable cost estimate of $0.759 per patient-day rather than $0.80 per patient-day as derived using the high-low method.

# GLOSSARY (APPENDIX 6A)

**Account analysis** A method for analyzing cost behavior in which an account is classified as either variable or fixed based on the analyst's prior knowledge of how the cost in the account behaves. (p 260)

**Dependent variable** A variable that responds to some causal factor; total cost is the dependent variable, as represented by the letter Y, in the equation $Y = a + bX$. (p 261)

**Engineering approach** A detailed analysis of cost behavior based on an industrial engineer's evaluation of the inputs that are required to carry out a particular activity and of the prices of those inputs. (p 260)

**High-low method** A method of separating a mixed cost into its fixed and variable elements by analyzing the change in cost between the high and low activity levels. (p 261)

**Independent variable** A variable that acts as a causal factor; activity is the independent variable, as represented by the letter X, in the equation $Y = a + bX$. (p 261)

**Least-squares regression method** A method of separating a mixed cost into its fixed and variable elements by fitting a regression line that minimizes the sum of the squared errors. (p 262)

**Linear cost behavior** Cost behavior is said to be linear whenever a straight line is a reasonable approximation for the relation between cost and activity. (p 261)

**$R^2$** A measure of goodness of fit in least-squares regression analysis. It is the percentage of the variation in the dependent variable that is explained by variation in the independent variable. (p 270)

## connect  APPENDIX 6A: EXERCISES AND PROBLEMS

**EXERCISE 6A–1   High-Low Method** LO6–10

The Cheyenne Hotel in Big Sky, Montana, has accumulated records of the total electrical costs of the hotel and the number of occupancy-days over the last year. An occupancy-day represents a room rented for one day. The hotel's business is highly seasonal, with peaks occurring during the ski season and in the summer.

| Month | Occupancy-Days | Electrical Costs |
|---|---|---|
| January .............. | 1,736 | $4,127 |
| February.............. | 1,904 | $4,207 |
| March ............... | 2,356 | $5,083 |
| April ................ | 960 | $2,857 |
| May.................. | 360 | $1,871 |
| June ................ | 744 | $2,696 |
| July ................. | 2,108 | $4,670 |
| August .............. | 2,406 | $5,148 |
| September........... | 840 | $2,691 |
| October ............. | 124 | $1,588 |
| November ........... | 720 | $2,454 |
| December ........... | 1,364 | $3,529 |

**Required:**

1.  Using the high-low method, estimate the fixed cost of electricity per month and the variable cost of electricity per occupancy-day. Round off the fixed cost to the nearest whole dollar and the variable cost to the nearest whole cent.
2.  What other factors in addition to occupancy-days are likely to affect the variation in electrical costs from month to month?

**EXERCISE 6A–2   Least-Squares Regression** LO6–11

Bargain Rental Car offers rental cars in an off-airport location near a major tourist destination in California. Management would like to better understand the variable and fixed portions of its car washing costs. The company operates its own car wash facility in which each rental car that is returned is thoroughly cleaned before being released for rental to another customer. Management believes that the variable portion of its car washing costs relates to the number of rental returns. Accordingly, the following data have been compiled:

| Month | Rental Returns | Car Wash Costs |
|---|---|---|
| January ............... | 2,380 | $10,825 |
| February.............. | 2,421 | $11,865 |
| March ................ | 2,586 | $11,332 |
| April ................. | 2,725 | $12,422 |
| May.................. | 2,968 | $13,850 |
| June ................. | 3,281 | $14,419 |
| July .................. | 3,353 | $14,935 |
| August ............... | 3,489 | $15,738 |
| September............ | 3,057 | $13,563 |
| October .............. | 2,876 | $11,889 |
| November ............ | 2,735 | $12,683 |
| December ............ | 2,983 | $13,796 |

*Required:*

1.  Prepare a scattergraph plot. (Place car wash costs on the vertical axis and rental returns on the horizontal axis.)
2.  Using least-squares regression, estimate the variable cost per rental return and the monthly fixed cost incurred to wash cars. The total fixed cost should be estimated to the nearest dollar and the variable cost per rental return to the nearest cent.

### EXERCISE 6A–3   Cost Behavior; High-Low Method LO6–10

Hoi Chong Transport, Ltd., operates a fleet of delivery trucks in Singapore. The company has determined that if a truck is driven 105,000 kilometers during a year, the average operating cost is 11.4 cents per kilometer. If a truck is driven only 70,000 kilometers during a year, the average operating cost increases to 13.4 cents per kilometer.

*Required:*

1.  Using the high-low method, estimate the variable operating cost per kilometer and the annual fixed operating cost associated with the fleet of trucks.
2.  Express the variable and fixed costs in the form $Y = a + bX$.
3.  If a truck were driven 80,000 kilometers during a year, what total operating cost would you expect to be incurred?

### EXERCISE 6A–4   High-Low Method; Scattergraph Analysis LO6–10

Archer Company is a wholesaler of custom-built air-conditioning units for commercial buildings. It gathered the following monthly data relating to units shipped and total shipping expense:

| Month | Units Shipped | Total Shipping Expense |
|---|---|---|
| January .............. | 3 | $1,800 |
| February.............. | 6 | $2,300 |
| March ................ | 4 | $1,700 |
| April ................ | 5 | $2,000 |
| May.................. | 7 | $2,300 |
| June ................. | 8 | $2,700 |
| July.................. | 2 | $1,200 |

*Required:*

1.  Prepare a scattergraph using the data given above. Plot cost on the vertical axis and activity on the horizontal axis. Is there an approximately linear relationship between shipping expense and the number of units shipped?
2.  Using the high-low method, estimate the cost formula for shipping expense. Draw a straight line through the high and low data points shown in the scattergraph that you prepared in requirement (1). Make sure your line intersects the Y-axis.
3.  Comment on the accuracy of your high-low estimates assuming a least-squares regression analysis estimated the total fixed costs to be $910.71 per month and the variable cost to be $217.86 per unit. How would the straight line that you drew in requirement 2 differ from a straight line that minimizes the sum of the squared errors?
4.  What factors, other than the number of units shipped, are likely to affect the company's shipping expense? Explain.

### EXERCISE 6A–5   Least-Squares Regression LO6–11

George Caloz & Frères, located in Grenchen, Switzerland, makes luxury custom watches in small lots. One of the company's products, a platinum diving watch, goes through an etching process. The company has recorded etching costs as follows over the last six weeks:

For planning purposes, management would like to know the variable etching cost per unit and the total fixed etching cost per week.

| Week | Units | Total Etching Cost |
|------|-------|--------------------|
| 1 .................... | 4 | $ 18 |
| 2 .................... | 3 | 17 |
| 3 .................... | 8 | 25 |
| 4 .................... | 6 | 20 |
| 5 .................... | 7 | 24 |
| 6 .................... | 2 | 16 |
|      | 30 | $120 |

**Required:**
1. Prepare a scattergraph plot. (Plot etching costs on the vertical axis and units on the horizontal axis.)
2. Using the least-squares regression method, estimate the variable etching cost per unit and the total fixed etching cost per week. Express these estimates in the form $Y = a + bX$.
3. If the company processes five units next week, what would be the expected total etching cost? (Round your answer to the nearest cent.)

**PROBLEM 6A–6  Least-Squares Regression; Scattergraph; Comparison of Activity Bases LO6–11**

The Hard Rock Mining Company is developing cost formulas for management planning and decision-making purposes. The company's cost analyst has concluded that utilities cost is a mixed cost, and he is attempting to find a base that correlates with the cost. The controller has suggested that tons mined might be a good base to use in developing a cost formula. The production superintendent disagrees; she thinks that direct labor-hours would be a better base. The cost analyst has decided to try both bases and has assembled the following information:

| Quarter | Tons Mined | Direct Labor-Hours | Utilities Cost |
|---------|-----------|--------------------|----------------|
| Year 1: | | | |
| First..................... | 15,000 | 5,000 | $50,000 |
| Second.................. | 11,000 | 3,000 | $45,000 |
| Third ................... | 21,000 | 4,000 | $60,000 |
| Fourth.................. | 12,000 | 6,000 | $75,000 |
| Year 2: | | | |
| First..................... | 18,000 | 10,000 | $100,000 |
| Second.................. | 25,000 | 9,000 | $105,000 |
| Third ................... | 30,000 | 8,000 | $85,000 |
| Fourth.................. | 28,000 | 11,000 | $120,000 |

**Required:**
1. Using tons mined as the independent variable, prepare a scattergraph that plots tons mined on the horizontal axis and utilities cost on the vertical axis. Using the least-squares regression method, estimate the variable utilities cost per ton mined and the total fixed utilities cost per quarter. Express these estimates in the form $Y = a + bX$.
2. Using direct labor-hours as the independent variable, prepare a scattergraph that plots direct labor-hours on the horizontal axis and utilities cost on the vertical axis. Using the least-squares regression method, estimate the variable utilities cost per direct labor-hour and the total fixed utilities cost per quarter. Express these estimates in the form $Y = a + bX$.
3. Would you recommend that the company use tons mined or direct labor-hours as a base for planning utilities cost?

**PROBLEM 6A–7  Cost Behavior; High-Low Method; Contribution Format Income Statement LO6–10**

Morrisey & Brown, Ltd., of Sydney is a merchandising company that is the sole distributor of a product that is increasing in popularity among Australian consumers. The company's income statements for the three most recent months follow:

| Morrisey & Brown, Ltd.<br>Income Statements<br>For the Three Months Ended September 30 | | | |
|---|---|---|---|
| | July | August | September |
| Sales in units.................................... | 4,000 | 4,500 | 5,000 |
| Sales........................................ | $400,000 | $450,000 | $500,000 |
| Cost of goods sold........................... | 240,000 | 270,000 | 300,000 |
| Gross margin................................ | 160,000 | 180,000 | 200,000 |
| Selling and administrative expenses: | | | |
|   Advertising expense ....................... | 21,000 | 21,000 | 21,000 |
|   Shipping expense ......................... | 34,000 | 36,000 | 38,000 |
|   Salaries and commissions ................... | 78,000 | 84,000 | 90,000 |
|   Insurance expense......................... | 6,000 | 6,000 | 6,000 |
|   Depreciation expense...................... | 15,000 | 15,000 | 15,000 |
| Total selling and administrative expenses......... | 154,000 | 162,000 | 170,000 |
| Net operating income ....................... | $ 6,000 | $ 18,000 | $ 30,000 |

**Required:**
1. By analyzing the data from the company's income statements, classify each of its expenses (including cost of goods sold) as either variable, fixed, or mixed.
2. Using the high-low method, separate each mixed expense into variable and fixed elements. Express the variable and fixed portions of each mixed expense in the form $Y = a + bX$.
3. Redo the company's income statement at the 5,000-unit level of activity using the contribution format.

**PROBLEM 6A–8  High-Low Method; Predicting Cost LO6–10**
Nova Company's total overhead cost at various levels of activity are presented below:

| Month | Machine-Hours | Total<br>Overhead Cost |
|---|---|---|
| April ................. | 70,000 | $198,000 |
| May................... | 60,000 | $174,000 |
| June ................. | 80,000 | $222,000 |
| July.................. | 90,000 | $246,000 |

Assume that the total overhead cost above consists of utilities, supervisory salaries, and maintenance. The breakdown of these costs at the 60,000 machine-hour level of activity is:

| | |
|---|---|
| Utilities (variable) ............................. | $ 48,000 |
| Supervisory salaries (fixed) .................... | 21,000 |
| Maintenance (mixed) ........................ | 105,000 |
| Total overhead cost ......................... | $174,000 |

Nova Company's management wants to break down the maintenance cost into its variable and fixed cost elements.

**Required:**
1. Estimate how much of the $246,000 of overhead cost in July was maintenance cost. (*Hint:* to do this, it may be helpful to first determine how much of the $246,000 consisted of utilities and supervisory salaries. Think about the behavior of variable and fixed costs.)
2. Using the high-low method, estimate a cost formula for maintenance in the form $Y = a + bX$.
3. Express the company's *total* overhead cost in the form $Y = a + bX$.
4. What *total* overhead cost would you expect to be incurred at an activity level of 75,000 machine-hours?

**PROBLEM 6A–9  High-Low Method; Contribution Format Income Statement LO6–10**
Milden Company is a distributor who wants to start using a contribution format income statement for planning purposes. The company has analyzed its expenses and developed the following cost formulas:

| Cost | Cost Formula |
|---|---|
| Cost of good sold................. | $35 per unit sold |
| Advertising expense ............... | $210,000 per quarter |
| Sales commissions................. | 6% of sales |
| Shipping expense ................. | ? |
| Administrative salaries ............. | $145,000 per quarter |
| Insurance expense................. | $9,000 per quarter |
| Depreciation expense.............. | $76,000 per quarter |

Because shipping expense is a mixed cost, the company needs to estimate the variable shipping expense per unit sold and the fixed shipping expense per quarter using the following data:

| Quarter | Units Sold | Shipping Expense |
|---|---|---|
| **Year 1:** | | |
| First................. | 10,000 | $119,000 |
| Second............. | 16,000 | $175,000 |
| Third................ | 18,000 | $190,000 |
| Fourth.............. | 15,000 | $164,000 |
| **Year 2:** | | |
| First................. | 11,000 | $130,000 |
| Second............. | 17,000 | $185,000 |
| Third................ | 20,000 | $210,000 |
| Fourth.............. | 13,000 | $147,000 |

**Required:**
1. Using the high-low method, estimate a cost formula for shipping expense in the form $Y = a + bX$.
2. In the first quarter of Year 3, the company plans to sell 12,000 units at a selling price of $100 per unit. Prepare a contribution format income statement for the quarter.

**PROBLEM 6A–10  Least-Squares Regression Method; Scattergraph; Cost Behavior LO6–11**
Professor John Morton has just been appointed chairperson of the Finance Department at Westland University. In reviewing the department's cost records, Professor Morton has found the following total cost associated with Finance 101 over the last five terms:

| Term | Number of Sections Offered | Total Cost |
|---|---|---|
| Fall, last year.............. | 4 | $10,000 |
| Winter, last year ........... | 6 | $14,000 |
| Summer, last year ......... | 2 | $7,000 |
| Fall, this year ............. | 5 | $13,000 |
| Winter, this year ........... | 3 | $9,500 |

Professor Morton knows that there are some variable costs, such as amounts paid to graduate assistants, associated with the course. He would like to have the variable and fixed costs separated for planning purposes.

**Required:**
1. Prepare a scattergraph plot. (Plot total cost on the vertical axis and number of sections offered on the horizontal axis.)
2. Using the least-squares regression method, estimate the variable cost per section and the total fixed cost per term for Finance 101. Express these estimates in the form $Y = a + bX$.
3. Assume that because of the small number of sections offered during the Winter Term this year, Professor Morton will have to offer eight sections of Finance 101 during the Fall Term. Compute the expected total cost for Finance 101. Can you see any problem with using the cost formula from (2) above to derive this total cost figure? Explain.

**PROBLEM 6A–11  Mixed Cost Analysis and the Relevant Range** LO6–10

The Ramon Company is a manufacturer that is interested in developing a cost formula to estimate the variable and fixed components of its monthly manufacturing overhead costs. The company wishes to use machine-hours as its measure of activity and has gathered the data below for this year and last year:

| | Last Year | | This Year | |
|---|---|---|---|---|
| **Month** | **Machine-Hours** | **Overhead Costs** | **Machine-Hours** | **Overhead Costs** |
| January ........... | 21,000 | $84,000 | 21,000 | $86,000 |
| February........... | 25,000 | $99,000 | 24,000 | $93,000 |
| March ............. | 22,000 | $89,500 | 23,000 | $93,000 |
| April .............. | 23,000 | $90,000 | 22,000 | $87,000 |
| May ............... | 20,500 | $81,500 | 20,000 | $80,000 |
| June .............. | 19,000 | $75,500 | 18,000 | $76,500 |
| July ............... | 14,000 | $70,500 | 12,000 | $67,500 |
| August ........... | 10,000 | $64,500 | 13,000 | $71,000 |
| September......... | 12,000 | $69,000 | 15,000 | $73,500 |
| October ........... | 17,000 | $75,000 | 17,000 | $72,500 |
| November ......... | 16,000 | $71,500 | 15,000 | $71,000 |
| December ......... | 19,000 | $78,000 | 18,000 | $75,000 |

The company leases all of its manufacturing equipment. The lease arrangement calls for a flat monthly fee up to 19,500 machine-hours. If the machine-hours used exceeds 19,500, then the fee becomes strictly variable with respect to the total number of machine-hours consumed during the month. Lease expense is a major element of overhead cost.

**Required:**

1. Using the high-low method, estimate a manufacturing overhead cost formula in the form $Y = a + bX$.
2. Prepare a scattergraph using all of the data for the two-year period. Fit a straight line or lines to the plotted points using a ruler. Describe the cost behavior pattern revealed by your scattergraph plot.
3. Assume a least-squares regression analysis using all of the given data points estimated the total fixed cost to be $40,102 and the variable cost to be $2.13 per machine-hour. Do you have any concerns about the accuracy of the high-low estimates that you have computed or the least-squares regression estimates that have been provided?
4. Assume that the company consumes 22,500 machine-hours during a month. Using the high-low method, estimate the total overhead cost that would be incurred at this level of activity. Be sure to consider only the data points contained in the relevant range of activity when performing your computations.
5. Comment on the accuracy of your high-low estimates assuming a least-squares regression analysis using only the data points in the relevant range of activity estimated the total fixed cost to be $10,090 and the variable cost to be $3.53 per machine-hour.

**PROBLEM 6A–12  Analysis of Mixed Costs in a Pricing Decision** LO6–11

Maria Chavez owns a catering company that serves food and beverages at parties and business functions. Chavez's business is seasonal, with a heavy schedule during the summer months and holidays and a lighter schedule at other times.

One of the major events Chavez's customers request is a cocktail party. She offers a standard cocktail party and has estimated the cost per guest as follows:

| | |
|---|---|
| Food and beverages............................ | $15.00 |
| Labor (0.5 hrs. @ $10.00/hr.) ................... | 5.00 |
| Overhead (0.5 hrs. @ $13.98/hr.) ............... | 6.99 |
| Total cost per guest........................... | $26.99 |

The standard cocktail party lasts three hours and Chavez hires one worker for every six guests, so that works out to one-half hour of labor per guest. These workers are hired only as needed and are paid only for the hours they actually work.

When bidding on cocktail parties, Chavez adds a 15% markup to yield a price of about $31 per guest. She is confident about her estimates of the costs of food and beverages and labor but is not as comfortable with the estimate of overhead cost. The $13.98 overhead cost per labor-hour was determined by dividing total overhead expenses for the last 12 months by total labor-hours for the same period. Monthly data concerning overhead costs and labor-hours follow:

| Month | Labor-Hours | Overhead Expenses |
|---|---|---|
| January | 2,500 | $ 55,000 |
| February | 2,800 | 59,000 |
| March | 3,000 | 60,000 |
| April | 4,200 | 64,000 |
| May | 4,500 | 67,000 |
| June | 5,500 | 71,000 |
| July | 6,500 | 74,000 |
| August | 7,500 | 77,000 |
| September | 7,000 | 75,000 |
| October | 4,500 | 68,000 |
| November | 3,100 | 62,000 |
| December | 6,500 | 73,000 |
| Total | 57,600 | $805,000 |

Chavez has received a request to bid on a 180-guest fundraising cocktail party to be given next month by an important local charity. (The party would last the usual three hours.) She would like to win this contract because the guest list for this charity event includes many prominent individuals that she would like to secure as future clients. Maria is confident that these potential customers would be favorably impressed by her company's services at the charity event.

*Required:*
1. Prepare a scattergraph plot that puts labor-hours on the X-axis and overhead expenses on the Y-axis. What insights are revealed by your scattergraph?
2. Use the least-squares regression method to estimate the fixed and variable components of overhead expenses. Express these estimates in the form $Y = a + bX$.
3. If Chavez charges her usual price of $31 per guest for the 180-guest cocktail party, how much contribution margin will she earn by serving this event?
4. How low could Chavez bid for the charity event in terms of a price per guest and still break even on the event itself?
5. The individual who is organizing the charity's fundraising event has indicated that he has already received a bid under $30 from another catering company. Do you think Chavez should bid below her normal $31 per guest price for the charity event? Why or why not?

(CMA, adapted)

**A LOOK BACK**

Chapter 6 explained how to compute a break-even point and how to determine the sales needed to achieve a desired profit. We also described how to compute and use the margin of safety and operating leverage.

**A LOOK AT THIS CHAPTER**

This chapter explains how to use the contribution format to create variable costing income statements for manufacturers and segmented income statements. It also contrasts variable costing income statements and absorption income statements.

**A LOOK AHEAD**

Chapter 8 describes the budgeting process.

# 7 Variable Costing and Segment Reporting: Tools for Management

## CHAPTER OUTLINE

**Overview of Variable and Absorption Costing**

- Variable Costing
- Absorption Costing
- Selling and Administrative Expenses

**Variable and Absorption Costing—An Example**

- Variable Costing Contribution Format Income Statement
- Absorption Costing Income Statement

**Reconciliation of Variable Costing with Absorption Costing Income**

**Advantages of Variable Costing and the Contribution Approach**

- Enabling CVP Analysis
- Explaining Changes in Net Operating Income
- Supporting Decision Making

**Segmented Income Statements and the Contribution Approach**

- Traceable and Common Fixed Costs and the Segment Margin

- Identifying Traceable Fixed Costs
- Traceable Fixed Costs Can Become Common Fixed Costs

**Segmented Income Statements—An Example**

- Levels of Segmented Income Statements

**Segmented Income Statements—Decision Making and Break-Even Analysis**

- Decision Making
- Break-Even Analysis

**Segmented Income Statements—Common Mistakes**

- Omission of Costs
- Inappropriate Methods for Assigning Traceable Costs among Segments
- Arbitrarily Dividing Common Costs among Segments

**Income Statements—An External Reporting Perspective**

- Companywide Income Statements
- Segmented Financial Information

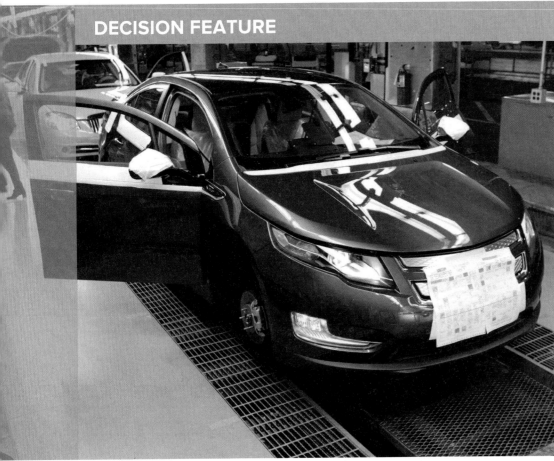

*After studying Chapter 7, you should be able to:*

**LO7–1** Explain how variable costing differs from absorption costing and compute unit product costs under each method.

**LO7–2** Prepare income statements using both variable and absorption costing.

**LO7–3** Reconcile variable costing and absorption costing net operating incomes and explain why the two amounts differ.

**LO7–4** Prepare a segmented income statement that differentiates traceable fixed costs from common fixed costs and use it to make decisions.

**LO7–5** Compute company-wide and segment break-even points for a company with traceable fixed costs.

# Misguided Incentives in the Auto Industry

When the economy tanks, automakers, such as **General Motors** and **Chrysler**, often "flood the market" with a supply of vehicles that far exceeds customer demand. They pursue this course of action even though it tarnishes their brand image and increases their auto storage costs, tire replacement costs, customer rebate costs, and advertising costs. This begs the question why would managers knowingly produce more vehicles than are demanded by customers?

In the auto industry, a manager's bonus is often influenced by the company's reported profits; thus, there is a strong incentive to boost profits by producing more units. How can this be done you ask? It would seem logical that producing more units would have no impact on profits unless the units were sold, right? Wrong! As we will discover in this chapter, absorption costing—the most widely used method of determining unit product costs—can artificially increase profits when managers choose to increase the quantity of units produced.

Source: Segarra, Marielle, "Lots of Trouble," *CFO,* March 2012, pp. 29–30.

his chapter describes two applications of the contribution format income statement that was introduced in earlier chapters. First, it explains how manufacturing companies can prepare *variable costing* income statements, which rely on the contribution format, for internal decision making purposes. The variable costing approach will be contrasted with *absorption costing* income statements, which are generally used for external reports. Ordinarily, variable costing and absorption costing produce different net operating income figures, and the difference can be quite large. In addition to showing how these two methods differ, we will describe the advantages of variable costing for internal reporting purposes and we will show how management decisions can be affected by the costing method chosen.

Second, the chapter explains how the contribution format can be used to prepare segmented income statements. In addition to companywide income statements, managers need to measure the profitability of individual *segments* of their organizations. A **segment** is a part or activity of an organization about which managers would like cost, revenue, or profit data. This chapter explains how to create contribution format income statements that report profit data for business segments, such as divisions, individual stores, geographic regions, customers, and product lines.

# OVERVIEW OF VARIABLE AND ABSORPTION COSTING

As you begin to read about variable and absorption costing income statements in the coming pages, focus your attention on three key concepts. First, both income statement formats include product costs and period costs, although they define these cost classifications differently. Second, variable costing income statements are grounded in the contribution format. They categorize expenses based on cost behavior—variable expenses are reported separately from fixed expenses. Absorption costing income statements ignore variable and fixed cost distinctions. Third, as mentioned in the paragraph above, variable and absorption costing net operating incomes often differ from one another. The reason for the difference always relates to the fact that variable costing and absorption costing income statements account for fixed manufacturing overhead differently. *Pay very close attention to the two different ways that variable costing and absorption costing account for fixed manufacturing overhead.*

## Variable Costing

Under **variable costing**, only those manufacturing costs that vary with output are treated as product costs. This would usually include direct materials, direct labor, and the variable portion of manufacturing overhead. Fixed manufacturing overhead is not treated as a product cost under this method. Rather, fixed manufacturing overhead is treated as a period cost and, like selling and administrative expenses, it is reported as an expense on the income statement in its entirety each period. Consequently, the cost of a unit of product in inventory or in cost of goods sold under the variable costing method does not contain any fixed manufacturing overhead cost. Variable costing is sometimes referred to as *direct costing* or *marginal costing*.

## Absorption Costing

**Absorption costing** treats *all* manufacturing costs as product costs, regardless of whether they are variable or fixed. The cost of a unit of product under the absorption costing method consists of direct materials, direct labor, and *both* variable and fixed manufacturing overhead. Thus, absorption costing allocates a portion of fixed manufacturing overhead cost to each unit of product, along with the variable manufacturing costs. Because absorption costing includes all manufacturing costs in product costs, it is frequently referred to as the *full cost* method.

## Selling and Administrative Expenses

Selling and administrative expenses are never treated as product costs, regardless of the costing method. Thus, under absorption and variable costing, variable and fixed selling and administrative expenses are always treated as period costs and are reported as expenses on the income statement as incurred.

**EXHIBIT 7–1** Variable Costing versus Absorption Costing

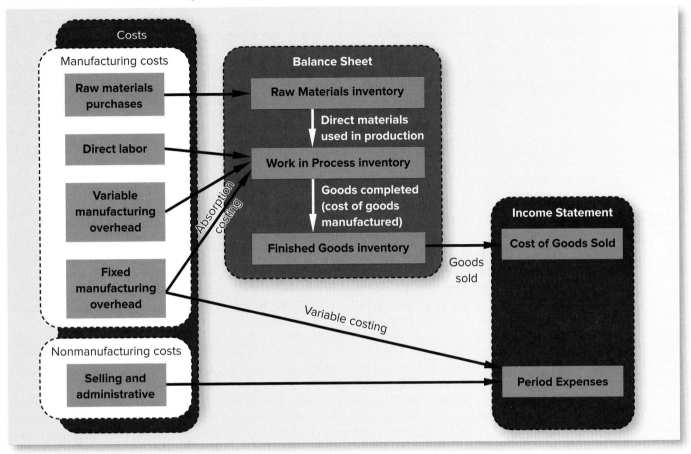

**Summary of Differences** The reason variable costing and absorption costing often report different net operating incomes, as illustrated in Exhibit 7–1, is because the two methods account for fixed manufacturing overhead costs differently—all other costs have the same effect on net operating income under the two methods. In absorption costing, fixed manufacturing overhead costs are included in work in process inventory. When units are completed, these costs are transferred to finished goods and only when the units are sold do these costs flow through to the income statement as part of cost of goods sold. In variable costing, fixed manufacturing overhead costs are considered to be period costs—just like selling and administrative costs—and are taken immediately to the income statement as period expenses.

HELPFUL HINT

In this chapter all differences in net operating income between variable costing and absorption costing will be caused by the accounting for fixed manufacturing overhead. Variable costing treats fixed manufacturing overhead as a period cost. This means that the entire amount of fixed manufacturing overhead incurred each period is recorded as an expense on the income statement within that period. Fixed manufacturing overhead is not attached to units of production. Absorption costing treats fixed manufacturing overhead as a product cost. This means that the entire amount of fixed manufacturing overhead incurred each period is attached to the units produced during that period. The fixed manufacturing overhead attached to units of production is recorded as an expense on the income statement only when the units are sold.

1. Which of the following statements is false? (You may select more than one answer.)
   a. Under variable costing, only those manufacturing costs that vary with output are treated as product costs.
   b. Under variable costing, variable selling and administrative expenses are treated as product costs.
   c. Under absorption costing, fixed manufacturing overhead is treated as a product cost.
   d. Under absorption costing, fixed selling and administrative expenses are treated as period costs.

# VARIABLE AND ABSORPTION COSTING—AN EXAMPLE

We will be making three simplifying assumptions throughout the forthcoming example and the entire chapter. First, this chapter uses *actual costing* rather than the *normal costing* approach that was used in the job-order costing chapters. In other words, rather than relying on predetermined overhead rates to apply overhead costs to products, this chapter assigns *actual* variable and fixed manufacturing overhead costs to products. Second, this chapter always uses the actual *number of units produced* as the allocation base for assigning actual fixed manufacturing overhead costs to products. Third, this chapter always assumes that the variable manufacturing costs per unit and the total fixed manufacturing overhead cost per period remain constant.

Having stated those assumptions, now let's illustrate the difference between variable costing and absorption costing by considering Weber Light Aircraft, a company that produces light recreational aircraft. Data concerning the company's operations appear below:

|  | Per Aircraft | Per Month |
|---|---|---|
| Selling price. | $100,000 | |
| Direct materials. | $19,000 | |
| Direct labor | $5,000 | |
| Variable manufacturing overhead | $1,000 | |
| Fixed manufacturing overhead | | $70,000 |
| Variable selling and administrative expense | $10,000 | |
| Fixed selling and administrative expense | | $20,000 |

|  | January | February | March |
|---|---|---|---|
| Beginning inventory. | 0 | 0 | 1 |
| Units produced | 1 | 2 | 4 |
| Units sold. | 1 | 1 | 5 |
| Ending inventory. | 0 | 1 | 0 |

As you review the data above, it is important to realize that for the months of January, February, and March, the selling price per aircraft, variable costs per aircraft, and total monthly fixed expenses never change. The only data that change in this example are the number of units produced (January = 1 unit produced; February = 2 units produced; March = 4 units produced) and the number of units sold (January = 1 unit sold; February = 1 unit sold; March = 5 units sold).

We will first construct the company's variable costing income statements for January, February, and March. Then we will show how the company's net operating income would be determined for the same months using absorption costing.

# Variable Costing Contribution Format Income Statement

To prepare the company's variable costing income statements for January, February, and March we begin by computing the unit product cost. Under variable costing, the unit product cost consists solely of variable production costs as shown below:

**LEARNING OBJECTIVE 7–2**

Prepare income statements using both variable and absorption costing.

| Variable Costing Unit Product Cost | |
|---|---|
| Direct materials | $19,000 |
| Direct labor | 5,000 |
| Variable manufacturing overhead | 1,000 |
| Unit product cost | $25,000 |

Because each month's unit product cost is $25,000 per aircraft, the variable costing cost of goods sold for all three months can be computed as follows:

| Variable Costing Cost of Goods Sold | January | February | March |
|---|---|---|---|
| Unit product cost (a) | $25,000 | $25,000 | $ 25,000 |
| Units sold (b) | 1 | 1 | 5 |
| Variable cost of goods sold (a) × (b) | $25,000 | $25,000 | $125,000 |

And the company's total selling and administrative expense would be derived as follows:

| Selling and Administrative Expenses | January | February | March |
|---|---|---|---|
| Variable selling and administrative expense (@ $10,000 per unit sold) | $10,000 | $10,000 | $50,000 |
| Fixed selling and administrative expense | 20,000 | 20,000 | 20,000 |
| Total selling and administrative expense | $30,000 | $30,000 | $70,000 |

Putting it all together, the variable costing income statements would appear as shown in Exhibit 7–2. Notice, the contribution format has been used in these income statements. Also, the monthly fixed manufacturing overhead cost ($70,000) has been recorded as a period expense in the month incurred.

| Variable Costing Contribution Format Income Statements | January | February | March |
|---|---|---|---|
| Sales | $100,000 | $100,000 | $500,000 |
| Variable expenses: | | | |
|   Variable cost of goods sold | 25,000 | 25,000 | 125,000 |
|   Variable selling and administrative expense | 10,000 | 10,000 | 50,000 |
| Total variable expenses | 35,000 | 35,000 | 175,000 |
| Contribution margin | 65,000 | 65,000 | 325,000 |
| Fixed expenses: | | | |
|   Fixed manufacturing overhead | 70,000 | 70,000 | 70,000 |
|   Fixed selling and administrative expense | 20,000 | 20,000 | 20,000 |
| Total fixed expenses | 90,000 | 90,000 | 90,000 |
| Net operating income (loss) | $ (25,000) | $ (25,000) | $235,000 |

**EXHIBIT 7–2**
Variable Costing Income Statements

A simple method for understanding how Weber Light Aircraft computed its variable costing net operating income for each month is to focus on the contribution margin per aircraft sold, which is computed as follows:

| Contribution Margin per Aircraft Sold | | |
|---|---|---|
| Selling price per aircraft | | $100,000 |
| Variable cost of goods sold per aircraft | $25,000 | |
| Variable selling and administrative expense per aircraft | 10,000 | 35,000 |
| Contribution margin per aircraft | | $ 65,000 |

*The variable costing net operating income for each period can always be computed by multiplying the number of units sold by the contribution margin per unit and then subtracting total fixed expenses.* For Weber Light Aircraft these computations would appear as follows:

| | January | February | March |
|---|---|---|---|
| Number of aircraft sold | 1 | 1 | 5 |
| Contribution margin per aircraft | × $ 65,000 | × $ 65,000 | × $ 65,000 |
| Total contribution margin | $ 65,000 | $ 65,000 | $325,000 |
| Total fixed expenses | 90,000 | 90,000 | 90,000 |
| Net operating income (loss) | $(25,000) | $(25,000) | $235,000 |

Notice, January and February have the same net operating loss. This occurs because one aircraft was sold in each month and, as previously mentioned, the selling price per aircraft, variable costs per aircraft, and total monthly fixed expenses remain constant.

## HELPFUL HINT

When students prepare variable costing income statements they often mistakenly assume that variable selling and administrative expense is a product cost. The confusion arises because variable selling and administrative expense is included in the calculation of contribution margin; however, it is not a product cost. Variable selling and administrative expense is always a period cost and the total amount of this expense included in the income statement is always derived by multiplying the variable selling and administrative expense per unit by the number of units sold—not the number of units produced.

 CONCEPT CHECK

2. Smith Company produces and sells one product for $40 per unit. The company has no beginning inventories. Its variable manufacturing cost per unit is $18 and the variable selling and administrative expense per unit is $4. The fixed manufacturing overhead and fixed selling and administrative expense total $80,000 and $20,000, respectively. If Smith Company produces 8,000 units and sells 7,500 units during the year, then its net operating income under variable costing would be
   a. $65,000
   b. $41,250
   c. $40,000
   d. $35,000

# Absorption Costing Income Statement

As we begin the absorption costing portion of the example, remember that the only reason absorption costing income differs from variable costing is that the two methods account for fixed manufacturing overhead differently. Under absorption costing, fixed manufacturing overhead is included in product costs. In variable costing, fixed manufacturing overhead is not included in product costs and instead is treated as a period expense just like selling and administrative expenses.

The first step in preparing Weber's absorption costing income statements for January, February, and March is to determine the company's unit product costs for each month as follows:

| Absorption Costing Unit Product Cost | | | |
| --- | --- | --- | --- |
| | January | February | March |
| Direct materials..................................... | $19,000 | $19,000 | $19,000 |
| Direct labor ...................................... | 5,000 | 5,000 | 5,000 |
| Variable manufacturing overhead.................. | 1,000 | 1,000 | 1,000 |
| Fixed manufacturing overhead ($70,000 ÷ 1 unit produced in January; $70,000 ÷ 2 units produced in February; $70,000 ÷ 4 units produced in March).... | 70,000 | 35,000 | 17,500 |
| Unit product cost ................................ | $95,000 | $60,000 | $42,500 |

Notice that in each month, Weber's fixed manufacturing overhead cost of $70,000 is divided by the number of units produced to determine the fixed manufacturing overhead cost per unit.

**HELPFUL HINT**

Compute the unit product cost for each period mentioned in a problem before attempting to create the income statements. To compute absorption costing unit product costs, always take the fixed manufacturing overhead incurred in each period and divide it by the number of units produced during that period. Do not use the number of units sold to calculate unit product costs. The number of units sold is used to calculate the cost of goods sold for an income statement; however, the number of units produced is used to compute unit product costs.

Given these unit product costs, the company's absorption costing net operating income in each month would be determined as shown in Exhibit 7–3.

| Absorption Costing Income Statements | | | |
| --- | --- | --- | --- |
| | January | February | March |
| Sales ........................................ | $100,000 | $100,000 | $500,000 |
| Cost of goods sold ($95,000 × 1 unit; $60,000 × 1 unit; $60,000 × 1 unit + $42,500 × 4 units) ........................ | 95,000 | 60,000 | 230,000 |
| Gross margin ................................ | 5,000 | 40,000 | 270,000 |
| Selling and administrative expenses ........... | 30,000 | 30,000 | 70,000 |
| Net operating income (loss) ................. | $ (25,000) | $ 10,000 | $200,000 |

**EXHIBIT 7–3**
Absorption Costing Income Statements

The sales for all three months in Exhibit 7–3 are the same as the sales shown in the variable costing income statements. The January cost of goods sold consists of one unit produced during January at a cost of $95,000 according to the absorption costing system. The February cost of goods sold consists of one unit produced during February at a cost of $60,000 according to the absorption costing system. The March cost of goods sold ($230,000) consists of one unit produced during February at an absorption cost of $60,000 plus four units produced in March with a total absorption cost of $170,000 (= 4 units produced × $42,500 per unit). The selling and administrative expenses equal the amounts reported in the variable costing income statements; however they are reported as one amount rather than being separated into variable and fixed components.

Note that even though sales were exactly the same in January and February and the cost structure did not change, net operating income was $35,000 higher in February than in January under absorption costing. This occurs because one aircraft produced in February is not sold until March. This aircraft has $35,000 of fixed manufacturing overhead attached to it that was incurred in February, but will not be recorded as part of cost of goods sold until March.

Contrasting the variable costing and absorption costing income statements in Exhibits 7–2 and 7–3, note that net operating income is the same in January under variable costing and absorption costing, but differs in the other two months. We will discuss this in more depth shortly. Also note that the format of the variable costing income statement differs from the absorption costing income statement. An absorption costing income statement categorizes costs by function—manufacturing versus selling and administrative. All of the manufacturing costs flow through the absorption costing cost of goods sold and all of the selling and administrative expenses are listed separately as period expenses. In contrast, in the contribution approach, costs are categorized according to how they behave. All of the variable expenses are listed together and all of the fixed expenses are listed together. The variable expenses category includes manufacturing costs (i.e., variable cost of goods sold) as well as selling and administrative expenses. The fixed expenses category also includes both manufacturing costs and selling and administrative expenses.

## HELPFUL HINT

Be careful computing the cost of goods sold under absorption costing when the units that have been sold were produced in more than one period. For example, if a company produces 8,000 units and sells 10,000 units in year 2, it is wrong to compute the cost of goods sold for year 2 by multiplying 10,000 units by the unit product cost for units produced in year 2. Logically speaking, it is impossible for this solution to be correct because only 8,000 units were produced in year 2. Assuming there is no ending inventory at the end of year 2, the correct cost of goods sold figure would include 8,000 units multiplied by the unit product cost for units produced in year 2 plus 2,000 units multiplied by the unit product cost for units produced in year 1.

CONCEPT CHECK

3.  Smith Company produces and sells one product for $40 per unit. The company has no beginning inventories. Its variable manufacturing cost per unit is $18 and the variable selling and administrative expense per unit is $4. The fixed manufacturing overhead and fixed selling and administrative expense total $80,000 and $20,000, respectively. If Smith Company produces 8,000 units and sells 7,500 units during the year, then its net operating income under absorption costing would be.
    a.  $65,000
    b.  $41,250
    c.  $40,000
    b.  $35,000

## Super Glue: The Variable Overhead Cost That Holds Our Products Together

Adhesives are gradually replacing welds, rivets, screws, and bolts in automobiles and airplanes. For companies that manufacture structural adhesives, such as **Henkel AG**, **Dow Chemical**, and **3M**, the 4%–5% annual growth rate in this $2 billion market is good news. Automakers are replacing heavy metal fasteners with lighter adhesives in an effort to meet tougher fuel-economy standards. For example, the **Ford Motor Company**'s F-150 pickup truck is using three times as much adhesive as prior models. In the aerospace industry, the **Boeing** 787 Dreamliner uses between 200,000 and 250,000 fewer metal fasteners than conventional airplanes thanks to its reliance on structural adhesives, which in turn lightens the plane and lowers fuel costs.

Source: Hagerty, James R., and Ramsey, Mike, "Super Glues, Not Bolts, Hold Cars Together," *The Wall Street Journal*, September 9, 2014, pp. B1 and B4.

# RECONCILIATION OF VARIABLE COSTING WITH ABSORPTION COSTING INCOME

As noted earlier, variable costing and absorption costing net operating incomes may not be the same. In the case of Weber Light Aircraft, the net operating incomes are the same in January, but differ in the other two months. These differences occur because under absorption costing some fixed manufacturing overhead is capitalized in inventories (i.e., included in product costs) rather than being immediately expensed on the income statement. If inventories increase during a period, under absorption costing some of the fixed manufacturing overhead of the current period will be *deferred* in ending inventories. For example, in February two aircraft were produced and each carried with it $35,000 (= $70,000 ÷ 2 aircraft produced) in fixed manufacturing overhead. Since only one aircraft was sold, $35,000 of this fixed manufacturing overhead was on February's absorption costing income statement as part of cost of goods sold, whereas the other $35,000 attached to the unsold aircraft would be included in February's ending finished goods inventory on the balance sheet. In contrast, under variable costing *all* of the $70,000 of fixed manufacturing overhead appeared on the February income statement as a period expense. Consequently, net operating income was higher under absorption costing than under variable costing by $35,000 in February. This was reversed in March when four units were produced, but five were sold. In March, under absorption costing $105,000 of fixed manufacturing overhead was included in cost of goods sold ($35,000 for the unit produced in February and sold in March plus $17,500 for each of the four units produced and sold in March), but only $70,000 was recognized as a period expense under variable costing. Hence, the net operating income in March was $35,000 lower under absorption costing than under variable costing.

In general, when the units produced exceed the units sold and hence inventories increase, net operating income is higher under absorption costing than under variable costing. This occurs because some of the fixed manufacturing overhead of the period is *deferred* in inventories under absorption costing. In contrast, when the units sold exceed the units produced and hence inventories decrease, net operating income is lower under absorption costing than under variable costing. This occurs because some of the fixed manufacturing overhead of previous periods is *released* from inventories under absorption costing. When the units produced and the units sold are equal, no change in inventories occurs and absorption costing and variable costing net operating incomes are the same.[1]

---

[1]These general statements about the relation between variable costing and absorption costing net operating income assume LIFO is used to value inventories. Even when LIFO is not used, the general statements tend to be correct. Although U.S. GAAP allows LIFO and FIFO inventory flow assumptions, International Financial Reporting Standards do not allow a LIFO inventory flow assumption.

Variable costing and absorption costing net operating incomes can be reconciled by determining how much fixed manufacturing overhead was deferred in, or released from, inventories during the period:

| Fixed Manufacturing Overhead Deferred in, or Released from, Inventories under Absorption Costing | | | |
|---|---|---|---|
| | January | February | March |
| Fixed manufacturing overhead in ending inventories . . . . . . . . . . . . . . . . . . . . . . . . . . . . . | $0 | $35,000 | $ 0 |
| Deduct: Fixed manufacturing overhead in beginning inventories . . . . . . . . . . . . . . . . . . . . . . . . . | 0 | 0 | 35,000 |
| Fixed manufacturing overhead deferred in (released from) inventories . . . . . . . . . . . . . . . . . . . . . | $0 | $35,000 | $(35,000) |

In equation form, the fixed manufacturing overhead that is deferred in or released from inventories can be determined as follows:

$$\begin{array}{c}\text{Manufacturing overhead} \\ \text{deferred in} \\ \text{(released from) inventory}\end{array} = \begin{array}{c}\text{Fixed manufacturing} \\ \text{overhead in} \\ \text{ending inventories}\end{array} - \begin{array}{c}\text{Fixed manufacturing} \\ \text{overhead in} \\ \text{beginning inventories}\end{array}$$

The reconciliation would then be reported as shown in Exhibit 7–4.

**EXHIBIT 7–4**
Reconciliation of Variable
Costing and Absorption Costing
Net Operating Incomes

| Reconciliation of Variable Costing and Absorption Costing Net Operating Incomes | | | |
|---|---|---|---|
| | January | February | March |
| Variable costing net operating income (loss) . . . . . . . . . | $(25,000) | $(25,000) | $235,000 |
| Add (deduct) fixed manufacturing overhead deferred in (released from) inventory under absorption costing . . . . . . . . . . . . . . . . . . . . . . | 0 | 35,000 | (35,000) |
| Absorption costing net operating income (loss) . . . . . . | $(25,000) | $ 10,000 | $200,000 |

Again note that the difference between variable costing net operating income and absorption costing net operating income is entirely due to the amount of fixed manufacturing overhead that is deferred in, or released from, inventories during the period under absorption costing. Changes in inventories affect absorption costing net operating income—they do not affect variable costing net operating income, providing that variable manufacturing costs per unit are stable.

The reasons for differences between variable and absorption costing net operating incomes are summarized in Exhibit 7–5. When the units produced equal the units sold, as in January for Weber Light Aircraft, absorption costing net operating income will equal variable costing net operating income. This occurs because when production equals sales, all of the fixed manufacturing overhead incurred in the current period flows through to the income statement under both methods. For companies that use Lean Production, the number of units produced tends to equal the number of units sold. This occurs because goods are produced in response to customer orders, thereby eliminating finished goods inventories and reducing work in process inventory to almost nothing. So, when a company uses Lean Production differences in variable costing and absorption costing net operating income will largely disappear.

When the units produced exceed the units sold, absorption costing net operating income will exceed variable costing net operating income. This occurs because inventories have increased; therefore, under absorption costing some of the fixed manufacturing overhead incurred in the current period is deferred in ending inventories on the balance

**EXHIBIT 7-5**   Comparative Income Effects—Absorption and Variable Costing

| Relation between Production and Sales for the Period | Effect on Inventories | Relation between Absorption and Variable Costing Net Operating Incomes |
|---|---|---|
| Units produced = Units sold | No change in inventories | Absorption costing net operating income = Variable costing net operating income |
| Units produced > Units sold | Inventories increase | Absorption costing net operating income > Variable costing net operating income* |
| Units produced < Units sold | Inventories decrease | Absorption costing net operating income < Variable costing net operating income† |

*Net operating income is higher under absorption costing because fixed manufacturing overhead cost is *deferred* in inventory under absorption costing as inventories increase.
†Net operating income is lower under absorption costing because fixed manufacturing overhead cost is *released* from inventory under absorption costing as inventories decrease.

sheet, whereas under variable costing all of the fixed manufacturing overhead incurred in the current period flows through to the income statement. In contrast, when the units produced are less than the units sold, absorption costing net operating income will be less than variable costing net operating income. This occurs because inventories have decreased; therefore, under absorption costing fixed manufacturing overhead that had been deferred in inventories during a prior period flows through to the current period's income statement together with all of the fixed manufacturing overhead incurred during the current period. Under variable costing, just the fixed manufacturing overhead of the current period flows through to the income statement.

## Inventory Management is a Delicate Balancing Act                IN BUSINESS

Manufacturers are constantly striving to maintain optimal inventories. If they make too many units, it ties up working capital, whereas if they make too few units it can lead to lengthy customer delivery times and lost sales. The same challenges hold true for merchandisers such as Seattle-based web retailer **Zulily**. The company had been ordering items from vendors only after its customers ordered them. While this approach helped Zulily avoid the need to store inventories, it also led to order delivery times ranging from 14–18 days—which pales in comparison to **Amazon.com**, **QVC**, and **overstock.com** whose order delivery times range from 2–5 days.

To shorten its delivery times. Zulily decided to order and store items from vendors prior to their sale to end consumers. Although the items will reside in Zulily's warehouses, the goods will not be recorded on the company's balance sheet. The vendors will continue to own the merchandise stored in Zulily's warehouses until it is sold to end consumers.

Source: Ng, Serena, "Zulily Nips Business Model in the Bud," *The Wall Street Journal*, March 24, 2015, p. B4.

In its first year of operations, Kelley Company produced 10,000 units and sold 7,000 units. Its direct materials, direct labor, variable manufacturing overhead, and variable selling and administrative unit costs were $12, $8, $2, and $1, respectively. Its total fixed manufacturing overhead for the year was $50,000.

4.  What is the amount of cost of goods sold under variable costing?
    a. $220,000.
    b. $161,000.
    c. $154,000.
    d. $230,000.
5.  What is the amount of cost of goods sold under absorption costing?
    a. $189,000.
    b. $196,000.
    c. $179,000.
    d. $186,000.
6.  When comparing Kelley's absorption costing net operating income to its variable costing net operating income, which of the following will be true?
    a. Its absorption costing net operating income will be $35,000 lower than its variable costing net operating income.
    b. Its absorption costing net operating income will be $35,000 higher than its variable costing net operating income.
    c. Its absorption costing net operating income will be $15,000 lower than its variable costing net operating income.
    d. Its absorption costing net operating income will be $15,000 higher than its variable costing net operating income.

# ADVANTAGES OF VARIABLE COSTING AND THE CONTRIBUTION APPROACH

Variable costing, together with the contribution approach, offers appealing advantages for internal reports. This section discusses three of those advantages.

## Enabling CVP Analysis

Cost-volume-profit (CVP) analysis requires that we break costs down into their variable and fixed components. Because variable costing income statements categorize costs as variable and fixed, it is much easier to use this income statement format to perform CVP analysis than attempting to use the absorption costing format, which mixes together variable and fixed costs.

Moreover, absorption costing net operating income may or may not agree with the results of CVP analysis. For example, let's suppose that you are interested in computing the sales that would be necessary to attain a target profit of $235,000 at Weber Light Aircraft. A CVP analysis based on the January variable costing income statement from Exhibit 7–2 would proceed as follows:

| | |
|---|---|
| Sales (a) ............................. | $100,000 |
| Contribution margin (b) ................. | $65,000 |
| Contribution margin ratio (b) ÷ (a) ........ | 65% |
| Total fixed expenses .................... | $90,000 |

$$\text{Dollar sales to attain target profit } = \frac{\text{Target profit} + \text{Fixed expenses}}{\text{CM ratio}}$$

$$= \frac{\$235,000\ +\ \$90,000}{0.65} = \$500,000$$

Thus, a CVP analysis based on the January variable costing income statement predicts that the net operating income would be $235,000 when sales are $500,000. And indeed, the net operating income under variable costing *is* $235,000 when the sales are $500,000 in March. However, the net operating income under absorption costing is *not* $235,000 in March, even though the sales are $500,000. Why is this? The reason is that under absorption costing, net operating income can be distorted by changes in inventories. In March, inventories decreased, so some of the fixed manufacturing overhead that had been deferred in February's ending inventories was released to the March income statement, resulting in a net operating income that is $35,000 lower than the $235,000 predicted by CVP analysis. If inventories had increased in March, the opposite would have occurred—the absorption costing net operating income would have been higher than the $235,000 predicted by CVP analysis.

## Explaining Changes in Net Operating Income

The variable costing income statements in Exhibit 7–2 are clear and easy to understand. All other things the same, when sales go up, net operating income goes up. When sales go down, net operating income goes down. When sales are constant, net operating income is constant. The number of units produced does not affect net operating income.

Absorption costing income statements can be confusing and are easily misinterpreted. Look again at the absorption costing income statements in Exhibit 7–3. A manager might wonder why net operating income went up from January to February even though sales were exactly the same. Was it a result of lower selling costs, more efficient operations, or was it some other factor? In fact, it was simply because the number of units produced exceeded the number of units sold in February and so some of the fixed manufacturing overhead costs were deferred in inventories in that month. These costs have not gone away—they will eventually flow through to the income statement in a later period when inventories go down. There is no way to tell this from the absorption costing income statements.

To avoid mistakes when absorption costing is used, readers of financial statements should be alert to changes in inventory levels. Under absorption costing, if inventories increase, fixed manufacturing overhead costs are deferred in inventories, which in turn increases net operating income. If inventories decrease, fixed manufacturing overhead costs are released from inventories, which in turn decreases net operating income. Thus, when absorption costing is used, fluctuations in net operating income can be caused by changes in inventories as well as changes in unit sales.

## Supporting Decision Making

The variable costing method correctly identifies the additional variable costs that will be incurred to make one more unit. It also emphasizes the impact of fixed costs on profits. The total amount of fixed manufacturing costs appears explicitly on the income statement, highlighting that the whole amount of fixed manufacturing costs must be covered for the company to be truly profitable. In the Weber Light Aircraft example, the variable costing income statements correctly report that the cost of producing another unit is $25,000 and they explicitly recognize that $70,000 of fixed manufactured overhead must be covered to earn a profit.

Under absorption costing, fixed manufacturing overhead costs appear to be variable with respect to the number of units sold, but they are not. For example, in January, the absorption unit product cost at Weber Light Aircraft is $95,000, but the variable portion of this cost is only $25,000. The fixed overhead costs of $70,000 are commingled with variable production costs, thereby obscuring the impact of fixed overhead costs on profits. Because absorption unit product costs are stated on a per unit basis, managers may mistakenly believe that if another unit is produced, it will cost the company $95,000. But of course it would not. The cost of producing another unit would be only $25,000. Misinterpreting absorption unit product costs as variable can lead to many problems, including inappropriate pricing decisions and decisions to drop products that are in fact profitable.

---

**DECISION POINT**

## The Pricing Decision

Each year Webb Company produces and sells 20,000 units of its only product. The selling price for this product is $100 per unit and its direct materials, direct labor, and variable manufacturing overhead costs per unit are $25, $15, and $10, respectively. Webb's annual fixed manufacturing overhead expenses and fixed selling and administrative expenses are $400,000 and $150,000, respectively. It does not have any variable selling and administrative expenses.

The company's marketing manager believes a 10% price increase would lead to a 20% decline in the number of units sold. He claims that if the level of production stays at 20,000 units his price hike will increase gross margins and net operating income by $40,000. Would you support the price increase? Do you think it will increase profits?

---

# SEGMENTED INCOME STATEMENTS AND THE CONTRIBUTION APPROACH

In the remainder of the chapter, we'll learn how to use the contribution approach to construct income statements for business segments. These segmented income statements are useful for analyzing the profitability of segments, making decisions, and measuring the performance of segment managers.

## Traceable and Common Fixed Costs and the Segment Margin

You need to understand three new terms to prepare segmented income statements using the contribution approach—*traceable fixed cost, common fixed cost,* and *segment margin.*

A **traceable fixed cost** of a segment is a fixed cost that is incurred because of the existence of the segment—if the segment had never existed, the fixed cost would not have been incurred; and if the segment were eliminated, the fixed cost would disappear. Examples of traceable fixed costs include the following:

- The salary of the Fritos product manager at **PepsiCo** is a *traceable* fixed cost of the Fritos business segment of PepsiCo.
- The maintenance cost for the building in which Boeing 747s are assembled is a *traceable* fixed cost of the 747 business segment of **Boeing**.
- The liability insurance at Disney World is a *traceable* fixed cost of the Disney World business segment of **The Walt Disney Corporation**.

A **common fixed cost** is a fixed cost that supports the operations of more than one segment, but is not traceable in whole or in part to any one segment. Even if a segment were entirely eliminated, there would be no change in a true common fixed cost. For example:

- The salary of the CEO of **General Motors** is a *common* fixed cost of the various divisions of General Motors.
- The cost of heating a **Safeway** or **Kroger** grocery store is a *common* fixed cost of the store's various departments—groceries, produce, bakery, meat, and so forth.
- The cost of the receptionist's salary at an office shared by a number of doctors is a *common* fixed cost of the doctors. The cost is traceable to the office, but not to individual doctors.

To prepare a segmented income statement, variable expenses are deducted from sales to yield the contribution margin for the segment. The contribution margin tells us what happens to profits as sales volume changes—holding a segment's capacity and fixed costs constant. The contribution margin is especially useful in decisions involving temporary uses of capacity such as special orders. These types of decisions often involve only sales and variable costs—the two components of contribution margin.

The **segment margin** is obtained by deducting the traceable fixed costs of a segment from the segment's contribution margin. It represents the margin available after a segment has covered all of its own costs. *The segment margin is the best gauge of the long-run profitability of a segment* because it includes only those costs that are caused by the segment. If a segment can't cover its own costs, then that segment probably should be dropped (unless it has important side effects on other segments). Notice, common fixed costs are not allocated to segments.

From a decision-making point of view, the segment margin is most useful in major decisions that affect capacity such as dropping a segment. By contrast, as we noted earlier, the contribution margin is most useful in decisions involving short-run changes in sales volume, such as pricing special orders that involve temporary use of existing capacity.

## J. C. Penney Is Bringing Back Its Catalog

### IN BUSINESS

In 2010, **J.C. Penney** discontinued its catalog that was first published and distributed in 1963. However, once the company realized that many of its online sales came from customers responding to what they saw in print, it reintroduced the catalog in 2015. In other words, J.C. Penney realized that catalog shoppers and Internet shoppers are not independent customer segments. If retailers such as J.C. Penney separately analyze catalog sales and Internet sales, they may discontinue the catalog's segment while overlooking the adverse impact of this decision on Internet segment margins.

Source: Kapner, Suzanne, "Catalog Makes a Comeback at Penney," *The Wall Street Journal,* January 20, 2015, pp. B1 and B7.

©StockRocket/iStock/Getty Images RF

## Identifying Traceable Fixed Costs

The distinction between traceable and common fixed costs is crucial in segment reporting because traceable fixed costs are charged to segments and common fixed costs are not. In an actual situation, it is sometimes hard to determine whether a cost should be classified as traceable or common.

The general guideline is to treat as traceable costs *only those costs that would disappear over time if the segment itself disappeared.* For example, if one division within a company were sold or discontinued, it would no longer be necessary to pay that division manager's salary. Therefore the division manager's salary would be classified as a traceable fixed cost of the division. On the other hand, the president of the company undoubtedly would continue to be paid even if one of many divisions was dropped. In fact, he or she might even be paid more if dropping the division was a good idea. Therefore, the president's salary is common to the company's divisions and should not be charged to them.

When assigning costs to segments, the key point is to resist the temptation to allocate costs (such as depreciation of corporate facilities) that are clearly common and that will continue regardless of whether the segment exists or not. *Any allocation of common costs to segments reduces the value of the segment margin as a measure of long-run segment profitability and segment performance.*

## Traceable Fixed Costs Can Become Common Fixed Costs

Fixed costs that are traceable to one segment may be a common cost of another segment. For example, **United Airlines** might want a segmented income statement that shows the segment margin for a particular flight from Chicago to Paris further broken down into first-class, business-class, and economy-class segment margins. The airline must pay a substantial landing fee at Charles DeGaulle airport in Paris. This fixed landing fee is a traceable cost of the flight, but it is a common cost of the first-class, business-class, and economy-class segments. Even if the first-class cabin is empty, the entire landing fee must be paid. So the landing fee is not a traceable cost of the first-class cabin. But on the other hand, paying the fee is necessary in order to have any first-class, business-class, or economy-class passengers. So the landing fee is a common cost of these three classes.

---

**IN BUSINESS**          ## Segment Reporting at the Vilar Performing Arts Center

The **Vilar Performing Arts Center** is a 535-seat theater located in Beaver Creek, Colorado, that presents an unusually wide variety of performances categorized into six business segments—Family Series, Broadway Series, Theatre/Comedy Series, Dance Series, Classical Series, and Concert Series. The executive director of the Vilar, Kris Sabel, must decide which shows to book, what financial terms to offer to the artists, what contributions are likely from underwriters (i.e., donors), and what prices to charge for tickets. He evaluates the profitability of the segments using segmented income statements that include traceable costs (such as the costs of transporting, lodging, and feeding the artists) and exclude common costs (such as his salary, the salaries of his staff, depreciation on the theater, and general marketing expenses).

Data concerning the Classical Series segment for one season appears below:

| | | |
|---|---:|---:|
| Number of shows | | 4 |
| Number of seats budgeted | | 863 |
| Number of seats sold | | 655 |
| Average seats sold per show | | 164 |
| Ticket sales | $46,800 | |
| Underwriting (donors) | 65,000 | |
| Total revenue | | $111,800 |
| Artists fees | $78,870 | |
| Other traceable expenses | 11,231 | |
| Total expenses | | 90,101 |
| Classical Series segment margin | | $ 21,699 |

(continued)

(concluded)

Although the Classical Series sold an average of only 164 seats per show, its overall segment margin ($21,699) is positive thanks to $65,000 of underwriting revenues from donors. Had common costs been allocated to the Classical Series, it may have appeared unprofitable and been discontinued—resulting in fewer shows during the season; less diverse programming; disappointment among a small, but dedicated, number of fans; and lower overall income for the Vilar due to the loss of its Classical Series segment margin.

## SEGMENTED INCOME STATEMENTS—AN EXAMPLE

ProphetMax, Inc., is a rapidly growing computer software company. Exhibit 7–6 shows its variable costing income statement for the most recent month. As the company has grown, its senior managers have asked for segmented income statements that could be used to make decisions and evaluate managerial performance. ProphetMax's controller responded by creating examples of contribution format income statements segmented by the company's divisions, product lines, and sales channels. She created Exhibit 7–7 to explain that ProphetMax's profits can be segmented into its two divisions—the Business Products Division and the Consumer Products Division. The Consumer Products Division's profits can be further segmented into the Clip Art and Computer Games product lines. Finally, the Computer Games product line's profits (within the Consumer Products Division) can be segmented into the Online Sales and Retail Stores sales channels.

**EXHIBIT 7–6**
ProphetMax, Inc. Variable Costing Income Statement

| ProphetMax, Inc. Variable Costing Income Statement | |
|---|---|
| Sales | $500,000 |
| Variable expenses: | |
| Variable cost of goods sold | 180,000 |
| Other variable expenses | 50,000 |
| Total variable expenses | 230,000 |
| Contribution margin | 270,000 |
| Fixed expenses | 256,500 |
| Net operating income | $ 13,500 |

## Levels of Segmented Income Statements

Exhibit 7–8 contains the controller's segmented income statements for the segments depicted in Exhibit 7–7. The contribution format income statement for the entire company appears at the very top of the exhibit under the column labeled Total Company. Notice, the net operating income shown in this column ($13,500) is the same as the net operating income shown in Exhibit 7–6. Immediately to the right of the Total Company column are two columns—one for each of the two divisions. We can see that the Business Products Division's traceable fixed expenses are $90,000 and the Consumer Products Division's are $81,000. These $171,000 of traceable fixed expenses (as shown in the Total Company column) plus the $85,500 of common fixed expenses not traceable to individual divisions equals ProphetMax's total fixed expenses ($256,500) as shown in Exhibit 7–6. We can also see that the Business Products Division's segment margin is $60,000 and the Consumer Products Division's is $39,000. These segment margins show the company's divisional managers how much each of their divisions is contributing to the company's profits.

EXHIBIT 7-7
ProphetMax, Inc.: Examples of
Business Segments

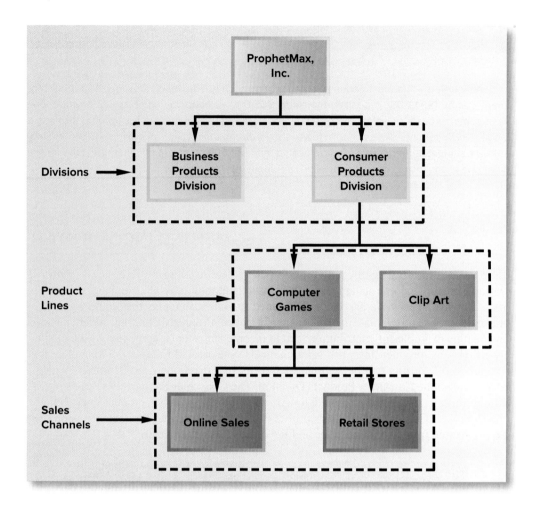

The middle portion of Exhibit 7–8 further segments the Consumer Products Division into its two product lines—Clip Art and Computer Games. The dual nature of some fixed costs can be seen in this portion of the exhibit. Notice, in the top portion of Exhibit 7–8 when segments are defined as divisions, the Consumer Products Division has $81,000 in traceable fixed expenses. However, when we drill down to the product lines (in the middle portion of the exhibit), only $70,000 of the $81,000 expense that was traceable to the Consumer Products Division is traceable to the product lines. The other $11,000 becomes a common fixed expense of the two product lines of the Consumer Products Division.

Why would $11,000 of traceable fixed expense become a common fixed expense when the division is divided into product lines? The $11,000 is the monthly depreciation expense on a machine that is used to encase products in tamper-proof packages for the consumer market. The depreciation expense is a traceable cost of the Consumer Products Division as a whole, but it is a common cost of the division's two product lines. Even if one of the product lines were discontinued entirely, the machine would still be used to wrap the remaining products. Therefore, none of the depreciation expense can really be traced to individual products. Conversely, the $70,000 traceable fixed expense can be traced to the individual product lines because it consists of the costs of product-specific advertising. A total of $30,000 was spent on advertising clip art and $40,000 was spent on advertising computer programs.

The bottom portion of Exhibit 7–8 further segments the Computer Games product line into two sales channels—Online Sales and Retail Stores. The dual nature of some fixed costs can also be seen in this portion of the exhibit. In the middle portion of Exhibit 7–8 when segments are defined as product lines, the Computer Games product line has

**Segments Defined as Divisions**

|  | Total Company | Divisions | |
|---|---|---|---|
|  |  | Business Products Division | Consumer Products Division |
| Sales .................................... | $500,000 | $300,000 | $200,000 |
| Variable expenses: |  |  |  |
|   Variable cost of goods sold ............. | 180,000 | 120,000 | 60,000 |
|   Other variable expenses ............... | 50,000 | 30,000 | 20,000 |
| Total variable expenses .................. | 230,000 | 150,000 | 80,000 |
| Contribution margin ..................... | 270,000 | 150,000 | 120,000 |
| Traceable fixed expenses ................ | 171,000 | 90,000 | 81,000 |
| Divisional segment margin ............... | 99,000 | $ 60,000 | $ 39,000 |
| Common fixed expenses not |  |  |  |
|   traceable to individual divisions ......... | 85,500 |  |  |
| Net operating income .................... | $ 13,500 |  |  |

**Segments Defined as Product Lines of the Consumer Products Division**

|  | Consumer Products Division | Product Line | |
|---|---|---|---|
|  |  | Clip Art | Computer Games |
| Sales .................................... | $200,000 | $75,000 | $125,000 |
| Variable expenses: |  |  |  |
|   Variable cost of goods sold ............. | 60,000 | 20,000 | 40,000 |
|   Other variable expenses ............... | 20,000 | 5,000 | 15,000 |
| Total variable expenses .................. | 80,000 | 25,000 | 55,000 |
| Contribution margin ..................... | 120,000 | 50,000 | 70,000 |
| Traceable fixed expenses ................ | 70,000 | 30,000 | 40,000 |
| Product-line segment margin ............. | 50,000 | $20,000 | $ 30,000 |
| Common fixed expenses not |  |  |  |
|   traceable to individual product lines ..... | 11,000 |  |  |
| Divisional segment margin ................ | $ 39,000 |  |  |

**Segments Defined as Sales Channels for One Product Line, Computer Games, of the Consumer Products Division**

|  | Computer Games | Sales Channels | |
|---|---|---|---|
|  |  | Online Sales | Retail Stores |
| Sales .................................... | $125,000 | $100,000 | $25,000 |
| Variable expenses: |  |  |  |
|   Variable cost of goods sold ............. | 40,000 | 32,000 | 8,000 |
|   Other variable expenses ............... | 15,000 | 5,000 | 10,000 |
| Total variable expenses .................. | 55,000 | 37,000 | 18,000 |
| Contribution margin ..................... | 70,000 | 63,000 | 7,000 |
| Traceable fixed expenses ................ | 25,000 | 15,000 | 10,000 |
| Sales-channel segment margin ............ | 45,000 | $ 48,000 | $ (3,000) |
| Common fixed expenses not |  |  |  |
|   traceable to individual sales channels .... | 15,000 |  |  |
| Product-line segment margin ............. | $ 30,000 |  |  |

$40,000 in traceable fixed expenses. However, when we look at the sales channels in the bottom portion of the exhibit, only $25,000 of the $40,000 that was traceable to Computer Games is traceable to the sales channels. The other $15,000 becomes a common fixed expense of the two sales channels for the Computer Games product line.

# SEGMENTED INCOME STATEMENTS—DECISION MAKING AND BREAK-EVEN ANALYSIS

Once a company prepares contribution format segmented income statements, it can use those statements to make decisions and perform break-even analysis.

## Decision Making

Let's refer again to the bottom portion of Exhibit 7–8 to illustrate how segmented income statements support decision making. Notice that the Online Sales segment has a segment margin of $48,000 and the Retail Stores segment has a segment margin of $(3,000). Let's assume that ProphetMax wants to know the profit impact of discontinuing the sale of computer games through its Retail Stores sales channel. The company believes that Online Sales of its computer games will increase 10% if it discontinues the Retail Stores sales channel. It also believes that the Business Products Division and Clip Art product line will be unaffected by this decision. How would you compute the profit impact of this decision?

The first step is to calculate the profit impact of discontinuing the Retail Stores sales channel. If this sales channel is eliminated, we assume its sales, variable expenses, and traceable fixed expenses would all go away. The quickest way to summarize these financial impacts is to focus on the Retail Stores' segment margin. In other words, if the Retail Stores sales channel discontinued, then its negative segment margin of $3,000 would also be avoided. This would increase ProphetMax's net operating income by $3,000. The second step is to calculate the profit impact of increasing Online Sales of computer games by 10%. To perform this calculation, we assume that the Online Sales total traceable fixed expenses ($15,000) remain constant and its contribution margin ratio remains constant at 63% (= $63,000 ÷ $100,000). If Online Sales increase $10,000 (= $100,000 × 10%), then the Online Sales segment's contribution margin will increase by $6,300 (= $10,000 × 63%). The overall profit impact of discontinuing the Retail Stores sales channel can be summarized as follows:

| | |
|---|---|
| Avoidance of the Retail Stores' segment loss | $3,000 |
| Increase in Online Sales contribution margin | 6,300 |
| Increase in ProphetMax's net operating income | $9,300 |

## Break-Even Analysis

**LO7–5**

Compute companywide and segment break-even points for a company with traceable fixed costs.

In Chapter 6, we learned how to compute a companywide break-even point for a multiproduct company with no traceable fixed expenses. Now we are going to use the ProphetMax, Inc., data in Exhibit 7–8 to explain how to compute companywide and segment break-even points for a company with traceable fixed expenses. Beginning with the companywide perspective, the formula for computing the break-even point for a multiproduct company with traceable fixed expenses is as follows:

$$\text{Dollar sales for company to break even} = \frac{\text{Traceable fixed expenses} + \text{Common fixed expenses}}{\text{Overall CM ratio}}$$

In the case of ProphetMax, we should begin by reviewing the information in the Total Company column in the top portion of Exhibit 7–8. This column of data indicates that ProphetMax's total traceable fixed expenses are $171,000 and its total common fixed expenses are $85,500. Furthermore, the company's overall contribution margin of $270,000 divided by its total sales of $500,000 equals its overall CM ratio of 0.54. Given this information, ProphetMax's companywide break-even point is computed as follows:

$$\text{Dollar sales for company to break even} = \frac{\text{Traceable fixed expenses} + \text{Common fixed expenses}}{\text{Overall CM ratio}}$$

$$= \frac{\$171,000 + \$85,500}{0.54}$$

$$= \frac{\$256,500}{0.54}$$

$$= \$475,000$$

It is important to emphasize that this computation assumes a constant sales mix. In other words, in the ProphetMax example, it assumes that 60% of the total sales ($300,000 ÷ $500,000) will always come from the Business Products Division and 40% of the total sales ($200,000 ÷ $500,000) will always come from the Consumer Products Division.

To compute the break-even point for a business segment, the formula is as follows:

$$\text{Dollar sales for a segment to break even} = \frac{\text{Segment traceable fixed expenses}}{\text{Segment CM ratio}}$$

In the case of ProphetMax's Business Products Division, we should begin by reviewing the information in the Business Products Division column in the top portion of Exhibit 7–8. This column of data indicates that the Business Products Division's traceable fixed expenses are $90,000 and its CM ratio is 0.50 ($150,000 ÷ $300,000). Given this information, the Business Products Division's break-even point is computed as follows:

$$\text{Dollar sales for a segment to break even} = \frac{\text{Segment traceable fixed expenses}}{\text{Segment CM ratio}}$$

$$= \frac{\$90,000}{0.50}$$

$$= \$180,000$$

The same calculation can be performed for the Consumer Products Division using data from the Consumer Products Division column in the top portion of Exhibit 7–8. Given that the Consumer Products Division's traceable fixed expenses are $81,000 and its CM ratio is 0.60 ($120,000 ÷ $200,000), its break-even point is computed as follows:

$$\text{Dollar sales for a segment to break even} = \frac{\text{Segment traceable fixed expenses}}{\text{Segment CM ratio}}$$

$$= \frac{\$81,000}{0.60}$$

$$= \$135,000$$

Notice that the sum of the segment break-even sales figures of $315,000 ($180,000 + $135,000) is less than the companywide break-even point of $475,000. This occurs because the segment break-even calculations *do not include the company's common fixed expenses.* The exclusion of the company's common fixed expenses can be verified by preparing income statements based on each segment's break-even dollar sales as follows:

| | Total Company | Business Products Division | Consumer Products Division |
|---|---|---|---|
| Sales . . . . . . . . . . . . . . . . . . . . . . . . . . | $315,000 | $180,000 | $135,000 |
| Variable expenses . . . . . . . . . . . . . . . | 144,000 | 90,000 | 54,000 |
| Contribution margin . . . . . . . . . . . . . | 171,000 | 90,000 | 81,000 |
| Traceable fixed expenses . . . . . . . . . | 171,000 | 90,000 | 81,000 |
| Segment margin . . . . . . . . . . . . . . . . . | 0 | $ 0 | $ 0 |
| Common fixed expenses . . . . . . . . . | 85,500 | | |
| Net operating loss . . . . . . . . . . . . . . | $ (85,500) | | |

When each segment achieves its break-even point, the company's overall net operating loss of $85,500 equals its common fixed expenses of $85,500. This reality can often lead managers astray when making decisions. In an attempt to "cover the company's common fixed expenses," managers will often allocate common fixed expenses to business segments when performing break-even calculations and making decisions. *This is a mistake!* Allocating common fixed expenses to business segments artificially inflates each segment's break-even point. This may cause managers to erroneously discontinue business segments where the inflated break-even point appears unobtainable. The decision to retain or discontinue a business segment should be based on the sales and expenses that would disappear if the segment were dropped. Because common fixed expenses *will persist even if a business segment is dropped,* they should not be allocated to business segments when making decisions.

# SEGMENTED INCOME STATEMENTS—COMMON MISTAKES

All of the costs attributable to a segment—and only those costs—should be assigned to the segment. Unfortunately, companies often make mistakes when assigning costs to segments. They omit some costs, inappropriately assign traceable fixed costs, and arbitrarily allocate common fixed costs.

## Omission of Costs

The costs assigned to a segment should include all costs attributable to that segment from the company's entire value chain. All of these functions, from research and development, through product design, manufacturing, marketing, distribution, and customer service, are required to bring a product or service to the customer and generate sales.

However, only manufacturing costs are included in product costs under absorption costing, which is widely regarded as required for external financial reporting. To avoid having to maintain two costing systems and to provide consistency between internal and external reports, many companies also use absorption costing for their internal reports such as segmented income statements. As a result, such companies omit from their profitability analysis part or all of the "upstream" costs in the value chain, which consist of research and development and product design, and the "downstream" costs, which consist of marketing, distribution, and customer service. Yet these nonmanufacturing costs are just as essential in determining product profitability as are the manufacturing costs.

These upstream and downstream costs, which are usually included in selling and administrative expenses on absorption costing income statements, can represent half or more of the total costs of an organization. If either the upstream or downstream costs are omitted in profitability analysis, then the product is undercosted and management may unwittingly develop and maintain products that in the long run result in losses.

## Inappropriate Methods for Assigning Traceable Costs among Segments

In addition to omitting costs, many companies do not correctly handle traceable fixed expenses on segmented income statements. First, they do not trace fixed expenses to segments even when it is feasible to do so. Second, they use inappropriate allocation bases to allocate traceable fixed expenses to segments.

**Failure to Trace Costs Directly** Costs that can be traced directly to a specific segment should be charged directly to that segment and should not be allocated to other segments. For example, the rent for a branch office of an insurance company should be charged directly to the branch office rather than included in a companywide overhead pool and then spread throughout the company.

**Inappropriate Allocation Base** Some companies use arbitrary allocation bases to allocate costs to segments. For example, some companies allocate selling and administrative expenses on the basis of sales revenues. Thus, if a segment generates 20% of total company sales, it would be allocated 20% of the company's selling and administrative expenses as its "fair share." This same basic procedure is followed if cost of goods sold or some other measure is used as the allocation base.

Costs should be allocated to segments for internal decision-making purposes only when the allocation base actually drives the cost being allocated (or is very highly correlated with the real cost driver). For example, sales should be used to allocate selling and administrative expenses only if a 10% increase in sales will result in a 10% increase in selling and administrative expenses. To the extent that selling and administrative expenses are not driven by sales volume, these expenses will be improperly allocated—with a disproportionately high percentage of the selling and administrative expenses assigned to the segments with the largest sales.

## Arbitrarily Dividing Common Costs among Segments

The third business practice that leads to distorted segment costs is the practice of assigning nontraceable costs to segments. For example, some companies allocate the common costs of the corporate headquarters building to products on segment reports. However, in a multiproduct company, no single product is likely to be responsible for any significant amount of this cost. Even if a product were eliminated entirely, there would usually be no significant effect on any of the costs of the corporate headquarters building. In short, there is no cause-and-effect relation between the cost of the corporate headquarters building and the existence of any one product. As a consequence, any allocation of the cost of the corporate headquarters building to the products must be arbitrary.

Common costs like the costs of the corporate headquarters building are necessary, of course, to have a functioning organization. The practice of arbitrarily allocating common costs to segments is often justified on the grounds that "someone" has to "cover the common costs." While it is undeniably true that a company must cover its common costs to earn a profit, arbitrarily allocating common costs to segments does not ensure that this will happen. In fact, adding a share of common costs to the real costs of a segment may make an otherwise profitable segment appear to be unprofitable. If a manager eliminates the apparently unprofitable segment, the real traceable costs of the segment will be saved, but its sales will be lost. And what happens to the common fixed costs that were allocated to the segment? They don't disappear; they are reallocated to the remaining segments of the company. That makes all of the remaining segments appear to be less profitable—possibly resulting in dropping other segments. The net effect will be to reduce the overall profits of the company and make it even more difficult to "cover the common costs."

Additionally, common fixed costs are not manageable by the manager to whom they are arbitrarily allocated; they are the responsibility of higher-level managers. When common fixed costs are allocated to managers, they are held responsible for those costs even though they cannot control them.

**CONCEPT CHECK**

7. Which of the following statements is true? (You can select more than one answer.)
   a. A segment's contribution margin minus its traceable fixed expenses equals the segment margin.
   b. A company's common fixed costs should be evenly allocated to business segments when computing the dollar sales for a segment to break even.
   c. A segment's traceable fixed costs should include only those costs that would disappear over time if the segment disappeared.
   d. Fixed costs that are traceable to one segment may be a common cost of another segment.

# INCOME STATEMENTS—AN EXTERNAL REPORTING PERSPECTIVE

## Companywide Income Statements

Practically speaking, absorption costing is required for external reports according to U.S. generally accepted accounting principles (GAAP).[2] Furthermore, International Financial Reporting Standards (IFRS) explicitly require companies to use absorption costing. Probably because of the cost and possible confusion of maintaining two separate costing systems—one for external reporting and one for internal reporting—most companies use absorption costing for their external and internal reports.

With all of the advantages of the contribution approach, you may wonder why the absorption approach is used at all. While the answer is partly due to adhering to tradition, absorption costing is also attractive to many accountants and managers because they believe it better matches costs with sales. Advocates of absorption costing argue that *all* manufacturing costs must be assigned to products in order to properly match the costs of producing units of product with their sales. The fixed costs of depreciation, taxes, insurance, supervisory salaries, and so on, are just as essential to manufacturing products as are the variable costs.

Advocates of variable costing argue that fixed manufacturing costs are not really the costs of any particular unit of product. These costs are incurred to have the *capacity* to make products during a particular period and will be incurred even if nothing is made

---

[2]The Financial Accounting Standards Board (FASB) has created a single source of authoritative nongovernmental U.S. generally accepted accounting principles (GAAP) called the FASB Accounting Standards Codification (FASB codification). Although the FASB codification does not explicitly disallow variable costing, it does explicitly prohibit companies from excluding all manufacturing overhead costs from product costs. It also provides an in-depth discussion of fixed overhead allocation to products, thereby implying that absorption costing is required for external reports. Although some companies expense significant elements of fixed manufacturing costs on their external reports, practically speaking, U.S. GAAP requires absorption costing for external reports.

during the period. Moreover, whether a unit is made or not, the fixed manufacturing costs will be exactly the same. Therefore, variable costing advocates argue that fixed manufacturing costs are not part of the costs of producing a particular unit of product, and thus, the matching principle dictates that fixed manufacturing costs should be recognized as an expense in the current period.

## Segmented Financial Information

U.S. GAAP and IFRS require that publicly traded companies include segmented financial and other data in their annual reports and that the segmented reports prepared for external users *must use the same methods and definitions that the companies use in internal segmented reports that are prepared to aid in making operating decisions.* This is a very unusual stipulation because companies are not ordinarily required to report the same data to external users that are used for internal decision-making purposes. This requirement creates incentives for publicly traded companies to avoid using the contribution format for internal segmented reports. Segmented contribution format income statements contain vital information that companies are often very reluctant to release to the public (and hence competitors). In addition, this requirement creates problems in reconciling internal and external reports.

## SUMMARY

**LO7–1 Explain how variable costing differs from absorption costing and compute unit product costs under each method.**
Variable and absorption costing are alternative methods of determining unit product costs. Under variable costing, only variable manufacturing costs (direct materials, direct labor, and variable manufacturing overhead) are treated as product costs. Fixed manufacturing overhead is treated as a period cost and it is expensed on the income statement as incurred. By contrast, absorption costing treats fixed manufacturing overhead as a product cost, along with direct materials, direct labor, and variable overhead.

**LO7–2 Prepare income statements using both variable and absorption costing.**
The unit product costs under the two methods are different and so the cost of goods sold are different on the income statement. Additionally, fixed manufacturing overhead is expensed on

the income statement under variable costing, but is included in unit product costs under absorption costing. Under both costing methods, selling and administrative expenses are treated as period costs and are expensed on the income statement as incurred.

### LO7–3 Reconcile variable costing and absorption costing net operating incomes and explain why the two amounts differ.

Because absorption costing treats fixed manufacturing overhead as a product cost, a portion of fixed manufacturing overhead is assigned to each unit as it is produced. If units of product are unsold at the end of a period, then the fixed manufacturing overhead cost attached to those units is carried with them into the inventory account and deferred to a future period. When these units are later sold, the fixed manufacturing overhead cost attached to them is released from the inventory account and charged against income as part of cost of goods sold. Thus, under absorption costing, it is possible to defer a portion of the fixed manufacturing overhead cost from one period to a future period through the inventory account.

### LO7–4 Prepare a segmented income statement that differentiates traceable fixed costs from common fixed costs and use it to make decisions.

Segmented income statements provide information for evaluating the profitability and performance of divisions, product lines, sales territories, and other segments of a company. Under the contribution approach, variable costs and fixed costs are clearly distinguished from each other and only those costs that are traceable to a segment are assigned to the segment. A cost is considered traceable to a segment only if the cost is caused by the segment and could be avoided by eliminating the segment. Fixed common costs are not allocated to segments. The segment margin consists of revenues, less variable expenses, less traceable fixed expenses of the segment.

### LO7–5 Compute companywide and segment break-even points for a company with traceable fixed costs.

The dollar sales required for a segment to break even is computed by dividing the segment's traceable fixed expenses by its contribution margin ratio. A company's common fixed expenses should not be allocated to segments when performing break-even calculations because they will not change in response to segment-level decisions. Conversely, a company's common fixed expenses should be included when performing companywide break-even calculations.

## GUIDANCE ANSWERS TO DECISION POINT

**The Pricing Decision**

Under absorption costing, the fixed manufacturing overhead cost per unit is $20 ($400,000 ÷ 20,000 units). The absorption costing unit product cost is $70 ($25 + $15 + $10 + $20) and the gross margin per unit is $30 ($100 − $70). The variable costing unit product cost is $50 ($25 + $15 + $10) and the contribution margin per unit is $50 ($100 − $50). When the company produces and sells 20,000 units at a price of $100, it earns a total gross margin of $600,000 (20,000 units × $30) and a total contribution margin of $1,000,000 (20,000 units × $50).

A 10% price increase would raise the selling price to $110 per unit, whereas a 20% decline in unit sales would drop the sales volume to 16,000 units. In this scenario, the total gross margin earned is $640,000 (16,000 units × $40), which is $40,000 higher than the gross margin from the original scenario. This explains why the marketing manager thinks the price increase is a good idea. However, if the price increase is implemented the total contribution margin earned would become $960,000 (16,000 units × $60), which is $40,000 lower than the contribution margin from the original scenario. The price increase will lower profits by $40,000.

 ## GUIDANCE ANSWERS TO CONCEPT CHECKS

1.  **Choice b.** Under variable costing, variable selling and administrative expenses are treated as period costs.
2.  **Choice d.** The contribution margin per unit equals $18 ($40 − $18 − $4). The number of units sold (7,500 units) multiplied by the contribution margin per unit ($18 per unit) minus the total fixed costs ($100,000) equals the net operating income ($35,000).

3. **Choice c.** The unit product cost of $28 includes $18 of variable manufacturing costs and $10 of fixed manufacturing overhead ($80,000 ÷ 8,000 = $10 per unit). The gross margin per unit is $12 ($40 − $28) and the total gross margin is $90,000 (7,500 units × $12 = $90,000). The gross margin of $90,000 minus variable selling and administrative expense of $30,000 (7,500 units × $4 per unit = $30,000) and fixed selling and administrative expense of $20,000 equals net operating income of $40,000.

4. **Choice c.** The variable costing unit product cost is $22 ($12 + $8 + $2). The cost of goods sold is $154,000 (7,000 units sold × $22 per unit). The variable selling and administrative expense is a period cost, not a product cost.

5. **Choice a.** The absorption costing fixed manufacturing overhead cost per unit is $5 ($50,000 ÷ 10,000 units). The absorption costing unit product cost is $27 ($12 + $8 + $2 + 5). The cost of goods sold is $189,000 (7,000 units sold × $27 per unit).

6. **Choice d.** Absorption costing income is $15,000 higher because it defers $15,000 (3,000 units × $5 per unit) of fixed manufacturing overhead in inventory, whereas variable costing expenses the entire $50,000 of fixed manufacturing overhead during the current period.

7. **Choices a, c, and d.** Common fixed costs should not be allocated to business segments.

## REVIEW PROBLEM 1: CONTRASTING VARIABLE AND ABSORPTION COSTING

Dexter Corporation produces and sells a single product, a wooden hand loom for weaving small items such as scarves. Selected cost and operating data relating to the product for two years are given below:

| | |
|---|---|
| Selling price per unit | $50 |
| Manufacturing costs: | |
| Variable manufacturing cost per unit produced: | |
| Direct materials | $11 |
| Direct labor | $6 |
| Variable manufacturing overhead | $3 |
| Fixed manufacturing overhead per year | $120,000 |
| Selling and administrative expenses: | |
| Variable selling and administrative per unit sold | $4 |
| Fixed selling and administrative per year | $70,000 |

| | Year 1 | Year 2 |
|---|---|---|
| Units in beginning inventory | 0 | 2,000 |
| Units produced during the year | 10,000 | 6,000 |
| Units sold during the year | 8,000 | 8,000 |
| Units in ending inventory | 2,000 | 0 |

*Required:*
1. Assume the company uses absorption costing.
   a. Compute the unit product cost in each year.
   b. Prepare an income statement for each year.
2. Assume the company uses variable costing.
   a. Compute the unit product cost in each year.
   b. Prepare an income statement for each year.
3. Reconcile the variable costing and absorption costing net operating incomes.

**Solution to Review Problem 1**

1.  a.  Under absorption costing, all manufacturing costs, variable and fixed, are included in unit product costs:

|  | Year 1 | Year 2 |
|---|---|---|
| Direct materials.......................... | $11 | $11 |
| Direct labor............................. | 6 | 6 |
| Variable manufacturing overhead ....... | 3 | 3 |
| Fixed manufacturing overhead | | |
| ($120,000 ÷ 10,000 units)............ | 12 | |
| ($120,000 ÷ 6,000 units)............. | | 20 |
| Unit product cost..................... | $32 | $40 |

b.  The absorption costing income statements follow:

|  | Year 1 | Year 2 |
|---|---|---|
| Sales (8,000 units × $50 per unit) .................... | $400,000 | $400,000 |
| Cost of goods sold (8,000 units × $32 per unit); | | |
| (2,000 units × $32 per unit) + | | |
| (6,000 units × $40 per unit)...................... | 256,000 | 304,000 |
| Gross margin...................................... | 144,000 | 96,000 |
| Selling and administrative expenses | | |
| (8,000 units × $4 per unit + $70,000) ............. | 102,000 | 102,000 |
| Net operating income (loss)......................... | $ 42,000 | $ (6,000) |

2.  a.  Under variable costing, only the variable manufacturing costs are included in unit product costs:

|  | Year 1 | Year 2 |
|---|---|---|
| Direct materials........................... | $11 | $11 |
| Direct labor.............................. | 6 | 6 |
| Variable manufacturing overhead........... | 3 | 3 |
| Unit product cost........................ | $20 | $20 |

b.  The variable costing income statements follow:

|  | Year 1 | | Year 2 | |
|---|---|---|---|---|
| Sales (8,000 units × $50 per unit)............ | | $400,000 | | $400,000 |
| Variable expenses: | | | | |
| Variable cost of goods sold | | | | |
| (8,000 units × $20 per unit)............. | $160,000 | | $160,000 | |
| Variable selling and administrative | | | | |
| expenses (8,000 units × $4 per unit)..... | 32,000 | 192,000 | 32,000 | 192,000 |
| Contribution margin........................ | | 208,000 | | 208,000 |
| Fixed expenses: | | | | |
| Fixed manufacturing overhead ............ | $120,000 | | $120,000 | |
| Fixed selling and administrative | | | | |
| expenses............................. | 70,000 | 190,000 | 70,000 | 190,000 |
| Net operating income ...................... | | $ 18,000 | | $ 18,000 |

3. The reconciliation of the variable and absorption costing net operating incomes follows:

|  | Year 1 | Year 2 |
|---|---|---|
| Fixed manufacturing overhead in ending inventories (2,000 units × $12 per unit; 0 units × $20 per unit) ... | $24,000 | $      0 |
| Deduct: Fixed manufacturing overhead in beginning inventories (0; 2,000 units × $12 per unit) ... | 0 | 24,000 |
| Fixed manufacturing overhead deferred in (released from) inventories ...................... | $24,000 | $(24,000) |

|  | Year 1 | Year 2 |
|---|---|---|
| Variable costing net operating income ................. | $18,000 | $ 18,000 |
| Add: Fixed manufacturing overhead costs deferred in inventory under absorption costing (2,000 units × $12 per unit) .......................... | 24,000 | |
| Deduct: Fixed manufacturing overhead costs released from inventory under absorption costing (2,000 units × $12 per unit) ................... | | (24,000) |
| Absorption costing net operating income (loss)........... | $42,000 | $ (6,000) |

## REVIEW PROBLEM 2: SEGMENTED INCOME STATEMENTS

The business staff of the law firm Frampton, Davis & Smythe has constructed the following report that breaks down the firm's overall results for last month into two business segments—family law and commercial law:

|  | Company Total | Family Law | Commercial Law |
|---|---|---|---|
| Revenues from clients ........... | $1,000,000 | $400,000 | $600,000 |
| Variable expenses............... | 220,000 | 100,000 | 120,000 |
| Contribution margin ............. | 780,000 | 300,000 | 480,000 |
| Traceable fixed expenses ........ | 670,000 | 280,000 | 390,000 |
| Segment margin ................ | 110,000 | 20,000 | 90,000 |
| Common fixed expenses......... | 60,000 | 24,000 | 36,000 |
| Net operating income (loss)....... | $   50,000 | $  (4,000) | $  54,000 |

However, this report is not quite correct. The common fixed expenses such as the managing partner's salary, general administrative expenses, and general firm advertising have been allocated to the two segments based on revenues from clients.

**Required:**
1. Redo the segment report, eliminating the allocation of common fixed expenses. Would the firm be better off financially if the family law segment were dropped? (Note: Many of the firm's commercial law clients also use the firm for their family law requirements such as drawing up wills.)
2. The firm's advertising agency has proposed an ad campaign targeted at boosting the revenues of the family law segment. The ad campaign would cost $20,000, and the advertising agency claims it would increase family law revenues by $100,000. The managing partner of Frampton, Davis & Smythe believes this increase in business could be accommodated without any increase in fixed expenses. Estimate the effect this ad campaign would have on the family law segment margin and on the firm's overall net operating income.

3.  Compute the companywide break-even point in dollar sales and the dollar sales required for each business segment to break even.

**Solution to Review Problem 2**

1.  The corrected segmented income statement appears below:

|  | Company Total | Family Law | Commercial Law |
|---|---|---|---|
| Revenues from clients . . . . . . . . . . | $1,000,000 | $400,000 | $600,000 |
| Variable expenses. . . . . . . . . . . . . . | 220,000 | 100,000 | 120,000 |
| Contribution margin . . . . . . . . . . . . | 780,000 | 300,000 | 480,000 |
| Traceable fixed expenses . . . . . . . | 670,000 | 280,000 | 390,000 |
| Segment margin . . . . . . . . . . . . . . | 110,000 | $ 20,000 | $ 90,000 |
| Common fixed expenses . . . . . . . . | 60,000 | | |
| Net operating income. . . . . . . . . . | $   50,000 | | |

No, the firm would not be better off financially if the family law practice were dropped. The family law segment is covering all of its own costs and is contributing $20,000 per month to covering the common fixed expenses of the firm. While the segment margin for family law is much lower than for commercial law, it is still profitable. Moreover, family law may be a service that the firm must provide to its commercial clients in order to remain competitive.

2.  The ad campaign would increase the family law segment margin by $55,000 as follows:

| | |
|---|---|
| Increased revenues from clients . . . . . . . . . . . . . . . . . . . . . . . . . . | $100,000 |
| Family law contribution margin ratio ($300,000 ÷ $400,000). . . | × 75% |
| Increased contribution margin . . . . . . . . . . . . . . . . . . . . . . . . . . . | $75,000 |
| Less cost of the ad campaign . . . . . . . . . . . . . . . . . . . . . . . . . . . | 20,000 |
| Increased segment margin . . . . . . . . . . . . . . . . . . . . . . . . . . . . . | $55,000 |

Because there would be no increase in fixed expenses (including common fixed expenses), the increase in overall net operating income is also $55,000.

3.  The companywide break-even point is computed as follows:

$$\text{Dollar sales for company to break even} = \frac{\text{Traceable fixed expenses} + \text{Common fixed expenses}}{\text{Overall CM ratio}}$$

$$= \frac{\$670,000 + \$60,000}{0.78}$$

$$= \frac{\$730,000}{0.78}$$

$$= \$935,897 \text{ (rounded)}$$

The break-even point for the family law segment is computed as follows:

$$\text{Dollar sales for a segment to break even} = \frac{\text{Segment traceable fixed expenses}}{\text{Segment CM ratio}}$$

$$= \frac{\$280,000}{0.75}$$

$$= \$373,333 \text{ (rounded)}$$

The break-even point for the commercial law segment is computed as follows:

$$\text{Dollar sales for a segment to break even} = \frac{\text{Segment traceable fixed expenses}}{\text{Segment CM ratio}}$$

$$= \frac{\$390,000}{0.80}$$

$$= \$487,500$$

## GLOSSARY

**Absorption costing**   A costing method that includes all manufacturing costs—direct materials, direct labor, and both variable and fixed manufacturing overhead—in unit product costs. (p. 282)

**Common fixed cost**   A fixed cost that supports more than one business segment, but is not traceable in whole or in part to any one of the business segments. (p. 295)

**Segment**   Any part or activity of an organization about which managers seek cost, revenue, or profit data. (p. 282)

**Segment margin**   A segment's contribution margin less its traceable fixed costs. It represents the margin available after a segment has covered all of its own traceable costs. (p. 295)

**Traceable fixed cost**   A fixed cost that is incurred because of the existence of a particular business segment and that would be eliminated if the segment were eliminated. (p. 294)

**Variable costing**   A costing method that includes only variable manufacturing costs—direct materials, direct labor, and variable manufacturing overhead—in unit product costs. (p. 282)

## QUESTIONS

7–1   What is the difference between absorption costing and variable costing?

7–2   Are selling and administrative expenses treated as product costs or as period costs under variable costing?

7–3   Explain how fixed manufacturing overhead costs are shifted from one period to another under absorption costing.

7–4   What are the arguments in favor of treating fixed manufacturing overhead costs as product costs?

7–5   What are the arguments in favor of treating fixed manufacturing overhead costs as period costs?

7–6   If the units produced equals the units sold, which method would you expect to show the higher net operating income, variable costing or absorption costing? Why?

7–7   If the units produced exceed the units sold, which method would you expect to show the higher net operating income, variable costing or absorption costing? Why?

7–8   If fixed manufacturing overhead costs are released from inventory under absorption costing, what does this tell you about the level of production in relation to the level of unit sales?

7–9   Under absorption costing, how is it possible to increase net operating income without increasing sales?

7–10   How does Lean Production reduce or eliminate the difference in reported net operating income between absorption and variable costing?

7–11   What is a segment of an organization? Give several examples of segments.

7–12   What costs are assigned to a segment under the contribution approach?

7–13   Distinguish between a traceable fixed cost and a common fixed cost. Give several examples of each.

7–14   Explain how the contribution margin differs from the segment margin.

7–15   Why aren't common fixed costs allocated to segments under the contribution approach?

7–16   How is it possible for a fixed cost that is traceable to a segment to become a common fixed cost if the segment is divided into further segments?

7–17   Should a company allocate its common fixed costs to business segments when computing the break-even point for those segments? Why?

## ☰ connect   CHAPTER 7: APPLYING EXCEL

LO7–2

The Excel worksheet form that appears below is to be used to recreate portions of Review Problem 1 relating to Dexter Corporation. Download the workbook containing this form from Connect, where you will also receive instructions about how to use this worksheet form.

You should proceed to the requirements below only after completing your worksheet. The LIFO inventory flow assumption is used throughout this problem.

| | A | B | C | D | E | F |
|---|---|---|---|---|---|---|
| 1 | Chapter 7: Applying Excel | | | | | |
| 2 | | | | | | |
| 3 | **Data** | | | | | |
| 4 | Selling price per unit | $50 | | | | |
| 5 | Manufacturing costs: | | | | | |
| 6 | Variable per unit produced: | | | | | |
| 7 | Direct materials | $11 | | | | |
| 8 | Direct labor | $6 | | | | |
| 9 | Variable manufacturing overhead | $3 | | | | |
| 10 | Fixed manufacturing overhead per year | $120,000 | | | | |
| 11 | Selling and administrative expenses: | | | | | |
| 12 | Variable per unit sold | $4 | | | | |
| 13 | Fixed per year | $70,000 | | | | |
| 14 | | | | | | |
| 15 | | Year 1 | Year 2 | | | |
| 16 | Units in beginning inventory | 0 | | | | |
| 17 | Units produced during the year | 10,000 | 6,000 | | | |
| 18 | Units sold during the year | 8,000 | 8,000 | | | |
| 19 | | | | | | |
| 20 | Enter a formula into each of the cells marked with a ? below | | | | | |
| 21 | **Review Problem 1: Contrasting Variable and Absorption Costing** | | | | | |
| 22 | | | | | | |
| 23 | *Compute the Ending Inventory* | | | | | |
| 24 | | Year 1 | Year 2 | | | |
| 25 | Units in beginning inventory | 0 | ? | | | |
| 26 | Units produced during the year | ? | ? | | | |
| 27 | Units sold during the year | ? | ? | | | |
| 28 | Units in ending inventory | ? | ? | | | |
| 29 | | | | | | |
| 30 | *Compute the Absorption Costing Unit Product Cost* | | | | | |
| 31 | | Year 1 | Year 2 | | | |
| 32 | Direct materials | ? | ? | | | |
| 33 | Direct labor | ? | ? | | | |
| 34 | Variable manufacturing overhead | ? | ? | | | |
| 35 | Fixed manufacturing overhead | ? | ? | | | |
| 36 | Absorption costing unit product cost | ? | ? | | | |
| 37 | | | | | | |
| 38 | *Construct the Absorption Costing Income Statement* | | | | | |
| 39 | | Year 1 | Year 2 | | | |
| 40 | Sales | ? | ? | | | |
| 41 | Cost of goods sold | ? | ? | | | |
| 42 | Gross margin | ? | ? | | | |
| 43 | Selling and administrative expenses | ? | ? | | | |
| 44 | Net operating income | ? | ? | | | |
| 45 | | | | | | |
| 46 | *Compute the Variable Costing Unit Product Cost* | | | | | |
| 47 | | Year 1 | Year 2 | | | |
| 48 | Direct materials | ? | ? | | | |
| 49 | Direct labor | ? | ? | | | |
| 50 | Variable manufacturing overhead | ? | ? | | | |
| 51 | Variable costing unit product cost | ? | ? | | | |
| 52 | | | | | | |
| 53 | *Construct the Variable Costing Income Statement* | | | | | |
| 54 | | | Year 1 | | Year 2 | |
| 55 | Sales | | ? | | ? | |
| 56 | Variable expenses: | | | | | |
| 57 | Variable cost of goods sold | ? | | ? | | |
| 58 | Variable selling and administrative expenses | ? | ? | ? | ? | |
| 59 | Contribution margin | | ? | | ? | |
| 60 | Fixed expenses: | | | | | |
| 61 | Fixed manufacturing overhead | ? | | ? | | |
| 62 | Fixed selling and administrative expenses | ? | ? | ? | ? | |
| 63 | Net operating income | | ? | | ? | |
| 64 | | | | | | |

**Required:**

1.  Check your worksheet by changing the units sold in the Data to 6,000 for Year 2. The cost of goods sold under absorption costing for Year 2 should now be $240,000. If it isn't, check cell C41. The formula in this cell should be =IF(C26<C27,C26*C36+(C27-C26)*B36,C27*C36). If your worksheet is operating properly, the net operating income under both absorption costing and variable costing should be $(34,000) for Year 2. That is, the loss in Year 2 is $34,000 under both methods. If you do not get these answers, find the errors in your worksheet and correct them.

    Why is the absorption costing net operating income now equal to the variable costing net operating income in Year 2?

2. Enter the following data from a different company into your worksheet:

| Data | |
|---|---|
| Selling price per unit.... | $75 |
| Manufacturing costs: | |
| Variable per unit produced: | |
| Direct materials .... | $12 |
| Direct labor.... | $5 |
| Variable manufacturing overhead .... | $7 |
| Fixed manufacturing overhead per year.... | $150,000 |
| Selling and administrative expenses: | |
| Variable per unit sold .... | $1 |
| Fixed per year .... | $60,000 |

| | Year 1 | Year 2 |
|---|---|---|
| Units in beginning inventory .... | 0 | |
| Units produced during the year .... | 15,000 | 10,000 |
| Units sold during the year .... | 12,000 | 12,000 |

Is the net operating income under variable costing different in Year 1 and Year 2? Why or why not? Explain the relation between the net operating income under absorption costing and variable costing in Year 1. Explain the relation between the net operating income under absorption costing and variable costing in Year 2.

3. At the end of Year 1, the company's board of directors set a target for Year 2 of net operating income of $500,000 under absorption costing. If this target is met, a hefty bonus would be paid to the CEO of the company. Keeping everything else the same from part (2) above, change the units produced in Year 2 to 50,000 units. Would this change result in a bonus being paid to the CEO? Do you think this change would be in the best interests of the company? What is likely to happen in Year 3 to the absorption costing net operating income if sales remain constant at 12,000 units per year?

**connect THE FOUNDATIONAL 15**

Diego Company manufactures one product that is sold for $80 per unit in two geographic regions—the East and West regions. The following information pertains to the company's first year of operations in which it produced 40,000 units and sold 35,000 units.

LO7–1, LO7–2, LO7–3, LO7–4, LO7–5

| Variable costs per unit: | |
|---|---|
| Manufacturing: | |
| Direct materials .... | $24 |
| Direct labor.... | $14 |
| Variable manufacturing overhead .... | $2 |
| Variable selling and administrative.... | $4 |
| Fixed costs per year: | |
| Fixed manufacturing overhead.... | $800,000 |
| Fixed selling and administrative expenses.... | $496,000 |

The company sold 25,000 units in the East region and 10,000 units in the West region. It determined that $250,000 of its fixed selling and administrative expense is traceable to the West region, $150,000 is traceable to the East region, and the remaining $96,000 is a common fixed expense. The company will continue to incur the total amount of its fixed manufacturing overhead costs as long as it continues to produce any amount of its only product.

*Required:*

Answer each question independently based on the original data unless instructed otherwise. You do not need to prepare a segmented income statement until question 13.

1. What is the unit product cost under variable costing?
2. What is the unit product cost under absorption costing?
3. What is the company's total contribution margin under variable costing?
4. What is the company's net operating income under variable costing?
5. What is the company's total gross margin under absorption costing?
6. What is the company's net operating income under absorption costing?
7. What is the amount of the difference between the variable costing and absorption costing net operating incomes? What is the cause of this difference?
8. What is the company's break-even point in unit sales? Is it above or below the actual unit sales? Compare the break-even point in unit sales to your answer for question 6 and comment.
9. If the sales volumes in the East and West regions had been reversed, what would be the company's overall break-even point in unit sales?
10. What would have been the company's variable costing net operating income if it had produced and sold 35,000 units? You do not need to perform any calculations to answer this question.
11. What would have been the company's absorption costing net operating income if it had produced and sold 35,000 units? You do not need to perform any calculations to answer this question.
12. If the company produces 5,000 fewer units than it sells in its second year of operations, will absorption costing net operating income be higher or lower than variable costing net operating income in Year 2? Why? No calculations are necessary.
13. Prepare a contribution format segmented income statement that includes a Total column and columns for the East and West regions.
14. Diego is considering eliminating the West region because an internally generated report suggests the region's total *gross margin* in the first year of operations was $50,000 less than its traceable fixed selling and administrative expenses. Diego believes that if it drops the West region, the East region's sales will grow by 5% in Year 2. Using the contribution approach for analyzing segment profitability and assuming all else remains constant in Year 2, what would be the profit impact of dropping the West region in Year 2?
15. Assume the West region invests $30,000 in a new advertising campaign in Year 2 that increases its unit sales by 20%. If all else remains constant, what would be the profit impact of pursuing the advertising campaign?

## EXERCISES

**connect**

### EXERCISE 7–1  Variable and Absorption Costing Unit Product Costs LO7–1

Ida Sidha Karya Company is a family-owned company located in the village of Gianyar on the island of Bali in Indonesia. The company produces a handcrafted Balinese musical instrument called a gamelan that is similar to a xylophone. The gamelans are sold for $850. Selected data for the company's operations last year follow:

| | |
|---|---|
| Units in beginning inventory | 0 |
| Units produced | 250 |
| Units sold | 225 |
| Units in ending inventory | 25 |
| Variable costs per unit: | |
|     Direct materials | $100 |
|     Direct labor | $320 |
|     Variable manufacturing overhead | $40 |
|     Variable selling and administrative | $20 |
| Fixed costs: | |
|     Fixed manufacturing overhead | $60,000 |
|     Fixed selling and administrative | $20,000 |

*Required:*

1. Assume that the company uses absorption costing. Compute the unit product cost for one gamelan.
2. Assume that the company uses variable costing. Compute the unit product cost for one gamelan.

**EXERCISE 7–2  Variable Costing Income Statement; Explanation of Difference in Net Operating Income LO7–2**

Refer to the data in Exercise 7–1 for Ida Sidha Karya Company. The absorption costing income statement prepared by the company's accountant for last year appears as shown:

| | |
|---|---|
| Sales | $191,250 |
| Cost of goods sold | 157,500 |
| Gross margin | 33,750 |
| Selling and administrative expense | 24,500 |
| Net operating income | $ 9,250 |

**Required:**
1. Under absorption costing, how much fixed manufacturing overhead cost is included in the company's inventory at the end of last year?
2. Prepare an income statement for last year using variable costing. What is the amount of the difference in net operating income between the two costing methods?

**EXERCISE 7–3  Reconciliation of Absorption and Variable Costing Net Operating Incomes LO7–3**

Jorgansen Lighting, Inc., manufactures heavy-duty street lighting systems for municipalities. The company uses variable costing for internal management reports and absorption costing for external reports to shareholders, creditors, and the government. The company has provided the following data:

| | Year 1 | Year 2 | Year 3 |
|---|---|---|---|
| Inventories: | | | |
| Beginning (units) | 200 | 170 | 180 |
| Ending (units) | 170 | 180 | 220 |
| Variable costing net operating income | $1,080,400 | $1,032,400 | $996,400 |

The company's fixed manufacturing overhead per unit was constant at $560 for all three years.

**Required:**
1. Calculate each year's absorption costing net operating income. Present your answer in the form of a reconciliation report.
2. Assume in Year 4 that the company's variable costing net operating income was $984,400 and its absorption costing net operating income was $1,012,400.
   a. Did inventories increase or decrease during Year 4?
   b. How much fixed manufacturing overhead cost was deferred or released from inventory during Year 4?

**EXERCISE 7–4  Basic Segmented Income Statement LO7–4**

Royal Lawncare Company produces and sells two packaged products—Weedban and Greengrow. Revenue and cost information relating to the products follow:

| | Product | |
|---|---|---|
| | Weedban | Greengrow |
| Selling price per unit | $6.00 | $7.50 |
| Variable expenses per unit | $2.40 | $5.25 |
| Traceable fixed expenses per year | $45,000 | $21,000 |

Common fixed expenses in the company total $33,000 annually. Last year the company produced and sold 15,000 units of Weedban and 28,000 units of Greengrow.

**Required:**
Prepare a contribution format income statement segmented by product lines.

**EXERCISE 7–5   Companywide and Segment Break-Even Analysis LO7–5**

Piedmont Company segments its business into two regions—North and South. The company prepared the contribution format segmented income statement as shown below:

| | Total Company | North | South |
|---|---|---|---|
| Sales ......................... | $600,000 | $400,000 | $200,000 |
| Variable expenses................ | 360,000 | 280,000 | 80,000 |
| Contribution margin .............. | 240,000 | 120,000 | 120,000 |
| Traceable fixed expenses ......... | 120,000 | 60,000 | 60,000 |
| Segment margin ................. | 120,000 | $ 60,000 | $ 60,000 |
| Common fixed expenses.......... | 50,000 | | |
| Net operating income............. | $ 70,000 | | |

**Required:**

1. Compute the companywide break-even point in dollar sales.
2. Compute the break-even point in dollar sales for the North region.
3. Compute the break-even point in dollar sales for the South region.

**EXERCISE 7–6   Variable and Absorption Costing Unit Product Costs and Income Statements LO7–1, LO7–2**

Lynch Company manufactures and sells a single product. The following costs were incurred during the company's first year of operations:

| | |
|---|---|
| Variable costs per unit: | |
| Manufacturing: | |
| Direct materials ........................... | $6 |
| Direct labor................................ | $9 |
| Variable manufacturing overhead ........... | $3 |
| Variable selling and administrative.............. | $4 |
| Fixed costs per year: | |
| Fixed manufacturing overhead................ | $300,000 |
| Fixed selling and administrative.............. | $190,000 |

During the year, the company produced 25,000 units and sold 20,000 units. The selling price of the company's product is $50 per unit.

**Required:**

1. Assume that the company uses absorption costing:
   a. Compute the unit product cost.
   b. Prepare an income statement for the year.
2. Assume that the company uses variable costing:
   a. Compute the unit product cost.
   b. Prepare an income statement for the year.

**EXERCISE 7–7   Segmented Income Statement LO7–4**

Shannon Company segments its income statement into its North and South Divisions. The company's overall sales, contribution margin ratio, and net operating income are $500,000, 46%, and $10,000, respectively. The North Division's contribution margin and contribution margin ratio are $150,000 and 50%, respectively. The South Division's segment margin is $30,000. The company has $90,000 of common fixed expenses that cannot be traced to either division.

**Required:**

Prepare an income statement for Shannon Company that uses the contribution format and is segmented by divisions. In addition, for the company as a whole and for each segment, show each item on the segmented income statements as a percent of sales.

**EXERCISE 7–8  Deducing Changes in Inventories LO7–3**
Parker Products, Inc. is a manufacturer whose absorption costing income statement reported sales of $123 million and a net operating loss of $18 million. According to a CVP analysis prepared for management, the company's break-even point is $115 million in sales.

**Required:**
Assuming that the CVP analysis is correct, is it likely that the company's inventory level increased, decreased, or remained unchanged during the year? Explain.

**EXERCISE 7–9  Variable and Absorption Costing Unit Product Costs and Income Statements LO7–1, LO7–2, LO7–3**
Walsh Company manufactures and sells one product. The following information pertains to each of the company's first two years of operations:

| Variable costs per unit: | |
|---|---|
| Manufacturing: | |
| Direct materials | $25 |
| Direct labor | $15 |
| Variable manufacturing overhead | $5 |
| Variable selling and administrative | $2 |
| Fixed costs per year: | |
| Fixed manufacturing overhead | $250,000 |
| Fixed selling and administrative expenses | $80,000 |

During its first year of operations, Walsh produced 50,000 units and sold 40,000 units. During its second year of operations, it produced 40,000 units and sold 50,000 units. The selling price of the company's product is $60 per unit.

**Required:**
1. Assume the company uses variable costing:
   a. Compute the unit product cost for Year 1 and Year 2.
   b. Prepare an income statement for Year 1 and Year 2.
2. Assume the company uses absorption costing:
   a. Compute the unit product cost for Year 1 and Year 2.
   b. Prepare an income statement for Year 1 and Year 2.
3. Explain the difference between variable costing and absorption costing net operating income in Year 1. Also, explain why the two net operating incomes differ in Year 2.

**EXERCISE 7–10  Companywide and Segment Break-Even Analysis LO7–5**
Crossfire Company segments its business into two regions—East and West. The company prepared a contribution format segmented income statement as shown below:

| | Total Company | East | West |
|---|---|---|---|
| Sales | $900,000 | $600,000 | $300,000 |
| Variable expenses | 675,000 | 480,000 | 195,000 |
| Contribution margin | 225,000 | 120,000 | 105,000 |
| Traceable fixed expenses | 141,000 | 50,000 | 91,000 |
| Segment margin | 84,000 | $ 70,000 | $ 14,000 |
| Common fixed expenses | 59,000 | | |
| Net operating income | $ 25,000 | | |

**Required:**
1. Compute the companywide break-even point in dollar sales.
2. Compute the break-even point in dollar sales for the East region.
3. Compute the break-even point in dollar sales for the West region.

4.  Prepare a new segmented income statement based on the break-even dollar sales that you computed in requirements 2 and 3. Use the same format as shown above. What is Crossfire's net operating income (loss) in your new segmented income statement?
5.  Do you think that Crossfire should allocate its common fixed expenses to the East and West regions when computing the break-even points for each region? Why?

**EXERCISE 7–11    Segmented Income Statement LO7–4**
Wingate Company, a wholesale distributor of electronic equipment, has been experiencing losses for some time, as shown by its most recent monthly contribution format income statement:

| | |
|---|---:|
| Sales ................................... | $1,000,000 |
| Variable expenses ..................... | 390,000 |
| Contribution margin ................... | 610,000 |
| Fixed expenses ........................ | 625,000 |
| Net operating income (loss) ........... | $ (15,000) |

In an effort to resolve the problem, the company would like to prepare an income statement segmented by division. Accordingly, the Accounting Department has developed the following information:

| | Division East | Division Central | Division West |
|---|---:|---:|---:|
| Sales ....................................... | $250,000 | $400,000 | $350,000 |
| Variable expenses as a percentage of sales ......... | 52% | 30% | 40% |
| Traceable fixed expenses ........................ | $160,000 | $200,000 | $175,000 |

*Required:*
1.  Prepare a contribution format income statement segmented by divisions.
2.  The Marketing Department has proposed increasing the West Division's monthly advertising by $15,000 based on the belief that it would increase that division's sales by 20%. Assuming these estimates are accurate, how much would the company's net operating income increase (decrease) if the proposal is implemented?

**EXERCISE 7–12    Variable Costing Income Statement; Reconciliation LO7–2, LO7–3**
Whitman Company has just completed its first year of operations. The company's absorption costing income statement for the year follows:

| Whitman Company Income Statement | |
|---|---:|
| Sales (35,000 units × $25 per unit) ................... | $875,000 |
| Cost of goods sold (35,000 units × $16 per unit) ....... | 560,000 |
| Gross margin ....................................... | 315,000 |
| Selling and administrative expenses ................. | 280,000 |
| Net operating income ............................... | $ 35,000 |

The company's selling and administrative expenses consist of $210,000 per year in fixed expenses and $2 per unit sold in variable expenses. The $16 unit product cost given above is computed as follows:

| | |
|---|---:|
| Direct materials .......................................... | $ 5 |
| Direct labor ............................................. | 6 |
| Variable manufacturing overhead ......................... | 1 |
| Fixed manufacturing overhead ($160,000 ÷ 40,000 units) .... | 4 |
| Absorption costing unit product cost ...................... | $16 |

**Required:**
1. Redo the company's income statement in the contribution format using variable costing.
2. Reconcile any difference between the net operating income on your variable costing income statement and the net operating income on the absorption costing income statement above.

**EXERCISE 7–13 Inferring Costing Method; Unit Product Cost LO7–1**

Sierra Company incurs the following costs to produce and sell its only product.

| | |
|---|---|
| Variable costs per unit: | |
| Direct materials ..................................... | $9 |
| Direct labor ........................................ | $10 |
| Variable manufacturing overhead ................ | $5 |
| Variable selling and administrative expenses ...... | $3 |
| Fixed costs per year: | |
| Fixed manufacturing overhead ................... | $150,000 |
| Fixed selling and administrative expenses ......... | $400,000 |

During this year, 25,000 units were produced and 22,000 units were sold. The Finished Goods inventory account at the end of this year shows a balance of $72,000 for the 3,000 unsold units.

**Required:**
1. Calculate this year's ending balance in Finished Goods inventory two ways—using variable costing and using absorption costing. Does it appear that the company is using variable costing or absorption costing to assign costs to the 3,000 units in its Finished Goods inventory?
2. Assume that the company wishes to prepare this year's financial statements for its stockholders.
   a. Is Finished Goods inventory of $72,000 the correct amount to include on the balance sheet for external reporting purposes? Explain.
   b. What balance should be reported in the Finished Goods inventory account for external reporting purposes?

**EXERCISE 7–14 Variable Costing Unit Product Cost and Income Statement; Break-Even Analysis LO7–1, LO7–2**

Chuck Wagon Grills, Inc., makes a single product—a handmade specialty barbecue grill that it sells for $210. Data for last year's operations follow:

| | |
|---|---|
| Units in beginning inventory ...................... | 0 |
| Units produced ................................... | 20,000 |
| Units sold ....................................... | 19,000 |
| Units in ending inventory ......................... | 1,000 |
| Variable costs per unit: | |
| Direct materials ............................... | $ 50 |
| Direct labor ................................... | 80 |
| Variable manufacturing overhead ............... | 20 |
| Variable selling and administrative .............. | 10 |
| Total variable cost per unit ..................... | $160 |
| Fixed costs: | |
| Fixed manufacturing overhead ................... | $700,000 |
| Fixed selling and administrative ................. | 285,000 |
| Total fixed costs ............................... | $985,000 |

**Required:**
1. Assume that the company uses variable costing. Compute the unit product cost for one barbecue grill.
2. Assume that the company uses variable costing. Prepare a contribution format income statement for last year.
3. What is the company's break-even point in terms of the number of barbecue grills sold?

**EXERCISE 7–15  Absorption Costing Unit Product Cost and Income Statement LO7–1, LO7–2**

Refer to the data in Exercise 7–14 for Chuck Wagon Grills. Assume in this exercise that the company uses absorption costing.

**Required:**
1. Compute the unit product cost for one barbecue grill.
2. Prepare an income statement for last year.

**EXERCISE 7–16  Working with a Segmented Income Statement; Break-Even Analysis LO7–4, LO7–5**

Raner, Harris & Chan is a consulting firm that specializes in information systems for medical and dental clinics. The firm has two offices—one in Chicago and one in Minneapolis. The firm classifies the direct costs of consulting jobs as variable costs. A contribution format segmented income statement for the company's most recent year is given:

| | Total Company | | Office Chicago | | Minneapolis | |
|---|---|---|---|---|---|---|
| Sales | $450,000 | 100% | $150,000 | 100% | $300,000 | 100% |
| Variable expenses | 225,000 | 50% | 45,000 | 30% | 180,000 | 60% |
| Contribution margin | 225,000 | 50% | 105,000 | 70% | 120,000 | 40% |
| Traceable fixed expenses | 126,000 | 28% | 78,000 | 52% | 48,000 | 16% |
| Office segment margin | 99,000 | 22% | $ 27,000 | 18% | $ 72,000 | 24% |
| Common fixed expenses not traceable to offices | 63,000 | 14% | | | | |
| Net operating income | $ 36,000 | 8% | | | | |

**Required:**
1. Compute the companywide break-even point in dollar sales. Also, compute the break-even point for the Chicago office and for the Minneapolis office. Is the companywide break-even point greater than, less than, or equal to the sum of the Chicago and Minneapolis break-even points? Why?
2. By how much would the company's net operating income increase if Minneapolis increased its sales by $75,000 per year? Assume no change in cost behavior patterns.
3. Refer to the original data. Assume that sales in Chicago increase by $50,000 next year and that sales in Minneapolis remain unchanged. Assume no change in fixed costs.
   a. Prepare a new segmented income statement for the company using the above format. Show both amounts and percentages.
   b. Observe from the income statement you have prepared that the contribution margin ratio for Chicago has remained unchanged at 70% (the same as in the above data) but that the segment margin ratio has changed. How do you explain the change in the segment margin ratio?

**EXERCISE 7–17  Working with a Segmented Income Statement LO7–4**

Refer to the data in Exercise 7–16. Assume that Minneapolis' sales by major market are:

| | Minneapolis | | Market Chicago | | Dental | |
|---|---|---|---|---|---|---|
| Sales | $300,000 | 100% | $200,000 | 100% | $100,000 | 100% |
| Variable expenses | 180,000 | 60% | 128,000 | 64% | 52,000 | 52% |
| Contribution margin | 120,000 | 40% | 72,000 | 36% | 48,000 | 48% |
| Traceable fixed expenses | 33,000 | 11% | 12,000 | 6% | 21,000 | 21% |
| Market segment margin | 87,000 | 29% | $ 60,000 | 30% | $ 27,000 | 27% |
| Common fixed expenses not traceable to markets | 15,000 | 5% | | | | |
| Office segment margin | $ 72,000 | 24% | | | | |

The company would like to initiate an intensive advertising campaign in one of the two market segments during the next month. The campaign would cost $5,000. Marketing studies indicate that such a campaign would increase sales in the Medical market by $40,000 or increase sales in the Dental market by $35,000.

**Required:**

1. How much would the company's profits increase (decrease) if it implemented the advertising campaign in the Medical Market?
2. How much would the company's profits increase (decrease) if it implemented the advertising campaign in the Dental Market?
3. In which of the markets would you recommend that the company focus its advertising campaign?
4. In Exercise 7–16, Minneapolis shows $48,000 in traceable fixed expenses. What happened to the $48,000 in this exercise?

**≡connect** PROBLEMS

**PROBLEM 7–18  Variable and Absorption Costing Unit Product Costs and Income Statements LO7–1, LO7–2**

Haas Company manufactures and sells one product. The following information pertains to each of the company's first three years of operations:

| | |
|---|---:|
| Variable costs per unit: | |
| Manufacturing: | |
| Direct materials | $20 |
| Direct labor | $12 |
| Variable manufacturing overhead | $4 |
| Variable selling and administrative | $2 |
| Fixed costs per year: | |
| Fixed manufacturing overhead | $960,000 |
| Fixed selling and administrative expenses | $240,000 |

During its first year of operations, Haas produced 60,000 units and sold 60,000 units. During its second year of operations, it produced 75,000 units and sold 50,000 units. In its third year, Haas produced 40,000 units and sold 65,000 units. The selling price of the company's product is $58 per unit.

**Required:**

1. Compute the company's break-even point in unit sales.
2. Assume the company uses variable costing:
   a. Compute the unit product cost for Year 1, Year 2, and Year 3.
   b. Prepare an income statement for Year 1, Year 2, and Year 3.
3. Assume the company uses absorption costing:
   a. Compute the unit product cost for Year 1, Year 2, and Year 3.
   b. Prepare an income statement for Year 1, Year 2, and Year 3.
4. Compare the net operating incomes that you computed in requirements 2 and 3 to the break-even point in unit sales that you computed in requirement 1. Which net operating income figures (variable costing or absorption costing) seem counterintuitive? Why?

**PROBLEM 7–19  Variable Costing Income Statement; Reconciliation LO7–2, LO7–3**

During Heaton Company's first two years of operations, it reported absorption costing net operating income as follows:

| | Year 1 | Year 2 |
|---|---:|---:|
| Sales (@ $25 per unit) | $1,000,000 | $1,250,000 |
| Cost of goods sold (@ $18 per unit) | 720,000 | 900,000 |
| Gross margin | 280,000 | 350,000 |
| Selling and administrative expenses* | 210,000 | 230,000 |
| Net operating income | $ 70,000 | $ 120,000 |

*$2 per unit variable; $130,000 fixed each year.

The company's $18 unit product cost is computed as follows:

| | |
|---|---:|
| Direct materials ........................................... | $ 4 |
| Direct labor ............................................... | 7 |
| Variable manufacturing overhead ........................... | 1 |
| Fixed manufacturing overhead ($270,000 ÷ 45,000 units) .... | 6 |
| Absorption costing unit product cost ....................... | $18 |

Forty percent of fixed manufacturing overhead consists of wages and salaries; the remainder consists of depreciation charges on production equipment and buildings.

Production and cost data for the first two years of operations are:

| | Year 1 | Year 2 |
|---|---|---|
| Units produced ......... | 45,000 | 45,000 |
| Units sold ............. | 40,000 | 50,000 |

**Required:**
1. Using variable costing, what is the unit product cost for both years?
2. What is the variable costing net operating income in Year 1 and in Year 2?
3. Reconcile the absorption costing and the variable costing net operating income figures for each year.

**PROBLEM 7–20   Variable and Absorption Costing Unit Product Costs and Income Statements; Explanation of Difference in Net Operating Income** LO7–1, LO7–2, LO7–3
High Country, Inc., produces and sells many recreational products. The company has just opened a new plant to produce a folding camp cot that will be marketed throughout the United States. The following cost and revenue data relate to May, the first month of the plant's operation:

| | |
|---|---:|
| Beginning inventory ..................................... | 0 |
| Units produced ........................................ | 10,000 |
| Units sold ............................................ | 8,000 |
| Selling price per unit ................................. | $75 |
| **Selling and administrative expenses:** | |
| Variable per unit .................................... | $6 |
| Fixed (per month) ................................... | $200,000 |
| **Manufacturing costs:** | |
| Direct materials cost per unit ....................... | $20 |
| Direct labor cost per unit ........................... | $8 |
| Variable manufacturing overhead cost per unit ...... | $2 |
| Fixed manufacturing overhead cost (per month) ..... | $100,000 |

Management is anxious to assess the profitability of the new camp cot during the month of May.

**Required:**
1. Assume that the company uses absorption costing.
   a. Determine the unit product cost.
   b. Prepare an income statement for May.
2. Assume that the company uses variable costing.
   a. Determine the unit product cost.
   b. Prepare a contribution format income statement for May.
3. Explain the reason for any difference in the ending inventory balances under the two costing methods and the impact of this difference on reported net operating income.

**PROBLEM 7–21  Segment Reporting and Decision-Making LO7–4**

Vulcan Company's contribution format income statement for June is as follows:

| Vulcan Company Income Statement For the Month Ended June 30 | |
|---|---|
| Sales | $750,000 |
| Variable expenses | 336,000 |
| Contribution margin | 414,000 |
| Fixed expenses | 378,000 |
| Net operating income | $ 36,000 |

Management is disappointed with the company's performance and is wondering what can be done to improve profits. By examining sales and cost records, you have determined the following:

a. The company is divided into two sales territories—Northern and Southern. The Northern territory recorded $300,000 in sales and $156,000 in variable expenses during June; the remaining sales and variable expenses were recorded in the Southern territory. Fixed expenses of $120,000 and $108,000 are traceable to the Northern and Southern territories, respectively. The rest of the fixed expenses are common to the two territories.

b. The company is the exclusive distributor for two products—Paks and Tibs. Sales of Paks and Tibs totaled $50,000 and $250,000, respectively, in the Northern territory during June. Variable expenses are 22% of the selling price for Paks and 58% for Tibs. Cost records show that $30,000 of the Northern territory's fixed expenses are traceable to Paks and $40,000 to Tibs, with the remainder common to the two products.

**Required:**

1. Prepare contribution format segmented income statements first showing the total company broken down between sales territories and then showing the Northern territory broken down by product line. In addition, for the company as a whole and for each segment, show each item on the segmented income statements as a percent of sales.
2. Look at the statement you have prepared showing the total company segmented by sales territory. What insights revealed by this statement should be mentioned to management?
3. Look at the statement you have prepared showing the Northern territory segmented by product lines. What insights revealed by this statement should be mentioned to management?

**PROBLEM 7–22  Variable Costing Income Statements; Income Reconciliation LO7–1, LO7–2, LO7–3**

Denton Company manufactures and sells a single product. Cost data for the product are given:

| Variable costs per unit: | |
|---|---|
| Direct materials | $ 7 |
| Direct labor | 10 |
| Variable manufacturing overhead | 5 |
| Variable selling and administrative | 3 |
| Total variable cost per unit | $25 |
| Fixed costs per month: | |
| Fixed manufacturing overhead | $315,000 |
| Fixed selling and administrative | 245,000 |
| Total fixed cost per month | $560,000 |

The product sells for $60 per unit. Production and sales data for July and August, the first two months of operations, follow:

| | Units Produced | Units Sold |
|---|---|---|
| July .................... | 17,500 | 15,000 |
| August .................. | 17,500 | 20,000 |

The company's Accounting Department has prepared the following absorption costing income statements for July and August:

| | July | August |
|---|---|---|
| Sales ...................................... | $900,000 | $1,200,000 |
| Cost of goods sold ........................ | 600,000 | 800,000 |
| Gross margin ............................. | 300,000 | 400,000 |
| Selling and administrative expenses ......... | 290,000 | 305,000 |
| Net operating income ...................... | $ 10,000 | $ 95,000 |

*Required:*
1. Determine the unit product cost under:
   a. Absorption costing.
   b. Variable costing.
2. Prepare contribution format variable costing income statements for July and August.
3. Reconcile the variable costing and absorption costing net operating incomes.
4. The company's Accounting Department has determined the company's break-even point to be 16,000 units per month, computed as follows:

$$\frac{\text{Fixed cost per month}}{\text{Unit contribution margin}} = \frac{\$560,000}{\$35 \text{ per unit}} = 16,000 \text{ units}$$

"I'm confused," said the president. "The accounting people say that our break-even point is 16,000 units per month, but we sold only 15,000 units in July, and the income statement they prepared shows a $10,000 profit for that month. Either the income statement is wrong or the break-even point is wrong." Prepare a brief memo for the president, explaining what happened on the July absorption costing income statement.

**PROBLEM 7–23    Absorption and Variable Costing; Production Constant, Sales Fluctuate LO7–1, LO7–2, LO7–3**
Tami Tyler opened Tami's Creations, Inc., a small manufacturing company, at the beginning of the year. Getting the company through its first quarter of operations placed a considerable strain on Ms. Tyler's personal finances. The following income statement for the first quarter was prepared by a friend who has just completed a course in managerial accounting at State University.

| Tami's Creations, Inc. Income Statement For the Quarter Ended March 31 | | |
|---|---|---|
| Sales (28,000 units) ...................... | | $1,120,000 |
| Variable expenses: | | |
|   Variable cost of goods sold .............. | $462,000 | |
|   Variable selling and administrative ........ | 168,000 | 630,000 |
| Contribution margin ....................... | | 490,000 |
| Fixed expenses: | | |
|   Fixed manufacturing overhead ............ | 300,000 | |
|   Fixed selling and administrative ........... | 200,000 | 500,000 |
| Net operating loss ....................... | | $ (10,000) |

Ms. Tyler is discouraged over the loss shown for the quarter, particularly because she had planned to use the statement as support for a bank loan. Another friend, a CPA, insists that the company should be using absorption costing rather than variable costing and argues that if absorption costing had been used the company probably would have reported at least some profit for the quarter.

At this point, Ms. Tyler is manufacturing only one product—a swimsuit. Production and cost data relating to the swimsuit for the first quarter follow:

| | |
|---|---|
| Units produced ............................. | 30,000 |
| Units sold .................................... | 28,000 |
| Variable costs per unit: | |
| Direct materials ........................... | $3.50 |
| Direct labor .............................. | $12.00 |
| Variable manufacturing overhead ............ | $1.00 |
| Variable selling and administrative ........... | $6.00 |

**Required:**
1.  Complete the following:
    a.  Compute the unit product cost under absorption costing.
    b.  What is the company's absorption costing net operating income (loss) for the quarter?
    c.  Reconcile the variable and absorption costing net operating income (loss) figures.
2.  Was the CPA correct in suggesting that the company really earned a "profit" for the quarter? Explain.
3.  During the second quarter of operations, the company again produced 30,000 units but sold 32,000 units. (Assume no change in total fixed costs.)
    a.  What is the company's variable costing net operating income (loss) for the second quarter?
    b.  What is the company's absorption costing net operating income (loss) for the second quarter?
    c.  Reconcile the variable costing and absorption costing net operating incomes for the second quarter.

**PROBLEM 7–24  Companywide and Segment Break-Even Analysis; Decision Making  LO7–4, LO7–5**
Toxaway Company is a merchandiser that segments its business into two divisions—Commercial and Residential. The company's accounting intern was asked to prepare segmented income statements that the company's divisional managers could use to calculate their break-even points and make decisions. She took the prior month's companywide income statement and prepared the absorption format segmented income statement shown below:

| | Total Company | Commercial | Residential |
|---|---|---|---|
| Sales ...................................... | $750,000 | $250,000 | $500,000 |
| Cost of goods sold ....................... | 500,000 | 140,000 | 360,000 |
| Gross margin ............................. | 250,000 | 110,000 | 140,000 |
| Selling and administrative expenses ........ | 240,000 | 104,000 | 136,000 |
| Net operating income .................... | $ 10,000 | $ 6,000 | $ 4,000 |

In preparing these statements, the intern determined that Toxaway's only variable selling and administrative expense is a 10% sales commission on all sales. The company's total fixed expenses include $72,000 of common fixed expenses that would continue to be incurred even if the Commercial or Residential segments are discontinued, $55,000 of fixed expenses that would be avoided if the Commericial segment is dropped, and $38,000 of fixed expenses that would be avoided if the Residential segment is dropped.

**Required:**
1.  Do you agree with the intern's decision to use an absorption format for her segmented income statement? Why?
2.  Based on a review of the intern's segmented income statement:
    a.  How much of the company's common fixed expenses did she allocate to the Commercial and Residential segments?
    b.  Which of the following three allocation bases did she most likely use to allocate common fixed expenses to the Commercial and Residential segments: (a) sales, (b) cost of goods sold, or (c) gross margin?
3.  Do you agree with the intern's decision to allocate the common fixed expenses to the Commercial and Residential segments? Why?

Chapter 7

4. Redo the intern's segmented income statement using the contribution format.
5. Compute the companywide break-even point in dollar sales.
6. Compute the break-even point in dollar sales for the Commercial Division and for the Residential Division.
7. Assume the company decided to pay its sales representatives in the Commercial and Residential Divisions a total monthly salary of $15,000 and $30,000, respectively, and to lower its companywide sales commission percentage from 10% to 5%. Calculate the new break-even point in dollar sales for the Commercial Division and the Residential Division.

**PROBLEM 7–25   Prepare and Interpret Income Statements; Changes in Both Sales and Production; Lean Production LO7–1, LO7–2, LO7–3**

Starfax, Inc., manufactures a small part that is widely used in various electronic products such as home computers. Results for the first three years of operations were as follows (absorption costing basis):

|  | Year 1 | Year 2 | Year 3 |
|---|---|---|---|
| Sales | $800,000 | $640,000 | $800,000 |
| Cost of goods sold | 580,000 | 400,000 | 620,000 |
| Gross margin | 220,000 | 240,000 | 180,000 |
| Selling and administrative expenses | 190,000 | 180,000 | 190,000 |
| Net operating income (loss) | $ 30,000 | $ 60,000 | $ (10,000) |

In the latter part of Year 2, a competitor went out of business and in the process dumped a large number of units on the market. As a result, Starfax's sales dropped by 20% during Year 2 even though production increased during the year. Management had expected sales to remain constant at 50,000 units; the increased production was designed to provide the company with a buffer of protection against unexpected spurts in demand. By the start of Year 3, management could see that it had excess inventory and that spurts in demand were unlikely. To reduce the excessive inventories, Starfax cut back production during Year 3, as shown below:

|  | Year 1 | Year 2 | Year 3 |
|---|---|---|---|
| Production in units | 50,000 | 60,000 | 40,000 |
| Sales in units | 50,000 | 40,000 | 50,000 |

Additional information about the company follows:

a. The company's plant is highly automated. Variable manufacturing expenses (direct materials, direct labor, and variable manufacturing overhead) total only $2 per unit, and fixed manufacturing overhead expenses total $480,000 per year.
b. A new fixed manufacturing overhead rate is computed each year based that year's actual fixed manufacturing overhead costs divided by the actual number of units produced.
c. Variable selling and administrative expenses were $1 per unit sold in each year. Fixed selling and administrative expenses totaled $140,000 per year.
d. The company uses a FIFO inventory flow assumption. (FIFO means first-in first-out. In other words, it assumes that the oldest units in inventory are sold first.)

Starfax's management can't understand why profits doubled during Year 2 when sales dropped by 20% and why a loss was incurred during Year 3 when sales recovered to previous levels.

*Required:*
1. Prepare a contribution format variable costing income statement for each year.
2. Refer to the absorption costing income statements above.
   a. Compute the unit product cost in each year under absorption costing. Show how much of this cost is variable and how much is fixed.
   b. Reconcile the variable costing and absorption costing net operating income figures for each year.
3. Refer again to the absorption costing income statements. Explain why net operating income was higher in Year 2 than it was in Year 1 under the absorption approach, in light of the fact that fewer units were sold in Year 2 than in Year 1.
4. Refer again to the absorption costing income statements. Explain why the company suffered a loss in Year 3 but reported a profit in Year 1 although the same number of units was sold in each year.
5. a. Explain how operations would have differed in Year 2 and Year 3 if the company had been using Lean Production, with the result that ending inventory was zero.
   b. If Lean Production had been used during Year 2 and Year 3, what would the company's net operating income (or loss) have been in each year under absorption costing? No computations are necessary.

**PROBLEM 7–26   Restructuring a Segmented Income Statement** LO7–4

Millard Corporation is a wholesale distributor of office products. It purchases office products from manufacturers and distributes them in the West, Central, and East regions. Each of these regions is about the same size and each has its own manager and sales staff.

The company has been experiencing losses for many months. In an effort to improve performance, management has requested that the monthly income statement be segmented by sales region. The company's first effort at preparing a segmented income statement for May is given below.

| | Sales Region | | |
| --- | --- | --- | --- |
| | West | Central | East |
| Sales . . . . . . . . . . . . . . . . . . . . . . . . . . . . . . . . . . . . . . | $450,000 | $800,000 | $750,000 |
| Regional expenses (traceable): | | | |
| Cost of goods sold . . . . . . . . . . . . . . . . . . . . . . . . . | 162,900 | 280,000 | 376,500 |
| Advertising . . . . . . . . . . . . . . . . . . . . . . . . . . . . . | 108,000 | 200,000 | 210,000 |
| Salaries . . . . . . . . . . . . . . . . . . . . . . . . . . . . . . . . | 90,000 | 88,000 | 135,000 |
| Utilities . . . . . . . . . . . . . . . . . . . . . . . . . . . . . . . . . | 13,500 | 12,000 | 15,000 |
| Depreciation . . . . . . . . . . . . . . . . . . . . . . . . . . . . | 27,000 | 28,000 | 30,000 |
| Shipping expense . . . . . . . . . . . . . . . . . . . . . . . . . | 17,100 | 32,000 | 28,500 |
| Total regional expenses . . . . . . . . . . . . . . . . . . . . . . | 418,500 | 640,000 | 795,000 |
| Regional income (loss) before corporate expenses . . . . | 31,500 | 160,000 | (45,000) |
| Corporate expenses: | | | |
| Advertising (general) . . . . . . . . . . . . . . . . . . . . . . . | 18,000 | 32,000 | 30,000 |
| General administrative expense . . . . . . . . . . . . . . . . . | 50,000 | 50,000 | 50,000 |
| Total corporate expenses . . . . . . . . . . . . . . . . . . . . . | 68,000 | 82,000 | 80,000 |
| Net operating income (loss) . . . . . . . . . . . . . . . . . . . | $ (36,500) | $ 78,000 | $(125,000) |

The cost of goods sold and shipping expense are both variable. All other costs are fixed.

*Required:*
1.   List any weaknesses that you see in the company's segmented income statement given above.
2.   Explain the basis that is apparently being used to allocate the corporate expenses to the regions. Do you agree with these allocations? Explain.
3.   Prepare a new contribution format segmented income statement for May. Show a Total column as well as data for each region. In addition, for the company as a whole and for each sales region, show each item on the segmented income statement as a percent of sales.
4.   Analyze the statement that you prepared in part (3) above. What insights do those statements reveal that you would bring to management's attention?

**PROBLEM 7–27   Variable and Absorption Costing Unit Product Costs and Income Statements** LO7–1, LO7–2

O'Brien Company manufactures and sells one product. The following information pertains to each of the company's first three years of operations:

| | |
| --- | --- |
| Variable costs per unit: | |
| Manufacturing: | |
| Direct materials . . . . . . . . . . . . . . . . . . . . . . . . . . . . . . . . . . . . . | $32 |
| Direct labor. . . . . . . . . . . . . . . . . . . . . . . . . . . . . . . . . . . . . . . . | $20 |
| Variable manufacturing overhead . . . . . . . . . . . . . . . . . . . . . . . | $4 |
| Variable selling and administrative. . . . . . . . . . . . . . . . . . . . . . . | $3 |
| Fixed costs per year: | |
| Fixed manufacturing overhead. . . . . . . . . . . . . . . . . . . . . . . . . . | $660,000 |
| Fixed selling and administrative expenses. . . . . . . . . . . . . . . . . | $120,000 |

During its first year of operations, O'Brien produced 100,000 units and sold 80,000 units. During its second year of operations, it produced 75,000 units and sold 90,000 units. In its third year, O'Brien produced 80,000 units and sold 75,000 units. The selling price of the company's product is $75 per unit.

**Required:**

1. Assume the company uses variable costing and a FIFO inventory flow assumption (FIFO means first-in first-out. In other words, it assumes that the oldest units in inventory are sold first):
   a. Compute the unit product cost for Year 1, Year 2, and Year 3.
   b. Prepare an income statement for Year 1, Year 2, and Year 3.
2. Assume the company uses variable costing and a LIFO inventory flow assumption (LIFO means last-in first-out. In other words, it assumes that the newest units in inventory are sold first):
   a. Compute the unit product cost for Year 1, Year 2, and Year 3.
   b. Prepare an income statement for Year 1, Year 2, and Year 3.
3. Assume the company uses absorption costing and a FIFO inventory flow assumption (FIFO means first-in first-out. In other words, it assumes that the oldest units in inventory are sold first):
   a. Compute the unit product cost for Year 1, Year 2, and Year 3.
   b. Prepare an income statement for Year 1, Year 2, and Year 3.
4. Assume the company uses absorption costing and a LIFO inventory flow assumption (LIFO means last-in first-out. In other words, it assumes that the newest units in inventory are sold first):
   a. Compute the unit product cost for Year 1, Year 2, and Year 3.
   b. Prepare an income statement for Year 1, Year 2, and Year 3.

## connect  BUILDING YOUR SKILLS

**ETHICS CHALLENGE LO7–2**

Carlos Cavalas, the manager of Echo Products' Brazilian Division, is trying to set the production schedule for the last quarter of the year. The Brazilian Division had planned to sell 3,600 units during the year, but by September 30 only the following activity had been reported:

|  | Units |
|---|---|
| Inventory, January 1 | 0 |
| Production | 2,400 |
| Sales | 2,000 |
| Inventory, September 30 | 400 |

The division can rent warehouse space to store up to 1,000 units. The minimum inventory level that the division should carry is 50 units. Mr. Cavalas is aware that production must be at least 200 units per quarter in order to retain a nucleus of key employees. Maximum production capacity is 1,500 units per quarter.

Demand has been soft, and the sales forecast for the last quarter is only 600 units. Due to the nature of the division's operations, fixed manufacturing overhead is a major element of product cost.

**Required:**

1. Assume that the division is using variable costing. How many units should be scheduled for production during the last quarter of the year? (The basic formula for computing the required production for the quarter is: Required production = Expected sales + Desired ending inventory − Beginning inventory.) Show computations and explain your answer. Will the number of units scheduled for production affect the division's reported income or loss for the year? Explain.
2. Assume that the division is using absorption costing and that the divisional manager is given an annual bonus based on divisional operating income. If Mr. Cavalas wants to maximize his division's operating income for the year, how many units should be scheduled for production during the last quarter? [See the formula in (1) above.] Explain.
3. Identify the ethical issues involved in the decision Mr. Cavalas must make about the level of production for the last quarter of the year.

**ANALYTICAL THINKING LO7–4**

Diversified Products, Inc., has recently acquired a small publishing company that offers three books for sale—a cookbook, a travel guide, and a handy speller. Each book sells for $10. The publishing company's most recent monthly income statement is shown below.

| | Total Company | | Product Line | |
|---|---|---|---|---|
| | | Cookbook | Travel Guide | Handy Speller |
| Sales .................................. | $300,000 | $90,000 | $150,000 | $60,000 |
| Expenses: | | | | |
| Printing costs ..................... | 102,000 | 27,000 | 63,000 | 12,000 |
| Advertising ....................... | 36,000 | 13,500 | 19,500 | 3,000 |
| General sales .................... | 18,000 | 5,400 | 9,000 | 3,600 |
| Salaries .......................... | 33,000 | 18,000 | 9,000 | 6,000 |
| Equipment depreciation............. | 9,000 | 3,000 | 3,000 | 3,000 |
| Sales commissions ................. | 30,000 | 9,000 | 15,000 | 6,000 |
| General administration ............. | 42,000 | 14,000 | 14,000 | 14,000 |
| Warehouse rent ................... | 12,000 | 3,600 | 6,000 | 2,400 |
| Depreciation—office facilities ........ | 3,000 | 1,000 | 1,000 | 1,000 |
| Total expenses ..................... | 285,000 | 94,500 | 139,500 | 51,000 |
| Net operating income (loss) ........... | $ 15,000 | $ (4,500) | $ 10,500 | $ 9,000 |

The following additional information is available:

a. Only printing costs and sales commissions are variable; all other costs are fixed. The printing costs (which include materials, labor, and variable overhead) are traceable to the three product lines as shown in the income statement above. Sales commissions are 10% of sales.

b. The same equipment is used to produce all three books, so the equipment depreciation expense has been allocated equally among the three product lines. An analysis of the company's activities indicates that the equipment is used 30% of the time to produce cookbooks, 50% of the time to produce travel guides, and 20% of the time to produce handy spellers.

c. The warehouse is used to store finished units of product, so the rental cost has been allocated to the product lines on the basis of sales dollars. The warehouse rental cost is $3 per square foot per year. The warehouse contains 48,000 square feet of space, of which 7,200 square feet is used by the cookbook line, 24,000 square feet by the travel guide line, and 16,800 square feet by the handy speller line.

d. The general sales cost above includes the salary of the sales manager and other sales costs not traceable to any specific product line. This cost has been allocated to the product lines on the basis of sales dollars.

e. The general administration cost and depreciation of office facilities both relate to administration of the company as a whole. These costs have been allocated equally to the three product lines.

f. All other costs are traceable to the three product lines in the amounts shown on the income statement above.

The management of Diversified Products, Inc., is anxious to improve the publishing company's 5% return on sales.

**Required:**

1. Prepare a new contribution format segmented income statement for the month. Adjust allocations of equipment depreciation and of warehouse rent as indicated by the additional information provided.

2. Based on the segmented income statements given in the problem, management plans to eliminate the cookbook because it is not returning a profit, and to focus all available resources on promoting the travel guide. However, based on the new contribution format segmented income statement that you prepared:

   a. Do you agree with management's plan to eliminate the cookbook? Explain.

   b. Do you agree with the decision to focus all available resources on promoting the travel guide? Assume that an ample market is available for all three product lines. (*Hint:* Compute the contribution margin ratio for each product.)

**CASE LO7–4**

Music Teachers, Inc., is an educational association for music teachers that has 20,000 members. The association operates from a central headquarters but has local membership chapters throughout the United States.

Monthly meetings are held by the local chapters to discuss recent developments on topics of interest to music teachers. The association's magazine, *Teachers' Forum,* is issued monthly with features about recent developments in the field. The association publishes books and reports and also sponsors professional courses that qualify for continuing professional education credit. The association's statement of revenues and expenses for the current year is presented below.

| Music Teachers, Inc. Statement of Revenues and Expenses For the Year Ended November 30 | |
| --- | --- |
| Revenues .......................................... | $3,275,000 |
| Expenses: | |
| Salaries ......................................... | 920,000 |
| Personnel costs ................................. | 230,000 |
| Occupancy costs ................................. | 280,000 |
| Reimbursement of member costs to local chapters ..... | 600,000 |
| Other membership services ....................... | 500,000 |
| Printing and paper .............................. | 320,000 |
| Postage and shipping ............................ | 176,000 |
| Instructors' fees ................................ | 80,000 |
| General and administrative ...................... | 38,000 |
| Total expenses .................................. | 3,144,000 |
| Excess of revenues over expenses .................. | $  131,000 |

The board of directors of Music Teachers, Inc., has requested that a segmented income statement be prepared showing the contribution of each segment to the association. The association has four segments: Membership Division, Magazine Subscriptions Division, Books and Reports Division, and Continuing Education Division. Mike Doyle has been assigned responsibility for preparing the segmented income statement, and he has gathered the following data:

a.  The 20,000 members of the association pay dues of $100 per year, of which $20 covers a one-year subscription to the *Teachers' Forum.* Other benefits include membership in the association and chapter affiliation. The portion of the dues covering the magazine subscription ($20) should be assigned to the Magazine Subscriptions Division.
b.  A total of 2,500 one-year subscriptions to *Teachers' Forum* were also sold last year to nonmembers and libraries at $30 per subscription. In addition to subscriptions, the journal generated $100,000 in advertising revenues.
c.  The costs to produce the *Teachers' Forum* magazine included $7 per subscription for printing and paper and $4 per subscription for postage and shipping.
d.  A total of 28,000 technical reports and professional texts were sold by the Books and Reports Division at an average selling price per unit of $25. Average costs per publication were $4 for printing and paper and $2 for postage and shipping.
e.  The association offers a variety of continuing education courses to both members and nonmembers. The one-day courses had a tuition cost of $75 each and were attended by 2,400 students. A total of 1,760 students took two-day courses at a tuition cost of $125 for each student. Outside instructors were paid to teach some courses.

f. Salary costs and space occupied by division follow:

| | Salaries | Space Occupied (square feet) |
|---|---|---|
| Membership ................ | $210,000 | 2,000 |
| Magazine Subscriptions ....... | 150,000 | 2,000 |
| Books and Reports ........... | 300,000 | 3,000 |
| Continuing Education ......... | 180,000 | 2,000 |
| Corporate staff .............. | 80,000 | 1,000 |
| Total ...................... | $920,000 | 10,000 |

Personnel costs are 25% of salaries in the separate divisions as well as for the corporate staff. The $280,000 in occupancy costs includes $50,000 in rental cost for a warehouse used by the Books and Reports Division for storage purposes.

g. Printing and paper costs other than for magazine subscriptions and for books and reports relate to the Continuing Education Division.

h. General and administrative expenses include costs relating to overall administration of the association as a whole. The company's corporate staff does some mailing of materials for general administrative purposes.

The expenses that can be traced or assigned to the corporate staff, as well as any other expenses that are not traceable to the segments, will be treated as common costs. It is not necessary to distinguish between variable and fixed costs.

**Required:**

1. Prepare a segmented income statement for Music Teachers, Inc. This statement should show the segment margin for each division as well as results for the association as a whole.
2. Give arguments for and against allocating all costs of the association to the four divisions.

(CMA, adapted)

**A LOOK BACK**

Chapter 7 explained how the contribution format can be used to create variable costing income statements for manufacturers and segmented income statements that distinguish between traceable fixed costs and common fixed costs. It also contrasted variable costing with the absorption format.

**A LOOK AT THIS CHAPTER**

After discussing why organizations prepare budgets and the process they use to create a budget, Chapter 8 overviews each of the parts of a master budget including the cash budget, the budgeted income statement, and the budgeted balance sheet.

**A LOOK AHEAD**

In Chapter 9 we turn our attention from the planning process to management control, focusing on the use of flexible budgets and variance analysis.

# Master Budgeting

## CHAPTER OUTLINE

**Why and How Do Organizations Create Budgets?**

- Advantages of Budgeting
- Responsibility Accounting
- Choosing a Budget Period
- The Self-Imposed Budget
- Human Factors in Budgeting

**The Master Budget: An Overview**

- Seeing the Big Picture

**Preparing the Master Budget**

- The Beginning Balance Sheet
- The Budgeting Assumptions

- The Sales Budget
- The Production Budget
- Inventory Purchases—Merchandising Company
- The Direct Materials Budget
- The Direct Labor Budget
- The Manufacturing Overhead Budget
- The Ending Finished Goods Inventory Budget
- The Selling and Administrative Budget
- The Cash Budget
- The Budgeted Income Statement
- The Budgeted Balance Sheet

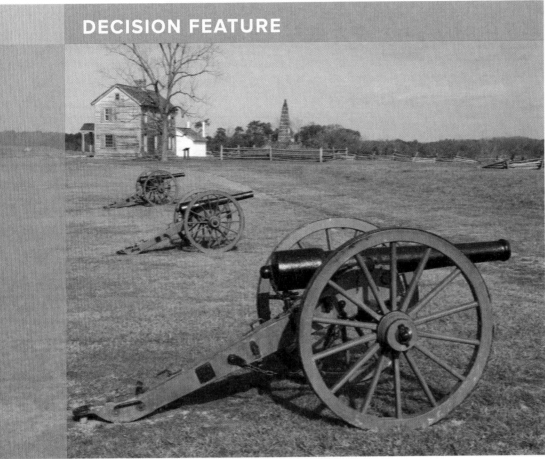

©Sandee Noreen

# Planning for a Crisis—Civil War Trust

The **Civil War Trust** (CWT) is a private, nonprofit organization with 70,000 members that works to preserve the nation's remaining Civil War battlefields—many of which are threatened by commercial development such as shopping centers, houses, industrial parks, and casinos. To forestall development, the CWT typically purchases the land or development rights to the land. The CWT has saved over 25,000 acres from development, including, for example, 698 acres of battlefield at Gettysburg.

The CWT is wholly supported by contributions from its members. When the economy stagnates it complicates the CWT's ability to predict the amount of future donations. The CWT responds to this uncertainty by creating an annual budget that contains three variations based on progressively pessimistic economic assumptions. The more pessimistic budgets were called contingent budgets. If member contributions decline somewhat due to economic woes, the CWT can switch to its first contingent budget. In the past, rolling to the contingent budget has required a number of actions to reduce costs including a hiring freeze and a salary freeze while maintaining an aggressive program of protecting battlefield acreage through purchases of land and development rights. In more dire circumstances, the CWT can switch to its most pessimistic budget—which would involve layoffs and other extraordinary cost-saving measures.

Instead of reacting in a panic mode to unfavorable developments, CWT uses the budgeting process to carefully plan in advance for a number of possible contingencies.

Sources: Communications with James Lighthizer, president, and David Duncan, director of membership and development, Civil War Trust; and the CWT website, www.civilwar.orgw

## LEARNING OBJECTIVES

*After studying Chapter 8, you should be able to:*

**LO8–1** Understand why organizations budget and the processes they use to create budgets.

**LO8–2** Prepare a sales budget, including a schedule of expected cash collections.

**LO8–3** Prepare a production budget.

**LO8–4** Prepare a direct materials budget, including a schedule of expected cash disbursements for purchases of materials.

**LO8–5** Prepare a direct labor budget.

**LO8–6** Prepare a manufacturing overhead budget.

**LO8–7** Prepare a selling and administrative expense budget.

**LO8–8** Prepare a cash budget.

**LO8–9** Prepare a budgeted income statement.

**LO8–10** Prepare a budgeted balance sheet.

**I**n **this chapter,** we describe how organizations strive to achieve their financial goals by preparing *budgets*. A **budget** is a detailed plan for the future that is usually expressed in formal quantitative terms. Individuals sometimes create household budgets that balance their income and expenditures for food, clothing, housing, and so on while providing for some savings. Once the budget is established, actual spending is compared to the budget to make sure the plan is being followed. Companies use budgets in a similar way, although the amount of work and underlying details far exceed a personal budget.

# WHY AND HOW DO ORGANIZATIONS CREATE BUDGETS?

Budgets are used for two distinct purposes—*planning* and *control*. **Planning** involves developing goals and preparing various budgets to achieve those goals. **Control** involves gathering feedback to ensure that the plan is being properly executed or modified as circumstances change. To be effective, a good budgeting system must provide for both planning and control. Good planning without effective control is a waste of time and effort.

## Advantages of Budgeting

Organizations realize many benefits from budgeting, including:

1. Budgets *communicate* management's plans throughout the organization.
2. Budgets force managers to *think about* and *plan* for the future. In the absence of the necessity to prepare a budget, many managers would spend all of their time dealing with day-to-day emergencies.
3. The budgeting process provides a means of *allocating resources* to those parts of the organization where they can be used most effectively.
4. The budgeting process can uncover potential *bottlenecks* before they occur.
5. Budgets *coordinate* the activities of the entire organization by *integrating* the plans of its various parts. Budgeting helps to ensure that everyone in the organization is pulling in the same direction.
6. Budgets define goals and objectives that can serve as *benchmarks* for evaluating subsequent performance.

## IN BUSINESS | A Critical Prespective of How Companies Use Budgets

©Morsa Images/Getty Images RF

Most, if not all, companies operate in dynamic environments where the only constant is change. The large majority of these companies also rely on annual budgets to manage themselves. The question becomes: at what point do changes in the business environment render an annual budget obsolete? When 152 business professionals were asked this question 13% of them said their company's annual budget becomes obsolete before the new budget year begins. Another 46% of respondents said the budget becomes obsolete before the second quarter of the budget year concludes, whereas 25% of those surveyed said the budget never becomes obsolete.

Given that approximately 60% of respondents expressed concerns over obsolescence, it begged a related question for the 152 respondents: how many "what if" forecasts does your company prepare in response to changing market conditions? About 20% of the respondents said their company did not evaluate any "what if" scenarios. Another 60% of respondents said their employers evaluated no more than six "what if" scenarios.

Source: Merchant, Kenneth A., "Companies Get Budgets All Wrong," *The Wall Street Journal,* July 22, 2013, p. R5.

# Responsibility Accounting

Most of what we say in this chapter and in the next three chapters is concerned with *responsibility accounting*. The basic idea underlying **responsibility accounting** is that a manager should be held responsible for those items—and *only* those items—that the manager can actually control to a significant extent. Each line item (i.e., revenue or cost) in the budget is the responsibility of a manager who is held responsible for subsequent deviations between budgeted goals and actual results. In effect, responsibility accounting *personalizes* accounting information by holding individuals responsible for revenues and costs. This concept is central to any effective planning and control system. Someone must be held responsible for each cost or else no one will be responsible and the cost will inevitably grow out of control.

What happens if actual results do not measure up to the budgeted goals? The manager is not necessarily penalized. However, the manager should take the initiative to understand the sources of significant favorable or unfavorable discrepancies, should take steps to correct unfavorable discrepancies and to exploit and replicate favorable discrepancies, and should be prepared to explain discrepancies and the steps taken to correct or exploit them to higher management. The point of an effective responsibility accounting system is to make sure that nothing "falls through the cracks," that the organization reacts quickly and appropriately to deviations from its plans, and that the organization learns from the feedback it gets by comparing budgeted goals to actual results. The point is *not* to penalize individuals for missing targets.

# Choosing a Budget Period

Operating budgets ordinarily cover a one-year period corresponding to the company's fiscal year. Many companies divide their budget year into four quarters. The first quarter is then subdivided into months, and monthly budgets are developed. The last three quarters may be carried in the budget as quarterly totals only. As the year progresses, the figures for the second quarter are broken down into monthly amounts, then the third-quarter figures are broken down, and so forth. This approach has the advantage of requiring periodic review and reappraisal of budget data throughout the year.

*Continuous* or *perpetual budgets* are sometimes used. A **continuous** or **perpetual budget** is a 12-month budget that rolls forward one month (or quarter) as the current month (or quarter) is completed. In other words, one month (or quarter) is added to the end of the budget as each month (or quarter) comes to a close. This approach keeps managers focused at least one year ahead so that they do not become too narrowly focused on short-term results.

In this chapter, we will look at one-year operating budgets. However, using basically the same techniques, operating budgets can be prepared for periods that extend over many years. It may be difficult to accurately forecast sales and other data much beyond a year, but even rough estimates can be invaluable in uncovering potential problems and opportunities that would otherwise be overlooked.

# The Self-Imposed Budget

The success of a budget program is largely determined by the way a budget is developed. Oftentimes, the budget is imposed from above, with little participation by lower-level managers. However, in the most successful budget programs, managers actively participate in preparing their own budgets. Imposing expectations from above and then penalizing employees who do not meet those expectations will generate resentment rather than cooperation and commitment. In fact, many managers believe that being empowered to create their own *self-imposed budgets* is the most effective method of budget preparation. A **self-imposed budget** or **participative budget** is a budget that is prepared with the full cooperation and participation of managers at all levels.

Self-imposed budgets have a number of advantages:

1. Individuals at all levels of the organization are recognized as members of the team whose views and judgments are valued by top management.
2. Budget estimates prepared by front-line managers are often more accurate and reliable than estimates prepared by top managers who have less intimate knowledge of markets and day-to-day operations.
3. Motivation is generally higher when individuals participate in setting their own goals than when the goals are imposed from above. Self-imposed budgets create commitment.
4. A manager who is not able to meet a budget that has been imposed from above can always say that the budget was unrealistic and impossible to meet. With a self-imposed budget, this claim cannot be made.

Self-imposed budgeting has two important limitations. First, lower-level managers may make suboptimal budgeting recommendations if they lack the broad strategic perspective possessed by top managers. Second, self-imposed budgeting may allow lower-level managers to create too much *budgetary slack*. Because the manager who creates the budget will be held accountable for actual results that deviate from the budget, the manager will have a natural tendency to submit a budget that is easy to attain (i.e., the manager will build slack into the budget). For this reason, budgets prepared by lower-level managers should be scrutinized by higher levels of management. Questionable items should be discussed and modified as appropriate. Without such a review, self-imposed budgets may fail to support the organization's strategy or may be too slack, resulting in suboptimal performance.

Unfortunately, many companies do not use self-imposed budgeting. Instead, top managers often initiate the budgeting process by issuing profit targets. Lower-level managers are directed to prepare budgets that meet those targets. The difficulty is that the targets set by top managers may be unrealistically high or may allow too much slack. If the targets are too high and employees know they are unrealistic, motivation will suffer. If the targets allow too much slack, waste will occur. Unfortunately, top managers often are not in a position to know whether the targets are appropriate. Admittedly, a self-imposed budgeting system may lack sufficient strategic direction and lower-level managers may be tempted to build slack into their budgets. Nevertheless, because of the motivational advantages of self-imposed budgets, top managers should be cautious about imposing inflexible targets from above.

## Human Factors in Budgeting

The success of a budget program also depends on whether top management uses the budget to pressure or blame employees. Using budgets to blame employees breeds hostility, tension, and mistrust rather than cooperation and productivity. Unfortunately, the budget is too often used as a pressure device and excessive emphasis is placed on "meeting the budget" under all circumstances. Rather than being used as a weapon, the budget should be used as a positive instrument to assist in establishing goals, measuring operating results, and isolating areas that need attention.

The budgeting process also is influenced by the fact that bonuses are often based on meeting and exceeding budgets. Typically, no bonus is paid unless the budget is met. The bonus often increases when the budget target is exceeded, but the bonus is usually capped out at some level. For obvious reasons, managers who have such a bonus plan or whose performance is evaluated based on meeting budget targets usually prefer to be evaluated based on highly achievable budgets. Moreover, highly achievable budgets may help build a manager's confidence and generate greater commitment to the budget while also reducing the likelihood that a manager will engage in undesirable behavior at the end of budgetary periods to secure bonus compensation. So, while some experts argue that budget targets should be very challenging and should require managers to stretch to meet their goals, in practice, most companies set their budget targets at "highly achievable" levels.

1. Which of the following statements is false? (You may select more than one answer.)
   a. Control involves gathering feedback to ensure that the plan is being properly executed or modified as circumstances change.
   b. Responsibility accounting is based on the belief that all managers should be held accountable for achieving the company's overall goals, even if this requires holding some managers responsible for items that are beyond their control.
   c. A self-imposed budget is prepared with the full cooperation and participation of managers at all levels of the organization.
   d. One limitation of self-imposed budgets is that lower-level managers may allow too much budgetary slack.

## THE MASTER BUDGET: AN OVERVIEW

For the remainder of the chapter, we are going to illustrate a type of integrated business plan known as a *master budget*. The **master budget** consists of a number of separate but interdependent budgets that formally lay out the company's sales, production, and financial goals. The master budget culminates in a cash budget, a budgeted income statement, and a budgeted balance sheet. Exhibit 8–1 provides an overview of the various parts of the master budget and how they are related.

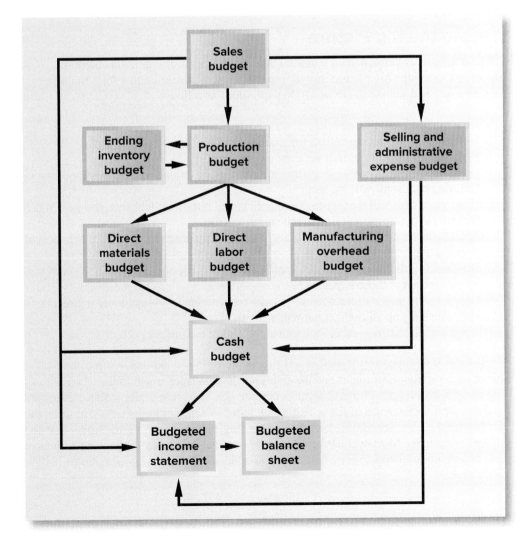

**EXHIBIT 8–1**
The Master Budget
Interrelationships

The first step in the budgeting process is preparing a **sales budget**, which is a detailed schedule showing the expected sales for the budget period. An accurate sales budget is the key to the entire budgeting process. As illustrated in Exhibit 8–1, all other parts of the master budget depend on the sales budget. If the sales budget is inaccurate, the rest of the budget will be inaccurate. The sales budget is based on the company's sales forecast, which may require the use of sophisticated mathematical models and statistical tools that are beyond the scope of this course.

The sales budget influences the variable portion of the selling and administrative expense budget and it feeds into the production budget, which defines how many units need to be produced during the budget period. The production budget in turn is used to determine the direct materials, direct labor, and manufacturing overhead budgets. Once a company has prepared these three manufacturing cost budgets, it can prepare the ending finished goods inventory budget.

The master budget concludes with the preparation of a cash budget, income statement, and balance sheet. Information from the sales budget, selling and administrative expense budget, and the manufacturing cost budgets all influence the preparation of the *cash budget*. A **cash budget** is a detailed plan showing how cash resources will be acquired and used. The budgeted income statement provides an estimate of net income for the budget period and it relies on information from the sales budget, ending finished goods inventory budget, selling and administrative expense budget, and the cash budget. The final schedule of the master budget is the balance sheet, which estimates a company's assets, liabilities, and stockholders' equity at the end of a budget period.

## Seeing the Big Picture

The 10 schedules contained in a master budget can be overwhelming; therefore, it is important to see the big picture in two respects. First, a master budget for a manufacturing company is designed to answer 10 key questions as follows:

1. How much sales will we earn?
2. How much cash will we collect from customers?
3. How much raw material will we need to purchase?
4. How much manufacturing cost (including direct materials, direct labor, and manufacturing overhead) will we incur?
5. How much cash will we pay to our suppliers and our direct laborers, and how much will we pay for manufacturing overhead resources?
6. What is the total cost that will be transferred from finished goods inventory to cost of goods sold?
7. How much selling and administrative expense will we incur and how much cash will we pay related to those expenses?
8. How much money will we borrow from or repay to lenders—including interest?
9. How much net operating income will we earn?
10. What will our balance sheet look like at the end of the budget period?

Second, it is important to understand that many of the schedules in a master budget hinge on a variety of estimates and assumptions that managers must make when preparing those schedules. Exhibit 8–2 summarizes the questions that underlie these estimates and assumptions for seven of the schedules included in a master budget. As you study the forthcoming budget schedules, keep these two "big picture" insights in mind—that the budget is designed to answer 10 key questions and that it is based on various estimates and assumptions—because they will help you understand *why* and *how* a master budget is created.

**Sales budget:**
1. What are the budgeted unit sales?
2. What is the budgeted selling price per unit?
3. What percentage of accounts receivable will be collected in the current and subsequent periods?

**Production budget:**
1. What percentage of next period's unit sales needs to be maintained in ending finished goods inventory?

**Direct materials budget:**
1. How many units of raw material are needed to make one unit of finished goods?
2. What is the budgeted cost for one unit of raw material?
3. What percentage of next period's production needs should be maintained in ending raw materials inventory?
4. What percentage of raw material purchases will be paid in the current and subsequent periods?

**Direct labor budget:**
1. How many direct labor-hours are required per unit of finished goods?
2. What is the budgeted direct labor wage rate per hour?

**Manufacturing overhead budget:**
1. What is the budgeted variable overhead cost per unit of the allocation base?
2. What is the total budgeted fixed overhead cost per period?
3. What is the budgeted depreciation expense on factory assets per period?

**Selling and administrative expense budget:**
1. What is the budgeted variable selling and administrative expense per unit sold?
2. What is the total budgeted fixed selling and administrative expense per period?
3. What is the budgeted depreciation expense on non-factory assets per period?

**Cash budget:**
1. What is the budgeted minimum cash balance?
2. What are our estimated expenditures for noncurrent asset purchases and dividends?
3. What is the estimated interest rate on borrowed funds?

**EXHIBIT 8–2**
Estimates and Assumptions for a Master Budget

# PREPARING THE MASTER BUDGET

Tom Wills is the majority stockholder and chief executive officer of Hampton Freeze, Inc., a company he started in 2016. The company makes premium popsicles using only natural ingredients and featuring exotic flavors such as tangy tangerine and minty mango. The company's business is highly seasonal, with most of the sales occurring in spring and summer.

In 2017, the company's second year of operations, a major cash crunch in the first and second quarters almost forced the company into bankruptcy. In spite of this cash crunch, 2017 turned out to be a very successful year in terms of both cash flow and net income. Partly as a result of that harrowing experience, Tom decided toward the end of 2017 to hire a professional financial manager. Tom interviewed several promising candidates for the job and settled on Larry Giano, who had considerable experience in the packaged foods industry. In the job interview, Tom questioned Larry about the steps he would take to prevent a recurrence of the 2017 cash crunch:

**Tom:** As I mentioned earlier, we are going to end 2017 with a very nice profit. What you may not know is that we had some very big financial problems this year.

**Larry:** Let me guess. You ran out of cash sometime in the first or second quarter.

*Tom:* How did you know?

*Larry:* Most of your sales are in the second and third quarter, right?

*Tom:* Sure, everyone wants to buy popsicles in the spring and summer, but nobody wants them when the weather turns cold.

*Larry:* So you don't have many sales in the first quarter?

*Tom:* Right.

*Larry:* And in the second quarter, which is the spring, you are producing like crazy to fill orders?

*Tom:* Sure.

*Larry:* Do your customers, the grocery stores, pay you the day you make your deliveries?

*Tom:* Are you kidding? Of course not.

*Larry:* So in the first quarter, you don't have many sales. In the second quarter, you are producing like crazy, which eats up cash, but you aren't paid by your customers until long after you have paid your employees and suppliers. No wonder you had a cash problem. I see this pattern all the time in food processing because of the seasonality of the business.

*Tom:* So what can we do about it?

*Larry:* The first step is to predict the magnitude of the problem before it occurs. If we can predict early in the year what the cash shortfall is going to be, we can go to the bank and arrange for credit before we really need it. Bankers tend to be leery of panicky people who show up begging for emergency loans. They are much more likely to make the loan if you look like you are in control of the situation.

*Tom:* How can we predict the cash shortfall?

*Larry:* You can put together a cash budget. In fact, while you're at it, you might as well do a master budget. You'll find it well worth the effort because we can use a master budget to estimate the financial statement implications of numerous "what if" questions. For example, with the click of a mouse we can answer questions such as: what if unit sales are 10% less than our original forecast, what will be the impact on profits? Or, what if we increase our selling price by 15% and unit sales drop by 5%, what will be the impact on profits?

*Tom:* That sounds great, Larry! Not only do we need a cash budget, but I would love to have a master budget that could quickly answer the types of "what if" questions that you just described. As far as I'm concerned, the sooner you get started, the better.

With the full backing of Tom Wills, Larry Giano set out to create a master budget for the company for the year 2018. In his planning for the budgeting process, Larry drew up the following list of documents that would be a part of the master budget:

1. A sales budget, including a schedule of expected cash collections.
2. A production budget (a merchandise purchases budget would be used in a merchandising company).
3. A direct materials budget, including a schedule of expected cash disbursements for purchases of materials.
4. A direct labor budget.
5. A manufacturing overhead budget.
6. An ending finished goods inventory budget.
7. A selling and administrative expense budget.
8. A cash budget.
9. A budgeted income statement.
10. A budgeted balance sheet.

Larry felt it was important to have everyone's cooperation in the budgeting process, so he asked Tom to call a companywide meeting to explain the budgeting process.

At the meeting there was initially some grumbling, but Tom was able to convince nearly everyone of the necessity for planning and getting better control over spending. It helped that the cash crisis earlier in the year was still fresh in everyone's minds. As much as some people disliked the idea of budgets, they liked their jobs more.

In the months that followed, Larry worked closely with all of the managers involved in the master budget, gathering data from them and making sure that they understood and fully supported the parts of the master budget that would affect them.

The interdependent documents that Larry Giano prepared for Hampton Freeze are Schedules 1 through 10 of the company's master budget. In this section, we will study these schedules as well as the beginning balance sheet and the budgeting assumptions that Larry included in his master budget to help answer the types of "what if" questions that he discussed with Tom Wills.

## The Beginning Balance Sheet

Exhibit 8–3 shows the first tab included in Larry's Microsoft Excel master budget file. It contains Hampton Freeze's beginning balance sheet as of December 31, 2017. Larry included this balance sheet in his master budget file so he could link some of this data to subsequent schedules. For example, as you'll eventually see, he used cell references

|  | A | B | C |
|---|---|---|---|
| 1 | **Hampton Freeze, Inc.** | | |
| 2 | **Balance Sheet** | | |
| 3 | **December 31, 2017** | | |
| 4 | | | |
| 5 | **Assets** | | |
| 6 | Current assets: | | |
| 7 | Cash | $ 42,500 | |
| 8 | Accounts receivable | 90,000 | |
| 9 | Raw materials inventory (21,000 pounds) | 4,200 | |
| 10 | Finished goods inventory (2,000 cases) | 26,000 | |
| 11 | Total current assets | | $ 162,700 |
| 12 | Plant and equipment: | | |
| 13 | Land | 80,000 | |
| 14 | Buildings and equipment | 700,000 | |
| 15 | Accumulated depreciation | (292,000) | |
| 16 | Plant and equipment, net | | 488,000 |
| 17 | Total assets | | $ 650,700 |
| 18 | | | |
| 19 | **Liabilities and Stockholders' Equity** | | |
| 20 | Current liabilities: | | |
| 21 | Accounts payable | | $ 25,800 |
| 22 | Stockholders' equity: | | |
| 23 | Common stock | $ 175,000 | |
| 24 | Retained earnings | 449,900 | |
| 25 | Total stockholders' equity | | 624,900 |
| 26 | Total liabilities and stockholders' equity | | $ 650,700 |
| 27 | | | |

Beginning Balance Sheet / Budgeting Assump

Source: Microsoft

within Excel to link the beginning accounts receivable balance of $90,000 to the schedule of expected cash collections. He also used cell references to link the beginning cash balance of $42,500 to the cash budget.

## The Budgeting Assumptions

Exhibit 8–4 shows the second tab included in Larry's master budget file. It is labeled Budgeting Assumptions and it contains all of Hampton Freeze's answers to the questions summarized in Exhibit 8–2. The data included in Exhibit 8–4 summarize the estimates and assumptions that provide the foundation for Hampton Freeze's entire master budget, so it is important to familiarize yourself with this information now. Beginning with the estimates underlying the sales budget, Exhibit 8–4 shows that Hampton Freeze's budgeted quarterly unit sales are 10,000, 30,000, 40,000, and 20,000 cases. Its budgeted selling price is $20 per case. The company expects to collect 70% of its credit sales in the

**EXHIBIT 8–4**    Hampton Freeze: Budgeting Assumptions

| | A | B | C | D | E | F |
|---|---|---|---|---|---|---|
| 1 | Hampton Freeze, Inc. | | | | | |
| 2 | Budgeting Assumptions | | | | | |
| 3 | For the Year Ended December 31, 2018 | | | | | |
| 4 | | | | | | |
| 5 | | All 4 Quarters | | Quarter | | |
| 6 | Sales Budget | | 1 | 2 | 3 | 4 |
| 7 | Budgeted sales in cases | | 10,000 | 30,000 | 40,000 | 20,000 |
| 8 | Selling price per case | $ 20.00 | | | | |
| 9 | Percentage of sales collected in the quarter of sale | 70% | | | | |
| 10 | Percentage of sales collected in the quarter after sale | 30% | | | | |
| 11 | | | | | | |
| 12 | Production Budget | | | | | |
| 13 | Percentage of next quarter's sales in ending finished goods inventory | 20% | | | | |
| 14 | | | | | | |
| 15 | Direct Materials Budget | | | | | |
| 16 | Pounds of sugar per case | 15 | | | | |
| 17 | Cost per pound of sugar | $ 0.20 | | | | |
| 18 | Percentage of next quarter's production needs in ending inventory | 10% | | | | |
| 19 | Percentage of purchases paid in the quarter purchased | 50% | | | | |
| 20 | Percentage of purchases paid in the quarter after purchase | 50% | | | | |
| 21 | | | | | | |
| 22 | Direct Labor Budget | | | | | |
| 23 | Direct labor-hours required per case | 0.40 | | | | |
| 24 | Direct labor cost per hour | $ 15.00 | | | | |
| 25 | | | | | | |
| 26 | Manufacturing Overhead Budget | | | | | |
| 27 | Variable manufacturing overhead per direct labor-hour | $ 4.00 | | | | |
| 28 | Fixed manufacturing overhead per quarter | $ 60,600 | | | | |
| 29 | Depreciation per quarter | $ 15,000 | | | | |
| 30 | | | | | | |
| 31 | | | | | | |
| 32 | Selling and Administrative Expense Budget | | | | | |
| 33 | Variable selling and administrative expense per case | $ 1.80 | | | | |
| 34 | Fixed selling and administrative expense per quarter: | | | | | |
| 35 | Advertising | $ 20,000 | | | | |
| 36 | Executive salaries | $ 55,000 | | | | |
| 37 | Insurance | $ 10,000 | | | | |
| 38 | Property tax | $ 4,000 | | | | |
| 39 | Depreciation | $ 10,000 | | | | |
| 40 | | | | | | |
| 41 | Cash Budget | | | | | |
| 42 | Minimum cash balance | $ 30,000 | | | | |
| 43 | Equipment purchases | | $ 50,000 | $ 40,000 | $ 20,000 | $ 20,000 |
| 44 | Dividends | $ 8,000 | | | | |
| 45 | Simple interest rate per quarter | 3% | | | | |
| 46 | | | | | | |

◄ ◄ ► ►│ Beginning Balance Sheet │ **Budgeting Assumptions** │ Schedule 1 │ Schedule 2 │ Sche ◄│

*For simplicity, we assume that all quarterly estimates, except quarterly unit sales and equipment purchases, will be the same for all four quarters.

Source: Microsoft

quarter of sale, and the remaining 30% of credit sales will be collected in the quarter after sale. The company's bad debts are negligible.

Exhibit 8–4 also shows that the production budget is based on the assumption that Hampton Freeze will maintain ending finished goods inventory equal to 20% of the next quarter's unit sales. In terms of the company's only direct material, high fructose sugar, it budgets 15 pounds of sugar per case of popsicles at a cost of $0.20 per pound.[1] It expects to maintain ending raw materials inventory equal to 10% of the raw materials needed to satisfy the following quarter's production. In addition, the company plans to pay for 50% of its material purchases within the quarter of purchase and the remaining 50% in the following quarter.

Continuing with a summary of Exhibit 8–4, the two key assumptions underlying the direct labor budget are that 0.40 direct labor-hours are required per case of popsicles and the direct labor cost per hour is $15. The manufacturing overhead budget is based on three underlying assumptions—the variable overhead cost per direct labor-hour is $4.00, the total fixed overhead per quarter is $60,600, and the quarterly depreciation on factory assets is $15,000. Exhibit 8–4 also shows that the budgeted variable selling and administrative expense per case of popsicles is $1.80 and the fixed selling and administrative expenses per quarter include advertising ($20,000), executive salaries ($55,000), insurance ($10,000), property tax ($4,000), and depreciation expense ($10,000). The remaining budget assumptions depicted in Exhibit 8–4 pertain to the cash budget. The company expects to maintain a minimum cash balance each quarter of $30,000; it plans to make quarterly equipment purchases of $50,000, $40,000, $20,000, and $20,000;[2] it plans to pay quarterly dividends of $8,000; and it expects to pay simple interest on borrowed money of 3% per quarter.

Before reading further, it is important to understand why Larry created the Budgeting Assumptions tab shown in Exhibit 8–4. He did it because it simplifies the process of using a master budget to answer "what if" questions. For example, assume that Larry wanted to answer the question: what if we increase the selling price per unit by $2 and expect sales to drop by 1,000 units per quarter; what would be the impact on profits? With a properly constructed Budgeting Assumptions tab, Larry would only need to make a few adjustments to the data within this tab and the formulas embedded in each of the budget schedules would automatically update the projected financial results. This is much simpler than attempting to adjust data inputs within each of the master budget schedules.

## The Sales Budget

Schedule 1 contains Hampton Freeze's sales budget for 2018. As you study this schedule, keep in mind that all of its numbers are derived from cell references to the Budgeting Assumptions tab and formulas—none of the numbers appearing in the schedule were actually keyed into their respective cells. Furthermore, it bears emphasizing that all remaining schedules in the master budget are prepared in the same fashion—they rely almost exclusively on cell references and formulas.

For the year, Hampton Freeze expects to sell 100,000 cases of popsicles at a price of $20 per case for total budgeted sales of $2,000,000. The budgeted unit sales for each quarter (10,000, 30,000, 40,000, and 20,000) come from cells C7 through F7 in the Budgeting Assumptions tab shown in Exhibit 8–4, and the selling price per case ($20.00) comes from cell B8 in the Budgeting Assumptions tab. Schedule 1 also shows that the company's expected cash collections for 2018 are $1,970,000. The accounts receivable balance of $90,000 that is collected in the first quarter comes from cell B8 of the beginning balance sheet shown in Exhibit 8–3. All other cash collections rely on the estimated cash collection percentages from cells B9 and B10 of the Budgeting Assumptions tab. For example, Schedule 1 shows that the budgeted sales for the first quarter equal

LEARNING OBJECTIVE 8–2

Prepare a sales budget, including a schedule of expected cash collections.

---

[1]While popsicle manufacturing is likely to involve other raw materials, such as popsicle sticks and packaging materials, for simplicity, we have limited our scope to high fructose sugar.
[2]For simplicity, we assume that depreciation on these newly acquired assets is included in the quarterly depreciation estimates included in the Budgeting Assumptions tab.

**SCHEDULE 1**

| | A | B | C | D | E | F |
|---|---|---|---|---|---|---|
| 1 | | \multicolumn{5}{c}{Hampton Freeze, Inc.} | | | | |
| 2 | | Sales Budget | | | | |
| 3 | | For the Year Ended December 31, 2018 | | | | |
| 4 | | | | | | |
| 5 | | | | Quarter | | |
| 6 | | 1 | 2 | 3 | 4 | Year |
| 7 | Budgeted unit sales (in cases) | 10,000 | 30,000 | 40,000 | 20,000 | 100,000 |
| 8 | Selling price per unit | $ 20.00 | $ 20.00 | $ 20.00 | $ 20.00 | $ 20.00 |
| 9 | Total sales | $200,000 | $600,000 | $800,000 | $400,000 | $2,000,000 |
| 10 | | | | | | |
| 11 | | 70% | 30% | | | |
| 12 | | \multicolumn{5}{c}{Schedule of Expected Cash Collections} | | | | |
| 13 | Beginning accounts receivable[1] | $ 90,000 | | | | $ 90,000 |
| 14 | First-quarter sales[2] | 140,000 | $ 60,000 | | | 200,000 |
| 15 | Second-quarter sales[3] | | 420,000 | $ 180,000 | | 600,000 |
| 16 | Third-quarter sales[4] | | | 560,000 | $ 240,000 | 800,000 |
| 17 | Fourth-quarter sales[5] | | - | - | 280,000 | 280,000 |
| 18 | Total cash collections[6] | $230,000 | $480,000 | $740,000 | $520,000 | $ 1,970,000 |

Budgeting Assumptions   **Schedule 1**   Schedule 2   Schedule 3   Sc

[1]Cash collections from last year's fourth-quarter sales. See the beginning balance sheet in Exhibit 8–3.
[2]$200,000 × 70%; $200,000 × 30%.
[3]$600,000 × 70%; $600,000 × 30%.
[4]$800,000 × 70%; $800,000 × 30%.
[5]$400,000 × 70%.
[6]Uncollected fourth-quarter sales ($120,000) appear as accounts receivable on the company's end-of-year budgeted balance sheet (see Schedule 10).

Source: Microsoft

$200,000. In the first quarter, Hampton Freeze expects to collect 70% of this amount, or $140,000. In the second quarter, the company expects to collect the remaining 30% of this amount, or $60,000.

CONCEPT CHECK ✓

2. March, April, and May sales are $100,000, $120,000, and $125,000, respectively. A total of 80% of all sales are credit sales and 20% are cash sales. A total of 60% of credit sales are collected in the month of the sale and 40% are collected in the next month. There are no bad debt expenses. What is the amount of cash collections for April?
   a. $89,600
   b. $111,600
   c. $113,600
   d. $132,600

3. Referring to the facts in question 2 above, what is the accounts receivable balance at the end of May?
   a. $40,000
   b. $50,000
   c. $72,000
   d. $80,000

## Budgeting for Sales Returns

In addition to preparing sales budgets, companies need to budget for the expense of managing sales returns. **Optoro**, a logistics provider, estimates that companies process $60 billion in customer returns during the holiday season. The **U.S. Postal Service** and **United Parcel Service** transport 3.2 million and 4 million returns, respectively, in the two weeks after Christmas. **Best Buy** estimates that returns, damaged goods, and replaced merchandise cost the company $400 million per year, or 10% of its revenue.

When it comes to internet commerce, 82% of shoppers say they are more likely to complete online purchases if the company offers free returns via pre-paid shipping labels or free in-store returns. For some high-end apparel retailers, the return rate for online purchases can reach 50% of the transactions processed.

Source: Stevens, Laura, "For Retailers, It's Many Unhappy Returns," *The Wall Street Journal*, December 27–28, 2014, p. B3.

## The Production Budget

The production budget is prepared after the sales budget. The **production budget** lists the number of units that must be produced to satisfy sales needs and to provide for the desired ending finished goods inventory. Production needs can be determined as follows:

| | |
|---|---|
| Budgeted unit sales .................................................... | XXXX |
| Add desired units of ending finished goods inventory ................ | XXXX |
| Total needs ........................................................... | XXXX |
| Less units of beginning finished goods inventory .................... | XXXX |
| Required production in units ......................................... | XXXX |

Note the production requirements are influenced by the desired level of the ending finished goods inventory. Inventories should be carefully planned. Excessive inventories tie up funds and create storage problems. Insufficient inventories can lead to lost sales or last-minute, high-cost production efforts.

Schedule 2 contains the production budget for Hampton Freeze. The budgeted sales data come from cells B7 through E7 of the sales budget. The desired ending finished goods inventory for the first quarter of 6,000 cases is computed by multiplying budgeted sales from the second quarter (30,000 cases) by the desired ending finished goods inventory percentage (20%) shown in cell B13 of the Budgeting Assumptions tab. The total needs for the first quarter (16,000 cases) are determined by adding together the budgeted sales of 10,000 cases for the quarter and the desired ending inventory of 6,000 cases. As discussed above, the ending inventory is intended to provide some cushion in the event that problems develop in production, or sales increase unexpectedly. Because the company already has 2,000 cases in beginning finished goods inventory (as shown in the beginning balance sheet in Exhibit 8–3), only 14,000 cases need to be produced in the first quarter.

Pay particular attention to the Year column to the right of the production budget in Schedule 2. In some cases (e.g., budgeted unit sales and required production in units), the amount listed for the year is the sum of the quarterly amounts for the item. In other cases, (e.g., desired units of ending finished goods inventory and units of beginning finished goods inventory), the amount listed for the year is not simply the sum of the quarterly amounts. From the standpoint of the entire year, the ending finished goods inventory, which Larry Giano assumed to be 3,000 units, is the same as the ending finished goods inventory for the fourth quarter—it is *not* the sum of the ending finished goods inventories for all four

**SCHEDULE 2**

| | A | B | C | D | E | F | |
|---|---|---|---|---|---|---|---|
| 3 | | Hampton Freeze, Inc. | | | | | |
| 4 | | Production Budget | | | | | |
| 5 | | For the Year Ended December 31, 2018 | | | | | |
| 6 | | (in cases) | | | | | |
| 7 | | | | | | Assumed | |
| 8 | | | | *Quarter* | | | |
| 9 | | 1 | 2 | 3 | 4 | *Year* | |
| 10 | Budgeted unit sales (Schedule 1) | 10,000 | 30,000 | 40,000 | 20,000 | 100,000 | |
| 11 | Add desired units of ending finished goods inventory* | 6,000 | 8,000 | 4,000 | 3,000 | 3,000 | |
| 12 | Total needs | 16,000 | 38,000 | 44,000 | 23,000 | 103,000 | |
| 13 | Less units of beginning finished goods inventory† | 2,000 | 6,000 | 8,000 | 4,000 | 2,000 | |
| 14 | Required production in units | 14,000 | 32,000 | 36,000 | 19,000 | 101,000 | |

Tabs: Budgeting Assumptions / Schedule 1 / **Schedule 2** / Schedule 3 / Schedul

*Twenty percent of next quarter's sales. For example, the second-quarter sales are 30,000 cases. Therefore, the desired ending inventory of finished goods for the first quarter would be 20% × 30,000 cases = 6,000 cases.

†The beginning inventory in each quarter is the same as the prior quarter's ending inventory.

Source: Microsoft

quarters. Similarly, from the standpoint of the entire year, the beginning finished goods inventory (2,000 units) is the same as the beginning finished goods inventory for the first quarter—it is *not* the sum of the beginning finished goods inventories for all four quarters. It is important to pay attention to such distinctions in all schedules that follow.

## Inventory Purchases—Merchandising Company

Hampton Freeze prepares a production budget because it is a *manufacturing* company. If it were a *merchandising* company, instead it would prepare a **merchandise purchases budget** showing the amount of goods to be purchased from suppliers during the period. The format of the merchandise purchases budget is shown below:

| | |
|---|---|
| Budgeted cost of goods sold | XXXX |
| Add desired ending merchandise inventory | XXXX |
| Total needs | XXXX |
| Less beginning merchandise inventory | XXXX |
| Required purchases | XXXX |

A merchandising company would prepare a merchandise purchases budget, such as the one above, for each item carried in stock. The merchandise purchases budget can be expressed in dollars (using the headings shown above) or in units. The top line of a merchandise purchases budget based on units would say Budgeted unit sales instead of Budgeted cost of goods sold.

A merchandise purchases budget is usually accompanied by a schedule of expected cash disbursements for merchandise purchases. The format of this schedule mirrors the approach used for the schedule of expected cash disbursements for purchases of materials that is illustrated at the bottom of Schedule 3.

4. If a company has a beginning merchandise inventory of $50,000, a desired ending merchandise inventory of $30,000, and a budgeted cost of goods sold of $300,000, what is the amount of required inventory purchases?
   a. $320,000
   b. $280,000
   c. $380,000
   d. $300,000

5. Budgeted unit sales for March, April, and May are 75,000, 80,000, and 90,000 units. Management desires to maintain an ending inventory equal to 30% of the next month's unit sales. How many units should be produced in April?
   a. 80,000 units
   b. 83,000 units
   c. 77,000 units
   d. 85,000 units

## The Direct Materials Budget

A *direct materials budget* is prepared after the production requirements have been computed. The **direct materials budget** details the raw materials that must be purchased to fulfill the production budget and to provide for adequate inventories. The required purchases of raw materials are computed as follows:

> **LEARNING OBJECTIVE 8–4**
>
> Prepare a direct materials budget, including a schedule of expected cash disbursements for purchases of materials.

| | |
|---|---|
| Required production in units of finished goods | XXXX |
| Units of raw materials needed per unit of finished goods | XXXX |
| Units of raw materials needed to meet production | XXXX |
| Add desired units of ending raw materials inventory | XXXX |
| Total units of raw materials needed | XXXX |
| Less units of beginning raw materials inventory | XXXX |
| Units of raw materials to be purchased | XXXX |
| Unit cost of raw materials | XXXX |
| Cost of raw materials to be purchased | XXXX |

Schedule 3 contains the direct materials budget for Hampton Freeze. The first line of this budget contains the required production for each quarter, which is taken directly from cells B14 through E14 of the production budget (Schedule 2). The second line of the direct materials budget recognizes that 15 pounds of sugar (see cell B16 from the Budgeting Assumptions tab) are required to make one case of popsicles. The third line of the budget presents the raw materials needed to meet production. For example, in the first quarter, the required production of 14,000 cases is multiplied by 15 pounds to equal 210,000 pounds of sugar needed to meet production. The fourth line shows the desired units of ending raw materials inventory. For the first quarter this amount is computed by multiplying the raw materials needed to meet production in the second quarter of 480,000 pounds by the desired ending inventory percentage of 10% as shown in cell B18 of the Budgeting Assumptions tab. The desired units of ending raw materials inventory of 48,000 pounds is added to 210,000 pounds to provide the total units of raw materials needed of 258,000 pounds. However, because the company already has 21,000 pounds of sugar in beginning inventory (as shown in cell A9 in the beginning

## SCHEDULE 3

| | A | B | C | D | E | F | G |
|---|---|---|---|---|---|---|---|
| 3 | | Hampton Freeze, Inc. | | | | | |
| 4 | | Direct Materials Budget | | | | | |
| 5 | | For the Year Ended December 31, 2018 | | | | | |
| 6 | | | | | | Assumed | |
| 7 | | Quarter | | | | | |
| 8 | | 1 | 2 | 3 | 4 | Year | |
| 9 | Required production in cases (Schedule 2) | 14,000 | 32,000 | 36,000 | 19,000 | 101,000 | |
| 10 | Units of raw materials needed per case | 15 | 15 | 15 | 15 | 15 | |
| 11 | Units of raw materials needed to meet production | 210,000 | 480,000 | 540,000 | 285,000 | 1,515,000 | |
| 12 | Add desired units of ending raw materials inventory[1] | 48,000 | 10% 54,000 | 10% 28,500 | 10% 22,500 | 22,500 | |
| 13 | Total units of raw materials needed | 258,000 | 534,000 | 568,500 | 307,500 | 1,537,500 | |
| 14 | Less units of beginning raw materials inventory | 21,000 | 48,000 | 54,000 | 28,500 | 21,000 | |
| 15 | Units of raw materials to be purchased | 237,000 | 486,000 | 514,500 | 279,000 | 1,516,500 | |
| 16 | Cost of raw materials per pound | $ 0.20 | $ 0.20 | $ 0.20 | $ 0.20 | $ 0.20 | |
| 17 | Cost of raw materials to be purchased | $47,400 | $97,200 | $102,900 | $55,800 | $ 303,300 | |
| 18 | | | | | | | |
| 19 | | 50% | 50% | | | | |
| 20 | Schedule of Expected Cash Disbursements for Purchases of Materials | | | | | | |
| 21 | | | | | | | |
| 22 | Beginning accounts payable[2] | $25,800 | | | | $ 25,800 | |
| 23 | First-quarter purchases[3] | 23,700 | $23,700 | | | 47,400 | |
| 24 | Second-quarter purchases[4] | | 48,600 | $ 48,600 | | 97,200 | |
| 25 | Third-quarter purchases[5] | | | 51,450 | $51,450 | 102,900 | |
| 26 | Fourth-quarter purchases[6] | | | | 27,900 | 27,900 | |
| 27 | Total cash disbursements for materials | $49,500 | $72,300 | $100,050 | $79,350 | $ 301,200 | |

Schedule 3 / Schedule 4 / Schedule 5 / Schedule 6 / Schedule 7 / S

[1]Ten percent of the next quarter's production needs. For example, the second-quarter production needs are 480,000 pounds. Therefore, the desired ending inventory for the first quarter would be 10% × 480,000 pounds = 48,000 pounds. The desired ending inventory for quarter 4 (22,500 pounds) assumes the first quarter production needs in 2019 are 225,000 pounds (= 225,000 pounds × 10% = 22,500 pounds).

[2]Cash payments for last year's fourth-quarter purchases. See the beginning-of-year balance sheet in Exhibit 8–3.

[3]$47,400 × 50%; $47,400 × 50%.

[4]$97,200 × 50%; $97,200 × 50%.

[5]$102,900 × 50%; $102,900 × 50%.

[6]$55,800 × 50%. Unpaid fourth-quarter purchases ($27,900) appear as accounts payable on the company's end-of-year budgeted balance sheet (see Schedule 10).

Source: Microsoft

balance sheet in Exhibit 8–3), only 237,000 pounds of sugar need to be purchased in the first quarter. Because the budgeted cost of raw materials per pound is $0.20 (see cell B17 from the Budgeting Assumptions tab), the cost of raw material to be purchased in the first quarter is $47,400. For the entire year, the company plans to purchase $303,300 of raw materials.

Schedule 3 also shows that the company's expected cash disbursements for material purchases for 2017 are $301,200. The accounts payable balance of $25,800 that is paid in the first quarter comes from cell C21 of the beginning balance sheet shown in Exhibit 8–3. All other cash disbursement computations rely on the estimated cash payment percentages (both of which are 50%) from cells B19 and B20 of the Budgeting Assumptions tab. For example, Schedule 3 shows that the budgeted raw material purchases for the first quarter equal $47,400. In the first quarter, Hampton Freeze expects to pay 50% of this amount, or $23,700. In the second quarter, the company expects to pay the remaining 50% of this amount, or $23,700.

Master Budgeting **349**

## HELPFUL HINT

The direct materials budget includes three different units of measure. It begins by defining the number of units of finished goods that need to be produced each period. It then defines the quantity of raw material inputs (measured in terms such as pounds or ounces) that need to be purchased to support production. It concludes by translating the quantity of raw materials to be purchased into the cost of raw materials to be purchased.

## IN BUSINESS

### Toyota Reduces Direct Materials Cost by Sharing Components

**Toyota Motor Corporation** is redesigning its manufacturing processes to enable sharing more component parts across all styles and sizes of its vehicles. In addition to realizing cost savings due to bulk purchases of common parts, Toyota also expects its redesigned modular assembly lines to be much smaller, thereby enabling a 40% reduction in initial plant investment costs compared to 2008. The company acknowledged that it lags **Volkswagen** when it comes to implementing modular manufacturing processes. Toyota hopes to produce half of its vehicles using modular assembly lines by 2020.

Source: Kubota, Yoko, "Toyota Adopts More Modular Design," *The Wall Street Journal,* March 27, 2015, p. B3.

©Tomohiro Ohsumi/Bloomberg/ Getty Images

## The Direct Labor Budget

The **direct labor budget** shows the direct labor-hours required to satisfy the production budget. By knowing in advance how much labor time will be needed throughout the budget year, the company can develop plans to adjust the labor force as the situation requires. Companies that neglect the budgeting process run the risk of facing labor shortages or having to hire and lay off workers at awkward times. Erratic labor policies lead to insecurity, low morale, and inefficiency.

The direct labor budget for Hampton Freeze is shown in Schedule 4. The first line in the direct labor budget consists of the required production for each quarter, which is taken

**LEARNING OBJECTIVE 8–5**

Prepare a direct labor budget.

**SCHEDULE 4**

|  | | Quarter | | | |
|---|---|---|---|---|---|
| Hampton Freeze, Inc. Direct Labor Budget For the Year Ended December 31, 2018 | | | | | |
|  | 1 | 2 | 3 | 4 | Year |
| Required production in cases (Schedule 2) | 14,000 | 32,000 | 36,000 | 19,000 | 101,000 |
| Direct labor-hours per case | 0.40 | 0.40 | 0.40 | 0.40 | 0.40 |
| Total direct labor-hours needed | 5,600 | 12,800 | 14,400 | 7,600 | 40,400 |
| Direct labor cost per hour | $ 15.00 | $ 15.00 | $ 15.00 | $ 15.00 | $ 15.00 |
| Total direct labor cost | $ 84,000 | $ 192,000 | $ 216,000 | $ 114,000 | $ 606,000 |

Schedule 1 / Schedule 2 / Schedule 3 / **Schedule 4** / Schedule 5 / Schedule

*This schedule assumes that the direct labor workforce will be fully adjusted to the total direct labor-hours needed each quarter.

Source: Microsoft

directly from cells B14 through E14 of the production budget (Schedule 2). The direct labor requirement for each quarter is computed by multiplying the number of units to be produced in each quarter by the 0.40 direct labor-hours required to make one unit (see cell B23 from the Budgeting Assumptions tab). For example, 14,000 cases are to be produced in the first quarter and each case requires 0.40 direct labor-hours, so a total of 5,600 direct labor-hours (14,000 cases × 0.40 direct labor-hours per case) will be required in the first quarter. The direct labor requirements are then translated into budgeted direct labor costs, which we will assume are paid in the quarter incurred. How this is done will depend on the company's labor policy. In Schedule 4, Hampton Freeze has assumed that the direct labor force will be adjusted as the work requirements change from quarter to quarter. In that case, the direct labor cost is computed by simply multiplying the direct labor-hour requirements by the direct labor rate of $15 per hour (see cell B24 from the Budgeting Assumptions tab). For example, the direct labor cost in the first quarter is $84,000 (5,600 direct labor-hours × $15 per direct labor-hour).

However, many companies have employment policies or contracts that prevent them from laying off and rehiring workers as needed. Suppose, for example, that Hampton Freeze has 25 workers who are classified as direct labor, but each of them is guaranteed at least 480 hours of pay each quarter at a rate of $15 per hour. In that case, the minimum direct labor cost for a quarter would be computed as follows:

25 workers × 480 hours per worker × $15 per hour = $180,000

Note that in this case the direct costs shown in the first and fourth quarters of Schedule 4 would have to be increased to $180,000.

## The Manufacturing Overhead Budget

The **manufacturing overhead budget** lists all costs of production other than direct materials and direct labor. Schedule 5 shows the manufacturing overhead budget for Hampton Freeze. At Hampton Freeze, manufacturing overhead is separated into variable and fixed components. As shown in the Budgeting Assumptions tab (Exhibit 8–4), the variable component is $4 per direct labor-hour and the fixed component is $60,600 per quarter. Because the variable component of manufacturing overhead depends on direct labor, the

**SCHEDULE 5**

| A | B | C | D | E | F |
|---|---|---|---|---|---|
| 1 | Hampton Freeze, Inc. | | | | |
| 2 | Manufacturing Overhead Budget | | | | |
| 3 | For the Year Ended December 31, 2018 | | | | |
| 4 | | | | | |
| 5 | | Quarter | | | |
| 6 | | 1 | 2 | 3 | 4 | Year |
| 7 Budgeted direct labor-hours (Schedule 4) | 5,600 | 12,800 | 14,400 | 7,600 | 40,400 |
| 8 Variable manufacturing overhead rate | $ 4.00 | $ 4.00 | $ 4.00 | $ 4.00 | $ 4.00 |
| 9 Variable manufacturing overhead | $ 22,400 | $ 51,200 | $ 57,600 | $ 30,400 | $ 161,600 |
| 10 Fixed manufacturing overhead | 60,600 | 60,600 | 60,600 | 60,600 | 242,400 |
| 11 Total manufacturing overhead | 83,000 | 111,800 | 118,200 | 91,000 | 404,000 |
| 12 Less depreciation | 15,000 | 15,000 | 15,000 | 15,000 | 60,000 |
| 13 Cash disbursements for manufacturing overhead | $ 68,000 | $ 96,800 | $ 103,200 | $ 76,000 | $ 344,000 |
| 14 | | | | | |
| 15 Total manufacturing overhead (a) | | | | | $ 404,000 |
| 16 Budgeted direct labor-hours (b) | | | | | 40,400 |
| 17 Predetermined overhead rate for the year (a)÷(b) | | | | | $10.00 |
| 18 | | | | | |
| 19 | | | | | |

H ◀ ▶ H   Schedule 3 / Schedule 4 / **Schedule 5** / Schedule 6 / Schedule 7 / Schedule 8

Source: Microsoft

first line in the manufacturing overhead budget consists of the budgeted direct labor-hours from cells B9 through E9 of the direct labor budget (Schedule 4). The budgeted direct labor-hours in each quarter are multiplied by the variable overhead rate to determine the variable component of manufacturing overhead. For example, the variable manufacturing overhead for the first quarter is $22,400 (5,600 direct labor-hours × $4.00 per direct labor-hour). This is added to the fixed manufacturing overhead for the quarter to determine the total manufacturing overhead for the quarter of $83,000 ($22,400 + $60,600).

The last line of Schedule 5 for Hampton Freeze shows the budgeted cash disbursements for manufacturing overhead. Because some of the overhead costs are not cash outflows, the total budgeted manufacturing overhead costs must be adjusted to determine the cash disbursements for manufacturing overhead. At Hampton Freeze, the only significant noncash manufacturing overhead cost is depreciation, which is $15,000 per quarter (see cell B29 in the Budgeting Assumptions tab). These noncash depreciation charges are deducted from the total budgeted manufacturing overhead to determine each quarter's expected cash disbursements. Hampton Freeze pays all overhead costs involving cash disbursements in the quarter incurred. Note that the company's predetermined overhead rate for the year is $10 per direct labor-hour, which is determined by dividing the total budgeted manufacturing overhead for the year ($404,000) by the total budgeted direct labor-hours for the year (40,400).

## The Ending Finished Goods Inventory Budget

After completing Schedules 1–5, Larry Giano had all of the data he needed to compute the absorption unit product cost for the units produced during the budget year. This computation was needed for two reasons: first, to help determine cost of goods sold on the budgeted income statement; and second, to value ending inventories on the budgeted balance sheet. The cost of unsold units is computed on the **ending finished goods inventory budget**.[3]

Schedule 6 shows that Hampton Freeze's absorption unit product cost is $13 per case of popsicles—consisting of $3 of direct materials, $6 of direct labor, and $4 of manufacturing overhead. Notice that manufacturing overhead has been applied to units of product using the rate of $10 per direct labor-hour from cell F17 of the Manufacturing Overhead budget. The budgeted carrying cost of the ending inventory is $39,000.

## The Selling and Administrative Expense Budget

The **selling and administrative expense budget** lists the budgeted expenses for areas other than manufacturing. In large organizations, this budget would be a compilation of many smaller, individual budgets submitted by department heads and other persons responsible for selling and administrative expenses. For example, the marketing manager would submit a budget detailing the advertising expenses for each budget period.

Schedule 7 contains the selling and administrative expense budget for Hampton Freeze. Like the manufacturing overhead budget, the selling and administrative expense budget is divided into variable and fixed cost components. Consequently, budgeted sales in cases for each quarter are entered at the top of the schedule. These data are taken from cells B7 through E7 of the sales budget (Schedule 1). The budgeted variable selling and administrative expenses are determined by multiplying the budgeted cases sold by the variable selling and administrative expense of $1.80 per case (see cell B33 from the Budgeting Assumptions tab). For example, the budgeted variable selling and administrative expense for the first quarter is $18,000 (10,000 cases × $1.80 per case). The fixed selling and administrative expenses of $99,000 per quarter (see cells B35 through B39 from the

[3]For simplicity, the beginning balance sheet and the ending finished goods inventory budget both report a unit product cost of $13. For purposes of answering "what if" questions, this schedule would assume a FIFO inventory flow. In other words, the ending inventory would consist solely of units that are produced during the budget year.

**SCHEDULE 6**

|  | A | B | C | D | E | F | G | H | I |
|---|---|---|---|---|---|---|---|---|---|
| 1 | | | Hampton Freeze, Inc. | | | | | | |
| 2 | | | Ending Finished Goods Inventory Budget | | | | | | |
| 3 | | | (absorption costing basis) | | | | | | |
| 4 | | | For the Year Ended December 31, 2018 | | | | | | |
| 5 | | | | | | | | | |
| 6 | *Item* | *Quantity* | | | *Cost* | | | *Total* | |
| 7 | Production cost per case: | | | | | | | | |
| 8 | Direct materials | 15.00 | pounds | | $ 0.20 | per pound | $ | 3.00 | |
| 9 | Direct labor | 0.40 | hours | | $15.00 | per hour | | 6.00 | |
| 10 | Manufacturing overhead | 0.40 | hours | | $10.00 | per hour | | 4.00 | |
| 11 | Unit product cost | | | | | | $ | 13.00 | |
| 12 | | | | | | | | | |
| 13 | Budgeted finished goods inventory: | | | | | | | | |
| 14 | Ending finished goods inventory in cases (Schedule 2) | | | | | | | 3,000 | |
| 15 | Unit product cost (see above) | | | | | | $ | 13.00 | |
| 16 | Ending finished goods inventory in dollars | | | | | | $ | 39,000 | |
| 17 | | | | | | | | | |

Schedule 3 / Schedule 4 / Schedule 5 / **Schedule 6** / Sch

**SCHEDULE 7**

|  | A | B | C | D | E | F |
|---|---|---|---|---|---|---|
| 1 | | Hampton Freeze, Inc. | | | | |
| 2 | | Selling and Administrative Expense Budget | | | | |
| 3 | | For the Year Ended December 31, 2018 | | | | |
| 4 | | | | | | |
| 5 | | | *Quarter* | | | |
| 6 | | *1* | *2* | *3* | *4* | *Year* |
| 7 | Budgeted units sales (Schedule 1) | 10,000 | 30,000 | 40,000 | 20,000 | 100,000 |
| 8 | Variable selling and administrative expense per case | $ 1.80 | $ 1.80 | $ 1.80 | $ 1.80 | $ 1.80 |
| 9 | Variable selling and administrative expense | $ 18,000 | $ 54,000 | $ 72,000 | $ 36,000 | $180,000 |
| 10 | Fixed selling and administrative expenses: | | | | | |
| 11 | Advertising | 20,000 | 20,000 | 20,000 | 20,000 | 80,000 |
| 12 | Executive salaries | 55,000 | 55,000 | 55,000 | 55,000 | 220,000 |
| 13 | Insurance | 10,000 | 10,000 | 10,000 | 10,000 | 40,000 |
| 14 | Property taxes | 4,000 | 4,000 | 4,000 | 4,000 | 16,000 |
| 15 | Depreciation | 10,000 | 10,000 | 10,000 | 10,000 | 40,000 |
| 16 | Total fixed selling and administrative expenses | 99,000 | 99,000 | 99,000 | 99,000 | 396,000 |
| 17 | Total selling and administrative expenses | 117,000 | 153,000 | 171,000 | 135,000 | 576,000 |
| 18 | Less depreciation | 10,000 | 10,000 | 10,000 | 10,000 | 40,000 |
| 19 | Cash disbursements for selling and administrative expenses | $107,000 | $143,000 | $161,000 | $125,000 | $536,000 |
| 20 | | | | | | |

Schedule 5 / Schedule 6 / **Schedule 7** / Schedule 8 / Schedule 9 / Schedule 10

Budgeting Assumptions tab) are then added to the variable selling and administrative expenses to arrive at the total budgeted selling and administrative expenses. Finally, to determine the cash disbursements for selling and administrative items, the total budgeted selling and administrative expense is adjusted by subtracting any noncash selling and administrative expenses (in this case, just depreciation).[4]

6.  Which of the following statements is true? (You may select more than one answer.)
    a.  The manufacturing overhead budget includes depreciation related to assets that support a company's selling and administrative functions.
    b.  The cash disbursements for selling and administrative expenses are reported in the budgeted income statement.
    c.  The selling and administrative expense budget includes depreciation related to manufacturing assets.
    d.  The total variable and fixed selling and administrative expenses incurred during a period are reported in the budgeted income statement.

## Budget Analyst

**DECISION POINT**

You have been hired as a budget analyst by a regional chain of Italian restaurants with attached bars. Management has had difficulty in the past predicting some of its costs; the assumption has always been that all operating costs are variable with respect to gross restaurant sales. What would you suggest doing to improve the accuracy of the budget forecasts?

## The Cash Budget

The cash budget is composed of four main sections:

**LEARNING OBJECTIVE 8–8**

Prepare a cash budget.

1.  The cash receipts section.
2.  The cash disbursements section.
3.  The cash excess or deficiency section.
4.  The financing section.

The receipts section lists all of the cash inflows, except from financing, expected during the budget period. Generally, the major source of receipts is from sales. The disbursements section summarizes all cash payments that are planned for the budget period. These payments include raw materials purchases, direct labor payments, manufacturing overhead costs, and so on, as contained in their respective budgets. In addition, other cash disbursements such as equipment purchases and dividends are listed.

The cash excess or deficiency section is computed as follows:

| | |
|---|---|
| Beginning cash balance | XXXX |
| Add cash receipts | XXXX |
| Total cash available | XXXX |
| Less cash disbursements | XXXX |
| Excess (deficiency) of cash available over disbursements | XXXX |

---

[4]Other adjustments might need to be made for differences between cash flows on the one hand and revenues and expenses on the other hand. For example, if property taxes are paid twice a year in installments of $8,000 each, the expense for property tax would have to be "backed out" of the total budgeted selling and administrative expenses and the cash installment payments added to the appropriate quarters to determine the cash disbursements. Similar adjustments might also need to be made in the manufacturing overhead budget. We generally ignore these complications in this chapter.

If a cash deficiency exists during any budget period or if there is a cash excess during any budget period that is less than the minimum required cash balance, the company will need to borrow money. Conversely, if there is a cash excess during any budget period that is greater than the minimum required cash balance, the company can invest the excess funds or repay principal and interest to lenders.

---

## IN BUSINESS                    Mismatched Cash Flows—Climbing the Hills and Valleys

©Eric Noreen

The **Washington Trails Association (WTA)** is a private, nonprofit organization primarily concerned with protecting and maintaining hiking trails in the state of Washington. Some 2,000 WTA volunteer workers donate more than 80,000 hours per year maintaining trails in rugged landscapes on federal, state, and private lands. The organization is supported by membership dues, voluntary contributions, grants, and some contract work for government.

The organization's income and expenses are erratic—although somewhat predictable—over the course of the year as shown in the following chart. Expenses tend to be highest in the spring and summer when most of the trail maintenance work is done. However, income spikes in December well after the expenses have been incurred. With cash outflows running ahead of cash inflows for much of the year, it is very important for the WTA to carefully plan its cash budget and to maintain adequate cash reserves to be able to pay its bills.

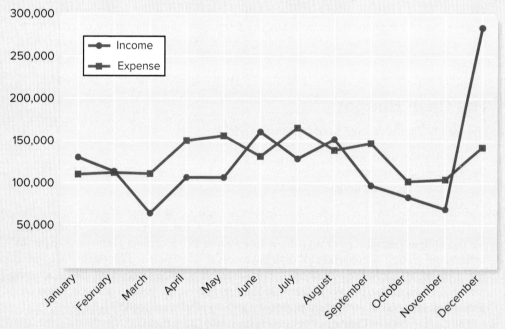

Note: Total income and total expense are approximately equal over the course of the year.

Sources: Conversation with Elizabeth Lunney, President of the Washington Trails Association; WTA documents; and the WTA website www.wta.org.

---

The financing section of the cash budget details the borrowings and principal and interest repayments projected to take place during the budget period. *In this chapter unless explicitly stated otherwise, we'll always assume that all borrowings take place on the first day of the borrowing period and all repayments take place on the last day of the final period included in the cash budget.* To calculate borrowings and interest payments, you'll need to pay attention to the company's desired minimum cash balance and to the terms of the company's loan agreement with the bank. For example, Hampton Freeze's desired minimum cash balance is $30,000 (see cell B42 in the Budgeting Assumptions tab). Furthermore, *we are going to assume that Hampton Freeze's loan agreement stipulates that* *it must borrow money in increments of $10,000* and that it must pay simple interest of 3% per quarter (as shown in cell B45 in Exhibit 8–4).[5]

The cash balances at both the beginning and end of the year may be adequate even though a serious cash deficit occurs at some point during the year. Consequently, the cash budget should be broken down into time periods that are short enough to capture major fluctuations in cash balances. While a monthly cash budget is most common, some organizations budget cash on a weekly or even daily basis. At Hampton Freeze, Larry Giano has prepared a quarterly cash budget that can be further refined as necessary. This budget appears in Schedule 8.[6]

The beginning cash balance in the first quarter of $42,500 agrees with cell B7 of the beginning balance sheet in Exhibit 8–3. Each quarter's collections from customers come from cells B18 through E18 of the schedule of expected cash collections in Schedule 1. Each quarter's beginning cash balance plus the collections from customers equals the total cash available. For example, in the first quarter, the beginning cash balance of $42,500 plus the collections from customers of $230,000 equals the total cash available of $272,500.

The disbursements section of the cash budget includes six types of cash disbursements. Each quarter's cash disbursements for direct materials come from cells B27 through E27 of the schedule of expected cash disbursements for materials (see Schedule 3). The quarterly cash payments for direct labor were calculated in cells B11 through E11 of the direct labor budget (see Schedule 4), whereas the quarterly cash payments related to manufacturing overhead were calculated in cells B13 through E13 of the manufacturing

## SCHEDULE 8

| | Schedule | 1 | 2 | 3 | 4 | Year |
|---|---|---|---|---|---|---|
| **Hampton Freeze, Inc.** | | | | | | |
| **Cash Budget** | | | | | | |
| **For the Year Ended December 31, 2018** | | | | | | |
| | | | | *Quarter* | | |
| 7 Beginning cash balance | | $ 42,500 | $ 36,000 | $ 33,900 | $ 165,650 | $ 42,500 |
| 8 Add cash receipts: | | | | | | |
| 9    Collections from customers | 1 | 230,000 | 480,000 | 740,000 | 520,000 | 1,970,000 |
| 10 Total cash available | | 272,500 | 516,000 | 773,900 | 685,650 | 2,012,500 |
| 11 Less cash disbursements: | | | | | | |
| 12    Direct materials | 3 | 49,500 | 72,300 | 100,050 | 79,350 | 301,200 |
| 13    Direct labor | 4 | 84,000 | 192,000 | 216,000 | 114,000 | 606,000 |
| 14    Manufacturing overhead | 5 | 68,000 | 96,800 | 103,200 | 76,000 | 344,000 |
| 15    Selling and administrative | 7 | 107,000 | 143,000 | 161,000 | 125,000 | 536,000 |
| 16    Equipment purchases | | 50,000 | 40,000 | 20,000 | 20,000 | 130,000 |
| 17    Dividends | | 8,000 | 8,000 | 8,000 | 8,000 | 32,000 |
| 18 Total cash disbursements | | 366,500 | 552,100 | 608,250 | 422,350 | 1,949,200 |
| 19 Excess (deficiency) of cash available over disbursements | | (94,000) | (36,100) | 165,650 | 263,300 | 63,300 |
| 20 Financing: | | | | | | |
| 21    Borrowings (at the beginnings of quarters) | | 130,000 | 70,000 | - | - | 200,000 |
| 22    Repayments (at end of the year) | | - | - | - | (200,000) | (200,000) |
| 23    Interest | | - | - | - | (21,900) | (21,900) |
| 24 Total financing | | 130,000 | 70,000 | - | (221,900) | (21,900) |
| 25 Ending cash balance | | $ 36,000 | $ 33,900 | $ 165,650 | $ 41,400 | $ 41,400 |

Source: Microsoft

[5]We use simple interest rather than compound interest throughout the chapter for simplicity.
[6]The format for the statement of cash flows, which is discussed in a later chapter, may also be used for the cash budget.

overhead budget (see Schedule 5). The quarterly cash payments for selling and administrative expenses come from cells B19 through E19 of the selling and administrative expense budget (see Schedule 7). So putting it all together, in the first quarter, the cash disbursements for direct materials ($49,500), direct labor ($84,000), manufacturing overhead ($68,000), selling and administrative expenses ($107,000), equipment purchases ($50,000), and the dividend ($8,000) (see cells C43 and B44 in Exhibit 8–4) equals the total cash disbursements of $366,500.

Each quarter's total cash available minus its total disbursements equals the excess (deficiency) of cash available over disbursements. For example, in the first quarter the total cash available of $272,500 minus the total disbursements of $366,500 results in a cash deficiency of $94,000. The excess or deficiency of cash directly influences whether Hampton Freeze will need to borrow money as shown in the financing section of the cash budget.

The first row in the financing section of the cash budget relates to projected borrowings. In any period where a company's excess of cash available over disbursements is greater than its desired minimum cash balance, the company will not need to borrow money during that period. In the case of Hampton Freeze, the company wants to maintain a minimum cash balance of $30,000; therefore, it will not need to borrow money in any quarter where its excess of cash available over disbursements is greater than $30,000. However, in the first quarter of 2018 Hampton Freeze estimates that it will have a cash deficiency of $94,000; consequently, the company's minimum required borrowings at the beginning of the first quarter would be computed as follows:

| Required Borrowings at the Beginning of the First Quarter: | |
|---|---|
| Desired ending cash balance ........................................ | $ 30,000 |
| Plus deficiency of cash available over disbursements ................ | 94,000 |
| Minimum required borrowings ........................................ | $124,000 |

Recall that the bank requires that loans be made in increments of $10,000. Because Hampton Freeze needs to borrow at least $124,000, it will have to borrow $130,000.

In the second quarter of 2018 Hampton Freeze estimates that it will have another cash deficiency of $36,100; therefore, the company's minimum required borrowings at the beginning of the second quarter would be computed as follows:

| Required Borrowings at the Beginning of the Second Quarter: | |
|---|---|
| Desired ending cash balance ........................................ | $30,000 |
| Plus deficiency of cash available over disbursements ................ | 36,100 |
| Minimum required borrowings ........................................ | $66,100 |

Again, recall that the bank requires loans be made in increments of $10,000. Because Hampton Freeze needs to borrow at least $66,100 at the beginning of the second quarter, the company will have to borrow $70,000 from the bank.

In the third and fourth quarters, Hampton Freeze has an excess of cash available over disbursements that is greater than $30,000, so it will not need to borrow money in these two quarters. Notice that in the third quarter Hampton Freeze has excess cash of $165,650, yet the cash budget does not include any principal or interest repayments during this quarter. This occurs because, unless stated otherwise, we always assume that the company will, as far as it is able, repay the loan plus accumulated interest on the *last day of the final period* included in the cash budget. Because Hampton Freeze has excess cash of $263,300 in the fourth quarter, on the last day of the fourth quarter, it would be able to repay the $200,000 that it borrowed from the lender plus $21,900 of interest computed as follows:

| Interest on the $130,000 borrowed at the beginning of the first quarter : | |
|---|---|
| $130,000 × 0.03 per quarter × 4 quarters* ................................... | $15,600 |
| Interest on the $70,000 borrowed at the beginning of the second quarter: | |
| $70,000 × 0.03 per quarter × 3 quarters* .................................... | 6,300 |
| Total interest accrued to the end of the fourth quarter ....................... | $21,900 |

*Simple, rather than compounded, interest is assumed for simplicity

The ending cash balance for each period is computed by taking the excess (deficiency) of cash available over disbursements plus the total financing. For example, in the first quarter, Hampton Freeze's cash deficiency of $(94,000) plus its total financing of $130,000 equals its ending cash balance of $36,000. The ending cash balance for each quarter then becomes the beginning cash balance for the next quarter. Also notice that the amounts under the Year column in the cash budget are not always the sum of the amounts for the four quarters. In particular, the beginning cash balance for the year is the same as the beginning cash balance for the first quarter and the ending cash balance for the year is the same as the ending cash balance for the fourth quarter.

## HELPFUL HINT

Students often incorrectly calculate the interest payments in the cash budget. To reduce your chances of making mistakes, remember that we always assume that money is borrowed on the first day of the period and that principal and interest payments are made on the last day of the period. This explains why Hampton Freeze will pay 12 months of interest on the $130,000 it plans to borrow on the first day of Quarter 1 (January 1, 2018) and repay on the last day of Quarter 4 (December 31, 2018). It also explains why Hampton Freeze will pay nine months of interest on the $70,000 it plans to borrow on the first day of Quarter 2 (April 1, 2018) and repay on the last day of Quarter 4 (December 31, 2018).

## Cinnabon Manages Seasonal Demand

### IN BUSINESS

**Cinnabon Inc.** has over 1,000 franchise locations worldwide including one of its most recent new store openings in Tripoli, Libya. The company's annual sales exceed $900 million with 60% of those revenues being earned in November and December. Seasonal demand impacts a variety of supporting schedules within a company's master budget. For example, materials and labor budgets are likely to differ in months with slack versus peak sales. In Cinnabon's case, the cash budget will show a spike in cash receipts during the last two months of the year with more modest cash inflows throughout the remainder of the year.

Source: Kwoh, Leslie, "Cinnabon Finds Sweet Success in Russia, Mideast," *The Wall Street Journal*, December 26, 2012, p. B5.

©AP Images/GDA

## The Budgeted Income Statement

**LEARNING OBJECTIVE 8–9**

Prepare a budgeted income statement.

Schedule 9 contains the budgeted income statement for Hampton Freeze. All of the sales and expenses shown on the budgeted income statement come from the data in the beginning balance sheet and the data developed in Schedules 1–8. The sales of $2,000,000 come from cell F9 of the sales budget (Schedule 1). Given that the unit product cost of the year's beginning inventory and the year's production both equal $13 per unit, the cost of goods sold of $1,300,000 can be computed by multiplying 100,000 units sold (see cell F7 from Schedule 1) by the unit product cost of $13 per unit (see cell H11

**SCHEDULE 9**

| | A | B | C |
|---|---|---|---|
| 1 | **Hampton Freeze, Inc.** | | |
| 2 | **Budgeted Income Statement** | | |
| 3 | **For the Year Ended December 31, 2018** | | |
| 4 | | | |
| 5 | | *Schedules* | |
| 6 | Sales | 1 | $ 2,000,000 |
| 7 | Cost of goods sold | 1, 6 | 1,300,000 |
| 8 | Gross margin | | 700,000 |
| 9 | Selling and administrative expenses | 7 | 576,000 |
| 10 | Net operating Income | | 124,000 |
| 11 | Interest expense | 8 | 21,900 |
| 12 | Net Income | | $  102,100 |
| 13 | | | |

Schedule 7 / Schedule 8 / **Schedule 9** / S

Source: Microsoft

in Schedule 6).[7] The selling and administrative expenses of $576,000 come from cell F17 of the selling and administrative expenses budget (Schedule 7). Finally, the interest expense of $21,900 comes from cell G23 of the cash budget (Schedule 8).

The budgeted income statement is one of the key schedules in the budget process. It shows the company's planned profit and serves as a benchmark against which subsequent company performance can be measured. Because Larry Giano created a Budgeting Assumptions tab in his Excel file (see Exhibit 8–4) and linked all of his budget schedules together using properly constructed Excel formulas, he can make changes to his underlying budgeting assumptions and instantly see the impact of the change on all of the schedules and on net income. For example, if Larry wanted to estimate the profit impact if fourth quarter sales are 18,000 cases instead of 20,000 cases, he would simply change the 20,000 cases shown in cell F7 of his Budgeting Assumptions worksheet to 18,000 cases. The revised net income of $87,045 would instantly appear in cell C12 of the budgeted income statement.

## The Budgeted Balance Sheet

**LEARNING OBJECTIVE 8–10**

Prepare a budgeted balance sheet.

The budgeted balance sheet is developed using data from the balance sheet from the beginning of the budget period (see Exhibit 8–3) and data contained in the various schedules. Hampton Freeze's budgeted balance sheet accompanied by explanations of how the numbers were derived is presented in Schedule 10.

**MANAGERIAL ACCOUNTING IN ACTION**

**THE WRAP-UP**

After completing the master budget, Larry Giano took the documents to Tom Wills, chief executive officer of Hampton Freeze, for his review.

**Larry:**  Here's the budget. Overall, the income is excellent, and the net cash flow for the entire year is positive.

**Tom:**  Yes, but I see on this cash budget that we have the same problem with negative cash flows in the first and second quarters that we had last year.

**Larry:**  That's true. I don't see any way around that problem. However, there is no doubt in my mind that if you take this budget to the bank today, they'll approve an open line of credit that will allow you to borrow enough money to make it through the first two quarters without any problem.

---

[7]Cost of goods sold can also be computed using equations introduced in earlier chapters. Manufacturing companies can use the equation: Cost of goods sold = Beginning finished goods inventory + Cost of goods manufactured – Ending finished goods inventory. Merchandising companies can use the equation: Cost of goods sold = Beginning merchandise inventory + Purchases – Ending merchandise inventory.

**SCHEDULE 10**

| | A | B | C | D | E |
|---|---|---|---|---|---|
| 1 | **Hampton Freeze, Inc.** | | | | |
| 2 | **Budgeted Balance Sheet** | | | | |
| 3 | **December 31, 2018** | | | | |
| 4 | | | | | |
| 5 | *Assets* | | | | |
| 6 | Current assets: | | | | |
| 7 | Cash | $ 41,400 | (a) | | |
| 8 | Accounts receivable | 120,000 | (b) | | |
| 9 | Raw materials inventory | 4,500 | (c) | | |
| 10 | Finished goods inventory | 39,000 | (d) | | |
| 11 | Total current assets | | | $ 204,900 | |
| 12 | Plant and equipment: | | | | |
| 13 | Land | 80,000 | (e) | | |
| 14 | Buildings and equipment | 830,000 | (f) | | |
| 15 | Accumulated depreciation | (392,000) | (g) | | |
| 16 | Plant and equipment, net | | | 518,000 | |
| 17 | Total assets | | | $ 722,900 | |
| 18 | | | | | |
| 19 | *Liabilities and Stockholders' Equity* | | | | |
| 20 | Current liabilities: | | | | |
| 21 | Accounts payable (raw materials) | | | $ 27,900 | (h) |
| 22 | Stockholders' equity: | | | | |
| 23 | Common stock, no par | $ 175,000 | (i) | | |
| 24 | Retained earnings | 520,000 | (j) | | |
| 25 | Total stockholders' equity | | | 695,000 | |
| 26 | Total liabilities and stockholders' equity | | | $ 722,900 | |
| 27 | | | | | |

Schedule 8 / Schedule 9 / **Schedule 10**

Source: Microsoft

Explanations of December 31, 2018, balance sheet figures:
(a) From cell G25 of the cash budget (Schedule 8).
(b) Thirty percent of fourth-quarter sales, from Schedule 1 ($400,000 × 30% = $120,000).
(c) From the direct materials budget (Schedule 3). Cell E12 multiplied by cell E16. In other words, 22,500 pounds × $0.20 per pound = $4,500.
(d) From cell H16 of the ending finished goods inventory budget (Schedule 6).
(e) From cell B13 of the beginning balance sheet (Exhibit 8–3).
(f) Cell B14 of the beginning balance sheet (Exhibit 8–3) plus cell G16 from the cash budget (Schedule 8). In other words, $700,000 + $130,000 = $830,000.
(g) The beginning balance of $292,000 (from cell B15 of the beginning balance sheet in Exhibit 8–3) plus the depreciation of $60,000 included in cell F12 of the manufacturing overhead budget (Schedule 5) plus depreciation expense of $40,000 included in cell F18 in the selling and administrative expense budget (Schedule 7). In other words, $292,000 + $60,000 + $40,000 = $392,000.
(h) One-half of fourth-quarter raw materials purchases, from Schedule 3 ($55,800 × 50% = $27,900).
(i) From cell B23 of the beginning balance sheet (Exhibit 8–3).
(j)

| | | |
|---|---|---|
| December 31, 2017, balance, from cell B24 of Exhibit 8–3 ........ | $449,900 | |
| Add net income, from cell C12 of Schedule 9...................... | 102,100 | |
| | 552,000 | |
| Deduct dividends paid, from cell G17 of Schedule 8 .............. | 32,000 | |
| December 31, 2018, balance ..................................... | $520,000 | |

*Tom:* Are you sure? They didn't seem very happy to see me last year when I came in for an emergency loan.

*Larry:* Did you repay the loan on time?

*Tom:* Sure.

*Larry:* I don't see any problem. You won't be asking for an emergency loan this time. The bank will have plenty of warning. And with this budget, you have a solid plan that shows when and how you are going to pay off the loan. Trust me, they'll go for it. Also, keep in mind that the master budget contains all the embedded formulas you'll need to answer the types of "what if" questions that we discussed earlier. If you want to calculate the financial impact of changing any of your master budget's underlying estimates or assumptions, you can do it with the click of a mouse!

*Tom:* This sounds fabulous Larry. Thanks for all of your work on this project.

## HELPFUL HINT

One of the most important equations that you should learn while studying accounting is shown in item (j) of Schedule 10 . The beginning balance in Retained Earnings plus net income minus dividends equals the ending balance in Retained Earnings. This equation highlights how the income statement and the balance sheet connect to one another. The net income from the income statement plugs into Retained Earnings on the balance sheet. This concept, which is formally referred to as articulated financial statements, is something that all business students must understand.

## SUMMARY

### LO8–1 Understand why organizations budget and the processes they use to create budgets.

Organizations budget for a variety of reasons, including to communicate management's plans throughout the organization, to force managers to think about and plan for the future, to allocate resources within the organization, to identify bottlenecks before they occur, to coordinate activities, and to provide benchmarks for evaluating subsequent performance.

Budgets should be developed with the full participation of all managers who will be subject to budgetary controls.

### LO8–2 Prepare a sales budget, including a schedule of expected cash collections.

The sales budget forms the foundation for the master budget. It provides details concerning the anticipated unit and dollar sales.

The schedule of expected cash collections is based on the sales budget, the expected breakdown between cash and credit sales, and the expected pattern of collections on credit sales.

### LO8–3 Prepare a production budget.

The production budget details how many units must be produced each budget period to satisfy expected sales and to provide for adequate levels of finished goods inventories.

### LO8–4 Prepare a direct materials budget, including a schedule of expected cash disbursements for purchases of materials.

The direct materials budget shows the materials that must be purchased each budget period to meet anticipated production requirements and to provide for adequate levels of materials inventories.

Cash disbursements for purchases of materials will depend on the amount of materials purchased in each budget period and the company's policies concerning payments to suppliers for materials bought on credit.

### LO8–5 Prepare a direct labor budget.

The direct labor budget shows the direct labor-hours that are required to meet the production schedule as detailed in the production budget. The direct labor-hour requirements are used to determine the direct labor cost in each budget period.

### LO8–6 Prepare a manufacturing overhead budget.

Manufacturing overhead consists of both variable and fixed manufacturing overhead. The variable manufacturing overhead depends on the number of units produced from the production budget. The variable and fixed manufacturing overhead costs are combined to determine the total manufacturing overhead. Any noncash manufacturing overhead such as depreciation is deducted from the total manufacturing overhead to determine the cash disbursements for manufacturing overhead.

### LO8–7 Prepare a selling and administrative expense budget.

Like manufacturing overhead, selling and administrative expenses consist of both variable and fixed expenses. The variable expenses depend on the number of units sold or some other measure of activity. The variable and fixed expenses are combined to determine the total selling and administrative expense. Any noncash selling and administrative expenses such as depreciation are deducted from the total to determine the cash disbursements for selling and administrative expenses.

### LO8–8 Prepare a cash budget.

The cash budget is a critical piece of the master budget. It permits managers to anticipate and plan for cash shortfalls.

The cash budget is organized into a receipts section, a disbursements section, a cash excess or deficiency section, and a financing section. The cash budget draws on information taken from nearly all of the other budgets and schedules including the schedule of cash collections, the schedule of cash disbursements for purchases of materials, the direct labor budget, the manufacturing overhead budget, and the selling and administrative expense budget.

### LO8–9 Prepare a budgeted income statement.

The budgeted income statement is constructed using data from the sales budget, the ending finished goods inventory budget, the manufacturing overhead budget, the selling and administrative budget, and the cash budget.

### LO8–10 Prepare a budgeted balance sheet.

The budgeted balance sheet is constructed using data from virtually all other parts of the master budget.

## GUIDANCE ANSWER TO DECISION POINT

**Budget Analyst**

Not all costs are variable with respect to gross restaurant sales. For example, assuming no change in the number of restaurant sites, rental costs are probably fixed. To more accurately forecast costs for the budget, costs should be separated into variable and fixed components. Furthermore, more appropriate activity measures should be selected for the variable costs. For example, gross restaurant sales may be divided into food sales and bar sales—each of which could serve as an activity measure for some costs. In addition, some costs (such as the costs of free dinner rolls) may be variable with respect to the number of diners rather than with respect to food or bar sales. Other activity measures may permit even more accurate cost predictions.

## GUIDANCE ANSWERS TO CONCEPT CHECKS

1. **Choice b.** Responsibility accounting focuses on holding managers accountable for only those items that they can control.
2. **Choice c.** Cash collections for April are calculated as follows: ($100,000 × 80% × 40%) + ($120,000 × 20%) + ($120,000 × 80% × 60%) = $113,600.
3. **Choice a.** The May 31 accounts receivable balance is $125,000 × 80% × 40% = $40,000.
4. **Choice b.** Required inventory purchases are calculated as follows: Cost of goods sold of $300,000 + Ending inventory of $30,000 − Beginning inventory of $50,000 = $280,000.
5. **Choice b.** 80,000 units sold in April + 27,000 units of desired ending inventory − 24,000 units of beginning inventory = 83,000 units.
6. **Choice d.** The manufacturing overhead budget includes depreciation on manufacturing assets. Cash disbursements for selling and administrative expenses are reported in the cash budget. The selling and administrative expense budget included depreciation related to assets that support a company's selling and administrative functions.

# REVIEW PROBLEM: BUDGET SCHEDULES

Mynor Corporation manufactures and sells a seasonal product that has peak sales in the third quarter. The following information concerns operations for Year 2—the coming year—and for the first two quarters of Year 3:

a.  The company's single product sells for $8 per unit. Budgeted unit sales for the next six quarters are as follows (all sales are on credit):

|  | Year 2 Quarter | | | | Year 3 Quarter | |
|---|---|---|---|---|---|---|
|  | 1 | 2 | 3 | 4 | 1 | 2 |
| Budgeted unit sales ......... | 40,000 | 60,000 | 100,000 | 50,000 | 70,000 | 80,000 |

b.  Sales are collected in the following pattern: 75% in the quarter the sales are made, and the remaining 25% in the following quarter. On January 1, Year 2, the company's balance sheet showed $65,000 in accounts receivable, all of which will be collected in the first quarter of the year. Bad debts are negligible and can be ignored.

c.  The company desires an ending finished goods inventory at the end of each quarter equal to 30% of the budgeted unit sales for the next quarter. On December 31, Year 1, the company had 12,000 units on hand.

d.  Five pounds of raw materials are required to complete one unit of product. The company requires ending raw materials inventory at the end of each quarter equal to 10% of the following quarter's production needs. On December 31, Year 1, the company had 23,000 pounds of raw materials on hand.

e.  The raw material costs $0.80 per pound. Raw material purchases are paid for in the following pattern: 60% paid in the quarter the purchases are made, and the remaining 40% paid in the following quarter. On January 1, Year 2, the company's balance sheet showed $81,500 in accounts payable for raw material purchases, all of which will be paid for in the first quarter of the year.

*Required:*
Prepare the following budgets and schedules for the year, showing both quarterly and total figures:
1.  A sales budget and a schedule of expected cash collections.
2.  A production budget.
3.  A direct materials budget and a schedule of expected cash payments for purchases of materials.

**Solution to Review Problem**
1.  The sales budget is prepared as follows:

|  | Year 2 Quarter | | | | |
|---|---|---|---|---|---|
|  | 1 | 2 | 3 | 4 | Year 2 |
| Budgeted unit sales ....... | 40,000 | 60,000 | 100,000 | 50,000 | 250,000 |
| Selling price per unit ...... | × $8 | × $8 | × $8 | × $8 | × $8 |
| Total sales ................. | $320,000 | $480,000 | $800,000 | $400,000 | $2,000,000 |

Based on the budgeted sales above, the schedule of expected cash collections is prepared as follows:

|  | Year 2 Quarter | | | | |
|---|---|---|---|---|---|
|  | 1 | 2 | 3 | 4 | Year 2 |
| Beginning accounts receivable ............................... | $ 65,000 | | | | $  65,000 |
| First-quarter sales ($320,000 × 75%, 25%) .................... | 240,000 | $ 80,000 | | | 320,000 |
| Second-quarter sales ($480,000 × 75%, 25%) ................ | | 360,000 | $120,000 | | 480,000 |
| Third-quarter sales ($800,000 × 75%, 25%) ................... | | | 600,000 | $200,000 | 800,000 |
| Fourth-quarter sales ($400,000 × 75%) ...................... | | | | 300,000 | 300,000 |
| Total cash collections ......................................... | $305,000 | $440,000 | $720,000 | $500,000 | $1,965,000 |

2. Based on the sales budget in units, the production budget is prepared as follows:

| | Year 2 Quarter | | | | | Year 3 Quarter | |
| --- | --- | --- | --- | --- | --- | --- | --- |
| | 1 | 2 | 3 | 4 | Year 2 | 1 | 2 |
| Budgeted unit sales | 40,000 | 60,000 | 100,000 | 50,000 | 250,000 | 70,000 | 80,000 |
| Add desired ending finished goods inventory* | 18,000 | 30,000 | 15,000 | 21,000† | 21,000 | 24,000 | |
| Total needs | 58,000 | 90,000 | 115,000 | 71,000 | 271,000 | 94,000 | |
| Less beginning finished goods inventory | 12,000 | 18,000 | 30,000 | 15,000 | 12,000 | 21,000 | |
| Required production | 46,000 | 72,000 | 85,000 | 56,000 | 259,000 | 73,000 | |

*30% of the following quarter's budgeted unit sales.
†30% of the budgeted Year 3 first-quarter sales.

3. Based on the production budget, raw materials will need to be purchased during the year as follows:

| | Year 2 Quarter | | | | | Year 3 Quarter |
| --- | --- | --- | --- | --- | --- | --- |
| | 1 | 2 | 3 | 4 | Year 2 | 1 |
| Required production in units of finished goods | 46,000 | 72,000 | 85,000 | 56,000 | 259,000 | 73,000 |
| Units of raw materials needed per unit of finished goods | × 5 | × 5 | × 5 | × 5 | × 5 | × 5 |
| Units of raw materials needed to meet production | 230,000 | 360,000 | 425,000 | 280,000 | 1,295,000 | 365,000 |
| Add desired units of ending raw materials inventory* | 36,000 | 42,500 | 28,000 | 36,500† | 36,500 | |
| Total units of raw materials needed | 266,000 | 402,500 | 453,000 | 316,500 | 1,331,500 | |
| Less units of beginning raw materials inventory | 23,000 | 36,000 | 42,500 | 28,000 | 23,000 | |
| Units of raw materials to be purchased | 243,000 | 366,500 | 410,500 | 288,500 | 1,308,500 | |
| Unit cost of raw materials | × $0.80 | × $0.80 | × $0.80 | × $0.80 | × $0.80 | |
| Cost of raw materials to be purchased | $194,400 | $293,200 | $328,400 | $230,800 | $1,046,800 | |

*10% of the following quarter's production needs in pounds.
†10% of the Year 3 first-quarter production needs in pounds.

Based on the raw material purchases above, expected cash payments are computed as follows:

| | Year 2 Quarter | | | | |
| --- | --- | --- | --- | --- | --- |
| | 1 | 2 | 3 | 4 | Year 2 |
| Beginning accounts payable | $ 81,500 | | | | $ 81,500 |
| First-quarter purchases ($194,400 × 60%, 40%) | 116,640 | $ 77,760 | | | 194,400 |
| Second-quarter purchases ($293,200 × 60%, 40%) | | 175,920 | $117,280 | | 293,200 |
| Third-quarter purchases ($328,400 × 60%, 40%) | | | 197,040 | $131,360 | 328,400 |
| Fourth-quarter purchases ($230,800 × 60%) | | | | 138,480 | 138,480 |
| Total cash disbursements | $198,140 | $253,680 | $314,320 | $269,840 | $1,035,980 |

# GLOSSARY

**Budget**   A detailed plan for the future that is usually expressed in formal quantitative terms. (p. 334)

**Cash budget**   A detailed plan showing how cash resources will be acquired and used over a specific time period. (p. 338)

**Continuous budget**   A 12-month budget that rolls forward one month as the current month is completed. (p. 335)

**Control**   The process of gathering feedback to ensure that a plan is being properly executed or modified as circumstances change. (p. 334)

**Direct labor budget**   A detailed plan that shows the direct labor-hours required to fulfill the production budget. (p. 349)

**Direct materials budget**   A detailed plan showing the amount of raw materials that must be purchased to fulfill the production budget and to provide for adequate inventories. (p. 347)

**Ending finished goods inventory budget**   A budget showing the dollar amount of unsold finished goods inventory that will appear on the ending balance sheet. (p. 351)

**Manufacturing overhead budget**   A detailed plan showing the production costs, other than direct materials and direct labor, that will be incurred over a specified time period. (p. 350)

**Master budget**   A number of separate but interdependent budgets that formally lay out the company's sales, production, and financial goals and that culminates in a cash budget, budgeted income statement, and budgeted balance sheet. (p. 337)

**Merchandise purchases budget**   A detailed plan used by a merchandising company that shows the amount of goods that must be purchased from suppliers during the period. (p. 346)

**Participative budget**   See *Self-imposed budget.* (p. 335)

**Perpetual budget**   See *Continuous budget.* (p. 335)

**Planning**   The process of establishing goals and specifying how to achieve them.  (p. 334)

**Production budget**   A detailed plan showing the number of units that must be produced during a period in order to satisfy both sales and inventory needs. (p. 345)

**Responsibility accounting**   A system of accountability in which managers are held responsible for those items of revenue and cost—and only those items—over which they can exert significant control. The managers are held responsible for differences between budgeted and actual results. (p. 335)

**Sales budget**   A detailed schedule showing expected sales expressed in both dollars and units. (p. 338)

**Self-imposed budget**   A method of preparing budgets in which managers prepare their own budgets. These budgets are then reviewed by higher-level managers, and any issues are resolved by mutual agreement. (p. 335)

**Selling and administrative expense budget**   A detailed schedule of planned expenses that will be incurred in areas other than manufacturing during a budget period. (p. 351)

# QUESTIONS

**8–1**   What is a budget? What is budgetary control?

**8–2**   Discuss some of the major benefits to be gained from budgeting.

**8–3**   What is meant by the term *responsibility accounting?*

**8–4**   What is a master budget? Briefly describe its contents.

**8–5**   Why is the sales forecast the starting point in budgeting?

**8–6**   "As a practical matter, planning and control mean exactly the same thing." Do you agree? Explain.

**8–7**   Why is it a good idea to create a "Budgeting Assumptions" tab when creating a master budget in Microsoft Excel?

**8–8**   What is a self-imposed budget? What are the major advantages of self-imposed budgets? What caution must be exercised in their use?

**8–9**   How can budgeting assist a company in planning its workforce staffing levels?

**8–10**   "The principal purpose of the cash budget is to see how much cash the company will have in the bank at the end of the year." Do you agree? Explain.

# APPLYING EXCEL        connect

**LO8–2, LO8–3, LO8–4**

The Excel worksheet form that appears below is to be used to recreate the Review Problem related to Mynor Corporation. Download the workbook containing this form from Connect, where you will also receive instructions about how to use this worksheet form.

| | A | B | C | D | E | F | G | H | I |
|---|---|---|---|---|---|---|---|---|---|
| 1 | Chapter 8: Applying Excel | | | | | | | | |
| 2 | | | | | | | | | |
| 3 | Data | | | Year 2 Quarter | | | Year 3 Quarter | | |
| 4 | | | 1 | 2 | 3 | 4 | 1 | 2 | |
| 5 | Budgeted unit sales | | 40,000 | 60,000 | 100,000 | 50,000 | 70,000 | 80,000 | |
| 6 | | | | | | | | | |
| 7 | • Selling price per unit | $8 | | | | | | | |
| 8 | • Accounts receivable, beginning balance | $65,000 | | | | | | | |
| 9 | • Sales collected in the quarter sales are made | 75% | | | | | | | |
| 10 | • Sales collected in the quarter after sales are made | 25% | | | | | | | |
| 11 | • Desired ending finished goods inventory is | 30% of the budgeted unit sales of the next quarter | | | | | | | |
| 12 | • Finished goods inventory, beginning | 12,000 units | | | | | | | |
| 13 | • Raw materials required to produce one unit | 5 pounds | | | | | | | |
| 14 | • Desired ending inventory of raw materials is | 10% of the next quarter's production needs | | | | | | | |
| 15 | • Raw materials inventory, beginning | 23,000 pounds | | | | | | | |
| 16 | • Raw material costs | $0.80 per pound | | | | | | | |
| 17 | • Raw materials purchases are paid | 60% in the quarter the purchases are made | | | | | | | |
| 18 | and | 40% in the quarter following purchase | | | | | | | |
| 19 | • Accounts payable for raw materials, beginning balance | $81,500 | | | | | | | |
| 20 | | | | | | | | | |
| 21 | Enter a formula into each of the cells marked with a ? below | | | | | | | | |
| 22 | Review Problem: Budget Schedules | | | | | | | | |
| 23 | | | | | | | | | |
| 24 | Construct the sales budget | | | Year 2 Quarter | | | Year 3 Quarter | | |
| 25 | | | 1 | 2 | 3 | 4 | 1 | 2 | |
| 26 | Budgeted unit sales | | ? | ? | ? | ? | ? | ? | |
| 27 | Selling price per unit | | ? | ? | ? | ? | ? | ? | |
| 28 | Total sales | | ? | ? | ? | ? | ? | ? | |
| 29 | | | | | | | | | |
| 30 | Construct the schedule of expected cash collections | | | Year 2 Quarter | | | | | |
| 31 | | | 1 | 2 | 3 | 4 | Year | | |
| 32 | Beginning balance accounts receivable | | ? | | | | ? | | |
| 33 | First-quarter sales | | ? | ? | | | ? | | |
| 34 | Second-quarter sales | | | ? | ? | | ? | | |
| 35 | Third-quarter sales | | | | ? | ? | ? | | |
| 36 | Fourth-quarter sales | | | | | ? | ? | | |
| 37 | Total cash collections | | ? | ? | ? | ? | ? | | |
| 38 | | | | | | | | | |
| 39 | Construct the production budget | | | Year 2 Quarter | | | | Year 3 Quarter | |
| 40 | | | 1 | 2 | 3 | 4 | Year | 1 | 2 |
| 41 | Budgeted unit sales | | ? | ? | ? | ? | ? | ? | ? |
| 42 | Add desired ending finished goods inventory | | ? | ? | ? | ? | ? | ? | |
| 43 | Total needs | | ? | ? | ? | ? | ? | ? | |
| 44 | Less beginning finished goods inventory | | ? | ? | ? | ? | ? | ? | |
| 45 | Required production in units | | ? | ? | ? | ? | ? | ? | |
| 46 | | | | | | | | | |
| 47 | Construct the raw materials purchases budget | | | Year 2 Quarter | | | | Year 3 Quarter | |
| 48 | | | 1 | 2 | 3 | 4 | Year | 1 | |
| 49 | Required production (units) | | ? | ? | ? | ? | ? | ? | |
| 50 | Raw materials required to produce one unit (pounds) | | ? | ? | ? | ? | ? | ? | |
| 51 | Production needs (pounds) | | ? | ? | ? | ? | ? | ? | |
| 52 | Add desired ending inventory of raw materials (pounds) | | ? | ? | ? | ? | ? | | |
| 53 | Total needs (pounds) | | ? | ? | ? | ? | ? | | |
| 54 | Less beginning inventory of raw materials (pounds) | | ? | ? | ? | ? | ? | | |
| 55 | Raw materials to be purchased (pounds) | | ? | ? | ? | ? | ? | | |
| 56 | Cost of raw materials per pound | | ? | ? | ? | ? | ? | | |
| 57 | Cost of raw materials to be purchased | | ? | ? | ? | ? | ? | | |
| 58 | | | | | | | | | |
| 59 | Construct the schedule of expected cash payments | | | Year 2 Quarter | | | | | |
| 60 | | | 1 | 2 | 3 | 4 | Year | | |
| 61 | Beginning balance accounts payable | | ? | | | | ? | | |
| 62 | First-quarter purchases | | ? | ? | | | ? | | |
| 63 | Second-quarter purchases | | | ? | ? | | ? | | |
| 64 | Third-quarter purchases | | | | ? | ? | ? | | |
| 65 | Fourth-quarter purchases | | | | | ? | ? | | |
| 66 | Total cash disbursements | | ? | ? | ? | ? | ? | | |
| 67 | | | | | | | | | |

⊮ ◀ ▶ ⊮  **Chapter 8 Form** / Filled in Chapter 8 Form / Chapter 8 Formulas / Chapter 8 Requirement ◀

You should proceed to the requirements below only after completing your worksheet.

*Required:*

1.  Check your worksheet by changing the budgeted unit sales in Quarter 2 of Year 2 in cell C5 to 75,000 units. The total expected cash collections for the year should now be $2,085,000. If you do not get this answer, find the errors in your worksheet and correct them. Have the total cash disbursements for the year changed? Why or why not?
2.  The company has just hired a new marketing manager who insists that unit sales can be dramatically increased by dropping the selling price from $8 to $7. The marketing manager would like to use the following projections in the budget:

|  | Year 2 Quarter | | | | Year 3 Quarter | |
|---|---|---|---|---|---|---|
|  | **1** | **2** | **3** | **4** | **1** | **2** |
| Budgeted unit sales ..... | 50,000 | 70,000 | 120,000 | 80,000 | 90,000 | 100,000 |
| Selling price per unit .... | $7 | | | | | |

a.  What are the total expected cash collections for the year under this revised budget?
b.  What is the total required production for the year under this revised budget?
c.  What is the total cost of raw materials to be purchased for the year under this revised budget?
d.  What are the total expected cash disbursements for raw materials for the year under this revised budget?
e.  After seeing this revised budget, the production manager cautioned that due to the limited availability of a complex milling machine, the plant can produce no more than 90,000 units in any one quarter. Is this a potential problem? If so, what can be done about it?

# THE FOUNDATIONAL 15  ■connect

**LO8–2, LO8–3, LO8–4, LO8–5, LO8–7, LO8–9, LO8–10**

Morganton Company makes one product and it provided the following information to help prepare the master budget:

a.  The budgeted selling price per unit is $70. Budgeted unit sales for June, July, August, and September are 8,400, 10,000, 12,000, and 13,000 units, respectively. All sales are on credit.
b.  Forty percent of credit sales are collected in the month of the sale and 60% in the following month.
c.  The ending finished goods inventory equals 20% of the following month's unit sales.
d.  The ending raw materials inventory equals 10% of the following month's raw materials production needs. Each unit of finished goods requires 5 pounds of raw materials. The raw materials cost $2.00 per pound.
e.  Thirty percent of raw materials purchases are paid for in the month of purchase and 70% in the following month.
f.  The direct labor wage rate is $15 per hour. Each unit of finished goods requires two direct labor-hours.
g.  The variable selling and administrative expense per unit sold is $1.80. The fixed selling and administrative expense per month is $60,000.

*Required:*

1.  What are the budgeted sales for July?
2.  What are the expected cash collections for July?
3.  What is the accounts receivable balance at the end of July?
4.  According to the production budget, how many units should be produced in July?
5.  If 61,000 pounds of raw materials are needed to meet production in August, how many pounds of raw materials should be purchased in July?
6.  What is the estimated cost of raw materials purchases for July?
7.  In July what are the total estimated cash disbursements for raw materials purchases? Assume the cost of raw material purchases in June is $88,880.
8.  What is the estimated accounts payable balance at the end of July?
9.  What is the estimated raw materials inventory balance at the end of July?
10. What is the total estimated direct labor cost for July assuming the direct labor workforce is adjusted to match the hours required to produce the forecasted number of units produced?

11. If we assume that there is no fixed manufacturing overhead and the variable manufacturing overhead is $10 per direct labor-hour, what is the estimated unit product cost?
12. What is the estimated finished goods inventory balance at the end of July?
13. What is the estimated cost of goods sold and gross margin for July?
14. What is the estimated total selling and administrative expense for July?
15. What is the estimated net operating income for July?

**connect**                    **EXERCISES**

### EXERCISE 8-1    Schedule of Expected Cash Collections LO8-2

Silver Company makes a product that is very popular as a Mother's Day gift. Thus, peak sales occur in May of each year, as shown in the company's sales budget for the second quarter given below:

|                                   | April    | May      | June     | Total      |
|-----------------------------------|----------|----------|----------|------------|
| Budgeted sales (all on account) . . . . . . . . . . . . . . . . . . | $300,000 | $500,000 | $200,000 | $1,000,000 |

From past experience, the company has learned that 20% of a month's sales are collected in the month of sale, another 70% are collected in the month following sale, and the remaining 10% are collected in the second month following sale. Bad debts are negligible and can be ignored. February sales totaled $230,000, and March sales totaled $260,000.

**Required:**
1. Using Schedule 1 as your guide, prepare a schedule of expected cash collections from sales, by month and in total, for the second quarter.
2. What is the accounts receivable balance on June 30th?

### EXERCISE 8-2    Production Budget LO8-3

Down Under Products, Ltd., of Australia has budgeted sales of its popular boomerang for the next four months as follows:

|         | Unit Sales |
|---------|------------|
| April . . . . . . . . . . . . . . . . . . | 50,000 |
| May . . . . . . . . . . . . . . . . . . | 75,000 |
| June . . . . . . . . . . . . . . . . . . | 90,000 |
| July . . . . . . . . . . . . . . . . . . | 80,000 |

The company is now in the process of preparing a production budget for the second quarter. Past experience has shown that end-of-month inventory levels must equal 10% of the following month's unit sales. The inventory at the end of March was 5,000 units.

**Required:**
Using Schedule 2 as your guide, prepare a production budget by month and in total, for the second quarter.

### EXERCISE 8-3    Direct Materials Budget LO8-4

Three grams of musk oil are required for each bottle of Mink Caress, a very popular perfume made by a small company in western Siberia. The cost of the musk oil is $1.50 per gram. Budgeted production of Mink Caress is given below by quarters for Year 2 and for the first quarter of Year 3:

|                                      |        | Year 2 |         |         | Year 3 |
|--------------------------------------|--------|--------|---------|---------|--------|
|                                      | First  | Second | Third   | Fourth  | First  |
| Budgeted production, in bottles . . . . . . . . . . . | 60,000 | 90,000 | 150,000 | 100,000 | 70,000 |

Musk oil has become so popular as a perfume ingredient that it has become necessary to carry large inventories as a precaution against stock-outs. For this reason, the inventory of musk oil at the end of a quarter must be equal to 20% of the following quarter's production needs. Some 36,000 grams of musk oil will be on hand to start the first quarter of Year 2.

**Required:**
Using Schedule 3 as your guide, prepare a direct materials budget for musk oil, by quarter and in total, for Year 2.

### EXERCISE 8–4  Direct Labor Budget LO8–5
The production manager of Rordan Corporation has submitted the following quarterly production forecast for the upcoming fiscal year:

|  | 1st Quarter | 2nd Quarter | 3rd Quarter | 4th Quarter |
|---|---|---|---|---|
| Units to be produced ............. | 8,000 | 6,500 | 7,000 | 7,500 |

Each unit requires 0.35 direct labor-hours, and direct laborers are paid $12.00 per hour.

**Required:**
1. Using Schedule 4 as your guide, prepare the company's direct labor budget for the upcoming fiscal year. Assume that the direct labor workforce is adjusted each quarter to match the number of hours required to produce the forecasted number of units produced.
2. Prepare the company's direct labor budget for the upcoming fiscal year, assuming that the direct labor workforce is not adjusted each quarter. Instead, assume that the company's direct labor workforce consists of permanent employees who are guaranteed to be paid for at least 2,600 hours of work each quarter. If the number of required direct labor-hours is less than this number, the workers are paid for 2,600 hours anyway. Any hours worked in excess of 2,600 hours in a quarter are paid at the rate of 1.5 times the normal hourly rate for direct labor.

### EXERCISE 8–5  Manufacturing Overhead Budget LO8–6
The direct labor budget of Yuvwell Corporation for the upcoming fiscal year contains the following details concerning budgeted direct labor-hours:

|  | 1st Quarter | 2nd Quarter | 3rd Quarter | 4th Quarter |
|---|---|---|---|---|
| Budgeted direct labor-hours ...... | 8,000 | 8,200 | 8,500 | 7,800 |

The company uses direct labor-hours as its overhead allocation base. The variable portion of its predetermined manufacturing overhead rate is $3.25 per direct labor-hour and its total fixed manufacturing overhead is $48,000 per quarter. The only noncash item included in fixed manufacturing overhead is depreciation, which is $16,000 per quarter.

**Required:**
1. Using Schedule 5 as your guide, prepare the company's manufacturing overhead budget for the upcoming fiscal year.
2. Compute the company's predetermined overhead rate (including both variable and fixed manufacturing overhead) for the upcoming fiscal year. Round off to the nearest whole cent.

### EXERCISE 8–6  Selling and Administrative Expense Budget LO8–7
Weller Company's budgeted unit sales for the upcoming fiscal year are provided below:

|  | 1st Quarter | 2nd Quarter | 3rd Quarter | 4th Quarter |
|---|---|---|---|---|
| Budgeted unit sales ................ | 15,000 | 16,000 | 14,000 | 13,000 |

The company's variable selling and administrative expense per unit is $2.50. Fixed selling and administrative expenses include advertising expenses of $8,000 per quarter, executive salaries of $35,000 per quarter, and depreciation of $20,000 per quarter. In addition, the company will make insurance payments of $5,000 in the first quarter and $5,000 in the third quarter. Finally, property taxes of $8,000 will be paid in the second quarter.

**Required:**
Using Schedule 7 as your guide, prepare the company's selling and administrative expense budget for the upcoming fiscal year.

### EXERCISE 8-7  Cash Budget LO8-8
Garden Depot is a retailer that is preparing its budget for the upcoming fiscal year. Management has prepared the following summary of its budgeted cash flows:

|  | 1st Quarter | 2nd Quarter | 3rd Quarter | 4th Quarter |
|---|---|---|---|---|
| Total cash receipts | $180,000 | $330,000 | $210,000 | $230,000 |
| Total cash disbursements | $260,000 | $230,000 | $220,000 | $240,000 |

The company's beginning cash balance for the upcoming fiscal year will be $20,000. The company requires a minimum cash balance of $10,000 and may borrow any amount needed from a local bank at a quarterly interest rate of 3%. The company may borrow any amount at the beginning of any quarter and may repay its loans, or any part of its loans, at the end of any quarter. Interest payments are due on any principal at the time it is repaid. For simplicity, assume that interest is not compounded.

**Required:**
Using Schedule 8 as your guide, prepare the company's cash budget for the upcoming fiscal year.

### EXERCISE 8-8  Budgeted Income Statement LO8-9
Gig Harbor Boating is the wholesale distributor of a small recreational catamaran sailboat. Management has prepared the following summary data to use in its annual budgeting process:

| | |
|---|---|
| Budgeted unit sales | 460 |
| Selling price per unit | $1,950 |
| Cost per unit | $1,575 |
| Variable selling and administrative expenses (per unit) | $75 |
| Fixed selling and administrative expenses (per year) | $105,000 |
| Interest expense for the year | $14,000 |

**Required:**
Using Schedule 9 as your guide, prepare the company's budgeted income statement for the year.

### EXERCISE 8-9  Budgeted Balance Sheet LO8-10
The management of Mecca Copy, a photocopying center located on University Avenue, has compiled the following data to use in preparing its budgeted balance sheet for next year:

| | Ending Balances |
|---|---|
| Cash | ? |
| Accounts receivable | $8,100 |
| Supplies inventory | $3,200 |
| Equipment | $34,000 |
| Accumulated depreciation | $16,000 |
| Accounts payable | $1,800 |
| Common stock | $5,000 |
| Retained earnings | ? |

The beginning balance of retained earnings was $28,000, net income is budgeted to be $11,500, and dividends are budgeted to be $4,800.

**Required:**
Prepare the company's budgeted balance sheet.

**EXERCISE 8-10    Production and Direct Materials Budgets** LO8-3, LO8-4

Pearl Products Limited of Shenzhen, China, manufactures and distributes toys throughout Southeast Asia. Three cubic centimeters (cc) of solvent H300 are required to manufacture each unit of Supermix, one of the company's products. The company now is planning raw materials needs for the third quarter, the quarter in which peak sales of Supermix occur. To keep production and sales moving smoothly, the company has the following inventory requirements:

a.  The finished goods inventory on hand at the end of each month must equal 3,000 units of Supermix plus 20% of the next month's sales. The finished goods inventory on June 30 is budgeted to be 10,000 units.

b.  The raw materials inventory on hand at the end of each month must equal one-half of the following month's production needs for raw materials. The raw materials inventory on June 30 is budgeted to be 54,000 cc of solvent H300.

c.  The company maintains no work in process inventories.

A monthly sales budget for Supermix for the third and fourth quarters of the year follows.

|  | **Budgeted Unit Sales** |
|---|---|
| July ............................. | 35,000 |
| August ......................... | 40,000 |
| September ..................... | 50,000 |
| October ........................ | 30,000 |
| November ...................... | 20,000 |
| December ...................... | 10,000 |

*Required:*

1.  Prepare a production budget for Supermix for the months July, August, September, and October.
2.  Examine the production budget that you prepared in (1) above. Why will the company produce more units than it sells in July and August, and fewer units than it sells in September and October?
3.  Prepare a direct materials budget showing the quantity of solvent H300 to be purchased for July, August, and September, and for the quarter in total.

**EXERCISE 8-11    Cash Budget Analysis** LO8-8

A cash budget, by quarters, is given below for a retail company (000 omitted). The company requires a minimum cash balance of at least $5,000 to start each quarter.

|  | | | Quarter | | |
|---|---|---|---|---|---|
|  | **1** | **2** | **3** | **4** | **Year** |
| Cash balance, beginning ....................... | $ 6 | $ ? | $ ? | $ ? | $ ? |
| Add collections from customers ............................. | ? | ? | 96 | ? | 323 |
| Total cash available ........................................... | 71 | ? | ? | ? | ? |
| Less disbursements: | | | | | |
| Purchase of inventory ..................................... | 35 | 45 | ? | 35 | ? |
| Selling and administrative expenses ...................... | ? | 30 | 30 | ? | 113 |
| Equipment purchases ...................................... | 8 | 8 | 10 | ? | 36 |
| Dividends ................................................. | 2 | 2 | 2 | 2 | ? |
| Total disbursements ........................................... | ? | 85 | ? | ? | ? |
| Excess (deficiency) of cash available over disbursements .... | (2) | ? | 11 | ? | ? |
| Financing: | | | | | |
| Borrowings .................................................. | ? | 15 | — | — | ? |
| Repayments (including interest)* ........................... | — | — | (?) | (17) | (?) |
| Total financing ................................................. | ? | ? | ? | ? | ? |
| Cash balance, ending ......................................... | $ ? | $ ? | $ ? | $ ? | $ ? |

*Interest will total $1,000 for the year.

**Required:**
Fill in the missing amounts in the above table.

**EXERCISE 8–12  Schedules of Expected Cash Collections and Disbursements; Income Statement; Balance Sheet** LO8–2, LO8–4, LO8–9, LO8–10

Beech Corporation is a merchandising company that is preparing a master budget for the third quarter of the calendar year. The company's balance sheet as of June 30th is shown below:

| Beech Corporation Balance Sheet June 30 | |
| --- | --- |
| **Assets** | |
| Cash ....................................................... | $ 90,000 |
| Accounts receivable ........................................ | 136,000 |
| Inventory .................................................. | 62,000 |
| Plant and equipment, net of depreciation .................... | 210,000 |
| Total assets .............................................. | $498,000 |
| **Liabilities and Stockholders' Equity** | |
| Accounts payable ........................................... | $ 71,100 |
| Common stock .............................................. | 327,000 |
| Retained earnings .......................................... | 99,900 |
| Total liabilities and stockholders' equity .................... | $498,000 |

Beech's managers have made the following additional assumptions and estimates:

1.  Estimated sales for July, August, September, and October will be $210,000, $230,000, $220,000, and $240,000, respectively.
2.  All sales are on credit and all credit sales are collected. Each month's credit sales are collected 35% in the month of sale and 65% in the month following the sale. All of the accounts receivable at June 30 will be collected in July.
3.  Each month's ending inventory must equal 30% of the cost of next month's sales. The cost of goods sold is 60% of sales. The company pays for 40% of its merchandise purchases in the month of the purchase and the remaining 60% in the month following the purchase. All of the accounts payable at June 30 will be paid in July.
4.  Monthly selling and administrative expenses are always $60,000. Each month $5,000 of this total amount is depreciation expense and the remaining $55,000 relates to expenses that are paid in the month they are incurred.
5.  The company does not plan to borrow money or pay or declare dividends during the quarter ended September 30. The company does not plan to issue any common stock or repurchase its own stock during the quarter ended September 30.

**Required:**

1.  Prepare a schedule of expected cash collections for July, August, and September. Also compute total cash collections for the quarter ended September 30.
2.  a. Prepare a merchandise purchases budget for July, August, and September. Also compute total merchandise purchases for the quarter ended September 30.
    b. Prepare a schedule of expected cash disbursements for merchandise purchases for July, August, and September. Also compute total cash disbursements for merchandise purchases for the quarter ended September 30.
3.  Using Schedule 9 as your guide, prepare an income statement for the quarter ended September 30.
4.  Prepare a balance sheet as of September 30.

**EXERCISE 8–13  Schedules of Expected Cash Collections and Disbursements; Income Statement; Balance Sheet** LO8–2, LO8–4, LO8–9, LO8–10

Refer to the data for Beech Corporation in Exercise 8–12. The company is considering making the following changes to the assumptions underlying its master budget:

1.  Each month's credit sales are collected 45% in the month of sale and 55% in the month following the sale.

2. Each month's ending inventory must equal 20% of the cost of next month's sales.
3. The company pays for 30% of its merchandise purchases in the month of the purchase and the remaining 70% in the month following the purchase.

All other information from Exercise 8–12 that is not mentioned above remains the same.

***Required:***

Using the new assumptions described above, complete the following requirements:

1. Prepare a schedule of expected cash collections for July, August, and September. Also compute total cash collections for the quarter ended September 30.
2. a. Prepare a merchandise purchases budget for July, August, and September. Also compute total merchandise purchases for the quarter ended September 30.
   b. Prepare a schedule of expected cash disbursements for merchandise purchases for July, August, and September. Also compute total cash disbursements for merchandise purchases for the quarter ended September 30.
3. Using Schedule 9 as your guide, prepare an income statement for the quarter ended September 30.
4. Prepare a balance sheet as of September 30.

**EXERCISE 8–14　Sales and Production Budgets LO8–2, LO8–3**

The marketing department of Jessi Corporation has submitted the following sales forecast for the upcoming fiscal year (all sales are on account):

| | 1st Quarter | 2nd Quarter | 3rd Quarter | 4th Quarter |
|---|---|---|---|---|
| Budgeted unit sales ............... | 11,000 | 12,000 | 14,000 | 13,000 |

The selling price of the company's product is $18.00 per unit. Management expects to collect 65% of sales in the quarter in which the sales are made, 30% in the following quarter, and 5% of sales are expected to be uncollectible. The beginning balance of accounts receivable, all of which is expected to be collected in the first quarter, is $70,200.

The company expects to start the first quarter with 1,650 units in finished goods inventory. Management desires an ending finished goods inventory in each quarter equal to 15% of the next quarter's budgeted sales. The desired ending finished goods inventory for the fourth quarter is 1,850 units.

***Required:***

1. Calculate the estimated sales for each quarter of the fiscal year and for the year as a whole. (*Hint:* Refer to Schedule 1 for guidance.)
2. Calculate the expected cash collections for each quarter of the fiscal year and for the year as a whole. (*Hint:* Refer to Schedule 1 for guidance.)
3. Calculate the required production in units of finished goods for each quarter of the fiscal year and for the year as a whole. (*Hint:* Refer to Schedule 2 for guidance.)

**EXERCISE 8–15　Direct Labor and Manufacturing Overhead Budgets LO8–5, LO8–6**

The Production Department of Hruska Corporation has submitted the following forecast of units to be produced by quarter for the upcoming fiscal year:

| | 1st Quarter | 2nd Quarter | 3rd Quarter | 4th Quarter |
|---|---|---|---|---|
| Units to be produced ............... | 12,000 | 10,000 | 13,000 | 14,000 |

Each unit requires 0.2 direct labor-hours and direct laborers are paid $12.00 per hour.

In addition, the variable manufacturing overhead rate is $1.75 per direct labor-hour. The fixed manufacturing overhead is $86,000 per quarter. The only noncash element of manufacturing overhead is depreciation, which is $23,000 per quarter.

***Required:***

1. Calculate the company's total estimated direct labor cost for each quarter of the the upcoming fiscal year and for the year as a whole. Assume that the direct labor workforce is adjusted each quarter to

match the number of hours required to produce the estimated number of units produced (*Hint:* Refer to Schedule 4 for guidance).

2.  Calculate the company's total estimated manufacturing overhead cost for each quarter of the upcoming fiscal year and for the year as a whole (*Hint:* Refer to Schedule 5 for guidance).

3.  Calculate the company's cash disbursements for manufacturing overhead for each quarter of the the upcoming fiscal year and for the year as a whole (*Hint:* Refer to Schedule 5 for guidance).

**EXERCISE 8-16  Direct Materials and Direct Labor Budgets** LO8-4, LO8-5

The production department of Zan Corporation has submitted the following forecast of units to be produced by quarter for the upcoming fiscal year:

|  | 1st Quarter | 2nd Quarter | 3rd Quarter | 4th Quarter |
|---|---|---|---|---|
| Units to be produced .............. | 5,000 | 8,000 | 7,000 | 6,000 |

In addition, 6,000 grams of raw materials inventory is on hand at the start of the 1st Quarter and the beginning accounts payable for the 1st Quarter is $2,880.

Each unit requires 8 grams of raw material that costs $1.20 per gram. Management desires to end each quarter with an inventory of raw materials equal to 25% of the following quarter's production needs. The desired ending inventory for the 4th Quarter is 8,000 grams. Management plans to pay for 60% of raw material purchases in the quarter acquired and 40% in the following quarter. Each unit requires 0.20 direct labor-hours and direct laborers are paid $11.50 per hour.

**Required:**

1.  Calculate the estimated grams of raw material that need to be purchased each quarter and for the year as a whole (*Hint:* Refer to Schedule 3 for guidance).

2.  Calculate the cost of raw material purchases for each quarter and for the year as a whole (*Hint:* Refer to Schedule 3 for guidance).

3.  Calculate the expected cash disbursements for purchases of materials for each quarter and for the year as a whole (*Hint:* Refer to Schedule 3 for guidance).

4.  Calculate the estimated direct labor cost for each quarter and for the year as a whole. Assume that the direct labor workforce is adjusted each quarter to match the number of hours required to produce the estimated number of units produced (*Hint:* Refer to Schedule 4 for guidance).

**EXERCISE 8-17  Cash Flows; Budgeted Income Statement and Balance Sheet** LO 8-2, LO 8-3, LO 8-4, LO8-9, LO8-10

Wheeling Company is a merchandiser that provided a balance sheet as of September 30 as shown below:

| Wheeling Company<br>Balance Sheet<br>September 30 | |
|---|---|
| **Assets** | |
| Cash ............................................... | $ 59,000 |
| Accounts receivable................................ | 90,000 |
| Inventory........................................... | 32,400 |
| Buildings and equipment, net of depreciation...... | 214,000 |
| Total assets ....................................... | $395,400 |
| **Liabilities and Stockholders' Equity** | |
| Accounts payable ................................... | $ 73,000 |
| Common stock ...................................... | 216,000 |
| Retained earnings .................................. | 106,400 |
| Total liabilities and stockholders' equity............ | $395,400 |

The company is in the process of preparing a budget for October and has assembled the following data:

1.  Sales are budgeted at $240,000 for October and $250,000 for November. Of these sales, 35% will be for cash; the remainder will be credit sales. Forty percent of a month's credit sales are collected in

the month the sales are made, and the remaining 60% is collected in the following month. All of the September 30 accounts receivable will be collected in October.

2.  The budgeted cost of goods sold is always 45% of sales and the ending merchandise inventory is always 30% of the following month's cost of goods sold.

3.  All merchandise purchases are on account. Thirty percent of all purchases are paid for in the month of purchase and 70% are paid for in the following month. All of the September 30 accounts payable to suppliers will be paid during October.

4.  Selling and administrative expenses for October are budgeted at $78,000, exclusive of depreciation. These expenses will be paid in cash. Depreciation is budgeted at $2,000 for the month.

**Required:**

1.  Using the information provided, calculate or prepare the following:
    a.  The budgeted cash collections for October.
    b.  The budgeted merchandise purchases for October.
    c.  The budgeted cash disbursements for merchandise purchases for October.
    d.  The budgeted net operating income for October.
    e.  A budgeted balance sheet at October 31.

2.  Assume the following changes to the underlying budgeting assumptions: (1) 50% of a month's credit sales are collected in the month the sales are made and the remaining 50% is collected in the following month, (2) the ending merchandise inventory is always 10% of the following month's cost of goods sold, and (3) 20% of all purchases are paid for in the month of purchase and 80% are paid for in the following month. Using these new assumptions, calculate or prepare the following:
    a.  The budgeted cash collections for October.
    b.  The budgeted merchandise purchases for October.
    c.  The budgeted cash disbursements for merchandise purchases for October.
    d.  Net operating income for the month of October.
    e.  A budgeted balance sheet at October 31.

3.  Compare your answers in requirement 1 to those that you obtained in requirement 2. If Wheeling Company is able to achieve the budgeted projections described in requirement 2, will it improve the company's financial performance relative to the projections that you derived in requirement 1?

**EXERCISE 8–18   Cash Flows; Budgeted Income Statement and Balance Sheet** LO 8–2, LO 8–3, LO8–9, LO8–10

Wolfpack Company is a merchandising company that is preparing a budget for the month of July. It has provided the following information:

| Wolfpack Company<br>Balance Sheet<br>June 30 | |
|---|---|
| **Assets** | |
| Cash | $ 75,000 |
| Accounts receivable | 50,000 |
| Inventory | 30,000 |
| Buildings and equipment, net of depreciation | 150,000 |
| Total assets | $305,000 |
| **Liabilities and Stockholders' Equity** | |
| Accounts payable | $ 35,300 |
| Common stock | 100,000 |
| Retained earnings | 169,700 |
| Total liabilities and stockholders' equity | $305,000 |

Budgeting Assumptions:

1.  All sales are on account. Thirty percent of the credit sales are collected in the month of sale and the remaining 70% are collected in the month subsequent to the sale. The accounts receivable at June 30 will be collected in July.

2.  All merchandise purchases are on account. Twenty percent of merchandise inventory purchases are paid in the month of the purchase and the remaining 80% is paid in the month after the purchase.

3.  The budgeted inventory balance at July 31 is $22,000.
4.  Depreciation expense is $3,000 per month. All other selling and administrative expenses are paid in full in the month the expense is incurred.
5.  The company's cash budget for July shows expected cash collections of $77,000, expected cash disbursements for merchandise purchases of $44,500, and cash paid for selling and administrative expenses of $15,000.

**Required:**
1.  For the month of July, calculate the following:
    a.  Budgeted sales
    b.  Budgeted merchandise purchases
    c.  Budgeted cost of goods sold
    d.  Budgeted net operating income
2.  Prepare a budgeted balance sheet as of July 31.

**connect**                    **PROBLEMS**

**PROBLEM 8–19    Cash Budget; Income Statement; Balance Sheet** LO8–2, LO8–4, LO8–8, LO8–9, LO8–10

Minden Company is a wholesale distributor of premium European chocolates. The company's balance sheet as of April 30 is given below:

| Minden Company Balance Sheet April 30 | |
|---|---|
| **Assets** | |
| Cash | $ 9,000 |
| Accounts receivable | 54,000 |
| Inventory | 30,000 |
| Buildings and equipment, net of depreciation | 207,000 |
| Total assets | $300,000 |
| **Liabilities and Stockholders' Equity** | |
| Accounts payable | $ 63,000 |
| Note payable | 14,500 |
| Common stock | 180,000 |
| Retained earnings | 42,500 |
| Total liabilities and stockholders' equity | $300,000 |

The company is in the process of preparing a budget for May and has assembled the following data:

a.  Sales are budgeted at $200,000 for May. Of these sales, $60,000 will be for cash; the remainder will be credit sales. One-half of a month's credit sales are collected in the month the sales are made, and the remainder is collected in the following month. All of the April 30 accounts receivable will be collected in May.

b.  Purchases of inventory are expected to total $120,000 during May. These purchases will all be on account. Forty percent of all purchases are paid for in the month of purchase; the remainder are paid in the following month. All of the April 30 accounts payable to suppliers will be paid during May.

c.  The May 31 inventory balance is budgeted at $40,000.

d.  Selling and administrative expenses for May are budgeted at $72,000, exclusive of depreciation. These expenses will be paid in cash. Depreciation is budgeted at $2,000 for the month.

e.  The note payable on the April 30 balance sheet will be paid during May, with $100 in interest. (All of the interest relates to May.)

f.  New refrigerating equipment costing $6,500 will be purchased for cash during May.

g.  During May, the company will borrow $20,000 from its bank by giving a new note payable to the bank for that amount. The new note will be due in one year.

*Required:*
1. Calculate the expected cash collections for May.
2. Calculate the expected cash disbursements for merchandise purchases for May.
3. Prepare a cash budget for May.
4. Using Schedule 9 as your guide, prepare a budgeted income statement for May.
5. Prepare a budgeted balance sheet as of May 31.

**PROBLEM 8–20   Cash Budget; Income Statement; Balance Sheet; Changing Assumptions** LO8–2, **LO8–4, LO8–8, LO8–9, LO8–10**

Refer to the data for Minden Company in Problem 8–19. The company is considering making the following changes to the assumptions underlying its master budget:
1. Sales are budgeted for $220,000 for May.
2. Each month's credit sales are collected 60% in the month of sale and 40% in the month following the sale.
3. The company pays for 50% of its merchandise purchases in the month of the purchase and the remaining 50% in the month following the purchase.
   All other information from Problem 8–19 that is not mentioned above remains the same.

*Required:*
   Using the new assumptions described above, complete the following requirements:
1. Calculate the expected cash collections for May.
2. Calculate the expected cash disbursements for merchandise purchases for May.
3. Prepare a cash budget for May.
4. Using Schedule 9 as your guide, prepare a budgeted income statement for May.
5. Prepare a budgeted balance sheet as of May 31.

**PROBLEM 8–21   Schedules of Expected Cash Collections and Disbursements** LO8–2, LO8–4, LO8–8

You have been asked to prepare a December cash budget for Ashton Company, a distributor of exercise equipment. The following information is available about the company's operations:

a.   The cash balance on December 1 is $40,000.
b.   Actual sales for October and November and expected sales for December are as follows:

|                      | October   | November  | December  |
|----------------------|-----------|-----------|-----------|
| Cash sales           | $65,000   | $70,000   | $83,000   |
| Sales on account     | $400,000  | $525,000  | $600,000  |

   Sales on account are collected over a three-month period as follows: 20% collected in the month of sale, 60% collected in the month following sale, and 18% collected in the second month following sale. The remaining 2% is uncollectible.
c.   Purchases of inventory will total $280,000 for December. Thirty percent of a month's inventory purchases are paid during the month of purchase. The accounts payable remaining from November's inventory purchases total $161,000, all of which will be paid in December.
d.   Selling and administrative expenses are budgeted at $430,000 for December. Of this amount, $50,000 is for depreciation.
e.   A new web server for the Marketing Department costing $76,000 will be purchased for cash during December, and dividends totaling $9,000 will be paid during the month.
f.   The company maintains a minimum cash balance of $20,000. An open line of credit is available from the company's bank to increase its cash balance as needed.

*Required:*
1. Calculate the expected cash collections for December.
2. Calculate the expected cash disbursements for merchandise purchases for December.
3. Prepare a cash budget for December. Indicate in the financing section any borrowing that will be needed during the month. Assume that any interest will not be paid until the following month.

**PROBLEM 8–22   Evaluating a Company's Budget Procedures** LO8–1

Springfield Corporation operates on a calendar-year basis. It begins the annual budgeting process in late August, when the president establishes targets for total sales dollars and net operating income before taxes for the next year.

The sales target is given to the Marketing Department, where the marketing manager formulates a sales budget by product line in both units and dollars. From this budget, sales quotas by product line in units and dollars are established for each of the corporation's sales districts.

The marketing manager also estimates the cost of the marketing activities required to support the target sales volume and prepares a tentative marketing expense budget.

The executive vice president uses the sales and profit targets, the sales budget by product line, and the tentative marketing expense budget to determine the dollar amounts that can be devoted to manufacturing and corporate office expense. The executive vice president prepares the budget for corporate expenses, and then forwards to the Production Department the product-line sales budget in units and the total dollar amount that can be devoted to manufacturing.

The production manager meets with the factory managers to develop a manufacturing plan that will produce the required units when needed within the cost constraints set by the executive vice president. The budgeting process usually comes to a halt at this point because the Production Department does not consider its allocated financial resources to be adequate.

When this standstill occurs, the vice president of finance, the executive vice president, the marketing manager, and the production manager meet to determine the final budgets for each of the areas. This normally results in a modest increase in the total amount available for manufacturing costs, while the marketing expense and corporate office expense budgets are cut. The total sales and net operating income figures proposed by the president are seldom changed. Although the participants are seldom pleased with the compromise, these budgets are final. Each executive then develops a new detailed budget for the operations in his or her area.

None of the areas has achieved its budget in recent years. Sales often run below the target. When budgeted sales are not achieved, each area is expected to cut costs so that the president's profit target can still be met. However, the profit target is seldom met because costs are not cut enough. In fact, costs often run above the original budget in all functional areas. The president is disturbed that Springfield has not been able to meet the sales and profit targets. He hired a consultant with considerable relevant industry experience. The consultant reviewed the budgets for the past four years. He concluded that the product-line sales budgets were reasonable and that the cost and expense budgets were adequate for the budgeted sales and production levels.

**Required:**

1.  Discuss how Springfield Corporation's budgeting process contributes to its failure to achieve the president's sales and profit targets.
2.  Suggest how Springfield Corporation's budgeting process could be revised to correct the problem.
3.  Should the functional areas be expected to cut their costs when sales volume falls below budget? Explain your answer.

(CMA, adapted)

**PROBLEM 8–23    Schedule of Expected Cash Collections; Cash Budget LO8–2, LO8–8**

The president of the retailer Prime Products has just approached the company's bank with a request for a $30,000, 90-day loan. The purpose of the loan is to assist the company in acquiring inventories. Because the company has had some difficulty in paying off its loans in the past, the loan officer has asked for a cash budget to help determine whether the loan should be made. The following data are available for the months April through June, during which the loan will be used:

a.  On April 1, the start of the loan period, the cash balance will be $24,000. Accounts receivable on April 1 will total $140,000, of which $120,000 will be collected during April and $16,000 will be collected during May. The remainder will be uncollectible.

b.  Past experience shows that 30% of a month's sales are collected in the month of sale, 60% in the month following sale, and 8% in the second month following sale. The other 2% is bad debts that are never collected. Budgeted sales and expenses for the three-month period follow:

|  | April | May | June |
|---|---|---|---|
| Sales (all on account) ........................ | $300,000 | $400,000 | $250,000 |
| Merchandise purchases ..................... | $210,000 | $160,000 | $130,000 |
| Payroll ........................................ | $20,000 | $20,000 | $18,000 |
| Lease payments ............................. | $22,000 | $22,000 | $22,000 |
| Advertising ................................... | $60,000 | $60,000 | $50,000 |
| Equipment purchases ........................ | — | — | $65,000 |
| Depreciation ................................. | $15,000 | $15,000 | $15,000 |

c.   Merchandise purchases are paid in full during the month following purchase. Accounts payable for merchandise purchases during March, which will be paid in April, total $140,000.

d.   In preparing the cash budget, assume that the $30,000 loan will be made in April and repaid in June. Interest on the loan will total $1,200.

**Required:**

1.   Calculate the expected cash collections for April, May, and June, and for the three months in total.
2.   Prepare a cash budget, by month and in total, for the three-month period.
3.   If the company needs a minimum cash balance of $20,000 to start each month, can the loan be repaid as planned? Explain.

**PROBLEM 8–24   Cash Budget with Supporting Schedules** LO8–2, LO8–4, LO8–8

Garden Sales, Inc., sells garden supplies. Management is planning its cash needs for the second quarter. The company usually has to borrow money during this quarter to support peak sales of lawn care equipment, which occur during May. The following information has been assembled to assist in preparing a cash budget for the quarter:

a.   Budgeted monthly absorption costing income statements for April–July are:

|  | April | May | June | July |
|---|---|---|---|---|
| Sales ........................................ | $600,000 | $900,000 | $500,000 | $400,000 |
| Cost of goods sold ......................... | 420,000 | 630,000 | 350,000 | 280,000 |
| Gross margin ............................... | 180,000 | 270,000 | 150,000 | 120,000 |
| Selling and administrative expenses: |  |  |  |  |
| Selling expense ......................... | 79,000 | 120,000 | 62,000 | 51,000 |
| Administrative expense* ................. | 45,000 | 52,000 | 41,000 | 38,000 |
| Total selling and administrative expenses ... | 124,000 | 172,000 | 103,000 | 89,000 |
| Net operating income ..................... | $ 56,000 | $ 98,000 | $ 47,000 | $ 31,000 |

*Includes $20,000 of depreciation each month.

b.   Sales are 20% for cash and 80% on account.

c.   Sales on account are collected over a three-month period with 10% collected in the month of sale; 70% collected in the first month following the month of sale; and the remaining 20% collected in the second month following the month of sale. February's sales totaled $200,000, and March's sales totaled $300,000.

d.   Inventory purchases are paid for in 15 days. Therefore, 50% of a month's inventory purchases are paid for in the month of purchase. The remaining 50% is paid in the following month. Accounts payable at March 31 for inventory purchases during March total $126,000.

e.   Each month's ending inventory must equal 20% of the cost of the merchandise to be sold in the following month. The merchandise inventory at March 31 is $84,000.

f.   Dividends of $49,000 will be declared and paid in April.

g.   Land costing $16,000 will be purchased for cash in May.

h.   The cash balance at March 31 is $52,000; the company must maintain a cash balance of at least $40,000 at the end of each month.

i.   The company has an agreement with a local bank that allows the company to borrow in increments of $1,000 at the beginning of each month, up to a total loan balance of $200,000. The interest rate on these loans is 1% per month and for simplicity we will assume that interest is not compounded. The company would, as far as it is able, repay the loan plus accumulated interest at the end of the quarter.

**Required:**

1.   Prepare a schedule of expected cash collections for April, May, and June, and for the quarter in total.
2.   Prepare the following for merchandise inventory:
    a.  A merchandise purchases budget for April, May, and June.
    b.  A schedule of expected cash disbursements for merchandise purchases for April, May, and June, and for the quarter in total.
3.   Prepare a cash budget for April, May, and June as well as in total for the quarter.

**PROBLEM 8–25    Cash Budget with Supporting Schedules; Changing Assumptions** LO8–2, LO8–4, LO8–8

Refer to the data for Garden Sales, Inc., in Problem 8–24. The company's president is interested in knowing how reducing inventory levels and collecting accounts receivable sooner will impact the cash budget. He revises the cash collection and ending inventory assumptions as follows:

1.  Sales continue to be 20% for cash and 80% on credit. However, credit sales from April, May, and June are collected over a three-month period with 25% collected in the month of sale, 65% collected in the month following sale, and 10% in the second month following sale. Credit sales from February and March are collected during the second quarter using the collection percentages specified in Problem 8–24.

2.  The company maintains its ending inventory levels for April, May, and June at 15% of the cost of merchandise to be sold in the following month. The merchandise inventory at March 31 remains $84,000 and accounts payable for inventory purchases at March 31 remains $126,000.

    All other information from Problem 8–24 that is not referred to above remains the same.

*Required:*

1.  Using the president's new assumptions in (1) above, prepare a schedule of expected cash collections for April, May, and June and for the quarter in total.
2.  Using the president's new assumptions in (2) above, prepare the following for merchandise inventory:
    a.  A merchandise purchases budget for April, May, and June.
    b.  A schedule of expected cash disbursements for merchandise purchases for April, May, and June and for the quarter in total.
3.  Using the president's new assumptions, prepare a cash budget for April, May, and June, and for the quarter in total.
4.  Prepare a brief memorandum for the president explaining how his revised assumptions affect the cash budget.

**PROBLEM 8–26    Behavioral Aspects of Budgeting; Ethics and the Manager** LO8–1

Norton Company, a manufacturer of infant furniture and carriages, is in the initial stages of preparing the annual budget for next year. Scott Ford has recently joined Norton's accounting staff and wants to learn as much as possible about the company's budgeting process. During a recent lunch with Marge Atkins, sales manager, and Pete Granger, production manager, Ford initiated the following conversation.

*Ford:*  Since I'm new around here and am going to be involved with the preparation of the annual budget, I'd be interested to learn how the two of you estimate sales and production numbers.

*Atkins:*  We start out very methodically by looking at recent history, discussing what we know about current accounts, potential customers, and the general state of consumer spending. Then, we add that usual dose of intuition to come up with the best forecast we can.

*Granger:*  I usually take the sales projections as the basis for my projections. Of course, we have to make an estimate of what this year's ending inventories will be, which is sometimes difficult.

*Ford:*  Why does that present a problem? There must have been an estimate of ending inventories in the budget for the current year.

*Granger:*  Those numbers aren't always reliable because Marge makes some adjustments to the sales numbers before passing them on to me.

*Ford:*  What kind of adjustments?

*Atkins:*  Well, we don't want to fall short of the sales projections so we generally give ourselves a little breathing room by lowering the initial sales projection anywhere from 5% to 10%.

*Granger:*  So, you can see why this year's budget is not a very reliable starting point. We always have to adjust the projected production rates as the year progresses and, of course, this changes the ending inventory estimates. By the way, we make similar adjustments to expenses by adding at least 10% to the estimates; I think everyone around here does the same thing.

*Required:*

1.  Marge Atkins and Pete Granger have described the use of what is sometimes called *budgetary slack.*
    a.  Explain why Atkins and Granger behave in this manner and describe the benefits they expect to realize from the use of budgetary slack.
    b.  Explain how the use of budgetary slack can adversely affect Atkins and Granger.
2.  As a management accountant, Scott Ford believes that the behavior described by Marge Atkins and Pete Granger may be unethical. By referring to the IMA's Statement of Ethical Professional Practice in the Prologue, explain why the use of budgetary slack may be unethical.

(CMA, adapted)

**PROBLEM 8–27   Cash Collections; Cash Disbursements; Budgeted Balance Sheet** LO8–2, LO8–3, LO8–4, LO8–10

Deacon Company is a merchandising company that is preparing a budget for the three-month period ended June 30. The following information is available:

| Deacon Company Balance Sheet March 31 | |
| --- | --- |
| **Assets** | |
| Cash | $ 55,000 |
| Accounts receivable | 36,000 |
| Inventory | 40,000 |
| Buildings and equipment, net of depreciation | 100,000 |
| Total assets | $231,000 |
| **Liabilities and Stockholders' Equity** | |
| Accounts payable | $ 51,300 |
| Common Stock | 70,000 |
| Retained earnings | 109,700 |
| Total liabilities and stockholders' equity | $231,000 |

| Budgeted Income Statements | April | May | June |
| --- | --- | --- | --- |
| Sales | $100,000 | $110,000 | $130,000 |
| Cost of goods sold | 60,000 | 66,000 | 78,000 |
| Gross margin | 40,000 | 44,000 | 52,000 |
| Selling and administrative expenses | 15,000 | 16,500 | 19,500 |
| Net operating income | $ 25,000 | $ 27,500 | $ 32,500 |

Budgeting Assumptions:

1.  Sixty percent of sales are cash sales and 40% of sales are credit sales. Twenty percent of all credit sales are collected in the month of sale and the remaining 80% are collected in the month subsequent to the sale.
2.  Budgeted sales for July are $140,000.
3.  Ten percent of merchandise inventory purchases are paid in cash at the time of the purchase. The remaining 90% of purchases are credit purchases. All purchases on credit are paid in the month subsequent to the purchase.
4.  Each month's ending merchandise inventory should equal $10,000 plus 50% of the next month's cost of goods sold.
5.  Depreciation expense is $1,000 per month. All other selling and administrative expenses are paid in full in the month the expense is incurred.

*Required:*

1.  Calculate the expected cash collections for April, May, and June.
2.  Calculate the budgeted merchandise purchases for April, May, and June.
3.  Calculate the expected cash disbursements for merchandise purchases for April, May, and June.
4.  Prepare a budgeted balance sheet at June 30. (*Hint:* You need to calculate the cash paid for selling and administrative expenses during April, May, and June to determine the cash balance in your June 30 balance sheet.)

**PROBLEM 8–28   Cash Budget with Supporting Schedules** LO8–2, LO8–4, LO8–7, LO8–8

Westex Products is a wholesale distributor of industrial cleaning products. When the treasurer of Westex Products approached the company's bank late in the current year seeking short-term financing, he was told that money was very tight and that any borrowing over the next year would have to be supported by a detailed statement of cash collections and disbursements. The treasurer also was told that it would be very helpful to the bank if borrowers would indicate the quarters in which they would be needing funds, as well as the amounts that would be needed, and the quarters in which repayments could be made.

Because the treasurer is unsure as to the particular quarters in which bank financing will be needed, he has assembled the following information to assist in preparing a detailed cash budget:

a. Budgeted sales and merchandise purchases for next year, as well as actual sales and purchases for the last quarter of the current year, are:

|  | Sales | Merchandise Purchases |
| --- | --- | --- |
| Current Year: | | |
| Fourth quarter actual.............. | $200,000 | $126,000 |
| Next Year: | | |
| First quarter estimated............. | $300,000 | $186,000 |
| Second quarter estimated......... | $400,000 | $246,000 |
| Third quarter estimated........... | $500,000 | $305,000 |
| Fourth quarter estimated.......... | $200,000 | $126,000 |

b. All sales are on account. The company normally collects 65% of a quarter's sales before the quarter ends and another 33% in the following quarter. The remainder is uncollectible. This pattern of collections is now being experienced in the current year's fourth-quarter actual data.

c. Eighty percent of a quarter's merchandise purchases are paid for within the quarter. The remainder is paid for in the following quarter.

d. Selling and administrative expenses for next year are budgeted at $50,000 per quarter plus 15% of sales. Of the fixed amount, $20,000 each quarter is depreciation.

e. The company will pay $10,000 in dividends each quarter.

f. Land purchases of $75,000 will be made in the second quarter, and purchases of $48,000 will be made in the third quarter. These purchases will be for cash.

g. The Cash account contained $10,000 at the end of the current year. The treasurer feels that this represents a minimum balance that must be maintained.

h. The company's bank allows borrowing in increments of $1,000 at the beginning of each quarter, up to a total loan balance of $100,000. The interest rate on these loans is 2.5% per quarter and for simplicity we will assume that interest is not compounded. The company would, as far as it is able, repay the loan plus accumulated interest at the end of the year.

i. At present, the company has no loans outstanding.

**Required:**
1. Calculate the expected cash collections by quarter and in total for next year.
2. Calculate the expected cash disbursements for merchandise purchases by quarter and in total for next year.
3. Calculate the expected cash disbursements for selling and administrative expenses, by quarter and in total for next year.
4. Prepare a cash budget by quarter and in total for next year.

**PROBLEM 8–29 Completing a Master Budget** LO8–2, LO8–4, LO8–7, LO8–8, LO8–9, LO8–10
The following data relate to the operations of Shilow Company, a wholesale distributor of consumer goods:

| Current assets as of March 31: | |
| --- | --- |
| Cash .............................. | $8,000 |
| Accounts receivable .............. | $20,000 |
| Inventory ......................... | $36,000 |
| Building and equipment, net ........ | $120,000 |
| Accounts payable ................... | $21,750 |
| Common stock ..................... | $150,000 |
| Retained earnings ................. | $12,250 |

382       Chapter 8

a.  The gross margin is 25% of sales.
b.  Actual and budgeted sales data:

| | |
|---|---|
| March (actual) .................. | $50,000 |
| April ........................... | $60,000 |
| May ........................... | $72,000 |
| June ........................... | $90,000 |
| July ........................... | $48,000 |

c.  Sales are 60% for cash and 40% on credit. Credit sales are collected in the month following sale. The accounts receivable at March 31 are a result of March credit sales.
d.  Each month's ending inventory should equal 80% of the following month's budgeted cost of goods sold.
e.  One-half of a month's inventory purchases is paid for in the month of purchase; the other half is paid for in the following month. The accounts payable at March 31 are the result of March purchases of inventory.
f.  Monthly expenses are as follows: commissions, 12% of sales; rent, $2,500 per month; other expenses (excluding depreciation), 6% of sales. Assume that these expenses are paid monthly. Depreciation is $900 per month (includes depreciation on new assets).
g.  Equipment costing $1,500 will be purchased for cash in April.
h.  Management would like to maintain a minimum cash balance of at least $4,000 at the end of each month. The company has an agreement with a local bank that allows the company to borrow in increments of $1,000 at the beginning of each month, up to a total loan balance of $20,000. The interest rate on these loans is 1% per month and for simplicity we will assume that interest is not compounded. The company would, as far as it is able, repay the loan plus accumulated interest at the end of the quarter.

**Required:**
Using the preceding data:

1.  Complete the following schedule:

**Schedule of Expected Cash Collections**

| | April | May | June | Quarter |
|---|---|---|---|---|
| Cash sales ........................................... | $36,000 | | | |
| Credit sales ......................................... | 20,000 | | | |
| Total collections ..................................... | $56,000 | | | |

2.  Complete the following:

**Merchandise Purchases Budget**

| | April | May | June | Quarter |
|---|---|---|---|---|
| Budgeted cost of goods sold ................. | $45,000* | $54,000 | | |
| Add desired ending inventory ............... | 43,200† | | | |
| Total needs ...................................... | 88,200 | | | |
| Less beginning inventory ..................... | 36,000 | | | |
| Required purchases .......................... | $52,200 | | | |

*For April sales: $60,000 sales × 75% cost ratio = $45,000.
†$54,000 × 80% = $43,200.

**Schedule of Expected Cash Disbursements—Merchandise Purchases**

|  | April | May | June | Quarter |
|---|---|---|---|---|
| March purchases | $21,750 | | | $21,750 |
| April purchases | 26,100 | $26,100 | | 52,200 |
| May purchases | | | | |
| June purchases | | | | |
| Total disbursements | $47,850 | | | |

3. Complete the following cash budget:

**Cash Budget**

|  | April | May | June | Quarter |
|---|---|---|---|---|
| Beginning cash balance | $ 8,000 | | | |
| Add cash collections | 56,000 | | | |
| Total cash available | 64,000 | | | |
| Less cash disbursements: | | | | |
| For inventory | 47,850 | | | |
| For expenses | 13,300 | | | |
| For equipment | 1,500 | | | |
| Total cash disbursements | 62,650 | | | |
| Excess (deficiency) of cash | 1,350 | | | |
| Financing: | | | | |
| Etc. | | | | |

4. Using Schedule 9 as your guide, prepare an absorption costing income statement for the quarter ended June 30.
5. Prepare a balance sheet as of June 30.

**PROBLEM 8–30  Integration of the Sales, Production, and Direct Materials Budgets** LO8–2, LO8–3, LO8–4

Milo Company manufactures beach umbrellas. The company is preparing detailed budgets for the third quarter and has assembled the following information to assist in the budget preparation:

a. The Marketing Department has estimated sales as follows for the remainder of the year (in units):

| July | 30,000 | October | 20,000 |
|---|---|---|---|
| August | 70,000 | November | 10,000 |
| September | 50,000 | December | 10,000 |

The selling price of the beach umbrellas is $12 per unit.

b. All sales are on account. Based on past experience, sales are collected in the following pattern:

30% in the month of sale
65% in the month following sale
5% uncollectible

Sales for June totaled $300,000.

c. The company maintains finished goods inventories equal to 15% of the following month's sales. This requirement will be met at the end of June.

d. Each beach umbrella requires 4 feet of Gilden, a material that is sometimes hard to acquire. Therefore, the company requires that the ending inventory of Gilden be equal to 50% of the following month's production needs. The inventory of Gilden on hand at the beginning and end of the quarter will be:

| | |
|---|---|
| June 30 ..................... | 72,000 feet |
| September 30 .............. | ?  feet |

e. Gilden costs $0.80 per foot. One-half of a month's purchases of Gilden is paid for in the month of purchase; the remainder is paid for in the following month. The accounts payable on July 1 for purchases of Gilden during June will be $76,000.

**Required:**
1. Calculate the estimated sales, by month and in total, for the third quarter (*Hint:* Refer to Schedule 1 for guidance).
2. Calculate the expected cash collections, by month and in total, for the third quarter (*Hint:* Refer to Schedule 1 for guidance).
3. Calculate the estimated quantity of beach umbrellas that need to be produced in July, August, September, and October (*Hint:* Refer to Schedule 2 for guidance).
4. Calculate the quantity of Gilden (in feet) that needs to be purchased by month and in total, for the third quarter (*Hint:* Refer to Schedule 3 for guidance).
5. Calculate the cost of the raw material (Gilden) purchases by month and in total, for the third quarter (*Hint:* Refer to Schedule 3 for guidance).
6. Calculate the expected cash disbursements for raw material (Gilden) purchases, by month and in total, for the third quarter (*Hint:* Refer to Schedule 3 for guidance).

**PROBLEM 8–31   Completing a Master Budget** LO8–2, LO8–4, LO8–7, LO8–8, LO8–9, LO8–10

Hillyard Company, an office supplies specialty store, prepares its master budget on a quarterly basis. The following data have been assembled to assist in preparing the master budget for the first quarter:

a. As of December 31 (the end of the prior quarter), the company's general ledger showed the following account balances:

| | Debits | Credits |
|---|---|---|
| Cash ........................................................ | $ 48,000 | |
| Accounts receivable .............................. | 224,000 | |
| Inventory ................................................ | 60,000 | |
| Buildings and equipment (net) .................... | 370,000 | |
| Accounts payable ..................................... | | $ 93,000 |
| Common stock ......................................... | | 500,000 |
| Retained earnings .................................... | | 109,000 |
| | $702,000 | $702,000 |

b. Actual sales for December and budgeted sales for the next four months are as follows:

| | |
|---|---|
| December (actual) .............. | $280,000 |
| January ......................... | $400,000 |
| February ....................... | $600,000 |
| March .......................... | $300,000 |
| April ........................... | $200,000 |

c.  Sales are 20% for cash and 80% on credit. All payments on credit sales are collected in the month following sale. The accounts receivable at December 31 are a result of December credit sales.

d.  The company's gross margin is 40% of sales. (In other words, cost of goods sold is 60% of sales.)

e.  Monthly expenses are budgeted as follows: salaries and wages, $27,000 per month; advertising, $70,000 per month; shipping, 5% of sales; other expenses, 3% of sales. Depreciation, including depreciation on new assets acquired during the quarter, will be $42,000 for the quarter.

f.  Each month's ending inventory should equal 25% of the following month's cost of goods sold.

g.  One-half of a month's inventory purchases is paid for in the month of purchase; the other half is paid in the following month.

h.  During February, the company will purchase a new copy machine for $1,700 cash. During March, other equipment will be purchased for cash at a cost of $84,500.

i.  During January, the company will declare and pay $45,000 in cash dividends.

j.  Management wants to maintain a minimum cash balance of $30,000. The company has an agreement with a local bank that allows the company to borrow in increments of $1,000 at the beginning of each month. The interest rate on these loans is 1% per month and for simplicity we will assume that interest is not compounded. The company would, as far as it is able, repay the loan plus accumulated interest at the end of the quarter.

**Required:**

Using the data above, complete the following statements and schedules for the first quarter:

1.  Schedule of expected cash collections:

|  | January | February | March | Quarter |
|---|---|---|---|---|
| Cash sales ............................. | $ 80,000 | | | |
| Credit sales ............................ | 224,000 | | | |
| Total cash collections ................... | $304,000 | | | |

2.  a. Merchandise purchases budget:

|  | January | February | March | Quarter |
|---|---|---|---|---|
| Budgeted cost of goods sold ........... | $240,000* | $360,000 | | |
| Add desired ending inventory .......... | 90,000† | | | |
| Total needs ............................. | 330,000 | | | |
| Less beginning inventory .............. | 60,000 | | | |
| Required purchases .................... | $270,000 | | | |

\*$400,000 sales × 60% cost ratio = $240,000.
†$360,000 × 25% = $90,000.

b.  Schedule of expected cash disbursements for merchandise purchases:

|  | January | February | March | Quarter |
|---|---|---|---|---|
| December purchases ........................... | $ 93,000 | | | $ 93,000 |
| January purchases .............................. | 135,000 | 135,000 | | 270,000 |
| February purchases ............................. | | — | | |
| March purchases ................................ | | — | | |
| Total cash disbursements for purchases ......... | $228,000 | | | |

3.  Cash budget:

|  | January | February | March | Quarter |
|---|---|---|---|---|
| Beginning cash balance ............ | $ 48,000 | | | |
| Add cash collections ................ | 304,000 | | | |
| Total cash available ................. | 352,000 | | | |
| Less cash disbursements: | | | | |
|    Inventory purchases .............. | 228,000 | | | |
|    Selling and administrative | | | | |
|       expenses ...................... | 129,000 | | | |
|    Equipment purchases ............ | — | | | |
|    Cash dividends .................. | 45,000 | | | |
| Total cash disbursements .......... | 402,000 | | | |
| Excess (deficiency) of cash .......... | (50,000) | | | |
| Financing: | | | | |
| Etc. | | | | |

4.  Using Schedule 9 as your guide, prepare an absorption costing income statement for the quarter ending March 31.
5.  Prepare a balance sheet as of March 31.

## CASES        ▪ connect

**ANALYTICAL THINKING LO8–1**

Tom Emory and Jim Morris strolled back to their plant from the administrative offices of Ferguson & Son Manufacturing Company. Tom is manager of the machine shop in the company's factory; Jim is manager of the equipment maintenance department.

The men had just attended the monthly performance evaluation meeting for plant department heads. These meetings had been held on the third Tuesday of each month since Robert Ferguson, Jr., the president's son, had become plant manager a year earlier.

As they were walking, Tom Emory spoke: "Boy, I hate those meetings! I never know whether my department's accounting reports will show good or bad performance. I'm beginning to expect the worst. If the accountants say I saved the company a dollar, I'm called 'Sir,' but if I spend even a little too much— boy, do I get in trouble. I don't know if I can hold on until I retire."

Tom had just been given the worst evaluation he had ever received in his long career with Ferguson & Son. He was the most respected of the experienced machinists in the company. He had been with Ferguson & Son for many years and was promoted to supervisor of the machine shop when the company expanded and moved to its present location. The president (Robert Ferguson, Sr.) had often stated that the company's success was due to the high-quality work of machinists like Tom. As supervisor, Tom stressed the importance of craftsmanship and told his workers that he wanted no sloppy work coming from his department.

When Robert Ferguson, Jr., became the plant manager, he directed that monthly performance comparisons be made between actual and budgeted costs for each department. The departmental budgets were intended to encourage the supervisors to reduce inefficiencies and to seek cost reduction opportunities. The company controller was instructed to have his staff "tighten" the budget slightly whenever a department attained its budget in a given month; this was done to reinforce the plant manager's desire to reduce costs. The young plant manager often stressed the importance of continued progress toward attaining the budget; he also made it known that he kept a file of these performance reports for future reference when he succeeded his father.

Tom Emory's conversation with Jim Morris continued as follows:

**Emory:** I really don't understand. We've worked so hard to meet the budget, and the minute we do so they tighten it on us. We can't work any faster and still maintain quality. I think my men are ready to quit trying. Besides, those reports don't tell the whole story. We always seem to be interrupting the big jobs for all those small rush orders. All that setup and machine adjustment time is killing us. And quite frankly, Jim, you were no help. When our hydraulic press broke down last month, your people were nowhere to be found. We had to take it apart ourselves and got stuck with all that idle time.

*Morris:* I'm sorry about that, Tom, but you know my department has had trouble making budget, too. We were running well behind at the time of that problem, and if we'd spent a day on that old machine, we would never have made it up. Instead we made the scheduled inspections of the forklift trucks because we knew we could do those in less than the budgeted time.

*Emory:* Well, Jim, at least you have some options. I'm locked into what the scheduling department assigns to me and you know they're being harassed by sales for those special orders. Incidentally, why didn't your report show all the supplies you guys wasted last month when you were working in Bill's department?

*Morris:* We're not out of the woods on that deal yet. We charged the maximum we could to other work and haven't even reported some of it yet.

*Emory:* Well, I'm glad you have a way of getting out of the pressure. The accountants seem to know everything that's happening in my department, sometimes even before I do. I thought all that budget and accounting stuff was supposed to help, but it just gets me into trouble. It's all a big pain. I'm trying to put out quality work; they're trying to save pennies.

**Required:**
1. Identify the problems that appear to exist in Ferguson & Son Manufacturing Company's budgetary control system and explain how the problems are likely to reduce the effectiveness of the system.
2. Explain how Ferguson & Son Manufacturing Company's budgetary control system could be revised to improve its effectiveness.

(CMA, adapted)

### CASE LO8–2, LO8–4, LO8–8, LO8–9, LO8–10

You have just been hired as a new management trainee by Earrings Unlimited, a distributor of earrings to various retail outlets located in shopping malls across the country. In the past, the company has done very little in the way of budgeting and at certain times of the year has experienced a shortage of cash. Since you are well trained in budgeting, you have decided to prepare a master budget for the upcoming second quarter. To this end, you have worked with accounting and other areas to gather the information assembled below.

The company sells many styles of earrings, but all are sold for the same price—$10 per pair. Actual sales of earrings for the last three months and budgeted sales for the next six months follow (in pairs of earrings):

| | | | |
|---|---|---|---|
| January (actual) | 20,000 | June (budget) | 50,000 |
| February (actual) | 26,000 | July (budget) | 30,000 |
| March (actual) | 40,000 | August (budget) | 28,000 |
| April (budget) | 65,000 | September (budget) | 25,000 |
| May (budget) | 100,000 | | |

The concentration of sales before and during May is due to Mother's Day. Sufficient inventory should be on hand at the end of each month to supply 40% of the earrings sold in the following month.

Suppliers are paid $4 for a pair of earrings. One-half of a month's purchases is paid for in the month of purchase; the other half is paid for in the following month. All sales are on credit. Only 20% of a month's sales are collected in the month of sale. An additional 70% is collected in the following month, and the remaining 10% is collected in the second month following sale. Bad debts have been negligible.

Monthly operating expenses for the company are given below:

| Variable: | |
|---|---|
| Sales commissions | 4% of sales |
| **Fixed:** | |
| Advertising | $200,000 |
| Rent | $18,000 |
| Salaries | $106,000 |
| Utilities | $7,000 |
| Insurance | $3,000 |
| Depreciation | $14,000 |

Insurance is paid on an annual basis, in November of each year.

The company plans to purchase $16,000 in new equipment during May and $40,000 in new equipment during June; both purchases will be for cash. The company declares dividends of $15,000 each quarter, payable in the first month of the following quarter.

The company's balance sheet as of March 31 is given below:

| Assets | |
| --- | --- |
| **Assets** | |
| Cash ...................................................................................... | $ 74,000 |
| Accounts receivable ($26,000 February sales; $320,000 March sales) ............. | 346,000 |
| Inventory ................................................................................. | 104,000 |
| Prepaid insurance ..................................................................... | 21,000 |
| Property and equipment (net) ..................................................... | 950,000 |
| Total assets ............................................................................. | $1,495,000 |
| **Liabilities and Stockholders' Equity** | |
| Accounts payable ..................................................................... | $ 100,000 |
| Dividends payable ..................................................................... | 15,000 |
| Common stock ......................................................................... | 800,000 |
| Retained earnings ..................................................................... | 580,000 |
| Total liabilities and stockholders' equity ........................................ | $1,495,000 |

The company maintains a minimum cash balance of $50,000. All borrowing is done at the beginning of a month; any repayments are made at the end of a month.

The company has an agreement with a bank that allows the company to borrow in increments of $1,000 at the beginning of each month. The interest rate on these loans is 1% per month and for simplicity we will assume that interest is not compounded. At the end of the quarter, the company would pay the bank all of the accumulated interest on the loan and as much of the loan as possible (in increments of $1,000), while still retaining at least $50,000 in cash.

**Required:**

Prepare a master budget for the three-month period ending June 30. Include the following detailed schedules:

1.  a.  A sales budget, by month and in total.
    b.  A schedule of expected cash collections, by month and in total.
    c.  A merchandise purchases budget in units and in dollars. Show the budget by month and in total.
    d.  A schedule of expected cash disbursements for merchandise purchases, by month and in total.
2.  A cash budget. Show the budget by month and in total. Determine any borrowing that would be needed to maintain the minimum cash balance of $50,000.
3.  A budgeted income statement for the three-month period ending June 30. Use the contribution approach.
4.  A budgeted balance sheet as of June 30.

**ETHICS CHALLENGE LO8–1**

Granger Stokes, managing partner of the venture capital firm of Halston and Stokes, was dissatisfied with the top management of PrimeDrive, a manufacturer of computer disk drives. Halston and Stokes had invested $20 million in PrimeDrive, and the return on their investment had been below expectations for several years. In a tense meeting of the board of directors of PrimeDrive, Stokes exercised his firm's rights as the major equity investor in PrimeDrive and fired PrimeDrive's chief executive officer (CEO). He then quickly moved to have the board of directors of PrimeDrive appoint himself as the new CEO.

Stokes prided himself on his hard-driving management style. At the first management meeting, he asked two of the managers to stand and fired them on the spot, just to show everyone who was in control of the company. At the budget review meeting that followed, he ripped up the departmental budgets that had been submitted for his review and yelled at the managers for their "wimpy, do nothing targets." He then ordered everyone to submit new budgets calling for at least a 40% increase in sales volume and announced that he would not accept excuses for results that fell below budget.

Keri Kalani, an accountant working for the production manager at PrimeDrive, discovered toward the end of the year that her boss had not been scrapping defective disk drives that had been returned by customers. Instead, he had been shipping them in new cartons to other customers to avoid booking losses. Quality control had deteriorated during the year as a result of the push for increased volume, and returns of defective disk drives were running as high as 15% of the new drives shipped. When she confronted her boss with her discovery, he told her to mind her own business. And then, to justify his actions, he said, "All of us managers are finding ways to hit Stokes's targets."

***Required:***
1. Is Granger Stokes using budgets as a planning and control tool?
2. What are the behavioral consequences of the way budgets are being used at PrimeDrive?
3. What, if anything, do you think Keri Kalani should do?

### COMMUNICATING IN PRACTICE LO8–1

In recent years, public universities have experienced major budget cuts due to reduced funding from their state governments. These budget cuts usually occur at the most inopportune time—during the school year when contractual commitments with faculty and staff had been signed, programs had been planned, and students were enrolled and taking classes.

***Required:***
1. Should the administration be "fair" to all affected and institute across-the-board cuts whenever the state announces a reduction in funding?
2. If not across-the-board cutbacks in programs, then would you recommend more focused reductions, and if so, what priorities would you establish for bringing spending in line with revenues?
3. Since these usually are not one-time-only cutbacks, how would you manage continuous, long-term reductions in budgets extending over a period of years?
4. Should the decision-making process be top-down (centralized with top administrators) or bottom-up (participative)? Why?
5. How should issues such as protect-your-turf mentality, resistance to change, and consensus building be dealt with?

**A LOOK BACK**

In Chapter 8, we discussed the budgeting process and each of the schedules in the master budget.

**A LOOK AT THIS CHAPTER**

Chapter 9 begins our discussion of management control and performance measures. We explain how to prepare flexible budgets and how to compare them to actual results for the purposes of computing revenue and spending variances. We also describe how standards are used to isolate the effects of various factors on actual results. In particular, we compute material, labor, and overhead variances.

**A LOOK AHEAD**

In Chapter 10, we continue the discussion of management control and performance measures by focusing on how decentralized organizations are managed.

# Flexible Budgets, Standard Costs, and Variance Analysis

©Michael Sears/MCT/Newscom

*After studying Chapter 9, you should be able to:*

**LO9–1** Prepare a planning budget and a flexible budget and understand how they differ from one another.

**LO9–2** Calculate and interpret revenue and spending variances.

**LO9–3** Prepare a flexible budget with more than one cost driver.

**LO9–4** Compute the direct materials price and quantity variances and explain their significance.

**LO9–5** Compute the direct labor rate and efficiency variances and explain their significance.

**LO9–6** Compute the variable manufacturing overhead rate and efficiency variances and explain their significance.

**LO9–7** (Appendix 9A) Compute and interpret the fixed overhead budget and volume variances.

**LO9–8** (Appendix 9B) Prepare an income statement using a standard cost system.

# Why Do Companies Need Flexible Budgets?

The difficulty of accurately predicting future financial performance can be readily understood by reading the annual report of any publicly traded company. For example, **Nucor Corporation**, a steel manufacturer headquartered in Charlotte, North Carolina, cites numerous reasons why its actual results may differ from expectations, including the following: (1) changes in the supply and cost of raw materials; (2) changes in the availability and cost of electricity and natural gas; (3) changes in the market demand for steel products; (4) fluctuations in currency conversion rates; (5) significant changes in laws or government regulations; and (6) the cyclical nature of the steel industry.

Source: *Form 10-K*, 8-13. Nucor Corporation, 2016

In the last chapter we explored how budgets are developed before a period begins. In this chapter, we explain how budgets can be adjusted to help guide actual operations and influence the performance evaluation process. For example, an organization's actual expenses will rarely equal its budgeted expenses as estimated at the beginning of the period. The reason is that the actual level of activity (such as unit sales) will rarely be the same as the budgeted activity; therefore, many actual expenses and revenues will naturally differ from what was budgeted. Should a manager be penalized for spending 10% more than budgeted for a variable expense like direct materials if unit sales are 10% higher than budgeted? Of course not. After studying this chapter, you'll know how to adjust a budget to enable meaningful comparisons to actual results.

# THE VARIANCE ANALYSIS CYCLE

Companies use the *variance analysis cycle,* as illustrated in Exhibit 9–1, to evaluate and improve performance. The cycle begins with the preparation of performance reports in the accounting department. These reports highlight variances, which are the differences between the actual results and what should have occurred according to the budget. The variances raise questions. Why did this variance occur? Why is this variance larger than it was last period? The significant variances are investigated so that their root causes can be either replicated or eliminated. Then, next period's operations are carried out and the cycle begins again with the preparation of a new performance report for the latest period. The emphasis should be on highlighting superior and unsatisfactory results, finding the root causes of these outcomes, and then replicating the sources of superior achievement and eliminating the sources of unsatisfactory performance. The variance analysis cycle should not be used to assign blame for poor performance.

Managers frequently use the concept of *management by exception* in conjunction with the variance analysis cycle. **Management by exception** is a management system that compares actual results to a budget so that significant deviations can be flagged as exceptions and investigated further. This approach enables managers to focus on the most important variances while bypassing trivial discrepancies between the budget and actual results. For example, a variance of $5 is probably not big enough to warrant attention, whereas a variance of $5,000 might be worth tracking down. Another clue is the size of the variance relative to the amount of spending. A variance that is only 0.1% of spending on an item is probably caused by random factors. On the other hand, a variance of 10% of spending is much more likely to be a signal that something is wrong. In addition to watching for unusually large variances, the pattern of the variances should be monitored. For example, a run of steadily mounting variances should trigger an investigation even though none of the variances is large enough by itself to warrant investigation.

**EXHIBIT 9–1**
The Variance Analysis Cycle

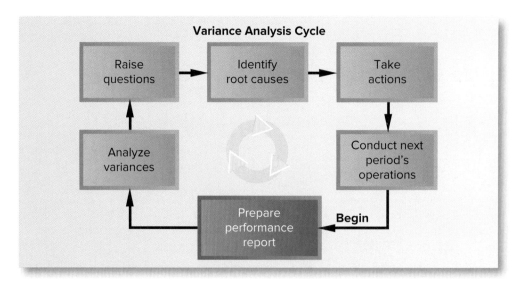

Next, we explain how service organizations use flexible budgets to analyze variances followed by a discussion of how companies can use standard costs for those same purposes.

## Characteristics of a Flexible Budget

The budgets that we explored in the last chapter were *planning budgets.* A **planning budget** is prepared before the period begins and is valid for only the planned level of activity. A static planning budget is suitable for planning but is inappropriate for evaluating how well costs are controlled. If the actual level of activity differs from what was planned, it would be misleading to compare actual costs to the static, unchanged planning budget. If activity is higher than expected, variable costs should be higher than expected; and if activity is lower than expected, variable costs should be lower than expected.

*Flexible budgets* take into account how changes in activity affect costs. A **flexible budget** is an estimate of what revenues and costs should have been, given the actual level of activity for the period. When a flexible budget is used in performance evaluation, actual costs are compared to what the costs *should have been for the actual level of activity during the period* rather than to the static planning budget. This is a very important distinction. If adjustments for the level of activity are not made, it is very difficult to interpret discrepancies between budgeted and actual costs.

> **LEARNING OBJECTIVE 9–1**
>
> Prepare a planning budget and a flexible budget and understand how they differ from one another.

1. Which of the following statements is true? (You may select more than one answer.)
    a. A planning budget is prepared before the period begins and it is based on the actual level of activity incurred during the period.
    b. A flexible budget is an estimate of what revenues and costs should have been, given the actual level of activity for the period.
    c. The variance analysis cycle includes analyzing differences between actual results and what should have occurred according to the budget.
    d. The management by exception approach enables managers to focus on the most important variances while bypassing trivial discrepancies.

CONCEPT CHECK

## Deficiencies of the Static Planning Budget

To illustrate the difference between a static planning budget and a flexible budget, consider Rick's Hairstyling, an upscale hairstyling salon located in Beverly Hills that is owned and managed by Rick Manzi. Recently Rick has been attempting to get better control of his revenues and costs, and at the urging of his accounting and business adviser, Victoria Kho, he has begun to prepare monthly budgets.

At the end of February, Rick prepared the March budget that appears in Exhibit 9–2. Rick believes that the number of customers served in a month (also known as the number of client-visits) is the best way to measure the overall level of activity in his salon. A customer who comes into the salon and has his or her hair styled is counted as one client-visit.

Note that the term *revenue* is used in the planning budget rather than *sales.* We use the term revenue throughout the chapter because some organizations have sources of revenue other than sales. For example, donations, as well as sales, are counted as revenue in nonprofit organizations.

Rick has identified eight major categories of costs—wages and salaries, hairstyling supplies, client gratuities, electricity, rent, liability insurance, employee health insurance, and miscellaneous. Client gratuities consist of flowers, candies, and glasses of champagne that Rick gives to his customers while they are in the salon.

EXHIBIT 9–2
Planning Budget

**Rick's Hairstyling**
**Planning Budget**
**For the Month Ended March 31**

| | |
|---|---:|
| *Budgeted* client-visits $(q)$. | 1,000 |
| Revenue $(\$180.00q)$ | $180,000 |
| Expenses: | |
|    Wages and salaries $(\$65,000 + \$37.00q)$ | 102,000 |
|    Hairstyling supplies $(\$1.50q)$ | 1,500 |
|    Client gratuities $(\$4.10q)$ | 4,100 |
|    Electricity $(\$1,500 + \$0.10q)$ | 1,600 |
|    Rent $(\$28,500)$ | 28,500 |
|    Liability insurance $(\$2,800)$ | 2,800 |
|    Employee health insurance $(\$21,300)$ | 21,300 |
|    Miscellaneous $(\$1,200 + \$0.20q)$ | 1,400 |
| Total expense | 163,200 |
| Net operating income | $ 16,800 |

Working with Victoria, Rick estimated a cost formula for each cost. For example, the cost formula for electricity is $\$1,500 + \$0.10q$, where $q$ equals the number of client-visits. In other words, electricity is a mixed cost with a $1,500 fixed element and a $0.10 per client-visit variable element. Once the budgeted level of activity was set at 1,000 client-visits, Rick computed the budgeted amount for each line item in the budget. For example, using the cost formula, he set the budgeted cost for electricity at $1,600 ($= \$1,500 + \$0.10 \times 1,000$). To finalize his budget, Rick computed his expected net operating income for March of $16,800.

At the end of March, Rick prepared the income statement in Exhibit 9–3, which shows that 1,100 clients actually visited his salon in March and that his actual net operating income for the month was $21,230. It is important to realize that the actual results are *not* determined by plugging the actual number of client-visits into the revenue and cost formulas. The formulas are simply estimates of what the revenues and costs should be for a given level of activity. What actually happens usually differs from what is supposed to happen.

EXHIBIT 9–3
Actual Results—Income
Statement

**Rick's Hairstyling**
**Income Statement**
**For the Month Ended March 31**

| | |
|---|---:|
| *Actual* client-visits | 1,100 |
| Revenue | $194,200 |
| Expenses: | |
|    Wages and salaries | 106,900 |
|    Hairstyling supplies | 1,620 |
|    Client gratuities | 6,870 |
|    Electricity | 1,550 |
|    Rent | 28,500 |
|    Liability insurance | 2,800 |
|    Employee health insurance | 22,600 |
|    Miscellaneous | 2,130 |
| Total expense | 172,970 |
| Net operating income | $ 21,230 |

The first thing Rick noticed when comparing Exhibits 9–2 and 9–3 is that the actual profit of $21,230 (from Exhibit 9–3) was substantially higher than the budgeted profit of $16,800 (from Exhibit 9–2). This was, of course, good news, but Rick wanted to know more. Business was up by 10%—the salon had 1,100 client-visits instead of the budgeted 1,000 client-visits. Could this alone explain the higher net operating income? The answer is no. An increase in net operating income of 10% would have resulted in net operating income of only $18,480 (= 1.1 × $16,800), not the $21,230 actually earned during the month. What is responsible for this better outcome? Higher prices? Lower costs? Something else? Whatever the cause, Rick would like to know the answer and then hopefully repeat the same performance next month.

In an attempt to analyze what happened in March, Rick prepared the report comparing actual to budgeted costs that appears in Exhibit 9–4. Note that most of the variances in this report are labeled unfavorable (U) rather than favorable (F) even though net operating income was actually higher than expected. For example, wages and salaries show an unfavorable variance of $4,900 because the actual wages and salaries expense was $106,900, whereas the budget called for wages and salaries of $102,000. The problem with the report, as Rick immediately realized, is that it compares revenues and costs at one level of activity (1,000 client-visits) to revenues and costs at a different level of activity (1,100 client-visits). This is like comparing apples to oranges. Because Rick had 100 more client-visits than expected, some of his costs should be higher than budgeted. From Rick's standpoint, the increase in activity was good; however, it appears to be having a negative impact on most of the costs in the report. Rick knew that something would have to be done to make the report more meaningful, but he was unsure of what to do. So he contacted his accountant, Victoria Kho, and asked her to analyze his salon's performance using the data in Exhibit 9–2 and 9–3.

**EXHIBIT 9–4**
Comparison of Actual Results to the Static Planning Budget

**Rick's Hairstyling**
**Comparison of Actual Results to the Planning Budget**
**For the Month Ended March 31**

| | Actual Results | Planning Budget | Variances* |
|---|---|---|---|
| Client-visits .......................... | 1,100 | 1,000 | |
| Revenue.............................. | $194,200 | $180,000 | $14,200 F |
| Expenses: | | | |
| Wages and salaries ................. | 106,900 | 102,000 | 4,900 U |
| Hairstyling supplies ................. | 1,620 | 1,500 | 120 U |
| Client gratuities..................... | 6,870 | 4,100 | 2,770 U |
| Electricity............................ | 1,550 | 1,600 | 50 F |
| Rent ............................... | 28,500 | 28,500 | 0 |
| Liability insurance................... | 2,800 | 2,800 | 0 |
| Employee health insurance .......... | 22,600 | 21,300 | 1,300 U |
| Miscellaneous....................... | 2,130 | 1,400 | 730 U |
| Total expense ....................... | 172,970 | 163,200 | 9,770 U |
| Net operating income ................ | $ 21,230 | $ 16,800 | $ 4,430 F |

*The revenue variance is labeled favorable (unfavorable) when the actual revenue is greater than (less than) the planning budget. The expense variances are labeled favorable (unfavorable) when the actual expense is less than (greater than) the planning budget.

**EXHIBIT 9–5**
Flexible Budget Based on Actual
Activity

| Rick's Hairstyling Flexible Budget For the Month Ended March 31 | |
| --- | --- |
| *Actual* client-visits *(q)* . . . . . . . . . . . . . . . . . . . . . . . . . . . . . . | 1,100 |
| Revenue ($180.00q) . . . . . . . . . . . . . . . . . . . . . . . . . . . . | $198,000 |
| Expenses: | |
| Wages and salaries ($65,000 + $37.00q) . . . . . . . . | 105,700 |
| Hairstyling supplies ($1.50q) . . . . . . . . . . . . . . . . . . . | 1,650 |
| Client gratuities ($4.10q) . . . . . . . . . . . . . . . . . . . . . | 4,510 |
| Electricity ($1,500 + $0.10q) . . . . . . . . . . . . . . . . . . . | 1,610 |
| Rent ($28,500) . . . . . . . . . . . . . . . . . . . . . . . . . . . . . . | 28,500 |
| Liability insurance ($2,800) . . . . . . . . . . . . . . . . . . . . | 2,800 |
| Employee health insurance ($21,300) . . . . . . . . . . . | 21,300 |
| Miscellaneous ($1,200 + $0.20q) . . . . . . . . . . . . . . | 1,420 |
| Total expense . . . . . . . . . . . . . . . . . . . . . . . . . . . . . . . . | 167,490 |
| Net operating income . . . . . . . . . . . . . . . . . . . . . . . . . . | $ 30,510 |

## How a Flexible Budget Works

Victoria responded to Rick's request by preparing the flexible budget shown in Exhibit 9–5. Her flexible budget shows what the *revenues and costs should have been given the actual level of activity* in March. She calculated the expenses in her flexible budget by using Rick's cost formulas from Exhibit 9–2 to estimate what each expense should have been for $1,100$ client-visits—the actual level of activity. For example, using the cost formula $1,500 + $0.10q$, the cost of electricity in March *should have been* $1,610 (= $1,500 + $0.10 \times 1,100$). Also, notice that the amounts of rent ($28,500), liability insurance ($2,800), and employee health insurance ($21,300) in Victoria's flexible budget equal the corresponding amounts included in Rick's planning budget. This occurs because fixed costs are not affected by the activity level.

We can see from the flexible budget that the net operating income in March *should have been* $30,510, but recall from Exhibit 9–3 that the net operating income was actually only $21,230. The results are not as good as we thought. Why? We will answer that question shortly.

To summarize to this point, Rick had budgeted for a profit of $16,800. The actual profit was quite a bit higher—$21,230. However, Victoria's analysis shows that given the actual number of client-visits in March, the profit should have been even higher—$30,510. What are the causes of these discrepancies? Rick would certainly like to build on the positive factors, while working to reduce the negative factors. But what are they?

**IN BUSINESS**

## On-Call Scheduling Draws the Attention of the New York Attorney General

The New York Attorney General has warned **Target, Gap,** and 11 other companies that their on-call employee scheduling practices may violate the law. These companies are using software programs to forecast immediate-term staffing needs based on real-time sales and customer traffic information. If a store is busy it requires its on-call employees to come to work, whereas if the store is not busy the employees do not come to work and they are not paid. In other words, the employees need to plan to be available even though they may or may not be called into work or get paid.

©Bloomberg/Getty Images

(continued)

From a flexible budgeting standpoint, the companies are trying to make their labor costs variable with respect to sales and customer traffic. From a legal standpoint, the attorney general noted that this compensation scheme leaves employees "too little time to make arrangements for family needs, let alone to find an alternative source of income to compensate for the lost pay."

Source: Weber, Lauren, "Retailers Under Fire for Work Schedules," *The Wall Street Journal*, April 13, 2015, B1–B2.

# FLEXIBLE BUDGET VARIANCES

Recall that the flexible budget based on the actual level of activity in Exhibit 9–5 shows what *should have happened given the actual level of activity*. Therefore, Victoria's next step was to compare actual results to the flexible budget—in essence comparing what actually happened to what should have happened. Her work is shown in Exhibit 9–6.

## Revenue Variances

Focusing first on revenue, the actual revenue totaled $194,200. However, the flexible budget indicates that, given the actual level of activity, revenue should have been $198,000. Consequently, revenue was $3,800 less than it should have been, given the actual number of client-visits for the month. This discrepancy is labeled as a $3,800 U (unfavorable) variance and is called a *revenue variance*. A **revenue variance** is the difference between the actual total revenue and what the total revenue should have been, given the

**EXHIBIT 9–6**
Revenue and Spending Variances from Comparing Actual Results to the Flexible Budget

**Rick's Hairstyling**
**Revenue and Spending Variances**
**For the Month Ended March 31**

| | Actual Results | Flexible Budget | Revenue and Spending Variances* | |
|---|---|---|---|---|
| Client-visits | 1,100 | 1,100 | | |
| Revenue ($180.00q) | $194,200 | $198,000 | $3,800 | U |
| Expenses: | | | | |
| Wages and salaries ($65,000 + $37.00q) | 106,900 | 105,700 | 1,200 | U |
| Hairstyling supplies ($1.50q) | 1,620 | 1,650 | 30 | F |
| Client gratuities ($4.10q) | 6,870 | 4,510 | 2,360 | U |
| Electricity ($1,500 + $0.10q) | 1,550 | 1,610 | 60 | F |
| Rent ($28,500) | 28,500 | 28,500 | 0 | |
| Liability insurance ($2,800) | 2,800 | 2,800 | 0 | |
| Employee health insurance ($21,300) | 22,600 | 21,300 | 1,300 | U |
| Miscellaneous ($1,200 + $0.20q) | 2,130 | 1,420 | 710 | U |
| Total expense | 172,970 | 167,490 | 5,480 | U |
| Net operating income | $ 21,230 | $ 30,510 | $9,280 | U |

*The revenue variance is labeled favorable (unfavorable) when the actual revenue is greater than (less than) the flexible budget. The expense variances are labeled favorable (unfavorable) when the actual expense is less than (greater than) the flexible budget.

actual level of activity for the period. If actual revenue exceeds what the revenue should have been, the variance is labeled favorable. If actual revenue is less than what the revenue should have been, the variance is labeled unfavorable. Why would actual revenue be less than or more than it should have been, given the actual level of activity? Basically, the revenue variance is favorable if the average selling price is greater than expected; it is unfavorable if the average selling price is less than expected. This could happen for a variety of reasons including a change in selling price, a different mix of products sold, a change in the amount of discounts given, poor accounting controls, and so on.

## IN BUSINESS

## The Sales Implications of the World Cup

Actual sales volumes can differ from planned sales volumes for many reasons. For example, some companies may fail to consider how sporting events such as the World Cup will affect their planned sales. **Corning** said TV sales were up 13% in Europe and 64% in Latin America during the World Cup and **Carrefour** reported a bump in sales of its beer, soft drinks, and meats during the same period. Conversely, **Whirlpool** reported lower demand for its washing machines (because the company claimed that customers were spending their disposable income on TVs) and Denny's reported a drop in full-service dining during the World Cup.

©Lars Baron - FIFA/FIFA/Getty Images

Source: Monga, Vipal, and Chasan, Emily, "When in Doubt, Blame It on the World Cup," *The Wall Street Journal*, July 31, 2014, B1 and B4.

## Spending Variances

Focusing next on costs, the actual electricity cost was $1,550; however, the flexible budget indicates that electricity costs should have been $1,610 for the 1,100 client-visits in March. Because the cost was $60 less than we would have expected for the actual level of activity during the period, it is labeled as a favorable variance, $60 F. This is an example of a *spending variance*. By definition, a **spending variance** is the difference between the actual amount of the cost and how much a cost should have been, given the actual level of activity. If the actual cost is greater than what the cost should have been, the variance is labeled as unfavorable. If the actual cost is less than what the cost should have been, the variance is labeled as favorable. Why would a cost have a favorable or unfavorable variance? There are many possible explanations including paying a higher price for inputs than should have been paid, using too many inputs for the actual level of activity, a change in technology, and so on. Later in the chapter we will explore these types of explanations in greater detail when we begin discussing standard costs.

Note from Exhibit 9–6 that the overall net operating income variance is $9,280 U (unfavorable). This means that given the actual level of activity for the period, the net operating income was $9,280 lower than it should have been. There are a number of reasons for this. The most prominent is the unfavorable revenue variance of $3,800. Next in line is the $2,360 unfavorable variance for client gratuities. Looking at this in another way, client gratuities were more than 50% larger than they should have been according to the flexible budget. This is a variance that Rick would almost certainly want to investigate further. He may find that this unfavorable variance is not necessarily a bad thing. It is possible, for example, that more lavish use of gratuities led to the 10% increase in client-visits.

Exhibit 9–6 also includes a $1,300 unfavorable variance related to employee health insurance, thereby highlighting how a fixed cost can have a spending variance. While fixed costs do not depend on the level of activity, the actual amount of a fixed cost can differ from the estimated amount included in a flexible budget. For example, perhaps Rick's employee health insurance premiums unexpectedly increased by $1,300 during March.

In conclusion, the revenue and spending variances in Exhibit 9–6 will help Rick better understand why his actual net operating income differs from what should have happened given the actual level of activity.

## Owner of Micro-Brewery

Hops is an essential ingredient in beer. The brewery's budget for the current month, which was based on the production of 800 barrels of beer, allowed for an expense of $960 for hops. The actual production for the month was 850 barrels of beer and the actual cost of the hops used to produce that beer was $1,020. Hops is a variable cost. Do you think the expense for hops for the month was too high?

## FLEXIBLE BUDGETS WITH MULTIPLE COST DRIVERS

At Rick's Hairstyling, we have thus far assumed that there is only one cost driver—the number of client-visits. However, in the activity-based costing chapter, we found that more than one cost driver might be needed to adequately explain all of the costs in an organization. For example, some of the costs at Rick's Hairstyling probably depend more on the number of hours that the salon is open for business than the number of client-visits. Specifically, most of Rick's employees are paid salaries, but some are paid on an hourly basis. None of the employees is paid on the basis of the number of customers actually served. Consequently, the cost formula for wages and salaries would be more accurate if it were stated in terms of the hours of operation rather than the number of client-visits. The cost of electricity is even more complex. Some of the cost is fixed—the heat must be kept at some minimum level even at night when the salon is closed. Some of the cost depends on the number of client-visits—the power consumed by hair dryers depends on the number of customers served. Some of the cost depends on the number of hours the salon is open—the costs of lighting the salon and heating it to a comfortable temperature. Consequently, the cost formula for electricity would be more accurate if it were stated in terms of both the number of client-visits and the hours of operation rather than just in terms of the number of client-visits.

Exhibit 9–7 shows a flexible budget in which these changes have been made. In that flexible budget, two cost drivers are listed—client-visits and hours of operation—where $q_1$ refers to client-visits and $q_2$ refers to hours of operation. For example, wages and salaries depend on the hours of operation and its cost formula is $65,000 + $220q_2$. Because the salon actually operated 190 hours, the flexible budget amount for wages and salaries is $106,800 (= $65,000 + $220 \times 190$). The electricity cost depends on both client-visits and the hours of operation and its cost formula is $390 + $0.10q_1 + $6.00q_2$. Because the

**EXHIBIT 9–7**
Flexible Budget Based on More than One Cost Driver

| Rick's Hairstyling<br>Flexible Budget<br>For the Month Ended March 31 | |
| --- | --- |
| *Actual* client-visits ($q_1$) | 1,100 |
| *Actual* hours of operation ($q_2$) | 190 |
| Revenue ($180.00q_1$) | $198,000 |
| Expenses: | |
| Wages and salaries ($65,000 + $220q_2$) | 106,800 |
| Hairstyling supplies ($1.50q_1$) | 1,650 |
| Client gratuities ($4.10q_1$) | 4,510 |
| Electricity ($390 + $0.10q_1 + $6.00q_2$) | 1,640 |
| Rent ($28,500) | 28,500 |
| Liability insurance ($2,800) | 2,800 |
| Employee health insurance ($21,300) | 21,300 |
| Miscellaneous ($1,200 + $0.20q_1$) | 1,420 |
| Total expense | 168,620 |
| Net operating income | $ 29,380 |

actual number of client-visits was 1,100 and the salon actually operated for 190 hours, the flexible budget amount for electricity is $1,640 (= $390 + $0.10 × 1,100 + $6.00 × 190). Notice that the net operating income in the flexible budget based on two cost drivers is $29,380, whereas the net operating income in the flexible budget based on one cost driver (see Exhibit 9–5) is $30,510. These two amounts differ because the flexible budget based on two cost drivers is more accurate than the flexible budget based on one driver.

The revised flexible budget based on both client-visits and hours of operation can be used exactly like we used the earlier flexible budget based on just client-visits to compute revenue and spending variances as in Exhibit 9–6. The difference is that because the cost formulas based on more than one cost driver are more accurate than the cost formulas based on just one cost driver, the variances will also be more accurate.

Beyond using more than one cost driver to improve its budgeting and performance analysis process, a company can also decompose its spending variances into two parts—a part that measures how well resources were used and a part that measures how well the acquisition prices of those resources were controlled. For example, at Rick's Hairstyling, an unfavorable spending variance for hairstyling supplies could be due to using too many supplies or paying too much for the supplies, or some combination of the two. *The remainder of the chapter explains how standard cost systems can be used to decompose spending variances into these two parts.* Shortly, we'll transition from our example involving Rick's Hairstyling to an example involving a manufacturing company called The Colonial Pewter Company. Because standard cost systems are frequently used in manufacturing companies, we are shifting our focus accordingly.

CONCEPT CHECK ✓

2. A five-star hotel buys bouquets of flowers to decorate its common areas and guest rooms. Its flexible budget for flowers is $325 per day of operations plus $7.20 per room-day. (A room-day is a room rented for one day; a room is decorated with flowers only if it is occupied.) If this month the hotel operated for 30 days and it had 7,680 room-days, what would be the flexible budget amount for flowers for the month?
   a. $55,296
   b. $65,046
   c. $9,750
   d. $332.20
3. Refer to the data in the above question. If the actual spending on flowers for the month was $61,978 and the hotel originally budgeted for 30 operating days and 7,500 room-days, what was the spending variance for the month?
   a. $3,068 Favorable
   b. $3,068 Unfavorable
   c. $1,772 Favorable
   d. $1,772 Unfavorable

## STANDARD COSTS—SETTING THE STAGE

A *standard* is a benchmark for measuring performance. Standards are found everywhere. Auto service centers like **Firestone** and **Sears**, for example, often set specific labor time standards for the completion of certain tasks, such as installing a carburetor or doing a valve job, and then measure actual performance against these standards. Fast-food outlets such as **McDonald's** and **Subway** have exacting standards for the quantity of meat going into a sandwich, as well as standards for the cost of the meat. Your doctor evaluates your weight using standards for individuals of your age, height, and gender. The buildings we live in conform to standards set in building codes.

Standards are also widely used in managerial accounting where they relate to the *quantity* and acquisition *price* of inputs used in manufacturing goods or providing services.[1] *Quantity standards* specify how much of an input should be used to make a product or provide a service. *Price standards* specify how much should be paid for each unit of the input. If either the quantity or acquisition price of an input departs significantly from the standard, managers investigate the discrepancy to find the cause of the problem and eliminate it.

Next we'll demonstrate how a company can establish quantity and price standards for direct materials, direct labor, and variable manufacturing overhead and then we'll discuss how those standards can be used to calculate variances and manage operations.

The Colonial Pewter Company makes only one product—an elaborate reproduction of an 18th century pewter statue. The statue is made largely by hand, using traditional metal-working tools. Consequently, the manufacturing process is labor intensive and requires a high level of skill.

Colonial Pewter has recently expanded its workforce to take advantage of unexpected demand for the statue as a gift. The company started with a small cadre of experienced pewter workers but has had to hire less experienced workers as a result of the expansion. The president of the company, J. D. Wriston, has called a meeting to discuss production problems. Attending the meeting are Tom Kuchel, the production manager; Janet Warner, the purchasing manager; and Terry Sherman, the corporate controller.

**MANAGERIAL ACCOUNTING IN ACTION**
**THE ISSUE**

Colonial
Pewter
Company

*J. D.:* I've got a feeling that we aren't getting the production we should out of our new people.

*Tom:* Give us a chance. Some of the new people have been with the company for less than a month.

*Janet:* Let me add that production seems to be wasting an awful lot of material—particularly pewter. That stuff is very expensive.

*Tom:* What about the shipment of defective pewter that you bought—the one with the iron contamination? That caused us major problems.

*Janet:* How was I to know it was off-grade? Besides, it was a great deal.

*J. D.:* Calm down everybody. Let's get the facts before we start attacking each other.

*Tom:* I agree. The more facts the better.

*J. D.:* Okay, Terry, it's your turn. Facts are the controller's department.

*Terry:* I'm afraid I can't provide the answers off the top of my head, but if you give me about a week I can set up a system that can routinely answer questions relating to worker productivity, material waste, and input prices.

*J. D.:* Let's mark it on our calendars.

---

[1]Throughout the chapter, we assume that "tight but attainable" practical standards are used rather than ideal standards that can only be attained by the most skilled and efficient employees working at peak effort 100% of the time.

## Setting Direct Materials Standards

Terry Sherman's first task was to prepare quantity and price standards for the company's only significant raw material, pewter ingots. The **standard quantity per unit** defines the amount of direct materials that should be used for each unit of finished product, including an allowance for normal inefficiencies, such as scrap and spoilage.[2] After consulting with the production manager, Tom Kuchel, Terry set the quantity standard for pewter at 3.0 pounds per statue.

The **standard price per unit** defines the price that should be paid for each unit of direct materials and it should reflect the final, delivered cost of those materials. After consulting with purchasing manager Janet Warner, Terry set the standard price of pewter at $4.00 per pound.

Once Terry established the quantity and price standards he computed the standard direct materials cost per statue as follows:

$$3.0 \text{ pounds per statue} \times \$4.00 \text{ per pound} = \$12.00 \text{ per statue}$$

---

### IN BUSINESS

## Managing Raw Material Costs in the Apparel Industry

©casadaphoto/123RF

A company's raw material costs can rise for numerous and often uncontrollable reasons. For example, severe weather in China, which is the world's largest producer of cotton, can influence the cotton prices paid by **Abercrombie & Fitch**. Rising fuel costs can influence what **Maidenform Brands** pays for its petroleum-based synthetic fabrics. When farmers stop producing cotton in favor of soybeans, it increases the price **Jones Apparel Group** pays for a shrinking supply of cotton.

When faced with rising raw material costs, companies can respond three ways. First, they can maintain existing selling prices and consequently operate with lower margins. Second, they can pass the cost increases along to customers in the form of higher prices. Third, they can try to lower their raw material costs. For example, **Hanesbrands** buys hedging contracts that lock in its cotton prices, thereby insulating the company from future cost increases. **J.C. Penney** is changing the blend of raw materials used in its garments, whereas Maidenform has started buying some of its raw materials from lower-cost producers in Bangladesh.

Source: Holmes, Elizabeth, and Dodes, Rachel, "Cotton Tale: Apparel Prices Set to Rise," *The Wall Street Journal*, May 19, 2010, B8.

---

## Setting Direct Labor Standards

Direct labor quantity and price standards are usually expressed in terms of labor-hours or a labor rate. The **standard hours per unit** defines the amount of direct labor-hours that should be used to produce one unit of finished goods. One approach used to determine this standard is for an industrial engineer to do a time and motion study, actually clocking the time required for each task. Throughout the chapter, we'll assume that "tight but attainable" labor standards are used rather than "ideal" standards that can only be attained by the most skilled and efficient employees working at peak effort 100% of the time. Therefore, after consulting with the production manager and considering

---

[2]Although companies often create "practical" rather than "ideal" materials quantity standards that include allowances for normal inefficiencies such as scrap, spoilage, and rejects, this practice is often criticized because it contradicts the zero defects goal that underlies many process improvement programs. If these types of allowances are built into materials quantity standards, they should be periodically reviewed and reduced over time to reflect improved processes, better training, and better equipment.

reasonable allowances for breaks, personal needs of employees, cleanup, and machine downtime, Terry set the standard hours per unit at 0.50 direct labor-hours per statue.[3]

The **standard rate per hour** defines the company's expected direct labor wage rate per hour, including employment taxes and fringe benefits. Using wage records and in consultation with the production manager, Terry Sherman established a standard rate per hour of $22.00. This standard rate reflects the expected "mix" of workers, even though the actual hourly wage rates may vary somewhat from individual to individual due to differing skills or seniority.

Once Terry established the time and rate standards, he computed the standard direct labor cost per statue as follows:

0.50 direct labor-hours per statue × $22.00 per direct labor-hour = $11.00 per statue

## Setting Variable Manufacturing Overhead Standards

As with direct labor, the quantity and price standards for variable manufacturing overhead are usually expressed in terms of hours and a rate. The *standard hours per unit* for variable overhead measures the amount of the allocation base from a company's predetermined overhead rate that is required to produce one unit of finished goods. In the case of Colonial Pewter, we will assume that the company uses direct labor-hours as the allocation base in its predetermined overhead rate. Therefore, the standard hours per unit for variable overhead is exactly the same as the standard hours per unit for direct labor—0.50 direct labor-hours per statue.

The *standard rate per unit* that a company expects to pay for variable overhead equals *the variable portion of the predetermined overhead rate*. At Colonial Pewter, the variable portion of the predetermined overhead rate is $6.00 per direct labor-hour. Therefore, Terry computed the standard variable manufacturing overhead cost per statue as follows:

0.50 direct labor-hours per statue × $6.00 per direct-labor hour = $3.00 per statue

This $3.00 per unit cost for variable manufacturing overhead appears along with direct materials ($12 per unit) and direct labor ($11 per unit) on the *standard cost card* in Exhibit 9–8. A **standard cost card** shows the standard quantity (or hours) and standard price (or rate) of the inputs required to produce a unit of a specific product. The **standard cost per unit** for all three variable manufacturing costs is computed the same way. The standard quantity (or hours) per unit is multiplied by the standard price (or rate) per unit to obtain the standard cost per unit.

| Inputs | (1) Standard Quantity or Hours | (2) Standard Price or Rate | Standard Cost (1) × (2) |
|---|---|---|---|
| Direct materials . . . . . . . . . . . . . . . | 3.0 pounds | $4.00 per pound | $12.00 |
| Direct labor. . . . . . . . . . . . . . . . . . . | 0.50 hours | $22.00 per hour | 11.00 |
| Variable manufacturing overhead . . . . . . . . . . . . . . . . . | 0.50 hours | $6.00 per hour | 3.00 |
| Total standard cost per unit. . . . . . | | | $26.00 |

**EXHIBIT 9–8**
Standard Cost Card—Variable Manufacturing Costs

---

[3]Labor quantity standards assume that the production process is labor-paced—if labor works faster, output will go up. However, output in many companies is determined by the processing speed of machines, not by labor efficiency.

## Using Standards in Flexible Budgets

Once Terry Sherman created the standard cost card shown in Exhibit 9–8, he was ready to use this information to calculate direct materials, direct labor, and variable manufacturing overhead variances. Therefore, he gathered the following data for the month of June:

| | |
|---|---|
| Actual output in June . . . . . . . . . . . . . . . . . . . . . . . . . . . . . . . . . . . . . . | 2,000 statues |
| Actual direct materials cost in June* . . . . . . . . . . . . . . . . . . . . . . | $24,700 |
| Actual direct labor cost in June . . . . . . . . . . . . . . . . . . . . . . . . . | $22,680 |
| Actual variable manufacturing overhead cost in June . . . . . . . | $7,140 |

*There were no beginning or ending inventories of raw materials in June; all materials purchased were used.

Using the above data and the standard cost data from Exhibit 9–8, Terry computed the spending variances shown in Exhibit 9–9. Notice that the actual results and flexible budget columns are each based on the actual output of 2,000 statues. The standard costs of $12.00 per unit for materials, $11.00 per unit for direct labor, and $3.00 per unit for variable manufacturing overhead are each multiplied by the actual output of 2,000 statues to compute the amounts in the flexible budget column. For example, the standard direct labor cost per unit of $11.00 multiplied by 2,000 statues equals the direct labor flexible budget of $22,000.

The spending variances shown in Exhibit 9–9 are computed by taking the amounts in the actual results column and subtracting the amounts in the flexible budget column. For all three variable manufacturing costs, this computation results in a positive number because the actual amount of the cost incurred to produce 2,000 statues exceeds the standard cost allowed for 2,000 statues. Because, in all three instances, the actual cost incurred exceeds the standard cost allowed for the actual level of output, the variance is labeled unfavorable (U). Had any of the actual costs incurred been less than the standard cost allowed for the actual level of output, the corresponding variances would have been labeled favorable (F).

While the information in Exhibit 9–9 is useful, it would be even more useful if the spending variances could be broken down into their price-related and quantity-related components. For example, the direct materials spending variance in the report is $700 unfavorable. This means that, given the actual level of production for the period, direct materials costs were too high by $700—at least according to the standard costs. Was this due to higher than expected prices for materials? Or was it due to too much material being used? The standard cost variances we will be discussing in the rest of the chapter are designed to answer these questions.

**EXHIBIT 9–9**
Spending Variances for Variable Manufacturing Costs

| **Colonial Pewter**<br>**Spending Variances—Variable Manufacturing Costs Only**<br>**For the Month Ended June 30** | Actual Results | Spending Variances | Flexible Budget |
|---|---|---|---|
| Statues produced (q). . . . . . . . . . . . . . . . . . . . . . . . . . . . . | 2,000 | | 2,000 |
| Direct materials ($12.00q). . . . . . . . . . . . . . . . . . . . . . | $24,700 | $700 U | $24,000 |
| Direct labor ($11.00q) . . . . . . . . . . . . . . . . . . . . . . . . . | $22,680 | $680 U | $22,000 |
| Variable manufacturing overhead ($3.00q) . . . . . . . . | $7,140 | $1,140 U | $6,000 |

# A GENERAL MODEL FOR STANDARD COST VARIANCE ANALYSIS

Standard cost variance analysis decomposes spending variances from the flexible budget into two elements—one due to the price paid for the input and the other due to the amount of the input that is used. A **price variance** is the difference between the actual amount paid for an input and the standard amount that should have been paid, multiplied by the actual amount of the input purchased. A **quantity variance** is the difference between how much of an input was actually used and how much should have been used and is stated in dollar terms using the standard price of the input.

Why are standards separated into two categories—price and quantity? Price variances and quantity variances usually have different causes. In addition, different managers are usually responsible for buying and using inputs. For example, in the case of a raw material, the purchasing manager is responsible for its price and the production manager is responsible for the amount of the raw material actually used to make products. Therefore, it is important to clearly distinguish between deviations from price standards (the responsibility of the purchasing manager) and deviations from quantity standards (the responsibility of the production manager).

Exhibit 9–10 presents a general model that can be used to decompose the spending variance for a variable cost into a *price variance* and a *quantity variance*.[4] Column (1) in this exhibit corresponds with the Actual Results column in Exhibit 9–9. Column (3) corresponds with the Flexible Budget column in Exhibit 9–9. Column (2) has been inserted into Exhibit 9–10 to enable separating the spending variance into a price variance and a quantity variance.

Three things should be noted from Exhibit 9–10. First, it can be used to compute a price variance and a quantity variance for each of the three variable cost elements—direct materials, direct labor, and variable manufacturing overhead—even though the variances have different names. A price variance is called a *materials price variance* in the case of direct materials, a *labor rate variance* in the case of direct labor, and a *variable overhead rate variance* in the case of variable manufacturing overhead. A quantity variance

**EXHIBIT 9–10**   A General Model for Standard Cost Variance Analysis—Variable Manufacturing Costs

---

[4]This general model can always be used to compute direct labor and variable manufacturing overhead variances. However, it can be used to compute direct materials variances only when the actual quantity of materials purchased equals the actual quantity of materials used in production. Later in the chapter, we will explain how to compute direct materials variances when these quantities differ.

is called a *materials quantity variance* in the case of direct materials, a *labor efficiency variance* in the case of direct labor, and a *variable overhead efficiency variance* in the case of variable manufacturing overhead.

Second, all three columns in the exhibit are based on the *actual amount of output* produced during the period. Even the flexible budget column depicts the standard cost allowed for the *actual amount of output* produced during the period. The key to understanding the flexible budget column in Exhibit 9–10 is to grasp the meaning of the term *standard quantity allowed (SQ)*. The **standard quantity allowed** (when computing direct materials variances) or **standard hours allowed** (when computing direct labor and variable manufacturing overhead variances) refers to the amount of an input *that should have been used* to manufacture the actual output of finished goods produced during the period. It is computed by multiplying the actual output by the standard quantity (or hours) per unit. The standard quantity (or hours) allowed is then multiplied by the standard price (or rate) per unit of the input to obtain the total cost according to the flexible budget. For example, if a company actually produced 100 units of finished goods during the period and its standard quantity per unit of finished goods for direct materials is 3 pounds, then its *standard quantity allowed (SQ)* would be 300 pounds (= 100 units × 3 pounds per unit). If the company's standard cost per pound of direct materials is $2.00, then the total direct materials cost in its flexible budget would be $600 (= 300 pounds × $2.00 per pound).

Third, the spending, price, and quantity variances—regardless of what they are called—are computed exactly the same way regardless of whether one is dealing with direct materials, direct labor, or variable manufacturing overhead. The spending variance is computed by taking the total cost in column (1) and subtracting the total cost in column (3). The price variance is computed by taking the total cost in column (1) and subtracting the total cost in column (2). The quantity variance is computed by taking the total cost in column (2) and subtracting the total cost in column (3). In all of these variance calculations, a positive number should be labeled as an unfavorable (U) variance and a negative number should be labeled as a favorable (F) variance. An unfavorable price variance indicates that the actual price (AP) per unit of the input was greater than the standard price (SP) per unit. A favorable price variance indicates that the actual price (AP) of the input was less than the standard price per unit (SP). An unfavorable quantity variance indicates that the actual quantity (AQ) of the input used was greater than the standard quantity allowed (SQ). Conversely, a favorable quantity variance indicates that the actual quantity (AQ) of the input used was less than the standard quantity allowed (SQ).

With this general model as the foundation, we will now calculate Colonial Pewter's price and quantity variances.

# USING STANDARD COSTS—DIRECT MATERIALS VARIANCES

**LEARNING OBJECTIVE 9–4**

Compute the direct materials price and quantity variances and explain their significance.

After determining Colonial Pewter Company's standard costs for direct materials, direct labor, and variable manufacturing overhead, Terry Sherman's next step was to compute the company's variances for June. As discussed in the preceding section, variances are computed by comparing actual costs to standard costs. Terry referred to the standard cost card in Exhibit 9–8 that shows the standard direct materials cost per statue was computed as follows:

3.0 pounds per statue × $4.00 per pound = $12.00 per statue

Colonial Pewter's records for June showed that the actual quantity (AQ) of pewter purchased was 6,500 pounds at an actual price (AP) of $3.80 per pound, for a total cost of $24,700. All of the material purchased was used during June to manufacture 2,000 statues.[5]

---

[5]Throughout this section, we assume zero beginning and ending inventories of materials and that all materials purchased during the period are used during that period. The more general case in which there are beginning and ending inventories of materials and materials are not necessarily used during the period in which they are purchased is considered later in the chapter.

**EXHIBIT 9–11**    Standard Cost Variance Analysis—Direct Materials
(Note: The quantity of materials purchased equals the quantity used in production.)

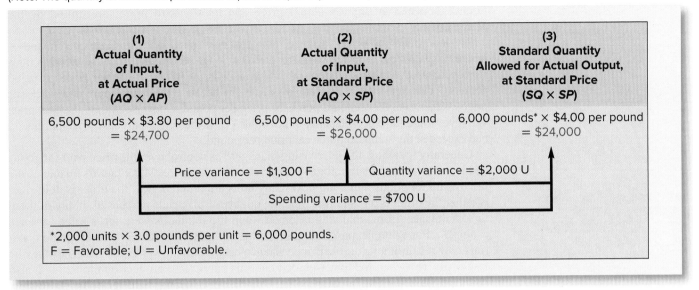

| (1)<br>**Actual Quantity**<br>**of Input,**<br>**at Actual Price**<br>**(AQ × AP)** | (2)<br>**Actual Quantity**<br>**of Input,**<br>**at Standard Price**<br>**(AQ × SP)** | (3)<br>**Standard Quantity**<br>**Allowed for Actual Output,**<br>**at Standard Price**<br>**(SQ × SP)** |
|---|---|---|
| 6,500 pounds × $3.80 per pound<br>= $24,700 | 6,500 pounds × $4.00 per pound<br>= $26,000 | 6,000 pounds* × $4.00 per pound<br>= $24,000 |

Price variance = $1,300 F         Quantity variance = $2,000 U

Spending variance = $700 U

*2,000 units × 3.0 pounds per unit = 6,000 pounds.
F = Favorable; U = Unfavorable.

Using these data and the standard costs from Exhibit 9–8, Terry computed the price and quantity variances shown in Exhibit 9–11.

Notice that the variances in this exhibit are based on three different total costs—$24,700, $26,000, and $24,000. The first, $24,700, is the actual amount paid for the actual amount of pewter purchased. The third total cost figure, $24,000, refers to how much should have been spent on pewter to produce the actual output of 2,000 statues. The standards call for 3 pounds of pewter per statue. Because 2,000 statues were produced, 6,000 pounds of pewter should have been used. This is referred to as the *standard quantity allowed* for the actual output and its computation can be stated in formula form as follows:

> Standard quantity allowed = Actual output × Standard quantity per unit

If 6,000 pounds of pewter had been purchased at the standard price of $4.00 per pound, the company would have spent $24,000. This is the amount that appears in the company's flexible budget for the month. The difference between the $24,700 actually spent and the $24,000 that should have been spent is the spending variance for the month of $700 U. This variance is unfavorable (denoted by U) because the amount that was actually spent exceeds the amount that should have been spent. Also note that this spending variance agrees with the direct materials spending variance in Exhibit 9–9.

The second total cost figure in Exhibit 9–11, $26,000, is the key that allows us to decompose the spending variance into two distinct elements—one due to price and one due to quantity. It represents how much the company should have spent if it had purchased the actual amount of input, 6,500 pounds, at the standard price of $4.00 a pound rather than the actual price of $3.80 a pound.

## The Materials Price Variance

Using the $26,000 total cost figure in column (2) of Exhibit 9–11, we can make two comparisons—one with the total cost of $24,700 in column (1) and one with the total cost of $24,000 in column (3). The difference between the $24,700 in column (1) and the $26,000 in column (2) is the *materials price variance* of $1,300, which is labeled as favorable (denoted by F). A **materials price variance** measures the difference between an input's actual price and its standard price, multiplied by the actual quantity purchased.

To understand the price variance, note that the actual price of $3.80 per pound of pewter is $0.20 less than the standard price of $4.00 per pound. Because 6,500 pounds were purchased, the total amount of the variance is $1,300 (= $0.20 per pound × 6,500 pounds). This variance is labeled favorable (F) because the actual purchase price per pound is less than the standard purchase price per pound. Conversely, the materials price variance would have been labeled unfavorable (U) if the actual purchase price per pound had exceeded the standard purchase price per pound.

Generally speaking, the purchasing manager has control over the price paid for goods and is therefore responsible for the materials price variance. Many factors influence the prices paid for goods including how many units are ordered, how the order is delivered, whether the order is a rush order, and the quality of materials purchased. If any of these factors deviates from what was assumed when the standards were set, a price variance can result. For example, purchasing second-grade materials rather than top-grade materials may result in a favorable price variance because the lower-grade materials may be less costly. However, the lower-grade materials may create production problems. It also bears emphasizing that someone other than the purchasing manager could be responsible for a materials price variance. For example, due to production problems beyond the purchasing manager's control, the purchasing manager may have to use express delivery. In these cases, the production manager should be held responsible for the resulting price variances.

## The Materials Quantity Variance

Referring again to Exhibit 9–11, the difference between the $26,000 in column (2) and the $24,000 in column (3) is the *materials quantity variance* of $2,000, which is labeled as unfavorable (denoted by U). The **materials quantity variance** measures the difference between the actual quantity of materials used in production and the standard quantity of materials allowed for the actual output, multiplied by the standard price per unit of materials. It is labeled as unfavorable (favorable) when the actual quantity of material used in production is greater than (less than) the quantity of material that should have been used according to the standard.

To understand the materials quantity variance, note that the actual amount of pewter used in production was 6,500 pounds. However, the standard amount of pewter allowed for the actual output is 6,000 pounds. Therefore, too much pewter was used to produce the actual output—by a total of 500 pounds. To express this in dollar terms, the 500 pounds is multiplied by the standard price of $4.00 per pound to yield the quantity variance of $2,000 U. Why is the standard price of pewter, rather than the actual price, used in this calculation? The production manager is ordinarily responsible for the quantity variance. If the actual price were used in the calculation of the quantity variance, the production manager's performance evaluation would be unfairly influenced by the efficiency or inefficiency of the purchasing manager.

Excessive materials usage can result from many factors, including faulty machines, inferior materials quality, untrained workers, and poor supervision. Generally speaking, it is the responsibility of the production manager to see that material usage is kept in line with standards. There may be times, however, when the *purchasing* manager is responsible for an unfavorable materials quantity variance. For example, if the purchasing manager buys inferior materials at a lower price, the materials may be unsuitable for use and may result in excessive waste. Thus, the purchasing manager rather than the production manager would be responsible for the quantity variance.

The Colonial Pewter Company's materials price and quantity variances can also be computed using the equations shown below where:

$AQ$ = Actual quantity of pounds purchased and used in production
$SQ$ = Standard quantity of pounds allowed for the actual output
$AP$ = Actual price per unit of the input
$SP$ = Standard price per unit of the input

*Materials Price Variance:*
Materials price variance = $(AQ \times AP) - (AQ \times SP)$
Materials price variance = $AQ (AP - SP)$
Materials price variance = 6,500 pounds ($3.80 per pound − $4.00 per pound)
Materials price variance = $1,300 F

The materials price variance is favorable because the actual price paid per pound was $0.20 less than the standard price per pound.

*Materials Quantity Variance:*
Materials quantity variance = $(AQ \times SP) - (SQ \times SP)$
Materials quantity variance = $SP (AQ - SQ)$
Materials quantity variance = $4.00 per pound (6,500 pounds − 6,000 pounds)
Materials quantity variance = $2,000 U

The materials quantity variance is unfavorable because the company used 500 more pounds than it should have to make 2,000 statues.

4.  Which of the following statements is true? (You may select more than one answer.)
    a.  The standard quantity per unit defines the amount of direct materials that should be used for each unit of finished goods.
    b.  The "standard quantity allowed for actual output" equals the actual output of finished goods multiplied by the standard quantity per unit.
    c.  The materials price variance measures the difference between an input's actual price and its standard price, multiplied by the standard quantity purchased.
    d.  The materials quantity variance measures the difference between the actual quantity of materials used in production and the standard quantity of materials allowed for the actual output, multiplied by the standard price per unit of materials.
5.  The standard and actual prices per pound of raw material are $4.00 and $4.50, respectively. A total of 10,500 pounds of raw material was purchased and then used to produce 5,000 units. The quantity standard allows two pounds of the raw material per unit produced. What is the materials price variance?
    a.  $5,250 favorable
    b.  $5,250 unfavorable
    c.  $5,000 unfavorable
    d.  $5,000 favorable
6.  Referring to the facts in question 5 above, what is the material quantity variance?
    a.  $5,000 unfavorable
    b.  $5,000 favorable
    c.  $2,000 favorable
    d.  $2,000 unfavorable

CONCEPT CHECK

# USING STANDARD COSTS—DIRECT LABOR VARIANCES

Terry Sherman's next step in determining Colonial Pewter's variances for June was to compute the direct labor variances for the month. Recall from Exhibit 9–8 that the standard direct labor cost per statue is $11, computed as follows:

$$0.50 \text{ hours per statue} \times \$22.00 \text{ per hour} = \$11.00 \text{ per statue}$$

In addition, Colonial Pewter's records for June showed that 1,050 direct labor-hours were actually worked. Given that the company paid its direct labor workers a total of $22,680 (including payroll taxes and fringe benefits), the average actual wage rate was $21.60 per hour (= $22,680 ÷ 1,050 hours). Using these data and the standard costs from Exhibit 9–8, Terry computed the direct labor rate and efficiency variances that appear in Exhibit 9–12.

Notice that the column headings in Exhibit 9–12 are the same as those used in Exhibits 9–10 and 9–11, except that in Exhibit 9–12 the terms *rate* and *hours* are used in place of the terms *price* and *quantity*.

## The Labor Rate Variance

Using the $23,100 total cost figure in column (2) of Exhibit 9–12, we can make two comparisons—one with the total cost of $22,680 in column (1) and one with the total cost of $22,000 in column (3). The difference between the $22,680 in column (1) and the $23,100 in column (2) is the *labor rate variance* of $420 F. The **labor rate variance** measures the difference between the actual hourly rate and the standard hourly rate, multiplied by the actual number of hours worked during the period.

To understand the labor rate variance, note that the actual hourly rate of $21.60 is $0.40 less than the standard rate of $22.00 per hour. Because 1,050 hours were actually worked, the total amount of the variance is $420 (= $0.40 per hour × 1,050 hours). The variance is labeled favorable (F) because the actual hourly rate is less than the standard hourly rate. If the actual hourly rate had been greater than the standard hourly rate, the variance would have been labeled unfavorable (U).

In most companies, the wage rates paid to workers are quite predictable. Nevertheless, rate variances can arise based on how production supervisors use their direct labor workers. Skilled workers with high hourly rates of pay may be given duties that require little skill and call for lower hourly rates of pay. This will result in an unfavorable labor

**EXHIBIT 9–12** Standard Cost Variance Analysis—Direct Labor

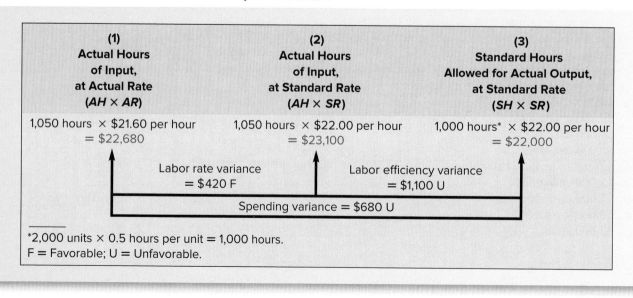

| (1) Actual Hours of Input, at Actual Rate (AH × AR) | (2) Actual Hours of Input, at Standard Rate (AH × SR) | (3) Standard Hours Allowed for Actual Output, at Standard Rate (SH × SR) |
|---|---|---|
| 1,050 hours × $21.60 per hour = $22,680 | 1,050 hours × $22.00 per hour = $23,100 | 1,000 hours* × $22.00 per hour = $22,000 |

Labor rate variance = $420 F          Labor efficiency variance = $1,100 U

Spending variance = $680 U

*2,000 units × 0.5 hours per unit = 1,000 hours.
F = Favorable; U = Unfavorable.

rate variance because the actual hourly rate of pay will exceed the standard rate specified for the particular task. In contrast, a favorable rate variance would result when workers who are paid at a rate lower than specified in the standard are assigned to the task. However, the lower-paid workers may not be as efficient. Finally, overtime work at premium rates will result in an unfavorable labor rate variance if the overtime premium is charged to the direct labor account.

## The Labor Efficiency Variance

Referring back to Exhibit 9–12, the difference between the $23,100 in column (2) and the $22,000 in column (3) is the *labor efficiency variance* of $1,100 unfavorable (U). The **labor efficiency variance** measures the difference between the actual hours used and the standard hours allowed for the actual output, multiplied by the standard hourly rate.

To understand Colonial Pewter's labor efficiency variance, note that the actual amount of hours used in production was 1,050 hours. However, the standard amount of hours allowed for the actual output is 1,000 hours. Therefore, the company used 50 more hours for the actual output than the standards allow. To express this in dollar terms, the 50 hours are multiplied by the standard rate of $22.00 per hour to yield the efficiency variance of $1,100 U.

Possible causes of an unfavorable labor efficiency variance include poorly trained or motivated workers; poor-quality materials, requiring more labor time; faulty equipment, causing breakdowns and work interruptions; poor supervision of workers; and inaccurate standards. The managers in charge of production would usually be responsible for control of the labor efficiency variance. However, the purchasing manager could be held responsible if the purchase of poor-quality materials resulted in excessive labor processing time.

Another important cause of an unfavorable labor efficiency variance may be insufficient demand for the company's products. Managers in some companies argue that it is difficult, and perhaps unwise, to constantly adjust the workforce in response to changes in the amount of work that needs to be done. In such companies, the direct labor workforce is essentially fixed in the short run. If demand is insufficient to keep everyone busy, workers are not laid off, which in turn creates an unfavorable labor efficiency variance.

If customer orders are insufficient to keep the workers busy, the work center manager has two options—either accept an unfavorable labor efficiency variance or build inventory. A central lesson of Lean Production is that building inventory with no immediate prospect of sale is a bad idea. Excessive inventory—particularly work in process inventory—leads to high defect rates, obsolete goods, and inefficient operations.

As a consequence, when the workforce is basically fixed in the short term, managers must be cautious about how labor efficiency variances are used. Some experts advocate eliminating labor efficiency variances in such situations—at least for the purposes of motivating and controlling workers on the shop floor.

## HELPFUL HINT

The Colonial Pewter Company's direct labor rate and efficiency variances can also be computed using the equations shown below where:

$AH$ = Actual quantity of hours used in production
$SH$ = Standard quantity of hours allowed for the actual output
$AR$ = Actual rate per direct labor-hour
$SR$ = Standard rate per direct labor-hour

*Labor Rate Variance:*
Labor rate variance = $(AH \times AR) - (AH \times SR)$
Labor rate variance = $AH(AR - SR)$
Labor rate variance = 1,050 hours ($21.60 per hour − $22.00 per hour)
Labor rate variance = $420 F

The labor rate variance is favorable because the actual hourly rate of $21.60 is $0.40 less than the standard hourly rate of $22.00.

*Labor Efficiency Variance:*
Labor efficiency variance = $(AH \times SR) - (SH \times SR)$
Labor efficiency variance = $SR(AH - SH)$
Labor efficiency variance = $22.00 per hour (1,050 hours − 1,000 hours)
Labor efficiency variance = $1,100 U

The labor efficiency variance is unfavorable because the company used 50 more hours than it should have to make 2,000 statues.

# USING STANDARD COSTS—VARIABLE MANUFACTURING OVERHEAD VARIANCES

**LEARNING OBJECTIVE 9–6**

Compute the variable manufacturing overhead rate and efficiency variances and explain their significance.

The final step in Terry Sherman's analysis of Colonial Pewter's variances for June was to compute the variable manufacturing overhead variances. The variable portion of manufacturing overhead can be analyzed using the same basic formulas that we used to analyze direct materials and direct labor. Recall from Exhibit 9–8 that the standard variable manufacturing overhead is $3.00 per statue, computed as follows:

0.50 hours per statue × $6.00 per hour = $3.00 per statue

Also recall that Colonial Pewter's cost records showed that the total actual variable manufacturing overhead cost for June was $7,140 and that 1,050 direct labor-hours were worked in June to produce 2,000 statues. Terry's analysis of this overhead data appears in Exhibit 9–13.

Notice the similarities between Exhibits 9–12 and 9–13. These similarities arise from the fact that direct labor-hours are being used as the base for allocating overhead cost to units of product; thus, the same hourly figures appear in Exhibit 9–13 for variable manufacturing overhead as in Exhibit 9–12 for direct labor. The main difference between the two exhibits is in the standard hourly rate being used, which in this company is much lower for variable manufacturing overhead than for direct labor.

**EXHIBIT 9–13**    Standard Cost Variance Analysis—Variable Manufacturing Overhead

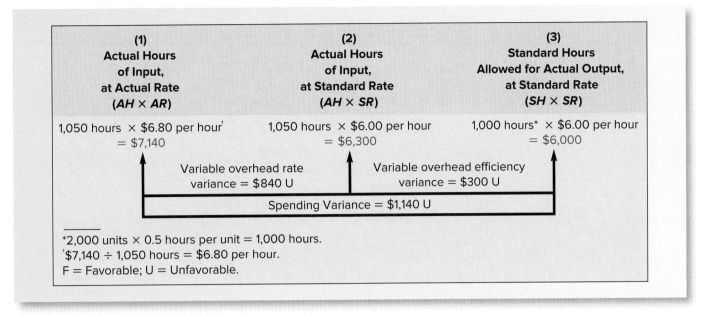

| (1) Actual Hours of Input, at Actual Rate (AH × AR) | (2) Actual Hours of Input, at Standard Rate (AH × SR) | (3) Standard Hours Allowed for Actual Output, at Standard Rate (SH × SR) |
|---|---|---|
| 1,050 hours × $6.80 per hour† = $7,140 | 1,050 hours × $6.00 per hour = $6,300 | 1,000 hours* × $6.00 per hour = $6,000 |

Variable overhead rate variance = $840 U

Variable overhead efficiency variance = $300 U

Spending Variance = $1,140 U

*2,000 units × 0.5 hours per unit = 1,000 hours.
†$7,140 ÷ 1,050 hours = $6.80 per hour.
F = Favorable; U = Unfavorable.

## The Variable Manufacturing Overhead Rate and Efficiency Variances

Using the $6,300 total cost figure in column (2) of Exhibit 9–13, we can make two comparisons—one with the total cost of $7,140 in column (1) and one with the total cost of $6,000 in column (3). The difference between the $7,140 in column (1) and the $6,300 in column (2) is the *variable overhead rate variance* of $840 U. The **variable overhead rate variance** measures the difference between the actual variable overhead cost incurred during the period and the standard cost that should have been incurred based on the actual activity of the period. The difference between the $6,300 in column (2) and the $6,000 in column (3) is the *variable overhead efficiency variance* of $300 U. The **variable overhead efficiency variance** measures the difference between the actual level of activity and the standard activity allowed for the actual output, multiplied by the variable part of the predetermined overhead rate.

To understand Colonial Pewter's variable overhead efficiency variance, note that the actual amount of hours used in production was 1,050 hours. However, the standard amount of hours allowed for the actual output is 1,000 hours. Therefore, the company used 50 more hours for the actual output than the standards allow. To express this in dollar terms, the 50 hours are multiplied by the variable part of the predetermined overhead rate of $6.00 per hour to yield the variable overhead efficiency variance of $300 U.

The interpretation of the variable overhead variances is not as clear as the direct materials and direct labor variances. In particular, the variable overhead efficiency variance is exactly the same as the direct labor efficiency variance except for one detail—the rate that is used to translate the variance into dollars. In both cases, the variance is the difference between the actual hours worked and the standard hours allowed for the actual output. In the case of the direct labor efficiency variance, this difference is multiplied by the standard direct labor rate. In the case of the variable overhead efficiency variance, this difference is multiplied by the variable portion of the predetermined overhead rate. So when direct labor is used as the base for overhead, whenever the direct labor efficiency variance is favorable, the variable overhead efficiency variance will also be favorable. And whenever the direct labor efficiency variance is unfavorable, the variable overhead efficiency variance will be unfavorable. Indeed, the variable overhead efficiency variance really doesn't tell us anything about how efficiently overhead resources were used. It depends solely on how efficiently direct labor was used.

The Colonial Pewter Company's variable overhead rate and efficiency variances can also be computed using the equations shown below where:

$AH$ = Actual quantity of hours used in production
$SH$ = Standard quantity of hours allowed for the actual output
$AR$ = Actual rate per direct labor-hour
$SR$ = Standard rate per direct labor-hour

*Variable Overhead Rate Variance:*
Variable overhead rate variance = $(AH \times AR) - (AH \times SR)$
Variable overhead rate variance = $AH(AR - SR)$
Variable overhead rate variance = $1{,}050$ hours ($\$6.80 - \$6.00$)
Variable overhead rate variance = $\$840$ U

*Variable Overhead Efficiency Variance:*
Variable overhead efficiency variance = $(AH \times SR) - (SH \times SR)$
Variable overhead efficiency variance = $SR(AH - SH)$
Variable overhead efficiency variance = $\$6.00$ per hour ($1{,}050$ hours $- 1{,}000$ hours)
Variable overhead efficiency variance = $\$300$ U

The variable overhead efficiency variance is unfavorable because the company used 50 more hours than it should have to make 2,000 statues.

In preparation for the scheduled meeting to discuss his analysis of Colonial Pewter's standard costs and variances, Terry summarized his manufacturing cost variances as follows:

| | | |
|---|---:|---|
| Materials price variance . . . . . . . . . . . . . . . . . . | $1,300 | F |
| Materials quantity variance. . . . . . . . . . . . . . . | 2,000 | U |
| Labor rate variance . . . . . . . . . . . . . . . . . . . . . | 420 | F |
| Labor efficiency variance . . . . . . . . . . . . . . . . | 1,100 | U |
| Variable overhead rate variance . . . . . . . . . . . | 840 | U |
| Variable overhead efficiency variance . . . . . . | 300 | U |
| Total of the variances. . . . . . . . . . . . . . . . . . . | $2,520 | U |

He distributed these results to the management group of Colonial Pewter, which included J. D. Wriston, the president of the company; Tom Kuchel, the production manager; and Janet Warner, the purchasing manager. J. D. Wriston opened the meeting with the following question:

**J. D.:** Terry, I think I understand what you have done, but just to make sure, would you mind summarizing the highlights of what you found?

**Terry:** As you can see, the biggest problems are the unfavorable materials quantity variance of $2,000 and the unfavorable labor efficiency variance of $1,100.

**J. D.:** Tom, you're the production boss. What do you think is causing the unfavorable labor efficiency variance?

**Tom:** It has to be the new production workers. Our experienced workers shouldn't have much problem meeting the standard of half an hour per unit. We all knew that there would be some inefficiency for a while as we brought new people on board. My plan for overcoming the problem is to pair up each of the new guys with one of our old-timers and have them work together for a while. It would slow down our older guys a bit, but I'll bet the unfavorable variance disappears and our new workers would learn a lot.

**J. D.:** Sounds good. Now, what about that $2,000 unfavorable materials quantity variance?

**Terry:** Tom, are the new workers generating a lot of scrap?

*Tom:* Yeah, I guess so.

*J. D.:* I think that could be part of the problem. Can you do anything about it?

*Tom:* I can watch the scrap closely for a few days to see where it's being generated. If it is the new workers, I can have the old-timers work with them on the problem when I team them up.

*J. D.:* Janet, the favorable materials price variance of $1,300 isn't helping us if it is contributing to the unfavorable materials quantity and labor efficiency variances. Let's make sure that our raw material purchases conform to our quality standards.

*Janet:* Will do.

*J. D.:* Good. Let's reconvene in a few weeks to see what has happened. Hopefully, we can get those unfavorable variances under control.

## AN IMPORTANT SUBTLETY IN THE MATERIALS VARIANCES

Most companies use the *quantity of materials purchased* to compute the materials price variance and the *quantity of materials used* in production to compute the materials quantity variance. There are two reasons for this practice. First, delaying the computation of the price variance until the materials are used would result in less timely variance reports. Second, computing the price variance when the materials are purchased allows materials to be carried in the inventory accounts at their standard cost. This greatly simplifies bookkeeping. (See Appendix 9B at the end of the chapter for an explanation of how to prepare an income statement using a standard costing system.)[6]

When we computed materials price and quantity variances for Colonial Pewter in Exhibit 9–11, we assumed that 6,500 pounds of materials were purchased and used in production. However, it is very common for a company's quantity of materials purchased to differ from its quantity used in production. When this happens, the materials price variance is computed using the *quantity of materials purchased,* whereas the materials quantity variance is computed using the *quantity of materials used* in production.

To illustrate, assume that during June Colonial Pewter purchased 7,000 pounds of materials at $3.80 per pound instead of 6,500 pounds as assumed earlier in the chapter. Also assume that the company continued to use 6,500 pounds of materials in production and that the standard price remained at $4.00 per pound.

Given these assumptions, Exhibit 9–14 shows how to compute the materials price variance of $1,400 F and the materials quantity variance of $2,000 U. Note that the price variance is based on the amount of the input purchased whereas the quantity variance is based on the quantity of the input used in production. Column (2) of Exhibit 9–14 contains two different total costs for this reason. When the price variance is computed, the total cost used from column (2) is $28,000—which is the cost of the input *purchased,* evaluated at the standard price. When the quantity variance is computed, the total cost used from column (2) is $26,000—which is the cost of the actual input *used,* evaluated at the standard price.

Exhibit 9–14 shows that the price variance is computed on the entire amount of material purchased (7,000 pounds), whereas the quantity variance is computed only on the amount of materials used in production during the month (6,500 pounds). What about the other 500 pounds of material that were purchased during the period, but that have not yet been used? When those materials are used in future periods, a quantity variance will be computed. However, a price variance will not be computed when the materials are finally used because the price variance was computed when the materials were purchased.

Because the price variance is based on the amount purchased and the quantity variance is based on the amount used, the two variances do not generally sum to the spending variance from the flexible budget, which is wholly based on the amount used. We would

---

[6] Standard cost systems are typically used as part of a company's financial reporting system. Therefore, standard cost variance reports are often prepared on a monthly basis as part of the financial closing process. As a consequence, the reports may be produced too infrequently to enable real-time operational improvements. To combat this problem, some companies are now reporting variances and other key operating data daily or even more frequently.

**EXHIBIT 9-14**    Standard Cost Variance Analysis—Direct Materials
(Note: The quantity of materials purchased does not equal the quantity used in production.)

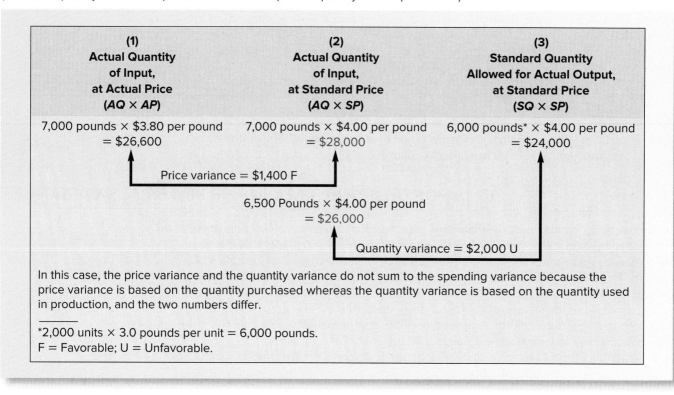

In this case, the price variance and the quantity variance do not sum to the spending variance because the price variance is based on the quantity purchased whereas the quantity variance is based on the quantity used in production, and the two numbers differ.

_____

\*2,000 units × 3.0 pounds per unit = 6,000 pounds.
F = Favorable; U = Unfavorable.

also like to emphasize that the approach shown in Exhibit 9–14 *can always be used to compute direct materials variances.* However, Exhibit 9–11 *can only be used in the special case when the quantity of materials purchased equals the quantity of materials used.*

## HELPFUL HINT

When Colonial Pewter purchases 7,000 pounds of materials and uses 6,500 pounds in production, the materials quantity and price variances can be computed using the equations shown below:

*Materials Price Variance:*
AQ = Actual quantity of pounds *purchased*
AP = Actual price per unit of the input
SP = Standard price per unit of the input

Materials price variance = (AQ × AP) − (AQ × SP)
Materials price variance = AQ(AP − SP)
Materials price variance = 7,000 pounds ($3.80 per pound − $4.00 per pound)
Materials price variance = $1,400 F

*Materials Quantity Variance:*
AQ = Actual quantity of pounds *used in production*
SQ = Standard quantity of pounds allowed for the actual output
SP = Standard price per unit of the input

Materials quantity variance = (AQ × SP) − (SQ × SP)
Materials quantity variance = SP(AQ − SQ)
Materials quantity variance = $4.00 per pound (6,500 pounds − 6,000 pounds)
Materials quantity variance = $2,000 U

**LO9–1 Prepare a planning budget and a flexible budget and understand how they differ from one another.**

A planning budget is prepared before the period begins and is valid for only the planned level of activity, whereas a flexible budget is a budget that is adjusted to the actual level of activity. The flexible budget provides the best estimate of what revenues and costs should have been, given the actual level of activity during the period.

**LO9–2 Calculate and interpret revenue and spending variances.**

When actual results are compared to the flexible budget, revenue and spending variances are the result. A favorable revenue variance indicates that revenue was larger than should have been expected, given the actual level of activity. An unfavorable revenue variance indicates that revenue was less than it should have been, given the actual level of activity. A favorable spending variance indicates that the actual cost was less than expected, given the actual level of activity. An unfavorable spending variance indicates that the actual cost was greater than expected, given the actual level of activity.

**LO9–3 Prepare a flexible budget with more than one cost driver.**

A cost may depend on more than one cost driver. If so, the flexible budget for that cost should be stated in terms of all of the cost drivers.

**LO9–4 Compute the direct materials price and quantity variances and explain their significance.**

The materials price variance is the difference between the actual price paid for materials and the standard price, multiplied by the quantity purchased. An unfavorable variance occurs whenever the actual price exceeds the standard price. A favorable variance occurs when the actual price is less than the standard price for the input.

The materials quantity variance is the difference between the amount of materials actually used and the amount that should have been used to produce the actual good output of the period, multiplied by the standard price per unit of the input. An unfavorable materials quantity variance occurs when the amount of materials actually used exceeds the amount that should have been used according to the materials quantity standard. A favorable variance occurs when the amount of materials actually used is less than the amount that should have been used according to the standard.

**LO9–5 Compute the direct labor rate and efficiency variances and explain their significance.**

The direct labor rate variance is the difference between the actual wage rate paid and the standard wage rate, multiplied by the hours worked. An unfavorable variance occurs whenever the actual wage rate exceeds the standard wage rate. A favorable variance occurs when the actual wage rate is less than the standard wage rate.

The labor efficiency variance is the difference between the hours actually worked and the hours that should have been used to produce the actual good output of the period, multiplied by the standard wage rate. An unfavorable labor efficiency variance occurs when the hours actually worked exceed the hours allowed for the actual output. A favorable variance occurs when the hours actually worked are less than hours allowed for the actual output.

**LO9–6 Compute the variable manufacturing overhead rate and efficiency variances and explain their significance.**

The variable manufacturing overhead rate variance is the difference between the actual variable manufacturing overhead cost incurred and the actual hours worked multiplied by the standard variable manufacturing overhead rate. The variable manufacturing overhead efficiency variance is the difference between the hours actually worked and the hours that should have been used to produce the actual good output of the period, multiplied by the standard variable manufacturing overhead rate.

# GUIDANCE ANSWERS TO DECISION POINT

**Owner of Micro-Brewery**

The cost of hops is a purely variable cost. Since the cost for producing 800 barrels of beer is $960, the cost of hops in one barrel of beer is $1.20 (= $960 ÷ 800 barrels). Therefore, if 850 barrels of beer are produced, the cost of the hops should be $1.20 per barrel times 850 barrels, or $1,020. Since that is how much was actually spent, there is no indication that too much or too little was spent on hops.

# GUIDANCE ANSWERS TO CONCEPT CHECKS

1. **Choices b, c, and d.** A planning budget is based on the planned level, not the actual level of activity.
2. **Choice b.** The cost for flowers according to the flexible budget is $65,046 (= $325 per operating day × 30 operating days + $7.20 per room-day × 7,680 room-days).
3. **Choice a.** The spending variance is $3,068 favorable (= $65,046 − $61,978).
4. **Choices a, b, and d.** The materials price variance is based on the actual quantity purchased.
5. **Choice b.** The materials price variance is ($4.50 actual price per pound − $4.00 standard price per pound) × 10,500 pounds purchased = $5,250 unfavorable.
6. **Choice d.** The materials quantity variance is (10,500 pounds used − 10,000 pounds allowed) × $4.00 per pound = $2,000 unfavorable.

# REVIEW PROBLEM 1: VARIANCE ANALYSIS USING A FLEXIBLE BUDGET

Harrald's Fish House is a family-owned restaurant that specializes in Scandinavian-style seafood. Data concerning the restaurant's monthly revenues and costs appear below ($q$ refers to the number of meals served):

| | Formula |
|---|---|
| Revenue................ | $16.50q$ |
| Cost of ingredients........ | $6.25q$ |
| Wages and salaries ...... | $10,400 |
| Utilities................ | $800 + $0.20q$ |
| Rent ................... | $2,200 |
| Miscellaneous........... | $600 + $0.80q$ |

*Required:*

1. Prepare the restaurant's planning budget for April assuming that 1,800 meals are served.
2. Assume that 1,700 meals were actually served in April. Prepare a flexible budget for this level of activity.
3. The actual results for April appear below. Compute the revenue and spending variances for the restaurant for April.

| | |
|---|---|
| Revenue................... | $27,920 |
| Cost of ingredients......... | $11,110 |
| Wages and salaries ........ | $10,130 |
| Utilities................... | $1,080 |
| Rent ................... | $2,200 |
| Miscellaneous............. | $2,240 |

**Solution to Review Problem**

1. The planning budget for April appears below:

| Harrald's Fish House<br>Planning Budget<br>For the Month Ended April 30 | |
| --- | --- |
| Budgeted meals served (q) | 1,800 |
| Revenue ($16.50q) | $29,700 |
| Expenses: | |
| Cost of ingredients ($6.25q) | 11,250 |
| Wages and salaries ($10,400) | 10,400 |
| Utilities ($800 + $0.20q) | 1,160 |
| Rent ($2,200) | 2,200 |
| Miscellaneous ($600 + $0.80q) | 2,040 |
| Total expense | 27,050 |
| Net operating income | $ 2,650 |

2. The flexible budget for April appears below:

| Harrald's Fish House<br>Flexible Budget<br>For the Month Ended April 30 | |
| --- | --- |
| Actual meals served (q) | 1,700 |
| Revenue ($16.50q) | $28,050 |
| Expenses: | |
| Cost of ingredients ($6.25q) | 10,625 |
| Wages and salaries ($10,400) | 10,400 |
| Utilities ($800 + $0.20q) | 1,140 |
| Rent ($2,200) | 2,200 |
| Miscellaneous ($600 + $0.80q) | 1,960 |
| Total expense | 26,325 |
| Net operating income | $ 1,725 |

3. The revenue and spending variances for April appear below:

| Harrald's Fish House<br>Revenue and Spending Variances<br>For the Month Ended April 30 | (1)<br>Actual<br>Results | Revenue<br>and Spending<br>Variances<br>(1) − (2) | (2)<br>Flexible<br>Budget |
| --- | --- | --- | --- |
| Meals served | 1,700 | | 1,700 |
| Revenue ($16.50q) | $27,920 | $130 U | $28,050 |
| Expenses: | | | |
| Cost of ingredients ($6.25q) | 11,110 | 485 U | 10,625 |
| Wages and salaries ($10,400) | 10,130 | 270 F | 10,400 |
| Utilities ($800 + $0.20q) | 1,080 | 60 F | 1,140 |
| Rent ($2,200) | 2,200 | 0 | 2,200 |
| Miscellaneous ($600 + $0.80q) | 2,240 | 280 U | 1,960 |
| Total expense | 26,760 | 435 U | 26,325 |
| Net operating income | $ 1,160 | $565 U | $ 1,725 |

# REVIEW PROBLEM 2: STANDARD COSTS

Xavier Company produces a single product. Variable manufacturing overhead is applied to products on the basis of direct labor-hours. The standard costs for one unit of product are as follows:

| | |
|---|---|
| Direct material: 6 ounces at $0.50 per ounce. . . . . . . . . . . . . . . . . . . . . | $  3.00 |
| Direct labor: 0.6 hours at $30.00 per hour . . . . . . . . . . . . . . . . . . . . . . | 18.00 |
| Variable manufacturing overhead: 0.6 hours at $10.00 per hour . . . . | 6.00 |
| Total standard variable cost per unit. . . . . . . . . . . . . . . . . . . . . . . . . . | $27.00 |

During June, 2,000 units were produced. The costs associated with June's operations were as follows:

| | |
|---|---|
| Material purchased: 18,000 ounces at $0.60 per ounce . . . . . . . . . . | $10,800 |
| Material used in production: 14,000 ounces. . . . . . . . . . . . . . . . . . . | — |
| Direct labor: 1,100 hours at $30.50 per hour. . . . . . . . . . . . . . . . . . | $33,550 |
| Variable manufacturing overhead costs incurred. . . . . . . . . . . . . . . | $12,980 |

*Required:*
Compute the direct materials, direct labor, and variable manufacturing overhead variances.

**Solution to Review Problem**

**Direct Materials Variances**

| Actual Quantity of Input, at Actual Price (AQ × AP) | Actual Quantity of Input at Standard Price (AQ × SP) | Standard Quantity Allowed for Actual Output, at Standard Price (SQ × SP) |
|---|---|---|
| 18,000 ounces × $0.60 per ounce = $10,800 | 18,000 ounces × $0.50 per ounce = $9,000 | 12,000 ounces* × $0.50 per ounce = $6,000 |

Price variance = $1,800 U

14,000 ounces × $0.50 per ounce = $7,000

Quantity variance = $1,000 U

*2,000 units × 6 ounces per unit = 12,000 ounces.

Using formulas, the same variances would be computed as follows:

$$\text{Materials price variance} = (AQ \times AP) - (AQ \times SP)$$
$$= AQ(AP - SP)$$
$$= 18,000 \text{ ounces } (\$0.60 \text{ per ounce} - \$0.50 \text{ per ounce})$$
$$= \$1,800 \text{ U}$$
$$\text{Materials quantity variance} = (AQ \times SP) - (SQ \times SP)$$
$$= SP(AQ - SQ)$$
$$= \$0.50 \text{ per ounce } (14,000 \text{ ounces} - 12,000 \text{ ounces})$$
$$= \$1,000 \text{ U}$$

**Direct Labor Variances**

| Actual Hours of Input, at Actual Rate ($AH \times AR$) | Actual Hours of Input, at Standard Rate ($AH \times SR$) | Standard Hours Allowed for Actual Output, at Standard Rate ($SH \times SR$) |
|---|---|---|
| 1,100 hours × $30.50 per hour = $33,550 | 1,100 hours × $30.00 per hour = $33,000 | 1,200 hours* × $30.00 per hour = $36,000 |

↑    Labor rate variance = $550 U    ↑    Labor efficiency variance = $3,000 F    ↑

Spending variance = $2,450 F

*2,000 units × 0.6 hours per unit = 1,200 hours.
F = Favorable; U = Unfavorable.

Using formulas, the same variances can be computed as follows:

$$\text{Labor rate variance} = (AH \times AR) - (AH \times SR)$$
$$= AH(AR - SR)$$
$$= 1{,}100 \text{ hours } (\$30.50 \text{ per hour} - \$30.00 \text{ per hour})$$
$$= \$550 \text{ U}$$

$$\text{Labor efficiency variance} = (AH \times SR) - (SH \times SR)$$
$$= SR(AH - SH)$$
$$= \$30.00 \text{ per hour } (1{,}100 \text{ hours} - 1{,}200 \text{ hours})$$
$$= \$3{,}000 \text{ F}$$

**Variable Manufacturing Overhead Variances**

| Actual Hours of Input, at Actual Rate ($AH \times AR$) | Actual Hours of Input, at Standard Rate ($AH \times SR$) | Standard Hours Allowed for Actual Output, at Standard Rate ($SH \times SR$) |
|---|---|---|
| 1,100 hours × $11.80[†] per hour[†] = $12,980 | 1,100 hours × $10.00 per hour = $11,000 | 1,200 hours* × $10.00 per hour = $12,000 |

↑    Variable overhead rate variance = $1,980 U    ↑    Variable overhead efficiency variance = $1,000 F    ↑

Spending variance = $980 U

*2,000 units × 0.6 hours per unit = 1,200 hours.
[†]$12,980 ÷ 1,100 hours = $11.80 per hour.
F = Favorable; U = Unfavorable.

Using formulas, the same variances can be computed as follows:

$$\text{Variable overhead rate variance} = (AH \times AR) - (AH \times SR)$$
$$= AH(AR - SR)$$
$$= 1{,}100 \text{ hours } (\$11.80 \text{ per hour} - \$10.00 \text{ per hour})$$
$$= \$1{,}980 \text{ U}$$

$$\text{Variable overhead efficiency variance} = (AH \times SR) - (SH \times SR)$$
$$= SR(AH - SH)$$
$$= \$10.00 \text{ per hour } (1{,}100 \text{ hours} - 1{,}200 \text{ hours})$$
$$= \$1{,}000 \text{ F}$$

# GLOSSARY

**Flexible budget**   A report showing estimates of what revenues and costs should have been, given the actual level of activity for the period. (p. 393)

**Labor efficiency variance**   The difference between the actual hours taken to complete a task and the standard hours allowed for the actual output, multiplied by the standard hourly labor rate. (p. 411)

**Labor rate variance**   The difference between the actual hourly labor rate and the standard rate, multiplied by the number of hours worked during the period. (p. 410)

**Management by exception**   A management system in which actual results are compared to a budget. Significant deviations from the budget are flagged as exceptions and investigated further. (p. 392)

**Materials price variance**   The difference between the actual unit price paid for an item and the standard price, multiplied by the quantity purchased. (p. 408)

**Materials quantity variance**   The difference between the actual quantity of materials used in production and the standard quantity allowed for the actual output, multiplied by the standard price per unit of materials. (p. 408)

**Planning budget**   A budget created at the beginning of the budgeting period that is valid only for the planned level of activity. (p. 393)

**Price variance**   A variance that is computed by taking the difference between the actual price and the standard price and multiplying the result by the actual quantity of the input. (p. 405)

**Quantity variance**   A variance that is computed by taking the difference between the actual quantity of the input used and the amount of the input that should have been used for the actual level of output and multiplying the result by the standard price of the input. (p. 405)

**Revenue variance**   The difference between how much the revenue should have been, given the actual level of activity, and the actual revenue for the period. A favorable (unfavorable) revenue variance occurs because the revenue is higher (lower) than expected, given the actual level of activity for the period. (p. 397)

**Spending variance**   The difference between how much a cost should have been, given the actual level of activity, and the actual amount of the cost. A favorable (unfavorable) spending variance occurs because the cost is lower (higher) than expected, given the actual level of activity for the period. (p. 398)

**Standard cost card**   A detailed listing of the standard amounts of inputs and their costs that are required to produce one unit of a specific product. (p. 403)

**Standard cost per unit**   The standard quantity allowed of an input per unit of a specific product, multiplied by the standard price of the input. (p. 403)

**Standard hours allowed for actual output**   The time that should have been taken to complete the period's output. It is computed by multiplying the actual number of units produced by the standard hours per unit. (p. 406)

**Standard hours per unit**   The amount of direct labor time that should be required to complete a single unit of product, including allowances for breaks, machine downtime, cleanup, rejects, and other normal inefficiencies. (p. 402)

**Standard price per unit**   The price that should be paid for an input. (p. 402)

**Standard quantity allowed for actual output**   The amount of an input that should have been used to complete the period's actual output. It is computed by multiplying the actual number of units produced by the standard quantity per unit. (p. 406)

**Standard quantity per unit**   The amount of an input that should be required to complete a single unit of product, including allowances for normal waste, spoilage, rejects, and other normal inefficiencies. (p. 402)

**Standard rate per hour**   The labor rate that should be incurred per hour of labor time, including employment taxes and fringe benefits. (p. 403)

**Variable overhead efficiency variance**   The difference between the actual level of activity (direct labor-hours, machine-hours, or some other base) and the standard activity allowed, multiplied by the variable part of the predetermined overhead rate. (p. 413)

**Variable overhead rate variance**   The difference between the actual variable overhead cost incurred during a period and the standard cost that should have been incurred based on the actual activity of the period. (p. 413)

# QUESTIONS

**9–1**   What is a static planning budget?

**9–2**   What is a flexible budget and how does it differ from a static planning budget?

**9–3**   What are some of the possible reasons that actual results may differ from what had been budgeted at the beginning of a period?

**9–4**   Why is it difficult to interpret a difference between how much expense was budgeted at the beginning of the period and how much was actually spent?

**9–5**   What is a revenue variance and what does it mean?

**9–6**  What is a spending variance and what does it mean?

**9–7**  What does a flexible budget enable that a simple comparison of the planning budget to actual results does not do?

**9–8**  How does a flexible budget based on two cost drivers differ from a flexible budget based on a single cost driver?

**9–9**  What is a quantity standard? What is a price standard?

**9–10**  Why are separate price and quantity variances computed?

**9–11**  Who is generally responsible for the materials price variance? The materials quantity variance? The labor efficiency variance?

**9–12**  The materials price variance can be computed at what two different points in time? Which point is better? Why?

**9–13**  If the materials price variance is favorable but the materials quantity variance is unfavorable, what might this indicate?

**9–14**  "Our workers are all under labor contracts; therefore, our labor rate variance is bound to be zero." Discuss.

**9–15**  What effect, if any, would you expect poor-quality materials to have on direct labor variances?

**9–16**  If variable manufacturing overhead is applied to production on the basis of direct labor-hours and the direct labor efficiency variance is unfavorable, will the variable overhead efficiency variance be favorable or unfavorable, or could it be either? Explain.

**9–17**  Why can undue emphasis on labor efficiency variances lead to excess inventories?

---

**connect    CHAPTER 9: APPLYING EXCEL**

The Excel worksheet form that appears below is to be used to recreate the main example in the text related to the Colonial Pewter Company. Download the workbook containing this form from Connect, where you will also receive instructions about how to use this worksheet form.

**LO9–4, LO9–5, LO9–6**

| | A | B | C | D | E | F | G |
|---|---|---|---|---|---|---|---|
| 1 | Chapter 9: Applying Excel | | | | | | |
| 2 | | | | | | | |
| 3 | **Data** | | | | | | |
| 4 | *Exhibit 9-8: Standard Cost Card* | | | | | | |
| 5 | Inputs | Standard Quantity | | Standard Price | | | |
| 6 | Direct materials | 3.0 | pounds | $4.00 | per pound | | |
| 7 | Direct labor | 0.50 | hours | $22.00 | per hour | | |
| 8 | Variable manufacturing overhead | 0.50 | hours | $6.00 | per hour | | |
| 9 | | | | | | | |
| 10 | Actual results: | | | | | | |
| 11 | Actual output | 2,000 | units | | | | |
| 12 | Actual variable manufacturing overhead cost | $7,140 | | | | | |
| 13 | | Actual Quantity | | Actual price | | | |
| 14 | Actual direct materials cost | 6,500 | pounds | $3.80 | per pound | | |
| 15 | Actual direct labor cost | 1,050 | hours | $21.60 | per hour | | |
| 16 | | | | | | | |
| 17 | *Enter a formula into each of the cells marked with a ? below* | | | | | | |
| 18 | **Main Example: Chapter 9** | | | | | | |
| 19 | | | | | | | |
| 20 | *Exhibit 9-11: Standard Cost Variance Analysis–Direct Materials* | | | | | | |
| 21 | Actual Quantity of Input, at Actual Price | ? | pounds × | ? | per pound = | ? | |
| 22 | Actual Quantity of Input, at Standard Price | ? | pounds × | ? | per pound = | ? | |
| 23 | Standard Quantity Allowed for the Actual Output, at Standard Price | ? | pounds × | ? | per pound = | ? | |
| 24 | Direct materials variances: | | | | | | |
| 25 | Materials price variance | ? | | | | | |
| 26 | Materials quantity variance | ? | | | | | |
| 27 | Materials spending variance | ? | | | | | |
| 28 | | | | | | | |
| 29 | *Exhibit 9-12: Standard Cost Variance Analysis–Direct Labor* | | | | | | |
| 30 | Actual Hours of Input, at Actual Rate | ? | hours × | ? | per hour = | ? | |
| 31 | Actual Hours of Input, at Standard Rate | ? | hours × | ? | per hour = | ? | |
| 32 | Standard Hours Allowed for the Actual Output, at Standard Rate | ? | hours × | ? | per hour = | ? | |
| 33 | Direct labor variances: | | | | | | |
| 34 | Labor rate variance | ? | | | | | |
| 35 | Labor efficiency variance | ? | | | | | |
| 36 | Labor spending variance | ? | | | | | |
| 37 | | | | | | | |
| 38 | *Exhibit 9-13: Standard Cost Variance Analysis–Variable Manufacturing Overhead* | | | | | | |
| 39 | Actual Hours of Input, at Actual Rate | ? | hours × | ? | per hour = | ? | |
| 40 | Actual Hours of Input, at Standard Rate | ? | hours × | ? | per hour = | ? | |
| 41 | Standard Hours Allowed for the Actual Output, at Standard Rate | ? | hours × | ? | per hour = | ? | |
| 42 | Variable overhead variances: | | | | | | |
| 43 | Variable overhead rate variance | ? | | | | | |
| 44 | Variable overhead efficiency variance | ? | | | | | |
| 45 | Variable overhead spending variance | ? | | | | | |
| 46 | | | | | | | |

Chapter 9 Form    Filled in Chapter 9 Form    C ...

You should proceed to the requirements below only after completing your worksheet.

**Required:**

1. Check your worksheet by changing the direct materials standard quantity in cell B6 to 2.9 pounds, the direct labor quantity standard quantity in cell B7 to 0.6 hours, and the variable manufacturing overhead in cell B8 to 0.6 hours. The materials spending variance should now be $1,500 U, the labor spending variance should now be $3,720 F, and the variable overhead spending variance should now be $60 F. If you do not get these answers, find the errors in your worksheet and correct them.
   a. What is the materials quantity variance? Explain this variance.
   b. What is the labor rate variance? Explain this variance.
2. Revise the data in your worksheet to reflect the results for the subsequent period:

**Data**
**Exhibit 9–8: Standard Cost Card**

| Inputs | Standard Quantity | Standard Price |
|---|---|---|
| Direct materials . . . . . . . . . . . . . . . . . . . . . . . . . . . . . | 3.0 pounds | $4.00 per pound |
| Direct labor . . . . . . . . . . . . . . . . . . . . . . . . . . . . . . . . | 0.50 hours | $22.00 per hour |
| Variable manufacturing overhead . . . . . . . . . . . . . . | 0.50 hours | $6.00 per hour |

Actual results:

| | | |
|---|---|---|
| Actual output . . . . . . . . . . . . . . . . . . . . . . . . . . . . . . | 2,100 units | |
| Actual variable manufacturing overhead cost . . | $5,100 | |

| | Actual Quantity | Actual Price |
|---|---|---|
| Actual direct materials cost . . . . . . . . . . . . . . . . . . | 6,350 pounds | $4.10 per pound |
| Actual direct labor cost . . . . . . . . . . . . . . . . . . . . . | 1,020 hours | $22.10 per hour |

   a. What is the materials quantity variance? What is the materials price variance?
   b. What is the labor efficiency variance? What is the labor rate variance?
   c. What is the variable overhead efficiency variance? What is the variable overhead rate variance?

# THE FOUNDATIONAL 15   connect

**LO9–1, LO9–2, LO9–4, LO9–5, LO9–6**

Preble Company manufactures one product. Its variable manufacturing overhead is applied to production based on direct labor-hours and its standard cost card per unit is as follows:

| | |
|---|---|
| Direct material: 5 pounds at $8.00 per pound . . . . . . . . . . . . . . . . . . . . . | $40.00 |
| Direct labor: 2 hours at $14 per hour . . . . . . . . . . . . . . . . . . . . . . . . . . . . | 28.00 |
| Variable overhead: 2 hours at $5 per hour . . . . . . . . . . . . . . . . . . . . . . . | 10.00 |
| Total standard variable cost per unit . . . . . . . . . . . . . . . . . . . . . . . . . . . . | $78.00 |

The company also established the following cost formulas for its selling expenses:

| | Fixed Cost per Month | Variable Cost per Unit Sold |
|---|---|---|
| Advertising . . . . . . . . . . . . . . . . . . . . . . . . | $200,000 | |
| Sales salaries and commissions . . . . . . | $100,000 | $12.00 |
| Shipping expenses . . . . . . . . . . . . . . . . . | | $3.00 |

The planning budget for March was based on producing and selling 25,000 units. However, during March the company actually produced and sold 30,000 units and incurred the following costs:

a.  Purchased 160,000 pounds of raw materials at a cost of $7.50 per pound. All of this material was used in production.
b.  Direct-laborers worked 55,000 hours at a rate of $15.00 per hour.
c.  Total variable manufacturing overhead for the month was $280,500.
d.  Total advertising, sales salaries and commissions, and shipping expenses were $210,000, $455,000, and $115,000, respectively.

***Required:***

1.  What raw materials cost would be included in the company's flexible budget for March?
2.  What is the materials quantity variance for March?
3.  What is the materials price variance for March?
4.  If Preble had purchased 170,000 pounds of materials at $7.50 per pound and used 160,000 pounds in production, what would be the materials quantity variance for March?
5.  If Preble had purchased 170,000 pounds of materials at $7.50 per pound and used 160,000 pounds in production, what would be the materials price variance for March?
6.  What direct labor cost would be included in the company's flexible budget for March?
7.  What is the direct labor efficiency variance for March?
8.  What is the direct labor rate variance for March?
9.  What variable manufacturing overhead cost would be included in the company's flexible budget for March?
10. What is the variable overhead efficiency variance for March?
11. What is the variable overhead rate variance for March?
12. What amounts of advertising, sales salaries and commissions, and shipping expenses would be included in the company's flexible budget for March?
13. What is the spending variance related to advertising?
14. What is the spending variance related to sales salaries and commissions?
15. What is the spending variance related to shipping expenses?

    **EXERCISES**

---

**EXERCISE 9–1   Prepare a Flexible Budget LO9–1**

Puget Sound Divers is a company that provides diving services such as underwater ship repairs to clients in the Puget Sound area. The company's planning budget for May appears below:

| Puget Sound Divers Planning Budget For the Month Ended May 31 | |
|---|---|
| Budgeted diving-hours (q) . . . . . . . . . . . . . . . . . . . . . . | 100 |
| Revenue ($365.00q) . . . . . . . . . . . . . . . . . . . . . . . . . | $36,500 |
| Expenses: | |
|    Wages and salaries ($8,000 + $125.00q) . . . . . . . | 20,500 |
|    Supplies ($3.00q) . . . . . . . . . . . . . . . . . . . . . . . . | 300 |
|    Equipment rental ($1,800 + $32.00q) . . . . . . . . . | 5,000 |
|    Insurance ($3,400) . . . . . . . . . . . . . . . . . . . . . . . | 3,400 |
|    Miscellaneous ($630 + $1.80q). . . . . . . . . . . . . . | 810 |
| Total expense. . . . . . . . . . . . . . . . . . . . . . . . . . . . . . | 30,010 |
| Net operating income. . . . . . . . . . . . . . . . . . . . . . . | $ 6,490 |

During May, the company's actual activity was 105 diving-hours.

***Required:***

Using Exhibit 9–5 as your guide, prepare a flexible budget for May.

**EXERCISE 9-2   Prepare a Report Showing Revenue and Spending Variances LO9-2**

Quilcene Oysteria farms and sells oysters in the Pacific Northwest. The company harvested and sold 8,000 pounds of oysters in August. The company's flexible budget for August appears below:

| Quilcene Oysteria<br>Flexible Budget<br>For the Month Ended August 31 | |
|---|---:|
| Actual pounds (*q*) | 8,000 |
| Revenue ($4.00*q*) | $32,000 |
| Expenses: | |
| Packing supplies ($0.50*q*) | 4,000 |
| Oyster bed maintenance ($3,200) | 3,200 |
| Wages and salaries ($2,900 + $0.30*q*) | 5,300 |
| Shipping ($0.80*q*) | 6,400 |
| Utilities ($830) | 830 |
| Other ($450 + $0.05*q*) | 850 |
| Total expense | 20,580 |
| Net operating income | $11,420 |

The actual results for August appear below:

| Quilcene Oysteria<br>Income Statement<br>For the Month Ended August 31 | |
|---|---:|
| Actual pounds | 8,000 |
| Revenue | $35,200 |
| Expenses: | |
| Packing supplies | 4,200 |
| Oyster bed maintenance | 3,100 |
| Wages and salaries | 5,640 |
| Shipping | 6,950 |
| Utilities | 810 |
| Other | 980 |
| Total expense | 21,680 |
| Net operating income | $13,520 |

*Required:*

Calculate the company's revenue and spending variances for August. (Hint: Refer to Exhibit 9–6.)

**EXERCISE 9-3   Prepare a Flexible Budget with More Than One Cost Driver LO9-3**

Alyeski Tours operates day tours of coastal glaciers in Alaska on its tour boat the Blue Glacier. Management has identified two cost drivers—the number of cruises and the number of passengers—that it uses in its budgeting and performance reports. The company publishes a schedule of day cruises that it may supplement with special sailings if there is sufficient demand. Up to 80 passengers can be accommodated on the tour boat. Data concerning the company's cost formulas appear below:

| | Fixed Cost per Month | Cost per Cruise | Cost per Passenger |
|---|---|---|---|
| Vessel operating costs | $5,200 | $480.00 | $2.00 |
| Advertising | $1,700 | | |
| Administrative costs | $4,300 | $24.00 | $1.00 |
| Insurance | $2,900 | | |

For example, vessel operating costs should be $5,200 per month plus $480 per cruise plus $2 per passenger. The company's sales should average $25 per passenger. In July, the company provided 24 cruises for a total of 1,400 passengers.

**Required:**
Using Exhibit 9–7 as your guide, prepare the company's flexible budget for July.

### EXERCISE 9–4    Direct Materials Variances LO9–4

Bandar Industries Berhad of Malaysia manufactures sporting equipment. One of the company's products, a football helmet for the North American market, requires a special plastic. During the quarter ending June 30, the company manufactured 35,000 helmets, using 22,500 kilograms of plastic. The plastic cost the company $171,000.

According to the standard cost card, each helmet should require 0.6 kilograms of plastic, at a cost of $8 per kilogram.

**Required:**
1. What is the standard quantity of kilograms of plastic (SQ) that is allowed to make 35,000 helmets?
2. What is the standard materials cost allowed (SQ × SP) to make 35,000 helmets?
3. What is the materials spending variance?
4. What is the materials price variance and the materials quantity variance?

### EXERCISE 9–5    Direct Labor Variances LO9–5

SkyChefs, Inc., prepares in-flight meals for a number of major airlines. One of the company's products is grilled salmon in dill sauce with baby new potatoes and spring vegetables. During the most recent week, the company prepared 4,000 of these meals using 960 direct labor-hours. The company paid its direct labor workers a total of $19,200 for this work, or $20.00 per hour.

According to the standard cost card for this meal, it should require 0.25 direct labor-hours at a cost of $19.75 per hour.

**Required:**
1. What is the standard labor-hours allowed (SH) to prepare 4,000 meals?
2. What is the standard labor cost allowed (SH × SR) to prepare 4,000 meals?
3. What is the labor spending variance?
4. What is the labor rate variance and the labor efficiency variance?

### EXERCISE 9–6    Variable Overhead Variances LO9–6

Logistics Solutions provides order fulfillment services for dot.com merchants. The company maintains warehouses that stock items carried by its dot.com clients. When a client receives an order from a customer, the order is forwarded to Logistics Solutions, which pulls the item from storage, packs it, and ships it to the customer. The company uses a predetermined variable overhead rate based on direct labor-hours.

In the most recent month, 120,000 items were shipped to customers using 2,300 direct labor-hours. The company incurred a total of $7,360 in variable overhead costs.

According to the company's standards, 0.02 direct labor-hours are required to fulfill an order for one item and the variable overhead rate is $3.25 per direct labor-hour.

**Required:**
1. What is the standard labor-hours allowed (SH) to ship 120,000 items to customers?
2. What is the standard variable overhead cost allowed (SH × SR) to ship 120,000 items to customers?
3. What is the variable overhead spending variance?
4. What is the variable overhead rate variance and the variable overhead efficiency variance?

### EXERCISE 9–7    Planning Budget LO9–1

Lavage Rapide is a Canadian company that owns and operates a large automatic car wash facility near Montreal. The following table provides data concerning the company's costs:

| | Fixed Cost per Month | Cost per Car Washed |
|---|---|---|
| Cleaning supplies............. | | $0.80 |
| Electricity.................... | $1,200 | $0.15 |
| Maintenance................. | | $0.20 |
| Wages and salaries............ | $5,000 | $0.30 |
| Depreciation.................. | $6,000 | |
| Rent........................ | $8,000 | |
| Administrative expenses....... | $4,000 | $0.10 |

For example, electricity costs are $1,200 per month plus $0.15 per car washed. The company expects to wash 9,000 cars in August and to collect an average of $4.90 per car washed.

**Required:**
Using Exhibit 9–2 as your guide, prepare the company's planning budget for August.

**EXERCISE 9–8  Flexible Budget LO9–1**
Refer to the data for Lavage Rapide in Exercise 9–7. The company actually washed 8,800 cars in August.

**Required:**
Using Exhibit 9–5 as your guide, prepare the company's flexible budget for August.

**EXERCISE 9–9  Prepare a Report Showing Revenue and Spending Variances LO9–2**
Refer to the data for Lavage Rapide in Exercise 9–7. Also assume that the company's actual operating results for August are as follows:

| Lavage Rapide<br>Income Statement<br>For the Month Ended August 31 | |
|---|---:|
| Actual cars washed............... | 8,800 |
| Revenue ........................ | $43,080 |
| Expenses: | |
| Cleaning supplies .............. | 7,560 |
| Electricity ..................... | 2,670 |
| Maintenance ................... | 2,260 |
| Wages and salaries............. | 8,500 |
| Depreciation.................... | 6,000 |
| Rent........................... | 8,000 |
| Administrative expenses ........ | 4,950 |
| Total expense................... | 39,940 |
| Net operating income............ | $ 3,140 |

**Required:**
Calculate the company's revenue and spending variances for August. (*Hint:* Refer to Exhibit 9–6.)

**EXERCISE 9–10  Direct Labor and Variable Manufacturing Overhead Variances LO9–5, LO9–6**
Erie Company manufactures a mobile fitness device called the Jogging Mate. The company uses standards to control its costs. The labor standards that have been set for one Jogging Mate are as follows:

| Standard<br>Hours | Standard Rate<br>per Hour | Standard<br>Cost |
|---|---|---|
| 18 minutes | $17.00 | $5.10 |

During August, 5,750 hours of direct labor time were needed to make 20,000 units of the Jogging Mate. The direct labor cost totaled $102,350 for the month.

**Required:**
1. What is the standard labor-hours allowed (SH) to makes 20,000 Jogging Mates?
2. What is the standard labor cost allowed (SH × SR) to make 20,000 Jogging Mates?
3. What is the labor spending variance?
4. What is the labor rate variance and the labor efficiency variance?
5. The budgeted variable manufacturing overhead rate is $4 per direct labor-hour. During August, the company incurred $21,850 in variable manufacturing overhead cost. Compute the variable overhead rate and efficiency variances for the month.

**EXERCISE 9–11  Working Backwards from Labor Variances LO9–5**
The auto repair shop of Quality Motor Company uses standards to control the labor time and labor cost in the shop. The standard labor cost for a motor tune-up is given below:

|  | Standard Hours | Standard Rate | Standard Cost |
|---|---|---|---|
| Motor tune-up . . . . . . . | 2.5 | $25.00 | $62.50 |

The record showing the time spent in the shop last week on motor tune-ups has been misplaced. However, the shop supervisor recalls that 50 tune-ups were completed during the week, and the controller recalls the following variance data relating to tune-ups:

| Labor rate variance. . . . . . . . . . . . . . . . . | $150 F |
|---|---|
| Labor spending variance . . . . . . . . . . . . | $200 U |

**Required:**
1. Determine the number of actual labor-hours spent on tune-ups during the week.
2. Determine the actual hourly rate of pay for tune-ups last week. (Round your answer to the nearest cent.)
(*Hint:* A useful way to proceed would be to work from known to unknown data by using the columnar format shown in Exhibit 9–12.)

**EXERCISE 9–12   Working with More Than One Cost Driver** LO9–1, LO9–2, LO9–3

The Gourmand Cooking School runs short cooking courses at its small campus. Management has identified two cost drivers it uses in its budgeting and performance reports—the number of courses and the total number of students. For example, the school might run two courses in a month and have a total of 50 students enrolled in those two courses. Data concerning the company's cost formulas appear below:

|  | Fixed Cost per Month | Cost per Course | Cost per Student |
|---|---|---|---|
| Instructor wages . . . . . . . . . . . . . . |  | $3,080 |  |
| Classroom supplies. . . . . . . . . . . |  |  | $260 |
| Utilities . . . . . . . . . . . . . . . . . . . . . | $870 | $130 |  |
| Campus rent. . . . . . . . . . . . . . . . | $4,200 |  |  |
| Insurance . . . . . . . . . . . . . . . . . . . | $1,890 |  |  |
| Administrative expenses . . . . . . . | $3,270 | $15 | $4 |

For example, administrative expenses should be $3,270 per month plus $15 per course plus $4 per student. The company's sales should average $800 per student.

The company planned to run three courses with a total of 45 students; however, it actually ran three courses with a total of only 42 students. The actual operating results for September appear below:

|  | Actual |
|---|---|
| Revenue . . . . . . . . . . . . . . . . . . | $32,400 |
| Instructor wages . . . . . . . . . . . | $9,080 |
| Classroom supplies. . . . . . . . . . | $8,540 |
| Utilities . . . . . . . . . . . . . . . . . . | $1,530 |
| Campus rent. . . . . . . . . . . . . . . | $4,200 |
| Insurance . . . . . . . . . . . . . . . . | $1,890 |
| Administrative expenses . . . . . | $3,790 |

**Required:**
1. Using Exhibit 9–2 as your guide, prepare the company's planning budget for September.
2. Using Exhibit 9–5 as your guide, prepare the company's flexible budget for September.
3. Calculate the revenue and spending variances for September. (*Hint:* Refer to Exhibit 9–6.)

**EXERCISE 9–13   Direct Materials and Direct Labor Variances** LO9–4, LO9–5
Huron Company produces a commercial cleaning compound known as Zoom. The direct materials and direct labor standards for one unit of Zoom are given below:

|  | Standard Quantity or Hours | Standard Price or Rate | Standard Cost |
|---|---|---|---|
| Direct materials . . . . . . . . . . | 4.6 pounds | $2.50 per pound | $11.50 |
| Direct labor. . . . . . . . . . . . . . | 0.2 hours | $18.00 per hour | $3.60 |

During the most recent month, the following activity was recorded:
a.  Twenty thousand pounds of material were purchased at a cost of $2.35 per pound.
b.  All of the material purchased was used to produce 4,000 units of Zoom.
c.  750 hours of direct labor time were recorded at a total labor cost of $14,925.

**Required:**
1.  Compute the materials price and quantity variances for the month.
2.  Compute the labor rate and efficiency variances for the month.

**EXERCISE 9–14    Direct Materials Variances LO9–4**
Refer to the data in Exercise 9–13. Assume that instead of producing 4,000 units during the month, the company produced only 3,000 units, using 14,750 pounds of material. (The rest of the material purchased remained in raw materials inventory.)

**Required:**
Compute the materials price and quantity variances for the month.

**EXERCISE 9–15    Flexible Budgets and Revenue and Spending Variances LO9–1, LO9–2**
Via Gelato is a popular neighborhood gelato shop. The company has provided the following cost formulas and actual results for the month of June:

|  | Fixed Element per Month | Variable Element per Liter | Actual Total for June |
|---|---|---|---|
| Revenue . . . . . . . . . . . . . . . |  | $12.00 | $71,540 |
| Raw materials. . . . . . . . . . . |  | $4.65 | $29,230 |
| Wages . . . . . . . . . . . . . . . . . | $5,600 | $1.40 | $13,860 |
| Utilities . . . . . . . . . . . . . . . | $1,630 | $0.20 | $3,270 |
| Rent . . . . . . . . . . . . . . . . . . | $2,600 |  | $2,600 |
| Insurance . . . . . . . . . . . . . . | $1,350 |  | $1,350 |
| Miscellaneous . . . . . . . . . . . | $650 | $0.35 | $2,590 |

While gelato is sold by the cone or cup, the shop measures its activity in terms of the total number of liters of gelato sold. For example, wages should be $5,600 plus $1.40 per liter of gelato sold and the actual wages for June were $13,860. Via Gelato expected to sell 6,000 liters in June, but actually sold 6,200 liters.

**Required:**
Calculate Via Gelato revenue and spending variances for June. (*Hint:* Refer to Exhibit 9–6.)

**EXERCISE 9–16    Flexible Budgets in a Cost Center LO9–1, LO9–2**
Packaging Solutions Corporation manufactures and sells a wide variety of packaging products. Performance reports are prepared monthly for each department. The planning budget and flexible budget for the Production Department are based on the following formulas, where $q$ is the number of labor-hours worked in a month:

|  | Cost Formulas |
|---|---|
| Direct labor. . . . . . . . . . . . . . . . . . . . . . | $15.80q |
| Indirect labor . . . . . . . . . . . . . . . . . . . . | $8,200 + $1.60q |
| Utilities . . . . . . . . . . . . . . . . . . . . . . . | $6,400 + $0.80q |
| Supplies . . . . . . . . . . . . . . . . . . . . . . | $1,100 + $0.40q |
| Equipment depreciation. . . . . . . . . . . . | $23,000 + $3.70q |
| Factory rent . . . . . . . . . . . . . . . . . . . . . | $8,400 |
| Property taxes . . . . . . . . . . . . . . . . . . . | $2,100 |
| Factory administration . . . . . . . . . . . . . | $11,700 + $1.90q |

The Production Department planned to work 8,000 labor-hours in March; however, it actually worked 8,400 labor-hours during the month. Its actual costs incurred in March are listed below:

| | Actual Cost Incurred in March |
|---|---|
| Direct labor.................. | $134,730 |
| Indirect labor ............... | $19,860 |
| Utilities ..................... | $14,570 |
| Supplies .................... | $4,980 |
| Equipment depreciation....... | $54,080 |
| Factory rent ................. | $8,700 |
| Property taxes ............... | $2,100 |
| Factory administration ........ | $26,470 |

**Required:**
1. Using Exhibit 9–2 as your guide, prepare the Production Department's planning budget for the month.
2. Using Exhibit 9–5 as your guide, prepare the Production Department's flexible budget for the month.
3. Calculate the spending variances for all expense items.(*Hint*: Refer to Exhibit 9–6.)

**EXERCISE 9–17   Direct Materials and Direct Labor Variances** LO9–4, LO9–5

Dawson Toys, Ltd., produces a toy called the Maze. The company has recently created a standard cost system to help control costs and has established the following standards for the Maze toy:

> Direct materials: 6 microns per toy at $1.50 per micron
> Direct labor: 1.3 hours per toy at $21 per hour

During July, the company produced 3,000 Maze toys. The toy's production data for the month are as follows:

*Direct materials:* 25,000 microns were purchased at a cost of $1.48 per micron. 5,000 of these microns were still in inventory at the end of the month.

*Direct labor:* 4,000 direct labor-hours were worked at a cost of $88,000.

**Required:**
1. Compute the following variances for July:
   a. The materials price and quantity variances.
   b. The labor rate and efficiency variances.
2. Prepare a brief explanation of the possible causes of each variance.

**PROBLEMS**

**PROBLEM 9–18   Comprehensive Variance Analysis** LO9–4, LO9–5, LO9–6

Miller Toy Company manufactures a plastic swimming pool at its Westwood Plant. The plant has been experiencing problems as shown by its June contribution format income statement below:

| | Flexible Budget | Actual |
|---|---|---|
| Sales (15,000 pools) ............................ | $675,000 | $675,000 |
| **Variable expenses:** | | |
| Variable cost of goods sold*..................... | 435,000 | 461,890 |
| Variable selling expenses ...................... | 20,000 | 20,000 |
| Total variable expenses ......................... | 455,000 | 481,890 |
| Contribution margin ............................. | 220,000 | 193,110 |
| **Fixed expenses:** | | |
| Manufacturing overhead ........................ | 130,000 | 130,000 |
| Selling and administrative ...................... | 84,000 | 84,000 |
| Total fixed expenses............................. | 214,000 | 214,000 |
| Net operating income (loss) ..................... | $   6,000 | $ (20,890) |

*Contains direct materials, direct labor, and variable manufacturing overhead.

Janet Dunn, who has just been appointed general manager of the Westwood Plant, has been given instructions to "get things under control." Upon reviewing the plant's income statement, Ms. Dunn has concluded that the major problem lies in the variable cost of goods sold. She has been provided with the following standard cost per swimming pool:

| | Standard Quantity or Hours | Standard Price or Rate | Standard Cost |
|---|---|---|---|
| Direct materials . . . . . . . . . . . . . . . . . . . . . | 3.0 pounds | $5.00 per pound | $15.00 |
| Direct labor. . . . . . . . . . . . . . . . . . . . . . . . | 0.8 hours | $16.00 per hour | 12.80 |
| Variable manufacturing overhead . . . . . | 0.4 hours* | $3.00 per hour | 1.20 |
| Total standard cost per unit. . . . . . . . . . | | | $29.00 |

*Based on machine-hours.

During June the plant produced 15,000 pools and incurred the following costs:

a.   Purchased 60,000 pounds of materials at a cost of $4.95 per pound.
b.   Used 49,200 pounds of materials in production. (Finished goods and work in process inventories are insignificant and can be ignored.)
c.   Worked 11,800 direct labor-hours at a cost of $17.00 per hour.
d.   Incurred variable manufacturing overhead cost totaling $18,290 for the month. A total of 5,900 machine-hours was recorded.

It is the company's policy to close all variances to cost of goods sold on a monthly basis.

*Required:*
1.   Compute the following variances for June:
a.   Materials price and quantity variances.
b.   Labor rate and efficiency variances.
c.   Variable overhead rate and efficiency variances.
2.   Summarize the variances that you computed in (1) above by showing the net overall favorable or unfavorable variance for the month. What impact did this figure have on the company's income statement? Show computations.
3.   Pick out the two most significant variances that you computed in (1) above. Explain to Ms. Dunn possible causes of these variances.

**PROBLEM 9–19   More than One Cost Driver** LO9–2, LO9–3
Milano Pizza is a small neighborhood pizzeria that has a small area for in-store dining as well as offering take-out and free home delivery services. The pizzeria's owner has determined that the shop has two major cost drivers—the number of pizzas sold and the number of deliveries made.
The pizzeria's cost formulas appear below:

| | Fixed Cost per Month | Cost per Pizza | Cost per Delivery |
|---|---|---|---|
| Pizza ingredients. . . . . . . . . . | | $3.80 | |
| Kitchen staff . . . . . . . . . . . . . | $5,220 | | |
| Utilities . . . . . . . . . . . . . . . . . | $630 | $0.05 | |
| Delivery person . . . . . . . . . . . | | | $3.50 |
| Delivery vehicle. . . . . . . . . . . | $540 | | $1.50 |
| Equipment depreciation. . . . | $275 | | |
| Rent . . . . . . . . . . . . . . . . . . . . | $1,830 | | |
| Miscellaneous . . . . . . . . . . . . | $820 | $0.15 | |

In November, the pizzeria budgeted for 1,200 pizzas at an average selling price of $13.50 per pizza and for 180 deliveries.

Data concerning the pizzeria's actual results in November appear below:

|  | Actual Results |
|---|---|
| Pizzas ..................... | 1,240 |
| Deliveries ................. | 174 |
| Revenue ................... | $17,420 |
| Pizza ingredients........... | $4,985 |
| Kitchen staff ............... | $5,281 |
| Utilities ................... | $984 |
| Delivery person ............ | $609 |
| Delivery vehicle............ | $655 |
| Equipment depreciation...... | $275 |
| Rent....................... | $1,830 |
| Miscellaneous ............. | $954 |

**Required:**
1. Compute the revenue and spending variances for the pizzeria for November. (*Hint*: Refer to Exhibit 9–6.)
2. Explain the revenue and spending variances.

**PROBLEM 9–20   Basic Variance Analysis; the Impact of Variances on Unit Costs** LO9–4, LO9–5, LO9–6

Koontz Company manufactures a number of products. The standards relating to one of these products are shown below, along with actual cost data for May.

|  | Standard Cost per Unit | Actual Cost per Unit |
|---|---|---|
| Direct materials: | | |
| Standard: 1.80 feet at $3.00 per foot............. | $5.40 | |
| Actual: 1.80 feet at $3.30 per foot .............. | | $5.94 |
| Direct labor: | | |
| Standard: 0.90 hours at $18.00 per hour ......... | 16.20 | |
| Actual: 0.92 hours at $17.50 per hour ........... | | 16.10 |
| Variable overhead: | | |
| Standard: 0.90 hours at $5.00 per hour .......... | 4.50 | |
| Actual: 0.92 hours at $4.50 per hour............. | | 4.14 |
| Total cost per unit ............................... | $26.10 | $26.18 |
| Excess of actual cost over standard cost per unit .... | $0.08 | |

The production superintendent was pleased when he saw this report and commented: "This $0.08 excess cost is well within the 2 percent limit management has set for acceptable variances. It's obvious that there's not much to worry about with this product."

Actual production for the month was 12,000 units. Variable overhead cost is assigned to products on the basis of direct labor-hours. There were no beginning or ending inventories of materials.

**Required:**
1. Compute the following variances for May:
   a. Materials price and quantity variances.
   b. Labor rate and efficiency variances.
   c. Variable overhead rate and efficiency variances.
2. How much of the $0.08 excess unit cost is traceable to each of the variances computed in (1) above.
3. How much of the $0.08 excess unit cost is traceable to apparent inefficient use of labor time?
4. Do you agree that the excess unit cost is not of concern?

**PROBLEM 9–21   Multiple Products, Materials, and Processes LO9–4, LO9–5**

Mickley Corporation produces two products, Alpha6s and Zeta7s, which pass through two operations, Sintering and Finishing. Each of the products uses two raw materials—X442 and Y661. The company uses a standard cost system, with the following standards for each product (on a per unit basis):

| Product | Raw Material | | Standard Labor Time | |
| --- | --- | --- | --- | --- |
| | X442 | Y661 | Sintering | Finishing |
| Alpha6.............. | 1.8 kilos | 2.0 liters | 0.20 hours | 0.80 hours |
| Zeta7 ............... | 3.0 kilos | 4.5 liters | 0.35 hours | 0.90 hours |

Information relating to materials purchased and materials used in production during May follows:

| Material | Purchases | Purchase Cost | Standard Price | Used in Production |
| --- | --- | --- | --- | --- |
| X442 ............ | 14,500 kilos | $52,200 | $3.50 per kilo | 8,500 kilos |
| Y661............. | 15,500 liters | $20,925 | $1.40 per liter | 13,000 liters |

The following additional information is available:

a.   The company recognizes price variances when materials are purchased.
b.   The standard labor rate is $19.80 per hour in Sintering and $19.20 per hour in Finishing.
c.   During May, 1,200 direct labor-hours were worked in Sintering at a total labor cost of $27,000, and 2,850 direct labor-hours were worked in Finishing at a total labor cost of $59,850.
d.   Production during May was 1,500 Alpha6s and 2,000 Zeta7s.

**Required:**

1.   Prepare a standard cost card for each product, showing the standard cost of direct materials and direct labor.
2.   Compute the materials price and quantity variances for each material.
3.   Compute the labor rate and efficiency variances for each operation.

**PROBLEM 9–22   Variance Analysis in a Hospital LO9–4, LO9–5, LO9–6**

John Fleming, chief administrator for Valley View Hospital, is concerned about the costs for tests in the hospital's lab. Charges for lab tests are consistently higher at Valley View than at other hospitals and have resulted in many complaints. Also, because of strict regulations on amounts reimbursed for lab tests, payments received from insurance companies and governmental units have not been high enough to cover lab costs.

Mr. Fleming has asked you to evaluate costs in the hospital's lab for the past month. The following information is available:

a.   Two types of tests are performed in the lab—blood tests and smears. During the past month, 1,800 blood tests and 2,400 smears were performed in the lab.
b.   Small glass plates are used in both types of tests. During the past month, the hospital purchased 12,000 plates at a cost of $56,400. 1,500 of these plates were unused at the end of the month; no plates were on hand at the beginning of the month.
c.   During the past month, 1,150 hours of labor time were recorded in the lab at a cost of $21,850.
d.   The lab's variable overhead cost last month totaled $7,820.

Valley View Hospital has never used standard costs. By searching industry literature, however, you have determined the following nationwide averages for hospital labs:

*Plates:* Two plates are required per lab test. These plates cost $5.00 each and are disposed of after the test is completed.
*Labor:* Each blood test should require 0.3 hours to complete, and each smear should require 0.15 hours to complete. The average cost of this lab time is $20 per hour.
*Overhead:* Overhead cost is based on direct labor-hours. The average rate for variable overhead is $6 per hour.

*Required:*

1.  Compute a materials price variance for the plates purchased last month and a materials quantity variance for the plates used last month.
2.  For labor cost in the lab:
    a.  Compute a labor rate variance and a labor efficiency variance.
    b.  In most hospitals, one-half of the workers in the lab are senior technicians and one-half are assistants. In an effort to reduce costs, Valley View Hospital employs only one-fourth senior technicians and three-fourths assistants. Would you recommend that this policy be continued? Explain.
3.  Compute the variable overhead rate and efficiency variances. Is there any relation between the variable overhead efficiency variance and the labor efficiency variance? Explain.

**PROBLEM 9–23  Flexible Budgets and Spending Variances LO9–1, LO9–2**

You have just been hired by FAB Corporation, the manufacturer of a revolutionary new garage door opening device. The president has asked that you review the company's costing system and "do what you can to help us get better control of our manufacturing overhead costs." You find that the company has never used a flexible budget, and you suggest that preparing such a budget would be an excellent first step in overhead planning and control.

After much effort and analysis, you determined the following cost formulas and gathered the following actual cost data for March:

|  | Cost Formula | Actual Cost in March |
| --- | --- | --- |
| Utilities | $20,600 + $0.10 per machine-hour | $24,200 |
| Maintenance | $40,000 + $1.60 per machine-hour | $78,100 |
| Supplies | $0.30 per machine-hour | $8,400 |
| Indirect labor | $130,000 + $0.70 per machine-hour | $149,600 |
| Depreciation | $70,000 | $71,500 |

During March, the company worked 26,000 machine-hours and produced 15,000 units. The company had originally planned to work 30,000 machine-hours during March.

*Required:*

1.  Using Exhibit 9–2 as your guide, prepare a flexible budget for March.
2.  Using Exhibit 9–6 as your guide, prepare a report showing the spending variances for March. Explain what these variances mean.

**PROBLEM 9–24  Comprehensive Variance Analysis LO9–4, LO9–5, LO9–6**

Marvel Parts, Inc., manufactures auto accessories. One of the company's products is a set of seat covers that can be adjusted to fit nearly any small car. The company uses a standard cost system for all of its products. According to the standards that have been set for the seat covers, the factory should work 2,850 hours each month to produce 1,900 sets of covers. The standard costs associated with this level of production are:

|  | Total | Per Set of Covers |
| --- | --- | --- |
| Direct materials | $42,560 | $22.40 |
| Direct labor | $51,300 | 27.00 |
| Variable manufacturing overhead (based on direct labor-hours) | $6,840 | 3.60 |
|  |  | $53.00 |

During August, the factory worked only 2,800 direct labor-hours and produced 2,000 sets of covers. The following actual costs were recorded during the month:

| | Total | Per Set of Covers |
|---|---|---|
| Direct materials (12,000 yards) . . . . . . . . . | $45,600 | $22.80 |
| Direct labor. . . . . . . . . . . . . . . . . . . . . . . . . | $49,000 | 24.50 |
| Variable manufacturing overhead . . . . . . | $7,000 | 3.50 |
| | | $50.80 |

At standard, each set of covers should require 5.6 yards of material. All of the materials purchased during the month were used in production.

**Required:**
Compute the following variances for August:
1.   The materials price and quantity variances.
2.   The labor rate and efficiency variances.
3.   The variable overhead rate and efficiency variances.

**PROBLEM 9–25   Direct Materials and Direct Labor Variances; Computations from Incomplete Data LO9–4, LO9–5**
Sharp Company manufactures a product for which the following standards have been set:

| | Standard Quantity or Hours | Standard Price or Rate | Standard Cost |
|---|---|---|---|
| Direct materials . . . . . . . . . . . | 3 feet | $11 per foot | $33 |
| Direct labor. . . . . . . . . . . . . . . | ? hours | ? per hour | ? |

During March, the company purchased direct materials at a cost of $111,300, all of which were used in the production of 3,200 units of product. In addition, 4,900 direct labor-hours were worked on the product during the month. The cost of this labor time was $95,550. The following variances have been computed for the month:

| | |
|---|---|
| Materials quantity variance . . . . . . . . . . . . . . . | $4,400 U |
| Labor spending variance . . . . . . . . . . . . . . . . . | $450 F |
| Labor efficiency variance. . . . . . . . . . . . . . . . . | $2,000 U |

**Required:**
1.   For direct materials:
   a.   Compute the actual cost per foot of materials for March.
   b.   Compute the price variance and the spending variance.
2.   For direct labor:
   a.   Compute the standard direct labor rate per hour.
   b.   Compute the standard hours allowed for the month's production.
   c.   Compute the standard hours allowed per unit of product.

(*Hint:* In completing the problem, it may be helpful to move from known to unknown data by the columnar format shown in Exhibits 9–11 and 9–12.)

**PROBLEM 9–26   Comprehensive Variance Analysis LO9–4, LO9–5, LO9–6**
Highland Company produces a lightweight backpack that is popular with college students. Standard variable costs relating to a single backpack are given below:

| | Standard Quantity or Hours | Standard Price or Rate | Standard Cost |
|---|---|---|---|
| Direct materials . . . . . . . . . . . . . . . . . . . . | ? | $6 per yard | $? |
| Direct labor. . . . . . . . . . . . . . . . . . . . . . . | ? | ? | ? |
| Variable manufacturing overhead . . . . | ? | $3 per direct labor-hour | ? |
| Total standard cost per unit. . . . . . . . . | | | $? |

Overhead is applied to production on the basis of direct labor-hours. During March, 1,000 backpacks were manufactured and sold. Selected information relating to the month's production is given below:

| | Materials Used | Direct Labor | Variable Manufacturing Overhead |
|---|---|---|---|
| Total standard cost allowed* . . . . . . . . . . . | $16,800 | $21,000 | $4,200 |
| Actual costs incurred . . . . . . . . . . . . . . . . . | $15,000 | ? | $3,600 |
| Materials price variance. . . . . . . . . . . . . . . | ? | | |
| Materials quantity variance . . . . . . . . . . . . | $1,200 U | | |
| Labor rate variance. . . . . . . . . . . . . . . . . . . | | ? | |
| Labor efficiency variance. . . . . . . . . . . . . . | | ? | |
| Variable overhead rate variance. . . . . . . . . | | | ? |
| Variable overhead efficiency variance. . . . | | | ? |

*For the month's production.

The following additional information is available for March's production:

| | |
|---|---|
| Actual direct labor-hours . . . . . . . . . . . . . . . . . . . . . . . . . . . . . . . . . . . . | 1,500 |
| Difference between standard and actual cost per backpack produced during March . . . . . . . . . . . . . . . . . . . . . | $0.15 F |

*Required:* (*Hint:* It may be helpful to complete a general model diagram for direct materials, direct labor, and variable manufacturing overhead before attempting to answer any of the requirements.)

1. What is the standard cost of a single backpack?
2. What was the actual cost per backpack produced during March?
3. How many yards of material are required at standard per backpack?
4. What was the materials price variance for March if there were no beginning or ending inventories of materials?
5. What is the standard direct labor rate per hour?
6. What was the labor rate variance for March? The labor efficiency variance?
7. What was the variable overhead rate variance for March? The variable overhead efficiency variance?
8. Prepare a standard cost card for one backpack.

## BUILDING YOUR SKILLS

**ETHICS CHALLENGE LO9–2**

Tom Kemper is the controller of the Wichita manufacturing facility of Prudhom Enterprises, Inc. The annual cost control report is one of the many reports that must be filed with corporate headquarters and is due at corporate headquarters shortly after the beginning of the New Year. Kemper does not like putting work off to the last minute, so just before Christmas he prepared a preliminary draft of the cost control report. Some adjustments would later be required for transactions that occur between

Christmas and New Year's Day. A copy of the preliminary draft report, which Kemper completed on December 21, follows:

### Wichita Manufacturing Facility
### Cost Control Report
### December 21 Preliminary Draft

| | Actual Results | Flexible Budget | Spending Variances |
|---|---|---|---|
| Labor-hours . . . . . . . . . . . . . . . . | 18,000 | 18,000 | |
| Direct labor. . . . . . . . . . . . . . . . | $ 326,000 | $ 324,000 | $ 2,000 U |
| Power . . . . . . . . . . . . . . . . . . . . | 19,750 | 18,000 | 1,750 U |
| Supplies . . . . . . . . . . . . . . . . . . | 105,000 | 99,000 | 6,000 U |
| Equipment depreciation. . . . . . . | 343,000 | 332,000 | 11,000 U |
| Supervisory salaries . . . . . . . . . | 273,000 | 275,000 | 2,000 F |
| Insurance . . . . . . . . . . . . . . . . . | 37,000 | 37,000 | 0 |
| Industrial engineering. . . . . . . . | 189,000 | 210,000 | 21,000 F |
| Factory building lease . . . . . . . . | 60,000 | 60,000 | 0 |
| Total expense. . . . . . . . . . . . . . . | $1,352,750 | $1,355,000 | $ 2,250 F |

Melissa Ilianovitch, the general manager at the Wichita facility, asked to see a copy of the preliminary draft report. Kemper carried a copy of the report to her office where the following discussion took place:

*Ilianovitch:* Wow! Almost all of the variances on the report are unfavorable. The only favorable variances are for supervisory salaries and industrial engineering. How did we have an unfavorable variance for depreciation?

*Kemper:* Do you remember that milling machine that broke down because the wrong lubricant was used by the machine operator?

*Ilianovitch:* Yes.

*Kemper:* We couldn't fix it. We had to scrap the machine and buy a new one.

*Ilianovitch:* This report doesn't look good. I was raked over the coals last year when we had just a few unfavorable variances.

*Kemper:* I'm afraid the final report is going to look even worse.

*Ilianovitch:* Oh?

*Kemper:* The line item for industrial engineering on the report is for work we hired Ferguson Engineering to do for us. The original contract was for $210,000, but we asked them to do some additional work that was not in the contract. We have to reimburse Ferguson Engineering for the costs of that additional work. The $189,000 in actual costs that appears on the preliminary draft report reflects only their billings up through December 21. The last bill they had sent us was on November 28, and they completed the project just last week. Yesterday I got a call from Laura Sunder over at Ferguson and she said they would be sending us a final bill for the project before the end of the year. The total bill, including the reimbursements for the additional work, is going to be . . .

*Ilianovitch:* I am not sure I want to hear this.

*Kemper:* $225,000

*Ilianovitch:* Ouch!

*Kemper:* The additional work added $15,000 to the cost of the project.

*Ilianovitch:* I can't turn in a report with an overall unfavorable variance! They'll kill me at corporate headquarters. Call up Laura at Ferguson and ask her not to send the bill until after the first of the year. We have to have that $21,000 favorable variance for industrial engineering on the report.

**Required:**

What should Tom Kemper do? Explain.

**ANALYTICAL THINKING LO9–2, LO9–4**

Southside Pizzeria wants to improve its ability to manage the ingredient costs associated with making and selling its pizzas. For the month of June, the company plans to make 1,000 pizzas. It has created a planning budget that includes a cost formula for mozzarella cheese of $2.40 per pizza. At the end of June, Southside actually sold 1,100 pizzas and the actual cost of the cheese that it used during the month was $2,632.

*Required:*

1. What is the mozzarella cheese spending variance for June?
2. Assume that the company establishes a price standard of $0.30 per ounce for mozzarella cheese and a quantity standard of eight ounces of cheese per pizza. Also, assume that Southside actually used 9,400 ounces of cheese during the month to make 1,100 pizzas.
   a. What is the materials price variance for mozzarella cheese for June?
   b. What is the materials quantity variance for mozzarella cheese for June?
   c. What is the materials spending variance for mozzarella cheese for June?

**CASE LO9–1, LO9–2, LO9–3**

The Little Theatre is a nonprofit organization devoted to staging plays for children. The theater has a very small full-time professional administrative staff. Through a special arrangement with the actors' union, actors and directors rehearse without pay and are paid only for actual performances.

The Little Theatre had tentatively planned to put on six different productions with a total of 108 performances. For example, one of the productions was *Peter Rabbit*, which had a six-week run with three performances on each weekend. The costs from the current year's planning budget appear below.

| The Little Theatre Costs from the Planning Budget For the Year Ended December 31 | |
|---|---|
| Budgeted number of productions | 6 |
| Budgeted number of performances | 108 |
| Actors and directors wages | $216,000 |
| Stagehands wages | 32,400 |
| Ticket booth personnel and ushers wages | 16,200 |
| Scenery, costumes, and props | 108,000 |
| Theater hall rent | 54,000 |
| Printed programs | 27,000 |
| Publicity | 12,000 |
| Administrative expenses | 43,200 |
| Total | $508,800 |

Some of the costs vary with the number of productions, some with the number of performances, and some are fixed and depend on neither the number of productions nor the number of performances. The costs of scenery, costumes, props, and publicity vary with the number of productions. It doesn't make any difference how many times *Peter Rabbit* is performed, the cost of the scenery is the same. Likewise, the cost of publicizing a play with posters and radio commercials is the same whether there are 10, 20, or 30 performances of the play. On the other hand, the wages of the actors, directors, stagehands, ticket booth personnel, and ushers vary with the number of performances. The greater the number of performances, the higher the wage costs will be. Similarly, the costs of renting the hall and printing the programs will vary with the number of performances. Administrative expenses are more difficult to analyze, but the best estimate is that approximately 75% of the budgeted costs are fixed, 15% depend on the number of productions staged, and the remaining 10% depend on the number of performances.

After the beginning of the year, the board of directors of the theater authorized expanding the theater's program to seven productions and a total of 168 performances. Not surprisingly, actual costs were considerably higher than the costs from the planning budget. (Grants from donors and ticket sales were also correspondingly higher, but are not shown here.) Data concerning the actual costs appear below:

| The Little Theatre<br>Actual Costs<br>For the Year Ended December 31 | |
|---|---:|
| Actual number of productions............... | 7 |
| Actual number of performances............. | 168 |
| Actors and directors wages................. | $341,800 |
| Stagehands wages........................ | 49,700 |
| Ticket booth personnel and ushers wages.... | 25,900 |
| Scenery, costumes, and props.............. | 130,600 |
| Theater hall rent......................... | 78,000 |
| Printed programs......................... | 38,300 |
| Publicity................................. | 15,100 |
| Administrative expenses................... | 47,500 |
| Total.................................... | $726,900 |

**Required:**

1. Using Exhibit 9–5 as your guide, prepare a flexible budget for The Little Theatre based on the actual activity of the year.
2. Using Exhibit 9–6 as your guide, prepare a report for the year that shows the spending variances for all expense items.
3. If you were on the board of directors of the theater, would you be pleased with how well costs were controlled during the year? Why, or why not?
4. The cost formulas provide figures for the average cost per production and average cost per performance. How accurate do you think these figures would be for predicting the cost of a new production or of an additional performance of a particular production?

# APPENDIX 9A: PREDETERMINED OVERHEAD RATES AND OVERHEAD ANALYSIS IN A STANDARD COSTING SYSTEM

**LEARNING OBJECTIVE 9–7**

Compute and interpret the fixed overhead budget and volume variances.

In this appendix, we explain how the predetermined overhead rates that were discussed in the job-order costing chapters can be used in a standard costing system. Throughout this appendix, we assume that an absorption costing system is used in which *all* manufacturing costs—both variable and fixed—are included in product costs.

## MicroDrive Corporation: An Example

Exhibit 9A–1 pertains to MicroDrive Corporation, a company that produces miniature electric motors. The data within this exhibit is divided into three sections. The first section summarizes the budgeted overhead costs and budgeted machine-hours included in the company's planning budget. Note that the company's planning budget is based on producing 25,000 motors. Given that two machine-hours are allowed per motor, the planning budget allows for 50,000 machine-hours. At this level of activity, the budgeted variable manufacturing overhead is $75,000 and the budgeted fixed manufacturing overhead is $300,000.

The second section includes information that MicroDrive will use to apply overhead costs to production. Notice that the company actually produced 20,000 motors instead

**EXHIBIT 9A–1**
MicroDrive Corporation Data

| Budgeted (Planned) Overhead: | | |
|---|---|---|
| Budgeted variable manufacturing overhead....... | $ 75,000 | |
| Budgeted fixed manufacturing overhead......... | 300,000 | |
| Total budgeted manufacturing overhead......... | $375,000 | |
| Budgeted production (a)....................... | 25,000 | motors |
| Standard machine-hours per motor (b)........... | 2 | machine-hours per motor |
| Budgeted machine-hours (a) × (b)............... | 50,000 | machine-hours |
| **Applying Overhead:** | | |
| Actual production (a).......................... | 20,000 | motors |
| Standard machine-hours per motor (b)........... | 2 | machine-hours per motor |
| Standard machine-hours allowed for the actual production (a) × (b).................... | 40,000 | machine-hours |
| **Actual Overhead and Machine-Hours:** | | |
| Actual variable manufacturing overhead.......... | $ 71,400 | |
| Actual fixed manufacturing overhead............ | 308,000 | |
| Total actual manufacturing overhead............ | $379,400 | |
| Actual machine-hours ......................... | 42,000 | machine-hours |

of the 25,000 motors included in the planning budget. Given that two machine-hours are allowed per motor, the standard machine-hours allowed for the actual production is 40,000 machine-hours. This is the quantity of machine-hours that the company will use to apply variable and fixed overhead costs to production.

The third section summarizes the company's actual variable and fixed manufacturing overhead costs for the period as well as its actual machine-hours used during the period. As we will describe in greater detail shortly, *it is very important to understand that in a standard cost system the actual hours (42,000 machine-hours) are not used to apply overhead costs to production. Variable and fixed overhead costs are applied to production using the standard hours allowed for the actual production (40,000 machine-hours).*

## Predetermined Overhead Rates

Recall from earlier chapters that the following formula is used to establish the predetermined overhead rate at the beginning of the period:

$$\text{Predetermined overhead rate} = \frac{\text{Estimated total manufacturing overhead cost}}{\text{Estimated total amount of the allocation base}}$$

The estimated total amount of the allocation base in the formula for the predetermined overhead rate is called the **denominator activity**.

Once the predetermined overhead rate has been established, it remains unchanged throughout the period, even if the actual level of activity differs from what was estimated. Consequently, the amount of overhead applied to each unit of product is the same regardless of when it is produced during the period.

As alluded to in Exhibit 9A–1, MicroDrive Corporation uses 50,000 budgeted machine-hours as its denominator activity in the predetermined overhead rate. Consequently, the company's predetermined overhead rate would be computed as follows:

$$\text{Predetermined overhead rate} = \frac{\$375,000}{50,000 \text{ MHs}} = \$7.50 \text{ per MH}$$

This predetermined overhead rate can be broken down into its variable and fixed components as follows:

$$\text{Variable component of the predetermined overhead rate} = \frac{\$75,000}{50,000 \text{ MHs}} = \$1.50 \text{ per MH}$$

$$\text{Fixed component of the predetermined overhead rate} = \frac{\$300,000}{50,000 \text{ MHs}} = \$6.00 \text{ per MH}$$

For every standard machine-hour recorded, work in process is charged with $7.50 of manufacturing overhead, of which $1.50 represents variable manufacturing overhead and $6.00 represents fixed manufacturing overhead. In total, MicroDrive Corporation would apply $300,000 of overhead to work in process as shown below:

$$\text{Overhead applied} = \text{Predetermined overhead rate} \times \text{Standard hours allowed for the actual output}$$
$$= \$7.50 \text{ per machine-hour} \times 40,000 \text{ machine-hours}$$
$$= \$300,000$$

## Overhead Application in a Standard Cost System

To understand fixed overhead variances, we first have to realize how overhead is applied to work in process in a standard cost system. Recall that in the job-order costing chapters we applied overhead to work in process on the basis of the actual level of activity (e.g., the actual direct labor-hours worked or the actual machine-hours used). This procedure was correct because at the time we were dealing with a normal cost system.[7] However, we are now dealing with a standard cost system. In such a system, overhead is applied to work in process on the basis of the *standard hours allowed for the actual output of the period* rather than on the basis of the actual number of hours worked. Exhibit 9A–2 illustrates this point. In a standard cost system, every unit of output is charged with the same amount of overhead cost, regardless of how much time the unit actually requires for processing.

**EXHIBIT 9A–2**
Applied Overhead Costs: Normal Cost System versus Standard Cost System

| Normal Cost System | | Standard Cost System | |
|---|---|---|---|
| **Manufacturing Overhead** | | **Manufacturing Overhead** | |
| Actual overhead costs incurred. | Applied overhead costs: Actual hours × Pre-determined overhead rate. | Actual overhead costs incurred. | Applied overhead costs: Standard hours allowed for actual output × Pre-determined overhead rate. |
| Underapplied or overapplied overhead | | Underapplied or overapplied overhead | |

## Budget Variance

Two fixed manufacturing overhead variances are computed in a standard costing system—a *budget variance* and a *volume variance*. These variances are computed in Exhibit 9A–3. The **budget variance** is simply the difference between the actual fixed manufacturing overhead and the budgeted fixed manufacturing overhead for the period. The formula is:

Budget variance = Actual fixed overhead − Budgeted fixed overhead

---

[7]Normal cost systems are defined in the Chapters 2 and 3 glossaries.

**EXHIBIT 9A–3** Fixed Overhead Variances

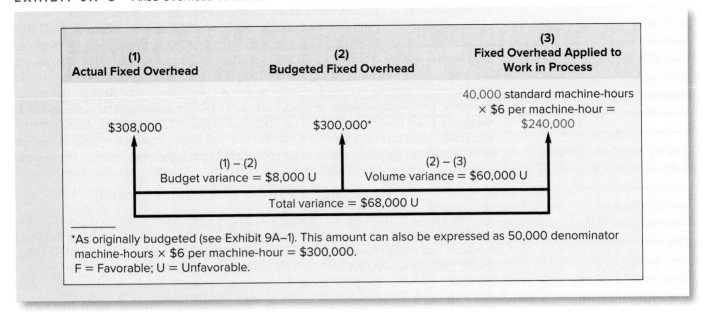

*As originally budgeted (see Exhibit 9A–1). This amount can also be expressed as 50,000 denominator machine-hours × $6 per machine-hour = $300,000.
F = Favorable; U = Unfavorable.

If the actual fixed overhead cost exceeds the budgeted fixed overhead cost, the budget variance is labeled unfavorable. If the actual fixed overhead cost is less than the budgeted fixed overhead cost, the budget variance is labeled favorable.

Applying the formula to the MicroDrive Corporation data, the budget variance is computed as follows:

$$\text{Budget variance} = \$308{,}000 - \$300{,}000 = \$8{,}000 \text{ U}$$

According to the budget, the fixed manufacturing overhead should have been $300,000, but it was actually $308,000. Because the actual cost exceeds the budget by $8,000, the variance is labeled as unfavorable; however, this label does not automatically signal ineffective managerial performance. For example, this variance may be the result of waste and inefficiency, or it may be due to an unforeseen yet prudent investment in fixed overhead resources that improves product quality or manufacturing cycle efficiency.

## Volume Variance

The **volume variance** is defined by the following formula:

$$\text{Volume variance} = \frac{\text{Budgeted fixed}}{\text{overhead}} - \frac{\text{Fixed overhead applied}}{\text{to work in process}}$$

When the budgeted fixed manufacturing overhead exceeds the fixed manufacturing overhead applied to work in process, the volume variance is labeled as unfavorable. When the budgeted fixed manufacturing overhead is less than the fixed manufacturing overhead applied to work in process, the volume variance is labeled as favorable. As we shall see, caution is advised when interpreting this variance.

To understand the volume variance, we need to understand how fixed manufacturing overhead is applied to work in process in a standard costing system. As discussed earlier, fixed manufacturing overhead is applied to work in process on the basis of the standard hours allowed for the actual output of the period. In the case of MicroDrive

Corporation, the company produced 20,000 motors and the standard for each motor is 2 machine-hours. Therefore, the standard hours allowed for the actual output is 40,000 machine-hours (= 20,000 motors × 2 machine-hours). As shown in Exhibit 9A–3, the predetermined fixed manufacturing overhead rate of $6.00 per machine-hour is multiplied by the 40,000 standard machine-hours allowed for the actual output to arrive at $240,000 of fixed manufacturing overhead applied to work in process. Another way to think of this is that the standard for each motor is 2 machine-hours. Because the predetermined fixed manufacturing overhead rate is $6.00 per machine-hour, each motor is assigned $12.00 (= 2 machine-hours × $6.00 per machine-hour) of fixed manufacturing overhead. Consequently, a total of $240,000 of fixed manufacturing overhead is applied to the 20,000 motors that are actually produced. Under either explanation, the volume variance according to the formula is:

$$\text{Volume variance} = \$300,000 - \$240,000 = \$60,000 \text{ U}$$

The key to interpreting the volume variance is to understand that it depends on the difference between the hours used in the denominator to compute the predetermined overhead rate and the standard hours allowed for the actual output of the period. In other words, the volume variance can also be computed using the following formula:

$$\frac{\text{Volume}}{\text{variance}} = \frac{\text{Fixed component of the}}{\text{predetermined overhead rate}} \times \left( \frac{\text{Denominator}}{\text{hours}} - \frac{\text{Standard hours allowed}}{\text{for the actual output}} \right)$$

In the case of MicroDrive Corporation, the volume variance can be computed using this formula as follows:

$$\text{Volume variance} = \frac{\$6.00 \text{ per}}{\text{machine-hour}} \times \left( \frac{50,000}{\text{machine-hours}} - \frac{40,000}{\text{machine-hours}} \right)$$
$$= \$6.00 \text{ per machine-hour} \times (10,000 \text{ machine-hours})$$
$$= \$60,000 \text{ U}$$

Note that this agrees with the volume variance computed using the earlier formula.

Focusing on this new formula, if the denominator hours exceed the standard hours allowed for the actual output, the volume variance is unfavorable. If the denominator hours are less than the standard hours allowed for the actual output, the volume variance is favorable. Stated differently, the volume variance is unfavorable if the actual level of activity is less than expected. The volume variance is favorable if the actual level of activity is greater than expected. It is important to note that the volume variance does not measure overspending or underspending. A company should incur the same dollar amount of fixed overhead cost regardless of whether the period's activity was above or below the planned (denominator) level.

The volume variance is often viewed as a measure of the utilization of facilities. If the standard hours allowed for the actual output are greater than (less than) the denominator hours, it signals efficient (inefficient) usage of facilities. However, other measures of utilization—such as the percentage of capacity utilized—are easier to compute and understand. Perhaps a better interpretation of the volume variance is that it is the error that occurs when the level of activity is incorrectly estimated and the costing system assumes fixed costs behave as if they are variable. This interpretation may be clearer in the next section that graphically analyzes the fixed manufacturing overhead variances.

## Graphic Analysis of Fixed Overhead Variances

Exhibit 9A–4 shows a graphic analysis that offers insights into the fixed overhead budget and volume variances. As shown in the graph, fixed overhead cost is applied to work in process at the predetermined rate of $6.00 for each standard hour of activity. (The

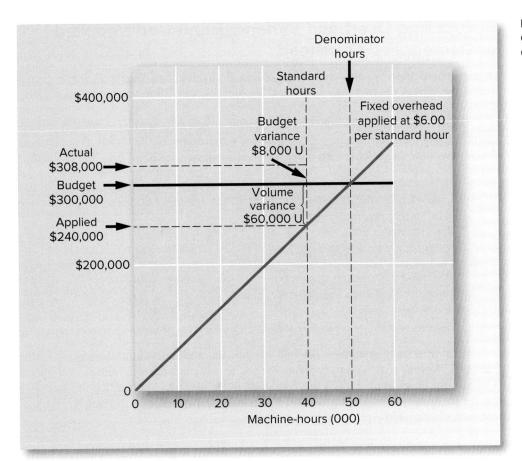

applied-cost line is the upward-sloping line on the graph.) Because a denominator level of 50,000 machine-hours was used in computing the $6.00 rate, the applied-cost line crosses the budget-cost line at exactly 50,000 machine-hours. If the denominator hours and the standard hours allowed for the actual output are the same, there is no volume variance. It is only when the standard hours differ from the denominator hours that a volume variance arises.

In MicroDrive's case, the standard hours allowed for the actual output (40,000 hours) are less than the denominator hours (50,000 hours). The result is an unfavorable volume variance because less cost was applied to production than was originally budgeted. If the situation had been reversed and the standard hours allowed for the actual output had exceeded the denominator hours, then the volume variance on the graph would have been favorable.

## Cautions in Fixed Overhead Analysis

A volume variance for fixed overhead arises because when applying the costs to work in process, we act *as if* the fixed costs are variable. The graph in Exhibit 9A–4 illustrates this point. Notice from the graph that fixed overhead costs are applied to work in process at a rate of $6 per hour *as if* they are variable. Treating these costs as if they are variable is necessary for product costing purposes, but some real dangers lurk here. Managers can easily be misled into thinking that fixed costs are *in fact* variable.

Keep clearly in mind that fixed overhead costs come in large chunks. Expressing fixed costs on a unit or per hour basis, though necessary for product costing for external reports, is artificial. Increases or decreases in activity in fact have no effect on total fixed costs within the relevant range of activity. Even though fixed costs are expressed on a unit or per hour basis, they are *not* proportional to activity. In a sense, the volume variance is the error that occurs as a result of treating fixed costs as variable costs in the costing system.

## Reconciling Overhead Variances and Underapplied or Overapplied Overhead

In a standard cost system, the underapplied or overapplied overhead for a period equals the sum of the overhead variances. To see this, we will return to the MicroDrive Corporation example.

As discussed earlier, in a standard cost system, overhead is applied to work in process on the basis of the standard hours allowed for the actual output of the period. The following table shows how the underapplied or overapplied overhead for MicroDrive is computed.

| | |
|---|---|
| Predetermined overhead rate (a) . . . . . . . . . . . . . . . . | $7.50 per machine-hour |
| Standard machine-hours allowed for the actual production [Exhibit 9A–1] (b) . . . . . . . . . . . | 40,000 machine-hours |
| Manufacturing overhead applied (a) × (b) . . . . . . . . | $300,000 |
| Total actual manufacturing overhead [Exhibit 9A–1] . . . . . . . . . . . . . . . . . . . . . . . . . . . . . . | $379,400 |
| Manufacturing overhead underapplied or overapplied . . . . . . . . . . . . . . . . . . . . . . . . . . . . | $79,400 underapplied |

We have already computed the budget variance and the volume variance for this company. We will also need to compute the variable manufacturing overhead variances. The data for these computations are contained in Exhibit 9A–1. Recalling the formulas for the variable manufacturing overhead variances from earlier in the chapter, we can compute the variable overhead rate and efficiency variances as follows:

$$\text{Variable overhead rate variance} = (AH \times AR) - (AH \times SR)$$
$$= AH(AR - SR)$$
$$= \begin{pmatrix} 42{,}000 \\ \text{machine-hours} \end{pmatrix} - \begin{pmatrix} \$1.70 \text{ per} \\ \text{machine-hour*} \end{pmatrix} - \begin{pmatrix} \$1.50 \text{ per} \\ \text{machine-hour} \end{pmatrix}$$
$$= \$8{,}400 \text{ U}$$

$$\text{Variable overhead efficiency variance} = (AH \times SR) - (SH \times SR)$$
$$= SR(AH - SH)$$
$$= \begin{pmatrix} \$1.50 \text{ per} \\ \text{machine-hour} \end{pmatrix} - \begin{pmatrix} 42{,}000 \\ \text{machine-hours} \end{pmatrix} - \begin{pmatrix} 40{,}000 \text{ per} \\ \text{machine-hours} \end{pmatrix}$$
$$= \$3{,}000 \text{ U}$$

We can now compute the sum of all of the overhead variances as follows:

| | |
|---|---|
| Variable overhead rate variance. . . . . . . . . . . . | $ 8,400 U |
| Variable overhead efficiency variance. . . . . . . . | 3,000 U |
| Fixed overhead budget variance . . . . . . . . . . . | 8,000 U |
| Fixed overhead volume variance . . . . . . . . . . . | 60,000 U |
| Total of the overhead variances . . . . . . . . . . . | $79,400 U |

Note that the total of the overhead variances is $79,400, which equals the underapplied overhead of $79,400. In general, if the overhead is underapplied, the total of the standard cost overhead variances is unfavorable. If the overhead is overapplied, the total of the standard cost overhead variances is favorable.

---

*AR = $71,400 ÷ 42,000 machine-hours = $1.70 per machine-hour.

## GLOSSARY

**Budget variance** The difference between the actual fixed overhead costs and the budgeted fixed overhead costs for the period. (p. 442)

**Denominator activity** The level of activity used to compute the predetermined overhead rate. (p. 441)

**Volume variance** The variance that arises whenever the standard hours allowed for the actual output of a period are different from the denominator activity level that was used to compute the predetermined overhead rate. It is computed by multiplying the fixed component of the predetermined overhead rate by the difference between the denominator hours and the standard hours allowed for the actual output. (p. 443)

## ■ connect  APPENDIX 9A: EXERCISES AND PROBLEMS

### EXERCISE 9A–1  Fixed Overhead Variances LO9–7

Primara Corporation has a standard cost system in which it applies overhead to products based on the standard direct labor-hours allowed for the actual output of the period. Data concerning the most recent year appear below:

| | |
|---|---|
| Total budgeted fixed overhead cost for the year..................... | $250,000 |
| Actual fixed overhead cost for the year............................ | $254,000 |
| Budgeted direct labor-hours (denominator level of activity) ........... | 25,000 |
| Actual direct labor-hours ........................................ | 27,000 |
| Standard direct labor-hours allowed for the actual output............. | 26,000 |

**Required:**

1. Compute the fixed portion of the predetermined overhead rate for the year.
2. Compute the fixed overhead budget variance and volume variance.

### EXERCISE 9A–2  Predetermined Overhead Rate; Overhead Variances LO9–6, LO9–7

Norwall Company's budgeted variable manufacturing overhead cost is $3.00 per machine-hour and its budgeted fixed manufacturing overhead is $300,000 per month.

The following information is available for a recent month:
a. The denominator activity of 60,000 machine-hours is used to compute the predetermined overhead rate.
b. At a denominator activity of 60,000 machine-hours, the company should produce 40,000 units of product.
c. The company's actual operating results were:

| | |
|---|---|
| Number of units produced..................... | 42,000 |
| Actual machine-hours......................... | 64,000 |
| Actual variable manufacturing overhead cost .... | $185,600 |
| Actual fixed manufacturing overhead cost....... | $302,400 |

**Required:**

1. Compute the predetermined overhead rate and break it down into variable and fixed cost elements.
2. Compute the standard hours allowed for the actual production.
3. Compute the variable overhead rate and efficiency variances and the fixed overhead budget and volume variances.

### EXERCISE 9A–3  Applying Overhead in a Standard Costing System LO9–7

Privack Corporation has a standard cost system in which it applies overhead to products based on the standard direct labor-hours allowed for the actual output of the period. Data concerning the most recent year appear below:

| | |
|---|---|
| Budgeted variable overhead cost per direct labor-hour .............. | $2 |
| Total budgeted fixed overhead cost per year....................... | $250,000 |
| Budgeted direct labor-hours (denominator level of activity) ........... | 40,000 |
| Actual direct labor-hours ......................................... | 39,000 |
| Standard direct labor-hours allowed for the actual output............. | 38,000 |

*Required:*

1. Compute the predetermined overhead rate for the year. Be sure to include the total budgeted fixed overhead and the total budgeted variable overhead in the numerator of your rate.
2. Compute the amount of overhead that would be applied to the output of the period.

### EXERCISE 9A–4  Fixed Overhead Variances LO9–7

Selected operating information on three different companies for a recent year is given below:

| | Company | | |
|---|---|---|---|
| | A | B | C |
| Full-capacity machine-hours .......................... | 10,000 | 18,000 | 20,000 |
| Budgeted machine-hours* ............................ | 9,000 | 17,000 | 20,000 |
| Actual machine-hours. ................................. | 9,000 | 17,800 | 19,000 |
| Standard machine-hours allowed for actual production. .............................. | 9,500 | 16,000 | 20,000 |

*Denominator activity for computing the predetermined overhead rate.

*Required:*

For each company, state whether the company would have a favorable or unfavorable volume variance and why.

### EXERCISE 9A–5  Using Fixed Overhead Variances LO9–7

The standard cost card for the single product manufactured by Cutter, Inc., is given below:

| Inputs | (1)<br>Standard Quantity<br>or Hours | (2)<br>Standard Price<br>or Rate | Standard<br>Cost<br>(1) × (2) |
|---|---|---|---|
| Direct materials. ................. | 3 yards | $6.00 per yard | $ 18 |
| Direct labor .................... | 4 hours | $15.50 per hour | 62 |
| Variable overhead .............. | 4 hours | $1.50 per hour | 6 |
| Fixed overhead. ................. | 4 hours | $5.00 per hour | 20 |
| Total standard cost per unit ...... | | | $106 |

Manufacturing overhead is applied to production on the basis of standard direct labor-hours. During the year, the company worked 37,000 hours and manufactured 9,500 units of product. Selected data relating to the company's fixed manufacturing overhead cost for the year are shown below:

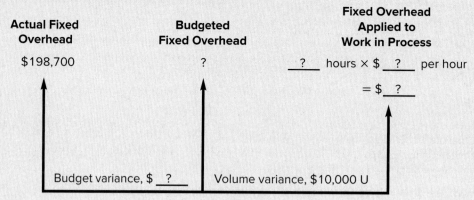

*Required:*

1. What were the standard hours allowed for the year's production?
2. What was the amount of budgeted fixed overhead cost for the year?
3. What was the fixed overhead budget variance for the year?
4. What denominator activity level did the company use in setting the predetermined overhead rate for the year?

### EXERCISE 9A–6  Predetermined Overhead Rate LO9–7

Lasser Company plans to produce 10,000 units next period at a denominator activity of 30,000 direct labor-hours. The direct labor wage rate is $12 per hour. The company's standards allow 2.5 yards of direct materials for each unit of product; the standard material cost is $8.60 per yard. The company's budget includes variable manufacturing overhead cost of $1.90 per direct labor-hour and fixed manufacturing overhead of $168,000 per period.

**Required:**

1. Using 30,000 direct labor-hours as the denominator activity, compute the predetermined overhead rate and break it down into variable and fixed elements.
2. Complete the standard cost card below for one unit of product:

| Inputs | (1) Standard Quantity or Hours | (2) Standard Price or Rate | Standard Cost (1) × (2) |
|---|---|---|---|
| Direct materials.................... | 2.5 yards | $8.60 per yard | $21.50 |
| Direct labor ...................... | ? | ? | ? |
| Variable manufacturing overhead......... | ? | ? | ? |
| Fixed manufacturing overhead .......... | ? | ? | ? |
| Total standard cost per unit ............ | | | $ ? |

### EXERCISE 9A–7   Relations Among Fixed Overhead Variances LO9–7

Selected information relating to Yost Company's operations for the most recent year is given below:

| | |
|---|---|
| **Activity:** | |
| Denominator activity (machine-hours) ......... | 45,000 |
| Standard hours allowed per unit.............. | 3 |
| Actual number of units produced.............. | 14,000 |
| **Costs:** | |
| Actual fixed overhead costs incurred .......... | $267,000 |
| Fixed overhead budget variance .............. | $3,000 F |

The company applies overhead cost to products on the basis of standard machine-hours.

**Required:**

1. What were the standard machine-hours allowed for the actual number of units produced?
2. What was the total budgeted fixed overhead cost for the period?
3. What was the fixed portion of the predetermined overhead rate?
4. What was the fixed overhead volume variance?

### PROBLEM 9A–8   Applying Overhead; Overhead Variances LO9–6, LO9–7

Lane Company manufactures a single product and applies overhead cost to that product using standard direct labor-hours. The budgeted variable manufacturing overhead is $2 per direct labor-hour and the budgeted fixed manufacturing overhead is $480,000 per year.

The standard quantity of materials is 3 pounds per unit and the standard cost is $7 per pound. The standard direct labor-hours per unit is 1.5 hours and the standard labor rate is $12 per hour.

The company planned to operate at a denominator activity level of 60,000 direct labor-hours and to produce 40,000 units of product during the most recent year. Actual activity and costs for the year were as follows:

| | |
|---|---|
| Actual number of units produced....................... | 42,000 |
| Actual direct labor-hours worked...................... | 65,000 |
| Actual variable manufacturing overhead cost incurred ..... | $123,500 |
| Actual fixed manufacturing overhead cost incurred ........ | $483,000 |

**Required:**

1. Compute the predetermined overhead rate for the year. Break the rate down into variable and fixed elements.
2. Prepare a standard cost card for the company's product; show the details for all manufacturing costs on your standard cost card.
3. Do the following:
   a. Compute the standard direct labor-hours allowed for the year's production.
   b. Complete the following Manufacturing Overhead T-account for the year:

**Manufacturing Overhead**

| ? | ? |
|---|---|
| ? | ? |

4.  Determine the reason for any underapplied or overapplied overhead for the year by computing the variable overhead rate and efficiency variances and the fixed overhead budget and volume variances.
5.  Suppose the company had chosen 65,000 direct labor-hours as the denominator activity rather than 60,000 hours. State which, if any, of the variances computed in (4) above would have changed, and explain how the variance(s) would have changed. No computations are necessary.

**PROBLEM 9A–9    Applying Overhead; Overhead Variances LO9–6, LO9–7**
Chilczuk, S.A., of Gdansk, Poland, is a major producer of classic Polish sausage. The company uses a standard cost system to help control costs. Manufacturing overhead is applied to production on the basis of standard direct labor-hours. According to the company's planning budget, the following manufacturing overhead costs should be incurred at an activity level of 35,000 labor-hours (the denominator activity level):

| | |
|---|---|
| Variable manufacturing overhead cost . . . . . | $ 87,500 |
| Fixed manufacturing overhead cost. . . . . . . | 210,000 |
| Total manufacturing overhead cost . . . . . . . | $297,500 |

During the most recent year, the following operating results were recorded:

| | |
|---|---|
| Activity: | |
| Actual labor-hours worked . . . . . . . . . . . . . . . . . . . . . . . . . . . . | 30,000 |
| Standard labor-hours allowed for the actual output . . . . . . . . | 32,000 |
| Cost: | |
| Actual variable manufacturing overhead cost incurred . . . . . | $78,000 |
| Actual fixed manufacturing overhead cost incurred. . . . . . . . | $209,400 |

At the end of the year, the company's Manufacturing Overhead account contained the following data:

**Manufacturing Overhead**

| Actual | 287,400 | Applied | 272,000 |
|---|---|---|---|
| | 15,400 | | |

Management would like to determine the cause of the $15,400 underapplied overhead.

**Required:**
1.  Compute the predetermined overhead rate. Break the rate down into variable and fixed cost elements.
2.  Show how the $272,000 Applied figure in the Manufacturing Overhead account was computed.
3.  Breakdown the $15,400 underapplied overhead into four components: (1) variable overhead rate variance, (2) variable overhead efficiency variance, (3) fixed overhead budget variance, and (4) fixed overhead volume variance.
4.  Explain the meaning of each variance that you computed in (3) above.

**PROBLEM 9A–10    Comprehensive Standard Cost Variances LO9–4, LO9–5, LO9–6, LO9–7**
"Wonderful! Not only did our salespeople do a good job in meeting the sales budget this year, but our production people did a good job in controlling costs as well," said Kim Clark, president of Martell Company. "Our $18,300 overall manufacturing cost variance is only 1.2% of the $1,536,000 standard cost of products made during the year. That's well within the 3% parameter set by management for acceptable variances. It looks like everyone will be in line for a bonus this year."
The company produces and sells a single product. The standard cost card for the product follows:

| Inputs | (1) Standard Quantity or Hours | (2) Standard Price or Rate | Standard Cost (1) × (2) |
|---|---|---|---|
| Direct materials. . . . . . . . . . . . . . . . | 2 feet | $8.45 per foot | $16.90 |
| Direct labor . . . . . . . . . . . . . . . . . . . | 1.4 hours | $16 per hour | 22.40 |
| Variable overhead . . . . . . . . . . . . . . | 1.4 hours | $2.50 per hour | 3.50 |
| Fixed overhead. . . . . . . . . . . . . . . | 1.4 hours | $6 per hour | 8.40 |
| Total standard cost per unit . . . . . . | | | $51.20 |

The following additional information is available for the year just completed:

a. The company manufactured 30,000 units of product during the year.

b. A total of 64,000 feet of material was purchased during the year at a cost of $8.55 per foot. All of this material was used to manufacture the 30,000 units produced. There were no beginning or ending inventories for the year.

c. The company worked 43,500 direct labor-hours during the year at a direct labor cost of $15.80 per hour.

d. Overhead is applied to products on the basis of standard direct labor-hours. Data relating to manufacturing overhead costs follow:

| | |
|---|---|
| Denominator activity level (direct labor-hours)................. | 35,000 |
| Budgeted fixed overhead costs ............................. | $210,000 |
| Actual variable overhead costs incurred...................... | $108,000 |
| Actual fixed overhead costs incurred ........................ | $211,800 |

**Required:**

1. Compute the materials price and quantity variances for the year.
2. Compute the labor rate and efficiency variances for the year.
3. For manufacturing overhead compute:
   a. The variable overhead rate and efficiency variances for the year.
   b. The fixed overhead budget and volume variances for the year.
4. Total the variances you have computed and compare the net amount with the $18,300 mentioned by the president. Do you agree that bonuses should be given to everyone for good cost control during the year? Explain.

**PROBLEM 9A–11 Comprehensive Standard Cost Variances LO9–4, LO9–5, LO9–6, LO9–7**

Flandro Company uses a standard cost system and sets its predetermined overhead rate on the basis of direct labor-hours. The following data are taken from the company's planning budget for the current year:

| | |
|---|---|
| Denominator activity (direct labor-hours) .................. | 5,000 |
| Variable manufacturing overhead cost .................... | $25,000 |
| Fixed manufacturing overhead cost....................... | $59,000 |

The standard cost card for the company's only product is given below:

| Inputs | (1) Standard Quantity or Hours | (2) Standard Price or Rate | Standard Cost (1) × (2) |
|---|---|---|---|
| Direct materials................. | 3 yards | $4.40 per yard | $13.20 |
| Direct labor .................... | 1 hour | $12 per hour | 12.00 |
| Manufacturing overhead......... | 1 hour | $16.80 per hour | 16.80 |
| Total standard cost per unit ...... | | | $42.00 |

During the year, the company produced 6,000 units of product and incurred the following actual results:

| | |
|---|---|
| Materials purchased, 24,000 yards at $4.80 per yard ....... | $115,200 |
| Materials used in production (in yards) ................... | 18,500 |
| Direct labor cost incurred, 5,800 hours at $13 per hour...... | $75,400 |
| Variable manufacturing overhead cost incurred ............ | $29,580 |
| Fixed manufacturing overhead cost incurred............... | $60,400 |

**Required:**

1. Create a new standard cost card that separates the variable manufacturing overhead per unit and the fixed manufacturing overhead per unit.
2. Compute the materials price and quantity variances. Also, compute the labor rate and efficiency variances.
3. Compute the variable overhead rate and efficiency variances. Also, compute the fixed overhead budget and volume variances.
4. What effect, if any, does the choice of a denominator activity level have on unit standard costs? Is the volume variance a controllable variance from a spending point of view? Explain.

**PROBLEM 9A–12  Selection of a Denominator; Overhead Analysis; Standard Cost Card LO9–6, LO9–7**

Morton Company's budgeted variable manufacturing overhead is $4.50 per direct labor-hour and its budgeted fixed manufacturing overhead is $270,000 per year.

The company manufactures a single product whose standard direct labor-hours per unit is 2 hours. The standard direct labor wage rate is $15 per hour. The standards also allow 4 feet of raw material per unit at a standard cost of $8.75 per foot.

Although normal activity is 30,000 direct labor-hours each year, the company expects to operate at a 40,000-hour level of activity this year.

*Required:*
1.  Assume that the company chooses 30,000 direct labor-hours as the denominator level of activity. Compute the predetermined overhead rate, breaking it down into variable and fixed cost elements.
2.  Assume that the company chooses 40,000 direct labor-hours as the denominator level of activity. Compute the predetermined overhead rate, breaking it down into variable and fixed cost elements.
3.  Complete two standard cost cards as outlined below.

| Inputs | (1) Standard Quantity or Hours | (2) Standard Price or Rate | Standard Cost (1) × (2) |
|---|---|---|---|
| Denominator Activity: 30,000 Direct Labor-Hours | | | |
| Direct materials .............................. | 4 feet | $8.75 per foot | $35.00 |
| Direct labor.................................. | ? | ? | ? |
| Variable manufacturing overhead.............. | ? | ? | ? |
| Fixed manufacturing overhead ............... | ? | ? | ? |
| Total standard cost per unit .................. | | | $  ? |
| Denominator Activity: 40,000 Direct Labor-Hours | | | |
| Direct materials............................. | $4 feet | $8.75 per foot | $35.00 |
| Direct labor ................................. | ? | ? | ? |
| Variable manufacturing overhead.............. | ? | ? | ? |
| Fixed manufacturing overhead ............... | ? | ? | ? |
| Total standard cost per unit .................. | | | $  ? |

4.  Assume that the company actually produces 18,000 units and works 38,000 direct labor-hours during the year. Actual manufacturing overhead costs for the year are:

| | |
|---|---|
| Variable manufacturing overhead cost ..... | $174,800 |
| Fixed manufacturing overhead cost........ | 271,600 |
| Total manufacturing overhead cost ........ | $446,400 |

Do the following:
a.  Compute the standard direct labor-hours allowed for this year's production.
b.  Complete the Manufacturing Overhead T-account below. Assume that the company uses 30,000 direct labor-hours (normal activity) as the denominator activity in computing predetermined overhead rates, as you have done in (1) above.

**Manufacturing Overhead**

| Actual costs | 446,400 | Applied costs | ? |
|---|---|---|---|
| | ? | | ? |

c.  Determine the cause of the underapplied or overapplied overhead for the year by computing the variable overhead rate and efficiency variances and the fixed overhead budget and volume variances.
5.  Looking at the variances you have computed, what appears to be the major disadvantage of using normal activity rather than expected actual activity as a denominator in computing the predetermined overhead rate? What advantages can you see to offset this disadvantage?

# APPENDIX 9B: STANDARD COST SYSTEMS: A FINANCIAL REPORTING PERSPECTIVE USING MICROSOFT EXCEL

The main body of Chapter 9 and Appendix 9A focused on calculating standard cost variances for management control purposes. This appendix explains how to use a standard cost system to create a balance sheet and an income statement for financial reporting purposes. We purposely use Microsoft Excel to create these two financial statements because it enables us to teach you a valuable managerial skill—how to evaluate a transaction's impact on the balance sheet.

To set the stage for the forthcoming example, we need to review two fundamental accounting equations and specify four important assumptions.

## Fundamental Accounting Equations

A company's balance sheet is based on the following accounting equation that is the bedrock of double-entry bookkeeping:

$$\text{Assets} = \text{Liabilities} + \text{Stockholders' Equity}$$

In the Excel spreadsheets that we'll be using in this appendix, one column will always be populated with an "=" sign. The accounts on the left-hand side of the "=" sign will be asset accounts and the accounts on the right-hand side will be liability and equity accounts. After we record every transaction, the amounts on the left-hand side of the "=" sign must equal the amounts on the right-hand side.

The second foundational equation relates to the Retained Earnings account on a company's balance sheet. The ending balance in retained earnings is computed using the following equation:

$$\text{Ending balance in retained earnings} = \text{Beginning balance in retained earnings} + \text{Net operating income} - \text{Dividends}$$

This equation highlights the connection between the balance sheet and the income statement. It explicitly recognizes the fact that net operating income from the income statement plugs into Retained Earnings on the balance sheet. In this appendix, we will not include any dividends; therefore, the only transactions that will be recorded in the Retained Earnings account will be those transactions that affect net operating income. Any transactions involving the recording of sales or the recognition of expenses will be recorded in the Retained Earnings column of the balance sheet. This approach highlights the critically important idea that a company's income statement is embedded within the Retained Earnings account in its balance sheet.

## Four Key Assumptions

The first assumption that we use in this appendix is that Raw Materials, Work in Process, and Finished Goods are always carried at their *standard cost.* In other words, the standard prices paid for inputs and the standard quantities of inputs allowed for the actual level of production *will be used to flow costs through the inventory accounts.* The actual prices paid for inputs and the actual quantities of inputs that are used in production *will not affect the costs recorded in the inventory accounts.*

This approach to standard costing greatly simplifies the bookkeeping process. To enable this simplification, we will always close all standard cost variances to Cost of Goods Sold rather than closing them to the various inventory accounts *and* Cost of Goods Sold. When the closing entry increases Cost of Goods Sold we will decrease Retained Earnings. We do this because increasing Cost of Goods Sold lowers net operating income, which in turn, lowers Retained Earnings. Conversely, when the closing entry decreases Cost of Goods Sold we will increase Retained Earnings. We do this because decreasing Cost of Goods Sold increases net operating income, which in turn, increases Retained Earnings.

The second assumption relates to the *clearing accounts* that we use to record standard cost variances. Clearing accounts always begin and end each accounting period with a zero balance. In our Excel spreadsheets, each variance will always have its own clearing account that appears on the right-hand side of the "=" sign. Putting these clearing accounts on the right-hand side of the "=" sign (rather than the left-hand side) enables us to record all favorable variances as *increases* to their respective clearing accounts and all unfavorable variances as *decreases* to their accounts. Once all variances have been recorded, the final transaction of the period will close each clearing account to Cost of Goods Sold and record the resulting change in net operating income within the Retained Earnings account.

The third assumption relates to restricting the number of general ledger accounts used in this appendix. In terms of asset accounts, we will always limit the scope of our accounts to include Cash, Raw Materials, Work in Process, Finished Goods, and Property, Plant, and Equipment, net of accumulated depreciation (which may be abbreviated as PP&E, net). With respect to liability and equity accounts, we will always use only one account—Retained Earnings.[8]

Our fourth assumption is that we'll record transactions within Microsoft Excel by using positive numbers to increase accounts and negative numbers (shown in parentheses) to decrease accounts. This is a slightly different approach than relying on the language of debits and credits. Instead of recording debits and credits, we'll identify the accounts affected by each transaction and then record increases or decreases in those accounts.

## Standard Cost Systems: An Example

Dylan Corporation manufactures only one product and uses a standard cost system for internal management and financial reporting purposes. The company uses a *plantwide predetermined overhead rate* that relies on direct labor-hours as the allocation base. All of the company's manufacturing overhead costs are fixed—it does not incur any variable manufacturing overhead costs. The predetermined overhead rate is based on a cost formula that estimated $1,875,000 of fixed manufacturing overhead for an estimated allocation base of 75,000 labor-hours.

The company wants to create an ending balance sheet and an income statement for the current year. Its beginning balance sheet is shown in Exhibit 9B–1(all numbers are in thousands). Work in Process does not appear on the beginning balance sheet because Dylan Corporation does not maintain any beginning or ending work in process inventory. A standard cost card for the company's only product is shown in Exhibit 9B–2.

## Summary of Transactions

During the year Dylan completed the following transactions:

a.　Purchased 380,000 pounds of raw material for cash at a price of $4.75 per pound.

b.　Added 365,000 pounds of raw material to work in process to produce 88,000 units.

c.　Assigned direct labor costs to work in process. The direct laborers (who were paid in cash) worked 72,000 hours at an average cost of $14.50 per hour to manufacture 88,000 units.

d.　Applied fixed overhead to work in process using the predetermined overhead rate multiplied by the number of labor-hours allowed to manufacture 88,000 units. Actual fixed overhead costs for the year were $1,750,000. Of this total, $900,000 related to items such as insurance, utilities, and indirect labor salaries that were all paid in cash and $850,000 related to depreciation of manufacturing equipment.

e.　Transferred 88,000 units from work in process to finished goods.

f.　Sold (for cash) 85,000 units to customers at a price of $62.00 per unit.

g.　Transferred the standard cost associated with the 85,000 units sold from finished goods to cost of goods sold.

h.　Paid $450,000 of selling and administrative expenses.

i.　Closed all standard cost variances to cost of goods sold.

---

[8] Ordinarily we would include a Common Stock account within the Stockholders' Equity section of the balance sheet. However, to minimize the number of columns in our spreadsheets, this appendix omits the Common Stock account and uses the term Liabilities and Equity rather than Liabilities and Stockholders' Equity.

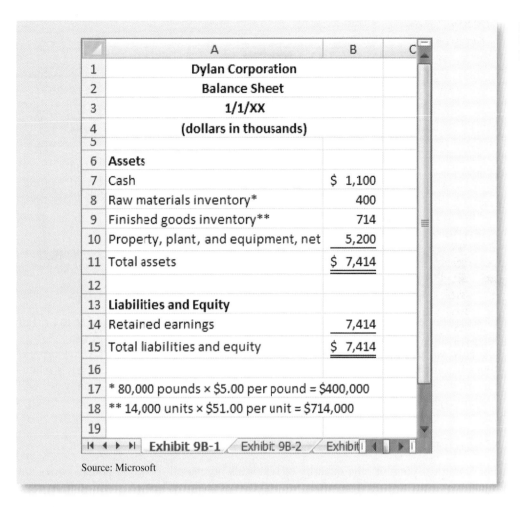

Source: Microsoft

**EXHIBIT 9B–1**
Dylan Corporation: Beginning Balance Sheet

**EXHIBIT 9B–2**
Dylan Corporation: Standard Cost Card

Exhibit 9B–3 shows the spreadsheet that we'll be using to record Dylan Corporation's transactions. Notice that cell A7 depicts the beginning balance for the period (1/1) and cell A17 depicts the ending balance (12/31). In between the beginning and ending balances, rows 8 through 16 will be used to record transactions *a* through *i*. Also, note that the beginning balances shown in row 7 of the spreadsheet (in thousands) correspond to the amounts shown in the balance sheet in Exhibit 9B–1. Finally, we want to emphasize that columns H through M represent the clearing accounts that correspond to the six variances that we'll be computing shortly. Each variance account in these six columns starts with a beginning balance of zero and concludes the period with an ending balance

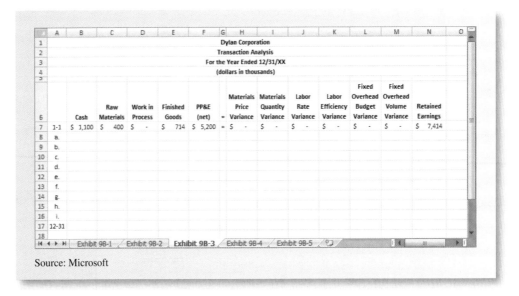

Source: Microsoft

of zero. They each record a variance for the period and then close that variance to Cost of Goods Sold at the end of the period, thereby ensuring an ending balance of zero.

Now we are ready to demonstrate a three-step process for preparing Dylan Corporation's income statement. First, we are going to compute all six of the company's manufacturing cost variances. Second, we will record transactions *a* through *i*. Finally, we will prepare Dylan's income statement for the year.

## Calculating the Variances

For Dylan Corporation, the quantity of materials purchased (380,000 pounds) does not equal the quantity used in production (365,000 pounds); therefore, the materials price variance will be based on the *quantity of materials purchased* and the materials quantity variance will be based on the *quantity of materials used in production.* The computations of these two variances are as follows:

**Materials price variance:**

Materials price variance $= (AQ \times AP) - (AQ \times SP)$

Materials price variance $= AQ(AP - SP)$

Materials price variance = 380,000 pounds ($4.75 per pound − $5.00 per pound)

Materials price variance = $95,000 F

**Materials quantity variance:**

Materials quantity variance $= (AQ \times SP) - (SQ \times SP)$

Materials quantity variance $= SP(AQ - SQ)$

Materials quantity variance = $5.00 per pound (365,000 pounds − 369,600 pounds*)

Materials quantity variance = $23,000 F

*SQ = 88,000 units produced × 4.2 pounds per unit = 369,600 pounds.

The materials price variance is favorable because the actual price per pound ($4.75) is less than the standard price per pound ($5.00). The materials quantity variance is favorable because the 365,000 pounds used in production are less than the 369,600 pounds (= 88,000 units × 4.2 pounds per unit) that the standards allow for the actual level of output.

The direct labor rate and efficiency variances are computed as follows:

**Labor rate variance:**

Labor rate variance = $(AH \times AR) - (AH \times SR)$

Labor rate variance = $AH(AR - SR)$

Labor rate variance = 72,000 hours ($14.50 per hour − $15.00 per hour)

Labor rate variance = $36,000 F

**Labor efficiency variance:**

Labor efficiency variance = $(AH \times SR) - (SH \times SR)$

Labor efficiency variance = $SR(AH - SH)$

Labor efficiency variance = $15.00 per hour (72,000 hours − 66,000 hours*)

Labor efficiency variance = $90,000 U

*SQ = 88,000 units produced x 0.75 hours per unit = 66,000 hours.

The labor rate variance is favorable because the actual labor rate ($14.50) is less than the standard labor rate ($15.00). The labor efficiency variance is unfavorable because the 72,000 hours actually worked are greater than the 66,000 hours (= 88,000 units × 0.75 hours per unit) that the standards allow for the actual level of output.

The fixed overhead budget and volume variances are computed as follows:

**Budget variance:**

Budget variance = Actual fixed overhead − Budgeted fixed overhead

Budget variance = $1,750,000 − $1,875,000

Budget variance = $125,000 F

**Volume variance:**

Volume variance = Budgeted fixed overhead − Fixed overhead applied to work in process

Volume variance = $1,875,000 − $1,650,000*

Volume variance = $225,000 U

*Fixed overhead applied to work in process = 66,000 hours allowed for the actual output × $25 per hour = $1,650,000.

The fixed overhead budget variance of $125,000 is favorable (F) because the actual amount of fixed overhead ($1,750,000) is less than the budgeted amount of fixed overhead ($1,875,000), whereas the fixed overhead volume variance of $225,000 is unfavorable (U) because the budgeted fixed overhead ($1,875,000) is greater than the fixed overhead applied to work in process ($1,650,000). The fixed overhead applied to work in process is calculated by multiplying the predetermined overhead rate ($25.00) by the *number of direct labor-hours allowed for the actual level of production* (66,000 hours). Fixed overhead is *not* applied to production using the actual direct labor-hours worked!

## Recording the Transactions

Exhibit 9B–4 shows how to properly record all of the transactions for Dylan Corporation (all amounts are in thousands). You'll notice that all favorable variances (in columns H through M) are recorded without parentheses and all unfavorable variances (in columns H through M) are recorded with parentheses. This occurs because favorable variances increase net operating income (and retained earnings) when they are closed to cost of goods sold and unfavorable variances decrease net operating income (and retained

**EXHIBIT 9B–4**
Dylan Corporation: Transaction Analysis

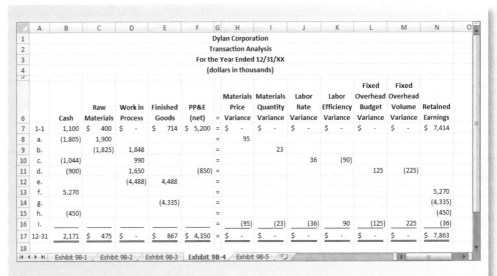

Dylan Corporation
Transaction Analysis
For the Year Ended 12/31/XX
(dollars in thousands)

| | Cash | Raw Materials | Work in Process | Finished Goods | PP&E (net) | = | Materials Price Variance | Materials Quantity Variance | Labor Rate Variance | Labor Efficiency Variance | Fixed Overhead Budget Variance | Fixed Overhead Volume Variance | Retained Earnings |
|---|---|---|---|---|---|---|---|---|---|---|---|---|---|
| 1-1 | 1,100 | $ 400 | $ - | $ 714 | $ 5,200 | = | $ - | $ - | $ - | $ - | $ - | $ - | $ 7,414 |
| a. | (1,805) | 1,900 | | | | = | 95 | | | | | | |
| b. | | (1,825) | 1,848 | | | = | | 23 | | | | | |
| c. | (1,044) | | 990 | | | = | | | 36 | (90) | | | |
| d. | (900) | | 1,650 | | (850) | = | | | | | 125 | (225) | |
| e. | | | (4,488) | 4,488 | | = | | | | | | | |
| f. | 5,270 | | | | | = | | | | | | | 5,270 |
| g. | | | | (4,335) | | = | | | | | | | (4,335) |
| h. | (450) | | | | | = | | | | | | | (450) |
| i. | | | | | | = | (95) | (23) | (36) | 90 | (125) | 225 | (36) |
| 12-31 | 2,171 | $ 475 | $ - | $ 867 | $ 4,350 | = | $ - | $ - | $ - | $ - | $ - | $ - | $ 7,863 |

Exhibit 9B-1 | Exhibit 9B-2 | Exhibit 9B-3 | **Exhibit 9B-4** | Exhibit 9B-5

The explanations for transactions *a* through *i* (as recorded above) are as follows:

a. Cash decreases by the actual cost of the raw materials purchased, which is AQ × AP (380,000 × $4.75 = $1,805,000). Raw Materials increase by the standard cost of the raw materials purchased, which is AQ × SP (380,000 × 5 = $1,900,000). The materials price variance is $95,000 F.

b. Raw Materials decrease by the standard cost of the raw materials used in production, which is AQ × SP (365,000 × $5.00 = $1,825,000). Work in Process increases by the standard cost of the standard quantity of raw materials allowed for the actual output, which is SQ × SP (369,600 × $5.00 = $1,848,000). The materials quantity variance is $23,000 F.

c. Cash decreases by the actual amount paid to direct laborers, which is AH × AR (72,000 × $14.50 = $1,044,000). Work in Process increases by the standard cost of the standard amount of hours allowed for the actual output, which is SH × SR (66,000 × $15.00 = $990,000). The labor rate variance is $36,000 F and the labor efficiency variance is $90,000 U.

d. Cash decreases by the actual amount paid for various fixed overhead costs, which is $900,000. Work in Process increases by the standard amount of hours allowed for the actual output multiplied by the predetermined overhead rate, which is 66,000 hours × $25.00 per hour = $1,650,000. PP&E (net) decreases by the amount of depreciation for the period, which is $850,000. The fixed overhead budget variance is $125,000 F and the fixed overhead volume variance is $225,000 U.

e. Work in process decreases by the number of units transferred to Finished Goods multiplied by the standard cost per unit, which is 88,000 units × $51.00 per unit = $4,488,000. Finished Goods increases by the same amount.

f. Cash increases by the number of units sold multiplied by the selling price per unit, which is 85,000 units sold × $62.00 per unit = $5,270,000. Retained Earnings increases by the same amount.

g. Finished Goods decrease by the number of units sold multiplied by their standard cost per unit, which is 85,000 units sold × $51.00 per unit = $4,335,000. Retained Earnings decreases by the same amount.

h. Cash and Retained Earnings decrease by $450,000 to record the selling and administrative expenses.

i. All variance accounts take their balance to zero as they are closed to Cost of Goods Sold. The net effect of closing all of these variances is to increase Cost of Goods Sold by $36,000. The equation supporting this logic is as follows: $(95,000) + $(23,000) + $(36,000) + $90,000 + $(125,000) + $225,000 = $36,000. Because Cost of Goods Sold increases by $36,000, it lowers net operating income and Retained Earnings by the same amount.

Source: Microsoft

earnings) when they are closed to cost of goods sold. For example, the materials price variance of $95,000 F appears in cell H8 without parentheses. To close this variance, we record $(95,000) in cell H16, thereby bringing the ending balance in the Materials Price Variance clearing account to zero. The $(95,000) in cell H16 is offset by adding $95,000 to Retained Earnings. When all six variances are closed to Cost of Goods Sold, their combined effect is to reduce net operating income and Retained Earnings by the $(36,000) shown in cell N16.

Once all transactions are recorded, Microsoft Excel can quickly compute the ending balances for all balance sheet accounts as shown in row 17 of Exhibit 9B–4. Notice that all of the variance accounts (in columns H through M) have an ending balance of zero because they all serve as clearing accounts. Also note that the inventory accounts in the ending balance sheet are valued using *standard costs*. For example, the ending balance in Raw Materials ($475,000) consists of 95,000 pounds of materials each carried in inventory at a standard cost of $5.00 per pound. The ending balance in Finished Goods ($867,000) consists of 17,000 units each valued at a standard cost of $51.00 per unit.

## Preparing the Income Statement

Exhibit 9B–5 shows Dylan Corporation's income statement that is derived from the Retained Earnings column of Exhibit 9B–4. The sales in the income statement of $5,270,000 come from cell N13 in Exhibit 9B–4. The cost of goods sold at standard ($4,335,000) comes from cell N14 of Exhibit 9B–4. Finally, the sum of the variance adjustments ($36,000) and the selling and administrative expenses ($450,000) come from cells N16 and N15, respectively. Although all of the numbers in Exhibit 9B–5 are shown as positive numbers, the cost of goods sold at standard ($4,335,000), the selling and administrative expenses ($450,000), and the variance adjustments ($36,000) are shown as negative numbers in column N of Exhibit 9B–4 to recognize that they each reduce retained earnings.

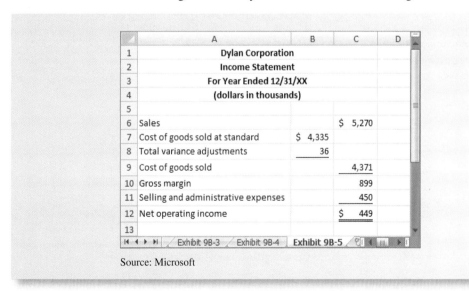

Source: Microsoft

**EXHIBIT 9B–5**
Dylan Corporation: Income Statement

# APPENDIX 9B: EXERCISES AND PROBLEMS

**EXERCISE 9B–1   Standard Cost Flows; Income Statement Preparation LO9–8**
Forsyth Company manufactures one product, it does not maintain any beginning or ending inventories, and its uses a standard cost system. During the year, the company produced and sold 10,000 units at a price of $135 per unit. Its standard cost per unit produced is $105 and its selling and administrative expenses

totaled $235,000. Forsyth does not have any variable manufacturing overhead costs and it recorded the following variances during the year:

| | |
|---|---|
| Materials price variance ....................... | $6,500 F |
| Materials quantity variance..................... | $10,200 U |
| Labor rate variance ........................... | $3,500 U |
| Labor efficiency variance ...................... | $4,400 F |
| Fixed overhead budget variance................ | $2,500 F |
| Fixed overhead volume variance ............... | $12,000 F |

**Required:**
1. When Forsyth closes its standard cost variances, the cost of goods sold will increase (decrease) by how much?
2. Using Exhibit 9B–5 as a guide, prepare an income statement for the year.

**EXERCISE 9B–2   Standard Cost Flows; Income Statement Preparation** LO9–8
Swain Company manufactures one product, it does not maintain any beginning or ending inventories, and its uses a standard cost system. The company's beginning balance in Retained Earnings is $70,000. It sells one product for $165 per unit and it generated total sales during the period of $577,500 while incurring selling and administrative expenses of $54,000. Swain Company does not have any variable manufacturing overhead costs and its standard cost card for its only product is as follows:

| | (1)<br>Standard Quantity<br>or Hours | (2)<br>Standard Price<br>or Rate | Standard<br>Cost<br>(1) × (2) |
|---|---|---|---|
| Direct materials................. | 7.0 pounds | $9 per pound | $ 63 |
| Direct labor .................... | 2.5 hours | $12 per hour | 30 |
| Fixed manufacturing overhead ... | 2.5 hours | $20 per hour | 50 |
| Total standard cost per unit ...... | | | $143 |

During the period, Swain recorded the following variances:

| | |
|---|---|
| Materials price variance ....................... | $3,400 U |
| Materials quantity variance..................... | $9,000 F |
| Labor rate variance ........................... | $3,900 U |
| Labor efficiency variance ...................... | $6,600 U |
| Fixed overhead budget variance................ | $1,300 U |
| Fixed overhead volume variance ............... | $5,500 F |

**Required:**
1. When Swain closes its standard cost variances, the cost of goods sold will increase (decrease) by how much?
2. Using Exhibit 9B–5 as a guide, prepare an income statement for the year.
3. What is Swain's ending balance in Retained Earnings?

**EXERCISE 9B–3   Standard Cost Flows** LO9–8
Bowen Company manufactures one product, it does not maintain any beginning or ending inventories, and its uses a standard cost system. Its predetermined overhead rate includes $1,000,000 of fixed overhead in the numerator and 50,000 direct labor-hours in the denominator. The company purchased (with cash) and used 30,000 yards of raw materials at a cost of $9.80 per yard. Its direct laborers worked 20,000 hours and

were paid a total of $290,000. The company started and completed 8,100 units of finished goods during the period. Bowen's standard cost card for its only product is as follows:

| Inputs | (1)<br>Standard Quantity<br>or Hours | (2)<br>Standard Price<br>or Rate | Standard<br>Cost<br>(1) × (2) |
|---|---|---|---|
| Direct materials. . . . . . . . . . . . . . . . | 3.0 yards | $10.00 per yard | $ 30.00 |
| Direct labor . . . . . . . . . . . . . . . . . . . | 2.4 hours | $14.00 per hour | 33.60 |
| Fixed manufacturing overhead . . . | 2.4 hours | $20.00 per hour | 48.00 |
| Total standard cost per unit . . . . . . | | | $111.60 |

*Required:*
1. When recording the raw material purchases:
   a. The Raw Materials inventory will increase (decrease) by how much?
   b. The Cash will increase (decrease) by how much?
2. When recording the raw materials used in production:
   a. The Raw Materials inventory will increase (decrease) by how much?
   b. The Work in Process inventory will increase (decrease) by how much?
3. When recording the direct labor costs added to production:
   a. The Work in Process inventory will increase (decrease) by how much?
   b. The Cash will increase (decrease) by how much?
4. When applying fixed manufacturing overhead to production, the Work in Process inventory will increase (decrease) by how much?
5. When transferring manufacturing costs from Work in Process to Finished Goods, the Finished Goods inventory will increase (decrease) by how much?

**EXERCISE 9B–4    Standard Cost Flows LO9–8**
Hartwell Company manufactures one product, it does not maintain any beginning or ending inventories, and its uses a standard cost system. Its predetermined overhead rate includes $1,760,000 of fixed manufacturing overhead in the numerator and 44,000 direct labor-hours in the denominator. The actual fixed manufacturing overhead for the period was $1,780,000.

The company purchased (with cash) and used 60,000 yards of raw materials at a cost of $11.00 per yard. Its direct laborers worked 40,000 hours and were paid a total of $600,000. The company started and completed 28,000 units of finished goods during the period. Bowen's standard cost card for its only product is as follows:

| Inputs | (1)<br>Standard Quantity<br>or Hours | (2)<br>Standard Price<br>or Rate | Standard<br>Cost<br>(1) × (2) |
|---|---|---|---|
| Direct materials. . . . . . . . . . . . . . . . | 2 yards | $12.00 per yard | $ 24.00 |
| Direct labor . . . . . . . . . . . . . . . . . . . | 1.5 hours | $15.00 per hour | 22.50 |
| Fixed manufacturing overhead . . . | 1.5 hours | $40.00 per hour | 60.00 |
| Total standard cost per unit . . . . . . | | | $106.50 |

*Required:*
1. When recording the raw material purchases (on account):
   a. The Raw Materials inventory will increase (decrease) by how much?
   b. The Cash will increase (decrease) by how much?
   c. The materials price variance will be favorable or unfavorable and by how much?
2. When recording the raw materials used in production:
   a. The Raw Materials inventory will increase (decrease) by how much?
   b. The Work in Process inventory will increase (decrease) by how much?
   c. The materials quantity variance will be favorable or unfavorable and by how much?

3.  When recording the direct labor costs added to production:
    a.  The Work in Process inventory will increase (decrease) by how much?
    b.  The Cash will increase (decrease) by how much?
    c.  The labor rate and efficiency variances will be favorable or unfavorable and by how much?
4.  When applying fixed manufacturing overhead to production:
    a.  The Work in Process inventory will increase (decrease) by how much?
    b.  The fixed overhead budget and volume variances will be favorable or unfavorable and by how much?
5.  When transferring costs from Work in Process to Finished Goods, the Finished Goods inventory will increase (decrease) by how much?

**PROBLEM 9B–5   Transaction Analysis; Income Statement Preparation** LO9–4, LO9–5, LO9–7, LO9–8

Wallis Company manufactures only one product and uses a standard cost system. The company uses a predetermined plantwide overhead rate that relies on direct labor-hours as the allocation base. All of the company's manufacturing overhead costs are fixed—it does not incur any variable manufacturing overhead costs. The predetermined overhead rate is based on a cost formula that estimated $2,880,000 of fixed manufacturing overhead for an estimated allocation base of 288,000 direct labor-hours. Wallis does not maintain any beginning or ending work in process inventory.

The company's beginning balance sheet is as follows:

**Wallis Company**
**Balance Sheet**
**1/1/XX**
**(dollars in thousands)**

**Assets**

| | |
|---|---|
| Cash | $   700 |
| Raw materials inventory | 150 |
| Finished goods inventory | 270 |
| Property, plant, and equipment, net | 8,500 |
| Total assets | $9,620 |

**Liabilities and Equity**

| | |
|---|---|
| Retained earnings | $9,620 |
| Total liabilities and equity | $9,620 |

The company's standard cost card for its only product is as follows:

| Inputs | (1) Standard Quantity or Hours | (2) Standard Price or Rate | Standard Cost (1) × (2) |
|---|---|---|---|
| Direct materials | 2 pounds | $30.00 per pound | $  60.00 |
| Direct labor | 3.00 hours | $15.00 per hour | 45.00 |
| Fixed manufacturing overhead | 3.00 hours | $10.00 per hour | 30.00 |
| Total standard cost per unit | | | $135.00 |

During the year Wallis completed the following transactions:
a.  Purchased (with cash) 230,000 pounds of raw material at a price of $29.50 per pound.
b.  Added 215,000 pounds of raw material to work in process to produce 95,000 units.
c.  Assigned direct labor costs to work in process. The direct laborers (who were paid in cash) worked 245,000 hours at an average cost of $16.00 per hour to manufacture 95,000 units.
d.  Applied fixed overhead to work in process inventory using the predetermined overhead rate multiplied by the number of direct labor-hours allowed to manufacture 95,000 units. Actual fixed overhead costs

for the year were $2,740,000. Of this total, $1,340,000 related to items such as insurance, utilities, and salaried indirect laborers that were all paid in cash and $1,400,000 related to depreciation of equipment.

e.  Transferred 95,000 units from work in process to finished goods.

f.  Sold (for cash) 92,000 units to customers at a price of $170 per unit.

g.  Transferred the standard cost associated with the 92,000 units sold from finished goods to cost of goods sold.

h.  Paid $2,120,000 of selling and administrative expenses.

i.  Closed all standard cost variances to cost of goods sold.

### Required:

1.  Compute all direct materials, direct labor, and fixed overhead variances for the year.
2.  Using Exhibit 9B–3 as a guide, record transactions *a* through *i* for Wallis Company.
3.  Compute the ending balances for Wallis Company's balance sheet.
4.  Using Exhibit 9B–5 as a guide, prepare Wallis Company's income statement for the year.

**PROBLEM 9B–6   Transaction Analysis; Income Statement Preparation** LO9–4, LO9–5, LO9–6, LO9–7, LO9–8

Phoenix Company manufactures only one product and uses a standard cost system. The company uses a plantwide predetermined overhead rate that relies on direct labor-hours as the allocation base. The predetermined overhead rate is based on a cost formula that estimated $2,880,000 of fixed and variable manufacturing overhead for an estimated allocation base of 240,000 direct labor-hours. Phoenix does not maintain any beginning or ending work in process inventory.

The company's beginning balance sheet is as follows:

| Phoenix Company Balance Sheet 1/1/XX (dollars in thousands) | |
| --- | --- |
| **Assets** | |
| Cash | $ 1,200 |
| Raw materials inventory | 300 |
| Finished goods inventory | 540 |
| All other assets | 12,000 |
| Total assets | $14,040 |
| | |
| **Liabilities and Equity** | |
| Retained earnings | $14,040 |
| Total liabilities and equity | $14,040 |

The company's standard cost card for its only product is as follows:

| Inputs | (1) Standard Quantity or Hours | (2) Standard Price or Rate | Standard Cost (1) × (2) |
| --- | --- | --- | --- |
| Direct materials | 3 pounds | $25.00 per pound | $ 75.00 |
| Direct labor | 2.00 hours | $16.00 per hour | 32.00 |
| Variable manufacturing overhead | 2.00 hours | $2.00 per hour | 4.00 |
| Fixed manufacturing overhead | 2.00 hours | $10.00 per hour | 20.00 |
| Total standard cost per unit | | | $131.00 |

During the year Phoenix completed the following transactions:

a.  Purchased (with cash) 460,000 pounds of raw material at a price of $26.50 per pound.

b.  Added 430,000 pounds of raw material to work in process to produce 125,000 units.

c.  Assigned direct labor costs to work in process. The direct laborers (who were paid in cash) worked 265,000 hours at an average cost of $15.00 per hour to manufacture 125,000 units.

d.  Applied variable manufacturing overhead to work in process inventory using the variable portion of the predetermined overhead rate multiplied by the number of direct labor-hours allowed to manufacture 125,000 units. Actual variable manufacturing overhead costs for the year (all paid in cash) were $480,000.

e.  Applied fixed manufacturing overhead to work in process inventory using the fixed portion of the predetermined overhead rate multiplied by the number of direct labor-hours allowed to manufacture 125,000 units. Actual fixed manufacturing overhead costs for the year were $2,450,000. Of this total, $1,300,000 related to items such as insurance, utilities, and salaried indirect laborers that were all paid in cash and $1,150,000 related to depreciation of equipment.

f.  Transferred 125,000 units from work in process to finished goods.

g.  Sold (for cash) 123,000 units to customers at a price of $175 per unit.

h.  Transferred the standard cost associated with the 123,000 units sold from finished goods to cost of goods sold.

i.  Paid $3,300,000 of selling and administrative expenses.

j.  Closed all standard cost variances to cost of goods sold.

**Required:**

1.  Compute all direct materials, direct labor, variable overhead, and fixed overhead variances for the year.

2.  Using Exhibit 9B–3 as a guide, record transactions *a* through *j* for Phoenix Company.

3.  Compute the ending balances for Phoenix Company's balance sheet.

4.  Using Exhibit 9B–5 as a guide, prepare Phoenix Company's income statement for the year.

## A LOOK BACK

In Chapter 9, we looked at flexible budgets and spending variances. Standards were used to isolate the effects of various factors on actual results. In particular, we computed material, labor, and overhead variances.

## A LOOK AT THIS CHAPTER

In Chapter 10 we continue our coverage of performance measurement. Return on investment and residual income measures are used to motivate managers and monitor progress. The balanced scorecard is an integrated set of performance measures that are derived from and support the organization's strategy.

## A LOOK AHEAD

In Chapter 11, we concentrate on the identification of differential costs and benefits to aid decision making.

# 10

# Performance Measurement in Decentralized Organizations

## CHAPTER OUTLINE

**Decentralization in Organizations**

- Advantages and Disadvantages of Decentralization

**Responsibility Accounting**

- Cost, Profit, and Investment Centers

**Evaluating Investment Center Performance—Return on Investment**

- The Return on Investment (ROI) Formula
- Net Operating Income and Operating Assets Defined
- Understanding ROI
- Criticisms of ROI

**Residual Income**

- Motivation and Residual Income
- Divisional Comparison and Residual Income

**Operating Performance Measures**

- Throughput (Manufacturing Cycle) Time
- Delivery Cycle Time
- Manufacturing Cycle Efficiency (MCE)

**Balanced Scorecard**

- Common Characteristics of Balanced Scorecards
- A Company's Strategy and the Balanced Scorecard
- Tying Compensation to the Balanced Scorecard

©Luke Sharrett/Bloomberg/Getty Images

# A Strategy of Scarcity

**Old Rip Van Winkle Distillery** employs two people: Julian Van Winkle III and his son Preston. Its annual sales of $2 million pale in comparison to larger competitors such as **Makers' Mark** and **Wild Turkey**. Although the company could easily triple its sales volume, it chooses to limit sales to 7,000 cases of bourbon per year. Given that the company's 20-year-old aged whiskey once achieved an unprecedented "99" rating from the **Beverage Tasting Institute of Chicago**, demand for the company's products far exceeds its supply—thereby enabling regular price increases. For example, a fifth of 20-year-old Pappy Van Winkle bourbon sells for $110. As you'll learn in this chapter, the Old Rip Van Winkle Distillery purposely foregoes turnover in favor of earning large margins on its award-winning products.

Source: Dumaine, Brian, "Creating the Ultimate Cult Brand," *Fortune,* February 28, 2011, 21–24.

**E**xcept in very small organizations, a company's owners and its top managers must delegate decision-making authority to others. When a company's owners (e.g., stockholders) delegate decision-making authority to top managers, they employ *corporate governance systems* to direct and control the actions of those managers. When properly implemented, corporate governance systems provide incentives and feedback mechanisms to help ensure that a company's board of directors and top managers pursue goals that align with the owners' interests.[1] Similarly, when a company's top managers delegate decision-making authority to subordinates, they employ *management control systems* to direct and control the actions of those subordinates. When properly implemented, management control systems provide incentives and feedback mechanisms to help ensure that all of a company's employees pursue goals that align with its interests.

This chapter explains a variety of performance measures that a company can use to align its employees' incentives and actions with its overall interests. First, it discusses the advantages and disadvantages of decentralization. Next, it provides a brief overview of responsibility accounting systems followed by a discussion of two performance measures commonly used within those systems—return on investment (ROI) and residual income. The chapter concludes with an overview of operating performance measures and the balanced scorecard.

# DECENTRALIZATION IN ORGANIZATIONS

In a **decentralized organization,** decision-making authority is spread throughout the organization rather than being confined to a few top executives. As noted above, out of necessity all large organizations are decentralized to some extent. Organizations do differ, however, in the extent to which they are decentralized. In strongly centralized organizations, decision-making authority is reluctantly delegated to lower-level managers who have little freedom to make decisions. In strongly decentralized organizations, even the lowest-level managers are empowered to make as many decisions as possible. Most organizations fall somewhere between these two extremes.

## Advantages and Disadvantages of Decentralization

The major advantages of decentralization include:

1. By delegating day-to-day problem solving to lower-level managers, top-level managers can concentrate on bigger issues, such as overall strategy.
2. Empowering lower-level managers to make decisions puts the decision-making authority in the hands of those who tend to have the most detailed and up-to-date information about day-to-day operations.
3. By eliminating layers of decision making and approvals, organizations can respond more quickly to customers and to changes in the operating environment.
4. Granting decision-making authority helps train lower-level managers for higher-level positions.
5. Empowering lower-level managers to make decisions can increase their motivation and job satisfaction.

The major disadvantages of decentralization include:

1. Lower-level managers may make decisions without fully understanding the company's overall strategy.
2. If lower-level managers make their own decisions independently of each other, coordination may be lacking.

---

[1]These comments on corporate governance were adapted from the 2004 report titled OECD Principles of Corporate Governance published by the Organization for Economic Co-Operation and Development.

3. Lower-level managers may have objectives that clash with the objectives of the entire organization.[2] For example, a manager may be more interested in increasing the size of his or her department, leading to more power and prestige, than in increasing the department's effectiveness.

4. Spreading innovative ideas may be difficult in a decentralized organization. Someone in one part of the organization may have a terrific idea that would benefit other parts of the organization, but without strong central direction the idea may not be shared with, and adopted by, other parts of the organization.

# RESPONSIBILITY ACCOUNTING

Decentralized organizations need *responsibility accounting systems* that link lower-level managers' decision-making authority with accountability for the outcomes of those decisions. The term **responsibility center** is used for any part of an organization whose manager has control over and is accountable for cost, profit, or investments. The three primary types of responsibility centers are *cost centers, profit centers,* and *investment centers.*

## Cost, Profit, and Investment Centers

**Cost Center**   The manager of a **cost center** has control over costs, but not over revenue or the use of investment funds. Service departments such as accounting, finance, general administration, legal, and personnel are usually classified as cost centers. In addition, manufacturing facilities are often treated as cost centers. The managers of cost centers are expected to minimize costs while providing the level of products and services needed by other parts of the organization. For example, the manager of a manufacturing facility would be evaluated at least in part by comparing actual costs to how much costs should have been for the actual level of output during the period. Standard cost variances and flexible budget variances, such as those discussed in earlier chapters, are often used to evaluate cost center performance.

**Profit Center**   The manager of a **profit center** has control over both costs and revenue, but not over the use of investment funds. For example, the manager in charge of a **Six Flags** amusement park would be responsible for both the revenues and costs, and hence the profits, of the amusement park, but may not have control over major investments in the park. Profit center managers are often evaluated by comparing actual profit to targeted or budgeted profit.

**Investment Center**   The manager of an **investment center** has control over cost, revenue, and investments in operating assets. For example, **General Motors'** vice president of manufacturing in North America would have a great deal of discretion over investments in manufacturing—such as investing in equipment to produce more fuel-efficient engines. Once General Motors' top-level managers and board of directors approve the vice president's investment proposals, he is held responsible for making them pay off. As discussed in the next section, investment center managers are often evaluated using return on investment (ROI) or residual income measures.

---

[2]Similar problems exist with top-level managers as well. The shareholders of the company delegate their decision-making authority to the top managers. Unfortunately, top managers may abuse that trust by rewarding themselves and their friends too generously, spending too much company money on palatial offices, and so on. The issue of how to ensure that top managers act in the best interests of the company's owners continues to challenge experts. To a large extent, the owners rely on performance evaluation using return on investment and residual income measures, as discussed later in the chapter, and on bonuses and stock options. The stock market is also an important disciplining mechanism. If top managers squander the company's resources, the price of the company's stock will almost surely fall—possibly resulting in a loss of prestige, bonuses, and a job. And, of course, particularly outrageous self-dealing may land a CEO in court.

1. Managers in which of the following responsibility centers are held responsible for profits? (You may select more than one answer.)
   a. Revenue centers
   b. Cost centers
   c. Profit centers
   d. Investment centers

# EVALUATING INVESTMENT CENTER PERFORMANCE—RETURN ON INVESTMENT

**LEARNING OBJECTIVE 10–1**

Compute return on investment (ROI) and show how changes in sales, expenses, and assets affect ROI.

An investment center is responsible for earning an adequate return on investment. The following two sections present two methods for evaluating this aspect of an investment center's performance. The first method, covered in this section, is called *return on investment* (ROI). The second method, covered in the next section, is called *residual income.*

## The Return on Investment (ROI) Formula

**Return on investment (ROI)** is defined as net operating income divided by average operating assets:

$$\text{ROI} = \frac{\text{Net operating income}}{\text{Average operating assets}}$$

The higher a business segment's return on investment (ROI), the greater the profit earned per dollar invested in the segment's operating assets.

## Net Operating Income and Operating Assets Defined

Note that *net operating income,* rather than net income, is used in the ROI formula. **Net operating income** is income before interest and taxes and is sometimes referred to as EBIT (earnings before interest and taxes). Net operating income is used in the formula because the base (i.e., denominator) consists of *operating assets.* To be consistent, we use net operating income in the numerator.

Operating assets include cash, accounts receivable, inventory, plant and equipment, and all other assets held for operating purposes. Examples of assets that are not included in operating assets (i.e., examples of nonoperating assets) include land held for future use, an investment in another company, or a building rented to someone else. These assets are not held for operating purposes and therefore are excluded from operating assets. The operating assets base used in the formula is typically computed as the average of the operating assets between the beginning and the end of the year.

Most companies use the net book value (i.e., acquisition cost less accumulated depreciation) of depreciable assets to calculate average operating assets. This approach has drawbacks. An asset's net book value decreases over time as the accumulated depreciation increases. This decreases the denominator in the ROI calculation, thus increasing ROI. Consequently, ROI mechanically increases over time. Moreover, replacing old depreciated equipment with new equipment increases the book value of depreciable assets and decreases ROI. Hence, using net book value in the calculation of average operating assets results in a predictable pattern of increasing ROI over time as accumulated depreciation grows and discourages replacing old equipment with new, updated equipment. An alternative to using net book value is the gross cost of the asset, which ignores accumulated depreciation. Gross cost stays constant over time because depreciation is ignored;

therefore, ROI does not grow automatically over time, and replacing a fully depreciated asset with a comparably priced new asset will not adversely affect ROI.

Nevertheless, most companies use the net book value approach to computing average operating assets because it is consistent with their financial reporting practices of recording the net book value of assets on the balance sheet and including depreciation as an operating expense on the income statement. In this text, we will use the net book value approach unless a specific exercise or problem directs otherwise.

## Understanding ROI

The equation for ROI, net operating income divided by average operating assets, does not provide much help to managers interested in taking actions to improve their ROI. It only offers two levers for improving performance—net operating income and average operating assets. Fortunately, ROI can also be expressed in terms of **margin** and **turnover** as follows:

$$ROI = Margin \times Turnover$$

where

$$Margin = \frac{Net\ operating\ income}{Sales}$$

and

$$Turnover = \frac{Sales}{Average\ operating\ assets}$$

Note that the sales terms in the margin and turnover formulas cancel out when they are multiplied together, yielding the original formula for ROI stated in terms of net operating income and average operating assets. So either formula for ROI will give the same answer. However, the margin and turnover formulation provides some additional insights.

Margin and turnover are important concepts in understanding how a manager can affect ROI. All other things the same, margin is ordinarily improved by increasing selling prices, reducing operating expenses, or increasing unit sales. Increasing selling prices and reducing operating expenses both increase net operating income and therefore margin. Increasing unit sales also ordinarily increases the margin because of operating leverage. As discussed in a previous chapter, because of operating leverage, a given percentage increase in unit sales usually leads to an even larger percentage increase in net operating income. Therefore, an increase in unit sales ordinarily has the effect of increasing margin. Some managers tend to focus too much on margin and ignore turnover. However, turnover incorporates a crucial area of a manager's responsibility—the investment in operating assets. Excessive funds tied up in operating assets (e.g., cash, accounts receivable, inventories, plant and equipment, and other assets) depress turnover and lower ROI. In fact, excessive operating assets can be just as much of a drag on ROI as excessive operating expenses, which depress margin.

### HELPFUL HINT

To better understand the concepts of margin and turnover, link them to actual companies. For example, the local jewelry store in your hometown relies more on margin than turnover to generate a satisfactory return on investment (ROI). It completes a small number of transactions each day, so to be profitable it needs to earn a high margin per transaction. Conversely, Walmart relies more on turnover than margin to generate its ROI. Walmart completes an enormous number of transactions each day so, even though each transaction earns a very small margin, the company's extraordinary turnover creates a favorable ROI.

## Home Remodeling ROI Is Less Than You Might Think

©Irina Mos/Shutterstock.com RF

When it comes to home remodeling the return on investment (ROI) is calculated by taking the increase in a home's resale value due to the remodel divided by the cost of the remodeling project. While realtors often claim that remodeling projects have an ROI of at least 100% (meaning the increase in the home's resale value equals or exceeds the cost of the remodeling project), research from *Remodeling* magazine suggests otherwise. The table below summarizes the ROI of six types of remodeling projects. In each case the data indicate that homeowners would be better off selling their homes without investing in the remodeling project.

| Project | (a) Increase in Resale Value | (b) Investment in Project | ROI (a) ÷ (b) |
|---|---|---|---|
| Deck addition . . . . . . . . . . . . . . . . . . . . . . . . . | $20,532 | $34,403 | 59.7% |
| Roofing replacement . . . . . . . . . . . . . . . . . . . . | $19,194 | $33,880 | 56.7% |
| Garage addition . . . . . . . . . . . . . . . . . . . . . . . | $ 44,034 | $80,511 | 54.7% |
| Master-suite addition . . . . . . . . . . . . . . . . . . . | $114,569 | $220,086 | 52.1% |
| Major kitchen remodel . . . . . . . . . . . . . . . . . . | $64,113 | $107,406 | 59.7% |
| Siding replacement (fiber-cement) . . . . . . . . . | $10,379 | $13,083 | 79.3% |

Source: Tanaka, Sanette, "After the Remodel, It's Payback Time," *The Wall Street Journal*, April 26, 2013, M12.

Many actions involve combinations of changes in sales, expenses, and operating assets. For example, a manager may make an investment in (i.e., increase) operating assets to reduce operating expenses or increase sales. Whether the net effect is favorable or not is judged in terms of its overall impact on ROI.

For example, suppose that the Montvale Burger Grill expects the following operating results next month:

| | |
|---|---|
| Sales . . . . . . . . . . . . . . . . . . . . . . . . . . . . | $100,000 |
| Operating expenses . . . . . . . . . . . . . . . | $90,000 |
| Net operating income . . . . . . . . . . . . . . | $10,000 |
| Average operating assets . . . . . . . . . . | $50,000 |

The expected return on investment (ROI) for the month is computed as follows:

$$\text{ROI} = \text{Margin} \times \text{Turnover}$$

$$\text{ROI} = \frac{\text{Net operating income}}{\text{Sales}} \times \frac{\text{Sales}}{\text{Average operating assets}}$$

$$= \frac{\$10,000}{\$100,000} \times \frac{\$100,000}{\$50,000}$$

$$= 10\% \times 2 = 20\%$$

Suppose that the manager of the Montvale Burger Grill is considering investing $2,000 in a state-of-the-art soft-serve ice cream machine that can dispense a number of different flavors. This new machine would boost sales by $4,000, but would require additional operating expenses of $1,000. Thus, net operating income would increase by $3,000, to $13,000. The new ROI would be:

$$\text{ROI} = \text{Margin} \times \text{Turnover}$$

$$\text{ROI} = \frac{\text{Net operating income}}{\text{Sales}} \times \frac{\text{Sales}}{\text{Average operating assets}}$$

$$= \frac{\$13,000}{\$104,000} \times \frac{\$104,000}{\$52,000}$$

$$= 12.5\% \times 2 = 25\% \text{ (as compared to 20\% originally)}$$

In this particular example, the investment increases ROI, but that will not always happen.

**E.I. du Pont de Nemours and Company** (better known as DuPont) pioneered the use of ROI and recognized the importance of looking at both margin and turnover in assessing a manager's performance. ROI is now widely used as the key measure of investment center performance. ROI reflects in a single figure many aspects of the manager's responsibilities. It can be compared to the returns of other investment centers in the organization, the returns of other companies in the industry, and to the past returns of the investment center itself. DuPont also developed the diagram that appears in Exhibit 10–1. This exhibit helps managers understand how they can improve ROI.

**EXHIBIT 10–1**   Elements of Return on Investment (ROI)

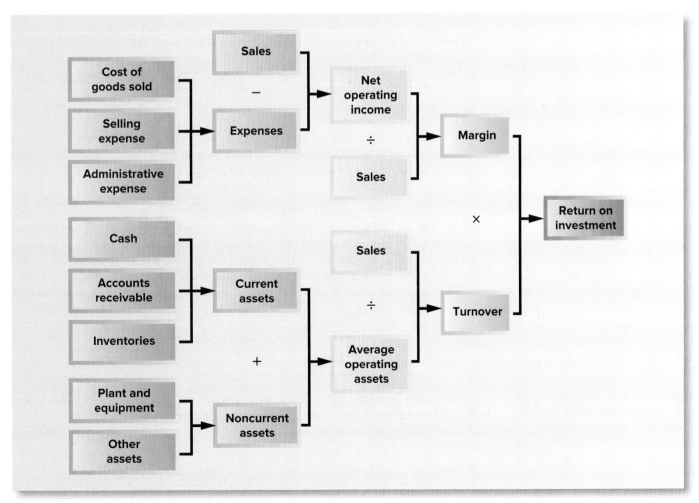

## Whirlpool Chooses Margin Rather Than Turnover

**Whirlpool Corporation** has an industry-leading 40% market share in the United States when it comes to selling washers, dryers, refrigerators, dishwashers, and cooking equipment. Rather than using deep discounts to generate sales volume, the company relies on product innovations that enable price premiums and higher margins. In a recent quarter, Whirlpool's profits jumped 44% from the same quarter in the prior year due to fatter margins. In addition to margin expansion, the company also plans to boost profits by reducing capacity and cutting costs by $175 million.

Source: Tita, Bob, "Whirlpool Shuns Discounts," *The Wall Street Journal,* April 25, 2013, B6.

## Criticisms of ROI

Although ROI is widely used in evaluating performance, it is subject to the following criticisms:

1. Just telling managers to increase ROI may not be enough. Managers may not know how to increase ROI; they may increase ROI in a way that is inconsistent with the company's strategy; or they may take actions that increase ROI in the short run but harm the company in the long run (such as cutting back on research and development). This is why ROI is best used as part of a balanced scorecard, as discussed later in this chapter. A balanced scorecard can provide concrete guidance to managers, making it more likely that their actions are consistent with the company's strategy and reducing the likelihood that they will boost short-run performance at the expense of long-term performance.

2. A manager who takes over a business segment typically inherits many committed costs over which the manager has no control. These committed costs may be relevant in assessing the performance of the business segment as an investment but they make it difficult to fairly assess the performance of the manager.

3. As discussed in the next section, a manager who is evaluated based on ROI may reject investment opportunities that are profitable for the whole company but would have a negative impact on the manager's performance evaluation.

**CONCEPT CHECK**

2. Which of the following statements is false? (You may select more than one answer.)
   a. Margin equals net operating income divided by sales.
   b. Turnover equals sales divided by average operating assets.
   c. Return on investment (ROI) equals margin divided by turnover.
   d. Return on investment (ROI) equals net operating income divided by average operating assets.

## RESIDUAL INCOME

*Residual income* is another approach to measuring an investment center's performance. **Residual income** is the net operating income that an investment center earns above the minimum required return on its operating assets. In equation form, residual income is calculated as follows:

$$\text{Residual income} = \text{Net operating income} - \left( \text{Average operating assets} \times \text{Minimum required rate of return} \right)$$

**Economic Value Added (EVA®)** is an adaptation of residual income that has been adopted by many companies.[3] Under EVA, companies often modify their accounting principles in various ways. For example, funds used for research and development are often treated as investments rather than as expenses.[4] These complications are best dealt with in a more advanced course; in this text we will not draw any distinction between residual income and EVA.

When residual income or EVA is used to measure performance, the objective is to maximize the total amount of residual income or EVA, not to maximize ROI. This is an important distinction. If the objective were to maximize ROI, then every company should divest all of its products except the single product with the highest ROI.

A wide variety of organizations have embraced some version of residual income or EVA, including **Bausch & Lomb, Best Buy, Boise Cascade, Coca-Cola, Dun and Bradstreet, Eli Lilly, Federal Mogul, Georgia-Pacific, Hershey Foods, Husky Injection Molding, J.C. Penney, Kansas City Power & Light, Olin, Quaker Oats, Silicon Valley Bank, Sprint, Toys R Us, Tupperware,** and the **United States Postal Service.**

For purposes of illustration, consider the following data for an investment center—the Ketchikan Division of Alaskan Marine Services Corporation.

| Alaskan Marine Services Corporation<br>Ketchikan Division<br>Basic Data for Performance Evaluation | |
| --- | --- |
| Average operating assets ................. | $100,000 |
| Net operating income .................... | $20,000 |
| Minimum required rate of return ........... | 15% |

Alaskan Marine Services Corporation has long had a policy of using ROI to evaluate its investment center managers, but it is considering switching to residual income. The controller of the company, who is in favor of the change to residual income, has provided the following table that shows how the performance of the division would be evaluated under each of the two methods:

| Alaskan Marine Services Corporation<br>Ketchikan Division | Alternative<br>Performance Measures | |
| --- | --- | --- |
| | **ROI** | **Residual<br>Income** |
| Average operating assets (a) .................... | $100,000 | $100,000 |
| Net operating income (b) ....................... | $ 20,000 | $ 20,000 |
| ROI, (b) ÷ (a) ................................. | 20% | |
| Minimum required return (15% × $100,000) ........ | | 15,000 |
| Residual income ............................... | | $ 5,000 |

---

[3]The basic idea underlying residual income and economic value added has been around for over 100 years. Economic value added has been popularized and trademarked by the consulting firm Stern, Stewart & Co.

[4]Over 100 different adjustments could be made for deferred taxes, LIFO reserves, provisions for future liabilities, mergers and acquisitions, gains or losses due to changes in accounting rules, operating leases, and other accounts, but most companies make only a few. For further details, see John O'Hanlon and Ken Peasnell, "Wall Street's Contribution to Management Accounting: The Stern Stewart EVA® Financial Management System," *Management Accounting Research* 9, 1998, pp. 421–444.

The reasoning underlying the residual income calculation is straightforward. The company is able to earn a rate of return of at least 15% on its investments. Because the company has invested $100,000 in the Ketchikan Division in the form of operating assets, the company should be able to earn at least $15,000 (15% × $100,000) on this investment. Because the Ketchikan Division's net operating income is $20,000, the residual income above and beyond the minimum required return is $5,000. If residual income is adopted as the performance measure to replace ROI, the manager of the Ketchikan Division would be evaluated based on the growth in residual income from year to year.

## Motivation and Residual Income

One of the primary reasons why the controller of Alaskan Marine Services Corporation would like to switch from ROI to residual income relates to how managers view new investments under the two performance measurement methods. The residual income approach encourages managers to make investments that are profitable for the entire company but that would be rejected by managers who are evaluated using the ROI formula.

To illustrate this problem with ROI, suppose that the manager of the Ketchikan Division is considering purchasing a computerized diagnostic machine to aid in servicing marine diesel engines. The machine would cost $25,000 and is expected to generate additional operating income of $4,500 a year. From the standpoint of the company, this would be a good investment because it promises a rate of return of 18% ($4,500 ÷ $25,000), which exceeds the company's minimum required rate of return of 15%.

If the manager of the Ketchikan Division is evaluated based on residual income, she would be in favor of the investment in the diagnostic machine as shown below:

**Alaskan Marine Services Corporation**
**Ketchikan Division**
**Performance Evaluated Using Residual Income**

|  | Present | New Project | Overall |
|---|---|---|---|
| Average operating assets | $100,000 | $25,000 | $125,000 |
| Net operating income | $20,000 | $4,500 | $24,500 |
| Minimum required return | 15,000 | 3,750* | 18,750 |
| Residual income | $ 5,000 | $ 750 | $ 5,750 |

*$25,000 × 15% = $3,750.

Because the project would increase the residual income of the Ketchikan Division by $750, the manager would choose to invest in the new diagnostic machine.

Now suppose that the manager of the Ketchikan Division is evaluated based on ROI. The effect of the diagnostic machine on the division's ROI is computed below:

**Alaskan Marine Services Corporation**
**Ketchikan Division**
**Performance Evaluated Using ROI**

|  | Present | New Project | Overall |
|---|---|---|---|
| Average operating assets (a) | $100,000 | $25,000 | $125,000 |
| Net operating income (b) | $20,000 | $4,500 | $24,500 |
| ROI, (b) ÷ (a) | 20% | 18% | 19.6% |

The new project reduces the division's ROI from 20% to 19.6%. This happens because the 18% rate of return on the new diagnostic machine, while above the company's 15% minimum required rate of return, is below the division's current ROI of 20%. Therefore, the new diagnostic machine would decrease the division's ROI even though it would be a good investment from the standpoint of the company as a whole. If the manager of the division is evaluated based on ROI, she will be reluctant to even propose such an investment.

Generally, a manager who is evaluated based on ROI will reject any project whose rate of return is below the division's current ROI even if the rate of return on the project is above the company's minimum required rate of return. In contrast, managers who are evaluated using residual income will pursue any project whose rate of return is above the minimum required rate of return because it will increase their residual income. Because it is in the best interests of the company as a whole to accept any project whose rate of return is above the minimum required rate of return, managers who are evaluated based on residual income will tend to make better decisions concerning investment projects than managers who are evaluated based on ROI.

## HELPFUL HINT

When managers are evaluated and rewarded based on return on investment (ROI), it can create situations where managers make decisions that are not in the company's best interest. For example, assume that the company establishes a minimum required return of 15%, thereby implying that the company wants its managers to pursue investment opportunities that can earn a return equal to or greater than 15%. However, let's also assume that the manager has historically earned an ROI of 20% and that her bonus is based on her ability to meet or exceed this 20% threshold.

In this situation, the manager and the company will both want to bypass investment opportunities with an ROI less than 15%. They will both want to pursue investment opportunities with an ROI greater than 20%. The problem arises with investment opportunities that earn greater than 15% but less than 20%. The company will want the manager to pursue these opportunities, whereas the manager will want to bypass them because they will reduce her historical ROI and lower her chances of earning a bonus. This problem can be resolved by using residual income to evaluate managerial performance because it would reward the manager for pursuing all investments that exceed the minimum required return of 15%.

## Divisional Comparison and Residual Income

The residual income approach has one major disadvantage. It can't be used to compare the performance of divisions of different sizes. Larger divisions often have more residual income than smaller divisions, not necessarily because they are better managed but simply because they are bigger.

As an example, consider the following residual income computations for the Wholesale Division and the Retail Division of Sisal Marketing Corporation:

| | Wholesale Division | Retail Division |
|---|---|---|
| Average operating assets (a) .............. | $1,000,000 | $250,000 |
| Net operating income .................... | $120,000 | $40,000 |
| Minimum required return: 10% × (a) ........ | 100,000 | 25,000 |
| Residual income ......................... | $ 20,000 | $15,000 |

Observe that the Wholesale Division has slightly more residual income than the Retail Division, but that the Wholesale Division has $1,000,000 in operating assets as compared to only $250,000 in operating assets for the Retail Division. Thus, the Wholesale Division's greater residual income is probably due to its larger size rather than the quality of its management. In fact, it appears that the smaller division may be better managed because it has been able to generate nearly as much residual income with only one-fourth as much in operating assets. When comparing investment centers, it is probably better to focus on the percentage change in residual income from year to year rather than on the absolute amount of the residual income.

**CONCEPT CHECK**

3. Last year sales were $300,000, net operating income was $75,000, and average operating assets were $500,000. If sales next year remain the same as last year and expenses and average operating assets are reduced by 5%, what will be the return on investment next year?
   a. 12.2%
   b. 18.2%
   c. 0.2%
   d. 25.2%
4. Referring to the facts in question 3 above, if the minimum required rate of return is 12%, what will be the residual income next year?
   a. $26,250
   b. $27,250
   c. $28,250
   d. $29,250

## Shoe Store Manager

You are the manager of a shoe store in a busy shopping mall. The store is part of a national chain that evaluates its store managers on the basis of return on investment (ROI). As the manager of the store, you have control over costs, pricing, and the inventory you carry. The ROI of your store was 17.21% last year and is projected to be 17.00% this year unless some action Is taken. The projected ROI has been computed as follows:

| | |
|---|---|
| Average operating assets (a) | $2,000,000 |
| Net operating income (b) | $340,000 |
| ROI, (b) ÷ (a) | 17.00% |

Your bonus this year will depend on improving your ROI performance over last year. The minimum required rate of return on investment for the national chain is 15%. You are considering two alternatives for improving this year's ROI:

a. Cut inventories (and average operating assets) by $500,000. This will unfortunately result in a reduction in sales, with a negative impact on net operating income of $79,000.
b. Add a new product line that would increase average operating assets by $200,000, but would increase net operating income by $33,000.

Which alternative would result in your earning a bonus for the year? Which alternative is in the best interests of the national chain?

## OPERATING PERFORMANCE MEASURES

In addition to financial performance measures, organizations use many nonfinancial performance measures. While financial measures reflect the *results* of what people in the organization do, they do not measure what *drives* organizational performance. For example, activity and revenue variances summarize the results of efforts aimed at increasing sales, but they do not measure the actions that actually drive sales such as improving quality, exposing more potential customers to the product, filling customer orders on time, and so on. Consequently, many organizations use a variety of nonfinancial performance measures in addition to financial measures. In this section we will discuss three examples of such measures that are critical to success in many organizations—throughput time, delivery cycle time, and manufacturing cycle efficiency (MCE). Note that while these examples focus on manufacturers, very similar measures can be used by any service organization that experiences a delay between receiving a customer request and responding to that request.

**LEARNING OBJECTIVE 10–3**

Compute throughput time, delivery cycle time, and manufacturing cycle efficiency (MCE).

### Throughput (Manufacturing Cycle) Time

The elapsed time from when production is started until finished goods are shipped to customers is called **throughput time**, or *manufacturing cycle time*. The goal is to continuously reduce this measure and the formula for computing it is as follows:

$$\text{Throughput (manufacturing cycle) time} = \text{Process time} + \text{Inspection time} + \text{Move time} + \text{Queue time}$$

*Process time* is the amount of time work is actually done on the product. *Inspection time* is the amount of time spent ensuring that the product is not defective. *Move time* is the time required to move materials or partially completed products from workstation to workstation. *Queue time* is the amount of time a product spends waiting to be worked on, to be moved, to be inspected, or to be shipped. Only one of these four activities adds value to the product—process time. The other three activities—inspecting, moving, and queuing—add no value and should be eliminated as much as possible.

### Delivery Cycle Time

The elapsed time from when a customer order is received until the finished goods are shipped is called **delivery cycle time**. The goal is to reduce this measure and the formula for computing it is as follows:

$$\text{Delivery cycle time} = \text{Wait time} + \text{Throughput time}$$

*Wait time* is the elapsed time from when a customer order is received until production of the order is started. This is a non–value-added activity that should be reduced or eliminated. When companies succeed in drastically reducing or eliminating wait time plus the non–value-added components of throughput time it often enables them to increase customer satisfaction and profits. The relation between throughput (manufacturing cycle) time and delivery cycle time is illustrated in Exhibit 10–2.

### Manufacturing Cycle Efficiency (MCE)

Through concerted efforts to eliminate the *non–value-added* activities of inspecting, moving, and queuing, some companies have reduced their throughput time to only a

**EXHIBIT 10-2**    Throughput (Manufacturing Cycle) Time and Delivery Cycle Time

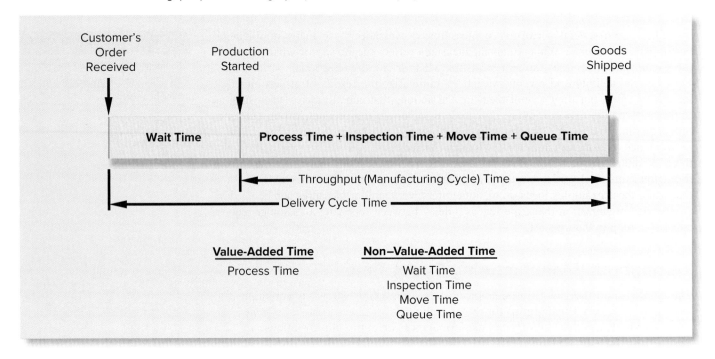

fraction of previous levels. In turn, this has helped to reduce the delivery cycle time from months to only weeks or hours. Throughput time, which is a key measure in delivery performance, can be put into better perspective by computing the **manufacturing cycle efficiency (MCE)**. The MCE is computed by relating the value-added time to the throughput time. The goal is to increase this measure and the formula for computing it is as follows:

$$MCE = \frac{\text{Value-added time (Process time)}}{\text{Throughput (manufacturing cycle) time}}$$

Any non–value-added time results in an MCE of less than 1. An MCE of 0.5, for example, would mean that half of the total production time consists of inspection, moving, and similar non–value-added activities. In many manufacturing companies, the MCE is less than 0.1 (10%), which means that 90% of the time a unit is in process is spent on activities that do not add value to the product. Monitoring the MCE helps companies to reduce non–value-added activities and thus get products into the hands of customers more quickly and at a lower cost.

**Example**    To provide an example of these measures, consider the following data for Novex Company:

Novex Company keeps careful track of the time to complete customer orders. During the most recent quarter, the following average times were recorded per order:

|  | Days |
|---|---|
| Wait time . . . . . . . . . . . . . . . . . . . . . | 17.0 |
| Inspection time . . . . . . . . . . . . . . . . | 0.4 |
| Process time . . . . . . . . . . . . . . . . . | 2.0 |
| Move time . . . . . . . . . . . . . . . . . . . . | 0.6 |
| Queue time . . . . . . . . . . . . . . . . . . . | 5.0 |

Goods are shipped as soon as production is completed.

**REQUIRED:**

1. Compute the throughput time.
2. Compute the manufacturing cycle efficiency (MCE).
3. What percentage of the production time is spent in non–value-added activities?
4. Compute the delivery cycle time.

## Solution

1. Throughput time = Process time + Inspection time + Move time + Queue time

$$= 2.0 \text{ days} + 0.4 \text{ days} + 0.6 \text{ days} + 5.0 \text{ days}$$
$$= 8.0 \text{ days}$$

2. Only process time represents value-added time; therefore, MCE would be computed as follows:

$$\text{MCE} = \frac{\text{Value-added time}}{\text{Throughput time}} = \frac{2.0 \text{ days}}{8.0 \text{ days}}$$
$$= 0.25$$

Thus, once put into production, a typical order is actually being worked on only 25% of the time.

3. Because the MCE is 25%, 75% (100% − 25%) of total production time is spent in non–value-added activities.

4. Delivery cycle time = Wait time + Throughput time

$$= 17.0 \text{ days} + 8.0 \text{ days}$$
$$= 25.0 \text{ days}$$

5. Which of the following statements is false? (You may select more than one answer.)
   a. The delivery cycle time will always be equal to or greater than the throughput (manufacturing cycle) time.
   b. A manufacturing cycle efficiency of 1.0 is better than a manufacturing cycle efficiency of 0.1.
   c. The throughput (manufacturing cycle) time increases when the wait time increases.
   d. The delivery cycle time is unaffected by queue time.

CONCEPT CHECK

## UPS Looks to Shrink Delivery Times and Save Money

IN BUSINESS

**The United Parcel Service** (UPS) has invested more than 10 years and hundreds of millions of dollars developing a computer platform called Orion that is designed to identify optimal delivery routes for its drivers. The human mind cannot possibly evaluate the most efficient way for a driver to deliver 120 packages per day, so UPS has turned to 50 engineers to develop the computerized algorithms and heuristics embedded in the Orion platform.

Given that UPS drivers complete 55,000 routes per day in the U.S., if Orion can shave one mile per day off of each of these routes, it saves the company $50 million per year. Since the drivers already using Orion are actually saving seven to eight miles per day, UPS estimates that Orion will save the company $300 to $400 million per year.

©B Christopher/Alamy Stock Photo

Source: Rosenbush, Steven, and Stevens, Laura, "At UPS, the Algorithm is the Driver," *The Wall Street Journal,* February 17, 2015, B1 and B4.

# BALANCED SCORECARD

**LEARNING OBJECTIVE 10–4**

Understand how to construct and use a balanced scorecard.

Financial measures, such as ROI and residual income, and operating measures, such as those discussed in the previous section, may be included in a *balanced scorecard.* A **balanced scorecard** consists of an integrated set of performance measures that are derived from and support a company's strategy. A strategy is essentially a theory about how to achieve the organization's goals. For example, **Southwest Airlines'** strategy is to offer an *operational excellence* customer value proposition that has three key components—low ticket prices, convenience, and reliability. The company operates only one type of aircraft, the Boeing 737, to reduce maintenance and training costs and simplify scheduling. It further reduces costs by not offering meals, seat assignments, or baggage transfers and by booking a large portion of its passenger revenue over the Internet. Southwest also uses point-to-point flights rather than the hub-and-spoke approach of its larger competitors, thereby providing customers convenient, nonstop service to their final destination. Because Southwest serves many less-congested airports such as Chicago Midway, Burbank, Manchester, Oakland, and Providence, it offers quicker passenger check-ins and reliable departures, while maintaining high asset utilization (i.e., the company's average gate turnaround time of 25 minutes enables it to function with fewer planes and gates). Overall, the company's strategy has worked, as Southwest Airlines continues to earn substantial profits.

Under the balanced scorecard approach, top management translates its strategy into performance measures that employees can understand and influence. For example, the amount of time passengers have to wait in line to have their baggage checked might be a performance measure for the supervisor in charge of the Southwest Airlines check-in counter at the Burbank airport. This performance measure is easily understood by the supervisor, and can be improved by the supervisor's actions.

## Common Characteristics of Balanced Scorecards

Performance measures used in balanced scorecards tend to fall into the four groups illustrated in Exhibit 10–3: financial, customer, internal business processes, and learning and growth. Internal business processes are what the company does in an attempt to satisfy customers. For example, in a manufacturing company, assembling a product is an internal business process. In an airline, handling baggage is an internal business process. The idea underlying these groupings (as indicated by the vertical arrows in Exhibit 10–3) is that learning is necessary to improve internal business processes; improving business processes is necessary to improve customer satisfaction; and improving customer satisfaction is necessary to improve financial results.

Note that the emphasis in Exhibit 10–3 is on *improvement*—not on just attaining some specific objective such as profits of $10 million. In the balanced scorecard approach, continual improvement is encouraged. If an organization does not continually improve, it will eventually lose out to competitors that do.

Financial performance measures appear at the top of Exhibit 10–3. Ultimately, most companies exist to provide financial rewards to owners. There are exceptions. Some companies—for example, **The Body Shop**—may have loftier goals such as providing environmentally friendly products to consumers. However, even nonprofit organizations must generate enough financial resources to stay in operation.

For several reasons, financial performance measures are not sufficient in themselves—they should be integrated with nonfinancial measures in a well-designed balanced scorecard. First, financial measures are lag indicators that report on the results of past actions. In contrast, nonfinancial measures of key success drivers such as customer satisfaction are leading indicators of future financial performance. Second, top managers are ordinarily responsible for the financial performance measures—not lower-level managers. The supervisor in charge of checking in passengers can be held responsible for how long passengers have to wait in line. However, this supervisor cannot reasonably

**EXHIBIT 10-3**    From Strategy to Performance Measures: The Balanced Scorecard

*Performance Measures*

What are our financial goals?

**Financial**
"Has our financial performance improved?"

Vision and Strategy

What customers do we want to serve and how are we going to win and retain them?

**Customer**
"Do customers recognize that we are delivering more value?"

What internal business processes are critical to providing value to customers?

**Internal Business Processes**
"Have we improved key business processes so that we can deliver more value to customers?"

**Learning and Growth**
"Are we maintaining our ability to change and improve?"

be held responsible for the entire company's profit. That is the responsibility of the airline's top managers.

Exhibit 10–4 lists some examples of performance measures that can be found on the balanced scorecards of companies. However, few companies, if any, would use all of these performance measures, and almost all companies would add other performance measures. Managers should carefully select performance measures for their own company's balanced scorecard, keeping the following points in mind. First and foremost, the performance measures should be consistent with, and follow from, the company's strategy. If the performance measures are not consistent with the company's strategy, people will find themselves working at cross-purposes. Second, the performance measures should be understandable and controllable to a significant extent by those being evaluated. Third, the performance measures should be reported on a frequent and timely basis. For example, data about defects should be reported to the responsible manager at least once a day so that problems can be resolved quickly. Fourth, the scorecard should not have too many performance measures. This can lead to a lack of focus and confusion.

While the entire organization will have an overall balanced scorecard, each responsible individual will have his or her own personal scorecard as well. This scorecard should consist of items the individual can personally influence that relate directly to the performance measures on the overall balanced scorecard. The performance measures on this personal scorecard should not be overly influenced by actions taken by others in the company or by events that are outside of the individual's control. And, focusing on the performance measure should not lead an individual to take actions that are counter to the organization's objectives.

EXHIBIT 10–4
Examples of Performance
Measures for Balanced
Scorecards

| Customer Perspective | |
|---|---|
| **Performance Measure** | **Desired Change** |
| Customer satisfaction as measured by survey results | + |
| Number of customer complaints | − |
| Market share | + |
| Product returns as a percentage of sales | − |
| Percentage of customers retained from last period | + |
| Number of new customers | + |

| Internal Business Processes Perspective | |
|---|---|
| **Performance Measure** | **Desired Change** |
| Percentage of sales from new products | + |
| Time to introduce new products to market | − |
| Percentage of customer calls answered within 20 seconds | + |
| On-time deliveries as a percentage of all deliveries | + |
| Work in process inventory as a percentage of sales | − |
| Unfavorable standard cost variances | − |
| Defect-free units as a percentage of completed units | + |
| Delivery cycle time | − |
| Throughput time | − |
| Manufacturing cycle efficiency | + |
| Quality costs | − |
| Setup time | − |
| Time from call by customer to repair of product | − |
| Percent of customer complaints settled on first contact | + |
| Time to settle a customer claim | − |

| Learning and Growth Perspective | |
|---|---|
| **Performance Measure** | **Desired Change** |
| Suggestions per employee | + |
| Employee turnover | − |
| Hours of in-house training per employee | + |

With those broad principles in mind, we will now take a look at how a company's strategy affects its balanced scorecard.

## A Company's Strategy and the Balanced Scorecard

Returning to the performance measures in Exhibit 10–3, each company must decide which customers to target and what internal business processes are crucial to attracting and retaining those customers. Different companies, having different strategies, will target different customers with different kinds of products and services. Take the automobile industry as an example. **BMW** stresses engineering and handling; **Volvo**, safety; **Jaguar**, luxury detailing; and **Honda**, reliability. Because of these differences in emphasis, a one-size-fits-all approach to performance measurement won't work even within this one industry. Performance measures must be tailored to the specific strategy of each company.

Suppose, for example, that Jaguar's strategy is to offer distinctive, richly finished luxury automobiles to wealthy individuals who prize handcrafted, individualized products. To deliver this customer intimacy value proposition to its wealthy target customers, Jaguar might create such a large number of options for details, such as leather seats, interior and exterior color combinations, and wooden dashboards, that each car becomes virtually one of a kind. For example, instead of just offering tan or blue leather seats in standard cowhide, the company may offer customers the choice of an almost infinite palette of colors in any of a number of different exotic leathers. For such a system to work effectively, Jaguar would have to be able to deliver a completely customized car within a reasonable amount of time—and without incurring more cost for this customization than the customer is willing to pay. Exhibit 10–5 suggests how Jaguar might reflect this strategy in its balanced scorecard.

If the balanced scorecard is correctly constructed, the performance measures should be linked together on a cause-and-effect basis. Each link can then be read as a hypothesis in the form: "If we improve this performance measure, then this other performance

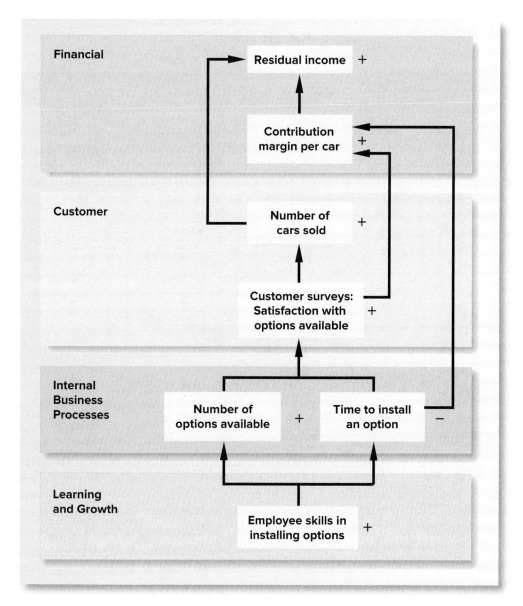

**EXHIBIT 10–5**
A Possible Strategy at Jaguar and the Balanced Scorecard

measure should also improve." Starting from the bottom of Exhibit 10–5, we can read the links between performance measures as follows. If employees acquire the skills to install new options more effectively, then the company can offer more options and the options can be installed in less time. If more options are available and they are installed in less time, then customer surveys should show greater satisfaction with the range of options available. If customer satisfaction improves, then the number of cars sold should increase. In addition, if customer satisfaction improves, the company should be able to maintain or increase its selling prices, and if the time to install options decreases, the costs of installing the options should decrease. Together, this should result in an increase in the contribution margin per car. If the contribution margin per car increases and more cars are sold, the result should be an increase in residual income.

In essence, the balanced scorecard lays out a theory of how the company can take concrete actions to attain its desired outcomes (financial, in this case). The strategy laid out in Exhibit 10–5 seems plausible, but it should be regarded as only a theory. For example, if the company succeeds in increasing the number of options available and in decreasing the time required to install options and yet there is no increase in customer satisfaction, the number of cars sold, the contribution margin per car, or residual income, the strategy would have to be reconsidered. One of the advantages of the balanced scorecard is that it continually tests the theories underlying management's strategy. If a strategy is not working, it should become evident when some of the predicted effects (i.e., more car sales) don't occur. Without this feedback, the organization may drift on indefinitely with an ineffective strategy based on faulty assumptions.

## IN BUSINESS

### Employee Wellness Drives Employee Productivity

©JGI/Tom Grill/Getty Images RF

When a company's employees are sick or suffering from emotional stress, it can affect their absenteeism and productivity rates. Survey results from the **Financial Fitness Group** indicate that 80% of workers in the United States and Puerto Rico are under moderate to high levels of financial stress. To reduce these stress levels, some companies are implementing financial wellness programs that "include finance classes, counseling sessions, and even video games designed to help staffers pay down debt, stick to a budget, and invest for their retirement."

**Meredith Corporation** encourages its employees to complete a financial wellness questionnaire or take a course on refinancing their mortgage in exchange for points that make them eligible for lower health care premiums. The company estimates that 88% of its workers who reported less money stress used no sick days in the prior year, whereas only 78% of employees who reported higher levels of stress used no sick days.

Source: Feintzeig, Rachel, "Can Companies Solve Workers' Money Woes," *The Wall Street Journal*, April 8, 2015, B1 and B6.

## Tying Compensation to the Balanced Scorecard

Incentive compensation for employees, such as bonuses, can, and probably should, be tied to balanced scorecard performance measures. However, this should be done only after the organization has been successfully managed with the scorecard for some time—perhaps a year or more. Managers must be confident that the performance measures are reliable, sensible, understood by those who are being evaluated, and not easily manipulated. As Robert Kaplan and David Norton, the originators of the balanced scorecard concept point out, "compensation is such a powerful lever that you have to be pretty confident that you have the right measures and have good data for the measures before making the link."[5]

---

[5]Lori Calabro, "On Balance: A CFO Interview," *CFO*, February 2001, pp. 73–78.

6.  Which of the following statements is true? (You may select more than one answer.)
    a.  The balanced scorecard contains four categories of performance measures.
    b.  The balanced scorecard focuses on nonfinancial performance measures and excludes financial performance measures.
    c.  The performance measures in a balanced scorecard should be linked together on a cause-and-effect basis.
    d.  The balanced scorecard is derived from and supports a company's strategy.

CONCEPT CHECK

## SUMMARY

**LO10–1 Compute return on investment (ROI) and show how changes in sales, expenses, and assets affect ROI.**

Return on investment (ROI) is defined as net operating income divided by average operating assets. Alternatively, it can be defined as the product of margin and turnover, where margin is net operating income divided by sales and turnover is sales divided by average operating assets.

The relations among sales, expenses, assets, and ROI are complex. The effect of a change in any one variable on the others will depend on the specific circumstances. Nevertheless, an increase in sales often leads to an increase in ROI via the effect of sales on net operating income. If the organization has significant fixed costs, then a given percentage increase in sales is likely to have an even larger percentage effect on net operating income.

**LO10–2 Compute residual income and understand its strengths and weaknesses.**

Residual income is the difference between net operating income and the minimum required return on average operating assets. The minimum required return on average operating assets is computed by applying the minimum rate of return to the average operating assets.

A major advantage of residual income over ROI is that it encourages investment in projects whose rates of return are above the minimum required rate of return for the entire organization, but below the segment's current ROI.

**LO10–3 Compute throughput time, delivery cycle time, and manufacturing cycle efficiency (MCE).**

In addition to financial measures, companies use operating performance measures to assess their performance. The amount of time required to turn raw materials into completed products is called throughput time. The delivery cycle time is the amount of time from when a customer order is received to when the completed order is shipped. The manufacturing cycle efficiency (MCE) measures the value-added time divided by the throughput time. Any non–value-added time results in an MCE of less than 1.

**LO10–4 Understand how to construct and use a balanced scorecard.**

A balanced scorecard is an integrated system of performance measures designed to support an organization's strategy. The various measures in a balanced scorecard should be linked on a plausible cause-and-effect basis from the very lowest level up through the organization's ultimate objectives. The balanced scorecard is essentially a theory about how specific actions taken by various people in the organization will further the organization's objectives. The theory should be viewed as tentative and subject to change if the actions do not in fact result in improvements in the organization's financial and other goals. If the theory changes, then the performance measures on the balanced scorecard should also change. The balanced scorecard is a dynamic measurement system that evolves as an organization learns more about what works and what doesn't work and refines its strategy accordingly.

# GUIDANCE ANSWER TO DECISION POINT

### Shoe Store Manager

The effects of the two alternatives on your store's ROI for the year can be computed as follows:

|  | Present | Alternative (a) | Overall |
|---|---|---|---|
| Average operating assets (a) . . . . . . . . . . . . . . . . . . | $2,000,000 | $(500,000) | $1,500,000 |
| Net operating income (b) . . . . . . . . . . . . . . . . . . . . | $340,000 | $(79,000) | $261,000 |
| ROI, (b) ÷ (a). . . . . . . . . . . . . . . . . . . . . . . . . . . . . | 17.00% | 15.80% | 17.40% |

|  | Present | Alternative (b) | Overall |
|---|---|---|---|
| Average operating assets (a) . . . . . . . . . . . . . . . . . . | $2,000,000 | $200,000 | $2,200,000 |
| Net operating income (b) . . . . . . . . . . . . . . . . . . . . | $340,000 | $33,000 | $373,000 |
| ROI, (b) ÷ (a). . . . . . . . . . . . . . . . . . . . . . . . . . . . . | 17.00% | 16.50% | 16.95% |

Alternative (a) would increase your store's ROI to 17.40%—beating last year's ROI and hence earning you a bonus. Alternative (b) would actually decrease your store's ROI and would result in no bonus for the year. So to earn the bonus, you would select Alternative (a). However, this alternative is not in the best interests of the national chain since the ROI of the lost sales is 15.8%, which exceeds the national chain's minimum required rate of return of 15%. Rather, it would be in the national chain's interests to adopt Alternative (b)—the addition of a new product line. The ROI on these sales would be 16.5%, which exceeds the minimum required rate of return of 15%.

## GUIDANCE ANSWERS TO CONCEPT CHECKS

1. **Choices c and d.** Both profit and investment center managers are held responsible for profits. In addition, an investment center manager is held responsible for earning an adequate return on investment or residual income.
2. **Choice c.** Return on investment equals margin times turnover.
3. **Choice b.** The net operating income would be $300,000 − ($225,000 × 95%) = $86,250. The return on investment would be ($86,250 ÷ ($500,000 × 95%) = 18.2%.
4. **Choice d.** The residual income would be $86,250 − ($475,000 × 12%) = $29,250.
5. **Choices c and d.** The throughput (manufacturing cycle) time is unaffected by the wait time. The delivery cycle time is influenced by the queue time.
6. **Choices a, c, and d.** The balanced scorecard includes financial measures.

# REVIEW PROBLEM: RETURN ON INVESTMENT (ROI) AND RESIDUAL INCOME

The Magnetic Imaging Division of Medical Diagnostics, Inc., has reported the following results for last year's operations:

| | |
|---|---|
| Sales. . . . . . . . . . . . . . . . . . . . . . . . | $25 million |
| Net operating income . . . . . . . . . . | $3 million |
| Average operating assets. . . . . . . | $10 million |

*Required:*
1. Compute the Magnetic Imaging Division's margin, turnover, and ROI.
2. Top management of Medical Diagnostics, Inc., has set a minimum required rate of return on average operating assets of 25%. What is the Magnetic Imaging Division's residual income for the year?

**Solution to Review Problem**

1. The required calculations follow:

$$\text{Margin} = \frac{\text{Net operating income}}{\text{Sales}}$$

$$= \frac{\$3,000,000}{\$25,000,000}$$

$$= 12\%$$

$$\text{Turnover} = \frac{\text{Sales}}{\text{Average operating assets}}$$

$$= \frac{\$25,000,000}{\$10,000,000}$$

$$= 2.5$$

$$\text{ROI} = \text{Margin} \times \text{Turnover}$$

$$= 12\% \times 2.5$$

$$= 30\%$$

2. The Magnetic Imaging Division's residual income is computed as follows:

| | |
|---|---:|
| Average operating assets.......................... | $10,000,000 |
| Net operating income ............................ | $3,000,000 |
| Minimum required return (25% × $10,000,000)...... | 2,500,000 |
| Residual income................................. | $ 500,000 |

# GLOSSARY

**Balanced scorecard**   An integrated set of performance measures that are derived from and support the organization's strategy. (p. 482)

**Cost center**   A business segment whose manager has control over cost but has no control over revenue or investments in operating assets. (p. 469)

**Decentralized organization**   An organization in which decision-making authority is not confined to a few top executives but rather is spread throughout the organization. (p. 468)

**Delivery cycle time**   The elapsed time from when a customer order is received until the finished goods are shipped. (p. 479)

**Economic Value Added (EVA)**   A concept similar to residual income in which a variety of adjustments may be made to GAAP financial statements for performance evaluation purposes. (p. 475)

**Investment center**   A business segment whose manager has control over cost, revenue, and investments in operating assets. (p. 469)

**Manufacturing cycle efficiency (MCE)**   Process (value-added) time as a percentage of throughput time. (p. 480)

**Margin**   Net operating income divided by sales. (p. 471)

**Net operating income**   Income before interest and income taxes have been deducted. (p. 470)

**Operating assets**   Cash, accounts receivable, inventory, plant and equipment, and all other assets held for operating purposes. (p. 470)

**Profit center**   A business segment whose manager has control over cost and revenue but has no control over investments in operating assets. (p. 469)

**Residual income**   The net operating income that an investment center earns above the minimum required return on its operating assets. (p. 474)

**Responsibility center**   Any business segment whose manager has control over costs, revenues, or investments in operating assets. (p. 469)

**Return on investment (ROI)**   Net operating income divided by average operating assets. It also equals margin multiplied by turnover. (p. 470)

**Throughput time**   The elapsed time from when production is started until finished goods are shipped. (p. 479)

**Turnover**   Sales divided by average operating assets. (p. 471)

## QUESTIONS

10–1   What is meant by the term *decentralization?*
10–2   What benefits result from decentralization?
10–3   Distinguish between a cost center, a profit center, and an investment center.
10–4   What is meant by the terms *margin* and *turnover* in ROI calculations?
10–5   What is meant by residual income?
10–6   In what way can the use of ROI as a performance measure for investment centers lead to bad decisions? How does the residual income approach overcome this problem?
10–7   What is the difference between delivery cycle time and throughput time? What four elements make up throughput time? What elements of throughput time are value-added and what elements are non–value-added?
10–8   What does a manufacturing cycle efficiency (MCE) of less than 1 mean? How would you interpret an MCE of 0.40?
10–9   Why do the measures used in a balanced scorecard differ from company to company?
10–10  Why does the balanced scorecard include financial performance measures as well as measures of how well internal business processes are doing?

## CHAPTER 10: APPLYING EXCEL   ██ connect

LO10–1, LO10–2

The Excel worksheet form that appears below is to be used to recreate the Review Problem pertaining to the Magnetic Imaging Division of Medical Diagnostics, Inc. Download the workbook containing this form from Connect, where you will also receive instructions about how to use this worksheet form.

| | A | B | C | D | E | F |
|---|---|---|---|---|---|---|
| 1 | Chapter 10: Applying Excel | | | | | |
| 2 | | | | | | |
| 3 | Data | | | | | |
| 4 | Sales | $25,000,000 | | | | |
| 5 | Net operating income | $3,000,000 | | | | |
| 6 | Average operating assets | $10,000,000 | | | | |
| 7 | Minimum required rate of return | 25% | | | | |
| 8 | | | | | | |
| 9 | Enter a formula into each of the cells marked with a ? below | | | | | |
| 10 | Review Problem: Return on Investment (ROI) and Residual Income | | | | | |
| 11 | | | | | | |
| 12 | Compute the ROI | | | | | |
| 13 | Margin | ? | | | | |
| 14 | Turnover | ? | | | | |
| 15 | ROI | ? | | | | |
| 16 | | | | | | |
| 17 | Compute the residual income | | | | | |
| 18 | Average operating assets | ? | | | | |
| 19 | Net operating income | ? | | | | |
| 20 | Minimum required return | ? | | | | |
| 21 | Residual income | ? | | | | |
| 22 | | | | | | |

Chapter 10 Form    Filled in ...   ⊕

You should proceed to the requirements below only after completing your worksheet.

*Required:*

1.   Check your worksheet by changing the average operating assets in cell B6 to $8,000,000. The ROI should now be 38% and the residual income should now be $1,000,000. If you do not get these answers, find the errors in your worksheet and correct them.

     Explain why the ROI and the residual income both increase when the average operating assets decrease.

2. Revise the data in your worksheet as follows:

| Data | |
| --- | --- |
| Sales.................................. | $1,200 |
| Net operating income ................. | $72 |
| Average operating assets.............. | $500 |
| Minimum required rate of return ........ | 15% |

a. What is the ROI?
b. What is the residual income?
c. Explain the relationship between the ROI and the residual income.

**■ connect** **THE FOUNDATIONAL 15**

Westerville Company reported the following results from last year's operations:

LO10–1, LO10–2

| Sales........................... | $1,000,000 |
| --- | --- |
| Variable expenses ............... | 300,000 |
| Contribution margin.............. | 700,000 |
| Fixed expenses................... | 500,000 |
| Net operating income ............ | $ 200,000 |
| Average operating assets......... | $ 625,000 |

At the beginning of this year, the company has a $120,000 investment opportunity with the following cost and revenue characteristics:

| Sales........................... | $200,000 |
| --- | --- |
| Contribution margin ratio ....... | 60% of sales |
| Fixed expenses.................. | $90,000 |

The company's minimum required rate of return is 15%.

**Required:**
1. What is last year's margin?
2. What is last year's turnover?
3. What is last year's return on investment (ROI)?
4. What is the margin related to this year's investment opportunity?
5. What is the turnover related to this year's investment opportunity?
6. What is the ROI related to this year's investment opportunity?
7. If the company pursues the investment opportunity and otherwise performs the same as last year, what margin will it earn this year?
8. If the company pursues the investment opportunity and otherwise performs the same as last year, what turnover will it earn this year?
9. If the company pursues the investment opportunity and otherwise performs the same as last year, what ROI will it earn this year?
10. If Westerville's chief executive officer will earn a bonus only if her ROI from this year exceeds her ROI from last year, would she pursue the investment opportunity? Would the owners of the company want her to pursue the investment opportunity?
11. What is last year's residual income?
12. What is the residual income of this year's investment opportunity?
13. If the company pursues the investment opportunity and otherwise performs the same as last year, what residual income will it earn this year?

14. If Westerville's chief executive officer will earn a bonus only if her residual income from this year exceeds her residual income from last year, would she pursue the investment opportunity?

15. Assume that the contribution margin ratio of the investment opportunity was 50% instead of 60%. If Westerville's chief executive officer will earn a bonus only if her residual income from this year exceeds her residual income from last year, would she pursue the investment opportunity? Would the owners of the company want her to pursue the investment opportunity?

# EXERCISES

connect

**EXERCISE 10–1    Compute the Return on Investment (ROI) LO10–1**

Alyeska Services Company, a division of a major oil company, provides various services to the operators of the North Slope oil field in Alaska. Data concerning the most recent year appear below:

| | |
|---|---|
| Sales.............................. | $7,500,000 |
| Net operating income ............. | $600,000 |
| Average operating assets.......... | $5,000,000 |

**Required:**

1. Compute the margin for Alyeska Services Company.
2. Compute the turnover for Alyeska Services Company.
3. Compute the return on investment (ROI) for Alyeska Services Company.

**EXERCISE 10–2    Residual Income LO10–2**

Juniper Design Ltd. of Manchester, England, is a company specializing in providing design services to residential developers. Last year the company had net operating income of $600,000 on sales of $3,000,000. The company's average operating assets for the year were $2,800,000 and its minimum required rate of return was 18%.

**Required:**

Compute the company's residual income for the year.

**EXERCISE 10–3    Measures of Internal Business Process Performance LO10–3**

Management of Mittel Rhein AG of Köln, Germany, would like to reduce the amount of time between when a customer places an order and when the order is shipped. For the first quarter of operations during the current year the following data were reported:

| | |
|---|---|
| Inspection time................................ | 0.3 days |
| Wait time (from order to start of production) ....... | 14.0 days |
| Process time.................................... | 2.7 days |
| Move time ..................................... | 1.0 days |
| Queue time .................................... | 5.0 days |

**Required:**

1. Compute the throughput time.
2. Compute the manufacturing cycle efficiency (MCE) for the quarter.
3. What percentage of the throughput time was spent in non–value-added activities?
4. Compute the delivery cycle time.
5. If by using Lean Production all queue time during production is eliminated, what will be the new MCE?

**EXERCISE 10–4    Building a Balanced Scorecard LO10–4**

Lost Peak ski resort was for many years a small, family-owned resort serving day skiers from nearby towns. Lost Peak was recently acquired by Western Resorts, a major ski resort operator. The new owners have plans to upgrade the resort into a destination resort for vacationers. As part of this plan, the new owners would like to make major improvements in the Powder 8 Lodge, the resort's on-the-hill cafeteria. The menu at the lodge is very limited—hamburgers, hot dogs, chili, tuna fish sandwiches, pizzas, french fries, and packaged snacks. With little competition, the previous owners of the resort felt no urgency to upgrade the food service at the lodge. If skiers want lunch on the mountain, the only alternatives are the Powder 8 Lodge or a brown bag lunch brought from home.

As part of the deal when acquiring Lost Peak, Western Resorts agreed to retain all of the current employees of the resort. The manager of the lodge, while hardworking and enthusiastic, has very little experience in the restaurant business. The manager is responsible for selecting the menu, finding and training employees, and overseeing daily operations. The kitchen staff prepare food and wash dishes. The dining room staff take orders, serve as cashiers, and clean the dining room area.

Shortly after taking over Lost Peak, management of Western Resorts held a day-long meeting with all of the employees of the Powder 8 Lodge to discuss the future of the ski resort and the new management's plans for the lodge. At the end of this meeting, management and lodge employees created a balanced score-card for the lodge that would help guide operations for the coming ski season. Almost everyone who partici-pated in the meeting seemed to be enthusiastic about the scorecard and management's plans for the lodge.

The following performance measures were included on the balanced scorecard for the Powder 8 Lodge:

a. Weekly Powder 8 Lodge sales
b. Weekly Powder 8 Lodge profit
c. Number of menu items
d. Dining area cleanliness as rated by a representative from Western Resorts management
e. Customer satisfaction with menu choices as measured by customer surveys
f. Customer satisfaction with service as measured by customer surveys
g. Average time to take an order
h. Average time to prepare an order
i. Percentage of kitchen staff completing a basic cooking course at the local community college
j. Percentage of dining room staff completing a basic hospitality course at the local community college

Western Resorts will pay for the costs of staff attending courses at the local community college.

***Required:***
1. Using the above performance measures, construct a balanced scorecard for the Powder 8 Lodge. Use Exhibit 10–5 as a guide. Use arrows to show causal links and indicate with a + or − whether the performance measure should increase or decrease.
2. What hypotheses are built into the balanced scorecard for the Powder 8 Lodge? Which of these hypotheses do you believe are most questionable? Why?
3. How will management know if one of the hypotheses underlying the balanced scorecard is false?

**EXERCISE 10–5  Return on Investment (ROI) LO10–1**
Provide the missing data in the following table for a distributor of martial arts products:

|  | Division | | |
|---|---|---|---|
|  | **Alpha** | **Bravo** | **Charlie** |
| Sales.................................... | $    ? | $11,500,000 | $    ? |
| Net operating income .................. | $    ? | $    920,000 | $210,000 |
| Average operating assets.............. | $800,000 | $    ? | $    ? |
| Margin ............................... | 4% | ? | 7% |
| Turnover............................. | 5 | ? | ? |
| Return on investment (ROI)............. | ? | 20% | 14% |

**EXERCISE 10–6  Contrasting Return on Investment (ROI) and Residual Income LO10–1, LO10–2**
Meiji Isetan Corp. of Japan has two regional divisions with headquarters in Osaka and Yokohama. Selected data on the two divisions follow:

|  | Division | |
|---|---|---|
|  | **Osaka** | **Yokohama** |
| Sales............................. | $3,000,000 | $9,000,000 |
| Net operating income ............. | $210,000 | $720,000 |
| Average operating assets.......... | $1,000,000 | $4,000,000 |

*Required:*

1.  For each division, compute the return on investment (ROI) in terms of margin and turnover. Where necessary, carry computations to two decimal places.
2.  Assume that the company evaluates performance using residual income and that the minimum required rate of return for any division is 15%. Compute the residual income for each division.
3.  Is Yokohama's greater amount of residual income an indication that it is better managed? Explain.

**EXERCISE 10–7   Creating a Balanced Scorecard** LO10–4

Ariel Tax Services prepares tax returns for individual and corporate clients. As the company has gradually expanded to 10 offices, the founder Max Jacobs has begun to feel as though he is losing control of operations. In response to this concern, he has decided to implement a performance measurement system that will help control current operations and facilitate his plans of expanding to 20 offices.

Jacobs describes the keys to the success of his business as follows:

"Our only real asset is our people. We must keep our employees highly motivated and we must hire the 'cream of the crop.' Interestingly, employee morale and recruiting success are both driven by the same two factors—compensation and career advancement. In other words, providing superior compensation relative to the industry average coupled with fast-track career advancement opportunities keeps morale high and makes us a very attractive place to work. It drives a high rate of job offer acceptances relative to job offers tendered."

"Hiring highly qualified people and keeping them energized ensures operational success, which in our business is a function of productivity, efficiency, and effectiveness. Productivity boils down to employees being billable rather than idle. Efficiency relates to the time required to complete a tax return. Finally, effectiveness is critical to our business in the sense that we cannot tolerate errors. Completing a tax return quickly is meaningless if the return contains errors."

"Our growth depends on acquiring new customers through word-of-mouth from satisfied repeat customers. We believe that our customers come back year after year because they value error-free, timely, and courteous tax return preparation. Common courtesy is an important aspect of our business! We call it service quality, and it all ties back to employee morale in the sense that happy employees treat their clients with care and concern."

"While sales growth is obviously important to our future plans, growth without a corresponding increase in profitability is useless. Therefore, we understand that increasing our profit margin is a function of cost-efficiency as well as sales growth. Given that payroll is our biggest expense, we must maintain an optimal balance between staffing levels and the revenue being generated. As I alluded to earlier, the key to maintaining this balance is employee productivity. If we can achieve cost-efficient sales growth, we should eventually have 20 profitable offices!"

*Required:*

1.  Create a balanced scorecard for Ariel Tax Services. Link your scorecard measures using the framework from Exhibit 10–5. Indicate whether each measure is expected to increase or decrease. Feel free to create measures that may not be specifically mentioned in the chapter, but make sense given the strategic goals of the company.
2.  What hypotheses are built into the balanced scorecard for Ariel Tax Services? Which of these hypotheses do you believe are most questionable and why?
3.  Discuss the potential advantages and disadvantages of implementing an internal business process measure called *total dollar amount of tax refunds generated*. Would you recommend using this measure in Ariel's balanced scorecard?
4.  Would it be beneficial to attempt to measure each office's individual performance with respect to the scorecard measures that you created? Why or why not?

**EXERCISE 10–8   Computing and Interpreting Return on Investment (ROI)** LO10–1

Selected operating data for two divisions of Outback Brewing, Ltd., of Australia are given below:

|  | Division | |
| --- | --- | --- |
|  | **Queensland** | **New South Wales** |
| Sales..................................... | $4,000,000 | $7,000,000 |
| Average operating assets................ | $2,000,000 | $2,000,000 |
| Net operating income ................... | $360,000 | $420,000 |
| Property, plant, and equipment (net)....... | $950,000 | $800,000 |

**Required:**
1.   Compute the rate of return for each division using the return on investment (ROI) formula stated in terms of margin and turnover.
2.   Which divisional manager seems to be doing the better job? Why?

**EXERCISE 10–9   Return on Investment (ROI) and Residual Income Relations** LO10–1, LO10–2

A family friend has asked your help in analyzing the operations of three anonymous companies operating in the same service sector industry. Supply the missing data in the table below:

| | Company | | |
|---|---|---|---|
| | **A** | **B** | **C** |
| Sales..................................... | $9,000,000 | $7,000,000 | $4,500,000 |
| Net operating income ..................... | $    ? | $  280,000 | $    ? |
| Average operating assets.................. | $3,000,000 | $    ? | $1,800,000 |
| Return on investment (ROI)................. | 18% | 14% | ? |
| Minimum required rate of return: | | | |
|    Percentage ............................ | 16% | ? | 15% |
|    Dollar amount.......................... | $    ? | $  320,000 | $    ? |
| Residual income.......................... | $    ? | $    ? | $   90,000 |

**EXERCISE 10–10   Cost-Volume-Profit Analysis and Return on Investment (ROI)** LO10–1

Posters.com is a small Internet retailer of high-quality posters. The company has $1,000,000 in operating assets and fixed expenses of $150,000 per year. With this level of operating assets and fixed expenses, the company can support sales of up to $3,000,000 per year. The company's contribution margin ratio is 25%, which means that an additional dollar of sales results in additional contribution margin, and net operating income, of 25 cents.

**Required:**
1.   Complete the following table showing the relation between sales and return on investment (ROI).

| Sales | Net Operating Income | Average Operating Assets | ROI |
|---|---|---|---|
| $2,500,000 | $475,000 | $1,000,000 | ? |
| $2,600,000 | $    ? | $1,000,000 | ? |
| $2,700,000 | $    ? | $1,000,000 | ? |
| $2,800,000 | $    ? | $1,000,000 | ? |
| $2,900,000 | $    ? | $1,000,000 | ? |
| $3,000,000 | $    ? | $1,000,000 | ? |

2.   What happens to the company's return on investment (ROI) as sales increase? Explain.

**EXERCISE 10–11   Effects of Changes in Profits and Assets on Return on Investment (ROI)** LO10–1

Fitness Fanatics is a regional chain of health clubs. The managers of the clubs, who have authority to make investments as needed, are evaluated based largely on return on investment (ROI). The company's Springfield Club reported the following results for the past year:

| | |
|---|---|
| Sales................................. | $1,400,000 |
| Net operating income ................. | $70,000 |
| Average operating assets.............. | $350,000 |

**Required:**
The following questions are to be considered independently. Carry out all computations to two decimal places.
1.   Compute the Springfield club's return on investment (ROI).

2. Assume that the manager of the club is able to increase sales by $70,000 and that, as a result, net operating income increases by $18,200. Further assume that this is possible without any increase in average operating assets. What would be the club's return on investment (ROI)?

3. Assume that the manager of the club is able to reduce expenses by $14,000 without any change in sales or average operating assets. What would be the club's return on investment (ROI)?

4. Assume that the manager of the club is able to reduce average operating assets by $70,000 without any change in sales or net operating income. What would be the club's return on investment (ROI)?

**EXERCISE 10–12  Evaluating New Investments Using Return on Investment (ROI) and Residual Income** LO10–1, LO10–2

Selected sales and operating data for three divisions of different structural engineering firms are given as follows:

|  | Division A | Division B | Division C |
|---|---|---|---|
| Sales...................................... | $12,000,000 | $14,000,000 | $25,000,000 |
| Average operating assets..................... | $3,000,000 | $7,000,000 | $5,000,000 |
| Net operating income ....................... | $600,000 | $560,000 | $800,000 |
| Minimum required rate of return .............. | 14% | 10% | 16% |

**Required:**

1. Compute the return on investment (ROI) for each division using the formula stated in terms of margin and turnover.

2. Compute the residual income for each division.

3. Assume that each division is presented with an investment opportunity that would yield a 15% rate of return.
   a. If performance is being measured by ROI, which division or divisions will probably accept the opportunity? Reject? Why?
   b. If performance is being measured by residual income, which division or divisions will probably accept the opportunity? Reject? Why?

**EXERCISE 10–13  Effects of Changes in Sales, Expenses, and Assets on ROI** LO10–1

CommercialServices.com Corporation provides business-to-business services on the Internet. Data concerning the most recent year appear below:

| Sales............................... | $3,000,000 |
|---|---|
| Net operating income ............... | $150,000 |
| Average operating assets............ | $750,000 |

**Required:**

Consider each question below independently. Carry out all computations to two decimal places.

1. Compute the company's return on investment (ROI).

2. The entrepreneur who founded the company is convinced that sales will increase next year by 50% and that net operating income will increase by 200%, with no increase in average operating assets. What would be the company's ROI?

3. The chief financial officer of the company believes a more realistic scenario would be a $1,000,000 increase in sales, requiring a $250,000 increase in average operating assets, with a resulting $200,000 increase in net operating income. What would be the company's ROI in this scenario?

**PROBLEMS**          connect

**PROBLEM 10–14  Measures of Internal Business Process Performance** LO10–3

DataSpan, Inc., automated its plant at the start of the current year and installed a flexible manufacturing system. The company is also evaluating its suppliers and moving toward Lean Production. Many adjustment problems have been encountered, including problems relating to performance measurement. After much study, the company has decided to use the performance measures below, and it has gathered data relating to these measures for the first four months of operations.

|                                          |       | Mon   | th    |       |
|------------------------------------------|-------|-------|-------|-------|
|                                          | **1** | **2** | **3** | **4** |
| Throughput time (days)...............    | ?     | ?     | ?     | ?     |
| Delivery cycle time (days)..............  | ?     | ?     | ?     | ?     |
| Manufacturing cycle efficiency (MCE)....  | ?     | ?     | ?     | ?     |
| Percentage of on-time deliveries........  | 91%   | 86%   | 83%   | 79%   |
| Total sales (units) .....................  | 3,210 | 3,072 | 2,915 | 2,806 |

Management has asked for your help in computing throughput time, delivery cycle time, and MCE. The following average times have been logged over the last four months:

|                                                   |       | Average per Month (in days) |       |       |
|---------------------------------------------------|-------|------|------|------|
|                                                   | **1** | **2** | **3** | **4** |
| Move time per unit...........................      | 0.4   | 0.3  | 0.4  | 0.4  |
| Process time per unit.........................     | 2.1   | 2.0  | 1.9  | 1.8  |
| Wait time per order before start of production.... | 16.0  | 17.5 | 19.0 | 20.5 |
| Queue time per unit..........................      | 4.3   | 5.0  | 5.8  | 6.7  |
| Inspection time per unit.......................    | 0.6   | 0.7  | 0.7  | 0.6  |

**Required:**
1. For each month, compute the following:
   a. The throughput time.
   b. The delivery cycle time.
   c. The manufacturing cycle efficiency (MCE).
2. Evaluate the company's performance over the last four months.
3. Refer to the move time, process time, and so forth, given above for month 4.
   a. Assume that in month 5 the move time, process time, and so forth, are the same as in month 4, except that through the use of Lean Production the company is able to completely eliminate the queue time during production. Compute the new throughput time and MCE.
   b. Assume in month 6 that the move time, process time, and so forth, are again the same as in month 4, except that the company is able to completely eliminate both the queue time during production and the inspection time. Compute the new throughput time and MCE.

**PROBLEM 10–15   Return on Investment (ROI) and Residual Income** LO10–1, LO10–2
Financial data for Joel de Paris, Inc., for last year follow:

| Joel de Paris, Inc. Balance Sheet | | |
|---|---|---|
|  | **Beginning Balance** | **Ending Balance** |
| **Assets** | | |
| Cash ........................................ | $ 140,000 | $ 120,000 |
| Accounts receivable ....................... | 450,000 | 530,000 |
| Inventory ................................... | 320,000 | 380,000 |
| Plant and equipment, net .................. | 680,000 | 620,000 |
| Investment in Buisson, S.A. ............... | 250,000 | 280,000 |
| Land (undeveloped) ....................... | 180,000 | 170,000 |
| Total assets ................................ | $2,020,000 | $2,100,000 |
| **Liabilities and Stockholders' Equity** | | |
| Accounts payable .......................... | $ 360,000 | $ 310,000 |
| Long-term debt ........................... | 1,500,000 | 1,500,000 |
| Stockholders' equity ...................... | 160,000 | 290,000 |
| Total liabilities and stockholders' equity......... | $2,020,000 | $2,100,000 |

| Joel de Paris, Inc. Income Statement | | |
|---|---|---|
| Sales........................................ | | $4,050,000 |
| Operating expenses ......................... | | 3,645,000 |
| Net operating income ....................... | | 405,000 |
| Interest and taxes: | | |
| Interest expense.......................... | $150,000 | |
| Tax expense ............................. | 110,000 | 260,000 |
| Net income ................................ | | $  145,000 |

The company paid dividends of $15,000 last year. The "Investment in Buisson, S.A.," on the balance sheet represents an investment in the stock of another company. The company's minimum required rate of return is 15%.

*Required:*

1.  Compute the company's average operating assets for last year.
2.  Compute the company's margin, turnover, and return on investment (ROI) for last year. (*Hint:* Should you use net income or net operating income in your calculations?)
3.  What was the company's residual income last year?

**PROBLEM 10–16   Creating a Balanced Scorecard LO10–4**

Mason Paper Company (MPC) manufactures commodity grade papers for use in computer printers and photocopiers. MPC has reported net operating losses for the last two years due to intense price pressure from much larger competitors. The MPC management team—including Kristen Townsend (CEO), Mike Martinez (VP of Manufacturing), Tom Andrews (VP of Marketing), and Wendy Chen (CFO)—is contemplating a change in strategy to save the company from impending bankruptcy. Excerpts from a recent management team meeting are shown below:

**Townsend:** As we all know, the commodity paper manufacturing business is all about economies of scale. The largest competitors with the lowest cost per unit win. The limited capacity of our older machines prohibits us from competing in the high-volume commodity paper grades. Furthermore, expanding our capacity by acquiring a new paper-making machine is out of the question given the extraordinarily high price tag. Therefore, I propose that we abandon cost reduction as a strategic goal and instead pursue manufacturing flexibility as the key to our future success.

**Chen:** Manufacturing flexibility? What does that mean?

**Martinez:** It means we have to abandon our "crank out as many tons of paper as possible" mentality. Instead, we need to pursue the low-volume business opportunities that exist in the nonstandard, specialized paper grades. To succeed in this regard, we'll need to improve our flexibility in three ways. First, we must improve our ability to switch between paper grades. Right now, we require an average of four hours to change over to another paper grade. Timely customer deliveries are a function of changeover performance. Second, we need to expand the range of paper grades that we can manufacture. Currently, we can only manufacture three paper grades. Our customers must perceive that we are a "one-stop shop" that can meet all of their paper grade needs. Third, we will need to improve our yields (e.g., tons of acceptable output relative to total tons processed) in the nonstandard paper grades. Our percentage of waste within these grades will be unacceptably high unless we do something to improve our processes. Our variable costs will go through the roof if we cannot increase our yields!

**Chen:** Wait just a minute! These changes are going to destroy our equipment utilization numbers!

**Andrews:** You're right Wendy; however, equipment utilization is not the name of the game when it comes to competing in terms of flexibility. Our customers don't care about our equipment utilization. Instead, as Mike just alluded to, they want just-in-time delivery of smaller quantities of a full range of paper grades. If we can shrink the elapsed time from order placement to order delivery and expand our product offerings, it will increase sales from current customers and bring in new customers. Furthermore, we will be able to charge a premium price because of the limited competition within this niche from our cost-focused larger competitors. Our contribution margin per ton should drastically improve!

**Martinez:** Of course, executing the change in strategy will not be easy. We'll need to make a substantial investment in training because ultimately it is our people who create our flexible manufacturing capabilities.

**Chen:** If we adopt this new strategy, it is definitely going to impact how we measure performance. We'll need to create measures that motivate our employees to make decisions that support our flexibility goals.

**Townsend:** Wendy, you hit the nail right on the head. For our next meeting, could you pull together some potential measures that support our new strategy?

*Required:*
1. Contrast MPC's previous manufacturing strategy with its new manufacturing strategy.
2. Generally speaking, why would a company that changes its strategic goals need to change its performance measurement system as well? What are some examples of measures that would have been appropriate for MPC prior to its change in strategy? Why would those measures fail to support MPC's new strategy?
3. Construct a balanced scorecard that would support MPC's new manufacturing strategy. Use arrows to show the causal links between the performance measures and show whether the performance measure should increase or decrease over time. Feel free to create measures that may not be specifically mentioned in the chapter, but nonetheless make sense given the strategic goals of the company.
4. What hypotheses are built into MPC's balanced scorecard? Which of these hypotheses do you believe are most questionable and why?

**PROBLEM 10–17  Comparison of Performance Using Return on Investment (ROI) LO10–1**
Comparative data on three companies in the same service industry are given below:

| | A | B | C |
|---|---|---|---|
| Sales.................... | $600,000 | $500,000 | $? |
| Net operating income......... | $ 84,000 | $ 70,000 | $? |
| Average operating assets...... | $300,000 | $ ? | $1,000,000 |
| Margin ................ | ? | ? | 3.5% |
| Turnover................ | ? | ? | 2 |
| ROI ................... | ? | 7% | ? |

Header: **Company** spans A, B, C.

*Required:*
1. What advantages are there to breaking down the ROI computation into two separate elements, margin and turnover?
2. Fill in the missing information above, and comment on the relative performance of the three companies in as much detail as the data permit. Make *specific recommendations* about how to improve the ROI.

(Adapted from National Association of Accountants, *Research Report No. 35,* p. 34)

**PROBLEM 10–18  Return on Investment (ROI) and Residual Income LO10–1, LO10–2**
"I know headquarters wants us to add that new product line," said Dell Havasi, manager of Billings Company's Office Products Division. "But I want to see the numbers before I make any move. Our division's return on investment (ROI) has led the company for three years, and I don't want any letdown."

Billings Company is a decentralized wholesaler with five autonomous divisions. The divisions are evaluated on the basis of ROI, with year-end bonuses given to the divisional managers who have the highest ROIs. Operating results for the company's Office Products Division for this year are given below:

| | |
|---|---|
| Sales........................ | $10,000,000 |
| Variable expenses............... | 6,000,000 |
| Contribution margin........... | 4,000,000 |
| Fixed expenses................ | 3,200,000 |
| Net operating income......... | $ 800,000 |
| Divisional average operating assets....... | $ 4,000,000 |

The company had an overall return on investment (ROI) of 15% this year (considering all divisions). Next year the Office Products Division has an opportunity to add a new product line that would require an additional investment that would increase average operating assets by $1,000,000. The cost and revenue characteristics of the new product line per year would be:

| | |
|---|---|
| Sales.......................... | $2,000,000 |
| Variable expenses.............. | 60% of sales |
| Fixed expenses................. | $640,000 |

**Required:**
1. Compute the Office Products Division's ROI for this year.
2. Compute the Office Products Division's ROI for the new product line by itself.
3. Compute the Office Products Division's ROI for next year assuming that it performs the same as this year and adds the new product line.
4. If you were in Dell Havasi's position, would you accept or reject the new product line? Explain.
5. Why do you suppose headquarters is anxious for the Office Products Division to add the new product line?
6. Suppose that the company's minimum required rate of return on operating assets is 12% and that performance is evaluated using residual income.
   a. Compute the Office Products Division's residual income for this year.
   b. Compute the Office Products Division's residual income for the new product line by itself.
   c. Compute the Office Products Division's residual income for next year assuming that it performs the same as this year and adds the new product line.
   d. Using the residual income approach, if you were in Dell Havasi's position, would you accept or reject the new product line? Explain.

**PROBLEM 10–19 Internal Business Process Performance Measures LO10–3**
Tombro Industries is in the process of automating one of its plants and developing a flexible manufacturing system. The company is finding it necessary to make many changes in operating procedures. Progress has been slow, particularly in trying to develop new performance measures for the factory.

In an effort to evaluate performance and determine where improvements can be made, management has gathered the following data relating to activities over the last four months:

| | Month | | | |
|---|---|---|---|---|
| | **1** | **2** | **3** | **4** |
| Quality control measures: | | | | |
|   Number of defects..................................... | 185 | 163 | 124 | 91 |
|   Number of warranty claims......................... | 46 | 39 | 30 | 27 |
|   Number of customer complaints.................... | 102 | 96 | 79 | 58 |
| Material control measures: | | | | |
|   Purchase order lead time .......................... | 8 days | 7 days | 5 days | 4 days |
|   Scrap as a percent of total cost.................... | 1% | 1% | 2% | 3% |
| Machine performance measures: | | | | |
|   Machine downtime as a percentage of availability .... | 3% | 4% | 4% | 6% |
|   Use as a percentage of availability.................. | 95% | 92% | 89% | 85% |
|   Setup time (hours) ................................ | 8 | 10 | 11 | 12 |
| Delivery performance measures: | | | | |
|   Throughput time..................................... | ? | ? | ? | ? |
|   Manufacturing cycle efficiency (MCE)................ | ? | ? | ? | ? |
|   Delivery cycle time................................. | ? | ? | ? | ? |
|   Percentage of on-time deliveries .................. | 96% | 95% | 92% | 89% |

The president has read in industry journals that throughput time, MCE, and delivery cycle time are important measures of performance, but no one is sure how they are computed. You have been asked to assist the company, and you have gathered the following data relating to these measures:

| | Average per Month (in days) | | | |
|---|---|---|---|---|
| | **1** | **2** | **3** | **4** |
| Wait time per order before start of production ...................... | 9.0 | 11.5 | 12.0 | 14.0 |
| Inspection time per unit .............. | 0.8 | 0.7 | 0.7 | 0.7 |
| Process time per unit ................ | 2.1 | 2.0 | 1.9 | 1.8 |
| Queue time per unit ................. | 2.8 | 4.4 | 6.0 | 7.0 |
| Move time per unit .................. | 0.3 | 0.4 | 0.4 | 0.5 |

**Required:**

1. For each month, compute the following performance measures:
   a. Throughput time.
   b. MCE.
   c. Delivery cycle time.
2. Using the performance measures given in the main body of the problem and the performance measures computed in (1) above, do the following:
   a. Identify areas where the company seems to be improving.
   b. Identify areas where the company seems to be deteriorating.
3. Refer to the inspection time, process time, and so forth, given for month 4.
   a. Assume that in month 5 the inspection time, process time, and so forth, are the same as for month 4, except that the company is able to completely eliminate the queue time during production using Lean Production. Compute the new throughput time and MCE.
   b. Assume that in month 6 the inspection time, process time, and so forth, are the same as in month 4, except that the company is able to eliminate both the queue time during production and the inspection time using Lean Production. Compute the new throughput time and MCE.

**PROBLEM 10–20   Return on Investment (ROI) Analysis LO10–1**

The contribution format income statement for Huerra Company for last year is given below:

| | Total | Unit |
|---|---|---|
| Sales.......................... | $4,000,000 | $80.00 |
| Variable expenses .............. | 2,800,000 | 56.00 |
| Contribution margin............. | 1,200,000 | 24.00 |
| Fixed expenses.................. | 840,000 | 16.80 |
| Net operating income ........... | 360,000 | 7.20 |
| Income taxes @ 30%............. | 108,000 | 2.16 |
| Net income .................... | $ 252,000 | $ 5.04 |

The company had average operating assets of $2,000,000 during the year.

**Required:**

1. Compute the company's return on investment (ROI) for the period using the ROI formula stated in terms of margin and turnover.
   For each of the following questions, indicate whether the margin and turnover will increase, decrease, or remain unchanged as a result of the events described, and then compute the new ROI figure. Consider each question separately, starting in each case from the data used to compute the original ROI in (1) above.
2. Using Lean Production, the company is able to reduce the average level of inventory by $400,000. (The released funds are used to pay off short-term creditors.)
3. The company achieves a cost savings of $32,000 per year by using less costly materials.
4. The company issues bonds and uses the proceeds to purchase machinery and equipment that increases average operating assets by $500,000. Interest on the bonds is $60,000 per year. Sales remain unchanged. The new, more efficient equipment reduces production costs by $20,000 per year.

5.  As a result of a more intense effort by salespeople, sales are increased by 20%; operating assets remain unchanged.

6.  At the beginning of the year, obsolete inventory carried on the books at a cost of $40,000 is scrapped and written off as a loss.

7.  At the beginning of the year, the company uses $200,000 of cash (received on accounts receivable) to repurchase and retire some of its common stock.

**PROBLEM 10–21   Creating Balanced Scorecards that Support Different Strategies LO10–4**

The Midwest Consulting Group (MCG) helps companies build balanced scorecards. As part of its marketing efforts, MCG conducts an annual balanced scorecard workshop for prospective clients. As MCG's newest employee, your boss has asked you to participate in this year's workshop by explaining to attendees how a company's strategy determines the measures that are appropriate for its balanced scorecard. Your boss has provided you with the excerpts below from the annual reports of two current MCG clients. She has asked you to use these excerpts in your portion of the workshop.

Excerpt from Applied Pharmaceuticals' annual report:

> The keys to our business are consistent and timely new product introductions and manufacturing process integrity. The new product introduction side of the equation is a function of research and development (R&D) yield (e.g., the number of marketable drug compounds created relative to the total number of potential compounds pursued). We seek to optimize our R&D yield and first-to-market capability by investing in state-of-the-art technology, hiring the highest possible percentage of the "best and the brightest" engineers that we pursue, and providing world-class training to those engineers. Manufacturing process integrity is all about establishing world-class quality specifications and then relentlessly engaging in prevention and appraisal activities to minimize defect rates. Our customers must have an awareness of and respect for our brand image of being "first to market and first in quality." If we deliver on this pledge to our customers, then our financial goal of increasing our return on stockholders' equity should take care of itself.

Excerpt from Destination Resorts International's annual report:

> Our business succeeds or fails based on the quality of the service that our front-line employees provide to customers. Therefore, it is imperative that we strive to maintain high employee morale and minimize employee turnover. In addition, it is critical that we train our employees to use technology to create one seamless worldwide experience for our repeat customers. Once an employee enters a customer preference (e.g., provide two extra pillows in the room, deliver fresh brewed coffee to the room at 8:00 A.M., etc.) into our database, our worldwide workforce strives to ensure that a customer will never need to repeat it at any of our destination resorts. If we properly train and retain a motivated workforce, we should see continuous improvement in our percentage of error-free repeat customer check-ins, the time taken to resolve customer complaints, and our independently assessed room cleanliness. This in turn should drive improvement in our customer retention, which is the key to meeting our revenue growth goals.

***Required:***

1.  Based on the excerpts above, compare and contrast the strategies of Applied Pharmaceuticals and Destination Resorts International.

2.  Select balanced scorecard measures for each company and link the scorecard measures using the framework from Exhibit 10-5. Use arrows to show the causal links between the performance measures and show whether the performance measure should increase or decrease over time. Feel free to create measures that may not be specifically mentioned in the chapter, but nonetheless make sense given the strategic goals of each company.

3.  What hypotheses are built into each balanced scorecard? Why do the hypotheses differ between the two companies?

**PROBLEM 10–22   Perverse Effects of Some Performance Measures LO10–4**

There is often more than one way to improve a performance measure. Unfortunately, some of the actions taken by managers to make their performance look better may actually harm the organization. For example, suppose the marketing department is held responsible only for increasing the performance measure "total revenues." Increases in total revenues may be achieved by working harder and smarter, but they can also usually be achieved by simply cutting prices. The increase in volume from cutting prices almost always results in greater total revenues; however, it does not always lead to greater total profits. Those who design performance measurement systems need to keep in mind that managers who are under pressure to perform may take actions to improve performance measures that have negative consequences elsewhere.

***Required:***

For each of the following situations, describe actions managers might take to show improvement in the performance measure but which do not actually lead to improvement in the organization's overall performance.

1. Concerned with the slow rate at which new products are brought to market, top management of a consumer electronics company introduces a new performance measure—speed-to-market. The research and development department is given responsibility for this performance measure, which measures the average amount of time a product is in development before it is released to the market for sale.

2. The CEO of an airline company is dissatisfied with the amount of time her ground crews are taking to unload luggage from airplanes. To solve the problem, she decides to measure the average elapsed time from when an airplane parks at the gate to when all pieces of luggage are unloaded from the airplane. For each month that an airport's ground crew can lower its "average elapsed time" relative to the prior month, the CEO pays a lump-sum bonus to be split equally among members of the crew.

3. A manufacturing company has been plagued by the chronic failure to ship orders to customers by the promised date. To solve this problem, the production manager has been given the responsibility of increasing the percentage of orders shipped on time. When a customer calls in an order, the production manager and the customer agree to a delivery date. If the order is not completed by that date, it is counted as a late shipment.

4. Concerned with the productivity of employees, the board of directors of a large multinational corporation has dictated that the manager of each subsidiary will be held responsible for increasing the revenue per employee of his or her subsidiary.

**connect BUILDING YOUR SKILLS**

**CASE LO10–4**

Haglund Department Store is located in the downtown area of a small city. While the store had been profitable for many years, it is facing increasing competition from large national chains that have set up stores on the outskirts of the city. Recently the downtown area has been undergoing revitalization, and the owners of Haglund Department Store are somewhat optimistic that profitability can be restored.

In an attempt to accelerate the return to profitability, management of Haglund Department Store is in the process of designing a balanced scorecard for the company. Management believes the company should focus on two key problems. First, customers are taking longer and longer to pay the bills they incur using the department store's charge card, and the company has far more bad debts than are normal for the industry. If this problem were solved, the company would have more cash to make much needed renovations. Investigation has revealed that much of the problem with late payments and unpaid bills results from customers disputing incorrect charges on their bills. These incorrect charges usually occur because salesclerks incorrectly enter data on the charge account slip. Second, the company has been incurring large losses on unsold seasonal apparel. Such items are ordinarily resold at a loss to discount stores that specialize in such distress items.

The meeting in which the balanced scorecard approach was discussed was disorganized and ineffectively led—possibly because no one other than one of the vice presidents had read anything about how to build a balanced scorecard. Nevertheless, a number of potential performance measures were suggested by various managers. These potential performance measures are:

a. Percentage of charge account bills containing errors.
b. Percentage of salesclerks trained to correctly enter data on charge account slips.
c. Average age of accounts receivables.
d. Profit per employee.
e. Customer satisfaction with accuracy of charge account bills from monthly customer survey.
f. Total sales revenue.
g. Sales per employee.
h. Travel expenses for buyers for trips to fashion shows.
i. Unsold inventory at the end of the season as a percentage of total cost of sales.
j. Courtesy shown by junior staff members to senior staff members based on surveys of senior staff.
k. Percentage of suppliers making just-in-time deliveries.
l. Sales per square foot of floor space.
m. Written-off accounts receivable (bad debts) as a percentage of sales.
n. Quality of food in the staff cafeteria based on staff surveys.
o. Percentage of employees who have attended the city's cultural diversity workshop.
p. Total profit.

*Required:*

1.  As someone with more knowledge of the balanced scorecard than almost anyone else in the company, you have been asked to build an integrated balanced scorecard. In your scorecard, use only performance measures listed previously. You do not have to use all of the performance measures suggested by the managers, but you should build a balanced scorecard that reveals a strategy for dealing with the problems with accounts receivable and with unsold merchandise. Construct the balanced scorecard following the format used in Exhibit 10–5. Do not be concerned with whether a specific performance measure falls within the learning and growth, internal business process, customer, or financial perspective. However, use arrows to show the causal links between performance measures within your balanced scorecard and explain whether the performance measures should show increases or decreases.

2.  Assume the company adopts your balanced scorecard. After operating for a year, some performance measures show improvements, but not others. What should management do next?

3.  a. Suppose customers express greater satisfaction with the accuracy of their charge account bills but the performance measures for the average age of accounts receivable and for bad debts do not improve. Explain why this might happen.

    b. Suppose the performance measures for the average age of accounts receivable, bad debts, and unsold inventory improve, but total profits do not. Explain why this might happen. Assume in your answer that the explanation lies within the company.

**COMMUNICATING IN PRACTICE** LO10–1, LO10–2, LO10–3

How do the performance measurement and compensation systems of service companies compare with those of manufacturers? Ask the manager of your local McDonald's, Wendy's, Burger King, or other fast-food chain if he or she could spend some time discussing the performance measures that the company uses to evaluate store managers and how the performance measures tie in with their compensation.

*Required:*

After asking the following questions, write a brief memorandum to your instructor that summarizes what you discovered during your interview with the manager of the franchise.

1.  What are the national chain's goals, that is, the broad, long-range plans of the company (e.g., to increase market share)?

2.  What performance measures are used to help motivate the store managers and monitor progress toward achieving the corporation's goals?

3.  Are the performance measures consistent with the store manager's compensation plan?

**A LOOK BACK**

We concluded our coverage of performance measures in Chapter 10 by focusing on decentralized organizations. Return on investment (ROI) and residual income are used to motivate the managers of investment centers and to monitor the performance of these centers.

**A LOOK AT THIS CHAPTER**

We continue our coverage of decision making in Chapter 11 by focusing on the use of differential analysis when analyzing alternatives. In general, only those costs and benefits that differ between alternatives are relevant in a decision. This basic idea is applied in a wide variety of situations in this chapter.

**A LOOK AHEAD**

In Chapter 12, we discuss common approaches to making major investment decisions, which can have significant long-term implications for any organization.

# 11 Differential Analysis: The Key to Decision Making

## CHAPTER OUTLINE

**Decision Making: Six Key Concepts**

- Key Concept #1
- Key Concept #2
- Key Concept #3
- Key Concept #4
- Key Concept #5
- Key Concept #6

**Identifying Relevant Costs and Benefits: An Example**

**Decision Analysis: The Total Cost and Differential Cost Approaches**

- Why Isolate Relevant Costs?

**Adding and Dropping Product Lines and Other Segments**

- An Illustration of Cost Analysis
- A Comparative Format

- Beware of Allocated Fixed Costs

**Make or Buy Decisions**

- Strategic Aspects of the Make or Buy Decision
- An Example of a Make or Buy Decision
- Opportunity Cost

**Special Order Decisions**

**Volume Trade-Off Decisions**

- What is a Constraint?
- Utilizing a Constrained Resource to Maximize Profits
- Managing Constraints

**Joint Product Costs and Sell or Process Further Decisions**

- Santa Maria Wool Cooperative: An Example

**Activity-Based Costing and Relevant Costs**

©Ian Dagnall/Alamy Stock Photo

# Understanding the Qualitative Aspects of Decision Making

**SAS** is a privately held $3.2 billion company located in Cary, North Carolina. The company maintains a beautifully landscaped 200-acre campus that includes walking and biking trails for its employees. It also has an on-site medical facility that is staffed by doctors, nurse practitioners, physical therapists, and a nutritionist as well as a subsidized child care center, a recreation center, on-site vendor services (such as massage, hair care, shoe/watch repair, and tax preparation), and free snacks and beverages in the employee break rooms.

Although it may be difficult for SAS to quantify the benefits of providing these perks to its employees, the company chooses to make the investments because it believes that retaining happy and healthy employees is instrumental to its financial success.

Sources: *2017 Fortune's 100 Best Companies to Work For* (http://beta.fortune.com/best-companies/sas-15) and www.sas.com.

This chapter discusses what may be a manager's most important responsibility—making decisions. Examples of decisions include deciding what products to sell, whether to make or buy component parts, what prices to charge, what channels of distribution to use, and whether to accept special orders at special prices. Making such decisions is often a difficult task that is complicated by numerous alternatives and massive amounts of data; however, in this chapter you will learn how to narrow your focus to the information that matters.

# DECISION MAKING: SIX KEY CONCEPTS

**LEARNING OBJECTIVE 11–1**

Identify relevant and irrelevant costs and benefits in a decision.

There are six key concepts that you need to understand to make intelligent decisions. This section discusses each of those concepts and then concludes by introducing some additional terminology that was created to help you solve the exercises and problems at the end of the chapter.

## Key Concept #1

Every decision involves choosing from among at least two alternatives. Therefore, the first step in decision making is to define the alternatives being considered. For example, if a company is deciding whether to make a component part or buy it from an outside supplier, the alternatives are *make* or *buy* the component part. Similarly, if a company is considering discontinuing a particular product, the alternatives are *keep* or *drop* the product.

## Key Concept #2

Once you have defined the alternatives, you need to identify the criteria for choosing among them. The key to choosing among alternatives is distinguishing between *relevant* and *irrelevant* costs and benefits. **Relevant costs** and **relevant benefits** should be considered when making decisions. *Irrelevant costs* and *irrelevant benefits* should be ignored when making decisions. This is an important concept for two reasons. First, being able to ignore irrelevant data saves decision makers tremendous amounts of time and effort. Second, bad decisions can easily result from erroneously including irrelevant costs and benefits when analyzing alternatives.

## Key Concept #3

The key to effective decision making is *differential analysis*—focusing on the future costs and benefits that differ between the alternatives. Everything else is irrelevant and should be ignored. A future cost that differs between any two alternatives is known as a **differential cost**. Differential costs are always relevant costs. Future revenue that differs between any two alternatives is known as **differential revenue**. Differential revenue is an example of a relevant benefit.

   The terms *incremental cost* and *avoidable cost* are often used to describe differential costs. An **incremental cost** is an increase in cost between two alternatives. For example, if you are choosing between buying the standard model or the deluxe model of your favorite automobile, the costs of the upgrades contained in the deluxe model are incremental costs. An **avoidable cost** is a cost that can be eliminated by choosing one alternative over another. For example, assume that you have decided to watch a movie tonight; however, you are trying to choose between two alternatives—going to the movie theater or renting a movie. The cost of the ticket to get into the movie theater is an avoidable cost. You would avoid this cost by renting a movie. Similarly, the movie rental fee is an avoidable cost because you could avoid it by going to the movie theater. Avoidable costs (and incremental costs) are always relevant costs.

Differential costs and benefits can be qualitative or quantitative in nature. While qualitative differences between alternatives can have an important impact on decisions, and therefore, should not be ignored; our goal in this chapter is to hone your quantitative analysis skills. Therefore, our primary focus will be on analyzing quantitative differential costs and benefits—those that have readily measurable impacts on future cash flows.

## Key Concept #4

*Sunk costs* are always irrelevant when choosing among alternatives. A **sunk cost** is a cost that has already been incurred and cannot be changed regardless of what a manager decides to do. Sunk costs have no impact on future cash flows and they remain the same no matter what alternatives are being considered; therefore, they are irrelevant and should be ignored when making decisions.

For example, suppose a company purchased a five-year-old truck for $12,000. The amount paid for the truck is a sunk cost because it has already been incurred and the transaction cannot be undone. The $12,000 paid for the truck is irrelevant in making decisions such as whether to keep, sell, or replace the truck. Furthermore, any accounting depreciation expense related to the truck is irrelevant in making decisions. This is true because accounting depreciation is a noncash expense that has no effect on future cash flows. It simply spreads the sunk cost of the truck over its useful life.

## Key Concept #5

Future costs and benefits that *do not differ between alternatives* are irrelevant to the decision-making process. So, continuing with the movie example, assume that you plan to buy a **Papa John's** pizza after watching a movie. If you are going to buy the same pizza regardless of your movie-watching venue, the cost of the pizza is irrelevant when choosing between the theater and the rental. The cost of the pizza is *not* a sunk cost because it has not yet been incurred. Nonetheless, the cost of the pizza is irrelevant to the choice of venue because it is a future cost that does not differ between the alternatives.

## Key Concept #6

*Opportunity costs* also need to be considered when making decisions. An **opportunity cost** is the potential benefit that is given up when one alternative is selected over another. For example, if you were considering giving up a high-paying summer job to travel overseas, the forgone wages would be an opportunity cost of traveling abroad. Opportunity costs are not usually found in accounting records, but they are a type of differential cost that must be explicitly considered in every decision a manager makes.

This chapter covers various decision contexts, such as keep or drop decisions, make or buy decisions, special order decisions, and sell or process further decisions. While tackling these diverse decision contexts may seem a bit overwhelming, keep in mind that they all share a unifying theme—choosing between alternatives based on their differential costs and benefits. To emphasize this common theme, many end-of-chapter exercises and problems that span a variety of learning objectives will often use the same terminology—financial advantage (disadvantage)—when asking you to choose between alternatives. For example, numerous exercises and problems will ask questions such as:

1. What is the financial advantage (disadvantage) of closing the store?
2. What is the financial advantage (disadvantage) of buying the component part from a supplier rather than making it?
3. What is the financial advantage (disadvantage) of accepting the special order?
4. What is the financial advantage (disadvantage) of further processing the intermediate product?

In all of these various contexts, a financial advantage exists if pursuing an alternative, such as closing a store or accepting a special order, passes the cost/benefit test. In other words, it exists if the alternative's differential benefits (i.e., its future cash inflows) exceed its differential costs (i.e., its future cash outflows). Conversely, a financial (disadvantage) exists when an alternative fails the cost/benefit test—its differential benefits are less than its differential costs.[1]

# IDENTIFYING RELEVANT COSTS AND BENEFITS: AN EXAMPLE

Cynthia is currently a student in an MBA program in Boston and would like to visit a friend in New York City over the weekend. She is trying to decide whether to drive or take the train. Because she is on a tight budget, she wants to carefully consider the costs of the two alternatives. If one alternative is far less expensive than the other, that may be decisive in her choice. By car, the distance between her apartment in Boston and her friend's apartment in New York City is 230 miles. Cynthia has compiled the following list of items to consider:

| | **Automobile Costs** | | |
|---|---|---|---|
| | Item | Annual Cost of Fixed Items | Cost per Mile (based on 10,000 miles per year) |
| (a) | Annual straight-line depreciation on car [($24,000 original cost − $10,000 estimated resale value in 5 years)/5 years]............... | $2,800 | $0.280 |
| (b) | Cost of gasoline ($2.40 per gallon ÷ 24 miles per gallon).................................... | | 0.100 |
| (c) | Annual cost of auto insurance and license........ | $1,380 | 0.138 |
| (d) | Maintenance and repairs....................... | | 0.065 |
| (e) | Parking fees at school ($45 per month × 8 months).................................... | $360 | 0.036 |
| (f) | Total average cost per mile..................... | | $0.619 |

| | **Additional Data** | |
|---|---|---|
| | Item | |
| (g) | Reduction in the resale value of car due solely to wear and tear................................ | $0.080 per mile |
| (h) | Cost of round-trip train ticket from Boston to New York City...................................... | $114 |
| (i) | Benefit of relaxing and being able to study during the train ride rather than having to drive........ | ? |
| (j) | Cost of putting the dog in a kennel while gone..... | $80 |
| (k) | Benefit of having a car available in New York City .. | ? |
| (l) | Hassle of parking the car in New York City......... | ? |
| (m) | Cost of parking the car in New York City........... | $25 per day |

---

[1]Over the life of a company, cumulative net cash flows equal cumulative net income. Therefore, if a decision maximizes future net cash flows, it will also maximize future cumulative net income. However, because of accruals, in any particular period net income will usually be different from net cash flow. A decision that is based on maximizing future net cash flows might, in the short run, reduce net income, but in the long run cumulative net income will be higher than it otherwise would have been.

Which costs and benefits are relevant in this decision? Remember, only the differential costs and benefits are relevant—everything else is irrelevant and can be ignored.

Start at the top of the list with item (a): the original cost of the car is a sunk cost. This cost has already been incurred and therefore can never differ between alternatives. Consequently, it is irrelevant and should be ignored. The same is true of the accounting depreciation of $2,800 per year, which simply spreads the sunk cost across five years.

Item (b), the cost of gasoline consumed by driving to New York City, is a relevant cost. If Cynthia takes the train, she would avoid the cost of the gasoline. Hence, the cost differs between alternatives and is therefore relevant.

Item (c), the annual cost of auto insurance and license, is not relevant. Whether Cynthia takes the train or drives on this particular trip, her annual auto insurance premium and her auto license fee will remain the same.[2]

Item (d), the cost of maintenance and repairs, is relevant. While maintenance and repair costs have a large random component, over the long run they should be more or less proportional to the number of miles the car is driven. Thus, the average cost of $0.065 per mile is a reasonable estimate to use.

Item (e), the monthly fee that Cynthia pays to park at her school during the academic year is not relevant. Regardless of which alternative she selects—driving or taking the train—she will still need to pay for parking at school.

Item (f) is the total average cost of $0.619 per mile. As discussed above, some elements of this total are relevant, but some are not relevant. Because it contains some irrelevant costs, it would be incorrect to estimate the cost of driving to New York City and back by simply multiplying the $0.619 by 460 miles (230 miles each way × 2). This erroneous approach would yield a cost of driving of $284.74. Unfortunately, such mistakes are often made in both personal life and in business. Because the total cost is stated on a per-mile basis, people are easily misled. Often people think that if the cost is stated as $0.619 per mile, the cost of driving 100 miles is $61.90. But it is not. Many of the costs included in the $0.619 cost per mile are sunk and/or fixed and will not increase if the car is driven another 100 miles. The $0.619 is an average cost, not a differential cost. Beware of such unitized costs (i.e., costs stated in terms of a dollar amount per unit, per mile, per direct labor-hour, per machine-hour, and so on)—they are often misleading.

Item (g), the decline in the resale value of the car that occurs as a consequence of driving more miles, is relevant in the decision. Because she uses the car, its resale value declines, which is a real cost of using the car that should be taken into account. Cynthia estimated this cost by accessing the *Kelley Blue Book* website at www.kbb.com. The reduction in resale value of an asset through use or over time is often called *real* or *economic depreciation*. This is different from accounting depreciation, which attempts to match the sunk cost of an asset with the periods that benefit from that cost.

Item (h), the $114 cost of a round-trip ticket on the train, is relevant in this decision. If she drives, she would avoid the cost of the ticket.

Item (i) is relevant to the decision, even if it is difficult to put a dollar value on relaxing and being able to study while on the train. It is relevant because it is a benefit that is available under one alternative but not under the other.

Item (j), the cost of putting Cynthia's dog in the kennel while she is gone, is irrelevant in this decision. Whether she takes the train or drives to New York City, she will still need to put her dog in a kennel.

Like item (i), items (k) and (l) are relevant to the decision even if it is difficult to measure their dollar impacts.

Item (m), the cost of parking in New York City, is relevant to the decision.

---

[2] If Cynthia has an accident while driving to New York City or back, this might affect her insurance premium when the policy is renewed. The increase in the insurance premium would be a relevant cost of this particular trip, but the normal amount of the insurance premium is not relevant in any case.

Bringing together all of the relevant data, Cynthia would estimate the relevant costs of driving and taking the train as follows:

**Relevant financial cost of driving to New York City:**

| | |
|---|---|
| Gasoline (460 miles × $0.100 per mile) . . . . . . . . . . . . . . . . . . . . . . . . . . . . . . . . | $ 46.00 |
| Maintenance and repairs (460 miles × $0.065 per mile) . . . . . . . . . . . . . . . . | 29.90 |
| Reduction in the resale value of car due solely to wear and tear (460 miles × $0.080 per mile) . . . . . . . . . . . . . . . . . . . . . . . . . . . . . . . . . . . | 36.80 |
| Cost of parking the car in New York City (2 days × $25 per day) . . . . . . . . . | 50.00 |
| Total . . . . . . . . . . . . . . . . . . . . . . . . . . . . . . . . . . . . . . . . . . . . . . . . . . . . . . . . . . . . . . | $162.70 |

**Relevant financial cost of taking the train to New York City:**

| | |
|---|---|
| Cost of round-trip train ticket from Boston to New York City . . . . . . . . . . . . . | $114.00 |

What should Cynthia do? From a purely financial standpoint, it would be cheaper by $48.70 ($162.70 − $114.00) to take the train than to drive. Cynthia has to decide if the convenience of having a car in New York City outweighs the additional cost and the disadvantages of being unable to relax and study on the train and the hassle of finding parking in the city.

## DECISION ANALYSIS: THE TOTAL COST AND DIFFERENTIAL COST APPROACHES

The example that we just completed focused on identifying the relevant costs and benefits of taking the train versus driving—everything else was ignored. This method of decision analysis is called the *differential approach* because it focuses solely on the relevant costs and benefits. Another method of decision analysis, called the *total cost approach*, includes all of the costs and benefits—relevant or not. When done correctly, the two methods always provide the same correct answer.

To compare and contrast these two methods, let's consider Oak Harbor Woodworks, a company that is contemplating renting a new labor-saving machine for $3,000 per year.

The machine will be used on the company's butcher block production line. Data concerning the company's annual sales and costs of butcher blocks with and without the new machine are shown below:

| | Current Situation | Situation with the New Machine |
|---|---|---|
| Units produced and sold . . . . . . . . . . . . . . . . . . . . . . . . . . . . | 5,000 | 5,000 |
| Selling price per unit. . . . . . . . . . . . . . . . . . . . . . . . . . . . . . | $40 | $40 |
| Direct materials cost per unit . . . . . . . . . . . . . . . . . . . . . . | $14 | $14 |
| Direct labor cost per unit . . . . . . . . . . . . . . . . . . . . . . . . . . | $8 | $5 |
| Variable overhead cost per unit . . . . . . . . . . . . . . . . . . . . | $2 | $2 |
| Fixed expenses, other . . . . . . . . . . . . . . . . . . . . . . . . . . . . | $62,000 | $62,000 |
| Fixed expenses, rental of new machine . . . . . . . . . . . . . . | — | $3,000 |

Given the data above, the net operating income for the product under the two alternatives can be computed, using the *total cost approach,* as shown in the first two columns of Exhibit 11–1. The net operating income in the current situation is $18,000 and the net operating income with the new machine is $30,000. The difference in the net operating incomes in these two columns indicates a $12,000 (= $30,000 – $18,000) financial advantage associated with renting the new machine. The irrelevant items (which includes sales, direct materials, variable overhead, and fixed expenses, other) appear in both columns, so they cancel each other out when isolating the $12,000 difference in favor of renting the machine.

| | Current Situation | Situation with New Machine | Differential Costs and Benefits |
|---|---|---|---|
| Sales (5,000 units × $40 per unit) . . . . . . . . . . . . . . . | $200,000 | $200,000 | $      0 |
| Variable expenses: | | | |
| Direct materials (5,000 units × $14 per unit). . . . . | 70,000 | 70,000 | 0 |
| Direct labor (5,000 units × $8 per unit; | | | |
| 5,000 units × $5 per unit) . . . . . . . . . . . . . . . . . | 40,000 | 25,000 | 15,000 |
| Variable overhead (5,000 units × $2 per unit) . . . . | 10,000 | 10,000 | 0 |
| Total variable expenses . . . . . . . . . . . . . . . . . . . . . . . | 120,000 | 105,000 | |
| Contribution margin . . . . . . . . . . . . . . . . . . . . . . . . . . | 80,000 | 95,000 | |
| Fixed expenses: | | | |
| Other. . . . . . . . . . . . . . . . . . . . . . . . . . . . . . . . . . . . | 62,000 | 62,000 | 0 |
| Rental of new machine. . . . . . . . . . . . . . . . . . . . . . . | 0 | 3,000 | (3,000) |
| Total fixed expenses. . . . . . . . . . . . . . . . . . . . . . . . . . | 62,000 | 65,000 | |
| Net operating income. . . . . . . . . . . . . . . . . . . . . . . . . | $ 18,000 | $ 30,000 | $12,000 |

**EXHIBIT 11–1**
Total and Differential Costs

The third column in Exhibit 11–1 uses the *differential cost approach* to derive the same financial advantage of $12,000 (= $15,000 + $(3,000)) that is associated with renting the new machine. A positive number in the Differential Costs and Benefits column indicates that the difference between the alternatives favors the new machine; a negative number indicates that the difference favors the current situation. A zero in that column simply means that the total amount for the item is exactly the same for both alternatives. If we properly account for the costs and benefits that do not differ between the alternatives, they will cancel out when we compare the alternatives; hence, they can be ignored.

Rather than setting up comparative income statements, we could have arrived at the same solution much more quickly by completely ignoring the irrelevant costs and benefits.

- The selling price per unit and the number of units sold do not differ between the alternatives. Therefore, the total sales revenues are exactly the same for the two alternatives as shown in Exhibit 11–1. Because the sales revenues are exactly the same, they have no effect on the difference in net operating income between the two alternatives. That is shown in the last column in Exhibit 11–1, which shows a $0 differential benefit.

- The direct materials cost per unit, the variable overhead cost per unit, and the number of units produced and sold do not differ between the alternatives. Consequently, the total direct materials cost and the total variable overhead cost are the same for the two alternatives and can be ignored.

- The "other" fixed expenses do not differ between the alternatives, so they can be ignored as well.

Indeed, the only costs that do differ between the alternatives are direct labor costs and the fixed rental cost of the new machine. Therefore, the two alternatives can be compared based only on these relevant costs:

| **Financial Advantage of Renting the New Machine** | |
| --- | --- |
| Decrease in direct labor costs (5,000 units at a cost savings of $3 per unit)... | $15,000 |
| Increase in fixed expenses ............................................. | (3,000) |
| Financial advantage of renting the new machine ......................... | $12,000 |

If we focus on just the relevant costs and benefits, we get exactly the same answer ($12,000 in favor of renting the new machine) as when we listed all of the costs and benefits as shown in Exhibit 11–1—including those that do not differ between the alternatives. We get the same answer because the only costs and benefits that matter in the final comparison are those items that differ between the two alternatives and, hence, are not zero in the last column of Exhibit 11–1.

## Why Isolate Relevant Costs?

In the preceding example, we used the total cost approach and the differential cost approach to derive the exact same answer. Thus, it would be natural to ask, "Why bother to isolate relevant costs when total costs will do the job just as well?" Isolating relevant costs is desirable for at least two reasons.

First, only rarely will enough information be available to prepare a detailed income statement for both alternatives. Assume, for example, that you are asked to make a decision relating to a portion of a single business process in a multidepartment, multiproduct company. Under these circumstances, it would be virtually impossible to prepare an income statement of any type. You would have to rely on your ability to recognize which costs are relevant and which are not in order to assemble the data necessary to make a decision.

Second, mingling irrelevant costs with relevant costs may cause confusion and distract attention from the information that is really critical. Furthermore, the danger always exists that an irrelevant piece of data may be used improperly, resulting in an incorrect decision. The best approach is to ignore irrelevant data and base the decision entirely on relevant data.

1. Which of the following statements is false? (You may select more than one answer.)
   a. Under some circumstances, a sunk cost may be a relevant cost.
   b. Future costs that do not differ between alternatives are irrelevant.
   c. The same cost may be relevant or irrelevant depending on the decision context.
   d. Only variable costs are relevant costs. Fixed costs cannot be relevant costs.
2. Assume that in October you bought a $450 nonrefundable airline ticket to Telluride, Colorado, for a 5-day/4-night winter ski vacation. You now have an opportunity to buy an airline ticket for a 5-day/4-night winter ski vacation in Stowe, Vermont, for $400 that includes a free ski lift ticket. The price of your lift ticket for the Telluride vacation would be $300. The price of a hotel room in Telluride is $180 per night. The price of a hotel room in Stowe is $150 per night. Which of the following costs is not relevant in a decision of whether to proceed with the planned trip to Telluride or to change to a trip to Stowe?
   a. The $450 airline ticket to Telluride.
   b. The $400 airline ticket to Stowe.
   c. The $300 lift ticket for the Telluride vacation.
   d. The $180 per night hotel room in Telluride.
3. Based on the facts in question 2 above, does a differential cost analysis favor Telluride or Stowe, and by how much?
   a. Stowe by $470.
   b. Stowe by $20.
   c. Telluride by $70.
   d. Telluride by $20.

## ADDING AND DROPPING PRODUCT LINES AND OTHER SEGMENTS

Decisions relating to whether product lines or other segments of a company should be dropped and new ones added are among the most difficult that a manager has to make. In such decisions, many qualitative and quantitative factors must be considered. Ultimately, however, any final decision to drop a business segment or to add a new one hinges primarily on its financial impact. To assess this impact, costs must be carefully analyzed.

> **LEARNING OBJECTIVE 11–2**
>
> Prepare an analysis showing whether a product line or other business segment should be added or dropped.

### An Illustration of Cost Analysis

Exhibit 11–2 provides sales and cost information for the preceding month for the Discount Drug Company and its three major product lines—drugs, cosmetics, and housewares. A quick review of this exhibit suggests that dropping the housewares segment would increase the company's overall net operating income by $8,000. However, this would be a flawed conclusion because the data in Exhibit 11–2 do not distinguish between fixed expenses that can be avoided if a product line is dropped and common fixed expenses that cannot be avoided by dropping any particular product line.

In this scenario, the two alternatives under consideration are whether to *keep* the housewares product line or *drop* it. If the housewares line is dropped, then the company will lose $20,000 per month in contribution margin because all of this segment's sales and variable expenses will be eliminated. However, by dropping the housewares line it may be possible to avoid some fixed costs such as salaries or advertising costs. If dropping the housewares line enables the company to avoid more in fixed costs than it loses in contribution margin, then it would be financially advantageous to eliminate the product line. On the other hand, if the company is not able to avoid as much in fixed costs as it loses in contribution margin, then the housewares line should be kept. Thus, the company's managers need to focus their attention on identifying the

**EXHIBIT 11–2**
Discount Drug Company Product Lines

| | Total | Product Line Drugs | Cosmetics | Housewares |
|---|---|---|---|---|
| Sales .......................... | $250,000 | $125,000 | $75,000 | $50,000 |
| Variable expenses............. | 105,000 | 50,000 | 25,000 | 30,000 |
| Contribution margin ........... | 145,000 | 75,000 | 50,000 | 20,000 |
| Fixed expenses: | | | | |
| Salaries................... | 50,000 | 29,500 | 12,500 | 8,000 |
| Advertising................ | 15,000 | 1,000 | 7,500 | 6,500 |
| Utilities ................... | 2,000 | 500 | 500 | 1,000 |
| Depreciation—fixtures ....... | 5,000 | 1,000 | 2,000 | 2,000 |
| Rent....................... | 20,000 | 10,000 | 6,000 | 4,000 |
| Insurance ................. | 3,000 | 2,000 | 500 | 500 |
| General administrative....... | 30,000 | 15,000 | 9,000 | 6,000 |
| Total fixed expenses........... | 125,000 | 59,000 | 38,000 | 28,000 |
| Net operating income (loss)..... | $ 20,000 | $ 16,000 | $12,000 | $ (8,000) |

costs that differ between the two alternatives (i.e., that can be avoided by dropping the housewares product line). They should be asking themselves—"What costs can we avoid if we drop this product line?"—while purposely ignoring any costs that do not differ between the alternatives.

As we have seen from our earlier discussion, not all costs are avoidable. For example, some of the costs associated with a product line may be sunk costs. Other costs may be allocated fixed costs that will not differ in total regardless of whether the product line is dropped or retained.

To show how to proceed in a product-line analysis, suppose that Discount Drug Company has analyzed the fixed costs being charged to the three product lines and determined the following:

1. The salaries expense represents salaries paid to employees working directly on the product. All of the employees working in housewares would be discharged if the product line is dropped.
2. The advertising expense represents advertisements that are specific to each product line and are avoidable if the line is dropped.
3. The utilities expense represents utilities costs for the entire company. The amount charged to each product line is an allocation based on space occupied and is not avoidable if the product line is dropped.
4. The depreciation expense represents depreciation on previously purchased fixtures that are used to display the various product lines. Although the fixtures are nearly new, they are custom-built and will have no resale value if the housewares line is dropped.
5. The rent expense represents rent on the entire building housing the company; it is allocated to the product lines on the basis of sales dollars. The monthly rent of $20,000 is fixed under a long-term lease agreement.
6. The insurance expense is for insurance carried on inventories within each of the three product lines. If housewares is dropped, the related inventories will be liquidated and the insurance premiums will decrease proportionately.
7. The general administrative expense represents the costs of accounting, purchasing, and general management, which are allocated to the product lines on the basis of sales dollars. These costs will not change if the housewares line is dropped.

With this information, management can determine that $15,000 of the fixed expenses associated with the housewares product line are avoidable and $13,000 are not:

| Fixed Expenses | Total Cost Assigned to Housewares | Not Avoidable* | Avoidable |
|---|---|---|---|
| Salaries | $ 8,000 | | $ 8,000 |
| Advertising | 6,500 | | 6,500 |
| Utilities | 1,000 | $ 1,000 | |
| Depreciation—fixtures | 2,000 | 2,000 | |
| Rent | 4,000 | 4,000 | |
| Insurance | 500 | | 500 |
| General administrative | 6,000 | 6,000 | |
| Total | $28,000 | $13,000 | $15,000 |

*These fixed costs represent either sunk costs or future costs that will not change whether the housewares line is retained or discontinued.

As stated earlier, if the housewares product line were dropped, the company would lose the product's contribution margin of $20,000, but would save its associated avoidable fixed expenses. We now know that those avoidable fixed expenses total $15,000. Therefore, the financial disadvantage of dropping the housewares product line is $(5,000) as shown below:

| | |
|---|---|
| Contribution margin lost if the housewares product line is discontinued (see Exhibit 11–2) | $(20,000) |
| Fixed expenses that can be avoided if the housewares product line is discontinued (see above) | 15,000 |
| Financial disadvantage of dropping the housewares product line | $ (5,000) |

In this case, the fixed costs that can be avoided by dropping the housewares product line ($15,000) are less than the contribution margin that will be lost ($20,000). Therefore, based on the data given, the housewares line should not be discontinued unless a more profitable use can be found for the floor and counter space that it is occupying.

## HELPFUL HINT

Use the following three steps to quantify the financial advantage (disadvantage) of discontinuing a business segment:

Step 1: Calculate the contribution margin that would disappear if the segment is dropped. Put this number in parentheses to denote it as a cash outflow.

Step 2: Calculate the fixed costs that would be avoided if the segment is dropped. Do not put this number in parentheses (thereby denoting it as a cash inflow).

Step 3: Add the amounts from steps 1 and 2. If the result is a negative number (a net cash outflow), then do not drop the segment. If it is a positive number (a net cash inflow), then choose to drop the segment.

While you may need to add additional steps when solving complex problems, these three steps will help organize your analysis.

## A Comparative Format

This decision can also be approached by preparing comparative income statements showing the effects of either keeping or dropping the product line. Exhibit 11–3

EXHIBIT 11–3
A Comparative Format for
Product-Line Analysis

| | Keep Housewares | Drop Housewares | Difference: Net Operating Income Increase (or Decrease) |
|---|---|---|---|
| Sales . . . . . . . . . . . . . . . . . . . . . . . . . . . | $50,000 | $ 0 | $(50,000) |
| Variable expenses. . . . . . . . . . . . . . . . . . | 30,000 | 0 | 30,000 |
| Contribution margin . . . . . . . . . . . . . . . . | 20,000 | 0 | (20,000) |
| Fixed expenses: | | | |
| Salaries. . . . . . . . . . . . . . . . . . . . . . . . | 8,000 | 0 | 8,000 |
| Advertising. . . . . . . . . . . . . . . . . . . . . | 6,500 | 0 | 6,500 |
| Utilities . . . . . . . . . . . . . . . . . . . . . . . . | 1,000 | 1,000 | 0 |
| Depreciation—fixtures . . . . . . . . . . . . | 2,000 | 2,000 | 0 |
| Rent. . . . . . . . . . . . . . . . . . . . . . . . . . . | 4,000 | 4,000 | 0 |
| Insurance . . . . . . . . . . . . . . . . . . . . . . | 500 | 0 | 500 |
| General administrative. . . . . . . . . . . . | 6,000 | 6,000 | 0 |
| Total fixed expenses. . . . . . . . . . . . . . . . | 28,000 | 13,000 | 15,000 |
| Net operating loss. . . . . . . . . . . . . . . . . . | $ (8,000) | $(13,000) | $ (5,000) |

contains such an analysis for the Discount Drug Company. As shown in the last column of the exhibit, if the housewares line is dropped, then overall company net operating income will decrease by $5,000 each period. This is the same answer, of course, as we obtained when we focused just on the lost contribution margin and avoidable fixed costs.

## Beware of Allocated Fixed Costs

Go back to Exhibit 11–2. Does this exhibit suggest that the housewares product line should be kept—as we have just concluded? No, it does not. Exhibit 11–2 suggests that the housewares product line is losing money. Why keep a product line that is showing a loss? The explanation for this apparent inconsistency lies in part with the common fixed costs that are being allocated to the product lines. One of the great dangers in allocating common fixed costs is that such allocations can make a product line (or other business segment) look less profitable than it really is. In this instance, allocating the common fixed costs among all product lines makes the housewares product line appear to be unprofitable. However, as we have just shown, there is a $5,000 financial *disadvantage* associated with dropping the product line. This point can be seen clearly if we redo Exhibit 11–2 by eliminating the allocation of the common fixed costs. Exhibit 11–4 uses the segmented approach from Chapter 7 to estimate the profitability of the product lines.

Exhibit 11–4 gives us a much different perspective of the housewares line than does Exhibit 11–2. As shown in Exhibit 11–4, the housewares line is covering all of its own traceable fixed costs and generating a $3,000 segment margin toward covering the common fixed costs of the company. Unless another product line can be found that will generate a segment margin greater than $3,000, the company would be better off keeping the housewares line rather than dropping it.

Additionally, managers may choose to retain an unprofitable product line if it helps sell other products, or if it serves as a "magnet" to attract customers. Bread, for example, may not be an especially profitable line in some food stores, but customers expect it to be available, and many of them would undoubtedly shift their buying elsewhere if a particular store decided to stop carrying it.

**EXHIBIT 11–4**
Discount Drug Company Product
Lines—Recast in Contribution
Format (from Exhibit 11–2)

|  | Total | Product Line | | |
|---|---|---|---|---|
|  |  | Drugs | Cosmetics | Housewares |
| Sales . . . . . . . . . . . . . . . . . . . . . . . . . . . | $250,000 | $125,000 | $75,000 | $50,000 |
| Variable expenses . . . . . . . . . . . . . . . | 105,000 | 50,000 | 25,000 | 30,000 |
| Contribution margin. . . . . . . . . . . . . | 145,000 | 75,000 | 50,000 | 20,000 |
| Traceable fixed expenses: |  |  |  |  |
|    Salaries. . . . . . . . . . . . . . . . . . . . . . | 50,000 | 29,500 | 12,500 | 8,000 |
|    Advertising . . . . . . . . . . . . . . . . . . | 15,000 | 1,000 | 7,500 | 6,500 |
|    Depreciation—fixtures. . . . . . . . . . | 5,000 | 1,000 | 2,000 | 2,000 |
|    Insurance. . . . . . . . . . . . . . . . . . . . . | 3,000 | 2,000 | 500 | 500 |
| Total traceable fixed expenses . . . . | 73,000 | 33,500 | 22,500 | 17,000 |
| Product-line segment margin . . . . . | 72,000 | $ 41,500 | $27,500 | $ 3,000* |
| Common fixed expenses: |  |  |  |  |
|    Utilities . . . . . . . . . . . . . . . . . . . . . . | 2,000 |  |  |  |
|    Rent. . . . . . . . . . . . . . . . . . . . . . . . . | 20,000 |  |  |  |
|    General administrative . . . . . . . . . | 30,000 |  |  |  |
| Total common fixed expenses. . . . . | 52,000 |  |  |  |
| Net operating income . . . . . . . . . . . | $ 20,000 |  |  |  |

*If the housewares line is dropped, the company will lose the $3,000 segment margin generated by this product line. In addition, we have seen that the $2,000 depreciation on the fixtures is a sunk cost that cannot be avoided. The sum of these two figures (= $3,000 + $2,000) equals the financial disadvantage of $5,000 associated with discontinuing the housewares product line. Of course, the company may later choose to drop the product if circumstances change—such as a pending decision to replace the fixtures.

4. Which of the following statements is true? (You may select more than one answer.)
   a. Common fixed costs should be allocated to business segments when making decisions because all of a company's costs need to be covered to be profitable.
   b. When making decisions, common fixed costs should be allocated to business segments based on each segment's sales revenue because this reflects each segment's "ability to bear" additional costs.
   c. Common fixed costs should not be allocated to business segments for decision-making purposes.
   d. When making decisions, allocating common fixed costs to segments may understate the true profitability of those segments.

CONCEPT
CHECK

## Delphi Closes 42 Factories

IN BUSINESS

More than a decade ago, **Delphi Automotive** earned revenues of $30 billion per year and employed 47,000 people. Now the company's U.S. workforce has dropped to 5,000 employees as it has closed 42 of its 47 factories. The company has dropped low-margin businesses, such as its heating and cooling segment, to focus its manufacturing efforts on auto safety, navigation systems, fuel economy, and self-driving technologies. It appears that Wall Street investors agree with Delphi's efforts to trim its product lines given that the company's stock price has more than tripled since it emerged from a four-year bankruptcy.

Source: Bennett, Jeff, "Delphi Sale Signals New Era for Car Suppliers," *The Wall Street Journal,* February 19, 2015, B1 and B8.

# MAKE OR BUY DECISIONS

Providing a product or service to a customer involves many steps. For example, consider all of the steps that are necessary to develop and sell a product such as a **Fitbit** fitness watch. First, engineers need to develop the underlying electronics that provide customers with capabilities such as real-time GPS tracking, heart rate monitoring, and activity monitoring. In addition, they need to design a wrist watch that not only houses the electronic circuitry, but that also meets the customers' needs in terms of aesthetics, durability, and functionality. Second, the watches need to be assembled, tested, individually packaged, and then boxed in larger quantities to enable shipping. Third, the finished goods need to be transported to retail sales locations and eventually sold to customers. Finally, the company needs to provide after-sale service such as Internet and phone-based help lines, warranty claims, and product returns. All of these activities, from development, to production, to after-sales service are called a *value chain.*

Separate companies may carry out each of the activities in the value chain or a single company may carry out several. When a company is involved in more than one activity in the entire value chain, it is **vertically integrated**. Some companies control all of the activities in the value chain from producing basic raw materials right up to the final distribution of finished goods and provision of after-sales service. Other companies are content to integrate on a smaller scale by purchasing many of the parts and materials that go into their finished products. A decision to carry out one of the activities in the value chain internally, rather than to buy externally from a supplier, is called a **make or buy decision**. Quite often these decisions involve whether to buy a particular part or to make it internally. Make or buy decisions also involve decisions concerning whether to outsource development tasks, after-sales service, or other activities.

## Strategic Aspects of the Make or Buy Decision

Vertical integration provides certain advantages. An integrated company is less dependent on its suppliers and may be able to ensure a smoother flow of parts and materials for production than a nonintegrated company. For example, a strike against a major parts supplier can interrupt the operations of a nonintegrated company for many months, whereas an integrated company that is producing its own parts would be able to continue operations. Also, some companies feel that they can control quality better by producing their own parts and materials, rather than by relying on the quality control standards of outside suppliers. In addition, an integrated company realizes profits from the parts and materials that it is "making" rather than "buying," as well as profits from its regular operations.

The advantages of vertical integration are counterbalanced by the advantages of using external suppliers. By pooling demand from a number of companies, a supplier may be able to enjoy economies of scale. These economies of scale can result in higher quality and lower costs than would be possible if the company were to attempt to make the parts or provide the service on its own. A company must be careful, however, to retain control over activities that are essential to maintaining its competitive position. For example, **Hewlett-Packard** controls the software for laser printers that it makes in cooperation with **Canon Inc.** of Japan. The present trend appears to be toward less vertical integration, with companies like **Oracle** and Hewlett-Packard concentrating on hardware and software design and relying on outside suppliers for almost everything else in the value chain.

## An Example of a Make or Buy Decision

To provide an illustration of a make or buy decision, consider Mountain Goat Cycles. The company is currently making the heavy-duty gear shifters that it installs on its most popular line of mountain bikes. The company's Accounting Department reports the following costs of making 8,000 shifters each year:

| | Per Unit | 8,000 Units |
|---|---|---|
| Direct materials | $ 6 | $ 48,000 |
| Direct labor | 4 | 32,000 |
| Variable overhead | 1 | 8,000 |
| Supervisor's salary | 3 | 24,000 |
| Depreciation of special equipment | 2 | 16,000 |
| Allocated general overhead | 5 | 40,000 |
| Total cost | $21 | $ 168,000 |

An outside supplier has offered to sell 8,000 shifters a year to Mountain Goat Cycles for a price of only $19 each, or a total of $152,000 (= 8,000 shifters × $19 each). Should the company stop making the shifters internally and buy them from the outside supplier? As always, the decision should depend on the relevant costs—those that differ between the alternatives. And the costs that differ between the alternatives consist of the costs that could be avoided by buying the shifters from the outside supplier. If the costs that can be avoided by buying the shifters from the outside supplier total less than $152,000, then the company should continue to make its own shifters and reject the outside supplier's offer. On the other hand, if the costs that can be avoided by buying the shifters from the outside supplier total more than $152,000 the outside supplier's offer should be accepted.

## Ashley Furniture Manages its Own Fleet of Delivery Trucks

**IN BUSINESS**

Many manufacturers choose to outsource truck deliveries in the name of cost savings. However, **Ashley Furniture Industries** in Arcadia, Wisconsin, takes a different approach. It owns 800 delivery trucks and employs 3,000 people in warehousing and transportation based on the belief that delivering furniture from its warehouses to the retailers that sell its products improves customer relations and service. Ashley pays its drivers an average of $70,000 per year and it strives to provide them with predictable delivery schedules that enable them to be home more often. Ashley's vice-president of transportation, Larry Corey, says that he needs to review 100 applications to find one good truck driver. Keith Koenig, who owns furniture stores in southern Florida says that Ashley's delivery times and reliability are unbeatable.

©AP Images/Imaginechina

Source: Hagerty, James R., "A Radical Idea: Own Your Supply Chain," *The Wall Street Journal*, April 30, 2015, B1–B2.

Exhibit 11–5 contains the relevant cost analysis of the make or buy decision related to the gear shifters. The direct materials ($48,000), direct labor ($32,000), and variable overhead ($8,000) are all relevant costs because each cost could be avoided by purchasing the shifters from the outside supplier. In other words, Mountain Goat Cycles would no longer incur these variable manufacturing costs if it stopped making the shifters. In addition, we will assume that the supervisor of the gear shifter manufacturing process would not be retained if the company stops making the shifters; thus, the supervisory salary of $24,000 would be avoided if the company decides to buy the gear shifters from an outside supplier. [3]

---

[3]Many companies adhere to a "no layoffs" policy because they believe it improves employee morale, organizational learning, customer satisfaction, and financial results. Furthermore, in some countries, such as France, Germany, and Japan, labor regulations and cultural norms may limit management's ability to reduce the size of the labor force. In these contexts, it would be incorrect to assume that direct labor and supervision are automatically avoidable costs in make or buy decisions. Nonetheless, for the sake of consistency, within this chapter you should assume that direct labor and supervisory salaries are avoidable costs when analyzing make or buy decisions unless you are explicitly told otherwise.

**EXHIBIT 11-5**
Mountain Goat Cycles Make or
Buy Analysis

| | Total Relevant Costs—8,000 units | |
|---|---|---|
| | **Make** | **Buy** |
| Direct materials (8,000 units × $6 per unit) . . . . . . . . . . . . . . . . . | $48,000 | |
| Direct labor (8,000 units × $4 per unit) . . . . . . . . . . . . . . . . . . . . | 32,000 | |
| Variable overhead (8,000 units × $1 per unit) . . . . . . . . . . . . . . | 8,000 | |
| Supervisor's salary . . . . . . . . . . . . . . . . . . . . . . . . . . . . . . . . . . . . | 24,000 | |
| Depreciation of special equipment (not relevant) . . . . . . . . . . . . | | |
| Allocated general overhead (not relevant) . . . . . . . . . . . . . . . . . | | |
| Outside purchase price . . . . . . . . . . . . . . . . . . . . . . . . . . . . . . . . | | $152,000 |
| Total cost. . . . . . . . . . . . . . . . . . . . . . . . . . . . . . . . . . . . . . . . . . . . | $112,000 | $152,000 |
| Financial advantage of making the gear shifters. . . . . . . . . . . . . | $40,000 | |

The depreciation of special equipment of $16,000 (as shown in the original data) is an irrelevant cost because the equipment has already been purchased; thus, the cost incurred to buy the equipment is a sunk cost. The depreciation charge of $16,000 simply spreads this sunk cost over the equipment's useful life. If the equipment could be sold, its salvage value would be relevant. Or if the equipment could be used to make other products, this could be relevant as well. However, we will assume that the equipment has no salvage value and that it has no other use except making the heavy-duty gear shifters.

The allocated general overhead of $40,000 (as shown in the original data) is also an irrelevant cost in this decision context. We draw this conclusion because we are assuming that these allocated costs are common to all items produced in the factory and would continue unchanged even if the shifters were bought from an outside supplier. Throughout this chapter, you should assume that these types of allocated common costs are irrelevant to the decision unless you are explicitly told otherwise. If you are explicitly told that a portion of allocated common costs can be avoided by choosing one alternative over another, then by all means, treat the explicitly identified avoidable costs as relevant costs. Otherwise, err on the side of ignoring allocated common costs when choosing between alternatives.

Because the avoidable costs related to making the shifters is $40,000 less than the total amount that would be paid to buy them from the outside supplier, Mountain Goat Cycles should reject the outside supplier's offer. However, the company may wish to consider one additional factor before coming to a final decision—the opportunity cost of the space that it currently uses to produce the shifters.

## HELPFUL HINT

Use the following three steps to quantify the financial advantage (disadvantage) of a make or buy decision:

Step 1: Calculate the total amount that would be paid to the supplier if the buy option is chosen.

Step 2: Calculate the total differential manufacturing costs. These are the variable manufacturing costs and traceable fixed manufacturing costs that will be incurred if the company chooses to make, but avoided if the company chooses to buy.

Step 3: Calculate the difference between the amounts from steps 1 and 2. If the amount from step 1 exceeds the amount from step 2, then choose the make option. If the amount from step 1 is less than the amount from step 2, then choose the buy option.

While you may need to add additional steps when solving complex problems, these three steps will help organize your analysis.

## Opportunity Cost

If the space now being used to produce the shifters *would otherwise be idle*, then Mountain Goat Cycles should continue to make its own shifters and the supplier's offer should be rejected, as stated above. Idle space that has no alternative use has an opportunity cost of zero.

But what if the space now being used to make shifters could be used for some other purpose? In that case, the space would have an opportunity cost equal to the segment margin that could be derived from the best alternative use of the space.

To illustrate, assume that the space now being used to make shifters could be used to produce a new cross-country bike that would generate a segment margin of $60,000 per year. Under these conditions, Mountain Goat Cycles would be $20,000 better off by choosing to buy the shifters from the outside supplier (rather than making them) and using the newly available space to produce the cross-country bike:

| | Make | Buy |
|---|---|---|
| Total annual cost (see Exhibit 11–5) ....................... | $112,000 | $152,000 |
| Opportunity cost—segment margin forgone on a potential new product line ....................................... | 60,000 | |
| Total cost........................................... | $172,000 | $152,000 |
| Financial advantage of buying the gear shifters from the outside supplier............................................ | | $20,000 |

Opportunity costs are not recorded in the organization's general ledger because they do not represent actual dollar outlays. Rather, they represent economic benefits that are *forgone* as a result of pursuing some course of action. The opportunity cost for Mountain Goat Cycles is sufficiently large in this case to change the decision.

## Vice President of Production

DECISION POINT

You are faced with a make or buy decision. The company currently makes a component for one of its products but is considering whether it should instead purchase the component. If the offer from an outside supplier were accepted, the company would no longer need to rent the machinery currently being used to manufacture the component. You realize that the annual rental cost is a fixed cost, but recall some sort of warning about fixed costs. Is the annual rental cost relevant to this make or buy decision?

## SPECIAL ORDER DECISIONS

Managers must often evaluate whether a *special order* should be accepted, and if the order is accepted, the price that should be charged. A **special order** is a one-time order that is not considered part of the company's normal ongoing business. To illustrate, Mountain Goat Cycles has just received a request from the Seattle Police Department to produce 100 specially modified mountain bikes at a price of $558 each. The bikes would be used to patrol some of the more densely populated residential sections of the city. Mountain Goat Cycles can easily modify its City Cruiser model to fit the specifications of the Seattle Police. The normal selling price of the City Cruiser bike is $698, and its unit product cost is $564 as shown below:

**LEARNING OBJECTIVE 11–4**

Prepare an analysis showing whether a special order should be accepted.

| | |
|---|---|
| Direct materials ................... | $372 |
| Direct labor...................... | 90 |
| Manufacturing overhead .......... | 102 |
| Unit product cost................ | $564 |

The variable portion of the above manufacturing overhead is $12 per unit. The order would have no effect on the company's total fixed manufacturing overhead costs.

The modifications requested by the Seattle Police Department consist of welded brackets to hold radios, nightsticks, and other gear. These modifications would require $34 in incremental variable costs. In addition, the company would have to pay a graphics design studio $2,400 to design and cut stencils that would be used for spray painting the Seattle Police Department's logo and other identifying marks on the bikes. The company's managers believe that this order will have no effect on the company's other sales and it can be produced without disrupting any of the company's regular scheduled production.

To quantify the financial advantage (disadvantage) of accepting the Seattle Police Department's order, Mountain Goat Cycles should focus its attention on the incremental costs and benefits associated with the order. Because the existing fixed manufacturing overhead costs would not be affected by the order, they are not relevant. The financial advantage (disadvantage) of the special order would be computed as follows:

| | Per Unit | Total 100 Bikes |
|---|---|---|
| Incremental revenue (a) | $558 | $55,800 |
| Less incremental costs: | | |
| Variable costs: | | |
| Direct materials | 372 | 37,200 |
| Direct labor | 90 | 9,000 |
| Variable manufacturing overhead | 12 | 1,200 |
| Special modifications | 34 | 3,400 |
| Total variable cost | $508 | 50,800 |
| Fixed cost: | | |
| Purchase of stencils | | 2,400 |
| Total incremental cost (b) | | 53,200 |
| Financial advantage of accepting the order (a) − (b) | | $ 2,600 |

Therefore, even though the $558 price on the special order is below the normal $564 unit product cost and the order would require additional costs, the company is still better off accepting the order. In general, a special order should be accepted if the incremental revenue from the special order exceeds the incremental costs of the order. However, it is important to make sure that there is indeed idle capacity and that the special order does not cut into normal unit sales or undercut prices on normal sales. For example, if the company was operating at capacity, opportunity costs would have to be taken into account, as well as the incremental costs that have already been detailed above.

## HELPFUL HINT

Use the following three steps to quantify the financial advantage (disadvantage) of accepting a special order:

Step 1: Calculate the total revenue generated by the special order.

Step 2: Calculate the total incremental costs that will be incurred to produce the special order.

Step 3: Take the amount in step 1 and subtract from it the amount in step 2. If the result is a positive number, then accept the special order. If it is a negative number, then reject the special order.

While you may need to add additional steps when solving complex problems, these three steps will help organize your analysis.

## VOLUME TRADE-OFF DECISIONS

Companies are forced to make *volume trade-off decisions* when they do not have enough capacity to produce all of the products and sales volumes demanded by their customers. In these situations, companies must trade off, or sacrifice production of some products in favor of others in an effort to maximize profits. The key questions become: how should companies manage those trade-offs? Which products should they produce and sell and which sales opportunities should they intentionally bypass?

To answer these questions, our discussion of volume trade-off decisions will proceed in three steps. First, we'll define the meaning of a constraint. Second, we'll explain how to determine the most profitable use of a constrained resource. Third, we'll discuss how to determine the value of obtaining more of a constrained resource and how to manage constraints to increase profits.

## What Is a Constraint?

A **constraint** is anything that prevents you from getting more of what you want. Every individual and every organization faces at least one constraint, so it is not difficult to find examples of constraints.[5] You may not have enough time to study thoroughly for every subject *and* to go out with your friends on the weekend, so time is your constraint. **United Airlines** has only a limited number of loading gates available at its busy Chicago O'Hare hub, so its constraint is loading gates. **Vail Resorts** has only a limited amount of land to develop as homesites and commercial lots at its ski areas, so its constraint is land.

As an example, long waiting periods for surgery are a chronic problem in the **National Health Service (NHS)**, the government-funded provider of health care in the United Kingdom. The diagram in Exhibit 11–6 illustrates a simplified version of the steps followed by a surgery patient. The number of patients who can be processed through each step in a day is indicated in the exhibit. For example, appointments for outpatient visits can be made for as many as 100 referrals from general practitioners in a day.

The constraint, or **bottleneck**, in the system is determined by the step that limits total output because it has the smallest capacity—in this case surgery. The total number of patients processed through the entire system cannot exceed 15 per day—the maximum number of patients who can be treated in surgery. No matter how hard managers, doctors, and nurses try to improve the processing rate elsewhere in the system, they will never succeed in driving down wait lists until the capacity of surgery is increased. In fact, improvements elsewhere in the system—particularly before the constraint—are likely to result in even longer waiting times and more frustrated patients and health care providers. Thus, to be effective, improvement efforts must be focused on the constraint.

**EXHIBIT 11–6**   Processing Surgery Patients at an NHS Facility (simplified)

Source: This diagram originally appeared in the February 1999 issue of the U.K. magazine *Health Management.*

---

[5]In this chapter, we always assume that the company has only one constraint. When companies have more than one constraint, the optimal production mix can be found using a quantitative method known as linear programming, which is covered in more advanced courses.

A business process, such as the process for serving surgery patients, is like a chain. If you want to increase the strength of a chain, what is the most effective way to do this? Should you concentrate your efforts on strengthening the strongest link, all the links, or the weakest link? Clearly, focusing your effort on the weakest link will bring the biggest benefit.

The procedure to follow to strengthen the chain is clear. First, identify the weakest link, which is the constraint. In the case of the NHS, the constraint is surgery. Second, do not place a greater strain on the system than the weakest link can handle—if you do, the chain will break. In the case of the NHS, more referrals than surgery can accommodate lead to unacceptably long waiting lists. Third, concentrate improvement efforts on strengthening the weakest link. In the case of the NHS, this means finding ways to increase the number of surgeries that can be performed in a day. Fourth, if the improvement efforts are successful, eventually the weakest link will improve to the point where it is no longer the weakest link. At that point, the new weakest link (i.e., the new constraint) must be identified, and improvement efforts must be shifted over to that link. This simple sequential process provides a powerful strategy for optimizing business processes.

## Utilizing a Constrained Resource to Maximize Profits

**LEARNING OBJECTIVE 11–5**

Determine the most profitable use of a constrained resource.

Managers routinely face the challenge of managing constrained resources in a manner that maximizes profits. A department store, for example, has a limited amount of floor space and therefore cannot stock every product that may be available. A manufacturer has a limited number of machine-hours and a limited number of direct labor-hours at its disposal. When companies face these types of constraints their managers must decide which products or services make the most profitable use of those limited resources. Because fixed costs remain the same regardless of how a constrained resource is used, managers should ignore them when making volume trade-off decisions and instead focus their attention on identifying the mix of products that maximizes the total contribution margin.

Given that some products must be cut back when a constraint exists, the key to maximizing the total contribution margin may seem obvious—favor the products with the highest unit contribution margins. Unfortunately, that is not quite correct. Rather, the correct solution is to favor the products that provide the highest *contribution margin per unit of the constrained resource.* To illustrate, in addition to its other products, Mountain Goat Cycles makes saddlebags for bicycles called *panniers.* These panniers come in two models—a touring model and a mountain model. Cost and revenue data for the two models of panniers follow:

| | Mountain Pannier | Touring Pannier |
|---|---|---|
| Selling price per unit................... | $25 | $30 |
| Variable cost per unit.................. | 10 | 18 |
| Contribution margin per unit........... | $15 | $12 |
| Contribution margin (CM) ratio.......... | 60% | 40% |

The mountain pannier appears to be much more profitable than the touring pannier. It has a $15 per unit contribution margin as compared to only $12 per unit for the touring model, and it has a 60% CM ratio as compared to only 40% for the touring model.

But now let us add one more piece of information—the plant that makes the panniers is operating at capacity. This does not mean that every machine and every person in the plant is working at the maximum possible rate. Because machines have different capacities, some machines will be operating at less than 100% of capacity. However, if the plant as a whole cannot produce any more units, some machine or process must be operating at capacity. The machine or process that is limiting overall output is called the bottleneck—it is the constraint.

At Mountain Goat Cycles, the bottleneck (i.e., constraint) is a stitching machine. The mountain pannier requires two minutes of stitching time per unit, and the touring pannier requires one minute of stitching time per unit. The stitching machine is available for 12,000 minutes per month, and the company can sell up to 4,000 mountain panniers and 7,000 touring panniers per month. Producing up to this demand for both products would require 15,000 minutes, as shown below:

| | Mountain Pannier | Touring Pannier | Total |
|---|---|---|---|
| Monthly demand (a) | 4,000 units | 7,000 units | |
| Stitching machine time required to produce one unit (b) | 2 minutes | 1 minute | |
| Total stitching time required (a) × (b) | 8,000 minutes | 7,000 minutes | 15,000 minutes |

Producing up to demand would require 15,000 minutes, but only 12,000 minutes are available. This simply confirms that the stitching machine is the bottleneck. By definition, because the stitching machine is a bottleneck, the stitching machine does not have enough capacity to satisfy the existing demand for mountain panniers and touring panniers. Therefore, some orders for the products will have to be turned down. Naturally, managers will want to know which product is less profitable. To answer this question, they should focus on the contribution margin per unit of the constrained resource. This figure is computed by dividing a product's contribution margin per unit by the amount of the constrained resource required to make a unit of that product. These calculations are carried out below for the mountain and touring panniers:

| | Mountain Pannier | Touring Pannier |
|---|---|---|
| Contribution margin per unit (a) | $15.00 | $12.00 |
| Stitching machine time required to produce one unit (b) | 2 minutes | 1 minute |
| Contribution margin per unit of the constrained resource, (a) ÷ (b) | $7.50 per minute | $12.00 per minute |

It is now easy to decide which product is less profitable and should be deemphasized. Each minute on the stitching machine that is devoted to the touring pannier results in an increase of $12.00 in contribution margin and profits. The comparable figure for the mountain pannier is only $7.50 per minute. Therefore, the touring model should be emphasized. Even though the mountain model has the larger contribution margin per unit and the larger CM ratio, the touring model provides the larger contribution margin in relation to the constrained resource.

To verify that the touring model is indeed the more profitable product, suppose an hour of additional stitching time is available and that unfilled orders exist for both products. The additional hour on the stitching machine could be used to make either 30 mountain panniers

(60 minutes ÷ 2 minutes per mountain pannier) or 60 touring panniers (60 minutes ÷ 1 minute per touring pannier), with the following profit implications:

|  | Mountain Pannier | Touring Pannier |
|---|---|---|
| Contribution margin per unit (a) .................... | $ 15 | $ 12 |
| Additional units that can be processed in one hour (b) ....................... | × 30 | × 60 |
| Additional contribution margin (a) × (b) ............. | $450 | $720 |

Because the additional contribution margin would be $720 for the touring panniers and only $450 for the mountain panniers, the touring panniers make the most profitable use of the company's constrained resource—the stitching machine.

The stitching machine is available for 12,000 minutes per month, and producing the touring panniers is the most profitable use of the stitching machine. Therefore, to maximize profits, the company should produce all of the touring panniers the market will demand (7,000 units) and use any remaining capacity to produce mountain panniers. The computations to determine how many mountain panniers can be produced are as follows:

| | |
|---|---|
| Monthly demand for touring panniers (a)............................. | 7,000 units |
| Stitching machine time required to produce one touring pannier (b)...... | 1 minute |
| Total stitching time required to produce touring panniers (a) × (b) ........ | 7,000 minutes |
| Remaining stitching time available (12,000 minutes − 7,000 minutes) (c) ............................. | 5,000 minutes |
| Stitching machine time required to produce one mountain pannier (d).... | 2 minutes |
| Production of mountain panniers (c) ÷ (d) ............................. | 2,500 units |

Therefore, profit would be maximized by producing 7,000 touring panniers and then using the remaining capacity to produce 2,500 mountain panniers. With this product mix the company can earn a total contribution margin of $121,500 computed as follows:

|  | Mountain Pannier | Touring Pannier | Total |
|---|---|---|---|
| Contribution margin per unit (a) .................. | $15 | $12 | |
| Number of units produced (b).................... | 2,500 | 7,000 | |
| Contribution margin (a) × (b) ..................... | $37,500 | $84,000 | $121,500 |

This example clearly shows that looking at each product's unit contribution margin alone is not enough; the contribution margin must be viewed in relation to the amount of the constrained resource each product requires.

## HELPFUL HINT

Use the following four steps to help determine the most profitable use of a constrained resource:

Step 1: Calculate each product's contribution margin per unit.

Step 2: Identify the constraining resource and the quantity of that resource that is consumed to make one unit of each product.

Step 3: Calculate each product's contribution margin per unit of the constraining resource.

Step 4: Rank the products from the highest contribution margin per unit of the constraining resource to the lowest.

If you start by completing these four steps, it will help you compute the most profitable use of a constrained resource.

## Subaru Responds to a Production Constraint

When demand for **Subaru**'s vehicles jumped unexpectedly, the automaker missed many sales opportunities because of insufficient production capacity. The company responded by expanding its Japanese production capacity by 15% and investing $400 million to increase the output of its U.S. plant in Lafayette, Indiana, by 76%. Subaru is contemplating building a new plant that could produce 200,000 more vehicles; however, because this volume represents more than 25% of Subaru's global output, it presents some risks. If sales take a downturn, Subaru could be left with a large amount of unused capacity costs.

Source: Takahashi, Yoshio, and Koh, Yoree, "Subaru's Got a Big Problem: It's Selling Too Many Cars," *The Wall Street Journal,* August 21, 2013, B1 and B2.

©Kristoffer Tripplaar/Alamy Stock Photo

## Managing Constraints

Effectively managing an organization's constraints is a key to increasing profits. As discussed above, when a constraint exists in the production process, managers can increase profits by producing the products with the highest contribution margin per unit of the constrained resource. However, they can also increase profits by increasing the capacity of the bottleneck operation.

When a manager increases the capacity of the bottleneck, it is called **relaxing (or elevating) the constraint**. In the case of Mountain Goat Cycles, the company is currently working one eight-hour shift. To relax the constraint, the stitching machine operator could be asked to work overtime. No one else would have to work overtime. Because all of the other operations involved in producing panniers have excess capacity, up to a point, the additional panniers processed through the stitching machine during overtime could be finished during normal working hours in the other operations.

The benefits from relaxing the constraint are often enormous and can be easily quantified—the key is the contribution margin per unit of the constrained resource that we have already computed. This number, which was originally stated in terms of minutes in the Mountain Goat Cycles example, is restated below in terms of hours for easier interpretation:

|  | Mountain Pannier | Touring Pannier |
|---|---|---|
| Contribution margin per minute of the constrained resource (a) . . . . . . . . . . . . . . . . . | $7.50 per minute | $12.00 per minute |
| Minutes per hour (b) . . . . . . . . . . . . . . . . . . . . . . . | 60 minutes | 60 minutes |
| Contribution margin per hour of the constrained resource (a) × (b) . . . . . . . . . . . . | $450 per hour | $720 per hour |

So what is the value of relaxing the constraint—the time on the stitching machine? The manager should first ask, "What would I do with additional capacity at the bottleneck if it were available?" If the time were to be used to make additional mountain panniers, it would be worth $450 per hour. If the time were to be used to make additional touring panniers, it would be worth $720 per hour. In this latter case, the company should be willing to pay an overtime *premium* to the stitching machine operator of up to $720 per hour! Suppose, for example, that the stitching machine operator is paid $20 per hour during normal working hours and time-and-a-half, or $30 per hour, for overtime. In this case, the premium for overtime is only $10 per hour, whereas in principle, the company should be willing to pay a premium of up to $720 per hour. The difference between what the company should be willing to pay as a premium, $720 per hour, and what it would actually have to pay, $10 per hour, is pure profit of $710 per hour.

To reinforce this concept, suppose that there are only unfilled orders for the mountain pannier. How much would it be worth to the company to run the stitching machine overtime in this situation? Because the additional capacity would be used to make the mountain pannier, the value of that additional capacity would drop to $7.50 per minute or $450 per hour. Nevertheless, the value of relaxing the constraint would still be quite high and the company should be willing to pay an overtime premium of up to $450 per hour.

These calculations indicate that managers should pay great attention to the bottleneck operation. If a bottleneck machine breaks down or is ineffectively utilized, the losses to the company can be quite large. In our example, for every minute the stitching machine is down due to breakdowns or setups, the company loses between $7.50 and $12.00.[6] The losses on an hourly basis are between $450 and $720! In contrast, there is no such loss of contribution margin if time is lost on a machine that is not a bottleneck—such machines have excess capacity anyway.

The implications are clear. Managers should focus much of their attention on managing the bottleneck. As we have discussed, managers should emphasize products that make the most profitable use of the constrained resource. They should also make sure that products are processed smoothly through the bottleneck, with minimal lost time due to breakdowns and setups. And they should try to find ways to increase the capacity at the bottleneck.

The capacity of a bottleneck can be effectively increased in a number of ways, including:

- Working overtime on the bottleneck.
- Subcontracting some of the processing that would ordinarily be done at the bottleneck.
- Investing in additional machines at the bottleneck.
- Shifting workers from processes that are not bottlenecks to the process that is the bottleneck.
- Focusing business process improvement efforts on the bottleneck.
- Reducing defective units. Each defective unit that is processed through the bottleneck and subsequently scrapped takes the place of a good unit that could have been sold.

The last three methods of increasing the capacity of the bottleneck are particularly attractive because they are essentially free and may even yield additional cost savings.

CONCEPT CHECK ✓

5. A company has received a special order from a customer to make 5,000 units of a customized product. The direct materials cost per unit of the customized product is $15, the direct labor cost per unit is $5, and the manufacturing overhead per unit is $18, including $6 of variable manufacturing overhead. If the company has sufficient available manufacturing capacity, what is the minimum price that can be accepted for the special order?
   a. $24
   b. $26
   c. $32
   d. $38

(continued)

---

[6]Setups are required when production switches from one product to another. For example, consider a company that makes automobile side panels. The panels are painted before shipping them to an automobile manufacturer for final assembly. The customer might require 100 blue panels, 50 black panels, and 20 yellow panels. Each time the color is changed, the painting equipment must be purged of the old paint color, cleaned with solvents, and refilled with the new paint color. This takes time. In fact, some equipment may require such lengthy and frequent setups that it is unavailable for actual production more often than not.

6. Refer to the facts from question 5; however, in answering this question assume that the company is operating at 100% of its capacity without the special order. If the company normally manufactures only one product that has a contribution margin of $20 per unit and that consumes 2 minutes of the constrained resource per unit, what is the opportunity cost (stated in terms of forgone contribution margin) of accepting the special order? Assume the special order would require 1.5 minutes of the constrained resource per unit.
   a. $25,000
   b. $50,000
   c. $75,000
   d. $100,000
7. When a company has a constraint and wishes to maximize profits, it should favor the products that have the highest
   a. Gross margin per unit.
   b. Gross margin per unit of the constraining resource.
   c. Contribution margin per unit.
   d. Contribution margin per unit of the constraining resource.

CONCEPT
CHECK

(concluded)

# JOINT PRODUCT COSTS AND SELL OR PROCESS FURTHER DECISIONS

In some industries, two or more products, known as **joint products**, are produced from a single raw material input. For example, in the petroleum refining industry a large number of joint products are extracted from crude oil, including gasoline, jet fuel, home heating oil, lubricants, asphalt, and various organic chemicals. The point in a manufacturing process where joint products (such as gasoline and jet fuel) can be recognized as separate products is referred to as the **split-off point**.

> **LEARNING OBJECTIVE 11–7**
>
> Prepare an analysis showing whether joint products should be sold at the split-off point or processed further.

Quite often joint products can be sold at the split-off point or they can be processed further and sold for a higher price. A decision as to whether a joint product should be sold at the split-off point or processed further is known as a **sell or process further decision**. To make these decisions, managers need to follow a three step process. First, they should always ignore all **joint costs**, which include all costs incurred up to the split-off point. These costs should be ignored because they remain the same under both alternatives—whether the manager chooses to sell a joint product at the split-off point or process it further.

The second step is to determine the incremental revenue that is earned by further processing the joint product. This computation is performed by taking the revenue earned after further processing the joint product and subtracting the revenue that could be earned by selling the joint product at the split-off point.

The third step is to take the incremental revenue from step two and subtract the incremental costs associated with processing the joint product beyond the split-off point. If the resulting answer is positive, then the joint product should be processed further and sold for a higher price. If the answer is negative, then the joint product should be sold at the split-off point without any further processing.

## Santa Maria Wool Cooperative: An Example

Santa Maria Wool Cooperative buys raw wool from local sheepherders, separates the wool into three grades—coarse, fine, and superfine—and then dyes the wool using traditional methods that rely on pigments from local materials. Exhibit 11–7 contains a diagram of the company's production process.

**EXHIBIT 11–7** Santa Maria Wool Cooperative

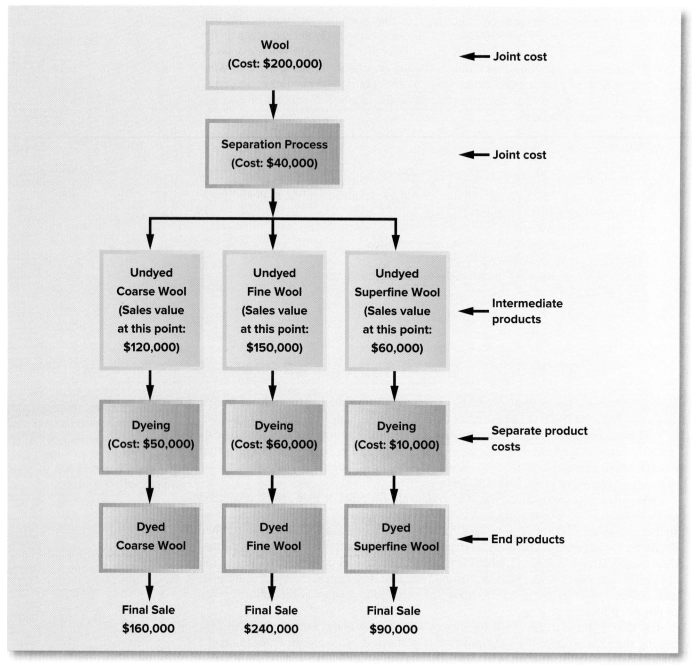

The company's joint costs include $200,000 for the raw wool and $40,000 for separating the raw wool into three intermediate products. The three types of undyed wool are called intermediate products because they are not finished at this point. Nevertheless, a market does exist for undyed wool—although at a significantly lower price than finished, dyed wool. More specifically and as shown in Exhibit 11–7, the undyed course wool, undyed fine wool, and undyed superfine wool each can be sold at the split-off point for $120,000, $150,000, and $60,000 respectively.

Exhibit 11–7 also shows that the cost of further processing the undyed coarse wool, undyed fine wool, and undyed superfine wool is $50,000, $60,000, and $10,000 respectively. Furthermore, the sales values of dyed coarse wool, dyed fine wool, and dyed superfine wool are $160,000, $240,000, and $90,000, respectively.

If Santa Maria Wool Cooperative chooses to further process all three of its intermediate products, it will earn a profit of $130,000 as shown below:

**Analysis of the profitability of the overall operation:**

| | | |
|---|---:|---:|
| Combined final sales value ($160,000 + $240,000 + $90,000) . . . | | $490,000 |
| Less costs of producing the end products: | | |
| Cost of wool . . . . . . . . . . . . . . . . . . . . . . . . . . . . . . . . . . . . . . . . . . . . . . . . | $200,000 | |
| Cost of separating wool . . . . . . . . . . . . . . . . . . . . . . . . . . . . . . . . . . . . | 40,000 | |
| Combined costs of dyeing ($50,000 + $60,000 + $10,000) . . . . | 120,000 | 360,000 |
| Profit . . . . . . . . . . . . . . . . . . . . . . . . . . . . . . . . . . . . . . . . . . . . . . . . . . . . . . | | $130,000 |

Note that the joint costs of buying the wool ($200,000) and separating the wool ($40,000) are relevant when considering the profitability of the entire operation. This is because these joint costs could be avoided if the entire operation were shut down.

While Santa Maria can make a profit of $130,000 if it further processes all three products, the questions we want to explore further are: should the company further process all three products? Could the company be financially better off by selling one or more of the three products at the split-off point?

The appropriate way to answer these sell-or-process-further questions is to compare the incremental revenues and incremental costs for each of the joint products as follows:

**Analysis of sell or process further:**

| | Coarse Wool | Fine Wool | Superfine Wool |
|---|---:|---:|---:|
| Final sales value after further processing . . . . . . . . . | $160,000 | $240,000 | $90,000 |
| Less sales value at the split-off point . . . . . . . . . . . . | 120,000 | 150,000 | 60,000 |
| Incremental revenue from further processing . . . . . | 40,000 | 90,000 | 30,000 |
| Less cost of further processing (dyeing) . . . . . . . . . . | 50,000 | 60,000 | 10,000 |
| Financial advantage (disadvantage) of further processing . . . . . . . . . . . . . . . . . . . . . . . . . . . . . . . . . . . | $ (10,000) | $ 30,000 | $20,000 |

As this analysis shows, the company would be better off selling the undyed coarse wool at the split-off point rather than processing it further. The other two products should be processed further and dyed before selling them.

Note that the joint costs of the wool ($200,000) and of the wool separation process ($40,000) play no role in the decision to sell or further process the intermediate products. These joint costs are relevant in a decision of whether to buy wool and to run the wool separation process, but they are not relevant in decisions about what to do with the intermediate products once they have been separated.

Finally, we can recompute Santa Maria's overall profitability if it chooses to sell the undyed coarse wool at the split-off point and to further process the dyed fine wool and the dyed superfine wool as follows:

**Analysis of the profitability of the overall operation:**

| | | |
|---|---:|---:|
| Combined final sales value ($120,000 + $240,000 + $90,000) . . . | | $450,000 |
| Less costs of producing the end products: | | |
| Cost of wool . . . . . . . . . . . . . . . . . . . . . . . . . . . . . . . . . . . . . . . . . . . . . . . | $200,000 | |
| Cost of separating wool . . . . . . . . . . . . . . . . . . . . . . . . . . . . . . . . . . . . | 40,000 | |
| Combined costs of dyeing ($60,000 + $10,000) . . . . . . . . . . . . . . . | 70,000 | 310,000 |
| Profit . . . . . . . . . . . . . . . . . . . . . . . . . . . . . . . . . . . . . . . . . . . . . . . . . . . . . . | | $140,000 |

Notice that the revised profit of $140,000 is $10,000 higher than the profit of $130,000 that was computed earlier when the company further processes all three products. This $10,000 increase in profit equals the $10,000 financial disadvantage of further processing coarse wool that was computed earlier.

For each end product, use the following three steps to calculate the financial advantage (disadvantage) associated with sell or process further decisions:

Step 1: Calculate the sales value if processed further minus the sales value at the split-off point.

Step 2: Determine the cost of further processing beyond the split-off point.

Step 3: Take the amount in step 1 and subtract from it the amount in step 2. If the result is a positive number, then choose to process further. If it is a negative number, then choose to sell at the split-off point.

While you may need to add additional steps when solving complex problems, these three steps will help organize your analysis.

**CONCEPT CHECK**

8. It is profitable to continue processing a joint product after the split-off point so long as
   a. the incremental revenue from such processing exceeds the incremental processing costs incurred after the split-off point.
   b. the incremental revenue from such processing exceeds the incremental processing costs incurred before the split-off point.
   c. the incremental revenue from such processing exceeds the allocated joint costs attributable to the product.
   d. the incremental revenue from such processing exceeds the sum of the allocated joint costs attributable to the product and the incremental processing costs incurred after the split-off point.

## ACTIVITY-BASED COSTING AND RELEVANT COSTS

As discussed in an earlier chapter, activity-based costing can be used to help identify potentially relevant costs for decision-making purposes. Activity-based costing improves the traceability of costs by focusing on the activities caused by a product or other segment. However, managers should exercise caution against reading more into this "traceability" than really exists. People have a tendency to assume that if a cost is traceable to a segment, then the cost is automatically an avoidable cost. That is not true because the costs provided by a well-designed activity-based costing system are only *potentially* relevant. Before making a decision, managers must still decide which of the potentially relevant costs are actually avoidable. Only those costs that are avoidable are relevant and the others should be ignored.

To illustrate, refer again to the data relating to the housewares line in Exhibit 11–4. The $2,000 fixtures depreciation is a traceable cost of the housewares lines because it directly relates to activities in that department. We found, however, that the $2,000 is not avoidable if the housewares line is dropped. The key lesson here is that the method used to assign a cost to a product or other segment does not change the basic nature of the cost. A sunk cost such as depreciation of old equipment is still a sunk cost regardless of whether it is traced directly to a particular segment on an activity basis, allocated to all segments on the basis of labor-hours, or treated in some other way in the costing process. Regardless of the method used to assign costs to products or other segments, the principles discussed in this chapter must be applied to determine the costs that are avoidable in each situation.

### LO11–1  Identify relevant and irrelevant costs and benefits in a decision.

Every decision involves a choice from among at least two alternatives. Only those costs and benefits that differ in total between the alternatives are relevant; costs and benefits that are the same for all alternatives are not affected by the decision and can be ignored. Only future costs that differ between alternatives are relevant. Sunk costs are always irrelevant.

### LO11–2  Prepare an analysis showing whether a product line or other business segment should be added or dropped.

A decision of whether a product line or other segment should be dropped should focus on the differences in the costs and benefits between dropping or retaining the product line or segment. Caution should be exercised when using reports in which common fixed costs have been allocated among segments. If these common fixed costs are unaffected by the decision of whether to add or drop the segment, they are irrelevant and should be removed before determining the real profitability of a segment.

### LO11–3  Prepare a make or buy analysis.

When deciding whether to make or buy a component, focus on the costs and benefits that differ between those two alternatives. As in other decisions, sunk costs—such as the depreciation on old equipment—should be ignored. Future costs that do not differ between alternatives—such as allocations of common fixed costs like general overhead—should be ignored.

### LO11–4  Prepare an analysis showing whether a special order should be accepted.

When deciding whether to accept or reject a special order, focus on the benefits and costs that differ between those two alternatives. Specifically, a special order should be accepted when the incremental revenue from the sale exceeds the incremental cost. As always, sunk costs and future costs that do not differ between the alternatives are irrelevant.

### LO11–5  Determine the most profitable use of a constrained resource.

When demand for a company's products and services exceeds its ability to supply them, the company has a bottleneck. The bottleneck, whether it is a particular material, skilled labor, or a specific machine, is a constrained resource. Since the company is unable to make everything it could sell, managers must decide what the company will make and what the company will not make. In this situation, the profitability of a product is best measured by its contribution margin per unit of the constrained resource. The products with the highest contribution margin per unit of the constrained resource should be favored.

### LO11–6  Determine the value of obtaining more of the constrained resource.

Managers should focus their attention on effectively managing the constraint. This involves making the most profitable use of the constrained resource and increasing the amount of the constrained resource that is available. The value of relaxing the constraint is determined by the contribution margin per unit of the constrained resource for the work that would be done if more of the resource were available.

### LO11–7  Prepare an analysis showing whether joint products should be sold at the split-off point or processed further.

Managers should recommend further processing of an intermediate product so long as the incremental revenue from such processing exceeds the incremental processing cost incurred after the split-off point. Joint costs are irrelevant in decisions regarding what to do with a product from the split-off point forward. Once the split-off point is reached, the joint costs have already been incurred and nothing can be done to avoid them.

## GUIDANCE ANSWERS TO DECISION POINT

**Vice President of Production**

The annual rental cost for the machinery is an avoidable fixed cost. An avoidable fixed cost is a cost that can be eliminated in whole or in part by choosing one alternative over another. Because the annual rental cost of the machinery can be avoided if the company purchases the components from an outside supplier, it is relevant to this decision.

GUIDANCE ANSWERS TO CONCEPT CHECKS

1. **Choices a and d.** Sunk costs are always irrelevant. Fixed costs can be relevant costs.
2. **Choice a.** The cost of the airline ticket to Telluride is a sunk cost; it has already been incurred and the ticket is nonrefundable.
3. **Choice b.** The cost of going to Stowe would be $1,000 [$400 + ($150 per night × 4 nights)] whereas the incremental cost of going to Telluride would be $1,020 [$300 + ($180 per night × 4 nights)]. Note that the $450 cost of flying to Telluride is irrelevant at this point because it is a sunk cost. The analysis favors Stowe by $20.
4. **Choices c and d.** Common fixed costs should not be allocated to segments when making decisions. Doing so will understate the true profitability of each segment.
5. **Choice b.** The minimum price would be $15 direct materials + $5 direct labor + $6 variable manufacturing overhead = $26.
6. **Choice c.** The special order requires 7,500 minutes (5,000 units × 1.5 minutes per unit). Accepting the special order would require sacrificing 3,750 units (7,500 minutes ÷ 2 minutes per unit) of the regular product. The forgone contribution margin would be 3,750 units × $20 per unit = $75,000.
7. **Choice d.** Gross margin includes fixed costs that are not relevant to this situation. The contribution margin per unit overlooks the constraining resource.
8. **Choice a.** Any costs incurred before the split-off point are not relevant to sell or process further decisions.

## REVIEW PROBLEM: DIFFERENTIAL ANALYSIS

Charter Sports Equipment manufactures round, rectangular, and octagonal trampolines. Sales and expense data for the past month follow:

|  | Total | Trampoline | | |
|  |  | Round | Rectangular | Octagonal |
| --- | --- | --- | --- | --- |
| Sales ............................ | $1,000,000 | $140,000 | $500,000 | $360,000 |
| Variable expenses.................. | 410,000 | 60,000 | 200,000 | 150,000 |
| Contribution margin ................ | 590,000 | 80,000 | 300,000 | 210,000 |
| Fixed expenses: |  |  |  |  |
| Advertising—traceable............. | 216,000 | 41,000 | 110,000 | 65,000 |
| Depreciation of special equipment .. | 95,000 | 20,000 | 40,000 | 35,000 |
| Line supervisors' salaries........... | 19,000 | 6,000 | 7,000 | 6,000 |
| General factory overhead*......... | 200,000 | 28,000 | 100,000 | 72,000 |
| Total fixed expenses................ | 530,000 | 95,000 | 257,000 | 178,000 |
| Net operating income (loss).......... | $ 60,000 | $ (15,000) | $ 43,000 | $ 32,000 |

*A common fixed cost that is allocated on the basis of sales dollars.

Management is concerned about the continued losses shown by the round trampolines and wants a recommendation as to whether or not the line should be discontinued. The special equipment used to produce the trampolines has no resale value. If the round trampoline model is dropped, the two line supervisors assigned to the model would be discharged.

**Required:**

1. What is the financial advantage (disadvantage) of discontinuing the round trampolines? The company has no other use for the capacity now being used to produce the round trampolines. Show computations to support your answer.
2. Recast the above data in a format that would be more useful to management in assessing the profitability of the various product lines.

**Solution to Review Problem**

1. No, production and sale of the round trampolines should not be discontinued. Computations to support this answer follow:

| | | |
|---|---|---|
| Contribution margin lost if the round trampolines are discontinued ............................................ | | $(80,000) |
| Less fixed expenses that can be avoided: | | |
| Advertising—traceable....................................... | $41,000 | |
| Line supervisors' salaries.................................... | 6,000 | 47,000 |
| Financial (disadvantage) of discontinuing the round trampolines..... | | $(33,000) |

The depreciation of the special equipment is a sunk cost, and, therefore, it is not relevant to the decision. The general factory overhead is allocated and will presumably continue regardless of whether or not the round trampolines are discontinued; thus, it is not relevant.

2. If management wants a clearer picture of the profitability of the segments, the general factory overhead should not be allocated. It is a common cost and, therefore, should be deducted from the total product-line segment margin. A more useful income statement format would be as follows:

| | Total | Round | Rectangular | Octagonal |
|---|---|---|---|---|
| | | **Trampoline** | | |
| Sales ................................ | $1,000,000 | $140,000 | $500,000 | $360,000 |
| Variable expenses.................... | 410,000 | 60,000 | 200,000 | 150,000 |
| Contribution margin .................. | 590,000 | 80,000 | 300,000 | 210,000 |
| Traceable fixed expenses: | | | | |
| Advertising—traceable.............. | 216,000 | 41,000 | 110,000 | 65,000 |
| Depreciation of special equipment ... | 95,000 | 20,000 | 40,000 | 35,000 |
| Line supervisors salaries ............ | 19,000 | 6,000 | 7,000 | 6,000 |
| Total traceable fixed expenses......... | 330,000 | 67,000 | 157,000 | 106,000 |
| Product-line segment margin .......... | 260,000 | $ 13,000 | $143,000 | $104,000 |
| Common fixed expenses.............. | 200,000 | | | |
| Net operating income................. | $ 60,000 | | | |

## GLOSSARY

**Avoidable cost** A cost that can be eliminated by choosing one alternative over another in a decision. This term is synonymous with *differential cost* and *relevant cost*. (p. 508)

**Bottleneck** A machine or some other part of a process that limits the total output of the entire system. (p. 525)

**Constraint** A limitation under which a company must operate, such as limited available machine time or raw materials, that restricts the company's ability to satisfy demand. (p. 525)

**Differential cost** A future cost that differs between any two alternatives. (p. 508)

**Differential revenue** Future revenue that differs between any two alternatives. (p. 508)

**Incremental cost** An increase in cost between two alternatives. (p. 508)

**Joint costs**   Costs that are incurred up to the split-off point in a process that produces joint products. (p. 531)

**Joint products**   Two or more products that are produced from a common input. (p. 531)

**Make or buy decision**   A decision concerning whether an item should be produced internally or purchased from an outside supplier. (p. 520)

**Opportunity cost**   The potential benefit that is given up when one alternative is selected over another. (p. 509)

**Relaxing (or elevating) the constraint**   An action that increases the amount of a constrained resource. Equivalently, an action that increases the capacity of the bottleneck. (p. 529)

**Relevant benefit**   A benefit that should be considered when making decisions. (p. 508)

**Relevant cost**   A cost that should be considered when making decisions.  (p. 508)

**Sell or process further decision**   A decision as to whether a joint product should be sold at the split-off point or sold after further processing. (p. 531)

**Special order**   A one-time order that is not considered part of the company's normal ongoing business. (p. 523)

**Split-off point**   That point in the manufacturing process where some or all of the joint products can be recognized as individual products. (p. 531)

**Sunk cost**   A cost that has already been incurred and that cannot be changed by any decision made now or in the future. (p. 509)

**Vertical integration**   The involvement by a company in more than one of the activities in the entire value chain from development through production, distribution, sales, and after-sales service. (p. 520)

## QUESTIONS

**11–1**  What is a *relevant cost?*

**11–2**  Define the following terms: *incremental cost, opportunity cost,* and *sunk cost.*

**11–3**  Are variable costs always relevant costs? Explain.

**11–4**  "Sunk costs are easy to spot—they're the fixed costs associated with a decision." Do you agree? Explain.

**11–5**  "Variable costs and differential costs mean the same thing." Do you agree? Explain.

**11–6**  "All future costs are relevant in decision making." Do you agree? Why?

**11–7**  Prentice Company is considering dropping one of its product lines. What costs of the product line would be relevant to this decision? What costs would be irrelevant?

**11–8**  "If a product is generating a loss, then it should be discontinued." Do you agree? Explain.

**11–9**  What is the danger in allocating common fixed costs among products or other segments of an organization?

**11–10**  How does opportunity cost enter into a make or buy decision?

**11–11**  Give at least four examples of possible constraints.

**11–12**  How will relating product contribution margins to the amount of the constrained resource they consume help a company maximize its profits?

**11–13**  Define the following terms: *joint products, joint costs,* and *split-off point.*

**11–14**  From a decision-making point of view, should joint costs be allocated among joint products?

**11–15**  What guideline should be used in determining whether a joint product should be sold at the split-off point or processed further?

**11–16**  Airlines sometimes offer reduced rates during certain times of the week to members of a businessperson's family if they accompany him or her on trips. How does the concept of relevant costs enter into the decision by the airline to offer reduced rates of this type?

## CHAPTER 11: APPLYING EXCEL   connect

**LO11–7**

The Excel worksheet form that appears below is to be used to recreate the example in the text related to Santa Maria Wool Cooperative. Download the workbook containing this form from Connect, where you will also receive instructions about how to use this worksheet form.

| | A | B | C | D | E |
|---|---|---|---|---|---|
| 1 | Chapter 11: Applying Excel | | | | |
| 2 | | | | | |
| 3 | Data | | | | |
| 4 | Exhibit 11-7 Santa Maria Wool Cooperative | | | | |
| 5 | Cost of wool | $200,000 | | | |
| 6 | Cost of separation process | $40,000 | | | |
| 7 | Sales value of intermediate products at split-off point: | | | | |
| 8 |   Undyed coarse wool | $120,000 | | | |
| 9 |   Undyed fine wool | $150,000 | | | |
| 10 |   Undyed superfine wool | $60,000 | | | |
| 11 | Costs of further processing (dyeing) intermediate products: | | | | |
| 12 |   Undyed coarse wool | $50,000 | | | |
| 13 |   Undyed fine wool | $60,000 | | | |
| 14 |   Undyed superfine wool | $10,000 | | | |
| 15 | Sales value of end products: | | | | |
| 16 |   Dyed coarse wool | $160,000 | | | |
| 17 |   Dyed fine wool | $240,000 | | | |
| 18 |   Dyed superfine wool | $90,000 | | | |
| 19 | | | | | |
| 20 | Enter a formula into each of the cells marked with a ? below | | | | |
| 21 | Example: Joint Product Costs and the Contribution Approach | | | | |
| 22 | | | | | |
| 23 | Analysis of the profitability of the overall operation: | | | | |
| 24 | Combined final sales value | | ? | | |
| 25 | Less costs of producing the end products: | | | | |
| 26 |   Cost of wool | ? | | | |
| 27 |   Cost of separation process | ? | | | |
| 28 |   Combined costs of dyeing | ? | ? | | |
| 29 | Profit | | ? | | |
| 30 | | | | | |
| 31 | Analysis of sell or process further: | | | | |
| 32 | | Coarse | Fine | Superfine | |
| 33 | | Wool | Wool | Wool | |
| 34 | Final sales value after further processing | ? | ? | ? | |
| 35 | Less sales value at the split-off point | ? | ? | ? | |
| 36 | Incremental revenue from further processing | ? | ? | ? | |
| 37 | Less cost of further processing (dyeing) | ? | ? | ? | |
| 38 | Financial advantage (disadvantage) of further processing | ? | ? | ? | |
| 39 | | | | | |

Chapter 11 Form     Chapter 11 Fo ...

You should proceed to the requirements below only after completing your worksheet.

**Required:**

1. Check your worksheet by changing the cost of further processing undyed coarse wool in cell B12 to $30,000. The overall profit from processing all intermediate products into final products should now be $150,000 and the financial advantage of further processing coarse wool should now be $10,000. If you do not get these answers, find the errors in your worksheet and correct them.

   How should operations change in response to this change in cost?

2. In industries that process joint products, the costs of the raw materials inputs and the sales values of intermediate and final products are often volatile. Change the data area of your worksheet to match the following:

**Data**
**Exhibit 11–7 Santa Maria Wool Cooperative**

| | |
|---|---|
| Cost of wool............................................................. | $290,000 |
| Cost of separation process ............................................ | $40,000 |
| Sales value of intermediate products at split-off point: | |
|   Undyed coarse wool...................................................... | $100,000 |
|   Undyed fine wool ........................................................ | $110,000 |
|   Undyed superfine wool ................................................. | $90,000 |

(continued)

(concluded)

**Data**

**Exhibit 11–7 Santa Maria Wool Cooperative**

Costs of further processing (dyeing) intermediate products:

| | |
|---|---|
| Undyed coarse wool.............................................. | $50,000 |
| Undyed fine wool ................................................ | $60,000 |
| Undyed superfine wool .......................................... | $10,000 |
| Sales value of end products: | |
| Dyed coarse wool................................................ | $180,000 |
| Dyed fine wool................................................... | $210,000 |
| Dyed superfine wool ............................................ | $90,000 |

    a. What is the overall profit if all intermediate products are processed into final products?

    b. What is the financial advantage (disadvantage) from further processing each of the intermediate products?

    c. With these new costs and selling prices, what recommendations would you make concerning the company's operations? If your recommendation is followed, what should be the overall profit of the company?

# THE FOUNDATIONAL 15   ■ connect

**LO11–2, LO11–3, LO11–4, LO11–5, LO11–6**

Cane Company manufactures two products called Alpha and Beta that sell for $120 and $80, respectively. Each product uses only one type of raw material that costs $6 per pound. The company has the capacity to annually produce 100,000 units of each product. Its average cost per unit for each product at this level of activity are given below:

| | Alpha | Beta |
|---|---|---|
| Direct materials ................................. | $ 30 | $12 |
| Direct labor..................................... | 20 | 15 |
| Variable manufacturing overhead ................. | 7 | 5 |
| Traceable fixed manufacturing overhead .......... | 16 | 18 |
| Variable selling expenses ....................... | 12 | 8 |
| Common fixed expenses.......................... | 15 | 10 |
| Total cost per unit ............................. | $100 | $68 |

The company considers its traceable fixed manufacturing overhead to be avoidable, whereas its common fixed expenses are unavoidable and have been allocated to products based on sales dollars.

***Required:***

(Answer each question independently unless instructed otherwise.)

1. What is the total amount of traceable fixed manufacturing overhead for each of the two products?
2. What is the company's total amount of common fixed expenses?
3. Assume that Cane expects to produce and sell 80,000 Alphas during the current year. One of Cane's sales representatives has found a new customer who is willing to buy 10,000 additional Alphas for a price of $80 per unit. What is the financial advantage (disadvantage) of accepting the new customer's order?
4. Assume that Cane expects to produce and sell 90,000 Betas during the current year. One of Cane's sales representatives has found a new customer who is willing to buy 5,000 additional Betas for a price of $39 per unit. What is the financial advantage (disadvantage) of accepting the new customer's order?
5. Assume that Cane expects to produce and sell 95,000 Alphas during the current year. One of Cane's sales representatives has found a new customer who is willing to buy 10,000 additional Alphas for a price of $80 per unit; however pursuing this opportunity will decrease Alpha sales to regular customers by 5,000 units. What is the financial advantage (disadvantage) of accepting the new customer's order?
6. Assume that Cane normally produces and sells 90,000 Betas per year. What is the financial advantage (disadvantage) of discontinuing the Beta product line?

7. Assume that Cane normally produces and sells 40,000 Betas per year. What is the financial advantage (disadvantage) of discontinuing the Beta product line?

8. Assume that Cane normally produces and sells 60,000 Betas and 80,000 Alphas per year. If Cane discontinues the Beta product line, its sales representatives could increase sales of Alpha by 15,000 units. What is the financial advantage (disadvantage) of discontinuing the Beta product line?

9. Assume that Cane expects to produce and sell 80,000 Alphas during the current year. A supplier has offered to manufacture and deliver 80,000 Alphas to Cane for a price of $80 per unit. What is the financial advantage (disadvantage) of buying 80,000 units from the supplier instead of making those units?

10. Assume that Cane expects to produce and sell 50,000 Alphas during the current year. A supplier has offered to manufacture and deliver 50,000 Alphas to Cane for a price of $80 per unit. What is the financial advantage (disadvantage) of buying 50,000 units from the supplier instead of making those units?

11. How many pounds of raw material are needed to make one unit of each of the two products?

12. What contribution margin per pound of raw material is earned by each of the two products?

13. Assume that Cane's customers would buy a maximum of 80,000 units of Alpha and 60,000 units of Beta. Also assume that the raw material available for production is limited to 160,000 pounds. How many units of each product should Cane produce to maximize its profits?

14. If Cane follows your recommendation in requirement 13, what total contribution margin will it earn?

15. If Cane uses its 160,000 pounds of raw materials as you recommended in requirement 13, up to how much should it be willing to pay per pound for additional raw materials?

    **EXERCISES**

### EXERCISE 11–1  Identifying Relevant Costs LO11–1

Svahn, AB, is a Swedish manufacturer of sailing yachts. The company has assembled the information shown below that pertains to two independent decision-making contexts called Case A and Case B:

Case A:

The company chronically has no idle capacity and the old Model B100 machine is the company's constraint. Management is considering purchasing a Model B300 machine to use in addition to the company's present Model B100 machine. The old Model B100 machine will continue to be used to capacity as before, with the new Model B300 machine being used to expand production. This will increase the company's production and sales. The increase in volume will be large enough to require increases in fixed selling expenses and in general administrative overhead, but not in the fixed manufacturing overhead.

Case B:

The old Model B100 machine is not the company's constraint, but management is considering replacing it with a new Model B300 machine because of the potential savings in direct materials with the new machine. The Model B100 machine would be sold. This change will have no effect on production or sales, other than some savings in direct materials costs due to less waste.

***Required:***

Copy the information below onto your answer sheet and place an X in the appropriate column to indicate whether each item is relevant or irrelevant to the decision context described in Case A and Case B.

| | Case A | | Case B | |
|---|---|---|---|---|
| Item | Relevant | Irrelevant | Relevant | Irrelevant |
| a. Sales revenue . . . . . . . . . . . . . . . . . . . . . . . . . . . . | | | | |
| b. Direct materials . . . . . . . . . . . . . . . . . . . . . . . . . . | | | | |
| c. Direct labor. . . . . . . . . . . . . . . . . . . . . . . . . . . . . . | | | | |
| d. Variable manufacturing overhead . . . . . . . . . . . . | | | | |
| e. Depreciation—Model B100 machine. . . . . . . . . . | | | | |
| f. Book value—Model B100 machine . . . . . . . . . . . | | | | |
| g. Disposal value—Model B100 machine . . . . . . . . | | | | |
| h. Market value—Model B300 machine (cost) . . . . | | | | |
| i. Fixed manufacturing overhead (general) . . . . . . | | | | |
| j. Variable selling expense . . . . . . . . . . . . . . . . . . . | | | | |
| k. Fixed selling expense. . . . . . . . . . . . . . . . . . . . . . | | | | |
| l. General administrative overhead . . . . . . . . . . . . . | | | | |

**EXERCISE 11–2    Dropping or Retaining a Segment LO11–2**

The Regal Cycle Company manufactures three types of bicycles—a dirt bike, a mountain bike, and a racing bike. Data on sales and expenses for the past quarter follow:

| | Total | Dirt Bikes | Mountain Bikes | Racing Bikes |
|---|---|---|---|---|
| Sales . . . . . . . . . . . . . . . . . . . . . . . . . . . . . . . . . . . . . | $300,000 | $90,000 | $150,000 | $60,000 |
| Variable manufacturing and selling expenses . . . . | 120,000 | 27,000 | 60,000 | 33,000 |
| Contribution margin . . . . . . . . . . . . . . . . . . . . . . . . | 180,000 | 63,000 | 90,000 | 27,000 |
| Fixed expenses: | | | | |
|    Advertising, traceable. . . . . . . . . . . . . . . . . . . . . | 30,000 | 10,000 | 14,000 | 6,000 |
|    Depreciation of special equipment . . . . . . . . . . | 23,000 | 6,000 | 9,000 | 8,000 |
|    Salaries of product-line managers . . . . . . . . . . . | 35,000 | 12,000 | 13,000 | 10,000 |
|    Allocated common fixed expenses* . . . . . . . . . . | 60,000 | 18,000 | 30,000 | 12,000 |
| Total fixed expenses . . . . . . . . . . . . . . . . . . . . . . . . | 148,000 | 46,000 | 66,000 | 36,000 |
| Net operating income (loss). . . . . . . . . . . . . . . . . . | $ 32,000 | $17,000 | $ 24,000 | $ (9,000) |

*Allocated on the basis of sales dollars.

Management is concerned about the continued losses shown by the racing bikes and wants a recommendation as to whether or not the line should be discontinued. The special equipment used to produce racing bikes has no resale value and does not wear out.

**Required:**
1.  What is the financial advantage (disadvantage) per quarter of discontinuing the racing bikes?
2.  Should the production and sale of racing bikes be discontinued?
3.  Prepare a properly formatted segmented income statement that would be more useful to management in assessing the long-run profitability of the various product lines.

**EXERCISE 11–3    Make or Buy Decision LO11–3**

Troy Engines, Ltd., manufactures a variety of engines for use in heavy equipment. The company has always produced all of the necessary parts for its engines, including all of the carburetors. An outside supplier has offered to sell one type of carburetor to Troy Engines, Ltd., for a cost of $35 per unit. To evaluate this offer, Troy Engines, Ltd., has gathered the following information relating to its own cost of producing the carburetor internally:

| | Per Unit | 15,000 Units per Year |
|---|---|---|
| Direct materials . . . . . . . . . . . . . . . . . . . . . . . . . . . . . . . . . . . . . | $14 | $210,000 |
| Direct labor. . . . . . . . . . . . . . . . . . . . . . . . . . . . . . . . . . . . . . . . . | 10 | 150,000 |
| Variable manufacturing overhead . . . . . . . . . . . . . . . . . . . . . . . . | 3 | 45,000 |
| Fixed manufacturing overhead, traceable . . . . . . . . . . . . . . . . . | 6* | 90,000 |
| Fixed manufacturing overhead, allocated. . . . . . . . . . . . . . . . . . | 9 | 135,000 |
| Total cost. . . . . . . . . . . . . . . . . . . . . . . . . . . . . . . . . . . . . . . . . . . | $42 | $630,000 |

*One-third supervisory salaries; two-thirds depreciation of special equipment (no resale value).

**Required:**
1.  Assuming the company has no alternative use for the facilities that are now being used to produce the carburetors, what would be the financial advantage (disadvantage) of buying 15,000 carburetors from the outside supplier?
2.  Should the outside supplier's offer be accepted?
3.  Suppose that if the carburetors were purchased, Troy Engines, Ltd., could use the freed capacity to launch a new product. The segment margin of the new product would be $150,000 per year. Given this new assumption, what would be the financial advantage (disadvantage) of buying 15,000 carburetors from the outside supplier?
4.  Given the new assumption in requirement 3, should the outside supplier's offer be accepted?

**EXERCISE 11–4  Special Order Decision** LO11–4

Imperial Jewelers manufactures and sells a gold bracelet for $189.95. The company's accounting system says that the unit product cost for this bracelet is $149.00 as shown below:

| | |
|---|---|
| Direct materials . . . . . . . . . . . . . . . . . . . . . . . . . . . . | $ 84.00 |
| Direct labor. . . . . . . . . . . . . . . . . . . . . . . . . . . . . . . | 45.00 |
| Manufacturing overhead . . . . . . . . . . . . . . . . . . . | 20.00 |
| Unit product cost. . . . . . . . . . . . . . . . . . . . . . . . . . | $149.00 |

The members of a wedding party have approached Imperial Jewelers about buying 20 of these gold bracelets for the discounted price of $169.95 each. The members of the wedding party would like special filigree applied to the bracelets that would require Imperial Jewelers to buy a special tool for $250 and that would increase the direct materials cost per bracelet by $2.00. The special tool would have no other use once the special order is completed.

To analyze this special order opportunity, Imperial Jewelers has determined that most of its manufacturing overhead is fixed and unaffected by variations in how much jewelry is produced in any given period. However, $4.00 of the overhead is variable with respect to the number of bracelets produced. The company also believes that accepting this order would have no effect on its ability to produce and sell jewelry to other customers. Furthermore, the company could fulfill the wedding party's order using its existing manufacturing capacity.

**Required:**
1. What is the financial advantage (disadvantage) of accepting the special order from the wedding party?
2. Should the company accept the special order?

**EXERCISE 11–5  Volume Trade-Off Decisions** LO11–5

Outdoor Luggage, Inc., makes high-end, hard-sided luggage for sports equipment. Data concerning three of the company's most popular models appear below.

| | Ski Guard | Golf Guard | Fishing Guard |
|---|---|---|---|
| Selling price per unit. . . . . . . . . . . . . . . . . . . . . . . . . | $200 | $300 | $255 |
| Variable cost per unit . . . . . . . . . . . . . . . . . . . . . . . . | $60 | $140 | $55 |
| Plastic injection molding machine processing time required to produce one unit . . . . . . . . . . . . . . . . . | 2 minutes | 5 minutes | 4 minutes |
| Pounds of plastic pellets per unit . . . . . . . . . . . . . . . | 7 pounds | 4 pounds | 8 pounds |

**Required:**
1. If we assume that the total time available on the plastic injection molding machine is the constraint in the production process, how much contribution margin per minute of the constrained resource is earned by each product?
2. Which product offers the most profitable use of the plastic injection molding machine?
3. If we assume that a severe shortage of plastic pellets has required the company to cut back its production so much that its new constraint has become the total available pounds of plastic pellets, how much contribution margin per pound of the constrained resource is earned by each product?
4. Which product offers the most profitable use of the plastic pellets?
5. Which product has the largest contribution margin per unit? Why wouldn't this product be the most profitable use of the constrained resource in either case?

**EXERCISE 11–6  Managing a Constrained Resource** LO11–6

Portsmouth Company makes fine colonial reproduction furniture. Upholstered furniture is one of its major product lines and the bottleneck on this production line is time in the upholstery shop. Upholstering is a craft that takes years of experience to master and the demand for upholstered furniture far exceeds the company's capacity in the upholstering shop. The company's only variable cost is direct materials. Information concerning three of its upholstered chairs appears below:

| | Recliner | Sofa | Love Seat |
|---|---|---|---|
| Selling price per unit. . . . . . . . . . . . . . . . . . . . . . . . . . . . . . . | $1,400 | $1,800 | $1,500 |
| Variable cost per unit . . . . . . . . . . . . . . . . . . . . . . . . . . . . . . | $800 | $1,200 | $1,000 |
| Upholstery shop time required to produce one unit. . . . . . . . . | 8 hours | 10 hours | 5 hours |

*Required:*

1.  More time could be made available in the upholstery shop by asking the employees who work in this shop to work overtime. Assuming that this extra time would be used to produce sofas, up to how much of a premium should the company be willing to pay in terms of an overtime premium per hour to keep the upholstery shop open after normal working hours?
2.  A small nearby upholstering company has offered to upholster furniture for Portsmouth at a fixed charge of $45 per hour. The management of Portsmouth is confident that this upholstering company's work is high quality and their craftsmen can work as quickly as Portsmouth's own craftsmen on the simpler upholstering jobs such as the Love Seat. How much additional contribution margin per hour can Portsmouth earn if it provides the raw materials to the nearby company and then hires it to upholster the Love Seats?
3.  Should Portsmouth hire the nearby upholstering company? Explain.

### EXERCISE 11–7   Sell or Process Further Decisions LO11–7

Dorsey Company manufactures three products from a common input in a joint processing operation. Joint processing costs up to the split-off point total $350,000 per quarter. For financial reporting purposes, the company allocates these costs to the joint products on the basis of their relative sales value at the split-off point. Unit selling prices and total output at the split-off point are as follows:

| Product | Selling Price | Quarterly Output |
|---|---|---|
| A.................. | $16 per pound | 15,000 pounds |
| B.................. | $8 per pound | 20,000 pounds |
| C.................. | $25 per gallon | 4,000 gallons |

Each product can be processed further after the split-off point. Additional processing requires no special facilities. The additional processing costs (per quarter) and unit selling prices after further processing are given below:

| Product | Additional Processing Costs | Selling Price |
|---|---|---|
| A.............. | $63,000 | $20 per pound |
| B.............. | $80,000 | $13 per pound |
| C.............. | $36,000 | $32 per gallon |

*Required:*

1.  What is the financial advantage (disadvantage) of further processing each of the three products beyond the split-off point?
2.  Based on your analysis in requirement 1, which product or products should be sold at the split-off point and which product or products should be processed further?

### EXERCISE 11–8   Volume Trade-Off Decisions LO11–5, LO11–6

Barlow Company manufactures three products—A, B, and C. The selling price, variable costs, and contribution margin for one unit of each product follow:

|  | Product | | |
|---|---|---|---|
|  | A | B | C |
| Selling price ..................................... | $180 | $270 | $240 |
| Variable expenses: | | | |
|    Direct materials ............................. | 24 | 80 | 32 |
|    Other variable expenses .................... | 102 | 90 | 148 |
| Total variable expenses ........................ | 126 | 170 | 180 |
| Contribution margin .......................... | $ 54 | $100 | $ 60 |
| Contribution margin ratio..................... | 30% | 37% | 25% |

The same raw material is used in all three products. Barlow Company has only 6,000 pounds of raw material on hand and will not be able to obtain any more of it for several weeks due to a strike in its supplier's plant. Management is trying to decide which product(s) to concentrate on next week in filling its backlog of orders. The material costs $8 per pound.

**Required:**
1. Calculate the contribution margin per pound of the constraining resource for each product.
2. Assuming that Barlow has unlimited demand for each of its three products, what is the maximum contribution margin the company can earn when using the 6,000 pounds of raw material on hand?
3. Assuming that Barlow's estimated customer demand is 500 units per product line, what is the maximum contribution margin the company can earn when using the 6,000 pounds of raw material on hand?
4. A foreign supplier could furnish Barlow with additional stocks of the raw material at a substantial premium over the usual price. Assuming Barlow's estimated customer demand is 500 units per product line and that the company has used its 6,000 pounds of raw material in an optimal fashion, what is the highest price Barlow Company should be willing to pay for an additional pound of materials? Explain.

### EXERCISE 11–9 Special Order Decision LO11–4

Delta Company produces a single product. The cost of producing and selling a single unit of this product at the company's normal activity level of 60,000 units per year is:

| | |
|---|---|
| Direct materials | $5.10 |
| Direct labor | $3.80 |
| Variable manufacturing overhead | $1.00 |
| Fixed manufacturing overhead | $4.20 |
| Variable selling and administrative expense | $1.50 |
| Fixed selling and administrative expense | $2.40 |

The normal selling price is $21 per unit. The company's capacity is 75,000 units per year. An order has been received from a mail-order house for 15,000 units at a special price of $14.00 per unit. This order would not affect regular sales or the company's total fixed costs.

**Required:**
1. What is the financial advantage (disadvantage) of accepting the special order?
2. As a separate matter from the special order, assume the company's inventory includes 1,000 units of this product that were produced last year and that are inferior to the current model. The units must be sold through regular channels at reduced prices. What unit cost is relevant for establishing a minimum selling price for these units? Explain.

### EXERCISE 11–10 Make or Buy Decision LO11–3

Futura Company purchases the 40,000 starters that it installs in its standard line of farm tractors from a supplier for the price of $8.40 per unit. Due to a reduction in output, the company now has idle capacity that could be used to produce the starters rather than buying them from an outside supplier. However, the company's chief engineer is opposed to making the starters because the production cost per unit is $9.20 as shown below:

| | Per Unit | Total |
|---|---|---|
| Direct materials | $3.10 | |
| Direct labor | 2.70 | |
| Supervision | 1.50 | $60,000 |
| Depreciation | 1.00 | $40,000 |
| Variable manufacturing overhead | 0.60 | |
| Rent | 0.30 | $12,000 |
| Total production cost | $9.20 | |

If Futura decides to make the starters, a supervisor would have to be hired (at a salary of $60,000) to oversee production. However, the company has sufficient idle tools and machinery such that no new equipment would have to be purchased. The rent charge above is based on space utilized in the plant. The total rent on the plant is $80,000 per period. Depreciation is due to obsolescence rather than wear and tear.

***Required:***
What is the financial advantage (disadvantage) of making the 40,000 starters instead of buying them from an outside supplier?

### EXERCISE 11–11 Make or Buy Decision LO11–3
Han Products manufactures 30,000 units of part S-6 each year for use on its production line. At this level of activity, the cost per unit for part S-6 is:

| | |
|---|---|
| Direct materials | $ 3.60 |
| Direct labor | 10.00 |
| Variable manufacturing overhead | 2.40 |
| Fixed manufacturing overhead | 9.00 |
| Total cost per part | $25.00 |

An outside supplier has offered to sell 30,000 units of part S-6 each year to Han Products for $21 per part. If Han Products accepts this offer, the facilities now being used to manufacture part S-6 could be rented to another company at an annual rental of $80,000. However, Han Products has determined that two-thirds of the fixed manufacturing overhead being applied to part S-6 would continue even if part S-6 were purchased from the outside supplier.

***Required:***
What is the financial advantage (disadvantage) of accepting the outside supplier's offer?

### EXERCISE 11–12 Volume Trade-Off Decisions LO11–5
Benoit Company produces three products—A, B, and C. Data concerning the three products follow (per unit):

| | Product A | B | C |
|---|---|---|---|
| Selling price | $80 | $56 | $70 |
| Variable expenses: | | | |
| Direct materials | 24 | 15 | 9 |
| Other variable expenses | 24 | 27 | 40 |
| Total variable expenses | 48 | 42 | 49 |
| Contribution margin | $32 | $14 | $21 |
| Contribution margin ratio | 40% | 25% | 30% |

The company estimates that it can sell 800 units of each product per month. The same raw material is used in each product. The material costs $3 per pound with a maximum of 5,000 pounds available each month.

***Required:***
1. Calculate the contribution margin per pound of the constraining resource for each product.
2. Which orders would you advise the company to accept first, those for A, B, or C? Which orders second? Third?
3. What is the maximum contribution margin that the company can earn per month if it makes optimal use of its 5,000 pounds of materials?

### EXERCISE 11–13 Sell or Process Further Decision LO11–7
Wexpro, Inc., produces several products from processing 1 ton of clypton, a rare mineral. Material and processing costs total $60,000 per ton, one-fourth of which is allocated to product X15. Seven thousand units of product X15 are produced from each ton of clypton. The units can either be sold at the split-off point for $9 each, or processed further at a total cost of $9,500 and then sold for $12 each.

**Required:**
1. What is the financial advantage (disadvantage) of further processing product X15?
2. Should product X15 be processed further or sold at the split-off point?

**EXERCISE 11–14   Identification of Relevant Costs** LO11–1
Kristen Lu purchased a used automobile for $8,000 at the beginning of last year and incurred the following operating costs:

| | |
|---|---|
| Depreciation ($8,000 ÷ 5 years)........... | $1,600 |
| Insurance ............................. | $1,200 |
| Garage rent ........................... | $360 |
| Automobile tax and license.............. | $40 |
| Variable operating cost .................. | $0.14 per mile |

The variable operating cost consists of gasoline, oil, tires, maintenance, and repairs. Kristen estimates that, at her current rate of usage, the car will have zero resale value in five years, so the annual straight-line depreciation is $1,600. The car is kept in a garage for a monthly fee.

**Required:**
1. Kristen drove the car 10,000 miles last year. Compute the average cost per mile of owning and operating the car.
2. Kristen is unsure about whether she should use her own car or rent a car to go on an extended cross-country trip for two weeks during spring break. What costs above are relevant in this decision? Explain.
3. Kristen is thinking about buying an expensive sports car to replace the car she bought last year. She would drive the same number of miles regardless of which car she owns and would rent the same parking space. The sports car's variable operating costs would be roughly the same as the variable operating costs of her old car. However, her insurance and automobile tax and license costs would go up. What costs are relevant in estimating the incremental cost of owning the more expensive car? Explain.

**EXERCISE 11–15   Dropping or Retaining a Segment** LO11–2
Thalassines Kataskeves, S.A., of Greece makes marine equipment. The company has been experiencing losses on its bilge pump product line for several years. The most recent quarterly contribution format income statement for the bilge pump product line follows:

| Thalassines Kataskeves, S.A. Income Statement—Bilge Pump For the Quarter Ended March 31 | | |
|---|---|---|
| Sales ................................................. | | $850,000 |
| Variable expenses: | | |
| Variable manufacturing expenses ......................... | $330,000 | |
| Sales commissions ...................................... | 42,000 | |
| Shipping .............................................. | 18,000 | |
| Total variable expenses ................................... | | 390,000 |
| Contribution margin ....................................... | | 460,000 |
| Fixed expenses: | | |
| Advertising (for the bilge pump product line)................ | 270,000 | |
| Depreciation of equipment (no resale value)................ | 80,000 | |
| General factory overhead ................................ | 105,000* | |
| Salary of product-line manager........................... | 32,000 | |
| Insurance on inventories ................................. | 8,000 | |
| Purchasing department ................................... | 45,000† | |
| Total fixed expenses...................................... | | 540,000 |
| Net operating loss........................................ | | $ (80,000) |

*Common costs allocated on the basis of machine-hours.
†Common costs allocated on the basis of sales dollars.

Discontinuing the bilge pump product line would not affect sales of other product lines and would have no effect on the company's total general factory overhead or total Purchasing Department expenses.

**Required:**
What is the financial advantage (disadvantage) of discontinuing the bilge pump product line?

### EXERCISE 11–16  Identification of Relevant Costs LO11–1
Bill has just returned from a duck hunting trip. He brought home eight ducks. Bill's friend, John, disapproves of duck hunting, and to discourage Bill from further hunting, John presented him with the following cost estimate per duck:

| | |
|---|---:|
| Camper and equipment: | |
| Cost, $12,000; usable for eight seasons; 10 hunting trips per season......... | $150 |
| Travel expense (pickup truck): | |
| 100 miles at $0.31 per mile (gas, oil, and tires—$0.21 per mile; depreciation and insurance—$0.10 per mile)....................................... | 31 |
| Shotgun shells (two boxes per hunting trip).................................... | 20 |
| Boat: | |
| Cost, $2,320, usable for eight seasons; 10 hunting trips per season........... | 29 |
| Hunting license: | |
| Cost, $30 for the season; 10 hunting trips per season ...................... | 3 |
| Money lost playing poker: | |
| Loss, $24 (Bill plays poker every weekend whether he goes hunting or stays at home)........................................... | 24 |
| Bottle of whiskey: | |
| Cost, $15 per hunting trip (used to ward off the cold)....................... | 15 |
| Total cost................................................................ | $272 |
| Cost per duck ($272 ÷ 8 ducks)........................................... | $ 34 |

**Required:**
1.  Assuming the duck hunting trip Bill has just completed is typical, what costs are relevant to a decision as to whether Bill should go duck hunting again this season?
2.  Suppose Bill gets lucky on his next hunting trip and shoots 10 ducks using the same amount of shotgun shells he used on his previous hunting trip to bag 8 ducks. How much would it have cost him to shoot the last two ducks? Explain.
3.  Which costs are relevant in a decision of whether Bill should give up hunting? Explain.

### EXERCISE 11–17  Dropping or Retaining a Segment LO11–2
Bed & Bath, a retailing company, has two departments—Hardware and Linens. The company's most recent monthly contribution format income statement follows:

| | | Department | |
|---|---:|---:|---:|
| | Total | Hardware | Linens |
| Sales ...................................... | $4,000,000 | $3,000,000 | $1,000,000 |
| Variable expenses......................... | 1,300,000 | 900,000 | 400,000 |
| Contribution margin ....................... | 2,700,000 | 2,100,000 | 600,000 |
| Fixed expenses............................ | 2,200,000 | 1,400,000 | 800,000 |
| Net operating income (loss)................ | $ 500,000 | $ 700,000 | $ (200,000) |

A study indicates that $340,000 of the fixed expenses being charged to Linens are sunk costs or allocated costs that will continue even if the Linens Department is dropped. In addition, the elimination of the Linens Department will result in a 10% decrease in the sales of the Hardware Department.

**Required:**
What is the financial advantage (disadvantage) of discontinuing the Linens Department?

**connect**     **PROBLEMS**

**PROBLEM 11–18  Relevant Cost Analysis in a Variety of Situations** LO11–2, LO11–3, LO11–4

Andretti Company has a single product called a Dak. The company normally produces and sells 60,000 Daks each year at a selling price of $32 per unit. The company's unit costs at this level of activity are given below:

| | | |
|---|---|---|
| Direct materials | $10.00 | |
| Direct labor | 4.50 | |
| Variable manufacturing overhead | 2.30 | |
| Fixed manufacturing overhead | 5.00 | ($300,000 total) |
| Variable selling expenses | 1.20 | |
| Fixed selling expenses | 3.50 | ($210,000 total) |
| Total cost per unit | $26.50 | |

A number of questions relating to the production and sale of Daks follow. Each question is independent.

**Required:**

1. Assume that Andretti Company has sufficient capacity to produce 90,000 Daks each year without any increase in fixed manufacturing overhead costs. The company could increase its unit sales by 25% above the present 60,000 units each year if it were willing to increase the fixed selling expenses by $80,000. What is the financial advantage (disadvantage) of investing an additional $80,000 in fixed selling expenses? Would the additional investment be justified?

2. Assume again that Andretti Company has sufficient capacity to produce 90,000 Daks each year. A customer in a foreign market wants to purchase 20,000 Daks. If Andretti accepts this order it would have to pay import duties on the Daks of $1.70 per unit and an additional $9,000 for permits and licenses. The only selling costs that would be associated with the order would be $3.20 per unit shipping cost. What is the break-even price per unit on this order?

3. The company has 1,000 Daks on hand that have some irregularities and are therefore considered to be "seconds." Due to the irregularities, it will be impossible to sell these units at the normal price through regular distribution channels. What is the unit cost figure that is relevant for setting a minimum selling price? Explain.

4. Due to a strike in its supplier's plant, Andretti Company is unable to purchase more material for the production of Daks. The strike is expected to last for two months. Andretti Company has enough material on hand to operate at 30% of normal levels for the two-month period. As an alternative, Andretti could close its plant down entirely for the two months. If the plant were closed, fixed manufacturing overhead costs would continue at 60% of their normal level during the two-month period and the fixed selling expenses would be reduced by 20% during the two-month period.
   a. How much total contribution margin will Andretti forgo if it closes the plant for two months?
   b. How much total fixed cost will the company avoid if it closes the plant for two months?
   c. What is the financial advantage (disadvantage) of closing the plant for the two-month period?
   d. Should Andretti close the plant for two months?

5. An outside manufacturer has offered to produce 60,000 Daks and ship them directly to Andretti's customers. If Andretti Company accepts this offer, the facilities that it uses to produce Daks would be idle; however, fixed manufacturing overhead costs would be reduced by 75%. Because the outside manufacturer would pay for all shipping costs, the variable selling expenses would be only two-thirds of their present amount. What is Andretti's avoidable cost per unit that it should compare to the price quoted by the outside manufacturer?

**PROBLEM 11–19  Dropping or Retaining a Segment** LO11–2

Jackson County Senior Services is a nonprofit organization devoted to providing essential services to seniors who live in their own homes within the Jackson County area. Three services are provided for seniors—home nursing, Meals On Wheels, and housekeeping. Data on revenue and expenses for the past year follow.

| | Total | Home Nursing | Meals On Wheels | House-keeping |
|---|---|---|---|---|
| Revenues ......................... | $900,000 | $260,000 | $400,000 | $240,000 |
| Variable expenses.................. | 490,000 | 120,000 | 210,000 | 160,000 |
| Contribution margin ................ | 410,000 | 140,000 | 190,000 | 80,000 |
| Fixed expenses: | | | | |
|   Depreciation...................... | 68,000 | 8,000 | 40,000 | 20,000 |
|   Liability insurance ................ | 42,000 | 20,000 | 7,000 | 15,000 |
|   Program administrators' salaries .... | 115,000 | 40,000 | 38,000 | 37,000 |
|   General administrative overhead* ... | 180,000 | 52,000 | 80,000 | 48,000 |
| Total fixed expenses................ | 405,000 | 120,000 | 165,000 | 120,000 |
| Net operating income (loss).......... | $ 5,000 | $ 20,000 | $ 25,000 | $ (40,000) |

*Allocated on the basis of program revenues.

The head administrator of Jackson County Senior Services, Judith Miyama, considers last year's net operating income of $5,000 to be unsatisfactory; therefore, she is considering the possibility of discontinuing the housekeeping program.

The depreciation in housekeeping is for a small van that is used to carry the housekeepers and their equipment from job to job. If the program were discontinued, the van would be donated to a charitable organization. None of the general administrative overhead would be avoided if the housekeeping program were dropped, but the liability insurance and the salary of the program administrator would be avoided.

**Required:**

1. What is the financial advantage (disadvantage) of discontinuing the Housekeeping program? Should the Housekeeping program be discontinued? Explain.
2. Prepare a properly formatted segmented income statement that would be more useful to management in assessing the long-run financial viability of its various services.

**PROBLEM 11–20   Sell or Process Further Decision LO11–7**
(Prepared from a situation suggested by Professor John W. Hardy.) Lone Star Meat Packers is a major processor of beef and other meat products. The company has a large amount of T-bone steak on hand, and it is trying to decide whether to sell the T-bone steaks as they are initially cut or to process them further into filet mignon and the New York cut.

If the T-bone steaks are sold as initially cut, the company figures that a 1-pound T-bone steak would yield the following profit:

| | |
|---|---|
| Selling price ($7.95 per pound)............................................ | $7.95 |
| Less joint costs incurred up to the split-off point where T-bone steak | |
|   can be identified as a separate product.................................. | 3.80 |
| Profit per pound ....................................................... | $4.15 |

If the company were to further process the T-bone steaks, then cutting one side of a T-bone steak provides the filet mignon and cutting the other side provides the New York cut. One 16-ounce T-bone steak cut in this way will yield one 6-ounce filet mignon and one 8-ounce New York cut; the remaining ounces are waste. It costs $0.55 to further process one T-bone steak into the filet mignon and New York cuts. The filet mignon can be sold for $12.00 per pound, and the New York cut can be sold for $8.80 per pound.

**Required:**

1. What is the financial advantage (disadvantage) of further processing one T-bone steak into filet mignon and New York cut steaks?
2. Would you recommend that the T-bone steaks be sold as initially cut or processed further? Why?

## PROBLEM 11–21 Dropping or Retaining a Flight LO11–2

Profits have been decreasing for several years at Pegasus Airlines. In an effort to improve the company's performance, the company is thinking about dropping several flights that appear to be unprofitable.

A typical income statement for one round-trip of one such flight (flight 482) is as follows:

| | | |
|---|---:|---:|
| Ticket revenue (175 seats × 40% occupancy × $200 ticket price) . . . . . . . . . . . . . . . . . . . . . . . . . . . . . . . . . . . | $14,000 | 100.0% |
| Variable expenses ($15 per person) . . . . . . . . . . . . . . . . . . . . . . . . . . . | 1,050 | 7.5 |
| Contribution margin . . . . . . . . . . . . . . . . . . . . . . . . . . . . . . . . . . . . . . . | 12,950 | 92.5% |
| Flight expenses: | | |
| Salaries, flight crew. . . . . . . . . . . . . . . . . . . . . . . . . . . . . . . . . . . . . . | 1,800 | |
| Flight promotion . . . . . . . . . . . . . . . . . . . . . . . . . . . . . . . . . . . . . . . | 750 | |
| Depreciation of aircraft. . . . . . . . . . . . . . . . . . . . . . . . . . . . . . . . . . . . | 1,550 | |
| Fuel for aircraft. . . . . . . . . . . . . . . . . . . . . . . . . . . . . . . . . . . . . . . . . | 5,800 | |
| Liability insurance . . . . . . . . . . . . . . . . . . . . . . . . . . . . . . . . . . . . . . | 4,200 | |
| Salaries, flight assistants . . . . . . . . . . . . . . . . . . . . . . . . . . . . . . . . | 1,500 | |
| Baggage loading and flight preparation . . . . . . . . . . . . . . . . . . . . . . | 1,700 | |
| Overnight costs for flight crew and assistants at destination. . . . . . . . . . . . . . . . . . . . . . . . . . . . . . . . . . . . . . . | 300 | |
| Total flight expenses. . . . . . . . . . . . . . . . . . . . . . . . . . . . . . . . . . . . . | 17,600 | |
| Net operating loss. . . . . . . . . . . . . . . . . . . . . . . . . . . . . . . . . . . . . . . | $ (4,650) | |

The following additional information is available about flight 482:
a. Members of the flight crew are paid fixed annual salaries, whereas the flight assistants are paid based on the number of round trips they complete.
b. One-third of the liability insurance is a special charge assessed against flight 482 because in the opinion of the insurance company, the destination of the flight is in a "high-risk" area. The remaining two-thirds would be unaffected by a decision to drop flight 482.
c. The baggage loading and flight preparation expense is an allocation of ground crews' salaries and depreciation of ground equipment. Dropping flight 482 would have no effect on the company's total baggage loading and flight preparation expenses.
d. If flight 482 is dropped, Pegasus Airlines has no authorization at present to replace it with another flight.
e. Aircraft depreciation is due entirely to obsolescence. Depreciation due to wear and tear is negligible.
f. Dropping flight 482 would not allow Pegasus Airlines to reduce the number of aircraft in its fleet or the number of flight crew on its payroll.

**Required:**
1. What is the financial advantage (disadvantage) of discontinuing flight 482?
2. The airline's scheduling officer has been criticized because only about 50% of the seats on Pegasus' flights are being filled compared to an industry average of 60%. The scheduling officer has explained that Pegasus' average seat occupancy could be improved considerably by eliminating about 10% of its flights, but that doing so would reduce profits. Explain how this could happen.

## PROBLEM 11–22 Special Order Decisions LO11–4

Polaski Company manufactures and sells a single product called a Ret. Operating at capacity, the company can produce and sell 30,000 Rets per year. Costs associated with this level of production and sales are given below:

| | Unit | Total |
|---|---:|---:|
| Direct materials . . . . . . . . . . . . . . . . . . | $15 | $ 450,000 |
| Direct labor. . . . . . . . . . . . . . . . . . . . . . | 8 | 240,000 |
| Variable manufacturing overhead . . | 3 | 90,000 |
| Fixed manufacturing overhead. . . . . | 9 | 270,000 |
| Variable selling expense . . . . . . . . . | 4 | 120,000 |
| Fixed selling expense. . . . . . . . . . . . | 6 | 180,000 |
| Total cost. . . . . . . . . . . . . . . . . . . . . . | $45 | $1,350,000 |

The Rets normally sell for $50 each. Fixed manufacturing overhead is $270,000 per year within the range of 25,000 through 30,000 Rets per year.

**Required:**

1.  Assume that due to a recession, Polaski Company expects to sell only 25,000 Rets through regular channels next year. A large retail chain has offered to purchase 5,000 Rets if Polaski is willing to accept a 16% discount off the regular price. There would be no sales commissions on this order; thus, variable selling expenses would be slashed by 75%. However, Polaski Company would have to purchase a special machine to engrave the retail chain's name on the 5,000 units. This machine would cost $10,000. Polaski Company has no assurance that the retail chain will purchase additional units in the future. What is the financial advantage (disadvantage) of accepting the special order?

2.  Refer to the original data. Assume again that Polaski Company expects to sell only 25,000 Rets through regular channels next year. The U.S. Army would like to make a one-time-only purchase of 5,000 Rets. The Army would pay a fixed fee of $1.80 per Ret, and it would reimburse Polaski Company for all costs of production (variable and fixed) associated with the units. Because the army would pick up the Rets with its own trucks, there would be no variable selling expenses associated with this order. What is the financial advantage (disadvantage) of accepting the U.S. Army's special order?

3.  Assume the same situation as described in (2) above, except that the company expects to sell 30,000 Rets through regular channels next year. Thus, accepting the U.S. Army's order would require giving up regular sales of 5,000 Rets. Given this new information, what is the financial advantage (disadvantage) of accepting the U.S. Army's special order?

**PROBLEM 11–23   Make or Buy Decision LO11–3**

Silven Industries, which manufactures and sells a highly successful line of summer lotions and insect repellents, has decided to diversify in order to stabilize sales throughout the year. A natural area for the company to consider is the production of winter lotions and creams to prevent dry and chapped skin.

After considerable research, a winter products line has been developed. However, Silven's president has decided to introduce only one of the new products for this coming winter. If the product is a success, further expansion in future years will be initiated.

The product selected (called Chap-Off) is a lip balm that will be sold in a lipstick-type tube. The product will be sold to wholesalers in boxes of 24 tubes for $8 per box. Because of excess capacity, no additional fixed manufacturing overhead costs will be incurred to produce the product. However, a $90,000 charge for fixed manufacturing overhead will be absorbed by the product under the company's absorption costing system.

Using the estimated sales and production of 100,000 boxes of Chap-Off, the Accounting Department has developed the following manufacturing cost per box:

| | |
|---|---:|
| Direct material . . . . . . . . . . . . . . . . . . . . . . . . . . . . . . | $3.60 |
| Direct labor. . . . . . . . . . . . . . . . . . . . . . . . . . . . . . . . . | 2.00 |
| Manufacturing overhead . . . . . . . . . . . . . . . . . . . . . . | 1.40 |
| Total cost. . . . . . . . . . . . . . . . . . . . . . . . . . . . . . . . . . . | $7.00 |

The costs above relate to making both the lip balm and the tube that contains it. As an alternative to making the tubes for Chap-Off, Silven has approached a supplier to discuss the possibility of buying the tubes. The purchase price of the supplier's empty tubes would be $1.35 per box of 24 tubes. If Silven Industries stops making the tubes and buys them from the outside supplier, its direct labor and variable manufacturing overhead costs per box of Chap-Off would be reduced by 10% and its direct materials costs would be reduced by 25%.

**Required:**

1.  If Silven buys its tubes from the outside supplier, how much of its own Chap-Off manufacturing costs per box will it be able to avoid? (*Hint:* You need to separate the manufacturing overhead of $1.40 per box that is shown above into its variable and fixed components to derive the correct answer.)

2.  What is the financial advantage (disadvantage) per box of Chap-Off if Silven buys its tubes from the outside supplier?

3.  What is the financial advantage (disadvantage) in total (not per box) if Silven buys 100,000 boxes of tubes from the outside supplier?

4.  Should Silven Industries make or buy the tubes?

5.  What is the maximum price that Silven should be willing to pay the outside supplier for a box of 24 tubes? Explain.

6.  Instead of sales of 100,000 boxes, revised estimates show a sales volume of 120,000 boxes. At this higher sales volume, Silven would need to rent extra equipment at a cost of $40,000 per year to make the additional 20,000 boxes of tubes. Assuming that the outside supplier will not accept an order for less than 120,000 boxes, what is the financial advantage (disadvantage) in total (not per box) if Silven buys 120,000 boxes of tubes from the outside supplier? Given this new information, should Silven Industries make or buy the tubes?

7.  Refer to the data in (6) above. Assume that the outside supplier will accept an order of any size for the tubes at a price of $1.35 per box. How many boxes of tubes should Silven make? How many boxes of tubes should it buy from the outside supplier?

8.  What qualitative factors should Silven Industries consider in determining whether they should make or buy the tubes?

(CMA, adapted)

### PROBLEM 11–24   Shutting Down or Continuing to Operate a Plant LO11–2

Birch Company normally produces and sells 30,000 units of RG-6 each month. The selling price is $22 per unit, variable costs are $14 per unit, fixed manufacturing overhead costs total $150,000 per month, and fixed selling costs total $30,000 per month.

Employment-contract strikes in the companies that purchase the bulk of the RG-6 units have caused Birch Company's sales to temporarily drop to only 8,000 units per month. Birch Company estimates that the strikes will last for two months, after which time sales of RG-6 should return to normal. Due to the current low level of sales, Birch Company is thinking about closing down its own plant during the strike, which would reduce its fixed manufacturing overhead costs by $45,000 per month and its fixed selling costs by 10%. Start-up costs at the end of the shutdown period would total $8,000. Because Birch Company uses Lean Production methods, no inventories are on hand.

### Required:

1.  What is the financial advantage (disadvantage) if Birch closes its own plant for two months?
2.  Should Birch close the plant for two months? Explain.
3.  At what level of unit sales for the two-month period would Birch Company be indifferent between closing the plant or keeping it open? (*Hint:* This is a type of break-even analysis, except that the fixed cost portion of your break-even computation should include only those fixed costs that are relevant [i.e., avoidable] over the two-month period.)

### PROBLEM 11–25   Volume Trade-Off Decisions LO11–5, LO11–6

The Walton Toy Company manufactures a line of dolls and a sewing kit. Demand for the company's products is increasing, and management requests assistance from you in determining an economical sales and production mix for the coming year. The company has provided the following data:

| Product | Demand Next Year (units) | Selling Price per Unit | Direct Materials | Direct Labor |
|---|---|---|---|---|
| Debbie. . . . . . . . . . . . . . . . . . . . . . | 50,000 | $16.70 | $4.30 | $6.40 |
| Trish. . . . . . . . . . . . . . . . . . . . . . | 42,000 | $7.50 | $1.10 | $4.00 |
| Sarah. . . . . . . . . . . . . . . . . . . . . . | 35,000 | $26.60 | $6.44 | $11.20 |
| Mike. . . . . . . . . . . . . . . . . . . . . . | 40,000 | $14.00 | $2.00 | $8.00 |
| Sewing kit. . . . . . . . . . . . . . . . . . . . | 325,000 | $9.60 | $3.20 | $3.20 |

The following additional information is available:

a.  The company's plant has a capacity of 130,000 direct labor-hours per year on a single-shift basis. The company's present employees and equipment can produce all five products.

b.  The direct labor rate of $16 per hour is expected to remain unchanged during the coming year.

c.  Fixed manufacturing costs total $520,000 per year. Variable overhead costs are $2 per direct labor-hour.

d.  All of the company's nonmanufacturing costs are fixed.

e.  The company's finished goods inventory is negligible and can be ignored.

### Required:

1.  How many direct labor hours are used to manufacture one unit of each of the company's five products?

2.  How much variable overhead cost is incurred to manufacture one unit of each of the company's five products?
3.  What is the contribution margin per direct labor-hour for each of the company's five products?
4.  Assuming that direct labor-hours is the company's constraining resource, what is the highest total contribution margin that the company can earn if it makes optimal use of its constrained resource?
5.  Assuming that the company has made optimal use of its 130,000 direct labor-hours, what is the highest direct labor rate per hour that Walton Toy Company would be willing to pay for additional capacity (that is, for added direct labor time)?
6.  Identify changes that the company could make to enable it to satisfy the customers' demand for *all* of its products.

(CMA, adapted)

**PROBLEM 11–26   Close or Retain a Store LO11–2**
Superior Markets, Inc., operates three stores in a large metropolitan area. A segmented absorption costing income statement for the company for the last quarter is given below:

| Superior Markets, Inc.<br>Income Statement<br>For the Quarter Ended September 30 | | | | |
|---|---|---|---|---|
| | Total | North Store | South Store | East Store |
| Sales | $3,000,000 | $720,000 | $1,200,000 | $1,080,000 |
| Cost of goods sold | 1,657,200 | 403,200 | 660,000 | 594,000 |
| Gross margin | 1,342,800 | 316,800 | 540,000 | 486,000 |
| Selling and administrative expenses: | | | | |
| Selling expenses | 817,000 | 231,400 | 315,000 | 270,600 |
| Administrative expenses | 383,000 | 106,000 | 150,900 | 126,100 |
| Total expenses | 1,200,000 | 337,400 | 465,900 | 396,700 |
| Net operating income (loss) | $ 142,800 | $ (20,600) | $ 74,100 | $ 89,300 |

The North Store has consistently shown losses over the past two years. For this reason, management is giving consideration to closing the store. The company has asked you to make a recommendation as to whether the store should be closed or kept open. The following additional information is available for your use:

a.  The breakdown of the selling and administrative expenses that are shown above is as follows:

| | Total | North Store | South Store | East Store |
|---|---|---|---|---|
| Selling expenses: | | | | |
| Sales salaries | $239,000 | $ 70,000 | $ 89,000 | $ 80,000 |
| Direct advertising | 187,000 | 51,000 | 72,000 | 64,000 |
| General advertising* | 45,000 | 10,800 | 18,000 | 16,200 |
| Store rent | 300,000 | 85,000 | 120,000 | 95,000 |
| Depreciation of store fixtures | 16,000 | 4,600 | 6,000 | 5,400 |
| Delivery salaries | 21,000 | 7,000 | 7,000 | 7,000 |
| Depreciation of delivery equipment | 9,000 | 3,000 | 3,000 | 3,000 |
| Total selling expenses | $817,000 | $231,400 | $315,000 | $270,600 |

*Allocated on the basis of sales dollars.

| | Total | North Store | South Store | East Store |
|---|---|---|---|---|
| **Administrative expenses:** | | | | |
| Store managers' salaries . . . . . . . . . . . . . . | $ 70,000 | $ 21,000 | $ 30,000 | $ 19,000 |
| General office salaries* . . . . . . . . . . . . . . . . | 50,000 | 12,000 | 20,000 | 18,000 |
| Insurance on fixtures and inventory. . . . . . | 25,000 | 7,500 | 9,000 | 8,500 |
| Utilities . . . . . . . . . . . . . . . . . . . . . . . . . . . | 106,000 | 31,000 | 40,000 | 35,000 |
| Employment taxes. . . . . . . . . . . . . . . . . . . | 57,000 | 16,500 | 21,900 | 18,600 |
| General office—other* . . . . . . . . . . . . . . . | 75,000 | 18,000 | 30,000 | 27,000 |
| Total administrative expenses. . . . . . . . . . . . | $383,000 | $106,000 | $150,900 | $126,100 |

*Allocated on the basis of sales dollars.

b.  The lease on the building housing the North Store can be broken with no penalty.
c.  The fixtures being used in the North Store would be transferred to the other two stores if the North Store were closed.
d.  The general manager of the North Store would be retained and transferred to another position in the company if the North Store were closed. She would be filling a position that would otherwise be filled by hiring a new employee at a salary of $11,000 per quarter. The general manager of the North Store would continue to earn her normal salary of $12,000 per quarter. All other managers and employees in the North store would be discharged.
e.  The company has one delivery crew that serves all three stores. One delivery person could be discharged if the North Store were closed. This person's salary is $4,000 per quarter. The delivery equipment would be distributed to the other stores. The equipment does not wear out through use, but does eventually become obsolete.
f.  The company pays employment taxes equal to 15% of their employees' salaries.
g.  One-third of the insurance in the North Store is on the store's fixtures.
h.  The "General office salaries" and "General office—other" relate to the overall management of Superior Markets, Inc. If the North Store were closed, one person in the general office could be discharged because of the decrease in overall workload. This person's compensation is $6,000 per quarter.

**Required:**
1.  How much employee salaries will the company avoid if it closes the North Store?
2.  How much employment taxes will the company avoid if it closes the North Store?
3.  What is the financial advantage (disadvantage) of closing the North Store?
4.  Assuming that the North Store's floor space can't be subleased, would you recommend closing the North Store?
5.  Assume that the North Store's floor space can't be subleased. However, let's introduce three more assumptions. First, assume that if the North Store were closed, one-fourth of its sales would transfer to the East Store, due to strong customer loyalty to Superior Markets. Second, assume that the East Store has enough capacity to handle the increased sales that would arise from closing the North Store. Third, assume that the increased sales in the East Store would yield the same gross margin as a percentage of sales as present sales in the East store. Given these new assumptions, what is the financial advantage (disadvantage) of closing the North Store?

### PROBLEM 11–27  Sell or Process Further Decisions LO11–7

Come-Clean Corporation produces a variety of cleaning compounds and solutions for both industrial and household use. While most of its products are processed independently, a few are related, such as the company's Grit 337 and its Sparkle silver polish.

Grit 337 is a coarse cleaning powder with many industrial uses. It costs $1.60 a pound to make, and it has a selling price of $2.00 a pound. A small portion of the annual production of Grit 337 is retained in the factory for further processing. It is combined with several other ingredients to form a paste that is marketed as Sparkle silver polish. The silver polish sells for $4.00 per jar.

This further processing requires one-fourth pound of Grit 337 per jar of silver polish. The additional direct variable costs involved in the processing of a jar of silver polish are:

| | |
|---|---|
| Other ingredients ...................... | $0.65 |
| Direct labor........................... | 1.48 |
| Total direct cost ...................... | $2.13 |

Overhead costs associated with processing the silver polish are:

| | |
|---|---|
| Variable manufacturing overhead cost ..................... | 25% of direct labor cost |
| Fixed manufacturing overhead cost (per month): | |
| Production supervisor ................................. | $3,000 |
| Depreciation of mixing equipment....................... | $1,400 |

The production supervisor has no duties other than to oversee production of the silver polish. The mixing equipment is special-purpose equipment acquired specifically to produce the silver polish. It can produce up to 15,000 jars of polish per month. Its resale value is negligible and it does not wear out through use.

Advertising costs for the silver polish total $4,000 per month. Variable selling costs associated with the silver polish are 7.5% of sales.

Due to a recent decline in the demand for silver polish, the company is wondering whether its continued production is advisable. The sales manager feels that it would be more profitable to sell all of the Grit 337 as a cleaning powder.

**Required:**
1. How much incremental revenue does the company earn per jar of polish by further processing Grit 337 rather than selling it as a cleaning powder?
2. How much incremental contribution margin does the company earn per jar of polish by further processing Grit 337 rather than selling it as a cleaning powder?
3. How many jars of silver polish must be sold each month to exactly offset the avoidable fixed costs incurred to produce and sell the polish? Explain.
4. If the company sells 9,000 jars of polish, what is the financial advantage (disadvantage) of choosing to further process Grit 337 rather than selling is as a cleaning powder?
5. If the company sells 11,500 jars of polish, what is the financial advantage (disadvantage) of choosing to further process Grit 337 rather than selling is as a cleaning powder?

(CMA, adapted)

**PROBLEM 11–28    Make or Buy Decisions LO11–3**
"In my opinion, we ought to stop making our own drums and accept that outside supplier's offer," said Wim Niewindt, managing director of Antilles Refining, N.V., of Aruba. "At a price of $18 per drum, we would be paying $5 less than it costs us to manufacture the drums in our own plant. Since we use 60,000 drums a year, that would be an annual cost savings of $300,000." Antilles Refining's current cost to manufacture one drum is given below (based on 60,000 drums per year):

| | |
|---|---|
| Direct materials ........................................... | $10.35 |
| Direct labor.............................................. | 6.00 |
| Variable overhead......................................... | 1.50 |
| Fixed overhead ($2.80 general company overhead, $1.60 depreciation, and $0.75 supervision)........ | 5.15 |
| Total cost per drum....................................... | $23.00 |

A decision about whether to make or buy the drums is especially important at this time because the equipment being used to make the drums is completely worn out and must be replaced. The choices facing the company are:

*Alternative 1:* Rent new equipment and continue to make the drums. The equipment would be rented for $135,000 per year.
*Alternative 2:* Purchase the drums from an outside supplier at $18 per drum.

The new equipment would be more efficient than the equipment that Antilles Refining has been using and, according to the manufacturer, would reduce direct labor and variable overhead costs by 30%. The old equipment has no resale value. Supervision cost ($45,000 per year) and direct materials cost per drum would not be affected by the new equipment. The new equipment's capacity would be 90,000 drums per year.

The company's total general company overhead would be unaffected by this decision.

**Required:**

1. Assuming that 60,000 drums are needed each year, what is the financial advantage (disadvantage) of buying the drums from an outside supplier?
2. Assuming that 75,000 drums are needed each year, what is the financial advantage (disadvantage) of buying the drums from an outside supplier?
3. Assuming that 90,000 drums are needed each year, what is the financial advantage (disadvantage) of buying the drums from an outside supplier?
4. What other factors would you recommend that the company consider before making a decision?

**connect** BUILDING YOUR SKILLS

**CASE LO11–7**

The Scottie Sweater Company produces sweaters under the "Scottie" label. The company buys raw wool and processes it into wool yarn from which the sweaters are woven. One spindle of wool yarn is required to produce one sweater. The costs and revenues associated with the sweaters are given below:

|  | Per Sweater | |
|---|---|---|
| Selling price | | $30.00 |
| Cost to manufacture: | | |
| Raw materials: | | |
| Buttons, thread, lining | $ 2.00 | |
| Wool yarn | 16.00 | |
| Total raw materials | 18.00 | |
| Direct labor | 5.80 | |
| Manufacturing overhead | 8.70 | 32.50 |
| Manufacturing profit (loss) | | $ (2.50) |

Originally, all of the wool yarn was used to produce sweaters, but in recent years a market has developed for the wool yarn itself. The yarn is purchased by other companies for use in production of wool blankets and other wool products. Since the development of the market for the wool yarn, a continuing dispute has existed in the Scottie Sweater Company as to whether the yarn should be sold simply as yarn or processed into sweaters. Current cost and revenue data on the yarn are given below:

|  | Per Spindle of Yarn | |
|---|---|---|
| Selling price | | $20.00 |
| Cost to manufacture: | | |
| Raw materials (raw wool) | $7.00 | |
| Direct labor | 3.60 | |
| Manufacturing overhead | 5.40 | 16.00 |
| Manufacturing profit | | $ 4.00 |

The market for sweaters is temporarily depressed, due to unusually warm weather in the western states where the sweaters are sold. This has made it necessary for the company to discount the selling price of the sweaters to $30 from the normal $40 price. Since the market for wool yarn has remained strong, the dispute has again surfaced over whether the yarn should be sold outright rather than processed into sweaters. The sales manager thinks that the production of sweaters should be discontinued; she is upset about having to sell sweaters at a $2.50 loss when the yarn could be sold for a $4.00 profit. However, the production superintendent does not want to close down a large portion of the factory. He argues that the company is in the sweater business, not the yarn business, and the company should focus on its core strength.

All of the manufacturing overhead costs are fixed and would not be affected even if sweaters were discontinued. Manufacturing overhead is assigned to products on the basis of 150% of direct labor cost. Materials and direct labor costs are variable.

***Required:***

1. What is the financial advantage (disadvantage) of further processing one spindle of wool yarn into a sweater?
2. Would you recommend that the wool yarn be sold outright or processed into sweaters? Explain.
3. What is the lowest price that the company should accept for a sweater? Support your answer with appropriate computations and explain your reasoning.

### ETHICS CHALLENGE LO11–2

Haley Romeros had just been appointed vice president of the Rocky Mountain Region of the Bank Services Corporation (BSC). The company provides check processing services for small banks. The banks send checks presented for deposit or payment to BSC, which records the data on each check in a computerized database. BSC then sends the data electronically to the nearest Federal Reserve Bank check-clearing center where the appropriate transfers of funds are made between banks. The Rocky Mountain Region has three check processing centers, which are located in Billings, Montana; Great Falls, Montana; and Clayton, Idaho. Prior to her promotion to vice president, Ms. Romeros had been the manager of a check processing center in New Jersey.

Immediately after assuming her new position, Ms. Romeros requested a complete financial report for the just-ended fiscal year from the region's controller, John Littlebear. Ms. Romeros specified that the financial report should follow the standardized format required by corporate headquarters for all regional performance reports. That report follows:

**Bank Services Corporation (BSC)**
**Rocky Mountain Region**
**Financial Performance**

| | Total | Check Processing Centers | | |
| --- | --- | --- | --- | --- |
| | | Billings | Great Falls | Clayton |
| Sales | $50,000,000 | $20,000,000 | $18,000,000 | $12,000,000 |
| Operating expenses: | | | | |
| Direct labor | 32,000,000 | 12,500,000 | 11,000,000 | 8,500,000 |
| Variable overhead | 850,000 | 350,000 | 310,000 | 190,000 |
| Equipment depreciation | 3,900,000 | 1,300,000 | 1,400,000 | 1,200,000 |
| Facility expense* | 2,800,000 | 900,000 | 800,000 | 1,100,000 |
| Local administrative expense† | 450,000 | 140,000 | 160,000 | 150,000 |
| Regional administrative expense‡ | 1,500,000 | 600,000 | 540,000 | 360,000 |
| Corporate administrative expense§ | 4,750,000 | 1,900,000 | 1,710,000 | 1,140,000 |
| Total operating expense | 46,250,000 | 17,690,000 | 15,920,000 | 12,640,000 |
| Net operating income (loss) | $ 3,750,000 | $ 2,310,000 | $ 2,080,000 | $ (640,000) |

*Includes building rental expense for the Billings and Great Falls locations and building depreciation for the Clayton location.
†Local administrative expenses are the administrative expenses incurred at the check processing centers.
‡Regional administrative expenses are allocated to the check processing centers based on sales.
§Corporate administrative expenses are charged to segments of the company such as the Rocky Mountain Region and the check processing centers at the rate of 9.5% of their sales.

Upon seeing this report, Ms. Romeros summoned John Littlebear for an explanation.

*Romeros:* What's the story on Clayton? It didn't have a loss the previous year did it?

*Littlebear:* No, the Clayton facility has had a nice profit every year since it opened six years ago, but Clayton lost a big contract this year.

*Romeros:* Why?

*Littlebear:* One of our national competitors entered the local market and bid very aggressively on the contract. We couldn't afford to meet the bid. Clayton's costs—particularly their facility expenses—are just too high. When Clayton lost the contract, we had to lay off a lot of employees, but we could not reduce the fixed costs of the Clayton facility.

*Romeros:* Why is Clayton's facility expense so high? It's a smaller facility than either Billings or Great Falls and yet its facility expense is higher.

*Littlebear:* The problem is that we are able to rent suitable facilities very cheaply at Billings and Great Falls. No such facilities were available at Clayton; we had them built. Unfortunately, there were big cost overruns. The contractor we hired was inexperienced at this kind of work and in fact went bankrupt before the project was completed. After hiring another contractor to finish the work, we were way over budget. The large depreciation charges on the facility didn't matter at first because we didn't have much competition at the time and could charge premium prices.

*Romeros:* Well we can't do that anymore. The Clayton facility will obviously have to be shut down. Its business can be shifted to the other two check processing centers in the region.

*Littlebear:* I would advise against that. The $1,100,000 in facility depreciation at the Clayton location is misleading. That facility should last indefinitely with proper maintenance. And it has no resale value; there is no other commercial activity around Clayton.

*Romeros:* What about the other costs at Clayton?

*Littlebear:* If we shifted Clayton's sales over to the other two processing centers in the region, we wouldn't save anything on direct labor or variable overhead costs. We might save $90,000 or so in local administrative expense, but we would not save any regional administrative expense and corporate headquarters would still charge us 9.5% of our sales as corporate administrative expense.

In addition, we would have to rent more space in Billings and Great Falls in order to handle the work transferred from Clayton; that would probably cost us at least $600,000 a year. And don't forget that it will cost us something to move the equipment from Clayton to Billings and Great Falls. And the move will disrupt service to customers.

*Romeros:* I understand all of that, but a money-losing processing center on my performance report is completely unacceptable.

*Littlebear:* And if you shut down Clayton, you are going to throw some loyal employees out of work.

*Romeros:* That's unfortunate, but we have to face hard business realities.

*Littlebear:* And you would have to write off the investment in the facilities at Clayton.

*Romeros:* I can explain a write-off to corporate headquarters; hiring an inexperienced contractor to build the Clayton facility was my predecessor's mistake. But they'll have my head at headquarters if I show operating losses every year at one of my processing centers. Clayton has to go. At the next corporate board meeting, I am going to recommend the Clayton facility be closed.

**Required:**
1. From the standpoint of the company as a whole, what is the financial advantage (disadvantage) of closing the Clayton processing center and redistributing its work to other processing centers in the region? Explain.
2. Why might it be in Haley Romeros's self-interest to shut down the Clayton facility? Do you think Haley Romeros is conducting herself in an ethical fashion? Explain.
3. What influence should the depreciation on the facilities at Clayton have on prices charged by Clayton for its services?

**ANALYTICAL THINKING LO11–1, LO11–3, LO11–5**

TufStuff, Inc., sells a wide range of drums, bins, boxes, and other containers that are used in the chemical industry. One of the company's products is a heavy-duty corrosion-resistant metal drum, called the WVD drum, used to store toxic wastes. Production is constrained by the capacity of an automated welding machine that is used to make precision welds. A total of 2,000 hours of welding time is available annually on the machine. Because each drum requires 0.4 hours of welding machine time, annual production is limited to 5,000 drums. At present, the welding machine is used exclusively to make the WVD drums. The accounting department has provided the following financial data concerning the WVD drums:

| WVD Drums | | |
|---|---:|---:|
| Selling price per drum .............................. | | $149.00 |
| Cost per drum: | | |
| Direct materials .................................. | $52.10 | |
| Direct labor ($18 per hour) ...................... | 3.60 | |
| Manufacturing overhead ......................... | 4.50 | |
| Selling and administrative expense................ | 29.80 | 90.00 |
| Margin per drum .................................. | | $ 59.00 |

Management believes 6,000 WVD drums could be sold each year if the company had sufficient manufacturing capacity. As an alternative to adding another welding machine, management has considered buying additional drums from an outside supplier. Harcor Industries, Inc., a supplier of quality products, would be able to provide up to 4,000 WVD-type drums per year at a price of $138 per drum, which Tuf-Stuff would resell to its customers at its normal selling price after appropriate relabeling.

Megan Flores, TufStuff's production manager, has suggested the company could make better use of the welding machine by manufacturing bike frames, which would require only 0.5 hours of welding machine time per frame and yet sell for far more than the drums. Megan believes that TufStuff could sell up to 1,600 bike frames per year to bike manufacturers at a price of $239 each. The accounting department has provided the following data concerning the proposed new product:

| Bike Frames | | |
|---|---:|---:|
| Selling price per frame..................... | | $239.00 |
| Cost per frame: | | |
| Direct materials ......................... | $99.40 | |
| Direct labor ($18 per hour) ............... | 28.80 | |
| Manufacturing overhead ................. | 36.00 | |
| Selling and administrative expense........ | 47.80 | 212.00 |
| Margin per frame.......................... | | $ 27.00 |

The bike frames could be produced with existing equipment and personnel. Manufacturing overhead is allocated to products on the basis of direct labor-hours. Most of the manufacturing overhead consists of fixed common costs such as rent on the factory building, but some of it is variable. The variable manufacturing overhead has been estimated at $1.35 per WVD drum and $1.90 per bike frame. The variable manufacturing overhead cost would not be incurred on drums acquired from the outside supplier.

Selling and administrative expenses are allocated to products on the basis of revenues. Almost all of the selling and administrative expenses are fixed common costs, but it has been estimated that variable selling and administrative expenses amount to $0.75 per WVD drum whether made or purchased and would be $1.30 per bike frame.

All of the company's employees—direct and indirect—are paid for full 40-hour work weeks and the company has a policy of laying off workers only in major recessions.

*Required:*

1.  Would you be comfortable relying on the financial data provided by the accounting department for making decisions related to the WVD drums and bike frames? Why?
2.  Assuming direct labor is a fixed cost, compute the contribution margin per unit for:
    a.  Purchased WVD drums.
    b.  Manufactured WVD drums.
    c.  Manufactured bike frames.
3.  Assuming direct labor is a fixed cost, compute the contribution margin per welding hour for:
    a.  Manufactured WVD drums.
    b.  Manufactured bike frames.

4.  Assuming direct labor is a fixed cost, determine the number of WVD drums (if any) that should be purchased and the number of WVD drums and/or bike frames (if any) that should be manufactured. What is the increase (decrease) in net operating income that would result from this plan over current operations?

    As soon as your analysis was shown to the top management team at TufStuff, several managers got into an argument concerning how direct labor costs should be treated when making this decision. One manager argued that direct labor is always treated as a variable cost in textbooks and in practice and has always been considered a variable cost at TufStuff. After all, "direct" means you can directly trace the cost to products. "If direct labor is not a variable cost, what is?" Another manager argued just as strenuously that direct labor should be considered a fixed cost at TufStuff. No one had been laid off in over a decade, and for all practical purposes, everyone at the plant is on a monthly salary. Everyone classified as direct labor works a regular 40-hour workweek and overtime has not been necessary since the company adopted Lean Production techniques. Whether the welding machine is used to make drums or frames, the total payroll would be exactly the same. There is enough slack, in the form of idle time, to accommodate any increase in total direct labor time that the bike frames would require.

5.  Assuming direct labor is a variable cost, compute the contribution margin per unit for:
    a.  Purchased WVD drums.
    b.  Manufactured WVD drums.
    c.  Manufactured bike frames.

6.  Assuming direct labor is a variable cost, compute the contribution margin per welding hour for:
    a.  Manufactured WVD drums.
    b.  Manufactured bike frames.

7.  Assuming direct labor is a variable cost, determine the number of WVD drums (if any) that should be purchased and the number of WVD drums and/or bike frames (if any) that should be manufactured. What is the increase (decrease) in net operating income that would result from this plan over current operations?

8.  What do you think is the correct way to treat direct labor cost in this situation—as variable or as fixed? Explain.

**A LOOK BACK**

Chapter 11 used the basic decision-making framework, which focuses on differential costs and benefits, to analyze a wide variety of situations.

**A LOOK AT THIS CHAPTER**

Chapter 12 expands coverage of decision making by focusing on decisions about investments in long-term projects. It illustrates a variety of techniques used by managers faced with these decisions.

**A LOOK AHEAD**

Chapter 13 covers the statement of cash flows. It addresses how to classify various types of cash inflows and outflows along with the interpretation of information reported on that financial statement.

# 12 Capital Budgeting Decisions

## CHAPTER OUTLINE

©Tim Graham/Getty Images

# Investing in a Vineyard: A Cash Flows Perspective

When Michael Evans was contemplating moving to Buenos Aires, Argentina, to start a company called the **Vines of Mendoza**, he had to estimate the project's initial cash outlays and compare them to its future net cash inflows. The initial cash outlays included $2.9 million to buy 1,046 acres of land and to construct a tasting room, $300,000 for a well and irrigation system, $30,000 for underground power lines, and $285,000 for 250,000 grape plants. The annual operating costs included $1,500 per acre for pruning, mowing, and irrigation and $114 per acre for harvesting.

In terms of future cash inflows, Evans hopes to sell his acreage to buyers who want to grow their own grapes and make their own wine while avoiding the work involved with doing so. He intends to charge buyers a one-time fee of $55,000 per planted acre. The buyers also would reimburse Evans for his annual operating costs per acre plus a 25% markup. In a good year, buyers should be able to get 250 cases of wine from their acre of grapevines.

Source: Coster, Helen, "Planting Roots," *Forbes*, March 1, 2010, 42–44.

LEARNING OBJECTIVES

*After studying Chapter 12, you should be able to:*

**LO12–1** Determine the payback period for an investment.

**LO12–2** Evaluate the acceptability of an investment project using the net present value method.

**LO12–3** Evaluate the acceptability of an investment project using the internal rate of return method.

**LO12–4** Evaluate an investment project that has uncertain cash flows.

**LO12–5** Rank investment projects in order of preference.

**LO12–6** Compute the simple rate of return for an investment.

**LO12–7** (*Appendix 12A*) Understand present value concepts and the use of present value tables.

**M**anagers often consider decisions that involve an investment today in the hope of realizing future profits. For example, **Yum! Brands, Inc.,** makes an investment when it opens a new Pizza Hut restaurant. **L. L. Bean** makes an investment when it installs a new computer to handle customer billing. **Ford** makes an investment when it redesigns a vehicle such as the F-150 pickup truck. **Merck & Co.** invests in medical research. **Amazon.com** makes an investment when it redesigns its website. All of these investments require spending money now to realize future net cash inflows.

The term **capital budgeting** is used to describe how managers plan significant investments in projects that have long-term implications such as the purchase of new equipment or the introduction of new products. Most companies have many more potential projects than they can actually fund. Hence, managers must carefully select those projects that promise the greatest future return. How well managers make these capital budgeting decisions is a critical factor in the long-run financial health of the organization. This chapter discusses four methods for making capital budgeting decisions—the *payback method,* the *net present value method,* the *internal rate of return method,* and the *simple rate of return method.*

# CAPITAL BUDGETING—AN OVERVIEW

## Typical Capital Budgeting Decisions

Any decision that involves a cash outlay now to obtain a future return is a capital budgeting decision. Typical capital budgeting decisions include:

1. Cost reduction decisions. Should new equipment be purchased to reduce costs?
2. Expansion decisions. Should a new plant, warehouse, or other facility be acquired to increase capacity and sales?
3. Equipment selection decisions. Which of several available machines should be purchased?
4. Lease or buy decisions. Should new equipment be leased or purchased?
5. Equipment replacement decisions. Should old equipment be replaced now or later?

Capital budgeting decisions fall into two broad categories—*screening decisions* and *preference decisions.* **Screening decisions** relate to whether a proposed project is acceptable—whether it passes a preset hurdle. For example, a company may have a policy of accepting projects only if they provide a return of at least 20% on the investment. The required rate of return is the minimum rate of return a project must yield to be acceptable. **Preference decisions**, by contrast, relate to selecting from among several acceptable alternatives. To illustrate, a company may be considering several different machines to replace an existing machine on the assembly line. The choice of which machine to purchase is a preference decision.

## Cash Flows versus Net Operating Income

The first three capital budgeting methods discussed in the chapter—the payback method, the net present value method, and internal rate of return method—all focus on analyzing the *cash flows* associated with capital investment projects, whereas the simple rate of return method focuses on *incremental net operating income.* To better prepare you to apply the payback, net present value, and internal rate of return methods, we'd like to define the most common types of cash outflows and cash inflows that accompany capital investment projects.

**Typical Cash Outflows**    Most projects have at least three types of cash outflows. First, they often require an immediate cash outflow in the form of an initial investment in equipment, other assets, and installation costs. Any salvage value realized from the sale of old equipment can be recognized as a reduction in the initial investment or as a cash inflow. Second, some projects require a company to expand its working capital. **Working capital** is current assets (e.g., cash, accounts receivable, and inventory) less current liabilities. When a company takes on a new project, the balances in the current asset accounts often increase. For example, opening a new **Nordstrom**'s department store requires additional cash in sales registers and more inventory. These additional working capital needs are treated as part of the initial investment in a project. Third, many projects require periodic outlays for repairs and maintenance and additional operating costs.

**Typical Cash Inflows** Most projects also have at least three types of cash inflows. First, a project will normally increase revenues or reduce costs. Either way, the amount involved should be treated as a cash inflow for capital budgeting purposes. Notice that from a cash flow standpoint, a reduction in costs is equivalent to an increase in revenues. Second, cash inflows are also frequently realized from selling equipment for its salvage value when a project ends, although the company actually may have to pay to dispose of some low-value or hazardous items. Third, any working capital that was tied up in the project can be released for use elsewhere at the end of the project and should be treated as a cash inflow at that time. Working capital is released, for example, when a company sells off its inventory or collects its accounts receivable.

## The Time Value of Money

Beyond defining a capital project's cash outflows and inflows, it is also important to consider when those cash flows occur. For example, if someone offered to give you $1,000 dollars today that you could save toward your eventual retirement or $1,000 dollars a year from now that you could save toward your future retirement, which alternative would you choose? In all likelihood, you would choose to receive $1,000 today because you could invest it and have more than $1,000 dollars a year from now. This simple example illustrates an important capital budgeting concept known as *the time value of money*. The **time value of money** recognizes that a dollar today is worth more than a dollar a year from now if for no other reason than you could put the dollar in a bank today and have more than a dollar a year from now. Because of the time value of money, capital investments that promise earlier cash flows are preferable to those that promise later cash flows.

Although the payback method focuses on cash flows, it does not recognize the time value of money. In other words, it treats a dollar received today as being of equal value to a dollar received at any point in the future. Conversely, the net present value and internal rate of return methods not only focus on cash flows, but they also recognize the time value of those cash flows. These two methods use a technique called *discounting cash flows* to translate the value of future cash flows to their present value. If you are not familiar with the concept of discounting cash flows and the use of present value tables, you should read Appendix 12A: The Concept of Present Value, at the end of the chapter, before studying the net present value and internal rate of return methods.

## HELPFUL HINT

The simple rate of return method uses net operating income to evaluate capital budgeting proposals, whereas the payback, net present value, and internal rate of return methods are cash flow-based modes of analysis. The payback method ignores the time value of money. Conversely, the net present value and internal rate of return methods acknowledge the time value of money by discounting cash flows to their present value.

# THE PAYBACK METHOD

**LEARNING OBJECTIVE 12–1**

Determine the payback period for an investment.

The payback method of evaluating capital budgeting projects focuses on the *payback period*. The **payback period** is the length of time that it takes for a project to recover its initial cost from the net cash inflows that it generates. This period is sometimes referred to as "the time that it takes for an investment to pay for itself." The basic premise of the payback method is that the more quickly the cost of an investment can be recovered, the more desirable is the investment.

The payback period is expressed in years. *When the annual net cash inflow is the same every year,* the following formula can be used to compute the payback period:

$$\text{Payback period} = \frac{\text{Investment required}}{\text{Annual net cash inflow}} \tag{1}$$

To illustrate the payback method, consider the following data:

**Example A:** York Company needs a new milling machine. The company is considering two machines: machine A and machine B. Machine A costs $15,000, has a useful life of ten years, and will reduce operating costs by $5,000 per year. Machine B costs only $12,000, will also reduce operating costs by $5,000 per year, but has a useful life of only five years.

**Required:**
Which machine should be purchased according to the payback method?

$$\text{Machine A payback period} = \frac{\$15,000}{\$5,000} = 3.0 \text{ years}$$

$$\text{Machine B payback period} = \frac{\$12,000}{\$5,000} = 2.4 \text{ years}$$

According to the payback calculations, York Company should purchase machine B because it has a shorter payback period than machine A.

## Evaluation of the Payback Method

The payback method is not a true measure of the profitability of an investment. Rather, it simply tells a manager how many years are required to recover the original investment. Unfortunately, a shorter payback period does not always mean that one investment is more desirable than another.

To illustrate, refer back to Example A. Machine B has a shorter payback period than machine A, but it has a useful life of only 5 years rather than 10 years for machine A. Machine B would have to be purchased twice—once immediately and then again after the fifth year—to provide the same service as just one machine A. Under these circumstances, machine A would probably be a better investment than machine B, even though machine B has a shorter payback period. Unfortunately, the payback method ignores all cash flows that occur after the payback period.

A further criticism of the payback method is that it does not consider the time value of money. A cash inflow to be received several years in the future is weighed the same as a cash inflow received right now. To illustrate, assume that for an investment of $8,000 you can purchase either of the two following streams of cash inflows:

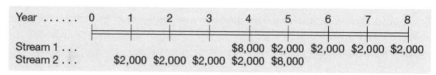

Which stream of cash inflows would you prefer to receive in return for your $8,000 investment? Each stream has a payback period of 4.0 years. Therefore, if payback alone is used to make the decision, the streams would be considered equally desirable. However, from a time value of money perspective, stream 2 is much more desirable than stream 1.

On the other hand, under certain conditions the payback method can be very useful. For one thing, it can help identify which investment proposals are in the "ballpark." That is, it can be used as a screening tool to help answer the question, "Should I consider this proposal further?" If a proposal doesn't provide a payback within some specified period, then there may be no need to consider it further. In addition, the payback period is often important to new companies that are "cash poor." When a company is cash poor, a project with a short payback period but a low rate of return might be preferred over another project with a high rate of return but a long payback period. The reason is that the company may simply need a faster return of its cash investment. And finally, the payback method is sometimes used in industries where products become obsolete very rapidly—such as consumer electronics. Because products may last only a year or two, the payback period on investments must be very short.

## An Extended Example of Payback

As shown by formula (1) from earlier in the chapter, the payback period is computed by dividing the investment in a project by the project's annual net cash inflows. If new equipment is replacing old equipment, then any salvage value to be received when disposing of the old equipment should be deducted from the cost of the new equipment, and only the *incremental* investment should be used in the payback computation. In addition, any depreciation deducted in arriving at the project's net operating income must be added back to obtain the project's expected annual net cash inflow. To illustrate, consider the following data:

**Example B:** Goodtime Fun Centers, Inc., operates amusement parks. Some of the vending machines in one of its parks provide very little revenue, so the company is considering removing the machines and installing equipment to dispense soft ice cream. The equipment would cost $80,000 and have an eight-year useful life with no salvage value. Incremental annual revenues and costs associated with the sale of ice cream would be as follows:

| | |
|---|---:|
| Sales......................... | $150,000 |
| Variable expenses............ | 90,000 |
| Contribution margin........... | 60,000 |
| Fixed expenses: | |
|    Salaries ................... | 27,000 |
|    Maintenance............... | 3,000 |
|    Depreciation.............. | 10,000 |
| Total fixed expenses .......... | 40,000 |
| Net operating income ......... | $ 20,000 |

The vending machines can be sold for a $5,000 scrap value. The company will not purchase the equipment unless it has a payback period of three years or less. Does the ice cream dispenser pass this hurdle?

Exhibit 12–1 computes the payback period for the ice cream dispenser. Several things should be noted. First, depreciation is added back to net operating income to obtain the annual net cash inflow from the new equipment. Depreciation is not a cash outlay; thus, it must be added back to adjust net operating income to a cash basis. Second, the payback

Step 1: *Compute the annual net cash inflow.* Because the annual net cash inflow is not given, it must be computed before the payback period can be determined:

| | |
|---|---:|
| Net operating income . . . . . . . . . . . . . . . . . . . . . . . . . . . . . | $20,000 |
| Add: Noncash deduction for depreciation. . . . . . . . . . . | 10,000 |
| Annual net cash inflow . . . . . . . . . . . . . . . . . . . . . . . . . . . | $30,000 |

Step 2: *Compute the payback period.* Using the annual net cash inflow from above, the payback period can be determined as follows:

| | |
|---|---:|
| Cost of the new equipment . . . . . . . . . . . . . . . . . . . . . . . | $80,000 |
| Less salvage value of old equipment . . . . . . . . . . . . . . | 5,000 |
| Investment required. . . . . . . . . . . . . . . . . . . . . . . . . . . . . | $75,000 |

$$\text{Payback period} = \frac{\text{Investment required}}{\text{Annual net cash inflow}}$$

$$= \frac{\$75,000}{\$30,000} = 2.5 \text{ years}$$

computation deducts the salvage value of the old machines from the cost of the new equipment so that only the incremental investment is used in computing the payback period.

Because the proposed equipment has a payback period of less than three years, the company's payback requirement has been met.

## Payback and Uneven Cash Flows

When the cash flows associated with an investment project change from year to year, the simple payback formula that we outlined earlier cannot be used. Instead, the payback period can be computed as follows (assuming that cash inflows occur evenly throughout the year): Payback period = Number of years up to the year in which the investment is paid off + (Unrecovered investment at the beginning of the year in which the investment is paid off ÷ Cash inflow in the period in which the investment is paid off). To illustrate how to apply this formula, consider the following data:

| Year | Investment | Cash Inflow |
|---|---|---|
| 1 . . . . . . . . . . . . . . | $4,000 | $1,000 |
| 2 . . . . . . . . . . . . . . | | $0 |
| 3 . . . . . . . . . . . . . . | | $2,000 |
| 4 . . . . . . . . . . . . . . | $2,000 | $1,000 |
| 5 . . . . . . . . . . . . . . | | $500 |
| 6 . . . . . . . . . . . . . . | | $3,000 |
| 7 . . . . . . . . . . . . . . | | $2,000 |

What is the payback period on this investment? The answer is 5.5 years, computed as follows: 5 + ($1,500 ÷ $3,000) = 5.5 years. In essence, we are tracking the unrecovered investment year by year as shown in Exhibit 12–2. By the middle of the sixth year, sufficient cash inflows will have been realized to recover the entire investment of $6,000 ($4,000 + $2,000).

| Year | Investment | Cash Inflow | Unrecovered Investment* |
|---|---|---|---|
| 1 ............................. | $4,000 | $1,000 | $3,000 |
| 2 ............................. | | $0 | $3,000 |
| 3 ............................. | | $2,000 | $1,000 |
| 4 ............................. | $2,000 | $1,000 | $2,000 |
| 5 ............................. | | $500 | $1,500 |
| 6 ............................. | | $3,000 | $0 |
| 7 ............................. | | $2,000 | $0 |

*Year X unrecovered investment = Year X−1 unrecovered investment + Year X investment − Year X cash inflow

**EXHIBIT 12–2**
Payback and Uneven Cash Flows

1. Which of the following statements is true? (You may select more than one answer.)
   a. The time value of money recognizes that a dollar received today is worth more than a dollar received a year from now.
   b. Working capital is noncurrent assets minus current assets.
   c. The simple rate of return method focuses on incremental net operating income.
   d. The cost of capital is the average rate of return the company must pay to its long-term creditors and its shareholders for the use of their funds.
2. Which of the following statements is true? (You may select more than one answer.)
   a. The payback period increases as the cost of capital increases.
   b. The payback period is the length of time that it takes for a project to recover its initial cost from the net cash inflows that it generates.
   c. The equation for computing the payback period includes a company's net operating income.
   d. The payback method relies on discounted cash flows.

CONCEPT CHECK

# THE NET PRESENT VALUE METHOD

As previously mentioned, the *net present value method* and the *internal rate of return method* use discounted cash flows to analyze capital budgeting decisions. The net present value method is discussed in this section followed by a discussion of the internal rate of return method.

**LEARNING OBJECTIVE 12–2**

Evaluate the acceptability of an investment project using the net present value method.

## The Net Present Value Method Illustrated

The net present value method compares the present value of a project's cash inflows to the present value of its cash outflows. The difference between the present value of these cash flows, called the **net present value**, determines whether or not a project is an acceptable investment.

When performing net present value analysis, managers usually make two important assumptions. First, they assume that all cash flows other than the initial investment occur at the end of periods. This assumption is somewhat unrealistic because cash flows typically occur *throughout* a period rather than just at its end; however, it simplifies the computations considerably. Second, managers assume that all cash flows generated by an investment project are immediately reinvested at a rate of return equal to the rate used to discount the future cash flows, also known as the *discount rate*. If this condition is not met, the net present value computations will not be accurate.

To illustrate net present analysis, consider the following data:

**Example C:** Harper Company is contemplating buying a new machine that will cost $50,000 and last for five years. The new machine will enable the company to reduce its labor costs by $18,000 per year. At the end of the five-year period, the company will sell the machine for its salvage value of $5,000. Harper Company requires a minimum pretax return of 18% on all investment projects.

Should the machine be purchased? Harper Company must determine whether a cash investment now of $50,000 can be justified if it will result in an $18,000 cost reduction in each of the next five years. The answer may seem obvious given that the total cost savings is $90,000 ($18,000 per year × 5 years); however, the company can earn an 18% return by investing its money elsewhere. It is not enough that the annual cost reductions cover just the original cost of the machine; they must also yield a return of at least 18% or the company would be better off investing the money elsewhere.

To determine whether the investment is desirable, the stream of annual $18,000 cost savings and the machine's salvage value of $5,000 should be discounted to their present values and then compared to the cost of the new machine. Exhibits 12–3, 12–4, and 12–5 demonstrate three distinct but equivalent ways of performing these calculations. The approaches in Exhibit 12–3 and 12–4 rely on the discount factors shown in Appendix 12B that have been rounded to three decimal places. The method shown in Exhibit 12–5 derives its answer using unrounded discount factors.

Cell B8 of Exhibit 12–3 calculates the present value of Harper Company's initial cash outlay of $(50,000) by multiplying $(50,000) by 1.000, the present value factor for any cash flow that occurs immediately. Cell C8 calculates the present value of the annual cost savings of $56,286 by multiplying $18,000 by 3.127, the present value factor of a five-year annuity at the discount rate of 18% (see Exhibit 12B–2). Cell D8 calculates the present value of the machine's salvage value of $2,185 by multiplying $5,000 by 0.437, the present value factor of a single sum to be received in five years at the discount rate of 18% (see Exhibit 12B–1). Finally, cells B8 through D8 are added together to derive the net present value in cell B9 of $8,471.

**EXHIBIT 12–3**
Net Present Value Analysis Using Discount Factors from Exhibits 12B–1 and 12B–2 in Appendix 12B

| | A | B | C | D |
|---|---|---|---|---|
| 1 | | | Year(s) | |
| 2 | | Now | 1-5 | 5 |
| 3 | Initial investment | $ (50,000) | | |
| 4 | Annual cost savings | | $ 18,000 | |
| 5 | Salvage value of the new machine | | | $ 5,000 |
| 6 | Total cash flows (a) | $ (50,000) | $ 18,000 | $ 5,000 |
| 7 | Discount factor (18%) (b) | 1.000 | 3.127 | 0.437 |
| 8 | Present value of the cash flows (a) × (b) | $ (50,000) | $ 56,286 | $ 2,185 |
| 9 | Net present value (SUM B8:D8) | $ 8,471 | | |
| 10 | | | | |
| 11 | Note: The discount factors come from Exhibits 12B-1 and 12B-2 in Appendix 12B. | | | |
| 12 | | | | |

Exhibit 12-3   Exhibit 12-4   Exhibit 12-5   Exhibit 12-6   Exhi

Source: Microsoft

Exhibit 12–4 shows another way to calculate the net present value of $8,471. Under this approach Cell B8 calculates the present value of the initial cash outlay of $(50,000) by multiplying $(50,000) by 1.000—just as was done in Exhibit 12–3. However, rather than calculating the present value of the annual cost savings using a discount factor of 3.127 from Exhibit 12B–2, the approach used in Exhibit 12–4 discounts the annual cost savings in Years 1–5 *and* the machine's salvage value in Year 5 to their present values using the discount factors from Exhibit 12B–1. For example, the $18,000 cost savings in Year 3 (cell

E6) is multiplied by the discount factor of 0.609 (cell E7) to derive this future cash flow's present value of $10,962 (cell E8). As another example, the $23,000 of total cash flows in Year 5 (cell G6) is multiplied by the discount factor of 0.437 (cell G7) to determine these future cash flows' present value of $10,051 (cell G8). The present values in cells B8 through G8 are then added together to compute the project's net present value of $8,471 (cell B9).

| | A | B | C | D | E | F | G |
|---|---|---|---|---|---|---|---|
| 1 | | | | | Year | | |
| 2 | | Now | 1 | 2 | 3 | 4 | 5 |
| 3 | Initial investment | $ (50,000) | | | | | |
| 4 | Annual labor cost savings | | $ 18,000 | $ 18,000 | $ 18,000 | $ 18,000 | $ 18,000 |
| 5 | Salvage value of new machine | | | | | | $ 5,000 |
| 6 | Total cash flows (a) | $ (50,000) | $ 18,000 | $ 18,000 | $ 18,000 | $ 18,000 | $ 23,000 |
| 7 | Discount factor (18%) (b) | 1.000 | 0.847 | 0.718 | 0.609 | 0.516 | 0.437 |
| 8 | Present value of cash flows (a) × (b) | $ (50,000) | $ 15,246 | $ 12,924 | $ 10,962 | $ 9,288 | $ 10,051 |
| 9 | Net present value (SUM B8:G8) | $ 8,471 | | | | | |
| 10 | | | | | | | |
| 11 | Note: The discount factors come from Exhibits 12B-1 in Appendix 12B. | | | | | | |
| 12 | | | | | | | |

Exhibit 12-3 | **Exhibit 12-4** | Exhibit 12-5 | Exhibit 12-6 | Ex

Source: Microsoft

**EXHIBIT 12–4**
Net Present Value Analysis Using Discount Factors from Exhibit 12B–1 in Appendix 12B

The methods described in Exhibits 12–3 and 12–4 are mathematically equivalent—they both produced a net present value of $8,471. The only difference between these two exhibits relates to the discounting of the annual labor cost savings. In Exhibit 12–3, the labor cost savings are discounted to their present value using the annuity factor of 3.127, whereas in Exhibit 12–4, these cost savings are discounted using five separate factors that sum to 3.127 (0.847 + 0.718 + 0.609 + 0.516 + 0.437 = 3.127).

It bears reemphasizing that the net present values in Exhibits 12–3 and 12–4 are calculated using the *rounded* discount factors from Appendix 12B. However, net present value calculations can also be performed using *unrounded* discount factors. One approach to using unrounded discount factors would be to replace the rounded discount factors shown in row 7 of Exhibits 12–3 and 12–4 with formulas that compute unrounded discount factors. Another approach, as shown in Exhibit 12–5, is to use Microsoft Excel's NPV function to perform the calculations. The NPV function automatically calculates the net present value after specifying three parameters—the discount rate (0.18), the annual cash flows (C6:G6), and the initial cash outlay (+B6). Notice that the net present value in Exhibit 12–5 of $8,475 is $4 higher than the net present value shown in Exhibits 12–3 and 12–4. The trivial $4 difference arises because Microsoft Excel's NPV function uses unrounded discount factors.

| | A | B | C | D | E | F | G |
|---|---|---|---|---|---|---|---|
| 1 | | | | | Year | | |
| 2 | | Now | 1 | 2 | 3 | 4 | 5 |
| 3 | Initial investment | $ (50,000) | | | | | |
| 4 | Annual labor cost savings | | $ 18,000 | $ 18,000 | $ 18,000 | $ 18,000 | $ 18,000 |
| 5 | Salvage value of new machine | | | | | | $ 5,000 |
| 6 | Total cash flows (a) | $ (50,000) | $ 18,000 | $ 18,000 | $ 18,000 | $ 18,000 | $ 23,000 |
| 7 | Net present value (SUM B8:G8) | $ 8,475 | | | | | |
| 8 | | | | | | | |
| 9 | Note: The net present value is computed using the formula: =NPV(0.18,C6:G6)+B6 | | | | | | |
| 10 | | | | | | | |

Exhibit 12-3 | Exhibit 12-4 | **Exhibit 12-5** | Exhibit 12-6 | Ex

Source: Microsoft

**EXHIBIT 12–5**
Net Present Value Analysis Using Microsoft Excel's NPV Function

During your career you should feel free to use any of the methods discussed thus far to perform net present value calculations. However, throughout this chapter and its forthcoming exercises and problems, we'll be using the approaches illustrated in Exhibit 12–3 and 12-4 accompanied by the rounded discount factors in Appendix 12B.

Once you have computed a project's net present value, you'll need to interpret your findings. For example, because Harper Company's proposed project has a positive net present value of $8,471, it implies that the company should purchase the new machine. A positive net present value indicates that the project's return exceeds the discount rate. A negative net present value indicates that the project's return is less than the discount rate. Therefore, if the company's minimum required rate of return is used as the discount rate, a project with a positive net present value has a return that exceeds the minimum required rate of return and is acceptable. Conversely, a project with a negative net present value has a return that is less than the minimum required rate of return and is unacceptable. In sum:

| If the Net Present Value Is . . . . . | Then the Project Is . . . |
|---|---|
| Positive. . . . . . . . . . . . . . . . . . . . . . | Acceptable because its return is greater than the required rate of return. |
| Zero . . . . . . . . . . . . . . . . . . . . . . . | Acceptable because its return is equal to the required rate of return. |
| Negative . . . . . . . . . . . . . . . . . . . . | Not acceptable because its return is less than the required rate of return. |

A company's *cost of capital* is usually regarded as its minimum required rate of return. The **cost of capital** is the average rate of return that the company must pay to its long-term creditors and its shareholders for the use of their funds. If a project's rate of return is less than the cost of capital, the company does not earn enough to compensate its creditors and shareholders. Therefore, any project with a rate of return less than the cost of capital should be rejected.

The cost of capital serves as a *screening device.* When the cost of capital is used as the discount rate in net present value analysis, any project with a negative net present value does not cover the company's cost of capital and should be discarded as unacceptable.

## Recovery of the Original Investment

The net present value method automatically provides for return of the original investment. Whenever the net present value of a project is positive, the project will recover the original cost of the investment plus sufficient excess cash inflows to compensate the organization for tying up funds in the project. To demonstrate this point, consider the following situation:

**Example D:** Carver Hospital is considering the purchase of an attachment for its X-ray machine that will cost $3,170. The attachment will be usable for four years, after which time it will have no salvage value. It will increase net cash inflows by $1,000 per year in the X-ray department. The hospital's board of directors requires a rate of return of at least 10% on such investments.

A net present value analysis of the desirability of purchasing the X-ray attachment (using a discount factor of 3.170 from Exhibit 12B–2) is presented in Exhibit 12–6. Notice that the attachment has exactly a 10% return on the original investment because the net present value is zero at a 10% discount rate.

Each annual $1,000 cash inflow arising from use of the attachment is made up of two parts. One part represents a recovery of a portion *of* the original $3,170 paid for the attachment, and the other part represents a return *on* this investment. The breakdown of each year's $1,000 cash inflow between recovery *of* investment and return *on* investment is shown in Exhibit 12–7.

| | | A | B | C |
|---|---|---|---|---|
| 1 | | | | Years |
| 2 | | | Now | 1-4 |
| 3 | Initial investment | | $ (3,170) | |
| 4 | Annual cost savings | | | $ 1,000 |
| 5 | Total cash flows (a) | | $ (3,170) | $ 1,000 |
| 6 | Discount factor (10%) (b) | | 1.000 | 3.170 |
| 7 | Present value of the cash flows (a) × (b) | | $ (3,170) | $ 3,170 |
| 8 | Net present value (SUM B7:C7) | | $ 0 | |
| 9 | | | | |
| 10 | Note: The discount factor comes from Exhibits 12B-2 in Appendix 12B. | | | |
| 11 | | | | |

Exhibit 12-6 / Exhibit 12-7

Source: Microsoft

**EXHIBIT 12–7**
Carver Hospital—Breakdown of
Annual Cash Inflows

| | A | B | C | D | E | F |
|---|---|---|---|---|---|---|
| 1 | | (1) | (2) | (3) | (4) | (5) |
| 2 | Year | Investment Outstanding during the Year | Cash Inflow | Return on Investment (1) × 10% | Recovery of Investment during the Year (2) – (3) | Unrecovered Investment at the End of the Year (1) – (4) |
| 3 | 1 | $3,170 | $1,000 | $317 | $683 | $2,487 |
| 4 | 2 | $2,487 | $1,000 | $249 | $751 | $1,736 |
| 5 | 3 | $1,736 | $1,000 | $173 | $827 | $909 |
| 6 | 4 | $909 | $1,000 | $91 | $909 | $0 |
| 7 | Total investment recovered | | | | $3,170 | |
| 8 | | | | | | |

Exhibit 12-6 Exhibit 12-7 / Exhibit 12-8 , Exhibit 12-9 Ex

Source: Microsoft

The first year's $1,000 cash inflow consists of a return *on* investment of $317 (a 10% return *on* the $3,170 original investment), plus a $683 return *of* that investment. Because the amount of the unrecovered investment decreases each year, the dollar amount of the return on investment also decreases each year. By the end of the fourth year, all $3,170 of the original investment has been recovered.

## Cooling Servers Naturally

IN BUSINESS

**Google** consumes more than 2 terawatt hours of electricity per year, which is greater than the annual electricity consumption of 200,000 American homes. A large part of Google's electricity consumption relates to running and cooling its huge number of servers. In an effort to lower its electricity bill, Google invested €200 million to build a server storage facility in the Baltic Sea coastal community of Hamina, Finland. Hamina's low electricity rates coupled with its persistently low ambient air temperatures will lower Google's annual electricity bills considerably. Shortly after Google's facility opened in Hamina, **Facebook** opened a five-acre data center in Luleå, Sweden, where the average temperature is 35 degrees Fahrenheit.

Source: Grunberg, Sven, and Rolander, Niclas, "For Data Center, Google Goes for the Cold," *The Wall Street Journal*, September 12, 2011, B10.

## An Extended Example of the Net Present Value Method

Example E provides an extended example of how the net present value method is used to analyze a proposed project. This example helps tie together and reinforce many of the ideas discussed thus far.

**Example E:** Under a special licensing arrangement, Swinyard Corporation has an opportunity to market a new product for a five-year period. The product would be purchased from the manufacturer, with Swinyard responsible for promotion and distribution costs. The licensing arrangement could be renewed at the end of the five-year period. After careful study, Swinyard estimated the following costs and revenues for the new product:

| | |
|---|---:|
| Cost of equipment needed.......................... | $60,000 |
| Working capital needed ............................ | $100,000 |
| Overhaul of the equipment in four years .............. | $5,000 |
| Salvage value of the equipment in five years ........... | $10,000 |
| | |
| Annual revenues and costs: | |
|    Sales revenues.................................... | $200,000 |
|    Cost of goods sold................................ | $125,000 |
|    Out-of-pocket operating costs (for salaries, | |
|       advertising, and other direct costs)............. | $35,000 |

At the end of the five-year period, if Swinyard decides not to renew the licensing arrangement the working capital would be released for investment elsewhere. Swinyard uses a 14% discount rate. Would you recommend that the new product be introduced?

This example involves a variety of cash inflows and cash outflows. The solution (using discount factors from Exhibit 12B–1) is given in Exhibit 12–8.

Notice how the working capital is handled in this exhibit. It is counted as a cash outflow at the beginning of the project (cell B4) and as a cash inflow when it is released

**EXHIBIT 12–8**   The Net Present Value Method—An Extended Example

| | A | B | C | D | E | F | G |
|---|---|---|---|---|---|---|---|
| 2 | | Now | 1 | 2 | 3 | 4 | 5 |
| 3 | Purchase of equipment | $ (60,000) | | | | | |
| 4 | Investment in working capital | $ (100,000) | | | | | |
| 5 | Sales | | $ 200,000 | $ 200,000 | $ 200,000 | $ 200,000 | $ 200,000 |
| 6 | Cost of goods sold | | $(125,000) | $(125,000) | $(125,000) | $(125,000) | $(125,000) |
| 7 | Out-of-pocket costs for salaries, advertising, etc. | | $ (35,000) | $ (35,000) | $ (35,000) | $ (35,000) | $ (35,000) |
| 8 | Overhaul of equipment | | | | | $ (5,000) | |
| 9 | Salvage value of the equipment | | | | | | $ 10,000 |
| 10 | Working capital released | | | | | | $ 100,000 |
| 11 | Total cash flows (a) | $ (160,000) | $ 40,000 | $ 40,000 | $ 40,000 | $ 35,000 | $ 150,000 |
| 12 | Discount factor (14%) (b) | 1.000 | 0.877 | 0.769 | 0.675 | 0.592 | 0.519 |
| 13 | Present value of cash flows (a) × (b) | $ (160,000) | $ 35,080 | $ 30,760 | $ 27,000 | $ 20,720 | $ 77,850 |
| 14 | Net present value (SUM B13:G13) | $ 31,410 | | | | | |
| 15 | | | | | | | |
| 16 | Note: The discount factors come from Exhibit 12B-1 in Appendix 12B. | | | | | | |
| 17 | | | | | | | |

Exhibit 12-3   Exhibit 12-4   Exhibit 12-5   Exhibit 12-6   Exhibit 12-7   **Exhibit 12-8**   Exhibit

Source: Microsoft

at the end of the project (cell G10). Also notice how the sales revenues, cost of goods sold, and out-of-pocket costs are handled. **Out-of-pocket costs** are actual cash outlays for salaries, advertising, and other operating expenses.

Because the net present value of the proposal is positive, the new product is acceptable.

---

### Should Egg Farmers Invest in Cage-Free Facilities or Bigger Cages?

**IN BUSINESS**

Egg farmers are facing an interesting capital budgeting question: should they invest in building cage-free facilities for their hens or should they buy bigger cages? Investing in bigger cages costs less than cage-free farming and it complies with new animal welfare laws; however, it does not satisfy the demands of many customers and animal-rights advocates. For example, **Nestlé**, **Starbucks**, **Burger King**, and **Aramark** have pledged to eliminate the use of eggs from caged hens.

**Rose Acre Farms** has committed to raising all of its hens in cage-free facilities. Farmers estimate that building a cage-free farm for 100,000 birds costs $1 million more than it would cost to build a large-cage facility for these same birds. Since only 6% of the U.S. flock is currently cage-free, egg farmers can command a price premium for eggs produced in a free-roaming farm.

Source: Kesmodel, David, "Flap Over Eggs: Whether to Go Cage-Free," *The Wall Street Journal,* March 16, 2015, B1–B2.

---

## THE INTERNAL RATE OF RETURN METHOD

The **internal rate of return** is the rate of return of an investment project over its useful life. The internal rate of return is computed by finding the discount rate that equates the present value of a project's cash outflows with the present value of its cash inflows. In other words, the internal rate of return is the discount rate that results in a net present value of zero.

### The Internal Rate of Return Method Illustrated

To illustrate the internal rate of return method, consider the following data:

**Example F:** Glendale School District is considering the purchase of a large tractor-pulled lawn mower. At present, the lawn is mowed using a small hand-pushed gas mower. The large, tractor-pulled mower will cost $16,950 and will have a useful life of 10 years. It will have a negligible scrap value, which can be ignored. The tractor-pulled mower would do the job faster than the old mower, resulting in labor savings of $3,000 per year.

To compute the internal rate of return of the new mower, we must find the discount rate that will result in a zero net present value. How do we do this? The simplest and most direct approach *when the net cash inflow is the same every year* is to divide the investment in the project by the expected annual net cash inflow. This computation yields a factor from which the internal rate of return can be determined. The formula is as follows:

$$\text{Factor of the internal rate of return} = \frac{\text{Investment required}}{\text{Annual net cash inflow}} \qquad (2)$$

EXHIBIT 12–9
Evaluation of the Mower
Using a 12% Discount Rate

| | A | B | C |
|---|---|---|---|
| 1 | | | Years |
| 2 | | Now | 1-10 |
| 3 | Initial investment | $ (16,950) | |
| 4 | Annual cost savings | | $ 3,000 |
| 5 | Total cash flows (a) | $ (16,950) | $ 3,000 |
| 6 | Discount factor (12%) (b) | 1.000 | 5.650 |
| 7 | Present value of the cash flows (a) × (b) | $ (16,950) | $ 16,950 |
| 8 | Net present value (SUM B7:C7) | $ 0 | |
| 9 | | | |
| 10 | Note: The discount factor comes from Exhibits 12B-2 in Appendix 12B. | | |
| 11 | | | |

Exhibit 12-8 | Exhibit 12-9 | Exhibit

Source: Microsoft

The factor derived from formula (2) is then located in Exhibit 12B–2 in Appendix 12B to see what rate of return it represents. Using formula (2) and the data for the Glendale School District's proposed project, we get:

$$\frac{\text{Investment required}}{\text{Annual net cash inflow}} = \frac{\$16,950}{\$3,000} = 5.650$$

Thus, the discount factor that will equate a series of $3,000 cash inflows with a present investment of $16,950 is 5.650. Now we need to find this factor in Exhibit 12B–2 in Appendix 12B to see what rate of return it represents. We should use the 10-period line in Exhibit 12B–2 because the cash flows for the project continue for 10 years. If we scan along the 10-period line, we find that a factor of 5.650 represents a 12% rate of return. Therefore, the internal rate of return of the mower project is 12%. We can verify this by computing the project's net present value using a 12% discount rate as shown in Exhibit 12–9.

Notice from Exhibit 12–9 that using a 12% discount rate equates the present value of the annual cost savings with the present value of the initial investment required for the project, leaving a zero net present value. The 12% rate therefore represents the internal rate of return of the project.

Once the Glendale School District computes the project's internal rate of return of 12%, it would accept or reject the project by comparing this percentage to the school district's minimum required rate of return. If the internal rate of return is equal to or greater than the required rate of return, then the project is acceptable. If the internal rate of return is less than the required rate of return, then the project is rejected. For example, if we assume that Glendale's minimum required rate of return is 15%, then the school district would reject this project because the 12% internal rate of return does not clear the 15% *hurdle rate*.

## Comparison of the Net Present Value and Internal Rate of Return Methods

This section compares the net present value and internal rate of return methods in three ways. First, both methods use the cost of capital to screen out undesirable investment projects. When the internal rate of return method is used, the cost of capital is used as the hurdle rate that a project must clear for acceptance. If the internal rate of return of a project is not high enough to clear the cost of capital hurdle, then the project is ordinarily rejected. When the net present value method is used, the cost of capital is the discount rate used to compute the net present value of a proposed project. Any project yielding a negative net present value is rejected unless other factors are significant enough to warrant its acceptance.

Second, the net present value method is often simpler to use than the internal rate of return method, particularly when a project does not have identical cash flows every year. For example, if a project has some salvage value at the end of its life in addition to its annual cash inflows, the internal rate of return method requires a trial-and-error process to find the rate of return that will result in a net present value of zero. While computer software can be used to perform this trial-and-error process in seconds, it is still a little more complex than using spreadsheet software to perform net present value analysis.

Third, the internal rate of return method makes a questionable assumption. Both methods assume that cash flows generated by a project during its useful life are immediately reinvested elsewhere. However, the two methods make different assumptions concerning the rate of return that is earned on those cash flows. The net present value method assumes the rate of return is the discount rate, whereas the internal rate of return method assumes the rate of return earned on cash flows is the internal rate of return on the project. Specifically, if the internal rate of return of the project is high, this assumption may not be realistic. It is generally more realistic to assume that cash inflows can be reinvested at a rate of return equal to the discount rate—particularly if the discount rate is the company's cost of capital or an opportunity rate of return. For example, if the discount rate is the company's cost of capital, this rate of return can be actually realized by paying off the company's creditors and buying back the company's stock with cash flows from the project. In short, when the net present value method and the internal rate of return method do not agree concerning the attractiveness of a project, it is best to go with the net present value method. Of the two methods, it makes the more realistic assumption about the rate of return that can be earned on cash flows from the project.

## EXPANDING THE NET PRESENT VALUE METHOD

So far, all of our examples have involved an evaluation of a single investment project. In the following section we use the *total-cost approach* to explain how the net present value method can be used to evaluate two alternative projects.

The total-cost approach is the most flexible method for comparing competing projects. To illustrate the mechanics of the approach, consider the following data:

**Example G:** Harper Ferry Company operates a high-speed passenger ferry service across the Mississippi River. One of its ferryboats is in poor condition. This ferry can be renovated at an immediate cost of $200,000. Further repairs and an overhaul of the motor will be needed three years from now at a cost of $80,000. In all, the ferry will be usable for 5 years if this work is done. At the end of 5 years, the ferry will have to be scrapped at a salvage value of $60,000. The scrap value of the ferry right now is $70,000. It will cost $300,000 each year to operate the ferry, and revenues will total $400,000 annually.

As an alternative, Harper Ferry Company can purchase a new ferryboat at a cost of $360,000. The new ferry will have a life of 5 years, but it will require some repairs costing $30,000 at the end of 3 years. At the end of 5 years, the ferry will have a scrap value of $60,000. It will cost $210,000 each year to operate the ferry, and revenues will total $400,000 annually.

Harper Ferry Company requires a return of at least 14% on all investment projects.

Should the company purchase the new ferry or renovate the old ferry? Exhibit 12–10 shows the solution using the total-cost approach and discount factors from Exhibit 12B–1.

Two points should be noted from the exhibit. First, *all* cash inflows and *all* cash outflows are included in the solution under each alternative. No effort has been made to isolate those cash flows that are relevant to the decision and those that are irrelevant. The inclusion of all cash flows associated with each alternative gives the approach its name—the *total-cost* approach.

**EXHIBIT 12–10** The Total-Cost Approach to Project Selection

| | A | B | C | D | E | F | G |
|---|---|---|---|---|---|---|---|
| 1 | Keep the old ferry: | | | | Year | | |
| 2 | | Now | 1 | 2 | 3 | 4 | 5 |
| 3 | Renovation | $(200,000) | | | | | |
| 4 | Annual revenues | | $ 400,000 | $ 400,000 | $ 400,000 | $ 400,000 | $ 400,000 |
| 5 | Annual cash operating costs | | $(300,000) | $(300,000) | $(300,000) | $(300,000) | $(300,000) |
| 6 | Repairs in three years | | | | $ (80,000) | | |
| 7 | Salvage value of old ferry | | | | | | $ 60,000 |
| 8 | Total cash flows (a) | $(200,000) | $ 100,000 | $ 100,000 | $ 20,000 | $ 100,000 | $ 160,000 |
| 9 | Discount factor (14%) (b) | 1.000 | 0.877 | 0.769 | 0.675 | 0.592 | 0.519 |
| 10 | Present value of cash flows (a) × (b) | $(200,000) | $ 87,700 | $ 76,900 | $ 13,500 | $ 59,200 | $ 83,040 |
| 11 | Net present value (SUM B10:G10) | $ 120,340 | | | | | |
| 12 | | | | | | | |
| 13 | Buy the new ferry: | | | | Year | | |
| 14 | | Now | 1 | 2 | 3 | 4 | 5 |
| 15 | Initial investment | $(360,000) | | | | | |
| 16 | Salvage value of the old ferry | $ 70,000 | | | | | |
| 17 | Annual revenues | | $ 400,000 | $ 400,000 | $ 400,000 | $ 400,000 | $ 400,000 |
| 18 | Annual cash operating costs | | $(210,000) | $(210,000) | $(210,000) | $(210,000) | $(210,000) |
| 19 | Repairs in three years | | | | $ (30,000) | | |
| 20 | Salvage value of new ferry | | | | | | $ 60,000 |
| 21 | Total cash flows (a) | $(290,000) | $ 190,000 | $ 190,000 | $ 160,000 | $ 190,000 | $ 250,000 |
| 22 | Discount factor (14%) (b) | 1.000 | 0.877 | 0.769 | 0.675 | 0.592 | 0.519 |
| 23 | Present value of cash flows (a) × (b) | $(290,000) | $ 166,630 | $ 146,110 | $ 108,000 | $ 112,480 | $ 129,750 |
| 24 | Net present value (SUM B23:G23) | $ 372,970 | | | | | |
| 25 | | | | | | | |
| 26 | Net present value in favor of buying the new ferry (B24-B11) | $ 252,630 | | | | | |
| 27 | | | | | | | |
| 28 | Note: The discount factors come from Exhibit 12B-1 in Appendix 12B. | | | | | | |
| 29 | | | | | | | |

Exhibit 12-5  Exhibit 12-6  Exhibit 12-7  Exhibit 12-8  Exhibit 12-9

Source: Microsoft

Second, notice that a net present value is computed for each alternative. This is a strength of the total-cost approach because an unlimited number of alternatives can be compared side by side to determine the best option. For example, another alternative for Harper Ferry Company would be to get out of the ferry business entirely. If management desired, the net present value of this alternative could be computed to compare with the alternatives shown in Exhibit 12–10. Still other alternatives might be available to the company. In the case at hand, given only two alternatives, the data indicate that the net present value in favor of buying the new ferry is $252,630.[1]

## Least-Cost Decisions

Some decisions do not involve any revenues. For example, a company may be trying to decide whether to buy or lease an executive jet. The choice would be made on the basis of which alternative—buying or leasing—would be least costly. In situations such as these, where no revenues are involved, the most desirable alternative is the one with the *least total cost* from a present value perspective. Hence, these are known as least-cost decisions. To illustrate a least-cost decision, consider the following data:

**Example H:** Val-Tek Company is considering replacing an old threading machine with a new threading machine that would substantially reduce annual operating costs. Selected data relating to the old and new machines are presented below:

---

[1]The alternative with the highest net present value is not always the best choice, although it is the best choice in this case. For further discussion, see the section Preference Decisions—The Ranking of Investment Projects.

| | Old Machine | New Machine |
|---|---|---|
| Purchase cost when new . . . . . . . . . . | $200,000 | $250,000 |
| Salvage value now. . . . . . . . . . . . . . . | $30,000 | — |
| Annual cash operating costs . . . . . . . | $150,000 | $90,000 |
| Overhaul needed immediately. . . . . . . | $40,000 | — |
| Salvage value in six years. . . . . . . . . . | $0 | $50,000 |
| Remaining life . . . . . . . . . . . . . . . . . . . | 6 years | 6 years |

Val-Tek Company uses a 10% discount rate.

Exhibit 12–11 analyzes the alternatives using the total-cost approach and discount factors from Exhibits 12B-1 and 12B-2. Because this is a least-cost decision, the present values are negative for both alternatives. However, the present value of the alternative of buying the new machine is $109,500 lower than the other alternative. Therefore, buying the new machine is the less costly alternative.

3. Which of the following statements is false? (You may select more than one answer.)
   a. The total-cost and incremental-cost approaches to net present value analysis can occasionally lead to conflicting results.
   b. Least-cost decisions do not involve any revenues.
   c. The present value of a dollar increases as the time of receipt extends further into the future.
   d. The higher the discount rate, the lower the present value of a dollar received in the future.

CONCEPT CHECK

**EXHIBIT 12–11**
Least-Cost Decision: A Net Present Value Analysis

| | A | B | C | D |
|---|---|---|---|---|
| 1 | Keep the old machine: | | Year(s) | |
| 2 | | Now | 1-6 | 6 |
| 3 | Overhaul needed now | $ (40,000) | | |
| 4 | Annual cash operating costs | | $(150,000) | |
| 5 | Total cash flows (a) | $ (40,000) | $(150,000) | |
| 6 | Discount factor (10%) (b) | 1.000 | 4.355 | |
| 7 | Present value of the cash flows (a) × (b) | $ (40,000) | $(653,250) | |
| 8 | Net present value (SUM B7:C7) | $(693,250) | | |
| 9 | | | | |
| 10 | Buy the new machine: | | Year(s) | |
| 11 | | Now | 1-6 | 6 |
| 12 | Initial investment | $(250,000) | | |
| 13 | Salvage value of old machine | $ 30,000 | | |
| 14 | Annual cash operating costs | | $ (90,000) | |
| 15 | Salvage value of new machine | | | $50,000 |
| 16 | Total cash flows (a) | $(220,000) | $ (90,000) | $50,000 |
| 17 | Discount factor (10%) (b) | 1.000 | 4.355 | 0.564 |
| 18 | Present value of the cash flows (a) × (b) | $(220,000) | $(391,950) | $28,200 |
| 19 | Net present value (SUM B18:D18) | $(583,750) | | |
| 20 | | | | |
| 21 | Net present value in favor of buying the new machine | $ 109,500 | | |
| 22 | | | | |

Exhibit 12-8 | Exhibit 12-9 | Exhibit 12-10 | Exhibit 12-11

Source: Microsoft

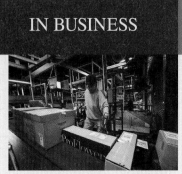

## IN BUSINESS

### United Parcel Service Focuses its Attention on December 22nd

When **United Parcel Service** (UPS) failed to deliver millions of packages by Christmas Day, it needed to devise a solution so that the same problems would not be repeated next year. The company's answer was a $500 million capital investment in an automated system that it calls the "Next Generation Sort Aisle." The new system rapidly identifies zip codes, thereby enabling employees to process 15% more packages per day. The system can also quickly reroute packages in the event of bad weather. UPS hopes that its new automated system also will enable it to save $500 million per year on employee training. But, perhaps more importantly, the company also hopes that the new system will enable it to deliver the 34 million packages that it receives on December 22 to its anxious recipients by Christmas Day.

Source: Stevens, Laura, "One Day, 34 Million Packages at UPS," *The Wall Street Journal,* December 22, 2014, B1–B2.

## UNCERTAIN CASH FLOWS

Thus far, we have assumed that all future cash flows are known with certainty. However, future cash flows are often uncertain or difficult to estimate. A number of techniques are available for handling this complication. Some of these techniques are quite technical—involving computer simulations or advanced mathematical skills—and are beyond the scope of this book. However, we can provide some very useful information to help managers deal with uncertain cash flows without getting too technical.

### An Example

As an example of difficult-to-estimate future cash flows, consider the case of investments in automated equipment. The up-front costs of automated equipment and the tangible benefits, such as reductions in operating costs and waste, tend to be relatively easy to estimate. However, the intangible benefits, such as greater reliability, greater speed, and higher quality, are more difficult to quantify in terms of future cash flows. These intangible benefits certainly impact future cash flows—particularly in terms of increased sales and perhaps higher selling prices—but the cash flow effects are difficult to estimate. What can be done?

A fairly simple procedure can be followed when the intangible benefits are likely to be significant. Suppose, for example, that a company with a 12% discount rate is considering purchasing automated equipment that would have a 10-year useful life. Also suppose that a discounted cash flow analysis of just the tangible costs and benefits shows a negative net present value of $226,000. Clearly, if the intangible benefits are large enough, they could turn this negative net present value into a positive net present value. In this case, the amount of additional cash flow per year from the intangible benefits that would be needed to make the project financially attractive can be computed as follows:

| | |
|---|---:|
| Net present value excluding the intangible benefits (negative) | $(226,000) |
| Present value factor for an annuity at 12% for 10 periods (from Exhibit 12B–2 in Appendix 12B) | 5.650 |

$$\frac{\text{Negative net present value to be offset, } \$226{,}000}{\text{Present value factor, } 5.650} = \$40{,}000$$

Thus, if the intangible benefits of the automated equipment are worth at least $40,000 a year to the company, then the automated equipment should be purchased. If, in the judgment of management, these intangible benefits are not worth $40,000 a year, then the automated equipment should not be purchased.

This technique can be used in other situations in which future cash flows are difficult to estimate. For example, this technique can be used when the salvage value is difficult to estimate. To illustrate, suppose that all of the cash flows from an investment in a super-tanker have been estimated—other than its salvage value in 20 years. Using a discount rate of 12%, management has determined that the net present value of all of these cash flows is a negative $1.04 million. This negative net present value would be offset by the salvage value of the supertanker. How large would the salvage value have to be to make this investment attractive?

| | |
|---|---|
| Net present value excluding salvage value (negative)............................................ | $(1,040,000) |
| Present value factor at 12% for 20 periods (from Exhibit 12B–1 in Appendix 12B).................... | 0.104 |

$$\frac{\text{Negative net present value to be offset, } \$1,040,000}{\text{Present value factor, } 0.104} = \$10,000,000$$

Thus, if the salvage value of the tanker in 20 years is at least $10 million, its net present value would be positive and the investment should be made. However, if management believes the salvage value is unlikely to be as large as $10 million, the investment should not be made.

## Financing the Sports Car

DECISION POINT

Assume you would like to buy a new sports car that can be purchased for $21,495 in cash or acquired from the dealer via a leasing arrangement. Under the terms of the lease, you would have to make a payment of $2,078 when the lease is signed and then monthly payments of $300 for 24 months. At the end of the 24-month lease, you can choose to buy the car you have leased for an additional payment of $13,776. If you do not make that final payment, the car reverts to the dealer.

You have enough cash to make the initial payment on the lease, but not enough to buy the car for cash. However, you could borrow the additional cash from a credit union for 1% per month. Do you think you should borrow money from a credit union to purchase the car or should you sign a lease with the dealer?

Hints: The net present value of the cash purchase option, including any payments to the credit union, is $21,495 using 1% per month as the discount rate. (Accept this statement as true; don't try to do the computations to verify it.) Determine the net present value of the lease, using 1% per month as the discount rate. The present value of an annuity of $1 for 24 periods at 1% per period is 21.243 and the present value of a single payment of $1 at the end of 24 periods at 1% per period is 0.788.

## PREFERENCE DECISIONS—THE RANKING OF INVESTMENT PROJECTS

Recall that when considering investment opportunities, managers must make two types of decisions—screening decisions and preference decisions. Screening decisions, which come first, pertain to whether or not a proposed investment is acceptable. Preference decisions come *after* screening decisions and attempt to answer the following question: "How do the remaining investment proposals, all of which have been screened and provide an acceptable rate of return, rank in terms of preference? That is, which one(s) would be *best* for the company to accept?"

**LEARNING OBJECTIVE 12–5**

Rank investment projects in order of preference.

Sometimes preference decisions are called rationing decisions, or ranking decisions. Limited investment funds must be rationed among many competing alternatives. Hence, the alternatives must be ranked. Either the internal rate of return method or the net present value method can be used in making preference decisions. However, as discussed earlier, if the two methods are in conflict, it is best to use the net present value method, which is more reliable.

## Internal Rate of Return Method

When using the internal rate of return method to rank competing investment projects, the preference rule is: *The higher the internal rate of return, the more desirable the project.* An investment project with an internal rate of return of 18% usually is considered preferable to another project that has a return of only 15%. Internal rate of return is widely used to rank projects.

## Net Present Value Method

The net present value of one project cannot be directly compared to the net present value of another project unless the initial investments are equal. For example, assume that a company is considering two competing investments, as shown below:

| | Investment A | Investment B |
|---|---|---|
| Investment required.............. | $(10,000) | $(5,000) |
| Present value of cash inflows....... | 11,000 | 6,000 |
| Net present value................ | $ 1,000 | $ 1,000 |

Although each project has a net present value of $1,000, the projects are not equally desirable if the funds available for investment are limited. The project requiring an investment of only $5,000 is much more desirable than the project requiring an investment of $10,000. This fact can be highlighted by dividing the net present value of the project by the investment required. The result, shown below in equation form, is called the **project profitability index**.

$$\text{Project profitability index} = \frac{\text{Net present value of the project}}{\text{Investment required}} \qquad (3)$$

The project profitability indexes for the two investments above would be computed as follows:

| | Investment A | Investment B |
|---|---|---|
| Net present value (a)........................... | $1,000 | $1,000 |
| Investment required (b)......................... | $10,000 | $5,000 |
| Project profitability index, (a) ÷ (b).............. | 0.10 | 0.20 |

When using the project profitability index to rank competing investments projects, the preference rule is: *The higher the project profitability index, the more desirable the project.*[2] Applying this rule to the two investments above, investment B should be chosen over investment A.

The project profitability index is an application of the techniques for utilizing constrained resources discussed in an earlier chapter. In this case, the constrained resource is the limited funds available for investment, and the project profitability index is similar to the contribution margin per unit of the constrained resource.

A few details should be clarified with respect to the computation of the project profitability index. The "Investment required" refers to any cash outflows that occur at the beginning of the project, reduced by any salvage value recovered from the sale of old equipment. The "Investment required" also includes any investment in working capital that the project may need.

# THE SIMPLE RATE OF RETURN METHOD

The **simple rate of return** method is the final capital budgeting technique discussed in the chapter. This method also is often referred to as the accounting rate of return or the unadjusted rate of return. We will begin by explaining how to compute the simple rate of return followed by a discussion of this method's limitations and its impact on the behavior of investment center managers.

**LEARNING OBJECTIVE 12–6**

Compute the simple rate of return for an investment.

To obtain the simple rate of return, the annual incremental net operating income generated by a project is divided by the initial investment in the project, as shown below.

$$\text{Simple rate of return} = \frac{\text{Annual incremental net operating income}}{\text{Initial investment}} \quad (4)$$

The annual incremental net operating income included in the numerator should be reduced by the depreciation charges that result from making the investment. Furthermore, the initial investment shown in the denominator should be reduced by any salvage value realized from the sale of old equipment.

> **Example I:** Brigham Tea, Inc., is a processor of low-acid tea. The company is contemplating purchasing equipment for an additional processing line that would increase revenues by $90,000 per year. Incremental cash operating expenses would be $40,000 per year. The equipment would cost $180,000 and have a nine-year life with no salvage value.

To apply the formula for the simple rate of return, we must first determine the annual incremental net operating income from the project:

| | | |
|---|---:|---:|
| Annual incremental revenues . . . . . . . . . . . . . . . . . . . . . . | | $90,000 |
| Annual incremental cash operating expenses . . . . . . . . | $40,000 | |
| Annual depreciation ($180,000 − $0) ÷ 9 . . . . . . . . . . . . | 20,000 | |
| Annual incremental expenses . . . . . . . . . . . . . . . . . . . . . . | | 60,000 |
| Annual incremental net operating income. . . . . . . . . . . . | | $30,000 |

---

[2]Because of the "lumpiness" of projects, the project profitability index ranking may not be perfect. Nevertheless, it is a good starting point.

Given that the annual incremental net operating income from the project is $30,000 and the initial investment is $180,000, the simple rate of return is 16.7% as shown below:

$$\text{Simple rate of return} = \frac{\text{Annual incremental net operating income}}{\text{Initial investment}}$$

$$= \frac{\$30,000}{\$180,000}$$

$$= 16.7\%$$

**Example J:** Midwest Farms, Inc., hires people on a part-time basis to sort eggs. The cost of hand sorting is $30,000 per year. The company is investigating an egg-sorting machine that would cost $90,000 and have a 15-year useful life. The machine would have negligible salvage value, and it would cost $10,000 per year to operate and maintain. The egg-sorting equipment currently being used could be sold now for a scrap value of $2,500.

This project is slightly different from the preceding project because it involves cost reductions with no additional revenues. Nevertheless, the annual incremental net operating income can be computed by treating the annual cost savings as if it were incremental revenues as follows:

| | | |
|---|---|---|
| Annual incremental cost savings.................... | | $30,000 |
| Annual incremental cash operating expenses......... | $10,000 | |
| Annual depreciation ($90,000 − $0) ÷ 15............ | 6,000 | |
| Annual incremental expenses ...................... | | 16,000 |
| Annual incremental net operating income............ | | $14,000 |

Thus, even though the new equipment would not generate any additional revenues, it would reduce costs by $14,000 a year. This would have the effect of increasing net operating income by $14,000 a year.

Finally, the salvage value of the old equipment offsets the initial cost of the new equipment as follows:

| | |
|---|---|
| Cost of the new equipment ....................... | $90,000 |
| Less salvage value of the old equipment............. | 2,500 |
| Initial investment................................ | $87,500 |

Given the annual incremental net operating income of $14,000 and the initial investment of $87,500, the simple rate of return is 16.0% computed as follows:

$$\text{Simple rate of return} = \frac{\text{Annual incremental net operating income}}{\text{Initial investment}}$$

$$= \frac{\$14,000}{\$87,500}$$

$$= 16.0\%$$

The simple rate of return suffers from two important limitations. First, it focuses on accounting net operating income rather than cash flows. Thus, if a project does not have constant incremental revenues and expenses over its useful life, the simple rate of return will fluctuate from year to year, thereby possibly causing the same project to appear desirable in some years and undesirable in others. Second, the simple rate of return method does not involve discounting cash flows. It considers a dollar received 10 years from now to be as valuable as a dollar received today.

Given these limitations, it is reasonable to wonder why we bothered discussing this method. First of all, in spite of its limitations, some companies use the simple rate of return to evaluate capital investment proposals. Therefore, you should be familiar with this approach so you can properly critique it in the event that you encounter it in practice. More importantly, you need to understand how the simple rate of return method influences the behavior of investment center managers who are evaluated and rewarded based on their return on investment (ROI).

For example, assume the following three facts. First, assume you are an investment center manager whose pay raises are based solely on ROI. Second, assume that last year your division had an ROI of 20%. Third, assume your division has the chance to pursue a capital budgeting project that will have a positive net present value and a simple rate of return of 17%. Given these three assumptions, would you choose to accept this project or reject it? Although the company would want you to accept it because of its positive net present value, you would probably choose to reject it because the simple rate of return of 17% is less than your prior year's ROI of 20%. This basic example illustrates how a project's simple rate of return can influence the decisions made by investment center managers. It also highlights an important challenge faced by organizations, namely designing performance measurement systems that align employee actions with organizational goals.

## HELPFUL HINT

When a capital budgeting project involves replacing an old piece of equipment with a new piece of equipment, remember to subtract any salvage value realized from the old equipment from the cost of the new equipment to determine the amount of the initial investment.

## CONCEPT CHECK

4. If a $300,000 investment has a project profitability index of 0.25, what is the net present value of the project?
   a. $75,000
   b. $225,000
   c. $25,000
   d. $275,000
5. Which of the following statements is true? (You may select more than one answer.)
   a. The project profitability index is used to make screening decisions.
   b. The internal rate of return is the rate of return promised by an investment over its useful life.
   c. A project's simple rate of return can fluctuate from year to year.
   d. The simple rate of return typically equals a company's cost of capital.

# POSTAUDIT OF INVESTMENT PROJECTS

After an investment project has been approved and implemented, a *postaudit* should be conducted. A **postaudit** involves checking whether or not expected results are actually realized. This is a key part of the capital budgeting process because it helps keep managers honest in their investment proposals. Any tendency to inflate the benefits or downplay the costs in a proposal should become evident after a few postaudits have been conducted.

The postaudit also provides an opportunity to reinforce and possibly expand successful projects and to cut losses on floundering projects.

The same capital budgeting method should be used in the postaudit as was used in the original approval process. That is, if a project was approved on the basis of a net present value analysis, then the same procedure should be used in performing the post-audit. However, the data used in the postaudit analysis should be *actual observed data* rather than estimated data. This gives management an opportunity to make a side-by-side comparison to see how well the project has succeeded. It also helps assure that estimated data received on future proposals will be carefully prepared because the persons submitting the data knows that their estimates will be compared to actual results in the postaudit process. Actual results that are far out of line with original estimates should be carefully reviewed.

## IN BUSINESS

### Macy's Plans to Increase its Capital Expenditures

**Macy's** hopes that $1.2 billion in capital expenditures will reverse a four-year slide in its sales growth rate. The capital investment projects will focus on developing new store formats, integrating its brick-and-mortar stores with its online operations, and expanding the presence of its Macy's and **Bloomingdale's** nameplates outside the United States. Some of the funds to support these capital investments will come from laying off more than 2,000 workers. The company's Chief Financial Officer, Karen Hoguet, advised investors that these capital projects will take 2–3 years to earn satisfactory returns on the initial investments.

Source: Kapner, Suzanne, "With Sales Sluggish, Macy's Boosts Spending," *The Wall Street Journal*, February 25, 2015, B3.

©NetPhotos/Alamy Stock Photo

## SUMMARY

**LO12–1 Determine the payback period for an investment.**
The payback period is the number of periods that are required to recover the investment in a project from the project's net cash inflows. The payback period is most useful for projects whose useful lives are short and uncertain. Generally speaking it is not a reliable method for evaluating investment opportunities because it ignores the time value of money and all cash flows that occur after the investment has been recovered.

**LO12–2 Evaluate the acceptability of an investment project using the net present value method.**
Investment decisions should take into account the time value of money because a dollar today is more valuable than a dollar received in the future. In the net present value method, future cash flows are discounted to their present value so that they can be compared with current cash outlays. The difference between the present value of the cash inflows and the present value of the cash outflows is called the project's net present value. If the net present value of the project is negative, the project is rejected. The company's cost of capital is often used as the discount rate in the net present value method.

**LO12–3 Evaluate the acceptability of an investment project using the internal rate of return method.**
The internal rate of return is the rate of return that equates the present value of the cash inflows and the present value of the cash outflows, resulting in a zero net present value. If the internal rate of return is less than a company's minimum required rate of return, the project is rejected.

**LO12–4 Evaluate an investment project that has uncertain cash flows.**
Future cash flows are often uncertain or difficult to estimate. Fairly simple procedures can be used to estimate the intangible benefits or salvage value required to raise a project's net present value to zero, thereby making it an acceptable investment alternative.

## LO12–5 Rank investment projects in order of preference.

After screening out projects whose net present values are negative, the company may still have more acceptable projects than can be supported with available funds. The remaining projects can be ranked using the project profitability index, which is computed by dividing the net present value of the project by the required initial investment.

## LO12–6 Compute the simple rate of return for an investment.

The simple rate of return is determined by dividing a project's accounting net operating income by the initial investment in the project. The simple rate of return is not a reliable guide for evaluating potential projects because it ignores the time value of money. While this method has important limitations, it can influence the decision-making process of investment center managers who are evaluated and rewarded based on their return on investment (ROI).

# GUIDANCE ANSWER TO DECISION POINT

**Financing the Sports Car**

The formal analysis, using the least-cost approach, appears below:

| Item | Month(s) | Amount of Cash Flows | 1% Factor | Present Value of Cash Flows |
|---|---|---|---|---|
| Pay cash for the car: | | | | |
| Cash payment........................ | Now | $(21,495) | 1.000 | $(21,495) |
| Net present value...................... | | | | $(21,495) |
| Lease the car: | | | | |
| Cash payment on lease signing........... | Now | $(2,078) | 1.000 | $ (2,078) |
| Monthly lease payment.................. | 1–24 | $(300) | 21.243 | (6,373) |
| Final payment......................... | 24 | $(13,776) | 0.788 | (10,855) |
| Net present value...................... | | | | $(19,306) |
| Net present value in favor of leasing ........ | | | | $ 2,189 |

The leasing alternative is $2,189 less costly, in terms of net present value, than the cash purchase alternative. In addition, the leasing alternative has the advantage that you can choose to not make the final payment of $13,776 at the end of 24 months if for some reason you decide you do not want to keep the car. For example, if the resale value of the car at that point is far less than $13,776, you may choose to return the car to the dealer and save the $13,776. If, however, you had purchased the car outright, you would not have this option—you could only realize the resale value. Because of this "real option," the leasing alternative is even more valuable than the net present value calculations indicate. Therefore, you should lease the car rather than pay cash (and borrow from the credit union).

# GUIDANCE ANSWERS TO CONCEPT CHECKS

1. **Choices a, c, and d.** Working capital is current assets minus current liabilities.
2. **Choice b.** The payback method focuses on cash flows rather than net operating income and it does not discount those cash flows; therefore, it is not affected by the cost of capital.
3. **Choices a and c.** The total-cost and incremental-cost approaches to net present value analysis produce the same results. The present value of a dollar decreases as the time of receipt extends farther into the future.
4. **Choice a.** The net present value of the project is $300,000 × 0.25 = $75,000.
5. **Choices b and c.** The project profitability index is used to make preference decisions. The simple rate of return is unrelated to a company's cost of capital.

## REVIEW PROBLEM: COMPARISON OF CAPITAL BUDGETING METHODS

Lamar Company is considering a project that would have a five-year life and require a $2,400,000 investment in equipment. At the end of five years, the project would terminate and the equipment would have no salvage value. The project would provide net operating income each year as follows:

| | | |
|---|---|---|
| Sales.............................. | | $3,200,000 |
| Variable expenses................... | | 1,800,000 |
| Contribution margin.................. | | 1,400,000 |
| Fixed expenses: | | |
| Advertising, salaries, and other fixed out-of-pocket costs ......... | $700,000 | |
| Depreciation..................... | 300,000 | |
| Total fixed expenses ................ | | 1,000,000 |
| Net operating income ............... | | $ 400,000 |

The company's discount rate is 12%.

**Required:**
1. Compute the annual net cash inflow from the project.
2. Compute the project's net present value. Is the project acceptable?
3. Find the project's internal rate of return to the nearest whole percent.
4. Compute the project's payback period.
5. Compute the project's simple rate of return.

**Solution to Review Problem**
1. The annual net cash inflow can be computed by deducting the cash expenses from sales:

| | |
|---|---|
| Sales.............................. | $3,200,000 |
| Variable expenses..................... | 1,800,000 |
| Contribution margin.................... | 1,400,000 |
| Advertising, salaries, and other fixed out-of-pocket costs .................... | 700,000 |
| Annual net cash inflow ................. | $ 700,000 |

Or the annual net cash inflow can be computed by adding depreciation back to net operating income:

| | |
|---|---|
| Net operating income ......................... | $400,000 |
| Add: Noncash deduction for depreciation ......... | 300,000 |
| Annual net cash inflow ....................... | $700,000 |

2. The net present value is computed as follows:

| | A | B | C | D | E | F | G |
|---|---|---|---|---|---|---|---|
| 1 | | | | | Year | | |
| 2 | | Now | 1 | 2 | 3 | 4 | 5 |
| 3 | Initial investment | $ (2,400,000) | | | | | |
| 4 | Sales | | $ 3,200,000 | $ 3,200,000 | $ 3,200,000 | $ 3,200,000 | $ 3,200,000 |
| 5 | Variable expenses | | $(1,800,000) | $(1,800,000) | $(1,800,000) | $(1,800,000) | $(1,800,000) |
| 6 | Fixed out-of-pocket costs | _____ | $ (700,000) | $ (700,000) | $ (700,000) | $ (700,000) | $ (700,000) |
| 7 | Total cash flows (a) | $ (2,400,000) | $ 700,000 | $ 700,000 | $ 700,000 | $ 700,000 | $ 700,000 |
| 8 | Discount factor (12%) (b) | 1.000 | 0.893 | 0.797 | 0.712 | 0.636 | 0.567 |
| 9 | Present value of cash flows (a) × (b) | $ (2,400,000) | $ 625,100 | $ 557,900 | $ 498,400 | $ 445,200 | $ 396,900 |
| 10 | Net present value (SUM B9:H9) | $ 123,500 | | | | | |
| 11 | | | | | | | |
| 12 | Note: The discount factors comes from Exhibit 12B-1 in Appendix 12B. | | | | | | |

Sheet1　Sheet2　Sheet3

Or, it can also be computed as follows:

| | A | B | C |
|---|---|---|---|
| 1 | | | Years |
| 2 | | Now | 1-5 |
| 3 | Initial investment | $(2,400,000) | |
| 4 | Sales | | $ 3,200,000 |
| 5 | Variable expenses | | $ (1,800,000) |
| 6 | Fixed out-of-pocket costs | | $ (700,000) |
| 7 | Total cash flows (a) | $(2,400,000) | $ 700,000 |
| 8 | Discount factor (12%) (b) | 1.000 | 3.605 |
| 9 | Present value of the cash flows (a) × (b) | $(2,400,000) | $2,523,500 |
| 10 | Net present value (SUM B7:C7) | $123,500 | |
| 11 | | | |
| 12 | Note: The discount factor comes from Exhibit 12B-2 in Appendix 12B. | | |
| 13 | | | |

| Sheet1 | **Sheet2** | Sheet3 |

Yes, the project is acceptable because it has a positive net present value.

3. The formula for computing the factor of the internal rate of return is:

$$\text{Factor of the internal rate of return} = \frac{\text{Investment required}}{\text{Annual net cash flow}}$$

$$= \frac{\$2,400,000}{\$700,000} = 3.429$$

Looking in Exhibit 12B–2 in Appendix 12B at the end of the chapter and scanning along the 5-period line, we find that a factor of 3.429 is closest to a factor of 3.433, which corresponds to a rate of return of 14%.

4. The formula for the payback period is:

$$\text{Payback period} = \frac{\text{Investment required}}{\text{Annual net cash flow}}$$

$$= \frac{\$2,400,000}{\$700,000}$$

$$= 3.4 \text{ years (rounded)}$$

5. The formula for the simple rate of return is:

$$\text{Simple rate of return} = \frac{\text{Annual incremental net operating income}}{\text{Initial investment}}$$

$$= \frac{\$400,000}{\$2,400,000}$$

$$= 16.7\%$$

## GLOSSARY

**Capital budgeting**  The process of planning significant investments in projects that have long-term implications such as the purchase of new equipment or the introduction of a new product. (p. 564)

**Cost of capital**  The average rate of return a company must pay to its long-term creditors and shareholders for the use of their funds. (p. 572)

**Internal rate of return**   The discount rate at which the net present value of an investment project is zero; the rate of return of a project over its useful life. (p. 575)

**Net present value**   The difference between the present value of an investment project's cash inflows and the present value of its cash outflows. (p. 569)

**Out-of-pocket costs**   Actual cash outlays for salaries, advertising, repairs, and similar costs. (p. 574)

**Payback period**   The length of time that it takes for a project to fully recover its initial cost out of the net cash inflows that it generates. (p. 566)

**Postaudit**   The follow-up after a project has been approved and implemented to determine whether expected results were actually realized. (p. 585)

**Preference decision**   A decision in which the acceptable alternatives must be ranked. (p. 564)

**Project profitability index**   The ratio of the net present value of a project's cash flows to the investment required. (p. 582)

**Screening decision**   A decision as to whether a proposed investment project is acceptable. (p. 564)

**Simple rate of return**   The rate of return computed by dividing a project's annual incremental net operating income by the initial investment required. (p. 583)

**Time value of money**   The concept that a dollar today is worth more than a dollar a year from now. (p. 565)

**Working capital**   Current assets less current liabilities. (p. 565)

## QUESTIONS

**12–1**   What is the difference between capital budgeting screening decisions and capital budgeting preference decisions?

**12–2**   What is meant by the term *time value of money?*

**12–3**   What is meant by the term *discounting?*

**12–4**   Why isn't accounting net income used in the net present value and internal rate of return methods of making capital budgeting decisions?

**12–5**   Why are discounted cash flow methods of making capital budgeting decisions superior to other methods?

**12–6**   What is net present value? Can it ever be negative? Explain.

**12–7**   Identify two simplifying assumptions associated with discounted cash flow methods of making capital budgeting decisions.

**12–8**   If a company has to pay interest of 14% on long-term debt, then its cost of capital is 14%. Do you agree? Explain.

**12–9**   What is meant by an investment project's internal rate of return? How is the internal rate of return computed?

**12–10**   Explain how the cost of capital serves as a screening tool when using (*a*) the net present value method and (*b*) the internal rate of return method.

**12–11**   As the discount rate increases, the present value of a given future cash flow also increases. Do you agree? Explain.

**12–12**   Refer to Exhibit 12–8. Is the return on this investment proposal exactly 14%, more than 14%, or less than 14%? Explain.

**12–13**   How is the project profitability index computed, and what does it measure?

**12–14**   What is meant by the term *payback period?* How is the payback period determined? How can the payback method be useful?

**12–15**   What is the major criticism of the payback and simple rate of return methods of making capital budgeting decisions?

## APPLYING EXCEL          ■ connect

**LO12–2, LO12–3**

The Excel worksheet form that appears below is to be used to recreate Example E and Exhibit 12–8. Download the workbook containing this form from Connect, where you will also receive instructions about how to use this worksheet form.

| | A | B | C | D | E | F | G |
|---|---|---|---|---|---|---|---|
| 1 | Chapter 12: Applying Excel | | | | | | |
| 2 | | | | | | | |
| 3 | Data | | | | | | |
| 4 | Example E | | | | | | |
| 5 | Cost of equipment needed | $60,000 | | | | | |
| 6 | Working capital needed | $100,000 | | | | | |
| 7 | Overhaul of equipment in four years | $5,000 | | | | | |
| 8 | Salvage value of the equipment in five years | $10,000 | | | | | |
| 9 | Annual revenues and costs: | | | | | | |
| 10 | Sales revenues | $200,000 | | | | | |
| 11 | Cost of goods sold | $125,000 | | | | | |
| 12 | Out-of-pocket operating costs | $35,000 | | | | | |
| 13 | Discount rate | 14% | | | | | |
| 14 | | | | | | | |
| 15 | Enter a formula into each of the cells marked with a ? below | | | | | | |
| 16 | Exhibit 12-8 | | | | | | |
| 17 | | | | | Years | | |
| 18 | | Now | 1 | 2 | 3 | 4 | 5 |
| 19 | Purchase of equipment | ? | | | | | |
| 20 | Investment in working capital | ? | | | | | |
| 21 | Sales | | ? | ? | ? | ? | ? |
| 22 | Cost of goods sold | | ? | ? | ? | ? | ? |
| 23 | Out-of-pocket operating costs | | ? | ? | ? | ? | ? |
| 24 | Overhaul of equipment | | | | | ? | |
| 25 | Salvage value of the equipment | | | | | | ? |
| 26 | Working capital released | | | | | | ? |
| 27 | Total cash flows (a) | ? | ? | ? | ? | ? | ? |
| 28 | Discount factor (14%) (b) | ? | ? | ? | ? | ? | ? |
| 29 | Present value of cash flows (a) x (b) | ? | ? | ? | ? | ? | ? |
| 30 | Net present value | ? | | | | | |
| 31 | | | | | | | |
| 32 | *Use the formulas from Appendix 12B: | | | | | | |
| 33 | Present value of $1 = 1/(1+r)^n | | | | | | |
| 34 | Present value of an annuity of $1 = (1/r)*(1-(1/(1+r)^n)) | | | | | | |
| 35 | where n is the number of years and r is the discount rate | | | | | | |
| 36 | | | | | | | |

Chapter 12 Form | Filled in Chapter 12 Form | ... | + | | |

You should proceed to the requirements below only after completing your worksheet. Note that you may get a slightly different net present value from that shown in the text due to the precision of the calculations.

**Required:**

1. Check your worksheet by changing the discount rate to 10%. The net present value should now be between $56,495 and $56,518—depending on the precision of the calculations. If you do not get an answer in this range, find the errors in your worksheet and correct them.

   Explain why the net present value has increased as a result of reducing the discount rate from 14% to 10%.

2. The company is considering another project involving the purchase of new equipment. Change the data area of your worksheet to match the following:

| Data | |
|---|---|
| **Example E** | |
| Cost of equipment needed . . . . . . . . . . . . . . . . . . | $120,000 |
| Working capital needed . . . . . . . . . . . . . . . . . . . . | $80,000 |
| Overhaul of equipment in four years . . . . . . . . | $40,000 |
| Salvage value of the equipment in five years . . . | $20,000 |
| Annual revenues and costs: | |
| Sales revenues . . . . . . . . . . . . . . . . . . . . . . . . . | $255,000 |
| Cost of goods sold . . . . . . . . . . . . . . . . . . . . . . | $160,000 |
| Out-of-pocket operating costs . . . . . . . . . . . . . | $50,000 |
| Discount rate . . . . . . . . . . . . . . . . . . . . . . . . . . . . | 14% |

a.  What is the net present value of the project?
b.  Experiment with changing the discount rate in one percent increments (e.g., 13%, 12%, 15%, etc.). At what interest rate does the net present value turn from negative to positive?
c.  The internal rate of return is between what two whole discount rates (e.g., between 10% and 11%, between 11% and 12%, between 12% and 13%, between 13% and 14%, etc.)?
d.  Reset the discount rate to 14%. Suppose the salvage value is uncertain. How large would the salvage value have to be to result in a positive net present value?

# THE FOUNDATIONAL 15     connect

**LO12–1, LO12–2, LO12–3, LO12–5, LO12–6**

Cardinal Company is considering a five-year project that would require a $2,975,000 investment in equipment with a useful life of five years and no salvage value. The company's discount rate is 14%. The project would provide net operating income in each of five years as follows:

| | |
|---|---:|
| Sales ..................................... | $2,735,000 |
| Variable expenses ......................... | 1,000,000 |
| Contribution margin ....................... | 1,735,000 |
| Fixed expenses: | |
| Advertising, salaries, and other fixed out-of-pocket costs .................... $735,000 | |
| Depreciation .......................... 595,000 | |
| Total fixed expenses ...................... | 1,330,000 |
| Net operating income ..................... | $ 405,000 |

*Required:*
(Answer each question by referring to the original data unless instructed otherwise.)
1.  Which item(s) in the income statement shown above will not affect cash flows?
2.  What are the project's annual net cash inflows?
3.  What is the present value of the project's annual net cash inflows?
4.  What is the project's net present value?
5.  What is the project profitability index for this project? (Round your answer to the nearest whole percent.)
6.  What is the project's internal rate of return to the nearest whole percent?
7.  What is the project's payback period?
8.  What is the project's simple rate of return for each of the five years?
9.  If the company's discount rate was 16% instead of 14%, would you expect the project's net present value to be higher than, lower than, or the same as your answer to requirement 4? No computations are necessary.
10. If the equipment had a salvage value of $300,000 at the end of five years, would you expect the project's payback period to be higher than, lower than, or the same as your answer to requirement 7? No computations are necessary.
11. If the equipment had a salvage value of $300,000 at the end of five years, would you expect the project's net present value to be higher than, lower than, or the same as your answer to requirement 3? No computations are necessary.
12. If the equipment had a salvage value of $300,000 at the end of five years, would you expect the project's simple rate of return to be higher than, lower than, or the same as your answer to requirement 8? No computations are necessary.
13. Assume a postaudit showed that all estimates (including total sales) were exactly correct except for the variable expense ratio, which actually turned out to be 45%. What was the project's actual net present value?
14. Assume a postaudit showed that all estimates (including total sales) were exactly correct except for the variable expense ratio, which actually turned out to be 45%. What was the project's actual payback period?
15. Assume a postaudit showed that all estimates (including total sales) were exactly correct except for the variable expense ratio, which actually turned out to be 45%. What was the project's actual simple rate of return?

**■ connect**          **EXERCISES**

**EXERCISE 12–1   Payback Method** LO12–1
The management of Unter Corporation, an architectural design firm, is considering an investment with the following cash flows:

| Year | Investment | Cash Inflow |
|------|-----------|-------------|
| 1 ....... | $15,000 | $1,000 |
| 2 ....... | $8,000 | $2,000 |
| 3 ....... | | $2,500 |
| 4 ....... | | $4,000 |
| 5 ....... | | $5,000 |
| 6 ....... | | $6,000 |
| 7 ....... | | $5,000 |
| 8 ....... | | $4,000 |
| 9 ....... | | $3,000 |
| 10 ....... | | $2,000 |

*Required:*
1. Determine the payback period of the investment.
2. Would the payback period be affected if the cash inflow in the last year were several times as large?

**EXERCISE 12–2   Net Present Value Analysis** LO12–2
The management of Kunkel Company is considering the purchase of a $27,000 machine that would reduce operating costs by $7,000 per year. At the end of the machine's five-year useful life, it will have zero salvage value. The company's required rate of return is 12%.

*Required:*
1. Determine the net present value of the investment in the machine.
2. What is the difference between the total, undiscounted cash inflows and cash outflows over the entire life of the machine?

**EXERCISE 12–3   Internal Rate of Return** LO12–3
Wendell's Donut Shoppe is investigating the purchase of a new $18,600 donut-making machine. The new machine would permit the company to reduce the amount of part-time help needed, at a cost savings of $3,800 per year. In addition, the new machine would allow the company to produce one new style of donut, resulting in the sale of 1,000 dozen more donuts each year. The company realizes a contribution margin of $1.20 per dozen donuts sold. The new machine would have a six-year useful life.

*Required:*
1. What would be the total annual cash inflows associated with the new machine for capital budgeting purposes?
2. What discount factor should be used to compute the new machine's internal rate of return?
3. Using Exhibit 12B–2 in Appendix 12B as a reference, what is the new machine's internal rate of return to the nearest whole percent?
4. In addition to the data given previously, assume that the machine will have a $9,125 salvage value at the end of six years. Under these conditions, what is the internal rate of return to the nearest whole percent? (*Hint:* You may find it helpful to use the net present value approach; find the discount rate that will cause the net present value to be closest to zero.)

**EXERCISE 12–4   Uncertain Future Cash Flows** LO12–4
Lukow Products is investigating the purchase of a piece of automated equipment that will save $400,000 each year in direct labor and inventory carrying costs. This equipment costs $2,500,000 and is expected to have a 15-year useful life with no salvage value. The company's required rate of return is 20% on all equipment purchases. Management anticipates that this equipment will provide intangible benefits such as greater flexibility and higher-quality output that will result in additional future cash inflows.

**Required:**
1. What is the net present value of the piece of equipment *before* considering its intangible benefits?
2. What minimum dollar value per year must be provided by the equipment's intangible benefits to justify the $2,500,000 investment?

**EXERCISE 12–5   Preference Ranking** LO12–5
Information on four investment proposals is given below:

| | Investment Proposal | | | |
| --- | --- | --- | --- | --- |
| | A | B | C | D |
| Investment required . . . . . . . . . . . . . . . | $(90,000) | $(100,000) | $(70,000) | $(120,000) |
| Present value of cash inflows . . . . . . . . | 126,000 | 138,000 | 105,000 | 160,000 |
| Net present value . . . . . . . . . . . . . . . . . | $ 36,000 | $ 38,000 | $ 35,000 | $ 40,000 |
| Life of the project . . . . . . . . . . . . . . . . . | 5 years | 7 years | 6 years | 6 years |

**Required:**
1. Compute the project profitability index for each investment proposal.
2. Rank the proposals in terms of preference.

**EXERCISE 12–6   Simple Rate of Return Method** LO12–6
The management of Ballard MicroBrew is considering the purchase of an automated bottling machine for $120,000. The machine would replace an old piece of equipment that costs $30,000 per year to operate. The new machine would cost $12,000 per year to operate. The old machine currently in use could be sold now for a salvage value of $40,000. The new machine would have a useful life of 10 years with no salvage value.

**Required:**
1. What is the annual depreciation expense associated with the new bottling machine?
2. What is the annual incremental net operating income provided by the new bottling machine?
3. What is the amount of the initial investment associated with this project that should be used for calculating the simple rate of return?
4. What is the simple rate of return on the new bottling machine?

**EXERCISE 12–7   Net Present Value Analysis of Two Alternatives** LO12–2
Perit Industries has $100,000 to invest. The company is trying to decide between two alternative uses of the funds. The alternatives are:

| | Project A | Project B |
| --- | --- | --- |
| Cost of equipment required . . . . . . . . . . . . . . . . . . | $100,000 | $0 |
| Working capital investment required . . . . . . . . . . | $0 | $100,000 |
| Annual cash inflows . . . . . . . . . . . . . . . . . . . . . . . . | $21,000 | $16,000 |
| Salvage value of equipment in six years . . . . . . . | $8,000 | $0 |
| Life of the project . . . . . . . . . . . . . . . . . . . . . . . . . . | 6 years | 6 years |

The working capital needed for project B will be released at the end of six years for investment elsewhere. Perit Industries' discount rate is 14%.

**Required:**
1. Compute the net present value of Project A.
2. Compute the net present value of Project B.
3. Which investment alternative (if either) would you recommend that the company accept?

**EXERCISE 12–8   Payback Period and Simple Rate of Return** LO12–1, LO12–6
Nick's Novelties, Inc., is considering the purchase of new electronic games to place in its amusement houses. The games would cost a total of $300,000, have an eight-year useful life, and have a total salvage

value of $20,000. The company estimates that annual revenues and expenses associated with the games would be as follows:

| | | |
|---|---|---|
| Revenues | | $200,000 |
| Less operating expenses: | | |
| Commissions to amusement houses | $100,000 | |
| Insurance | 7,000 | |
| Depreciation | 35,000 | |
| Maintenance | 18,000 | 160,000 |
| Net operating income | | $ 40,000 |

**Required:**
1. What is the payback period for the new electronic games? Assume that Nick's Novelties, Inc., will not purchase new games unless they provide a payback period of five years or less. Would the company purchase the new games?
2. What is the simple rate of return promised by the games? If the company requires a simple rate of return of at least 12%, will the games be purchased?

**EXERCISE 12–9  Net Present Value Analysis and Simple Rate of Return LO12–2, LO12–6**

Derrick Iverson is a divisional manager for Holston Company. His annual pay raises are largely determined by his division's return on investment (ROI), which has been above 20% each of the last three years. Derrick is considering a capital budgeting project that would require a $3,000,000 investment in equipment with a useful life of five years and no salvage value. Holston Company's discount rate is 15%. The project would provide net operating income each year for five years as follows:

| | | |
|---|---|---|
| Sales | | $2,500,000 |
| Variable expenses | | 1,000,000 |
| Contribution margin | | 1,500,000 |
| Fixed expenses: | | |
| Advertising, salaries, and other fixed out-of-pocket costs | $600,000 | |
| Depreciation | 600,000 | |
| Total fixed expenses | | 1,200,000 |
| Net operating income | | $ 300,000 |

**Required:**
1. Compute the project's net present value.
2. Compute the project's simple rate of return.
3. Would the company want Derrick to pursue this investment opportunity? Would Derrick be inclined to pursue this investment opportunity? Explain.

**EXERCISE 12–10  Net Present Value Analysis LO12–2**

Kathy Myers frequently purchases stocks and bonds, but she is uncertain how to determine the rate of return that she is earning. For example, three years ago she paid $13,000 for 200 shares of Malti Company's common stock. She received a $420 cash dividend on the stock at the end of each year for three years. At the end of three years, she sold the stock for $16,000. Kathy would like to earn a return of at least 14% on all of her investments. She is not sure whether the Malti Company stock provide a 14% return and would like some help with the necessary computations.

**Required:**
1. Compute the net present value that Kathy earned on her investment in Malti Company stock. Round your answer to the nearest whole dollar.
2. Did the Malti Company stock provide a 14% return?

**EXERCISE 12–11   Preference Ranking of Investment Projects** LO12–5

Oxford Company has limited funds available for investment and must ration the funds among four competing projects. Selected information on the four projects follows:

| Project | Investment Required | Net Present Value | Life of the Project (years) | Internal Rate of Return |
|---|---|---|---|---|
| A . . . . . . . . . . . . . . . | $160,000 | $44,323 | 7 | 18% |
| B . . . . . . . . . . . . . . . | $135,000 | $42,000 | 12 | 16% |
| C . . . . . . . . . . . . . . . | $100,000 | $35,035 | 7 | 20% |
| D . . . . . . . . . . . . . . . | $175,000 | $38,136 | 3 | 22% |

The net present values above have been computed using a 10% discount rate. The company wants your assistance in determining which project to accept first, second, and so forth.

**Required:**
1. Compute the project profitability index for each project.
2. In order of preference, rank the four projects in terms of:
   a. Net present value.
   b. Project profitability index.
   c. Internal rate of return.
3. Which ranking do you prefer? Why?

**EXERCISE 12–12   Uncertain Cash Flows** LO12–4

The Cambro Foundation, a nonprofit organization, is planning to invest $104,950 in a project that will last for three years. The project will produce net cash inflows as follows:

| | |
|---|---|
| Year 1 . . . . . . . . . . . . . . . . . . . . . . . . . . . . . . . . . . . . | $30,000 |
| Year 2 . . . . . . . . . . . . . . . . . . . . . . . . . . . . . . . . . . . . | $40,000 |
| Year 3 . . . . . . . . . . . . . . . . . . . . . . . . . . . . . . . . . . . . | ? |

**Required:**
Assuming that the project will yield exactly a 12% rate of return, what is the expected net cash inflow for Year 3?

**EXERCISE 12–13   Payback Period and Simple Rate of Return Computations** LO12–1, LO12–6

A piece of labor-saving equipment has just come onto the market that Mitsui Electronics, Ltd., could use to reduce costs in one of its plants in Japan. Relevant data relating to the equipment follow:

| | |
|---|---|
| Purchase cost of the equipment . . . . . . . . . . . . | $432,000 |
| Annual cost savings that will be provided by the equipment . . . . . . . . . . . . . . | $90,000 |
| Life of the equipment . . . . . . . . . . . . . . . . . . . . . . | 12 years |

**Required:**
1. What is the payback period for the equipment? If the company requires a payback period of four years or less, would the equipment be purchased?
2. What is the simple rate of return on the equipment? Use straight-line depreciation based on the equipment's useful life. Would the equipment be purchased if the company's required rate of return is 14%?

**EXERCISE 12–14   Comparison of Projects Using Net Present Value** LO12–2

Labeau Products, Ltd., of Perth, Australia, has $35,000 to invest. The company is trying to decide between two alternative uses for the funds as follows:

| | Invest in Project X | Invest in Project Y |
|---|---|---|
| Investment required .......................... | $35,000 | $35,000 |
| Annual cash inflows ......................... | $12,000 | |
| Single cash inflow at the end of 6 years ....... | | $90,000 |
| Life of the project ........................... | 6 years | 6 years |

The company's discount rate is 18%.

**Required:**
1.  Compute the net present value of Project X.
2.  Compute the net present value of Project Y.
3.  Which project would you recommend the company accept?

**EXERCISE 12–15  Internal Rate of Return and Net Present Value** LO12–2, LO12–3

Henrie's Drapery Service is investigating the purchase of a new machine for cleaning and blocking drapes. The machine would cost $137,320, including freight and installation. Henrie's estimated the new machine would increase the company's cash inflows, net of expenses, by $40,000 per year. The machine would have a five-year useful life and no salvage value.

**Required:**
1.  What is the machine's internal rate of return to the nearest whole percent?
2.  Using a discount rate of 14%, what is the machine's net present value? Interpret your results.
3.  Suppose the new machine would increase the company's annual cash inflows, net of expenses, by only $37,150 per year. Under these conditions, what is the internal rate of return to the nearest whole percent?

 **connect**    PROBLEMS

**PROBLEM 12–16  Net Present Value Analysis** LO12–2

Windhoek Mines, Ltd., of Namibia, is contemplating the purchase of equipment to exploit a mineral deposit on land to which the company has mineral rights. An engineering and cost analysis has been made, and it is expected that the following cash flows would be associated with opening and operating a mine in the area:

| | |
|---|---|
| Cost of new equipment and timbers ................... | $275,000 |
| Working capital required ............................. | $100,000 |
| Annual net cash receipts ............................ | $120,000* |
| Cost to construct new roads in three years ............. | $40,000 |
| Salvage value of equipment in four years ............... | $65,000 |

*Receipts from sales of ore, less out-of-pocket costs for salaries, utilities, insurance, and so forth.

The mineral deposit would be exhausted after four years of mining. At that point, the working capital would be released for reinvestment elsewhere. The company's required rate of return is 20%.

**Required:**
What is the net present value of the proposed mining project? Should the project be accepted? Explain.

**PROBLEM 12–17  Net Present Value Analysis; Internal Rate of Return; Simple Rate of Return**
LO12–2, LO12–3, LO12–6

Casey Nelson is a divisional manager for Pigeon Company. His annual pay raises are largely determined by his division's return on investment (ROI), which has been above 20% each of the last three years. Casey is considering a capital budgeting project that would require a $3,500,000 investment in equipment with a useful life of five years and no salvage value. Pigeon Company's discount rate is 16%. The project would provide net operating income each year for five years as follows:

| | | |
|---|---|---|
| Sales ..................................... | | $3,400,000 |
| Variable expenses ........................... | | 1,600,000 |
| Contribution margin ......................... | | 1,800,000 |
| Fixed expenses: | | |
| Advertising, salaries, and other fixed out-of-pocket costs ................... | $700,000 | |
| Depreciation ............................ | 700,000 | |
| Total fixed expenses ....................... | | 1,400,000 |
| Net operating income ...................... | | $ 400,000 |

**Required:**
1. What is the project's net present value?
2. What is the project's internal rate of return to the nearest whole percent?
3. What is the project's simple rate of return?
4. Would the company want Casey to pursue this investment opportunity? Would Casey be inclined to pursue this investment opportunity? Explain.

**PROBLEM 12–18   Net Present Value Analysis LO12–2**
Oakmont Company has an opportunity to manufacture and sell a new product for a four-year period. The company's discount rate is 15%. After careful study, Oakmont estimated the following costs and revenues for the new product:

| | |
|---|---|
| Cost of equipment needed ............................... | $130,000 |
| Working capital needed .................................. | $60,000 |
| Overhaul of the equipment in two years .................. | $8,000 |
| Salvage value of the equipment in four years .............. | $12,000 |
| Annual revenues and costs: | |
| Sales revenues ........................................ | $250,000 |
| Variable expenses ..................................... | $120,000 |
| Fixed out-of-pocket operating costs ..................... | $70,000 |

When the project concludes in four years the working capital will be released for investment elsewhere within the company.

**Required:**
Calculate the net present value of this investment opportunity.

**PROBLEM 12–19   Simple Rate of Return; Payback Period LO12–1, LO12–6**
Paul Swanson has an opportunity to acquire a franchise from The Yogurt Place, Inc., to dispense frozen yogurt products under The Yogurt Place name. Mr. Swanson has assembled the following information relating to the franchise:

a.   A suitable location in a large shopping mall can be rented for $3,500 per month.
b.   Remodeling and necessary equipment would cost $270,000. The equipment would have a 15-year life and an $18,000 salvage value. Straight-line depreciation would be used, and the salvage value would be considered in computing depreciation.
c.   Based on similar outlets elsewhere, Mr. Swanson estimates that sales would total $300,000 per year. Ingredients would cost 20% of sales.
d.   Operating costs would include $70,000 per year for salaries, $3,500 per year for insurance, and $27,000 per year for utilities. In addition, Mr. Swanson would have to pay a commission to The Yogurt Place, Inc., of 12.5% of sales.

*Required:*
1. Prepare a contribution format income statement that shows the expected net operating income each year from the franchise outlet.
2. Compute the simple rate of return promised by the outlet. If Mr. Swanson requires a simple rate of return of at least 12%, should he acquire the franchise?
3. Compute the payback period on the outlet. If Mr. Swanson wants a payback of four years or less, will he acquire the franchise?

**PROBLEM 12–20    Net Present Value Analysis; Uncertain Cash Flows** LO12–2, LO12–4

"I'm not sure we should lay out $250,000 for that automated welding machine," said Jim Alder, president of the Superior Equipment Company. "That's a lot of money, and it would cost us $80,000 for software and installation, and another $36,000 per year just to maintain the thing. In addition, the manufacturer admits it would cost $45,000 more at the end of three years to replace worn-out parts."

"I admit it's a lot of money," said Franci Rogers, the controller. "But you know the turnover problem we've had with the welding crew. This machine would replace six welders at a cost savings of $108,000 per year. And we would save another $6,500 per year in reduced material waste. When you figure that the automated welder would last for six years, I'm sure the return would be greater than our 16% required rate of return."

"I'm still not convinced," countered Mr. Alder. "We can only get $12,000 scrap value out of our old welding equipment if we sell it now, and in six years the new machine will only be worth $20,000 for parts. But have your people work up the figures and we'll talk about them at the executive committee meeting tomorrow."

*Required:*
1. Compute the annual net cost savings promised by the automated welding machine.
2. Using the data from (1) above and other data from the problem, compute the automated welding machine's net present value. Would you recommend purchasing the automated welding machine? Explain.
3. Assume that management can identify several intangible benefits associated with the automated welding machine, including greater flexibility in shifting from one type of product to another, improved quality of output, and faster delivery as a result of reduced throughput time. What minimum dollar value per year would management have to attach to these intangible benefits in order to make the new welding machine an acceptable investment?

**PROBLEM 12–21    Preference Ranking of Investment Projects** LO12–5

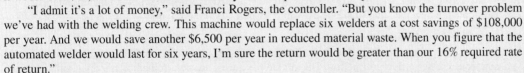

The management of Revco Products is exploring four different investment opportunities. Information on the four projects under study follows:

|  | Project Number | | | |
|---|---|---|---|---|
|  | 1 | 2 | 3 | 4 |
| Investment required | $(270,000) | $(450,000) | $(360,000) | $(480,000) |
| Present value of cash inflows at a 10% discount rate | 336,140 | 522,970 | 433,400 | 567,270 |
| Net present value | $ 66,140 | $ 72,970 | $ 73,400 | $ 87,270 |
| Life of the project | 6 years | 3 years | 12 years | 6 years |
| Internal rate of return | 18% | 19% | 14% | 16% |

Because the company's required rate of return is 10%, a 10% discount rate has been used in the present value computations above. Limited funds are available for investment, so the company can't accept all of the available projects.

*Required:*
1. Compute the project profitability index for each investment project.
2. Rank the four projects according to preference, in terms of:
   a. Net present value
   b. Project profitability index
   c. Internal rate of return
3. Which ranking do you prefer? Why?

**PROBLEM 12–22    Net Present Value Analysis LO12–2**

The Sweetwater Candy Company would like to buy a new machine that would automatically "dip" choco-lates. The dipping operation currently is done largely by hand. The machine the company is considering costs $120,000. The manufacturer estimates that the machine would be usable for five years but would require the replacement of several key parts at the end of the third year. These parts would cost $9,000, including installation. After five years, the machine could be sold for $7,500.

    The company estimates that the cost to operate the machine will be $7,000 per year. The present method of dipping chocolates costs $30,000 per year. In addition to reducing costs, the new machine will increase production by 6,000 boxes of chocolates per year. The company realizes a contribution margin of $1.50 per box. A 20% rate of return is required on all investments.

**Required:**
1. What are the annual net cash inflows that will be provided by the new dipping machine?
2. Compute the new machine's net present value. Round all dollar amounts to the nearest whole dollar.

**PROBLEM 13–23    Comprehensive Problem LO12–1, LO12–2, LO12–3, LO12–5, LO12–6**

Lou Barlow, a divisional manager for Sage Company, has an opportunity to manufacture and sell one of two new products for a five-year period. His annual pay raises are determined by his division's return on investment (ROI), which has exceeded 18% each of the last three years. He has computed the cost and revenue estimates for each product as follows:

|  | Product A | Product B |
|---|---|---|
| **Initial investment:** | | |
| Cost of equipment (zero salvage value) . . . . . . . | $170,000 | $380,000 |
| **Annual revenues and costs:** | | |
| Sales revenues . . . . . . . . . . . . . . . . . . . . . . . . . . | $250,000 | $350,000 |
| Variable expenses . . . . . . . . . . . . . . . . . . . . . . . | $120,000 | $170,000 |
| Depreciation expense . . . . . . . . . . . . . . . . . . . . . | $34,000 | $76,000 |
| Fixed out-of-pocket operating costs . . . . . . . . . . | $70,000 | $50,000 |

The company's discount rate is 16%.

**Required:**
1. Calculate the payback period for each product.
2. Calculate the net present value for each product.
3. Calculate the internal rate of return for each product.
4. Calculate the project profitability index for each product.
5. Calculate the simple rate of return for each product.
6. Which of the two products should Lou's division pursue? Why?

**PROBLEM 12–24    Simple Rate of Return; Payback Period; Internal Rate of Return LO12–1, LO12–3, LO12–6**

The Elberta Fruit Farm of Ontario always has hired transient workers to pick its annual cherry crop. Janessa Wright, the farm manager, just received information on a cherry picking machine that is being purchased by many fruit farms. The machine is a motorized device that shakes the cherry tree, caus-ing the cherries to fall onto plastic tarps that funnel the cherries into bins. Ms. Wright has gathered the following information to decide whether a cherry picker would be a profitable investment for the Elberta Fruit Farm:

a.  Currently, the farm is paying an average of $40,000 per year to transient workers to pick the cherries.
b.  The cherry picker would cost $94,500, and it would have an estimated 12-year useful life. The farm uses straight-line depreciation on all assets and considers salvage value in computing depreciation expense. The estimated salvage value of the cherry picker is $4,500.
c.  Annual out-of-pocket costs associated with the cherry picker would be: cost of an operator and an assistant, $14,000; insurance, $200; fuel, $1,800; and a maintenance contract, $3,000.

**Required:**
1. Determine the annual savings in cash operating costs that would be realized if the cherry picker was purchased.

2. Compute the simple rate of return expected from the cherry picker. Would the cherry picker be purchased if Elberta Fruit Farm's required rate of return is 16%?

3. Compute the payback period on the cherry picker. The Elberta Fruit Farm will not purchase equipment unless it has a payback period of five years or less. Would the cherry picker be purchased?

4. Compute (to the nearest whole percent) the internal rate of return promised by the cherry picker. Based on this computation, does it appear that the simple rate of return is an accurate guide in investment decisions?

### PROBLEM 12–25   Net Present Value Analysis of a Lease or Buy Decision LO12–2

The Riteway Ad Agency provides cars for its sales staff. In the past, the company has always purchased its cars from a dealer and then sold the cars after three years of use. The company's present fleet of cars is three years old and will be sold very shortly. To provide a replacement fleet, the company is considering two alternatives:

*Purchase alternative:*  The company can purchase the cars, as in the past, and sell the cars after three years of use. Ten cars will be needed, which can be purchased at a discounted price of $17,000 each. If this alternative is accepted, the following costs will be incurred on the fleet as a whole:

| | |
|---|---|
| Annual cost of servicing, taxes, and licensing . . . . . | $3,000 |
| Repairs, first year . . . . . . . . . . . . . . . . . . . . . . . . . . . | $1,500 |
| Repairs, second year . . . . . . . . . . . . . . . . . . . . . . . . | $4,000 |
| Repairs, third year . . . . . . . . . . . . . . . . . . . . . . . . . . | $6,000 |

At the end of three years, the fleet could be sold for one-half of the original purchase price.

*Lease alternative:*  The company can lease the cars under a three-year lease contract. The lease cost would be $55,000 per year (the first payment due at the end of Year 1). As part of this lease cost, the owner would provide all servicing and repairs, license the cars, and pay all the taxes. Riteway would be required to make a $10,000 security deposit at the beginning of the lease period, which would be refunded when the cars were returned to the owner at the end of the lease contract.

Riteway Ad Agency's required rate of return is 18%.

#### Required:

1. What is the net present value of the cash flows associated with the purchase alternative? Round all dollar amounts to the nearest whole dollar.
2. What is the net present value of the cash flows associated with the lease alternative? Round all dollar amounts to the nearest whole dollar.
3. Which alternative should the company accept?

### PROBLEM 12–26   Simple Rate of Return; Payback LO12–1, LO12–6

Sharkey's Fun Center contains a number of electronic games as well as a miniature golf course and various rides located outside the building. Paul Sharkey, the owner, would like to construct a water slide on one portion of his property. Mr. Sharkey gathered the following information about the slide:

a. Water slide equipment could be purchased and installed at a cost of $330,000. According to the manufacturer, the slide would be usable for 12 years after which it would have no salvage value.
b. Mr. Sharkey would use straight-line depreciation on the slide equipment.
c. To make room for the water slide, several rides would be dismantled and sold. These rides are fully depreciated, but they could be sold for $60,000 to an amusement park in a nearby city.
d. Mr. Sharkey concluded that about 50,000 more people would use the water slide each year than have been using the rides. The admission price would be $3.60 per person (the same price the Fun Center has been charging for the old rides).
e. Based on experience at other water slides, Mr. Sharkey estimates that annual incremental operating expenses for the slide would be: salaries, $85,000; insurance, $4,200; utilities, $13,000; and maintenance, $9,800.

#### Required:

1. Prepare an income statement showing the expected net operating income each year from the water slide.
2. Compute the simple rate of return expected from the water slide. Based on this computation, would the water slide be constructed if Mr. Sharkey requires a simple rate of return of at least 14% on all investments?

3.  Compute the payback period for the water slide. If Mr. Sharkey accepts any project with a payback period of five years or less, would the water slide be constructed?

**PROBLEM 12–27    Net Present Value Analysis LO12–2**

In five years, Kent Duncan will retire. He is exploring the possibility of opening a self-service car wash. The car wash could be managed in the free time he has available from his regular occupation, and it could be closed easily when he retires. After careful study, Mr. Duncan determined the following:

a.  A building in which a car wash could be installed is available under a five-year lease at a cost of $1,700 per month.
b.  Purchase and installation costs of equipment would total $200,000. In five years the equipment could be sold for about 10% of its original cost.
c.  An investment of an additional $2,000 would be required to cover working capital needs for cleaning supplies, change funds, and so forth. After five years, this working capital would be released for investment elsewhere.
d.  Both a wash and a vacuum service would be offered. Each customer would pay $2.00 for a wash and $1.00 for access to a vacuum cleaner.
e.  The only variable costs associated with the operation would be 20 cents per wash for water and 10 cents per use of the vacuum for electricity.
f.  In addition to rent, monthly costs of operation would be: cleaning, $450; insurance, $75; and maintenance, $500.
g.  Gross receipts from the wash would be about $1,350 per week. According to the experience of other car washes, 60% of the customers using the wash would also use the vacuum.

Mr. Duncan will not open the car wash unless it provides at least a 10% return.

***Required:***

1.  Assuming the car wash will be open 52 weeks a year, compute the expected annual net cash receipts (gross cash receipts less cash disbursements) from its operation. (Do not include the cost of the equipment, the working capital, or the salvage value in these computations.)
2.  What is the net present value of the investment in the car wash? Would you advise Mr. Duncan to open the car wash? Round all dollar figures to the nearest whole dollar.

**PROBLEM 12–28    Net Present Value Analysis LO12–2**

Bilboa Freightlines, S.A., of Panama, has a small truck that it uses for intracity deliveries. The truck is worn out and must be either overhauled or replaced with a new truck. The company has assembled the following information:

|  | Present Truck | New Truck |
|---|---|---|
| Purchase cost (new) . . . . . . . . . . . . . . . . | $21,000 | $30,000 |
| Remaining book value . . . . . . . . . . . . . . . | $11,500 | |
| Overhaul needed now . . . . . . . . . . . . . . . | $7,000 | |
| Annual cash operating costs . . . . . . . . . | $10,000 | $6,500 |
| Salvage value-now . . . . . . . . . . . . . . . . . | $9,000 | |
| Salvage value-five years from now . . . . | $1,000 | $4,000 |

If the company keeps and overhauls its present delivery truck, then the truck will be usable for five more years. If a new truck is purchased, it will be used for five years, after which it will be traded in on another truck. The new truck would be diesel-operated, resulting in a substantial reduction in annual operating costs, as shown above.

The company computes depreciation on a straight-line basis. All investment projects are evaluated using a 16% discount rate.

***Required:***

1.  What is the net present value of the "keep the old truck" alternative? Round to the nearest whole dollar.
2.  What is the net present value of the "purchase the new truck" alternative? Round to the nearest whole dollar.
3.  Should Bilboa Freightlines keep the old truck or purchase the new one?

**PROBLEM 12–29    Net Present Value Analysis LO12–2**

Linda Clark received $175,000 from her mother's estate. She placed the funds into the hands of a broker, who purchased the following securities on Linda's behalf:

a.  Common stock was purchased at a cost of $95,000. The stock paid no dividends, but it was sold for $160,000 at the end of three years.
b.  Preferred stock was purchased at its par value of $30,000. The stock paid a 6% dividend (based on par value) each year for three years. At the end of three years, the stock was sold for $27,000.
c.  Bonds were purchased at a cost of $50,000. The bonds paid annual interest of $6,000. After three years, the bonds were sold for $52,700.

The securities were all sold at the end of three years so that Linda would have funds available to open a new business venture. The broker stated that the investments had earned more than a 16% return, and he gave Linda the following computations to support his statement:

| | |
|---|---:|
| Common stock: | |
| Gain on sale ($160,000 − $95,000) . . . . . . . . . | $65,000 |
| Preferred stock: | |
| Dividends paid (6% × $30,000 × 3 years) . . . . | 5,400 |
| Loss on sale ($27,000 − $30,000) . . . . . . . . . . | (3,000) |
| Bonds: | |
| Interest paid ($6,000 × 3 years) . . . . . . . . . . . . | 18,000 |
| Gain on sale ($52,700 − $50,000) . . . . . . . . . . | 2,700 |
| Net gain on all investments . . . . . . . . . . . . . . . . | $88,100 |

$$\frac{\$88,100 \div 3 \text{ years}}{\$175,000} = 16.8\%$$

**Required:**

1.  Using a 16% discount rate, compute the net present value of each of the three investments. On which investment(s) did Linda earn a 16% rate of return? (Round computations to the nearest whole dollar.)
2.  Considering all three investments together, did Linda earn a 16% rate of return? Explain.
3.  Linda wants to use the $239,700 proceeds ($160,000 + $27,000 + $52,700 = $239,700) from sale of the securities to open a retail store under a 12-year franchise contract. What minimum annual net cash inflow must the store generate for Linda to earn a 14% return over the 12-year period? Round computations to the nearest whole dollar.

**PROBLEM 12–30    Net Present Value Analysis; Uncertain Future Cash Flows; Postaudit LO12–2, LO12–4**

Saxon Products, Inc., is investigating the purchase of a robot for use on the company's assembly line. Selected data relating to the robot are provided below:

| | |
|---|---:|
| Cost of the robot . . . . . . . . . . . . . . . . . . . . . . . . . . . . . . . . . | $1,600,000 |
| Installation and software . . . . . . . . . . . . . . . . . . . . . . . . . . . | $450,000 |
| Annual savings in inventory carrying costs . . . . . . . . . . . | $210,000 |
| Annual increase in power and maintenance costs . . . . . . | $30,000 |
| Salvage value in 5 years . . . . . . . . . . . . . . . . . . . . . . . . . . . | $70,000 |
| Useful life . . . . . . . . . . . . . . . . . . . . . . . . . . . . . . . . . . . . . . . | 5 years |

In addition to the data above, engineering studies suggest that use of the robot will result in a savings of 25,000 direct labor-hours each year. The labor rate is $16 per hour. Also, the smoother work flow made possible by the use of automation will allow the company to reduce the amount of inventory on hand by $400,000. This inventory reduction will take place at the end of the first year of operation; the released funds will be available for use elsewhere in the company. Saxon Products has a 20% required rate of return.

***Required:***

1. Determine the *annual net* cost savings if the robot is purchased. (Do not include the $400,000 inventory reduction or the salvage value in this computation.)

2. Compute the net present value of the proposed investment in the robot. Based on these data, would you recommend that the robot be purchased? Explain.

3. Assume that the robot is purchased. However, due to unforeseen problems, software and installation costs were $75,000 more than estimated and direct labor could only be reduced by 22,500 hours per year, rather than the original estimate of 25,000 hours. Assuming that all other cost data is accurate, what would a postaudit suggest is the actual net present value of this investment? Does it appear that the company made a wise investment?

4. Upon seeing your analysis in (3) above, Saxon's president stated, "That robot is the worst investment we've ever made. And now we'll be stuck with it for years."

   a. Explain to the president what benefits other than cost savings might accrue from using the new automated equipment.

   b. Compute for the president the minimum dollar amount of annual cash inflow that would be needed from the benefits in (a) above for the automated equipment to yield a 20% rate of return.

## CASES

### ETHICS CHALLENGE

The Fore Corporation is an integrated food processing company that has operations in over two dozen countries. Fore's corporate headquarters are in Chicago, and the company's executives frequently travel to visit Fore's foreign and domestic facilities.

Fore has a fleet of aircraft that consists of two business jets with international range and six smaller turboprop aircraft that are used on shorter flights. Company policy is to assign aircraft to trips on the basis of minimizing cost; however, the practice has been to assign the aircraft based on the organizational rank of the traveler. Fore offers its aircraft for short-term lease or for charter by other organizations whenever Fore itself does not plan to use the aircraft. Fore surveys the market often in order to keep its lease and charter rates competitive.

William Earle, Fore's vice president of finance, has claimed that a third business jet can be justified financially. However, some people in the controller's office have surmised that the real reason for a third business jet was to upgrade the aircraft used by Earle. Presently, the people outranking Earle keep the two business jets busy with the result that Earle usually flies in smaller turboprop aircraft.

The third business jet would cost $11 million. A capital expenditure of this magnitude requires a formal proposal with projected cash flows and net present value computations using Fore's minimum required rate of return. If Fore's president and the finance committee of the board of directors approve the proposal, it will be submitted to the full board of directors. The board has final approval on capital expenditures exceeding $5 million and has established a firm policy of rejecting any discretionary proposal that has a negative net present value.

Earle asked Rachel Arnett, assistant corporate controller, to prepare a proposal on a third business jet. Arnett gathered the following data:

- Acquisition cost of the aircraft, including instrumentation and interior furnishing.
- Operating cost of the aircraft for company use.
- Projected avoidable commercial airfare and other avoidable costs from company use of the plane.
- Projected value of executive time saved by using the third business jet.
- Projected contribution margin from incremental lease and charter activity.
- Estimated resale value of the aircraft.

When Earle reviewed Arnett's completed proposal and saw the large negative net present value figure, he returned the proposal to Arnett. With a glare, Earle commented, "You must have made an error. The proposal should look better than that."

Feeling some pressure, Arnett went back and checked her computations; she found no errors. However, Earle's message was clear. Arnett discarded her projections that she believed were reasonable and replaced them with figures that had a remote chance of actually occurring but were more favorable to the proposal. For example, she used first-class airfares to refigure the avoidable commercial airfare costs, even though company policy was to fly coach. She found revising the proposal to be distressing.

The revised proposal still had a negative net present value. Earle's anger was evident as he told Arnett to revise the proposal again, and to start with a $100,000 positive net present value and work backwards to compute supporting projections.

**Required:**
1. Explain whether Rachel Arnett's revision of the proposal was in violation of the IMA's Statement of Ethical Professional Practice.
2. Was William Earle in violation of the IMA's Statement of Ethical Professional Practice by telling Arnett specifically how to revise the proposal? Explain your answer.
3. Identify specific internal controls that Fore Corporation could implement to prevent unethical behavior on the part of the vice president of finance.

(CMA, adapted)

**CASE LO12–2**
Matheson Electronics has just developed a new electronic device it believes will have broad market appeal. The company has performed marketing and cost studies that revealed the following information:

a. New equipment would have to be acquired to produce the device. The equipment would cost $315,000 and have a six-year useful life. After six years, it would have a salvage value of about $15,000.
b. Sales in units over the next six years are projected to be as follows:

| Year | Sales in Units |
|---|---|
| 1 | 9,000 |
| 2 | 15,000 |
| 3 | 18,000 |
| 4–6 | 22,000 |

c. Production and sales of the device would require working capital of $60,000 to finance accounts receivable, inventories, and day-to-day cash needs. This working capital would be released at the end of the project's life.
d. The devices would sell for $35 each; variable costs for production, administration, and sales would be $15 per unit.
e. Fixed costs for salaries, maintenance, property taxes, insurance, and straight-line depreciation on the equipment would total $135,000 per year. (Depreciation is based on cost less salvage value.)
f. To gain rapid entry into the market, the company would have to advertise heavily. The advertising costs would be:

| Year | Amount of Yearly Advertising |
|---|---|
| 1–2 | $180,000 |
| 3 | $150,000 |
| 4–6 | $120,000 |

g. The company's required rate of return is 14%.

**Required:**
1. Compute the net cash inflow (incremental contribution margin minus incremental fixed expenses) anticipated from sale of the device for each year over the next six years.
2. Using the data computed in (1) above and other data provided in the problem, determine the net present value of the proposed investment. Would you recommend that Matheson accept the device as a new product?

# APPENDIX 12A: THE CONCEPT OF PRESENT VALUE

A dollar received today is more valuable than a dollar received a year from now for the simple reason that if you have a dollar today, you can put it in the bank and have more than a dollar a year from now. Because dollars today are worth more than dollars in the future, cash flows that are received at different times must be valued differently.

## The Mathematics of Interest

If a bank pays 5% interest, then a deposit of $100 today will be worth $105 one year from now. This can be expressed as follows:

$$F_1 = P(1 + r) \tag{1}$$

where $F_1$ = the balance at the end of one period, $P$ = the amount invested now, and $r$ = the rate of interest per period.

In the case where $100 is deposited in a savings account that earns 5% interest, $P = \$100$ and $r = 0.05$. Under these conditions, $F_1 = \$105$.

The $100 present outlay is called the **present value** of the $105 amount to be received in one year. It is also known as the *discounted value* of the future $105 receipt. The $100 represents the value in present terms of $105 to be received a year from now when the interest rate is 5%.

**Compound Interest**   What if the $105 is left in the bank for a second year? In that case, by the end of the second year the original $100 deposit will have grown to $110.25:

| | |
|---|---:|
| Original deposit .................................. | $100.00 |
| Interest for the first year: | |
| $100 × 0.05 .................................... | 5.00 |
| Balance at the end of the first year .................. | 105.00 |
| Interest for the second year: | |
| $105 × 0.05 .................................... | 5.25 |
| Balance at the end of the second year .............. | $110.25 |

Notice that the interest for the second year is $5.25, as compared to only $5.00 for the first year. This difference arises because interest is being paid on interest during the second year. That is, the $5.00 interest earned during the first year has been left in the account and has been added to the original $100 deposit when computing interest for the second year. This is known as **compound interest**. In this case, the compounding is annual. Interest can be compounded on a semiannual, quarterly, monthly, or even more frequent basis. The more frequently compounding is done, the more rapidly the balance will grow.

We can determine the balance in an account after $n$ periods of compounding using the following equation:

$$F_n = P(1 + r)^n \tag{2}$$

where $n$ = the number of periods of compounding.

If $n = 2$ years and the interest rate is 5% per year, then the balance in two years will be computed as follows:

$$F_2 = \$100(1 + 0.05)^2$$
$$F_2 = \$110.25$$

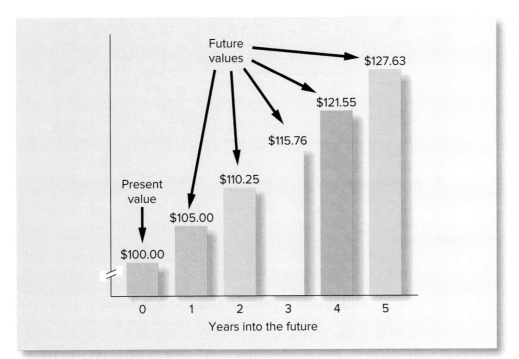

**Present Value and Future Value**   Exhibit 12A–1 shows the relationship between present value and future value. As shown in the exhibit, if $100 is deposited in a bank at 5% interest compounded annually, it will grow to $127.63 by the end of five years.

## Computation of Present Value

An investment can be viewed in two ways—either in terms of its future value or in terms of its present value. We have seen from our computations above that if we know the present value of a sum (such as our $100 deposit), the future value in $n$ years can be computed by using equation (2). But what if the situation is reversed and we know the *future* value of some amount but we do not know its present value?

For example, assume that you are to receive $200 two years from now. You know that the future value of this sum is $200 because this is the amount that you will be receiving in two years. But what is the sum's present value—what is it worth *right now?* The present value of any sum to be received in the future can be computed by turning equation (2) around and solving for $P$:

$$P = \frac{F_n}{(1 + r)^n} \qquad (3)$$

In our example, $F_n = \$200$ (the amount to be received in the future), $r = 0.05$ (the annual rate of interest), and $n = 2$ (the number of years in the future that the amount will be received).

$$P = \frac{\$200}{(1 + 0.05)^2}$$

$$P = \frac{\$200}{1.1025}$$

$$P = \$181.40$$

As shown by the computation above, the present value of a $200 amount to be received two years from now is $181.40 if the interest rate is 5%. In effect, $181.40 received *right now* is equivalent to $200 received two years from now.

The process of finding the present value of a future cash flow, which we have just completed, is called **discounting**. We have *discounted* the $200 to its present value of $181.40.

| Year | Factor at 12% (Exhibit 12B–1) | Interest Received | Present Value |
|------|------|------|------|
| 1 | 0.893 | $15,000 | $13,395 |
| 2 | 0.797 | $15,000 | 11,955 |
| 3 | 0.712 | $15,000 | 10,680 |
| 4 | 0.636 | $15,000 | 9,540 |
| 5 | 0.567 | $15,000 | 8,505 |
| | | | $54,075 |

The 5% interest we used to find this present value is called the **discount rate**. Discounting future sums to their present value is a common practice in business, particularly in capital budgeting decisions.

If you have a power key ($y^x$) on your calculator, the above calculations are fairly easy. However, some of the present value formulas we will be using are more complex. Fortunately, tables are available in which many of the calculations have already been done. For example, Exhibit 12B–1 in Appendix 12B shows the discounted present value of $1 to be received at various periods in the future at various interest rates. The table indicates that the present value of $1 to be received two periods from now at 5% is 0.907. Because in our example we want to know the present value of $200 rather than just $1, we need to multiply the factor in the table by $200:

$$\$200 \times 0.907 = \$181.40$$

This answer is the same as we obtained earlier using the formula in equation (3).

## Present Value of a Series of Cash Flows

Although some investments involve a single sum to be received (or paid) at a single point in the future, other investments involve a *series* of cash flows. A series of identical cash flows is known as an **annuity**. To provide an example, assume that a company has just purchased some government bonds. The bonds will yield interest of $15,000 each year and will be held for five years. What is the present value of the stream of interest receipts from the bonds? As shown in Exhibit 12A–2, if the discount rate is 12%, the present value of this stream is $54,075. The discount factors used in this exhibit were taken from Exhibit 12B–1 in Appendix 12B.

Exhibit 12A–2 illustrates two important points. First, the present value of the $15,000 interest declines the further it is into the future. The present value of $15,000 received a year from now is $13,395, as compared to only $8,505 if received five years from now. This point underscores the time value of money.

The second point is that the computations used in Exhibit 12A–2 involved unnecessary work. The same present value of $54,075 could have been obtained more easily by referring to Exhibit 12B–2 in Appendix 12B. Exhibit 12B–2 contains the present value of $1 to be received each year over a *series* of years at various interest rates. Exhibit 12B–2 has been derived by simply adding together the factors from Exhibit 12B–1, as follows:

| Year | Factors at 12% (from Exhibit 12B–1) |
|------|------|
| 1 | 0.893 |
| 2 | 0.797 |
| 3 | 0.712 |
| 4 | 0.636 |
| 5 | 0.567 |
| | 3.605 |

The sum of these five factors is 3.605. Notice from Exhibit 12B–2 that the factor for $1 to be received each year for five years at 12% is also 3.605. If we use this factor and multiply it by the $15,000 annual cash inflow, then we get the same $54,075 present value that we obtained earlier in Exhibit 12A–2.

$$\$15,000 \times 3.605 = \$54,075$$

Therefore, when computing the present value of a series of equal cash flows that begins at the end of period 1, Exhibit 12B–2 should be used.

To summarize, the present value tables in Appendix 12B should be used as follows:

Exhibit 12B–1: This table should be used to find the present value of a single cash flow (such as a single payment or receipt) occurring in the future.

Exhibit 12B–2: This table should be used to find the present value of a series of identical cash flows beginning at the end of the current period and continuing into the future.

The use of both of these tables is illustrated in various exhibits in the main body of the chapter. *When a present value factor appears in an exhibit, you should take the time to trace it back into either Exhibit 12B–1 or Exhibit 12B–2 to get acquainted with the tables and how they work.*

# APPENDIX 12A: REVIEW PROBLEM: BASIC PRESENT VALUE COMPUTATIONS

Each of the following situations is independent. Work out your own solution to each situation, and then check it against the solution provided.

1.  John plans to retire in 12 years. Upon retiring, he would like to take an extended vacation, which he expects will cost at least $40,000. What lump-sum amount must he invest now to have $40,000 at the end of 12 years if the rate of return is:
    a.  Eight percent?
    b.  Twelve percent?
2.  The Morgans would like to send their daughter to a music camp at the end of each of the next five years. The camp costs $1,000 a year. What lump-sum amount would have to be invested now to have $1,000 at the end of each year if the rate of return is:
    a.  Eight percent?
    b.  Twelve percent?
3.  You have just received an inheritance from a relative. You can either receive a $200,000 lump-sum amount at the end of 10 years or receive $14,000 at the end of each year for the next 10 years. If your discount rate is 12%, which alternative would you prefer?

**Solution to Review Problem**
1.  a.  The amount that must be invested now would be the present value of the $40,000, using a discount rate of 8%. From Exhibit 12B–1 in Appendix 12B, the factor for a discount rate of 8% for 12 periods is 0.397. Multiplying this discount factor by the $40,000 needed in 12 years will give the amount of the present investment required: $40,000 × 0.397 = $15,880.
    b.  We will proceed as we did in (*a*) above, but this time we will use a discount rate of 12%. From Exhibit 12B–1 in Appendix 12B, the factor for a discount rate of 12% for 12 periods is 0.257. Multiplying this discount factor by the $40,000 needed in 12 years will give the amount of the present investment required: $40,000 × 0.257 = $10,280.
    Notice that as the discount rate (desired rate of return) increases, the present value decreases.
2.  This part differs from (1) above in that we are now dealing with an annuity rather than with a single future sum. The amount that must be invested now is the present value of the $1,000 needed at the end of each year for five years. Because we are dealing with an annuity, or a series of annual cash flows, we must refer to Exhibit 12B–2 in Appendix 12B for the appropriate discount factor.

a. From Exhibit 12B–2 in Appendix 12B, the discount factor for 8% for five periods is 3.993. Therefore, the amount that must be invested now to have $1,000 available at the end of each year for five years is $1,000 × 3.993 = $3,993.

b. From Exhibit 12B–2 in Appendix 12B, the discount factor for 12% for five periods is 3.605. Therefore, the amount that must be invested now to have $1,000 available at the end of each year for five years is $1,000 × 3.605 = $3,605.

Again, notice that as the discount rate increases, the present value decreases. When the rate of return increases, less must be invested today to yield a given amount in the future.

3.  For this part we will need to refer to both Exhibits 12B–1 and 12B–2 in Appendix 12B. From Exhibit 12B–1, we will need to find the discount factor for 12% for 10 periods, then apply it to the $200,000 lump sum to be received in 10 years. From Exhibit 12B–2, we will need to find the discount factor for 12% for 10 periods, then apply it to the series of $14,000 payments to be received over the 10-year period. Whichever alternative has the higher present value is the one that should be selected.

$$\$200,000 \times 0.322 = \$64,400$$
$$\$14,000 \times 5.650 = \$79,100$$

Thus, you should prefer to receive the $14,000 per year for 10 years rather than the $200,000 lump sum. This means that you could invest the $14,000 received at the end of each year at 12% and have *more* than $200,000 at the end of 10 years.

# GLOSSARY (APPENDIX 12A)

**Annuity**   A series of identical cash flows. (p. 608)
**Compound interest**   The process of paying interest on interest in an investment. (p. 606)
**Discount rate**   The rate of return that is used to find the present value of a future cash flow. (p. 608)
**Discounting**   The process of finding the present value of a future cash flow. (p. 607)
**Present value**   The value now of an amount that will be received in some future period. (p. 606)

# APPENDIX 12A: EXERCISES   connect

### EXERCISE 12A–1   Basic Present Value Concepts LO12–7
Annual cash inflows that will arise from two competing investment projects are given below:

| Year | Investment A | Investment B |
|------|-------------|-------------|
| 1 ................. | $ 3,000 | $12,000 |
| 2 ................. | 6,000 | 9,000 |
| 3 ................. | 9,000 | 6,000 |
| 4 ................. | 12,000 | 3,000 |
| | $30,000 | $30,000 |

The discount rate is 18%.

*Required:*
Compute the present value of the cash inflows for each investment.

### EXERCISE 12A–2   Basic Present Value Concepts LO12–7
Julie has just retired. Her company's retirement program has two options as to how retirement benefits can be received. Under the first option, Julie would receive a lump sum of $150,000 immediately as her full retirement benefit. Under the second option, she would receive $14,000 each year for 20 years plus a lump-sum payment of $60,000 at the end of the 20-year period.

*Required:*
If she can invest money at 12%, which option would you recommend that she accept? Use present value analysis.

**EXERCISE 12A–3   Basic Present Value Concepts LO12–7**
In three years, when he is discharged from the Air Force, Steve wants to buy an $8,000 power boat.

*Required:*
What lump-sum amount must Steve invest now to have the $8,000 at the end of three years if he can invest money at:
1.   Ten percent?
2.   Fourteen percent?

**EXERCISE 12A–4   Basic Present Value Concepts LO12–7**
Fraser Company will need a new warehouse in five years. The warehouse will cost $500,000 to build.

*Required:*
What lump-sum amount should the company invest now to have the $500,000 available at the end of the five-year period? Assume that the company can invest money at:
1.   Ten percent.
2.   Fourteen percent.

**EXERCISE 12A–5   Basic Present Value Concepts LO12–7**
The Atlantic Medical Clinic can purchase a new computer system that will save $7,000 annually in billing costs. The computer system will last for eight years and have no salvage value.

*Required:*
What is the maximum price (i.e., the price that exactly equals the present value of the annual savings in billing costs) that the Atlantic Medical Clinic should be willing to pay for the new computer system if the clinic's required rate of return is:
1.   Sixteen percent?
2.   Twenty percent?

**EXERCISE 12A–6   Basic Present Value Concepts LO12–7**
The Caldwell Herald newspaper reported the following story: Frank Ormsby of Caldwell is the state's newest millionaire. By choosing the six winning numbers on last week's state lottery, Mr. Ormsby won the week's grand prize totaling $1.6 million. The State Lottery Commission indicated that Mr. Ormsby will receive his prize in 20 annual installments of $80,000 each.

*Required:*
1.   If Mr. Ormsby can invest money at a 12% rate of return, what is the present value of his winnings?
2.   Is it correct to say that Mr. Ormsby is the "state's newest millionaire"? Explain your answer.

# APPENDIX 12B: PRESENT VALUE TABLES

EXHIBIT 12B-1   Present Value of $1; $\frac{1}{(1+r)^n}$

| Periods | 4% | 5% | 6% | 7% | 8% | 9% | 10% | 11% | 12% | 13% | 14% | 15% | 16% | 17% | 18% | 19% | 20% | 21% | 22% | 23% | 24% | 25% |
|---|---|---|---|---|---|---|---|---|---|---|---|---|---|---|---|---|---|---|---|---|---|---|
| 1 | 0.962 | 0.952 | 0.943 | 0.935 | 0.926 | 0.917 | 0.909 | 0.901 | 0.893 | 0.885 | 0.877 | 0.870 | 0.862 | 0.855 | 0.847 | 0.840 | 0.833 | 0.826 | 0.820 | 0.813 | 0.806 | 0.800 |
| 2 | 0.925 | 0.907 | 0.890 | 0.873 | 0.857 | 0.842 | 0.826 | 0.812 | 0.797 | 0.783 | 0.769 | 0.756 | 0.743 | 0.731 | 0.718 | 0.706 | 0.694 | 0.683 | 0.672 | 0.661 | 0.650 | 0.640 |
| 3 | 0.889 | 0.864 | 0.840 | 0.816 | 0.794 | 0.772 | 0.751 | 0.731 | 0.712 | 0.693 | 0.675 | 0.658 | 0.641 | 0.624 | 0.609 | 0.593 | 0.579 | 0.564 | 0.551 | 0.537 | 0.524 | 0.512 |
| 4 | 0.855 | 0.823 | 0.792 | 0.763 | 0.735 | 0.708 | 0.683 | 0.659 | 0.636 | 0.613 | 0.592 | 0.572 | 0.552 | 0.534 | 0.516 | 0.499 | 0.482 | 0.467 | 0.451 | 0.437 | 0.423 | 0.410 |
| 5 | 0.822 | 0.784 | 0.747 | 0.713 | 0.681 | 0.650 | 0.621 | 0.593 | 0.567 | 0.543 | 0.519 | 0.497 | 0.476 | 0.456 | 0.437 | 0.419 | 0.402 | 0.386 | 0.370 | 0.355 | 0.341 | 0.328 |
| 6 | 0.790 | 0.746 | 0.705 | 0.666 | 0.630 | 0.596 | 0.564 | 0.535 | 0.507 | 0.480 | 0.456 | 0.432 | 0.410 | 0.390 | 0.370 | 0.352 | 0.335 | 0.319 | 0.303 | 0.289 | 0.275 | 0.262 |
| 7 | 0.760 | 0.711 | 0.665 | 0.623 | 0.583 | 0.547 | 0.513 | 0.482 | 0.452 | 0.425 | 0.400 | 0.376 | 0.354 | 0.333 | 0.314 | 0.296 | 0.279 | 0.263 | 0.249 | 0.235 | 0.222 | 0.210 |
| 8 | 0.731 | 0.677 | 0.627 | 0.582 | 0.540 | 0.502 | 0.467 | 0.434 | 0.404 | 0.376 | 0.351 | 0.327 | 0.305 | 0.285 | 0.266 | 0.249 | 0.233 | 0.218 | 0.204 | 0.191 | 0.179 | 0.168 |
| 9 | 0.703 | 0.645 | 0.592 | 0.544 | 0.500 | 0.460 | 0.424 | 0.391 | 0.361 | 0.333 | 0.308 | 0.284 | 0.263 | 0.243 | 0.225 | 0.209 | 0.194 | 0.180 | 0.167 | 0.155 | 0.144 | 0.134 |
| 10 | 0.676 | 0.614 | 0.558 | 0.508 | 0.463 | 0.422 | 0.386 | 0.352 | 0.322 | 0.295 | 0.270 | 0.247 | 0.227 | 0.208 | 0.191 | 0.176 | 0.162 | 0.149 | 0.137 | 0.126 | 0.116 | 0.107 |
| 11 | 0.650 | 0.585 | 0.527 | 0.475 | 0.429 | 0.388 | 0.350 | 0.317 | 0.287 | 0.261 | 0.237 | 0.215 | 0.195 | 0.178 | 0.162 | 0.148 | 0.135 | 0.123 | 0.112 | 0.103 | 0.094 | 0.086 |
| 12 | 0.625 | 0.557 | 0.497 | 0.444 | 0.397 | 0.356 | 0.319 | 0.286 | 0.257 | 0.231 | 0.208 | 0.187 | 0.168 | 0.152 | 0.137 | 0.124 | 0.112 | 0.102 | 0.092 | 0.083 | 0.076 | 0.069 |
| 13 | 0.601 | 0.530 | 0.469 | 0.415 | 0.368 | 0.326 | 0.290 | 0.258 | 0.229 | 0.204 | 0.182 | 0.163 | 0.145 | 0.130 | 0.116 | 0.104 | 0.093 | 0.084 | 0.075 | 0.068 | 0.061 | 0.055 |
| 14 | 0.577 | 0.505 | 0.442 | 0.388 | 0.340 | 0.299 | 0.263 | 0.232 | 0.205 | 0.181 | 0.160 | 0.141 | 0.125 | 0.111 | 0.099 | 0.088 | 0.078 | 0.069 | 0.062 | 0.055 | 0.049 | 0.044 |
| 15 | 0.555 | 0.481 | 0.417 | 0.362 | 0.315 | 0.275 | 0.239 | 0.209 | 0.183 | 0.160 | 0.140 | 0.123 | 0.108 | 0.095 | 0.084 | 0.074 | 0.065 | 0.057 | 0.051 | 0.045 | 0.040 | 0.035 |
| 16 | 0.534 | 0.458 | 0.394 | 0.339 | 0.292 | 0.252 | 0.218 | 0.188 | 0.163 | 0.141 | 0.123 | 0.107 | 0.093 | 0.081 | 0.071 | 0.062 | 0.054 | 0.047 | 0.042 | 0.036 | 0.032 | 0.028 |
| 17 | 0.513 | 0.436 | 0.371 | 0.317 | 0.270 | 0.231 | 0.198 | 0.170 | 0.146 | 0.125 | 0.108 | 0.093 | 0.080 | 0.069 | 0.060 | 0.052 | 0.045 | 0.039 | 0.034 | 0.030 | 0.026 | 0.023 |
| 18 | 0.494 | 0.416 | 0.350 | 0.296 | 0.250 | 0.212 | 0.180 | 0.153 | 0.130 | 0.111 | 0.095 | 0.081 | 0.069 | 0.059 | 0.051 | 0.044 | 0.038 | 0.032 | 0.028 | 0.024 | 0.021 | 0.018 |
| 19 | 0.475 | 0.396 | 0.331 | 0.277 | 0.232 | 0.194 | 0.164 | 0.138 | 0.116 | 0.098 | 0.083 | 0.070 | 0.060 | 0.051 | 0.043 | 0.037 | 0.031 | 0.027 | 0.023 | 0.020 | 0.017 | 0.014 |
| 20 | 0.456 | 0.377 | 0.312 | 0.258 | 0.215 | 0.178 | 0.149 | 0.124 | 0.104 | 0.087 | 0.073 | 0.061 | 0.051 | 0.043 | 0.037 | 0.031 | 0.026 | 0.022 | 0.019 | 0.016 | 0.014 | 0.012 |
| 21 | 0.439 | 0.359 | 0.294 | 0.242 | 0.199 | 0.164 | 0.135 | 0.112 | 0.093 | 0.077 | 0.064 | 0.053 | 0.044 | 0.037 | 0.031 | 0.026 | 0.022 | 0.018 | 0.015 | 0.013 | 0.011 | 0.009 |
| 22 | 0.422 | 0.342 | 0.278 | 0.226 | 0.184 | 0.150 | 0.123 | 0.101 | 0.083 | 0.068 | 0.056 | 0.046 | 0.038 | 0.032 | 0.026 | 0.022 | 0.018 | 0.015 | 0.013 | 0.011 | 0.009 | 0.007 |
| 23 | 0.406 | 0.326 | 0.262 | 0.211 | 0.170 | 0.138 | 0.112 | 0.091 | 0.074 | 0.060 | 0.049 | 0.040 | 0.033 | 0.027 | 0.022 | 0.018 | 0.015 | 0.012 | 0.010 | 0.009 | 0.007 | 0.006 |
| 24 | 0.390 | 0.310 | 0.247 | 0.197 | 0.158 | 0.126 | 0.102 | 0.082 | 0.066 | 0.053 | 0.043 | 0.035 | 0.028 | 0.023 | 0.019 | 0.015 | 0.013 | 0.010 | 0.008 | 0.007 | 0.006 | 0.005 |
| 25 | 0.375 | 0.295 | 0.233 | 0.184 | 0.146 | 0.116 | 0.092 | 0.074 | 0.059 | 0.047 | 0.038 | 0.030 | 0.024 | 0.020 | 0.016 | 0.013 | 0.010 | 0.009 | 0.007 | 0.006 | 0.005 | 0.004 |
| 26 | 0.361 | 0.281 | 0.220 | 0.172 | 0.135 | 0.106 | 0.084 | 0.066 | 0.053 | 0.042 | 0.033 | 0.026 | 0.021 | 0.017 | 0.014 | 0.011 | 0.009 | 0.007 | 0.006 | 0.005 | 0.004 | 0.003 |
| 27 | 0.347 | 0.268 | 0.207 | 0.161 | 0.125 | 0.098 | 0.076 | 0.060 | 0.047 | 0.037 | 0.029 | 0.023 | 0.018 | 0.014 | 0.011 | 0.009 | 0.007 | 0.006 | 0.005 | 0.004 | 0.003 | 0.002 |
| 28 | 0.333 | 0.255 | 0.196 | 0.150 | 0.116 | 0.090 | 0.069 | 0.054 | 0.042 | 0.033 | 0.026 | 0.020 | 0.016 | 0.012 | 0.010 | 0.008 | 0.006 | 0.005 | 0.004 | 0.003 | 0.002 | 0.002 |
| 29 | 0.321 | 0.243 | 0.185 | 0.141 | 0.107 | 0.082 | 0.063 | 0.048 | 0.037 | 0.029 | 0.022 | 0.017 | 0.014 | 0.011 | 0.008 | 0.006 | 0.005 | 0.004 | 0.003 | 0.002 | 0.002 | 0.002 |
| 30 | 0.308 | 0.231 | 0.174 | 0.131 | 0.099 | 0.075 | 0.057 | 0.044 | 0.033 | 0.026 | 0.020 | 0.015 | 0.012 | 0.009 | 0.007 | 0.005 | 0.004 | 0.003 | 0.003 | 0.002 | 0.002 | 0.001 |
| 40 | 0.208 | 0.142 | 0.097 | 0.067 | 0.046 | 0.032 | 0.022 | 0.015 | 0.011 | 0.008 | 0.005 | 0.004 | 0.003 | 0.002 | 0.001 | 0.001 | 0.001 | 0.000 | 0.000 | 0.000 | 0.000 | 0.000 |

EXHIBIT 12B–2    Present Value of an Annuity of \$1 in Arrears; $\dfrac{1}{r}\left[1 - \dfrac{1}{(1+r)^n}\right]$

| Periods | 4% | 5% | 6% | 7% | 8% | 9% | 10% | 11% | 12% | 13% | 14% | 15% | 16% | 17% | 18% | 19% | 20% | 21% | 22% | 23% | 24% | 25% |
|---|---|---|---|---|---|---|---|---|---|---|---|---|---|---|---|---|---|---|---|---|---|---|
| 1 | 0.962 | 0.952 | 0.943 | 0.935 | 0.926 | 0.917 | 0.909 | 0.901 | 0.893 | 0.885 | 0.877 | 0.870 | 0.862 | 0.855 | 0.847 | 0.840 | 0.833 | 0.826 | 0.820 | 0.813 | 0.806 | 0.800 |
| 2 | 1.886 | 1.859 | 1.833 | 1.808 | 1.783 | 1.759 | 1.736 | 1.713 | 1.690 | 1.668 | 1.647 | 1.626 | 1.605 | 1.585 | 1.566 | 1.547 | 1.528 | 1.509 | 1.492 | 1.474 | 1.457 | 1.440 |
| 3 | 2.775 | 2.723 | 2.673 | 2.624 | 2.577 | 2.531 | 2.487 | 2.444 | 2.402 | 2.361 | 2.322 | 2.283 | 2.246 | 2.210 | 2.174 | 2.140 | 2.106 | 2.074 | 2.042 | 2.011 | 1.981 | 1.952 |
| 4 | 3.630 | 3.546 | 3.465 | 3.387 | 3.312 | 3.240 | 3.170 | 3.102 | 3.037 | 2.974 | 2.914 | 2.855 | 2.798 | 2.743 | 2.690 | 2.639 | 2.589 | 2.540 | 2.494 | 2.448 | 2.404 | 2.362 |
| 5 | 4.452 | 4.329 | 4.212 | 4.100 | 3.993 | 3.890 | 3.791 | 3.696 | 3.605 | 3.517 | 3.433 | 3.352 | 3.274 | 3.199 | 3.127 | 3.058 | 2.991 | 2.926 | 2.864 | 2.803 | 2.745 | 2.689 |
| 6 | 5.242 | 5.076 | 4.917 | 4.767 | 4.623 | 4.486 | 4.355 | 4.231 | 4.111 | 3.998 | 3.889 | 3.784 | 3.685 | 3.589 | 3.498 | 3.410 | 3.326 | 3.245 | 3.167 | 3.092 | 3.020 | 2.951 |
| 7 | 6.002 | 5.786 | 5.582 | 5.389 | 5.206 | 5.033 | 4.868 | 4.712 | 4.564 | 4.423 | 4.288 | 4.160 | 4.039 | 3.922 | 3.812 | 3.706 | 3.605 | 3.508 | 3.416 | 3.327 | 3.242 | 3.161 |
| 8 | 6.733 | 6.463 | 6.210 | 5.971 | 5.747 | 5.535 | 5.335 | 5.146 | 4.968 | 4.799 | 4.639 | 4.487 | 4.344 | 4.207 | 4.078 | 3.954 | 3.837 | 3.726 | 3.619 | 3.518 | 3.421 | 3.329 |
| 9 | 7.435 | 7.108 | 6.802 | 6.515 | 6.247 | 5.995 | 5.759 | 5.537 | 5.328 | 5.132 | 4.946 | 4.772 | 4.607 | 4.451 | 4.303 | 4.163 | 4.031 | 3.905 | 3.786 | 3.673 | 3.566 | 3.463 |
| 10 | 8.111 | 7.722 | 7.360 | 7.024 | 6.710 | 6.418 | 6.145 | 5.889 | 5.650 | 5.426 | 5.216 | 5.019 | 4.833 | 4.659 | 4.494 | 4.339 | 4.192 | 4.054 | 3.923 | 3.799 | 3.682 | 3.571 |
| 11 | 8.760 | 8.306 | 7.887 | 7.499 | 7.139 | 6.805 | 6.495 | 6.207 | 5.938 | 5.687 | 5.453 | 5.234 | 5.029 | 4.836 | 4.656 | 4.486 | 4.327 | 4.177 | 4.035 | 3.902 | 3.776 | 3.656 |
| 12 | 9.385 | 8.863 | 8.384 | 7.943 | 7.536 | 7.161 | 6.814 | 6.492 | 6.194 | 5.918 | 5.660 | 5.421 | 5.197 | 4.988 | 4.793 | 4.611 | 4.439 | 4.278 | 4.127 | 3.985 | 3.851 | 3.725 |
| 13 | 9.986 | 9.394 | 8.853 | 8.358 | 7.904 | 7.487 | 7.103 | 6.750 | 6.424 | 6.122 | 5.842 | 5.583 | 5.342 | 5.118 | 4.910 | 4.715 | 4.533 | 4.362 | 4.203 | 4.053 | 3.912 | 3.780 |
| 14 | 10.563 | 9.899 | 9.295 | 8.745 | 8.244 | 7.786 | 7.367 | 6.982 | 6.628 | 6.302 | 6.002 | 5.724 | 5.468 | 5.229 | 5.008 | 4.802 | 4.611 | 4.432 | 4.265 | 4.108 | 3.962 | 3.824 |
| 15 | 11.118 | 10.380 | 9.712 | 9.108 | 8.559 | 8.061 | 7.606 | 7.191 | 6.811 | 6.462 | 6.142 | 5.847 | 5.575 | 5.324 | 5.092 | 4.876 | 4.675 | 4.489 | 4.315 | 4.153 | 4.001 | 3.859 |
| 16 | 11.652 | 10.838 | 10.106 | 9.447 | 8.851 | 8.313 | 7.824 | 7.379 | 6.974 | 6.604 | 6.265 | 5.954 | 5.668 | 5.405 | 5.162 | 4.938 | 4.730 | 4.536 | 4.357 | 4.189 | 4.033 | 3.887 |
| 17 | 12.166 | 11.274 | 10.477 | 9.763 | 9.122 | 8.544 | 8.022 | 7.549 | 7.120 | 6.729 | 6.373 | 6.047 | 5.749 | 5.475 | 5.222 | 4.990 | 4.775 | 4.576 | 4.391 | 4.219 | 4.059 | 3.910 |
| 18 | 12.659 | 11.690 | 10.828 | 10.059 | 9.372 | 8.756 | 8.201 | 7.702 | 7.250 | 6.840 | 6.467 | 6.128 | 5.818 | 5.534 | 5.273 | 5.033 | 4.812 | 4.608 | 4.419 | 4.243 | 4.080 | 3.928 |
| 19 | 13.134 | 12.085 | 11.158 | 10.336 | 9.604 | 8.950 | 8.365 | 7.839 | 7.366 | 6.938 | 6.550 | 6.198 | 5.877 | 5.584 | 5.316 | 5.070 | 4.843 | 4.635 | 4.442 | 4.263 | 4.097 | 3.942 |
| 20 | 13.590 | 12.462 | 11.470 | 10.594 | 9.818 | 9.129 | 8.514 | 7.963 | 7.469 | 7.025 | 6.623 | 6.259 | 5.929 | 5.628 | 5.353 | 5.101 | 4.870 | 4.657 | 4.460 | 4.279 | 4.110 | 3.954 |
| 21 | 14.029 | 12.821 | 11.764 | 10.836 | 10.017 | 9.292 | 8.649 | 8.075 | 7.562 | 7.102 | 6.687 | 6.312 | 5.973 | 5.665 | 5.384 | 5.127 | 4.891 | 4.675 | 4.476 | 4.292 | 4.121 | 3.963 |
| 22 | 14.451 | 13.163 | 12.042 | 11.061 | 10.201 | 9.442 | 8.772 | 8.176 | 7.645 | 7.170 | 6.743 | 6.359 | 6.011 | 5.696 | 5.410 | 5.149 | 4.909 | 4.690 | 4.488 | 4.302 | 4.130 | 3.970 |
| 23 | 14.857 | 13.489 | 12.303 | 11.272 | 10.371 | 9.580 | 8.883 | 8.266 | 7.718 | 7.230 | 6.792 | 6.399 | 6.044 | 5.723 | 5.432 | 5.167 | 4.925 | 4.703 | 4.499 | 4.311 | 4.137 | 3.976 |
| 24 | 15.247 | 13.799 | 12.550 | 11.469 | 10.529 | 9.707 | 8.985 | 8.348 | 7.784 | 7.283 | 6.835 | 6.434 | 6.073 | 5.746 | 5.451 | 5.182 | 4.937 | 4.713 | 4.507 | 4.318 | 4.143 | 3.981 |
| 25 | 15.622 | 14.094 | 12.783 | 11.654 | 10.675 | 9.823 | 9.077 | 8.422 | 7.843 | 7.330 | 6.873 | 6.464 | 6.097 | 5.766 | 5.467 | 5.195 | 4.948 | 4.721 | 4.514 | 4.323 | 4.147 | 3.985 |
| 26 | 15.983 | 14.375 | 13.003 | 11.826 | 10.810 | 9.929 | 9.161 | 8.488 | 7.896 | 7.372 | 6.906 | 6.491 | 6.118 | 5.783 | 5.480 | 5.206 | 4.956 | 4.728 | 4.520 | 4.328 | 4.151 | 3.988 |
| 27 | 16.330 | 14.643 | 13.211 | 11.987 | 10.935 | 10.027 | 9.237 | 8.548 | 7.943 | 7.409 | 6.935 | 6.514 | 6.136 | 5.798 | 5.492 | 5.215 | 4.964 | 4.734 | 4.524 | 4.332 | 4.154 | 3.990 |
| 28 | 16.663 | 14.898 | 13.406 | 12.137 | 11.051 | 10.116 | 9.307 | 8.602 | 7.984 | 7.441 | 6.961 | 6.534 | 6.152 | 5.810 | 5.502 | 5.223 | 4.970 | 4.739 | 4.528 | 4.335 | 4.157 | 3.992 |
| 29 | 16.984 | 15.141 | 13.591 | 12.278 | 11.158 | 10.198 | 9.370 | 8.650 | 8.022 | 7.470 | 6.983 | 6.551 | 6.166 | 5.820 | 5.510 | 5.229 | 4.975 | 4.743 | 4.531 | 4.337 | 4.159 | 3.994 |
| 30 | 17.292 | 15.372 | 13.765 | 12.409 | 11.258 | 10.274 | 9.427 | 8.694 | 8.055 | 7.496 | 7.003 | 6.566 | 6.177 | 5.829 | 5.517 | 5.235 | 4.979 | 4.746 | 4.534 | 4.339 | 4.160 | 3.995 |
| 40 | 19.793 | 17.159 | 15.046 | 13.332 | 11.925 | 10.757 | 9.779 | 8.951 | 8.244 | 7.634 | 7.105 | 6.642 | 6.233 | 5.871 | 5.548 | 5.258 | 4.997 | 4.760 | 4.544 | 4.347 | 4.166 | 3.999 |

## A LOOK BACK

Capital budgeting decisions involve significant investments in long-term projects. Chapter 12 covered various techniques used for capital budgeting decisions.

## A LOOK AT THIS CHAPTER

The statement of cash flows provides invaluable information. After addressing the classification of various types of cash inflows and outflows, we discuss how to prepare the statement of cash flows and how to interpret it.

## A LOOK AHEAD

Chapter 14 explains how managers use financial statements to assess the financial health of their companies. It describes how to prepare comparative and common-size form financial statements and how to compute and interpret financial ratios.

# 13

# Statement of Cash Flows

## CHAPTER OUTLINE

**The Statement of Cash Flows: Key Concepts**

- Organizing the Statement of Cash Flows

- Operating Activities: Direct or Indirect Method?

- The Indirect Method: A Three-Step Process

- Investing and Financing Activities: Gross Cash Flows

- Summary of Key Concepts

**An Example of a Statement of Cash Flows**

- Operating Activities

- Investing Activities

- Financing Activities

- Seeing the Big Picture

**Interpreting the Statement of Cash Flows**

- Consider a Company's Specific Circumstances

- Consider the Relationships among Numbers

**Appendix 13A: The Direct Method of Determining the Net Cash Provided by Operating Activities**

- Similarities and Differences in the Handling of Data

- Specific Rules—Direct and Indirect Methods

©Bloomberg/Getty Images

*After studying Chapter 13, you should be able to:*

**LO13–1** Classify cash inflows and outflows as relating to operating, investing, or financing activities.

**LO13–2** Prepare a statement of cash flows using the indirect method to determine the net cash provided by operating activities.

**LO13–3** Compute free cash flow.

**LO13–4** (*Appendix 13A*) Use the direct method to determine the net cash provided by operating activities.

# Understanding Cash Flows

In 2015, **The Kroger Company**, the largest food and drug retailer in the United States, reported net income of $2.0 billion. During the same year the company spent $3.3 billion for plant and equipment, paid dividends totaling $385 million, paid off $1.2 billion of long-term debt, and spent $703 million to purchase shares of its own common stock. At first glance, these figures may seem confusing because Kroger is spending amounts of money that far exceed its net income. In this chapter you'll learn about the statement of cash flows that explains the relationship between a company's net income and its cash inflows and outflows.

Source: The Kroger Company, 2015 Form 10-K Annual Report, www.sec.gov/edgar/searchedgar/companysearch.html.

**T**hree major financial statements are required for external reports—an income statement, a balance sheet, and a statement of cash flows. The **statement of cash flows** highlights the major activities that impact cash flows and, hence, affect the overall cash balance. Managers focus on cash for a very good reason—without sufficient cash at the right times, a company may miss golden investment opportunities or may even go bankrupt.

The statement of cash flows answers questions that cannot be easily answered by looking at the income statement and balance sheet. For example, where did **Delta Airlines** get the cash to pay a dividend of nearly $140 million in a year in which, according to its income statement, it lost more than $1 billion? How was **The Walt Disney Company** able to invest nearly $800 million to expand and renovate its theme parks despite a loss of more than $500 million on its investment in EuroDisney? Where did **The Kroger Company** get $3.3 billion to invest in plant and equipment in a year when its net income was only $2.0 billion? The answers to such questions can be found on the statement of cash flows.

The statement of cash flows is a valuable analytical tool for managers as well as for investors and creditors, although managers tend to be more concerned with forecasted statements of cash flows that are prepared as part of the budgeting process. The statement of cash flows can be used to answer crucial questions such as:

1. Is the company generating sufficient positive cash flows from its ongoing operations to remain viable?
2. Will the company be able to repay its debts?
3. Will the company be able to pay its usual dividend?
4. Why do net income and net cash flow differ?
5. To what extent will the company have to borrow money in order to make needed investments?

Managers prepare the statement of cash flows by applying a fundamental principle of double-entry bookkeeping—the change in the cash balance must equal the changes in all other balance sheet accounts besides cash.[1] This principle ensures that properly analyzing the changes in all noncash balance sheet accounts always quantifies the cash inflows and outflows that explain the change in the cash balance. Our goal in this chapter is to translate this fairly complex principle into a small number of concepts and steps that simplify the process of preparing and interpreting a statement of cash flows.

Before delving into the specifics of how to prepare the statement of cash flows, we need to review two basic equations that apply to all asset, contra-asset, liability, and stockholders' equity accounts:

> *Basic Equation for Asset Accounts*
> Beginning balance + Debits − Credits = Ending balance
>
> *Basic Equation for Contra-Asset, Liability, and Stockholders' Equity Accounts*
> Beginning balance − Debits + Credits = Ending balance

These equations will help you compute various cash inflows and outflows that are reported in the statement of cash flows and they'll be referred to throughout the chapter.

---

[1]The statement of cash flows is based on the following fundamental balance sheet and income statement equations:
(1) Change in cash + Changes in noncash assets = Changes in liabilities + Changes in stockholders' equity
(2) Net cash flow = Change in cash
(3) Changes in stockholders' equity = Net income − Dividends + Changes in capital stock
These three equations can be used to derive the following equation:
(4) Net cash flow = Net income − Changes in noncash assets + Changes in liabilities − Dividends + Changes in capital stock
Essentially, the statement of cash flows, which explains net cash flow, is constructed by starting with net income and then adjusting it for changes in noncash balance sheet accounts.

## THE STATEMENT OF CASH FLOWS: KEY CONCEPTS

The statement of cash flows summarizes all of a company's cash inflows and outflows during a period, thereby explaining the change in its cash balance. In a statement of cash flows, cash is broadly defined to include both cash and cash equivalents. **Cash equivalents** consist of short-term, highly liquid investments such as Treasury bills, commercial paper, and money market funds that are made solely for the purpose of generating a return on temporarily idle funds. Most companies invest their excess cash reserves in these types of interest-bearing assets that can be easily converted into cash. Because such assets are equivalent to cash, they are included with cash in a statement of cash flows.

The remainder of this section discusses four key concepts that you'll need to understand to prepare a statement of cash flows. These four concepts include organizing the statement of cash flows, distinguishing between the direct and indirect methods of preparing a portion of the statement of cash flows, completing the three-step process underlying the indirect method, and recording gross cash flows where appropriate within a statement of cash flows.[2]

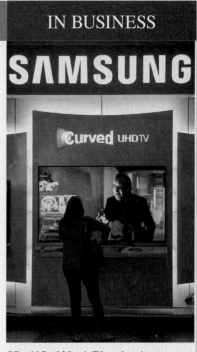

### IN BUSINESS

### Samsung's Enviable Cash Flows

**Samsung**'s cash and cash equivalents have reached $40 billion. The company is likely to use its cash for various purposes including research and development, marketing, making acquisitions in software and medical equipment, funding an increase in dividend payments, and buying back shares of its own stock. Samsung's cash hoard mirrors the types of enormous cash balance maintained by **Apple**. Apple's investors eventually pressured the company to increase its dividend per share and its stock repurchases.

Source: Wakabayashi, Daisuke, and Lee, Min-Jeong, "Samsung's Sweet Problem? Nearly $40 Billion in Cash," *The Wall Street Journal*, May 8, 2013, B1, B4.

©David Paul Morris/Bloomberg/ Getty Images

## Organizing the Statement of Cash Flows

To make it easier to compare data from different companies, U.S. generally accepted accounting principles (GAAP) and International Financial Reporting Standards (IFRS) require companies to follow prescribed rules when preparing the statement of cash flows. One of these rules requires organizing the statement into three sections that report cash

**LEARNING OBJECTIVE 13–1**

Classify cash inflows and outflows as relating to operating, investing, or financing activities.

---

[2]Another concept that relates to the statement of cash flows is direct exchange transactions, which refer to transactions where noncurrent balance sheet items are swapped. For example, a company might issue common stock in a direct exchange for property. Direct exchange transactions are not reported on the statement of cash flows; however, they are disclosed in a separate schedule that accompanies the statement. More advanced accounting courses cover this topic in greater detail. We will not include direct exchange transactions in this chapter.

| | Cash Inflow | Cash Outflow |
|---|:---:|:---:|
| **Operating activities** | | |
| Collecting cash from customers .......................... | √ | |
| Paying suppliers for inventory purchases .................... | | √ |
| Paying bills to insurers, utility providers, etc. ................ | | √ |
| Paying wages and salaries to employees ................... | | √ |
| Paying taxes to governmental bodies ...................... | | √ |
| Paying interest to lenders ................................ | | √ |
| **Investing activities** | | |
| Buying property, plant, and equipment ..................... | | √ |
| Selling property, plant, and equipment ..................... | √ | |
| Buying stocks and bonds as a long-term investment .......... | | √ |
| Selling stocks and bonds held for long-term investment ....... | √ | |
| Lending money to another entity .......................... | | √ |
| Collecting the principal on a loan to another entity ........... | √ | |
| **Financing activities** | | |
| Borrowing money from a creditor .......................... | √ | |
| Repaying the principal amount of a debt ................... | | √ |
| Collecting cash from the sale of common stock .............. | √ | |
| Paying cash to repurchase your own common stock .......... | | √ |
| Paying a dividend to stockholders ......................... | | √ |

flows resulting from *operating activities, investing activities,* and *financing activities.* **Operating activities** generate cash inflows and outflows related to revenue and expense transactions that affect net income. **Investing activities** generate cash inflows and outflows related to acquiring or disposing of noncurrent assets such as property, plant, and equipment, long-term investments, and loans to another entity. **Financing activities** generate cash inflows and outflows related to borrowing from and repaying principal to creditors and completing transactions with the company's owners, such as selling or repurchasing shares of common stock and paying dividends. The most common types of cash inflows and outflows resulting from these three activities are summarized in Exhibit 13–1.[3]

## Operating Activities: Direct or Indirect Method?

U.S. GAAP and IFRS allow companies to compute the net amount of cash inflows and outflows resulting from operating activities, which is known formally as the **net cash provided by operating activities,** using either the *direct* or *indirect* method. Both of these methods have the same purpose, which is to translate accrual-based net income to a cash basis. However, they approach this task in two different ways.

Under the **direct method,** the income statement is reconstructed on a cash basis from top to bottom. For example, cash collected from customers is listed instead of sales, and payments to suppliers is listed instead of cost of goods sold. In essence, cash receipts are counted as sales and cash disbursements pertaining to operating activities are counted as expenses. The difference between the cash receipts and cash disbursements is the net cash provided by operating activities.

Under the **indirect method,** net income is adjusted to a cash basis. That is, rather than directly computing cash sales, cash expenses, and so forth, these amounts are derived *indirectly* by removing from net income any items that do not affect cash flows.

---

[3]Operating cash inflows can also include interest income and dividend income; however, in this chapter we will limit our scope to cash receipts from sales to customers.

The indirect method has an advantage over the direct method because it shows the reasons for any differences between net income and net cash provided by operating activities.

Although both methods result in the same amount of net cash provided by operating activities, the overwhelming majority of companies uses the indirect method for external reporting purposes. If a company uses the direct method to prepare its statement of cash flows, then it must also provide a supplementary report that uses the indirect method. However, if a company chooses to use the indirect method, there is no requirement that it also report results using the direct method. Because the direct method requires more work, very few companies choose this approach. Therefore, we will explain the direct method in Appendix 13A, and we will cover the indirect method in the main body of the chapter.

CONCEPT CHECK

1.  Which of the following statements is true about the basic equation for asset accounts? (You may select more than one answer.)
    a.  Debits are added to the beginning balance.
    b.  Debits are subtracted from the beginning balance.
    c.  Credits are added to the beginning balance.
    d.  Credits are subtracted from the beginning balance.
2.  Which of the following is not a cash equivalent? (You may select more than one answer.)
    a.  Accounts receivable
    b.  Treasury bills
    c.  Commercial paper
    d.  Money market funds
3.  Which of the following statements is true? (You may select more than one answer.)
    a.  The direct method of preparing the operating activities section of the statement of cash flows starts with net income and adjusts it to a cash basis.
    b.  The basic equations for contra-assets and liabilities are the same.
    c.  Investing activities generate cash inflows and outflows related to acquiring or disposing of noncurrent assets.
    d.  Financing activities include paying dividends.

## The Indirect Method: A Three-Step Process

The indirect method adjusts net income to net cash provided by operating activities using a three-step process.

**Step 1**   The first step is to *add depreciation charges* to net income. Depreciation charges are the credits to the Accumulated Depreciation account during the period—the sum total of the entries that have increased Accumulated Depreciation. Why do we do this? Because Accumulated Depreciation is a noncash balance sheet account and we must adjust net income for all of the changes in the noncash balance sheet accounts that have occurred during the period.

To compute the credits to the Accumulated Depreciation account we use the equation for contra-assets that was mentioned earlier:

*Basic Equation for Contra-Asset Accounts*
Beginning balance – Debits + Credits = Ending balance

For example, assume the Accumulated Depreciation account had beginning and ending balances of $300 and $500, respectively. Also, assume that the company sold equipment with accumulated depreciation of $70 during the period. Given that we use debits to the Accumulated Depreciation account to record accumulated depreciation on assets that have been sold or retired, the depreciation that needs to be added to net income is computed as follows:

$$\text{Beginning balance} - \text{Debits} + \text{Credits} = \text{Ending balance}$$

$$\$300 - \$70 + \text{Credits} = \$500$$

$$\text{Credits} = \$500 - \$300 + \$70$$

$$\text{Credits} = \$270$$

The same logic can be depicted using an Accumulated Depreciation T-account. Given that we know the account's beginning and ending balances and the amount of the debit that would have been recorded for the sale of equipment, the credit side of the T-account must equal $270.

**Accumulated Depreciation**

|                        |    |           |        |
|------------------------|----|-----------|--------|
|                        |    | Beg. Bal. | $300   |
| Sale of equipment      | 70 |           | 270    |
|                        |    | End. Bal. | $500   |

For service and merchandising companies, the credits to the Accumulated Depreciation T-account equal the debits to the Depreciation Expense account. For these companies, the adjustment in step one consists of adding depreciation expense to net income. However, for manufacturing companies, some of the credits to the Accumulated Depreciation T-account relate to depreciation on production assets that are debited to work in process inventories rather than depreciation expense. For these companies, the depreciation charges do not simply equal depreciation expense.

Because depreciation is added back to net income on the statement of cash flows, some people erroneously conclude that a company can increase its cash flow by simply increasing its depreciation expense. This is false; a company cannot increase its net cash provided by operating activities by increasing its depreciation expense. If it increases its depreciation expense by X dollars, then net income will decline by X dollars and the amount of the adjustment in step one of this process will increase by X dollars. The decline in net income and the increase in the amount of the adjustment in step one exactly offset each other, resulting in zero impact on the net cash provided by operating activities.

### HELPFUL HINT

When completing step one in the indirect method, do not assume that the change in the balance of the Accumulated Depreciation account equals the amount of the required adjustment. Instead, you must check to see if any depreciable assets were sold during the period. If so, the amount of accumulated depreciation on the asset that was sold needs to be included in the basic equation for contra-asset accounts or included on the debit side of the Accumulated Depreciation T-account when determining the amount of the adjustment.

**Step 2**   The second step is to *analyze net changes in noncash balance sheet accounts that impact net income*. Exhibit 13–2 provides general guidelines for how to analyze current asset and current liability accounts.[4] For each account shown in the exhibit, you'll begin by referring to the balance sheet to compute the change in the account balance from the beginning to the end of the period. Then, you will either add each of these

---

[4]Other accounts such as Interest Payable can impact these computations. However, for simplicity, in this chapter we will focus on the accounts shown in Exhibit 13–2.

| | Increase in Account Balance | Decrease in Account Balance |
|---|---|---|
| **Current Assets** | | |
| Accounts receivable ...................... | Subtract | Add |
| Inventory ................................ | Subtract | Add |
| Prepaid expenses ........................ | Subtract | Add |
| **Current Liabilities** | | |
| Accounts payable......................... | Add | Subtract |
| Accrued liabilities........................ | Add | Subtract |
| Income taxes payable .................... | Add | Subtract |

**EXHIBIT 13–2**
General Guidelines for Analyzing How Changes in Noncash Balance Sheet Accounts Affect Net Income on the Statement of Cash Flows

amounts to net income or subtract them from net income as shown in Exhibit 13–2. Notice that changes in all current asset accounts (Accounts Receivable, Inventory, and Prepaid Expenses) result in the same type of adjustment to net income. If an asset account balance increases during the period, then the amount of the increase is subtracted from net income. If an asset account balance decreases during the period, then the amount of the decrease is added to net income. The current liability accounts (Accounts Payable, Accrued Liabilities, and Income Taxes Payable) are handled in the opposite fashion. If a liability account balance increases, then the amount of the increase is added to net income. If a liability account balance decreases, then the amount of the decrease is subtracted from net income.

Keep in mind that the purpose of these adjustments is to translate net income to a cash basis. For example, the change in the Accounts Receivable balance measures the difference between credit sales and cash collections from customers who purchased on account. When the Accounts Receivable balance increases it means that the amount of credit sales exceeds the amount of cash collected from customers. In this case, the change in the Accounts Receivable balance is subtracted from net income because it reflects the amount by which credit sales exceeds cash collections from customers. When the Accounts Receivable balance decreases it means that cash collected from customers exceeds credit sales. In this case, the change in the Accounts Receivable balance is added to net income because it reflects the amount by which cash collections from customers exceeds credit sales.

The other accounts shown in Exhibit 13–2 have a similar underlying logic. The Inventory and Accounts Payable adjustments translate cost of goods sold to cash paid for inventory purchases. The Prepaid Expenses and Accrued Liabilities adjustments translate selling and administrative expenses to a cash basis. The Income Taxes Payable adjustment translates income tax expense to a cash basis.

## HELPFUL HINT

Beyond memorizing the adjustments shown in Exhibit 13–2, you should understand the reasons for them. The adjustment pertaining to accounts receivable quantifies the difference between sales, as reported on the income statement, and cash collections from customers. The adjustments related to inventory and accounts payable quantify the difference between cost of goods sold and cash paid to suppliers. The adjustments related to prepaid expenses and accrued liabilities help quantify the difference between selling and administrative expenses and cash paid for those expenses. Finally, the adjustment pertaining to income taxes payable quantifies the difference between income tax expense and income tax payments.

**Step 3** The third step in computing the net cash provided by operating activities is to *adjust for gains/losses* included in the income statement. Under U.S. GAAP and IFRS rules, the cash proceeds from the sale of noncurrent assets must be included in the investing activities section of the statement of cash flows. To comply with these rules, the gains and losses pertaining to the sale of noncurrent assets must be removed from net income as reported in the operating activities section of the statement of cash flows. To make this adjustment, subtract gains from net income and add losses to net income in the operating activities section.

**CONCEPT CHECK**

4. Which of the following statements is false? (You may select more than one answer.)
   a. Depreciation charges are subtracted from net income.
   b. An increase in inventory is subtracted from net income.
   c. A loss on the sale of an asset is subtracted from net income.
   d. A decrease in accrued liabilities is subtracted from net income.
5. Assume that a company's beginning and ending balances in its Accumulated Depreciation account are $2,000 and $2,900, respectively. Also assume that the company sold a piece of equipment that had an original cost of $400 and accumulated depreciation of $350 for cash proceeds of $75. How much depreciation would the company add to net income in the operating activities section of its statement of cash flows?
   a. $550
   b. $500
   c. $1,300
   d. $1,250
6. Refer to the data in question 5 above. Which of the following choices is true?
   a. The company should subtract a gain of $25 from net income.
   b. The company should add a gain of $25 to net income.
   c. The company should subtract a loss of $25 from net income.
   d. The company should add a loss of $25 to net income.

---

**IN BUSINESS**

## Sears' Suppliers Want Their Money Sooner

Some of **Sears'** suppliers want to be paid in 15 days instead of their usual norms of 30–60 days. The suppliers are seeking quicker payments to compensate them for the risk of selling merchandise to the troubled retailer who is experiencing annual losses in excess of $1 billion. From a cash flow perspective, faster payments to suppliers will decrease Sears' accounts payable balance, which in turn lowers its net cash provided by operating activities.

Source: Kapner, Suzanne, "Jittery Suppliers Press Sears to Pay Up Faster," *The Wall Street Journal*, March 19, 2015, B1–B2.

---

## Investing and Financing Activities: Gross Cash Flows

U.S. GAAP and IFRS require that the investing and financing sections of the statement of cash flows disclose gross cash flows. To illustrate, suppose **Macy's Department Stores** purchases $50 million in property during the year and sells other property for $30 million. Instead of showing the net change of $20 million, the company must show the gross amounts of both the purchases and sales. The $50 million purchase would be disclosed as a cash outflow and the $30 million sale would be reported as a cash inflow in the investing section of the statement of cash flows. Similarly, if **Alcoa** receives $80 million from selling long-term bonds and then pays out $30 million to retire other bonds, the two transactions must be reported separately in the financing section of the statement of cash flows rather than being netted against each other.

The gross method of reporting cash flows is not used in the operating activities section of the statement of cash flows, where debits and credits are netted against each other. For example, if **Sears** adds $600 million to its accounts receivable as a result of sales during

| | Increase in Account Balance | Decrease in Account Balance |
|---|---|---|
| **Noncurrent Assets (Investing activities)** | | |
| Property, plant, and equipment . . . . . . . . . . . . . . | Subtract | Add |
| Long-term investments . . . . . . . . . . . . . . . . . . . . . | Subtract | Add |
| Loans to other entities. . . . . . . . . . . . . . . . . . . . . | Subtract | Add |
| **Liabilities and Stockholders' Equity (Financing activities)** | | |
| Bonds payable . . . . . . . . . . . . . . . . . . . . . . . . . . . | Add | Subtract |
| Common stock . . . . . . . . . . . . . . . . . . . . . . . . . . . | Add | Subtract |
| Retained earnings . . . . . . . . . . . . . . . . . . . . . . . . | * | * |

*Requires further analysis to quantify cash dividends paid.

**EXHIBIT 13–3**
General Guidelines for Analyzing How Changes in Noncash Balance Sheet Accounts Affect the Investing and Financing Sections of the Statement of Cash Flows

the year and $520 million of accounts receivable are collected, only the net increase of $80 million is reported on the statement of cash flows.

To compute gross cash flows for the investing and financing activities sections of the statement of cash flows, you'll begin by calculating the changes in the balance of each applicable balance sheet account. As with the current assets, when a noncurrent asset account balance (including Property, Plant, and Equipment; Long-Term Investments; and Loans to Other Entities) increases, it signals the need to subtract cash outflows in the investing activities section of the statement of cash flows. If the balance in a noncurrent asset account decreases during the period, then it signals the need to add cash inflows. The liability and equity accounts (Bonds Payable and Common Stock) are handled in the opposite fashion. If a liability or equity account balance increases, then it signals a need to add cash inflows to the financing activities section of the statement of cash flows. If a liability or equity account balance decreases, then it signals a need to subtract cash outflows. Exhibit 13–3 summarizes these general guidelines.

While these guidelines provide a helpful starting point, to properly calculate each account's *gross* cash inflows and outflows you'll need to analyze the transactions that occurred within that account during the period. We will illustrate how to do this using Property, Plant, and Equipment and Retained Earnings.

**Property, Plant, and Equipment**   When a company purchases property, plant, or equipment it debits the Property, Plant, and Equipment account for the amount of the purchase. When it sells or disposes of these kinds of assets, it credits the Property, Plant, and Equipment account for the original cost of the asset. To compute the cash outflows related to Property, Plant, and Equipment we use the basic equation for assets mentioned earlier:

*Basic Equation for Asset Accounts*
Beginning balance + Debits − Credits = Ending balance

For example, assume a company's beginning and ending balances in its Property, Plant, and Equipment account are $1,000 and $1,800, respectively. In addition, during the period the company sold a piece of equipment for $40 cash that originally cost $100 and had accumulated depreciation of $70. The company recorded a gain on the sale of $10, which had been included in net income.

We start by calculating the $800 increase in the Property, Plant, and Equipment account. This increase signals the need to subtract cash outflows in the investing activities section of the statement of cash flows. In fact, it may be tempting to conclude that the proper way to analyze Property, Plant, and Equipment in this instance is to record an $800 cash outflow corresponding with the $800 increase in the account balance. However, that would only be correct if the company did not sell any property, plant, and equipment during the year. Because the company did sell equipment, we must use the basic equation for asset accounts to compute the cash outflows as follows:

$$\text{Beginning balance} + \text{Debits} - \text{Credits} = \text{Ending balance}$$

$$\$1{,}000 + \text{Debits} - \$100 = \$1{,}800$$

$$\text{Debits} = \$1{,}800 - \$1{,}000 + \$100$$

$$\text{Debits} = \$900$$

The same logic can be depicted using a Property, Plant, and Equipment T-account. Given that we know the account's beginning and ending balances and the amount of the credit that would have been recorded to write off the *original cost* of the equipment that was sold, the additions to the account, as summarized on the debit side of the T-account, must equal $900.

**Property, Plant, and Equipment**

| Beg. Bal. | $1,000 | | |
|---|---|---|---|
| Additions | 900 | Sale of equipment | 100 |
| End. Bal. | $1,800 | | |

So, instead of reporting an $800 cash outflow pertaining to Property, Plant, and Equipment in the investing activities section of the statement of cash flows, the proper accounting requires subtracting the $10 gain on the sale of equipment from net income in the operating activities section of the statement. It also requires disclosing a $40 cash inflow from the sale of equipment and a $900 cash outflow for additions to Property, Plant, and Equipment in the investing activities section of the statement.

CONCEPT
CHECK

7. Assume that a company's beginning and ending balances in its Property, Plant, and Equipment account are $5,000 and $6,000, respectively. Also assume that the company sold a piece of equipment that originally cost $700 and had accumulated depreciation of $450 for cash proceeds of $500. Based solely on the available information, what is the company's net cash provided by (used in) investing activities?
   a. $1,200
   b. $1,500
   c. $(1,200)
   d. $(1,500)

**Retained Earnings**   When a company earns net income it credits the Retained Earnings account and when it pays a dividend it debits the Retained Earnings account. To compute the amount of a cash dividend payment we use the basic equation for stockholders' equity accounts mentioned earlier:

*Basic Equation for Stockholders' Equity Accounts*
Beginning balance − Debits + Credits = Ending balance

For example, assume a company's beginning and ending balances in its Retained Earnings account are $2,000 and 3,000, respectively. In addition, the company reported net income of $1,200 and paid a cash dividend. To determine the amount of the dividend, we start by calculating the $1,000 increase in the Retained Earnings account. However, given that this amount reflects the net income earned during the period as well as the amount of the dividend payment, we must use the equation above to calculate the amount of the dividend payment as follows:

$$\text{Beginning balance} - \text{Debits} + \text{Credits} = \text{Ending balance}$$

$$\$2,000 - \text{Debits} + \$1,200 = \$3,000$$

$$\$3,200 = \$3,000 + \text{Debits}$$

$$\text{Debits} = \$200$$

The same logic can be depicted using a Retained Earnings T-account. Given that we know the account's beginning and ending balances and the net income that would have been recorded on the credit side of the T-account, the dividend, as reported on the debit side of the T-account, must equal $200.

**Retained Earnings**

|  |  |  |  |
|---|---|---|---|
|  |  | Beg. Bal. | $2,000 |
| Dividend | 200 | Net income | 1,200 |
|  |  | End. Bal. | $3,000 |

So, instead of erroneously reporting a $1,000 cash flow pertaining to the overall change in Retained Earnings, the proper accounting requires disclosing net income of $1,200 within the operating activities section of the statement of cash flows and a $200 cash dividend in the financing activities section of the statement.

**HELPFUL HINT**

Net income is the first number recorded on a statement of cash flows prepared using the indirect method. However, how would you determine net income if it was not explicitly disclosed within an exercise or problem? The secret is to use the basic equation for stockholders' equity accounts to determine the credit to the Retained Earnings account. Input into this equation the beginning and ending balances in Retained Earnings as well as the debit pertaining to cash dividends and then solve for the credit to the account—which corresponds to net income.

## Summary of Key Concepts

Exhibit 13–4 summarizes the four key concepts just discussed. The first key concept is that the statement of cash flows is divided into three sections: operating activities, investing activities, and financing activities. The net cash used or provided by these three types of activities is combined to derive the net increase/decrease in cash and cash equivalents, which explains the change in the cash balance. The second key concept is that the operating activities section of the statement of cash flows can be prepared using the direct or indirect method. The direct method translates sales, cost of goods sold, selling and administrative expenses, and income tax expense to a cash basis. The indirect method begins with accrual-based net income and adjusts it to a cash basis. The third key concept is that the indirect method requires three steps to compute net cash provided by operating activities. The first step is to add back depreciation to net income. The second step is to analyze net changes in noncash balance sheet accounts that impact net income. The third step is to adjust for gains or losses included in the income statement. The fourth key concept is to record gross (rather than net) cash inflows and outflows in the investing and financing activities sections of the statement of cash flows.[5]

[5]This chapter adopts two simplifications related to common stock transactions. First, it always assumes that companies issue no-par value common stock, thus the chapter excludes Additional Paid-In Capital. Second, the chapter assumes that stock repurchases are recorded with a debit to the Common Stock account rather than a debit to the contra-equity account called Treasury Stock.

**EXHIBIT 13–4** Summary of Key Concepts Needed to Prepare a Statement of Cash Flows

| Key Concept #1 | | Key Concept #2 | |
|---|---|---|---|
| The statement of cash flows is divided into three sections: | | U.S. GAAP and IFRS allow two methods for preparing the operating activities section of the statement of cash flows: | |
| **Operating activities** | | **Direct Method (Appendix 13A)** | |
| Net cash provided by (used in) operating activities | $xx | Cash receipts from customers | $xx |
| **Investing activities** | | Cash paid for inventory purchases | (xx) |
| Net cash provided by (used in) investing activities | xx | Cash paid for selling and administrative expenses | (xx) |
| **Financing activities** | | Cash paid for income taxes | (xx) |
| Net cash provided by (used in) financing activities | xx | Net cash provided by (used in) operating activities | $xx |
| | | **Indirect Method** | |
| Net increase/decrease in cash and cash equivalents | xx | Net income | $xx |
| Beginning cash and cash equivalents | xx | Various adjustments (+/−) | xx |
| Ending cash and cash equivalents | $xx | Net cash provided by (used in) operating activities | $xx |

| Key Concept #3 | | Key Concept #4 | |
|---|---|---|---|
| Computing the net cash provided by operating activities using the indirect method is a three step process: | | The investing and financing sections of the statement of cash flows must report gross cash flows: | |
| **Operating activities** | | Net cash provided by (used in) operating activities | $xx |
| Net income | $xx | **Investing activities** | |
| Adjustments to convert net income to a cash basis: | | Purchase of property, plant, and equipment | (xx) |
| | | Sale of property, plant, and equipment | xx |
| | | Purchase of long-term investments | (xx) |
| Step 1 { Add: Depreciation | xx | Sale of long-term investments | xx |
| | | Net cash provided by (used in) investing activities | (xx) |
| Analyze net changes in noncash balance sheet accounts: | | **Financing activities** | |
| Step 2 { Increase in current asset accounts | (xx) | Issuance of bonds payable | xx |
| Decrease in current asset accounts | xx | Repaying principal on bonds payable | (xx) |
| Increase in current liability accounts | xx | Issuance of common stock | xx |
| Decrease in current liability accounts | (xx) | Purchase own shares of common stock | (xx) |
| | | Paying a dividend | (xx) |
| Adjust for gains/losses: | | Net cash provided by (used in) financing activities | xx |
| Step 3 { Gain on sale | (xx) | Net increase/decrease in cash and cash equivalents | xx |
| Loss on sale | xx | Beginning cash and cash equivalents | xx |
| Net cash provided by (used in) operating activities | $xx | Ending cash and cash equivalents | $xx |

# AN EXAMPLE OF A STATEMENT OF CASH FLOWS

To illustrate the ideas introduced in the preceding section, we will now construct a statement of cash flows for a merchandising company called Apparel, Inc. The company's income statement and balance sheet are shown in Exhibits 13–5 and 13–6.

Let's also assume the following facts with respect to Apparel, Inc.:

1. The company sold a store that had an original cost of $15 million and accumulated depreciation of $10 million. The cash proceeds from the sale were $8 million. The gain on the sale was $3 million.
2. The company did not issue any new bonds during the year.
3. The company did not repurchase any of its own common stock during the year.
4. The company paid a cash dividend during the year.

EXHIBIT 13–5
Apparel, Inc., Income Statement

**Apparel, Inc.**
**Income Statement**
**(dollars in millions)**

| | |
|---|---:|
| Sales.................................... | $3,638 |
| Cost of goods sold......................... | 2,469 |
| Gross margin............................. | 1,169 |
| Selling and administrative expenses .......... | 941 |
| Net operating income ..................... | 228 |
| Nonoperating items: Gain on sale of store ..... | 3 |
| Income before taxes ...................... | 231 |
| Income taxes............................. | 91 |
| Net income .............................. | $ 140 |

EXHIBIT 13–6
Apparel, Inc., Balance Sheet

**Apparel, Inc.**
**Comparative Balance Sheet**
**(dollars in millions)**

| | Ending Balance | Beginning Balance | Change |
|---|---:|---:|---:|
| **Assets** | | | |
| Current assets: | | | |
|   Cash and cash equivalents ............... | $ 91 | $ 29 | +62 |
|   Accounts receivable .................... | 637 | 654 | −17 |
|   Inventory .............................. | 586 | 537 | +49 |
| Total current assets ....................... | 1,314 | 1,220 | |
| Property, plant, and equipment .............. | 1,517 | 1,394 | +123 |
|   Less accumulated depreciation ........... | 654 | 561 | +93 |
| Net property, plant, and equipment .......... | 863 | 833 | |
| Total assets .............................. | $2,177 | $2,053 | |
| **Liabilities and Stockholders' Equity** | | | |
| Current liabilities: | | | |
|   Accounts payable ...................... | $ 264 | $ 220 | +44 |
|   Accrued liabilities ...................... | 193 | 190 | +3 |
|   Income taxes payable ................... | 75 | 71 | +4 |
| Total current liabilities ..................... | 532 | 481 | |
| Bonds payable ........................... | 479 | 520 | −41 |
| Total liabilities ........................... | 1,011 | 1,001 | |
| Stockholders' equity: | | | |
|   Common stock......................... | 157 | 155 | +2 |
|   Retained earnings ...................... | 1,009 | 897 | +112 |
| Total stockholders' equity ................. | 1,166 | 1,052 | |
| Total liabilities and stockholders' equity ...... | $2,177 | $2,053 | |

Notice that the balance sheet in Exhibit 13–6 includes the amount of the change in each balance sheet account. For example, the beginning and ending balances in Cash and Cash Equivalents are $29 million and $91 million, respectively. This is a $62 million increase in the account balance. A similar computation is performed for all other balance sheet accounts. Study the changes in these account balances because we will be referring to them later. For example, keep in mind that the purpose of Apparel's statement of cash flows is to disclose the operating, investing, and financing cash flows underlying the $62 million increase in Cash and Cash Equivalents shown in Exhibit 13–6. *Also, please be advised that although the changes in account balances are computed for you in*

*Exhibit 13–6, you'll ordinarily need to compute these amounts yourself before attempting to construct the statement of cash flows.*

## Operating Activities

This section uses the three-step process explained earlier to construct Apparel's operating activities section of the statement of cash flows.

**Step 1** The first step in computing Apparel's net cash provided by operating activities is to *add depreciation* to net income. The balance sheet in Exhibit 13–6 shows Apparel's Accumulated Depreciation account had beginning and ending balances of $561 million and $654 million, respectively. We also know from the assumptions mentioned earlier that Apparel sold a store during the year that had $10 million of accumulated depreciation. Given these facts, we can use the basic equation for contra-assets to determine that Apparel needs to add $103 million of depreciation to its net income:

$$\text{Beginning balance} - \text{Debits} + \text{Credits} = \text{Ending balance}$$

$$\$561 \text{ million} - \$10 \text{ million} + \text{Credits} = \$654 \text{ million}$$

$$\text{Credits} = \$654 \text{ million} - \$561 \text{ million} + \$10 \text{ million}$$

$$\text{Credits} = \$103 \text{ million}$$

**Step 2** The second step in computing net cash provided by operating activities is to *analyze net changes in noncash balance sheet accounts* that impact net income. Exhibit 13–7 explains the five adjustments Apparel needs to make to complete this step. For your ease of reference, the top half of Exhibit 13–7 reproduces an excerpt of the general guidelines for completing this step that were previously summarized in Exhibit 13–2. The bottom half of Exhibit 13–7 applies the general guidelines from the top half of the exhibit to Apparel's balance sheet. For example, Exhibit 13–6 shows that Apparel's Accounts Receivable balance decreased by $17 million. The top half of Exhibit 13–7 says that decreases in accounts receivable are added to net income. This explains why the bottom half of Exhibit 13–7 includes a plus sign in front of

**EXHIBIT 13–7**
Apparel, Inc.: Analyzing How Net Changes in Noncash Balance Sheet Accounts Affect Net Income on the Statement of Cash Flows

| | Increase in Account Balance | Decrease in Account Balance |
|---|---|---|
| **General Guidelines from Exhibit 13–2** | | |
| Current Assets: | | |
| Accounts receivable ................. | Subtract | Add |
| Inventory ........................... | Subtract | Add |
| Current Liabilities: | | |
| Accounts payable..................... | Add | Subtract |
| Accrued liabilities.................... | Add | Subtract |
| Income taxes payable ................. | Add | Subtract |
| | **Increase in Account Balance** | **Decrease in Account Balance** |
| **Apparel's Account Analysis** | | |
| Current Assets: | | |
| Accounts receivable .................. | | +17 |
| Inventory ........................... | −49 | |
| Current Liabilities: | | |
| Accounts payable..................... | +44 | |
| Accrued liabilities.................... | +3 | |
| Income taxes payable ................. | +4 | |

Apparel's $17 million decrease in Accounts Receivable. Similarly, Exhibit 13–6 shows that Apparel's Inventory balance increased by $49 million. When inventory increases, the amount of the increase is subtracted from net income. This explains why the bottom half of Exhibit 13–7 includes a minus sign in front of Apparel's $49 million increase in Inventory. Similar logic can be used to explain why the increases from Exhibit 13–6 in Accounts Payable (+44), Accrued Liabilities (+3), and Income Taxes Payable (+4) all result in the additions to Apparel's net income that are shown in the bottom half of Exhibit 13–7.

**Step 3**   The third step in computing the net cash provided by operating activities is to *adjust for gains/losses* included in the income statement. Apparel reported a $3 million gain on its income statement in Exhibit 13–5; therefore, this amount needs to be subtracted from net income. Subtracting the gain on sale removes the gain from the operating activities section of the statement of cash flows. The entire amount of the cash proceeds related to this sale will be recorded in the investing activities section of the statement.

Exhibit 13–8 shows the operating activities section of Apparel's statement of cash flows. Take a moment to trace each of the numbers that we just computed to this exhibit. The total amount of the adjustments to net income is $119 million, which results in net cash provided by operating activities of $259 million.

## Investing Activities

Apparel's investing cash flows pertain to its Property, Plant, and Equipment account, which according to Exhibit 13–6 had beginning and ending balances of $1,394 million and $1,517 million, respectively, for an increase of $123 million. This increase suggests that Apparel purchased equipment; however, it does not capture the gross cash flows that need to be reported in the statement of cash flows.

The previously defined assumptions say that Apparel sold a store that had an original cost of $15 million for $8 million in cash. The cash inflow from this sale needs to be recorded in the investing activities section of the statement of cash flows. To compute the cash outflows related to purchases of property, plant, and equipment we use the basic equation for assets that was mentioned in the beginning of the chapter:

$$\text{Beginning balance} + \text{Debits} - \text{Credits} = \text{Ending balance}$$
$$\$1,394 \text{ million} + \text{Debits} - \$15 \text{ million} = \$1,517 \text{ million}$$
$$\text{Debits} = \$1,517 \text{ million} - \$1,394 \text{ million} + \$15 \text{ million}$$
$$\text{Debits} = \$138 \text{ million}$$

Notice the credits in the equation above include the original cost of the store that was sold. When the cash outflows of $138 million for purchases of property, plant, and equipment are combined with the $8 million of cash proceeds from the sale of the store, Apparel's net cash used in investing activities is $130 million.

| Apparel, Inc. (dollars in millions) | | |
|---|---|---|
| **Operating Activities** | | |
| Net income | | $140 |
| Adjustments to convert net income to a cash basis: | | |
| Step 1 → Depreciation | $103 | |
| Decrease in accounts receivable | 17 | |
| Increase in inventory | (49) | |
| Step 2 → Increase in accounts payable | 44 | |
| Increase in accrued liabilities | 3 | |
| Increase in income taxes payable | 4 | |
| Step 3 → Gain on sale of store | (3) | 119 |
| Net cash provided by (used in) operating activities | | $259 |

**EXHIBIT 13–8**
Apparel, Inc.: Operating Activities Section of the Statement of Cash Flows

## Financing Activities

Exhibit 13–9 explains how to compute Apparel's financing cash flows related to its Bonds Payable and Common Stock balance sheet accounts. The top half of the exhibit reproduces an excerpt of the general guidelines for analyzing financing cash flows that was previously summarized in Exhibit 13–3. The bottom half of Exhibit 13–9 applies the general guidelines from the top half of the exhibit to these two accounts from Apparel's balance sheet. We will analyze each account in turn.

Exhibit 13–6 shows that Apparel's Bonds Payable balance decreased by $41 million. Because, as stated earlier, Apparel did not issue any bonds during the year, we can conclude that the $41 million decrease in the account is due solely to retiring bonds payable. The top half of Exhibit 13–9 says that a decrease in Bonds Payable signals the need to subtract cash outflows in the investing activities section of the statement of cash flows. This explains why the bottom half of the exhibit includes a minus sign in front of Apparel's $41 million decrease in Bonds Payable. Similarly, Exhibit 13–6 shows that Apparel's Common Stock balance increased by $2 million. Because, as stated earlier, Apparel did not repurchase any of its own stock during the year, we can conclude that the $2 million increase in the account is due solely to issuing common stock. The top half of Exhibit 13–9 says that increases in common stock signal the need to add cash inflows in the investing activities section of the statement of cash flows. This explains why the bottom half of the exhibit includes a plus sign in front of Apparel's $2 million increase in Common Stock.

The final financing cash outflow for Apparel is its dividend payment to common stockholders. The dividend payment can be computed using the basic equation for stockholders' equity accounts mentioned at the beginning of the chapter:

$$\text{Beginning balance} - \text{Debits} + \text{Credits} = \text{Ending balance}$$

$$\$897 \text{ million} - \text{Debits} + \$140 \text{ million} = \$1{,}009 \text{ million}$$

$$\$1{,}037 \text{ million} = \$1{,}009 \text{ million} + \text{Debits}$$

$$\text{Debits} = \$28 \text{ million}$$

When the cash outflows of $69 million (= $41 million + $28 million) are combined with the cash inflows of $2 million, Apparel's net cash used in financing activities is $67 million.

Exhibit 13–10 shows Apparel's statement of cash flows. The operating activities section of this statement is carried over from Exhibit 13–8. Take a moment to trace the investing

**EXHIBIT 13–9**
Apparel, Inc.: Analyzing How Changes in Noncash Balance Sheet Accounts Affect Financing Cash Flows on the Statement of Cash Flows

**EXHIBIT 13–10**
Apparel, Inc. Statement of
Cash Flows

| Apparel, Inc. Statement of Cash Flows—Indirect Method (dollars in millions) | | |
|---|---|---|
| **Operating Activities** | | |
| Net income .............................................. | | $140 |
| Adjustments to convert net income to a cash basis: | | |
| Depreciation .......................................... | $103 | |
| Decrease in accounts receivable ............................ | 17 | |
| Increase in inventory ....................................... | (49) | |
| Increase in accounts payable................................ | 44 | |
| Increase in accrued liabilities................................ | 3 | |
| Increase in income taxes payable............................ | 4 | |
| Gain on sale of store ....................................... | (3) | 119 |
| Net cash provided by (used in) operating activities ................ | | 259 |
| **Investing Activities** | | |
| Additions to property, plant, and equipment...................... | (138) | |
| Proceeds from sale of store .................................. | 8 | |
| Net cash provided by (used in) investing activities................. | | (130) |
| **Financing Activities** | | |
| Retirement of bonds payable................................. | (41) | |
| Issuance of common stock................................... | 2 | |
| Cash dividends paid ....................................... | (28) | |
| Net cash provided by (used in) financing activities ............... | | (67) |
| Net increase in cash and cash equivalents ...................... | | 62 |
| Beginning cash and cash equivalents .......................... | | 29 |
| Ending cash and cash equivalents ............................ | | $ 91 |

and financing cash flows just discussed to Exhibit 13–10. Notice that the net change in cash and cash equivalents ($62 million) is calculated using the following equation:

$$\text{Net change in cash and cash equivalents} = \begin{array}{c} \text{Net cash provided} \\ \text{by (used in)} \\ \text{operating activities} \end{array} + \begin{array}{c} \text{Net cash provided} \\ \text{by (used in)} \\ \text{investing activities} \end{array} + \begin{array}{c} \text{Net cash provided} \\ \text{by (used in)} \\ \text{financing activities} \end{array}$$

$$\text{Net change in cash and cash equivalents} = \$259 \text{ million} + \$(130) \text{ million} + \$(67) \text{ million}$$

$$\text{Net change in cash and cash equivalents} = \$62 \text{ million}$$

This amount agrees with the $62 million change in the Cash and Cash Equivalents account shown on the balance sheet in Exhibit 13–6.

## Seeing the Big Picture

In the beginning of the chapter, we mentioned that a statement of cash flows is prepared by analyzing the changes in noncash balance sheet accounts. We then presented a method of preparing a statement of cash flows. This method simplified the process of creating the statement of cash flows, and now we will show that it is equivalent to analyzing the changes in noncash balance sheet accounts.

Exhibit 13–11 uses T-accounts to summarize how the changes in Apparel, Inc.'s noncash balance sheet accounts quantify the cash inflows and outflows that explain the change in

**EXHIBIT 13–11** T-Accounts after Posting of Account Changes—Apparel, Inc. (in millions)

**Cash**

| | | | | |
|---|---|---|---|---|
| Net income | (1) | 140 | 49 | (4) Increase in inventory |
| Depreciation | (2) | 103 | 3 | (12) Gain on sale of store |
| Decrease in accounts receivable | (3) | 17 | | |
| Increase in accounts payable | (5) | 44 | | |
| Increase in accrued liabilities | (6) | 3 | | |
| Increase in income taxes payable | (7) | 4 | | |
| Net cash provided by operating activities | | 259 | | |
| Proceeds from sale of store | (12) | 8 | 138 | (8) Additions to property, plant, and equipment |
| Increase in common stock | (11) | 2 | 41 | (9) Decrease in bonds payable |
| | | | 28 | (10) Cash dividends paid |
| Net increase in cash and cash equivalents | | 62 | | |

**Accounts Receivable**

| | | | |
|---|---|---|---|
| Bal. | 654 | | |
| | | 17 | (3) |
| Bal. | 637 | | |

**Inventory**

| | | |
|---|---|---|
| Bal. | 537 | |
| (4) | 49 | |
| Bal. | 586 | |

**Property, Plant, and Equipment**

| | | | | |
|---|---|---|---|---|
| Bal. | 1,394 | | | |
| (8) | 138 | 15 | (12) | |
| Bal. | 1,517 | | | |

**Accumulated Depreciation**

| | | | |
|---|---|---|---|
| | | 561 | Bal. |
| (12) | 10 | 103 | (2) |
| | | 654 | Bal. |

**Accounts Payable**

| | | |
|---|---|---|
| | 220 | Bal. |
| | 44 | (5) |
| | 264 | Bal. |

**Accrued Liabilities**

| | | |
|---|---|---|
| | 190 | Bal. |
| | 3 | (6) |
| | 193 | Bal. |

**Income Taxes Payable**

| | | |
|---|---|---|
| | 71 | Bal. |
| | 4 | (7) |
| | 75 | Bal. |

**Bonds Payable**

| | | | |
|---|---|---|---|
| | | 520 | Bal. |
| (9) | 41 | | |
| | | 479 | Bal. |

**Common Stock**

| | | |
|---|---|---|
| | 155 | Bal. |
| | 2 | (11) |
| | 157 | Bal. |

**Retained Earnings**

| | | | |
|---|---|---|---|
| | | 897 | Bal. |
| (10) | 28 | 140 | (1) |
| | | 1,009 | Bal. |

its cash balance. The top portion of the exhibit is Apparel's Cash T-account and the bottom portion provides T-accounts for the company's remaining balance sheet accounts. Notice that the net cash provided by operating activities of $259 million and the net increase in cash and cash equivalents of $62 million shown in the Cash T-account agree with the corresponding figures in the statement of cash flows shown in Exhibit 13–10.

We will explain Exhibit 13–11 in five steps. Entry (1) records Apparel's net income of $140 million in the credit side of the Retained Earnings account and the debit side of the Cash account. The net income of $140 million shown in the Cash T-account will be adjusted until it reflects the $62 million net increase in cash and cash equivalents. Entry (2) adds the depreciation of $103 million to net income. Entries (3) through (7) adjust net income for the changes in the current asset and current liability accounts. Entries (8) through (11) summarize the cash outflows and inflows related to the additions to property, plant, and equipment, the retirement of bonds payable, the payment of the cash dividend, and the issuance of common stock. Entry (12) records the sale of the store.

Notice that the gain on the sale of $3 million is recorded in the credit side of the Cash T-account. This is equivalent to subtracting the gain from net income so that the entire amount of the cash proceeds from the sale of $8 million can be recorded in the investing activities section of the statement of cash flows.

## INTERPRETING THE STATEMENT OF CASH FLOWS

Managers can derive many useful insights by studying the statement of cash flows. In this section, we will discuss two guidelines managers should use when interpreting the statement of cash flows.

### Consider a Company's Specific Circumstances

A statement of cash flows should be evaluated in the context of a company's specific circumstances. To illustrate this point, let's consider two examples related to start-up companies and companies with growing versus declining sales. Start-up companies usually are unable to generate positive cash flows from operations; therefore, they rely on issuing stock and taking out loans to fund investing activities. This means that start-up companies often have negative net cash provided by operating activities and large spikes in net cash used for investing activities and net cash provided by financing activities. However, as a start-up company matures, it should begin generating enough cash to sustain day-to-day operations and maintain its plant and equipment without issuing additional stock or borrowing money. This means the net cash provided by operating activities should swing from a negative to a positive number. The net cash used for investing activities should decline somewhat and stabilize and the net cash provided by financing activities should decrease.

A company with growing sales would understandably have an increase in its accounts receivable, inventory, and accounts payable balances. On the other hand, if a company with declining sales has increases in these account balances, it could signal trouble. Perhaps accounts receivable is increasing because the company is attempting to boost sales by selling to customers who can't pay their bills. Perhaps the increase in inventory suggests the company is stuck with large amounts of obsolete inventory. Accounts payable may be increasing because the company is deferring payments to suppliers in an effort to inflate its net cash provided by operating activities. Notice that the plausible interpretations of these changes in account balances depend on the company's circumstances.

---

### Owner

DECISION POINT

You are the owner of a small manufacturing company. The company started selling its products internationally this year, which has resulted in a very significant increase in sales revenue and net income during the last two months of the year. The operating activities section of the company's statement of cash flows shows a negative number (that is, cash was used rather than provided by operations). Would you be concerned?

### Consider the Relationships among Numbers

While each number in a statement of cash flows provides useful information, managers derive the most meaningful insights by examining the relationships among numbers.

For example, some managers study their company's trends in cash flow margins by comparing the net cash provided by operating activities to sales. The goal is to continuously increase the operating cash flows earned per sales dollar. If we refer back to Apparel's income statement in Exhibit 13–5 and its statement of cash flows in Exhibit 13–10, we can determine that its cash flow margin is about $0.07 per dollar of sales (= $259 ÷ $3,638). Managers also compare the net cash provided by operating activities to the ending balance of current liabilities. If the net cash provided by operating activities is greater than (less than) the current liabilities, it indicates the company did (did not) generate enough operating cash flow to pay its bills at the end of the period. Apparel's net cash provided by operating activities of $259 million (see Exhibit 13–10) was not enough to pay its year-end current liabilities of $532 million (see Exhibit 13–6).

As a third example, managers compare the additions to property, plant, and equipment in the investing activities section of the statement of cash flows to the depreciation included in the operating activities section of the statement. If the additions to property, plant, and equipment are consistently less than depreciation, it suggests the company is not investing enough money to maintain its noncurrent assets. If we refer back to Apparel's statement of cash flows in Exhibit 13–10, its additions to property, plant, and equipment ($138 million) are greater than its depreciation ($103 million). This suggests that Apparel is investing more than enough money to maintain its noncurrent assets.

**LEARNING OBJECTIVE 13–3**

Compute free cash flow.

**Free Cash Flow** *Free cash flow* is a measure used by managers to look at the relationship among three numbers from the statement of cash flows—net cash provided by operating activities, additions to property, plant, and equipment (also called capital expenditures), and dividends. **Free cash flow** measures a company's ability to fund its capital expenditures for property, plant, and equipment and its cash dividends from its net cash provided by operating activities.[6] The equation for computing free cash flow is as follows:

$$\text{Free cash flow} = \begin{array}{c}\text{Net cash provided} \\ \text{by operating} \\ \text{activities}\end{array} - \text{Capital expenditures} - \text{Dividends}$$

Using this equation and the statement of cash flows shown in Exhibit 13–10, we can compute Apparel's free cash flow (in millions) as follows:

$$\text{Free cash flow} = \$259 - \$138 - \$28$$
$$= \$93$$

The interpretation of free cash flow is straightforward. A positive number indicates that the company generated enough cash flow from its operating activities to fund its capital expenditures and dividend payments. A negative number suggests that the company needed to obtain cash from other sources, such as borrowing money from lenders or issuing shares of common stock, to fund its investments in property, plant, and equipment and its dividend payments. Negative free cash flow does not automatically signal poor performance. As previously discussed, a new company with enormous growth prospects would be expected to have negative free cash flow during its start-up phase. However, even new companies will eventually need to generate positive free cash flow to survive.

**Earnings Quality** Managers and investors often look at the relationship between net income and net cash provided by operating activities to help assess the extent to which a company's earnings truly reflects operational performance. Managers generally perceive that earnings are of higher quality, or more indicative of operational performance, when the earnings (1) are not unduly influenced by inflation, (2) are computed using conservative accounting principles and estimates, and (3) are correlated with net cash provided

---

[6]For a summary of alternative definitions of free cash flow, see John Mills, Lynn Bible, and Richard Mason, "Defining Free Cash Flow," *CPA Journal,* January 2002, pp. 36–42.

by operating activities. When a company's net income and net cash provided by operating activities move in tandem with one another (in other words, are correlated with one another), it suggests that earnings result from changes in sales and operating expenses. Conversely, if a company's net income is steadily increasing and its net cash provided by operating activities is declining, it suggests that net income is being influenced by factors unrelated to operational performance, such as nonrecurring transactions or aggressive accounting principles and estimates.

**CONCEPT CHECK**

8. Which of the following statements is true with respect to earnings quality? (You may select more than one answer.)
   a. Managers generally perceive that earnings are of higher quality when earnings are not unduly influenced by inflation.
   b. Managers generally perceive that earnings are of higher quality when earnings are computed using aggressive estimates.
   c. Managers generally perceive that earnings are of higher quality when earnings move in the opposite direction to net cash provided by operating activities.
   d. Managers generally perceive that earnings are of higher quality when earnings are computed using conservative accounting principles.

## Panera Increases Its Stock Buyback

**IN BUSINESS**

**Panera Bread Company** announced plans to spend $750 million to repurchase shares of its own stock. The company intends to take on $500 million in new debt and it plans to sell 73 of its 925 company-owned stores to fund the stock repurchase. When Panera's plans were made public its stock price jumped 12% to $182.89. The company also plans to bolster its financial performance by taking steps to grow sales outside the lunch hour and by implementing operational efficiencies that reduce food preparation time and the length of the lines at its checkout counters.

Source: Brat, Ilan, "Panera to Expand Buyback and Sell Some Stores," *The Wall Street Journal*, April 17, 2015, B3.

©Helen Sessions/Alamy Stock Photo

## SUMMARY

**LO13–1 Classify cash inflows and outflows as relating to operating, investing, or financing activities.**

The statement of cash flows is organized into three sections: operating activities, investing activities, and financing activities. Operating activities generate cash inflows and outflows related to revenue and expense transactions that affect net income. Investing activities generate cash inflows and outflows related to acquiring or disposing of noncurrent assets. Financing activities generate cash inflows and outflows related to borrowing from and repaying principal to creditors and completing transactions with the company's owners.

**LO13–2 Prepare a statement of cash flows using the indirect method to determine the net cash provided by operating activities.**

The net cash provided by operating activities can be depicted using either the direct or indirect method. Under the direct method, the income statement is reconstructed on a cash basis from top to bottom. For example, cash collected from customers is listed instead of revenue, and payments to suppliers is listed instead of cost of goods sold. Under the indirect method, net income is adjusted to a cash basis. That is, rather than directly computing cash sales, cash expenses, and so forth, these amounts are derived indirectly by removing from net income any items that do not affect cash flows.

The indirect method adjusts net income to net cash provided by operating activities using a three-step process. The first step is to add depreciation charges to net income. The second step is to analyze net changes in noncash balance sheet accounts that impact net income. The third step is to adjust for gains/losses included in the income statement.

The investing and financing sections of the statement of cash flows record gross cash flows rather than net cash flows. The net increase in cash and cash equivalents shown on the statement of cash flows agrees with the change in the Cash account shown on the balance sheet.

### LO13–3 Compute free cash flow.

Free cash flow is the net cash provided by operating activities less capital expenditures and dividends.

## GUIDANCE ANSWERS TO DECISION POINT

### Owner

Even though the company reported net income, the net effect of the company's operations was to consume rather than generate cash during the year. Cash disbursements relating to the company's operations exceeded the amount of cash receipts from operations. If the company generated a significant amount of sales just before the end of the year, it is quite possible that cash has not yet been received from the customers. In fact, given that the additional sales were international, a longer collection period would be expected. Nevertheless, as owner, you probably would want to ensure that the company's credit-granting policies and procedures were adhered to when these sales were made, and you should also monitor the length of time it takes to collect accounts receivable.

## GUIDANCE ANSWERS TO CONCEPT CHECKS

1.  **Choices a and d.** Debits are added to the beginning balance and credits are subtracted.
2.  **Choice a.** Accounts receivable is a current asset, but it is not a cash equivalent.
3.  **Choices b, c, and d.** The indirect method starts with net income and adjusts it to a cash basis.
4.  **Choices a and c.** Depreciation charges are added to net income. A loss on the sale of an asset should be added to net income.
5.  **Choice d.** Using the basic equation for contra assets, $2,000 − $350 + Credits = $2,900. The credits = $1,250.
6.  **Choice a.** The cash proceeds from the sale of the asset were $75 and the book value of the asset that was sold is $50 (= $400 − $350). The $25 difference between these two amounts is the gain on the sale of the asset and it should be subtracted from net income in the operating activities section of the statement of cash flows.
7.  **Choice c.** Using the basic equation for assets, $5,000 + Debits − $700 = $6,000. The debits equal $1,700 and this amount relates to purchases of noncurrent assets. Since the company sold an asset for $500 and it purchased noncurrent assets for $1,700, its net cash provided by (used in) investing activities is $(1,200).
8.  **Choices a and d.** Earnings quality is higher when managers use conservative estimates. It is also higher when earnings move in the same direction as net cash provided by operating activities.

Rockford Company's comparative balance sheets for this year and last year and the company's income statement for this year follow:

**Rockford Company**
**Comparative Balance Sheet**
**(dollars in millions)**

|  | This Year | Last Year |
|---|---|---|
| **Assets** | | |
| Current assets: | | |
| Cash and cash equivalents | $ 26 | $ 10 |
| Accounts receivable | 180 | 270 |
| Inventory | 205 | 160 |
| Prepaid expenses | 17 | 20 |
| Total current assets | 428 | 460 |
| Property, plant, and equipment | 430 | 309 |
| Less accumulated depreciation | 218 | 194 |
| Net property, plant, and equipment | 212 | 115 |
| Long-term investments | 60 | 75 |
| Total assets | $700 | $650 |
| **Liabilities and Stockholders' Equity** | | |
| Current liabilities: | | |
| Accounts payable | $230 | $310 |
| Accrued liabilities | 70 | 60 |
| Income taxes payable | 15 | 8 |
| Total current liabilities | 315 | 378 |
| Bonds payable | 135 | 40 |
| Total liabilities | 450 | 418 |
| Stockholders' equity: | | |
| Common stock | 140 | 140 |
| Retained earnings | 110 | 92 |
| Total stockholders' equity | 250 | 232 |
| Total liabilities and stockholders' equity | $700 | $650 |

**Rockford Company**
**Income Statement**
**For This Year Ended December 31**
**(dollars in millions)**

| | |
|---|---|
| Sales | $1,000 |
| Cost of goods sold | 530 |
| Gross margin | 470 |
| Selling and administrative expenses | 352 |
| Net operating income | 118 |
| Nonoperating items: | |
| Loss on sale of equipment | 4 |
| Income before taxes | 114 |
| Income taxes | 48 |
| Net income | $ 66 |

Additional data:
1.  This year Rockford paid a cash dividend.
2.  The $4 million loss on sale of equipment reflects a transaction in which equipment with an original cost of $12 million and accumulated depreciation of $5 million was sold for $3 million in cash.
3.  Rockford did not purchase any long-term investments during the year. There was no gain or loss on the sale of long-term investments.
4.  This year Rockford did not retire any bonds payable, or issue or repurchase any common stock.

*Required:*
1.  Using the indirect method, determine the net cash provided by operating activities for this year.
2.  Construct a statement of cash flows for this year.

### Solution to Review Problem

The first task you should complete before turning your attention to the problem's specific requirements is to compute the changes in each balance sheet account as shown below (all amounts are in millions):

| Rockford Company<br>Comparative Balance Sheet<br>(dollars in millions) | This Year | Last Year | Change |
|---|---|---|---|
| **Assets** | | | |
| Current assets: | | | |
|     Cash and cash equivalents................ | $ 26 | $ 10 | +16 |
|     Accounts receivable ..................... | 180 | 270 | −90 |
|     Inventory ............................... | 205 | 160 | +45 |
|     Prepaid expenses ........................ | 17 | 20 | −3 |
| Total current assets ......................... | 428 | 460 | |
| Property, plant, and equipment .............. | 430 | 309 | +121 |
|     Less accumulated depreciation............ | 218 | 194 | +24 |
| Net property, plant, and equipment .......... | 212 | 115 | |
| Long-term investments ...................... | 60 | 75 | −15 |
| Total assets ................................ | $700 | $650 | |
| **Liabilities and Stockholders' Equity** | | | |
| Current liabilities: | | | |
|     Accounts payable........................ | $230 | $310 | −80 |
|     Accrued liabilities...................... | 70 | 60 | +10 |
|     Income taxes payable .................... | 15 | 8 | +7 |
| Total current liabilities ..................... | 315 | 378 | |
| Bonds payable ............................. | 135 | 40 | +95 |
| Total liabilities ............................. | 450 | 418 | |
| Stockholders' equity: | | | |
|     Common stock........................... | 140 | 140 | +0 |
|     Retained earnings ...................... | 110 | 92 | +18 |
| Total stockholders' equity................... | 250 | 232 | |
| Total liabilities and stockholders' equity....... | $700 | $650 | |

*Requirement 1:*
You should perform three steps to compute the net cash provided by operating activities.

Step 1: Add depreciation to net income.
      To complete this step, apply the following equation:

$$\text{Beginning balance} - \text{Debits} + \text{Credits} = \text{Ending balance}$$

$$\$194 \text{ million} - \$5 \text{ million} + \text{Credits} = \$218 \text{ million}$$

$$\text{Credits} = \$218 \text{ million} - \$194 \text{ million} + \$5 \text{ million}$$

$$\text{Credits} = \$29 \text{ million}$$

Step 2: Analyze net changes in noncash balance sheet accounts that affect net income.
To complete this step, apply the logic from Exhibit 13–2 as follows:

| | Increase in Account Balance | Decrease in Account Balance |
|---|---|---|
| **Current Assets:** | | |
| Accounts receivable ................. | | +90 |
| Inventory .......................... | −45 | |
| Prepaid expenses ................... | | +3 |
| **Current Liabilities:** | | |
| Accounts payable ................... | | −80 |
| Accrued liabilities ................... | +10 | |
| Income taxes payable ................ | +7 | |

Step 3: Adjust for gains/losses included in the income statement.
Rockford's $4 million loss on the sale of equipment must be added to net income.

Having completed these three steps, the operating activities section of the statement of cash flows would appear as follows:

| Rockford Company<br>Statement of Cash Flows—Indirect Method<br>For This Year Ended December 31<br>(dollars in millions) | | |
|---|---|---|
| **Operating Activities** | | |
| Net income ......................................... | | $66 |
| Adjustments to convert net income to a cash basis: | | |
| Depreciation ...................................... | $29 | |
| Decrease in accounts receivable .................... | 90 | |
| Increase in inventory .............................. | (45) | |
| Decrease in prepaid expenses ...................... | 3 | |
| Decrease in accounts payable ...................... | (80) | |
| Increase in accrued liabilities ...................... | 10 | |
| Increase in income taxes payable ................... | 7 | |
| Loss on sale of equipment .......................... | 4 | 18 |
| Net cash provided by (used in) operating activities ........ | | $84 |

*Requirement 2:*
To finalize the statement of cash flows, we must complete the investing and financing sections of the statement. This requires analyzing the Property, Plant, and Equipment, Long-Term Investments, Bonds Payable, Common Stock, and Retained Earnings accounts. The table below is based on Exhibit 13–3 and it captures the changes in four account balances for Rockford.

| | Increase in Account Balance | Decrease in Account Balance |
|---|---|---|
| **Noncurrent Assets (Investing activities)** | | |
| Property, plant, and equipment ................... | −121 | |
| Long-term investments ......................... | | +15 |
| **Liabilities and Stockholders' Equity**<br>**(Financing activities)** | | |
| Bonds payable ................................ | +95 | |
| Common stock ................................ | No change | No change |
| Retained earnings ............................. | * | * |

*Requires further analysis to quantify cash dividends paid.

The data at the beginning of the problem state that Rockford did not purchase any long-term investments during the year and that there was no gain or loss on the sale of long-term investments. This means that the $15 million decrease in Long-Term Investments corresponds with a $15 million cash inflow from the sale of long-term investments that is recorded in the investing section of the statement of cash flows. The data also state that Rockford did not retire any bonds payable during the year; therefore, the $95 million increase in Bonds Payable must be due to issuing bonds payable. This cash inflow is recorded in the financing section of the statement of cash flows.

The Common Stock account had no activity during the period, so it does not impact the statement of cash flows. This leaves two accounts that require further analysis—Property, Plant, and Equipment and Retained Earnings.

The company sold equipment that had an original cost of $12 million for $3 million in cash. The cash proceeds from the sale need to be recorded in the investing activities section of the statement of cash flows. The cash outflows related to Rockford's investing activities can be computed using the following equation:

$$\text{Beginning balance} + \text{Debits} - \text{Credits} = \text{Ending balance}$$
$$\$309 \text{ million} + \text{Debits} - \$12 \text{ million} = \$430 \text{ million}$$
$$\text{Debits} = \$430 \text{ million} - \$309 \text{ million} + \$12 \text{ million}$$
$$\text{Debits} = \$133 \text{ million}$$

Rockford's Retained Earnings account and the basic equation for stockholders' equity can be used to compute the company's dividend payment as follows:

$$\text{Beginning balance} - \text{Debits} + \text{Credits} = \text{Ending balance}$$
$$\$92 \text{ million} - \text{Debits} + \$66 \text{ million} = \$110 \text{ million}$$
$$\$158 \text{ million} = \$110 \text{ million} + \text{Debits}$$
$$\text{Debits} = \$48 \text{ million}$$

The company's complete statement of cash flows is shown below. Notice that the net increase in cash and cash equivalents of $16 million equals the change in the Cash and Cash Equivalents account balance.

| Rockford Company<br>Statement of Cash Flows—Indirect Method<br>For This Year Ended December 31<br>(dollars in millions) | | |
|---|---:|---:|
| **Operating Activities** | | |
| Net income | | $ 66 |
| Adjustments to convert net income to a cash basis: | | |
| Depreciation | $ 29 | |
| Decrease in accounts receivable | 90 | |
| Increase in inventory | (45) | |
| Decrease in prepaid expenses | 3 | |
| Decrease in accounts payable | (80) | |
| Increase in accrued liabilities | 10 | |
| Increase in income taxes payable | 7 | |
| Loss on sale of equipment | 4 | 18 |
| Net cash provided by (used in) operating activities | | 84 |
| **Investing Activities** | | |
| Additions to property, plant, and equipment | (133) | |
| Proceeds from sale of long-term investments | 15 | |
| Proceeds from sale of equipment | 3 | |
| Net cash provided by (used in) investing activities | | (115) |
| **Financing Activities** | | |
| Issuance of bonds | 95 | |
| Cash dividends paid | (48) | |
| Net cash provided by (used in) financing activities | | 47 |
| Net increase in cash and cash equivalents | | 16 |
| Beginning cash and cash equivalents | | 10 |
| Ending cash and cash equivalents | | $ 26 |

**Cash equivalents**   Short-term, highly liquid investments such as Treasury bills, commercial paper, and money market funds, that are made solely for the purpose of generating a return on temporarily idle funds. (p. 617)

**Direct method**   A method of computing the net cash provided by operating activities in which the income statement is reconstructed on a cash basis from top to bottom. (p. 618)

**Financing activities**   These activities generate cash inflows and outflows related to borrowing from and repaying principal to creditors and completing transactions with the company's owners, such as selling or repurchasing shares of common stock and paying dividends. (p. 618)

**Free cash flow**   A measure that assesses a company's ability to fund its capital expenditures and dividends from its net cash provided by operating activities. (p. 634)

**Indirect method**   A method of computing the net cash provided by operating activities that starts with net income and adjusts it to a cash basis. (p. 618)

**Investing activities**   These activities generate cash inflows and outflows related to acquiring or disposing of noncurrent assets such as property, plant, and equipment, long-term investments, and loans to another entity. (p. 618)

**Net cash provided by operating activities**   The net result of the cash inflows and outflows arising from day-to-day operations. (p. 618)

**Operating activities**   These activities generate cash inflows and outflows related to revenue and expense transactions that affect net income. (p. 618)

**Statement of cash flows**   A financial statement that highlights the major activities that impact cash flows and, hence, affect the overall cash balance. (p. 616)

**13–1**   What is the purpose of a statement of cash flows?

**13–2**   What are *cash equivalents,* and why are they included with cash on a statement of cash flows?

**13–3**   What are the three major sections on a statement of cash flows, and what type of cash inflows and outflows should be included in each section?

**13–4**   What general guidelines can you provide for interpreting the statement of cash flows?

**13–5**   If an asset is sold at a gain, why is the gain subtracted from net income when computing the net cash provided by operating activities under the indirect method?

**13–6**   Why aren't transactions involving accounts payable considered to be financing activities?

**13–7**   Assume that a company repays a $300,000 loan from its bank and then later in the same year borrows $500,000. What amount(s) would appear on the statement of cash flows?

**13–8**   How do the direct and the indirect methods differ in their approach to computing the net cash provided by operating activities?

**13–9**   A business executive once stated, "Depreciation is one of our biggest operating cash inflows." Do you agree? Explain.

**13–10**   If the Accounts Receivable balance increases during a period, how will this increase be recognized using the indirect method of computing the net cash provided by operating activities?

**13–11**   Would a sale of equipment for cash be considered a financing activity or an investing activity? Why?

**13–12**   What is the difference between net cash provided by operating activities and free cash flow?

**connect** THE FOUNDATIONAL 15

LO13–1, LO13–2

Ravenna Company is a merchandiser that uses the indirect method to prepare the operating activities section of its statement of cash flows. Its balance sheet for this year is as follows:

| | Ending Balance | Beginning Balance |
|---|---|---|
| Cash and cash equivalents . . . . . . . . . . . . . . . . . . . | $ 48,000 | $ 57,000 |
| Accounts receivable . . . . . . . . . . . . . . . . . . . . . . . | 41,000 | 44,000 |
| Inventory . . . . . . . . . . . . . . . . . . . . . . . . . . . . . . . | 55,000 | 50,000 |
| Total current assets . . . . . . . . . . . . . . . . . . . . . . | 144,000 | 151,000 |
| Property, plant, and equipment . . . . . . . . . . . . . . | 150,000 | 140,000 |
|    Less accumulated depreciation . . . . . . . . . . . . . | 50,000 | 35,000 |
| Net property, plant, and equipment . . . . . . . . . . . | 100,000 | 105,000 |
| Total assets . . . . . . . . . . . . . . . . . . . . . . . . . . . . . | $244,000 | $256,000 |
| Accounts payable . . . . . . . . . . . . . . . . . . . . . . . . . | $ 32,000 | $ 57,000 |
| Income taxes payable . . . . . . . . . . . . . . . . . . . . . | 25,000 | 28,000 |
| Bonds payable . . . . . . . . . . . . . . . . . . . . . . . . . . . | 60,000 | 50,000 |
| Common stock . . . . . . . . . . . . . . . . . . . . . . . . . . . | 70,000 | 60,000 |
| Retained earnings . . . . . . . . . . . . . . . . . . . . . . . . | 57,000 | 61,000 |
| Total liabilities and stockholders' equity . . . . . . . . | $244,000 | $256,000 |

During the year, Ravenna paid a $6,000 cash dividend and it sold a piece of equipment for $3,000 that had originally cost $6,000 and had accumulated depreciation of $4,000. The company did not retire any bonds or repurchase any of its own common stock during the year.

**Required:**
1. What is the amount of the net increase or decrease in cash and cash equivalents that would be shown on the company's statement of cash flows?
2. What net income would the company include on its statement of cash flows?
3. How much depreciation would the company add to net income on its statement of cash flows?
4. (To help answer this question, create an Accounts Receivable T-account and insert the beginning and ending balances.) If the company debited Accounts Receivable and credited Sales for $600,000 during the year, what is the total amount of credits recorded in Accounts Receivable during the year? What does the amount of these credits represent?
5. What is the amount and direction (+ or −) of the accounts receivable adjustment to net income in the operating activities section of the statement of cash flows? What does this adjustment represent?
6. (To help answer this question, create T-accounts for Inventory and Accounts Payable and insert their beginning and ending balances.) If the company debited Cost of Goods Sold and credited Inventory for $400,000 during the year, what is the total amount of inventory purchases recorded on the debit side of the Inventory T-account and the credit side of the Accounts Payable T-account? What is the total amount of the debits recorded in the Accounts Payable T-account during the year? What does the amount of these debits represent?
7. What is the combined amount and direction (+ or −) of the inventory and accounts payable adjustments to net income in the operating activities section of the statement of cash flows? What does this amount represent?
8. (To help answer this question, create an Income Taxes Payable T-account and insert the beginning and ending balances.) If the company debited Income Tax Expense and credited Income Taxes Payable $700 during the year, what is the total amount of the debits recorded in the Income Taxes Payable account? What does the amount of these debits represent?
9. What is the amount and direction (+ or −) of the income taxes payable adjustment to net income in the operating activities section of the statement of cash flows? What does this adjustment represent?
10. Would the operating activities section of the company's statement of cash flows contain an adjustment for a gain or a loss? What would be the amount and direction (+ or −) of the adjustment?
11. What is the amount of net cash provided by operating activities in the company's statement of cash flows?
12. What is the amount of gross cash outflows reported in the investing section of the company's statement of cash flows?
13. What is the company's net cash provided by (used in) investing activities?
14. What is the amount of gross cash inflows reported in the financing section of the company's statement of cash flows?
15. What is the company's net cash provided by (used in) financing activities?

**EXERCISE 13–1  Classifying Transactions LO13–1**
Below are certain events that took place at Hazzard, Inc., last year:

a. Collected cash from customers.
b. Paid cash to repurchase its own stock.
c. Borrowed money from a creditor.
d. Paid suppliers for inventory purchases.
e. Repaid the principal amount of a debt.
f. Paid interest to lenders.
g. Paid a cash dividend to stockholders.
h. Sold common stock.
i. Loaned money to another entity.
j. Paid taxes to the government.
k. Paid wages and salaries to employees.
l. Purchased equipment with cash.
m. Paid bills to insurers and utility providers.

*Required:*
Prepare an answer sheet with the following headings:

| | Activity | | |
| --- | --- | --- | --- |
| Transaction | Operating | Investing | Financing |
| a. | | | |
| b. | | | |
| Etc. | | | |

Enter the cash inflows and outflows above on your answer sheet and indicate how each of them would be classified on a statement of cash flows. Place an X in the Operating, Investing, or Financing column as appropriate.

**EXERCISE 13–2  Net Cash Provided by Operating Activities LO13–2**
For the just completed year, Hanna Company had net income of $35,000. Balances in the company's current asset and current liability accounts at the beginning and end of the year were as follows:

| | December 31 | |
| --- | --- | --- |
| | End of Year | Beginning of Year |
| Current assets: | | |
| Cash and cash equivalents ........ | $30,000 | $40,000 |
| Accounts receivable ............. | $125,000 | $106,000 |
| Inventory ...................... | $213,000 | $180,000 |
| Prepaid expenses .............. | $6,000 | $7,000 |
| Current liabilities: | | |
| Accounts payable ............... | $210,000 | $195,000 |
| Accrued liabilities ............... | $4,000 | $6,000 |
| Income taxes payable ............ | $34,000 | $30,000 |

The Accumulated Depreciation account had total credits of $20,000 during the year. Hanna Company did not record any gains or losses during the year.

*Required:*
Using the indirect method, determine the net cash provided by operating activities for the year.

**EXERCISE 13–3   Calculating Free Cash Flow LO13–3**

Apex Company prepared the statement of cash flows for the current year that is shown below:

| Apex Company<br>Statement of Cash Flows—Indirect Method | | |
|---|---:|---:|
| **Operating activities** | | |
| Net income ........................................ | | $ 40,000 |
| Adjustments to convert net income to cash basis: | | |
| Depreciation ..................................... | $ 22,000 | |
| Increase in accounts receivable .................. | (60,000) | |
| Increase in inventory ............................ | (25,000) | |
| Decrease in prepaid expenses .................. | 9,000 | |
| Increase in accounts payable .................... | 55,000 | |
| Decrease in accrued liabilities ................... | (12,000) | |
| Increase in income taxes payable ................ | 5,000 | (6,000) |
| Net cash provided by (used in) operating activities .... | | 34,000 |
| **Investing activities** | | |
| Proceeds from the sale of equipment .............. | 14,000 | |
| Loan to Thomas Company ........................ | (40,000) | |
| Additions to plant and equipment .................. | (110,000) | |
| Net cash provided by (used in) investing activities ..... | | (136,000) |
| **Financing activities** | | |
| Increase in bonds payable ........................ | 90,000 | |
| Increase in common stock ........................ | 40,000 | |
| Cash dividends ................................... | (30,000) | |
| Net cash provided by (used in) financing activities .... | | 100,000 |
| Net decrease in cash and cash equivalents ......... | | (2,000) |
| Beginning cash and cash equivalents .............. | | 27,000 |
| Ending cash and cash equivalents ................. | | $ 25,000 |

*Required:*

Compute Apex Company's free cash flow for the current year.

**EXERCISE 13–4   Prepare a Statement of Cash Flows LO13–1, LO13–2**

The following changes took place last year in Pavolik Company's balance sheet accounts:

| Asset and Contra-Asset Accounts | | | Liabilities and Stockholders' Equity Accounts | | |
|---|---:|---|---|---:|---|
| Cash and cash equivalents ........ | $5 | D | Accounts payable ........ | $35 | I |
| Accounts receivable ............. | $110 | I | Accrued liabilities ........ | $4 | D |
| Inventory ....................... | $70 | D | Income taxes payable .... | $8 | I |
| Prepaid expenses ............... | $9 | I | Bonds payable .......... | $150 | I |
| Long-term investments ........... | $6 | D | Common stock .......... | $80 | D |
| Property, plant, and equipment .... | $185 | I | Retained earnings ....... | $54 | I |
| Accumulated depreciation ........ | $60 | I | | | |

D = Decrease; I = Increase

Long-term investments that cost the company $6 were sold during the year for $16 and land that cost $15 was sold for $9. In addition, the company declared and paid $30 in cash dividends during the year. Besides the sale of land, no other sales or retirements of plant and equipment took place during the year. Pavolik did not retire any bonds during the year or issue any new common stock.

The company's income statement for the year follows:

| | | |
|---|---|---|
| Sales | | $700 |
| Cost of goods sold | | 400 |
| Gross margin | | 300 |
| Selling and administrative expenses | | 184 |
| Net operating income | | 116 |
| Nonoperating items: | | |
| Loss on sale of land | $ (6) | |
| Gain on sale of investments | 10 | 4 |
| Income before taxes | | 120 |
| Income taxes | | 36 |
| Net income | | $ 84 |

The company's beginning cash balance was $90 and its ending balance was $85.

**Required:**
1. Use the indirect method to determine the net cash provided by operating activities for the year.
2. Prepare a statement of cash flows for the year.

**EXERCISE 13–5  Net Cash Provided by Operating Activities LO13–2**
Changes in various accounts and gains and losses on the sale of assets during the year for Argon Company are given below:

| Item | Amount |
|---|---|
| Accounts receivable | $90,000 decrease |
| Inventory | $120,000 increase |
| Prepaid expenses | $3,000 decrease |
| Accounts payable | $65,000 decrease |
| Accrued liabilities | $8,000 increase |
| Income taxes payable | $12,000 increase |
| Sale of equipment | $7,000 gain |
| Sale of long-term investments | $10,000 loss |

**Required:**
Prepare an answer sheet using the following column headings:

| Item | Amount | Add | Subtract |
|---|---|---|---|

For each item, place an X in the Add or Subtract column to indicate whether the dollar amount should be added to or subtracted from net income under the indirect method when computing the net cash provided by operating activities for the year.

**EXERCISE 13–6  Prepare a Statement of Cash Flows; Free Cash Flow LO13–1, LO13–2, LO13–3**
Comparative financial statement data for Carmono Company follow:

| | This Year | Last Year |
|---|---|---|
| **Assets** | | |
| Cash and cash equivalents | $ 3 | $ 6 |
| Accounts receivable | 22 | 24 |
| Inventory | 50 | 40 |
| Total current assets | 75 | 70 |
| Property, plant, and equipment | 240 | 200 |
| Less accumulated depreciation | 65 | 50 |
| Net property, plant, and equipment | 175 | 150 |
| Total assets | $250 | $220 |
| **Liabilities and Stockholders' Equity** | | |
| Accounts payable | $ 40 | $ 36 |
| Common stock | 150 | 145 |
| Retained earnings | 60 | 39 |
| Total liabilities and stockholders' equity | $250 | $220 |

For this year, the company reported net income as follows:

| | |
|---|---:|
| Sales | $275 |
| Cost of goods sold | 150 |
| Gross margin | 125 |
| Selling and administrative expenses | 90 |
| Net income | $ 35 |

This year Carmono declared and paid a cash dividend. There were no sales of property, plant, and equipment during this year. The company did not repurchase any of its own stock this year.

**Required:**
1. Using the indirect method, prepare a statement of cash flows for this year.
2. Compute Carmono's free cash flow for this year.

**PROBLEMS**      **⬛ connect**

**PROBLEM 13–7    Prepare a Statement of Cash Flows** LO13–1, LO13–2
Comparative financial statements for Weaver Company follow:

**Weaver Company**
**Comparative Balance Sheet**
**at December 31**

| | This Year | Last Year |
|---|---:|---:|
| **Assets** | | |
| Cash and cash equivalents | $ 9 | $ 15 |
| Accounts receivable | 340 | 240 |
| Inventory | 125 | 175 |
| Prepaid expenses | 10 | 6 |
| Total current assets | 484 | 436 |
| Property, plant, and equipment | 610 | 470 |
| Less accumulated depreciation | 93 | 85 |
| Net property, plant, and equipment | 517 | 385 |
| Long-term investments | 16 | 19 |
| Total assets | $1,017 | $840 |
| **Liabilities and Stockholders' Equity** | | |
| Accounts payable | $ 310 | $230 |
| Accrued liabilities | 60 | 72 |
| Income taxes payable | 40 | 34 |
| Total current liabilities | 410 | 336 |
| Bonds payable | 290 | 180 |
| Total liabilities | 700 | 516 |
| Common stock | 210 | 250 |
| Retained earnings | 107 | 74 |
| Total stockholders' equity | 317 | 324 |
| Total liabilities and stockholders' equity | $1,017 | $840 |

| Weaver Company |
| Income Statement |
| For This Year Ended December 31 |

| | | |
|---|---:|---:|
| Sales .................................. | | $800 |
| Cost of goods sold ................... | | 500 |
| Gross margin ......................... | | 300 |
| Selling and administrative expenses ... | | 213 |
| Net operating income ................ | | 87 |
| Nonoperating items: | | |
|    Gain on sale of investments ......... | $7 | |
|    Loss on sale of equipment .......... | (4) | 3 |
| Income before taxes ................. | | 90 |
| Income taxes ........................ | | 27 |
| Net income .......................... | | $ 63 |

During this year, Weaver sold some equipment for $20 that had cost $40 and on which there was accumulated depreciation of $16. In addition, the company sold long-term investments for $10 that had cost $3 when purchased several years ago. Weaver paid a cash dividend this year and the company repurchased $40 of its own stock. This year Weaver did not retire any bonds.

**Required:**
1. Using the indirect method, determine the net cash provided by operating activities for this year.
2. Using the information in (1) above, along with an analysis of the remaining balance sheet accounts, prepare a statement of cash flows for this year.

**PROBLEM 13–8    Classification of Transactions LO13–1**
Below are several transactions that took place in Seneca Company last year:

a.  Paid suppliers for inventory purchases.
b.  Bought equipment for cash.
c.  Paid cash to repurchase its own stock.
d.  Collected cash from customers.
e.  Paid wages to employees.
f.  Equipment was sold for cash.
g.  Common stock was sold for cash to investors.
h.  Cash dividends were declared and paid.
i.  A long-term loan was made to a supplier.
j.  Income taxes were paid to the government.
k.  Interest was paid to a lender.
l.  Bonds were retired by paying the principal amount due.

**Required:**
Prepare an answer sheet with the following headings:

| | Activity | | | Cash | Cash |
|---|---|---|---|---|---|
| Transaction | Operating | Investing | Financing | Inflow | Outflow |
| a. | | | | | |
| b. | | | | | |
| Etc. | | | | | |

Enter the transactions above on your answer sheet and indicate how each of them would be classified on a statement of cash flows. As appropriate, place an X in the Operating, Investing, or Financing column. Also, place an X in the Cash Inflow or Cash Outflow column.

**PROBLEM 13–9   Understanding a Statement of Cash Flows** LO13–1, LO13–2

Brock Company is a merchandiser that prepared the statement of cash flows and income statement provided below:

### Brock Company
### Statement of Cash Flows—Indirect Method

| | | |
|---|---:|---:|
| **Operating Activities** | | |
| Net income ........................................ | | $275 |
| Adjustments to convert net income to a cash basis: | | |
| Depreciation .................................... | $140 | |
| Increase in accounts receivable ................... | (24) | |
| Decrease in inventory ........................... | 39 | |
| Decrease in accounts payable ................... | (45) | |
| Decrease in accrued liabilities ................... | (5) | |
| Increase in income taxes payable ................ | 6 | |
| Gain on sale of equipment ...................... | (4) | 107 |
| Net cash provided by (used in) operating activities ... | | 382 |
| **Investing Activities** | | |
| Additions to property, plant, and equipment ......... | (150) | |
| Proceeds from sale of equipment .................. | 19 | |
| Net cash provided by (used in) investing activities .... | | (131) |
| **Financing Activities** | | |
| Issuance of bonds payable ........................ | 40 | |
| Issuance of common stock ........................ | 4 | |
| Cash dividends paid ............................. | (35) | |
| Net cash provided by (used in) financing activities ... | | 9 |
| Net increase in cash and cash equivalents .......... | | 260 |
| Beginning cash and cash equivalents .............. | | 170 |
| Ending cash and cash equivalents ................. | | $430 |

### Brock Company
### Income Statement

| | |
|---|---:|
| Sales ......................................... | $5,200 |
| Cost of goods sold ............................. | 2,980 |
| Gross margin ................................... | 2,220 |
| Selling and administrative expenses ............. | 1,801 |
| Net operating income .......................... | 419 |
| Nonoperating items: Gain on sale of equipment ... | 4 |
| Income before taxes ........................... | 423 |
| Income taxes ................................... | 148 |
| Net income .................................... | $ 275 |

**Required:**

Assume you have been asked to teach a workshop to the employees within Brock Company's Marketing Department. The purpose of your workshop is to explain how the statement of cash flows differs from the income statement. Your audience is expecting you to explain the logic underlying each number included in the statement of cash flows. Prepare a memo that explains the format of the statement of cash flows and the rationale for each number included in Brock's statement of cash flows.

**PROBLEM 13–10    Prepare a Statement of Cash Flows; Free Cash Flow** LO13–1, LO13–2, LO13–3

Joyner Company's income statement for Year 2 follows:

| | |
|---|---:|
| Sales | $900,000 |
| Cost of goods sold | 500,000 |
| Gross margin | 400,000 |
| Selling and administrative expenses | 328,000 |
| Net operating income | 72,000 |
| Nonoperating items: | |
| Gain on sale of equipment | 8,000 |
| Income before taxes | 80,000 |
| Income taxes | 24,000 |
| Net income | $ 56,000 |

Its balance sheet amounts at the end of Years 1 and 2 are as follows:

| | Year 2 | Year 1 |
|---|---:|---:|
| **Assets** | | |
| Cash and cash equivalents | $ 4,000 | $ 21,000 |
| Accounts receivable | 250,000 | 170,000 |
| Inventory | 310,000 | 260,000 |
| Prepaid expenses | 7,000 | 14,000 |
| Total current assets | 571,000 | 465,000 |
| Property, plant, and equipment | 510,000 | 400,000 |
| Less accumulated depreciation | 132,000 | 120,000 |
| Net property, plant, and equipment | 378,000 | 280,000 |
| Loan to Hymans Company | 40,000 | 0 |
| Total assets | $989,000 | $745,000 |
| **Liabilities and Stockholders' Equity** | | |
| Accounts payable | $310,000 | $250,000 |
| Accrued liabilities | 20,000 | 30,000 |
| Income taxes payable | 45,000 | 42,000 |
| Total current liabilities | 375,000 | 322,000 |
| Bonds payable | 190,000 | 70,000 |
| Total liabilities | 565,000 | 392,000 |
| Common stock | 300,000 | 270,000 |
| Retained earnings | 124,000 | 83,000 |
| Total stockholders' equity | 424,000 | 353,000 |
| Total liabilities and stockholders' equity | $989,000 | $745,000 |

Equipment that had cost $40,000 and on which there was accumulated depreciation of $30,000 was sold during Year 2 for $18,000. The company declared and paid a cash dividend during Year 2. It did not retire any bonds or repurchase any of its own stock.

***Required:***
1. Using the indirect method, compute the net cash provided by operating activities for Year 2.
2. Prepare a statement of cash flows for Year 2.
3. Compute the free cash flow for Year 2.
4. Briefly explain why cash declined so sharply during the year.

**PROBLEM 13–11   Missing Data; Statement of Cash Flows** LO13–1, LO13–2

Yoric Company listed the net changes in its balance sheet accounts for the past year as follows:

| | Debits ><br>Credits by: | Credits ><br>Debits by: |
|---|---|---|
| Cash and cash equivalents . . . . . . . . . . . . . . . . . . | $ 17,000 | |
| Accounts receivable . . . . . . . . . . . . . . . . . . . . . . | 110,000 | |
| Inventory . . . . . . . . . . . . . . . . . . . . . . . . . . . . . . . | | $ 65,000 |
| Prepaid expenses . . . . . . . . . . . . . . . . . . . . . . . . | | 8,000 |
| Long-term loans to subsidiaries . . . . . . . . . . . . . | | 30,000 |
| Long-term investments. . . . . . . . . . . . . . . . . . . . . | 80,000 | |
| Plant and equipment. . . . . . . . . . . . . . . . . . . . . . . | 220,000 | |
| Accumulated depreciation . . . . . . . . . . . . . . . . . . | | 5,000 |
| Accounts payable . . . . . . . . . . . . . . . . . . . . . . . . | | 32,000 |
| Accrued liabilities . . . . . . . . . . . . . . . . . . . . . . . . | 9,000 | |
| Income taxes payable . . . . . . . . . . . . . . . . . . . . . | | 16,000 |
| Bonds payable . . . . . . . . . . . . . . . . . . . . . . . . . . . | | 400,000 |
| Common stock . . . . . . . . . . . . . . . . . . . . . . . . . . . | 170,000 | |
| Retained earnings. . . . . . . . . . . . . . . . . . . . . . . . . | | 50,000 |
| | $606,000 | $606,000 |

The following additional information is available about last year's activities:

a. Net income for the year was $ _____?_____ .
b. The company sold equipment during the year for $15,000. The equipment originally cost $50,000 and it had $37,000 in accumulated depreciation at the time of sale.
c. Cash dividends of $20,000 were declared and paid during the year.
d. The beginning and ending balances in the Plant and Equipment and Accumulated Depreciation accounts are given below:

| | Beginning | Ending |
|---|---|---|
| Plant and equipment . . . . . . . . . . . . . . . . . . | $1,580,000 | $1,800,000 |
| Accumulated depreciation . . . . . . . . . . . . . | $675,000 | $680,000 |

e. The balance in the Cash account at the beginning of the year was $23,000; the balance at the end of the year was $ _____?_____ .
f. If data are not given explaining the change in an account, make the most reasonable assumption as to the cause of the change.

***Required:***
Using the indirect method, prepare a statement of cash flows for the year.

**PROBLEM 13–12  Prepare a Statement of Cash Flows** LO13–1, LO13–2

A comparative balance sheet and an income statement for Burgess Company are given below:

**Burgess Company**
**Comparative Balance Sheet**
**(dollars in millions)**

| | Ending Balance | Beginning Balance |
|---|---|---|
| **Assets** | | |
| Current assets: | | |
| Cash and cash equivalents | $ 49 | $ 79 |
| Accounts receivable | 645 | 580 |
| Inventory | 660 | 615 |
| Total current assets | 1,354 | 1,274 |
| Property, plant, and equipment | 1,515 | 1,466 |
| Less accumulated depreciation | 765 | 641 |
| Net property, plant, and equipment | 750 | 825 |
| Total assets | $2,104 | $2,099 |
| **Liabilities and Stockholders' Equity** | | |
| Current liabilities: | | |
| Accounts payable | $ 250 | $ 155 |
| Accrued liabilities | 190 | 165 |
| Income taxes payable | 76 | 70 |
| Total current liabilities | 516 | 390 |
| Bonds payable | 450 | 620 |
| Total liabilities | 966 | 1,010 |
| Stockholders' equity: | | |
| Common stock | 161 | 161 |
| Retained earnings | 977 | 928 |
| Total stockholders' equity | 1,138 | 1,089 |
| Total liabilities and stockholders' equity | $2,104 | $2,099 |

**Burgess Company**
**Income Statement**
**(dollars in millions)**

| | |
|---|---|
| Sales | $3,600 |
| Cost of goods sold | 2,550 |
| Gross margin | 1,050 |
| Selling and administrative expenses | 875 |
| Net operating income | 175 |
| Nonoperating items: Gain on sale of equipment | 3 |
| Income before taxes | 178 |
| Income taxes | 63 |
| Net income | $ 115 |

Burgess also provided the following information:
1. The company sold equipment that had an original cost of $13 million and accumulated depreciation of $8 million. The cash proceeds from the sale were $8 million. The gain on the sale was $3 million.
2. The company did not issue any new bonds during the year.
3. The company paid a cash dividend during the year.
4. The company did not complete any common stock transactions during the year.

***Required:***

1. Using the indirect method, prepare a statement of cash flows for the year.
2. Assume that Burgess had sales of $3,800, net income of $135, and net cash provided by operating activities of $150 in the prior year (all numbers are stated in millions). Prepare a memo that summarizes your interpretations of Burgess's financial performance.

**PROBLEM 13–13   Prepare and Interpret a Statement of Cash Flows; Free Cash Flow** LO13–1, LO13–2, LO13–3

Mary Walker, president of Rusco Company, considers $14,000 to be the minimum cash balance for operating purposes. As can be seen from the following statements, only $8,000 in cash was available at the end of this year. Since the company reported a large net income for the year, and also issued both bonds and common stock, the sharp decline in cash is puzzling to Ms. Walker.

**Rusco Company**
**Comparative Balance Sheet**
**at July 31**

|  | This Year | Last Year |
|---|---|---|
| **Assets** | | |
| Current assets: | | |
| Cash and cash equivalents . . . . . . . . . . . . | $  8,000 | $ 21,000 |
| Accounts receivable  . . . . . . . . . . . . . . . . . | 120,000 | 80,000 |
| Inventory  . . . . . . . . . . . . . . . . . . . . . . . . . . | 140,000 | 90,000 |
| Prepaid expenses  . . . . . . . . . . . . . . . . . | 5,000 | 9,000 |
| Total current assets  . . . . . . . . . . . . . . . . . | 273,000 | 200,000 |
| Long-term investments . . . . . . . . . . . . . . . | 50,000 | 70,000 |
| Plant and equipment . . . . . . . . . . . . . . . . . | 430,000 | 300,000 |
| Less accumulated depreciation . . . . . . . . | 60,000 | 50,000 |
| Net plant and equipment  . . . . . . . . . . . . . | 370,000 | 250,000 |
| Total assets . . . . . . . . . . . . . . . . . . . . . . . . | $693,000 | $520,000 |
| **Liabilities and Stockholders' Equity** | | |
| Current liabilities: | | |
| Accounts payable . . . . . . . . . . . . . . . . . . . | $123,000 | $ 60,000 |
| Accrued liabilities . . . . . . . . . . . . . . . . . . . | 8,000 | 17,000 |
| Income taxes payable  . . . . . . . . . . . . . . | 20,000 | 12,000 |
| Total current liabilities  . . . . . . . . . . . . . . . | 151,000 | 89,000 |
| Bonds payable  . . . . . . . . . . . . . . . . . . . . . | 70,000 | 0 |
| Total liabilities  . . . . . . . . . . . . . . . . . . . . . | 221,000 | 89,000 |
| Stockholders' equity: | | |
| Common stock  . . . . . . . . . . . . . . . . . . . . . | 366,000 | 346,000 |
| Retained earnings  . . . . . . . . . . . . . . . . . . | 106,000 | 85,000 |
| Total stockholders' equity  . . . . . . . . . . . | 472,000 | 431,000 |
| Total liabilities and stockholders' equity . . . | $693,000 | $520,000 |

**Rusco Company**
**Income Statement**
**For This Year Ended July 31**

| | | |
|---|---|---|
| Sales . . . . . . . . . . . . . . . . . . . . . . . . . . . . . . . . . . . . . | | $500,000 |
| Cost of goods sold . . . . . . . . . . . . . . . . . . . . . . . . . | | 300,000 |
| Gross margin . . . . . . . . . . . . . . . . . . . . . . . . . . . . . . | | 200,000 |
| Selling and administrative expenses  . . . . . . . . . . | | 158,000 |
| Net operating income  . . . . . . . . . . . . . . . . . . . . . . | | 42,000 |
| Nonoperating items: | | |
| Gain on sale of investments . . . . . . . . . . . . . . . . | $10,000 | |
| Loss on sale of equipment  . . . . . . . . . . . . . . . . | (2,000) | 8,000 |
| Income before taxes  . . . . . . . . . . . . . . . . . . . . . . | | 50,000 |
| Income taxes . . . . . . . . . . . . . . . . . . . . . . . . . . . . . . | | 20,000 |
| Net income  . . . . . . . . . . . . . . . . . . . . . . . . . . . . . . . | | $ 30,000 |

The following additional information is available for this year.

a. The company declared and paid a cash dividend.
b. Equipment was sold during the year for $8,000. The equipment originally cost $20,000 and had accumulated depreciation of $10,000.
c. Long-term investments that cost $20,000 were sold during the year for $30,000.
d. The company did not retire any bonds payable or repurchase any of its common stock.

**Required:**
1. Using the indirect method, compute the net cash provided by operating activities for this year.
2. Using the data from (1) above, and other data from the problem as needed, prepare a statement of cash flows for this year.
3. Compute free cash flow for this year.
4. Explain the major reasons for the decline in the company's cash balance.

**PROBLEM 13–14  Prepare and Interpret a Statement of Cash Flows LO13–1, LO13–2**
A comparative balance sheet for Lomax Company containing data for the last two years is as follows:

| Lomax Company Comparative Balance Sheet | This Year | Last Year |
|---|---|---|
| **Assets** | | |
| Current assets: | | |
| Cash and cash equivalents . . . . . . . . . . . . . | $ 61,000 | $ 40,000 |
| Accounts receivable . . . . . . . . . . . . . . . . . | 710,000 | 530,000 |
| Inventory . . . . . . . . . . . . . . . . . . . . . . . . . | 848,000 | 860,000 |
| Prepaid expenses . . . . . . . . . . . . . . . . . . | 10,000 | 5,000 |
| Total current assets . . . . . . . . . . . . . . . . . | 1,629,000 | 1,435,000 |
| Property, plant, and equipment . . . . . . . . . . | 3,170,000 | 2,600,000 |
| Less accumulated depreciation . . . . . . . . . | 810,000 | 755,000 |
| Net property, plant, and equipment . . . . . . . | 2,360,000 | 1,845,000 |
| Long-term investments . . . . . . . . . . . . . . . . | 60,000 | 110,000 |
| Loans to subsidiaries . . . . . . . . . . . . . . . . . | 214,000 | 170,000 |
| Total assets . . . . . . . . . . . . . . . . . . . . . . . . | $4,263,000 | $3,560,000 |
| **Liabilities and Stockholders' Equity** | | |
| Current liabilities: | | |
| Accounts payable . . . . . . . . . . . . . . . . . . . | $ 970,000 | $ 670,000 |
| Accrued liabilities . . . . . . . . . . . . . . . . . . . | 65,000 | 82,000 |
| Income taxes payable . . . . . . . . . . . . . . . . | 95,000 | 80,000 |
| Total current liabilities . . . . . . . . . . . . . . . . | 1,130,000 | 832,000 |
| Bonds payable . . . . . . . . . . . . . . . . . . . . . . | 820,000 | 600,000 |
| Total liabilities . . . . . . . . . . . . . . . . . . . . . . | 1,950,000 | 1,432,000 |
| Stockholders' equity: | | |
| Common stock . . . . . . . . . . . . . . . . . . . . . | 1,740,000 | 1,650,000 |
| Retained earnings . . . . . . . . . . . . . . . . . . | 573,000 | 478,000 |
| Total stockholders' equity . . . . . . . . . . . . . . | 2,313,000 | 2,128,000 |
| Total liabilities and stockholders' equity . . . . | $4,263,000 | $3,560,000 |

The following additional information is available about the company's activities during this year:
a. The company declared and paid a cash dividend this year.
b. Bonds with a principal balance of $350,000 were repaid during this year.
c. Equipment was sold during this year for $70,000. The equipment cost $130,000 and had $40,000 in accumulated depreciation on the date of sale.

d.  Long-term investments were sold during the year for $110,000. These investments cost $50,000 when purchased several years ago.
e.  The subsidiaries did not repay any outstanding loans during the year.
f.  Lomax did not repurchase any of its own stock during the year.

The company reported net income this year as follows:

| | | |
|---|---:|---:|
| Sales | | $2,000,000 |
| Cost of goods sold | | 1,300,000 |
| Gross margin | | 700,000 |
| Selling and administrative expenses | | 490,000 |
| Net operating income | | 210,000 |
| Nonoperating items: | | |
| Gain on sale of investments | $60,000 | |
| Loss on sale of equipment | (20,000) | 40,000 |
| Income before taxes | | 250,000 |
| Income taxes | | 80,000 |
| Net income | | $ 170,000 |

**Required:**
1.  Using the indirect method, prepare a statement of cash flows for this year.
2.  What problems relating to the company's activities are revealed by the statement of cash flows that you have prepared?

## BUILDING YOUR SKILLS    connect

**COMMUNICATING IN PRACTICE LO13–2, LO13–3**
Use an online yellow pages directory to find a company in your area that has a website on which it has an annual report, including a statement of cash flows. Make an appointment with the controller or chief financial officer of the company. Before your meeting, find out as much as you can about the organization's operations from its website.

**Required**
After asking the following questions, write a brief memorandum to your instructor that summarizes the information obtained from the company's website and addresses what you found out during your interview.
1.  Does the company use the direct method or the indirect method to determine the net cash provided by operating activities when preparing its statement of cash flows? Why?
2.  How is the information reported on the statement of cash flows used for decision-making purposes?

## APPENDIX 13A:    THE DIRECT METHOD OF DETERMINING THE NET CASH PROVIDED BY OPERATING ACTIVITIES

**LEARNING OBJECTIVE 13–4**

Use the direct method to determine the net cash provided by operating activities.

To compute the net cash provided by operating activities under the direct method, we must reconstruct the income statement on a cash basis from top to bottom. Exhibit 13A–1 shows the adjustments that must be made to adjust sales, expenses, and so forth, to a cash basis. To illustrate, we have included in the exhibit the Apparel, Inc., data from the chapter.

Note that the net cash provided by operating activities of $259 million agrees with the amount computed in the chapter by the indirect method. The two amounts agree because the direct and indirect methods are just different roads to the same destination. The investing and financing activities sections of the statement will be exactly the same as shown for the indirect method in Exhibit 13–10. The only difference between the indirect and direct methods is in the operating activities section.

## Similarities and Differences in the Handling of Data

Although we arrive at the same destination under either the direct or indirect method, not all data are handled the same way in the two adjustment processes. Stop for a moment, flip back to the bottom half of Exhibit 13–7 and compare the adjustments described in that exhibit to the adjustments made for the direct method in Exhibit 13A–1. The adjustments for accounts that affect sales (which includes only accounts receivable in our example) are handled the same way in the two methods. In either case, increases in the accounts are subtracted and decreases are added. However, the adjustments for accounts that affect expenses (which include all remaining accounts in Exhibit 13–7) are handled in opposite ways in the indirect and direct methods. This is because under the indirect method the adjustments are made to *net income,* whereas under the direct method the adjustments are made to the *expense accounts* themselves.

To illustrate this difference, note the handling of inventory and depreciation in the indirect and direct methods. Under the indirect method (Exhibit 13–7), an increase in the inventory account ($49) is *subtracted* from net income in computing the amount of net cash provided by operating activities. Under the direct method (Exhibit 13A–1), an increase in inventory is *added* to cost of goods sold. The reason for the difference can be explained as follows: An increase in inventory means that the period's inventory purchases exceeded the cost of goods sold included in the income statement. Therefore, to adjust net income to a cash basis, we must either subtract this increase from net income (indirect method) or we must add this increase to cost of goods sold (direct method). Either way, we will end up with the same figure for net cash provided by operating activities. Similarly, depreciation is added to net income under the indirect method to cancel

**EXHIBIT 13A–1**
General Model: Direct Method of Determining the Net Cash Provided by Operating Activities

| Revenue or Expense Item | Add (+) or Deduct (−) to Adjust to a Cash Basis | Illustration— Apparel, Inc. (in millions) | |
|---|---|---|---|
| Sales (as reported) | | $3,638 | |
| Adjustments to a cash basis: | | | |
| Increase in accounts receivable | − | | |
| Decrease in accounts receivable | + | +17 | $3,655 |
| Cost of goods sold (as reported) | | 2,469 | |
| Adjustments to a cash basis: | | | |
| Increase in inventory | + | +49 | |
| Decrease in inventory | − | | |
| Increase in accounts payable | − | −44 | |
| Decrease in accounts payable | + | | 2,474 |
| Selling and administrative expenses (as reported) | | 941 | |
| Adjustments to a cash basis: | | | |
| Increase in prepaid expenses | + | | |
| Decrease in prepaid expenses | − | | |
| Increase in accrued liabilities | − | −3 | |
| Decrease in accrued liabilities | + | | |
| Depreciation | − | −103 | 835 |
| Income tax expense (as reported) | | 91 | |
| Adjustments to a cash basis: | | | |
| Increase in income taxes payable | − | −4 | |
| Decrease in income taxes payable | + | | 87 |
| Net cash provided by (used in) operating activities | | | $ 259 |

out its effect (Exhibit 13–8), whereas it is subtracted from selling and administrative expenses under the direct method to cancel out its effect (Exhibit 13A–1). These differences in the handling of data are true for all other expense items in the two methods.

In the matter of gains and losses on sale of assets, no adjustments are needed under the direct method. These gains and losses are simply ignored because they are not part of sales, cost of goods sold, selling and administrative expenses, or income taxes. Observe that in Exhibit 13A–1, Apparel's $3 million gain on the sale of the store is not listed as an adjustment in the operating activities section.

## Special Rules—Direct and Indirect Methods

As stated earlier, when the direct method is used, U.S. GAAP and IFRS require a reconciliation between net income and the net cash provided by operating activities, as determined by the indirect method. Thus, *when a company elects to use the direct method, it must also present the indirect method* in a separate schedule accompanying the statement of cash flows.

On the other hand, if a company elects to use the indirect method to compute the net cash provided by operating activities, then it also must provide a special breakdown of data. The company must provide a separate disclosure of the amount of interest and the amount of income taxes paid during the year. This separate disclosure is required so that users can take the data provided by the indirect method and make estimates of what the amounts for sales, income taxes, and so forth, would have been if the direct method had been used instead.

---

## APPENDIX 13A:    EXERCISES AND PROBLEMS    ☐ connect

**EXERCISE 13A–1    Adjust Net Income to a Cash Basis LO13–4**
Refer to the data for Pavolik Company in Exercise 13–4.

***Required:***
Use the direct method to convert the company's income statement to a cash basis.

**EXERCISE 13A–2    Net Cash Provided by Operating Activities LO13–4**
Wiley Company's income statement for Year 2 follows:

| | |
|---|---:|
| Sales | $150,000 |
| Cost of goods sold | 90,000 |
| Gross margin | 60,000 |
| Selling and administrative expenses | 40,000 |
| Income before taxes | 20,000 |
| Income taxes | 8,000 |
| Net income | $ 12,000 |

The company's selling and administrative expense for Year 2 includes $7,500 of depreciation expense. Selected balance sheet accounts for Wiley at the end of Years 1 and 2 are as follows:

| | Year 2 | Year 1 |
|---|---:|---:|
| **Current Assets** | | |
| Accounts receivable | $40,000 | $30,000 |
| Inventory | $54,000 | $45,000 |
| Prepaid expenses | $8,000 | $6,000 |
| **Current Liabilities** | | |
| Accounts payable | $35,000 | $28,000 |
| Accrued liabilities | $5,000 | $8,000 |
| Income taxes payable | $2,000 | $2,500 |

*Required:*
1. Using the direct method, convert the company's income statement to a cash basis.
2. Assume that during Year 2 Wiley had a $9,000 gain on sale of investments and a $3,000 loss on the sale of equipment. Explain how these two transactions would affect your computations in (1) above.

**EXERCISE 13A–3    Net Cash Provided by Operating Activities LO13–4**
Refer to the data for Carmono Company in Exercise 13–6.

*Required:*
Using the direct method, convert the company's income statement to a cash basis.

**EXERCISE 13A–4    Net Cash Provided by Operating Activities LO13–4**
Refer to the data for Hanna Company in Exercise 13–2. The company's income statement for the year appears below:

| | |
|---|---:|
| Sales ...................................... | $350,000 |
| Cost of goods sold ......................... | 140,000 |
| Gross margin .............................. | 210,000 |
| Selling and administrative expenses .......... | 160,000 |
| Income before taxes ....................... | 50,000 |
| Income taxes .............................. | 15,000 |
| Net income ............................... | $ 35,000 |

*Required:*
Using the direct method (and the data from Exercise 13–2), convert the company's income statement to a cash basis.

**PROBLEM 13A–5    Prepare and Interpret a Statement of Cash Flows LO13–1, LO13–4**
Refer to the financial statements for Rusco Company in Problem 13–13. Because the Cash account decreased so dramatically during this year, the company's executive committee is anxious to see how the income statement would appear on a cash basis.

*Required:*
1. Using the direct method, adjust the company's income statement for this year to a cash basis.
2. Using the data from (1) above, and other data from the problem as needed, prepare a statement of cash flows for this year.
3. Briefly explain the major reasons for the sharp decline in cash during this year.

**PROBLEM 13A–6    Prepare a Statement of Cash Flows LO13–1, LO13–4**
Refer to the financial statement data for Weaver Company in Problem 13–7.

*Required:*
1. Using the direct method, adjust the company's income statement for this year to a cash basis.
2. Using the information obtained in (1) above, along with an analysis of the remaining balance sheet accounts, prepare a statement of cash flows for this year.

**PROBLEM 13A–7    Prepare and Interpret a Statement of Cash Flows LO13–1, LO13–4**
Refer to the financial statement data for Joyner Company in Problem 13–10. Sam Conway, president of the company, considers $15,000 to be the minimum cash balance for operating purposes. As can be seen from the balance sheet data, only $4,000 in cash was available at the end of the current year. The sharp decline is puzzling to Mr. Conway, particularly because sales and profits are at a record high.

*Required:*
1. Using the direct method, adjust the company's income statement to a cash basis for Year 2.
2. Using the data from (1) above and other data from the problem as needed, prepare a statement of cash flows for Year 2.
3. Explain why cash declined so sharply during the year.

**A LOOK BACK**

In Chapter 13 we showed how to construct the statement of cash flows and discussed how to interpret it.

**A LOOK AT THIS CHAPTER**

In Chapter 14 we focus on how managers analyze financial statements to better understand the financial health of their companies. We discuss the use of trend data, comparisons with other organizations, and financial ratios.

# 14

# Financial Statement Analysis

## CHAPTER OUTLINE

**Limitations of Financial Statement Analysis**

- Comparing Financial Data across Companies
- Looking beyond Ratios

**Statements in Comparative and Common-Size Form**

- Dollar and Percentage Changes on Statements
- Common-Size Statements

**Ratio Analysis—Liquidity**

- Working Capital
- Current Ratio
- Acid-Test (Quick) Ratio

**Ratio Analysis—Asset Management**

- Accounts Receivable Turnover
- Inventory Turnover
- Operating Cycle
- Total Asset Turnover

**Ratio Analysis—Debt Management**

- Times Interest Earned Ratio
- Debt-to-Equity Ratio
- Equity Multiplier

**Ratio Analysis—Profitability**

- Gross Margin Percentage
- Net Profit Margin Percentage
- Return of Total Assets
- Return on Equity

**Ratio Analysis—Market Performance**

- Earnings per Share
- Price-Earnings Ratio
- Dividend Payout and Yield Ratios
- Book Value per Share

**Summary of Ratios and Sources of Comparative Ratio Data**

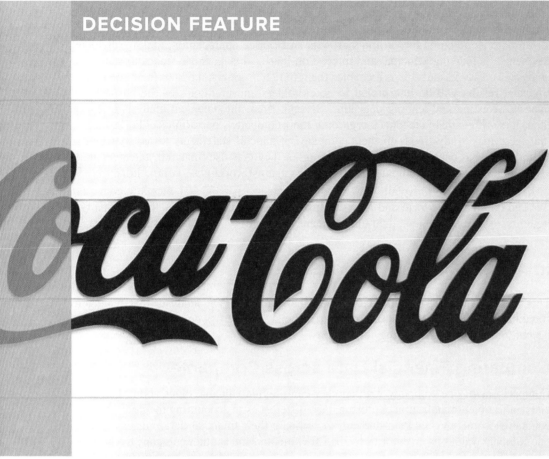

©Lionel Bonaventure/AFP/Getty Images

*After studying Chapter 14, you should be able to:*

**LO14–1** Prepare and interpret financial statements in comparative and common-size form.

**LO14–2** Compute and interpret financial ratios that managers use to assess liquidity.

**LO14–3** Compute and interpret financial ratios that managers use for asset management purposes.

**LO14–4** Compute and interpret financial ratios that managers use for debt management purposes.

**LO14–5** Compute and interpret financial ratios that managers use to assess profitability.

**LO14–6** Compute and interpret financial ratios that managers use to assess market performance.

## Coca-Cola Looks to Trim the Fat

**Coca-Cola's** operating expenses as a percentage of sales is 39%, which compares unfavorably with the likes of **Colgate** (35%), **Nestlé** (32%), **Proctor & Gamble** (31%), and **Anheuser-Busch InBev** (27%). The company plans to cut $3 billion in costs over five years by pursuing a variety of actions such as eliminating 1,000–2,000 jobs, dropping its lavish Christmas party, and tightening its travel and entertainment budget. Coke also plans to implement zero-based budgeting, which requires managers to justify all proposed annual expenditures rather than having to merely justify increases in spending relative to the prior year. Investors are skeptical whether Coke, which has historically focused on sales growth, can shift gears and reduce its spending. When Coke announced its cost-cutting plan its share price dropped 2.2%.

Source: Esterl, Mike, "Austerity Is the New Flavor at Coca-Cola," *The Wall Street Journal,* December 24, 2014, B1–B2.

S tockholders, creditors, and managers are examples of stakeholders that use *financial statement analysis* to evaluate a company's financial health and future prospects. Stockholders and creditors analyze a company's financial statements to estimate its potential for earnings growth, stock price appreciation, making dividend payments, and paying principal and interest on loans. Managers use financial statement analysis for two reasons. First, it enables them to better understand how their company's financial results will be interpreted by stockholders and creditors for the purposes of making investing and lending decisions. Second, financial statement analysis provides managers with valuable feedback regarding their company's performance. For example, managers may study trends in their company's financial statements to assess whether performance has been improving or declining, or they may use financial statement analysis to benchmark their company's performance against world-class competitors.

In this chapter, we'll explain how managers prepare financial statements in comparative and common-size form and how they use financial ratios to assess their company's liquidity, asset management, debt management, profitability, and market performance.

## LIMITATIONS OF FINANCIAL STATEMENT ANALYSIS

This section discusses two limitations of financial statement analysis that managers should always keep in mind—comparing financial data across companies and looking beyond ratios when formulating conclusions.

### Comparing Financial Data across Companies

Comparisons of one company with another can provide valuable clues about the financial health of an organization. Unfortunately, differences in accounting methods between companies sometimes make it difficult to compare their financial data. For example, if one company values its inventories by the LIFO method and another company by the average cost method, then direct comparisons of their financial data such as inventory valuations and cost of goods sold may be misleading. Sometimes enough data are presented in footnotes to the financial statements to restate data to a comparable basis. Otherwise, managers should keep in mind any lack of comparability. Even with this limitation in mind, comparing key ratios with other companies and with industry averages often helps managers identify opportunities for improvement.

### Looking beyond Ratios

Ratios should not be viewed as an end, but rather as a *starting point*. They raise many questions and point to opportunities for further analysis, but they rarely answer any questions by themselves. In addition to financial ratios, managers should consider various internal factors, such as employee learning and growth, business process performance, and customer satisfaction as well as external factors like industry trends, technological changes, changes in consumer tastes, and changes in broad economic indicators.

## STATEMENTS IN COMPARATIVE AND COMMON-SIZE FORM

**LEARNING OBJECTIVE 14–1**

Prepare and interpret financial statements in comparative and common-size form.

An item on a balance sheet or income statement has little meaning by itself. Suppose a company's sales for a year were $250 million. In isolation, that is not particularly useful information. How does that stack up against last year's sales? How do the sales relate to the cost of goods sold? In making these kinds of comparisons, three analytical techniques are widely used:

1. Dollar and percentage changes on statements (*horizontal analysis*).
2. Common-size statements (*vertical analysis*).
3. Ratios.

The first and second techniques are discussed in this section; the third technique is discussed in the remainder of the chapter. Throughout the chapter, we will illustrate these analytical techniques using the financial statements of Brickey Electronics, a producer of specialized electronic components.

## Dollar and Percentage Changes on Statements

**Horizontal analysis** (also known as **trend analysis**) involves analyzing financial data over time, such as computing year-to-year dollar and percentage changes within a set of financial statements. Exhibits 14–1 and 14–2 show Brickey Electronics' financial

**EXHIBIT 14–1**

**Brickey Electronics**
**Comparative Balance Sheet**
**(dollars in thousands)**

| | This Year | Last Year | Increase (Decrease) Amount | Increase (Decrease) Percent |
|---|---|---|---|---|
| **Assets** | | | | |
| Current assets: | | | | |
| Cash . . . . . . . . . . . . . . . . . . . . . . . . . . . . | $ 1,200 | $ 2,350 | $(1,150) | (48.9)%* |
| Accounts receivable, net . . . . . . . . . . . . | 6,000 | 4,000 | 2,000 | 50.0% |
| Inventory . . . . . . . . . . . . . . . . . . . . . . . . | 8,000 | 10,000 | (2,000) | (20.0)% |
| Prepaid expenses. . . . . . . . . . . . . . . . . | 300 | 120 | 180 | 150.0% |
| Total current assets . . . . . . . . . . . . . . . . | 15,500 | 16,470 | (970) | (5.9)% |
| Property and equipment: | | | | |
| Land . . . . . . . . . . . . . . . . . . . . . . . . . . . . | 4,000 | 4,000 | 0 | 0.0% |
| Buildings and equipment, net. . . . . . . . | 12,000 | 8,500 | 3,500 | 41.2% |
| Total property and equipment . . . . . . . . . | 16,000 | 12,500 | 3,500 | 28.0% |
| Total assets . . . . . . . . . . . . . . . . . . . . . . . . | $31,500 | $28,970 | $ 2,530 | 8.7% |
| **Liabilities and Stockholders' Equity** | | | | |
| Current liabilities: | | | | |
| Accounts payable . . . . . . . . . . . . . . . . . . | $ 5,800 | $ 4,000 | $ 1,800 | 45.0% |
| Accrued liabilities . . . . . . . . . . . . . . . . . | 900 | 400 | 500 | 125.0% |
| Notes payable, short term . . . . . . . . . . . | 300 | 600 | (300) | (50.0)% |
| Total current liabilities . . . . . . . . . . . . . . | 7,000 | 5,000 | 2,000 | 40.0% |
| Long-term liabilities: | | | | |
| Bonds payable, 8% . . . . . . . . . . . . . . . . | 7,500 | 8,000 | (500) | (6.3)% |
| Total liabilities . . . . . . . . . . . . . . . . . . . . . | 14,500 | 13,000 | 1,500 | 11.5% |
| Stockholders' equity: | | | | |
| Common stock, $12 par . . . . . . . . . . . . | 6,000 | 6,000 | 0 | 0.0% |
| Additional paid-in capital . . . . . . . . . . . . | 3,000 | 3,000 | 0 | 0.0% |
| Total paid-in capital . . . . . . . . . . . . . . . . | 9,000 | 9,000 | 0 | 0.0% |
| Retained earnings . . . . . . . . . . . . . . . . . | 8,000 | 6,970 | 1,030 | 14.8% |
| Total stockholders' equity . . . . . . . . . . . . | 17,000 | 15,970 | 1,030 | 6.4% |
| Total liabilities and stockholders' equity. . . . . . . . . . . . . . . | $31,500 | $28,970 | $ 2,530 | 8.7% |

*The changes between this year and last year are expressed as a percentage of the dollar amount for last year. For example, Cash decreased by $1,150 between this year and last year. This decrease expressed in percentage form is computed as follows: $1,150 ÷ $2,350 = 48.9%. Other percentage figures in this exhibit and Exhibit 14–2 are computed in the same way.

**EXHIBIT 14-2**

| | | | Increase (Decrease) | |
|---|---|---|---|---|
| | This Year | Last Year | Amount | Percent |

**Brickey Electronics**
**Comparative Income Statement and Reconciliation of Retained Earnings**
**(dollars in thousands)**

| | This Year | Last Year | Amount | Percent |
|---|---|---|---|---|
| Sales | $52,000 | $48,000 | $4,000 | 8.3% |
| Cost of goods sold | 36,000 | 31,500 | 4,500 | 14.3% |
| Gross margin | 16,000 | 16,500 | (500) | (3.0)% |
| Selling and administrative expenses: | | | | |
| Selling expenses | 7,000 | 6,500 | 500 | 7.7% |
| Administrative expenses | 5,860 | 6,100 | (240) | (3.9)% |
| Total selling and administrative expenses | 12,860 | 12,600 | 260 | 2.1% |
| Net operating income | 3,140 | 3,900 | (760) | (19.5)% |
| Interest expense | 640 | 700 | (60) | (8.6)% |
| Net income before taxes | 2,500 | 3,200 | (700) | (21.9)% |
| Income taxes (30%) | 750 | 960 | (210) | (21.9)% |
| Net income | 1,750 | 2,240 | $ (490) | (21.9)% |
| Dividends to common stockholders, $1.44 per share | 720 | 720 | | |
| Net income added to retained earnings | 1,030 | 1,520 | | |
| Beginning retained earnings | 6,970 | 5,450 | | |
| Ending retained earnings | $ 8,000 | $ 6,970 | | |

statements in this *comparative form.* The dollar changes highlight the changes that are the most important economically; the percentage changes highlight the changes that are the most unusual.

Horizontal analysis can be even more useful when data from a number of years are used to compute *trend percentages.* To compute **trend percentages**, a base year is selected and the data for all years are stated as a percentage of that base year. To illustrate, consider the sales and net income of **McDonald's Corporation,** the world's largest food service retailer, with more than 31,000 restaurants worldwide:

| | 2006 | 2007 | 2008 | 2009 | 2010 | 2011 | 2012 | 2013 | 2014 | 2015 |
|---|---|---|---|---|---|---|---|---|---|---|
| Sales (millions) | $20,895 | $22,787 | $23,522 | $22,745 | $24,075 | $27,006 | $27,567 | $28,106 | $27,441 | $25,413 |
| Net income (millions) | $3,544 | $2,395 | $4,313 | $4,551 | $4,946 | $5,503 | $5,465 | $5,586 | $4,758 | $4,529 |

By simply looking at these data, you can see that sales increased every year except 2009, 2014, and 2015 and net income increased every year except 2007, 2012, 2014, and 2015. However, recasting these data into trend percentages aids interpretation:

| | 2006 | 2007 | 2008 | 2009 | 2010 | 2011 | 2012 | 2013 | 2014 | 2015 |
|---|---|---|---|---|---|---|---|---|---|---|
| Sales | 100% | 109% | 113% | 109% | 115% | 129% | 132% | 135% | 131% | 122% |
| Net income | 100% | 68% | 122% | 128% | 140% | 155% | 154% | 158% | 134% | 128% |

In the above table, both sales and net income have been restated as a percentage of the 2006 sales and net income. For example, the 2008 sales of $23,522 are 113% of the 2006 sales of $20,895. This trend analysis is easier to analyze when the data are plotted as in Exhibit 14–3. McDonald's experienced modest but reasonably constant sales growth through 2013 and then sales dropped in 2014 and 2015. Net income plummeted in 2007, fully recovered in 2008, reached a record-high in 2013, and then dipped again in 2014 and 2015.

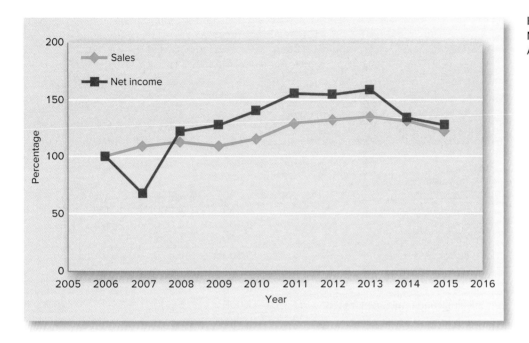

**EXHIBIT 14–3**
McDonald's Corporation: Trend Analysis of Sales and Net Income

## Common-Size Statements

Horizontal analysis, which was discussed in the previous section, examines changes in financial statement accounts over time. **Vertical analysis** focuses on the relations among financial statement accounts at a given point in time. A **common-size financial statement** is a vertical analysis in which each financial statement account is expressed as a percentage. In income statements, all items are usually expressed as a percentage of sales. In balance sheets, all items are usually expressed as a percentage of total assets. Exhibit 14–4 contains Brickey Electronics' common-size balance sheet and Exhibit 14–5 contains its common-size income statement.

Notice from Exhibit 14–4 that placing all assets in common-size form clearly shows the relative importance of the current assets as compared to the noncurrent assets. It also shows that significant changes have taken place in the composition of the current assets over the last year. For example, accounts receivable have increased in relative importance and both cash and inventory have declined in relative importance. Judging from the sharp increase in accounts receivable, the deterioration in the cash balance may be a result of an inability to collect from customers.

The common-size income statement in Exhibit 14–5 states each line item as a percentage of sales. For example, the administrative expenses were 12.7% of sales last year and 11.3% of sales this year. If the quality and efficiency of Brickey's administrative services is holding constant or improving over time, then these two percentages suggest that this year Brickey managed its administrative resources more cost-effectively than last year. Beyond administrative expenses, managers also have a keen interest in other percentages disclosed in a common-size income statement and those will be discussed in a later section related to profitability ratios.

## HELPFUL HINT

Common-size balance sheets express each balance sheet account as a percentage of total assets. Common-size income statements express each income statement account as a percentage of sales.

**EXHIBIT 14–4**

**Brickey Electronics**
**Common-Size Comparative Balance Sheet**
**(dollars in thousands)**

| | This Year | Last Year | Common-Size Percentages This Year | Common-Size Percentages Last Year |
|---|---|---|---|---|
| **Assets** | | | | |
| Current assets: | | | | |
| Cash ............................... | $ 1,200 | $ 2,350 | 3.8%* | 8.1% |
| Accounts receivable, net............. | 6,000 | 4,000 | 19.0% | 13.8% |
| Inventory ......................... | 8,000 | 10,000 | 25.4% | 34.5% |
| Prepaid expenses................... | 300 | 120 | 1.0% | 0.4% |
| Total current assets ................... | 15,500 | 16,470 | 49.2% | 56.9% |
| Property and equipment: | | | | |
| Land .............................. | 4,000 | 4,000 | 12.7% | 13.8% |
| Buildings and equipment, net......... | 12,000 | 8,500 | 38.1% | 29.3% |
| Total property and equipment........... | 16,000 | 12,500 | 50.8% | 43.1% |
| Total assets .......................... | $31,500 | $28,970 | 100.0% | 100.0% |
| **Liabilities and Stockholders' Equity** | | | | |
| Current liabilities: | | | | |
| Accounts payable................... | $ 5,800 | $ 4,000 | 18.4% | 13.8% |
| Accrued liabilities .................. | 900 | 400 | 2.9% | 1.4% |
| Notes payable, short term ........... | 300 | 600 | 1.0% | 2.1% |
| Total current liabilities................. | 7,000 | 5,000 | 22.2% | 17.3% |
| Long-term liabilities: | | | | |
| Bonds payable, 8%.................. | 7,500 | 8,000 | 23.8% | 27.6% |
| Total liabilities ....................... | 14,500 | 13,000 | 46.0% | 44.9% |
| Stockholders' equity: | | | | |
| Common stock, $12 par ............. | 6,000 | 6,000 | 19.0% | 20.7% |
| Additional paid-in capital............. | 3,000 | 3,000 | 9.5% | 10.4% |
| Total paid-in capital ................. | 9,000 | 9,000 | 28.6% | 31.1% |
| Retained earnings................... | 8,000 | 6,970 | 25.4% | 24.0% |
| Total stockholders' equity ............. | 17,000 | 15,970 | 54.0% | 55.1% |
| Total liabilities and stockholders' equity ............................. | $31,500 | $28,970 | 100.0% | 100.0% |

*Each asset account on a common-size statement is expressed as a percentage of total assets, and each liability and equity account is expressed as a percentage of total liabilities and stockholders' equity. For example, the percentage figure above for this year's Cash balance is computed as follows: $1,200 ÷ $31,500 = 3.8%. All common-size percentages have been rounded to one decimal place; therefore, the figures as shown may not fully reconcile down each column.

EXHIBIT 14-5

**Brickey Electronics**
**Common-Size Comparative Income Statement**
**(dollars in thousands)**

| | This Year | Last Year | Common-Size Percentages* This Year | Common-Size Percentages* Last Year |
|---|---|---|---|---|
| Sales.................................. | $52,000 | $48,000 | 100.0% | 100.0% |
| Cost of goods sold.................... | 36,000 | 31,500 | 69.2% | 65.6% |
| Gross margin......................... | 16,000 | 16,500 | 30.8% | 34.4% |
| Selling and administrative expenses: | | | | |
| Selling expenses ................... | 7,000 | 6,500 | 13.5% | 13.5% |
| Administrative expenses ............. | 5,860 | 6,100 | 11.3% | 12.7% |
| Total selling and administrative | | | | |
| expenses.......................... | 12,860 | 12,600 | 24.7% | 26.3% |
| Net operating income................. | 3,140 | 3,900 | 6.0% | 8.1% |
| Interest expense..................... | 640 | 700 | 1.2% | 1.5% |
| Net income before taxes .............. | 2,500 | 3,200 | 4.8% | 6.7% |
| Income taxes (30%) .................. | 750 | 960 | 1.4% | 2.0% |
| Net income.......................... | $ 1,750 | $ 2,240 | 3.4% | 4.7% |

*Note that the percentage figures for each year are expressed as a percentage of total sales for the year. For example, the percentage figure for this year's cost of goods sold is computed as follows: $36,000 ÷ $52,000 = 69.2%. All common-size percentages have been rounded to one decimal place; therefore, the figures as shown may not fully reconcile down each column.

# RATIO ANALYSIS—LIQUIDITY

*Liquidity* refers to how quickly an asset can be converted to cash. Liquid assets can be converted to cash quickly, whereas ill-liquid assets cannot. Companies need to continuously monitor the amount of their liquid assets relative to the amount that they owe short-term creditors, such as suppliers. If a company's liquid assets are not enough to support timely payments to short-term creditors, this presents an important management problem that, if not remedied, can lead to bankruptcy.

**LEARNING OBJECTIVE 14-2**

Compute and interpret financial ratios that managers use to assess liquidity.

This section uses Brickey Electronics' financial statements to explain one measure and two ratios that managers use to analyze their company's liquidity and its ability to pay short-term creditors. *As you proceed through this section, keep in mind that all calculations are performed for this year rather than last year.*

## Working Capital

The excess of current assets over current liabilities is known as **working capital.**

Working capital = Current assets − Current liabilities

The working capital for Brickey Electronics is computed as follows:

Working capital = $15,500,000 − $7,000,000 = $8,500,000

Managers need to interpret working capital from two perspectives. On one hand, if a company has ample working capital, it provides some assurance that the company can pay its creditors in full and on time. On the other hand, maintaining large amounts of working capital isn't free. Working capital must be financed with long-term debt and equity—both of which are expensive. Furthermore, a large and growing working capital balance may indicate troubles, such as excessive growth in inventories. Therefore, managers often want to minimize working capital while retaining the ability to pay short-term creditors.

## Current Ratio

A company's working capital is frequently expressed in ratio form. A company's current assets divided by its current liabilities is known as the **current ratio:**

$$\text{Current ratio} = \frac{\text{Current assets}}{\text{Current liabilities}}$$

For Brickey Electronics, the current ratio is computed as follows:

$$\text{Current ratio} = \frac{\$15,500,000}{\$7,000,000} = 2.21$$

Although widely regarded as a measure of short-term debt-paying ability, the current ratio must be interpreted with great care. A *declining* ratio might be a sign of a deteriorating financial condition, or it might be the result of eliminating obsolete inventories or other stagnant current assets. An *improving* ratio might be the result of stockpiling inventory, or it might indicate an improving financial situation. In short, the current ratio is useful, but tricky to interpret.

The general rule of thumb calls for a current ratio of at least 2. However, many companies successfully operate with a current ratio below 2. The adequacy of a current ratio depends heavily on the *composition* of the assets. For example, as we see in the table below, both Worthington Corporation and Greystone, Inc., have current ratios of 2. However, they are not in comparable financial condition. Greystone is more likely to have difficulty meeting its current financial obligations because almost all of its current assets consist of inventory rather than more liquid assets such as cash and accounts receivable.

| | Worthington Corporation | Greystone, Inc. |
|---|---|---|
| Current assets: | | |
| Cash | $ 25,000 | $ 2,000 |
| Accounts receivable, net | 60,000 | 8,000 |
| Inventory | 85,000 | 160,000 |
| Prepaid expenses | 5,000 | 5,000 |
| Total current assets (a) | $175,000 | $175,000 |
| Current liabilities (b) | $ 87,500 | $ 87,500 |
| Current ratio, (a) ÷ (b) | 2 | 2 |

## Acid-Test (Quick) Ratio

The **acid-test (quick) ratio** is a more rigorous test of a company's ability to meet its short-term debts than the current ratio. Inventories and prepaid expenses are excluded from total current assets, leaving only the more liquid (or "quick") assets to be divided by current liabilities.

$$\text{Acid-test ratio} = \frac{\text{Cash + Marketable securities + Accounts receivable + Short-term notes receivable}}{\text{Current liabilities}}$$

The acid-test ratio measures how well a company can meet its obligations without having to liquidate or depend too heavily on its inventory. Ideally, each dollar of liabilities should be backed by at least $1 of quick assets. However, acid-test ratios as low as 0.3 are common.

The acid-test ratio for Brickey Electronics is computed below:

$$\text{Acid-test ratio} = \frac{\$1,200,000 + \$0 + \$6,000,000 + \$0}{\$7,000,000} = 1.03$$

Although Brickey Electronics' acid-test ratio is within the acceptable range, a manager might be concerned about several trends revealed in the company's balance sheet. Notice in Exhibit 14–1 that short-term debts are rising, while the cash balance is declining. Perhaps the lower cash balance is a result of the substantial increase in accounts receivable. In short, as with the current ratio, the acid-test ratio should be interpreted with one eye on its basic components.

# RATIO ANALYSIS—ASSET MANAGEMENT

A company's assets are funded by lenders and stockholders, both of whom expect those assets to be deployed efficiently and effectively. In this section, we'll describe various measures and ratios that managers use to assess their company's asset management performance. *All forthcoming calculations will be performed for this year.*

**LEARNING OBJECTIVE 14–3**

Compute and interpret financial ratios that managers use for asset management purposes.

## Accounts Receivable Turnover

The *accounts receivable turnover* and *average collection period* ratios measure how quickly credit sales are converted into cash. The **accounts receivable turnover** is computed by dividing sales on account (i.e., credit sales) by the average accounts receivable balance for the year:

$$\text{Accounts receivable turnover} = \frac{\text{Sales on account}}{\text{Average accounts receivable balance}}$$

Assuming that all of Brickey Electronics' sales were on account, its accounts receivable turnover is computed as follows:

$$\text{Accounts receivable turnover} = \frac{\$52,000,000}{(\$6,000,000 + \$4,000,000)/2} = 10.4$$

The accounts receivable turnover can then be divided into 365 days to determine the average number of days required to collect an account (known as the **average collection period**).

$$\text{Average collection period} = \frac{365 \text{ days}}{\text{Accounts receivable turnover}}$$

The average collection period for Brickey Electronics is computed as follows:

$$\text{Average collection period} = \frac{365 \text{ days}}{10.4} = 35.1 \text{ days}$$

This means that on average it takes 35 days to collect a credit sale. Whether this is good or bad depends on the credit terms Brickey Electronics is offering its customers. Many customers will tend to withhold payment for as long as the credit terms allow. If the credit terms are 30 days, then a 35-day average collection period would usually be viewed as very good. On the other hand, if the company's credit terms are 10 days, then a 35-day average collection period is worrisome. A long collection period may result from having too many old uncollectible accounts, failing to bill promptly or follow up on late accounts, lax credit checks, and so on. In practice, average collection periods ranging all the way from 10 days to 180 days are common, depending on the industry.

## Inventory Turnover

The **inventory turnover ratio** measures how many times a company's inventory has been sold and replaced during the year. It is computed by dividing the cost of goods sold by the average level of inventory [(Beginning inventory balance + Ending inventory balance) ÷ 2]:

$$\text{Inventory turnover} = \frac{\text{Cost of goods sold}}{\text{Average inventory balance}}$$

Brickey's inventory turnover is computed as follows:

$$\text{Inventory turnover} = \frac{\$36,000,000}{(\$8,000,000 + \$10,000,000)/2} = 4.0$$

The number of days needed on average to sell the entire inventory (called the **average sale period**) can be computed by dividing 365 by the inventory turnover:

$$\text{Average sale period} = \frac{365 \text{ days}}{\text{Inventory turnover}}$$

$$= \frac{365 \text{ days}}{4 \text{ times}} = 91.3 \text{ days}$$

The average sale period varies from industry to industry. Grocery stores, with significant perishable stocks, tend to turn over their inventory quickly. On the other hand, jewelry stores tend to turn over their inventory slowly. In practice, average sale periods of 10 days to 90 days are common, depending on the industry.

A company whose inventory turnover ratio is much slower than the average for its industry may have too much inventory or the wrong sorts of inventory. Some managers argue that they must buy in large quantities to take advantage of quantity discounts. But these discounts must be compared to the added costs of insurance, taxes, financing, and risks of obsolescence and deterioration that result from carrying added inventories.

## HELPFUL HINT

When the numerator of a financial ratio contains an amount from the income statement and the denominator contains an amount derived from the balance sheet, the denominator must be expressed as an average. This averaging process is done because the income statement summarizes performance for a period of time, whereas the balance sheet reflects a company's financial position at a point in time. The average for a balance sheet account is typically computed by taking the account's beginning balance plus its ending balance and dividing this sum by two.

## Operating Cycle

The **operating cycle** measures the elapsed time from when inventory is received from suppliers to when cash is received from customers. It is computed as follows:

$$\text{Operating cycle} = \text{Average sale period} + \text{Average collection period}$$

Brickey Electronics' operating cycle is computed as follows:

Operating cycle = 91.3 days + 35.1 days = 126.4 days

A manager's goal is to reduce the operating cycle because it puts cash receipts in the company's possession sooner. In fact, if a company can shrink its operating cycle to fewer days than its average payment period for suppliers, it means the company is receiving cash from customers before it has to pay suppliers for inventory purchases. For example, if a company's operating cycle is 10 days and its average payment period to suppliers is 30 days, the company is receiving cash from customers 20 days before it pays its suppliers. In this example, the company could earn interest income on cash collections for 20 days before paying a portion of those receipts to suppliers. Conversely, if a company's operating cycle is much longer than its average payment period for suppliers, it creates the need to borrow money to fund its inventories and accounts receivable. In the case of Brickey Electronics, its operating cycle is very high, thereby suggesting that it needs to borrow money to fund its working capital.

1. Jones Company's sales are $1,000,000 and 80% of those sales are on credit. The beginning and ending accounts receivable balances are $100,000 and $140,000, respectively. What is the company's accounts receivable turnover?
   a. 3.33
   b. 6.67
   c. 8.33
   d. 10.67
2. Jones Company's sales are $1,000,000 and the gross margin percentage is 60%. The beginning and ending inventory balances are $240,000 and $260,000, respectively. What is the inventory turnover?
   a. 1.60
   b. 2.40
   c. 3.40
   d. 3.60
3. Based on the information in question 2, what is Jones Company's average sale period?
   a. 152 days
   b. 140 days
   c. 228 days
   d. 175 days
4. Based on the information in questions 1–3, what is Jones Company's operating cycle?
   a. 295 days
   b. 283 days
   c. 243 days
   d. 307 days

CONCEPT CHECK

## Total Asset Turnover

The **total asset turnover** is a ratio that compares total sales to average total assets. It measures how efficiently a company's assets are being used to generate sales. This ratio expands beyond current assets to include noncurrent assets, such as property, plant, and equipment. It is computed as follows:

$$\text{Total asset turnover} = \frac{\text{Sales}}{\text{Average total assets}}$$

Brickey Electronics' total asset turnover is computed as follows:

$$\text{Total asset turnover} = \frac{\$52,000,000}{(\$31,500,000 + \$28,970,000)/2} = 1.72$$

A company's goal is to increase its total asset turnover. To do so, it must either increase sales or reduce its investment in assets. If a company's accounts receivable turnover and inventory turnover are increasing, but its total asset turnover is decreasing, it suggests the problem may relate to noncurrent asset utilization and efficiency. It also bears emphasizing that if all else holds constant, a company's total asset turnover will increase over time simply because the accumulated depreciation on plant and equipment grows over time.

## RATIO ANALYSIS—DEBT MANAGEMENT

Managers need to evaluate their company's debt management choices from the vantage point of two stakeholders—long-term creditors and common stockholders. Long-term creditors are concerned with a company's ability to repay its loans over the long-run. For example, if a company paid out all of its available cash in the form of dividends, then nothing would be left to pay back creditors. Consequently, creditors often seek protection by requiring that borrowers agree to various restrictive covenants, or rules. These restrictive covenants typically include restrictions on dividend payments as well as rules stating that the company must maintain certain financial ratios at specified levels. Although restrictive covenants are widely used, they do not ensure that creditors will be paid when loans come due. The company still must generate sufficient earnings to cover payments.

Stockholders look at debt from a *financial leverage* perspective. **Financial leverage** refers to borrowing money to acquire assets in an effort to increase sales and profits. A company can have either positive or negative financial leverage depending on the difference between its rate of return on total assets and the rate of return that it must pay its creditors. If the company's rate of return on total assets exceeds the rate of return the company pays its creditors, *financial leverage is positive.* If the rate of return on total assets is less than the rate of return the company pays its creditors, *financial leverage is negative.* We will explore whether Brickey Electronics has positive or negative financial leverage later in the chapter. For now, you need to understand that if a company has positive financial leverage, having debt can substantially benefit common stockholders. Conversely, if a company has negative financial leverage, common stockholders suffer. Given the potential benefits of maintaining positive financial leverage, managers do not try to avoid debt, rather they often seek to maintain a level of debt that is considered to be normal within their industry.

In this section, we explain three ratios that managers use for debt management purposes, times interest earned ratio, debt-to-equity ratio, and the equity multiplier. *All calculations are performed for this year.*

### Times Interest Earned Ratio

The most common measure of a company's ability to provide protection to its long-term creditors is the **times interest earned ratio.** It is computed by dividing earnings before interest expense and income taxes (i.e., net operating income) by interest expense:

$$\text{Times interest earned ratio} = \frac{\text{Earnings before interest expense and income taxes}}{\text{Interest expense}}$$

For Brickey Electronics, the times interest earned ratio for this year is computed as follows:

$$\text{Times interest earned} = \frac{\$3,140,000}{\$640,000} = 4.91$$

The times interest earned ratio is based on earnings before interest expense and income taxes because that is the amount of earnings that is available for making interest payments. Interest expenses are deducted *before* income taxes are determined; creditors have first claim on the earnings before taxes are paid.

A times interest earned ratio of less than 1 is inadequate because interest expense exceeds the earnings that are available for paying that interest. In contrast, a times interest earned ratio of 2 or more may be considered sufficient to protect long-term creditors.

## Debt-to-Equity Ratio

The **debt-to-equity ratio** is one type of leverage ratio that indicates the relative proportions of debt and equity at one point in time on a company's balance sheet. As the debt-to-equity ratio increases, it indicates that a company is increasing its financial leverage. In other words, it is relying on a greater proportion of debt rather than equity to fund its assets. The debt-to-equity ratio is measured as follows:

$$\text{Debt-to-equity ratio} = \frac{\text{Total liabilities}}{\text{Stockholders' equity}}$$

Brickey's debt-to-equity ratio for this year is computed as follows:

$$\text{Debt-to-equity ratio} = \frac{\$14,500,000}{\$17,000,000} = 0.85$$

At the end of this year, Brickey Electronics' creditors were providing 85 cents for each $1 being provided by stockholders.

Creditors and stockholders have different views about the optimal debt-to-equity ratio. Ordinarily, stockholders would like a lot of debt to take advantage of positive financial leverage. On the other hand, because equity represents the excess of total assets over total liabilities, and hence a buffer of protection for creditors, creditors would like to see less debt and more equity. In practice, debt-to-equity ratios from 0.0 (no debt) to 3.0 are common. Generally speaking, in industries with little financial risk, managers maintain high debt-to-equity ratios. In industries with more financial risk, managers maintain lower debt-to-equity ratios.

## Equity Multiplier

The **equity multiplier** is another type of leverage ratio that indicates the portion of a company's assets funded by equity. Similar to the debt-to-equity ratio, as the equity multiplier increases, it indicates that a company is increasing its financial leverage. In other words, it is relying on a greater proportion of debt rather than equity to fund its assets. Instead of measuring amounts in the numerator and denominator at one point in time (as is done with the debt-to-equity ratio), the equity multiplier focuses on average amounts maintained throughout the year and it is measured as follows:

$$\text{Equity multiplier} = \frac{\text{Average total assets}}{\text{Average stockholders' equity}}$$

Brickey's equity multiplier for this year is computed as follows:

$$\text{Equity multiplier} = \frac{(\$31,500,000 + \$28,970,000)/2}{(\$17,000,000 + \$15,970,000)/2} = 1.83$$

The debt-to-equity ratio and the equity multiplier provide signals about how a company is managing its mix of debt and equity. We have introduced the equity multiplier because it will be used in the next section of the chapter to provide further insight into how companies measure and interpret what will be defined as return on equity (ROE).

5.  Total assets are $1,500,000 and stockholders' equity is $900,000. What is the debt-to-equity ratio?
    a. 0.33
    b. 0.50
    c. 0.60
    d. 0.67

# RATIO ANALYSIS—PROFITABILITY

Managers pay close attention to the amount of profits that their companies earn. However, when analyzing ratios, they tend to focus on the amount of profit earned relative to some other amount such as sales, total assets, or total stockholder's equity. When profits are stated as a percentage of another number, such as sales, it helps managers draw informed conclusions about how the organization is performing over time. For example, if a company had profits in Years 1 and 2 of $10 and $20, respectively, it would be naïve to immediately assume that the company's performance has improved. In other words, if we further assume that sales in Year 1 are $100 and sales in Year 2 are $1,000, it would be troubling to see that the company converted $900 of additional sales into only $10 dollars of additional profit. In this section, we develop this idea further by discussing four profitability ratios commonly used by managers—gross margin percentage, net profit margin percentage, return on total assets, and return on equity. *All forthcoming calculations are performed for this year.*

## Gross Margin Percentage

Exhibit 14–5 shows that Brickey's cost of goods sold as a percentage of sales increased from 65.6% last year to 69.2% this year. Or looking at this from a different viewpoint, the *gross margin percentage* declined from 34.4% last year to 30.8% this year. Managers and investors pay close attention to this measure of profitability. The **gross margin percentage** is computed as follows:

$$\text{Gross margin percentage} = \frac{\text{Gross margin}}{\text{Sales}}$$

The gross margin percentage should be more stable for retailing companies than for other companies because the cost of goods sold in retailing excludes fixed costs. When fixed costs are included in the cost of goods sold, the gross margin percentage should increase and decrease with sales volume. With increases in sales volume, fixed costs are spread across more units and the gross margin percentage should improve.

## Has Abercrombie & Fitch Lost Its Cachet?

Over the past five years, **Abercrombie & Fitch** (A&F) has earned gross margin percentages in the low-to-mid 60% range, whereas **American Eagle Outfitters** and **Aéropostale** have earned gross margin percentages below 40%. Part of the reason for A&F's huge margins has been its strong brand recognition among teenagers, who were willing to pay high prices for apparel donning the company's logo. However, now that the fickle teen market has declared logos a fashion faux pas, it presents A&F with an interesting challenge—maintaining its margins by selling logo-less apparel. The financial stakes are high given that each 1% drop in the company's gross margin percentage translates to a 14% drop in net operating income.

Source: Gottfried, Miriam, "Abercrombie's Margins Aren't Cool," *The Wall Street Journal*, December 9, 2014, C10.

## Net Profit Margin Percentage

Exhibit 14–5 shows that Brickey's *net profit margin percentage* decreased from 4.7% last year to 3.4% this year. The **net profit margin percentage** is widely used by managers and it is computed as follows:

$$\text{Net profit margin percentage} = \frac{\text{Net income}}{\text{Sales}}$$

The gross profit margin percentage and the net profit margin percentage state the gross margin and net income as a percentage of sales. The gross margin percentage focuses on only one type of expense (cost of goods sold) and its impact on performance, whereas the net profit margin percentage also looks at how selling and administrative expenses, interest expense, and income tax expense have influenced performance. The remaining ratios in this section look at profitability relative to amounts reported on the balance sheet rather than sales.

### Allegiant Travel Company Thrives Serving Small Cities

IN BUSINESS

**Allegiant Travel Company** earns the highest profit margins in the U.S. airline industry by flying customers from 75 small city markets, such as Minot, North Dakota, Allentown, Pennsylvania, and Casper, Wyoming, to 14 warm-weather destinations, such as Tampa, Florida, Honolulu, Hawaii, and Las Vegas, Nevada. Over a five-year span, Allegiant's stock price has risen by over 360% and in a recent quarter, the company earned a pre-tax profit margin of 18.5% on sales of $900 million.

Its enviable financial results are accompanied by the industry's worst on-time arrival rating—with more than 30% of its flights arriving late to their destinations. These contradictory statistics raise an interesting question: how can a company with the worst on-time arrival rate in the airline industry achieve market-leading profit margins? Perhaps part of the answer to this question is that Allegiant's small-city strategy removes competitors from 186 of its 203 routes.

©Mark Summerfield/Alamy Stock Photo

Source: Nicas, Jack, "From Toledo to Profitability," *The Wall Street Journal*, June 5, 2013, B1, B7.

## Return on Total Assets

The **return on total assets** is a measure of operating performance that is defined as follows:

$$\text{Return on total assets} = \frac{\text{Net income} + [\text{Interest expense} \times (1 - \text{Tax rate})]}{\text{Average total assets}}$$

Interest expense is added back to net income to show what earnings would have been if the company had no debt. With this adjustment, a manager can evaluate his company's return on total assets over time without the analysis being influenced by changes in the company's mix of debt and equity over time. Furthermore, this adjustment enables managers to draw more meaningful comparisons with other companies that have differing amounts of debt. Notice that the interest expense is placed on an after-tax basis by multiplying it by the factor (1 − Tax rate).

The return on total assets for Brickey Electronics is computed as follows (from Exhibits 14–1 and 14–2):

$$\text{Return on total assets} = \frac{\$1,750,000 + [\$640,000 \times (1 - 0.30)]}{(\$31,500,000 + \$28,970,000)/2} = 7.3\%$$

Brickey Electronics has earned a return of 7.3% on average total assets employed during this year.

## Return on Equity

The return on total assets looks at profits relative to total assets, whereas the *return on equity* looks at profits relative to the book value of stockholders' equity. The **return on equity** is computed as follows:

$$\text{Return on equity} = \frac{\text{Net income}}{\text{Average stockholders' equity}}$$

Brickey Electronics' return on equity for this year would be computed as follows:

$$\text{Return on equity} = \frac{\$1,750,000}{(\$17,000,000 + \$15,970,000)/2} = 10.6\%$$

Now that we have computed return on total assets and return on equity, we can take a moment to see financial leverage in operation for Brickey Electronics. Notice from Exhibit 14–1 that the company pays 8% interest on its bonds payable. The after-tax interest cost of these bonds is only 5.6% [8% interest rate × (1 − 0.30) = 5.6%]. As shown earlier, the company's after-tax return on total assets is 7.3%. Because the return on total assets of 7.3% is greater than the 5.6% after-tax interest cost of the bonds, leverage is positive and the difference goes to the stockholders. This explains in part why the return on equity of 10.6% is greater than the return on total assets of 7.3%.

It also bears emphasizing that many managers and investors take a more in-depth look at return on equity using principles pioneered by **E.I. du Pont de Nemours and Company** (better known as DuPont). This approach recognizes that return on equity is influenced by three elements—operating efficiency (as measured by net profit margin percentage), asset usage efficiency (as measured by total asset turnover), and financial leverage (as measured by the equity multiplier). The following equation computes Brickey Electronics' return on equity using these three elements:

$$\frac{\text{Return on}}{\text{equity}} = \frac{\text{Net profit margin}}{\text{percentage}} \times \frac{\text{Total asset}}{\text{turnover}} \times \frac{\text{Equity}}{\text{multiplier}}$$

$$\text{Return on equity} = \frac{\text{Net income}}{\text{Sales}} \times \frac{\text{Sales}}{\text{Average total assets}} \times \frac{\text{Average total assets}}{\text{Average stockholders' equity}}$$

$$\text{Return on equity} = 3.37\% \times 1.72 \times 1.83 = 10.6\%$$

Notice that the sales and average total asset figures cancel, so we are left with net income divided by average stockholders' equity. While this equation is a little bit more complex, its return on equity of 10.6% agrees with the initial return on equity computation performed earlier. Also notice that this equation uses a net profit margin percentage of 3.37% rather than the rounded net profit margin percentage of 3.4% shown in Exhibit 14–5. The total asset turnover of 1.72 and the equity multiplier of 1.83 were previously computed earlier in the chapter.

CONCEPT CHECK

6. Orvil Company's net profit margin percentage is 4.5%, its total asset turnover is 2.4, and its equity multiplier is 1.5. What is the company's return on equity?
   a. 2.8%
   b. 7.2%
   c. 16.2%
   d. 10.7%

# RATIO ANALYSIS—MARKET PERFORMANCE

This section summarizes five ratios that common stockholders use to assess a company's performance. Given that common stockholders are the ones who own the company, it logically follows that managers should have a thorough understanding of the measures that their owners will use to judge their performance. *All calculations are performed for this year.*

**LEARNING OBJECTIVE 14–6**

Compute and interpret financial ratios that managers use to assess market performance.

## Earnings per Share

An investor buys a stock in the hope of realizing a return in the form of either dividends or future increases in the value of the stock. Because earnings form the basis for dividend payments and future increases in the value of shares, investors are interested in a company's *earnings per share.*

**Earnings per share** is computed by dividing net income by the average number of common shares outstanding during the year.

$$\text{Earnings per share} = \frac{\text{Net income}}{\text{Average number of common shares outstanding}}$$

Using the data in Exhibits 14–1 and 14–2, Brickey Electronics' earnings per share would be computed as follows:

$$\text{Earnings per share} = \frac{\$1,750,000}{(500,000 \text{ shares* } + 500,000 \text{ shares})/2} = \$3.50 \text{ per share}$$

*$6,000,000 total par value ÷ $12 par value per share = 500,000 shares.

---

## HELPFUL HINT

The number of common shares outstanding is calculated by taking the dollar amount of common stock shown in the balance sheet and dividing it by the common stock's par value per share.

---

## McDonald's Faces Financial Challenges

**IN BUSINESS**

**McDonald's** posted a 4.6% drop in monthly same-store sales—its biggest such decline in more than 14 years. The fast-food chain is losing customers to fast-casual chains such as **Chick-fil-A** and **Five Guys Holdings** that offer fewer menu items and faster service. A survey of investment analysts showed that they expect McDonald's sales to drop by 3% and its earnings per share to drop by 9%.

McDonald's U.S.A, President Mike Andres said, "What has worked for McDonald's U.S. for the past decade is not sufficient to propel the business forward in the future." In that spirit, McDonald's has taken steps to better serve local tastes by creating a new organizational structure that divides the United States into four geographic regions. The new structure acknowledges that menu-item preferences can differ by geographic region and that McDonald's should be responsive to these differences.

©RosaIreneBetancourt 10/Alamy Stock Photo

Source: Jargon, Julie, "Sales Drop at McDonald's Worsens," *The Wall Street Journal*, December 9, 2014, B2.

## Price-Earnings Ratio

The **price-earnings ratio** expresses the relationship between a stock's market price per share and its earnings per share. If we assume that Brickey Electronics' stock has a market price of $40 per share at the end of this year, then its price-earnings ratio would be computed as follows:

$$\text{Price-earnings ratio} = \frac{\text{Market price per share}}{\text{Earnings per share}}$$

$$= \frac{\$40 \text{ per share}}{\$3.50 \text{ per share}} = 11.43$$

The price-earnings ratio is 11.43; that is, the stock is selling for about 11.43 times its current earnings per share.

A high price-earnings ratio means that investors are willing to pay a premium for the company's stock—presumably because the company is expected to have higher than average future earnings growth. Conversely, if investors believe a company's future earnings growth prospects are limited, the company's price-earnings ratio would be relatively low. In the late 1990s, the stock prices of some dot.com companies—particularly those with little or no earnings—were selling at levels that resulted in huge and nearly unprecedented price-earnings ratios. Many commentators cautioned that these price-earnings ratios were unsustainable in the long run—and they were right. The stock prices of almost all dot.com companies subsequently crashed.

## Dividend Payout and Yield Ratios

Investors in a company's stock make money in two ways—increases in the market value of the stock and dividends. In general, earnings should be retained in a company and not paid out in dividends as long as the rate of return on funds invested inside the company exceeds the rate of return that stockholders could earn on alternative investments outside the company. Therefore, companies with excellent prospects of profitable growth often pay little or no dividend. Companies with little opportunity for profitable growth, but with steady, dependable earnings, tend to pay out a higher percentage of their cash flow from operations as dividends.

**The Dividend Payout Ratio**   The **dividend payout ratio** quantifies the percentage of current earnings being paid out in dividends. This ratio is computed by dividing the dividends per share by the earnings per share for common stock:

$$\text{Dividend payout ratio} = \frac{\text{Dividends per share}}{\text{Earnings per share}}$$

For Brickey Electronics, the dividend payout ratio is computed as follows:

$$\text{Dividend payout ratio} = \frac{\$1.44 \text{ per share (see Exhibit 14–2)}}{\$3.50 \text{ per share}} = 41.1\%$$

There is no such thing as a "right" dividend payout ratio, although the ratio tends to be similar for companies within the same industry. As noted above, companies with ample growth opportunities at high rates of return tend to have low payout ratios, whereas companies with limited reinvestment opportunities tend to have higher payout ratios.

**The Dividend Yield Ratio**   The **dividend yield ratio** is computed by dividing the current dividends per share by the current market price per share:

$$\text{Dividend yield ratio} = \frac{\text{Dividends per share}}{\text{Market price per share}}$$

Because the market price for Brickey Electronics' stock is $40 per share, the dividend yield is computed as follows:

$$\text{Dividend yield ratio} = \frac{\$1.44 \text{ per share}}{\$40 \text{ per share}} = 3.6\%$$

The dividend yield ratio measures the rate of return (in the form of cash dividends only) that would be earned by an investor who buys common stock at the current market price. A low dividend yield ratio is neither bad nor good by itself.

## Book Value per Share

**Book value per share** measures the amount that would be distributed to holders of each share of common stock if all assets were sold at their balance sheet carrying amounts (i.e., book values) and if all creditors were paid off. Book value per share is based entirely on historical costs. The formula for computing it is:

$$\text{Book value per share} = \frac{\text{Total stockholders' equity}}{\text{Number of common shares outstanding}}$$

The book value per share of Brickey Electronics' common stock is computed as follows:

$$\text{Book value per share} = \frac{\$17,000,000}{500,000 \text{ shares}} = \$34 \text{ per share}$$

If this book value is compared with the $40 market value of Brickey Electronics' stock, then the stock may appear to be overpriced. However, as we discussed earlier, market prices reflect expectations about future earnings and dividends, whereas book value largely reflects the results of events that have occurred in the past. Ordinarily, the market value of a stock exceeds its book value. For example, in one year, **Microsoft**'s common stock often traded at over 4 times its book value, and **Coca-Cola**'s market value was over 17 times its book value.

## Portfolio Manager

DECISION POINT

Assume that you work for a mutual fund and have the responsibility of selecting stocks to include in its investment portfolio. You have been analyzing the financial statements of a chain of retail clothing stores and noticed that the company's current ratio has increased, but its acid-test (quick) ratio has decreased. In addition, the company's accounts receivable turnover has decreased and its inventory turnover ratio has decreased. Finally, the company's price-earnings ratio is at an all-time high. Would you recommend buying stock in this company?

## SUMMARY OF RATIOS AND SOURCES OF COMPARATIVE RATIO DATA

Exhibit 14–6 contains a summary of the ratios discussed in this chapter. The formula for each ratio and a summary comment on each ratio's significance are included in the exhibit.

Exhibit 14–7 contains a listing of public sources that provide comparative ratio data organized by industry. These sources are used extensively by managers, investors, and analysts. The **EDGAR** database listed in Exhibit 14–7 is a particularly rich source of data. It contains copies of all reports filed by companies with the SEC since about 1995—including annual reports filed as Form 10-K.

**EXHIBIT 14–6**    Summary of Ratios

| Ratio | Formula | Significance |
|---|---|---|
| **Liquidity:** | | |
| Working capital | Current assets − Current liabilities | Measures the company's ability to repay current liabilities using only current assets |
| Current ratio | Current assets ÷ Current liabilities | Test of short-term debt-paying ability |
| Acid-test ratio | (Cash + Marketable securities + Accounts receivable + Short-term notes receivable) ÷ Current liabilities | Test of short-term debt-paying ability without having to rely on inventory |
| **Asset Management:** | | |
| Accounts receivable turnover | Sales on account ÷ Average accounts receivable balance | Measures how many times a company's accounts receivable have been turned into cash during the year |
| Average collection period | 365 days ÷ Accounts receivable turnover | Measures the average number of days taken to collect an account receivable |
| Inventory turnover | Cost of goods sold ÷ Average inventory balance | Measures how many times a company's inventory has been sold during the year |
| Average sale period | 365 days ÷ Inventory turnover | Measures the average number of days taken to sell the inventory one time |
| Operating cycle | Average sale period + Average collection period | Measures the elapsed time from when inventory is received from suppliers to when cash is received from customers |
| Total asset turnover | Sales ÷ Average total assets | Measures how efficiently assets are being used to generate sales |
| **Debt Management:** | | |
| Times interest earned ratio | Earnings before interest expense and income taxes ÷ Interest expense | Measures the company's ability to make interest payments |
| Debt-to-equity ratio | Total liabilities ÷ Stockholders' equity | Measures the amount of assets being provided by creditors for each dollar of assets being provided by the stockholders |
| Equity multiplier | Average total assets ÷ Average stockholders' equity | Measures the portion of a company's assets funded by equity |
| **Profitability:** | | |
| Gross margin percentage | Gross margin ÷ Sales | Measures profitability before selling and administrative expenses |
| Net profit margin percentage | Net income ÷ Sales | A broad measure of profitability |
| Return on total assets | {Net income + [Interest expense × (1 − Tax rate)]} ÷ Average total assets | Measures how well assets have been employed by management |
| Return on equity | Net income ÷ Average stockholders' equity | When compared to the return on total assets, measures the extent to which financial leverage is working for or against common stockholders |
| **Market Performance:** | | |
| Earnings per share | Net income ÷ Average number of common shares outstanding | Affects the market price per share, as reflected in the price-earnings ratio |
| Price-earnings ratio | Market price per share ÷ Earnings per share | An index of whether a stock is relatively cheap or relatively expensive in relation to current earnings |
| Dividend payout ratio | Dividends per share ÷ Earnings per share | An index showing whether a company pays out most of its earnings in dividends or reinvests the earnings internally |
| Dividend yield ratio | Dividends per share ÷ Market price per share | Shows the return in terms of cash dividends being provided by a stock |
| Book value per share | Total stockholders' equity ÷ Number of common shares outstanding | Measures the amount that would be distributed to common stockholders if all assets were sold at their balance sheet carrying amounts and if all creditors were paid off |

**EXHIBIT 14–7**    Sources of Financial Ratios

| Source | Content |
|---|---|
| *Almanac of Business and Industrial Financial Ratios,* Aspen Publishers; published annually | An exhaustive source that contains common-size income statements and financial ratios by industry and by the size of companies within each industry. |
| *AMA Annual Statement Studies,* Risk Management Association; published annually | A widely used publication that contains common-size statements and financial ratios on individual companies; the companies are arranged by industry. |
| *EDGAR,* Securities and Exchange Commission; website that is continually updated; www.sec.gov | An exhaustive Internet database that contains reports filed by companies with the SEC; these reports can be downloaded. |
| *Hoover's Online,* Hoovers, Inc.; website that is continually updated; www.hoovers.com | A site that provides capsule profiles for 10,000 U.S. companies with links to company websites, annual reports, stock charts, news articles, and industry information. |
| *Industry Norms & Key Business Ratios,* Dun & Bradstreet; published annually | Fourteen commonly used financial ratios are computed for over 800 major industry groupings. |
| *Mergent Industrial Manual and Mergent Bank and Finance Manual;* published annually | An exhaustive source that contains financial ratios on all companies listed on the New York Stock Exchange, the American Stock Exchange, and regional American exchanges. |
| *Standard & Poor's Industry Survey,* Standard & Poor's; published annually | Various statistics, including some financial ratios, are given by industry and for leading companies within each industry grouping. |

# SUMMARY

## LO14–1 Prepare and interpret financial statements in comparative and common-size form.

Raw data from financial statements should be standardized so that the data can be compared over time and across companies. For example, all of the financial data for a company can be expressed as a percentage of the data in some base year. This makes it easier to spot trends over time. To make it easier to compare companies, common-size financial statements are often used in which income statement data are expressed as a percentage of sales and balance sheet data are expressed as a percentage of total assets.

## LO14–2 Compute and interpret financial ratios that managers use to assess liquidity.

Managers need to be concerned with their company's ability to repay its debts in the near future. Consequently, they focus on the relation between current assets and current liabilities using measures such as working capital, the current ratio, and the acid-test (quick) ratio.

## LO14–3 Compute and interpret financial ratios that managers use for asset management purposes.

Managers need to ensure that their companies use current and noncurrent assets efficiently. The accounts receivable turnover, inventory turnover, and operating cycle help managers assess how quickly their companies are able to translate inventories and credit sales into cash. The total asset turnover is another measure of efficiency that compares sales to the average total assets used to generate those sales.

**LO14–4 Compute and interpret financial ratios that managers use for debt management purposes.**

Managers need to ensure that their companies can repay long-term creditors. They often track the times interest earned ratio to assess the company's ability to use current operations to make interest payments to those lenders. They also measure the debt-to-equity ratio and the equity multiplier to better understand their company's use of financial leverage.

**LO14–5 Compute and interpret financial ratios that managers use to assess profitability.**

Profitability is a fundamental measure of organizational performance. The gross margin percentage states the gross margin as a percentage of sales. Similarly, the net profit margin percentage states the net income as a percentage of sales. The return on total assets and return on equity look at net income relative to information contained on the balance sheet—either average total assets or average total stockholders' equity. Generally speaking, companies seek to continually increase all of these measures.

**LO14–6 Compute and interpret financial ratios that managers use to assess market performance.**

Managers need to understand their company's performance through the eyes of common stockholders. They assess stock market performance using measures such as earnings per share, price-earnings ratio, dividend payout and dividend yield ratios, and book value per share. Generally speaking, the higher these ratios, the better it is for the company and its common stockholders.

## GUIDANCE ANSWER TO DECISION POINT

**Portfolio Manager**

All of the ratios—current ratio, acid-test (quick) ratio, accounts receivable turnover, and inventory turnover ratio—indicate deteriorating operations. And yet the company's price-earnings ratio is at an all-time high, suggesting that the stock market is optimistic about the company's future and its stock price. It would be risky to invest in this company without digging deeper and finding out what has caused the deteriorating operating ratios.

## GUIDANCE ANSWERS TO CONCEPT CHECKS

1. **Choice b.** The accounts receivable turnover is $800,000 of credit sales ÷ $120,000 average accounts receivable balance = 6.67.
2. **Choice a.** First, calculate the cost of goods sold as follows: $1,000,000 × (1 − 0.60) = $400,000. Next, the inventory turnover is calculated as follows: $400,000 of cost of goods sold ÷ $250,000 average inventory = 1.60.
3. **Choice c.** The inventory turnover is 1.60. So, 365 days divided by 1.60 = 228 days (rounded).
4. **Choice b.** The accounts receivable turnover is 6.67. So, the average collection period is 365 days divided by 6.67, or approximately 55 days. The average sale period of 228 days plus the average collection period of 55 days equal the operating cycle of 283 days.
5. **Choice d.** Total assets of $1,500,000 − $900,000 of stockholders' equity = $600,000 of total liabilities. The debt-to-equity ratio is $600,000 ÷ $900,000 = 0.67.
6. **Choice c.** The net profit margin percentage of 4.5% times the total asset turnover of 2.4 times the equity multiplier of 1.5 equals the return on equity of 16.2%.

## REVIEW PROBLEM: SELECTED RATIOS AND FINANCIAL LEVERAGE

Mulligan Corporation's financial statements are as follows:

### Mulligan Corporation
### Comparative Balance Sheet
### (dollars in millions)

| | This Year | Last Year |
|---|---|---|
| **Assets** | | |
| Current assets: | | |
| Cash | $ 281 | $ 313 |
| Marketable securities | 157 | 141 |
| Accounts receivable | 288 | 224 |
| Inventories | 692 | 636 |
| Other current assets | 278 | 216 |
| Total current assets | 1,696 | 1,530 |
| Property and equipment, net | 2,890 | 2,288 |
| Other assets | 758 | 611 |
| Total assets | $5,344 | $4,429 |
| **Liabilities and Stockholders' Equity** | | |
| Current liabilities: | | |
| Accounts payable | $ 391 | $ 341 |
| Short-term bank loans | 710 | 700 |
| Accrued liabilities | 757 | 662 |
| Other current liabilities | 298 | 233 |
| Total current liabilities | 2,156 | 1,936 |
| Long-term liabilities | 904 | 265 |
| Total liabilities | 3,060 | 2,201 |
| Stockholders' equity: | | |
| Common stock and additional paid-in capital | 40 | 40 |
| Retained earnings | 2,244 | 2,188 |
| Total stockholders' equity | 2,284 | 2,228 |
| Total liabilities and stockholders' equity | $5,344 | $4,429 |

### Mulligan Corporation
### Income Statement
### (dollars in millions)

| | This Year |
|---|---|
| Sales | $9,411 |
| Cost of goods sold | 3,999 |
| Gross margin | 5,412 |
| Selling and administrative expenses: | |
| Store operating expenses | 3,216 |
| Other operating expenses | 294 |
| Depreciation and amortization | 467 |
| General and administrative expenses | 489 |
| Total selling and administrative expenses | 4,466 |
| Net operating income | 946 |
| Plus interest and other income | 110 |
| Interest expense | 0 |
| Net income before taxes | 1,056 |
| Income taxes (about 36%) | 384 |
| Net income | $ 672 |

*Required:*
1. Compute the return on total assets.
2. Compute the return on equity.
3. Is Mulligan's financial leverage positive or negative? Explain.
4. Compute the current ratio.
5. Compute the acid-test ratio.
6. Compute the inventory turnover.
7. Compute the average sale period.
8. Compute the debt-to-equity ratio.
9. Compute the total asset turnover.
10. Compute the net profit margin percentage.

**Solution to Review Problem**
1.   Return on total assets:

$$\text{Return on total assets} = \frac{\text{Net income} + [\text{Interest expense} \times (1 - \text{Tax rate})]}{\text{Average total assets}}$$

$$= \frac{\$672 + [\$0 \times (1 - 0.36)]}{(\$5,344 + \$4,429)/2} = 13.8\% \text{ (rounded)}$$

2.   Return on equity:

$$\text{Return on equity} = \frac{\text{Net income}}{\text{Average stockholders' equity}}$$

$$= \frac{\$672}{(\$2,284 + \$2,228)/2} = 29.8\% \text{ (rounded)}$$

3.   The company has positive financial leverage because the return on equity of 29.8% is greater than the return on total assets of 13.8%. The positive financial leverage was obtained from current and long-term liabilities.
4.   Current ratio:

$$\text{Current ratio} = \frac{\text{Current assets}}{\text{Current liabilities}}$$

$$= \frac{\$1,696}{\$2,156} = 0.79 \text{ (rounded)}$$

5.   Acid-test ratio:

$$\text{Acid-test ratio} = \frac{\text{Cash} + \text{Marketable securities} + \text{Accounts receivable} + \text{Short-term notes receivable}}{\text{Current liabilities}}$$

$$= \frac{\$281 + \$157 + \$288 + \$0}{\$2,156} = 0.34 \text{ (rounded)}$$

6.   Inventory turnover:

$$\text{Inventory turnover} = \frac{\text{Cost of goods sold}}{\text{Average inventory balance}}$$

$$= \frac{\$3,999}{(\$692 + \$636)/2} = 6.0 \text{ (rounded)}$$

7.   Average sale period:

$$\text{Average sale period} = \frac{365 \text{ days}}{\text{Inventory turnover}}$$

$$= \frac{365 \text{ days}}{6.0} = 60.8 \text{ days (rounded)}$$

8.   Debt-to-equity ratio:

$$\text{Debt-to-equity ratio} = \frac{\text{Total liabilities}}{\text{Stockholders' equity}}$$

$$= \frac{\$3,060}{\$2,284} = 1.34 \text{ (rounded)}$$

9. Total asset turnover:

$$\text{Total asset turnover} = \frac{\text{Sales}}{\text{Average total assets}}$$

$$\text{Total asset turnover} = \frac{\$9,411}{(\$5,344 + \$4,429)/2} = 1.93 \text{ (rounded)}$$

10. Net profit margin percentage:

$$\text{Net profit margin percentage} = \frac{\text{Net income}}{\text{Sales}}$$

$$\text{Net profit margin percentage} = \frac{\$672}{\$9,411} = 7.1\% \text{ (rounded)}$$

## GLOSSARY

(Note: Definitions and formulas for all financial ratios are shown in Exhibit 14–6. These definitions and formulas are not repeated here.)

**Common-size financial statements**   A statement that shows the items appearing on it in percentage form as well as in dollar form. On the income statement, the percentages are based on total sales revenue; on the balance sheet, the percentages are based on total assets. (p. 663)

**Financial leverage**   A difference between the rate of return on assets and the rate paid to creditors. (p. 670)

**Horizontal analysis**   A side-by-side comparison of two or more years' financial statements. (p. 661)

**Trend analysis**   See *Horizontal analysis*. (p. 661)

**Trend percentages**   Several years of financial data expressed as a percentage of performance in a base year. (p. 661)

**Vertical analysis**   The presentation of a company's financial statements in common-size form. (p. 663)

## QUESTIONS

**14–1**   Distinguish between horizontal and vertical analysis of financial statement data.

**14–2**   What is the basic purpose for examining trends in a company's financial ratios and other data? What other kinds of comparisons might an analyst make?

**14–3**   Assume that two companies in the same industry have equal earnings. Why might these companies have different price-earnings ratios? If a company has a price-earnings ratio of 20 and reports earnings per share for the current year of $4, at what price would you expect to find the stock selling on the market?

**14–4**   Would you expect a company in a rapidly growing technological industry to have a high or low dividend payout ratio?

**14–5**   What is meant by the dividend yield on a common stock investment?

**14–6**   What is meant by the term financial leverage?

**14–7**   The president of a plastics company was quoted in a business journal as stating, "We haven't had a dollar of interest-paying debt in over 10 years. Not many companies can say that." As a stockholder in this company, how would you feel about its policy of not taking on debt?

**14–8**   If a stock's market value exceeds its book value, then the stock is overpriced. Do you agree? Explain.

**14–9**   A company seeking a line of credit at a bank was turned down. Among other things, the bank stated that the company's 2 to 1 current ratio was not adequate. Give reasons why a 2 to 1 current ratio might not be adequate.

**■ connect** THE FOUNDATIONAL 15

Markus Company's common stock sold for $2.75 per share at the end of this year. The company paid a common stock dividend of $0.55 per share this year. It also provided the following *data excerpts* from this year's financial statements:

LO14–2, LO14–3, LO14–4, LO14–5, LO14–6

| | Ending Balance | Beginning Balance |
|---|---|---|
| Cash...................................... | $35,000 | $30,000 |
| Accounts receivable...................... | $60,000 | $50,000 |
| Inventory................................. | $55,000 | $60,000 |
| Current assets ........................... | $150,000 | $140,000 |
| Total assets............................. | $450,000 | $460,000 |
| Current liabilities ....................... | $60,000 | $40,000 |
| Total liabilities.......................... | $130,000 | $120,000 |
| Common stock, $1 par value ............. | $120,000 | $120,000 |
| Total stockholders' equity ................ | $320,000 | $340,000 |
| Total liabilities and stockholders' equity ..... | $450,000 | $460,000 |

| | This Year |
|---|---|
| Sales (all on account) ..................... | $700,000 |
| Cost of goods sold ....................... | $400,000 |
| Gross margin ............................. | $300,000 |
| Net operating income..................... | $140,000 |
| Interest expense ......................... | $8,000 |
| Net income............................... | $92,400 |

*Required:*
1. What is the earnings per share?
2. What is the price-earnings ratio?
3. What is the dividend payout ratio and the dividend yield ratio?
4. What is the return on total assets (assuming a 30% tax rate)?
5. What is the return on equity?
6. What is the book value per share at the end of this year?
7. What is the amount of working capital and the current ratio at the end of this year?
8. What is the acid-test ratio at the end of this year?
9. What is the accounts receivable turnover and the average collection period?
10. What is the inventory turnover and the average sale period?
11. What is the company's operating cycle?
12. What is the total asset turnover?
13. What is the times interest earned ratio?
14. What is the debt-to-equity ratio at the end of this year?
15. What is the equity multiplier?

## EXERCISES     connect

**EXERCISE 14–1    Common-Size Income Statement LO14–1**

A comparative income statement is given below for McKenzie Sales, Ltd., of Toronto:

| McKenzie Sales, Ltd. Comparative Income Statement | | |
|---|---|---|
| | This Year | Last Year |
| Sales .............................. | $8,000,000 | $6,000,000 |
| Cost of goods sold ................. | 4,984,000 | 3,516,000 |
| Gross margin ...................... | 3,016,000 | 2,484,000 |
| Selling and administrative expenses: | | |
|   Selling expenses ................. | 1,480,000 | 1,092,000 |
|   Administrative expenses ........... | 712,000 | 618,000 |
| Total expenses .................... | 2,192,000 | 1,710,000 |
| Net operating income .............. | 824,000 | 774,000 |
| Interest expense .................. | 96,000 | 84,000 |
| Net income before taxes ........... | $ 728,000 | $ 690,000 |

Members of the company's board of directors are surprised to see that net income increased by only $38,000 when sales increased by $2,000,000.

**Required:**

1. Express each year's income statement in common-size percentages. Carry computations to one decimal place.
2. Comment briefly on the changes between the two years.

### EXERCISE 14–2   Financial Ratios for Assessing Liquidity LO14–2

Comparative financial statements for Weller Corporation, a merchandising company, for the year ending December 31 appear below. The company did not issue any new common stock during the year. A total of 800,000 shares of common stock were outstanding. The interest rate on the bond payable was 12%, the income tax rate was 40%, and the dividend per share of common stock was $0.75 last year and $0.40 this year. The market value of the company's common stock at the end of this year was $18. All of the company's sales are on account.

| Weller Corporation<br>Comparative Balance Sheet<br>(dollars in thousands) | | |
|---|---|---|
| | **This Year** | **Last Year** |
| **Assets** | | |
| Current assets: | | |
| Cash .......................................... | $ 1,280 | $ 1,560 |
| Accounts receivable, net ................... | 12,300 | 9,100 |
| Inventory .................................... | 9,700 | 8,200 |
| Prepaid expenses ........................... | 1,800 | 2,100 |
| Total current assets ......................... | 25,080 | 20,960 |
| Property and equipment: | | |
| Land ........................................ | 6,000 | 6,000 |
| Buildings and equipment, net .............. | 19,200 | 19,000 |
| Total property and equipment ............... | 25,200 | 25,000 |
| Total assets ................................. | $50,280 | $45,960 |
| **Liabilities and Stockholders' Equity** | | |
| Current liabilities: | | |
| Accounts payable .......................... | $ 9,500 | $ 8,300 |
| Accrued liabilities ......................... | 600 | 700 |
| Notes payable, short term ................. | 300 | 300 |
| Total current liabilities ..................... | 10,400 | 9,300 |
| Long-term liabilities: | | |
| Bonds payable ............................. | 5,000 | 5,000 |
| Total liabilities .............................. | 15,400 | 14,300 |
| Stockholders' equity: | | |
| Common stock ............................. | 800 | 800 |
| Additional paid-in capital ................. | 4,200 | 4,200 |
| Total paid-in capital ........................ | 5,000 | 5,000 |
| Retained earnings .......................... | 29,880 | 26,660 |
| Total stockholders' equity .................. | 34,880 | 31,660 |
| Total liabilities and stockholders' equity ........ | $50,280 | $45,960 |

| Weller Corporation<br>Comparative Income Statement and Reconciliation<br>(dollars in thousands) | | |
| :--- | ---: | ---: |
| | **This Year** | **Last Year** |
| Sales ..................................... | $79,000 | $74,000 |
| Cost of goods sold ...................... | 52,000 | 48,000 |
| Gross margin ........................... | 27,000 | 26,000 |
| Selling and administrative expenses: | | |
|    Selling expenses ...................... | 8,500 | 8,000 |
|    Administrative expenses ............... | 12,000 | 11,000 |
| Total selling and administrative expenses .. | 20,500 | 19,000 |
| Net operating income .................... | 6,500 | 7,000 |
| Interest expense ........................ | 600 | 600 |
| Net income before taxes ................. | 5,900 | 6,400 |
| Income taxes ........................... | 2,360 | 2,560 |
| Net income ............................. | 3,540 | 3,840 |
| Dividends to common stockholders ........ | 320 | 600 |
| Net income added to retained earnings .... | 3,220 | 3,240 |
| Beginning retained earnings .............. | 26,660 | 23,420 |
| Ending retained earnings ................ | $29,880 | $26,660 |

*Required:*

Compute the following financial data and ratios for this year:
1. Working capital.
2. Current ratio.
3. Acid-test ratio.

**EXERCISE 14–3    Financial Ratios for Asset Management** LO14–3

Refer to the data in Exercise 14-2 for Weller Corporation.

*Required:*

Compute the following financial data for this year:
1. Accounts receivable turnover. (Assume that all sales are on account.)
2. Average collection period.
3. Inventory turnover.
4. Average sale period.
5. Operating cycle.
6. Total asset turnover.

**EXERCISE 14–4    Financial Ratios for Debt Management** LO14–4

Refer to the data in Exercise 14-2 for Weller Corporation.

*Required:*

Compute the following financial ratios for this year:
1. Times interest earned ratio.
2. Debt-to-equity ratio.
3. Equity multiplier.

**EXERCISE 14–5    Financial Ratios for Assessing Profitability** LO14–5

Refer to the data in Exercise 14-2 for Weller Corporation.

*Required:*

Compute the following financial data for this year:
1. Gross margin percentage.
2. Net profit margin percentage.
3. Return on total assets.
4. Return on equity.

**EXERCISE 14–6    Financial Ratios for Assessing Market Performance** LO14–6

Refer to the data in Exercise 14-2 for Weller Corporation.

**Required:**

Compute the following financial data for this year:
1.  Earnings per share.
2.  Price-earnings ratio.
3.  Dividend payout ratio.
4.  Dividend yield ratio.
5.  Book value per share.

**EXERCISE 14–7    Trend Percentages** LO14–1

Rotorua Products, Ltd., of New Zealand markets agricultural products for the burgeoning Asian consumer market. The company's current assets, current liabilities, and sales over the last five years (Year 5 is the most recent year) are as follows:

|  | Year 1 | Year 2 | Year 3 | Year 4 | Year 5 |
|---|---|---|---|---|---|
| Sales | $1,800,000 | $1,980,000 | $2,070,000 | $2,160,000 | $2,250,000 |
| Cash | $     50,000 | $     65,000 | $     48,000 | $     40,000 | $     30,000 |
| Accounts receivable, net | 300,000 | 345,000 | 405,000 | 510,000 | 570,000 |
| Inventory | 600,000 | 660,000 | 690,000 | 720,000 | 750,000 |
| Total current assets | $ 950,000 | $1,070,000 | $1,143,000 | $1,270,000 | $1,350,000 |
| Current liabilities | $ 400,000 | $ 440,000 | $ 520,000 | $ 580,000 | $ 640,000 |

**Required:**

1.  Express all of the asset, liability, and sales data in trend percentages. (Show percentages for each item.) Use Year 1 as the base year and carry computations to one decimal place.
2.  Comment on the results of your analysis.

**EXERCISE 14–8    Selected Financial Ratios** LO14–2, LO14–3, LO14–4

The financial statements for Castile Products, Inc., are given below:

**Castile Products, Inc.**
**Balance Sheet**
**December 31**

**Assets**

Current assets:

| | |
|---|---|
| Cash | $   6,500 |
| Accounts receivable, net | 35,000 |
| Merchandise inventory | 70,000 |
| Prepaid expenses | 3,500 |
| Total current assets | 115,000 |
| Property and equipment, net | 185,000 |
| Total assets | $300,000 |

**Liabilities and Stockholders' Equity**

Liabilities:

| | |
|---|---|
| Current liabilities | $ 50,000 |
| Bonds payable, 10% | 80,000 |
| Total liabilities | 130,000 |

Stockholders' equity:

| | |
|---|---|
| Common stock, $5 per value | 30,000 |
| Retained earnings | 140,000 |
| Total stockholders' equity | 170,000 |
| Total liabilities and stockholders' equity | $300,000 |

| Castile Products, Inc. Income Statement For the Year Ended December 31 | |
|---|---:|
| Sales .................................... | $420,000 |
| Cost of goods sold ........................ | 292,500 |
| Gross margin ............................ | 127,500 |
| Selling and administrative expenses ....... | 89,500 |
| Net operating income ..................... | 38,000 |
| Interest expense ......................... | 8,000 |
| Net income before taxes .................. | 30,000 |
| Income taxes (30%) ...................... | 9,000 |
| Net income ............................. | $ 21,000 |

Account balances at the beginning of the year were: accounts receivable, $25,000; and inventory, $60,000. All sales were on account.

*Required:*
Compute the following financial data and ratios:
1. Working capital.
2. Current ratio.
3. Acid-test ratio.
4. Debt-to-equity ratio.
5. Times interest earned ratio.
6. Average collection period.
7. Average sale period.
8. Operating cycle.

**EXERCISE 14–9   Financial Ratios for Assessing Profitability and Managing Debt** LO14–4, LO14–5
Refer to the financial statements for Castile Products, Inc., in Exercise 14-8. Assets at the beginning of the year totaled $280,000, and the stockholders' equity totaled $161,600.

*Required:*
Compute the following:
1. Gross margin percentage.
2. Net profit margin percentage.
3. Return on total assets.
4. Return on equity.
5. Was financial leverage positive or negative for the year? Explain.

**EXERCISE 14–10   Financial Ratios for Assessing Market Performance** LO14–6
Refer to the financial statements for Castile Products, Inc., in Exercise 14-8. In addition to the data in these statements, assume that Castile Products, Inc., paid dividends of $2.10 per share during the year. Also assume that the company's common stock had a market price of $42 at the end of the year and there was no change in the number of outstanding shares of common stock during the year.

*Required:*
Compute financial ratios as follows:
1. Earnings per share.
2. Dividend payout ratio.
3. Dividend yield ratio.
4. Price-earnings ratio.
5. Book value per share.

**EXERCISE 14–11   Financial Ratios for Assessing Profitability and Managing Debt** LO14–4, LO14–5
Selected financial data from the June 30 year-end statements of Safford Company are given below:

| | |
|---|---:|
| Total assets ........................... | $3,600,000 |
| Long-term debt (12% interest rate) ........ | $500,000 |
| Total stockholders' equity ............... | $2,400,000 |
| Interest paid on long-term debt .......... | $60,000 |
| Net income ........................... | $280,000 |

Total assets at the beginning of the year were $3,000,000; total stockholders' equity was $2,200,000. The company's tax rate is 30%.

*Required:*
1. Compute the return on total assets.
2. Compute the return on equity.
3. Is financial leverage positive or negative? Explain.

**EXERCISE 14–12  Selected Financial Measures for Assessing Liquidity** LO14–2

Norsk Optronics, ALS, of Bergen, Norway, had a current ratio of 2.5 on June 30 of the current year. On that date, the company's assets were:

| | |
|---|---:|
| Cash ..................................... | $    90,000 |
| Accounts receivable, net .............. | 260,000 |
| Inventory ............................. | 490,000 |
| Prepaid expenses ...................... | 10,000 |
| Plant and equipment, net ............... | 800,000 |
| Total assets ......................... | $1,650,000 |

*Required:*
1. What was the company's working capital on June 30?
2. What was the company's acid-test ratio on June 30?
3. The company paid an account payable of $40,000 immediately after June 30.
   a. What effect did this transaction have on working capital? Show computations.
   b. What effect did this transaction have on the current ratio? Show computations.

**■ connect®**                                               **PROBLEMS**

**PROBLEM 14–13  Effects of Transactions on Various Financial Ratios** LO14–2, LO14–3, LO14–4, LO14–5, LO14–6

In the right-hand column below, certain financial ratios are listed. To the left of each ratio is a business transaction or event relating to the operating activities of Delta Company (each transaction should be considered independently).

| Business Transaction or Event | Ratio |
|---|---|
| 1. Declared a cash dividend. | Current ratio |
| 2. Sold inventory on account at cost. | Acid-test ratio |
| 3. Issued bonds with an interest rate of 8%. The company's return on assets is 10%. | Return on equity |
| 4. Net income decreased by 10% between last year and this year. Long-term debt remained unchanged. | Times interest earned |
| 5. Paid a previously declared cash dividend. | Current ratio |
| 6. The market price of the company's common stock dropped from $24.50 to $20.00. The dividend paid per share remained unchanged. | Dividend payout ratio |
| 7. Obsolete inventory totaling $100,000 was written off as a loss. | Inventory turnover ratio |
| 8. Sold inventory for cash at a profit. | Debt-to-equity ratio |
| 9. Changed customer credit terms from 2/10, n/30 to 2/15, n/30 to comply with a change in industry practice. | Accounts receivable turnover ratio |
| 10. Issued a stock dividend to common stockholders. | Book value per share |
| 11. The market price of the company's common stock increased from $24.50 to $30.00. | Book value per share |
| 12. Paid $40,000 on accounts payable. | Working capital |
| 13. Issued a stock dividend to common stockholders. | Earnings per share |
| 14. Paid accounts payable. | Debt-to-equity ratio |
| 15. Purchased inventory on account. | Acid-test ratio |
| 16. Wrote off an uncollectible account against the Allowance for Bad Debts. | Current ratio |
| 17. The market price of the company's common stock increased from $24.50 to $30.00. Earnings per share remained unchanged. | Price-earnings ratio |
| 18. The market price of the company's common stock increased from $24.50 to $30.00. The dividend paid per share remained unchanged. | Dividend yield ratio |

*Required:*

Indicate the effect that each business transaction or event would have on the ratio listed opposite to it. State the effect in terms of increase, decrease, or no effect on the ratio involved, and give the reason for your answer. In all cases, assume that the current assets exceed the current liabilities both before and after the event or transaction. Use the following format for your answers:

| Effect on Ratio | Reason for Increase, Decrease, or No Effect |
|---|---|
| 1. | |
| Etc. | |

**PROBLEM 14–14  Effects of Transactions on Various Ratios LO14–2**

Denna Company's working capital accounts at the beginning of the year follow:

| | |
|---|---|
| Cash | $50,000 |
| Marketable securities | $30,000 |
| Accounts receivable, net | $200,000 |
| Inventory | $210,000 |
| Prepaid expenses | $10,000 |
| Accounts payable | $150,000 |
| Notes due within one year | $30,000 |
| Accrued liabilities | $20,000 |

During the year, Denna Company completed the following transactions:

*Ex.* Paid a cash dividend previously declared, $12,000.
a. Issued additional shares of common stock for cash, $100,000.
b. Sold inventory costing $50,000 for $80,000, on account.
c. Wrote off uncollectible accounts in the amount of $10,000, reducing the accounts receivable balance accordingly.
d. Declared a cash dividend, $15,000.
e. Paid accounts payable, $50,000.
f. Borrowed cash on a short-term note with the bank, $35,000.
g. Sold inventory costing $15,000 for $10,000 cash.
h. Purchased inventory on account, $60,000.
i. Paid off all short-term notes due, $30,000.
j. Purchased equipment for cash, $15,000.
k. Sold marketable securities costing $18,000 for cash, $15,000.
l. Collected cash on accounts receivable, $80,000.

*Required:*

1. Compute the following amounts and ratios as of the beginning of the year:
   a. Working capital.
   b. Current ratio.
   c. Acid-test ratio.
2. Indicate the effect of each of the transactions given above on working capital, the current ratio, and the acid-test ratio. Give the effect in terms of increase, decrease, or none. Item *Ex* is given below as an example of the format to use:

| | The Effect on | | |
|---|---|---|---|
| Transaction | Working Capital | Current Ratio | Acid-Test Ratio |
| *Ex.* Paid a cash dividend previously declared | None | Increase | Increase |

**PROBLEM 14–15  Comprehensive Ratio Analysis LO14–2, LO14–3, LO14–4, LO14–5, LO14–6**

You have just been hired as a financial analyst for Lydex Company, a manufacturer of safety helmets. Your boss has asked you to perform a comprehensive analysis of the company's financial statements, including comparing Lydex's performance to its major competitors. The company's financial statements for the last two years are as follows:

## Lydex Company
## Comparative Balance Sheet

|  | This Year | Last Year |
|---|---|---|
| **Assets** | | |
| Current assets: | | |
| Cash ................................ | $ 960,000 | $ 1,260,000 |
| Marketable securities ................ | 0 | 300,000 |
| Accounts receivable, net ............. | 2,700,000 | 1,800,000 |
| Inventory ........................... | 3,900,000 | 2,400,000 |
| Prepaid expenses .................... | 240,000 | 180,000 |
| Total current assets .................... | 7,800,000 | 5,940,000 |
| Plant and equipment, net ................. | 9,300,000 | 8,940,000 |
| Total assets ........................... | $17,100,000 | $14,880,000 |
| **Liabilities and Stockholders' Equity** | | |
| Liabilities: | | |
| Current liabilities ...................... | $ 3,900,000 | $ 2,760,000 |
| Note payable, 10% ................... | 3,600,000 | 3,000,000 |
| Total liabilities ........................ | 7,500,000 | 5,760,000 |
| Stockholders' equity: | | |
| Common stock, $78 par value ......... | 7,800,000 | 7,800,000 |
| Retained earnings ................... | 1,800,000 | 1,320,000 |
| Total stockholders' equity .............. | 9,600,000 | 9,120,000 |
| Total liabilities and stockholders' equity .... | $17,100,000 | $14,880,000 |

## Lydex Company
## Comparative Income Statement and Reconciliation

|  | This Year | Last Year |
|---|---|---|
| Sales (all on account) ................... | $15,750,000 | $12,480,000 |
| Cost of goods sold .................... | 12,600,000 | 9,900,000 |
| Gross margin ......................... | 3,150,000 | 2,580,000 |
| Selling and administrative expenses ..... | 1,590,000 | 1,560,000 |
| Net operating income .................. | 1,560,000 | 1,020,000 |
| Interest expense ...................... | 360,000 | 300,000 |
| Net income before taxes .............. | 1,200,000 | 720,000 |
| Income taxes (30%) ................... | 360,000 | 216,000 |
| Net income ........................... | 840,000 | 504,000 |
| Common dividends ................... | 360,000 | 252,000 |
| Net income retained .................. | 480,000 | 252,000 |
| Beginning retained earnings ............ | 1,320,000 | 1,068,000 |
| Ending retained earnings .............. | $ 1,800,000 | $ 1,320,000 |

To begin your assignment you gather the following financial data and ratios that are typical of companies in Lydex Company's industry:

| | |
|---|---|
| Current ratio ............................ | 2.3 |
| Acid-test ratio .......................... | 1.2 |
| Average collection period ................. | 30 days |
| Average sale period ...................... | 60 days |
| Return on assets ........................ | 9.5% |
| Debt-to-equity ratio ..................... | 0.65 |
| Times interest earned ratio ................ | 5.7 |
| Price-earnings ratio ..................... | 10 |

*Required:*

1. You decide first to assess the company's performance in terms of debt management and profitability. Compute the following for both this year and last year:
   a. The times interest earned ratio.
   b. The debt-to-equity ratio.
   c. The gross margin percentage.
   d. The return on total assets. (Total assets at the beginning of last year were $12,960,000.)
   e. The return on equity. (Stockholders' equity at the beginning of last year totaled $9,048,000. There has been no change in common stock over the last two years.)
   f. Is the company's financial leverage positive or negative? Explain.
2. You decide next to assess the company's stock market performance. Assume that Lydex's stock price at the end of this year is $72 per share and that at the end of last year it was $40. For both this year and last year, compute:
   a. The earnings per share.
   b. The dividend yield ratio.
   c. The dividend payout ratio.
   d. The price-earnings ratio. How do investors regard Lydex Company as compared to other companies in the industry? Explain.
   e. The book value per share of common stock. Does the difference between market value per share and book value per share suggest that the stock at its current price is a bargain? Explain.
3. You decide, finally, to assess the company's liquidity and asset management. For both this year and last year, compute:
   a. Working capital.
   b. The current ratio.
   c. The acid-test ratio.
   d. The average collection period. (The accounts receivable at the beginning of last year totaled $1,560,000.)
   e. The average sale period. (The inventory at the beginning of last year totaled $1,920,000.)
   f. The operating cycle.
   g. The total asset turnover. (The total assets at the beginning of last year totaled $12,960,000.)
4. Prepare a brief memo that summarizes how Lydex is performing relative to its competitors.

**PROBLEM 14–16    Common-Size Financial Statements LO14–1**
Refer to the financial statement data for Lydex Company given in Problem 14-15.

*Required:*
For both this year and last year:
1. Present the balance sheet in common-size format.
2. Present the income statement in common-size format down through net income.
3. Comment on the results of your analysis.

**PROBLEM 14–17    Interpretation of Financial Ratios LO14–2, LO14–3, LO14–6**
Pecunious Products, Inc.'s financial results for the past three years are summarized below:

|  | Year 3 | Year 2 | Year 1 |
|---|---|---|---|
| Sales trend ..................... | 128.0 | 115.0 | 100.0 |
| Current ratio .................... | 2.5 | 2.3 | 2.2 |
| Acid-test ratio .................. | 0.8 | 0.9 | 1.1 |
| Accounts receivable turnover ...... | 9.4 | 10.6 | 12.5 |
| Inventory turnover ............... | 6.5 | 7.2 | 8.0 |
| Dividend yield ................... | 7.1% | 6.5% | 5.8% |
| Dividend payout ratio ............. | 40% | 50% | 60% |
| Dividends paid per share* ......... | $1.50 | $1.50 | $1.50 |

*There have been no changes in common stock outstanding over the three-year period.

Your boss has asked you to review these results and then answer the following questions:

a. Is it becoming easier for the company to pay its bills as they come due?
b. Are customers paying their accounts at least as fast now as they were in Year 1?
c. Is the total of the accounts receivable increasing, decreasing, or remaining constant?
d. Is the level of inventory increasing, decreasing, or remaining constant?

e. Is the market price of the company's stock going up or down?
f. Is the earnings per share increasing or decreasing?
g. Is the price-earning ratio going up or down?

**Required:**
Provide answers to each of the questions raised by your boss.

**PROBLEM 14–18  Common-Size Statements and Financial Ratios for a Loan Application LO14–1, LO14–2, LO14–3, LO14–4**

Paul Sabin organized Sabin Electronics 10 years ago to produce and sell several electronic devices on which he had secured patents. Although the company has been fairly profitable, it is now experiencing a severe cash shortage. For this reason, it is requesting a $500,000 long-term loan from Gulfport State Bank, $100,000 of which will be used to bolster the Cash account and $400,000 of which will be used to modernize equipment. The company's financial statements for the two most recent years follow:

| Sabin Electronics<br>Comparative Balance Sheet | This Year | Last Year |
|---|---|---|
| **Assets** | | |
| Current assets: | | |
| Cash | $ 70,000 | $ 150,000 |
| Marketable securities | 0 | 18,000 |
| Accounts receivable, net | 480,000 | 300,000 |
| Inventory | 950,000 | 600,000 |
| Prepaid expenses | 20,000 | 22,000 |
| Total current assets | 1,520,000 | 1,090,000 |
| Plant and equipment, net | 1,480,000 | 1,370,000 |
| Total assets | $3,000,000 | $2,460,000 |
| **Liabilities and Stockholders' Equity** | | |
| Liabilities: | | |
| Current liabilities | $ 800,000 | $ 430,000 |
| Bonds payable, 12% | 600,000 | 600,000 |
| Total liabilities | 1,400,000 | 1,030,000 |
| Stockholders' equity: | | |
| Common stock, $15 par | 750,000 | 750,000 |
| Retained earnings | 850,000 | 680,000 |
| Total stockholders' equity | 1,600,000 | 1,430,000 |
| Total liabilities and stockholders' equity | $3,000,000 | $2,460,000 |

| Sabin Electronics<br>Comparative Income Statement and Reconciliation | This Year | Last Year |
|---|---|---|
| Sales | $5,000,000 | $4,350,000 |
| Cost of goods sold | 3,875,000 | 3,450,000 |
| Gross margin | 1,125,000 | 900,000 |
| Selling and administrative expenses | 653,000 | 548,000 |
| Net operating income | 472,000 | 352,000 |
| Interest expense | 72,000 | 72,000 |
| Net income before taxes | 400,000 | 280,000 |
| Income taxes (30%) | 120,000 | 84,000 |
| Net income | 280,000 | 196,000 |
| Common dividends | 110,000 | 95,000 |
| Net income retained | 170,000 | 101,000 |
| Beginning retained earnings | 680,000 | 579,000 |
| Ending retained earnings | $ 850,000 | $ 680,000 |

During the past year, the company introduced several new product lines and raised the selling prices on a number of old product lines in order to improve its profit margin. The company also hired a new sales manager, who has expanded sales into several new territories. Sales terms are 2/10, n/30. All sales are on account.

*Required:*

1. To assist in approaching the bank about the loan, Paul has asked you to compute the following ratios for both this year and last year:
   a. The amount of working capital.
   b. The current ratio.
   c. The acid-test ratio.
   d. The average collection period. (The accounts receivable at the beginning of last year totaled $250,000.)
   e. The average sale period. (The inventory at the beginning of last year totaled $500,000.)
   f. The operating cycle.
   g. The total asset turnover. (The total assets at the beginning of last year were $2,420,000.)
   h. The debt-to-equity ratio.
   i. The times interest earned ratio.
   j. The equity multiplier. (The total stockholders' equity at the beginning of last year totaled $1,420,000.)
2. For both this year and last year:
   a. Present the balance sheet in common-size format.
   b. Present the income statement in common-size format down through net income.
3. Paul Sabin has also gathered the following financial data and ratios that are typical of companies in the electronics industry:

| | |
|---|---|
| Current ratio | 2.5 |
| Acid-test ratio | 1.3 |
| Average collection period | 18 days |
| Average sale period | 60 days |
| Debt-to-equity ratio | 0.90 |
| Times interest earned ratio | 6.0 |

Comment on the results of your analysis in (1) and (2) above and compare Sabin Electronics' performance to the benchmarks from the electronics industry. Do you think that the company is likely to get its loan application approved?

**PROBLEM 14–19   Financial Ratios for Assessing Profitability and Market Performance LO14–5, LO14–6**

Refer to the financial statements and other data in Problem 14-18. Assume Paul Sabin has asked you to assess his company's profitability and stock market performance.

*Required:*

1. You decide first to assess the company's stock market performance. For both this year and last year, compute:
   a. The earnings per share. There has been no change in common stock over the last two years.
   b. The dividend yield ratio. The company's stock is currently selling for $40 per share; last year it sold for $36 per share.
   c. The dividend payout ratio.
   d. The price-earnings ratio. How do investors regard Sabin Electronics as compared to other companies in the industry if the industry norm for the price-earnings ratio is 12? Explain.
   e. The book value per share of common stock. Does the difference between market value and book value suggest that the stock is overpriced? Explain.
2. You decide next to assess the company's profitability. Compute the following for both this year and last year:
   a. The gross margin percentage.
   b. The net profit margin percentage.
   c. The return on total assets. (Total assets at the beginning of last year were $2,420,000.)

  d. The return on equity. (Stockholders' equity at the beginning of last year was $1,420,000.)

  e. Is the company's financial leverage positive or negative? Explain.

3. Comment on the company's profit performance and stock market performance over the two-year period.

## BUILDING YOUR SKILLS

**ETHICS CHALLENGE LO14–2, LO14–4**

Venice InLine, Inc., was founded by Russ Perez to produce a specialized in-line skate he had designed for doing aerial tricks. Up to this point, Russ has financed the company with his own savings and with cash generated by his business. However, Russ now faces a cash crisis. In the year just ended, an acute shortage of high-impact roller bearings developed just as the company was beginning production for the Christmas season. Russ had been assured by his suppliers that the roller bearings would be delivered in time to make Christmas shipments, but the suppliers were unable to fully deliver on this promise. As a consequence, Venice InLine had large stocks of unfinished skates at the end of the year and was unable to fill all of the orders that had come in from retailers for the Christmas season. Consequently, sales were below expectations for the year, and Russ does not have enough cash to pay his creditors.

  Well before the accounts payable were due, Russ visited a local bank and inquired about obtaining a loan. The loan officer at the bank assured Russ that there should not be any problem getting a loan to pay off his accounts payable—providing that on his most recent financial statements the current ratio was above 2.0, the acid-test ratio was above 1.0, and net operating income was at least four times the interest on the proposed loan. Russ promised to return later with a copy of his financial statements.

  Russ would like to apply for a $80,000 six-month loan bearing an interest rate of 10% per year. The unaudited financial reports of the company appear below:

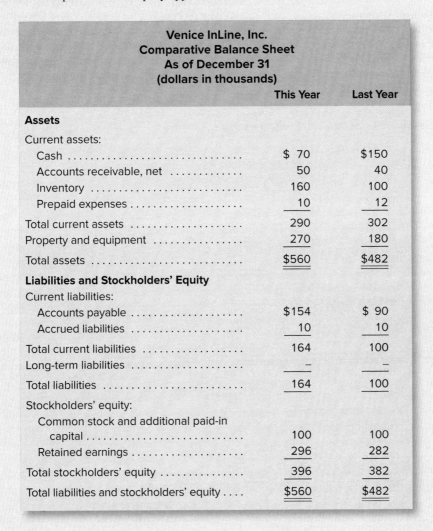

| Venice InLine, Inc.<br>Comparative Balance Sheet<br>As of December 31<br>(dollars in thousands) | This Year | Last Year |
|---|---|---|
| **Assets** | | |
| Current assets: | | |
|  Cash | $ 70 | $150 |
|  Accounts receivable, net | 50 | 40 |
|  Inventory | 160 | 100 |
|  Prepaid expenses | 10 | 12 |
| Total current assets | 290 | 302 |
| Property and equipment | 270 | 180 |
| Total assets | $560 | $482 |
| **Liabilities and Stockholders' Equity** | | |
| Current liabilities: | | |
|  Accounts payable | $154 | $ 90 |
|  Accrued liabilities | 10 | 10 |
| Total current liabilities | 164 | 100 |
| Long-term liabilities | – | – |
| Total liabilities | 164 | 100 |
| Stockholders' equity: | | |
|  Common stock and additional paid-in | | |
|   capital | 100 | 100 |
|  Retained earnings | 296 | 282 |
| Total stockholders' equity | 396 | 382 |
| Total liabilities and stockholders' equity | $560 | $482 |

**Venice InLine, Inc.**
**Income Statement**
**For the Year Ended December 31**
**(dollars in thousands)**

|  | This Year |
|---|---|
| Sales (all on account) . . . . . . . . . . . . . . . . . . . . . . | $420 |
| Cost of goods sold . . . . . . . . . . . . . . . . . . . . . . . | 290 |
| Gross margin . . . . . . . . . . . . . . . . . . . . . . . . . . . | 130 |
| Selling and administrative expenses: |  |
|     Selling expenses . . . . . . . . . . . . . . . . . . . . . | 42 |
|     Administrative expenses . . . . . . . . . . . . . . . | 68 |
| Total selling and administrative expenses . . . | 110 |
| Net operating income . . . . . . . . . . . . . . . . . . . . . | 20 |
| Interest expense . . . . . . . . . . . . . . . . . . . . . . . . . | – |
| Net income before taxes . . . . . . . . . . . . . . . . . . | 20 |
| Income taxes (30%) . . . . . . . . . . . . . . . . . . . . . | 6 |
| Net income . . . . . . . . . . . . . . . . . . . . . . . . . . . . | $ 14 |

***Required:***
1. Based on the unaudited financial statements and the statement made by the loan officer, would the company qualify for the loan?
2. Last year Russ purchased and installed new, more efficient equipment to replace an older plastic injection molding machine. Russ had originally planned to sell the old machine but found that it is still needed whenever the plastic injection molding process is a bottleneck. When Russ discussed his cash flow problems with his brother-in-law, he suggested to Russ that the old machine be sold or at least reclassified as inventory on the balance sheet because it could be readily sold. At present, the machine is carried in the Property and Equipment account and could be sold for its net book value of $45,000. The bank does not require audited financial statements. What advice would you give to Russ concerning the machine?

**ANALYTICAL THINKING** LO14–2, LO14–3, LO14–4, LO14–5, LO14–6
Incomplete financial statements for Pepper Industries follow:

**Pepper Industries**
**Balance Sheet**
**March 31**

| | |
|---|---|
| Current assets: | |
|     Cash . . . . . . . . . . . . . . . . . . . . . . . . . . . . . . . | $    ? |
|     Accounts receivable, net . . . . . . . . . . . . . . . | ? |
|     Inventory . . . . . . . . . . . . . . . . . . . . . . . . . . . . | ? |
| Total current assets . . . . . . . . . . . . . . . . . . . . . | ? |
| Plant and equipment, net . . . . . . . . . . . . . . . . . | ? |
| Total assets . . . . . . . . . . . . . . . . . . . . . . . . . . . | $    ? |
| Liabilities: | |
|     Current liabilities . . . . . . . . . . . . . . . . . . . . . . | $ 320,000 |
|     Bonds payable, 10% . . . . . . . . . . . . . . . . . . . | ? |
| Total liabilities . . . . . . . . . . . . . . . . . . . . . . . . . | ? |
| Stockholders' equity: | |
|     Common stock, $5 par value . . . . . . . . . . . . | ? |
|     Retained earnings . . . . . . . . . . . . . . . . . . . . . | ? |
| Total stockholders' equity . . . . . . . . . . . . . . . . | ? |
| Total liabilities and stockholders' equity . . . . . | $    ? |

**Pepper Industries**
**Income Statement**
**For the Year Ended March 31**

| | |
|---|---|
| Sales . . . . . . . . . . . . . . . . . . . . . . . . . . . . . . . . . . . . | $4,200,000 |
| Cost of goods sold . . . . . . . . . . . . . . . . . . . . . . | ? |
| Gross margin . . . . . . . . . . . . . . . . . . . . . . . . . . . | ? |
| Selling and administrative expenses . . . . . . . | ? |
| Net operating income . . . . . . . . . . . . . . . . . . . . | ? |
| Interest expense . . . . . . . . . . . . . . . . . . . . . . . . . | 80,000 |
| Net income before taxes . . . . . . . . . . . . . . . . . | ? |
| Income taxes (30%) . . . . . . . . . . . . . . . . . . . . . | ? |
| Net income . . . . . . . . . . . . . . . . . . . . . . . . . . . . | $      ? |

The following additional information is available about the company:

a. All sales during the year were on account.
b. There was no change in the number of shares of common stock outstanding during the year.
c. The interest expense on the income statement relates to the bonds payable; the amount of bonds outstanding did not change during the year.
d. Selected balances at the *beginning* of the current year were:

| | |
|---|---|
| Accounts receivable . . . . . | $270,000 |
| Inventory . . . . . . . . . . . . . . | $360,000 |
| Total assets . . . . . . . . . . . . | $1,800,000 |

e. Selected financial ratios computed from the statements above for the current year are:

| | |
|---|---|
| Earnings per share . . . . . . . . . . . . | $2.30 |
| Debt-to-equity ratio . . . . . . . . . . . | 0.875 |
| Accounts receivable turnover . . . | 14.0 |
| Current ratio . . . . . . . . . . . . . . . . . | 2.75 |
| Return on total assets . . . . . . . . . | 18.0% |
| Times interest earned ratio . . . . . | 6.75 |
| Acid-test ratio . . . . . . . . . . . . . . . . | 1.25 |
| Inventory turnover . . . . . . . . . . . . | 6.5 |

**Required:**

Compute the missing amounts on the company's financial statements. (*Hint:* What's the difference between the acid-test ratio and the current ratio?)

**TEAMWORK IN ACTION** LO14–2, LO14–3, LO14–4, LO14–5, LO14–6

Obtain the most recent annual report or SEC filing 10-K of a publicly traded company that interests you. It may be a local company or it may be a company in an industry that you would like to know more about. Using the annual report, compute as many of the financial ratios covered in this chapter as you can for at least the past two years. This may pose some difficulties—particularly because companies often use different terms for many income statement and balance sheet items than were shown in the chapter. Nevertheless, do the best that you can. After you have computed the financial ratios, summarize the company's performance for the current year. Has it improved, gotten worse, or remained about the same? Do the ratios indicate any potential problems or any areas that have shown significant improvement? What recommendations, if any, would you make to a bank about extending short-term credit to this company? What recommendations, if any, would you make to an insurance company about extending long-term credit to this company? What recommendations, if any, would you make to an investor about buying or selling this company's stock?

# Integration Exercises:
# An Overview

Successful managers rely on an integrated set of managerial accounting competencies to solve complex real-world problems. Therefore, we have created 12 integration exercises to help you develop these critically important managerial skills. This collective group of exercises will enable you to see how the learning objectives throughout the book interrelate with one another. As you begin to understand how it all fits together, you will start the exciting evolution from "number cruncher" to a manager-in-training.

## INTEGRATION EXERCISES    ⬛ connect

**INTEGRATION EXERCISE 1    Different Costs for Different Purposes, Cost-Volume-Profit-Relationships** LO 1–1, LO 1–2, LO 1–3, LO 1–4, LO 1–5, LO 1–6, LO 6–1, LO 6–3, LO 6–5, LO 6–7, LO 6–8

Hixson Company manufactures and sells one product for $34 per unit. The company maintains no beginning or ending inventories and its relevant range of production is 20,000 units to 30,000 units. When Hixson produces and sells 25,000 units, its unit costs are as follows:

|  | Amount Per Unit |
|---|---|
| Direct materials. . . . . . . . . . . . . . . . . . . . . . . . . | $8.00 |
| Direct labor . . . . . . . . . . . . . . . . . . . . . . . . . . . . | $5.00 |
| Variable manufacturing overhead. . . . . . . . . . | $1.00 |
| Fixed manufacturing overhead . . . . . . . . . . . . | $6.00 |
| Fixed selling expense . . . . . . . . . . . . . . . . . . . . | $3.50 |
| Fixed administrative expense. . . . . . . . . . . . . . | $2.50 |
| Sales commissions. . . . . . . . . . . . . . . . . . . . . . | $4.00 |
| Variable administrative expense . . . . . . . . . . . | $1.00 |

**Required:**

1. For financial accounting purposes, what is the total amount of product costs incurred to make 25,000 units? What is the total amount of period costs incurred to sell 25,000 units?
2. If 24,000 units are produced, what is the variable manufacturing cost per unit produced? What is the average fixed manufacturing cost per unit produced?
3. If 26,000 units are produced, what is the variable manufacturing cost per unit produced? What is the average fixed manufacturing cost per unit produced?
4. If 27,000 units are produced, what are the total amounts of direct and indirect manufacturing costs incurred to support this level of production?
5. What total incremental manufacturing cost will Hixson incur if it increases production from 25,000 to 25,001 units?
6. What is Hixson's contribution margin per unit? What is its contribution margin ratio?
7. What is Hixson's Break-Even point in unit sales? What is its Break-Even point in dollar sales?
8. How much will Hixson's net operating income increase if it can grow production and sales from 25,000 units to 26,500 units?
9. What is Hixson's margin of safety at a sales volume of 25,000 units?
10. What is Hixson degree of operating leverage at a sales volume of 25,000 units?

**INTEGRATION EXERCISE 2    Absorption Costing, Variable Costing, Cost-Volume-Profit-Relationships** LO 6–4, LO 6–5, LO 6–7, LO 7–1, LO 7–2

Newton Company manufactures and sells one product. The company assembled the following projections for its first year of operations:

| Variable costs per unit: | |
|---|---|
| Manufacturing: | |
| Direct materials. . . . . . . . . . . . . . . . . . . . . . . . . . . . . . . . . . . . . . | $20 |
| Direct labor . . . . . . . . . . . . . . . . . . . . . . . . . . . . . . . . . . . . . . . | $16 |
| Variable manufacturing overhead. . . . . . . . . . . . . . . . . . | $4 |
| Variable selling and administrative . . . . . . . . . . . . . . . . . | $2 |
| Fixed costs per year: | |
| Fixed manufacturing overhead . . . . . . . . . . . . . . . . . . . . | $450,000 |
| Fixed selling and administrative expenses . . . . . . . . . | $70,000 |

During its first year of operations, Newton expects to produce 25,000 units and sell 20,000 units. The budgeted selling price of the company's only product is $66 per unit.

**Required** *(answer each question independently by referring to the original data):*
1. Assuming that Newton's projections are accurate, what will be its absorption costing net operating income in its first year of operations?
2. Newton is considering investing in a higher quality raw material that will increase its direct materials cost by $1 per unit. It estimates that the higher quality raw material will increase sales by 1,000 units. What will be the company's revised absorption costing net operating income if it invests in the higher quality raw material and continues to *produce* 25,000 units?
3. Newton is considering raising its selling price by $1.00 per unit with an expectation that it will lower unit sales by 1,500 units. What will be the company's revised absorption costing net operating income if it raises its price by $1.00 and continues to *produce* 25,000 units?
4. Assuming that Newton's projections are accurate, what will be its variable costing net operating income in its first year of operations?
5. Newton is considering investing in a higher quality raw material that will increase its direct materials cost by $1 per unit. It estimates that the higher quality raw material will increase sales by 1,000 units. What will be the company's revised variable costing net operating income if it invests in the higher quality raw material and continues to *produce* 25,000 units?
6. Newton is considering raising its selling price by $1.00 per unit with an expectation that it will lower unit sales by 1,500 units. What will be the company's revised variable costing net operating income if it raises its price by $1.00 and continues to *produce* 25,000 units?
7. What is Newton's Break-Even point in unit sales? What is its Break-Even point in dollar sales?
8. What is the company's projected margin of safety in its first year of operations?

**INTEGRATION EXERCISE 3   Cash Budget, Income Statement, Balance Sheet, Statement of Cash Flows, Ratio Analysis** LO 8–2, LO 8–3, LO 8–4, LO 8–8, LO 8–9, LO 8–10, LO 13–2, LO 14–3

Millen Corporation is a merchandiser that is preparing a master budget for the month of July. The company's balance sheet as of June 30 is shown below:

| Millen Corporation<br>Balance Sheet<br>June 30 | |
|---|---|
| **Assets** | |
| Cash . . . . . . . . . . . . . . . . . . . . . . . . . . . . . . . . . . . . . . . . . . | $120,000 |
| Accounts receivable . . . . . . . . . . . . . . . . . . . . . . . . . . . . | 166,000 |
| Inventory . . . . . . . . . . . . . . . . . . . . . . . . . . . . . . . . . . . . . | 37,200 |
| Plant and equipment, net of depreciation . . . . . . . . . | 554,800 |
| Total assets . . . . . . . . . . . . . . . . . . . . . . . . . . . . . . . . . . . | $878,000 |
| **Liabilities and Stockholders' Equity** | |
| Accounts payable. . . . . . . . . . . . . . . . . . . . . . . . . . . . . . | $ 93,000 |
| Common stock . . . . . . . . . . . . . . . . . . . . . . . . . . . . . . . . | 586,000 |
| Retained earnings . . . . . . . . . . . . . . . . . . . . . . . . . . . . . | 199,000 |
| Total liabilities and stockholders' equity. . . . . . . . . . . | $878,000 |

Millen's managers have made the following additional assumptions and estimates:
1. Estimated sales for July and August are $310,000 and $330,000, respectively.
2. Each month's sales are 20% cash sales and 80% credit sales. Each month's credit sales are collected 30% in the month of sale and 70% in the month following the sale. All of the accounts receivable at June 30 will be collected in July.
3. Each month's ending inventory must equal 20% of the cost of next month's sales. The cost of goods sold is 60% of sales. The company pays for 40% of its merchandise purchases in the month of the purchase and the remaining 60% in the month following the purchase. All of the accounts payable at June 30 will be paid in July.
4. Monthly selling and administrative expenses are always $70,000. Each month $10,000 of this total amount is depreciation expense and the remaining $60,000 relates to expenses that are paid in the month they are incurred.
5. The company does not plan to buy or sell any plant and equipment during July. It will not borrow any money, pay a dividend, issue any common stock, or repurchase any of its own common stock during July.

*Required:*
1. Calculate the expected cash collections for July.
2. Calculate the expected cash disbursements for merchandise purchases for July.
3. Prepare a cash budget for July.
4. Prepare a budgeted income statement for the month ended July 31. Use an absorption format.
5. Prepare a budgeted balance sheet as of July 31.
6. Calculate the estimated accounts receivable turnover and inventory turnover for the month of July.
7. Calculate the estimated operating cycle for the month of July. (*Hint:* Use 30 days in the numerator to calculate the average collection period and the average sales period.)
8. Using the indirect method, calculate the estimated net cash provided by operating activities for July.

**INTEGRATION EXERCISE 4   Statement of Cash Flows; Ratio Analysis LO 13–1, LO 13–2, LO 13–3, LO 14–2, LO 14–3, LO 14–4, LO 14–5, LO 14–6**
A comparative balance sheet and an income statement for Rowan Company are given below:

| Rowan Company Comparative Balance Sheet (dollars in millions) | | |
| --- | --- | --- |
| | **Ending Balance** | **Beginning Balance** |
| **Assets** | | |
| *Current assets:* | | |
| Cash and cash equivalents.................... | $    70 | $    91 |
| Accounts receivable ........................... | 536 | 572 |
| Inventory ...................................... | 620 | 580 |
| Total current assets ......................... | 1,226 | 1,243 |
| Property, plant, and equipment.................... | 1,719 | 1,656 |
| Less accumulated depreciation................... | 640 | 480 |
| Net property, plant, and equipment ................ | 1,079 | 1,176 |
| Total assets ..................................... | $2,305 | $2,419 |
| **Liabilities and Stockholders' Equity** | | |
| *Current liabilities:* | | |
| Accounts payable............................ | $  205 | $  180 |
| Accrued liabilities.......................... | 94 | 105 |
| Income taxes payable ....................... | 72 | 88 |
| Total current liabilities ...................... | 371 | 373 |
| Bonds payable ................................ | 180 | 310 |
| Total liabilities ................................ | 551 | 683 |
| Stockholders' equity:............................ | | |
| Common stock ............................. | 800 | 800 |
| Retained earnings ........................... | 954 | 936 |
| Total stockholders' equity...................... | 1,754 | 1,736 |
| Total liabilities and stockholders' equity............. | $2,305 | $2,419 |

**Rowan Company**
**Income Statement**
**For the Year Ended December 31**
**(dollars in millions)**

| | |
|---|---:|
| Sales..................................................... | $4,350 |
| Cost of goods sold........................................ | 3,470 |
| Gross margin.............................................. | 880 |
| Selling and administrative expenses .................... | 820 |
| Net operating income .................................... | 60 |
| Nonoperating items: Gain on sale of equipment ....... | 4 |
| Income before taxes ..................................... | 64 |
| Income taxes.............................................. | 22 |
| Net income .............................................. | $ 42 |

Rowan also provided the following information:
1. The company sold equipment that had an original cost of $16 million and accumulated depreciation of $9 million. The cash proceeds from the sale were $11 million. The gain on the sale was $4 million.
2. The company did not issue any new bonds during the year.
3. The company paid a cash dividend during the year.
4. The company did not complete any common stock transactions during the year.

*Required:*
1. Using the indirect method, prepare a statement of cash flows for the year.
2. Calculate the free cash flow for the year.
3. To help Rowan assess its liquidity at the end of the year, calculate the following:
   a. Current ratio.
   b. Acid-test (quick) ratio.
4. To help Rowan assess its asset management, calculate the following:
   a. Average collection period (assuming all sales are on account).
   b. Average sale period.
5. To help Rowan assess its debt management, calculate the following:
   a. Debt-to-equity ratio at the end of the year.
   b. Equity multiplier.
6. To help Rowan assess its profitability, calculate the following:
   a. Net profit margin percentage.
   b. Return on equity.
7. To help Rowan assess its market performance, calculate the following (assume the par value of the company's common stock is $10 per share):
   a. Earnings per share.
   b. Dividend payout ratio.

**INTEGRATION EXERCISE 5   Plantwide and Departmental Overhead Allocation; Activity-Based Costing; Segmented Income Statements** LO 2–1, LO 2–2, LO 2–3, LO 2–4, LO 4–1, LO 4–2, LO 4–3, LO 4–4

Koontz Company manufactures two models of industrial components—a Basic model and an Advanced Model. The company considers all of its manufacturing overhead costs to be fixed and it uses plantwide manufacturing overhead cost allocation based on direct labor-hours. Koontz's controller prepared the segmented income statement that is shown below for the most recent year (he allocated selling and administrative expenses to products based on sales dollars):

| | Basic | Advanced | Total |
|---|---:|---:|---:|
| Number of units produced and sold............... | 20,000 | 10,000 | 30,000 |
| Sales........................................ | $3,000,000 | $2,000,000 | $5,000,000 |
| Cost of goods sold............................. | 2,300,000 | 1,350,000 | 3,650,000 |
| Gross margin.................................. | 700,000 | 650,000 | 1,350,000 |
| Selling and administrative expenses .............. | 720,000 | 480,000 | 1,200,000 |
| Net operating income (loss)..................... | $ (20,000) | $ 170,000 | $ 150,000 |

Direct laborers are paid $20 per hour. Direct materials cost $40 per unit for the Basic model and $60 per unit for the Advanced model. Koontz is considering a change from plantwide overhead allocation to a departmental approach. The overhead costs in the company's Molding Department would be allocated based on machine-hours and the overhead costs in its Assemble and Pack Department would be allocated based on direct labor-hours. To enable further analysis, the controller gathered the following information:

| | Molding | Assemble and Pack | Total |
|---|---|---|---|
| Manufacturing overhead costs ........... | $787,500 | $562,500 | $1,350,000 |
| Direct labor-hours: | | | |
| Basic..... | 10,000 | 20,000 | 30,000 |
| Advanced | 5,000 | 10,000 | 15,000 |
| Machine-hours: | | | |
| Basic..... | 12,000 | — | 12,000 |
| Advanced | 10,000 | — | 10,000 |

**Required:**
1. Using the plantwide approach:
   a. Calculate the plantwide overhead rate.
   b. Calculate the amount of overhead that would be assigned to each product.
2. Using a departmental approach:
   a. Calculate the departmental overhead rates.
   b. Calculate the total amount of overhead that would be assigned to each product.
   c. Using your departmental overhead cost allocations, redo the controller's segmented income statement (continue to allocate selling and administrative expenses based on sales dollars).
3. Koontz's production manager has suggested using activity-based costing instead of either the plantwide or departmental approaches. To facilitate the necessary calculations, she assigned the company's total manufacturing overhead cost to four activity cost pools as follows:

| Activity Cost Pool | Activity Measure | Manufacturing Overhead |
|---|---|---|
| Machining ............... | Machine-hours in molding | $ 417,500 |
| Assemble and pack......... | Direct labor-hours in assemble and pack | 282,500 |
| Order processing........... | Number of customer orders | 310,000 |
| Setups ................... | Setup hours | 340,000 |
| | | $1,350,000 |

She also determined that the average order size for the Basic and Advanced models is 400 units and 50 units, respectively. The molding machines require a setup for each order. One setup hour is required for each customer order of the Basic model and three hours are required to setup for an order of the Advanced model.

Using the additional information provided by the production manager, calculate:
   a. An activity rate for each activity cost pool.
   b. The total manufacturing overhead cost allocated to the Basic model and the Advanced model using the activity-based approach.
4. The company pays a sales commissions of 5% for the Basic model and 10% for the Advanced model. Its traceable fixed advertising expenses include $150,000 for the Basic model and $200,000 for the Advanced model. The remainder of the company's selling and administrative costs are common fixed expenses.
   Prepare a contribution format segmented income statement that is adapted from Exhibit 7-8. Organize all of the company's costs into three categories: variable expenses, traceable fixed expenses, and common fixed expenses. Use your activity-based cost assignments from requirement 3 to assign the manufacturing costs included in your traceable fixed expenses.

5. Using your contribution format segmented income statement from requirement 5, calculate the break-even point in dollar sales for the Advanced model.
6. Explain how Koontz's activity-based costing approach differs from its plantwide and departmental approaches. Also, explain how the controller's allocation of the selling and administrative expenses differs from how you accounted for these expenses within your contribution format segmented income statement.

**INTEGRATION EXERCISE 6    Normal Costing versus Actual Costing** LO 2–1, LO 2–2, LO 2–3, LO 3–3, LO 3–4, LO 7–1, LO 7–2

Darwin Company manufactures only one product that it sells for $200 per unit. The company uses plant-wide overhead cost allocation based on the number of units produced. It provided the following estimates at the beginning of the year:

| | |
|---|---|
| Number of units produced . . . . . . . . . . . . . . . . . . . . . . . . . . . . . . . . . . . . | 50,000 |
| Total fixed manufacturing overhead costs . . . . . . . . . . . . . . . . . . . . | $1,000,000 |
| Variable manufacturing overhead per unit produced . . . . . . . . . . | $12 |

During the year, the company had no beginning inventories of any kind and no ending raw materials or work in process inventories. All raw materials were used in production as direct materials. An unexpected business downturn caused annual sales to drop to 38,000 units. In response to the decline in sales, Darwin decreased its annual production to 40,000 units. The company's actual costs for the year were as follows:

| | |
|---|---|
| Variable costs per unit: | |
| *Manufacturing:* | |
| Direct materials. . . . . . . . . . . . . . . . . . . . . . . . . . . . . . . . . . . . . | $78 |
| Direct labor . . . . . . . . . . . . . . . . . . . . . . . . . . . . . . . . . . . . . . . . . | $60 |
| Variable manufacturing overhead . . . . . . . . . . . . . . . . . . . | $12 |
| Variable selling and administrative . . . . . . . . . . . . . . . . . . | $15 |
| Fixed costs per year: | |
| Fixed manufacturing overhead . . . . . . . . . . . . . . . . . . . . . . | $1,000,000 |
| Fixed selling and administrative expenses . . . . . . . . . . . | $350,000 |

*Required:*
1. Assuming the company uses normal costing (as described in Chapters 2 and 3):
   a. Compute the plantwide predetermined overhead rate.
   b. Compute the unit product cost for each unit produced during the year.
   c. Prepare a schedule of cost of goods manufactured and a schedule of cost of goods sold. Assume that any underapplied or overapplied overhead is closed entirely to cost of goods sold.
   d. Compute absorption costing net operating income for the year.
2. Assuming the company uses actual costing (as described in Chapter 7):
   a. Compute the unit product cost for each unit produced during the year.
   b. Compute absorption costing net operating income for the year.
3. Are your normal costing and actual costing net operating incomes the same? Why? Support your answer with computations.

**INTEGRATION EXERCISE 7    Capital Budgeting, Return on Investment, Residual Income** LO 10–1, LO 10–2, LO 12–2

Simmons Company is a merchandiser with multiple store locations. One of its store managers is considering a shift in her store's product mix in anticipation of a strengthening economy. Her store would invest $800,000 in more expensive merchandise (an increase in its working capital) with the expectation that it would increase annual sales and variable expenses by $400,000 and $250,000, respectively for three years. At the end of the three-year period, the store manager believes that the economic surge will subside; therefore, she will release the additional investment in working capital. The store manager's pay raises are largely determined by her store's return on investment (ROI), which has exceeded 22% each of the last three years.

**Required:**
1. Assuming the company's discount rate is 16%, calculate the net present value of the store manager's investment opportunity.
2. Calculate the annual margin, turnover, and return on investment (ROI) provided by the store manager's investment opportunity.
3. Assuming that the company's minimum required rate of return is 16%, calculate the residual income earned by the store manager's investment opportunity for each of years 1 through 3.
4. Do you think the store manager would choose to pursue this investment opportunity? Do you think the company would want the store manager to pursue it? Why?
5. Using a discount rate of 16%, calculate the present value of your residual incomes for years 1 through 3. Is your answer greater than, less than, or equal to the net present value that you computed in (1) above? Why? Support your explanation with computations.

**INTEGRATION EXERCISE 8   Master Budgeting** LO 8–2, LO 8–3, LO 8–4, LO 8–5, LO 8–6, LO 8–7, LO 8–8, LO 8–9, LO 8–10

Endless Mountain Company manufactures a single product that is popular with outdoor recreation enthusiasts. The company sells its product to retailers throughout the northeastern quadrant of the United States. It is in the process of creating a master budget for 2017 and reports a balance sheet at December 31, 2016, as follows:

|   | A | B | C |
|---|---|---|---|
| 1 | **Endless Mountain Company** | | |
| 2 | **Balance Sheet** | | |
| 3 | **December 31, 2016** | | |
| 4 | | | |
| 5 | **Assets** | | |
| 6 | Current assets: | | |
| 7 | Cash | $   46,200 | |
| 8 | Accounts receivable | 260,000 | |
| 9 | Raw materials inventory (4,500 yards) | 11,250 | |
| 10 | Finished goods inventory (1,500 units) | 32,250 | |
| 11 | Total current assets | | $349,700 |
| 12 | Plant and equipment: | | |
| 13 | Buildings and equipment | 900,000 | |
| 14 | Accumulated depreciation | (292,000) | |
| 15 | Plant and equipment, net | | 608,000 |
| 16 | Total assets | | $957,700 |
| 17 | | | |
| 18 | **Liabilities and Stockholders' Equity** | | |
| 19 | Current liabilities: | | |
| 20 | Accounts payable | | $158,000 |
| 21 | Stockholders' equity: | | |
| 22 | Common stock | $ 419,800 | |
| 23 | Retained earnings | 379,900 | |
| 24 | Total stockholders' equity | | 799,700 |
| 25 | Total liabilities and stockholders' equity | | $957,700 |
| 26 | | | |

I◄ ◀ ▶ ▶I   Beginning Balance Sheet ╱ Budgeting Assum ◀

The company's chief financial officer (CFO), in consultation with various managers across the organization has developed the following set of assumptions to help create the 2017 budget:

1. The budgeted unit sales are 12,000 units, 37,000 units, 15,000 units, and 25,000 units for quarters 1-4, respectively. Notice that the company experiences peak sales in the second and fourth quarters. The budgeted selling price for the year is $32 per unit. The budgeted unit sales for the first quarter of 2018 is 13,000 units.

2. All sales are on credit. Uncollectible accounts are negligible and can be ignored. Seventy-five percent of all credit sales are collected in the quarter of the sale and 25% are collected in the subsequent quarter.
3. Each quarter's ending finished goods inventory should equal 15% of the next quarter's unit sales.
4. Each unit of finished goods requires 3.5 yards of raw material that costs $3.00 per yard. Each quarter's ending raw materials inventory should equal 10% of the next quarter's production needs. The estimated ending raw materials inventory on December 31, 2017, is 5,000 yards.
5. Seventy percent of each quarter's purchases are paid for in the quarter of purchase. The remaining 30% of each quarter's purchases are paid in the following quarter.
6. Direct laborers are paid $18 an hour and each unit of finished goods requires 0.25 direct labor-hours to complete. All direct labor costs are paid in the quarter incurred.
7. The budgeted variable manufacturing overhead per direct labor-hour is $3.00. The quarterly fixed manufacturing overhead is $150,000 including $20,000 of depreciation on equipment. The number of direct labor-hours is used as the allocation base for the budgeted plantwide overhead rate. All overhead costs (excluding depreciation) are paid in the quarter incurred.
8. The budgeted variable selling and administrative expense is $1.25 per unit sold. The fixed selling and administrative expenses per quarter include advertising ($25,000), executive salaries ($64,000), insurance ($12,000), property tax ($8,000), and depreciation expense ($8,000). All selling and administrative expenses (excluding depreciation) are paid in the quarter incurred.
9. The company plans to maintain a minimum cash balance at the end of each quarter of $30,000. Assume that any borrowings take place on the first day of the quarter. To the extent possible, the company will repay principal and interest on any borrowings on the last day of the fourth quarter. The company's lender imposes a simple interest rate of 3% per quarter on any borrowings.
10. Dividends of $15,000 will be declared and paid in each quarter.
11. The company uses a last-in, first-out (LIFO) inventory flow assumption. This means that the most recently purchased raw materials are the "first-out" to production and the most recently completed finished goods are the "first-out" to customers.

**Required:**

The company's CFO has asked you to use Microsoft Excel to prepare the 2017 master budget. Your Excel file should include a tab that contains the December 31, 2016, balance sheet, a tab that summarizes the budgeting assumptions, and tabs corresponding to the following budget schedules and financial statements:

1. Quarterly sales budget including a schedule of expected cash collections.
2. Quarterly production budget.
3. Quarterly direct materials budget including a schedule of expected cash disbursements for purchases of materials.
4. Quarterly direct labor budget.
5. Quarterly manufacturing overhead budget.
6. Ending finished goods inventory budget at December 31, 2017.
7. Quarterly selling and administrative expense budget.
8. Quarterly cash budget.
9. Income statement for the year ended December 31, 2017.
10. Balance sheet at December 31, 2017.

**INTEGRATION EXERCISE 9    Statement of Cash Flows** LO 13–1, 13–2
Refer to the information pertaining to Endless Mountain Company that is provided in Integration Exercise 8. In addition to the budget schedules that you prepared in Integration Exercise 8, insert a new tab in your Microsoft Excel worksheet titled "Statement of Cash Flows."

**Required:**
1. Using the indirect method, calculate Endless Mountain Company's estimated net cash provided by operating activities for 2017.
2. Prepare the company's budgeted statement of cash flows for the year ended December 31, 2017.

**INTEGRATION EXERCISE 10    Financial Statement Ratio Analysis** LO 14–2, LO 14–3, LO 14–4, LO 14–5
Refer to the information pertaining to Endless Mountain Company that is provided in Integration Exercise 8. In addition to the budget schedules that you prepared in Integration Exercise 8, insert a new tab in your Microsoft Excel worksheet titled "Ratio Analysis."

***Required*** *(For all questions, be sure to use formulas that link to the other tabs in your Microsoft Excel worksheet when performing your calculations):*

1. To help assess the company's liquidity, calculate the following at December 31, 2017:
   a. Working capital.
   b. Current ratio.
2. To help assess the company's asset management, calculate the following for 2017:
   a. Accounts receivable turnover.
   b. Average collection period.
   c. Inventory turnover.
   d. Average sale period.
   e. Operating cycle.
3. To help assess the company's debt management, calculate the following for 2017:
   a. Times interest earned ratio.
   b. Equity multiplier.
4. To help assess the company's profitability, calculate the following for 2017:
   a. Net profit margin percentage.
   b. Return on equity.
5. For each of the measures and ratios that you computed in requirements 1 through 4, indicate whether, generally speaking, management would prefer to see it increase or decrease over time. Support each answer with an explanation.

## INTEGRATION EXERCISE 11   Cost-Volume-Profit Relationships, Variable Costing LO 1–4, LO 6–5, LO 6–7, LO 6–8, LO 7–1, LO 7–2, LO 7–3

Refer to the information pertaining to Endless Mountain Company that is provided in Integration Exercise 8. In addition to the budget schedules that you prepared in Integration Exercise 8, insert two new tabs in your Microsoft Excel worksheet titled "CVP Analysis" and "Variable Costing."

***Required*** *(For all questions, be sure to use formulas that link to the other tabs in your Microsoft Excel worksheet when performing your calculations):*
1. Calculate the following budgeted figures for 2017:
   a. The total fixed cost.
   b. The variable cost per unit sold.
   c. The contribution margin per unit sold.
   d. The break-even point in unit sales and dollar sales.
   e. The margin of safety.
   f. The degree of operating leverage.
2. Calculate the following budgeted figures for 2017:
   a. A variable costing income statement. Stop your computations at net operating income.
   b. A reconciliation that explains the difference in the absorption costing and variable costing net operating incomes.

## INTEGRATION EXERCISE 12   Master Budgeting, Statement of Cash Flows, Ratio Analysis, Cost-Volume-Profit Relationships, Variable Costing LO 6–5, LO 7–2, LO 8–5, LO 8–6, LO 8–8, LO 8–9, LO 8–10, LO 13–2, LO 14–3

Refer to the information pertaining to Endless Mountain Company that is provided in Integration Exercise 8 as well as the schedules that you prepared in answering Integration Exercises 8 through 11.

***Required:***
1. Assume that the company expects to collect all of its credit sales in the quarter of sale rather than the original assumption that it will collect 75% of credit sales in the quarter of sale and the remaining 25% in the subsequent quarter. *Without changing any of the underlying assumptions in your budgeting assumptions tab,* calculate the following revised figures related to the 2017 budget:
   a. Net income (absorption basis).
   b. Accounts receivable turnover.
   c. Net cash provided by operating activities.
2. Go to the Budgeting Assumptions tab in your Microsoft Excel worksheet. Change the percentage of sales that are collected in the quarter of sale to 100% and the percentage of sales that are collected in the quarter after sale to 0%. Do your answers to 1a through 1c match the numbers that appear in your Excel worksheet? If not, why?

3. Refer to the original budgeting assumptions from Integration Exercise 8. Assume that the company expects to pay its direct laborers $19 per hour instead of the original estimate of $18 per hour. *Without changing any of the underlying assumptions in your budgeting assumptions tab,* calculate the following revised figures related to the 2017 budget:

   a. Ending finished goods inventory at December 31, 2017.

   b. The Break-Even point in unit sales.

   c. Variable costing net operating income.

4. Go to the Budgeting Assumptions tab in your Microsoft Excel worksheet. Change the direct labor cost per hour from $18 to $19. Do your answers to 3a through 3c match the numbers that appear in your Excel worksheet? If not, why?

# INDEX